Annual Abstract
of Statistics

CARDIFF
CAERDYDD

No 147
2011 Edition

About us

The Office for National Statistics

ONS is the executive office of the UK Statistics Authority, a non-ministerial department which reports directly to Parliament. ONS is the UK government's single largest statistical producer. It compiles information about the UK's society and economy, and provides the evidence-base for policy and decision-making, the allocation of resources, and public accountability. The Director-General of ONS reports directly to the National Statistician who is the Authority's Chief Executive and the Head of the Government Statistical Service.

The Government Statistical Service

The Government Statistical Service (GSS) is a network of professional statisticians and their staff operating both within the Office for National Statistics and across more than 30 other government departments and agencies.

Copyright and reproduction

Contacts

For information about the content of this publication, contact the Measuring National Well-being Tel: 01329 455851
Email: ctu@ons.gsi.gov.uk

Other customer enquiries

ONS Customer Contact Centre

Tel: 0845 601 3034
International: +44 (0)845 601 3034
Minicom: 01633 815044
Email: info@statistics.gsi.gov.uk
Fax: 01633 652747
Post: Room 1.101, Government Buildings, Cardiff Road,
Newport, South Wales NP10 8XG
www.ons.gov.uk

Media enquiries

Tel: 0845 604 1858
Email: press.office@ons.gsi.gov.uk

Publications orders

To obtain the print version of this publication, please contact
Dandy Booksellers Limited
Tel: 0207 624 2993
Email: dandybooksellers@btconnect.com
Fax: 0207 624 5049
Post: Unit 3&4, 31-33 Priory Park Road
London, NW6 7UP
www.dandybooksellers.com

Contents

Contents

6: External trade and investment

7: Research and development

8: Personal income, expenditure & wealth

9: Lifestyles

Page:

10: Environment

11: Housing

12: Banking and Finance

Contents

13: Service industry

14: Defence

15: Population and vital statistics

Page:

16: Health

17: Prices

18: Production

Contents

Contents

24:Agriculture

Units of measurement

Length

1 millimetre (mm)	= 0.03937 inch	
1 centimetre (cm)	= 10 millimetres	= 0.3937 inch
1 metre (m)	= 1,000 millimetres	= 1.094 yards
1 kilometre (km)	= 1,000 metres	= 0.6214 mile
1 inch (in.)		= 25.40 millimetres or 2.540 centimetres
1 foot (ft.)	= 12 inches	= 0.3048 metre
1 yard (yd.)	= 3 feet	= 0.9144 metre
1 mile	= 1,760 yards	= 1.609 kilometres

Area

1 square millimetre (mm2)		= 0.001550 square inch
1 square metre (m2)	= one million square millimetres	= 1.196 square yards
1 hectare (ha)	= 10,000 square metres	= 2.471 acres
1 square kilometre (km2)	= one million square metres	= 247.1 acres
1 square inch (sq. in.)		= 645.2 square millimetres or 6.452 square centimetres
1 square foot (sq. ft.)	= 144 square inches	= 0.09290 square metre or 929.0 square centimetres
1 square yard (sq. yd.)	= 9 square feet	= 0.8361 square metre
1 acre	= 4,840 square yards	= 4,046 square metres or 0.4047 hectare
1 square mile (sq. mile)	= 640 acres	= 2.590 square kilometres or 259.0 hectares

Volume

1 cubic centimetre (cm3)		= 0.06102 cubic inch
1 cubic decimetre (dm3)	= 1,000 cubic centimetres	= 0.03531 cubic foot
1 cubic metre (m3)	= one million cubic centimetres	= 1.308 cubic yards
1 cubic inch (cu.in.)		=16.39 cubic centimetres
1 cubic foot (cu. ft.)	= 1,728 cubic inches	= 0.02832 cubic metre or 28.32 cubic decimetres
1 cubic yard (cu. yd.)	= 27 cubic feet	= 0.7646 cubic metre

Capacity

1 litre (l)	= 1 cubic decimetre	= 0.2200 gallon
1 hectolitre (hl)	= 100 litres	= 22.00 gallons
1 pint		= 0.5682 litre
1 quart	= 2 pints	= 1.137 litres
1 gallon	= 8 pints	= 4.546 litres
1 bulk barrel	= 36 gallons (gal.)	= 1.637 hectolitres

Weight

1 gram (g)		= 0.03527 ounce avoirdupois
1 hectogram (hg)	= 100 grams	= 3.527 ounces or 0.2205 pound
1 kilogram (kg)	= 1,000 grams or 10 hectograms	= 2.205 pounds
1 tonne (t)	= 1,000 kilograms	= 1.102 short tons or 0.9842 long ton
1 ounce avoirdupois (oz.)	= 437.5 grains	= 28.35 grams
1 pound avoirdupois (lb.)	= 16 ounces	= 0.4536 kilogram
1 hundredweight (cwt.)	= 112 pounds	= 50.80 kilograms
1 short ton	= 2,000 pounds	= 907.2 kilograms or 0.9072 tonne
1 long ton (referred to as ton)	= 2,240 pounds	= 1,016 kilograms or 1.016 tonnes
1 ounce troy	= 480 grains	= 31.10 grams

Energy

British thermal unit (Btu)	= 0.2520 kilocalorie (kcal) = 1.055 kilojoule (kj)
Therm	= 105 British thermal units = 25,200 kcal = 105,506 kj
Megawatt hour (MWh)	= 106 watt hours (Wh)
Gigawatt hour (GWh)	= 106 kilowatt hours = 34,121 therms

Food and drink

Butter	23,310 litres milk	= 1 tonne butter (average)
Cheese	10,070 litres milk	= 1 tonne cheese
Condensed milk	2,550 litres milk	= 1 tonne full cream condensed milk
	2,953 litres skimmed milk	= 1 tonne skimmed condensed milk
Milk	1 million litres	= 1,030 tonnes
Milk powder	8,054 litres milk	= 1 tonne full cream milk powder
	10,740 litres skimmed milk	= 1 tonne skimmed milk powder
Eggs	17,126 eggs	= 1 tonne (approximate)
Sugar	100 tonnes sugar beet	= 92 tonnes refined sugar
	100 tonnes cane sugar	= 96 tonnes refined sugar

Shipping

Gross tonnage	= The total volume of all the enclosed spaces of a vessel, the unit of measurement being a 'ton' of 100 cubic feet.
Deadweight tonnage	= Deadweight tonnage is the total weight in tons of 2,240 lb. that a ship can legally carry, that is the total weight of cargo, bunkers, stores and crew.

Introduction

Welcome to the 2011 edition of the Annual Abstract of Statistics. This compendium draws together statistics from a wide range of official and other authoritative sources.

Regional information, supplementary to the national figures in Annual Abstract, appear in Regional Trends online. The latest edition of Regional Trends is available electronically on the ONS website free of charge. This can be accessed at:

http://www.ons.gov.uk/ons/rel/regional-trends/regional-trends/no--43--2011-edition/index.html

Current data for many of the series appearing in this Annual Abstract are contained in other ONS publications, such as Economic & Labour Market Review, Population Trends, Health Statistics Quarterly and Financial Statistics. These titles can be purchased through Dandy Booksellers.

Other ONS publications which contain related data are the Monthly Digest of Statistics and Social Trends.

These publications can be found at:
http://www.ons.gov.uk

The name (and telephone number, where this is available) of the organisation providing the statistics are shown under each table. In addition, a list of Sources is given at the back of the book, which sets out the official publications or other sources to which further reference can be made.

Identification codes

The four-letter identification code at the top of each data column, or at the side of each row is the ONS reference for this series of data on our database. Please quote the relevant code if you contact us requiring any further information about the data. On some tables it is not possible to include these codes, so please quote the table number in these cases.

Definitions and classification

Time series
So far as possible annual totals are given throughout, but quarterly or monthly figures are given where these are more suitable to the type of series.

Explanatory notes
Most sections are preceded by explanatory notes which should be read in conjunction with the tables. Definitions and explanatory notes for many of the terms occurring in the Annual Abstract are also given in the Annual Supplement to the Monthly Digest of Statistics, published in the January edition. Detailed notes on items which appear in both the Annual Abstract and Financial Statistics are given in an annual supplement to the latter entitled Financial Statistics Explanatory Handbook. The original sources listed in the Sources may also be consulted.

Standard Industrial Classification

A Standard Industrial Classification (SIC) was first introduced into the UK in 1948 for use in classifying business establishments and other statistical units by the type of economic activity in which they are engaged. The classification provides a framework for the collection, tabulation, presentation and analysis of data about economic activities. Its use promotes uniformity of data collected by various government departments and agencies.

Since 1948 the classification has been revised in 1958, 1968, 1980, 1992, 2003 and 2007. One of the principal objectives of the 1980 revision was to eliminate differences from the activity classification issued by the Statistical Office of the European Communities (Eurostat) and entitled 'Nomenclature générale des activités économiques dans les Communautés Européennes', usually abbreviated to NACE.

In 1990 the European Communities introduced a new statistical classification of economic activities (NACE Rev 1) by regulation. The regulation made it obligatory for the UK to introduce a new Standard Industrial Classification SIC(92), based on NACE Rev 1. UK SIC(92) was based exactly on NACE Rev 1 but, where it was thought necessary or helpful, a fifth digit was added to form subclasses of the NACE 1 four digit system. Classification systems need to be revised periodically because, over time, new products, processes and industries emerge. In January 2003 a minor revision of NACE Rev 1, known as NACE Rev 1.1, was published in the Official Journal of the European Communities.

Consequently, the UK was obliged to introduce a new Standard Industrial Classification, SIC(2003) consistent with NACE Rev 1.1. The UK took the opportunity of the 2003 revision also to update the national Subclasses. Full details are available in UK Standard Industrial Classification of Economic Activities 2003 and the Indexes to the UK Standard Industrial Classification of Economic Activities 2003. These are the most recent that are currently used. The most up to date version is the UK Standard Industrial Classification of Economic activities 2007 (SIC2007). It will be implemented in five stages and came into effect on 1 January 2008.

- For reference year 2008, the Annual Business Inquiry (parts 1 & 2) will be based on SIC 2007

- PRODCOM will also be based on SIC 2007 from reference year 2008

- Other annual outputs will be based on SIC 2007 from reference year 2009, unless otherwise determined by regulation

- Quarterly and monthly surveys will be based on SIC 2007 from the first reference period in 2010, unless otherwise determined by regulation

- National Accounts will move to SIC 2007 in September 2011

Symbols and conventions used

Change of basis
Where consecutive figures have been compiled on different bases and are not strictly comparable, a footnote is added indicating the nature of the difference.

Geographic coverage
Statistics relate mainly to the UK. Where figures relate to other areas, this is indicated on the table.

Units of measurement
The various units of measurement used are listed after the Contents.

Rounding of figures
In tables where figures have been rounded to the nearest final digit, the constituent items may not add up exactly to the total.

Symbols
The following symbols have been used throughout:

.. = not available or not applicable (also information
    supressed to avoid disclosure)

- = nil or less than half the final digit shown

Office for National Statistics online:
www.ons.gov.uk

Web-based access to time series, cross-sectional data and metadata from across the Government Statistical Service (GSS), is available using the site search function from the homepage. Download many datasets, in whole or in part, or consult directory information for all GSS statistical resources, including censuses, surveys, periodicals and enquiry services. Information is posted as PDF electronic documents or in XLS and CSV formats, compatible with most spreadsheet packages.

Contact point

ONS welcomes any feedback on the content of the Annual Abstract, including comments on the format of the data and the selection of topics. Comments and requests for general information should be addressed to:

Measuring National Well-being
Room 2.164
Office for National Statistics
Government Buildings

Cardiff Road
Newport
South Wales
NP10 8XG
or
Email: info@statistics.gov.uk

March 2012

Area

Chapter 1

Area

The United Kingdom (UK) comprises Great Britain and Northern Ireland. Great Britain comprises England, Wales and Scotland.

Physical Features

The United Kingdom (UK) constitutes the greater part of the British Isles. The largest of the islands is Great Britain. The next largest comprises Northern Ireland and the Irish Republic. Western Scotland is fringed by the large island chain known as the Hebrides, and to the north east of the Scottish mainland are the Orkney and Shetland Islands. All these, along with the Isle of Wight, Anglesey and the Isles of Scilly, form part of the UK, but the Isle of Man, in the Irish Sea and the Channel Islands, between Great Britain and France are largely self-governing and are not part of the UK. The UK is one of the 27 member states of the European Union. With an area of about 243 000 sq km (about 94 000 sq miles), the UK is just under 1 000 km (about 600 miles) from the south coast to the extreme north of Scotland and just under 500 km (around 300 miles) across at the widest point.

- Highest mountain: Ben Nevis, in the highlands of Scotland, at 1 343 m (4 406 ft)
- Longest river: the Severn, 354 km (220 miles) long, which rises in central Wales and flows through Shrewsbury, Worcester and Gloucester in England to the Bristol Channel
- Largest lake: Lough Neagh, Northern Ireland, at 396 sq km (153 sq miles)
- Deepest lake: Loch Morar in the Highlands of Scotland, 310 m (1 017 ft) deep
- Highest waterfall: Eas a'Chual Aluinn, from Glas Bheinn, in the highlands of Scotland, with a drop of 200 m (660 ft)
- Deepest cave: Ogof Ffynnon Ddu, Wales, at 308 m (1 010 ft) deep
- Most northerly point on the British mainland: Dunnet Head, north-east Scotland
- Most southerly point on the British mainland: Lizard Point, Cornwall
- Closest point to mainland continental Europe: Dover, Kent. The Channel Tunnel, which links England and France, is a little over 50 km (31 miles) long, of which nearly 38 km (24 miles) are actually under the Channel

1.1 Area of the United Kingdom[1,2],2009

	sq km		sq km
United Kingdom	242495	Shropshire	3197
		Staffordshire	2620
Great Britain[3]	228937	Warwickshire	1975
		West Midlands (Met County)	902
England and Wales	151012	Worcestershire	1741
		East of England	19109
England	130279	Luton UA	43
		Peterborough UA	343
North East	8573	Southend-on-Sea UA	42
		Thurrock UA	163
Darlington UA	197		
Hartlepool UA	94	Bedfordshire	1192
Middlesbrough UA	54	Cambridgeshire	3046
Redcar and Cleveland UA	245	Essex	3465
Stockton-on-Tees UA	204	Hertfordshire	1643
		Norfolk	5371
Durham	2226	Suffolk	3800
Northumberland	5013		
Tyne and Wear (Met County)	540	**London**	1572
North West	14106	Inner London	319
		Outer London	1253
Blackburn with Darwen UA	137		
Blackpool UA	35	**South East**	19069
Halton UA	79		
Warrington UA	181	Bracknell Forest UA	109
		Brighton and Hove UA	83
Cheshire	2083	Isle of Wight UA	380
Cumbria	6768	Medway UA	192
Greater Manchester (Met County)	1276	Milton Keynes UA	309
Lancashire	2903	Portsmouth UA	40
Merseyside (Met County)	645	Reading UA	40
		Slough UA	33
Yorkshire and The Humber	15408	Southampton UA	50
		West Berkshire UA	704
East Riding of Yorkshire UA	2408	Windsor and Maidenhead UA	197
Kingston upon Hull, City of UA	71	Wokingham UA	179
North East Lincolnshire UA	192		
North Lincolnshire UA	846	Buckinghamshire	1565
York UA	272	East Sussex	1709
		Hampshire	3679
North Yorkshire	8038	Kent	3544
South Yorkshire (Met County)	1552	Oxfordshire	2605
West Yorkshire (Met County)	2029	Surrey	1663
		West Sussex	1991
East Midlands	15607	**South West**	23837
Derby UA	78	Bath and North East Somerset UA	346
Leicester UA	73	Bournemouth UA	46
Nottingham UA	75	Bristol, City of UA	110
Rutland UA	382	North Somerset UA	374
		Plymouth UA	80
Derbyshire	2547	Poole UA	65
Leicestershire	2083	South Gloucestershire UA	497
Lincolnshire	5921	Swindon UA	230
Northamptonshire	2364	Torbay UA	63
Nottinghamshire	2085		
		Cornwall and the Isles of Scilly	3563
West Midlands	12998	Devon	6564
		Dorset	2542
Herefordshire, County of UA	2180	Gloucestershire	2653
Stoke-on-Trent UA	93	Somerset	3451
Telford and Wrekin UA	290	Wiltshire	3255

1.1 Area of the United Kingdom[1,2], 2009

	sq km		sq km
Wales	20733	Dumfries & Galloway	6426
		Dundee City	60
Blaenau Gwent	109	East Ayrshire	1262
Bridgend	251	East Dunbartonshire	175
Caerphilly	277	East Lothian	679
Cardiff	140		
Carmarthenshire	2371	East Renfrewshire	174
		Edinburgh, City of	264
Ceredigion	1785	Eilean Siar[4]	3071
Conwy	1126	Falkirk	297
Denbighshire	837	Fife	1325
Flintshire	437		
Gwynedd	2535	Glasgow City	175
		Highland	25659
Isle of Anglesey	711	Inverclyde	160
Merthyr Tydfil	111	Midlothian	354
Monmouthshire	849	Moray	2238
Neath Port Talbot	441		
Newport	190	North Ayrshire	885
Pembrokeshire	1619	North Lanarkshire	470
		Orkney Islands	990
Powys	5181	Perth & Kinross	5286
Rhondda, Cynon, Taff	424	Renfrewshire	262
Swansea	378	Scottish Borders	4732
Torfaen	126		
The Vale of Glamorgan	331	Shetland Islands	1466
Wrexham	504	South Ayrshire	1222
		South Lanarkshire	1772
		Stirling	2187
Scotland	77925	West Dunbartonshire	159
		West Lothian	427
Aberdeen City	186		
Aberdeenshire	6313		
Angus	2182	**Northern Ireland[5]**	13576
Argyll & Bute	6909		
Clackmannanshire	159		

Source: Office for National Statistics

1 Figures relate to land area only.

2 The area measurements are a definitive set derived from boundaries maintained by Ordnance Survey and Ordnance Survey of Northern Ireland. The current measurements may differ from those published previously in tables, publications or other statistical outputs, even allowing for boundary changes or changes to the physical structure of the land because of improvements to the source of the data.

3 Excludes inland water for all countries.

4 Formerly known as the Western Isles.

5 Differences in areas such as NI are attributable to the measurement not including all waters.

Parliamentary elections

Chapter 2

Parliamentary elections

This chapter covers parliamentary elections, by-elections and devolved assembly elections in the UK, Wales, Scotland and Northern Ireland.

Parliamentary elections (Table 2.1)

Information is supplied on the total electorate, average electorate and valid votes as a percentage of electorate. The number of seats by party is also listed.

Parliamentary by-elections (Table 2.2)

Information can be found on the votes recorded for each party and General Elections and subsequent by-elections between General Elections.

Devolved assembly elections (Tables 2.3 and 2.4)

Table 2.2 provides information on the devolved assembly elections in Wales and Scotland, listing information on the total electorate, average electorate and valid votes as a percentage of electorate. The number of seats by party is also listed. Table 2.4 provides information on the devolved assembly elections in Northern Ireland, listing information on the total electorate, average electorate and valid votes as a percentage of electorate. The number of seats by party is also listed.

2.1 Parliamentary elections[1]

United Kingdom

Thousands and percentages

		15-Oct 1964	31-Mar 1966	18-Jun 1970[1]	28-Feb 1974		10-Oct 1974	03-May 1979	09-Jun 1983	11-Jun 1987	09-Apr 1992	01-May 1997	07-Jun 2001	05-May 2005	06-May 2010
United Kingdom															
Electorate	DZ5P	35894	35957	39615	40256	DZ6V	40256	41573	42704	43666	43719	43846	44403	44246	45597
Average-electors per seat	DZ5T	57	57.1	62.9	63.4	DZ6R	63.4	65.5	66.7	67.2	67.2	66.5	67.4	68.5	70.1
Valid votes counted	DZ5X	27657	27265	28345	31340	DZ6N	29189	31221	30671	32530	33614	31286	26367	27149	29688
As percentage of electorate	DZ63	77.1	75.8	71.5	77.9	DZ6J	72.5	75.1	71.8	74.5	76.7	71.4	59.4	61.4	65.1
England and Wales															
Electorate	DZ5Q	31610	31695	34931	35509	DZ6W	35509	36695	37708	38568	38648	38719	39228	39266	40565
Average-electors per seat	DZ5U	57.8	57.9	63.9	64.3	DZ6S	64.3	66.5	67.2	68.8	68.8	68	68.9	69	70.8
Valid votes counted	DZ5Y	24384	24116	24877	27735	DZ6O	25729	27609	27082	28832	29897	27679	23243	24097	26548
As percentage of electorate	DZ64	77.1	76.1	71.2	78.1	DZ6K	72.5	75.2	71.8	74.8	77.5	71.5	59.3	61.4	65.4
Scotland															
Electorate	DZ5R	3393	3360	3659	3705	DZ6X	3705	3837	3934	3995	3929	3949	3984	3840	3863
Average-electors per seat	DZ5V	47.8	47.3	51.5	52.2	DZ6T	52.2	54	54.6	55.5	54.6	54.8	55.3	65.1	65.5
Valid votes counted	DZ5Z	2635	2553	2688	2887	DZ6P	2758	2917	2825	2968	2931	2817	2313	2334	2466
As percentage of electorate	DZ65	77.6	76	73.5	77.9	DZ6L	74.5	76	71.8	74.3	74.2	71.3	58.1	60.8	63.8
Northern Ireland															
Electorate	DZ5S	891	902	1025	1027	DZ6Y	1037	1028	1050	1090	1141	1178	1191	1140	1169
Average-electors per seat	DZ5W	74.2	75.2	85.4	85.6	DZ6U	86.4	85.6	61.8	64.1	67.1	65.4	66.2	63.3	65
Valid votes counted	DZ62	638	596	779	718	DZ6Q	702	696	765	730	785	791	810	718	674
As percentage of electorate	DZ66	71.7	66.1	76	69.9	DZ6M	67.7	67.7	72.9	67	68.8	67.1	68	62.9	57.6
Members of Parliament elected: (numbers)	DZV7	630	630	630	635	DZV8	635	635	650	650	651	659	659	646	650
Conservative	DZ67	303	253	330	296	DZ6D	276	339	396	375	336	165	166	198	306
Labour	DZ68	317	363	287	301	DZ6E	319	268	209	229	271	418	412	355	258
Liberal Democrat[2]	DZ69	9	12	6	14	DZ6F	13	11	23	22	20	46	52	62	57
Scottish National Party	DZ6A	–	–	1	7	DZ6G	11	2	2	3	3	6	5	6	6
Plaid Cymru	DZ6B	–	–	–	2	DZ6H	3	2	2	3	4	4	4	3	3
Other[3]	DZ6C	1	2	6	15	DZ6I	13	13	18	18	17	20	20	22	20

1 The Representation of the People Act 1969 lowered the minimum voting age from 21 to 18 years with effect from 16 February 1970.
2 Liberal before 1992. The figures for 1983 and 1987 include six and five MPs respectively who were elected for the Social Democratic Party.
3 Including the Speaker.

Source: British Electoral Facts 1832-2006
University of Plymouth for the Electoral Commission: 01752 233207

2.2 Parliamentary by-elections

United Kingdom

	May 1997 - June 2001	General[1,2] Election May 1997	June 2001 - November 2004	General[1] Election June 2001	May 2005 - November 2009	General[1] Election May 2005
Numbers of by-elections	17		6		14	
Votes recorded						
By party (percentages)						
Conservative	27	25.1	17.7	21.2	27.7	25.7
Labour	29.7	40.1	40.8	58.3	29.3	35.7
Liberal Democrat	22.1	14.4	31.3	13.7	20	20.6
Scottish National Party	6	4.1	-	-	9.5	6.2
Plaid Cymru	2.5	2.3	2.7	2.1	0.4	0.1
Other	12.7	14.1	7.4	4.7	13	11.7
Total votes recorded (percentages)	100	100	100	100	100	100
(thousands)	435	723	140	205	436	586

1 Votes recorded in the same seats in the previous General Election.
2 Proportions of 'other' votes inflated by the fact that votes were cast for the retiring Speaker as 'The Speaker seeking re-election' and not as a party

Source: University of Plymouth for the Electoral Commission: 01752 233207

2.3 Devolved assembly elections

Wales and Scotland

Thousands and percentages

		06-May 1999	01-May 2003	03-May 2007
Welsh Assembly				
Electorate	E28K	2205	2230	2248
Average-electors per seat[1]	E28N	55.1	55.7	56.2
Valid votes counted	E28Q	1023	850	978
As percentage of electorate	E28T	46.4	38.1	43.5
Members elected:[2] (numbers)	E2XI	60	60	60
Conservative	E2WG	9	11	12
Labour	E2WU	28	30	26
Liberal Democrat	E2WW	6	6	6
Plaid Cymru	E2X3	17	12	15
Other	E2WY	–	1	1
Scottish Parliament				
Electorate	E28L	4024	3879	3899
Average-electors per seat[1]	E28O	55.1	53.1	53.4
Valid votes counted	E28R	2342	1916	2017
As percentage of electorate	E28U	58.2	49.4	51.7
Members elected:[3] (numbers)	E2XJ	129	129	129
Conservative	E2WH	18	18	17
Labour	E2WV	56	50	46
Liberal Democrat	E2WX	17	17	16
Scottish National Party	E2X4	35	27	47
Other	E2WZ	3	17	3

1 This is the average in each first-past-the-post constituency. Additional members are then elected on the basis of a regional 'list' vote.

2 Comprising 40 from constituencies and 20 from the regional 'list'.

3 Comprising 73 from constituencies and 56 from the regional 'list'.

Sources: British Electoral Facts 1832-2006;
University of Plymouth for the Electoral Commission: 01752 233207

2.4 Devolved assembly elections

Northern Ireland

Thousands and percentages

		25-Jun 1998	26-Nov 2003	08-Mar 2007
Electorate	E28M	1179	1098	1108
Average-electors per seat[1]	E28P	65.5	61	61.6
Valid votes counted	E28S	810	692	692
As percentage of electorate	E28V	68.7	63	63
Members elected: (numbers)	E2XK	108	108	108
Alliance Party	E2X5	6	6	7
SDLP	E2X6	24	18	16
Sinn Fein	E2X7	18	24	28
Democratic Unionist Party	E2X8	20	30	36
UK Unionist Party	E2X9	5	1	–
Ulster Unionist Party	E2XA	28	27	18
Other	E2X2	7	2	3

1 This is the average in each Westminster constituency. Six members are elected by single transferable vote (STV) in each constituency.

Sources: British Electoral Facts 1832-2006;
University of Plymouth for the Electoral Commission: 01752 233207

International development

Chapter 3

International development

Overseas development assistance

The Department for International Development (DFID) is the UK Government Department with lead responsibility for overseas development. DFID's aim is to eliminate poverty in poorer countries through achievement of the Millennium Development Goals (MDG's) by 2015. Statistics relating to international development are published on a financial year basis and on a calendar year basis. Statistics on a calendar year basis allow comparisons of aid expenditure with other donor countries. Aid flows can be measured before (gross) or after (net) deductions of repayments of principal on past loans. These tables show only the gross figures.

Aid is provided in two main ways: Bilateral funding is provided directly to partner countries while multilateral funding is provided through international organisations.

Funds can only be classified as multilateral if they are channelled through an organisation on a list in the OECD –

Development Assistance Committee (DAC) Statistical Reporting Directives – which identifies all multilateral organisations. This list also highlights some bodies that might appear to be multilateral but are actually bilateral (in particular this latter category includes some international non-governmental organisations such as the International Committee of the Red Cross and some Public-Private Partnerships). The DAC list of multilaterals is updated annually based on members nominations; organisations must be engaged in development work to be classified as multilateral aid channels although money may be classified as bilateral while a case is being made for a new multilateral organisation to be recognised.

While core funding to multilateral organisations is always classified as multilateral expenditure, additional funding channelled through multilaterals is often classified as bilateral expenditure. This would be the case in circumstances where a DFID country office transfers some money to a multilateral organisation (for example UN agency) for a particular programme in that country (or region). That is where DFID has control over what the money is being spent on and/or where it is being spent. Likewise, if DFID responds to an emergency appeal from an agency for a particular country or area, the funds will be allocated as bilateral spend to that country or region. As a result, some organisations, such as UN agencies have some of their DFID funding classified as bilateral and some as multilateral.

Table 3.1 shows the main groups of multilateral agencies, the International Development Association being the largest in the World Bank Group.

Bilateral assistance takes various forms:

Financial Aid – Poverty Reduction Budget Support (PRBS) – Funds provided to developing countries for them to spend in support of their expenditure programmes whose long-term objective is to reduce poverty; funds are spent using the overseas governments' own financial management, procurement and accountability systems to increase ownership and long term sustainability. PRBS can take the form of a general contribution to the overall budget – general budget support – or support with a more restricted focus which is earmarked for a specific sector – sector budget support.

Other Financial Aid – Funding of projects and programmes such as Sector Wide Programmes not classified as PRBS. Financial aid in its broader sense covers all bilateral aid expenditure other than technical cooperation and administrative costs but in SID we separately categorise this further.

Technical Co-operation – Activities designed to enhance the knowledge, intellectual skills, technical expertise or the productive capability of people in recipient countries. It also covers funding of services which contribute to the design or implementation of development projects and programmes.

This assistance is mainly delivered through research and development, the use of consultants, training (generally overseas partners visiting the UK or elsewhere for a training programme) and employment of 'other Personnel' (non-DFID experts on fixed term contracts). This latter category is growing less significant over time as existing contracted staff reach the end of their assignments.

Bilateral Aid Delivered Through a Multilateral Organisation – This category covers funding that is channelled through a multilateral organisation and DFID has control over the country, sector or theme that the funds will be spent on. For example, where a DFID country office transfers money to a multilateral organisation for a particular piece of work in that country. This also includes aid delivered through multi donor funds such as the United Nations Central Emergency Response Fund (CERF).

Bilateral Aid Delivered Through a Non-Governmental Organisation (NGO) – This category covers support to the international development work of UK and international not for profit organisations such as NGOs or Civil Society Organisations. This covers Partnership Programme Arrangements (PPAs), the Civil Society Challenge Fund and other grants.

Other Bilateral Aid – This category includes any aid not elsewhere classified such as funding to other donors for shared development purposes. More information on all of the above aid types is provided in the Glossary.

Humanitarian Assistance – Provides food, aid and other humanitarian assistance including shelter, medical care and advice in emergency situations and their aftermath. Work of the conflict pools is also included.

DFID Debt Relief – This includes sums for debt relief on DFID aid loans and cancellation of debt under the Commonwealth Debt Initiative (CDI). The non-CDI DFID debt relief is reported on the basis of the 'benefit to the recipient country'. This means that figures shown represent the money available to the country in the year in question that would otherwise have been spent on debt servicing. The CDI debt cancellation is reported on a 'lump sum' basis where all outstanding amounts on a loan are shown at the time the agreement to cancel is made.

CDC Gross Investments – **CDC Group PLC** is wholly government owned. Its investments must have a clear development objective. The net amount (that is equity purchase less equity sales) of

CDC investments in official development assistance (ODA)-eligible countries is reported as ODA and the gross amount (that is equity purchase only) is reported in GPEX.

Non-DFID Debt Relief – Comprises CDC Debt and ECGD Debt. CDC has a portfolio of loans to governments which can become eligible for debt relief under the Heavily Indebted Poor Countries (HIPC) or other debt relief deals. In 2005/06 £90 million of debts owed to CDC were reorganised. Export Credit Guarantee Department (ECGD) is the UK's official export credit agency providing insurance for exporters against the main risks in selling overseas and guarantees to banks providing export finance. It also negotiates debt relief arrangements on commercial debt.

The Foreign and Commonwealth Office (FCO) contributes to UK GPEX in a number of ways:

The FCO Strategic Programme Fund supports a range of the UK government's international goals. Where the programme funds projects which meet the required OECD definition these projects are included in UK GPEX statistics.

The FCO supports the British Council through grant-in-aid funding. This funding goes to support a range of initiatives including building the capacity and quality of English language teaching; supporting education systems; and using cultural exchange to improve economic welfare. UK GPEX statistics include the proportion of this work which is clearly focussed on delivering economic welfare and development in ODA eligible countries.

The British Council also manages, on behalf of the FCO, the Chevening Scholarships programme, which provides funding for postgraduate students or researchers from developing countries to study in UK universities. Funding from this scheme to students from ODA eligible countries are included in UK ODA and GPEX statistics.

The FCO makes annual contributions to UN and Commonwealth organisations. A proportion of these contributions are allowed to score as ODA in line with Annex 2 of the DAC Statistical Reporting Directives.

In addition to contributing directly to the Conflict Pool (see below) the FCO is also responsible for the UK contribution to the UN Department for Peacekeeping Operations (UNDPKO). In line with DAC rules 6 per cent of donor funding to UNDPKO is allowed to score as ODA. FCO also funds other bilateral peacekeeping missions including the Organisation for Security and Cooperation in Europe (OSCE) and the European Security and Defence Policy (ESDP) civilian missions; a proportion of which is reported as bilateral GPEX.

The Conflict Pool (CP) –is governed and jointly managed by DFID, the FCO and the Ministry of Defence (MoD) to bring together the UK government's development, diplomatic and defence interest and expertise to ensure a coherent response to conflict prevention. Some of the CP's expenditure is ODA eligible. All CP funds disbursed through DFID are included in GPEX and appear in these statistics as part of DFID expenditure. The remaining figures comprise the aggregate of FCO and MOD spending. Data on the ODA eligible CP funds disbursed by the FCO and MOD are collected by DFID in liaison with programme officers in the relevant departments.

Other –includes contributions from other government departments including: Department of Energy and Climate Change; Department of Health; Department for Environment, Food & Rural

Affairs; Department for Culture, Media and Sport; Scottish Government; and the Welsh Assembly Government. It also includes estimates of the UK Border Agency's costs of supporting refugees in the UK; as well as estimates of gift aid to NGOs and other official funding to NGOs.

Further details on the UK's development assistance can be found in the Department for International Developments publication Statistics on International Development which can be found on the website www.dfid.gov.uk

Comparisons are available in the OECD Development Assistance Committee's annual report.

3.1 Gross public expenditure on aid (GPEX)[1]

United Kingdom

£ Thousand

		2005 /06	2006 /07	2007 /08	2008 /09	2009 /10
Bilateral Assistance						
Department for International Development:						
Poverty Reduction Budget Support (General)	**LUJS**	347,320	297,553	366,453	392,748	383,150
Poverty Reduction Budget Support (Sector)	**I4UJ**	128,232	166,064	268,631	255,920	250,951
Other Financial Aid	**LUJW**	465,098	450,565	456,657	516,431	518,817
Technical Co-operation Projects	**LUOS**	481,053	522,722	474,287	514,235	419,911
Bilateral Aid Delivered though a Multilateral Organisation[2]	**KB5I**	388,751	482,442	576,809	656,448	1,264,716
Bilateral Aid Delivered through a NGO	**KB5J**	296,383	310,607	300,515	462,597	599,434
Other Bilateral Aid[3]	**KB5K**	27,299	17,943	12,399	17,030	34,668
Humanitarian Assistance	**LUOU**	447,978	383,513	430,773	449,163	434,556
Debt Relief	**KB4I**	68,120	147,106	71,386	19,425	52,061
Total DFID Bilateral Programme	**KB5L**	**2,650,234**	**2,778,516**	**2,957,909**	**3,283,996**	**3,958,263**
Other UK Official Sources:						
CDC Gross Investments	**LUOX**	172,808	278,787	360,821	436,028	354,436
Debt Relief	**EQ4B**	1,588,414	1,866,591	3,760	280,337	7,237
FCO	**KB5M**	68,502	91,192	117,591	122,963	142,269
Conflict Pool	**KB5N**	29,530	51,289	17,173	97,357	103,645
Other[4]	**KB5O**	60,035	57,707	60,135	113,269	199,885
Total Bilateral Aid from other UK Official Sources	**KB5P**	**1,919,290**	**2,345,566**	**559,480**	**1,049,954**	**807,472**
Total Bilateral GPEX	**LUOZ**	4,569,523	5,124,082	3,517,389	4,333,951	4,765,735
Multilateral Assistance						
European Community	**LUPA**	1,191,961	1,123,215	1,200,319	1,407,901	1,424,089
World Bank Group	**LUPB**	364,909	493,333	493,387	573,652	559,785
UN Agencies	**LUPD**	252,745	245,019	296,940	308,154	278,619
Other	**LUPF**	105,892	360,443	256,348	310,659	486,273
Total Multilateral GPEX	**LUPG**	1,915,506	2,222,010	2,246,995	2,600,365	2,748,766
Administrative costs	**LUPH**	256,451	245,893	262,731	249,000	252,101
Total Gross Public Expenditure on Aid	**LUPI**	6,741,480	7,591,985	6,027,115	7,183,316	7,766,602
Total DFID programme	**KB4J**	4,521,810	5,023,805	5,195,776	5,799,253	6,628,999

Source: Department for International Development: 01355 843764

1 See chapter text.

2 This covers aid provided through multialteral organisations where the recipient country, region, sector, theme or specific project are known.

3 Other Bilateral Aid covers bilateral aid that does not fit into any other category.

4 Includes Department for Energy & Climate Change; costs of supporting refugees in the UK; Scottish Government; Gift Aid to NGOs; Colonial Pensions; Department for Health; Deparment for Environment, Food & Rural Affairs; Department for Culture, Media & Sport; and the Welsh Assembly. This also includes other official funding to UK NGOs.

3.2 Total bilateral gross public expenditure on aid (GPEX): by main recipient countries and regions[1]

United Kingdom

£ Thousand

		2005 /06	2006 /07	2007 /08	2008 /09	2009 /10
Main recipients						
Afghanistan	**C224**	126,949	123,011	146,818	197,687	205,701
Bangladesh	**LUPM**	128,258	109,313	129,725	135,686	151,176
Burma	**KB5Q**	6,483	7,610	8,915	57,601	29,019
Congo, Dem Republic	**C223**	58,832	79,283	82,910	99,645	116,783
Ethiopia	**C225**	62,562	90,506	140,011	168,607	215,688
Ghana	**LUPL**	96,315	93,147	93,076	103,728	96,749
India	**LUPJ**	270,065	293,706	312,751	402,239	356,490
Kenya	**EU5W**	65,486	67,054	52,135	109,829	75,685
Kyrgyzstan	**KB5R**	7,271	5,455	5,908	10,683	4,624
Liberia	**KB5S**	6,081	8,364	7,608	17,027	12,576
Malawi	**LUPP**	68,653	88,686	72,619	82,021	77,370
Mozambique	**LUPV**	56,540	56,273	67,799	66,365	68,301
Nepal	**KB4U**	34,548	46,543	55,274	58,518	68,487
Nigeria	**C227**	1,227,717	1,750,694	157,722	131,637	130,594
West Bank & Gaza	**KB5T**	15,058	15,196	45,191	42,557	62,603
Pakistan	**LUPY**	97,688	118,150	88,145	129,713	151,244
Rwanda	**KB4V**	70,427	16,799	52,769	70,570	53,702
Sierra Leone	**KB4W**	34,208	37,696	57,705	48,352	46,686
Somalia	**KB5U**	18,753	16,643	25,799	33,600	45,176
South Africa	**KB5V**	79,366	30,287	89,076	78,556	39,404
Sudan	**EU5S**	117,114	109,917	138,702	109,945	149,289
Tanzania	**LUPK**	114,134	115,023	125,353	142,299	146,029
Tagikistan	**KB5W**	2,768	7,363	3,340	5,372	5,054
Uganda	**LUPN**	72,064	79,035	77,231	72,131	78,131
Yemen	**KB5X**	11,616	21,545	12,279	20,313	30,660
Zambia	**LUPO**	101,707	63,412	41,942	49,466	50,353
Zimbabwe	**KB4Y**	35,376	34,096	46,660	57,332	70,323
Regional totals						
Africa	**LUQF**	2,425,879	3,071,676	1,552,123	1,761,343	1,914,233
America	**LUQG**	85,390	119,490	68,545	75,376	98,861
Asia	**LUQH**	1,356,414	1,091,487	1,116,528	1,733,696	1,353,553
Europe	**LUQI**	90,086	135,699	39,496	53,284	45,174
Pacific	**LUQJ**	3,823	2,669	2,842	4,007	3,142
World unallocated[2]	**LUQK**	607,930	703,058	737,855	706,246	1,350,770
Total Bilateral GPEX	**LUQL**	4,569,523	5,124,082	3,517,389	4,333,951	4,765,735
Total Multilateral GPEX	**KB4Z**	1,915,506	2,222,010	2,246,995	2,600,365	2,748,766
Total Admin	**KB52**	256,451	245,893	262,731	249,000	252,101
Total GPEX on Development	**KB53**	**6,741,480**	**7,591,985**	**6,027,115**	**7,183,316**	**7,766,602**

Source: Department for International Development: 01355 843764

1 See chapter text.
2 Includes global funding e.g. core grants to CSOs, Research Institutions etc

3.3 DFID Bilateral Expenditure

United Kingdom

£ Thousand

	2005 /06	2006 /07	2007 /08	2008 /09	2009 /10
Education:					
Education Poverty Reduction Budget Support	93,367	83,991	100,605	105,319	155,629
Education Unallocable/Unspecified	-	-	-	281	1,489
Education Policy and Administrative Management	63,786	93,233	78,577	63,585	53,549
Facilities and Training Education	43,415	36,580	31,945	43,243	34,929
Teacher Training	5,095	4,483	2,338	9,891	14,135
Primary Education	103,316	146,023	113,980	179,650	111,045
Basic Life Skills for Youth and Adults Education	9,093	13,316	8,612	11,248	3,749
Pre-School	393	614	1,383	1,164	4,717
Secondary Education	1,533	1,979	22,207	11,784	8,040
Vocational Training	558	1,083	587	4,411	4,820
Higher Education	821	1,272	1,323	20,075	2,677
Advanced Technical and Managerial Training	113	201	46	323	269
Education Total	**321,491**	**382,775**	**361,603**	**450,973**	**395,049**
Health:					
Health Poverty Reduction Budget Support	93,048	100,401	111,499	105,679	111,811
Health Unallocable/Unspecified	-	-	-	1,827	2,585
Health Policy and Administrative Management	29,482	30,850	42,888	48,784	46,829
Basic Health Care	41,682	60,379	75,595	99,652	91,566
Basic Nutrition	665	2,203	9,486	12,927	19,365
Infectious Disease Control	100,879	110,196	99,722	69,169	61,487
Health Education	12,933	11,466	16,297	19,842	19,919
Malaria Control	-	-	-	35,060	42,295
Tuberculosis Control	-	-	-	12,802	13,577
Health Personnel Development	4,436	5,033	8,709	10,918	10,368
Population Policy and Administrative Management	2,962	4,484	2,843	2,619	2,949
Reproductive Health Care	27,540	29,376	18,621	36,466	43,196
Maternal and Neonatal Health	18,740	21,898	34,394	61,645	49,376
Family Planning	-	-	-	8,075	15,252
HIV/AIDS including STD Prevention	130,915	128,698	134,229	147,863	122,036
HIV/AIDS including STD Treatment and Care	-	-	-	10,113	24,002
Personnel Development for Population and Reproductive Health	-	-	-	1,490	6,676
Health Total	**463,280**	**504,983**	**554,284**	**684,931**	**683,289**
Social Infrastructure and Services:					
Social Protection	50,522	34,962	45,458	68,656	156,911
Social Other	35,482	28,118	33,841	22,893	27,923
Employment Policy & Admin Management	-	-	-	150	623
Housing Policy and Admin Management	3,653	6,680	5,463	2,764	623
Low-cost Housing	-	-	-	564	2,226
Poverty Reduction Budget Support-Social infrastructure and services	18,016	12,878	16,250	18,647	23,319
Food Aid and Food Security Programmes	18,333	19,315	35,830	51,148	26,468
Social Infrastructure and Services Total	**126,006**	**101,952**	**136,842**	**164,822**	**283,093**
Water Supply and Sanitation:					
Water Resources Policy and Administrative Management	7,827	6,285	13,359	7,484	20,611
Water Resources Protection	-	-	-	384	1,323
Water Supply and Sanitation Large Systems	-	-	50	4,415	3,081
Water Supply – Large Systems	-	-	-	-	54
Basic Drinking Water	29,501	45,121	47,585	59,799	55,820
Basic drinking water supply	-	-	-	-	72
Basic sanitation	-	-	-	-	88
River Development	-	-	17	1,359	5,439
Waste Management and Disposal	-	-	-	110	2,900
Water Poverty Reduction Budget Support	10,816	8,950	10,610	13,325	15,556
Water Unallocable/Unspecified	-	-	-	484	718
Education and Training	-	-	8	1,108	250
Water Supply and Sanitation Total	**48,144**	**60,356**	**71,629**	**88,467**	**105,912**
Government and Civil Society:					
Government Poverty Reduction Budget Support	74,362	59,764	75,895	111,246	137,078
Government Unallocated/ Unspecified	-	-	-	11,017	26,082
Economic and Development Policy/Planning	168,858	160,380	200,057	135,931	114,791
Public Sector Financial Management	101,753	99,132	127,843	118,112	113,514
Corruption - Public Sector Financial Management	-	-	370	7,908	13,182
Legal and Judicial Development	9,721	11,670	18,025	19,147	18,469
National Government Administration	19,754	19,149	14,368	21,657	16,791
Local Government Administration	35,186	29,155	32,943	36,803	42,417
Strengthening Civil Society	123,074	143,686	153,268	172,757	89,251
Elections	16,718	13,791	21,680	30,456	18,539
Human Rights	7,249	6,405	12,308	11,591	9,084
Free Flow of Information	-	-	25	2,956	7,419
Women's Equality Organisations and Institutions	-	-	-	3,748	6,138
Culture and Recreation	-	-	-	-	143
Statistical Capacity Building	13,070	15,199	18,147	12,262	27,935

3.3 DFID Bilateral Expenditure
United Kingdom

£ Thousand

	2005 /06	2006 /07	2007 /08	2008 /09	2009 /10
Narcotics Control	36	43	30	-	46
Security System Management and Reform	15,676	7,572	14,430	13,050	13,338
Civilian Peace-Building, Conflict Prevention and Resolution	30,803	31,443	66,941	61,327	39,409
Post-Conflict Peace-Building (UN)	-	-	-	2,627	5,689
Reintegration and SALW Control	-	-	-	1,343	6,377
Land Mine Clearance	11,223	12,352	8,401	16,444	9,907
Child Soldiers (Prevention and Demobilisation)	-	-	-	375	261
Government and Civil Society Total	**627,485**	**609,742**	**764,733**	**790,756**	**715,860**

Economic:
Economic Infrastructure

	2005 /06	2006 /07	2007 /08	2008 /09	2009 /10
Transport Policy and Administrative Management	38,363	27,640	28,675	37,973	39,007
Road Transport: Excluding Rural Feeder Roads	-	-	-	623	36,408
Road Transport: Rural Feeder Roads	-	-	-	9,868	8,745
Other Transport	-	-	69	12,295	12,832
Communications Policy and Administrative Management	8,385	12,976	11,009	8,190	8,150
Telecommunications	-	-	-	73	9,439
Radio/Television/Print Media: Communications	-	-	-	788	1,872
Information and Communication Technology (ICT)	-	-	-	28	519
Energy Policy and Administrative Management	27,781	30,087	28,015	22,815	23,993
Power Generation/Non-Renewable Sources: Energy	-	-	-	23	7,439
Power Generation/Renewable Sources: Energy	-	-	-	5,023	23,513
Power generation/renewable sources: energy	-	-	-	5,020	0
Financial Policy and Administrative Management	30,359	57,333	93,991	30,268	24,223
Monetary Institutions	-	-	-	1,593	205,870
Formal Sector Financial Intermediaries	-	-	-	4,528	6,239
Informal/Semi-Formal Financial Intermediaries	-	-	-	4,105	6,250
Education/Training in Banking and Financial Services	-	-	-	1,297	2,382
Business Support Services and Institutions	-	-	28	2,912	16,947
Privatisation	27,469	18,330	26,399	17,009	5,765

Production Sectors

	2005 /06	2006 /07	2007 /08	2008 /09	2009 /10
Agriculture Policy and Administrative Management	14,729	24,493	22,739	27,519	43,937
Agricultural Development	4,612	6,844	4,755	18,122	26,089
Agricultural Land Resources	29,698	33,619	19,996	11,972	7,555
Livestock: Agriculture	1,255	3,439	3,108	4,914	3,231
Agricultural Services	-	-	-	82	1,287
Forestry Policy and Administrative Management	6,730	5,187	2,423	10,901	16,583
Forestry Development	8,788	10,433	4,930	10,962	15,320
Fishing Policy and Administrative Management	2,985	4,553	1,329	1,025	2,368
Fishery Development	1,374	1,301	543	330	201
Industrial Policy and Administrative Management	-	-	-	45	548
Industrial Development	1,723	1,109	945	126	934
Small and Medium-Sized Enterprises (SME): Development	27,441	28,652	31,006	31,730	24,765
Mineral/Mining Policy and Administrative Management	2,948	1,653	2,775	1,101	679
Construction Policy and Administrative Management	7,421	3,813	2,653	101	105
Production Poverty Reduction Budget Support	32,807	26,583	32,718	34,501	34,237
Trade Policy and Administrative Management	24,338	33,710	31,299	35,267	34,430
Trade Facilitation	-	-	-	4,015	29,745
Regional Trade Agreements (RTAs)	-	-	-	160	3,865
Multilateral Trade Negotiations	-	-	-	1,982	741
Trade Education/Training	-	-	-	31	360
Tourism Policy and Administrative Management	-	-	-	13	829
Non-Agricultural Alternative Development	28,143	4,552	252	211	550

Development Planning

	2005 /06	2006 /07	2007 /08	2008 /09	2009 /10
Poverty Reduction Budget Support for Econ. Infrastructure & Dev. Planning	66,361	59,462	71,286	83,370	108,985
Urban Development and Management	21,607	24,602	25,371	28,476	16,626
Rural Development	26,290	25,350	48,633	55,536	51,502
Economic Total	**441,607**	**445,721**	**494,945**	**526,925**	**865,063**

Environment Protection:

	2005 /06	2006 /07	2007 /08	2008 /09	2009 /10
Environmental Policy and Administrative Management	12,020	10,098	11,192	11,587	15,071
Bio-Diversity	424	153	206	1,533	1,869
Climate Change	848	3,063	6,914	30,043	54,926
Desertification	126	352	431	108	624
Site Preservation	-	-	-	10	15
Flood Prevention/Control	-	-	-	472	188
Environment: Poverty Reduction Budget Support	1,375	791	1,275	2,990	3,359
Environment Unallocable/Unspecified	-	-	-	217	38
Environmental Education/ Training	19,435	11,889	17,720	4,737	1,804
Disaster Prevention and Preparedness	-	-	-	8,838	21,450
Environment Protection Total	**34,227**	**26,347**	**37,738**	**60,536**	**99,344**

Research:

	2005 /06	2006 /07	2007 /08	2008 /09	2009 /10
Economic Research	4,182	5,369	8,016	12,182	9,784
Education Research	1,764	2,304	2,012	3,549	3,076

3.3 DFID Bilateral Expenditure
United Kingdom

£ Thousand

	2005 /06	2006 /07	2007 /08	2008 /09	2009 /10
Health Research	34,614	43,459	47,985	48,900	66,816
Water Supply and Sanitation Research	0	0	66	1,622	908
Governance Research	3,075	3,932	4,120	17,247	9,923
Social Research	3,673	5,377	9,231	10,774	11,529
Humanitarian Research	551	369	601	772	939
Renewable Natural Resources Research	32,580	26,381	26,827	29,978	20,000
Environment Research	217	3,998	5,858	4,538	5,044
Energy Research	-	-	-	26	17
Agricultural Research	-	-	-	3,141	11,397
Forestry Research	-	-	-	17	403
Fishery Research	-	-	-	0	70
Technological Research and Development	-	-	549	3,284	2,436
Unspecified/Unallocated Research	-	-	-	3,191	3,983
Research Total	**80,656**	**91,189**	**105,264**	**139,244**	**146,325**
Humanitarian Assistance:					
Material Relief Assistance and Services	313,553	288,208	302,165	174,831	232,635
Emergency Food Aid	55,687	18,073	11,591	80,354	96,986
Relief Coordination, Protection and Support Services	-	-	169	46,535	56,769
Reconstruction Relief and Rehabilitation	-	17,500	823	15,674	50,861
Humanitarian Assistance Total	**369,241**	**323,781**	**314,749**	**317,395**	**437,250**
Non Sector Allocable:					
Multilateral Capacity Building and Administration	-	-	-	1,893	27,836
Multilateral Institutions: Secondees to & Staffing of	-	-	-	485	1,163
Action Relating to Debt	60,492	110,538	86,025	19,619	50,992
Programme Partnership Agreements	-	-	-	0	129,557
Administrative Costs of Donors	-	-	53	902	559
Support to Non-Governmental Organisations (NGOs)	-	-	-	1,784	36,422
Aid to Refugees in Recipient Countries	13,480	19,881	25,281	19,479	2,348
Promotion of Development Awareness	1,176	1,981	2,453	15,279	28,372
Non Sector Allocable Total	**75,148**	**132,399**	**113,812**	**59,440**	**277,249**

Source: Department for International Development: 01355 843764

Labour market

Chapter 4

Labour Market

Labour Force Survey (Tables 4.1–4.3 and 4.7–4.11)

Background

The Labour Force Survey (LFS) is the largest regular household survey in the UK. LFS interviews are conducted continuously throughout the year. In any three-month period, nationally representative samples of approximately 110,000 people aged 16 and over in around 50,000 households are interviewed. Each household is interviewed five times, at three-monthly intervals. The initial interview is done face-to-face by an interviewer visiting the address, except for residents north of the Caledonian Canal in Scotland. The other interviews are done by telephone wherever possible. The survey asks a series of questions about respondents' personal circumstances and their labour market activity. Most questions refer to activity in the week before the interview.

The LFS collects information on a sample of the population. To convert this information to give estimates for the population, the data must be grossed. This is achieved by calculating weighting factors (often referred to simply as weights) which can be applied to each sampled individual in such a way that the weighted-up results match estimates or projections of the total population in terms of age distribution, sex, and region of residence. There is a considerable amount of ongoing research to improve methodologies. Whenever methodologies are implemented the estimates may be revised.

The concepts and definitions used in the LFS are agreed by the International Labour Organisation (ILO) – an agency of the United Nations. The definitions are used by European Union member countries and members of the Organisation for Economic Co-operation and Development (OECD). The LFS was carried out every two years from 1973 to 1983. The ILO definition was first used in 1984. This was also the first year in which the survey was conducted on an annual basis with results available for every spring quarter (representing an average of the period from March to May). The survey moved to a continuous basis in spring 1992 in Great Britain and in winter 1994/95 in Northern Ireland, with average quarterly results published four times a year for seasonal quarters: spring (March to May), summer (June to August), autumn (September to November) and winter (December to February). From April 1998, results are published 12 times a year for the average of three consecutive months.

Strengths and limitations of the LFS

The LFS produces coherent labour market information on the basis of internationally standard concepts and definitions. It is a rich source of data on a wide variety of labour market and personal characteristics. It is the most suitable source for making comparisons between countries. The LFS is designed so that households interviewed in each three month period constitute a representative sample of UK households. The survey covers those living in private households and nurses in

National Health Service accommodation. Students living in halls of residence have been included since 1992, as information about them is collected at their parents' address.

However the LFS has its limitations. It is a sample survey and is therefore subject to sampling variability. The survey does not include people living in institutions such as hostels, hotels, boarding houses, mobile home sites or residential homes. 'Proxy' reporting (when members of the household are not present at the interview, another member of the household answers the questions on their behalf) can affect the quality of information on topics such as earnings, hours worked, benefit receipt and qualifications. Around a third of interviews are conducted 'by proxy', usually by a spouse or partner but sometimes by a parent or other near relation. LFS estimates are also potentially affected by non-response.

Sampling Variability

Survey estimates are prone to sampling variability. The easiest way to explain this concept is by example. In the September to November 1997 period, ILO unemployment in Great Britain (seasonally adjusted) stood at 1,847,000. If we drew another sample for the same period we could get a different result, perhaps 1,900,000 or 1,820,000.

In theory, we could draw many samples, and each would give a different result. This is because each sample would be made up of different people who would give different answers to the questions. The spread of these results is the sampling variability. Sampling variability is determined by a number of factors including the sample size, the variability of the population from which the sample is drawn and the sample design. Once we know the sampling variability we can calculate a range of values about the sample estimate that represents the expected variation with a given level of assurance. This is called a confidence interval. For a 95 per cent confidence interval we expect that in 95 per cent of the samples (19 times out of 20) the confidence interval will contain the true value that would be obtained by surveying the entire population. For the example given above, we can be 95 per cent confident that the true value was in the range 1,791,000 to 1,903,000.

Unreliable estimates

Estimates of small numbers have relatively wide confidence intervals making them unreliable. For this reason, the Office for National Statistics (ONS) does not currently publish LFS estimates below 10,000.

Non-response

All surveys are subject to non-response – that is respondents in the sample who either refuse to take part in the survey or who cannot be contacted. Non-response can introduce bias to a survey, particularly if the people not responding have characteristics that are different from those who do respond.

The LFS has a response rate of around 65 per cent to the first interview, and over 90 per cent of those who are interviewed once go on to complete all five interviews. These are relatively high levels for a household survey.

Any bias from non-response is minimised by weighting the results. Weighting (or grossing) converts sample data to represent the full population. In the LFS, the data are weighted separately by age, sex and area of residence to population estimates based on the census. Weighting also adjusts for people not in the survey and thus minimises non-response bias.

LFS concepts and definitions

Discouraged worker - A sub-group of the economically inactive population who said although they would like a job their main reason for not seeking work was because they believed there were no jobs available.

Economically active – People aged 16 and over who are either in employment or unemployed.

Economic activity rate – The number of people who are in employment or unemployed expressed as a percentage of the relevant population.

Economically inactive – People who are neither in employment nor unemployed. These include those who want a job but have not been seeking work in the last four weeks, those who want a job and are seeking work but not available to start, and those who do not want a job.

Employment – People aged 16 and over who did at least one hour of paid work in the reference week (as an employee or self-employed), those who had a job that they were temporarily away from, those on government-supported training and employment programmes, and those doing unpaid family work.

Employees – The division between employees and self employed is based on survey respondents' own assessment of their employment status.

Full Time – The classification of employees, self-employed and unpaid family workers in their main job as full-time or part-time is on the basis of self-assessment. However, people on government supported employment and training programmes that are at college in the reference week are classified, by convention, as part-time.

Government -supported training and employment programmes – Comprise all people aged 16 and over participating in one of the government's employment and training programmes (Youth Training, Training for Work and Community Action), together with those on similar programmes administered by Training and Enterprise Councils in England and Wales, or Local Enterprise Companies in Scotland.

Hours worked – Respondents to the LFS are asked a series of questions enabling the identification of both their usual hours and their actual hours. Total hours include overtime (paid and unpaid) and exclude lunch breaks.

Actual Hours Worked – Actual hours worked statistics measure how many hours were actually worked. These statistics are directly affected by changes in the number of people in employment and in the number of hours that individual works.

Usual Hours Worked – Usual hours worked statistics measure how many hours people usually work per week. Compared with actual hours worked, they are not affected by absences and so can provide a better measure of normal working patterns.

Unemployment – The number of unemployed people in the UK is measured through the LFS following the internationally agreed definition recommended by the International Labour Organisation (ILO), an agency of the United Nations.

Unemployed people are:

Without a job, have actively sought work in the last four weeks and are available to start work in the next two weeks, or

Out of work, have found a job and are waiting to start in the next two weeks

Unemployment (rate) – The number of unemployed people expressed as a percentage of the relevant economically active population.

Unemployment (duration) – The duration of respondents unemployment is defined as the shorter of the following two periods:

Duration of active search for work

Length of time since employment

Part-time – see full-time.

Second jobs – Jobs which LFS respondents hold in addition to a main full-time or part-time job.

Self-employment – See Employees.

Temporary employees – In the LFS these are defined as those employees who say that their main job is non permanent in one of the following ways: fixed period contract, agency temping, casual work, seasonal work or other temporary work.

Unpaid family workers – Persons doing unpaid work for a business they own or for a business that a relative owns.

International Employment Comparisons (Table 4.5)

All employment rates for European Union (EU) countries published by Eurostat (including the rate for the UK) are based on the population aged 15–64. The rates for Canada and Japan are also based on the population aged 15–64, but the rate for the US is for those aged 16–64. The employment rate for the UK published by ONS is based on the working age population aged 16–64 (men) and 16–59 (women) and therefore takes into account both the current school leaving age and state pension ages.

The unemployment rate published by Eurostat for most EU countries (but not for the UK), are calculated by extrapolating from the most recent LFS data using monthly registered unemployment data. A standard population basis (15–74) is used by Eurostat except for Spain and the UK (16–74). The unemployment rate for the US is based on those aged 16 and over, but the rates for Canada and Japan are for those aged 15 and over. All unemployment rates are seasonally adjusted.

The unemployment rate for the UK published by Eurostat is based on the population aged 16–74 while the unemployment rate for the UK published by ONS is based on those aged 16 and over. There are other minor definitional differences.

Jobseekers allowance claimant count (Tables 4.9 and 4.10)

This is a count of all those people who are claiming Jobseeker's Allowance (JSA) at Jobcentre Plus local offices. People claiming JSA must declare that they are:

- out of work
- capable of work
- available for work
- actively seeking work

during the week in which the claim is made.

All people claiming JSA on the day of the monthly count are included in the claimant count, irrespective of whether they are actually receiving benefits. Also see table 5.6 in Social protection chapter.

Annual Survey of Hours and Earnings (Tables 4.12, 4.13, 4.15 and 4.16)

The Annual Survey of Hours and Earnings (ASHE) is based on a one per cent sample of employee jobs taken from HM Revenue & Customs (HMRC) PAYE records. Information on earnings and paid hours worked is obtained from employers and treated confidentially. ASHE does not cover the self-employed nor does it cover employees not paid during the reference period.

The headline statistics for ASHE are based on the median rather than the mean. The median is the value below which 50 per cent of employees fall. It is ONS's preferred measure of average earnings as it is less affected by a relatively small number of very high earners and the skewed distribution of earnings. It therefore gives a better indication of typical pay than the mean.

The earnings information presented relates to gross pay before tax, National Insurance or other deductions, and excludes payments in kind. With the exception of annual earnings, the results are restricted to earnings relating to the survey pay period and so exclude payments of arrears from another period made during the survey period; any payments due as a result of a pay settlement but not yet paid at the time of the survey will also be excluded.

More detailed information is available on the National Statistics web site at:

www.statistics.gov.uk/StatBase/Product.asp?vlnk=13101

Average Weekly Earnings (Tables 4.13 and 4.14)

The Average Weekly Earnings (AWE) indicator measures changes in the level of earnings in Great Britain. Average earnings are calculated as the total wages and salaries paid by firms, divided by the number of employees paid. It is given as a level, in pounds per employee per week. Annual growth rates are derived from the level of average weekly earnings.

Statistics are published at two levels:

Table 4.13: this includes the whole economy, the private sector, the public sector (both including and excluding financial services) and five selected sectors. The data are published including bonuses only, and are available both unadjusted and seasonally adjusted.

Table 4.14: by 24 industry groups, broadly equivalent to SIC Section level. The data are not seasonally adjusted, available both including and excluding bonuses, and available both as levels and single month annual growth rates.

The AWE data are now published on a SIC 2007 basis, and the historic time series have been re-estimated as a result. For more information, see the article available at:

www.statistics.gov.uk/downloads/theme_labour/average-week-earnings-sic2007.pdf

AWE is based on the Monthly wages and Salaries Survey (MWSS). As such, it is a timely indicator of changes in the level of earnings. The survey does not cover businesses with fewer than 20 employees; an adjustment is made to AWE to reflect these businesses. Note that the survey does not include Northern Ireland.

Unlike the previous measure of average earnings (the Average Earnings Index), changes in the composition of the workforce have an impact on AWE. If a high-paying sector of the economy employs more people, other things staying the same, average earnings will increase.

Average Weekly Earnings, like AEI before it, is a measure based on earnings per employee. If the number of paid hours worked per employee change, average earnings will also change.

Trade unions (Table 4.17)

The statistics relate to all organisations of workers known to the Certification Officer with head offices in Great Britain that fall within the appropriate definition of a trade union in the Trade Union and Labour Relations (Consolidation) Act 1992. Included in the data are home and overseas membership figures of contributory and non-contributory members. Employment status of members is not provided and the figures may therefore include some people who are self-employed, unemployed or retired.

4.1 Labour force summary:[1] by sex United Kingdom

At Quarter[2] each year[2]. Seasonally adjusted

	All aged 16 & over	Total economically active	Total in employment	Total unemployed	Economically inactive	Economic activity rate(%)	Employment rate[2] (%)	Unemployment rate[3] (%)	Economic inactivity rate[4] (%)
People									
	MGSL	MGSF	MGRZ	MGSC	MGSI	MGWG	MGSR	MGSX	YBTC
2002	46786	29450	27922	1528	17336	63.0	59.7	5.2	37.0
2003	47086	29676	28186	1489	17411	63.0	59.9	5.0	37.0
2004	47448	29909	28485	1424	17538	63.0	60.0	4.8	37.0
2005	47871	30240	28775	1466	17631	63.2	60.1	4.8	36.8
2006	48280	30699	29027	1672	17581	63.6	60.1	5.4	36.4
2007	48694	30878	29225	1652	17816	63.4	60.0	5.3	36.6
2008	49084	31221	29440	1780	17864	63.6	60.0	5.7	36.4
2009	49468	31372	28978	2394	18095	63.4	58.6	7.7	36.6
2010	49855	31518	29043	2476	18337	63.2	58.2	7.8	36.8
Men									
	MGSM	MGSG	MGSA	MGSD	MGSJ	MGWH	MGSS	MGSY	YBTD
2002	22600	16018	15098	920	6582	70.8	66.8	5.8	29.1
2003	22775	16160	15261	899	6614	71.0	67.0	5.6	29.0
2004	22978	16240	15405	836	6738	70.7	67.1	5.1	29.3
2005	23214	16398	15536	862	6816	70.6	66.9	5.3	29.4
2006	23440	16629	15661	968	6811	70.9	66.8	5.8	29.1
2007	23672	16762	15817	944	6911	70.8	66.8	5.6	29.2
2008	23896	16951	15900	1051	6945	70.9	66.5	6.2	29.1
2009	24104	16961	15496	1465	7143	70.3	64.3	8.6	29.6
2010	24318	17016	15539	1478	7302	70.0	63.9	8.7	30.0
Women									
	MGSN	MGSH	MGSB	MGSE	MGSK	MGWI	MGST	MGSZ	YBTE
2002	24186	13432	12824	609	10754	55.5	53.0	4.5	44.5
2003	24311	13515	12925	590	10796	55.6	53.1	4.4	44.4
2004	24469	13669	13081	588	10800	55.8	53.5	4.3	44.2
2005	24657	13843	13240	603	10815	56.1	53.7	4.3	43.9
2006	24840	14070	13366	704	10770	56.7	53.8	5.0	43.3
2007	25022	14116	13408	708	10906	56.4	53.6	5.0	43.6
2008	25189	14270	13541	730	10918	56.7	53.8	5.1	43.3
2009	25364	14412	13483	929	10952	56.8	53.1	6.4	43.2
2010	25537	14502	13504	998	11034	56.8	52.9	6.9	43.2

	All aged 16 to 59/64	Total economically active	Total in employment	Total unemployed	Economically inactive	Economic activity rate(%)	Employment rate(%)	Unemployment rate(%)	Economic inactivity rate(%)
People									
	YBTF	YBSK	YBSE	YBSH	YBSN	MGSO	MGSU	YBTI	YBTL
2002	36304	28542	27034	1509	7762	78.6	74.5	5.3	21.4
2003	36514	28712	27240	1472	7801	78.6	74.6	5.2	21.3
2004	36773	28893	27486	1407	7880	78.6	74.7	4.9	21.4
2005	37089	29149	27705	1444	7940	78.6	74.7	5.0	21.4
2006	37365	29510	27864	1645	7856	79.0	74.6	5.6	21.0
2007	37564	29631	28002	1629	7934	78.9	74.6	5.5	21.1
2008	37737	29874	28119	1755	7863	79.2	74.5	5.9	20.8
2009	37922	29956	27597	2359	7967	79.0	72.8	7.9	21.0
2010	38102	30003	27564	2440	8099	78.7	72.3	8.1	21.3
Men									
	YBTG	YBSL	YBSF	YBSI	YBSO	MGSP	MGSV	YBTJ	YBTM
2002	18727	15712	14801	911	3015	83.9	79.0	5.8	16.1
2003	18855	15822	14932	890	3032	83.9	79.2	5.6	16.1
2004	19010	15894	15068	826	3115	83.6	79.2	5.2	16.4
2005	19198	16027	15174	852	3170	83.5	79.1	5.3	16.5
2006	19380	16228	15271	958	3152	83.8	78.8	5.9	16.2
2007	19551	16346	15411	935	3204	83.6	78.8	5.7	16.4
2008	19691	16496	15457	1040	3195	83.8	78.5	6.3	16.2
2009	19807	16502	15053	1450	3305	83.3	76.0	8.8	16.7
2010	19914	16502	15042	1461	3412	82.9	75.5	8.9	17.1
Women									
	YBTH	YBSM	YBSG	YBSJ	YBSP	MGSQ	MGSW	YBTK	YBTN
2002	17577	12830	12232	598	4747	73.0	69.6	4.6	27.0
2003	17660	12890	12308	582	4769	73.0	69.7	4.5	27.0
2004	17763	12998	12419	580	4765	73.2	69.9	4.4	26.8
2005	17891	13123	12530	592	4768	73.3	70.0	4.5	26.7
2006	17985	13279	12590	688	4706	73.8	70.0	5.2	26.1
2007	18014	13284	12590	694	4730	73.7	69.9	5.2	26.3
2008	18046	13376	12660	716	4670	74.1	70.2	5.3	25.9
2009	18116	13452	12542	910	4664	74.3	69.2	6.8	25.7
2010	18188	13501	12524	978	4686	74.2	68.8	7.2	25.8

1. The Labour Force Survey (LFS) is a survey of the population of private households, student halls of residence and NHS accommodation.
2. The headline employment rate is the number of working age people (aged 16 to 59 for women and 16 to 64 for men) in employment divided by the working age population.

3. The headline unemployment rate is the number unemployed people (aged 16+) divided by the economically active population (aged 16+). The economically active population is defined as those in employment plus those who are unemployed.
4. The headline inactivity rate is the number of working age inactive people (aged 16 to 59 for women and 16 to 64 for men) divided by the work population.

Sources: Labour Force Survey: Office for National Statistics
Helpline: 01633 456901

4.2 Employment status: full-time, part-time and temporary employees United Kingdom

United Kingdom
Seasonally adjusted

	All in employment					Total employment[1]		Employees[1]		Self-employed[1]		
	Total	Employees	Self employed	Unpaid family workers	Government supported training and employment programmes	Full-time	Part-time	Full-time	Part-time	Full-time	Part-time	Workers with jobs
People												
	MGRZ	MGRN	MGRQ	MGRT	MGRW	YCBE	YCBH	YCBK	YCBN	YCBQ	YCBT	YCBW
2002	27922	24386	3337	95	103	20809	7112	18173	6213	2564	772	1150
2003	28186	24427	3565	94	100	20915	7271	18116	6311	2730	834	1116
2004	28485	24645	3618	97	124	21131	7354	18264	6380	2788	830	1073
2005	28775	24928	3636	96	114	21484	7290	18596	6332	2811	825	1058
2006	29027	25097	3738	97	98	21642	7388	18711	6386	2864	874	1054
2007	29225	25208	3808	101	110	21802	7424	18844	6364	2892	915	1100
2008	29440	25407	3826	101	108	21933	7509	18964	6443	2912	914	1123
2009	28978	24937	3850	87	106	21362	7618	18422	6515	2887	963	1138
2010	29043	24862	3961	94	128	21178	7865	18196	6665	2929	1032	1108
Men												
	MGSA	MGRO	MGRR	MGRU	MGRX	YCBF	YCBI	YCBL	YCBO	YCBR	YCBU	YCBX
2002	15098	12558	2444	33	63	13606	1492	11430	1129	2131	313	480
2003	15261	12566	2604	34	58	13691	1570	11388	1178	2259	345	461
2004	15405	12634	2659	39	73	13776	1628	11413	1222	2313	346	456
2005	15536	12768	2666	35	66	13887	1648	11517	1250	2322	344	455
2006	15661	12856	2711	38	58	13976	1688	11578	1278	2355	356	452
2007	15817	12954	2764	39	61	14074	1745	11654	1301	2380	383	455
2008	15900	13017	2780	37	67	14078	1824	11648	1370	2394	386	461
2009	15496	12657	2747	34	59	13635	1862	11253	1404	2351	396	488
2010	15539	12630	2794	40	76	13547	1992	11152	1478	2362	431	459
Women												
	MGSB	MGRP	MGRS	MGRV	MGRY	YCBG	YCBJ	YCBM	YCBP	YCBS	YCBV	YCBY
2002	12824	11827	893	62	40	7203	5620	6743	5084	434	459	670
2003	12925	11861	960	60	42	7224	5700	6728	5133	471	490	656
2004	13081	12011	960	58	51	7354	5726	6852	5159	476	484	617
2005	13240	12161	970	61	48	7598	5642	7079	5082	489	480	603
2006	13366	12240	1028	60	40	7666	5700	7133	5107	510	518	602
2007	13408	12253	1044	62	48	7728	5680	7190	5063	512	532	645
2008	13541	12390	1046	64	42	7856	5685	7317	5073	517	528	662
2009	13483	12280	1103	53	46	7726	5756	7168	5111	536	567	650
2010	13504	12232	1167	54	52	7631	5873	7044	5188	566	601	649

	Temporary employees (reason for temporary working)							Part-time workers (reasons for working part-time)[2]					
	Total	Total as % of all employees	Could not find permanent job	% that could not find permanent job	Did not want a permanent job	Had a contract with period of training	Some other reason	Total[3]	Could not find full-time job	% that could not find full-time job	Did not want a full time job	ill or disabled	Student or at school
People													
	YCBZ	YCCC	YCCF	YCCI	YCCL	YCCO	YCCR	YCCU	YCCX	YCDA	YCDD	YCDG	YCDJ
2002	1587	6.5	423	26.7	467	82	613	6985	570	8.2	5148	138	1100
2003	1516	6.2	398	26.3	455	86	576	7145	567	8	5255	156	1134
2004	1509	6.1	384	25.5	430	98	597	7211	549	7.6	5291	176	1163
2005	1444	5.8	362	25	389	100	593	7157	588	8.2	5222	167	1147
2006	1479	5.9	374	25.3	428	102	576	7260	639	8.8	5221	181	1180
2007	1500	5.9	396	26.4	428	93	583	7280	690	9.4	5228	175	1152
2008	1399	5.5	360	25.7	404	85	550	7357	716	9.7	5246	197	1154
2009	1430	5.7	452	31.6	376	82	520	7478	971	12.9	5163	186	1114
2010	1537	6.2	562	36.6	363	86	526	7697	1120	14.6	5231	166	1134
Men													
	YCCA	YCCD	YCCG	YCCJ	YCCM	YCCP	YCCS	YCCV	YCCY	YCDB	YCDE	YCDH	YCDK
2002	721	5.8	233	32.3	186	43	260	1442	233	16.2	650	60	488
2003	697	5.5	225	32.2	185	38	250	1523	249	16.4	705	69	489
2004	709	5.6	222	31.3	175	47	264	1567	246	15.7	745	69	498
2005	681	5.3	204	30	169	52	256	1594	236	14.8	769	74	504
2006	678	5.2	197	29	177	52	252	1634	264	16.1	775	74	511
2007	700	5.4	211	30.1	186	44	258	1685	284	16.9	819	74	495
2008	641	4.9	184	28.8	164	44	248	1756	308	17.5	853	76	503
2009	677	5.3	243	36	152	43	240	1800	432	24	795	78	478
2010	736	5.8	296	40.2	153	45	242	1908	490	25.6	840	70	496
Women													
	YCCB	YCCE	YCCH	YCCK	YCCN	YCCQ	YCCT	YCCW	YCCZ	YCDC	YCDF	YCDI	YCDL
2002	866	7.3	190	22	282	40	354	5544	337	6.1	4498	78	611
2003	819	6.9	174	21.2	270	49	326	5622	318	5.6	4550	86	645
2004	800	6.7	162	20.3	254	51	332	5644	302	5.3	4546	108	666
2005	763	6.2	158	20.7	220	48	338	5562	353	6.4	4454	93	643
2006	802	6.6	177	22.1	251	50	324	5625	376	6.7	4446	106	670
2007	801	6.6	186	23.1	242	49	325	5595	406	7.2	4408	100	658
2008	758	6.1	176	23.1	240	41	301	5602	409	7.3	4393	120	651
2009	753	6.1	209	27.8	224	40	280	5678	540	9.5	4368	108	637
2010	801	6.6	266	33.2	210	41	284	5788	631	10.9	4391	96	638

1. The split between full-time and part-time employment is based on repondents self-classification

2. These series cover employees and self-employed only.

3. The total inculdes those who did not give a reason for working part-time

4.3 Employment: by sex and age United Kingdom

Seasonally adjusted

Thousands and percentages

	All aged 16 and over	16-59/64	16-17	18-24	25-34	35-49	50-64 (m) 50-59 (w)	65+ (m) 60+ (w)
In Employment								
People								
	MGRZ	YBSE	YBTO	YBTR	YBTU	YBTX	MGUW	MGUZ
2003	28186	27240	652	3414	6362	10592	6221	946
2004	28485	27486	642	3527	6283	10742	6293	998
2005	28775	27705	607	3538	6297	10886	6379	1070
2006	29027	27864	559	3617	6260	10976	6452	1166
2007	29225	28002	535	3656	6256	11040	6516	1224
2008	29440	28119	524	3653	6292	11060	6590	1324
2009	28978	27597	429	3449	6222	10916	6580	1383
2010	29043	27564	376	3418	6366	10775	6632	1476
Men								
	MGSA	YBSF	YBTP	YBTS	YBTV	YBTY	MGUX	MGVA
2003	15261	14932	316	1802	3473	5658	3682	330
2004	15405	15068	309	1868	3417	5743	3730	337
2005	15536	15174	293	1879	3432	5781	3789	361
2006	15661	15271	260	1912	3422	5845	3830	390
2007	15817	15411	257	1942	3446	5880	3886	406
2008	15900	15457	260	1923	3455	5869	3949	443
2009	15496	15053	196	1788	3404	5744	3920	443
2010	15539	15042	170	1789	3494	5668	3920	497
Women								
	MGSB	YBSG	YBTQ	YBTT	YBTW	YBTZ	MGUY	MGVB
2003	12925	12308	336	1612	2889	4933	2539	616
2004	13081	12419	333	1659	2866	4999	2562	661
2005	13240	12530	314	1659	2865	5105	2589	709
2006	13366	12590	298	1705	2838	5130	2619	776
2007	13408	12590	278	1714	2811	5160	2627	818
2008	13541	12660	264	1730	2837	5190	2639	881
2009	13483	12542	233	1661	2818	5172	2658	940
2010	13504	12524	206	1630	2872	5106	2710	980
Employment rates(%)								
People								
	MGSR	MGSU	YBUA	YBUD	YBUG	YBUJ	YBUM	YBUP
2003	59.9	74.6	42.7	66.5	79.5	82.1	69.6	8.9
2004	60.0	74.7	41.2	66.9	79.7	82.2	70.0	9.4
2005	60.1	74.7	38.6	65.5	80.2	82.4	70.4	9.9
2006	60.1	74.6	35.6	65.5	80.1	82.3	70.8	10.7
2007	60.0	74.6	33.7	64.8	80.3	82.3	71.3	11.0
2008	60.0	74.5	33.1	63.8	80.3	82.4	71.8	11.6
2009	58.6	72.8	27.6	59.5	78.3	81.5	71.3	12.0
2010	58.2	72.3	24.8	58.6	78.4	80.9	71.2	12.6
Men								
	MGSS	MGSV	YBUB	YBUE	YBUH	YBUK	YBUN	YBUQ
2003	67.0	79.2	40.3	69.8	87.6	88.7	71.6	8.4
2004	67.1	79.2	38.7	70.1	87.4	89.0	72.0	8.5
2005	66.9	79.1	36.4	68.8	88.2	88.5	72.4	9.0
2006	66.8	78.8	32.2	68.2	88.1	88.7	72.3	9.6
2007	66.8	78.8	31.5	67.7	88.7	88.8	72.6	9.9
2008	66.5	78.5	32.0	66.0	87.9	88.6	73.0	10.6
2009	64.3	76.0	24.6	60.7	85.1	86.9	71.8	10.3
2010	63.9	75.5	21.9	60.3	85.3	86.3	71.2	11.3
Women								
	MGST	MGSW	YBUC	YBUF	YBUI	YBUL	YBUO	YBUR
2003	53.1	69.7	45.1	63.1	71.6	75.6	66.8	9.2
2004	53.5	69.9	43.8	63.7	72.1	75.7	67.2	9.9
2005	53.7	70.0	41.0	62.2	72.3	76.4	67.8	10.5
2006	53.8	70.0	39.0	62.7	72.2	76.0	68.6	11.3
2007	53.6	69.9	36.1	62.0	72.0	75.9	69.5	11.7
2008	53.8	70.2	34.2	61.5	72.7	76.3	70.2	12.4
2009	53.1	69.2	30.8	58.2	71.4	76.2	70.4	13.0
2010	52.9	68.8	27.9	56.7	71.4	75.8	71.1	13.4

1. See chapter text.
Denominator = all persons in the relevant age group

Sources: Labour Force Survey, Office for National Statistics;
Helpline: 01633 456901

4.4a Employee jobs: by industry[1,2] Standard Industrial Classification 2007

At June each year. Not seasonally adjusted

Thousands

	SIC 2007	United Kingdom					Great Britain				
		2006	2007	2008	2009	2010	2006	2007	2008	2009	2010
All sections	A-S	27,273	27,418	27,645	27,053	26,627	26,568	26,699	26,912	26,344	25,932
Index of production and construction industries	B-F										
Index of production industries	B-E										
of which, manufacturing industries	C										
Service industries	G-S	22,605	22,787	23,111	22,714	22,393	22,046	22,217	22,527	22,138	21,824
Agriculture, forestry and fishing	A	236	230	232	213	257	224	218	220	201	245
Agriculture hunting & related activities	01	220	214	213	199	243	208	202	202	187	232
Forestry and logging	02	10	10	12	10	9	10	10	12	10	8
Fishing and aquaculture	03	6	6	7	5	5	6	6	7	5	5
Mining and quarrying	B	57	60	59	56	51	55	58	56	54	49
Mining of coal and lignite; extraction of crude petrol/gas	05-06	17	19	18	18	14	17	19	18	18	14
Mining of metal ores; other mining and quarrying	07-08	23	24	23	20	18	21	22	20	18	16
Mining support service activities	09	17	17	18	18	19	17	17	18	18	19
Manufacturing	C	2,780	2,739	2,643	2,442	2,363	2,697	2,655	2,559	2,366	2,290
Processing and preserving of meat products	10.1-5	..	..	..	..	..	153	153	147	132	132
Manufacture of grain mill, bakery and other food products	10.6-8	..	..	..	..	..	192	190	183	179	194
Manufacture of prepared animal feeds	10.9	..	..	..	..	..	12	13	13	13	13
Manufacture of beverages and tobacco	11-12	45	45	44	41	42	44	43	42	40	40
Manufacture of textiles	13	67	63	59	54	61	65	61	57	52	60
Manufacture of wearing apparel	14	40	39	35	28	26	38	37	34	27	25
Manufacture of leather and related products	15	11	9	10	9	7	11	9	10	9	7
Manufacture of wood and wood and cork products	16	74	79	72	63	64	70	75	69	60	61
Manufacture of paper and paper products	17	67	65	60	52	49	65	63	58	51	47
Printing and reproduction of recorded media	18	165	161	149	134	125	163	159	147	133	123
Manufacture of coke and refined petroleum products	19	8	9	9	9	8	8	9	9	9	8
Manufacture of chemicals and chemical products	20	132	126	113	106	102	131	124	111	104	101
Manufacture of basic pharmaceutical products	21	55	50	44	36	32	53	48	43	35	30
Manufacture of rubber and plastic products	22	197	186	177	155	168	190	179	170	149	161
Manufacture of other non-metallic mineral products	23	107	106	103	93	96	101	100	97	88	91
Manufacture of basic metals	24	86	83	83	81	65	86	83	82	81	64
Manufacture of fabricated metal products	25	314	314	323	316	300	306	306	315	309	293

4.4b Employee jobs: by industry[1,2] Standard Industrial Classification 2007

At June each year. Not seasonally adjusted

Thousands

	SIC 2007	United Kingdom					Great Britain				
		2006	2007	2008	2009	2010	2006	2007	2008	2009	2010
Manufacture of computer, electronic and optical products	26	149	155	146	127	118	144	150	141	123	115
Manufacture of electrical equipment	27	98	96	89	76	69	94	91	85	73	65
Manufacture of machinery and equipment not elsewhere classified	28	210	217	205	167	151	205	211	199	163	147
Manufacture of motor vehicles, trailers and semi-trailers	29	181	168	165	138	133	177	165	162	135	130
Manufacture of other transport equipment	30	111	118	119	130	127	103	111	112	123	120
Manufacture of furniture	31	89	90	84	85	82	86	87	81	82	80
Other manufacturing	32	92	90	88	92	89	90	89	86	90	88
Repair and installation of machinery and equipment	33	109	98	108	107	96	109	98	108	107	95
Electricity, gas, steam and air conditioning supply	D	75	83	80	107	132	73	81	79	106	130
Water supply, sewerage, waste and remediation activities	E	151	150	159	156	147	146	146	154	151	143
Water collection, treatment and supply	36	28	33	32	33	25	27	32	31	33	25
Sewerage	37	18	18	18	16	21	17	17	18	16	21
Waste collection, treatment and disposal; Remediation	38-39	106	99	109	107	101	102	96	105	103	97
Construction	F	1,370	1,369	1,361	1,365	1,284	1,327	1,324	1,316	1,327	1,250
Development of building projects	41.1	..	..	..	..	..	78	78	83	74	79
Construction of residential and non-residential buildings	41.2	..	..	..	..	..	294	300	256	316	274
Civil engineering	42	250	252	253	234	187	242	243	243	225	179
Specialised construction activities	43	735	727	756	730	735	713	704	734	712	718
Services	G-S	22,605	22,787	23,111	22,714	22,393	22,046	22,217	22,527	22,138	21,824
Wholesale and retail trade; repair of motor vehicles and motorcycles	G	4,510	4,530	4,567	4,426	4,301	4,388	4,405	4,438	4,299	4,180
Sale of motor vehicles	45.1	..	..	..	..	..	208	212	187	157	171
Maintenance and repair of motor vehicles	45.2	..	..	..	..	..	170	168	182	175	172
Sale of motor vehicle parts; sale and repair of motorcycles	45.3-4	..	..	..	..	..	117	118	114	112	98
Wholesale on a fee or contract basis	46.1	..	..	..	..	..	64	69	67	51	54
Wholesale of agricultural raw materials and live animals	46.2	..	..	..	..	..	19	19	20	26	25
Wholesale of food beverages & tobacco	46.3	..	..	..	..	..	195	194	206	192	184
Wholesale of household goods	46.4	..	..	..	..	..	266	266	261	262	238
Wholesale of information and communication equipment	46.5	..	..	..	..	..	81	82	82	83	82
Wholesale of other machinery, equipment and supplies	46.6	..	..	..	..	..	154	157	156	154	155
Other specialised wholesale	46.7	..	..	..	..	..	240	252	256	248	258
Non-specialised wholesale trade	46.9	..	..	..	..	..	87	85	81	69	80

4.4c Employee jobs: by industry[1,2] Standard Industrial Classification 2007

At June each year. Not seasonally adjusted

Thousands

	SIC 2007	United Kingdom					Great Britain				
		2006	2007	2008	2009	2010	2006	2007	2008	2009	2010
Retail sale in non-specialised stores with food, beverages and tobacco	47.11	..	..	..	..	..	977	970	1,002	1,031	1,024
Other retail in non-specialised stores	47.19	..	..	..	..	..	210	223	226	235	248
Retail sale of food, beverages and tobacco in specialised stores	47.2	..	..	..	..	..	173	154	148	145	123
Retail sale of automotive fuel in specialised stores	47.3	..	..	..	..	..	52	49	45	30	31
Retail sale of information and communication equipment	47.4	..	..	..	..	..	62	57	59	66	70
Retail sale of other household equipment in specialised stores	47.5	..	..	..	..	..	299	302	303	267	235
Retail sale of cultural and recreation goods in specialised stores	47.6	..	..	..	..	..	137	142	140	131	127
Retail sale of clothing, footwear and leather goods in specialised stores	47.71-72	..	..	..	..	..	413	431	429	416	383
Retail sale of other goods in specialised stores	47.73-89	..	..	..	..	..	381	379	389	371	347
Retail trade not in stores, stalls or markets	47.9	..	..	..	..	..	83	75	85	77	75
Transport and storage	H	1,259	1,279	1,283	1,239	1,216	1,235	1,254	1,258	1,214	1,191
Passenger rail transport, interurban; freight rail transport	49.1-2	..	..	..	..	..	52	54	53	51	51
Other passenger land transport	49.3	..	..	..	..	..	217	219	213	236	214
Freight transport by road and removal services; transport via pipeline	49.4-5	..	..	..	..	..	264	270	271	226	190
Water transport	50	17	17	17	16	14	17	17	16	15	14
Air transport	51	88	89	82	75	71	88	89	81	74	70
Warehousing and support activities for transportation	52	336	347	369	350	342	333	343	364	345	337
Postal and courier services	53	271	268	265	272	320	265	263	260	267	314
Accommodation and food service activities	I	1,862	1,841	1,885	1,828	1,747	1,819	1,798	1,842	1,786	1,705
Hotels and similar accommodation	55.1	..	..	..	..	..	322	328	320	298	301
Holiday and other short stay accommodation	55.2-9	..	..	..	..	..	64	63	61	65	64
Restaurants and mobile food service activities	56.1	..	..	..	..	..	646	636	662	669	638
Event catering and other food service activities	56.2	..	..	..	..	..	238	225	261	228	195
Beverage serving activities	56.3	..	..	..	..	..	549	546	538	525	507
Information and communication	J	1,013	1,016	1,025	1,013	954	998	1,000	1,009	998	939
Publishing activities	58	161	159	151	156	147	159	157	149	154	145
Motion picture, video and television; sound and music recording	59	85	87	92	83	82	84	86	90	82	81
Programming and broadcasting activities	60	26	28	28	23	23	25	27	26	22	22
Telecommunications	61	221	217	204	212	198	217	213	200	209	195
Computer programming, consultancy and related activities	62	465	466	492	481	439	458	459	484	473	432
Information service activities	63	56	58	58	58	66	55	57	58	58	66
Financial and insurance activities	K	1,099	1,108	1,128	1,105	1,044	1,080	1,089	1,108	1,085	1,025
Monetary intermediation	64.1	..	..	..	..	..	478	471	481	468	434
Activities of holding companies; trust funds; other financial activities	64.2-9	..	..	..	..	..	140	128	136	109	85

4.4d Employee jobs: by industry[1,2] Standard Industrial Classification 2007

At June each year. Not seasonally adjusted

Thousands

	SIC 2007	United Kingdom					Great Britain				
		2006	2007	2008	2009	2010	2006	2007	2008	2009	2010
Insurance, reinsurance and pension funding	65	163	165	137	121	93	161	162	135	119	91
Activities auxiliary to financial services and insurance activities	66	304	331	361	394	419	301	327	357	390	415
Real estate activities	L	325	351	388	397	389	318	344	381	390	382
Buying and selling of own real estate	68.1-2	..	..	..	..	..	163	166	187	198	183
Real estate activities on a fee or contract basis	68.3	..	..	..	..	..	155	178	194	192	199
Professional, scientific and technical activities	M	1,724	1,790	1,840	1,831	1,827	1,701	1,767	1,816	1,808	1,804
Legal activities	69.1	..	..	..	..	..	281	296	283	257	238
Accounting, bookkeeping and auditing activities; tax consultancy	69.2	..	..	..	..	..	228	242	230	238	233
Activities of head offices; management consultancy	70	412	421	457	478	529	410	419	455	476	527
Architectural and engineering activities; technical testing and analysis	71	352	372	407	412	395	347	367	400	406	390
Scientific research and development	72	107	114	112	123	115	105	113	110	121	113
Advertising and market research	73	138	147	148	139	133	137	146	147	138	132
Other professional, scientific and technical activities	74	152	146	153	132	130	151	144	151	130	129
Veterinary activities	75	44	42	41	42	44	42	40	40	41	43
Administrative and support service activities	N	2,163	2,258	2,324	2,069	2,040	2,126	2,219	2,280	2,028	2,000
Rental and leasing activities	77	168	166	161	138	133	166	164	159	136	131
Activities of employment placement agencies	78.1	..	..	..	..	..	152	180	214	151	161
Temporary employment agency activities; other human resources	78.2-3	..	..	..	..	..	601	621	659	571	580
Travel agency, tour operator, reservation services and related activities	79	114	113	110	97	72	113	112	108	96	71
Security and investigation activities	80	175	179	187	190	195	171	174	182	184	190
Services to buildings and landscape activities	81	558	564	593	603	599	549	555	582	592	589
Office administrative, office support and other business support	82	380	418	383	305	287	375	412	376	298	279
Public administration and defence; compulsory social security	O	1,553	1,548	1,512	1,535	1,525	1,493	1,490	1,454	1,476	1,466
Education	P	2,437	2,438	2,447	2,474	2,477	2,364	2,364	2,376	2,401	2,403
Human health and social work activities	Q	3,377	3,372	3,448	3,572	3,684	3,267	3,258	3,333	3,456	3,568
Human health activities	86	1,959	1,940	2,001	2,082	2,114	1,889	1,868	1,930	2,010	2,042
Residential care activities	87	637	654	632	616	627	626	643	620	604	615
Social work activities without accommodation	88	781	778	814	874	943	751	747	783	842	912
Arts, entertainment and recreation	R	679	658	675	655	657	666	644	661	640	642
Creative, arts and entertainment activities	90	90	84	81	68	65	89	83	80	68	64
Libraries, archives, museums and other cultural activities	91	112	113	113	108	103	110	111	110	105	101
Gambling and betting activities	92	105	103	102	91	84	103	100	100	88	82
Sports activities and amusement and recreation activities	93	371	358	379	388	405	363	350	371	379	396
Other service activities	S	604	598	587	570	532	590	585	573	556	519
Activities of membership organisations	94	241	226	211	225	237	232	218	203	216	229
Repair of computers and personal and household goods	95	41	42	39	40	41	41	42	39	40	40
Washing and (dry-) cleaning of textile and fur products	96.01	..	..	..	..	..	44	41	36	30	24
Hairdressing and other beauty treatment	96.02	..	..	..	..	..	102	114	118	112	96
Funeral and related activities	96.03	..	..	..	..	..	24	23	23	25	20
Physical well-being activities; other personal service activities	96.04-9	..	..	..	..	..	148	147	154	132	110

Note. Because the figures have been rounded independently totals may differ from the sum of the components. Also the totals may include some employees whose industrial classification could not be ascertained.
1. See chapter text. The data in this table have not been adjusted to reflect the 2001 Census population data.
2. All figures have been revised. For further information see: http://www.statistics.gov.uk/StatBase/Product.asp?vlnk=9765

Sources: Employer surveys and Labour Force Survey
Business Statistics Division, ONS: 01633 456776

4.5 International comparisons
Employment and unemployment rates[1,2]

		2007 Q3	2007 Q4	2008 Q1	2008 Q2	2008 Q3	2008 Q4	2009 Q1	2009 Q2	2009 Q3	2009 Q4	2010 Q1	2010 Q2	2010 Q3	2010 Q4
EUROSTAT Employment rates															
Austria	**YXSN**	72.5	71.3	71	72.3	72.8	72.2	70.8	71.7	72.3	71.6	70.6	71.4	72.6	..
Belgium	**YXSO**	62.1	62.7	62.6	62	62.6	62.4	61.7	61.5	61.4	61.8	61.9	61.5	62	..
Bulgaria	**A495**	62.7	62.9	62.6	63.9	65	64.3	62.6	63.3	63.1	61.2	58.8	60.2	60.6	..
Cyprus	**A4AC**	71.3	71.5	70.2	71.1	71	71.1	69.5	70.2	70	70	68.8	69.8	70	..
Czech Republic	**A4AD**	66.3	66.5	66.1	66.6	66.7	66.8	65.6	65.4	65.2	65.3	64.1	64.9	65.4	..
Denmark	**YXSP**	77.1	77.4	76.8	78.3	78.5	78.1	76.2	76.2	76.3	74.2	73	74.1	73.8	72.9
Estonia	**A4AE**	70.2	69.1	69.5	69.8	70.4	69.6	65.3	63.8	63.4	61.7	58.9	59.5	62.1	..
Finland	**YXSQ**	71.7	69.9	69.5	72.3	72.1	70.3	68.5	69.8	69.3	67.3	66.5	69.2	69.3	..
France	**YXSR**	64.9	64.5	64.6	65.1	65.3	64.7	64.1	64.5	64.4	63.5	63.6	64.2	64.4	..
Germany	**YXSS**	69.9	70	70	70.3	71.3	71.3	70.4	70.8	71	71.6	70.2	71	71.5	..
Greece	**YXST**	61.8	61.5	61.3	62.2	62.2	61.7	61	61.6	61.7	60.8	60.1	60.1	59.7	..
Hungary	**A4AF**	57.7	57.1	56.1	56.5	57.3	56.7	55.1	55.6	55.5	55.5	54.5	55.3	56	..
Ireland	**YXSU**	70	69	68.5	68.1	68	65.6	62.8	62.2	61.8	60.6	59.7	60.4	60.3	..
Italy	**YXSV**	59.1	58.7	58.3	59.2	59	58.5	57.4	57.9	57.5	57.1	56.6	57.2	56.7	..
Latvia	**A4AG**	69	70.3	69.6	69.5	69	66.5	64.3	61.4	59.8	58.4	57.7	58.9	60.6	..
Lithuania	**A4AH**	66.1	64.4	63.9	64.6	65	63.8	61	60.3	60.4	58.7	56.8	56.7	58.5	59.2
Luxembourg	**YXSW**	64.7	64.4	62.8	64.4	63.9	62.6	64.5	65.7	65.8	64.8	64.8	64.6	66.1	..
Malta	**A4AI**	54.9	54.5	54.7	55.2	56.1	55	54.9	54.9	55.1	54.9	55.3	55.9	56.8	..
Netherlands	**YXSX**	76.5	76.4	76.4	77.2	77.5	77.6	77.4	77	77	76.5	75.8	76.3	74.9	..
Poland	**A4AJ**	57.8	58.1	58	58.9	60	60	58.9	59.3	59.9	59.4	58.2	59.3	60	..
Portugal	**YXSY**	68.1	68.1	68.1	68.6	68.1	67.9	67	66.7	65.8	65.7	65.8	65.7	65.5	65.2
Romania	**A494**	60.5	57.9	57.7	59.7	60.5	58.3	57.4	59.2	60.4	57.4	57	60.1	60.2	..
Slovak Republic	**A4AK**	60.7	61.6	61.3	61.7	63.1	62.9	61	60.4	60.1	59.2	58	58.6	59.2	..
Slovenia	**A4AL**	69	67.7	67.1	68.3	70.1	68.8	66.7	67.6	68.3	67.5	66.3	66.5	66.3	..
Spain	**YXSZ**	66	65.5	65.1	65	64.5	62.8	60.4	59.9	59.7	59	58.3	58.6	58.9	58.4
Sweden	**YXTA**	75.7	74	73.4	74.8	75.7	73.4	71.9	72.7	72.9	71.3	71	72.9	74.1	72.9
United Kingdom	**ANZ6**	71.6	71.9	71.6	71.6	71.5	71.3	70.4	69.6	69.8	69.7	69	69.3	70	..
Total EU3	**A496**	66	65.7	65.5	66	66.4	65.8	64.6	64.8	64.8	64.3	63.6	64.3	64.6	..
Eurozone[3]	**YXTC**	66.1	65.9	65.7	66.2	66.4	65.8	64.7	64.9	64.8	64.5	63.8	64.3	64.4	..
National Statistical Offices Employment Rates															
Canada	**IUUK**	74.5	73.6	72.5	74.2	74.5	73.3	70.7	71.9	72.1	71.2	69.9	72.1	72.5	71.7
Japan	**YXTF**	70.8	70.9	70	71.3	70.8	70.9	69.8	70.2	70.1	70	69.6	70.2	70.3	70.3
United Kingdom	**MGSU**	74.6	74.8	74.8	74.8	74.4	74	73.5	72.7	72.5	72.4	72	72.4	72.6	72.3
United States	**YXTE**	71.6	71.5	71.7	71.4	70.7	69.8	68.7	68	67.3	66.5	66.7	66.9	66.7	66.4

4.5 International comparisons
Employment and unemployment rates[1,2]

		2009 Dec	2010 Jan	2010 Feb	2010 Mar	2010 Apr	2010 May	2010 Jun	2010 Jul	2010 Aug	2010 Sep	2010 Oct	2010 Nov	2010 Dec	2011 Jan
EUROSTAT Unemployment rates															
Austria	ZXDS	4.6	4.5	4.6	4.6	4.6	4.5	4.4	4.4	4.4	4.3	4.2	4.2	4.2	4.3
Belgium	ZXDI	8.2	8.3	8.4	8.4	8.4	8.4	8.4	8.5	8.4	8.3	8.3	8.2	8.1	8
Bulgaria	A492	8.6	9	9.4	9.7	9.9	10	10	10	10	10.1	10	10.1	10.1	10.2
Cyprus	A4AN	6.1	6.1	6.3	6.5	6.7	6.9	7	6.9	7	7	7.1	7.2	7.3	7.4
Czech Republic	A4AO	7.4	7.7	7.8	7.8	7.5	7.3	7.2	7.1	7.1	7.1	7.2	7.3	7.7	7.5
Denmark	ZXDJ	7.1	7.1	7.2	7.4	7.5	7.4	7.5	7.3	7.3	7.5	7.6	7.7	7.8	..
Estonia	A4AP	16.1	18.9	18.9	18.9	18	18	18	15.9	15.9	15.9	14.3	14.3	14.3	..
Finland	ZXDU	8.8	8.8	8.7	8.7	8.6	8.5	8.4	8.4	8.3	8.2	8.1	8	8	8
France	ZXDN	9.9	9.9	9.8	9.8	9.8	9.8	9.8	9.7	9.7	9.7	9.7	9.7	9.7	9.6
Germany	ZXDK	7.4	7.3	7.3	7.1	7	6.9	6.8	6.7	6.7	6.6	6.6	6.6	6.6	6.5
Greece	ZXDL	10.2	11	11	11	12.2	12.2	12.2	12.9	12.9	12.9	..	..	..	..
Hungary	A4AQ	10.8	11	11	11.1	11.2	11.1	11.2	11.2	11.1	11.2	11.4	11.5	11.8	12.6
Ireland	ZXDO	12.9	12.8	12.8	13	13.3	13.6	13.6	13.6	13.7	13.9	13.9	13.8	13.7	13.5
Italy	ZXDP	8.4	8.3	8.4	8.5	8.5	8.6	8.4	8.4	8.4	8.5	8.7	8.6	8.6	8.6
Latvia	A4AR	19.9	20	20	20	19.4	19.4	19.4	18.3	18.3	18.3	..	..	..	..
Lithuania	A4AS	15.9	17.3	17.3	17.3	18.2	18.2	18.2	18.3	18.3	18.3	17.4	17.4	17.4	
Luxembourg	ZXDQ	4.8	4.6	4.7	4.6	4.6	4.6	4.7	4.7	4.7	4.7	4.7	4.8	4.8	4.7
Malta	A4AT	7.3	7.2	7.2	7	7	7	6.7	6.6	6.6	6.4	6.4	6.2	6.2	6.1
Netherlands	ZXDR	4.4	4.5	4.5	4.5	4.5	4.5	4.5	4.6	4.5	4.4	4.4	4.4	4.3	4.3
Poland	A4AU	9.1	9.5	9.7	9.8	9.6	9.6	9.6	9.6	9.6	9.6	9.7	9.7	9.7	9.7
Portugal	ZXDT	10.2	10.5	10.5	10.7	10.9	11.1	11.1	11.1	11.1	11.2	11.2	11.2	11.2	11.2
Romania	A48Z	7.6	7.3	7.3	7.3	7.1	7.1	7.1	7.3	7.3	7.3	..	..	..	..
Slovak Republic	A4AV	14.3	14.5	14.6	14.6	14.5	14.5	14.5	14.4	14.4	14.5	14.5	14.5	14.5	14.5
Slovenia	A4AW	6.4	6.5	6.7	6.9	7.2	7.3	7.4	7.2	7.3	7.3	7.5	7.5	7.7	7.8
Spain	ZXDM	19.1	19.2	19.3	19.6	19.8	20	20.2	20.3	20.5	20.6	20.6	20.5	20.4	20.4
Sweden	ZXDV	9	8.9	8.8	8.5	9	8.7	8.1	8.4	8.2	8.2	8.1	7.8	7.8	7.9
United Kingdom	ZXDW	7.7	7.9	7.9	7.8	7.8	7.7	7.8	7.7	7.7	7.8	7.8	7.8	..	..
Total EU3	A493	9.5	9.5	9.6	9.6	9.6	9.6	9.6	9.6	9.6	9.6	9.6	9.6	9.6	9.5
Eurozone[3]	ZXDH	9.9	10	10	10	10	10.1	10	10	10	10	10.1	10	10	9.9
National Statistical Offices Unemployment Rates															
Canada	ZXDZ	8.5	8.3	8.2	8.2	8.1	8.1	7.9	8	8.1	8	7.8	7.6	7.6	7.8
Japan	ZXDY	5.2	4.9	4.8	5	5.1	5.2	5.3	5.2	5.1	5	5.1	5.1	4.9	4.9
United Kingdom	MGSX	7.8	7.9	8	7.9	7.8	7.8	7.8	7.7	7.7	7.9	7.9	7.9	..	..
United States	ZXDX	9.9	9.7	9.7	9.7	9.8	9.6	9.5	9.5	9.6	9.6	9.7	9.8	9.4	9

1. See chapter text.

2. The UK employment rate as published by the Office for National Statistics is seasonally adjusted. All other employment and unemployment rates are not seasonally adjusted.

3.The 'Total EU' series consists of all 27 EU countries. The Eurozone series consist of the following EU countries: Austria, Belgium, Cyprus, Finland, France, Germany, Greece, Ireland, Italy, Luxembourg, Malta, Netherlands, Portugal, Slovenia and Spain.

Sources: Office for National Statistics; Eurostat; StatsBLS; StatCan; Stat.go.JP;
Labour Market Statistics Helpline: 01633 456901

4.6 Civil Service employment by department[1]

Great Britain

Full-time equivalents, not seasonally adjusted

		2009 Q3	2009 Q4	2010 Q1	2010 Q2	2010 Q3
Attorney General's Departments	GB3F	9510	9650	9500	9270	9150
Business, Innovation and Skills	K9UH	10330	10480	10510	12210	12030
Cabinet Office	BBGD	1270	1270	1230	1600	1620
Chancellor's other departments	GB3I	1770	1890	1900	1250	1250
Charity Commission	GB3J	460	450	450	440	430
Communities and Local Government	YEGA	4990	4840	4790	4690	4600
Culture, Media and Sport	DMTC	570	580	590	600	580
Defence	BCDW	75670	75690	75230	74610	73590
Education	I44Z	3240	3180	2970	2890	2800
Energy and Climate Change	K9UG	970	990	1020	1060	1120
Environment, Food and Rural Affairs	LNFX	10430	10410	10370	9940	9670
Export Credits Guarantee Department	GB3L	210	210	210	210	200
Food Standards Agency	H6NX	720	710	700	1540	1420
Foreign and Commonwealth	BCDK	6090	6190	5970	5960	5970
Government Equalities Office	K9UI	100	90	120	120	110
Health	BAKR	3720	3660	3820	3770	3700
HM Revenue and Customs	GB3M	82520	80760	79300	72270	71320
HM Treasury	GB3H	1370	1350	1330	1350	1360
Home Office	BCDL	24780	24800	24990	29530	29070
International Development	DMUA	1630	1570	1570	1580	1600
Meat Hygiene Service	H6NY	960	920	870	-	-
Ministry of Justice	GB3K	81710	81250	80540	80110	79230
Northern Ireland Office	BBGG	110	110	110	130	120
Office for Standards in Education	GB3N	2150	2070	2060	1990	1500
Office of Qualifications and Examinations Regulation	K9UJ	-	-	-	180	170
Other Cabinet Office Agencies	GB3G	1270	1280	1240	1600	1520
Security and Intelligence Services	GB3O	5600	5640	5580	5590	5590
Transport	BCDR	18790	18800	18610	18610	18390
United Kingdom Statistics Authority	K9UK	3270	3290	3340	3670	3450
Work and Pensions	LNGA	121070	122910	120940	118360	115430
Central Governments Departments Total	**GB3P**	**475270**	**475050**	**469840**	**465110**	**456950**
Scottish Government	GB3Q	16780	16720	16770	16840	16800
Welsh Assembly	GB3R	6030	6020	5990	5900	5600
TOTAL	**BCDX**	498080	497780	492600	487840	479350

1. Numbers are rounded to the nearest ten.

Sources: Quarterly Public Sector Employment Survey, Office for National Statistics;

4.7a Duration of unemployment: by sex United Kingdom

Seasonally adjusted

| | All aged 16 and over | | | | | | All aged 16-59/64 | | | | | |
	All	Up to 6 months	Over 6 and up to 12 months	All over 12 months	% over 12 months	All over 24 months	All	Up to 6 months	Over 6 and up to 12 months	All over 12 months	% over 12 months	All over 24 months
Persons												
	MGSC	YBWF	YBWG	YBWH	YBWI	YBWL	YBSH	YBWO	YBWR	YBWU	YBWX	YBXA
2003	1489	956	216	317	21.3	156	1472	946	214	312	21.2	152
2004	1424	916	222	286	20.1	132	1407	905	220	282	20.1	129
2005	1466	927	231	307	20.9	144	1444	916	228	301	20.8	140
2006	1672	1012	288	371	22.2	175	1645	999	284	362	22.0	169
2007	1652	998	266	390	23.6	174	1629	984	262	382	23.5	170
2008	1780	1068	287	425	24.0	200	1755	1056	280	419	24.0	197
2009	2394	1324	484	586	24.5	238	2359	1308	476	575	24.3	231
2010	2476	1184	489	802	32.4	316	2440	1172	483	786	32.2	306
Men												
	MGSD	MGYK	MGYM	MGYO	YBWJ	YBWM	YBSI	YBWP	YBWS	YBWV	YBWY	YBXB
2003	899	535	139	226	25.1	118	890	530	138	222	25.0	116
2004	836	497	140	198	23.7	99	826	492	139	195	23.6	96
2005	862	504	142	216	25.1	106	852	500	141	212	24.8	103
2006	968	539	171	258	26.5	126	958	535	170	254	26.4	124
2007	944	522	156	266	28.2	124	935	518	155	262	28.0	122
2008	1051	589	168	294	28.1	146	1040	583	165	292	28.1	144
2009	1465	767	310	388	26.4	165	1450	760	306	383	26.4	162
2010	1478	638	294	546	37.0	224	1461	633	290	538	36.9	220
Women												
	MGSE	MGYL	MGYN	MGYP	YBWK	YBWN	YBSJ	YBWQ	YBWT	YBWW	YBWZ	YBXC
2003	590	422	77	91	15.5	38	582	416	75	90	15.4	37
2004	588	419	81	88	15.0	34	580	413	80	87	15.0	33
2005	603	423	89	90	15.0	37	592	417	87	88	15.0	36
2006	704	473	117	114	16.1	49	688	464	115	110	15.9	46
2007	708	476	109	123	17.4	50	694	467	107	121	17.4	48
2008	730	480	119	131	18.0	54	716	472	115	129	18.0	52
2009	929	557	174	199	21.3	73	910	548	170	192	21.1	68
2010	998	546	196	257	25.7	91	978	538	193	248	25.3	86

4.7b Duration of unemployment: by sex United Kingdom

Seasonally adjusted

	Ages 16-17						Ages 18-24					
	All	Up to 6 months	Over 6 and up to 12 months	All over 12 months	% over 12 months	All over 24 months	All	Up to 6 months	Over 6 and up to 12 months	All over 12 months	% over 12 months	All over 24 months
Persons												
	YBVH	YBXD	YBXG	YBXJ	YBXM	YBXP	YBVN	YBXS	YBXV	YBXY	YBYB	YBYE
2003	172	137	23	12	7.2	..	403	300	51	52	13	22
2004	175	138	27	..	..	..	409	292	62	54	13.3	19
2005	179	141	26	12	6.7	..	439	306	68	65	14.8	26
2006	182	137	30	15	8.1	..	505	343	84	78	15.4	32
2007	197	148	32	16	8.3	..	506	338	76	92	18.2	33
2008	185	141	32	13	6.8	..	558	370	84	104	18.7	39
2009	200	138	38	24	12.4	..	715	424	142	148	20.6	50
2010	200	134	40	25	12.6	..	730	396	142	192	26.4	69
Men												
	YBVI	YBXE	YBXH	YBXK	YBXN	YBXQ	YBVO	YBXT	YBXW	YBXZ	YBYC	YBYF
2003	100	79	14	..	..	..	244	171	36	37	15.2	16
2004	99	76	17	..	..	..	240	161	40	39	16.2	14
2005	100	76	16	..	..	..	270	178	43	49	18.2	22
2006	106	77	20	..	..	..	304	192	53	58	19.2	27
2007	110	80	19	..	..	..	305	190	49	66	21.8	26
2008	101	76	17	..	..	..	350	218	55	77	22	31
2009	110	73	22	14	13.2	..	444	245	96	104	23.2	38
2010	108	70	24	14	13.3	..	436	214	86	136	31.2	50
Women												
	YBVJ	YBXF	YBXI	YBXL	YBXO	YBXR	YBVP	YBXU	YBXX	YBYA	YBYD	YBYG
2003	72	58	..	..	..	..	160	128	16	15	9.6	..
2004	76	62	..	..	..	..	169	131	22	16	9.1	..
2005	78	65	..	..	..	..	168	128	25	15	9.1	..
2006	76	60	..	..	..	..	202	151	32	19	9.5	..
2007	87	69	13	..	..	..	202	148	27	26	12.9	..
2008	84	65	14	..	..	..	208	152	29	27	13.1	..
2009	90	64	16	..	..	..	270	180	46	44	16.4	13
2010	91	64	16	11	12.5	..	294	182	56	56	19.1	18

	Ages 25-49						Ages 50 and over					
	All	Up to 6 months	Over 6 and up to 12 months	All over 12 months	% over 12 months	All over 24 months	All	Up to 6 months	Over 6 and up to 12 months	All over 12 months	% over 12 months	All over 24 months
Persons												
	MGVI	YBYH	YBYK	YBYN	YBYQ	YBYT	YBVT	YBYW	YBYZ	YBZC	YBZF	YBZI
2003	684	410	105	170	24.9	85	229	110	36	82	36.0	48
2004	630	379	99	153	24.2	71	210	106	33	70	33.4	42
2005	632	380	104	148	23.5	67	216	101	34	81	37.7	49
2006	749	419	136	194	25.9	90	236	113	38	84	36.0	53
2007	706	394	118	194	27.5	93	242	116	40	86	35.6	47
2008	776	432	128	216	27.9	107	262	126	42	93	35.8	54
2009	1107	588	224	295	26.6	125	372	174	79	119	31.9	61
2010	1156	505	230	421	36.5	172	390	149	77	164	41.9	73
Men												
	MGVJ	YBYI	YBYL	YBYO	YBYR	YBYU	YBVU	YBYX	YBZA	YBZD	YBZG	YBZJ
2003	402	216	65	120	30.0	64	154	68	24	62	40.0	38
2004	355	192	61	101	28.4	52	142	67	22	52	37.2	33
2005	350	190	60	100	28.4	46	142	60	24	58	41.3	37
2006	410	209	74	127	30.9	60	148	61	25	62	42.1	40
2007	373	185	62	126	33.8	62	156	67	26	62	40.1	35
2008	427	218	68	140	33.0	73	173	76	28	70	40.8	42
2009	649	333	134	181	28.0	82	262	116	58	88	33.8	45
2010	666	258	131	276	41.6	118	267	96	53	119	44.5	54
Women												
	MGVK	YBYJ	YBYM	YBYP	YBYS	YBYV	YBVV	YBYY	YBZB	YBZE	YBZH	YBZK
2003	282	193	40	49	17.6	22	75	43	12	21	27.6	..
2004	276	186	38	52	18.8	20	68	39	11	17	25.4	..
2005	282	189	44	50	17.5	21	74	41	..	22	30.9	12
2006	339	210	62	67	19.8	30	87	52	13	22	25.8	13
2007	333	209	55	68	20.5	30	86	49	14	24	27.4	12
2008	349	213	60	76	21.7	34	89	50	15	23	26.3	12
2009	458	255	90	114	24.8	44	110	58	22	30	27.6	16
2010	490	247	98	145	29.6	53	123	53	24	45	36.4	19

See chapter text.

4.8 Unemployment rates: by region[1,2,3]

At Quarter 2 each year[4] . Seasonally adjusted[5]

Percentages

		2000	2001	2002	2003	2004	2005	2006	2007	2008	2009	2010
North East	**YCNC**	8.6	7.3	6.8	6.4	5.8	6.4	6.5	6.3	7.6	9.2	9.5
North West	**YCND**	5.5	5.3	5.4	4.9	4.5	4.6	5.3	5.9	6.7	8.4	8.1
Yorkshire and The Humber	**YCNE**	6.1	5.3	5.2	5.1	4.7	4.8	5.8	5.7	6.2	8.7	9.3
East Midlands	**YCNF**	4.8	4.7	4.7	4.3	4.3	4.4	5.4	5.3	5.8	7.2	7.7
West Midlands	**YCNG**	6	5.5	5.7	5.8	5.2	4.8	5.9	6.3	6.8	9.8	9
East	**YCNH**	3.7	3.7	3.8	4	3.7	4.1	4.8	4.7	4.8	6.3	6.7
London	**YCNI**	7.2	6.7	6.8	7.1	7.1	6.9	7.7	6.8	7	8.9	9.1
South East	**YCNJ**	3.3	3.3	3.8	3.9	3.7	3.9	4.5	4.5	4.4	5.9	6.2
South West	**YCNK**	4.1	3.6	3.8	3.4	3.3	3.6	3.8	3.9	4.1	6.3	6
Wales	**YCNM**	6.3	5.9	5.4	4.7	4.5	4.7	5.3	5.4	6	8.2	8.7
Scotland	**YCNN**	6.8	6.4	6.3	5.7	5.7	5.4	5.3	4.8	4.8	6.9	8.2
Northern Ireland	**ZSFB**	6.2	6	5.8	5.6	5	4.6	4.4	4	4.5	6.4	7.1

1. Total unemployed as a percentage of all economically active persons.

2. All aged 16 and over. See chapter text.

3. In August 2007, ONS published the mid-year population estimates for 2006.
These estimates have now been incorporated into the LFS estimates from 2001 onwards. Further details can be found at
http://www.statistics.gov.uk/cci/article.asp?id=1919

4. The Labour Force Survey has now moved to calendar quarters from May 2006. More information can be found on page 5 of the Concepts and Definitions
pdf by following this link:- www.statistics.gov.uk/downloads/theme_labour/Concepts_Definitions_HQS.pdf

5. Previously not seasonally adjusted data was shown

Sources: Labour Force Survey, Office for National Statistics;
Helpline: 01633 456901

4.9 Claimant count rates: by region[1]

Seasonally adjusted annual averages

Percentages

		2000	2001	2002	2003	2004	2005	2006	2007	2008	2009	2010
United Kingdom	**BCJE**	3.6	3.1	3.1	3.0	2.7	2.7	3.0	2.7	2.8	4.7	4.6
North East	**DPDM**	6.3	5.6	5.1	4.5	4.0	3.9	4.1	4.0	4.5	6.9	6.7
North West	**IBWC**	4.1	3.7	3.5	3.2	2.9	2.9	3.3	3.1	3.4	5.4	5.2
Yorkshire and the Humber	**DPBI**	4.3	3.9	3.6	3.3	2.8	2.9	3.3	3.0	3.3	5.7	5.6
East Midlands	**DPBJ**	3.3	3.1	2.9	2.8	2.5	2.5	2.8	2.6	2.8	4.9	4.6
West Midlands	**DPBN**	4.0	3.7	3.5	3.5	3.3	3.4	3.9	3.7	3.8	6.3	5.9
East	**DPDP**	2.4	2.0	2.1	2.1	2.0	2.1	2.3	2.1	2.2	4.0	3.8
London	**DPDQ**	3.7	3.3	3.6	3.6	3.5	3.4	3.5	3.0	2.8	4.3	4.5
South East	**DPDR**	1.8	1.5	1.6	1.7	1.6	1.6	1.9	1.6	1.7	3.3	3.1
South West	**DPBM**	2.5	2.0	1.9	1.9	1.6	1.6	1.8	1.6	1.7	3.4	3.1
England	**VASQ**	3.4	3.0	2.9	2.9	2.6	2.6	2.9	2.6	2.8	4.7	4.5
Wales	**DPBP**	4.4	3.9	3.5	3.3	3.0	3.0	3.1	2.8	3.2	5.5	5.2
Scotland	**DPBQ**	4.5	3.9	3.8	3.7	3.4	3.2	3.2	2.8	2.8	4.5	4.9
Northern Ireland	**DPBR**	5.3	4.9	4.4	4.2	3.6	3.3	3.2	2.8	3.1	5.5	6.3
Great Britain	**DPAJ**	3.5	3.1	3.0	3.0	2.7	2.7	2.9	2.7	2.8	4.7	4.6

1. The number of unemployment-related benefit claimants as a percentage of the estimated total workforce (the sum of claimants, employee jobs, self-employed,
participants on work-related government training programmes and HM Forces) at mid-year. Excluded are claimants under 18, consistent with current coverage.
See chapter text.

Source: Office for National Statistics: 01633 456901

4.10 Claimant count:[1] by region

Seasonally adjusted

Thousands

	North East	North West	Yorkshire and the Humber	East Midlands	West Midlands	East	London	South East	South West	England	Wales	Scotland	Great Britain	Northern Ireland	United Kingdom
	DPDG	IBWA	DPAX	DPAY	DPBC	DPDJ	DPDK	DPDL	DPBB	IBWK	DPBE	DPBF	DPAG	DPBG	BCJD
1994 Jan	145.6	325.1	233.7	174.7	262.3	210.0	451.4	296.7	203.6	2302.3	126.7	236.0	2665.8	100.2	2766.0
Apr	141.6	314.5	227.4	170.7	252.0	200.4	440.4	280.9	194.5	2221.7	123.3	231.7	2577.4	98.9	2676.3
Jul	139.1	304.2	222.7	166.3	242.3	191.0	428.1	268.1	188.1	2148.8	119.0	227.4	2496.3	97.2	2593.5
Oct	136.0	291.7	215.9	160.1	230.5	180.5	415.4	251.1	178.9	2059.0	112.9	218.1	2391.1	93.8	2484.9
1995 Jan	133.0	280.1	210.6	153.2	218.5	172.3	401.4	237.9	171.4	1977.5	108.3	209.3	2296.0	91.3	2387.3
Apr	130.0	270.8	206.8	148.1	211.0	167.1	395.0	229.7	166.0	1923.8	106.2	200.3	2231.0	88.6	2319.6
Jul	128.2	266.1	204.6	145.3	206.9	165.0	390.2	225.1	162.5	1892.8	106.7	195.3	2195.9	87.6	2283.5
Oct	126.4	260.9	200.7	142.3	201.3	160.7	383.2	219.1	159.4	1852.7	105.4	193.5	2152.9	85.8	2238.7
1996 Jan	123.1	255.8	197.0	140.0	196.5	157.2	376.8	213.3	155.6	1814.6	104.0	193.2	2112.5	85.9	2198.4
Apr	121.7	254.9	195.7	137.7	194.2	153.5	367.9	207.6	152.3	1785.1	104.6	194.9	2085.0	86.1	2171.1
Jul	116.9	248.2	188.8	131.8	187.6	146.8	357.5	198.9	146.8	1722.5	101.8	191.9	2017.0	86.4	2103.4
Oct	110.5	238.4	181.1	124.9	177.8	138.5	341.6	185.5	137.9	1635.0	98.2	186.3	1920.7	81.7	2002.4
1997 Jan	101.0	218.5	166.4	111.8	160.1	123.5	312.6	163.3	126.0	1483.2	90.3	173.8	1747.3	71.1	1818.4
Apr	95.2	201.3	154.7	102.4	147.3	110.6	284.9	144.4	112.1	1352.9	82.5	162.2	1597.6	65.0	1662.6
Jul	92.4	188.9	148.2	95.0	138.0	102.5	264.3	131.0	100.7	1261.0	78.1	153.6	1492.7	61.4	1554.1
Oct	90.4	177.6	142.0	87.6	131.7	94.3	246.4	120.4	93.0	1183.4	73.6	146.5	1403.6	60.6	1464.1
1998 Jan	87.6	170.6	137.2	82.8	126.1	88.5	234.3	112.3	88.7	1128.1	70.9	141.6	1340.6	59.9	1400.5
Apr	84.1	165.4	134.1	79.9	122.3	85.2	229.4	108.0	85.1	1093.5	69.3	138.7	1301.5	57.9	1359.4
Jul	81.8	163.7	133.3	80.0	121.4	83.7	225.2	105.5	84.1	1078.7	68.6	139.4	1286.7	57.3	1344.0
Oct	82.1	160.9	130.9	79.9	121.4	82.0	219.3	102.5	81.8	1060.8	68.1	136.9	1265.8	56.1	1321.9
1999 Jan	82.6	159.5	129.5	79.0	122.3	80.3	214.5	101.2	81.2	1050.4	67.8	135.6	1253.8	55.9	1309.7
Apr	82.5	157.2	127.0	78.2	123.1	79.1	207.8	98.8	78.4	1032.1	67.1	133.9	1233.1	55.0	1288.1
Jul	80.3	153.8	122.4	75.9	120.2	76.6	202.2	94.4	74.9	1000.7	63.8	130.2	1194.7	50.0	1244.7
Oct	76.7	150.0	118.3	73.6	115.9	73.6	196.5	91.1	71.4	967.1	61.0	126.1	1154.2	46.5	1200.7
2000 Jan	75.7	145.7	114.6	73.2	112.1	70.3	189.4	87.2	68.0	936.2	59.3	123.2	1118.7	44.2	1162.9
Apr	73.6	139.9	108.9	70.0	108.1	66.9	181.6	81.3	63.8	894.1	57.8	119.0	1070.9	42.4	1113.3
Jul	72.0	135.4	104.9	68.7	107.2	62.5	172.0	77.5	61.1	861.3	57.1	115.1	1033.5	41.2	1074.7
Oct	69.5	131.0	102.5	67.7	106.5	60.7	165.0	74.3	58.1	835.3	56.4	111.7	1003.4	41.3	1044.7
2001 Jan	66.2	127.4	99.9	66.6	104.0	57.2	158.2	69.7	54.9	804.1	54.9	108.8	967.8	40.8	1008.6
Apr	63.2	124.9	97.6	65.1	100.8	54.8	151.8	66.1	53.6	777.9	52.4	105.3	935.6	39.9	975.5
Jul	61.4	121.5	95.1	63.0	97.4	53.7	151.0	65.1	52.1	760.3	49.8	102.4	912.5	39.3	951.8
Oct	61.5	121.4	93.2	61.6	95.7	54.3	156.3	65.9	51.1	761.0	49.2	104.2	914.4	38.6	953.0
2002 Jan	60.9	121.3	91.4	60.6	95.4	55.4	163.1	68.6	51.1	767.8	48.1	104.3	920.2	38.0	958.2
Apr	59.2	119.4	89.4	59.4	93.6	56.4	166.2	71.0	50.9	765.5	47.5	104.4	917.4	37.5	954.9
Jul	58.5	118.1	89.1	58.6	93.4	57.5	167.3	72.3	50.1	764.9	46.8	101.9	913.6	36.4	950.0
Oct	55.9	116.1	87.6	57.9	93.7	57.2	167.6	72.3	49.3	757.6	46.7	100.1	904.4	35.1	939.5
2003 Jan	54.8	115.9	87.0	58.0	94.3	57.4	168.6	72.9	48.9	757.8	46.3	100.2	904.3	35.0	939.3
Apr	53.5	112.7	84.1	58.8	94.7	58.5	171.3	75.6	48.6	757.8	45.2	99.1	902.1	34.0	936.1
Jul	52.6	112.5	84.2	59.9	94.9	58.7	171.7	76.4	49.1	760.0	45.0	100.6	905.6	34.6	940.2
Oct	51.1	108.7	81.6	58.8	94.2	57.3	170.2	76.0	47.4	745.3	43.1	98.9	887.3	34.7	922.0
2004 Jan	49.8	104.6	78.3	56.2	93.0	56.7	167.8	75.0	45.3	726.7	42.0	97.0	865.7	33.5	899.2
Apr	47.5	101.3	75.6	53.7	89.7	56.0	165.5	72.3	42.7	704.3	41.4	94.4	840.1	31.8	871.9
Jul	45.4	96.7	71.6	51.1	86.7	54.6	162.0	68.5	40.4	677.0	39.5	90.0	806.5	29.9	836.4
Oct	45.1	96.5	71.1	50.9	86.0	55.0	158.8	69.2	40.6	673.2	39.2	89.5	801.9	29.6	831.5
2005 Jan	44.0	94.4	70.1	50.8	85.7	55.1	158.8	68.4	40.9	668.2	38.9	87.4	794.6	29.1	823.7
Apr	44.9	98.0	73.2	52.1	88.0	56.4	162.1	69.7	41.5	685.9	39.6	86.1	811.7	28.6	840.3
Jul	46.1	102.2	76.1	54.5	97.1	58.9	162.4	71.6	42.5	711.4	41.7	84.9	838.1	28.6	866.7
Oct	47.4	105.9	79.9	56.5	99.2	60.2	166.0	73.7	43.0	731.8	42.8	85.8	860.0	28.2	888.2
2006 Jan	47.2	109.4	84.2	59.1	102.6	62.2	168.2	78.5	44.3	755.7	43.9	85.7	885.4	28.2	913.7
Apr	49.4	115.0	86.9	62.1	109.2	64.9	167.8	81.2	47.7	784.3	45.1	88.1	917.5	28.0	945.5
Jul	50.8	117.0	88.3	62.5	109.8	65.9	168.4	83.5	49.2	795.4	44.3	89.0	928.8	28.0	956.7
Oct	51.6	118.2	89.0	63.3	110.2	68.0	166.4	82.5	49.7	799.0	44.3	87.3	930.6	28.0	958.6
2007 Jan	51.2	115.6	86.0	62.0	109.3	66.0	159.3	78.0	47.5	774.9	42.1	82.5	899.5	26.1	925.6
Apr	49.8	110.5	82.5	59.1	102.9	62.1	150.6	73.1	43.5	734.1	40.7	78.5	853.3	24.9	878.2
Jul	49.4	109.0	81.0	58.6	101.4	60.7	143.5	71.4	42.1	717.1	40.7	74.8	832.6	23.7	856.3
Oct	48.2	108.5	78.6	56.8	100.5	59.1	137.2	69.4	41.0	699.3	40.2	73.1	812.6	23.7	836.3
2008 Jan	46.9	105.2	75.3	52.5	94.5	55.4	131.5	64.6	38.0	663.9	38.0	69.3	771.2	23.6	794.8
Apr	48.0	106.3	75.7	52.3	93.4	54.2	126.8	63.6	37.3	657.6	39.2	69.4	766.2	24.4	790.6
Jul	52.0	117.0	85.4	59.8	103.3	61.0	133.3	74.2	44.8	730.8	44.5	76.1	851.4	26.8	878.2
Oct	59.7	132.9	99.9	69.5	116.8	72.1	145.8	89.0	55.8	841.5	51.1	88.5	981.1	31.3	1012.4
2009 Jan	72.2	159.9	122.7	87.9	143.6	92.6	170.4	115.9	73.5	1038.7	65.0	103.6	1207.3	39.0	1246.3
Apr	83.0	188.8	146.9	107.5	172.4	116.2	205.3	147.0	93.2	1260.3	77.0	121.9	1459.2	46.4	1505.6
Jul	86.4	198.7	154.7	112.0	179.3	120.2	218.8	155.4	95.5	1321.0	79.6	130.2	1530.8	50.8	1581.6
Oct	87.7	203.1	159.6	115.1	184.6	122.7	229.5	160.3	95.8	1358.4	81.1	134.5	1574.0	53.8	1627.8
2010 Jan	87.3	200.7	159.8	112.8	180.2	121.5	227.3	158.4	94.5	1342.5	79.8	139.0	1561.3	55.5	1616.8
Apr	81.1	185.5	150.8	103.6	166.2	112.7	218.6	144.0	84.8	1247.3	74.3	135.0	1456.6	55.4	1512.0
Jul	79.9	179.9	143.7	98.7	159.4	108.7	213.6	135.5	80.7	1200.4	71.3	135.4	1407.1	56.9	1464.0
Oct	81.1	179.9	144.2	97.0	158.0	108.9	215.4	132.8	81.7	1199.0	71.2	135.3	1405.5	58.4	1463.9
2011 Jan	80.0	177.0	144.7	96.9	157.2	107.0	215.2	130.2	81.4	1189.6	71.3	139.7	1400.6	59.1	1459.7

1. The figures are based on the number of claimants receiving unemployment related benefits and are adjusted for seasonality and discontinuities to be consistent with current coverage. See chapter text.

2. The latest national and regional seasonally adjusted claimant count figures are provisional and subject to revision in the following month.

Source: Office for National Statistics: 01633 456901

4.11 Median[1] weekly and hourly earnings of full-time employees[2] by industry division[3]: United Kingdom

April 2008 to 2010

	Agriculture, forestry and fishing	Mining and quarrying	Manufacturing	Electricity, gas, steam and air conditioning supply	Water supply, sewerage, waste management and remediation activities	Construction
SIC 2007[3] Divisions	A	B	C	D	E	F
Median gross weekly earnings (£)						
All						
	JR89	JR8A	JR8B	JR8C	JR8D	JR8E
2008	356.8	649.0	486.3	661.5	500.0	516.7
2009	386.6	683.2	484.1	596.5	517.8	530.9
2010	395.0	708.8	499.9	642.8	504.0	536.6
Men						
	JR8S	JR8T	JR8U	JR8V	JR8W	JR8X
2008	375.4	674.8	513.6	715.8	512.6	533.3
2009	402.5	701.1	509.9	639.5	528.6	550.0
2010	417.6	729.7	527.0	698.0	515.2	550.2
Women						
	JR9D	JR9E	JR9F	JR9G	JR9H	JR9I
2008	301.1	499.6	365.4	399.9	447.2	398.4
2009	345.0	567.9	369.1	407.7	467.9	400.0
2010	313.0	538.0	377.4	434.0	422.8	416.9
Median hourly earnings, excluding overtime (£)						
All						
	JR9W	JR9X	JR9Y	JR9Z	JRA2	JRA3
2008	7.69	15.27	11.44	16.12	10.94	11.79
2009	8.22	16.33	11.72	15.16	11.59	12.22
2010	8.32	16.18	11.83	15.87	11.28	12.34
Men						
	JRB9	JRC2	JRC3	JRC4	JRC5	JRC6
2008	7.83	15.30	11.95	17.09	10.92	12.00
2009	8.20	16.54	12.25	16.13	11.54	12.47
2010	8.40	16.25	12.30	17.10	11.30	12.50
Women						
	JRE4	JRE5	JRE6	JRE7	JRE8	JRE9
2008	7.21	15.07	9.20	10.53	11.03	10.49
2009	8.28	16.17	9.44	10.84	12.08	10.44
2010	7.38	14.40	9.58	11.29	11.23	10.91
Median total paid hours worked						
All						
	JS5P	JS5Q	JS5R	JS5S	JS5T	JS5U
2008	40.0	39.9	39.1	37.0	40.0	40.0
2009	40.0	37.5	39.0	37.0	40.0	40.0
2010	40.0	39.0	39.0	37.0	40.0	40.0
Men						
	JS6A	JS6B	JS6C	JS6D	JS6E	JS6F
2008	40.0	40.0	39.8	37.2	40.5	40.0
2009	40.5	39.4	39.0	37.0	40.5	40.0
2010	40.5	39.9	39.3	37.0	40.8	40.0
Women						
	JS6T	JS6U	JS6V	JS6W	JS6X	JS6Y
2008	40.0	37.5	37.8	37.0	37.2	37.5
2009	39.0	37.1	37.5	36.9	37.0	37.5
2010	39.0	37.3	37.5	37.0	37.0	37.5

4.11 Median[1] weekly and hourly earnings of full-time employees[2] by industry division[3]: United Kingdom

April 2008 to 2010

SIC 2007[3] Divisions	Wholesale and retail trade; repair of motor vehicles and motorcycles	Transport and storage	Accommodation and food service activities	Information and communication	Financial and insurance activities	Real estate activities	Professional, scientific and technical activities
	G	H	I	J	K	L	M
Median gross weekly earnings (£)							
All	JR8F	JR8G	JR8H	JR8I	JR8J	JR8K	JR8L
2008	380.0	470.6	296.8	634.8	597.2	451.9	579.7
2009	388.0	479.1	299.0	643.4	622.0	463.0	596.0
2010	393.5	495.6	304.0	651.6	630.3	465.2	607.6
Men	JR8Y	JR8Z	JR92	JR93	JR94	JR95	JR96
2008	421.6	480.1	316.2	687.8	766.6	528.8	680.4
2009	428.0	487.7	317.4	686.4	781.4	527.7	685.6
2010	430.1	504.5	320.9	699.3	784.4	515.4	689.9
Women	JR9J	JR9K	JR9L	JR9M	JR9N	JR9O	JR9P
2008	317.7	421.6	272.9	536.6	450.4	391.7	479.1
2009	325.2	436.0	277.9	542.5	484.9	407.8	498.3
2010	333.5	440.7	282.6	542.6	481.5	416.6	510.4
Median hourly earnings, excluding overtime (£)							
All	JRA4	JRA5	JRA6	JRA7	JRA8	JRA9	JRB2
2008	9.18	10.48	7.00	16.39	16.43	11.92	15.26
2009	9.46	10.99	7.10	16.71	17.19	12.19	15.83
2010	9.53	11.13	7.23	16.78	17.41	12.26	16.10
Men	JRC7	JRC8	JRC9	JRD2	JRD3	JRD4	JRD5
2008	9.88	10.46	7.25	17.50	20.90	13.64	17.50
2009	10.11	10.99	7.36	17.79	21.73	13.76	17.76
2010	10.10	11.10	7.48	17.92	21.86	13.37	18.06
Women	JRF2	JRF3	JRF4	JRF5	JRF6	JRF7	JRF8
2008	8.10	10.59	6.63	14.23	12.45	10.56	12.86
2009	8.37	11.00	6.89	14.56	13.55	10.93	13.42
2010	8.49	11.32	7.00	14.55	13.42	11.02	13.74
Median total paid hours worked							
All	JS5V	JS5W	JS5X	JS5Y	JS5Z	JS62	JS63
2008	39.1	40.0	40.0	37.5	35.0	37.4	37.5
2009	39.1	40.0	40.0	37.5	35.0	37.0	37.5
2010	39.1	40.0	40.0	37.5	35.0	37.0	37.5
Men	JS6G	JS6H	JS6I	JS6J	JS6K	JS6L	JS6M
2008	40.0	40.5	40.0	37.5	35.0	37.5	37.5
2009	40.0	40.0	40.0	37.5	35.0	37.4	37.5
2010	40.0	40.1	40.0	37.5	35.0	37.4	37.5
Women	JS6Z	JS72	JS73	JS74	JS75	JS76	JS77
2008	37.6	38.9	39.8	37.5	35.0	37.0	37.0
2009	37.5	37.5	39.5	37.5	35.0	37.0	37.0
2010	37.7	37.5	39.2	37.5	35.0	37.0	37.0

4.11 Median[1] weekly and hourly earnings of full-time employees[2] by industry division[3]: United Kingdom

April 2008 to 2010

	Administrative and support service activities	Public administration and defence	Education	Human health and social work activities	Arts, entertainment and recreation	Other service activities
SIC 2007[3] Divisions	N	O	P	Q	R	S
Median gross weekly earnings (£)						
All						
	JR8M	**JR8N**	**JR8O**	**JR8P**	**JR8Q**	**JR8R**
2008	383.6	533.5	525.6	458.4	380.6	414.7
2009	391.2	547.3	541.8	473.4	388.3	424.4
2010	395.8	581.6	552.5	486.2	395.8	431.2
Men						
	JR97	**JR98**	**JR99**	**JR9A**	**JR9B**	**JR9C**
2008	402.7	595.0	575.5	542.6	406.9	464.1
2009	414.5	604.4	586.6	567.5	403.5	472.4
2010	414.7	630.8	598.2	575.9	410.7	470.9
Women						
	JR9Q	**JR9R**	**JR9S**	**JR9T**	**JR9U**	**JR9V**
2008	350.0	443.9	484.5	433.8	351.9	361.5
2009	354.6	463.0	501.2	440.8	366.6	364.1
2010	359.4	500.5	518.4	454.4	371.5	371.8
Median hourly earnings, excluding overtime (£)						
All						
	JRB3	**JRB4**	**JRB5**	**JRB6**	**JRB7**	**JRB8**
2008	8.82	13.34	14.56	11.99	9.25	10.75
2009	9.21	13.83	15.07	12.34	9.78	11.09
2010	9.28	14.68	15.50	12.71	9.93	11.13
Men						
	JRD6	**JRD7**	**JRD8**	**JRD9**	**JRE2**	**JRE3**
2008	8.82	14.70	15.67	13.98	9.76	11.57
2009	9.31	14.97	16.25	14.58	10.05	11.98
2010	9.45	15.61	16.34	14.79	10.33	12.12
Women						
	JRF9	**JRG2**	**JRG3**	**JRG4**	**JRG5**	**JRG6**
2008	8.83	11.57	13.79	11.34	8.73	9.45
2009	9.08	12.22	14.33	11.49	9.41	9.51
2010	9.06	13.11	14.77	11.96	9.43	9.76
Median total paid hours worked						
All						
	JS64	**JS65**	**JS66**	**JS67**	**JS68**	**JS69**
2008	40.0	37.6	36.1	37.5	39.9	37.5
2009	39.9	37.2	36.1	37.5	39.4	37.5
2010	39.8	39.0	36.1	37.5	38.9	37.5
Men						
	JS6N	**JS6O**	**JS6P**	**JS6Q**	**JS6R**	**JS6S**
2008	40.0	39.9	36.9	37.5	40.0	38.6
2009	40.0	39.1	36.9	37.5	39.9	37.5
2010	40.0	40.0	37.0	37.5	39.8	37.5
Women						
	JS78	**JS79**	**JS7A**	**JS7B**	**JS7C**	**JS7D**
2008	37.5	37.0	35.0	37.5	38.3	37.5
2009	37.5	37.0	35.0	37.5	37.6	37.2
2010	37.5	37.0	35.0	37.5	37.5	37.0

1. Median values are less affected by extremes of earnings at either ends of the scale with half the employees earning above the stated amount and half below. Previous editions of Monthly Digest published means
2. Data relate to full-time employees on adult rates whose pay for the survey pay-period was not affected by absence.
3. Classification is based on Standard Industrial Classification 2007.

Source: Annual Survey of Hours and Earnings: 01633 456 120

4.12 Median[1] weekly and hourly earnings and total paid hours of full-time employees[2]: United Kingdom

April 2008 to 2010

SIC 2007[3]	Manufacturing industries				All industries and services			
			Hourly earnings(£)				Hourly earnings(£)	
	Gross weekly Earnings (£)	Total paid hours	Including overtime pay	Excluding overtime pay	Gross Weekly Earnings (£)	Total paid Hours	Including overtime pay	Excluding overtime pay
All								
	JR7J	**JR7K**	**JR7L**	**JR7M**	**JR7V**	**JR7W**	**JR7X**	**JR7Y**
2008	486.3	39.1	11.72	11.44	479.1	37.5	11.98	11.88
2009	484.1	39.0	11.91	11.72	488.5	37.5	12.42	12.33
2010	499.9	39.0	12.01	11.83	499.1	37.5	12.58	12.50
Men								
	JR7N	**JR7O**	**JR7P**	**JR7Q**	**JR7Z**	**JR82**	**JR83**	**JR84**
2008	513.6	39.8	12.21	11.95	522.0	39.0	12.63	12.50
2009	509.9	39.0	12.45	12.25	531.0	38.7	13.08	12.97
2010	527.0	39.3	12.53	12.30	538.3	39.0	13.15	13.01
Women								
	JR7R	**JR7S**	**JR7T**	**JR7U**	**JR85**	**JR86**	**JR87**	**JR88**
2008	365.4	37.8	9.25	9.20	412.4	37.1	10.94	10.92
2009	369.1	37.5	9.47	9.44	425.8	37.0	11.41	11.39
2010	377.4	37.5	9.67	9.58	439.2	37.0	11.72	11.69

1. Median values are less affected by extremes of earnings at either ends of the scale with half the employees earning above the stated amount and half below. Previous editions of Monthly Digest published means.
2. Data relate to full-time employees on adult rates whose pay for the survey pay-period was not affected by absence.
3. Classification is based on Standard Industrial Classification 2007.

Source: Annual Survey of Hours and Earnings: 01633 456 120

4.13 Average weekly earnings: main industrial sectors Great Britain

Great Britain
Standard Industrial Classification 2007

	Whole economy		Manufacturing		Construction		Services		Distribution Hotels and Restuarants	
	Actual	Seasonally adjusted	Actual	Seasonally adjusted	Actual	Seasonally adjusted	Actual	Seasonally adjusted	Actual	Seasonally adjusted
	KA46	**KAB9**	**K55I**	**K5CA**	**K55L**	**K5CD**	**K55O**	**K5BZ**	**K55R**	**K5CG**
2000	318	318	369	369	378	377	303	303	215	215
2001	335	334	383	382	407	407	320	320	223	223
2002	345	345	397	396	418	417	331	330	232	232
2003	356	356	412	411	436	436	342	341	237	237
2004	372	371	431	431	448	448	358	357	245	245
2005	389	388	447	446	461	461	375	375	254	254
2006	407	407	464	464	490	490	393	392	263	263
2007	427	426	483	482	522	522	413	412	279	279
2008	443	441	498	497	531	531	429	428	286	286
2009	442	441	503	503	536	535	427	427	290	290
2010	452	451	525	524	535	535	437	436	297	296

	Finance and Business Industries		Private Sector		Public Sector		Private Sector Excl Financial Services	
	Actual	Seasonally adjusted	Actual	Seasonally adjusted	Actual	Seasonally adjusted	Actual	Seasonally adjusted
	K55U	**K5C4**	**KA4O**	**KAC4**	**KA4R**	**KAC7**	**KA4U**	**KAD8**
2000	389	391	319	319	314	313	314	313
2001	417	418	335	335	331	329	331	329
2002	423	424	345	345	344	342	344	342
2003	434	434	355	355	360	358	360	358
2004	458	458	371	370	376	374	375	374
2005	485	485	387	387	396	394	395	394
2006	519	518	406	406	410	408	410	408
2007	546	544	428	428	424	421	424	421
2008	573	570	443	442	439	436	438	436
2009	552	553	439	438	452	451	450	448
2010	576	575	448	447	465	464	458	458

1 See chapter text.

Source: Office for National Statistics: 01633 456780

4.14a Average weekly earnings : by industry Great Britain

Not seasonally adjusted

£ per employee per week

	Agriculture, forestry and fishing	Mining and quarrying	Food products, beverages and tobacco	Textiles, leather and clothing	Chemicals and man-made fibres	Basic metals and metal products	Engineering and allied industries	Other manufacturing	Electricity, gas and water supply	Construction
Excluding bonuses SIC 2007										
	K53R	**K53S**	**K53T**	**K53U**	**K53V**	**K53W**	**K53X**	**K53Y**	**K53Z**	**K542**
2008	322	902	436	320	555	479	535	434	555	507
2009	332	939	446	331	594	477	535	446	568	516
2010	335	926	460	352	621	503	557	460	581	517
2007 Aug	298	873	421	331	554	448	518	419	528	502
Sep	293	852	418	329	556	450	518	423	529	510
Oct	296	871	426	326	559	457	523	427	541	502
Nov	297	877	422	314	568	456	524	429	537	506
Dec	294	889	431	314	563	450	523	430	549	503
2008 Jan	308	893	418	318	559	479	528	428	554	495
Feb	318	896	431	328	557	470	527	428	558	502
Mar	320	886	437	318	541	469	540	433	572	498
Apr	322	879	435	317	556	478	540	432	541	508
May	323	905	434	318	550	479	536	432	543	506
Jun	321	918	438	318	559	481	535	435	542	513
Jul	316	898	436	317	556	484	537	436	554	510
Aug	321	899	434	316	543	480	534	432	566	498
Sep	329	913	435	320	559	482	528	434	556	511
Oct	332	904	437	322	557	479	535	438	551	516
Nov	326	900	444	326	555	486	538	443	563	515
Dec	330	928	452	319	562	476	538	439	565	512
2009 Jan	331	916	446	325	563	473	530	441	561	518
Feb	320	934	440	329	559	468	529	439	560	514
Mar	334	932	448	327	574	469	533	441	566	518
Apr	327	946	446	332	581	474	534	441	560	516
May	340	937	447	329	598	472	529	445	565	513
Jun	335	937	445	325	616	483	531	449	570	509
Jul	319	946	443	327	609	470	528	445	570	513
Aug	327	932	434	329	602	474	534	446	569	512
Sep	337	948	442	326	603	480	533	449	571	515
Oct	330	946	439	336	602	482	543	451	572	522
Nov	343	946	438	341	604	487	544	453	580	521
Dec	346	950	478	343	616	490	548	453	576	521
2010 Jan	338	909	478	347	613	482	544	459	575	525
Feb	332	940	458	339	610	506	546	456	579	523
Mar	344	944	476	361	616	502	557	460	586	525
Apr	332	929	464	350	610	503	558	459	577	523
May	320	915	453	348	613	506	557	458	574	515
Jun	326	919	460	351	620	503	558	461	579	518
Jul	332	935	452	354	624	509	555	460	592	512
Aug	319	935	455	356	611	504	559	460	577	506
Sep	325	917	450	355	612	512	561	461	579	512
Oct	344	923	455	355	632	504	561	462	586	518
Nov	357	922	455	355	642	508	564	462	587	516
Dec	352	923	460	348	650	502	561	459	586	508

4.14a Average weekly earnings : by industry Great Britain

Not seasonally adjusted

£ per employee per week

	Agriculture, forestry and fishing	Mining and quarrying	Food products, beverages and tobacco	Textiles, leather and clothing	Chemicals and man-made fibres	Basic metals and metal products	Engineering and allied industries	Other manufacturing	Electricity, gas and water supply	Construction
Percentage change on the year										
	K592	**K593**	**K594**	**K595**	**K596**	**K597**	**K598**	**K599**	**K59A**	**K59B**
2008 Aug	7.4	3.0	3.0	-4.4	-1.9	7.0	3.0	3.2	7.3	-0.8
Sep	12.1	7.1	4.1	-2.4	0.4	7.2	1.9	2.6	4.9	0.2
Oct	12.3	3.8	2.7	-1.2	-0.4	4.8	2.3	2.6	1.8	2.7
Nov	9.7	2.8	5.1	3.8	-2.3	6.5	2.8	3.5	4.8	1.7
Dec	12.4	4.5	4.8	1.4	-0.1	5.9	2.8	2.0	2.9	1.8
2009 Jan	7.5	2.7	6.7	1.8	0.6	-1.1	0.3	2.9	1.2	4.6
Feb	0.8	4.3	2.1	-0.5	0.1	-0.2	0.3	2.7	0.2	2.3
Mar	4.3	6.3	2.5	2.6	5.5	0.3	-1.4	2.4	-0.5	4.0
Apr	1.8	7.5	2.5	3.7	4.0	-0.7	-1.2	2.3	3.7	1.7
May	5.6	3.4	3.1	2.8	8.6	-1.3	-1.4	2.8	4.0	1.5
Jun	4.7	2.0	1.7	2.3	10.0	0.5	-0.8	3.3	5.3	-0.7
Jul	1.1	5.2	1.6	2.4	9.5	-2.7	-1.8	2.0	3.0	0.6
Aug	2.0	3.6	0.1	3.5	10.7	-1.1	0.0	2.9	0.3	2.8
Sep	2.4	3.7	1.6	1.3	7.8	-0.3	0.9	3.2	2.8	0.8
Oct	-0.6	4.4	0.5	3.8	7.9	0.8	1.3	2.8	3.9	1.2
Nov	5.4	4.9	-1.3	3.9	8.7	0.5	1.0	2.1	3.0	1.2
Dec	4.8	2.3	5.7	6.9	9.2	3.1	1.8	3.7	2.0	1.8
2010 Jan	2.3	-0.7	7.3	6.8	8.9	2.0	2.8	3.9	2.5	1.4
Feb	3.8	0.7	4.0	3.0	9.1	7.9	3.2	3.9	3.4	1.8
Mar	3.0	1.3	6.3	10.3	7.4	7.1	4.6	4.2	3.5	1.4
Apr	1.6	-1.8	4.0	5.5	5.0	6.1	4.4	3.9	3.1	1.3
May	-5.9	-2.3	1.4	5.9	2.4	7.2	5.4	3.1	1.6	0.4
Jun	-2.8	-1.9	3.4	8.0	0.7	4.1	5.1	2.6	1.7	1.6
Jul	4.1	-1.2	2.1	8.3	2.4	8.2	5.0	3.3	3.8	-0.3
Aug	-2.4	0.3	4.8	8.2	1.5	6.4	4.7	3.2	1.4	-1.1
Sep	-3.6	-3.2	1.8	8.9	1.5	6.7	5.2	2.8	1.3	-0.5
Oct	4.3	-2.4	3.5	5.4	5.0	4.5	3.3	2.5	2.3	-0.8
Nov	4.2	-2.5	3.8	3.9	6.3	4.2	3.7	1.9	1.1	-1.0
Dec	1.9	-2.9	-3.7	1.5	5.5	2.4	2.4	1.2	1.6	-2.6

47

4.14b Average weekly earnings : by industry Great Britain

Not seasonally adjusted

	Wholesale trade	Retail trade and repairs	Accom-modation & Food Services	Trans-port and storage	Infor-mation and Comm-unication	Finan-cial & Insurance Activities	Real estate renting and business activities	Professional Scientific & Technical Activities	Administrative & support service activities	Public admini-stration	Educ-ation	Health and social work	Other ser-vices	Arts, Entert-ainment & Recreation
Excluding bonuses														
SIC 2007														
	K543	**K544**	**K545**	**K546**	**K5E5**	**K547**	**K548**	**K5E6**	**K5E7**	**K549**	**K54A**	**K54B**	**K54C**	**K5E8**
2008	458	235	208	474	655	657	417	592	320	496	380	380	370	292
2009	466	241	209	479	654	685	421	607	330	508	394	390	359	290
2010	465	247	215	492	668	728	440	618	325	524	396	395	349	305
2007 Aug	442	233	208	468	627	633	381	569	308	491	372	360	374	286
Sep	439	232	207	458	630	638	388	569	306	486	375	362	371	287
Oct	447	228	209	457	625	635	392	576	308	484	371	365	368	275
Nov	442	225	213	463	629	638	400	579	311	490	376	379	363	278
Dec	445	225	214	479	636	641	398	579	312	496	380	373	355	279
2008 Jan	456	233	205	465	642	642	411	574	311	496	369	373	357	297
Feb	453	229	206	468	645	657	406	585	316	496	370	373	357	295
Mar	458	232	213	479	650	659	396	579	315	490	371	374	365	304
Apr	459	240	206	477	650	653	413	592	319	496	375	377	373	289
May	457	237	210	489	654	653	411	587	318	493	376	375	375	293
Jun	458	236	208	481	662	662	413	591	321	494	375	377	375	286
Jul	457	234	208	467	659	669	416	596	322	496	378	381	386	293
Aug	455	237	212	468	661	655	426	606	325	497	382	389	380	296
Sep	462	238	209	468	658	652	417	602	323	495	386	381	374	283
Oct	460	235	208	473	658	662	428	599	323	494	385	384	371	286
Nov	460	231	204	472	658	657	432	601	323	506	398	386	363	287
Dec	464	234	210	482	663	667	429	593	321	503	396	387	364	291
2009 Jan	467	240	204	473	649	668	427	603	327	501	390	386	357	283
Feb	466	240	208	471	658	674	414	607	325	521	389	383	361	282
Mar	468	241	208	471	658	674	420	606	328	504	386	385	360	283
Apr	463	241	210	474	667	688	429	605	334	507	392	392	369	292
May	464	242	211	479	663	682	421	607	333	511	391	393	354	288
Jun	465	242	208	480	658	680	417	608	336	506	393	396	351	297
Jul	463	242	211	478	650	684	416	606	335	506	397	391	357	291
Aug	462	242	209	482	653	688	410	605	337	510	398	385	357	290
Sep	466	244	208	485	657	689	420	605	326	505	401	390	356	290
Oct	469	242	209	482	648	692	422	607	327	507	400	391	357	291
Nov	470	238	208	480	643	712	425	609	326	511	395	390	359	293
Dec	473	239	214	488	638	694	428	612	324	509	397	392	366	295
2010 Jan	470	245	209	482	653	701	428	614	332	519	392	388	385	305
Feb	464	243	214	483	651	719	441	615	320	519	391	391	354	299
Mar	474	247	214	488	658	725	438	623	330	519	391	388	348	298
Apr	469	247	213	487	658	718	436	620	330	521	395	396	349	294
May	467	247	213	488	666	725	440	618	332	521	393	398	343	296
Jun	465	251	212	489	668	736	439	619	326	521	393	398	352	298
Jul	467	250	212	494	673	744	447	603	324	529	395	396	348	309
Aug	462	250	221	495	677	732	440	615	322	524	397	395	347	315
Sep	464	252	218	498	675	727	441	618	321	526	403	397	345	317
Oct	460	245	223	497	677	736	442	617	323	528	400	396	337	310
Nov	461	246	213	501	681	733	444	624	320	530	400	398	341	309
Dec	462	245	220	505	678	739	449	625	315	531	400	397	344	312

4.14b Average weekly earnings : by industry Great Britain

Not seasonally adjusted

	Wholesale trade	Retail trade and repairs	Accom- modation & Food Services	Trans- port and storage	Infor- mation and Comm- unication	Finan- cial & Insurance Activities	Real estate renting and business activities	Professional Scientific & Technical Activities	Administrative & support service activities	Public admini- stration	Educ- ation	Health and social work	Other ser- vices	Arts, Entert- ainment & Recreation
Percentage change on the year														
	K59C	**K59D**	**K59E**	**K59F**	**K5EL**	**K59G**	**K59H**	**K5EM**	**K5EN**	**K59I**	**K59J**	**K59K**	**K59L**	**K5EO**
2008 Aug	3.1	1.4	1.9	-0.1	5.5	3.5	10.6	6.5	5.5	1.2	2.7	7.9	1.5	3.6
Sep	5.3	2.3	1.1	2.2	4.5	2.1	7.1	5.7	5.8	1.9	2.9	5.4	0.8	-1.3
Oct	2.8	3.0	-0.3	3.5	5.2	4.2	8.9	4.2	4.8	2.1	3.6	5.2	1.1	4.0
Nov	4.1	2.7	-4.2	1.9	4.5	3.0	7.9	3.8	3.8	3.4	5.8	1.7	0.5	3.4
Dec	4.4	4.0	-1.7	0.7	4.2	3.9	7.3	2.3	3.1	1.4	4.3	3.7	2.6	4.3
2009 Jan	2.4	3.1	-0.7	1.7	1.3	5.0	3.8	5.0	5.0	0.9	5.5	3.4	0.0	-4.7
Feb	3.0	4.9	1.0	0.8	2.2	4.5	2.0	3.9	2.8	5.0	5.2	2.6	0.9	-4.4
Mar	2.0	3.7	-2.3	-0.9	1.3	3.2	4.3	4.1	4.4	2.7	4.0	2.8	-1.4	-6.2
Apr	0.8	0.2	1.6	-0.5	2.7	5.3	3.6	2.3	4.6	2.3	4.5	3.7	-1.1	1.0
May	1.4	2.0	0.6	0.9	1.6	4.5	2.7	3.5	4.8	3.6	3.8	4.8	-5.8	-2.2
Jun	1.5	2.7	0.1	1.3	-0.7	2.9	1.0	2.8	4.8	2.4	4.8	4.9	-6.7	3.6
Jul	1.4	3.4	1.4	2.5	-1.2	2.1	-1.3	1.6	4.0	2.1	4.8	2.4	-7.6	-0.4
Aug	1.6	2.5	-1.3	3.0	-1.2	4.9	-3.6	-0.2	3.7	2.9	4.3	-1.0	-6.2	-2.0
Sep	0.9	2.6	-0.5	3.2	-0.1	5.7	1.0	0.7	0.6	1.9	3.8	2.2	-4.9	2.5
Oct	2.0	3.0	0.4	1.7	-1.3	4.5	-1.2	1.4	1.0	2.5	4.0	1.6	-3.9	1.6
Nov	2.1	2.8	1.9	1.5	-2.1	8.2	-1.3	1.5	0.7	0.9	-0.6	0.9	-1.3	1.8
Dec	2.0	2.0	1.7	2.3	-3.7	4.2	-0.2	2.9	1.2	1.3	0.2	1.2	1.0	1.6
2010 Jan	0.6	2.0	2.6	2.0	0.6	4.9	0.3	1.9	1.4	3.7	0.6	0.4	7.9	7.8
Feb	-0.5	1.3	2.8	2.6	-1.1	6.6	6.4	1.2	-1.4	-0.3	0.6	2.2	-1.8	6.0
Mar	1.4	2.6	3.0	3.6	-0.1	7.5	4.3	2.9	0.6	3.0	1.3	1.0	-3.1	5.0
Apr	1.3	2.7	1.8	2.7	-1.4	4.4	1.7	2.6	-1.2	2.7	0.7	1.1	-5.4	0.6
May	0.6	1.7	0.9	1.9	0.4	6.4	4.3	1.6	-0.4	1.9	0.6	1.1	-3.2	2.8
Jun	0.0	3.6	1.8	1.8	1.6	8.2	5.3	1.8	-3.0	2.9	0.0	0.7	0.3	0.4
Jul	0.8	3.4	0.4	3.4	3.5	8.7	7.5	-0.6	-3.3	4.6	-0.4	1.2	-2.5	6.0
Aug	-0.1	3.1	5.7	2.8	3.7	6.4	7.4	1.6	-4.6	2.7	-0.2	2.5	-2.5	8.5
Sep	-0.4	3.2	4.9	2.7	2.8	5.5	4.9	2.1	-1.6	4.3	0.6	1.9	-3.2	9.2
Oct	-1.9	1.3	6.7	3.1	4.4	6.3	4.7	1.7	-1.3	4.1	0.0	1.3	-5.8	6.5
Nov	-2.0	3.3	2.5	4.4	5.9	3.0	4.5	2.5	-1.7	3.7	1.1	2.0	-5.1	5.3
Dec	-2.4	2.6	3.0	3.5	6.4	6.4	4.8	2.2	-2.9	4.2	0.9	1.3	-6.1	5.5

4.14c Average weekly earnings : by industry Great Britain
Not seasonally adjusted

£ per employee per week

	Agriculture, forestry and fishing	Mining and quarrying	Food products, beverages and tobacco	Textiles, leather and clothing	Chemicals and man-made fibres	Basic metals and metal products	Engineering and allied industries	Other manufacturing	Electricity, gas and water supply	Construction
Including bonuses										
SIC 2007										
	K57A	**K57D**	**K57G**	**K57J**	**K57M**	**K57P**	**K57S**	**K57V**	**K57Y**	**K583**
2008	331	1014	460	337	592	502	556	449	587	531
2009	340	1035	465	347	631	495	555	459	601	536
2010	349	1042	484	367	662	527	577	476	616	535
2007 Aug	305	927	428	352	569	459	528	429	547	519
Sep	298	939	437	360	583	465	528	431	550	539
Oct	298	922	438	339	574	478	534	438	562	523
Nov	304	964	430	328	580	477	540	442	560	538
Dec	304	1009	461	333	606	499	559	456	574	567
2008 Jan	317	974	428	338	579	498	543	440	570	517
Feb	320	1005	469	341	595	491	566	442	577	524
Mar	331	1410	488	343	687	496	600	464	649	548
Apr	328	982	458	326	659	508	556	448	584	527
May	327	968	482	328	562	506	553	446	570	524
Jun	323	1017	456	365	585	503	552	449	587	532
Jul	318	974	462	328	573	524	552	452	588	530
Aug	329	936	443	321	551	494	543	442	585	514
Sep	338	989	458	333	569	493	540	443	588	536
Oct	337	949	446	338	568	506	547	449	570	532
Nov	328	959	450	338	580	500	550	453	584	537
Dec	370	1001	479	346	599	501	574	465	587	550
2009 Jan	339	1044	456	339	578	491	546	452	577	530
Feb	332	1022	457	344	595	491	563	449	581	528
Mar	341	1311	518	349	730	510	591	470	639	559
Apr	330	1044	462	346	690	495	562	453	599	535
May	342	989	456	340	610	485	545	456	589	525
Jun	337	996	459	361	639	500	544	461	636	526
Jul	330	992	459	336	623	490	540	456	618	530
Aug	330	995	441	335	609	481	544	455	588	524
Sep	346	988	463	335	611	486	544	459	590	531
Oct	335	1002	448	344	614	492	552	463	592	537
Nov	347	993	449	357	615	510	554	463	606	543
Dec	376	1045	514	375	663	513	576	476	594	559
2010 Jan	343	1021	487	367	639	502	557	469	595	540
Feb	358	1092	471	357	673	529	577	477	601	537
Mar	360	1583	581	400	823	591	627	505	670	592
Apr	340	1001	487	362	670	528	582	470	608	535
May	322	966	462	360	634	524	572	467	595	527
Jun	328	968	473	359	635	523	569	472	661	531
Jul	336	971	465	369	637	531	568	476	621	525
Aug	331	979	461	366	622	513	569	468	599	515
Sep	328	976	482	361	623	520	568	471	600	531
Oct	373	966	463	366	650	524	572	475	606	526
Nov	365	975	461	363	657	517	576	475	613	531
Dec	405	1009	512	368	682	516	588	484	620	533

4.14c Average weekly earnings : by industry Great Britain

Not seasonally adjusted

£ per employee per week

	Agriculture, forestry and fishing	Mining and quarrying	Food products, beverages and tobacco	Textiles, leather and clothing	Chemicals and man-made fibres	Basic metals and metal products	Engineering and allied industries	Other manufacturing	Electricity, gas and water supply	Construction
Percentage change on the year										
	K59M	**K59N**	**K59O**	**K59P**	**K59Q**	**K59R**	**K59S**	**K59T**	**K59U**	**K59V**
2008 Aug	7.8	1.0	3.5	-8.6	-3.1	7.7	2.8	3.0	6.9	-1.0
Sep	13.5	5.3	4.8	-7.7	-2.4	6.1	2.4	2.8	7.0	-0.6
Oct	13.1	2.9	1.9	-0.3	-1.2	6.0	2.5	2.5	1.5	1.7
Nov	8.1	-0.4	4.8	3.2	0.0	4.8	1.8	2.4	4.2	-0.3
Dec	21.5	-0.8	4.0	3.7	-1.1	0.4	2.7	2.0	2.3	-2.9
2009 Jan	6.9	7.2	6.5	0.4	-0.2	-1.5	0.6	2.8	1.2	2.5
Feb	4.0	1.7	-2.7	0.8	0.0	-0.1	-0.6	1.6	0.7	0.7
Mar	3.1	-7.0	6.2	1.8	6.3	2.8	-1.4	1.3	-1.5	2.1
Apr	0.6	6.3	1.0	6.1	4.7	-2.4	1.1	1.2	2.7	1.5
May	4.7	2.2	-5.4	3.6	8.4	-4.1	-1.5	2.4	3.3	0.3
Jun	4.4	-2.1	0.7	-1.1	9.1	-0.6	-1.4	2.6	8.4	-1.2
Jul	3.6	1.9	-0.8	2.3	8.7	-6.4	-2.1	0.8	5.0	-0.1
Aug	0.3	6.2	-0.5	4.3	10.5	-2.6	0.2	3.1	0.5	2.0
Sep	2.2	-0.1	1.1	0.5	7.3	-1.5	0.6	3.7	0.4	-0.9
Oct	-0.4	5.6	0.5	2.0	8.1	-2.8	0.9	3.0	3.8	0.9
Nov	5.6	3.5	-0.2	5.5	5.9	2.1	0.8	2.3	3.7	1.1
Dec	1.8	4.4	7.3	8.6	10.7	2.4	0.4	2.3	1.2	1.6
2010 Jan	1.0	-2.2	6.8	8.2	10.7	2.2	1.9	3.8	3.2	1.9
Feb	7.8	6.8	3.2	3.8	13.0	7.8	2.6	6.2	3.4	1.7
Mar	5.6	20.7	12.2	14.5	12.7	15.8	6.0	7.4	4.8	5.8
Apr	2.8	-4.1	5.5	4.6	-2.9	6.5	3.5	3.6	1.4	0.0
May	-5.9	-2.3	1.2	6.1	3.9	8.1	5.0	2.4	1.2	0.4
Jun	-2.9	-2.8	2.9	-0.5	-0.6	4.7	4.6	2.4	3.9	1.0
Jul	1.9	-2.2	1.3	9.8	2.3	8.3	5.1	4.4	0.5	-0.9
Aug	0.3	-1.5	4.5	9.3	2.2	6.7	4.5	2.9	1.9	-1.8
Sep	-5.1	-1.2	4.1	7.9	2.0	7.0	4.5	2.6	1.6	0.0
Oct	11.2	-3.6	3.4	6.3	5.9	6.4	3.7	2.7	2.4	-2.1
Nov	5.3	-1.8	2.7	1.9	6.9	1.4	3.9	2.6	1.2	-2.1
Dec	7.7	-3.5	-0.3	-2.0	2.8	0.7	2.0	1.7	4.4	-4.7

4.14d Average weekly earnings : by industry Great Britain

Not seasonally adjusted continued

	Wholesale trade	Retail trade and repairs	Accom- modation & Food Services	Transport and storage	Information and Comm- unication	Financial & Insurance Activities	Real estate activities	Professional Scientific & Technical Activities	Administrative & support service activities	Public admini- stration	Educ- ation	Health and social work	Other services	Arts, Entertainment & Recreation
Including bonuses SIC 2007														
	K586	**K589**	**K58C**	**K58F**	**K5E9**	**K58I**	**K58L**	**K5EC**	**K5EF**	**K58O**	**K58R**	**K58U**	**K58X**	**K5EI**
2008	503	250	213	490	732	966	454	625	334	500	381	380	382	305
2009	506	256	213	493	728	882	451	635	341	511	395	390	372	301
2010	510	264	220	503	740	954	470	652	337	527	397	395	365	317
2007 Aug	473	245	211	475	685	713	439	596	320	501	373	362	382	303
Sep	473	244	210	464	686	738	421	593	315	487	376	363	382	298
Oct	481	245	213	462	677	681	425	597	319	485	372	365	381	283
Nov	488	238	218	470	691	707	423	602	322	494	377	380	380	289
Dec	498	238	224	504	702	780	454	641	336	505	381	374	379	294
2008 Jan	502	244	208	472	704	1392	443	602	323	497	370	373	370	313
Feb	515	245	215	479	726	1974	439	618	330	498	371	373	371	307
Mar	543	261	224	498	780	1383	491	644	336	492	372	375	381	333
Apr	499	259	210	488	733	738	453	621	332	498	376	378	384	303
May	490	255	217	537	726	783	431	616	331	495	377	376	382	302
Jun	504	252	211	509	770	798	443	628	338	495	376	377	383	301
Jul	497	249	212	480	728	741	498	638	340	505	380	382	400	306
Aug	487	248	214	478	737	722	447	636	337	507	382	389	391	309
Sep	491	246	211	474	715	749	435	621	331	498	387	381	385	289
Oct	489	247	210	480	726	734	450	622	334	495	386	384	380	294
Nov	506	242	208	479	712	704	450	622	332	510	399	387	373	296
Dec	511	247	215	504	727	869	465	636	339	510	397	388	385	305
2009 Jan	518	252	206	480	710	1033	449	632	341	502	391	387	380	293
Feb	528	258	215	477	752	1229	430	638	337	524	390	384	376	291
Mar	537	265	213	490	803	1170	483	670	345	505	388	385	387	301
Apr	497	258	212	494	747	803	450	632	344	508	393	392	382	303
May	494	257	217	542	729	760	439	629	345	512	392	394	367	295
Jun	498	260	211	500	749	846	439	633	344	507	394	396	361	308
Jul	494	258	214	484	713	755	459	637	346	508	398	391	368	305
Aug	491	256	211	486	725	749	433	620	346	513	399	386	366	297
Sep	493	254	210	492	719	785	449	619	333	505	402	390	362	295
Oct	497	256	212	487	696	754	453	628	336	508	401	391	365	300
Nov	507	250	213	485	693	780	460	626	334	514	396	390	370	312
Dec	523	250	219	503	704	922	471	653	335	520	398	393	378	317
2010 Jan	512	258	213	488	713	899	456	637	343	521	393	388	401	322
Feb	523	266	222	491	746	1694	456	652	333	521	392	392	368	307
Mar	610	294	221	517	827	1438	521	719	353	521	393	390	411	333
Apr	503	270	217	497	704	789	451	648	342	522	395	397	365	302
May	496	261	221	496	725	887	454	635	341	522	394	398	353	304
Jun	497	267	215	521	782	869	463	641	334	524	394	399	360	309
Jul	501	265	215	500	728	804	481	634	339	532	397	396	356	319
Aug	489	261	223	499	736	780	466	635	332	535	398	395	359	325
Sep	489	260	221	501	728	839	468	636	330	528	404	397	352	323
Oct	490	257	226	503	722	793	473	645	334	529	401	396	345	315
Nov	490	258	220	507	729	787	474	655	329	533	400	398	354	317
Dec	521	256	228	515	742	871	482	683	328	539	401	398	354	326

4.14d Average weekly earnings : by industry Great Britain

Not seasonally adjusted continued

	Wholesale trade	Retail trade and repairs	Accom- modation & Food Services	Transport and storage	Information and Comm- unication	Financial & Insurance Activities	Real estate activities	Professional Scientific & Technical Activities	Administrative & support service activities	Public admini- stration	Educ- ation	Health and social work	Other services	Arts, Entertainment & Recreation

Percentage change on the year

	K59W	K59X	K59Y	K59Z	K5EP	K5A2	K5A3	K5EQ	K5ER	K5A4	K5A5	K5A6	K5A7	K5ES
2008 Aug	2.9	1.3	1.3	0.5	7.7	1.2	2.0	6.7	5.5	1.2	2.5	7.7	2.2	1.9
Sep	3.7	0.8	0.8	2.2	4.2	1.6	3.3	4.6	5.0	2.2	2.8	5.1	0.9	-3.0
Oct	1.5	0.7	-1.3	3.9	7.2	7.8	5.9	4.2	4.8	2.0	3.6	5.2	-0.2	3.8
Nov	3.7	2.0	-4.4	1.7	3.1	-0.4	6.2	3.3	3.1	3.3	5.9	1.9	-2.0	2.4
Dec	2.7	3.5	-3.8	0.1	3.6	11.3	2.5	-0.7	0.9	1.0	4.3	3.7	1.5	3.7
2009 Jan	3.2	3.1	-0.9	1.7	0.9	-25.8	1.4	5.0	5.5	0.9	5.5	3.5	2.8	-6.2
Feb	2.4	5.3	0.1	-0.5	3.5	-37.8	-2.1	3.2	2.1	5.3	5.0	2.8	1.6	-5.1
Mar	-1.2	1.7	-4.9	-1.5	3.0	-15.4	-1.8	4.0	2.7	2.7	4.1	2.8	1.7	-9.5
Apr	-0.2	-0.7	1.3	1.2	1.9	8.8	-0.6	1.7	3.7	2.0	4.4	3.8	-0.5	-0.1
May	0.8	0.9	0.2	0.8	0.4	-3.0	1.7	2.1	4.1	3.5	3.8	4.9	-3.9	-2.2
Jun	-1.1	3.1	0.0	-1.7	-2.8	6.0	-0.9	0.9	1.6	2.3	4.7	4.9	-5.6	2.6
Jul	-0.5	3.3	0.8	0.8	-2.0	1.9	-7.8	-0.2	1.9	0.8	4.6	2.4	-8.0	-0.4
Aug	0.8	3.3	-1.4	1.7	-1.6	3.8	-3.2	-2.5	2.8	1.3	4.4	-1.0	-6.2	-3.7
Sep	0.5	3.2	-0.5	3.7	0.5	4.7	3.3	-0.3	0.5	1.5	3.9	2.3	-5.8	1.9
Oct	1.7	3.7	0.7	1.4	-4.1	2.7	0.6	0.9	0.6	2.6	3.9	1.8	-4.1	1.9
Nov	0.1	3.2	2.4	1.4	-2.6	10.9	2.4	0.6	0.6	0.7	-0.7	0.9	-0.7	5.6
Dec	2.4	1.4	1.8	-0.2	-3.2	6.1	1.2	2.6	-1.2	1.9	0.1	1.3	-1.7	4.1
2010 Jan	-1.1	2.7	3.3	1.6	0.5	-13.0	1.5	0.8	0.6	3.8	0.6	0.4	5.7	9.8
Feb	-1.0	2.9	3.2	3.0	-0.8	37.9	6.0	2.2	-1.0	-0.6	0.5	2.2	-2.2	5.5
Mar	13.7	10.8	3.8	5.5	2.9	22.9	8.0	7.3	2.2	3.2	1.4	1.1	6.1	10.5
Apr	1.1	4.8	2.4	0.6	-5.8	-1.7	0.2	2.6	-0.7	2.7	0.7	1.2	-4.6	-0.2
May	0.3	1.3	1.5	-8.4	-0.6	16.8	3.4	1.0	-1.1	2.0	0.6	1.1	-3.7	3.1
Jun	-0.3	2.5	2.0	4.2	4.5	2.7	5.4	1.2	-2.8	3.4	0.0	0.7	-0.5	0.0
Jul	1.3	2.9	0.8	3.4	2.0	6.5	4.8	-0.4	-2.2	4.6	-0.3	1.2	-3.4	4.6
Aug	-0.2	1.8	5.8	2.7	1.5	4.1	7.7	2.4	-4.3	4.2	-0.2	2.5	-2.0	9.4
Sep	-0.8	2.5	5.2	2.0	1.3	6.9	4.1	2.7	-0.8	4.4	0.5	1.9	-2.8	9.5
Oct	-1.4	0.6	6.9	3.3	3.8	5.3	4.4	2.7	-0.5	4.1	0.0	1.2	-5.5	5.0
Nov	-3.3	3.1	3.1	4.4	5.2	0.8	3.0	4.7	-1.4	3.7	1.0	1.9	-4.3	1.6
Dec	-0.5	2.4	4.1	2.3	5.4	-5.5	2.3	4.6	-2.2	3.7	0.9	1.3	-6.3	2.6

See chapter text.

Source: Office for National Statistics: 01633 456780

4.15 Median[1] Gross weekly and hourly earnings of full-time employees[2] by sex: United Kingdom

April 2006 to 2010

£   £

	Gross weekly earnings						Gross hourly earnings				
	Lowest decile	Lower quartile	Median	Upper quartile	Highest decile		Lowest decile	Lower quartile	Median	Upper quartile	Highest decile
All											
	C5U9	C5UC	C5UF	C5UI	C5UL		C5UO	C5UR	C5UU	C5V2	C5UX
2006	243.8	315.2	443.6	630.5	881.6		6.24	7.93	11.12	16.39	23.49
2007	252.9	325.8	457.6	650.5	907.1		6.47	8.22	11.47	16.87	24.17
2008	262.2	338.8	479.1	677.9	950.7		6.67	8.51	11.98	17.59	25.12
2009	270.3	347.0	488.5	692.5	971.4		6.94	8.82	12.42	18.18	25.91
2010	275.7	354.6	498.8	705.3	984.2		7.02	8.95	12.57	18.49	26.26
Male											
	C5UA	C5UD	C5UG	C5UJ	C5UM		C5UP	C5US	C5UV	C5V3	C5UY
2006	264.5	346.0	484.3	687.5	980.5		6.50	8.37	11.76	17.38	25.64
2007	274.0	358.0	498.3	706.0	1,008.1		6.73	8.65	12.09	17.89	26.40
2008	283.0	371.5	522.0	737.7	1,055.5		6.96	8.95	12.63	18.69	27.54
2009	290.5	379.1	531.0	752.7	1,081.5		7.21	9.24	13.08	19.28	28.43
2010	295.3	384.6	538.2	765.0	1,091.0		7.27	9.33	13.14	19.49	28.62
Female											
	C5UB	C5UE	C5UH	C5UK	C5UN		C5UQ	C5UT	C5UW	C5V4	C5UZ
2006	226.3	282.1	383.3	550.0	724.9		5.98	7.42	10.16	14.92	20.39
2007	233.5	289.8	394.8	565.4	749.0		6.18	7.67	10.48	15.33	20.95
2008	241.0	302.9	412.4	590.8	777.9		6.37	7.95	10.94	16.01	21.65
2009	250.0	313.0	425.8	612.8	812.3		6.63	8.26	11.41	16.61	22.64
2010	255.2	321.1	439.0	628.2	826.5		6.75	8.46	11.71	17.08	23.10

1. Median values are less affected by extremes of earnings at either ends of the scale with half the employees earning above the stated amount and half below.

2. Data relate to full-time employees on adult rates whose pay for the survey pay-period was not affected by absence.

Source: Annual Survey of Hours and Earnings:
01633 456 120

4.16 Median[1] weekly and hourly earnings of full-time employees[2] by age group: United Kingdom April 2006 to 2010

£

	18-21	22-29	30-39	40-49	50-59	60+	All ages
Median gross weekly earnings							
All							
	JRG9	JRH2	JRH3	JRH4	JEH5	JRH6	JRH7
2006	250.6	376.5	496.1	502.5	465.4	400.0	443.6
2007	265.5	387.8	509.0	517.3	479.1	418.7	457.6
2008	271.6	400.0	532.7	539.9	504.1	437.5	479.1
2009	277.5	407.1	541.8	550.5	514.0	446.3	488.5
2010	277.4	411.2	547.8	559.6	528.2	457.3	498.8
Men							
	JRH8	JRH9	JRI2	JRI3	JRI4	JRI5	JRI6
2006	261.5	390.6	525.0	558.7	516.0	421.6	484.3
2007	275.9	402.5	539.0	574.9	534.4	440.9	498.3
2008	280.0	416.7	566.3	599.1	563.6	462.6	522.0
2009	285.7	421.6	571.1	605.2	569.7	469.0	531.0
2010	285.9	421.2	573.7	613.7	582.7	483.0	538.2
Women							
	JRI7	JRI8	JRI9	JRJ2	JRJ3	JRJ4	JRJ5
2006	240.4	362.7	444.0	410.2	385.0	343.7	383.3
2007	254.3	374.1	460.6	420.3	395.6	356.1	394.8
2008	258.8	384.7	480.9	437.3	419.7	376.4	412.4
2009	268.3	392.9	497.9	457.7	432.8	382.1	425.8
2010	268.3	401.3	507.9	472.2	440.9	389.0	439.0
Median hourly earnings (excluding overtime)							
All							
	JRJ6	JRJ7	JRJ8	JRJ9	JRK2	JRK3	JRK4
2006	6.31	9.50	12.43	12.49	11.50	9.72	11.03
2007	6.60	9.80	12.77	12.77	11.87	10.09	11.36
2008	6.75	10.12	13.34	13.31	12.53	10.57	11.88
2009	7.00	10.43	13.82	13.83	12.95	10.97	12.33
2010	7.00	10.34	13.91	14.01	13.19	11.18	12.50
Men							
	JRK5	JRK6	JRK7	JRK8	JRK9	JRL2	JRL3
2006	6.37	9.51	12.78	13.46	12.28	9.96	11.64
2007	6.65	9.80	13.10	13.77	12.79	10.31	11.97
2008	6.85	10.13	13.70	14.37	13.52	10.89	12.50
2009	7.09	10.45	14.15	14.95	13.91	11.25	12.97
2010	7.05	10.26	14.07	14.95	14.25	11.50	13.01
Women							
	JRL4	JRL5	JRL6	JRL7	JRL8	JRL9	JRM2
2006	6.24	9.48	11.87	10.95	10.24	9.17	10.14
2007	6.55	9.79	12.28	11.14	10.54	9.48	10.48
2008	6.64	10.12	12.78	11.57	11.10	9.82	10.92
2009	6.93	10.40	13.29	12.21	11.52	10.23	11.39
2010	6.90	10.48	13.66	12.54	11.84	10.40	11.68

1. Median values are less affected by extremes of earnings at either ends of the scale with half the employees earning above the stated amount and half below.
2. Data relate to full-time employees on adult rates whose pay for the survey pay-period was not affected by absence.

Source: Annual Survey of Hours and Earnings: 01633 456 120

4.17 Trade unions[1]

United Kingdom
Year ending 31st March[2]

Percentages

		2000 /01	2001 /02	2002 /03	2003 /04	2004 /05	2005 /06	2006 /07	2007 /08	2008 /09	2009 /10
Number of trade unions	**KCLB**	237	226	216	213	206	193	192	193	185	179
Analysis by number of members:											
Under 100 members	**KCLC**	18.6	22.1	19	20.7	19.9	17.6	17.7	17.1	17.8	19.6
100 and under 500	**KCLD**	20.7	18.1	18.5	18.8	17.5	20.7	18.2	19.2	17.3	16.8
500 and under 1,000	**KCLE**	9.3	9.3	11.6	10.3	10.7	9.3	9.9	10.9	13	12.3
1,000 and under 2,500	**KCLF**	14.3	12.4	10.2	10.8	11.7	13	12.5	11.4	10.8	9.5
2,500 and under 5,000	**KCLG**	9.7	9.3	11.6	10.8	10.7	10.9	11.5	12.4	12.4	11.7
5,000 and under 10,000	**KCLH**	5.1	5.3	4.2	4.7	5.3	5.7	6.3	6.2	5.9	6.1
10,000 and under 15,000	**KCLI**	1.7	1.8	2.8	3.3	2.4	2.1	1.6	1.6	1.1	2.2
15,000 and under 25,000	**KCLJ**	4.2	5.3	6	4.2	4.9	4.1	4.7	4.1	4.9	4.4
25,000 and under 50,000	**KCLK**	7.6	6.6	6.5	7	7.3	7.8	8.9	8.3	8.1	8.4
50,000 and under 100,000	**KCLL**	2.1	2.7	2.3	1.9	2.4	1.6	1.6	1	1.1	1.1
100,000 and under 250,000	**KCLM**	2.1	2.2	2.3	2.8	2.4	2.6	2.6	3.1	3.2	3.4
250,000 and over	**KCLN**	4.6	4.9	5.1	4.7	4.9	4.7	4.7	4.7	4.3	4.5
Membership											
Analysis by size of union:											
Under 100 members	**KCLQ**	–	–	–	–	–	–	–	–	–	–
100 and under 500	**KCLR**	0.2	0.2	0.2	0.2	0.1	0.1	0.1	0.1	0.1	0.1
500 and under 1,000	**KCLS**	0.2	0.2	0.2	0.2	0.2	0.2	0.2	0.2	0.2	0.2
1,000 and under 2,500	**KCLT**	0.7	0.6	0.5	0.5	0.5	0.6	0.5	0.5	0.4	0.4
2,500 and under 5,000	**KCLU**	1.1	1	1.2	1.1	1	1	1	1.1	1	1
5,000 and under 10,000	**KCLV**	1.2	1.1	0.9	0.9	1.1	1.2	1.2	1.2	1.1	1.1
10,000 and under 15,000	**KCLW**	0.7	0.6	0.9	1.1	0.8	0.6	0.5	0.5	0.3	0.8
15,000 and under 25,000	**KCLX**	2.3	2.9	3.3	2.2	2.5	1.9	2.2	2	2.3	2.2
25,000 and under 50,000	**KCLY**	7.8	6.6	6.3	6.7	6.9	7.1	8.1	7.4	7	7.2
50,000 and under 100,000	**KCLZ**	3.8	4.6	4	3.1	4.4	2.6	2.7	1.8	1.8	1.9
100,000 and under 250,000	**KCMA**	10	9.8	9.6	10.2	9	10.6	10.6	12.2	12.2	12.6
250,000 and over	**KCMB**	72.1	72.4	73	73.9	73.3	74.1	72.9	73	73.5	72.5
All sizes	**KCMC**	100	100	100	100	100	100	100	100	100	100
Total membership (thousands)	**KCMD**	7897519	7779393	7750990	7735983	7559062	7473000	7602842	7627693	7656156	7387898

1. See chapter text.
2. Data derived from trade union annual returns received during the reporting year.
The returns covered periods which ended between October and September of the preceding years,
 the majority, however, ended in December. In the case of year 2004/05, for example, the data derived from
annual returns with periods which ended between October 2003 and September
2004 - approximately 78% ended in December 2003.

Source: Certification Office

Social protection

Chapter 5

Social Protection

(Tables 5.2 to 5.11, 5.13 and 5.15 to 5.19)

Tables 5.2 to 5.6, 5.9 to 5.11 and 5.13 to 5.19 give details of contributors and beneficiaries under the National Insurance and Industrial Injury Acts, supplementary benefits and war pensions.

There are four classes of National Insurance Contributions (NICs):

Class 1 Earnings-related contributions paid on earnings from employment. Employees pay primary Class 1 contributions and employers pay secondary Class 1 contributions. Payment of Class 1 contributions builds up entitlement to contributory benefits which include Basic State Pension; Additional State Pension (State Earnings Related Pension Scheme SERPS and from April 2002, State Second Pension, S2P); Contribution Based Jobseeker's Allowance; Bereavement Benefits; Incapacity Benefit; and the new Employment and Support Allowance.

Primary class 1 contributions stop at State Pension age, but not Class 1 secondary contributions paid by employers. There are reduced contribution rates where the employee contracts out of S2P (previously SERPS). They still receive a Basic State Pension but an Occupational or Personal Pension instead of the Additional State Second Pension.

Class 2 Flat rate contributions paid by the self-employed whose profits are above the small earnings exception. Payment of Class 2 contributions builds up entitlement to the contributory benefits which include Basic State Pension; Bereavement Benefits; Maternity Allowance; Incapacity Benefit; and the Employment and Support Allowance, but not Additional State Second Pension or Contribution Based Jobseeker's Allowance (JSA).

Class 2 contributions stop at State Pension age.

Class 3 Flat rate voluntary contributions, which can be paid by someone whose contribution record is insufficient. Payment of Class 3 contributions builds up entitlement to contributory benefits which include Basic State Pension and Bereavement Benefits. (Tables 5.2 to 5.11, 5.13 and 5.15 to 5.19) Tables 5.2 to 5.6, 5.9 to 5.11 and 5.13 to 5.19 give details of contributors and beneficiaries under the National Insurance and Industrial Injury Acts, supplementary benefits and war pensions.

Class 4 Profit-related contributions paid by the self employed in addition to Class 2 contributions. Class 4 contributions stop at State Pension age. Under some circumstances people who are not in employment do not have to make voluntary contributions to accrue a qualifying year for Basic State Pension.

Home Responsibilities Protection

Home Responsibilities Protection (HRP) was introduced to help to protect the basic State Pension of those precluded from regular employment because they are caring for children or a sick or disabled person at home. To be entitled to HRP, a person must have been precluded from regular employment for a full tax year. HRP reduces the amount of qualifying years a person would otherwise need for a Basic State Pension. The scheme ceased on the 6th April 2010 and has been replaced by new weekly credits which can be claimed if qualifying criteria are met.

National Insurance Credits

In addition to paying, or being treated as having paid contributions, a person can be credited with National Insurance contributions (NIC) credits. Contribution credits help to protect people's rights to State Retirement Pension and other Social Security Benefits.

A person is likely to be entitled to contributions credits if they are: a student in full time education or training, in receipt of Jobseeker's Allowance, unable to work due to sickness or disability, entitled to Statutory Maternity Pay or Statutory Adoption Pay, or they have received Carer's Allowance.

Credits are automatically awarded for men aged 60 to 65 provided they are not liable to pay Class 1 or 2 NICs, and to young people for the tax years containing their 16th, 17th and 18th birthdays.

Jobseeker's Allowance (Table 5.6)

Jobseeker's Allowance (JSA) replaced Unemployment Benefit and Income Support for unemployed claimants on 7 October 1996. It is a unified benefit with two routes of entry: contribution-based, which depends mainly upon National Insurance contributions, and income-based, which depends mainly upon a means test. Some claimants can qualify by either route. In practice they receive income-based JSA but have an underlying entitlement to the contribution based element.

Employment and Support Allowance, Invalidity Benefit and Incapacity Benefit (Table 5.7)

Incapacity Benefit replaced Sickness Benefit and Invalidity Benefit from 13 April 1995. The first condition for entitlement to these contributory benefits is that the claimants are incapable of work because of illness or disablement. The second is that they satisfy the contribution conditions, which depend on contributions paid as an employed (Class 1) or self-employed person (Class 2). Under Sickness and Invalidity Benefits the contribution conditions were automatically treated as satisfied if a person was incapable of work because of an industrial accident or prescribed disease. Under Incapacity Benefit those who do not satisfy the contribution conditions do not have them treated as satisfied. Class 1A contributions paid by employers are in respect of the benefit of cars provided for the private use of employees, and the free fuel provided for private use. These contributions do not provide any type of benefit cover.

Since 6 April 1983, most people working for an employer and paying National Insurance contributions as employed persons receive Statutory Sick Pay (SSP) from their employer when they are off work sick. Until 5 April 1986 SSP was payable for a maximum of eight weeks, since this date SSP has been payable for 28 weeks. People who do not work for an employer, and employees who are excluded from the SSP scheme, or those who have run out of SSP before reaching the maximum of 28 weeks and are still sick, can claim benefit. Any period of SSP is excluded from the tables.

Spells of incapacity of three days or less do not count as periods of interruption of employment and are excluded from the tables. Exceptions are where people are receiving regular weekly treatment by dialysis or treatment by radiotherapy, chemotherapy or plasmapheresis where two days in any six consecutive days make up a period of interruption of employment, and those whose incapacity for work ends within three days of the end of SSP entitlement.

At the beginning of a period of incapacity, benefit is subject to three waiting days, except where there was an earlier spell of incapacity of more than three days in the previous eight weeks. Employees entitled to SSP for less than 28 weeks and who are still sick can get Sickness Benefit or Incapacity Benefit Short Term (Low) until they reach a total of 28 weeks provided they satisfy the conditions.

After 28 weeks of SSP and/or Sickness Benefit (SB), Invalidity Benefit (IVB) was payable up to pension age for as long as the incapacity lasted. From pension age, IVB was paid at the person's State Pension rate, until entitlement ceased when SP was paid, or until deemed pension age (70 for a man, 65 for a woman). People who were on Sickness or Invalidity Benefit on 12 April 1995 were automatically transferred to Incapacity Benefit, payable on the same basis as before.

For people on Incapacity Benefit under State Pension age there are two short-term rates: the lower rate is paid for the first 28 weeks of sickness and the higher rate for weeks 29 to 52. From week 53 the Long Term rate Incapacity Benefit is payable. The Short Term rate Incapacity Benefit is based on State Pension entitlement for people over State Pension age and is paid for up to a year if incapacity began before pension age.

The long-term rate of Incapacity Benefit applies to people under State Pension age who have been sick for more than a year. People with a terminal illness, or who are receiving the higher rate care component of Disability Living Allowance, will get the Long Term rate. The Long Term rate is not paid for people over pension age.

Under Incapacity Benefit, for the first 28 weeks of incapacity, people previously in work will be assessed on the 'own occupation' test – the claimant's ability to do their own job. Otherwise, incapacity will be based on a personal capability assessment, which will assess ability to carry out a range of work-related activities. The test will apply after 28 weeks of incapacity or from the start of the claim for people who did not previously have a job. Certain people will be exempted from this test.

The tables exclude all men aged over 65 and women aged over 60 who are in receipt of State Pension, and all people over deemed pension age (70 for a man and 65 for a woman), members of the armed forces, mariners while at sea, and married women and certain widows who have chosen not to be insured for sickness benefit. The tables include a number of individuals who were unemployed prior to incapacity.

levels. Also their IVB is not subject to tax. If they were over State Pension age on 12 April 1995 they may get Incapacity Benefit for up to five years beyond pension age.

Employment and Support Allowance (ESA) replaced Incapacity Benefit and Income Support paid on the grounds of incapacity for new claims from 27 October 2008. ESA consists of two phases. The first, the assessment phase rate, is paid for the first 13 weeks of the claim whilst a decision is made on the claimants capability through the 'Work Capability Asessment'. The second, or main phase begins after 14 weeks, but only if the 'Work Capability Assesment' has deemed the claimants illness or disability as a limitation on their ability to work.

Within the main phase there are two groups, 'The Work Related Activity Group' and 'The Support Group'. If a claimant is placed in the first, they are expected to take part in work focused interviews with a personal advisor. They will be given support to help them prepare for work and on gaining work will receive a work related activity component in addition to their basic rate. If the claimant is placed in the second group due to their illness or disability having a severe effect upon their ability to work, the claimant will not be expected to work at all, but can do so on a voluntary basis. These claimants will receive a support component in addition to their basic rate.

Child Benefits (Table 5.9a and 5.9b)

Child Benefit (CB) is paid to those responsible for children (aged under 16) or qualifying young people. The latter includes:
a) a person under the age of 19 in full-time non-advanced education or (from April 2006) on certain approved vocational training programmes
b) a person who is aged 19 who began their course of full-time, non-advanced education or approved training before reaching age 19 (note: those reaching 19 up to 9 April 2006 ceased to qualify on their 19th birthday)
c) a person who has reached the age of 16 until the 31 August following their 16th birthday
d) a person aged 16 or 17 who has left education and training who is registered with the Careers service or with Connexions and is awaiting a placement in employment or training for the limited period of up to 20 weeks from the date they left education or training. Entitlement for a qualifying young person continues until the terminal date following the date they leave full-time education or approved training. The terminal dates are at the end of August, November, February and May (there is a slight variation for Scotland). Entitlement is also maintained for a person who is entered for external examinations connected with their course throughout the period between a person leaving education or training and completing those examinations. Entitlement in all cases ceases when a person reaches the age of 20.

Guardian's Allowance is an additional allowance for people bringing up a child because one or both of their parents has died. They must be getting Child Benefit (CB) for the child. The table shows the number of families in the UK in receipt of CB. The numbers shown in the table are estimates based on a random 5 per cent sample of awards current at 31 August, and are therefore

Child and Working Tax Credits (CTC and WTC) replaced Working Families' Tax Credit (WFTC) from 6th April 2003. CTC and WTC are claimed by individuals, or jointly by couples, whether or not they have children.

CTC provides support to families for the children (up to the 31 August after their 16th birthday) and the 'qualifying' young people (in full-time non-advanced education until their 19th birthday) for which they are responsible. It is paid in addition to CB.

WTC tops up the earnings of families on low or moderate incomes. People working for at least 16 hours a week can claim it if they: (a) are responsible for at least one child or qualifying young person, (b) have a disability which puts them at a disadvantage in getting a job or, (c) in the first year of work, having returned to work aged at least 50 after a period of at least six months receiving out-of-work benefits. Other adults also qualify if they are aged at least 25 and work for at least 30 hours a week.

Widow's Benefit and Bereavement Benefit (Table 5.12 and 5.13)

Widow's Benefit is payable to women widowed on or after 11 April 1988 and up to and including 8 April 2001. There are three types of Widow's Benefits: Widow's Payment, Widowed Mother's Allowance and Widow's Pension. Women widowed before 11 April 1988 continue to receive Widow's Benefit based on the rules that existed before that date. Bereavement Benefit was introduced on 9 April 2001 as a replacement for Widow's Benefit, payable to both men and women widowed on or after 9 April 2001. There are three types of Bereavement Benefits available: Bereavement Payment, Widowed Parent's Allowance and Bereavement Allowance.

5.1 National Insurance Fund (Great Britain and Northern Ireland)

Years ended 31 March

£ million

		2000 /01	2001 /02	2002 /03	2003 /04	2004 /05	2005 /06	2006 /07	2007 /08	2008 /09	2009 /10
Receipts											
Opening balance	KJFB	14909	19868	24177	27267	27816	29804	34940	39243	50288	53046
Contributions	JXVM	55627	58050	59658	59827	62863	67786	69599	77224	74453	73817
State Scheme Premiums[1]	C59W	..	..	194	147	115	117	76	79	67	52
Grant from Consolidated Fund	KOTF	..	..	..	..	..	..	..	..	..	..
Compensation for SSP/SMP	KJQM	688	710	775	1346	1470	1392	1197	1919	1626	1684
Transfers from Great Britian	KOTG	200	110	350	260	270	185	630	452	505	395
Income from investments	KJFE	884	1146	1457	1292	1288	1399	1867	2453	1957	237
Other receipts	KJFF	112	67	80	82	72	66	54	57	50	49
Redundancy receipts	KIBQ	23	22	24	28	32	38	43	37	39	40
Total	JYJO	72442	79972	86716	90249	93926	100787	108406	121464	128985	129320
Expenditure											
Total benefits	JYJP	50960	54550	54201	56255	58572	61304	63695	67443	70487	75410
Jobseeker's Allowance (Contributory)	LUQW	449	478	519	512	455	497	493	435	703	1106
Incapacity	JYXL	6982	7074	7104	7116	6910	7028	7009	6945	6600	6177
Maternity	KETY	46	57	70	128	153	128	180	250	320	343
Bereavement Benefits	KEWU	1008	1132	1142	1033	946	903	826	759	683	647
Guardian's allowances and Child's special allowance[2]	KJFK	2	2	2	2	1	2	2	2	2	2
Retirement pensions[3]	JYJV	42350	45677	45240	47339	49979	52578	55053	58921	61301	66442
Other payments	KAAZ	21	29	27	34	30	33	40	61	97	126
Administration	KABE	1197	873	1280	1794	1521	1464	1473	1430	1326	1401
Transfers to Northern Ireland	KABF	200	110	350	260	270	185	630	452	505	395
Redundancy payments	KIBR	195	232	255	243	222	295	248	215	428	531
Personal Pensions	C59X	..	..	3336	3847	3508	2566	3076	2557	2629	2623
Total	JYJU	52574	55795	59449	62433	64123	65847	69161	72027	74594	79793
Accumulated funds	KABH	19868	24177	27267	27816	29804	34940	39245	50288	53046	48457

1 State Scheme Premiums are payable in respect of employed persons who cease to be covered, in certain circumstances, by a contracted out pension scheme.
2 Includes Child's special allowance for Northern Ireland
3 Includes personal pensions up to 2001/02.

Sources: HM Revenue and Customs
http://www.hmrc.gov.uk/about/ni-fundaccount09-10.pdf
Department for Work and Pensions:01253 856123 Ext 62436

5.2 Persons[1] who paid National Insurance contributions[2,3] in a tax year:[4] by sex United Kingdom

Millions

		Total					Men					Women			
		2005 /06	2006 /07	2007 /08	2008 /09		2005 /06	2006 /07	2007 /08	2008 /09		2005 /06	2006 /07	2007 /08	2008 /09
Total	**KABI**	29.02	28.91	28.98	29.39	**KEYF**	15.89	15.8	15.82	15.97	**KEYP**	13.13	13.08	13.17	13.42
Class 1	**KABJ**	24.5	24.5	24.77	25.21	**KEYG**	13.03	13.49	13.16	13.39	**KEYQ**	11.47	11.47	11.61	11.82
Not contracted out[5]	**KABK**	17.47	17.88	18.54	18.73	**KEYH**	9.69	9.64	10.35	10.43	**KEYR**	7.79	7.93	8.19	8.30
Contracted out	**KABL**	7.03	6.62	6.23	6.48	**KEYI**	3.35	3.34	2.81	2.96	**KEYS**	3.68	3.54	3.42	3.52
Mixed contracted in/out[6]	**KABM**	1.18	1.1	1.06	1.10	**KEYJ**	0.5	0.52	0.43	0.43	**KEYT**	0.68	0.63	0.63	0.67
Class 1 Reduced rate (including standard rate)	**KABO**	0.04	0.03	0.02	0.02	**KEYL**	–	–	–	–	**KEYV**	0.04	0.03	0.02	0.02
Class 2 exclusively[7]	**KABP**	2.38	2.4	2.36	2.32	**KEYM**	1.8	1.77	1.75	1.69	**KEYW**	0.59	0.6	0.62	0.63
Mixed Class 1 and Class 2	**KABQ**	0.71	0.7	0.7	0.69	**KEYN**	0.47	0.46	0.45	0.44	**KEYX**	0.24	0.25	0.25	0.26
Class 3 exclusively[8]	**KABR**	0.16	0.13	0.07	0.05	**KEYO**	0.07	0.06	0.03	0.02	**KEYY**	0.09	0.07	0.04	0.03
Mixed Class 1, 2 and 3[9]	**I6CH**	0.06	0.05	0.01	0.01	**I6CK**	0.02	0.02	–	–	**I6CN**	0.03	0.03	0.01	–

1 Based on all persons making contributions and not only if they have a qualfying year.
2 Estimates obtained from DWP Infor mation Directorate: Lifetime Labour Market Data Tabulation Tool which uses a 1% sample of the National Insurance Recording System (NIRS2) summer 2010 extract.
3 Components may not sum to totals as a result of rounding.
4 The tax year commences on 6 April and ends on 5 April the following year.

5 Includes those persons with an Appropriate Personal Pension (such persons pay contributions at the not contracted out rate but then receive a rebate paid directly to their scheme).
6 Not included in the above rows.
7 Persons who paid a mixture of Class 2 contributions and others are not included in this category.
8 Persons who paid a mixture of Class 3 contributions and others are not included in this category.
9 Persons with a mixture of class 1,2 or 3 contributions.
Source: HM:Revenue and Customs:020 7147 3045
Department for Work and Pensions;
Information Directorate

5.3 National Insurance contributions United Kingdom

	Employee's standard contibutions[1]		Employer's standard contributions[1]	
	not contracted-out rate	contracted-out rate[2]	not contracted-out rate	contracted-out rate[3]
Class 1 **Weekly earnings**				
2003/04				
Below 77.00 (LEL)	-	-	-	-
77.00-89.00 (PT/ST)	-	See note 4	-	See note 5
89.01-595.00 (UEL)	11.0%	9.4%	12.8%	9.3%
Above 595.00 (UEL)	1%	1%	12.8%	12.8%
2004/05				
Below 79.00 (LEL)	-	-	-	-
79.00-91.00 (PT/ST)	-	See note 4	-	See note 5
91.01-610.00 (UEL)	11.0%	9.4%	12.8%	9.3%
Above 610.00(UEL)	1.0%	1.0%	12.8%	12.8%
2005/06				
Below 82.00 (LEL)	-	-	-	-
82.00-94.00 (PT/ST)	-	See note 4	-	See note 5
94.01-630.00 (UEL)	11.0%	9.4%	12.8%	9.3%
Above 630.00(UEL)	1.0%	1.0%	12.8%	12.8%
2006/07				
Below 84.00 (LEL)	-	-	-	-
84.00-97.00 (PT/ST)	-	See note 4	-	See note 5
97.01-645.00 (UEL)	11.0%	9.4%	12.8%	9.3%
Above 645.00(UEL)	1.0%	1.0%	12.8%	12.8%
2007/08				
Below 87.00 (LEL)	-	-	-	-
87.00-100.00 (PT/ST)	-	See note 4	-	See note 6
100.01-670.00 (UEL)	11.0%	9.4%	12.8%	9.1%
Above 670.00(UEL)	1.0%	1.0%	12.8%	12.8%
2008/09				
Below 90.00 (LEL)	-	-	-	-
90.00-105.00 (PT/ST)	-	See note 4	-	See note 6
105.01-770.00 (UEL/UAP)	11.0%	9.4%	12.8%	9.1%
Above 770.00(UEL)	1.0%	1.0%	12.8%	12.8%
2009/10				
Below 95.00 (LEL)	-	-	-	-
95.00-110.00 (PT/ST)	-	See note 4	-	See note 6
110.01-770.00 (UAP)	11.0%	9.4%	12.8%	9.1%
770.01-844.00 (UEL)	11.0%	11.0%	12.8%	12.8%
Above 844.00	1.0%	1.0%	12.8%	12.8%
2010/11				
Below 97.00 (LEL)	-	-	-	-
97.00-110.00 (PT/ST)	-	See note 4	-	See note 6
110.01-770.00 (UAP)	11.0%	9.4%	12.8%	9.1%
770.01-844.00 (UEL)	11.0%	11.0%	12.8%	12.8%
Above 844.00	1.0%	1.0%	12.8%	12.8%
2011/12				
Below 102.00 (LEL)	-	-	-	-
102.00-136.00 (ST)	-	See note 4	-	See note 6
136.01-139.00 (PT)	-	See note 4	13.8%	10.1%
139.01-770.00 (UAP)	12.0%	10.4%	13.8%	10.1%
770.01-817.00 (UEL)	12.0%	12.0%	13.8%	13.8%
Above 817.00	2.0%	2.0%	13.8%	13.8%

5.3 National Insurance contributions United Kingdom

	2003/04	2004/05	2005/06	2006/07	2007/08	2008/09	2009/10	2010/11	2011/12
Class 2									
Flat rate weekly	£2.00	£2.05	£2.10	£2.10	£2.20	£2.30	£2.40	£2.40	£2.50
Small earnings exception[7] (per annum)	£4,095	£4,215	£4,345	£4,465	£4,635	£4,825	£5,075	£5,075	£5,315
Class 3									
Flat-rate voluntary weekly contributions	£6.95	£7.15	£7.35	£7.55	£7.80	£8.10	£12.05	£12.05	£12.60
Class 4 (Self-employed; profit-related)									
Rate on profits between LPL and UPL	8.0%	8.0%	8.0%	8.0%	8.0%	8.0%	8.0%	8.0%	9.00%
Rate on profits above UPL	1.0%	1.0%	1.0%	1.0%	1.0%	1.0%	1.0%	1.0%	2.00%
Lower profits limit (LPL)	£4,615	£4,745	£4,895	£5,035	£5,225	£5435	£5,715	£5,715	£7,225
Upper profits limit (UPL)	£30,940	£31,720	£32,760	£33,540	34,840	£40040	£43,875	£43,875	£42,475

Note:LEL: Lower Earnings Limit; UEL: Upper Earnings Limit. PT: Primary Threshold; ST: Secondary Threshold. UAP: Upper Accrual Point.

Source: HM Revenue and Customs

1 Married women opting to pay contributions at the reduced rate at 3.85% before 2003-04, 4.85% from 2003-04 and 5.85% from 2011-12 earn no entitlement to contributory National Insurance benefits as a result of these contributions. No women have been allowed to exercise this option since 1977, but around 15,000 women who have been continually married or widowed and in the labour market since that time have retained their right to pay the reduced rate.

2 The rates shown only apply to Contracted-Out Salary Related schemes (COSR). The employees' contracted-out rate applies only between the LEL and the UEL up to 2008-09, and between the LEL and UAP from 2009-10

3 The rates shown only apply to Contracted-Out Salary related schemes (COSR). The employers' contracted-out rate applies only between the LEL and the UEL up to 2008-09, and between the LEL and UAP from 2009-10.

4 The contracted-out rebate for primary contributions is 1.6% of earnings between the LEL and the UEL up to 2008-09 and between the LEL and UAP from 2009-10 for all forms of contracting-out.

5 The contracted-out rebate for secondary contributions is 3.5% of earnings between the LEL and the UEL up to 2006-07.

6 Since 2007-08 the contracted-out rebate for secondary contributions is 3.7% of earnings between the LEL and UEL up to 2008-09 and between the LEL and UAP from 2009-10.

7 If earnings from self-employment are below this annual limit and the contributor applies for and is granted a small earnings exception Class 2 contributions need not be paid. Class 2 or 3 contributions may be paid voluntarily.

5.4 Weekly rates of principal social security benefits[1]

Great Britain and Overseas (excluding Northern Ireland)

At April   £

		2001	2002	2003	2004	2005	2006	2007	2008	2009	2010
Jobseeker's Allowance:											
Personal allowances											
Single											
Aged under 18[2]	KXDH	31.95	32.5	32.9	33.5	33.85	34.6	35.65	47.95	50.95	51.85
Aged 18 - 24	KXDJ	42	42.7	43.25	44.05	44.5	45.5	46.85	47.95	50.95	51.85
Aged 25 or over	KXDK	53.05	53.95	54.65	55.65	56.2	57.45	59.15	60.5	64.3	65.45
Lone parent											
Aged under 18 - usual rate	F92E	31.95	32.5	32.9	33.5	33.85	34.6	35.65	47.95	50.95	51.85
Aged under 18 - higher rate payable in specific circumstances	F92F	42	42.7	43.25	44.05	44.5	45.5	46.85	47.95	50.95	51.85
Aged 18 or over	F92G	53.05	53.95	54.65	55.65	56.2	57.45	59.15	60.5	64.3	65.45
Couple											
Both aged under 18	KXDL	31.95	32.5	32.9	33.5	33.85	34.6	35.65	47.95	50.95	51.85
Both under 18, one disabled	KXDI	42	42.7	43.25	44.05	44.5	45.5	46.85	47.95	50.95	51.85
Both under 18, with a child	F92H	63.35	64.45	65.3	66.5	67.15	68.65	70.7	72.35	76.9	78.30
One under 18, one 18 - 24	KXDI	42	42.7	43.25	44.05	44.5	45.5	46.85	47.95	50.95	51.85
One under 18, one 25+	F92I	53.05	53.95	54.65	55.65	56.2	57.45	59.15	60.5	64.3	65.45
Both aged 18 or over	KXDM	83.25	84.65	85.75	87.3	88.15	90.1	92.8	94.95	100.95	102.75
Dependant children and young people											
Aged under 11 - 16	KXDN	31.45	33.5	38.5	42.27	43.88	45.58	47.45	52.59	56.11	57.57
Aged 16 - 18	KXDP	32.25	34.3	38.5	42.27	43.88	45.58	47.45	52.59	56.11	57.57
Invalidity allowance											
High rate	KJND	14.65	14.9	15.15	15.55	16.05	16.5	17.1	17.75	15.65	15.00
Middle rate	KJNE	9.3	9.5	9.7	10	10.3	10.6	11	11.4	9.1	8.40
Low rate	KJNF	4.65	4.75	4.85	5	5.15	5.3	5.5	5.7	5.35	5.45
Increase for dependants											
Adult	KJNG	41.75	42.45	43.15	44.35	45.7	46.95	48.65	50.55	53.1	53.10
Each child[3]	KJNH	11.35	11.35	11.35	11.35	11.35	11.35	11.35	11.35	11.35	11.35
Incapacity Benefit:											
Short term (Lower) Under pension age	KOSB	52.6	53.5	54.4	55.9	57.65	59.2	61.35	63.75	67.75	68.95
Increase for adult dependant	KOSC	32.55	33.1	33.65	34.6	35.65	36.6	37.9	39.4	41.35	41.35
Short term (Lower) Over pension age	KOSD	66.9	68.05	69.2	71.15	73.35	75.35	78.05	81.1	86.2	87.75
Increase for adult dependant	KOSE	40.1	42.45	41.5	42.65	43.95	45.15	46.8	48.65	51.1	51.10
Short term (Higher)	KOSF	62.2	63.25	64.35	66.15	68.2	70.05	72.55	75.4	80.15	81.60
Increase for dependants:											
Adult	KOSG	32.55	33.1	33.65	34.6	35.65	36.6	37.9	39.4	41.35	41.35
Child[3]	KOSH	11.35	11.35	11.35	11.35	11.35	11.35	11.35	11.35	11.35	11.35
Long term	KOSI	69.75	70.95	72.15	74.15	76.45	78.5	81.35	84.5	89.8	91.40
Increase for dependants:											
Adult	KOSJ	41.75	42.45	43.15	44.35	45.7	46.95	48.65	50.55	53.1	53.10
Child[3]	KOSK	11.35	11.35	11.35	11.35	11.35	11.35	11.35	11.35	11.35	11.35
Incapacity age addition:[4]											
Higher rate	KOSL	14.65	14.9	15.15	15.55	16.05	16.5	17.1	17.75	15.65	15.00
Lower rate	KOSM	7.35	7.45	7.6	7.8	8.05	8.25	8.55	8.9	6.55	5.80
Employment and Support Allowance:[5]											
Single Aged under 18[2]	JTM6	..	..	..	..	..	..	..	..	50.95	51.85
Aged 18 - 24	JTM7	..	..	..	..	..	..	..	..	50.95	51.85
Aged 25 and over	JTM8	..	..	..	..	..	..	..	..	64.3	65.45
Lone parent											
Aged under 18 - usual rate	JTM9	..	..	..	..	..	..	..	..	50.95	51.85
Aged 18 or over	JTN2	..	..	..	..	..	..	..	..	64.3	65.45
Couple											
Both aged under 18	JTN3	..	..	..	..	..	..	..	..	50.95	51.85
Both under 18, with a child	JTN4	..	..	..	..	..	..	..	..	76.9	78.30
Both aged under 18(main phase)	JTN5	..	..	..	..	..	..	..	..	64.3	65.45
Both under 18, with a child (main phase)	JTN6	..	..	..	..	..	..	..	..	100.95	102.75
One under 18, one 18-24	JTN7	..	..	..	..	..	..	..	..	50.95	51.85
One under 18, one 25+	JTN8	..	..	..	..	..	..	..	..	64.3	65.45
Both aged 18 or over	JTN9	..	..	..	..	..	..	..	..	100.95	102.75
Attendance Allowance:											
Higher rate	KJNI	55.3	56.25	57.2	58.8	60.6	62.25	64.5	67	70.35	71.40
Lower rate	KJNJ	37	37.65	38.3	39.35	40.55	41.65	43.15	44.85	47.1	47.80
Carer's Allowance											
Standard Rate	J8T6	..	..	43.15	44.35	45.7	46.95	48.65	50.55	53.1	53.90
Disability Living Allowance:											
Care component											
Higher rate	KXDC	55.3	56.25	57.2	58.8	60.6	62.25	64.5	67	70.35	71.40
Middle rate	KXDD	37	37.65	38.3	39.35	40.55	41.65	43.15	44.85	47.1	47.80
Lower rate	KXDE	14.65	14.9	15.15	15.55	16.05	16.5	17.1	17.75	18.65	18.95
Mobility component											
Higher rate	KXDF	38.65	39.3	39.95	41.05	42.3	43.45	45	46.75	49.1	49.85
Lower rate	KXDG	14.65	14.9	15.15	15.55	16.05	16.5	17.1	17.75	18.65	18.95

5.4 Weekly rates of principal social security benefits[1]
Great Britain and Overseas (excluding Northern Ireland)

At April continued

£

		2001	2002	2003	2004	2005	2006	2007	2008	2009	2010
Maternity Benefit:											
Maternity allowances for insured women[6]											
Standard rate	GPTJ	62.2	75	100	102.8	106	108.85	112.75	117.18	123.06	124.88
Threshold	GPTK	30	30	30	30	30	30	30	30	30	30.00
Guardian's Allowance	KJNN	11.35	11.35	11.55	11.85	12.2	12.5	12.95	13.45	14.1	14.30
Widow's Benefit:											
Widow's pension	KJNO	72.5	75.5	77.45	79.6	82.05	84.25	87.3	90.7	95.25	97.65
Widowed mother's allowance	KJNP	72.5	75.5	77.45	79.6	82.05	84.25	87.3	90.7	95.25	97.65
Addition for each child[3]	KJNQ	11.35	11.35	11.35	11.35	11.35	11.35	11.35	11.35	11.35	11.35
Bereavement Benefit:											
Bereavement allowance	WMPF	72.5	75.5	77.45	79.6	82.05	84.25	87.3	90.7	95.25	97.65
Widowed parent's allowance	WMOZ	72.5	72.5	77.45	79.6	82.05	84.25	87.3	90.7	95.25	97.65
Addition for each child[3]	WMPA	11.35	11.35	11.35	11.35	11.35	11.35	11.35	11.35	11.35	11.35
State Pension contributory:[7]											
Single person	KJNR	72.5	75.5	77.45	79.6	82.05	84.25	87.3	90.7	95.25	97.65
Married couple	KJNS	115.9	120.7	122.8	127.25	131.2	134.75	139.6	145.05	152.3	156.15
State Pension non contributory:											
Man or woman	KJNT	43.4	45.2	45.45	47.65	49.15	50.5	52.3	54.35	57.05	58.50
Married woman	KJNU	24.95	27	27.7	28.5	29.4	30.2	31.3	32.5	34.15	35.00
Industrial Injuries Benefit:											
Disablement pension at 100 per cent rate	KJNW	112.9	114.8	116.8	120.1	123.8	127.1	131.7	136.8	143.6	145.80
Widow's or widower's pension	KJNX	..	..	..	..	..	..	..	..	..	..
Child Benefit:											
First child	KJOA	15.5	15.75	16.05	16.5	17	17.45	18.1	18.8	20	20.30
Subsequent children	KETZ	10.35	10.55	10.75	11.05	11.4	11.7	12.1	12.55	13.2	13.40
War pension:											
Ex-private (100 per cent assessment)	KJOJ	116	119.8	121.79	123.9	127.38	130.2	133.6	138.34	152.4	154.70
War widow	KJOK	86.74	89.55	91	92.69	95.27	98.09	101.43	105.09	115.55	117.30
Income Support:											
Personal allowances[8]											
Single											
aged 16-17 usual rate	KJOW	31.95	32.50	32.9	33.5	33.85	34.6	35.65	47.95	50.95	51.85
aged 16-17 higher rate in specific circumstances	KABS	42.00	42.70	43.25	44.05	44.5	45.5	46.85	47.95	50.95	51.85
aged 18-24	KJOX	42.00	42.70	43.25	44.05	44.5	45.5	46.85	47.95	50.95	51.85
aged 25 or over	KJOY	53.05	53.95	54.65	55.65	56.2	57.45	59.15	60.5	64.3	65.45
Couple											
both aged under 18	KJOZ	31.95	32.50	32.9	33.5	33.85	34.6	35.65	47.95	50.95	51.85
both aged under 18, one disabled	F92J	42.00	42.70	43.25	44.05	44.5	45.5	46.85	47.95	50.95	51.85
both aged under 18, with a child	F92K	63.35	64.45	65.3	66.5	67.15	68.65	70.7	72.35	76.9	78.30
One aged under 18, one 18-24	F92L	42.00	42.70	43.25	44.05	44.5	45.5	46.85	47.95	50.95	51.85
One aged under 18, one 25+	F92M	53.05	53.95	54.65	55.65	56.2	57.45	59.15	60.5	64.3	65.45
Both aged 18 or over	KJPA	83.25	84.65	85.75	87.3	88.15	90.1	92.8	94.95	100.95	102.75
Lone parent											
aged 16-17 usual rate	KJPB	31.95	32.50	32.9	33.5	33.85	34.6	35.65	47.95	50.95	51.85
aged 16-17 higher rate in specific circumstances	KABT	42.00	42.70	43.25	44.05	44.5	45.5	46.85	47.95	50.95	51.85
aged 18 or over	KJPC	53.05	53.95	54.65	55.65	56.2	57.45	59.15	60.5	64.3	65.45
Pension Credit[9]											
Standard minimum guarantee:											
single	C59Y	..	..	102.1	105.45	109.45	114.05	119.05	124.05	130	132.60
couple	C59Z	..	..	155.8	160.95	167.05	174.05	181.7	189.35	198.45	202.40
Additional amount for severe disability											
single	C5A2	..	..	42.95	44.15	45.5	46.75	48.45	50.35	52.85	53.65
couple (one qualifies)	C5A3	..	..	42.95	44.15	45.5	46.75	48.45	50.35	52.85	53.65
couple (both qualifies)	C5A4	..	..	85.9	88.3	91	93.5	96.9	100.7	105.7	107.30
Additional amount for carers	C5A8	..	..	25.1	25.55	25.8	26.35	27.15	27.75	29.5	30.05
savings credit											
threshold single	C5A9	..	..	77.45	79.6	82.05	84.25	87.3	91.2	96	98.40
threshold couple	C5AA	..	..	123.8	127.25	131.2	134.75	139.6	145.8	153.4	157.25
maximum single	C5AB	..	..	14.79	15.51	16.44	17.88	19.05	19.71	20.4	20.52
maximum couple	C5AC	..	..	19.2	20.22	21.51	23.58	25.26	26.13	27.03	27.09

1 See chapter text.

2 Persons under 18 are entitled to the appropriate adult rate.

3 The rate of child dependency increase is adjusted where it is payable for the eldest child for whom child benefit (ChB) is also paid. The weekly rate in such cases is reduced by the difference (less £3.65) between the ChB rates for the eldest and subsequent children.

4 The rate of age addition depends on age at date of onset of incapacity: higher rate for under age 35 and lower rate for age 35-44.

5 Employment and Support Allowance (ESA) replaced Incapacity Benefit and Income Support paid on the grounds of incapacity for new claims from 27 October 2008.

6 Following an EU Directive, employee's maternity benefit is aligned with the state benefit they would receive if off work sick.

7 Retirement pensioners over 80 receive 25p addition.

8 In addition to personal allowances, a claimant may also be entitled to premiums. The types of premiums are family, lone parent, pensioner, higher pensioner, disability, sev ere disability and disabled child.

9 Pension Credit replaced Minimum Income Guarantee (MIG) for Income Support for those aged 60 and over on 6th Ocotober 2003.

Sources: Department for Work and Pensions;
Information Directorate;
HM Revenue and Customs: 020 7438 7370;
Ministry of Defence/DASA (Pay & Pensions): 020 7218 4271

5.5 Social Security Acts: number of persons receiving benefit[1]
Great Britain and Overseas (excluding Northern Ireland)

At any one time

Thousands

		2000	2001	2002	2003	2004	2005	2006	2007	2008	2009	2010
Persons receiving:												
Jobseeker's Allowance[3]	JYXM	1037.01	909.15	877.38	885.78	777.4	800.66	895.88	807.27	787.87	1443	1354.62
Employment and Support Allowance[4]	JTM5	..	..	..	..	..	..	..	..	..	288.27	527.12
Incapacity benefit[2,4,5]	KXDT	2352.52	2420.88	2471.14	2494.89	2508.77	2490.85	2449.99	2417.71	2382.01	2130.12	1892.99
Severe Disablement Allowance	J8T2	375.56	374.45	336.48	320.76	305.94	292.87	280.01	267.61	255.56	244.09	233.71
Attendance Allowance	KXDU	1556.1	1570.9	1290.77	1315.64	1377.35	1419.42	1465.59	1507.5	1546.68	1585.79	1614.27
Disability Living Allowance	KXDW	2193.1	2306.4	2424.35	2547.09	2644.28	2729.72	2799.16	2881.83	2973.54	3070.61	3157.31
Carers' Allowance	J8T3	..	..	..	..	421.18	441.03	453.54	464.67	480.73	507.97	536.90
Child Benefit[6]	J8T4	7305	7297.1	7296.1	7297.5	7301.3	7311.4	7365.4	7449.6	..	..	..
Widows' Benefits	KJHF	265.11	254.97	223.41	191.5	163.43	138.96	117.65	96.89	77.9	62.14	50.75
Bereavement Benefits	VQAA	..	..	41.49	47.68	51.18	55.24	57.66	58.54	59.85	61.91	63.31
National Insurance												
State pension contributory:												
Males[2]	KJHH	4039.4	4083.9	4149.16	4211.37	4275.67	4336.81	4374.18	4432.31	4520.56	4626.96	4752.13
Females[2]	KJHL	6928	6959.7	6972.2	7037.15	7117.78	7197.92	7245.71	7391.1	7529.4	7650.4	7760.16
Total[2]	KJHG	10967.4	11043.6	11121.4	11248.5	11393.5	11534.7	11619.9	11823.4	12050	12277.4	12512.30
State pension non contributory:												
Males	KJHI	5.2	5.1	5.26	5.37	5.39	5.34	5.36	5.68	6.23	6.67	7.23
Females	KJHJ	18	18.2	18.06	17.73	17.31	16.74	16.58	17.34	18.8	20.04	21.22
Total	KJHK	23.2	23.3	23.32	23.1	22.7	22.08	21.94	23.03	25.03	26.71	28.45
Industrial Injuries Disablement[2,7]												
Pensions assessments[5]	KJHN	274.6	275.4	273.7	267.13	266.48	267.12	266.45	264.88	262.73	260.55	265.77
Reduced Earnings Allowance/												
Retirement Allowance assessments[8]	KEYC	82.9	82.6	81	76.22	74.81	73.15	71.38	69.36	67.19	65.13	60.10
Income Support (Excluding MIG)	KABV	2237.13	2260.63	2238.76	2236.38	2192.64	2139.78	2114.77	2117.7	2091.52	1979.8	9.78
Minimum Income Guaranteed	J8T5	1607.48	1714.37	1737.53	1777.79	12.09	10.98	10.27	10.65	10.74	10.19	1842.49
Pension Credit	C5AP	..	..	..	..	2490.76	2682.73	2717.39	2733.5	2719.14	2730.56	2734.17
Housing Benefit and Council Tax Benefit[9,10]												
Housing Benefit Total	EW3X	4033.3	3874.4	3812.6	3796.4	3879.4	3957.1	3990	4031.81	..	4412.99	4751.53
Social Landlord[11]	KABY	3218.4	3131.1	3093.8	3081.67	3135.49	3165.89	3152.25	3108.73	..	3186.4	3293.63
Private Landlord	KABZ	815	743.3	718.83	714.75	743.93	790.93	837.79	923.07	..	1221.42	1455.26
Council tax benefit[12]	KJPO	4830.1	4673.4	4601.73	4627.78	4800.22	4959.69	5049.97	5076.94	..	5436.19	5780.09
War pensions[13]	KADG	295.67	284.33	272.78	260.79	247.59	235.3	223.85	212.54	201.27	190.75	180.40

1 See chapter text. Figures as at May each year unless otherwise stated.

2 Due to rounding errors several figures have been revised for May 2008.

3 Totals include 'credits only' cases.

4 Employment and Support Allowance (ESA) replaced Incapacity Benefit and Income Support paid on the grounds of incapacity for new claims from 27th October 2008.

5 Totals include 'credits only' cases.

6 Figures for Child Benefit in 2008 and 2009 are delayed due to extraction system up-dates.

7 Figures for IIDB include those receiving both IIDB and REA, at March.

8 Figures show REA only from 2000, at March.

9 The DWP have implemented an improvement to the way in which HB and CTB caseload statistics are compiled. Historic statistics for the period up to August 2008 are based on clerical returns made by Local Author ities (LAs) of the aggregate number of people claiming HB and CTB as a specific point in time. This has gradually transitioned into a monthly electronic scan of claimant level data direct from the LA computer systems. This data source (the Single Housing Benefit Extract (SHBE)) has been designed to provide sufficient information for all current and future statistical purposes and is now the single source of HB and CTB data.

10 Housing Benefit figures excludes any Extended Payment cases.

11 Social landlord figures include registered social landlord tenants.

12 Figure excludes Second Adult Rebate Claims.

13 Figures for War pensions are at March each year.

Sources: Department for Work and Pensions;
Information Directorate;
HM Revenue and Customs:0207 438 7370;
Ministry of Defence/DASA (Pay & Pensions):0207 218 4271

5.6 Jobseeker's Allowance[1,2,3] claimants: by benefit entitlement
Great Britain

As at May

Thousands

All Persons		2000	2001	2002	2003	2004	2005	2006	2007	2008	2009	2010
All with benefit - total	KXDX	945.1	818.7	790.4	797.9	699.6	728.3	812	730.8	718	1316.4	1237.3
Contribution-based JSA only	KXDY	144.0	141.9	155.3	160.4	131	139.5	134.6	113.6	127.8	341.8	205.3
Contribution based JSA & income-based JSA	KXDZ	18.4	17.6	18.5	18.1	13.5	13.5	13	11.9	12.8	34.6	21.1
Income-based JSA only payment	KXEA	782.6	659.2	616.6	619.4	555.1	575.3	664.5	605.3	577.4	940	1010.9
No benefit in payment	KXEB	91.9	90.4	87.0	87.9	77.8	72.4	83.9	76.4	69.9	126.6	117.3
Total	**KXEC**	1037.0	909.1	877.4	885.8	777.4	800.7	895.9	807.4	788	1443	1354.6
Males												
All with benefit - total	KXED	733.6	636.4	606.2	605.6	527.2	545.3	606.8	537.8	529.9	978.9	890.9
Contribution-based JSA only	KXEE	101.2	100.8	110.8	114.1	93.8	99.5	95.8	79.6	90.6	248.7	143.4
Contribution based JSA & income-based JSA	KXEF	16.7	16.2	16.7	15.9	12.3	12.6	12	10.7	11.7	31.2	18.1
Income-based JSA only payment	KXEG	615.6	519.4	478.7	475.6	421.1	433.2	498.9	447.5	427.6	698.9	729.5
No benefit in payment	KXEH	61.6	59.7	59.5	60.3	52.7	49.8	56.6	51.7	46.7	88.8	82.2
Total	**KXEI**	795.2	696.1	665.7	665.9	580	595.1	663.4	589.6	576.7	1067.7	973.1
Females												
All with benefit - total	KXEJ	211.5	182.3	184.2	192.3	172.4	182.9	205.3	193	188.1	337.6	346.4
Contribution-based JSA only	KXEK	42.8	41.0	44.5	46.3	37.2	40	38.7	34	37.2	93.1	61.9
Contribution based JSA & income-based JSA	KXEL	1.7	1.5	1.8	2.2	1.2	0.8	1	1.2	1.2	3.4	3.0
Income-based JSA only payment	KXEM	167.0	139.8	137.9	143.8	134	142.1	165.5	157.8	149.8	241.1	281.4
No benefit in payment	KXEN	30.3	30.7	27.5	27.6	25	22.6	27.2	24.8	23.2	37.7	35.1
Total	**KXEO**	241.8	213.1	211.7	219.8	197.4	205.5	232.5	217.8	211.3	375.3	381.5

1 See chapter text. Jobseeker's Allowance (JSA) has two routes of entry: contrbution-based which depends mainly upon national insurance contributions and income-based which depends mainly on a means test. Some claimants can qualify by either route. In practice they receive income-based JSA but have an under lying entitlement to the contribution-based element.

2 Figures are given at May each year and have been derived by applying 5% proportions to 100% totals taken from the DWP 100% Work and Pensions Longitudinal Study (WPLS).

3 Figures are rounded to the nearest hundred and quoted in thousands. They may not sum due to rounding.

Sources: Department for Work and Pensions;
Information Directorate

5.7 Employment and Support Allowance and Incapacity Benefit[1,2,3] claimants by sex, age and duration of spell
Great Britain and Overseas (excluding Northern Ireland).

At end of May   Thousands

		2000	2001	2002	2003	2004	2005	2006	2007	2008[4]	2009	2010
Males												
All durations: All ages	KJJA	1481.64	1512.24	1526.17	1525.02	1517.62	1492.38	1455.52	1428.65	1399.58	1419.43	1409.10
Under 20	KJJB	11.3	11.33	21.79	21.81	22.04	21.45	19.95	18.66	17.25	18.09	17.33
20-29	KJJC	122.62	129.02	133.83	138.54	142.68	143.24	141.8	146.07	149.47	159.1	160.91
30-39	KJJD	232.51	245.71	250.79	254.3	253.32	245.61	233.7	224.29	215.51	215.95	213.57
40-49	KJJE	287.37	298.04	304.47	311.85	318.04	320.77	319.77	320.24	319.22	330.96	335.93
50-59	KJJF	474.44	482.18	478.01	472.03	463.37	451.93	439.54	418.26	404.76	405.59	403.61
60-64	KJJG	353.22	345.87	337.22	326.45	318.12	309.36	300.73	301.1	293.33	289.57	277.30
65 and over	KJJH	0.17	0.09	0.05	0.05	0.05	0.04	0.02	0.03	0.04	0.17	0.46
Over six months: All ages	KJJI	1311.22	1338.11	1346.8	1359.53	1359.08	1347.43	1323.2	1291.32	1266.8	1253.91	1251.24
Under 20	KJJJ	4.99	3.52	6.91	13.4	13.78	13.51	12.85	11.7	10.9	10.42	10.50
20-29	KJJK	90.06	94.86	96.61	105.72	110.85	114.57	115.21	117.83	121.9	124.5	128.76
30-39	KJJL	195.96	207.75	213.19	217.05	217.81	213.91	205.36	195.22	188.25	182.41	180.52
40-49	KJJM	253.84	264.41	271.25	278.53	285.9	290.72	291.36	289.94	289.72	293.13	298.29
50-59	KJJN	431.52	439.78	438.55	434.04	427.06	418.6	409.46	387.76	374.75	368.48	367.26
60-64	KJJO	334.73	327.73	320.26	310.75	303.64	296.1	288.93	288.85	281.25	274.93	265.52
65 and over	KJJP	0.14	0.06	0.03	0.03	0.04	0.02	0.02	0.03	0.03	0.05	0.39
Females												
All durations: All ages	KJJQ	870.14	908.03	944.44	969.44	990.84	998.2	994.33	988.93	982.33	998.74	1007.13
Under 20	KJJR	14.62	13.68	21.51	21.49	21.48	20.51	18.92	17.86	16.79	15.68	14.54
20-29	KJJS	91.03	92.79	96.66	100.78	105.02	108.61	109.73	114.42	117.91	121.5	122.82
30-39	KJJT	165.07	172.04	175.37	177.7	177.91	173.45	167.36	162.39	156.95	156.85	157.74
40-49	KJJU	231.94	243.27	252.82	262.2	270.9	276.62	279.32	283.45	285.84	296.87	305.06
50-59	KJJV	367.23	386.21	398.06	407.24	415.52	418.99	418.99	410.8	404.82	407.82	406.97
60 and over	KJJW	0.26	0.04	0.03	0.03	0.02	0.02	0.02	0.02	0.02	0.02	0.01
Over six months: All ages	KJJX	761.08	795.67	825.25	858.03	880.52	894.57	896.33	885.69	881.41	882.94	888.73
Under 20	KJJY	6.94	4.74	7.41	12.35	12.4	12.1	11.13	10.2	9.55	8.75	8.15
20-29	KJJZ	69.35	70.88	72.32	79.63	84.02	88.98	90.99	93.6	97.24	99.15	100.81
30-39	KJKA	141.41	148.19	151.59	154.19	154.95	152.48	148	142.28	137.59	134.9	134.29
40-49	KJKB	205.6	216.19	225.65	234.71	243.52	250.11	253.5	255.99	258.74	263.7	269.48
50-59	KJKC	337.54	355.64	368.25	377.12	385.61	390.88	392.69	383.6	378.27	376.43	375.99
60 and over	KJKD	0.26	0.04	0.03	0.03	0.02	0.02	0.02	0.02	0.02	0.02	0.02
Unknown Gender												
All durations	EW44	0.74	0.62	0.54	0.44	0.31	0.26	0.15	0.13	0.11	0.23	3.86
Over 6 months	EW45	0.33	0.28	0.29	0.21	0.16	0.13	0.1	0.09	0.09	0.1	3.67

Definitions and conventions. Caseload figures are rounded to the nearest ten and displayed in thousands. Totals may not sum due to rounding.

1 See chapter text. Figures are given at May each year.

2 Table includes Employment and Support Allowance and Incapacity Benefit ONLY claimants and not those claiming Severe Disablement Allowance (SDA).

3 From 27th October 2008, new claims to Incapacity Benefit can also be allocated, on incapacity grounds, to the newly introduced Employment and Support Allowance (ESA).

4 Due to rounding errors several figures have been revised for May 2008.

Sources: Department for Work and Pensions; Information and Analysis Directorate: 0191 225 7373

5.8 Attendance allowance - cases in payment[1]: Age and gender of claimant Great Britain

At May each year

Thousands

		2003	2004	2005	2006	2007	2008	2009	2010
Males: All ages	JT9Z	393.9	418.5	436.9	459.5	478.4	497.2	516.5	531.5
Unknown age	JTA2	–	–	–	–	–	–	–	–
65 - 69	JTA3	19.5	21.4	22	22.3	22.8	23.5	24.4	24.8
70 - 74	JTA4	56.6	59.8	61.6	64.2	66.8	70.2	73.7	74.9
75 - 79	JTA5	100.9	103.8	104.2	104.8	106.3	109.1	112.4	114.9
80 - 84	JTA6	110.1	121.7	125.3	130.4	133.1	135.4	137.8	139.9
85 - 89	JTA7	68.5	70.1	78.7	89.4	98.5	107.7	116	118.1
90 and over	JTA8	38.3	41.7	45.1	48.4	50.8	51.2	52.2	58.9
Females: All ages	JTA9	921.8	958.9	982.6	1006.2	1029.1	1049.5	1069.3	1082.8
Unknown age	JTB2	0.1	–	–	–	–	–	–	–
65 - 69	JTB3	25.1	27.3	27.7	28.3	28.4	29.1	30	30.3
70 - 74	JTB4	88.2	91.5	92	93.6	96.4	99.6	103.5	104.5
75 - 79	JTB5	189.1	190.9	189.1	186.8	185.8	186.7	188.4	188.4
80 - 84	JTB6	260.7	282.5	282	279.4	278.3	277.7	277.7	277.0
85 - 89	JTB7	206.1	204.7	221.4	241.6	259.3	276.7	290.9	286.6
90 and over	JTB8	152.6	162	170.4	176.4	180.9	179.6	178.8	196.0

1 Totals show the number of people in receipt of allowance, and exclude people with entitlement where the payment has been suspended, for example if they are in hospital.

Sources: Department for Work and Pensions; Information Directorate

5.9 Child benefits[1,2]

United Kingdom

Thousands

		United Kingdom As at 31 August										
		2000	2001	2002	2003	2004	2005	2006	2007	2008	2009	2010
Families receiving allowances:												
Total	VOWX	7340	7335	7336	7246	7296	7315	7413	7475	7583	7770	7842
With 1 child	VOWY	3128	3143	3162	3067	3165	3187	3266	3345	3468	3606	3671
2 children	VOWZ	2898	2891	2894	2907	2891	2891	2910	2904	2903	2936	2943
3 children	VOXA	977	970	954	947	926	921	919	910	899	906	906
4 or more children	VOXB	251	247	242	325	315	316	318	317	313	320	321
Families receiving Guardian's Allowance[3]	VOXH	2.5	2.3	2.5	2.6	2.9	2.8	3.2	3.3	..	..	..

1 See chapter text.
2 Data revised from 2003, updates to previous years not available.
3 Data no longer available

Source: HM Revenue and Customs: 020 7147 3021

5.9 Child benefits[1,2]

At August continued

August 2010

Area names	New Area Codes [1]	Number of families, by size					Number of children in these families, by age				
		Total	One child	Two children	Three children	Four or more children	Total	Under 5	5-10	11-15	16 and over
United Kingdom [2]	K02000001	7,841,675	3,671,115	2,942,985	906,310	321,265	13,685,250	3,789,470	4,187,695	3,697,020	2,011,065
Great Britain	K03000001	7,557,305	3,543,380	2,840,610	866,500	306,820	13,170,155	3,650,365	4,032,065	3,558,365	1,929,360
England and Wales	K04000001	6,935,695	3,229,910	2,612,410	803,680	289,690	12,138,365	3,367,825	3,711,025	3,263,120	1,796,390
England	E92000001	6,562,705	3,051,980	2,473,415	761,550	275,765	11,495,395	3,197,030	3,517,020	3,084,565	1,696,785
North East	E12000001	324,265	162,860	117,510	32,930	10,965	544,775	146,480	163,620	149,590	85,085
North West	E12000002	894,940	431,275	324,695	101,075	37,895	1,551,080	422,930	469,840	420,040	238,270
Yorkshire and the Humber	E12000003	657,700	310,775	244,165	73,865	28,895	1,147,440	318,380	349,880	310,080	169,100
East Midlands	E12000004	559,645	261,660	213,595	62,915	21,475	971,690	263,180	295,040	266,250	147,220
West Midlands	E12000005	705,640	325,990	259,290	84,695	35,665	1,257,180	343,525	385,585	339,980	188,085
East	E12000006	723,030	322,945	288,450	85,025	26,610	1,269,870	345,780	388,485	346,465	189,140
London	E12000007	1,028,265	486,995	359,955	126,870	54,445	1,831,965	564,805	572,010	453,975	241,175
South East	E12000008	1,051,885	469,790	421,305	123,370	37,420	1,843,465	505,235	566,705	498,575	272,950
South West	E12000009	617,340	279,685	244,455	70,805	22,395	1,077,930	286,710	325,850	299,610	165,760
Wales	W92000004	372,985	177,935	138,995	42,130	13,925	642,965	170,800	194,010	178,555	99,605
Scotland	S92000003	621,615	313,470	228,195	62,820	17,125	1,031,795	282,540	321,040	295,240	132,975
Northern Ireland	N92000002	240,985	105,190	86,965	35,560	13,275	443,110	119,795	132,410	119,610	71,295
Foreign and not known	n/a	43,385	22,545	15,415	4,255	1,170	71,985	19,310	23,220	19,050	10,410

1 New area codes to be implemented from 1 January 2011; in line with the new GSS Coding and Naming policy.
2 Includes Foreign and not known

5.10 Child Tax Credit or Working Tax Credit elements and thresholds

Annual rate (£), except where specified

	2003-04	2004-05	2005-06	2006-07	2007-08	2008-09	2009-10	2010-11
Child Tax Credit								
Family element	545	545	545	545	545	545	545	545
Family element, baby addition[1]	545	545	545	545	545	545	545	545
Child element[2]	1,445	1,625	1,690	1,765	1,845	2,085	2,235	2,300
Disabled child additional element[3]	2,215	2,215	2,285	2,350	2,440	2,540	2,670	2,715
Severely disabled child additional element[4]	865	890	920	945	980	1,020	1,075	1,095
Working Tax Credit								
Basic element	1,525	1,570	1,620	1,665	1,730	1,800	1,890	1,920
Couples and lone parent element	1,500	1,545	1,595	1,640	1,700	1,770	1,860	1,890
30 hour element[5]	620	640	660	680	705	735	775	790
Disabled worker element	2,040	2,100	2,165	2,225	2,310	2,405	2,530	2,570
Severely disabled adult element	865	890	920	945	980	1,020	1,075	1,095
50+ return to work payment[6]								
16 but less than 30 hours per week	1,045	1,075	1,110	1,140	1,185	1,235	1,300	1,320
at least 30 hours per week	1,565	1,610	1,660	1,705	1,770	1,840	1,935	1,965
Childcare element								
Maximum eligible costs allowed (£ per week)								
Eligible costs incurred for 1 child	135	135	175	175	175	175	175	175
Eligible costs incurred for 2+ children	200	200	300	300	300	300	300	300
Percentage of eligible costs covered	*70%*	*70%*	*70%*	*80%*	*80%*	*80%*	*80%*	*80%*
Common features								
First income threshold[7]	5,060	5,060	5,220	5,220	5,220	6,420	6,420	6,420
First withdrawal rate	*37%*	*37%*	*37%*	*37%*	*37%*	*39%*	*39%*	*39%*
Second income threshold[8]	50,000	50,000	50,000	50,000	50,000	50,000	50,000	50,000
Second withdrawal rate	*1 in 15*	*1 in 15*	*1 in 15*	*1 in 15*	*1 in 15*	*1 in 15*	*1 in 15*	*1 in 15*
First income threshold for those entitled to Child Tax Credit only[9]	13,230	13,480	13,910	14,155	14,495	15,575	16,040	16,190
Income increase disregard	2,500	2,500	2,500	25,000	25,000	25,000	25,000	25,000
Minimum award payable	26	26	26	26	26	26	26	26

1 Payable to families for any period during which they have one or more children aged under 1.

2 Payable for each child up to 31 August after their 16th birthday, and for each young person for any period in which they are aged under 20 (under 19 to 2005-06) and in full-time non-advanced education, or under 18 and in their first 20 weeks of registration with the Careers service or Connexions.

3 Payable in addition to the child element for each disabled child.

4 Payable in addition to the disabled child element for each severely disabled child.

5 Payable for any period during which normal hours worked (for a couple, summed over the two partners) is at least 30 per week.

6 Payable for each qualifying adult for the first 12 months following a return to work.

7 Income is net of pension contributions, and excludes Child Benefit, Housing benefit, Council tax benefit, maintenance and the first £300 of family income other than from work or benefits. The award is reduced by the excess of income over the first threshold, multiplied by the first withdrawal rate.

8 For those entitled to the Child Tax Credit, the award is reduced only down to the family element, plus the baby addition where relevant, less the excess of income over the second threshold multiplied by the second withdrawal rate.

9 Those also receiving Income Support, income-based Jobseeker's Allowance or Pension Credit are passported to maximum award with no tapering.

5.11 In-work families with Child Tax Credit or Working Tax Credit awards United Kingdom

As at December

		'2003[1]	'2004	'2005	'2006	'2007	'2008	'2009	'2010
In-work families with award:	**C5PF**	4423	4519	4538	4526	4541	4630	4712	4838
With children Receiving	**C5PG**	4208	4261	4218	4204	4189	4205	4200	4277
Receiving Working Tax Credit and Child Tax Credit	**C5PH**	1548	1492	1497	1596	1650	1763	1870	1975
Child Tax Credit only	**C5PI**	2660	2769	2721	2608	2539	2442	2330	2302
Without children									
Receiving Working Tax Credit	**C5PL**	215	258	320	323	352	426	511	561

1 Child and Working Tax Credits replaced Working Families' Tax Credit on 6th April 2003. Figures for 2003 are based on awards current at 5th January 2004. All other figures at December each year. See chapter text.

Source: HM Revenue and Customs: 020 7147 3083

5.12 Widows' Benefit (excluding bereavement payment[1,2,3]): by type of benefit Great Britain

Number in receipt of widows benefit as at May each year

Thousands

		2004	2005	2006	2007	2008	2009	2010
All Widows' Benefit (excluding bereavement allowance)								
All ages	KJGA	163.4	139	117.7	96.89	77.9	62.14	50.75
Unknown Age	EW4O	–	–	–	0.02	–	–	–
18 - 24	EW4P	–	–	–	–	–	–	–
25 - 29	EW4Q	0.2	0.1	0.1	0.04	0.02	0.01	–
30 - 34	EW4R	1.2	0.8	0.5	0.32	0.2	0.13	0.08
35 - 39	EW4S	3.9	2.9	2.1	1.53	1.08	0.74	0.50
40 - 44	EW4T	7.5	6.1	4.9	3.93	3.04	2.31	1.72
45 - 49	EW4U	13.2	11	9.1	7.58	6.26	5.14	4.20
50 - 54	EW4V	33.3	26.9	21.8	17.69	14.42	11.72	9.76
55 - 59	EW4W	77.7	66.9	57.3	45.78	36.86	30.37	24.62
60 - 64	EW4X	26.4	24.3	21.8	20.01	16.01	11.71	9.86
Widowed parents' allowance - with dependant children								
All ages	KJGG	28.2	23.2	19	15.6	12.6	9.98	7.91
Unknown Age	EW4Y	–	–	–	–	–	–	–
18 - 24	EW4Z	–	–	–	–	–	–	–
25 - 29	EW52	0.2	0.1	0.1	0.03	0.02	0.01	–
30 - 34	EW53	1.1	0.8	0.5	0.31	0.19	0.12	0.07
35 - 39	EW54	3.8	2.8	2.1	1.49	1.05	0.72	0.49
40 - 44	EW55	7	5.7	4.6	3.75	2.92	2.23	1.65
45 - 49	EW56	7.8	6.7	5.6	4.71	3.87	3.13	2.61
50 - 54	EW57	5.7	4.8	4.1	3.58	3.1	2.53	2.08
55 - 59	EW58	2.3	2	1.8	1.57	1.33	1.13	0.92
60 - 64	EW59	0.3	0.3	0.2	0.17	0.13	0.1	0.09
Widowed parents' allowance - without dependant children								
All ages	KJGM	1.4	1.1	0.8	0.69	0.54	0.46	0.39
Unknown Age	EW5A	–	–	–	–	–	–	–
18 - 24	EW5B	–	–	–	–	–	–	–
25 - 29	EW5C	–	–	–	–	–	–	–
30 - 34	EW5D	–	–	–	0.01	0.01	0.01	0.01
35 - 39	EW5E	0.1	0.1	0.1	0.04	0.03	0.02	0.02
40 - 44	EW5F	0.3	0.2	0.2	0.13	0.09	0.07	0.06
45 - 49	EW5G	0.4	0.3	0.2	0.21	0.17	0.15	0.12
50 - 54	EW5H	0.3	0.3	0.2	0.17	0.13	0.13	0.12
55 - 59	EW5I	0.2	0.2	0.1	0.11	0.1	0.07	0.06
60 - 64	EW5J	–	–	–	0.02	0.01	0.01	0.01
Age-related bereavement allowance								
All ages	KJGS	110.1	96.6	84	70.13	57.37	46.58	38.55
Unknown Age	EW5K	–	–	–	0.01	–	–	–
18 - 24	EW5L	–	–	–	–	–	–	–
25 - 29	EW5M	–	–	–	–	–	–	–
30 - 34	EW5N	–	–	–	–	–	–	–
35 - 39	EW5O	–	–	–	–	–	–	–
40 - 44	EW5P	0.2	0.2	0.1	0.06	0.03	0.01	–
45 - 49	EW5Q	5.1	4	3.3	2.66	2.23	1.86	1.47
50 - 54	EW5R	26.7	21.4	17.2	13.75	11.08	9.01	7.55
55 - 59	EW5S	66.3	59	50.9	40.57	32.61	26.83	21.74
60 - 64	EW5T	11.9	12	12.5	13.08	11.42	8.87	7.78
Bereavement allowance (Not age related)								
All ages	KJGW	23.7	18.1	13.9	10.47	7.39	5.12	3.90
Unknown Age	EW5U	–	–	–	–	–	–	–
18 - 24	EW5V	–	–	–	–	–	–	–
25 - 29	EW5W	–	–	–	–	–	–	–
30 - 34	EW5X	–	–	–	–	–	–	–
35 - 39	EW5Y	–	–	–	–	–	–	–
40 - 44	EW5Z	–	–	–	–	–	–	–
45 - 49	EW62	–	–	–	–	–	–	–
50 - 54	EW63	0.6	0.5	0.3	0.2	0.11	0.05	0.01
55 - 59	EW64	8.8	5.6	4.4	3.53	2.82	2.33	1.90
60 - 64	EW65	14.2	12	9.1	6.74	4.45	2.74	1.98

1 Definitions and Conventions: "-" Nil or Negligible; "." Not applicable;
Caseload figures are rounded to the nearest hundred and displayed in thousands.

2 Caseload (Thousands) All Claimants of Widows Benefit are female. No new claims for WB have been accepted since April 2001 when it was replaced by Bereavement Benefit.

3 Figures include overseas cases.

Sources: DWP Information Directorate: Work and Pensions Longitudinal Study
100% data;
Information Directorate

5.13 Bereavement Benefit[1,2] (excluding bereavement payment): by sex, type of benefit and age of widow/er Great Britain.

Thousands

		Males					Females			
		2007	2008	2009	2010		2007	2008	2009	2010
All Bereavement Benefit (excluding bereavement allowance)										
All ages	WLSX	17.77	17.82	18.6	18.67	WLTC	40.77	42.04	43.32	44.64
18 - 24	EVW9	–	–	–	–	EVY2	0.07	0.08	0.06	0.04
25 - 29	EVX2	0.05	0.06	0.06	0.05	EVY3	0.53	0.53	0.53	0.52
30 - 34	EVX3	0.28	0.25	0.25	0.26	EVY4	1.63	1.66	1.68	1.71
35 - 39	EVX4	1.15	1.11	1.06	0.99	EVY5	4.05	4.31	4.3	4.27
40 - 44	EVX5	2.5	2.5	2.47	2.32	EVY6	7.01	7.33	7.61	7.74
45 - 49	EVX6	3.61	3.69	3.92	3.98	EVY7	8.92	9.54	10.22	10.78
50 - 54	EVX7	3.47	3.51	3.68	3.77	EVY8	8.65	9.1	9.64	10.3
55 - 59	EVX8	3.43	3.33	3.38	3.42	EVY9	9.9	9.49	9.28	9.18
60 - 64	EVX9	3.29	3.36	3.77	3.87	EVZ2	–	–	–	0.11
Widowed parents' allowance - with dependant children										
All ages	WLUD	11.27	11.51	11.81	11.78	WLUH	26.86	29.18	31.08	32.47
18 - 24	EVZ3	–	–	–	–	EW24	0.07	0.08	0.06	0.04
25 - 29	EVZ4	0.05	0.06	0.06	0.05	EW25	0.52	0.52	0.53	0.52
30 - 34	EVZ5	0.28	0.25	0.25	0.26	EW26	1.61	1.64	1.66	1.7
35 - 39	EVZ6	1.14	1.11	1.06	0.99	EW27	4.01	4.27	4.26	4.24
40 - 44	EVZ7	2.48	2.49	2.46	2.31	EW28	6.93	7.25	7.54	7.69
45 - 49	EVZ8	3.13	3.26	3.39	3.47	EW29	7.23	7.99	8.7	9.22
50 - 54	EVZ9	2.36	2.48	2.62	2.67	EW2A	4.61	5.29	5.97	6.58
55 - 59	EW22	1.29	1.32	1.38	1.42	EW2B	1.89	2.14	2.36	2.47
60 - 64	EW23	0.53	0.54	0.59	0.61	EW2C	–	–	–	0.01
Widowed parents' allowance - without dependant children										
All ages	WLVK	0.05	0.04	0.04	0.04	WMMR	0.34	0.32	0.28	0.25
18 - 24	EW2D	–	–	–	–	EW2M	–	–	–	–
25 - 29	EW2E	–	–	–	–	EW2N	0.01	0.01	0.01	–
30 - 34	EW2F	–	–	–	–	EW2O	0.02	0.02	0.02	0.01
35 - 39	EW2G	0.01	–	–	–	EW2P	0.05	0.04	0.04	0.03
40 - 44	EW2H	0.02	0.01	0.01	0.01	EW2Q	0.08	0.08	0.06	0.05
45 - 49	EW2I	0.01	0.01	0.01	0.01	EW2R	0.08	0.09	0.08	0.07
50 - 54	EW2J	0.01	0.01	0.01	0.01	EW2S	0.06	0.05	0.05	0.04
55 - 59	EW2K	0.01	–	0.01	0.01	EW2T	0.04	0.04	0.03	0.03
60 - 64	EW2L	–	–	–	–	EW2U	–	–	–	–
Age-related bereavement allowance										
All ages	WMOB	1.71	1.59	1.74	1.76	WMOC	6.17	5.76	5.59	5.63
18 - 24	EW2V	–	–	–	–	EW36	–	–	–	–
25 - 29	EW2W	–	–	–	–	EW37	–	–	–	–
30 - 34	EW2X	–	–	–	–	EW38	–	–	–	–
35 - 39	EW2Y	–	–	–	–	EW39	–	–	–	–
40 - 44	EW2Z	–	–	–	–	EW3A	–	–	–	–
45 - 49	EW32	0.46	0.42	0.52	0.5	EW3B	1.61	1.46	1.45	1.48
50 - 54	EW33	1.1	1.03	1.06	1.1	EW3C	3.97	3.76	3.62	3.67
55 - 59	EW34	0.15	0.14	0.16	0.16	EW3D	0.58	0.54	0.52	0.47
60 - 64	EW35	–	–	–	–	EW3E	–	–	–	–
Bereavement allowance (not age related)										
All ages	WMOX	4.74	4.68	5.01	5.09	WMOY	7.39	6.77	6.36	6.3
18 - 24	EW3F	–	–	–	–	EW3O	–	–	–	–
25 - 29	EW3G	–	–	–	–	EW3P	–	–	–	–
30 - 34	EW3H	–	–	–	–	EW3Q	–	–	–	–
35 - 39	EW3I	–	–	–	–	EW3R	–	–	–	–
40 - 44	EW3J	–	–	–	–	EW3S	–	–	–	–
45 - 49	EW3K	–	–	–	–	EW3T	–	–	–	–
50 - 54	EW3L	–	–	–	–	EW3U	–	–	–	–
55 - 59	EW3M	1.98	1.86	1.83	1.83	EW3V	7.39	6.77	6.36	6.2
60 - 64	EW3N	2.76	2.81	3.18	3.26	EW3W	–	–	–	0.1

1 Figures include overseas cases.
2 Figures are given at May each year and are taken from the DWP 100% Work and Pensions Longitudinal Study (WPLS).

Sources: DWP Information Directorate: Work and Pensions Longitudinal Study 100% data; Information Directorate

5.14 Contributory and non-contributory retirement pensions:[1,2] by sex and age of claimant Great Britain and Overseas.

At May each year.

Thousands and percentages

		2002	2003	2004	2005	2006	2007	2008	2009	2010
Men:										
Age-groups:										
65-69	KJSB	1,308.60	1,330.18	1354.3	1364.1	1341.5	1332.77	1350.61	1389.85	1,441.17
Percentage	KJSC	*31.50*	*31.55*	31.6	31.4	30.6	30.03	29.84	29.99	*30.28*
70-74	KJSD	1,129.27	1,136.59	1140.3	1150	1160.1	1177.96	1205.7	1232.97	1,252.63
Percentage	KJSE	*27.18*	*26.95*	26.6	26.5	26.5	26.54	26.63	26.61	*26.32*
75-79	KJSF	864.14	867.13	875	887.1	903	918.47	932.17	942.03	958.54
Percentage	KJSG	*20.80*	*20.56*	20.4	20.4	20.6	20.7	20.59	20.33	*20.14*
80-84	KJSH	531.89	565.32	593.7	593.3	596.9	604.74	614.77	627.28	644.94
Percentage	KJSI	*12.80*	*13.41*	13.9	13.7	13.6	13.63	13.58	13.54	*13.55*
85-89	KJSJ	233.29	225.86	221.4	246.4	273.1	296.36	317.9	335.49	340.87
Percentage	KJSK	*5.62*	*5.36*	5.2	5.7	6.2	6.68	7.02	7.24	*7.16*
90 and over	KJSL	85.91	90.59	95.5	100.2	103.6	106.13	105.33	105.62	120.82
Percentage	KJSM	*2.07*	*2.15*	2.2	2.3	2.4	2.39	2.33	2.28	*2.54*
Unknown age	EW3Y	1.24	1.00	0.8	1.1	1.2	1.45	0.19	0.24	0.23
Percentage	EW3Z	*0.03*	*0.02*	–	–	–	–	–	–	–
Total all ages	KJSA	4,154.42	4,216.74	4281.1	4342.2	4379.5	4437.99	4526.79	4633.62	4,759.36
Women:										
Age-groups:										
60-64	KJSO	1,371.70	1,402.74	1451.3	1498.7	1524	1628.19	1695.88	1734.92	1,747.21
Percentage	KJSP	*19.62*	*19.88*	20.3	20.8	21	21.98	22.47	22.62	*22.45*
65-69	KJSQ	1,409.95	1,429.68	1452.7	1464.2	1453.1	1456.08	1484.8	1527.47	1,576.10
Percentage	KJSR	*20.17*	*20.27*	20.4	20.3	20	19.65	19.67	19.91	*20.25*
70-74	KJSS	1,333.61	1,329.08	1319.2	1314.5	1312.7	1322.14	1343.22	1366.91	1,382.42
Percentage	KJST	*19.08*	*18.84*	18.5	18.2	18.1	17.85	17.8	17.82	*17.77*
75-79	KJSU	1,175.18	1,161.86	1156.7	1158.6	1165.5	1168.86	1170.01	1166.2	1,168.83
Percentage	KJSV	*16.81*	*16.47*	16.2	16.1	16	15.78	15.5	15.2	*15.02*
80-84	KJSW	893.08	939.41	973.9	951.6	933.3	923.7	919.11	921.01	931.08
Percentage	KJSX	*12.78*	*13.32*	13.6	13.2	12.9	12.47	12.18	12.01	*11.97*
85-89	KJSY	514.23	491.33	473.1	511	552.7	587.91	621.15	643.5	634.29
Percentage	KJSZ	*7.36*	*6.96*	6.6	7.1	7.6	7.94	8.23	8.39	*8.15*
90 and over	KJTA	289.11	298.76	307.2	314.9	319.4	319.9	313.66	310.01	341.10
Percentage	KJTB	*4.14*	*4.23*	4.3	4.4	4.4	4.32	4.16	4.04	*4.38*
Unknown age	EW42	3.40	2.01	1.1	1.3	1.5	1.67	0.37	0.38	0.35
Percentage	EW43	*0.05*	*0.03*	–	–	–	–	–	–	–
Total all ages	KJSN	6,990.26	7,054.88	7135.1	7214.7	7262.3	7408.44	7548.2	7670.44	7,781.39

1 See chapter text.

2 Caseloads include both contributory and non-contributory state pensioners.

Source: Department for Work and Pensions;
Work and Pensions Longitudinal Study (WPLS);
Information Directorate

5.15 War pensions: estimated number of pensioners[1]
Great Britain

At 31 March each year

Thousands

		1999	2000	2001	2002	2003	2004	2005	'2006[2]	2007	2008	2009	2010
Disablement	KADH	248.93	240.76	231.62	221.8	212.18	201.55	191.75	182.8	173.85	165.17	157.13	148.95
Widows and dependants	KADI	55.85	54.92	52.71	50.98	48.61	46.04	43.55	41.05	38.69	36.1	33.62	31.45
Total	KADG	306.06	295.67	284.33	272.78	260.79	247.59	235.3	223.85	212.54	201.27	190.75	180.40

1 See chapter text. From 1914 war, 1939 war and later service.

2 The discontinuity between 2005 and 2006 is due to improvements in data processing.

Source: Ministry of Defence/DASA (Health Information): 01225 468599

5.16 Income support[1],[2] by statistical group[3]: number of claimants receiving weekly payment

Great Britain

Thousands[4]

		2003	2004	2005	2006	2007	2008	2009	2010
All income support claimants (including MIG from 2003)[5]	F8YY	4014.2	2204.7	2150.8	2125.1	2128.4	2102.3	1990.0	1852.3
Incapacity Benefits	F8YZ	1361.1	1214.2	1202.8	1191.7	1193.5	1191.4	1097.0	996.6
Lone Parent	F8Z2	855.8	823.3	789.3	774.9	765.6	738.6	720.5	679.2
Carer	F8Z3	118.0	79.9	80.5	81.7	84.3	87.3	93.8	103.9
Others on Income Related Benefits	F8Z4	1679.3	87.3	78.1	76.8	84.9	85.0	78.9	72.7

1 Figures are given at May each year and are taken from the DWP 100% Work and Pensions Longitudinal Study (WPLS).

2 From 27th October 2008, new claims to Income Support can also be allocated, on incapacity grounds, to the newly introduced Employment and Support Allowance (ESA).

3 Statistical groups are defined as follows:

Incapacity Benefits - claimants aged under 60 on Incapacity Benefit or Severe Disablement Allowance;

Lone Parent - single claimants aged under 60 with dependants not in receipt of IB/SDA;

Carer - claimants aged under 60 entitled to Carer's Allowance;

Other Income Related Benefit - claimants not in one of the above categories.

4 Figures are rounded to the nearest hundred and quoted in thousands.

5 Totals may not sum due to rounding.

Sources: Department for Work and Pensions; Information Directorate

5.17 Pension Credit[1]: number of claimants

Great Britain

End of May

Thousands[2]

		2004[5]	2005	2006	2007	2008	2009	2010
All Pension Credit	F8Z5	2490.8	2682.7	2717.4	2733.5	2719.1	2730.6	2734.2
Guarantee Credit Only	F8Z6	735.0	767.3	775.6	805.7	882.1	925.7	954.4
Guarantee Credit Only and Savings Credit	F8Z7	1269.5	1321.7	1343.2	1330.1	1246.2	1205.2	1202.4
Savings Credit	F8Z8	486.0	593.7	598.6	597.7	590.8	599.6	577.4

1 Source: DWP 100% Work and Pensions Longitudinal study (WPLS).

2 Figures are rounded to the nearest hundred and expressed in thousands.

Sources: Department for Work and Pensions; Information Directorate

5.18 Income support: average weekly amounts of benefit[1,2,3]

Great Britain

As at May

£ per week

		2003	2004	2005	2006	2007	2008	2009	2010
All income support claimants	F8ZF	73.04	91.14	85.89	83.54	82.45	82.55	85.17	85.01
Incapacity benefits[4]	F8ZG	76.13	77.84	77.12	78.35	80.04	81.85	89.22	91.81
Lone Parent[4]	F8ZH	116.50	114.96	102.85	94.88	89.70	87.37	82.79	79.02
Carer[4]	F8ZI	71.28	77.22	73.03	71.13	70.82	70.21	71.85	70.90
Others on income related benefits[4]	F8ZJ	48.51	64.24	62.81	62.78	62.47	63.02	66.35	67.87

1 Figures are given at May each year and are taken from the DWP 100% Work and Pensions Longitudinal Study (WPLS).

2 From 27th October 2008, new claims to Income Support can also be allocated, on incapacity grounds, to the newly introduced Employment and Support Allowance (ESA).

3 Average amounts are rounded to the nearest penny.

4 Statistical groups are defined as follows:

Incapacity Benefits - claimants under 60 on incapacity benefit or Severe Disablement Allowance;

Lone Parent - single claimants aged under 60 with dependants not in receipt of IB/SDA;

Carer - claimants aged under 60 entitled to Carer's Allowance;

Other Income Related Benefit- claimants not in one of the above categories.

Sources: Department for Work and Pensions; Information Directorate

5.19 Pension Credit: average weekly amounts of benefit[1]

Great Britain

As at May								£ per week[2]
		2004	2005	2006	2007	2008	2009	2010
All Pension Credit	**F8ZA**	42.30	43.62	46.75	50.04	52.69	55.56	57.39
Guarantee Credit Only	**F8ZB**	71.91	75.43	79.56	83.74	85.07	88.86	90.73
Guarantee Credit and Savings Credit	**F8ZC**	37.51	39.87	43.11	46.11	48.29	50.81	51.75
Savings Credit only	**F8ZD**	10.03	10.83	12.39	13.36	13.62	13.71	14.01

1 Figures are given in each May from 2000 - 2005 and are taken from the DWP 100% Work and Pensions Longitudinal Study (WPLS).

2 Average amounts are shown as pounds per week and rounded to the nearest penny.

Sources: Department for Work and Pensions; Information Directorate

External trade and investment

Chapter 6

External trade and investment

External trade (Table 6.1 and 6.3 to 6.6)

The statistics in this section are on the basis of Balance of Payments (BoP). They are compiled from information provided to HM Revenue and Customs (HMRC) by importers and exporters on the basis of Overseas Trade Statistics (OTS) which values exports 'f.o.b.' (free on board) and imports 'c.i.f.' (including insurance and freight). In addition to deducting these freight costs and insurance premiums from the OTS figures, coverage adjustments are made to convert the OTS data to a BoP basis. Adjustments are also made to the level of all exports and European Union (EU) imports to take account of estimated under-recording. The adjustments are set out and described in the annual United Kingdom *Balance of Payments Pink Book* (Office for National Statistics (ONS)). These adjustments are made to conform to the definitions in the 5th edition of the IMF Balance of Payments Manual.

Aggregate estimates of trade in goods, seasonally adjusted and on a BoP basis, are published monthly in the ONS statistical bulletin UK Trade. More detailed figures are available from time series data on the ONS website (www.ons.gov.uk) and are also published in the *Monthly Review of External Trade Statistics*. Detailed figures for EU and non-EU trade on an OTS basis are published in *Overseas trade statistics: United Kingdom trade with the European Community and the world* (HMRC).

A fuller description of how trade statistics are compiled can be found in Statistics on Trade in Goods (Government Statistical Service Methodological Series) available at: www.statistics.gov.uk/STATBASE/Product.asp?vlnk=14943

Overseas Trade Statistics

HMRC provide accurate and up to date information via the website: www.uktradeinfo.com
They also produce publications entitled 'Overseas Trade Statistics'.

Import penetration and export sales ratios (Table 6.2)

The ratios were first introduced in the August 1977 edition of *Economic Trends* in an article entitled 'The Home and Export Performance of United Kingdom Industries'. The article described the conceptual and methodological problems involved in measuring such variables as import penetration.

The industries are grouped according to the 2007 Standard Industrial Classification at 2-digit level.

Table 19.2a lists total UK manufacturers' sales, and tables 19.2b to 19.2e list the four different sets of ratios defined as follows:

Ratio 1:   percentage ratio of imports to home demand

Ratio 2:   percentage ratio of imports to home demand plus exports

Ratio 3:   percentage ratio of exports to total manufacturers' sales

Ratio 4:   percentage ratio of exports to total manufacturers' sales plus imports

Home demand is defined as total manufacturers' sales plus imports minus exports. This is only an approximate estimate as different sources are used for the total manufacturers' sales and the import and export data. Total manufacturers' sales are determined by the Products of the European Community inquiry and import and export data are provided by HMRC.

Ratio 1 is commonly used to describe the import penetration of the home market. Allowance is made for the extent of a domestic industry's involvement in export markets by using Ratio 2; this reduces as exports increase.

Similarly, Ratio 3 is the measure normally used to relate exports to total sales by UK producers and Ratio 4 makes an allowance for the extent to which imports of the same product are coming into the UK.

International trade in services (Tables 6.7 and 6.8)

These data relate to overseas trade in services and cover both production and non-production industries (excluding the public sector). In terms of the types of services traded these include royalties, various forms of consultancy, computing and telecommunications services, advertising and market research and other business services. A separate inquiry covers the film and television industries. The surveys cover receipts from the provision of services to residents of other countries (exports) and payments to residents of other countries for services rendered (imports).

Sources of data

The International Trade in Services (ITIS) surveys (which consist of a quarterly component addressed to the largest businesses and an annual component for the remainder) are based on a sample of companies derived from the Inter-departmental Business Register in addition to a reference list and from 2007 onwards a sample of approximately 5000 contributors from the Annual Business Inquiry (ABI). The companies are asked to show the amounts for their imports and exports against the geographical area to which they were paid or from which they were received, irrespective of where they were first earned.

The purpose of the ITIS survey is to record international transactions which impact on the UK's BoP. Exports and imports of goods are generally excluded, as they will have been counted in the estimate for trade in goods. However earnings from third country trade – that is, from arranging the sale of goods between two countries other than the UK and where the goods never physically enter the UK (known as merchanting) – are included. Earnings from commodity trading are also included. Together, these two comprise trade related services.

Royalties are a large part of the total trade in services collected in the ITIS survey. These cover transactions for items such as printed matter, sound recordings, performing rights, patents, licences, trademarks, designs, copyrights, manufacturing rights, the use of technical know-how and technical assistance.

Balance of Payments (Tables 6.9 to 6.12)

Tables 6.9 to 6.12 are derived from *United Kingdom Balance of Payments: The Pink Book* 2008 edition. The following general notes to the tables provide brief definitions and explanations of the figures and terms used. Further notes are included in the Pink Book.

Summary of Balance of Payments

The BoP consists of the current account, the capital account, the financial account and the International Investment Position (IIP). The current account consists of trade in goods and services, income, and current transfers. Income consists of investment income and compensation of employees. The capital account mainly consists of capital transfers and the financial account covers financial transactions. The IIP covers balance sheet levels of UK external assets and liabilities. Every credit entry in the balance of payments accounts should, in theory, be matched by a corresponding debit entry so that total current, capital and financial account credits should be equal to, and therefore offset by, total debits. In practice there is a discrepancy termed net errors and omissions.

Current account

Trade in goods

The goods account covers exports and imports of goods. Imports of motor cars from Japan, for example, are recorded as debits in the trade in goods account, whereas exports of vehicles manufactured in the UK are recorded as credits. Trade in goods forms a component of the expenditure measure of gross domestic product (GDP).

Trade in services

The services account covers exports and imports of services, for example civil aviation. Passenger tickets for travel on UK aircraft sold abroad, for example, are recorded as credits in the services account, whereas the purchases of airline tickets from foreign airlines by UK passengers are recorded as debits. Trade in services, along with trade in goods, forms a component of the expenditure measure of GDP.

Income

The income account consists of compensation of employees and investment income and is dominated by the latter. Compensation of employees covers employment income from cross-border and seasonal workers which is less significant in the UK than in other countries. Investment income covers earnings (for example, profits, dividends and interest payments and receipts) arising from cross-border investment in financial assets and liabilities. For example, earnings on foreign bonds and shares held by financial institutions based in the UK are recorded as credits in the investment income account, whereas earnings on UK company securities held abroad are recorded as investment income debits. Investment income forms a component of gross national income (GNI) but not GDP.

Current transfers

Current transfers are composed of central government transfers (for example, taxes and payments to and receipts from, the EU) and other transfers (for example gifts in cash or kind received by private individuals from abroad or receipts from the EU where the UK government acts as an agent for the ultimate beneficiary of the transfer). Current transfers do not form a component either of GDP or of GNI. For example, payments to the UK farming industry under the EU Agricultural Guarantee Fund are recorded as credits in the current transfers account, while payments of EU agricultural levies by the UK farming industry are recorded as debits in the current transfers account.

Capital account

Capital account transactions involve transfers of ownership of fixed assets, transfers of funds associated with acquisition or disposal of fixed assets and cancellation of liabilities by creditors without any counterparts being received in return. The main components are migrants transfers, EU transfers relating to fixed capital formation (regional development fund and agricultural guidance fund) and debt forgiveness. Funds brought into the UK by new immigrants would, for example, be recorded as credits in the capital account, while funds sent abroad by UK residents emigrating to other countries would be recorded as debits in the capital account. The size of capital account transactions are quite minor compared with the current and financial accounts.

Financial account

While investment income covers earnings arising from cross-border investments in financial assets and liabilities, the financial account of the balance of payments covers the flows of such investments. Earnings on foreign bonds and shares held by financial institutions based in the UK are, for example, recorded as credits in the investment income account, but the acquisition of such foreign securities by UK-based financial institutions are recorded as net debits in the financial account or portfolio investment abroad. Similarly, the acquisitions of UK company securities held by foreign residents are recorded in the financial account as net credits or portfolio investment in the UK.

International Investment Position

While the financial account covers the flows of foreign investments and financial assets and liabilities, the IIP records the levels of external assets and liabilities. While the acquisition of foreign securities by UK-based financial institutions are recorded in the financial account as net debits, the total holdings of foreign securities by UK-based financial institutions are recorded as levels of UK external assets. Similarly, the holdings of UK company securities held by foreign residents are recorded as levels of UK liabilities.

Foreign direct investment (Tables 6.13 to 6.18)

Direct investment refers to investment that adds to, deducts from, or acquires a lasting interest in an enterprise operating in an economy other than that of the investor – the investor's purpose being to have an effective voice in the management of the enterprise. (For the purposes of the statistical inquiry, an effective voice is taken as equivalent to a holding of 10 per cent or more in the foreign enterprise.) Other investments in which the investor does not have an effective voice in the management of the enterprise are mainly portfolio investments and these are not covered here.

Direct investment is a financial concept and is not the same as capital expenditure on fixed assets. It covers only the money invested in a related concern by the parent company and the concern will then decide how to use the money. A related concern may also raise money locally without reference to the parent company.

The investment figures are published on a net basis; that is they consist of investments net of disinvestments by a company into its foreign subsidiaries, associate companies and branches.

Definitional changes from 1997

The new European System of Accounts (ESA(95)) definitions were introduced from the 1997 estimates. The changes were as follows:

i.   Previously, for the measurement of direct investment, an effective voice in the management of an enterprise was taken as the equivalent of a 20 per cent shareholding. This is now 10 per cent

ii.   The Channel Islands and the Isle of Man have been excluded from the definition of the economic territory of the UK. Prior to 1987 these islands were considered to be part of the UK

iii.   Interest received or paid was replaced by interest accrued in the figures on earnings from direct investment. There is deemed to be little or no impact arising from this definitional change on the estimates

A further change caused by the move to ESA(95) is that withholding taxes payable on direct investment earnings are now measured. Earnings were shown gross of these taxes in the Balance of Payments 2005 Pink Book. However, for the purposes of this business monitor earnings are calculated net of tax, as before.

New register sources available from 1998 have led to revisions of the figures from that year onwards. These sources gave an improved estimate of the population satisfying the criteria for foreign direct investment.

From the 2005 surveys new data sources have allowed the inclusion of data for the previously excluded Private Property (outward & inward surveys) and Public Corporations (outward surveys) sectors. From the 2006 surveys the tax data previously excluded from the FDI surveys are now also included in the final earnings figures for both the outward & inward surveys. This now means that there are no coherence issues between the FDI annual surveys and the quarterly Balance of Payments figures as published in the latest Balance of Payments Pink Book.

Definitional changes have been introduced from 1997 and the register changes from 1998. Data prior to these years have not been reworked in Tables 6.13 to 6.18. For clarity, the Offshore Islands are identified separately on the tables. Breaks in the series for the other definitional changes are not quantified but are relatively small. More detailed information on the effect of these changes appears in the business monitor MA4 – Foreign Direct Investment 2002, which was published in February 2003 and is available from the ONS website.

Sources of data

The figures in Tables 6.13 to 6.18 are based on annual inquiries into foreign direct investment for 2009. These were sample surveys which involved sending approximately 1530 forms to UK businesses investing abroad, and 2370 forms to UK businesses in which foreign parents and associates had invested. The tables also contain some revisions to 2008 as a result of new information coming to light in the course of the latest surveys. Further details from the latest annual surveys, including analyses by industry and by components of direct investment, are available in business monitor MA4. Initial figures were published on the ONS website in a statistical bulletin Foreign Direct Investment 2009 in December 2010 Data for 2010 will be published in a statistical bulletin in December 2011, followed by the full business monitor MA4 in February 2012.

Country allocation

The analysis of inward investment is based on the country of ownership of the immediate parent company. Thus, inward investment in a UK company may be attributed to the country of the intervening overseas subsidiary, rather than the country of the ultimate parent. Similarly, the country analysis of outward investment is based on the country of ownership of the immediate subsidiary; for example, to the extent that overseas investment in the UK is channelled through holding companies in the Netherlands, the underlying flow of investment from this country is overstated and the inflow from originating countries is understated.

Further information

More detailed statistics on foreign direct investment are available on request from Richard Tonkin, Office for National Statistics, International Transactions Branch, Room 2.364, Government

Buildings, Cardiff Road, Newport, South Wales, United Kingdom, NP10 8XG. Telephone: +44 (0)1633 456082, fax: +44 (0)1633 812855, email Richard.tonkin@ons.gov.uk

6.1 Trade in goods[1]

United Kingdom
Balance of payments basis

£million and indices (2006=100)

		1999	2000	2001	2002	2003	2004	2005	2006	2007	2008	2009	2010
Value (£ million)													
Exports of goods	**BOKG**	166,166	187,936	189,093	186,524	188,320	190,874	211,608	243,633	220,858	252,086	227,645	266,079
Imports of goods	**BOKH**	195,217	220,912	230,305	234,229	236,927	251,774	280,197	319,945	310,612	345,202	310,010	363,278
Balance on trade in goods	**BOKI**	-29,051	-32,976	-41,212	-47,705	-48,607	-60,900	-68,589	-76,312	-89,754	-93,116	-82,365	-97,199
Price index numbers													
Exports of goods	**BQKR**	94	95	94	94	96	96	100	103	103	114	117	124
Imports of goods	**BQKS**	97	100	99	97	96	96	100	104	105	114	118	125
Terms of trade[2]	**BQKT**	97	95	95	97	100	100	100	99	99	100	100	99
Volume index numbers													
Exports of goods	**BQKU**	80	90	92	91	91	92	100	112	100	91	80	89
Imports of goods	**BQKV**	71	78	82	86	87	94	100	110	107	96	84	93

Source: Office for National Statistics: 01633 456294

1 See chapter text. Statistics of trade in goods on a balance of payments basis are obtained by making certain adjustments in respect of valuation and coverage to the statistics recorded in the Overseas Trade Statistics. These adjustments are described in detail in The Pink Book 2009.
2 Export price index as a percentage of the import price index.

6.2(a) Sales of products manufactured in the United Kingdom [1]

United Kingdom

£thousands

Ratio Totals	Sic Division[2]	2008	2009[3]
Other mining and quarrying	8	2508359	2115814
Manufacture of food products	10	58304930	58105182
Manufacture of beverages	11	10964805	11495079
Manufacture of tobacco products	12	1734853	1912092
Manufacture of textiles	13	4276677	3746388
Manufacture of wearing apparel	14	1883699	1674157
Manufacture of leather and related products	15	527027	454267
Manufacture of wood and of products of wood and cork, except furniture; Manufacture of articles of straw and plaiting materials	16	6259187	5352385
Manufacture of paper and paper products	17	9724978	8945207
Printing and reproduction of recorded media	18	8689512	8363097
Manufacture of chemicals and chemical products	20	24399400	23088160
Manufacture of basic pharmaceutical products and pharmaceutical preparations	21	10221170	12198397
Manufacture of rubber and plastic products	22	16728953	14939768
Manufacture of other non-metallic mineral products	23	11106311	9153607
Manufacture of fabricated metal products, except machinery and equipment	25	26245246	22839132
Manufacture of computer, electronic and optical products	26	12714431	12635900
Manufacture of electrical equipment	27	11306936	9453803
Manufacture of machinery and equipment n.e.c.	28	26799819	18836111
Manufacture of motor vehicles, trailers and semi-trailers	29	35953861	27247038
Manufacture of other transport equipment	30	18600066	19990401
Manufacture of furniture	31	6102024	5401594
Other manufacturing	32	4492713	4650926
Repair and installation of machinery and equipment	33	12467871	11803809
Publishing activities	58	16065476	14869480
Total		338078304	309271794

1 See chapter text

2 Division 07 (Mining of metal ores), Division 19 (manufacture of coke and refined petroleum products) and Division 24 (Manufacture of basic metals) do not form part of this analysis.

3 Provisional data

Source: Office for National Statistics: 01633 456743

6.2(b) Import penetration and export sales ratios for products of manufacturing industry [1]

United Kingdom
Standard Industrial Classification 2007

Ratio1 Imports/Home Demand	Sic Division[2]	2008	2009 [3]
Other mining and quarrying	8	180.362	155.143
Manufacture of food products	10	26.829	27.543
Manufacture of beverages	11	40.821	40.669
Manufacture of tobacco products	12	15.862	12.681
Manufacture of textiles	13	66.714	69.454
Manufacture of wearing apparel	14	110.86	113.149
Manufacture of leather and related products	15	114.813	118.207
Manufacture of wood and of products of wood and cork, except furniture; Manufacture of articles of straw and plaiting materials	16	34.801	35.045
Manufacture of paper and paper products	17	47.015	48.822
Printing and reproduction of recorded media	18	2.976	4.514
Manufacture of chemicals and chemical products	20	89.619	96.014
Manufacture of basic pharmaceutical products and pharmaceutical preparations	21	262.49	252.887
Manufacture of rubber and plastic products	22	42.102	44.264
Manufacture of other non-metallic mineral products	23	28.507	30.122
Manufacture of fabricated metal products, except machinery and equipment	25	32.747	34.792
Manufacture of computer, electronic and optical products	26	127.94	131.602
Manufacture of electrical equipment	27	83.756	86.41
Manufacture of machinery and equipment n.e.c.	28	91.289	104.873
Manufacture of motor vehicles, trailers and semi-trailers	29	71.614	71.81
Manufacture of other transport equipment	30	84.454	85.324
Manufacture of furniture	31	46.15	45.273
Other manufacturing	32	141.137	136.314
Repair and installation of machinery and equipment	33	.	.
Publishing activities	58	.	.
Total		68.853	71.152

1 See chapter text

2 Division 07 (Mining of metal ores), Division 19 (manufacture of coke and refined petroleum products) and Division 24 (Manufacture of basic metals) do not form part of this analysis.

3 Provisional data

Source: Office for National Statistics: 01633 456743

6.2(c) Import penetration and export sales ratios for products of manufacturing industry [1]

United Kingdom
Standard Industrial Classification 2007

Ratio 2 Imports/Home Demand plus Exports	Sic Division[2]	2008	2009 [3]
Other mining and quarrying	8	62.0192	60.3023
Manufacture of food products	10	24.3518	24.9123
Manufacture of beverages	11	28.5029	27.9966
Manufacture of tobacco products	12	12.3611	10.344
Manufacture of textiles	13	48.8619	50.9005
Manufacture of wearing apparel	14	87.3843	89.1198
Manufacture of leather and related products	15	89.2265	90.937
Manufacture of wood and of products of wood and cork, except furniture; Manufacture of articles of straw and plaiting materials	16	33.5106	33.7128
Manufacture of paper and paper products	17	39.717	40.9232
Printing and reproduction of recorded media	18	2.8773	4.3495
Manufacture of chemicals and chemical products	20	49.1791	49.3217
Manufacture of basic pharmaceutical products and pharmaceutical preparations	21	53.6831	53.4621
Manufacture of rubber and plastic products	22	33.1267	34.6526
Manufacture of other non-metallic mineral products	23	24.2451	25.7257
Manufacture of fabricated metal products, except machinery and equipment	25	27.1199	28.6822
Manufacture of computer, electronic and optical products	26	74.6926	74.0083
Manufacture of electrical equipment	27	52.4677	55.179
Manufacture of machinery and equipment n.e.c.	28	48.4598	51.6239
Manufacture of motor vehicles, trailers and semi-trailers	29	49.2866	49.2431
Manufacture of other transport equipment	30	46.3456	47.5355
Manufacture of furniture	31	42.5836	41.9905
Other manufacturing	32	70.4006	69.3144
Repair and installation of machinery and equipment	33	.	.
Publishing activities	58	.	.
Total		46.4387	47.274

Source: Office for National Statistics: 01633 456743

1 See chapter text

2 Division 07 (Mining of metal ores), Division 19 (manufacture of coke and refined petroleum products) and Division 24 (Manufacture of basic metals) do not form part of this analysis.

3 Provisional data

6.2(d) Import penetration and export sales ratios for products of manufacturing industry[1]

United Kingdom
Standard Industrial Classification 2007

Ratio 3 Exports/Sales	Sic Division[2]	2008	2009[3]
Other mining and quarrying	8	172.756	153.992
Manufacture of food products	10	11.5	12.008
Manufacture of beverages	11	42.206	43.276
Manufacture of tobacco products	12	25.183	20.559
Manufacture of textiles	13	52.328	54.406
Manufacture of wearing apparel	14	167.856	195.186
Manufacture of leather and related products	15	206.853	254.546
Manufacture of wood and of products of wood and cork, except furniture; manufacture of articles of straw and plaiting materials	16	5.576	5.736
Manufacture of paper and paper products	17	25.75	27.387
Printing and reproduction of recorded media	18	0.31	0.309
Manufacture of chemicals and chemical products	20	88.79	95.96
Manufacture of basic pharmaceutical products and pharmaceutical preparations	21	171.748	169.452
Manufacture of rubber and plastic products	22	31.879	33.229
Manufacture of other non-metallic mineral products	23	19.735	19.651
Manufacture of fabricated metal products, except machinery and equipment	25	18.773	18.258
Manufacture of computer, electronic and optical products	26	164.454	168.376
Manufacture of electrical equipment	27	78.591	80.639
Manufacture of machinery and equipment n.e.c.	28	91.028	104.958
Manufacture of motor vehicles, trailers and semi-trailers	29	61.477	61.915
Manufacture of other transport equipment	30	84.1	84.415
Manufacture of furniture	31	13.458	12.499
Other manufacturing	32	169.324	160.176
Repair and installation of machinery and equipment	33	.	.
Publishing activities	58	.	.
Total		52.505	54.692

1 See chapter text

2 Division 07 (Mining of metal ores), Division 19 (manufacture of coke and refined petroleum products) and Division 24 (Manufacture of basic metals) do not form part of this analysis.

3 Provisional data

Source: Office for National Statistics: 01633 456743

6.2(e) Import penetration and export sales ratios for products of manufacturing industry [1]

United Kingdom
Standard Industrial Classification 2007

Ratio 4 Exports/Sales plus imports	SIC Division[2]	2008	2009[3]
Other mining and quarrying	8	65.614	61.1312
Manufacture of food products	10	8.8235	9.1445
Manufacture of beverages	11	30.176	31.1604
Manufacture of tobacco products	12	22.07	18.4319
Manufacture of textiles	13	26.76	26.7129
Manufacture of wearing apparel	14	21.176	21.2367
Manufacture of leather and related products	15	22.285	23.0696
Manufacture of wood and of products of wood and cork, except furniture; manufacture of articles of straw and plaiting materials	16	3.7071	3.8025
Manufacture of paper and paper products	17	15.523	16.1792
Printing and reproduction of recorded media	18	0.3093	0.3081
Manufacture of chemicals and chemical products	20	45.124	48.6307
Manufacture of basic pharmaceutical products and pharmaceutical preparations	21	79.549	78.8593
Manufacture of rubber and plastic products	22	21.319	21.7146
Manufacture of other non-metallic mineral products	23	14.95	14.5954
Manufacture of fabricated metal products, except machinery and equipment	25	14.482	14.0636
Manufacture of computer, electronic and optical products	26	41.619	43.7637
Manufacture of electrical equipment	27	37.356	36.1431
Manufacture of machinery and equipment n.e.c.	28	46.916	50.7747
Manufacture of motor vehicles, trailers and semi-trailers	29	31.177	31.4262
Manufacture of other transport equipment	30	45.123	44.2881
Manufacture of furniture	31	7.7272	7.2508
Other manufacturing	32	50.119	49.151
Repair and installation of machinery and equipment	33	.	.
Publishing activities	58	.	.
Total		29.982	30.8917

Source: Office for National Statistics: 01633 456743

1 See chapter text
2 Division 07 (Mining of metal ores), Division 19 (manufacture of coke and refined
petroleum products) and Division 24 (Manufacture of basic metals) do not form part of this analysis.
3 Provisional data

6.3 United Kingdom exports: by commodity[1,2]

Seasonally adjusted

£ million

		2000	2001	2002	2003	2004	2005	2006	2007	2008	2009	2010
0. Food and live animals	BOGG	5,827	5,491	5,693	6,478	6,461	6,552	6,770	7,374	8,703	9,167	10,092
01. Meat and meat preparations	BOGS	642	428	516	606	667	729	754	839	1,169	1,247	1,398
02. Dairy products and eggs	BQMS	660	614	625	760	780	718	712	807	887	837	1,036
04 & 08. Cereals and animal feeding stuffs	BQMT	1,604	1,383	1,444	1,681	1,553	1,554	1,587	1,791	2,290	2,364	2,592
05. Vegetables and fruit	BQMU	403	401	433	475	507	515	586	606	696	762	812
1. Beverages and tobacco	BQMZ	4,081	4,139	4,300	4,401	4,116	4,095	4,175	4,395	5,035	5,350	5,987
11. Beverages	BQNB	3,065	3,218	3,320	3,478	3,354	3,481	3,715	4,093	4,587	4,947	5,640
12. Tobacco	BQOW	1,016	921	980	923	762	614	460	302	448	403	347
2. Crude materials	BQOX	2,447	2,422	2,645	3,069	3,565	3,746	4,621	5,196	6,276	4,814	6,913
of which:												
24. Wood, lumber and cork	BQOY	72	70	81	106	117	131	146	144	126	84	109
25. Pulp and waste paper	BQOZ	78	81	106	180	244	283	338	417	482	356	546
26. Textile fibres	BQPA	496	440	472	492	520	516	542	499	544	575	675
28. Metal ores	BQPB	759	810	928	1,193	1,604	1,713	2,418	2,898	3,670	2,517	4,103
3. Fuels	BOPN	17,057	16,386	16,000	16,558	17,885	21,496	25,301	24,700	35,762	27,033	36,154
33. Petroleum and petroleum products	ELBL	15,584	14,815	14,321	14,608	16,200	19,794	23,173	22,756	32,212	24,671	32,316
32, 34 & 35. Coal, gas and electricity	BOQI	1,473	1,571	1,679	1,950	1,685	1,702	2,128	1,944	3,550	2,362	3,838
4. Animal and vegetable oils and fats	BQPI	156	149	210	266	205	235	271	327	361	378	431
5. Chemicals	ENDG	24,992	27,514	28,386	31,373	32,009	33,388	37,179	38,891	43,866	46,929	50,947
of which:												
51. Organic chemicals	BQPJ	5,718	6,090	5,698	6,070	6,040	6,702	8,009	7,601	8,405	9,093	8,938
52. Inorganic chemicals	BQPK	1,491	1,636	1,367	1,460	1,543	1,555	2,143	2,830	2,988	2,839	3,497
53. Colouring materials	CSCE	1,555	1,521	1,583	1,627	1,630	1,635	1,602	1,672	1,841	1,694	1,953
54. Medicinal products	BQPL	7,217	9,067	10,103	11,897	12,325	12,320	13,786	14,507	17,258	20,387	22,227
55. Toilet preparations	CSCF	2,597	2,714	2,823	3,122	3,105	3,219	3,443	3,689	3,953	4,133	4,306
57 & 58. Plastics	BQQA	3,366	3,416	3,526	3,703	3,847	4,298	4,445	4,612	4,869	4,397	5,323
6. Manufactures classified chiefly by material	BQQB	22,673	22,781	21,837	23,119	24,458	26,492	27,664	29,378	32,451	24,559	29,140
of which:												
63. Wood and cork manufactures	BQQC	255	261	270	322	291	255	273	272	244	222	221
64. Paper and paperboard manufactures	BQQD	2,096	2,081	2,019	2,097	1,996	2,043	2,014	2,124	2,341	2,278	2,333
65. Textile manufactures	BQQE	3,051	3,022	2,847	2,956	2,847	2,647	2,680	2,589	2,596	2,369	2,583
67. Iron and steel	BQQF	2,848	2,879	2,916	3,319	4,245	5,183	5,131	6,016	6,867	4,579	5,009
68. Non-ferrous metals	BQQG	3,171	3,033	2,552	2,567	3,228	3,862	4,827	5,778	6,874	3,974	5,848
69. Metal manufactures	BQQH	3,595	3,853	3,660	3,766	3,856	4,066	4,520	4,665	5,054	4,263	4,541
7. Machinery and transport equipment[3]	BQQI	87,812	87,240	84,395	79,650	78,376	89,379	110,393	82,713	89,328	79,638	92,836
71-716, 72, 73 & 74. Mechanical machinery	BQQK	22,140	24,244	22,704	24,231	23,808	25,795	28,244	28,969	32,315	29,371	32,921
716, 75, 76 & 77. Electrical machinery	BQQL	42,681	41,997	38,706	30,651	28,624	37,120	55,336	24,215	25,325	24,232	25,937
78. Road vehicles	BQQM	15,604	13,845	16,316	17,474	18,489	19,439	19,334	21,114	22,517	17,046	23,338
79. Other transport equipment	BQQN	7,387	7,154	6,669	7,294	7,455	7,025	7,479	8,415	9,171	8,989	10,640
8. Miscellaneous manufactures[3]	BQQO	21,206	21,948	21,985	22,543	22,917	25,105	25,973	26,695	28,512	27,755	31,353
of which:												
84. Clothing	CSCN	2,722	2,578	2,507	2,708	2,729	2,712	2,877	3,100	3,312	3,426	3,641
85. Footwear	CSCP	514	484	452	426	419	470	522	541	625	726	839
87 & 88. Scientific and photographic	BQQQ	7,333	7,775	7,212	7,281	7,040	7,245	7,344	7,063	8,073	8,303	9,285
9. Other commodities and transactions	BOQL	1,685	1,023	1,073	863	882	1,120	1,286	1,189	1,791	2,022	2,226
Total United Kingdom exports	BOKG	187,936	189,093	186,524	188,320	190,874	211,608	243,633	220,858	252,086	227,645	266,079

Source: Office for National Statistics: 01633 456294

1 See chapter text. The numbers on the left hand side of the table refer to the code numbers of the Standard International Trade Classification, Revision 3, which was introduced in January 1988.

2 Balance of payments consistent basis.

3 Sections 7 and 8 are shown by broad economic category in table G2 of the Monthly Review of External Trade Statistics.

6.4 United Kingdom imports: by commodity [1,2]

Seasonally adjusted

£ million

		2000	2001	2002	2003	2004	2005	2006	2007	2008	2009	2010
0. Food and live animals	BQQR	13,310	14,269	14,874	16,452	17,211	18,593	19,814	21,324	25,307	26,338	27,034
of which:												
01. Meat and meat preparations	BQQS	2,366	2,689	2,793	3,267	3,441	3,619	3,800	3,992	4,622	4,924	4,966
02. Dairy products and eggs	BQQT	1,165	1,245	1,291	1,501	1,609	1,700	1,808	1,837	2,283	2,313	2,447
04 & 08. Cereals and animal feeding stuffs	BQQU	1,762	1,957	1,985	2,219	2,307	2,363	2,497	2,918	3,816	3,928	3,951
05. Vegetables and fruit	BQQV	3,894	4,101	4,374	4,766	4,919	5,447	5,783	6,204	7,058	7,047	7,432
1. Beverages and tobacco	BQQW	4,350	4,216	4,501	4,735	4,939	5,102	5,199	5,423	5,834	5,968	6,395
11. Beverages	EGAT	2,910	2,854	3,028	3,237	3,474	3,625	3,701	3,942	4,321	4,386	4,626
12. Tobacco	EMAI	1,440	1,362	1,473	1,498	1,465	1,477	1,498	1,481	1,513	1,582	1,769
2. Crude materials	ENVB	5,816	5,921	5,420	5,525	5,716	6,129	7,116	8,663	9,598	6,539	9,126
of which:												
24. Wood, lumber and cork	ENVC	1,193	1,168	1,236	1,366	1,337	1,358	1,453	1,805	1,411	1,169	1,459
25. Pulp and waste paper	EQAH	763	606	488	489	480	477	512	503	595	438	575
26. Textile fibres	EQAP	412	393	361	337	339	314	298	315	335	285	358
28. Metalores	EHAA	1,811	1,997	1,448	1,430	1,647	1,999	2,672	3,790	4,659	2,258	3,911
3. Fuels	BQAT	10,016	10,795	10,279	12,311	17,547	25,921	30,888	31,928	48,589	35,113	45,418
33. Petroleum and petroleum products	ENXO	9,048	9,525	9,213	11,232	15,307	21,989	25,967	26,787	38,021	27,682	36,530
32, 34 & 35. Coal, gas and electricity	BPBI	968	1,270	1,066	1,079	2,240	3,932	4,921	5,141	10,568	7,431	8,888
4. Animal and vegetable oils and fats	EHAB	491	521	538	614	622	641	771	898	1,400	1,055	1,122
5. Chemicals	ENGA	20,633	22,745	23,987	26,139	27,929	29,208	31,727	34,645	37,955	38,944	44,656
of which:												
51. Organic chemicals	EHAC	5,374	5,529	5,673	6,102	6,802	7,183	7,692	8,620	8,466	8,279	9,444
52. Inorganic chemicals	EHAE	1,046	1,171	1,070	1,094	1,367	1,507	2,123	2,679	2,758	2,741	2,949
53. Colouring materials	CSCR	1,002	975	952	1,003	1,060	1,072	1,090	1,164	1,229	1,140	1,258
54. Medicinal products	EHAF	4,714	6,149	7,288	8,189	8,372	8,504	9,158	9,943	11,056	13,165	15,064
55. Toilet preparations	CSCS	2,005	2,261	2,499	2,745	2,881	3,035	3,336	3,448	3,918	4,163	4,422
57 & 58. Plastics	EHAG	4,144	4,096	4,063	4,403	4,749	5,038	5,409	5,699	6,224	5,560	6,825
6. Manufactures classified chiefly by material	EHAH	29,232	30,165	28,735	29,906	32,299	33,469	37,615	39,792	41,934	35,910	43,520
of which:												
63. Wood and cork manufactures	EHAI	1,245	1,340	1,436	1,449	1,585	1,505	1,575	1,733	1,732	1,476	1,660
64. Paper and paperboard manufactures	EHAJ	4,407	4,864	4,582	4,747	4,841	4,820	5,037	5,248	5,496	5,514	5,880
65. Textile manufactures	EHAK	4,365	4,303	4,149	4,089	4,124	3,844	4,018	4,084	4,075	3,815	4,275
67. Iron and steel	EHAL	2,731	3,051	3,047	3,237	4,199	4,402	4,981	5,958	6,579	3,855	5,169
68. Non-ferrous metals	EHAM	3,711	3,780	3,222	3,320	3,616	3,923	6,185	6,230	6,423	6,343	8,664
69. Metal manufactures	EHAN	4,065	4,324	4,501	4,765	4,977	5,355	5,852	6,563	6,989	5,983	6,868
7. Machinery and transport equipment[3]	EHAO	102,420	105,386	107,556	101,473	103,882	117,118	139,826	117,726	121,078	107,440	128,516
71 - 716, 72, 73 & 74. Mechanical machinery	EHAQ	17,867	18,618	18,901	18,951	19,725	21,848	22,613	25,776	28,932	24,271	28,381
716, 75, 76 & 77. Electrical machinery	EHAR	53,631	50,842	49,917	43,656	45,495	55,535	75,086	46,006	47,611	44,917	51,137
78. Road vehicles	EHAS	23,117	26,289	28,449	29,921	30,734	31,436	32,674	36,590	33,952	26,156	33,181
79. Other transport equipment	EHAT	7,805	9,637	10,289	8,945	7,928	8,299	9,453	9,354	10,583	12,096	15,817
8. Miscellaneous manufactures[3]	EHAU	32,798	35,023	36,889	38,168	39,822	42,175	44,919	47,939	50,940	49,974	54,624
of which:												
84. Clothing	CSDR	8,495	9,119	9,804	10,323	10,646	11,303	11,847	12,310	13,213	13,869	14,800
85. Footwear	CSDS	2,001	2,236	2,365	2,375	2,447	2,563	2,699	2,659	2,841	3,101	3,601
87 & 88. Scientific and photographic	EHAW	7,273	7,620	7,044	7,049	7,255	7,414	7,655	7,572	8,447	8,486	9,076
9. Other commodities and transactions	BQAW	1,846	1,264	1,450	1,604	1,807	1,841	2,070	2,274	2,567	2,729	2,867
Total United Kingdom imports	BOKH	220,912	230,305	234,229	236,927	251,774	280,197	319,945	310,612	345,202	310,010	363,278

Source: Office for National Statistics: 01633 456294

1 See chapter text. The numbers on the left hand side of the table refer to the code numbers of the Standard International Trade Classification, Revision 3,
which was introduced in January 1988.
2 Balance of payments consistent basis.
3 Sections 7 and 8 are shown by broad economic category in table G2 of the Monthly Review of External Trade Statistics.

6.5 United Kingdom exports: by area[1,2]

Seasonally adjusted

£ million

		2000	2001	2002	2003	2004	2005	2006	2007	2008	2009	2010
European Union:[3]	LGCK	112,459	114,406	114,737	111,286	111,650	121,486	152,357	127,813	141,831	124,423	142,449
EMU members:	QAKW	102,333	104,437	104,144	100,902	100,819	109,765	136,333	114,537	126,766	111,349	125,820
Austria	CHMY	1,146	1,224	1,265	1,264	1,095	1,332	1,699	1,376	1,474	1,288	1,474
Belgium & Luxembourg	CHNQ	10,322	9,893	10,552	11,374	10,510	11,394	15,082	12,122	13,619	11,060	13,653
Cyprus	BQGN	311	291	272	317	324	359	960	415	538	619	548
Finland	CHMZ	1,471	1,611	1,442	1,493	1,363	1,514	1,872	1,958	1,909	1,325	1,494
France	ENYL	18,577	19,249	18,757	18,885	18,562	19,931	28,693	18,103	18,168	17,171	19,290
Germany	ENYO	22,789	23,655	22,064	20,805	21,668	23,025	27,602	24,699	27,970	24,195	27,957
Greece	CHNT	1,267	1,156	1,234	1,286	1,408	1,367	1,469	1,350	1,659	1,626	1,360
Irish Republic	CHNS	12,372	13,835	15,422	12,224	14,134	16,294	17,480	17,801	19,124	15,917	16,928
Italy	CHNO	8,429	8,404	8,506	8,603	8,400	8,790	9,494	9,189	9,399	8,282	8,782
Malta	BQGY	206	215	228	260	259	240	319	362	449	401	391
Netherlands	CHNP	15,167	14,599	14,011	13,597	12,029	12,716	16,522	15,115	19,905	18,179	21,559
Portugal	CHNU	1,660	1,579	1,518	1,453	1,580	1,698	2,374	1,481	1,640	1,536	1,818
Slovakia	BQHB	157	203	201	237	224	259	272	382	457	380	466
Slovenia	BQHE	157	160	182	161	163	169	200	205	225	176	219
Spain	CHNV	8,302	8,363	8,490	8,943	9,100	10,677	12,295	9,979	10,230	9,194	9,881
Non-EMU members:[3]	BQIA	10,164	10,001	10,628	10,418	10,831	11,721	16,024	13,276	15,065	13,074	16,629
of which:												
Bulgaria	WYUF	85	122	134	154	155	220	237	202	253	198	244
Czech Rep	FKML	927	1,075	1,031	1,003	978	1,080	1,526	1,401	1,548	1,441	1,826
Denmark	CHNR	2,315	2,267	2,729	2,180	2,042	2,314	3,715	2,182	2,593	2,473	2,775
Estonia	AUEV	96	83	100	95	106	115	472	228	221	140	193
Hungary	QALC	613	612	750	856	934	834	855	863	1,011	849	1,100
Latvia	BQGQ	84	84	77	113	92	103	393	145	169	109	169
Lithuania	BQGU	131	137	149	189	142	167	238	311	283	171	224
Poland	ERDR	1,299	1,297	1,318	1,462	1,417	1,653	2,705	2,372	3,014	2,793	3,785
Romania	WMDB	381	341	432	509	609	647	637	668	759	690	779
Sweden	CHNA	4,211	3,951	3,873	3,823	4,356	4,588	5,246	4,904	5,213	4,210	5,534
Other Western Europe:	HCJD	7,223	6,786	6,334	6,629	7,031	9,730	9,221	9,232	10,756	9,635	12,086
of which:												
Iceland	EPLW	193	150	131	141	167	179	188	198	187	130	132
Norway	EPLX	2,018	1,813	1,696	1,886	1,939	2,211	2,125	2,697	2,849	2,805	3,055
Switzerland	EPLV	3,061	3,496	3,080	2,786	2,842	4,985	4,189	3,808	4,656	3,938	5,170
Turkey	EOBA	1,800	1,150	1,287	1,638	1,903	2,160	2,426	2,283	2,568	2,344	3,219
North America:	HBZQ	33,714	33,408	32,261	32,924	32,763	35,010	36,928	36,365	39,663	38,067	43,418
of which:												
Canada	EOBC	3,487	3,203	3,107	3,239	3,340	3,277	3,894	3,291	3,266	3,335	4,142
Mexico	EPJX	675	681	704	687	629	638	747	801	905	753	962
USA inc Puerto Rica	J9C5	29,549	29,519	28,452	28,997	28,794	31,095	32,287	32,274	35,471	33,979	38,272

6.5 United Kingdom exports: by area[1,2]

Seasonally adjusted

£ million

		2000	2001	2002	2003	2004	2005	2006	2007	2008	2009	2010
Other OECD countries:	**HCII**	8,028	7,542	7,469	7,824	8,226	8,577	8,716	8,778	9,948	9,026	10,442
of which:												
Australia	EPMA	2,699	2,298	2,114	2,289	2,455	2,580	2,488	2,630	3,103	2,953	3,354
Japan	EOBD	3,672	3,673	3,583	3,710	3,863	3,900	4,109	3,866	3,908	3,562	4,331
New Zealand	EPMB	305	309	311	348	418	415	373	364	385	348	415
South Korea	ERDM	1,350	1,262	1,461	1,468	1,481	1,677	1,746	1,914	2,552	2,163	2,342
Oil exporting countries:	**HDII**	6,031	6,474	6,229	7,615	7,996	10,850	9,060	9,716	11,618	11,421	12,452
of which:												
Brunei	QALF	96	59	61	127	67	43	79	870	65	61	158
UAE inc Dubai	J8YH	1,568	1,617	1,600	2,044	2,689	5,440	3,550	2,700	3,833	3,634	4,027
Indonesia	FKMR	404	313	324	452	397	366	311	289	385	359	455
Kuwait	QATB	338	359	308	373	354	426	438	450	543	469	548
Nigeria	QATE	524	686	711	738	773	799	821	1,043	1,513	1,307	1,410
Saudi Arabia	ERDI	1,557	1,525	1,388	1,819	1,611	1,559	1,644	1,857	2,191	2,341	2,467
Rest of the World	**HCHW**	20,481	20,477	19,494	22,042	23,208	25,955	27,351	28,954	38,269	35,073	45,232
of which:												
Brazil	FKMO	775	808	880	825	789	836	918	1,108	1,694	1,786	2,218
China	ERDN	1,468	1,709	1,493	1,924	2,366	2,811	3,264	3,860	5,084	5,399	7,607
Egypt	QALL	498	452	463	458	667	543	577	686	944	1,001	1,193
Hong Kong	ERDG	2,673	2,683	2,411	2,481	2,630	3,087	2,864	2,726	3,676	3,735	4,460
India	ERDJ	2,058	1,772	1,755	2,284	2,234	2,798	2,693	2,968	4,135	2,949	4,071
Israel	ERDL	1,516	1,357	1,428	1,359	1,386	1,352	1,308	1,257	1,341	1,140	1,394
Malaysia	ERDK	907	1,029	877	1,028	991	1,088	877	975	1,135	1,045	1,272
Pakistan	FKMU	207	229	240	291	343	461	488	423	475	474	458
Philippines	FKMX	273	392	352	377	315	279	242	251	245	272	287
Russia	ERDQ	668	893	981	1,420	1,465	1,869	2,063	2,893	4,274	2,403	3,596
Singapore	ERDH	1,625	1,592	1,445	1,582	1,708	2,078	2,318	2,467	2,820	2,958	3,450
South Africa	EPME	1,413	1,534	1,597	1,766	1,874	2,073	2,184	2,244	2,658	2,252	2,891
Taiwan	ERDP	1,015	875	848	897	950	939	911	957	892	796	1,110
Thailand	ERDO	582	594	529	572	637	638	567	613	757	914	1,135

Source: Office for National Statistics: 01633 456294

1 See chapter text.

2 Balance of payments consistent basis.

3 Includes Austria, Belgium, Bulgaria, Cyprus, Czech Republic, Denmark, Estonia, Finland, France, Germany, Greece, Hungary, Irish Republic, Italy,
Latvia, Lithuania, Luxemburg, Malta, Netherlands, Poland, Portugal, Romania, Slovakia, Slovenia, Spain and Sweden.

6.6 United Kingdom imports: by area[1,2]

Seasonally adjusted

£ million

		2000	2001	2002	2003	2004	2005	2006	2007	2008	2009	2010
European Union:[3]	LGDC	117,644	126,973	136,931	137,404	142,523	158,163	183,749	169,799	181,070	162,139	184,607
EMU members	QAKX	106,290	114,901	123,927	123,483	127,065	139,911	158,092	149,719	158,036	140,468	157,977
Austria	CHNB	1,410	1,888	2,396	2,776	2,354	2,461	2,786	2,488	2,345	2,283	2,613
Belgium & Luxembourg	CHNY	10,927	12,159	13,201	13,205	13,846	15,155	18,183	15,820	17,344	15,748	17,974
Cyprus	BQGO	208	243	247	251	205	272	1,445	193	157	124	102
Finland	CHNC	2,765	2,965	2,791	2,663	2,336	2,431	3,118	2,619	2,787	2,117	2,198
France	ENYP	18,644	20,127	20,798	20,389	20,133	21,984	26,376	21,896	23,199	20,472	21,704
Germany	ENYS	28,462	30,192	32,442	33,667	35,381	39,169	42,660	44,565	44,689	39,827	45,256
Greece	CHOB	459	476	555	613	637	703	790	640	655	539	695
Irish Republic	CHOA	10,261	12,141	13,176	9,920	10,131	10,411	10,770	11,338	12,250	12,457	12,942
Italy	CHNW	9,514	9,860	10,675	11,481	12,184	12,673	12,775	13,316	14,160	12,108	13,898
Malta	BQGZ	126	144	168	185	184	177	161	179	139	106	166
Netherlands	CHNX	15,380	15,395	16,143	16,692	18,196	20,436	22,275	23,079	25,840	21,952	26,408
Portugal	CHOC	1,735	1,625	1,761	1,966	1,928	2,018	3,054	1,506	1,745	1,428	1,752
Slovakia	BQHC	136	177	211	259	261	370	815	1,273	1,629	1,606	1,608
Slovenia	BQHN	122	149	173	169	169	201	740	318	314	251	358
Spain	CHOD	6,141	7,360	9,190	9,247	9,120	11,450	12,144	10,489	10,783	9,450	10,303
Non-EMU members:[3]	BQIB	11,362	12,072	13,004	13,921	15,458	18,252	25,657	20,080	23,034	21,671	26,630
of which:												
Bulgaria	WYUT	85	101	116	124	150	169	208	239	207	176	223
Czech Rep	FKMM	802	1,097	1,250	1,412	1,291	1,883	2,987	2,983	3,580	3,342	4,020
Denmark	CHNZ	2,630	2,922	3,595	3,399	3,357	4,393	6,439	3,444	3,924	3,849	4,104
Estonia	BQGL	309	283	327	264	379	363	2,100	226	145	126	162
Hungary	QALD	683	710	846	1,120	1,579	1,860	2,348	2,377	2,527	2,542	3,317
Latvia	BQGR	406	439	485	525	693	725	833	605	376	306	393
Lithuania	BQGV	247	235	268	285	270	273	274	299	349	368	562
Poland	ERED	905	1,166	1,265	1,545	1,835	2,320	3,622	3,695	4,312	4,679	6,038
Romania	WMDC	336	448	522	679	786	803	861	938	806	790	1,221
Sweden	CHND	4,951	4,671	4,330	4,568	5,118	5,463	5,985	5,274	6,808	5,493	6,590
Other Western Europe:	HBTS	13,040	12,240	12,523	13,331	15,754	20,072	23,417	24,359	32,436	26,491	34,087
of which:												
Iceland	EPMW	365	281	289	296	355	346	402	415	458	481	431
Norway	EPMX	5,563	5,523	5,258	6,423	8,495	12,077	14,453	14,316	21,609	15,913	20,785
Switzerland	EPMV	5,485	4,544	4,595	3,759	3,447	3,884	4,372	4,746	5,256	5,232	7,351
Turkey	EOBU	1,450	1,669	2,164	2,619	3,250	3,510	3,946	4,632	4,874	4,582	5,288
North America:	HCRB	33,460	34,617	29,811	27,480	27,130	27,133	31,228	32,472	32,627	29,897	34,624
of which:												
Canada	EOBW	4,009	3,664	3,563	3,664	4,194	4,157	4,954	5,793	5,824	4,528	5,908
Mexico	EPJY	613	680	505	490	411	446	444	582	794	765	1,056
USA inc Puerto Rica	J9C6	28,838	30,270	25,742	23,326	22,525	22,530	25,830	26,095	26,009	24,604	27,658

6.6 United Kingdom imports: by area[1,2]

Seasonally adjusted

		2000	2001	2002	2003	2004	2005	2006	2007	2008	2009	£ million 2010
Other OECD countries:	HDJQ	15,717	14,154	13,017	12,989	13,644	14,424	13,633	13,870	15,194	12,555	13,904
of which:												
Australia	EPNA	1,543	1,776	1,688	1,789	1,868	2,100	2,107	2,245	2,389	2,225	2,324
Japan	EOBX	10,214	9,080	8,079	8,085	8,109	8,669	7,857	7,885	8,547	6,659	8,160
New Zealand	EPNB	544	542	522	552	584	592	600	667	748	814	846
South Korea	ERDY	3,416	2,756	2,728	2,563	3,083	3,063	3,069	3,073	3,510	2,857	2,574
Oil exporting countries:	HCPC	4,258	3,969	3,780	3,923	4,866	6,017	6,992	6,387	7,995	7,642	11,401
of which:												
Brunei	QALG	95	35	33	51	63	25	70	57	27	47	19
UAE inc Dubai	J8YI	598	649	736	990	1,060	1,319	1,028	1,015	933	1,107	1,614
Indonesia	FKMS	1,081	1,128	1,006	875	918	839	958	925	1,184	1,195	1,366
Kuwait	QATC	314	296	271	313	396	367	741	696	1,090	731	1,004
Nigeria	QATF	89	65	90	83	106	152	206	271	911	632	874
Saudi Arabia	ERDU	977	933	677	715	1,158	1,714	1,232	821	673	596	752
Rest of the World	HCIF	36,793	38,352	38,167	41,800	47,857	54,388	60,926	63,725	75,880	71,286	84,655
of which:												
Brazil	FKMP	1,114	1,279	1,365	1,477	1,545	1,740	1,905	2,061	2,619	2,526	3,090
China	ERDZ	4,826	5,741	6,726	8,342	10,390	12,962	15,237	18,734	23,175	24,300	30,429
Egypt	QALM	411	406	416	432	495	349	662	538	640	679	654
Hong Kong	ERDS	5,917	5,754	5,561	5,500	5,761	6,602	7,338	6,939	8,080	7,661	8,128
India	ERDV	1,651	1,816	1,804	2,093	2,287	2,781	3,121	3,809	4,490	4,560	5,781
Israel	ERDX	1,025	939	880	861	920	1,002	965	1,045	1,155	1,082	1,554
Malaysia	ERDW	2,288	1,939	1,731	1,867	2,022	1,813	1,895	1,684	1,873	1,642	1,827
Pakistan	FKMV	363	421	472	519	554	487	511	512	630	692	806
Philippines	FKMY	1,155	1,155	944	713	655	712	742	717	629	394	524
Russia	EREC	1,496	2,047	1,950	2,454	3,506	5,010	5,740	5,248	6,928	4,608	5,240
Singapore	ERDT	2,395	2,067	1,959	2,672	3,379	3,828	3,756	4,247	4,007	3,541	4,127
South Africa	EPNE	2,553	2,841	2,685	2,949	3,272	3,937	3,904	3,060	4,739	3,800	4,396
Taiwan	EREB	3,561	2,784	2,385	2,198	2,341	2,226	2,339	2,418	2,598	2,240	3,092
Thailand	EREA	1,602	1,607	1,550	1,646	1,760	1,719	1,922	2,012	2,427	2,293	2,666

Source: Office for National Statistics: 01633 456294

1 See chapter text.

2 Balance of payments consistent basis.

3 Includes Austria, Belguim, Bulgaria, Cyprus, Czech Republic, Denmark, Estonia, Finland, France, Germany, Greece, Hungary, Irish Republic, Italy, Latvia, Lithuania, Luxemburg, Malta, Netherlands, Poland, Portugal, Romania, Slovakia, Slovenia, Spain and Sweden.

6.7 Services supplied (exports) and purchased (imports)[1,2]: 2008

		£ million	
	Exports	Imports	Net
Agricultural, Mining and On-site Processing services			
Agricultural	23	20	3
Mining	253	30	223
Waste treatment and depollution	11	25	-14
Other on-site processing services	490	98	392
Business and Professional services			
Accountancy, auditing, bookkeeping and tax consultancy	1,403	428	975
Advertising	2,210	1,631	579
Management consulting	1,303	565	738
Public relations services	259	131	128
Recruitment	635	184	451
Other Business Management	1,311	1,160	151
Legal Services	3,397	662	2,736
Market research and public opinion polling	488	353	135
Operational leasing services	468	591	-124
Procurement	158	286	-127
Property management	311	28	282
Research and development	5,826	4,325	1,501
Services between related enterprises	9,949	5,134	4,815
Other business and professional services	1,639	777	862
Communications services			
Postal and courier	811	446	365
Telecommunications	3,559	3,285	274
Computer services			
Computer	5,096	3,072	2,024
Information services			
News agency services	696	31	665
Publishing services	366	91	275
Other information provision services	1,426	429	997
Construction Goods and Services			
Construction in the UK	123	731	-608
Construction outside the UK	1,578	950	629
Financial services			
Financial	8,153	1,733	6,420
Insurance Services			
Auxiliary services	1,687	123	1,564
Freight Insurance - Claims	7	-	7
Freight Insurance - Premiums	-	30	-30
Life insurance and pension funding - Claims	0	-	0
Life insurance and pension funding - Premiums	-	3	-3
Reinsurance - Claims	16	-	16
Reinsurance - Premiums	-	92	-92
Other Direct insurance - Claims	38	-	38
Other Direct insurance - Premiums	-	183	-183
Merchanting and Other Trade related Services			
Merchanting	866	-	866
Other trade related services	1,580	428	1,152
Personal, Cultural and Recreational Services			
Audio-Visual and related services	280	67	213
Health services	55	47	7
Training and educational services	272	44	228
Other personal, cultural and recreational services	392	94	298
Royalties and Licenses			
Use of Franchise and similar rights fees	1,767	1,098	670
Other royalties and license fees	4,167	2,794	1,373
Purchases and sales of franchises and similar right	522	299	223
Purchases and sales of other royalties and licenses	538	816	-278
Technical services			
Architectural	375	21	354
Engineering	4,519	1,421	3,098
Surveying	167	66	101
Other technical services	1,327	466	861
Other Trade in Services			
Other Trade in services	2,105	1,249	856
World Total	72,623	36,536	36,087

Source: Office for National Statistics: 01633 456644

1 Due to rounding, the sum of constituent items may not always equal the total shown.
2 Data excludes the following industries: Financial, Film and TV, Travel and Transport,
Public Sector (including Education).

6.8 International trade in services:[1,2] by country, 2008

			£ million
	Receipts	Payments	Net
European Union			
Austria	584	154	430
Belgium	1,474	846	628
Bulgaria	61	45	16
Cyprus	145	97	48
Czech Republic	178	100	78
Denmark	753	248	505
Estonia	24	8	16
Finland	639	130	510
France	3,276	2,619	657
Germany	4,369	3,826	543
Greece	338	87	251
Hungary	221	129	92
Irish Republic	4,912	1,635	3,277
Italy	1,597	1,377	220
Latvia	26	8	18
Lithuania	23	14	9
Luxembourg	1,075	195	880
Malta	39	32	6
Netherlands	4,873	1,337	3,535
Poland	344	306	38
Portugal	273	77	196
Romania	156	42	114
Slovakia	142	19	123
Slovenia	..	..	..
Spain	1,520	793	727
Sweden	1,033	820	213
EU Institutions	..	..	..
Total European Union	**28,102**	**14,957**	**13,145**
EFTA			
Iceland	70	6	64
Liechtenstein	36	9	27
Norway	1,143	500	643
Switzerland	4,376	1,054	3,322
Total EFTA	**5,625**	**1,568**	**4,056**
Other European countries			
Russia	644	424	220
Channel Islands	1,367	213	1,154
Isle of Man	65	11	54
Turkey	232	74	158
Rest of Europe	327	153	175
Europe Unallocated	1,997	1,214	783
Total Europe	**38,359**	**18,615**	**19,744**
Africa			
Nigeria	596	305	292
South Africa	521	193	328
Rest of Africa	1,334	330	1,004
Africa Unallocated	150	34	116
Total Africa	**2,600**	**860**	**1,740**
America			
Brazil	218	135	84
Canada	845	495	350
Mexico	95	35	60
USA	15,523	8,271	7,252
Rest of America	2,626	1,157	1,470
America Unallocated	280	45	235
Total America	**19,587**	**10,136**	**9,451**

6.8 International trade in services:[1,2] by country, 2008

	Exports	Imports	Balances
			£ million
Asia			
China	478	360	117
Hong Kong	462	426	36
India	501	961	-460
Indonesia	70	22	48
Israel	193	176	16
Japan	1,386	1,465	-79
Malaysia	197	57	140
Pakistan	57	19	38
Phillippines	78	50	28
Saudi Arabia	1,289	494	795
Singapore	1,913	723	1,189
South Korea	411	111	300
Taiwan	146	196	-49
Thailand	129	45	84
Rest of Asia	2,991	1,123	1,868
Asia Unallocated	370	215	155
Total Asia	**10,671**	**6,444**	**4,227**
Australiasia and Oceania			
Australia	1,077	401	676
New Zealand	112	28	84
Rest of Australia and Oceania	27	10	17
Oceania Unallocated	8	4	4
Total Australasia and Oceania	**1,224**	**443**	**781**
Rest of World Unallocated and International Organisations	..	..	..
World Total	**72,623**	**36,536**	**36,087**
Economic Zones			
OECD	52,337	27,141	25,195.8
NAFTA	15,926	8,799	7,126.7
Central and EasternEurope	1,292	781	511.043
OPEC	3,920	1,477	2,442.75
ASEAN	2,445	918	1,526.85
CIS	1,339	641	698.178
NICs[1]	2,932	1,456	1,476.05
Offshore Financial centres	6,414	2,527	3,886.89
ACP	2,141	932	1,208.6

Source: Office for National Statistics: 01633 456644

1 Due to rounding, the sum of constituent items may not always equal the total shown.
2 Data excludes the following industries: Financial, Film and TV, Travel and Transport, Public Sector
(including Education) and Law Society Members

Note (-) Denotes disclosive data

6.9 Summary of balance of payments,[1] 2009

United Kingdom

£ million

	Credits	Debits
1. Current account		
A. Goods and services	388,838	421,315
1. Goods	227,670	309,460
2. Services	161,168	111,855
2.1. Transportation	21,348	18,177
2.2. Travel	19,292	31,117
2.3. Communications	5,199	4,585
2.4. Construction	1,472	1,644
2.5. Insurance	8,501	1,079
2.6. Financial	43,159	12,077
2.7. Computer and information	7,423	3,628
2.8. Royalties and licence fees	8,213	6,122
2.9. Other business	42,120	28,548
2.10. Personal, cultural and recreational	2,323	1,085
2.11. Government	2,118	3,793
B. Income	175,571	146,915
1. Compensation of employees	916	1,604
2. Investment income	174,655	145,311
2.1 Direct investment	77,519	26,073
2.2 Portfolio investment	54,593	59,539
2.3 Other investment (including earnings on reserve assets)	42,543	59,699
C. Current transfers	16,998	31,612
1. General government	6,158	17,348
2. Other sectors	10,840	14,264
Total current account	581,407	599,842
2. Capital and financial accounts		
A. Capital account	5,854	2,225
1. Capital transfers	4,251	1,339
2. Acquisition/disposal of non-produced, non-financial assets	1,603	886
B. Financial account	-162,373	-172,598
1. Direct investment	29,320	11,852
Abroad		11,852
1.1. Equity capital		4,631
1.2. Reinvested earnings		28,655
1.3. Other capital[2]		-21,434
In United Kingdom	29,320	
1.1. Equity capital	23,323	
1.2. Reinvested earnings	13,411	
1.3. Other capital[3]	-7,414	
2. Portfolio investment	188,299	154,396
Assets		154,396
2.1. Equity securities		13,655
2.2. Debt securities		140,741
Liabilities	188,299	
2.1. Equity securities	44,245	
2.2. Debt securities	144,054	
3. Financial derivatives (net)		-14,450
4. Other investment	-379,992	-330,159
Assets		-330,159
4.1 Trade credits		-96
4.2 Loans		-116,466
4.3 Currency and deposits		-213,738
4.4 Other assets		141
Liabilities	-379,992	
4.1. Trade credits	-	
4.2. Loans	-61,434	
4.3. Currency and deposits	-318,462	
4.4. Other liabilities	-96	
5. Reserve assets		5,763
5.1. Monetary gold	-	
5.2. Special drawing rights		8,522
5.3. Reserve position in the IMF		613
5.4. Foreign exchange		-3,282
Total capital and financial accounts	-156,519	-170,373
Total current, capital and financial accounts	424,888	429,469
Net errors and omissions	4,581	

1 See chapter text.

2 Other capital transaction on direct investment abroad represents claims on affiliated enterprises less liabilities to affiliated enterprises

3 Other capital transactions on direct investment in the United Kingdom represents liabilities to direct investors less claims on direct investors

Source: Office for National Statistics

6.10 Summary of balance of payments: balances (credits less debits)[1]
United Kingdom

£ million

	Current account									Capital account	Financial account	Net errors & omissions
	Trade in goods	Trade in services	Total goods and services	Compensation of employees	Investment income	Total income	Current transfers	Current balance	Current balance as % of GDP[2]	Capital account	Financial account	Net errors & omissions
	LQCT	KTMS	KTMY	KTMP	HMBM	HMBP	KTNF	HBOG	AA6H	FKMJ	HBNT	HHDH
1955	-315	42	-273	-27	149	122	43	-108	-0.6	-15	34	89
1956	50	26	76	-30	203	173	2	251	1.2	-13	-250	12
1957	-29	121	92	-32	223	191	-5	278	1.3	-13	-313	48
1958	34	119	153	-34	261	227	4	384	1.7	-10	-411	37
1959	-116	118	2	-37	233	196	-	198	0.8	-5	-68	-125
1960	-404	39	-365	-35	201	166	-6	-205	-0.8	-6	-7	218
1961	-144	51	-93	-35	223	188	-9	86	0.3	-12	23	-97
1962	-104	50	-54	-37	301	264	-14	196	0.7	-12	-195	11
1963	-123	4	-119	-38	364	326	-37	170	0.6	-16	-30	-124
1964	-551	-34	-585	-33	365	332	-74	-327	-1.0	-17	392	-48
1965	-263	-66	-329	-34	405	371	-75	-33	-0.1	-18	49	2
1966	-111	44	-67	-39	358	319	-91	161	0.4	-19	22	-164
1967	-601	157	-444	-39	354	315	-118	-247	-0.6	-25	179	93
1968	-708	341	-367	-48	303	255	-119	-231	-0.5	-26	688	-431
1969	-214	392	178	-47	468	421	-109	490	1.0	-23	-794	327
1970	-18	457	437	-56	527	471	-89	819	1.6	-22	-818	21
1971	205	617	822	-63	454	391	-90	1,123	2.0	-23	-1,330	230
1972	-736	722	-14	-52	350	298	-142	142	0.2	-35	477	-584
1973	-2,573	907	-1,666	-68	970	902	-336	-1,100	-1.5	-39	1,031	108
1974	-5,241	1,292	-3,949	-92	1,010	918	-302	-3,333	-4.0	-34	3,185	182
1975	-3,245	1,708	-1,537	-102	257	155	-313	-1,695	-1.6	-36	1,569	162
1976	-3,930	2,872	-1,058	-140	760	620	-534	-972	-0.8	-12	507	477
1977	-2,271	3,704	1,433	-152	-678	-830	-889	-286	-0.2	11	-3,286	3,561
1978	-1,534	4,215	2,681	-140	-300	-440	-1,420	821	0.5	-79	-2,655	1,913
1979	-3,326	4,573	1,247	-130	-342	-472	-1,777	-1,002	-0.5	-103	864	241
1980	1,329	4,414	5,743	-82	-2,268	-2,350	-1,653	1,740	0.8	-4	-2,157	421
1981	3,238	4,776	8,014	-66	-1,883	-1,949	-1,219	4,846	1.9	-79	-5,312	545
1982	1,879	4,261	6,140	-95	-2,336	-2,431	-1,476	2,233	0.8	6	-1,233	-1,006
1983	-1,618	5,406	3,788	-89	-1,050	-1,139	-1,391	1,258	0.4	75	-3,287	1,954
1984	-5,409	6,101	692	-94	-326	-420	-1,566	-1,294	-0.4	107	-7,130	8,317
1985	-3,416	8,499	5,083	-120	-2,609	-2,729	-2,924	-570	-0.2	185	-1,657	2,042
1986	-9,617	8,182	-1,435	-156	71	-85	-2,094	-3,614	-0.9	135	-122	3,601
1987	-11,698	8,604	-3,094	-174	-730	-904	-3,437	-7,435	-1.7	333	10,606	-3,504
1988	-21,553	6,388	-15,165	-64	-1,188	-1,252	-3,293	-19,710	-4.1	235	16,989	2,486
1989	-24,724	5,866	-18,858	-138	-2,309	-2,447	-4,228	-25,533	-4.9	270	13,614	11,649
1990	-18,707	6,643	-12,064	-110	-4,586	-4,696	-4,802	-21,562	-3.8	497	22,272	-1,207
1991	-10,223	6,312	-3,911	-63	-5,642	-5,705	-999	-10,615	-1.8	290	7,855	2,470
1992	-13,050	6,353	-6,697	-49	-1,037	-1,086	-5,228	-13,011	-2.1	421	16,311	-3,721
1993	-13,066	8,174	-4,892	35	-2,547	-2,512	-5,056	-12,460	-1.9	309	22,278	-10,127
1994	-11,126	8,161	-2,965	-170	1,521	1,351	-5,187	-6,801	-1.0	33	-3,240	10,008
1995	-12,023	11,165	-858	-296	-546	-842	-7,363	-9,063	-1.2	533	-1,717	10,247
1996	-13,722	14,312	590	93	-2,460	-2,367	-4,539	-6,316	-0.8	1,260	-940	5,996
1997	-12,342	16,801	4,459	83	241	324	-5,745	-962	-0.1	958	-7,294	7,298
1998	-21,813	15,003	-6,810	-10	11,813	11,803	-8,172	-3,179	-0.4	489	4,480	-1,790
1999	-29,051	15,562	-13,489	201	-1,244	-1,043	-7,322	-21,854	-2.4	747	29,505	-8,398
2000	-32,976	15,002	-17,974	150	1,812	1,962	-9,775	-25,787	-2.6	1,703	23,133	951
2001	-41,212	17,200	-24,012	66	9,359	9,425	-6,515	-21,102	-2.1	1,318	27,194	-7,410
2002	-47,705	19,632	-28,073	67	18,219	18,286	-8,870	-18,657	-1.7	932	24,204	-6,479
2003	-48,607	22,612	-25,995	59	17,464	17,523	-9,835	-18,307	-1.6	1,466	22,553	-5,712
2004	-60,900	28,414	-32,486	-494	18,339	17,845	-10,276	-24,917	-2.1	2,064	29,358	-6,505
2005	-68,589	25,742	-42,847	-610	22,465	21,855	-11,849	-32,841	-2.6	1,503	29,024	2,314
2006	-76,312	34,782	-41,530	-958	10,531	9,573	-11,885	-43,842	-3.3	975	38,225	1,985
2007	-89,754	44,807	-44,947	-734	21,509	20,775	-13,538	-37,710	-2.7	2,566	31,676	9,126
2008	-93,116	55,142	-38,239	-714	31,007	30,293	-14,029	-21,975	-1.5	3,241	15,182	-5,276
2009	-82,365	49,313	-32,477	-688	29,344	28,656	-14,614	-18,435	-1.3	3,629	10,225	-9,746
2010	-97,199	..	..	..	..	..	..	..	..	..	..	..

1 See chapter text.
2 Using series YBHA: GDP at current market prices.

Source: Office for National Statistics

6.11 Balance of payments:[1] current account

United Kingdom

£ million

		2000	2001	2002	2003	2004	2005	2006	2007	2008	2009	2010
Credits												
Exports of goods and services												
Exports of goods	LQAD	187,936	189,093	186,524	188,320	190,874	211,608	243,633	220,858	252,086	227,670	266,079
Exports of services	KTMQ	81,883	87,773	94,012	102,357	112,922	119,186	134,393	153,145	170,819	163,248	..
Total exports of goods and services	KTMW	269,819	276,866	280,536	290,677	303,796	330,794	378,026	374,003	422,905	390,893	..
Income												
Compensation of employees	KTMN	1,032	1,087	1,121	1,116	931	974	938	984	1,046	1,176	..
Investment income	HMBN	131,902	137,447	120,543	122,069	137,380	185,766	237,505	291,618	260,967	169,567	..
Total income	HMBQ	132,934	138,534	121,664	123,185	138,311	186,740	238,443	292,602	262,013	170,743	..
Current transfers												
General government	FJUM	2,465	4,991	3,663	3,968	4,177	4,294	4,383	4,318	5,652	6,252	..
Other sectors	FJUN	8,018	8,926	8,571	8,079	9,590	13,106	13,789	9,559	10,669	10,806	..
Total current transfers	KTND	10,483	13,917	12,234	12,047	13,767	17,400	18,172	13,877	16,321	17,058	..
Total	HBOE	413,236	429,317	414,434	425,909	455,874	534,934	634,641	680,482	701,239	578,694	..
Debits												
Imports of goods and services												
Imports of goods	LQBL	220,912	230,305	234,229	236,927	251,774	280,197	319,945	310,612	345,024	310,010	363,278
Imports of services	KTMR	66,881	70,573	74,380	79,745	84,508	93,444	99,618	106,347	115,463	110,570	..
Total imports of goods and services	KTMX	287,793	300,878	308,609	316,672	336,282	373,641	419,563	416,959	460,665	420,580	..
Income												
Compensation of employees	KTMO	882	1,021	1,054	1,057	1,425	1,584	1,896	1,718	1,761	1,432	..
Investment income	HMBO	130,090	128,088	102,324	104,605	119,041	163,301	228,066	270,864	232,217	148,759	..
Total income	HMBR	130,972	129,109	103,378	105,662	120,466	164,885	229,962	272,582	233,978	150,191	..
Current transfers												
General government	FJUO	7,778	7,340	9,085	10,657	12,225	13,637	13,874	14,082	14,726	17,303	..
Other sectors	FJUP	12,480	13,092	12,019	11,225	11,818	15,612	16,176	13,341	15,646	14,474	..
Total current transfers	KTNE	20,258	20,432	21,104	21,882	24,043	29,249	30,050	27,423	30,372	31,777	..
Total	HBOF	439,023	450,419	433,091	444,216	480,791	567,775	679,575	716,964	725,015	602,548	..
Balances												
Trade in goods and services												
Trade in goods	LQCT	-32,976	-41,212	-47,705	-48,607	-60,900	-68,589	-76,312	-89,754	-93,116	-82,365	-97,199
Trade in services	KTMS	15,002	17,200	19,632	22,612	28,414	25,742	34,782	44,807	55,142	49,313	..
Total trade in goods and services	KTMY	-17,974	-24,012	-28,073	-25,995	-32,486	-42,847	-41,530	-44,947	-38,239	-32,477	..
Income												
Compensation of employees	KTMP	150	66	67	59	-494	-610	-958	-734	-714	-688	..
Investment income	HMBM	1,812	9,359	18,219	17,464	18,339	22,465	10,531	21,509	31,007	29,344	..
Total income	HMBP	1,962	9,425	18,286	17,523	17,845	21,855	9,573	20,775	30,293	28,656	..
Current transfers												
General government	FJUQ	-5,313	-2,349	-5,422	-6,689	-8,048	-9,343	-9,498	-9,772	-9,093	11,190	..
Other sectors	FJUR	-4,462	-4,166	-3,448	-3,146	-2,228	-2,506	-2,387	-3,766	-4,936	-3,424	..
Total current transfers	KTNF	-9,775	-6,515	-8,870	-9,835	-10,276	-11,849	-11,885	-13,538	-14,029	-14,614	..
Total (Current balance)	HBOG	-25,787	-21,102	-18,657	-18,307	-24,917	-32,841	-43,842	-37,710	-21,975	-18,435	..

1 See chapter text.

Source: Office for National Statistics

6.12 Balance of payments:financial account and investment income[1] summary of international investment position,financial account and investment income

United Kingdom

£ billion

		1999	2000	2001	2002	2003	2004	2005	2006	2007	2008	2009
Investment abroad												
International investment position												
Direct investment	HBWD	438.3	618.8	616.9	637.2	691.1	678.1	705.9	7,331.1	899.8	1,046.1	1,033.6
Portfolio investment	HHZZ	838.3	906.1	937.4	844.0	935.8	1,092.1	1,360.9	1,531.1	1,697.3	1,664.3	1,874.5
Financial derivatives	JX96								853.7	1,378.1	4,040.2	2,201.5
Other investment	HLXV	1,097.3	1,379.7	1,521.9	1,545.2	1,813.7	2,118.0	2,714.8	2,916.6	3,744.5	4,193.6	3,529.9
Reserve assets	LTEB	22.2	28.8	25.6	25.5	23.8	23.2	24.7	22.9	26.7	36.3	40.1
Total	HBQA	2,396.1	2,933.4	3,101.9	3,051.9	3,464.5	3,911.4	4,806.3	6,057.4	7,746.4	10,980.5	8,679.7
Financial account transactions												
Direct investment	HJYP	125.6	155.6	42.8	35.0	40.9	51.5	44.0	45.0	162.6	87.6	28.5
Portfolio investment	HHZC	21.4	65.6	86.6	1.0	36.3	141.0	151.0	138.8	92.0	-123.5	163.3
Financial derivatives (net)	ZPNN	-2.7	-1.6	-8.4	-1.0	5.4	7.9	-9.6	-20.6	27.0	121.7	-29.1
Other investment	XBMM	41.5	241.7	170.7	70.4	260.4	325.2	501.3	395.9	742.4	-599.1	-336.3
Reserve assets	LTCV	-0.6	3.9	-3.1	-0.5	-1.6	0.2	0.7	-0.4	1.2	-1.3	5.8
Total	HBNR	185.2	465.2	288.5	105.0	341.4	525.8	687.3	558.7	1,025.2	-514.7	-167.8
Investment income												
Direct investment	HJYW	33.1	45.0	46.7	51.5	55.1	63.3	79.2	83.6	91.4	67.3	69.6
Portfolio investment	HLYX	25.9	33.0	34.9	32.5	32.5	36.7	45.4	55.1	66.1	67.6	54.6
Other investment	AIOP	40.6	52.9	54.9	35.8	33.6	36.7	60.5	98.1	133.5	125.3	44.6
Reserve assets	HHCB	1.2	1.0	1.0	0.8	0.8	0.7	0.7	0.6	0.6	0.8	0.8
Total	HMBN	100.7	131.9	137.4	120.5	122.1	137.4	185.8	237.5	291.6	261.0	169.6
Investment in the UK												
International investment position												
Direct investment	HBWI	250.2	310.4	363.5	340.6	355.5	383.3	494.2	577.3	613.8	668.5	652.3
Portfolio investment	HLXW	933.2	1,067.6	1,013.2	925.3	1,082.9	1,227.9	1,461.7	1,703.5	1,946.0	1,978.2	2,405.9
Financial derivatives	JX97								890.5	1,392.2	3,915.3	2,121.9
Other investment	HLYD	1,400.9	1,651.6	1,861.9	1,906.0	2,143.2	2,520.8	3,103.0	3,272.0	4,117.6	4,520.1	3,794.0
Total	HBQB	2,584.3	3,029.5	3,238.5	3,171.9	3,581.6	4,132.1	5,058.9	6,443.2	8,069.6	11,082.0	8,974.1
Financial account transactions												
Direct investment	HJYU	55.1	80.6	37.3	16.8	16.8	31.2	97.8	84.9	100.3	49.8	45.7
Portfolio investment	HHZF	106.3	172.2	40.8	49.7	105.6	97.3	129.0	152.5	217.9	200.5	195.0
Other investment	XBMN	53.3	235.6	237.6	62.6	241.5	426.6	489.5	363.3	731.8	-739.2	-378.2
Total	HBNS	214.7	488.3	315.7	129.2	364.0	555.2	716.3	600.7	1,050.0	-488.9	-137.5
Investment income												
Direct investment	HJYX	17.0	27.4	21.4	16.0	21.9	27.6	36.2	51.6	45.1	5.6	26.4
Portfolio investment	HLZC	32.2	32.4	36.1	33.3	32.9	38.7	47.6	57.6	66.8	74.5	60.3
Other investment	HLZN	52.7	70.2	70.5	53.0	49.8	52.7	79.6	118.9	159.0	152.1	62.0
Total	HMBO	102.0	130.1	128.1	102.3	104.6	119.0	163.3	228.1	270.9	232.2	148.8
Net investment												
International investment position												
Direct investment	HBWQ	188.1	308.4	253.5	296.6	335.6	294.7	211.7	155.8	285.9	377.6	381.3
Portfolio investment	CGNH	-94.9	-161.5	-75.7	-81.3	-147.0	-135.8	-100.8	-172.4	-248.7	-313.8	-531.4
Financial derivatives	JX98								-36.8	-14.1	124.9	79.6
Other investment	CGNG	-303.6	-271.9	-339.9	-360.8	-329.5	-402.9	-388.2	-355.4	-373.0	-326.5	-264.1
Reserve assets	LTEB	22.2	28.8	25.6	25.5	23.8	23.2	24.7	22.9	26.7	36.3	40.1
Net investment position	HBQC	-188.2	-96.2	-136.5	-120.0	-117.2	-220.7	-252.6	-385.8	-323.2	-101.5	-294.4
Financial account transactions												
Direct investment	HJYV	-70.5	-75.0	-5.5	-18.3	-24.1	-20.3	53.8	39.9	-62.3	-37.8	17.2
Portfolio investment	HHZD	84.9	106.6	-45.7	48.7	69.4	-43.7	-21.9	13.7	125.8	324.1	31.7
Financial derivatives	ZPNN	2.7	1.6	8.4	1.0	-5.4	-7.9	9.6	20.6	-27.0	-121.7	29.1
Other investment	HHYR	11.8	-6.1	66.9	-7.7	-18.9	101.4	-11.8	-32.6	-10.6	-140.1	-41.9
Reserve assets	LTCV	0.6	-3.9	3.1	0.5	1.6	-0.2	-0.7	0.4	-1.2	1.3	-5.8
Net transactions	HBNT	29.5	23.1	27.2	24.2	22.6	29.4	29.0	42.0	24.8	25.8	30.3
Investment income												
Direct investment	HJYE	16.1	17.6	25.3	35.5	33.2	35.7	43.0	32.0	46.3	61.7	43.2
Portfolio investment	HLZX	-6.4	0.5	-1.2	-0.8	-0.4	-2.0	-2.2	-2.4	-0.7	-6.9	-5.8
Other investment	CGNA	-12.2	-17.3	-15.7	-17.2	-16.1	-16.0	-19.0	-20.7	-25.5	-26.8	-17.4
Reserve assets	HHCB	1.2	1.0	1.0	0.8	0.8	0.7	0.7	0.6	0.6	0.8	0.8
Net earnings	HMBM	-1.2	1.8	9.4	18.2	17.5	18.3	22.5	9.4	20.8	28.8	20.8

1 See chapter text.

6.13 Net Foreign Direct Investment flows abroad analysed by area and main country[1,2]

						£ million
		2005	2006	2007	2008	2009
Europe	GQBX	12,105	16,899	90,683	50,863	14,367
EU27	IY6N	13,337	4,038	69,836	47,298	-8,502
Austria	CBJD	-301	-94	110	-159	437
Belgium	HIIL	970	-4,356	1,037	1,656	-906
Bulgaria	IY6O	11	-5	..	43	27
Cyprus	DG8D	69	98	365	294	62
Czech Republic	DG8O	24	-160	59	371	-83
Denmark	CAUW	391	1,529	539	2,774	-2,240
Estonia	DG8E	2	3	-3	-20	36
Finland	CBJE	707	106	268	63	-110
France	CAUX	3,138	1,175	4,536	5,979	-2,734
Germany	CAUY	-479	3,186	2,260	2,268	3,408
Greece	CAUZ	63	15	286	362	152
Hungary	DG8F	1,821	39	88	164	69
Irish Republic	CAVA	-1,181	5,161	3,995	-2,098	3,494
Italy	CAVB	191	-397	2,904	463	-3,970
Latvia	DG8G	-1	4	65	142	-51
Lithuania	DG8H	-4	1	-	-	-
Luxembourg	HIIM	-1,213	-14,131	25,453	6,094	4,502
Malta	DG8I	142	891	-1,952	..	..
Netherlands	CAVC	4,821	1,350	22,176	11,056	-14,859
Poland	DG8J	150	397	-500	-128	1,349
Portugal	CAVD	603	314	278	341	120
Romania	IY6P	101	40	117	211	52
Slovakia	DG8K	21	18	90	104	-42
Slovenia	DG8L	-5	14	9	12	8
Spain	CAVE	564	2,177	4,155	12,974	1,378
Sweden	CBJG	2,732	6,669	3,501	3,155	1,346
EFTA	CAVG	547	6,926	3,620	2,476	4,047
of which						
Norway	CBJF	-831	3	1,060	1,556	1,632
Switzerland	CBJH	1,330	6,948	2,653	1,054	2,512
Other European Countries	IY6Q	-1,779	5,935	17,227	1,088	18,823
of which						
Russia	GLAA	349	-13	1,334	3,919	-285
UK offshore islands[3]	GLAC	-2,341	5,023	14,752	-4,278	18,594
The Americas	GQBZ	20,689	19,100	53,837	33,574	-1,892
of which						
Bermuda	CBKZ	653	908	2,082	3,913	-2,196
Brazil	CBLA	48	354	791	832	377
Canada	CAVK	3,372	8,130	15,468	-1,075	-2,554
Chile	GQCA	790	25	110	-315	52
Colombia	GQCB	-687	315	126	157	294
Mexico	GLAD	168	334	128	409	-335
Panama	GLAE	27	7	-18	-4	37
USA	CAVJ	15,041	-1,803	30,820	27,568	6,331

6.13 Net Foreign Direct Investment flows abroad analysed by area and main country[1,2]

£ million

		2005	2006	2007	2008	2009
Asia	GQCI	5,399	7,992	7,734	6,364	5,538
Near and Middle East Countries	CBKF	398	1,219	2,044	2,884	1,138
of which						
Gulf Arabian countries[5]	GQCC	577	329	482	544	1,247
Other Asian Countries	GQCD	5,001	6,773	5,689	3,480	4,400
of which						
China	HIIN	598	374	1,138	290	311
Hong Kong	CAVN	1,547	1,674	1,503	305	-463
India	GLAF	616	104	650	437	747
Indonesia	GLAG	-116	196	-140	-68	596
Japan	CAVM	247	440	1,141	-140	1,068
Malaysia	CBKN	244	241	216	321	323
Singapore	CBKQ	-508	2,621	-1,265	183	-709
South Korea	GLAH	2,247	679	488	810	403
Thailand	GLAI	228	536	3	192	317
Australasia and Oceania	GQCE	423	3,132	2,149	7,662	-2,716
of which						
Australia	CBJO	444	2,743	2,012	6,590	-3,783
New Zealand	CBJP	-56	405	125	126	1,101
Africa	GQCF	5,843	-235	4,726	881	6,605
of which						
Kenya	GLAJ	73	62	97	67	99
Nigeria	CBJY	-108	44	56	273	859
South Africa	CAVO	4,368	1,466	1,734	1,317	954
Zimbabwe	CBKD	18	8	4	-6	1
World Total	CDQD	44,458	46,887	159,129	99,322	21,240
OECD	GQCG	35,305	21,276	125,975	83,393	-2,189
Central and Eastern Europe[4]	GQCH	158	76	-	53	41

Source: ONS foreign Direct Investments Surveys 01633 456082

1 Net foreign direct investment includes unremitted profits.

2 A minus sign indicates a net disinvestment abroad (ie a decrease in the amount due to the UK).

3 The UK Offshore Island consist of the Channel Islands & the Isle of Man, excluded from the definition of the economic territory of the UK from 1997.

4 From 2007 includes data for Bulgaria and Romania. Prior to 2003 also includes data for Czech Republic, Estonia, Hungary, Lithuania, Latvia, Poland, Slovakia and Slovenia.

5 Includes Abu Dhabi, Bahrain, Dubai, Iraq, Kuwait, Oman, Other Gulf States, Qatar, Saudi Arabia and Yemen.

6.14 Net Foreign Direct Investment international investment position abroad analysed by area and main country

£ million

		2005	2006	2007	2008	2009
Europe	GQCJ	387,324	402,593	527,997	600 375	553,060
EU27	IY6R	339,692	314,481	412,024	513 506	482,351
Austria	CDLZ	4,005	2,402	2,579	2,707	4,356
Belgium	HIIO	13,492	4,380	6,887	11,207	10,540
Bulgaria	IY6S	53	46	46	143	86
Cyprus	DG8Q	59	561	683	363	462
Czech Republic	DG8R	823	523	632	1,011	577
Denmark	CDLP	5,090	7,782	6,220	10,809	6,995
Estonia	DG8S	7	-1	7	25	19
Finland	CDMA	2,465	1,287	2,329	609	390
France	CDLQ	47,348	36,327	39,598	42 111	41,027
Germany	CDLR	20,753	17,602	19,766	30 550	29,372
Greece	CDLS	625	562	864	1,047	1,471
Hungary	DG8T	2,491	1,795	1,870	2,136	698
Irish Republic	CDLT	26,824	26,432	25,362	30 529	29,095
Italy	CDLU	10,872	7,924	12,786	10,734	11,698
Latvia	DG8U	22	27	..	95	27
Lithuania	DG8V	16	6	11	..	..
Luxembourg	HIIP	97,260	62,355	95,915	137 065	126,143
Malta	DG8W	-459	2,399	3,263	..	..
Netherlands	CDLV	64,511	92,783	138,769	160 172	154,767
Poland	DG8X	1,974	2,519	2,078	2,914	3,922
Portugal	CDLW	2,702	3,167	3,366	3,528	3,333
Romania	IY6T	356	247	402	675	541
Slovakia	DG8Y	93	136	184	392	266
Slovenia	DG8Z	3	53	..	52	52
Spain	CDLX	25,604	25,233	30,879	37 105	32,930
Sweden	CDMD	12,702	17,935	17,388	26 069	22,111
EFTA of which	CDLY	12,933	12,637	17,745	20 119	26,188
Norway	CDMC	4,498	2,116	2,370	3,927	5,326
Switzerland	CDME	7,979	10,239	15,124	15,790	20,443
Other European Countries of which	IY6U	34,700	75,475	98,228	66 750	44,521
Russia	GQAA	1,814	6,054	7,182	10,380	10,053
UK offshore islands[1]	GQAB	29,954	65,814	86,482	49 921	27,149
The Americas of which	GQCU	216,343	256,423	292,687	354 745	343,125
Bermuda	CDOA	10,604	13,889	13,839	24 027	15,509
Brazil	CDOB	3,220	2,824	3,717	6,502	4,956
Canada	CDML	12,812	19,188	28,980	29,216	29,462
Chile	GQCT	2,814	563	439	320	189
Colombia	GQCS	1,132	985	1,109	1,520	1,983
Mexico	GQAC	2,860	2,337	3,791	3,548	3,096
Panama	GQAD	166	..	..	168	..
USA	CDMM	164,405	180,629	202,117	246,063	252,269

6.14 Net Foreign Direct Investment international investment position abroad analysed by area and main country

		2005	2006	2007	2008	£ million 2009
Asia	**GQCL**	54,919	54,377	60,887	77,412	84,822
Near and Middle East Countries	**CDNH**	3,733	6,874	9,984	14,690	18,859
of which						
Gulf Arabian countries[3]	**GQCM**	3,013	4,756	6,320	8,926	13,142
Other Asian Countries	**GQCR**	51,187	47,503	50,903	62,723	65,963
of which						
China	**HIIQ**	2,685	2,228	2,719	4,571	4,474
Hong Kong	**CDNN**	20,432	22,256	25,517	28,666	29,398
India	**GQAE**	2,126	1,977	1,035	3,475	9,310
Indonesia	**GQAF**	1,168	982	825	1,035	1,865
Japan	**CDMP**	6,076	2,485	592	1,901	3,027
Malaysia	**CDNQ**	1,455	1,174	1,233	891	889
Singapore	**CDNT**	7,144	6,684	6,220	10,479	5,198
South Korea	**GQAG**	4,586	3,763	4,457	3,048	2,991
Thailand	**GQAH**	1,281	1,407	1,456	1,708	1,202
Australasia and Oceania	**GQCN**	16,694	12,665	16,173	19,930	18,933
of which						
Australia	**CDMO**	14,627	11,571	15,391	18,024	16,150
New Zealand	**CDMQ**	1,176	923	682	580	1,562
Africa	**GQCQ**	20,834	15,105	18,516	21,104	29,419
of which						
Kenya	**GQAI**	281	313	331	372	391
Nigeria	**CDNA**	924	1,011	744	1,349	2,177
South Africa	**CDMR**	13,733	8,255	9,533	10,994	14,277
Zimbabwe	**CDNF**	50	58	32	35	28
World Total	**CDOO**	696,113	741,163	916,261	1,073,613	1,029,674
OECD	**GQCO**	561,694	547,303	684,619	837,804	819,253
Central & Eastern Europe[2]	**GQCP**	640	515	65	275	307

Sources: ONS Foreign Direct Investment Surveys: 01633 456082;
Bank of England

1 The UK Offshore Islands consist of the Channel Islands & the Isle of Man excluded from the definition
of the economic territory of the UK from 1997.
2 Prior to 2007 includes data for Bulgaria and Romania. Prior to 2003 also includes data for Czech
Republic, Estonia, Hungary, Lithuania, Latvia, Poland, Slovenia and Slovakia
3 Includes Abu Dhabi, Bahrain, Dubai, Iraq, Kuwait, Oman, Other Gulf States, Qatar, Saudi Arabia and Yemen.

6.15 Net earnings from Foreign Direct Investment abroad analysed by area and main country[1,2]

					£ million	
		2005	2006	2007	2008	2009
Europe	GQCV	32,186	38,957	44,062	43,598	35,137
EU27	IY6V	23,904	28,337	34,284	37,521	29,249
Austria	CBLQ	301	186	247	169	222
Belgium	HIIR	818	875	1,312	1,568	1,412
Bulgaria	IY6W	9	3	-9	-3	5
Cyprus	DG94	37	171	366	92	54
Czech Republic	DG95	108	-64	72	-134	-123
Denmark	CAWI	387	411	580	530	176
Estonia	DG96	..	11	5	6	26
Finland	CBLR	103	69	281	131	126
France	CAWJ	2,957	3,344	3,007	1,769	1,168
Germany	CAWK	2,685	2,189	2,890	3,116	2,675
Greece	CAWL	160	151	223	102	199
Hungary	DG97	295	83	96	77	33
Irish Republic	CAWM	2,835	2,525	3,049	1,879	-1,869
Italy	CAWN	732	696	837	311	13
Latvia	DG98	..	5	4	-18	-26
Lithuania	DG99	-	-	2	-	-
Luxembourg	HIIS	4,006	7,626	8,030	13,185	11,420
Malta	DG9A	31	-185	-56	50	322
Netherlands	CAWO	5,344	7,251	9,725	9,460	8,408
Poland	DG9B	293	373	256	414	709
Portugal	CAWP	297	234	264	271	150
Romania	IY6X	26	43	76	111	95
Slovakia	DG9C	34	24	103	20	23
Slovenia	DG9D	17	5	11	14	5
Spain	CAWQ	1,023	918	1,021	1,083	813
Sweden	CBLT	1,395	1,395	1,896	3,325	3,218
EFTA	CAWS	3,334	3,759	4,987	4,765	3,238
of which						
Norway	CBLS	937	345	296	578	577
Switzerland	CBLU	2,396	3,411	4,377	3,872	2,383
Other European Countries	IY6Y	4,948	6,861	4,791	1,312	2,650
of which						
Russia	GQAJ	1,681	1,715	1,180	1,811	1,506
UK offshore islands[3]	GQAK	3,017	4,580	3,138	-993	433
The Americas	GQCX	26,585	26,461	28,527	9,871	15,186
of which						
Bermuda	CBNK	1,561	..	1,557	1,558	1,184
Brazil	CBNL	866	577	712	725	1,222
Canada	CAWW	1,895	1,769	1,653	-2,501	-470
Chile	GQCY	1,164	771	777	678	530
Colombia	GQCZ	414	274	190	320	138
Mexico	GQAL	536	531	563	293	261
Panama	GQAM	50	23	42	..	..
USA	CAWV	18,244	17,112	19,110	6,034	9,647

6.15 Net earnings from Foreign Direct Investment abroad analysed by area and main country[1,2]

						£ million
		2005	2006	2007	2008	2009
Asia	GQDA	10,975	11,621	11,389	9,129	11,449
Near and Middle East Countries	CBMS	1,053	1,430	2,563	2,341	1,676
of which						
Gulf Arabian countries[5]	GQDB	688	717	983	405	816
Other Asian Countries	GQDC	9,922	10,191	8,826	6,788	9,773
of which						
China	HIIT	580	445	504	265	570
Hong Kong	CAYB	3,553	3,786	4,163	1,448	2,163
India	GQAN	626	715	798	690	898
Indonesia	GQAO	226	336	153	105	370
Japan	CAWY	482	388	145	304	335
Malaysia	CBNA	508	494	595	526	713
Singapore	CBND	2,510	2,285	478	1,663	2,168
South Korea	GQAP	683	532	519	536	502
Thailand	GQAQ	171	-121	23	-132	190
Australasia and Oceania	GQDD	3,157	3,065	3,716	3,134	4,409
of which						
Australia	CBMB	2,681	2,665	3,294	2,734	4,071
New Zealand	CBMC	359	388	379	329	261
Africa	GQDE	5,764	3,488	4,548	3,765	3,203
of which						
Kenya	GQAR	70	88	89	100	125
Nigeria	CBML	197	133	78	212	97
South Africa	CAWZ	3,768	1,620	2,236	1,143	1,164
Zimbabwe	CBMQ	16	10	6	-5	-4
World Total	GLAB	78,667	83,591	92,242	69,500	69,552
OECD	GQDF	52,138	55,675	64,794	50,006	47,061
Central & Eastern Europe[4]	GQDG	76	62	-11	25	28

Sources: ONS Foreign Direct Investments Survey:01633 456082;
Bank of England

1 Net earnings equal profits of foreign branches plus UK companies' receipts of interest and their share of profits of foreign subsidiaries and associates. Earnings are after deduction of provisions for depreciation and foreign taxes on profits,dividends and interest.
2 A minus sign indicates net losses.
3 The UK Offshore Islands consists of the Channel Islands and the Isle of Man, excluded from the definition of the economic territory of the UK from 1997.
4 Prior to 2007 includes data for Bulgaria and Romania. Prior to 2003 also includes data for Czech Republic, Estonia, Hungary, Lithuania, Latvia, Poland, Slovenia and Slovakia.
5 Includes Abu Dhabi, Bahrain, Dubai, Iraq, Kuwait, Oman, Other Gulf States, Qatar, Saudi Arabia and Yemen.

6.16 Net Foreign Direct Investment flows into the United Kingdom analysed by area and main country[1,2]

£ million

		2005	2006	2007	2008	2009
Europe	GQDH	80,087	53,837	49,752	25, 258	27, 478
EU27	IY6Z	71,034	47,698	39,348	24, 122	21, 164
Austria	CBOB	171	-61	183	−170	−4
Belgium	HIIU	23	670	317	−547	1,812
Bulgaria	IY72	..	..	1	..	..
Cyprus	DG9G	7	18	75	30	16
Czech Republic	DG9H	-	..	1	1	
Denmark	CAYQ	-1,246	13	-18	1,577	−332
Estonia	DG9I	-	-	-	−	−
Finland	CBOC	238	44	21	−25	123
France	CAYR	9,643	2,356	-1,931	−2682	19,542
Germany	CAYS	7,279	5,566	16,616	4,454	4,734
Greece	CAYT	14	17	17	11	75
Hungary	DG9J	1	3	1	−	−
Irish Republic	CAYU	723	816	829	811	−191
Italy	CAYV	-42	282	288	−282	−1 393
Latvia	DG9K	..	..	-	..	..
Lithuania	DG9L	-	-	-	−	−
Luxembourg	HIIV	151	221	4,349	972	−1 648
Malta	DG9M	1	2	6	1	−14
Netherlands	CAYW	50,366	13,715	2,471	17 668	−7 988
Poland	DG9N	1	50	-29	7	..
Portugal	CAYX	-6	9	123	−79	14
Romania	IY73	..	..	4	−	−
Slovakia	DG9O	..	..	1	−	−
Slovenia	DG9P	..	..	3	−	−
Spain	CAYY	3,297	23,457	16,139	1,807	6 385
Sweden	CBOE	393	508	-117		45
EFTA	CAZB	9,050	5,321	8,793	575	2,000
of which						
Norway	CBOD	927	171	423	265	−148
Switzerland	CBOF	7,405	4,786	8,159	-3,094	1,901
Other European Countries	IY74	3	817	1,611	5,219	4,314
of which						
Russia	GQAS	..	..	332	1,769	45
UK offshore islands[3]	GQAT	-60	733	1,248	4,208	4,198
The Americas	GQDJ	17,422	17,242	32,460	18,614	20,549
of which						
Brazil	HP5A	6	..	2	1	..
Canada	CAZF	1,632	3,509	799	343	-1,262
USA	CAZE	15,589	12,313	27,975	18,135	19,126

6.16 Net Foreign Direct Investment flows into the United Kingdom analysed by area and main country[1,2]

		2005	2006	2007	2008	£ million 2009
Asia	**GQDK**	-4,168	11,806	9,938	4,026	-4,812
Near and Middle East Countries	**GQAU**	736	5,034	-979	-635	271
Other Asian Countries	**GQAV**	-4,904	6,772	10,919	4,662	-5,083
of which						
China	HP5B	13	12	16	-20	110
Hong Kong	GQAW	315	92	-1,919	737	133
India	HP5C	138	265	151	2,638	126
Japan	CAZH	-5,575	3,726	5,816	796	-5,749
Singapore	GQAX	46	..	6,749	268	274
South Korea	GQAY	175	-85	5	247	13
Australasia and Oceania	**GQDL**	3,396	1,869	540	-104	2,492
of which						
Australia	CBOJ	3,396	1,479	588	-66	2,529
New Zealand	CBOK	-	54	-48	-20	-37
Africa	**GQAZ**	66	131	459	1,083	-6
of which						
South Africa	CAZJ	25	101	438	1,053	..
World Total	**CBDH**	96,803	84,885	93,148	48,875	45,699
OECD	GQBA	95,187	73,961	83,165	39,384	37,753
Central & Eastern Europe[4]	GQBB	..	6	1	..	..

Sources: ONS Foreign Direct Investment Surveys: 01633 456082
Bank of England

1 Net investment includes unremmited profits.
2 A minus sign indicates net disinvestment in the United Kingdom (ie, a decrease in the amount due to overseas countries).
3 The UK Offshore Islands consist of the Channel Islands & the Isle of Man, excluded from the definition of the economic territory of the UK from 1997.
4 Prior to 2007 includes data for Bulgaria and Romania. Prior to 2003 also includes data for Czech Republic, Estonia, Hungary, Lithuania, Latvia, Poland, Slovakia and Slovenia.

6.17 Net Foreign Direct Investment international positions in the United Kingdom analysed by area and main country

£ million

		2005	2006	2007	2008	2009
Europe	GQDM	277,027	332,077	354,382	389 925	405,743
EU27	IY75	244,392	299,906	308,996	335 526	351, 544
Austria	CDPF	561	848	1,030	840	1, 000
Belgium	HIIW	4,481	5,609	4,545	4,121	5,125
Bulgaria	IY76	..	..	..	..	..
Cyprus	DG9S	100	162	437	494	326
Czech Republic	DG9T	3	..	8	18	14
Denmark	CDOV	1,404	4,344	5,530	8,706	5,550
Estonia	DG9U	-	-	..	..	-
Finland	CDPG	756	817	708	736	802
France	CDOW	56,309	59,998	54,303	51 838	73, 826
Germany	CDOX	51,469	54,382	64,558	71 755	68, 850
Greece	CDOY	103	121	174	221	434
Hungary	DG9V	9	12	12	20	5
Irish Republic	CDOZ	7,146	8,186	8,839	10,204	12, 124
Italy	CDPA	6,122	4,482	4,901	6,258	7,263
Latvia	DG9W	..	..	..	..	-
Lithuania	DG9X	-	-	-		-
Luxembourg	HIIX	7,880	16,021	20,399	26,833	30,733
Malta	DG9Y	12	12	62	69	48
Netherlands	CDPB	95,579	119,843	110,903	137, 248	110 ,587
Poland	DG9Z	21	96	75	76	30
Portugal	CDPC	111	122	222	308	613
Romania	IY77	..	..	..	..	..
Slovakia	DGA2	-	-	..	..	..
Slovenia	DGA3	..	..	9	13	..
Spain	CDPD	8,782	20,658	27,876	11,178	27,465
Sweden	CDPI	3,467	4,113	4,312	4,453	6,641
EFTA of which	CDPE	25,033	22,358	32,570	29,931	29,890
Norway	CDPH	1,085	969	1,522	1,789	1,742
Switzerland	CDPJ	21,624	19,033	28,936	26,783	27,089
Other European Countries of which	IY78	7,602	9,813	12,816	24,468	24,309
Russia	GQBC	..	..	179	1,581	779
UK offshore islands[1]	GQBD	7,059	9,111	11,963	22,026	23,080

6.17 Net Foreign Direct Investment international positions in the United Kingdom analysed by area and main country

£ million

		2005	2006	2007	2008	2009
The Americas	GQDU	174,037	200,709	202,062	209 792	195,260
of which						
Brazil	HP5D	77	134	21	9	1
Canada	CDPM	15,587	19,369	20,835	21,333	18,389
USA	CDPN	149,759	170,880	167,008	168,689	158,689
Asia	GQDO	24,101	39,436	53,166	50,419	38,932
Near and Middle East Countries	GQBE	2,970	10,160	6,449	5,389	3,818
Other Asian Countries	GQBF	21,131	29,275	46,717	45,030	35,113
of which						
China	HP5E	111	99	202	427	615
Hong Kong	GQBG	..	..	..	..	..
India	HP5F	518	798	1,376	3,591	1,841
Japan	CDPQ	10,513	14,766	25,479	30,643	21,251
Singapore	GQBH	1,034	4,046	12,197	1,555	2,978
South Korea	GQBI	638	798	779	914	787
Australasia and Oceania	GQDP	12,537	7,623	9,412	8,122	12,514
of which						
Australia	CDPP	12,313	7,093	8,974	7,842	12,261
New Zealand	CDPR	224	428	430	279	252
Africa	GQBJ	510	469	1,397	2,115	1,142
of which						
South Africa	CDPS	186	130	900	1,600	520
World Total	CDPZ	488,212	580,313	620,419	660,373	653,591
OECD	GQBK	458,185	535,218	564,201	594,466	592,407
Central & Eastern Europe[2]	GQBL	..	..	6	11	..

Sources: ONS Foreign Direct Investment Surveys 01633 456082;
Bank of England

1 The UK Offshore Islands consist of the Channel Islands & Isle of Man, excluded from the definition of the economic territory of the UK from 1997.
2 Prior to 2007 includes data for Bulgaria and Romania. Prior to 2003 also includes data for Czech Republic, Estonia, Hungary, Lithuania, Latvia, Poland, Slovenia and Slovakia.

6.18 Net earnings from Foreign Direct Investment in the United Kingdom analysed by area and main country[1,2]

					£ million	
		2005	2006	2007	2008	2009
Europe	**GQDQ**	17,592	27,447	26,174	-17,381	6,966
EU27	**IY79**	15,278	22,919	24,144	-3729	7,582
Austria	CBOR	60	207	211	-45	85
Belgium	HIIY	367	646	577	286	-221
Bulgaria	IY7A	-	-	..	..	..
Cyprus	DGA6	24	44	66	57	32
Czech Republic	DGA7	-	..	1	1	..
Denmark	CBDL	326	204	-70	-175	-247
Estonia	DGA8	-	-	..	..	–
Finland	CBOS	61	93	181	50	97
France	CBDM	5,121	5,329	3,489	1,351	9,717
Germany	CBDN	4,037	4,541	5,789	-823	-1 691
Greece	CBDO	49	70	104	212	196
Hungary	DGA9	1	3	1	–	..
Irish Republic	CBDP	724	1,012	1,202	-132	-1 639
Italy	CBDQ	483	477	577	466	-685
Latvia	DGB2	..	..	..	..	..
Lithuania	DGB3	1	1	-	–	–
Luxembourg	HIIZ	214	79	463	619	547
Malta	DGB4	-	3	7	28	21
Netherlands	CBDR	2,800	7,283	8,393	-7 297	-2 760
Poland	DGB5	1	8	6	3	1
Portugal	CBDS	30	48	54	50	139
Romania	IY7B	..	..	-	..	..
Slovakia	DGB6	5	5	3	..	..
Slovenia	DGB7	..	..	..	..	..
Spain	CBDT	773	2,536	2,696	1,255	3,649
Sweden	CBOU	182	316	386	368	347
EFTA of which	**CBDW**	1,495	3,366	264	-16,382	-2,324
Norway	CBOT	82	169	194	262	18
Switzerland	CBOV	1,320	2,933	-286	-15,112	-2,386
Other European Countries of which	**IY7C**	819	1,162	1,767	2,731	1,709
Russia	GQBM	..	..	7	-77	-21
UK offshore islands[3]	GQBN	757	1,107	1,752	2,891	1,682
The Americas of which	**GQDV**	16,460	20,154	17,158	21,033	17,714
Brazil	HP5G	-4	-4	6	-6	..
Canada	CBEA	1,348	1,458	-250	-2,856	672
USA	CBDZ	14,156	16,828	15,060	22,518	15,857

6.18 Net earnings from Foreign Direct Investment in the United Kingdom analysed by area and main country[1,2]

		2005	2006	2007	2008	£ million 2009
Asia	**GQDS**	937	2,710	447	-1,316	-403
Near and Middle East Countries	**GQBO**	354	564	237	216	99
Other Asian Countries	**GQBP**	583	2,145	210	-1,533	-502
of which						
China	HP5H	-63	-35	17	-38	35
Hong Kong	GQBQ	..	-597	..	-337	..
India	HP5I	65	132	140	261	111
Japan	CBEC	1,089	1,956	-216	-2,000	-1,087
Singapore	GQBS	85	259	609	166	94
South Korea	GQBT	72	104	125	134	62
Australasia and Oceania	**GQDT**	535	1,259	1,222	613	2,139
of which						
Australia	CBOZ	521	876	1,196	629	2,158
New Zealand	CBPA	13	46	25	-13	-18
Africa	**GQBU**	65	80	137	166	55
of which						
South Africa	CBED	25	31	82	..	69
World Total	**CBEV**	35,588	51,650	45,138	3,113	26,470
OECD	GQBV	33,927	47,476	40,242	-1,792	22,846
Central & Eastern Europe[4]	GQBW	..	..	1	..	..

Sources: ONS Foreign Direct Investment Surveys: 01633 456082;
Bank of England

1 Net earnings equal profits of United Kingdom branches plus overseas foreign investors' receipts of interest from, and their share of the profits of, United Kingdom subsidiaries and associates. Earnings are after deducting provisions for depreciation and UK tax.
2 A minus sign indicates net losses.
3 The UK Offshore Islands consist of the Channel Islands & the Isle of Man, excluded from the definition of the economic territory of the UK from 1997.
4 Prior to 2007 includes data for Bulgaria and Romania. Prior to 2003 also includes data for Czech Republic, Estonia, Hungary, Lithuania, Latvia, Poland, Slovenia and Slovakia.

Research and development

Chapter 7

Research and development

(Tables 7.1 to 7.5)

Research and experimental development (R&D) is defined for statistical purposes as 'creative work undertaken on a systematic basis in order to increase the stock of knowledge, including knowledge of man, culture and society, and the use of this stock of knowledge to devise new applications'.

R&D is financed and carried out mainly by businesses, the Government, and institutions of higher education. A small amount is performed by non-profit-making bodies. Gross Expenditure on R&D (GERD) is an indicator of the total amount of R&D performed within the UK: it has been approximately 2 per cent of GDP in recent years. Detailed figures are reported each year in a statistical bulletin published in March. Table 7.1 shows the main components of GERD.

ONS conducts an annual survey of expenditure and employment on R&D performed by government, and of government funding of R&D. The survey collects data for the reference period along with future estimates. Until 1993 the detailed results were reported in the *Annual Review of Government Funded R&D*. From 1997 the results have appeared in the Science, Engineering and Technology (SET) Statistics published by the Department for Business, Innovation and Skills (BIS). Table 7.2 gives some broad totals for gross expenditure by government (expenditure before deducting funds received by government for R&D). Table 7.3 gives a breakdown of net expenditure (receipts are deducted).

The ONS conducts an annual survey of R&D in business. Tables 7.4 and 7.5 give a summary of the main trends up to 2009. The latest set of results from the survey became available in a statistical bulletin dated 1 December 2010.

Revisions were made to the business data for the periods 2006, 2007 and 2008, and were published at the same time as the 2009 Business Enterprise R&D (BERD) Statistical Bulletin on 1 December 2010. The format of this report was used as it covers all aspects of the R&D data published by the Office for National Statistics (ONS).

Statistics on expenditure and employment on R&D in higher education institutions (HEIs) are based on information collected by Higher Education Funding Councils and the Higher Education Statistics Agency (HESA). In 1994 a new methodology was introduced to estimate expenditure on R&D in HEIs. This is based on the allocation of various Funding Council Grants. Full details of the new methodology are contained in science, engineering and technology (SET) Statistics available on the BIS website at: www.bis.gov.uk/policies/science/science-funding/set-stats

The most comprehensive international comparisons of resources devoted to R&D appear in Main Science and Technology Indicators published by the Organisation for Economic Co-operation and Development (OECD). The Statistical Office of the European Union and the United Nations also compile R&D statistics based on figures supplied by member states.

To make international comparisons more reliable the OECD have published a series of manuals giving guidance on how to measure various components of R&D inputs and outputs. The most important of these is the Frascati Manual, which defines R&D and recommends how resources for R&D should be measured. The UK follows the Frascati Manual as far as possible.

For information on available aggregated data on Research and Development please contact Mark Williams on 01633 456728 (e-mail Mark.Williams@ons.gsi.gov.uk).

7.1 Cost of research and development: by sector[1]

United Kingdom

	2002 £m	2002 %	2003 £m	2003 %	2004 £m	2004 %	2005 £m	2005 %	2006 £m	2006 %	2007 £m	2007 %	2008 £m	2008 %	2009 £m	2009 %
Sector carrying out the work **Cash terms (£ million)**																
Government	1053	5	1243	6	1240	6	1238	6	1252	5	1256	5	1281	5	1304	5
Research councils	713	4	825	4	930	5	1051	5	1061	5	1034	4	1041	4	1066	4
Business enterprise	12484	65	12505	63	12662	63	13734	62	14144	62	15676	63	16026	62	15624	60
Higher education	4618	24	4785	24	5004	25	5580	25	6022	26	6519	26	6798	26	7228	28
Private non-profit	374	2	369	2	406	2	502	2	513	2	557	2	605	2	642	2
Total	19243	100	19727	100	20242	100	22106	100	22993	100	25042	100	25751	100	25863	100
Sector providing the funds **Cash terms (£ million)**																
Government	2215	11	2650	13	2778	14	2584	12	2531	11	2986	12	2917	11	3177	12
Research councils	1713	9	1947	10	2084	10	2574	12	2709	12	2518	10	2740	11	2848	11
Higher education funding councils	1626	8	1665	8	1804	9	1928	9	2085	9	2234	9	2227	9	2395	9
Higher education	208	1	218	1	229	1	266	1	288	1	308	1	318	1	332	1
Business enterprise[2]	8384	44	8287	42	8914	44	9580	43	10377	45	11518	46	11772	46	11519	45
Private non-profit	962	5	931	5	961	5	1022	5	1076	5	1153	5	1247	5	1290	5
Abroad	4135	22	4029	20	3472	17	4152	19	3927	17	4326	17	4531	18	4304	17
Total	19243	100	19727	100	20242	100	22106	100	22993	100	25042	100	25751	100	25863	100

1 See chapter text.
2 Including research associations and public corporations.

Source: Office for National Statistics: 01633 456763

7.2 Gross central government expenditure on research and development[1]

United Kingdom

£

	2004/05 Intra-mural	2004/05 Extra-mural[2]	2005/06 Intra-mural	2005/06 Extra-mural[2]	2006/07 Intra-mural[2]	2006/07 Extra-mural	2007/08 Intra-mural[3]	2007/08 Extra-mural	2008/09 Intra-mural	2008/09 Extra-mural	2009/10 Intra-mural	2009/10 Extra-mural
Defence	357	2283	365	2223	361	1851	279	1941	262	1812	288	1542
Research councils	874	1752	1004	2034	1051	2135	1034	2005	1041	2297	1066	2434
Higher education institutes	-	1804	-	1928	-	2085	-	2234	-	2227	-	2395
Other programmes	327	870	316	1546	309	881	346	1418	351	1322	340	1619
Total (excluding NHS)	1558	6709	1685	7731	1721	6952	1659	7598	1654	7658	1694	7990

1 See chapter text.
2 Extramural Includes work performed overseas and excludes monies spent with other government departments.
3 2007/08 expenditure figure no longer includes VAT.

Source: Office for National Statistics 01633 456763

7.3 Net central government expenditure on research and development:[1] by European Union objectives for research and development expenditure

United Kingdom

£ million

		1999 /00	2000 /01	2001 /02	2002 /03	2003 /04	2004 /05	2005 /06	2006 /07	2007 /08	2008 /09	2009 /10
Exploration and exploitation of the earth	**KDVP**	79.5	85.5	106	138.3	176.8	193	239	241	228	254	261
Infrastructure and general planning of land-use	**KDVQ**	104.4	102.4	100.3	101	118.7	88	70	89	117	125	128
Control of environmental pollution	**KDVR**	147.0	151.1	129.1	126.5	150.1	149	158	158	220	260	259
Protection and promotion of human health (ex NHS)	**KDVS**	519.5	530.6	571.6	597.8	1163.7	1227.3	1258	1394	811	903	1012
Production, distribution and rational utilisation of energy	**KDVT**	29	31.9	36.8	40.3	28.4	35	21	43	56	69	101
Agricultural production and technology	**KDVU**	260.6	266.6	265.2	267.8	275.9	278	273	284	259	252	274
Industrial production and technology	**KDVV**	56.5	109.2	237	423.4	426.5	138.4	94	88	9	60	237
Social structures and relationships	**KDVW**	217.6	270.2	268.8	293.4	226.7	291.8	471	311	396	439	451
Exploration and exploitation of space	**KDVX**	142.7	146.3	139.8	155.5	168.6	168.9	192	153	177	205	182
Research financed from general university funds	**KDVY**	1157.1	1276.1	1473.5	1626.4	1664.6	1804.7	1933	2092	2234	2227	2395
Non-oriented research	**KDVZ**	700.5	789.3	918.2	1071.6	1290.9	1332	1658	1715	1925	1853	1896
Other civil research [2]	**KDWA**	20.6	22.3	19.7	36.3	39.9	38.4	38	45	-	-	-
Defence	**KDWB**	2275.9	2245.1	2063	2739.7	2682.2	2582.7	2528	2132	2150	2003	1776
Total (excluding NHS)	**KDWC**	5710.9	6026.6	6329	7618	8413.5	8327	8932	8745	8582	8650	8972

1 See chapter text.

2 Due to OECD changes to the NABS codes, from 2007 "Other Civil Research" no longer exists as a category.

Source: Office for National Statistics: 01633 456763

7.4 Intramural expenditure on Business Enterprise research and development:[1] by industry

United Kingdom
At Current and Constant 2009 Prices

£ million

		Total				Civil				Defence		
		2007	2008	2009		2007	2008	2009		2007	2008	2009
Current Prices												
Chemicals	KDWF	..	..	..	KDWP	4597	4979	5043	KDWZ	..	..	..
Mechanical engineering	KDWG	1123	879	984	KDWQ	634	462	478	KDXA	489	417	506
Electrical machinery	KJRT	1296	1338	1338	KJTC	934	957	936	KJUL	362	381	402
Aerospace	KDWJ	2070	1732	1468	KDWT	902	835	905	KDXD	1168	897	563
Transport equipment	KDWK	..	..	..	KDWU	983	1317	1197	KDXE	..	..	..
Other manufacturing	KDWL	1421	1483	1373	KDWV	1321	1358	1253	KDXF	100	125	120
Manufacturing: Total	KDWE	11611	11859	11550	KDWO	9372	9908	9812	KDWY	2239	1951	1738
Services	KDWM	3859	3934	3758	KDWW	3690	3797	3621	KDXG	169	137	137
Agriculture, hunting and forestry; fishing	HFRV	..	..	..	HFSA	..	88	112	MKFC	-	-	-
Extractive industries	HFRW	82	90	111	HFSB	82	90	111	MKFD	-	-	-
Electricity, gas and water supply	HFRX	35	40	75	HFSC	35	40	75	MKFE	-	-	-
Construction	HFRY	..	..	..	HFSE	..	14	18	MKFF	-	-	-
Other: Total	HFRU	205	232	316	HFRZ	205	232	316	MKFB	-	-	-
Total	KDWD	15677	16025	15624	KDWN	13268	13937	13749	KDWX	2409	2088	1875
2009 Prices												
Chemicals	HFXA	..	..	..	HFXJ	4803	5062	5043	HFYO	..	..	..
Mechanical engineering	HFXB	1173	894	984	HFXK	662	470	478	HFYP	511	424	506
Electrical machinery	HFXC	1354	1360	1338	HFYH	976	973	936	HFYQ	378	387	402
Aerospace	HFXD	2162	1761	1468	HFYI	942	849	905	HFYR	1220	912	563
Transport equipment	HFXE	..	..	..	HFYJ	1027	1339	1197	HFYS	..	..	..
Other manufacturing	HFXF	1484	1508	1373	HFYK	1380	1381	1253	HFYT	104	127	120
Manufacturing: Total	HFWZ	12130	12057	11550	HFXI	9791	10073	9812	HFYN	2339	1984	1738
Services	HFXG	4032	3999	3758	HFYL	3855	3860	3621	HFYU	177	139	137
Agriculture, hunting and forestry: fishing	HFSG	..	..	..	HFSL	..	89	112	MKFH	-	-	-
Extractive industries	HFSH	86	91	111	HFSM	86	91	111	MKFI	-	-	-
Electricity, gas and water supply	HFSI	37	41	75	HFSN	37	41	75	MKFJ	-	-	-
Construction	HFSJ	..	..	..	HFSO	..	14	18	MKFK			
Other: Total	HFSF	214	236	316	HFSK	214	236	316	MKFG	-	-	-
Total	HFWY	16378	16292	15624	HFXH	13861	14169	13749	HFYM	2517	2123	1875

1 See chapter text.

Source: Office for National Statistics 01633 456763

7.5 Sources of funds for research and development within Business Enterprises[1]

United Kingdom

		Total				Civil				Defence		
		2007	2008	2009		2007	2008	2009		2007	2008	2009
Cash terms (£ million)												
Government funds	**KDYM**	1072	1087	1233	**KDYU**	183	224	275	**KDZC**	889	863	958
Overseas funds	**KDYN**	3636	3720	3382	**KDYV**	2985	3188	3096	**KDZD**	652	532	254
Mainly own funds	**KDYO**	10968	11219	11009	**KDYW**	10100	10525	10378	**KDZE**	868	694	662
Total	**KDYL**	15676	16026	15624	**KDYT**	13268	13937	13749	**KDZB**	2409	2088	1875
Percentages												
Government funds	**KDYQ**	7	7	8	**KDYY**	1	2	2	**KDZG**	37	41	51
Overseas funds	**KDYR**	23	23	22	**KDYZ**	22	23	23	**KDZH**	27	25	14
Mainly own funds	**KDYS**	70	70	70	**KDZA**	76	76	75	**KDZI**	36	33	35
Total	**KDYP**	100	100	100	**KDYX**	100	100	100	**KDZF**	100	100	100

1 See chapter text

Source: Office for National Statistics 01633 456763

Income and wealth

Chapter 8

Personal income, expenditure and wealth

Distribution of total incomes (Table 8.1)

The information shown in Table 8.1 comes from the Survey of Personal Incomes, for the financial years 2000/01 to 2007/08. This is an annual survey covering approximately 600,000 individuals across the whole of the UK. It is based on administrative data held by HM Revenue & Customs (HMRC) on individuals who could be liable for tax.

The table relates only to those individuals who are taxpayers. The distributions only cover incomes as computed for tax purposes, and above a level which for each year corresponds approximately to the single person's allowance. Incomes below these levels are not shown because the information about them is incomplete.

Some components of investment income (for example interest and dividends), from which tax has been deducted at source, are not always held on HMRC business systems. Estimates of missing bank and building society interest and dividends from UK companies are included in these tables. The missing investment income is distributed to cases, so that the population as a whole has amounts consistent with evidence from other sources. For example, amounts of tax accounted for by deposit takers and the tendency to hold interest-bearing accounts as indicated by household surveys.

Superannuation contributions are estimated and included in total income. They have been distributed among earners in the Survey of Personal Incomes sample, by a method consistent with information about the number of employees who are contracted in or out of the State Earnings Related Pension Scheme (SERPS) and the proportion of their earnings contributed.

When comparing results of these surveys across years, it should be noted that the Survey of Personal Incomes is not a longitudinal survey. However, sample sizes have increased in recent years to increase precision.

Average incomes of households (Table 8.2)

Original income is the total income in cash of all the members of the household before receipt of Related Pension Scheme (SERPS) and the proportion of their earnings contributed.

When comparing results of these surveys across years, it should be noted that the Survey of Personal Incomes is not a longitudinal survey. However, sample sizes have increased in recent years to increase precision.

Average incomes of households (Table 8.2)

Original income is the total income in cash of all the members of the household before receipt of state benefits or the deduction of taxes. It includes income from employment, self-employment, investment income and occupational pensions. Gross income is original income plus cash benefits received from government (retirement pensions, child benefit, and so on). Disposal income is the income available for consumption; it is equal to gross income less direct taxes (which include income tax, national insurance contributions, and council tax). By further allowing for taxes paid on goods and services purchased, such as VAT, an estimate of post-tax income is derived. These income figures are derived from estimates made by the Office for National Statistics (ONS) based largely on information from the Living Costs and Food Survey (LFC) and published each year on the ONS website.

In Table 8.2, a retired household is defined as one where the combined income of retired members amounts to at least half the total gross income of the household; where a retired person is defined as anyone who describes themselves as retired, or anyone over the minimum National Insurance (NI) pension age describing themselves as 'unoccupied' or 'sick or injured but not intending to seek work.

Children are defined as persons aged under 16 or between 16 and 18, unmarried and receiving full-time non-advanced further education.

Living Costs and Food Survey (Tables 8.3–8.5)

The Living Costs and Food Survey (LCF) is a sample survey of 12,566 private households in the UK, with an achieved response of around 5,825 private households in 2009. The LCF sample is representative of all regions of the UK and of different types of households. The survey is continuous, with interviews spread evenly over the year to ensure that estimates are not biased by seasonal variation. The survey results show how households spend their money; how much goes on food, clothing and so on, how spending patterns vary depending upon income, household composition, and regional location of households. From January 2006 the survey has been conducted on a calendar-year basis, therefore the latest results refer to the January to December 2009 period.

One of the main purposes of the LCF is to define the 'basket of goods' for the Retail Prices Index (RPI) and the Consumer Prices Index (CPI). The RPI has a vital role in the up rating of state pensions and welfare benefits, while the CPI is a key instrument of the Government's monetary policy. Information from the survey is also a major source for estimates of household expenditure in the UK National Accounts. In addition, many other government departments use LCF data as a basis for policy making, for example in the areas of housing and transport. The Department for Environment, Food and Rural Affairs (Defra) uses LCF data to report on trends in food consumption and nutrient intake within the UK. Users of the LCF outside government include independent research institutes, academic researchers and business and market researchers. Like all surveys based on a sample of the population, its results are subject to sampling variability and potentially to some bias due to non-response. The results of the survey are published in an annual report the latest being The Family Spending 2010 edition. The report includes a list of definitions used in the survey, items on which information is collected, and a brief account of the fieldwork procedure.

8.1 Distribution of total income before and after tax

United Kingdom
Years ending 5 April

2004/2005 Annual Survey

Lower limit of range of income	Number of individuals (Thousands)	Total income before tax (£ million)	Total tax (£ million)	Total income after tax (£ million)
All incomes[1]	30,300	691,000	123,000	568,000
Income before tax (£)				
4,745	329	1,600	4	1,600
5,000	1,110	6,090	80	6,010
6,000	2,760	19,500	600	18,900
8,000	2,950	26,500	1,600	24,900
10,000	2,760	30,300	2,580	27,700
12,000	2,470	32,100	3,350	28,700
14,000	2,280	34,200	4,080	30,100
16,000	2,050	34,800	4,520	30,300
18,000	1,790	34,100	4,720	29,300
20,000	6,000	146,000	22,700	124,000
30,000	4,090	152,000	27,300	125,000
50,000	1,270	83,700	21,600	62,100
100,000	300	40,000	12,600	27,400
200,000 and over	111	49,500	17,300	32,200
Income after tax (£)				
4,745	364	1,770	5	11,770
5,000	1,220	6,830	98	6,730
6,000	3,270	24,100	902	23,200
8,000	3,600	34,800	2,510	32,300
10,000	3,280	40,000	3,920	36,000
12,000	2,920	43,000	5,050	37,900
14,000	2,540	43,700	5,730	38,000
16,000	2,180	43,200	6,090	37,100
18,000	1,850	41,400	6,210	35,200
20,000	5,320	154,000	25,100	129,000
30,000	2,840	131,000	27,100	104,000
50,000	681	63,200	18,300	44,800
100,000	143	28,400	9,420	19,000
200,000 and over	53	35,500	12,500	23,000

2005/06 Annual Survey

Lower limit of range of income	Number of individuals (Thousands)	Total income before tax (£ million)	Total tax (£ million)	Total income after tax (£ million)
All incomes[1]	31,100	756,000	138,000	618,000
Income before tax (£)				
4,895	112	555	-	555
5,000	1,040	5,750	62	5,690
6,000	2,540	18,000	522	17,500
8,000	2,920	26,200	1,450	24,800
10,000	2,810	30,900	2,500	24,800
12,000	2,550	33,100	3,380	29,700
14,000	2,340	35,000	4,140	30,900
16,000	2,100	35,700	4,610	31,100
18,000	1,880	35,700	4,930	30,800
20,000	6,200	152,000	23,400	128,000
30,000	4,540	170,000	29,900	140,000
50,000	1,500	98,800	25,000	73,700
100,000	366	49,300	15,300	34,000
200,000 and over	144	66,000	22,900	43,000
Income after tax (£)				
4,895	129	636	1	636
5,000	1,160	6,500	77	6,420
6,000	3,000	22,000	767	21,300
8,000	3,590	34,600	2,300	32,300
10,000	3,390	41,100	3,890	37,200
12,000	3,020	44,300	5,120	39,200
14,000	2,650	45,600	5,940	39,600
16,000	2,260	44,600	6,270	38,300
18,000	1,850	41,300	6,140	35,100
20,000	5,630	163,000	26,400	137,000
30,000	3,310	152,000	30,700	121,000
50,000	817	75,500	21,600	53,900
100,000	188	37,100	12,100	24,900
200,000 and over	69	47,900	16,800	31,000

8.1 Distribution of total income before and after tax

United Kingdom
Years ending 5 April

| | 2006/2007 Annual Survey | | | | | 2007/2008 Annual Survey | | | |
| | | £ million | | | | | £ million | | |
	Number of individuals (Thousands)	Total income before tax	Total tax	Total income after tax		Number of individuals (Thousands)	Total income before tax	Total tax	Total income after tax
Lower limit of range of income					**Lower limit of range of income**				
All incomes[1]	31,800	810,000	150,000	661,000	All incomes[1]	32,500	870,000	163,000	708,000
Income before tax (£)					**Income before tax (£)**				
5,035	919	5,090	43	5,050	5,225	719	4,050	27	4,020
6,000	2,440	17,200	451	16,800	6,000	2,210	15,600	371	15,200
8,000	2,920	26,200	1,330	24,900	8,000	2,760	24,800	1,140	23,700
10,000	2,790	30,600	2,390	28,200	10,000	2,720	30,000	2,190	27,800
12,000	2,570	33,400	3,310	30,100	12,000	2,650	34,400	3,230	31,100
14,000	2,400	36,000	4,180	31,800	14,000	2,420	36,300	4,050	32,200
16,000	2,140	36,300	4,630	31,700	16,000	2,220	37,800	4,690	33,100
18,000	1,970	37,300	5,110	32,200	18,000	2,020	38,400	5,140	33,200
20,000	6,530	160,000	24,460	135,000	20,000	6,850	168,000	25,500	142,000
30,000	4,900	184,000	32,000	152,000	30,000	5,340	201,000	34,500	167,000
50,000	1,670	110,000	27,400	82,600	50,000	1,900	125,000	30,700	94,100
100,000	406	54,700	16,700	38,000	100,000	456	61,600	18,800	42,800
200, 000 and over	170	79,700	27,400	52,300	200, 000 and over	192	93,900	32,400	61,500
Income after tax (£)					**Income after tax (£)**				
5,035	1,040	5,800	55	5,750	5,225	802	4,550	34	4,520
6,000	2,860	20,900	656	20,200	6,000	2,540	18,500	512	18,000
8,000	3,550	34,000	2,090	31,900	8,000	3,390	32,300	1,800	30,500
10,000	3,410	41,200	3,770	37,500	10,000	3,430	41,300	3,560	37,700
12,000	3,120	45,600	5,160	40,500	12,000	3,160	45,900	4,950	41,000
14,000	2,710	46,700	5,990	40,700	14,000	2,820	48,300	6,010	42,300
16,000	2,370	46,800	6,530	40,200	16,000	2,470	48,500	6,610	41,800
18,000	1,920	42,700	6,320	36,400	18,000	2,030	45,100	6,550	38,500
20,000	5,980	173,000	28,000	145,000	20,000	6,370	184,000	29,600	155,000
30,000	3,650	168,000	33,200	134,000	30,000	4,080	188,000	36,400	151,000
50,000	914	83,800	23,600	60,200	50,000	1,040	95,200	26,600	68,600
100,000	220	43,300	13,900	29,400	100,000	247	48,400	15,600	32,800
200, 000 and over	82	58,600	20,200	38,300	200, 000 and over	95	70,600	24,600	46,100

1 See chapter text. All figures have been independently rounded.

Source: Survey of Personal Incomes,
Board of HM Revenue & Customs: 020 7438 7055

8.2 Average incomes of households before and after taxes and benefits[1,2], 2009/10

United Kingdom

	Retired households		Non-retired households								
	1 adult	2 or more adults	1 adult[3]	2 adults[3]	3 or more adults[3]	1 adult with children	2 adults with 1 child	2 adults with 2 children	2 adults with 3 or more children	3 or more adults with children	All households
Number of households in the population (thousands)	3,750	3,223	3,880	5,607	2,098	1,251	2,271	2,089	833	1,051	26,053
Average per household (£ per year)											
Original income	5,648	12,962	22,050	43,116	52,791	10,050	45,867	49,652	37,624	50,298	30,924
Gross income	13,957	24,509	24,564	45,534	57,010	19,195	49,329	53,512	45,857	57,136	36,373
Disposable income	12,588	21,431	19,074	35,030	45,483	17,421	38,438	42,203	37,346	46,425	29,143
Post-tax income	10,623	17,301	16,071	29,477	37,944	14,004	32,588	35,770	31,321	38,770	24,400

1 See chapter text. Figures taken from the article "Effects of taxes and benefits on household income, 2009/10", published on the National Statistics website. (*www.statistics.gov.uk/taxesbenefits*).
2 Using the modified-OECD scale.
3 Without children.

Source: Office for National Statistics: 01633 455951
household.income.and.expenditure@ons.gsi.gov.uk

8.3 Sources of gross household income

United Kingdom

		1997 /98	1998[1] /99	1999 /00	2000 /01	2001[2] /02	2002 /03	2003 /04	2004 /05	2005 /06	2006[3]	2007	2008	2009
Weighted number of households (thousands)	GH92	24,560	24,660	25,330	25,030	24,450	24,350	24,670	24,430	24,800	25,440	25,350	25,690	25,980
Number of households supplying data	KPDA	6,409	6,630	7,097	6,637	7,473	6,927	7,048	6,798	6,785	6,650	6,140	5,850	5,830
Average weekly household income by source (£)														
Wages and salaries	KPCB	280	309	315	337	369	374	384	410	415	428	445	476	453
Self-employment	KPCC	33	37	46	45	43	45	50	49	51	55	54	66	57
Investments	KPCD	19	19	22	20	20	19	17	17	20	21	23	28	19
Annuities and pensions (other than social security benefits)	KPCE	29	30	33	35	37	40	41	42	45	44	48	49	52
Social security benefits[4]	KPCF	55	56	58	60	65	68	72	77	78	79	83	89	95
Other sources	KPCH	5	6	6	6	7	7	6	7	7	7	7	6	7
Total[5]	KPCI	421	457	480	503	541	552	570	601	616	635	659	713	683
Sources of household income as a percentage of total household income														
Wages and salaries	KPCJ	67	68	66	67	68	68	67	68	67	67	67	67	66
Self-employment	KPCK	8	8	10	9	8	8	9	8	8	9	8	9	8
Investments	KPCL	4	4	5	4	4	3	3	3	3	3	4	4	3
Annuities and pensions (other than social security benefits)	KPCM	7	7	7	7	7	7	7	7	7	7	7	7	8
Social security benefits[4]	KPCN	13	12	12	12	12	12	13	13	13	13	13	12	14
Other sources	KPCP	1	1	1	1	1	1	1	1	1	1	1	1	1
Total[5]	KPCQ	100	100	100	100	100	100	100	100	100	100	100	100	100

1 Based on weighted data from 1998/99.

2 From 2001/02 onwards, weighting is based on the population estimates from the 2001 census.

3 From this version of 2006, figures shown are based on weighted data using updated weights, with non and population figures based from the 1991 and 2001 Census.

4 Excluding housing benefit and council tax benefit (rates rebate in Northern Ireland) and their predecessors in earlier years.

5 Does not include imputed income from owner-occupied and rent free occupancy.

Sources: Living Costs and Food Survey;
(previously Expenditure and Food Survey);
Office for National Statistics;
01633 455678

8.4 Household expenditure based on FES classification[1]

United Kingdom

		1997 /98	1998[2] /99	1999 /00	2000 /01	2001[3] /02	2002 /03	2003 /04	2004 /05	2005 /06	2006[4]	2007	2008	2009
Weighted number of households (thousands)	GH92	24,560	24,660	25,330	25,030	24,450	24,350	24,670	24,430	24,800	25,440	25,350	25,690	25,980
Number of households supplying data	KPDA	6,409	6,630	7,097	6,637	7,473	6,927	7,048	6,798	6,785	6,650	6,140	5,850	5,830
Average weekly household expenditure commodities and services (£)														
Housing (Net)[5]	KPEV	51.50	57.20	57.00	63.90	65.90	66.70	69.90	76.70	80.90	83.20	92.00	94.00	85.20
Fuel and power	KPEW	12.70	11.70	11.30	11.90	11.70	11.70	12.00	12.50	13.90	15.80	17.20	18.90	21.30
Food and non-alcoholic drinks	KPEX	55.90	58.90	59.60	61.90	61.90	64.30	64.90	67.30	67.90	69.60	71.40	74.50	75.60
Alcoholic drink	KPEY	13.30	14.00	15.30	15.00	14.30	14.80	14.70	14.80	14.80	14.70	14.70	13.40	14.00
Tobacco	KPEZ	6.10	5.80	6.00	6.10	5.50	5.40	5.50	5.00	4.50	4.70	4.60	4.60	4.40
Clothing and footwear	KCWC	20.00	21.70	21.00	22.00	22.30	22.00	22.40	23.50	22.40	22.60	21.60	21.20	20.60
Household goods	KCWH	26.90	29.60	30.70	32.60	33.00	33.80	35.10	35.60	33.50	34.00	34.60	34.00	31.80
Household services	KCWI	17.90	18.90	18.90	22.00	23.60	23.30	24.90	26.30	27.10	26.40	26.50	27.30	26.70
Personal goods and services	KCWJ	12.50	13.30	13.90	14.70	14.90	15.20	16.20	16.00	16.90	17.50	17.80	17.20	17.70
Motoring	KCWK	46.60	51.70	52.60	55.10	57.90	61.70	62.40	62.60	63.80	61.10	62.00	63.60	60.00
Fares and other travel costs	KCWL	8.10	8.30	9.20	9.50	9.30	9.70	9.60	9.50	11.10	11.00	10.90	14.20	11.00
Leisure goods	KCWM	16.40	17.80	18.50	19.70	19.60	20.50	21.40	21.40	19.40	19.40	20.10	19.00	18.50
Leisure services	KCWN	38.80	41.90	43.90	50.60	51.90	53.60	55.00	59.60	63.00	65.30	61.70	65.90	63.40
Miscellaneous	KCWO	2.00	1.20	1.40	0.70	1.90	2.00	1.90	2.00	2.20	2.10	1.90	2.00	2.00
Total	KCWP	328.80	352.20	359.40	385.70	393.90	404.70	415.70	432.90	441.40	447.40	456.80	469.70	452.20
Expenditure on commodity or service as a percentage of total expenditure														
Housing (Net)[5]	KPFH	16	16	16	17	17	16	17	18	18	19	20	20	19
Fuel and power	KPFI	4	3	3	3	3	3	3	3	3	4	4	4	5
Food and non-alcoholic drinks	KPFJ	17	17	17	16	16	16	16	16	15	16	16	16	17
Alcoholic drink	KPFK	4	4	4	4	4	4	4	3	3	3	3	3	3
Tobacco	KPFL	2	2	2	2	1	1	1	1	1	1	1	1	1
Clothing and footwear	KPFM	6	6	6	6	6	5	5	5	5	5	5	5	5
Household goods	KCWQ	8	8	9	8	8	8	8	8	8	8	8	7	7
Household services	KCWR	5	5	5	6	6	6	6	6	6	6	6	6	6
Personal goods and services	KCWS	4	4	4	4	4	4	4	4	4	4	4	4	4
Motoring	KCWT	14	15	15	14	15	15	15	14	14	14	14	14	13
Fares and other travel costs	KCWU	2	2	2	2	2	2	2	2	3	2	2	3	2
Leisure goods	KCWV	5	5	5	5	5	5	5	5	4	4	4	4	4
Leisure services	KCWW	12	12	12	13	13	13	13	14	14	15	13	14	14
Miscellaneous	KPFR	1	0	-	-	-	-	-	-	-	-	-	-	-
Total	KPFS	100	100	100	100	100	100	100	100	100	100	100	100	100

1 Data are based on the Family Expenditure Survey (FES) classification and not the Living Costs and Food Survey (LCF) (formally Expenditure and Food Survey) (EFS) standard classification: Classification of Individual Consumption by Purpose (COICOP).
This has been done to preserve an historical time-series, as COICOP data are only available from 2001/02.
2 From 1998/99 figures shown are based on weighted data, including children's expenditure.
3 From 2001/02 onwards, weighting is based on population estimates from the 2001 Census.
4 From this version of 2006, figures shown are based on weighted data using updated weights, with non-response weights and population figures based on the 2001 Census.
5 An improvement to the imputation of mortgage interest payments was implemented for 2006 data which should lead to more accurate figures.
This will lead to a slight discontinuity. An error was discovered in the derivation of mortgage capital repayments which was leading to double counting.
This has been amended for the 2006 data onwards.

Source: Living Costs and Food Survey (previously Expenditure and Food Survey);
Office for National Statistics; 01633 455678

8.5 Percentage of households with certain durable goods
United Kingdom

		1997 /98	1998 [1] /99	1999 /00	2000 /01	2001[2] /02	2002 /03	2003 /04	2004 /05	2005 /06	2006[3]	2007	2008	2009
Weighted number of households (thousands)	GH92	24,560	24,660	25,330	25,030	24,450	24,350	24,670	24,430	24,800	25,440	25,350	25,690	25,980
Number of households supplying data	KPDA	6,409	6,630	7,097	6,637	7,473	6,927	7,048	6,798	6,785	6,650	6,140	5,850	5,830
Car/van	KPDB	70	72	71	72	74	74	75	75	74	74	75	74	76
One	KPDC	44	44	43	44	44	44	44	42	46	43	44	43	43
Two	KPDD	21	23	21	22	23	25	25	27	23	25	25	25	26
Three or more	KPDE	5	5	6	6	6	6	6	6	5	6	6	6	7
Central heating, full or partial	KPDF	89	89	90	91	92	93	94	95	94	95	95	95	95
Tumble dryer	J8O3	51	51	52	53	54	56	57	58	58	59	57	59	58
Washing machine	KPDG	91	92	91	92	93	94	94	95	95	96	96	96	96
Fridge/freezer or deep freezer	KPDI	90	92	91	94	95	96	96	96	97	97	97	97	97
Dishwasher	GPTL	22	23	23	25	27	29	31	33	35	37	37	37	39
Microwave	J8O4	77	79	80	84	86	87	89	90	91	91	91	92	93
Telephone	KPDL	94	95	95	93	94	94	92	93	92	91	89	90	88
Mobile phone	GH96	20	27	44	47	64	70	76	78	79	79	78	79	81
Home computer	KPDM	29	33	38	44	49	55	58	62	65	67	70	72	75
DVS player	J8O5	..	..	..	..	..	31	50	67	79	83	86	88	90
Video recorder	KPDN	84	85	86	87	90	90	90	88	86	82	75	70	61
CD player	J8O6	63	68	72	77	80	83	86	87	88	87	86	86	84
Digital television service[4]	GH97	26	28	32	40	43	45	49	58	65	70	77	82	86
Internet connection	ZBUZ	..	10	19	32	39	45	49	53	55	58	61	66	71

1 Based on weighted data from 1998/99.
2 From 2001/02 onwards, weighting is based on the population estimates from the 2001 Census.
3 From this version of 2006, figures shown are based on weighted data using updated weights, with non-response weights and population figures based on the 2001 Census.
4 Includes digital, satellite and cable receivers.

Source: Living Costs and Food Survey;
(previously Expenditure and Food Survey)
Office for National Statistics
01633 455678

Lifestyles

Chapter 9

Lifestyles

Expenditure by the Department for Culture, Media and Sport (Table 9.1)

The figures in this table are taken from the department's Annual Report and are outturn figures for each of the headings shown (later figures are the estimated outturn). The department's planned expenditure for future years is also shown.

International tourism and holidays abroad (Tables 9.8 and 9.9)

The figures in these tables are compiled using data from the International Passenger Survey (IPS). A holiday abroad is a visit made for holiday purposes. Business trips and visits to friends and relatives are excluded.

Domestic tourism (Table 9.10)

The figures in this table are compiled using data from the UK Tourism Survey (UKTS) and represent trips of one or more nights away from home. The UKTS changed survey methodology in 2000 and 2005. Data from 1995 to 1999 were reworked to allow comparisons to be made with 2000 to 2004 data. Data for 2004 should be used and interpreted with caution. Data for 2005 is not comparable with previous years.

Gambling (Table 9.12)

The National Lottery figures in this table are the latest figures released by The National Lottery Commission at the time of going to press. They represent ticket sales (money staked1) for each of the games which comprise the lottery. The figures have been adjusted to real terms using the Retail Prices Index (RPI).

The National Lottery started on the 19 November 1994 with the first instant ticket being sold in March 1995. The sum of the individual games may not agree exactly with the figures for total sales which also include the Easy Play games which started in 1998 but were dropped in 1999.

The other gambling figures in this table are obtained from the Gambling Commission (formerly the Gaming Board) and HM Revenue & Customs (HMRC). The figures have been adjusted to real terms using the Retail Prices Index (RPI).

9.1 Expenditure by the Department for Culture, Media and Sport[1]

£ Million

	Museums, galleries and libraries	The Arts (England)	Sports (UK)	Architecture and the Historic Environment (England)	The Royal Parks (UK)	Tourism (UK)	Broadcasting and media (UK)	Administration and research	Gambling and the National Lottery	Regional Cultural Consortiums	Total Resource Budget
	GQIF	KWFP	KWFQ	KWFR	LQYY	KWFS	KWFT	GQIG	SNKA	GLZ8	GM22
2004/05	340	367	83	159	25	50	2,644	42	668	2	4,380
2005/06	448	394	120	148	30	51	2,767	47	848	2	4,856
2006/07	492	387	134	179	18	55	2,919	54	851	2	5,092
2007/08	505	403	175	159	19	56	3,085	55	884	3	5,345
2008/09	451	405	171	172	20	55	3,001	57	1,012	2	5,346
2009/10[2,3]	521	417	154	181	19	51	3,158	57	1,002	0	5,558
2010/11[4]	621	407	200	175	19	43	3,321	57	1,092	0	5,935
2011/12[4]	587	378	253	145	17	37	3,372	55	929	0	5,772

Source: Department for Culture, Media and Sport: 020 7211 6121

1. It should be noted that it is not possible to compare the data in these tables with those previously published, due to the new financial regime put in place in 2010/11.
The Alignment project aims to improve current financial processes by bringing together as far as is reasonably possible, the present Treasury control (Budget) Parliamentary Approval (Estimates) and end year reporting Resource Accounts). The budgets have been restated across all years to remove the Cost of Capital, move Profit and Loss on the disposal of assets from Capital to Resource and Provisions from DEL to AME.
2. Figures are taken from the DCMS Resource Account 2009-10 for outturn years
3. Data was provided for the Final Outturn exercise recorded on the HM Treasury COINS database
4. Data are forecasts.

9.2 Estimates of Average Issue Readership of National Daily Newspapers
rolling 12 months' periods ending

		2007 Mar	2007 Jun	2007 Sep	2007 Sep	2008 Mar	2008 Jun	2008 Sep	2008 Dec	2009 Mar	2009 Jun	2009 Sep	2009 Dec	2010 Mar	2010 Jun	2010 Sep	2010 Dec	2011 Mar
The Sun	WSDV	7,840	7,768	7,931	7,980	7,897	8,031	7,949	7,872	7,870	7,860	7,798	7,761	7,751	7,694	7,700	7,722	7,722
Daily Mail	WSEI	5,253	5,197	5,239	5,230	5,293	5,347	5,212	5,062	4,949	4,846	4,936	4,934	4,881	4,896	4,739	4,741	4,775
Daily Mirror/Daily Record	WSEH	4,937	4,975	4,971	4,895	4,904	4,864	4,758	4,717	4,555	4,608	4,476	4,404	4,288	4,170	4,004	3,947	4,026
Daily Mirror	WSEM	3,844	3,880	3,868	3,789	3,748	3,685	3,623	3,600	3,489	3,566	3,477	3,425	3,381	3,244	3,117	3,087	3,163
The Daily Telegraph	WSEN	2,177	2,167	2,054	2,075	2,023	2,060	2,048	1,901	1,887	1,843	1,834	1,905	1,840	1,796	1,751	1,680	1,693
The Times	WSES	1,730	1,702	1,672	1,666	1,673	1,731	1,764	1,813	1,770	1,801	1,802	1,773	1,768	1,673	1,613	1,571	1,552
Daily Express	WSEP	1,742	1,694	1,687	1,678	1,621	1,598	1,605	1,571	1,557	1,624	1,546	1,577	1,617	1,586	1,551	1,565	1,504
Daily Star	WSEQ	1,620	1,701	1,690	1,597	1,500	1,484	1,417	1,427	1,451	1,471	1,598	1,577	1,529	1,463	1,423	1,427	1,488
The Guardian	WSET	1,239	1,226	1,193	1,121	1,169	1,165	1,240	1,240	1,206	1,205	1,142	1,147	1,124	1,132	1,130	1,103	1,154
The Independent	WSEU	767	774	787	745	733	702	722	688	649	679	636	671	635	607	556	532	562
Financial Times	WSEY	394	398	375	360	362	377	387	418	417	430	433	434	418	404	391	364	367
Any national morning	WSEZ	21,782	21,702	21,709	21,650	21,536	21,625	21,475	21,203	20,918	20,817	20,609	20,574	20,404	20,207	19,841	19,690	19,751

Source: National Readership Surveys Ltd.

9.3 Employment in creative industries, 2010[1]

Great Britain   Numbers

Sector	Employees in Creative Industries	Self-employed in Creative Industries	Employees doing creative jobs in other industries	Self-employed people doing creative jobs in other industries	Total Employment
Advertising	89,100	25,400	163,800	21,000	299,200
Architecture	63,300	35,300	26,300	3,500	128,400
Art & Antiques	6,600	3,200			9,800
Crafts			66,300	45,100	111,400
Design	35,000	56,600	113,500	20,400	225,400
Designer Fashion	2,500	3,700	3,200	400	9,700
Film, Video & Photography	26,000	13,300	10,700	10,500	60,500
Music & Visual and Performing Arts	67,200	136,300	33,300	69,000	305,800
Publishing	151,100	20,500	55,700	9,300	236,600
Software & Electronic Publishing	347,000	81,000	290,600	34,500	753,000
Digital & Entertainment Media	5,600	700			6,200
TV & Radio	77,300	37,300	10,500	7,200	132,300
Total	**870,600**	**413,200**	**774,000**	**220,700**	**2,278,500**

1 Data are at Q3 (July to September) 2010

Sources: Creative Industries Economic Estimates Statistical Bulletin;
Department for Culture, Media & Sport

9.4 Selected activities performed in free time:[1] by age, 2009/10

England   Percentages

	16-24	25-34	35-44	45-64	65 and over	All aged 16 and over
Watching television	88	85	88	89	92	89
Spending time with friends/family	87	85	85	83	82	84
Listening to music	90	78	76	74	69	76
Shopping	71	73	74	69	69	71
Reading	53	62	65	72	73	67
Eating out at restaurants	66	71	70	72	65	69
Days out	54	65	68	67	59	63
Internet/mailing	79	77	71	57	24	59
Sport/exercise	63	63	60	55	35	54
Gardening	16	36	51	64	62	49
Going to pubs/bars/clubs	59	63	50	44	33	48
Going to the cinema	72	61	55	42	21	48

Source: Taking Part: The National Survey of Culture, Leisure and Sport,

Media and Sport (2010)

1. Respondents were shown a list of activities and asked to pick the things they did in their free time in the last year prior to interview. The most popular activities performed by all adults aged 16 and over are shown in the table.

9.5 Films
United Kingdom

Numbers and £ million

	Production of UK films[1]		Expenditure on feature films (Current prices)		
	Films produced in the UK (numbers)	Production costs (current prices)	UK box office	Video[2] rental	Video[2] retail[3]
	KWGD	KWGE	KWHU	KWHV	KWHW
1998	83	389	547	n/a	n/a
1999	92	507	563	n/a	451
2000	80	578	583	n/a	601
2001	74	379	645	494	821
2002	119	551	755	492	1,175
2003	196	1,119	742	457	1,392
2004	173	875	770	458	1,557
2005	165	582	770	390	1,399
2006	136	826	762	327	1,302
2007	128	836	821	280	1,440
2008	134	691	850	202	1,454
2009	150	1,088	944	200	1,311

Source:UK Film Council RSU analysis of Official UK
Charts Company, Screen Digest and BVA data

1 Includes films with a production budget of £500,000 or more.
2 Video includes only rental and retail of physical discs, and does not include downloads.
3 In 2005 the British Video Association changed its methodology for producing market value which has necessitated a change to historical figures quoted.

9.6 Box office top 20 films released in the UK and Republic of Ireland, 2009

Rank		Country of origin	Box office gross £m[1]	Number of opening cinemas	Distributor
1	Avatar[2,3]	USA	83.27[2]	503	20th Century Fox
2	Harry Potter and the Half-Blood Prince	UK/USA	50.72	584	Warner Bros
3	Ice Age III	USA	35.02	526	20th Century Fox
4	Up	USA	34.59	511	Disney
5	Slumdog Millionaire	UK	31.66	324	Pathé
6	The Twilight Saga: New Moon	USA	27.47	497	E1 Films
7	Transformers: Revenge of the Fallen	USA	27.06	516	Paramount
8	Sherlock Holmes[1]	UK/USA	25.71	476	Warner Bros
9	Alvin and the Chipmunks 2: The Squeakquel[1]	USA	23.16	478	20th Century Fox
10	The Hangover	USA	22.12	422	Warner Bros
11	Star Trek	USA/Ger	21.4	499	Paramount
12	Monsters vs. Aliens	USA	21.37	520	Paramount
13	A Christmas Carol	USA	20.19	446	Disney
14	Night at the Museum 2	USA/Can	20.03	515	20th Century Fox
15	2012	USA	19.5	480	Sony Pictures
16	Angels and Demons	USA	18.79	506	Sony Pictures
17	Bolt	USA	17.94	496	Disney
18	X-Men Origins: Wolverine	USA	16.28	488	20th Century Fox
19	Brüno	USA	15.78	456	Universal
20	Marley and Me	USA	15.25	467	20th Century Fox

Source: Rentrak EDI, RSU analysis

1 Box office gross = cumulative total up to 21 February 2010
2 Films were still on release on 21 February 2010
3 At 4 April 2010 Avatar has grossed £91.4 million

9.7 Accomodation used by visitors from overseas during visit: 2010
Great Britain

	Number of trips (millions)	Number of nights spent (millions)	Expenditure at current prices (£millions)	Average nights spent (numbers)	Average expenditure per trip (£)
Paying guest in:					
Hotel/motel	39.0	82.9	9,274	2.1	237.9
Guest house	1.9	5.3	467	2.8	243.2
Farmhouse	0.6	2.7	152	4.5	253.3
Other private house/B&B	4.9	12.3	1,054	2.5	217.3
Self catering in:					
Rented flat/apartment	2.0	10.0	634	5.1	323.5
Rented house/villa/bungalow/chalet	5.1	29.1	1,668	5.7	328.3
Hotel/university/school	1.9	4.9	308	2.5	159.6
Hostel	1.5	3.7	241	2.4	156.5
Friend's/relatives home	43.5	131.9	3,926	3.0	90.2
Own second home/timeshare	1.1	4.3	149	3.9	136.7
Holiday camp/village					
Self catering	1.5	6.4	330	4.3	223.0
Serviced	0.3	1.3	70	4.2	233.3
Camping	4.7	15.9	548	3.4	117.3
Caravan					
Towed	4.8	21.6	656	4.5	138.1
Static owned	3.4	14.0	334	4.2	98.8
Static not owned	3.8	19.4	806	5.1	210.4
Boat	0.5	1.9	111	4.1	236.2
Sleeper cab of lorry/truck	0.4	0.9	61	2.0	138.6
Other/transit	2.1	8.6	276	4.1	132.7

Source: United Kingdom Tourism Survey: 02075781418

9.8 International tourism[1]

Thousands and £ million

	Visits to the UK by overseas residents (thousands)	Spending in the UK by overseas residents		Visits overseas by UK residents (thousands)	Spending overseas by UK residents	
		Current prices	Constant 1995 prices		Current prices	Constant 1995 prices
	GMAA	GMAK	CQPR	GMAF	GMAM	CQPS
1999	25,394	12,498	11,133	53,881	22,020	24,676
2000	25,209	12,805	11,102	56,837	24,251	27,281
2001	22,835	11,306	9,528	58,281	25,332	27,710
2002	24,180	11,737	9,641	59,377	26,962	29,311
2003	24,715	11,855	9,451	61,424	28,550	28,677
2004	27,755	13,047	10,146	64,194	30,285	30,444
2005	29,970	14,248	10,714	66,441	32,154	30,954
2006	32,713	16,002	11,641	69,536	34,411	30,904
2007	32,778	15,960	11,389	69,450	35,013	32,477
2008	31,888	16,323	11,276	69,011	36,838	28,657
2009	29,716	16,507	10,977	58,433	31,757	22,765
2010 [2]	29,641	16,723	10,679	54,934	30,931	21,589

1 See chapter text
2 Data for 2010 are provisional

Sources: International Passenger Survey
Office for National Statistics;
01633 456032

9.9 Holidays abroad:[1] by destination

Percentages

		1981	1991	2001	2002	2003	2004	2005	2006	2007	2008	2009	2010
Spain	JTKC	29.8	21.3	27.9	28.5	29.8	28.4	27.2	27.8	26.5	26.6	26.5	25.9
France	JTKD	18.1	25.8	18.3	19	18.1	17.3	16.6	15.9	16.7	16.7	18.6	18.3
Greece	JTKF	6.6	7.6	7.8	7	6.6	5.7	5.1	5.0	5.0	4.2	4.4	4.8
United States	JTKE	5.5	6.8	6.3	5.4	5.5	6.1	6.0	5.1	5.2	5.4	5.4	4.9
Italy	JTKG	5	3.5	4.3	4.6	5	5	5.4	5.4	5.6	5.2	4.7	4.6
Ireland	JTKI	3.7	3	4.1	4.1	3.7	3.8	3.8	4.0	3.3	3.2	3.2	2.5
Portugal	JTKH	4	4.8	3.6	4	4	3.5	3.6	3.7	4.1	4.8	4.1	4.4
Cyprus	JTKL	2.7	2.4	3.5	3	2.7	2.6	2.8	2.4	2.4	2.4	2.1	2.1
Netherlands	JTKK	2.6	3.5	2.6	2.8	2.6	2.6	2.5	2.7	2.4	2.1	2.2	2.2
Turkey	JTKJ	2.3	0.7	2	2.2	2.3	2.3	2.7	2.7	2.8	3.7	3.5	4.7
Belgium	JTKM	2.2	2.1	2.1	2	2.2	1.8	1.9	2.0	2.2	2.0	1.9	1.7
Germany	JTKN	1.2	2.7	1.4	1.5	1.2	1.6	1.7	1.7	2.0	1.9	1.7	1.7
Austria	JTKP	1.1	2.4	1.1	1.4	1.1	1.4	1.3	1.2	1.2	1.4	1.4	1.5
Malta	JTKO	1	1.7	1	1	1	1	1.1	1.0	0.9	0.9	0.8	1.0
Other countries	JTKQ	14.2	11.8	13.8	13.6	14.2	16.8	18.4	20	19.6	19.5	19.5	19.6

1 See chapter text.

Sources: International Passenger Survey, Office for National Statistics;
01633 456032

9.10 Domestic tourism[1]

United Kingdom

	Number of trips (millions)	Number of Nights Spent (millions)	Expenditure at current prices (£ million)	Average nights spent (numbers)	Average expenditure per trip (£)
	GQGY	GQGZ	GQHA	GQHB	GQHC
1999	173.1	568.6	25, 635	3.3	148.1
2000	175.4	576.4	26, 133	3.3	149.0
2001	163.1	529.6	26, 094	3.2	160.0
2002	167.3	531.9	26, 699	3.2	159.6
2003	151.0	490.5	26, 482	3.2	175.4
2004[2]	126.6	408.9	24, 357	3.2	192.4
2005[3]	138.7	442.3	22, 667	3.2	163.4
2006	126.3	400.1	20, 965	3.2	165.9
2007	123.5	394.4	21, 238	3.2	172.0
2008	117.7	378.4	21, 107	3.2	179.3
2009	126.0	398.8	21, 881	3.2	175.6
2010	119.4	373.3	20, 835	3.1	173.0

Source: United Kingdom Tourism Survey, Visit England: 020 75781418

1 See chapter text

2 There were concerns that data for 2004 was not truly representative of the UK
population. Data for 2004 should be used and interpreted with caution.

3 The UKTS under went a methological change in 2005 and results should not
be compared with previous years. The survey did not run between Jan-Apr 2005,
as a result full-year estimates were made using Jan-Apr 2003 data.

9.11 Domestic trips[1] for holidays and visiting friends and relatives: by country

United Kingdom

Millions

	England	Northern Ireland	Scotland	Wales	United Kingdom
Holidays					
2006	62.2	1.6	8.5	7.4	79.2
2007	60.9	1.4	8.6	6.5	76.8
2008	59.5	1.5	8.3	6.6	75.4
2009	67.4	1.6	8.9	7	84.3
Visiting friends and relatives					
2006	20.3	0.4	1.9	1.1	23.7
2007	21.2	0.4	1.9	1.3	24.7
2008	18	0.3	1.6	0.8	20.6
2009	18.1	0.4	1.4	1	20.8

1. Trips refer to a visit with at least one night's stay.

Source: Visit England, Visit Scotland, Visit Wales,
Northern Ireland Tourist Board (2010)

9.12 Gambling[1]

United Kingdom

£ million[2] and numbers

		1998 /99	1999 /00	2000 /01	2001 /02	2002 /03	2003 /04	2004 /05	2005 /06	2006 /07	2007 /08	2008 /09	2009 /10
Money staked on gambling													
National Lottery -Total[3]	C229	5,809	5,450	5,315	5,029	4,670	4,614	4,757	5,000	4,911	4,966	5,149	5,477
Lotto including on-line	C3PU	5,064	4,641	4,416	4,038	3,479	3,225	3,225	3,021	2,858	2,752	2,698	2,661
Instants[4]	C3PV	744	612	590	606	592	641	729	804	943	1,109	1,221	1,340
Thunderball	C3PW	..	197	257	254	287	351	343	355	329	309	297	286
Lottery Extra[7]	C3PX	..	..	51	131	90	78	77	57	12	0	-	-
HotPicks	C3PY	..	..	..	..	222	244	219	228	222	210	211	210
Euromillions	C3Q2	..	..	..	..	..	15	104	427	464	476	618	881
Daily Play	C3Q3	..	..	..	..	..	45	59	54	49	50	50	49
Dream number[8]		..	..	..	..	..	..	..	..	59	59	54	50
Lotteries (excluding the National Lottery)[5]	C3Q4	179	114	114	114	134	127	141	139	164	170	179	194
Bingo clubs[10]	C3Q5	1,159	1,179	1,190	1,221	1,256	1,381	1,783	1,826	1,820	1,620	1,428	1,359
Football pools	C3Q6	286	221	185	151	124	112	109	90	88	..	59	57
Off-course betting[6]	C3Q7	7,916	7,996	7,689	9,969	17,985	32,265	44,971	44,437	36,553	..	..	..
Number operating in GB:													
Casinos	JE55	116	118	117	122	126	131	138	140	138	144	145	141
Bingo clubs [10]	JE56	751	727	705	688	699	696	676	657	634	675	641	496
Gaming machines	JE57	250,000	250,000	250,000	255,000	25,000	250,000	244,000	235,000	234,000	261,000	248,000	..
Society Lotteries	JE58	634	646	657	678	651	644	647	660	651	562	469	515
on-course bookmakers[9]	JE59	..	..	..	..	..	..	..	..	..	579	714	681
off-course bookmakers[9]	JE5A	..	..	..	..	..	..	..	..	..	801	720	590
betting shops[9]	JE5B	..	..	..	..	..	..	..	..	..	8,800	8,862	8,822

1 See chapter text.

2 Adjusted to real terms using the Retail Prices Index.

3 Includes Easy Play tickets which are not shown separately.

4 From 2003/04 includes Inter-active games.

5 From 2002/03 includes Hotspot lotteries.

6 From 2001/02 includes Fixed Odds Betting Terminals.

7 Discontinued July 2006

8 Started July 2006

9 The Gambling Commission started regulating the betting industry from 1 September 2007, the number of betting shops is an ABB estimate.

10 Does not include money stake on gaming machines.

Sources: National Lottery Commission;
Gambling Commission: 0121 230 6666;
Department for Culture, Media and Sport: 020 7211 6451

9.13 Most Popular Boy and Girl Baby Names in England and Wales[1], 2009

Rank	Boys Names	Rank	Boys Names	Rank	Girls Names	Rank	Girls Names
1	OLIVER	51	MICHAEL	1	OLIVIA	51	ISABEL
2	JACK	52	CAMERON	2	RUBY	52	AMBER
3	HARRY	53	FREDDIE	3	CHLOE	53	BETHANY
4	ALFIE	54	AARON	4	EMILY	54	GRACIE
5	JOSHUA	55	THEO	5	SOPHIE	55	GEORGIA
6	THOMAS	56	HARLEY	6	JESSICA	56	ELEANOR
7	CHARLIE	57	TOBY	7	GRACE	57	AMELIE
8	WILLIAM	58	CHARLES	8	LILY	58	CAITLIN
9	JAMES	59	RHYS	9	AMELIA	59	MADISON
10	DANIEL	60	LEON	10	EVIE	60	ISOBEL
11	GEORGE	61	FINLAY	11	MIA	61	LAUREN
12	SAMUEL	62	MOHAMMAD	12	AVA	62	ROSIE
13	ETHAN	63	SEBASTIAN	13	ELLA	63	KEIRA
14	JOSEPH	64	DAVID	14	CHARLOTTE	64	ANNA
15	BENJAMIN	65	BEN	15	ISABELLA	65	PAIGE
16	MOHAMMED	66	LOUIS	16	LUCY	66	MAYA
17	LUCAS	67	ZACHARY	17	ISABELLE	67	LACEY
18	JACOB	68	KAI	18	DAISY	68	MADDISON
19	DYLAN	69	ASHTON	19	HOLLY	69	LEXIE
20	ARCHIE	70	EVAN	20	MEGAN	70	AIMEE
21	LEWIS	71	KIAN	21	FREYA	71	SKYE
22	ALEXANDER	72	LUCA	22	POPPY	72	TIA
23	OSCAR	73	AIDEN	23	PHOEBE	73	FAITH
24	LIAM	74	KYLE	24	SUMMER	74	SOFIA
25	MAX	75	GABRIEL	25	SCARLETT	75	ZARA
26	JAYDEN	76	REECE	26	MILLIE	76	NIAMH
27	JAKE	77	HAYDEN	27	ELLIE	77	REBECCA
28	CALLUM	78	AIDAN	28	AMY	78	LIBBY
29	RILEY	79	REUBEN	29	HANNAH	79	SARAH
30	RYAN	80	JOEL	30	ISLA	80	FLORENCE
31	TYLER	81	BAILEY	31	KATIE	81	MARTHA
32	NOAH	82	BRANDON	32	IMOGEN	82	HOLLIE
33	LUKE	83	JOHN	33	ERIN	83	ZOE
34	ADAM	84	LOUIE	34	MAISIE	84	JULIA
35	LOGAN	85	ELLIS	35	SOPHIA	85	EVELYN
36	MUHAMMAD	86	KIERAN	36	ABIGAIL	86	TILLY
37	HENRY	87	ELLIOT	37	JASMINE	87	ALEXANDRA
38	MATTHEW	88	SAM	38	EVA	88	NICOLE
39	HARVEY	89	TAYLOR	39	BROOKE	89	HARRIET
40	LEO	90	BRADLEY	40	MOLLY	90	EMILIA
41	ISAAC	91	ROBERT	41	EMMA	91	LYDIA
42	HARRISON	92	JOE	42	LOLA	92	EVE
43	FINLEY	93	ARTHUR	43	ELIZABETH	93	MARIA
44	EDWARD	94	CHRISTOPHER	44	LEAH	94	ROSE
45	MASON	95	EWAN	45	LILLY	95	ESME
46	CONNOR	96	FREDERICK	46	MATILDA	96	ALISHA
47	OWEN	97	MORGAN	47	LEXI	97	HEIDI
48	JAMIE	98	JUDE	48	LAYLA	98	FRANCESCA
49	NATHAN	99	STANLEY	49	SIENNA	99	SARA
50	ALEX	100	AUSTIN	50	ALICE	100	MYA

Source: Office for National Statistics

1. These rankings have been produced using the exact spelling of the name given at birth registration. Similar names with different spellings have been counted separately. Births where the name was not stated have been excluded from these figures. Of the 362,135 baby boys in the 2009 dataset, 15 were excluded for this reason. Names with a count of 2 or less have been redacted using S40 of the Freedom of Information Act in order to protect confidentiality of individuals.

9.14 Libraries overview (adults)

Great Britain

Percentages

	2005 /06	2006 /07	2007 /08	2008 /09	2009 /10
Has visited a public library in the last year	48.2	46.1	45.0	41.1	39.4
Reason for visit					
Own time					93.8
Paid work					3.1
Academic study					10.3
Frequency of attendance					
1-2 times a year	10.4	10.3	10.5	8.9	7.9
3-4 times a year	13.4	12.9	13.0	11.4	10.9
At least once a month	16.4	15.7	14.9	13.3	12.8
At least once a week	7.9	7.2	6.7	5.9	5.4
Has not visited	51.8	53.9	55.0	60.5	63.0

Source: DCMS

9.15 Museums and galleries overview (adults)

Great Britain

Percentages

	2005 /06	2006 /07	2007 /08	2008 /09	2009 /10
Has visited a museum, gallery in the last year	42.3	41.5	43.5	44.5	46.7
Frequency of attendance					
At least once a week	0.3	0.4	0.3	0.4	0.4
Less often than once a week but at least once a month	3.2	2.8	3.2	2.9	3.6
Less often than once a month but at least 3-4 times a year	13.2	12.9	13.8	13.9	14.1
1-2 times a year	25.6	25.3	26.3	26.1	27.9
Never	57.7	58.5	56.5	56.7	54.0

Source DCMS

9.16 Participation[1] in voluntary activities

England

	Formal volunteering[2]		Informal volunteering[3]	
	At least once a month	At least once a year	At least once a month	At least once a year
2001	27	39	34	67
2003	28	42	37	63
2005	29	44	37	68
2007/08	27	43	35	64
2008/09	26	41	35	62
2009/10	25	40	29	54

1. Participation by adults aged 16 and over.
2. Formal volunteering:giving unpaid help through groups, clubs or organisations to benefit other people or the environment.
3. Informal volunteering: giving unpaid help as an individual to people who are not relatives.

Source: Citizenship Survey, Department of Communities and Local Government (2010)

9.17 UK residents' visits to friends and relatives[1] abroad: by destination

United Kingdom

Percentages[2]

	1999	2003	2006	2009
Irish Republic	19	16	15	14
France	12	13	11	11
Poland	1	1	6	9
Spain	6	9	9	8
Germany	7	6	6	5
USA	9	7	6	5
India	3	3	3	4
Italy	3	4	4	4
Netherlands	5	4	3	3
Pakistan	2	3	3	3
Other countries	34	34	35	36
All destinations (=100%) (millions)	6.6	8.5	12.0	11.6

Source: International Passenger Survey,
Office for National Statistics

1 As a proportion of all visits to friends and relatives taken abroad by residents of the UK.
Excludes business trips and other miscellaneous visits.
2 Percentages may not add up to 100 per cent due to rounding.

9.18 The Internet

United Kingdom

Percentages

	Internet activities by age group 2010					
	16–24	25–44	45–54	55–64	65 plus	All
Finding information about goods or services	64	76	80	83	72	75
Sending/receiving emails	88	90	89	91	87	90
Using services related to travel and accommodation	50	64	70	72	62	63
Internet banking	45	63	54	53	34	54
Looking for information - education, training, courses	47	36	27	19	7	32
Reading or downloading online news, magazines	52	53	51	47	40	51
Looking for a job or sending job application	38	32	23	11	1	26
Seeking health-related information	27	42	39	44	36	39
Downloading software (other than games)	35	34	23	27	18	30
Selling of goods or services (eg. via auctions)	16	28	20	18	9	21
Consulting the Internet with the purpose of learning	47	34	34	30	27	35
Playing or downloading games, images, films or music	61	43	32	24	17	40
Listening to web radio or watching web TV	59	47	45	34	24	45
Uploading self created content	50	43	28	29	22	38
Posting messages to chat sites,blogs,newsgroups etc	75	49	31	19	8	43
Telephoning over the Internet/video calls(via webcam)	30	25	22	17	15	23
Doing an online course	11	8	7	5	3	8
Donating to charities online	10	13	15	13	7	12

	Internet purchases by age group: 2010					
	16–24	25–44	45–54	55–64	65 plus	All
Holiday, accommodation (eg hotels)	46	53	54	47	44	44
Films, music	50	50	33	27	25	47
Clothes, sports goods	58	45	46	43	38	52
Household goods (eg furniture, toys, etc)	52	41	46	39	37	43
Books, magazines or newspapers (including e-books)	40	43	39	41	40	39
Other travel arrangements (eg transport tickets, car hire)	36	42	48	35	32	36
Tickets for events	37	40	34	21	19	35
Electronic equipment (including cameras)	31	24	22	14	15	25
Video games software and upgrades	30	20	9	8	8	23
Computer software and upgrades	18	17	23	22	20	18
Food and groceries	32	25	16	17	17	24
Computer Hardware	13	15	14	11	10	13
Shares, financial services or insurance	24	23	18	13	11	20
e-learning material	8	5	2	2	2	6
Medicine	6	6	9	12	10	6
Telecommunication services	17	14	16	13	13	15
Other	4	6	7	5	5	5

	Households with access to the Internet 2006 to 2010		
	Internet access		
Year	Per cent	Number of households (millions)	Percentage change on previous year
2006	57	14.3	..
2007	61	15.2	7
2008	65	16.5	8
2009	70	18.3	11
2010	73	19.2	5

Source: Statistical Bulletin 2010, Office for National Statistics

9.19 Radio Listening

	Adult (15+) Population '000's	Weekly Reach '000's	Weekly Reach %	Average Hours Per Head	Average Hours Per Listener	Total Hours (000's)	Share of Listening
Quarterly Summary of Radio Listening - Period Mar 2011							
All Radio	51618	47266	91.6	20.5	22.4	1058098	100.0
All Commercial Radio	51618	34046	66.0	8.7	13.3	451178	42.6
All National Commercial	51618	15943	30.9	2.4	7.7	123363	11.7
All Local Commercial	51618	27305	52.9	6.4	12.0	327815	31.0
All BBC	51618	35074	67.9	11.3	16.6	581870	55.0
All BBC Network Radio	51618	31889	61.8	9.5	15.3	488535	46.2
BBC Local/Regional	51618	10197	19.8	1.8	9.2	93335	8.8
BBC Radio 1	51618	11825	22.9	1.8	7.8	92499	8.7
BBC Radio 2	51618	14537	28.2	3.3	11.6	169282	16.0
BBC Radio 3	51618	2258	4.4	0.3	6.1	13791	1.3
BBC Radio 4	51618	10829	21.0	2.5	12.0	130036	12.3
BBC Radio 5 Live	51618	6653	12.9	0.9	7.1	47148	4.5
FIVE live sports extra	51618	799	1.5	0.0	2.8	2262	0.2
BBC 6 Music	51618	1297	2.5	0.2	8.1	10448	1.0
BBC Radio7	51618	1159	2.2	0.1	5.7	6662	0.6
BBC Asian Network UK	51618	500	1.0	0.1	6.1	3051	0.3
BBC World Service	51618	1790	3.5	0.2	5.1	9154	0.9
1Xtra from the BBC	51618	892	1.7	0.1	4.7	4202	0.4

Radio Listening (UK): Average Weekly
Average hours per head (by age group).
Period ending Mar 2011

Age 10-14	9.9
Age 15-24	14.5
Age 25-34	17.5
Age 35-44	20.9
Age 45-54	22.5
Age 55-64	24.6
Age 65 and Over	22.8
Overall Average Weekly Listening Hours	19.8

Source: RAJAR / IpsosMori / RSMB

Environment

Chapter 10

Environment

Environmental taxes (Table 10.1)

In 2008 government revenue from environmental taxes was £38.5 billion. As a proportion of Gross Domestic Product (GDP) this amounts to 2.7 per cent. As a proportion of total taxes and social contributions, environmental taxes were 7.1 per cent in 2008. These proportions are lower than in previous years because growth in the economy and total taxes and social contributions has exceeded that of environmental taxes.

Air emissions (Table 10.2 to 10.8)

Emissions of air pollutants arise from a wide variety of sources. The National Atmospheric Emissions Inventory (NAEI) is prepared annually for the Government and the devolved administrations by AEA Energy and Environment, with the work being co-ordinated by the Department of Energy and Climate Change (DECC). Information is available for a range of point sources including the most significant polluters. However, a different approach has to be taken for diffuse sources such as transport and domestic emissions, where this type of information is not available. Estimates for these are derived from statistical information and from research on emission factors for stationary and mobile sources. Although for any given year considerable uncertainties surround the emission estimates for each pollutant, trends over time are likely to be more reliable.

UK national emission estimates are updated annually and any developments in methodology are applied retrospectively to earlier years. Adjustments in the methodology are made to accommodate new technical information and to improve international comparability.

Three different classification systems are used in the tables presented here; a National Accounts basis (Table 10.2), the format required by the Inter-governmental Panel on Climate Change (IPCC) (Table 10.3) and the National Communications (NC) categories (Tables 10.5-10.7).

The NC source categories are detailed below together with details of the main sources of these emissions:

Energy supply total: Power stations, refineries, manufacture of solid fuels and other energy industries, solid fuel transformation, exploration, production and transport of oils, offshore oil and gas – venting and flaring, power stations - FGD, coal mining and handling, and exploration, production and transport of gas.

Business total: Iron and steel – combustion, other industrial combustion, miscellaneous industrial and commercial combustion, energy recovery from waste fuels, refrigeration and air conditioning, foams, fire fighting, solvents, one components foams, and electronics, electrical insulation and sporting goods.

Transport total: Civil aviation (domestic, landing and take off, and cruise), passenger cars, light duty vehicles, buses, HGVs, mopeds & motorcycles, LPG emissions (all vehicles), other road vehicle engines, railways, railways – stationary combustion, national navigation, fishing vessels, military aircraft and shipping, and aircraft – support vehicles.

Residential total: Residential combustion, use of non aerosol consumer products, accidental vehicle fires, and aerosols and metered dose inhalers.

Agriculture total: Stationary and mobile combustion, breakdown of pesticides, enteric fermentation (cattle, sheep, goats, horses, pigs, and deer), wastes (cattle, sheep, goats, horses, pigs, poultry, and deer), manure liquid systems, manure solid storage and dry lot, other manure management, direct soil emission, and field burning of agricultural wastes.

Industrial process total: Sinter production, cement production, lime production, limestone and dolomite use, soda ash production and use, fletton bricks, ammonia production, iron and steel, nitric acid production, adipic acid production, other – chemical industry, halocarbon production, and magnesiun cover gas.

Land-use change: Forest land remaining forest land, forest land biomass burning, land converted to forest land, direct N2O emissions from N fertilisation of forest land, cropland liming, cropland remaining cropland, cropland biomass burning, land converted to cropland, N2O emissions from disturbance associated with land-use conversion to cropland, grassland biomass burning, grassland liming, grassland remaining grassland, land converted to grassland, wetlands remaining wetland, Non-CO2 emissions from drainage of soils and wetlands, settlements biomass burning, land converted to settlements, and harvested wood.

Waste management total: Landfill, waste-water handling, and waste incineration.

Atmospheric emissions on a National Accounts basis (Table 10.2)

The air and energy accounts are produced for ONS by AEA Technology plc based on data compiled for the National Atmospheric Emissions Inventory (NAEI)7 and UK Greenhouse Gas Inventory (GHGI)8. Every year a programme of development work is undertaken to optimise the methodologies employed in compiling the accounts. Assessments in previous years have indicated that a number of splits used to apportion road transport source data to more than one industry should be reviewed. The results of this review have been implemented in the 2011 UK Environmental Accounts for reference period 2009 and years back to 1990.

The industry breakdown used in the accounts has moved to using the Standard Industrial Classification 2007 (SIC 2007). Historically, the accounts were based on Environmental Accounts codes (EAcodes) based on SIC 2003. This change will allow the accounts which are broken down by industry to be more readily compared with other economic statistics. A methodology article that outlines this change in more detail was published on the ONS website in May 2011: http//www.statistics.gov.uk/cci/article.asp?id=2694. As a result while names given to the breakdown maybe similar they are not necessarily the same.

The National Accounts figures in Table 10.2 differ from those on an IPCC basis, in that they include estimated emissions from fuels purchased by UK resident households and companies either at home or abroad (including emissions from UK international shipping and aircraft operators), and exclude emissions in the UK resulting from the activities of non-residents. This allows for a more consistent comparison with key National Accounts indicators such as Gross Domestic Product (GDP).

Greenhouse gases include carbon dioxide, methane, nitrous oxide, hydro-fluorocarbons, perfluorocarbons and sulphur hexafluoride which are expressed in thousand tonnes of carbon dioxide equivalent.

Acid rain precursors include sulphur dioxide, nitrogen oxides and ammonia which are expressed as thousand tonnes of sulphur dioxide equivalent.

Estimated total emissions of greenhouse gases on an IPCC basis (Table 10.3)

The IPCC classification is used to report greenhouse gas emissions under the UN Framework Convention on Climate Change (UNFCCC) and includes Land Use Change and all emissions from Domestic aviation and shipping, but excludes International aviation and shipping bunkers. Estimates of the relative contribution to global warming of the main greenhouse gases, or classes of gases, are presented weighted by their global warming potential.

Greenhouse gas emissions bridging table (Table 10.4)
National Accounts measure to UNFCCC measure

The air and energy accounts are produced for ONS by AEA Technology plc based on data compiled for the National Atmospheric Emissions Inventory (NAEI)7 and UK Greenhouse Gas Inventory (GHGI)8. Every year a programme of development work is undertaken to optimise the methodologies employed in compiling the accounts. Assessments in previous years have indicated that a number of splits used to apportion road transport source data to more than one industry should be reviewed. The results of this review have been implemented in the 2011 UK Environmental Accounts for reference period 2009 and years back to 1990.

There are a number of formats for the reporting and recording of atmospheric emissions data, including those used by the Department of Energy and Climate Change (DECC) for reporting greenhouse gases under UNFCCC and the Kyoto Protocol, and for reporting air pollutant emissions to the UN Economic Commission for Europe (UNECE), which differ from the National Accounts consistent measure published by the Office for National Statistics (ONS).

Differences between the National Accounts measure and those for reporting under UNFCCC and the Kyoto Protocol, following the guidance of the IPCC, are shown in Table 10.4.

Emissions of carbon dioxide (Table 10.5)

Carbon dioxide is the main man-made contributor to global warming. The UK contributes about 2 per cent to global man-made emissions which, according to the IPCC, was estimated to be 38 billion tonnes of carbon dioxide in 2004. Carbon dioxide emissions accounted for about 84 per cent of the UK's man-made greenhouse gas emissions in 2009.

Emissions of methane (Table 10.6)

Weighted by global warming potential, methane accounted for about 8 per cent of the UK's greenhouse gas emissions in 2009. Methane emissions, excluding those from natural sources, were 61 per cent below 1990 levels. In 2009, the main sources of methane emissions were agriculture (41 per cent of the total) and landfill sites (37 per cent). Emissions from landfill have reduced by 72 per cent and emissions from agriculture by 19 per cent since 1990.

Emissions of nitrous oxide (Table 10.7)

Weighted by global warming potential, nitrous oxide emissions accounted for about 6 per cent of the UK's man-made greenhouse gas emissions in 2009. Nitrous oxide emissions fell by 49 per cent between 1990 and 2009. The largest reductions were in emissions from adipic acid production between 1998 and 1999 (down 95 per cent). This leaves agriculture as the main source in 2009, accounting for 79 per cent of emissions, mainly from agricultural soils.

Annual rainfall (Table 10.9)

Regional rainfall is derived by the Met Office's National Climate Information Centre for the National Hydrological Monitoring Programme at the Centre for Ecology and Hydrology. These monthly area rainfalls are based initially on a subset of rain gauges (circa 350) but are updated after four to five months with figures using the majority of the UK's rain gauge network.

The regions of England shown in this table correspond to the original nine English regions of the National Rivers Authority (NRA). The NRA became part of the Environment Agency on its creation in April 1996. The figures in this table relate to the country of Wales, not the Environment Agency Welsh Region.

UK weather summary (Table 10.10)

For 2010, initial averages use data available from about 200 observing sites available on 1 January 2011. They represent an initial assessment of the weather that was experienced across the UK during 2010 and how it compares with the 1961 to 1990 average.

For all other years, final averages use quality controlled data from the UK climate network of observing stations. They show the Met Office's best assessment of the weather that was experienced across the UK during the years and how it compares with the 1961 to 1990 average. The columns headed 'Anom' (anomaly) show the difference from, or percentage of, the 1961 to 1990 long-term average.

Biological and chemical quality of rivers and canals (Table 10.11)

The chemical quality of river and canal waters is monitored in a series of separate national surveys in England, Wales and Northern Ireland. The General Quality Assessment Headline Indicator (GQAHI) and General Quality Assessment (GQA) schemes are used in surveys to provide a rigorous and objective method for assessing the basic chemical quality of rivers and canals. In England the GQAHI survey is based on two determinants: dissolved oxygen and ammoniacal nitrogen. In previous years this assessment included biochemical oxygen demand however in 2007 this was removed from the assessment and the historic data recalculated. In Wales the GQA assessment is based on three determinants: dissolved oxygen, biochemical oxygen demand and ammoniacal nitrogen. The GQA grades river stretches into six categories (A-F) of chemical quality, and these in turn have been grouped into four broader groups: good (classes A and B), fair (C and D), poor (E) and bad (F)

To provide a more comprehensive picture of the health of rivers and canals, biological testing has also been carried out. The biological grading is based on the monitoring of tiny animals (invertebrates) which live in or on the bed of the river. Research has shown that there is a relationship between species composition and water quality. Using a procedure known as the River Invertebrate Prediction and Classification System, species groups recorded at a site were compared with those which would be expected to be present in the absence of pollution, allowing for the different environmental characteristics in different parts of the country. Two different summary statistics (known as ecological quality indices) were calculated and then the biological quality was assigned to one of six bands based on a combination of these two statistics.

From 2008, Northern Ireland uses a different classification system than that which was previously used. A unit of area known as a water body is now the classification unit rather than discrete stretches of individual rivers.

Water Framework Directive (WFD) classifications are based on chemical, physical and ecological parameters (referred to as quality elements). The indicators recorded here are just some of the WFD quality elements that are monitored in river water bodies.

It should be noted that the monitoring network only covers selected stretches which the Environment Agency are required to monitor. In England and Wales 32,000 km of river network are monitored out of an estimated total river length of 150,000 km. No canals are classified in Northern Ireland.

Biological and chemical quality of rivers and canals Scotland (Table 10.12)

Scotland's previous classification schemes focused on describing the pollution levels of the water environment. As required by the Water Framework Directive, the new classification scheme for surface waters now assesses:

• the quality of the aquatic ecosystems within rivers, lochs, estuaries and coastal waters

• the extent to which they have been adversely affected by the full range of pressures on the water environment – from water resources and physical habitat to pollution and invasive non-native species

This new scheme which started in 2007 assesses the condition of each river, loch, estuary and coastal water and assigns it a 'status' from of high, good, moderate, poor to bad.

The results on the current condition of our rivers, lochs, estuaries, coasts and ground waters are based primarily on monitoring data collected during 2007. However, as the new monitoring programmes have only been in place for one year, the Scottish Environment Protection Agency (SEPA) has supplemented the limited new monitoring data with data from previous assessments (where relevant and available). This is to ensure the classification results reflect the best current understanding of the status of the water environment. As more monitoring data are collected, SEPA expects its confidence in classification to progressively increase over the next five years.

Prior to 2007, river and canal water quality was based on the Scottish River Classification Scheme of 20 June 1997, which combined chemical, biological, nutrient and aesthetic quality using the following classes: excellent (A1), good (A2), fair (B), poor (C) and seriously polluted (D). The figures in the table are rounded to the nearest 10 km and may not sum to totals.

During 2000 a new digitised river network (DRN) was developed, based on 1:50,000 ordnance survey data digitised by the Institute of Hydrology. The DRN ensures consistency between all SEPA areas and includes the Scottish Islands which were not previously covered. Data based on this network were published for the first time in the 2004 edition of Annual Abstract of Statistics and are not consistent with data published previously. The DRN includes:

• All mainland and island rivers with a catchment area of 10 km2 or more. This is known as the 'baseline network'

• Mainland and island stream stretches with a catchment of less than 10 km2 which are classified as fair, poor or seriously polluted and have been monitored. These are added to the baseline network to give a 'classification network'

It is intended that future emphasis will be placed on the baseline network, which will be the reportable network for the purposes of the European Commission Water Framework Directive. Efforts to improve the quality of the downgraded smaller streams will continue, but once this has been sustainably achieved, their monitoring may be reduced. Many of these streams are the subject of current attention because of their influence on the quality of larger classification Network Rivers.

Using the DRN scheme, data for every routine sampling point are automatically applied to an identified river stretch of predetermined length. The loss in total river length in moving to the DRN (that is despite the first time inclusion of Island Rivers) arises mainly from the exclusion from classification of thousands of small remote headwater streams which were never monitored, but assumed to be of excellent quality. The smaller reduction in length of downgraded waters arises mainly from using 1:50,000 maps for the DRN; in the former system lengths were hand measured from 1:10,000 maps, so more minor channel bends were included.

Reservoir stocks in England and Wales (Table 10.13)

Data are collected for a network of major reservoirs (or reservoir groups) in England and Wales for the National Hydrological Monitoring Programme at the Centre for Ecology and Hydrology. Figures of usable capacity are supplied by the Water PLCs and the Environment Agency at the start of each month and are aggregated to provide an index of the total reservoir stocks for England and Wales.

Water industry expenditure (Table 10.14)

The data is taken from the annual regulatory accounts (and the June return submission to Ofwat) of water and sewerage companies and water companies of England and Wales.

Operating expenditure includes: employment costs, power, Environment Agency charges, bulk supply imports, general overheads, customer services, scientific services, local authority rates, local authority sewerage agencies, materials and consumables, charge for bad and doubtful debts, current cost depreciation and the infrastructure renewals charge.

Capital expenditure figures represent all capital additions (both maintenance and enhancement) but exclude infrastructure renewals expenditure. Figures quoted are before deducting grants and contributions, typically received from developers. Adopted assets at nil cost are not included.

Water pollution incidents (Table 10.15)

The Environment Agency responds to complaints and reported incidents of pollution in England and Wales. Each incident is then logged and categorised according to its severity. The category describes the impact of each incident on water, land and air. The impact of an incident on each medium is considered and reported separately. If no impact has occurred for a particular medium, the incident is reported as a category 4. Before 1999, the reporting system was used only for water pollution incidents; thus the total number of substantiated incidents was lower, as it did not include incidents not relating to the water environment.

Bathing waters (Table 10.16)

Under the EC Bathing Water Directive 76/160/EEC, 11 physical, chemical and microbiological parameters are measured including total and faecal coliforms which are generally considered to be the most important indicators of the extent to which water is contaminated by sewage. The mandatory value for total coliforms is 10,000 per 100 ml, and for faecal coliforms 2,000 per 100 ml. For a bathing water to comply with the coliform standards, the Directive requires that at least 95 per cent of samples taken for each of these parameters over the bathing season are less than or equal to the mandatory values. In the UK a minimum of 20 samples are normally taken at each site. In practice this means that where 20 samples are taken, a maximum of only one sample may exceed the mandatory value for the bathing water to comply, and where less than 20 samples are taken none may exceed the mandatory value for the bathing water to comply.

The bathing water season is from mid-May to end-September in England and Wales, but shorter in Scotland and Northern Ireland. Bathing waters which are closed for the season are excluded for that year.

The table shows Environment Agency regions for England and Wales, the boundaries of which are based on river catchment areas and not county borders. In particular, the figures shown for Wales are the Environment Agency Welsh Region, the boundary of which does not coincide with the boundary of Wales.

Surface and groundwater abstractions (Table 10.17)

Significant changes in the way data is collected and/or reported were made in 1991 (due to the Water Resources Act 1991) and 1999 (commission of National Abstraction Licensing Database). Figures are therefore not strictly comparable with those in previous/intervening years. From 1999, data have been stored and retrieved from one system nationally and are therefore more accurate and reliable. Some regions report licensed and actual abstracts for financial rather than calendar years. As figures represent an average for the whole year expressed as daily amounts, differences between amounts reported for financial and calendar years are small.

Under the Water Act 2003, abstraction of less than 20 m3/day became exempt from the requirement to hold a licence as of 1 April 2005. As a result over 22,000 licences were deregulated, mainly for agricultural or private water supply purposes. However, due to the small volumes involved, this has had a minimal affect on the estimated licensed and actual abstraction totals.

The following changes have occurred in the classification of individual sources:
• Spray irrigation: this category includes small amounts of non-agricultural spray irrigation
• Mineral washing: from 1999 this was not reported as a separate category; licences for 'Mineral washing' are now contained in 'Other industry'
• Private water supply: this was shown as separate category from 1992 and includes private abstractions for domestic use and individual households
• Fish farming, cress growing, amenity ponds: includes amenity ponds, but excludes miscellaneous from 1991

Estimates of remaining recoverable oil and gas reserves (Table 10.18)

Only a small proportion of the estimated remaining recoverable reserves of oil and gas are known with any degree of certainty. The latest oil and gas data for 2008 shows that the upper range of total UK oil reserves was estimated to be around 2.7 billion tonnes, while UK gas reserves were around 1950 billion cubic metres. Of these, proven reserves of oil were 0.4 billion tonnes and proven reserves of gas were 292 billion cubic metres. Compared with a year earlier, proven reserves were 9.7 per cent lower for oil and 14.9per cent lower for gas.

Local authority collected (Table 10.19)

Local authority collected includes household and non-household waste that is collected and disposed of by local authorities. It includes regular household collections, specific recycling collections, and special collections of bulky items, waste received at civic amenity sites, and waste collected from non-household sources that come under the control of local authorities.

Amounts of different materials from household sources collected for recycling (Table 10.20)

Household recycling includes those materials collected for recycling, composting or reuse by local authorities and those collected from household sources by 'private/voluntary' organisations where this material comes under the possession or control of local authorities. It includes residual waste from the household stream which was diverted for recycling by sorting or further treatment. 'Bring sites' are facilities where members of the public can bring recyclable materials (such as paper, glass, cans, textiles, shoes, etc). These are often located at supermarkets or similar locations, but exclude civic amenity sites.

'Civic Amenity sites' refers to household waste collected at sites provided by local authorities for the disposal of excess household and garden waste free of charge, as required by the Refuse Disposal (Amenity) Act 1978. These are also known as Household Waste Recycling Centres.

Noise incidents (Table 10.21)

The table shows trends in the number of incidents reported by local authority Environmental Health Officers (EHO). The figures are from those authorities making returns and are calculated per million people based on the population of the authorities making returns. Environmental health has changed from calculating complaints per million of population to incidents per million of the population in 2004/05. The reason for asking about incidents is to better reflect both the local noise environment and investigatory workloads during the reporting year, while avoiding the double counting which occurs with complaints (that is, multiple complaints about the same incident). This change is reflected in the data, which shows a drop in numbers across all categories.

Most complaints about traffic noise are addressed to highways authorities or Department for Transport (DfT) Regional Directors, and will not necessarily be included in the figures. Similarly, complaints about noise from civil aircraft are generally received by aircraft operators, the airport companies, the DfT or Civil Aviation Authority. Complaints about military flying are dealt with either by Station Commanding Officers or by Ministry of Defence headquarters. It is also true that railway noise will be reported elsewhere. Thus the figures in this table will not necessarily include these complaints and are likely to be considerably understated. Therefore, the information reported to the EHO is considered to give, at best, only a very approximate indication of the trend in noise complaints from these sources.

Over time some of the categories shown in this table have changed. These have included, up until 1996/97, Section 62 of the Control of Pollution Act 1974 which covered noise in the streets; it primarily included the chimes of ice-cream vendors and the use of loudspeakers other than for strictly defined purposes. From 1997/98, all complaints about noise in the street are included with 'vehicles machinery and equipment in streets'. From 1997/98, complaints about roadworks are included with 'vehicles machinery and equipment in streets'.

Material flows (Table 10.22)

Economy-wide material flow accounts record the total mass of natural resources and products that are used by the UK economy, either directly in the production and distribution of products and services, or indirectly through the movement of materials which are displaced in order for production to take place.

The direct movement of materials into the economy derives primarily from domestic extraction. This covers: biomass (agricultural harvest, timber, fish and animal grazing); fossil fuel extraction (such as coal, crude oil and natural gas); mineral extraction (metal ores, industrial minerals such as pottery clay; and construction material such as crushed rock, sand and gravel). This domestic extraction is supplemented by the imports of products, which may be raw materials such as unprocessed agricultural products, but can also be semi-manufactured or finished products. In a similar way the UK produces exports of raw materials, semi-manufactured and finished goods which can be viewed as inputs to the production and consumption of overseas economies.

Indirect flows of natural resources consist of the unused material resulting from domestic extraction, such as mining and quarrying overburden and the soil removed during construction and dredging activities. They also include the movement of used and unused material overseas which is associated with the production and delivery of imports. Water, except for that included directly in products, is excluded.

There are three main indicators used to measure inputs. The Direct Material Input measures the input of used materials into the economy that is all materials which are of economic value and are used in production and consumption activities (including the production of exports). Domestic Material Consumption measures the total amount of material directly used in the economy that is it includes imports but excludes exports. The Total Material Requirement (TMR) measures the total material basis of the economy that is the total primary resource requirements of all the production and consumption activities. It includes not only the direct use of resources for producing exports, but also indirect flows from the production of imports and the indirect flows associated with domestic extraction. Although TMR is widely favoured as a resource use indicator, the estimates of indirect flows are less reliable than those for materials directly used by the economy, and the indicator therefore needs to be considered alongside other indicators.

Between 2007 and 20082 the quantity of natural resources used by the UK economy, known as domestic material consumption, fell by 67 million tonnes (9.9 per cent) to 613 million tonnes. This is the largest recorded fall since records began in 1970. It follows 10 years where resource use has remained broadly unchanged. This means that, with rising levels of economic activity, UK material productivity has been increasing.

The fall in domestic material consumption mainly reflects decreases in the domestic extraction of minerals, with a decrease of 57 million tonnes (19.3 per cent) driven by a sharp fall in the extraction of primary aggregates – crushed stone, sand and gravel – as demand was impacted by the economic downturn. Imports of minerals also fell in 2008, by 10.9 per cent.

Much of the period 1990 to 2007 had seen strong economic growth in the UK and material productivity increased, with material use falling in relation to the level of economic activity. This in part reflects the increasing importance of the service industries in the UK economy. Gross Domestic Product overall continued to increase in 2008 (by 0.5 per cent) and material use fell. The fall in demand for primary aggregates coincides with the contraction in output of the construction industry in 2008.

10.1 Atmospheric emissions on a National Accounts basis[1], 2009

United Kingdom

	Green-house gases[1]	Acid rain precursors[2]	Emissions affecting air quality					Thousand tonnes			
	CO2 equivalent	SO2 equivalent	CO2	PM10[3]	CO	NMVOC[4]	Benzene	Butadiene	Lead	Cadmium	Mercury
Agriculture, forestry and fishing	51,042	475	5,680	20	58	82	0	0	0	0	0
Mining and quarrying	23,443	50	19,041	9	31	96	0	0	0	0	0
Manufacturing	90,583	303	86,862	24	507	281	2	1	41	1	4
Electricity, gas and air conditioning supply	188,324	362	164,909	8	87	52	1	0	3	0	2
Construction	9,803	37	9,039	5	54	48	0	0	0	0	0
Wholesale and retail trade	16,405	43	12,773	4	60	49	0	0	8	0	0
Transport and storage	86,438	672	84,929	37	160	35	3	0	3	1	0
Accommodation and food services	2,770	4	2,562	0	12	1	0	0	0	0	0
Financial and insurance activities	300	1	189	0	7	1	0	0	0	0	0
Real estate activities	5,639	9	5,072	1	30	3	0	0	0	0	0
Public administration and defence	6,503	37	6,254	1	32	4	0	0	0	0	0
Education	3,518	6	3,267	1	7	1	0	0	1	0	0
Human health and social work activites	4,313	5	3,977	0	7	1	0	0	0	0	0
Arts, entertainment and recreation	2,839	17	2,660	1	12	6	0	0	0	0	1
Activities of households as employers	222	0	220	0	47	4	0	0	0	0	0
Consumer expenditure	144,329	190	139,547	50	1,217	246	12	1	5	0	0
Total	636,472	2,211	546,982	162	2,333	933	20	2	63	4	7
of which, emissions from road transport	114,392	278	113,319	27	1,080	87	4	1	2	0	0

1 Carbon dioxide, methane, nitrous oxide, hydro-fluorocarbons, perfluorocarbons and sulphur hexafluoride expressed as thousand tonnes of carbon dioxide equivalent.

2 Sulphur dioxide, nitrogen oxides and ammonia expressed as thousand tonnes of sulphur dioxide equivalent.

3 PM10's are particulate matter arising from incomplete combustion.

4 Non-methane Volatile Compounds, including benzene and 1,3-butadiene.

Source: AEA Energy & Environment, ONS

10.2 Road Transport Emissions by Pollutant

United Kingdom

Thousand tonnes

Pollutant		1996	1997	1998	1999	2000	2001	2002	2003	2004	2005	2006	2007	2008	2009
Greenhouse gases[1] *of which*	I6BZ	117,979	120,082	119,685	120,650	119,806	119,521	121,859	121,444	122,228	122,615	122,943	124,007	119,242	114,392
Carbon dioxide	I6C2	115,939	118,069	117,693	118,691	117,910	117,738	120,150	119,819	120,671	121,135	121,508	122,623	118,038	113,319
Methane	I6C3	466	430	396	362	317	276	247	221	198	178	163	147	129	89
Nitrous oxide	I6C4	1,573	1,583	1,596	1,597	1,579	1,506	1,462	1,403	1,359	1,303	1,272	1,237	1,075	983
Acid rain precursors[2] *of which*	I6C5	680	660	642	614	586	548	517	487	463	434	406	376	339	278
Sulphur dioxide	I6C6	38	28	23	14	6	3	3	3	3	2	2	2	1	0
Nitrogen oxides	I6C7	625	610	592	569	536	504	476	449	428	402	376	349	315	256
Ammonia	I6C8	17	22	27	31	44	41	38	35	33	30	28	26	23	21
PM10	I6C9	47	46	45	44	39	38	36	35	34	33	32	31	29	27
Carbon monoxide	I6CA	5,365	5,012	4,835	4,487	3,919	3,527	3,144	2,803	2,493	2,169	1,929	1,729	1,554	1,080
NMVOCs	I6CB	750	684	629	563	481	411	348	293	247	208	179	156	137	87
Benzene	I6CC	22	22	21	20	13	13	12	11	10	9	8	7	6	4
1,3-Butadiene	I6CD	10	9	8	7	6	5	5	4	3	3	3	2	2	1

1 Greenhouse gases are made up of carbon dioxide, methane & nitrous oxide. Weight in carbon dioxide equivalent.

2 Acid rain precursors are made of sulphur dioxide, nitrogen & ammonia. Weight in sulphur dioxide equivalent.

Sources: AEA Energy & Environment;
Office for National Statistics;
environment.accounts@ons.gsi.gov.uk

10.3 Greenhouse gas emissions: weighted by global warming potential[1,3,4,5,6]

United Kingdom

Million tonnes (carbon dioxide equivalent[4])

		1995	1996	1997	1998	1999	2000	2001	2002	2003	2004	2005	2006	2007	2008	2009
Net CO_2 emissions (emissions minus removals)	JZCK	550.8	572.8	548.7	551.6	542.3	549.4	561.3	543.7	553.4	552.6	549.7	546.3	537.8	525.1	473.7
Methane (CH_4)	GXDO	90.1	87.1	81.6	76.9	71.6	66.7	60.9	57.9	52.0	50.2	48.6	47.2	45.7	44.5	43.6
Nitrous Oxide (N_2O)	GXDP	56.3	56.2	57.2	56.6	45.9	44.9	42.4	40.7	40.1	40.7	39.5	37.7	37.2	36.4	34.6
Hydrofluorocarbons (HFC)	JZCN	15.5	16.6	19.0	16.8	10.0	8.7	9.4	9.5	10.4	9.5	10.2	10.6	10.5	10.8	10.9
Perfluorocarbons (PFC)	JZCO	0.5	0.5	0.4	0.4	0.4	0.5	0.4	0.3	0.3	0.3	0.3	0.3	0.2	0.2	0.1
Sulphur hexafluoride (SF_6)	JZCP	1.2	1.3	1.2	1.3	1.4	1.8	1.4	1.5	1.3	1.1	1.1	0.9	0.8	0.7	0.7
Kyoto greenhouse gas basket[2]	F92X	712.3	732.4	706.1	702.0	670.2	671.2	675.5	654.2	658.2	656.0	651.4	645.0	634.7	620.5	566.3

1 Figures for each individual gas include the Land use, Land-Use Change and Forestry sector (LULUCF). These emissions cover the UK and Crown Dependencies,but exclude emissions from UK Overseas Territories.
2 Kyoto basket total differs slightly from sum of individual pollutants above as the basket uses a narrower definition for the LULUCF. This includes emissions from the UK, Crown Dependencies and UK Overseas Territories.
3 Kyoto base year consists of emissions of CO^2, CH^4, and N^2O in 1990 and of HFCs, PFCs and SF6 in 1995. Includes an allowance for net emissions from LULUCF in 1990.

4 The entire time series is revised each year to take account of methodological improvements in the UK emissions inventory.
5 Emissions are presented as carbon dioxide equivalent in line with international reporting and carbon trading. To convert Carbon dioxide into carbon equivalents, divide figures by 44/12.
6 Figures shown do not include any adjustment for the effect of the EU Emisions Trading Scheme (EUETS), which was introduced in 2005.

Source: AEA Department for Energy and Climate Change: 0300 060 4000

10.4 Greenhouse gas emissions bridging table

Environmental Accounts measure to UNFCC[1] measure

Thousand tonnes CO2 equivilent

		1990	2000	2001	2002	2003	2004	2005	2006	2007	2008	2009
Greenhouse gases- CO2, CH4, N2O, HFC, PFCs and SF62												
Environmental Accounts measure	JKRU	815,161	729,711	738,656	718,556	727,253	730,895	731,000	717,112	708,019	694,615	636,472
less												
Bunker emissions[3]	A43J	24,853	37,581	37,015	34,911	36,655	40,402	43,626	46,471	45,833	45,895	43,604
CO2 biomass[4]	A43K	2,980	6,716	7,388	7,633	8,484	9,594	10,903	10,901	11,655	12,909	13,338
Cross-boundary adjustment[5]	A43L	11,345	15,737	20,073	22,935	24,638	25,505	25,621	15,278	16,534	15,734	13,517
plus												
Crown Dependencies[6]	EQ44	1,740	1,905	1,654	1,612	1,501	1,514	1,610	1,641	1,753	1,662	1,691
Landuse change / forestry (LULUCF)[7]	A43M	3,876	369	-131	-1,000	-1,406	-2,486	-3,027	-3,201	-3,567	-4,005	-4,122
Overseas Territories (inc. net emissions from LULUCF)	JTL8	1,709	1,947	2,042	2,072	2,095	2,176	2,236	2,342	2,487	2,386	2,406
UNFCCC reported in the UK Greenhouse Gas Inventory[8]	A43N	783,308	673,900	677,745	655,760	659,667	656,598	651,669	645,244	634,670	620,121	565,987
Kyoto Greenhouse Gas Basket [9,10]	JTL9	778,289	671,196	675,473	654,161	658,211	656,009	651,376	644,989	634,665	620,462	566,327

1 United Nations Framework Convention on Climate Change.
2 Carbon dioxide, methane, nitrous oxide, hydrofluorocarbons, perfluorocarbon and sulphur hexafluoride expressed as thousand tonnes of carbon dioxide equivalent.
3 Bunker emissions include IPCC memo items International Aviation (source no.126) and international Shipping (source no.127).
4 Emissions arising from wood, straw, biogases and poultry litter combustion for energy production.
5 Emissions generated by UK households and businesses transport and travel abroad, net of emissions generated by non-residents travel and transport in the UK.

6 Revisions to the Crown Dependancies are due to a change in their treatment in the National Inventories and their inclusion in the UNFCCC total.
7 Emissions from deforestation, soils and changes in forest and other woody biomass.
8 http://www.airquality.co.uk/reports/cat07/1005070919_ukghgi-90-08_main_chapters_Issue3_Final.pdf
9 This is the UK total for the sum of 6 individual pollutants and differs slightly from the Kyoto Greenhouse Gas Basket totals which uses a narrower definition of LULUCF and includes emissions from the UK Overseas Territories (Gibraltar the Falkland Islands,the Cayman Islands, Montserrat, Bermuda).
10 http://www.decc.gov.uk/en/content/cms/statistics/climate_change/gg_emissions/uk_emissions/2008_final/2008_final.aspx

Source: AEA Energy & Environment, DECC, ONS

10.5 Estimated emissions[1] of carbon dioxide (CO_2)

United Kingdom

Million tonnes as CO_2

By source NC Category		1970	1980	1990	1997	1998	1999	2000	2001	2002	2003	2004	2005	2006	2007	2008	2009
Energy Supply Total	I6AH	259.8	261.5	241.2	198.1	202.4	191.8	201.8	212.4	209.5	216.8	215.1	216.1	219.9	215.9	209.4	185.3
Business Total	I6AI	205.0	132.0	109.8	102.9	102.9	103.9	104.1	104.2	93.9	95.6	93.6	93.8	91.3	89.2	87.4	75.9
Transport Total	I6AJ	72.5	87.9	120.0	126.0	125.1	126.2	125.2	125.3	127.9	127.5	128.8	129.3	129.6	130.7	126.0	120.8
Public Total	I6AK	23.8	19.9	14.0	14.3	12.7	12.4	11.7	12.1	10.3	10.1	11.1	11.0	10.0	9.3	9.3	8.2
Residential Total	I6AL	96.2	84.4	79.0	85.0	86.9	86.7	87.0	89.3	86.1	86.9	88.4	84.3	81.7	78.1	79.9	75.2
Agriculture Total	I6AM	6.2	5.3	5.2	5.3	5.1	5.1	4.8	4.8	4.8	4.8	4.6	4.5	4.3	4.1	4.1	4.1
Industrial Process Total	I6AN	20.9	14.1	16.2	15.6	15.6	15.5	14.7	13.4	12.5	13.4	13.8	14.0	13.2	14.5	13.4	8.8
Land Use Change	I6AO	-		3.1	1.1	0.5	0.3	-0.4	-0.9	-1.8	-2.1	-3.2	-3.7	-3.9	-4.3	-4.7	-4.8
Waste Management	I6AP	1.4	1.4	1.2	0.5	0.5	0.5	0.5	0.5	0.5	0.4	0.4	0.4	0.3	0.3	0.3	0.3
Total	I6AQ	685.9	606.4	589.7	548.7	551.6	542.3	549.4	561.3	543.7	553.4	552.6	549.7	546.3	537.8	525.1	473.7

1 The entire time series is revised each year to take account of methodological improvements in the UK emissions inventory.
2 These figures include emissions from the UK and Crown Dependancies, but exclude emissions from Overseas Territories.

Source: AEA Department for Energy and Climate Change: 0300 060 4000

10.6 Estimated emissions[1] of methane (CH_4)[2]

United Kingdom

Thousand tonnes

By source NC Category		1996	1997	1998	1999	2000	2001	2002	2003	2004	2005	2006	2007	2008	2009
Energy Supply Total	I6AR	1,018	970	884	791	725	697	686	549	536	484	451	409	395	399
Business Total	I6AS	16	16	16	16	16	15	13	14	14	14	14	13	13	11
Transport Total	I6AT	23	21	19	18	15	14	12	11	10	9	8	7	6	5
Public	I6AU	2	1	1	1	1	1	1	1	1	1	1	1	1	1
Residential Total	I6AV	41	38	40	42	32	29	24	22	21	19	20	21	23	22
Agriculture Total	I6AW	1,044	1,013	1,013	1,011	969	910	898	898	905	916	899	893	873	858
Industrial Process Total	I6AX	11	10	8	7	6	6	6	7	7	6	6	6	6	5
Land Use Change	I6AY	1	2	1	1	2	2	2	2	2	1	2	2	2	1
Waste Management Total	I6AZ	1,992	1,817	1,680	1,521	1,410	1,228	1,114	974	896	865	845	823	798	774
Grand Total	I6B2	4,149	3,888	3,662	3,408	3,177	2,901	2,756	2,477	2,391	2,314	2,245	2,176	2,117	2,076

1 The entire time series is revised each year to take account of methodological improvements in the UK emissions inventory.
2 These figures include emissions from the UK and Crown Dependancies, but exclude emissions from Overseas Territories.

Source: AEA Department for Energy and Climate Change: 0300 060 4000

10.7 Estimated emissions[1] of nitrous oxide (N_2O) [1,2]

United Kingdom

Thousand tonnes

By source NC Category		1995	1996	1997	1998	1999	2000	2001	2002	2003	2004	2005	2006	2007	2008	2009
Energy Supply Total	I6A7	5.5	5.4	4.9	5.1	4.7	5.1	5.4	5.4	5.4	5.2	5.4	5.6	5.2	4.8	4.4
Business Total	I6A8	4.7	4.6	4.4	4.3	4.3	4.2	4.2	4.1	4.1	4.2	4.2	4.2	4.2	4.1	3.5
Transport Total	I6A9	6.3	5.9	5.9	6.0	6.0	6.0	5.8	5.6	5.5	5.4	5.2	5.1	5.0	4.5	4.2
Public Total	I6AA	0.1	0.1	0.1	0.1	0.1	0.1	0.1	0.0	0.0	0.0	0.0	0.0	0.0	0.0	0.0
Residential Total	I6AB	0.7	0.8	0.7	0.7	0.7	0.6	0.6	0.5	0.5	0.4	0.4	0.4	0.4	0.4	0.4
Agriculture Total	I6AC	109.1	109.6	112.9	110.0	108.1	103.7	97.9	99.5	97.2	96.7	95.5	91.4	89.1	89.0	88.4
Industrial Process Total	I6AD	48.2	47.9	48.5	49.4	17.5	18.1	15.7	9.1	9.6	12.3	9.7	7.8	9.1	8.0	3.9
Land Use Change	I6AE	2.6	2.6	2.6	2.6	2.6	2.5	2.4	2.4	2.3	2.3	2.2	2.2	2.1	2.1	2.1
Waste Management Total	I6AF	4.3	4.4	4.4	4.4	4.4	4.6	4.6	4.6	4.6	4.6	4.7	4.7	4.7	4.5	4.6
Total	I6AG	181.5	181.2	184.4	182.5	148.2	144.8	136.6	131.4	129.3	131.2	127.4	121.5	119.9	117.5	111.5

1 The entire time series is revised each year to take account of methodological improvements in the UK emissions inventory.
2 These figures include emissions from the UK and Crown Dependencies, but exclude emissions from Overseas Territories.

Source: Department for Energy and Climate Control: 0300 060 4000

10.8 Material flows[1]

United Kingdom

Million tonnes

		1980	1985	1990	1995	2000	2001	2002	2003	2004	2005	2006	2007	2008	2009
Domestic extraction															
Biomass															
Agricultural harvest	JKUN	47	47	46	47	51	46	51	48	49	48	46	43	49	48
Timber	JKUO	4	5	6	8	8	8	8	8	8	9	8	9	8	8
Animal grazing	JKUP	49	48	47	45	43	43	43	43	43	43	43	43	43	43
Fish	JKUQ	1	1	1	1	1	1	1	1	1	1	1	1	1	1
Total biomass	JKUR	101	100	101	101	103	98	103	100	101	100	98	96	101	101
Minerals															
Ores	JKUS	1	1	0	0	0	0	0	0	0	0	0	0	0	0
Clay	JKUT	25	23	21	18	15	14	14	14	15	14	13	13	11	7
Other industrial minerals	JKUU	11	11	11	10	8	9	8	9	8	8	8	8	8	8
Sand and gravel	JKUV	110	112	128	106	106	105	98	95	102	99	97	98	90	70
Crushed stone	JKUW	150	160	212	200	176	183	173	170	175	169	173	176	152	125
Total minerals	JKUX	297	307	373	334	305	311	293	288	300	290	292	295	262	210
Fossil fuels															
Coal	JKUY	130	94	94	53	31	32	30	28	25	20	19	17	18	18
Natural gas	JKUZ	55	37	42	71	108	106	104	103	96	88	80	72	70	60
Crude oil	JKVA	80	128	92	130	126	117	116	106	95	85	77	77	73	69
Total fossil fuels	JKVB	266	259	228	254	266	254	250	237	217	193	175	166	161	147
Total domestic extraction	JKVC	664	666	702	688	673	663	645	626	618	584	565	557	524	458
Imports															
Biomass	JKVD	30	32	39	41	46	50	50	53	54	54	54	54	52	50
Minerals	JKVE	24	36	43	53	52	55	56	57	61	59	60	64	57	54
Fossil fuels	JKVF	76	80	95	82	93	109	105	113	138	148	159	158	152	148
Other Products	JKVG	10	9	10	11	16	16	16	16	16	16	16	16	16	16
Total imports	JKVH	141	157	187	188	208	230	227	240	269	278	290	292	278	268
Exports															
Biomass	JKVI	8	11	14	16	18	14	16	20	19	20	21	21	22	20
Minerals	JKVJ	26	22	26	39	45	44	42	45	48	49	51	50	48	44
Fossil fuels	JKVK	63	105	72	111	125	127	130	114	109	99	94	90	89	87
Other Products	JKVL	4	7	5	8	9	9	9	9	9	9	9	9	9	9
Total exports	JKVM	101	146	117	173	197	194	197	188	185	177	174	171	168	160
Domestic Material Consumption															
(domestic extraction + imports - exports)	JKVU	704	677	772	704	685	700	677	678	703	686	682	679	634	566
of which															
biomass	G9A8	123	121	126	126	130	133	137	133	136	134	132	129	132	130
minerals	G9A9	296	320	390	348	312	323	306	300	313	301	301	309	271	220
fossil fuels	G9AA	279	234	251	225	234	236	225	236	246	243	240	234	223	208
Indirect flows															
- from domestic extraction[2] (excl soil erosion)	JKVN	643	635	703	642	576	583	566	550	548	519	487	493	494	471
Of which:															
unused biomass	JKVO	32	36	37	37	41	35	40	38	39	38	36	34	39	38
fossil fuels	JKVP	297	281	319	282	234	244	228	212	206	180	151	152	162	165
minerals and ores	JKVQ	120	120	144	121	104	103	101	100	104	101	100	105	92	71
soil excavation and dredging	JKVR	195	199	203	201	197	200	197	200	199	200	201	201	201	197
- from production of raw materials and semi-natural products imported	JKVS	368	423	457	527	600	697	628	651	672	749	783	749	686	558
Other indicators															
Physical Trade Balance (imports-exports)[3]	DZ76	40	11	70	14	11	37	31	51	85	101	116	121	110	107
Direct Material Input (domestic extraction + imports)	JKVT	805	822	889	877	882	894	873	866	888	863	855	850	802	726
Total Material Requirement (direct material input + indirect flows)	JKVV	1816	1880	2049	2045	2057	2174	2067	2068	2107	2130	2126	2091	1982	1755

1 See chapter text. Components may not sum to totals due to rounding.
2 Indirect flows from domestic extraction relate to unused material which is moved during extraction, such as overburden from mining and quarrying.
3 A positive physical trade balance indicates a net import of material into the UK. This calculation of the PTB differs from the National Accounts formula (exports - imports) because flows of materials and products are considered the inverse of the flows of money recorded in the National Accounts.

Sources: Office for National Statistics; environment.accounts@ons.gsi.gov.uk

10.9 Annual rainfall: by region

United Kingdom

Millimetres and percentages

Region[1]		1971 - 2000[3] rainfall average (= 100%) millimetres	1999	2000	2001	2002	2003	2004	2005	2006	2007	2008	2009	2010
United Kingdom	JSJB	1084	114	123	97	118	83	112	100	108	110	120	112	88
North West	JSJC	1176	111	132	94	121	85	116	96	114	110	126	113	84
Northumbria	JSJD	831	106	132	106	124	80	120	111	101	105	134	116	105
Severn Trent	JSJE	759	120	132	104	119	81	110	92	103	123	121	102	84
Yorkshire	JSJF	814	110	136	99	125	82	114	96	110	115	130	105	91
Anglian	JSJG	603	113	129	124	118	86	115	89	102	118	116	99	97
Thames	JSLK	700	111	137	116	128	81	103	79	106	118	115	104	87
Southern	JSLL	782	105	148	114	129	85	97	79	101	106	108	109	94
Wessex	JSLM	866	118	136	100	132	83	98	89	100	113	116	107	79
South West	JSLN	1208	113	128	92	121	78	99	90	92	110	112	110	83
England	JSLO	819	113	133	105	123	82	109	91	103	114	120	107	89
Wales[2]	JSLP	1373	116	133	98	119	83	108	95	107	108	121	109	82
Scotland	JSLQ	1440	116	113	91	112	84	117	110	114	109	119	117	87
Northern Ireland	JSLR	1111	111	110	81	127	84	98	96	104	99	114	113	94

1 The regions of England shown in this table correspond to the original nine
English regions of the National Rivers Authority (NRA); the NRA became
part of the Environment Agency upon its creation in April 1996.
2 The figures in this table relate to the country of Wales, not the Environment Agency Welsh Region.
3 1971-2000 averages have been derived using arithmetic averages of Met Office areal rainfall.

Sources: The Met Office; Centre for Ecology and Hydrology

10.10 UK Annual Weather Summary

	Max Temp		Min Temp		Mean Temp		Sunshine		Rainfall	
	Actual (degrees celsius)	Anomaly (degrees celsius)	Actual (degrees celsius)	Anomaly (degrees celsius)	Actual (degrees celsius)	Anomaly (degrees celsius)	Actual (hours/ day)	Anomaly (%)	Actual (mm)	Anomaly (%)
	WLRL	WLRM	WLRO	WLRP	WLRR	WLRS	WLRX	WLRY	WLSH	WLSI
1989	13.1	1.2	5.5	0.7	9.3	1.0	1563.8	116.9	1018.5	92.6
1990	13.1	1.2	5.8	0.9	9.4	1.1	1490.7	111.4	1172.8	106.7
1991	12.1	0.3	5.1	0.2	8.6	0.3	1302.0	97.3	998.2	90.8
1992	12.3	0.4	5.2	0.4	8.7	0.4	1290.8	96.5	1186.8	107.9
1993	11.8	-0.1	5.0	0.1	8.4	0.0	1218.6	91.1	1121.1	102.0
1994	12.4	0.5	5.5	0.6	8.9	0.6	1366.9	102.2	1184.7	107.7
1995	13.0	1.1	5.4	0.6	9.2	0.9	1588.5	118.7	1023.7	93.1
1996	11.7	-0.1	4.7	-0.1	8.2	-0.2	1403.5	104.9	916.6	83.4
1997	13.1	1.3	5.8	1.0	9.4	1.1	1430.3	106.9	1024.0	93.1
1998	12.6	0.8	5.8	1.0	9.1	0.8	1268.4	94.8	1265.1	115.1
1999	13.0	1.1	5.9	1.0	9.4	1.1	1419.4	106.1	1239.1	112.5
2000	12.7	0.8	5.6	0.8	9.1	0.8	1367.5	102.2	1337.3	121.5
2001	12.4	0.6	5.3	0.5	8.8	0.5	1411.9	105.5	1052.8	95.5
2002	13.0	1.1	6.0	1.2	9.5	1.2	1304.0	97.5	1283.7	116.5
2003	13.5	1.6	5.6	0.7	9.5	1.2	1587.4	118.7	904.2	82.0
2004	13.0	1.2	6.0	1.2	9.5	1.2	1361.4	101.8	1210.1	110.1
2005	13.1	1.2	5.9	1.1	9.5	1.1	1399.2	104.6	1083.0	98.4
2006	13.4	1.5	6.1	1.3	9.7	1.4	1495.9	111.8	1175.9	106.8
2007	13.3	1.4	6.0	1.1	9.6	1.3	1450.7	108.4	1197.1	108.8
2008	12.7	0.8	5.5	0.6	9.1	0.7	1388.8	103.8	1295.0	117.7
2009	12.8	1.0	5.6	0.7	9.2	0.9	1467.4	109.7	1213.3	110.2
2010	11.7	-0.1	4.2	-0.6	8.0	-0.4	1456.0	108.8	950.5	86.4

Source: Met Office

10.11 Biological[1] and chemical[2] water quality of rivers and canals[3]
England, Wales and Northern Ireland

| | | Percentage of river surveyed (%) | | | | | | Percentage of total | |
| | | Good | | Fair | | Poor | Bad | Good or fair | Poor or bad |
	Years	A	B	C	D	E	F		
Biological quality									
North East	1990	35.8	28.9	12.4	7.3	10.0	5.6	84.4	15.6
	2009	50.6	23.5	12.2	7.9	5.6	0.3	94.1	5.9
North West	1990	14.4	26.2	18.7	6.2	14.1	20.3	65.6	34.4
	2009	26.4	38.0	16.6	9.8	7.8	1.3	90.9	9.1
Midlands	1990	10.6	25.4	27.8	19.4	11.4	5.4	83.2	16.8
	2009	25.0	34.7	24.4	7.9	6.0	2.1	92.0	8.0
Anglian	1990	13.1	37.2	36.5	9.2	2.7	1.3	96.0	4.0
	2009	39.8	43.6	10.3	5.6	0.4	0.2	99.3	0.7
Thames	1990	25.9	30.2	24.4	9.4	6.7	3.4	89.9	10.1
	2009	34.1	29.1	23.8	6.9	5.3	0.7	94.0	6.0
Southern	1990	37.3	30.1	24.4	6.3	1.8	-	98.2	1.8
	2009	49.0	34.1	13.5	2.4	0.9	0.0	99.1	0.9
South West	1990	42.4	35.8	14.6	4.0	2.8	0.5	96.7	3.3
	2009	65.0	27.5	6.7	0.7	0.1	0.0	99.9	0.1
England[4]	1990	28.6	34.0	19.7	7.5	6.5	3.6	89.9	10.1
	2009	39.9	32.7	16.0	6.4	4.2	0.9	94.9	5.1
Wales	1990	37.2	41.3	14.3	5.4	1.6	0.2	98.3	1.7
	2009	34.6	52.5	11.4	0.8	0.7	0.0	99.3	0.7
Chemical quality									
North East	1990	39.3	29.0	11.5	7.7	10.5	2.0	87.5	12.5
	2009	73.2	13.0	8.3	4.0	1.6	0.0	98.4	1.6
North West	1990	36.8	21.4	17.3	10.2	10.9	3.5	85.6	14.4
	2009	67.9	16.0	10.6	2.6	2.7	0.2	97.1	2.9
Midlands	1990	19.0	30.0	23.7	14.2	12.8	0.3	86.9	13.1
	2009	47.2	29.6	14.8	4.9	3.5	0.0	96.5	3.5
Anglian	1990	4.1	25.6	38.6	18.8	12.2	0.8	87.0	13.0
	2009	19.0	42.1	26.6	7.7	4.3	0.3	95.4	4.6
Thames	1990	17.6	35.3	21.9	11.3	13.6	0.3	86.1	13.9
	2009	55.6	27.6	11.1	3.9	1.7	0.0	98.3	1.7
Southern	1990	27.1	29.8	26.3	11.4	5.5	-	94.5	5.5
	2009	32.4	37.4	20.2	6.8	3.3	0.0	96.7	3.3
South West	1990	46.8	30.8	11.5	7.0	3.9	-	96.1	3.9
	2009	79.9	12.0	5.5	1.2	1.4	0.0	98.6	1.4
England[4]	1990	25.5	29.7	21.6	11.9	10.4	1.0	88.7	11.3
	2009	56.0	24.0	13.0	4.2	2.7	0.1	97.2	2.8
Wales	1990	51.9	34.4	7.6	3.7	1.6	0.8	97.6	2.4
	2009	75.1	19.6	3.1	0.8	1.3	0.1	98.6	1.4

Northern Ireland — Percentage of river waterbodies

	Years	High	Good	Moderate	Poor	Bad	No Data
Overall river quality[5]	2008	0.3	21.0	49.0	25.7	3.7	0.2
	2009	1.0	24.3	44.9	24.7	4.9	0.2

1 Based on the River invertebrate Prediction and Classification System (RIV-PACS).
2 Based on the General Quality Assessment Headline Indicator (GQAHI) scheme for England, and the General Quality Assessment (GQA) scheme for Wales.
3 See chapter text.
4 Figures for the English regions will not add to the national figure for England because a small amount of river lengths which are located along the border between England and Wales are counted in both the national figures for England and Wales.

5 Based on the Water Framework Directive (WFD) classification scheme
6 Based on WFD classification of Soluble Reactive Phosphorus, PH, Dissolved Oxygen and Ammonia.

Source: Environment Agency;
Northern Ireland Environment Agency

10.12 Overall status[1] of rivers and canals in Scotland, 2009[2]

Kilometres and percentages

	High	Maximum ecological potential[3]	Good	Good ecological potential[3]	Moderate	Moderate ecological potential[3]	Poor	Poor ecological potential[3]	Bad	Bad ecological potential[3]
Number of river water bodies	171	2	974	141	509	60	289	61	125	60
River length surveyed (km)	1309	35	9937	1337	6154	565	3036	579	1508	665
River length surveyed (percentages)	5.2	0.1	39.6	5.3	24.5	2.2	12.1	2.3	6.0	2.6
Change in percentage from 2007 results	5.2	0.1	39.6	5.3	24.5	2.2	12.1	2.3	6.0	2.6

Water quality[2, 4]

	High	Good	Moderate	Poor	Bad
Number of river water bodies	1118	729	475	61	9
River length surveyed (km)	11371	7611	5325	729	89
River length surveyed (percentages)	45.3	30.3	21.2	2.9	0.4

Source: Scottish Environment Protection Agency

1 Overall status includes results from tools sensitive to habitat changes, flow alteration and alien species.
2 From 2007 onwards the reporting for river quality is changing due to the move towards Water Framework Directive (WFD).
3 Ecological potential is used to classify artificial and heavily modified water bodies.
4 This is water quality only, so excludes results from tools sensitive to habitat changes, flow alteration and alien species.

10.13 Reservoir stocks in England and Wales:[1] by month

Percentages

		1999	2000	2001	2002	2003	2004	2005	2006	2007	2008	2009	2010
January	JTAS	95.8	95.8	94.8	86.5	95.1	79.9	91.2	85.9	92.2	89.8	92.4	90.2
February	JTAT	97.0	95.9	94.4	93.7	95.0	93.8	92.3	88.7	93.7	95.7	95.3	92.0
March	JTAU	96.5	97.4	95.0	95.5	92.1	92.1	92.1	91.2	96.7	95.6	93.3	91.4
April	JTAV	96.9	95.1	95.5	94.5	92.3	94.4	93.6	96.2	95.2	97.3	94.5	94.0
May	JTAW	97.0	97.0	96.7	91.9	88.6	94.7	95.0	93.4	91.9	95.1	92.0	91.9
June	JTAX	95.4	95.7	91.9	97.0	93.1	90.5	93.0	94.4	91.1	92.6	93.3	86.2
July	JTAY	92.0	93.7	85.1	94.9	87.0	84.8	85.6	88.4	94.4	90.6	88.6	78.9
August	JTAZ	82.6	88.5	80.7	91.1	81.1	78.5	77.9	77.2	93.5	92.0	91.0	77.3
September	JTBA	76.9	83.2	77.9	85.9	69.9	82.4	71.5	70.7	88.3	92.5	89.7	75.5
October	JTBB	79.7	88.0	77.0	77.3	60.4	84.2	67.4	67.8	86.1	90.9	84.0	81.0
November	JTBC	81.7	95.1	85.5	82.9	53.0	87.5	77.2	80.0	81.2	93.7	82.0	82.0
December	JTBD	84.9	96.7	87.9	91.8	60.9	86.2	83.8	89.8	82.4	93.1	92.6	86.9

1 Reservoir stocks are the percentage of useable capacity based on a representative
selection of reservoirs; the percentages relate to the beginning of each month.

Sources: Water PLCs;
Environment Agency;
Centre for Ecology and Hydrology: 01491 838800

10.14 Water industry expenditure[1]
England and Wales

£ million

		1998 /99	1999 /00	2000 /01	2001 /02	2002 /03	2003 /04	2004 /05	2005 /06	2006 /07	2007 /08	2008 /09	2009 /10
Operating expenditure													
Water supply	KQQX	2,386.1	2,448.1	2,391.0	2,426.9	2,544.2	2,676.5	2,690.7	2,942.7	3,118.6	3,244.9	3,377.5	3,405.3
Sewerage services	KQQY	1,971.3	2,069.8	2,087.1	2,167.6	2,265.2	2,319.4	2,499.3	2,708.1	2,876.2	3,049.0	3,110.9	3,213.3
Capital expenditure													
Water supply	KQSX	1,299.6	1,285.6	934.7	1,128.6	1,345.8	1,346.5	1,308.6	1,282.5	1,676.6	1,882.9	1,802.9	1,534.1
Sewerage	KQSY	443.3	454.1	322.0	306.5	469.5	590.6	575.5	476.2	585.3	583.5	604.5	582.8
Sewage treatment and disposal	KQSZ	1,386.9	1,435.4	1,046.3	999.7	1,068.0	1,235.4	1,185.6	1,046.1	1,289.6	1,542.3	1,467.3	1,148.8

1 See chapter text. All in outturn prices.

Source: Office of Water Services: 0121 644 1300

10.15 Water pollution incidents[1,3]
United Kingdom

Numbers

		1999[2]	2000[2]	2001[2]	2002[2]	2003[2]	2004[2]	2005[2]	2006[2]	2007[2]	2008[2]	2009[2]	2010
Categories 1 to 3													
Environment Agency Regions													
North West	**MKDB**	1668	1757	1734	1805	1534	1091	1056	913	932	861	864	..
North East	**MKDC**	1828	1822	1952	1789	1971	1692	1448	1132	993	823	1043	..
Midlands	**MKDD**	2804	3106	2862	2843	2464	1955	1890	1914	1671	1532	1498	..
Anglian	**MKDE**	1726	1369	1606	1716	1616	1418	1290	1223	1327	1765	1526	..
Thames	**MKDF**	1208	1379	1510	1630	1447	1211	1203	1159	1023	881	1047	..
Southern	**MKDG**	1317	1540	1585	1511	1543	1218	955	1020	887	768	932	..
South West	**MKDH**	2463	2294	2292	1929	1882	1689	1744	1539	1343	1076	1263	..
Welsh	**MKDI**	1360	1395	1475	1287	1356	1309	1260	1202	1193	954	1132	..
England and Wales	**MKDJ**	14374	14662	15016	14510	13813	11583	10846	10102	9369	8660	9305	..
Scotland[3]	**MKDK**	2306	2345	1829	1409	1708	1480	1377	1641	1782	1846	1793	1666
Northern Ireland	**MKDL**	1507	1705	1561	1517	1552	1227	1174	1133	1292	1237	1248	..
By category in England and Wales													
Category 1	**MKDM**	90	77	118	82	94	114	99	86	70	74	74	..
Category 2	**MKDN**	863	758	860	784	685	594	562	519	452	368	409	..
Category 3	**MKDO**	13421	13827	14038	13644	13034	10875	10 185	9497	8847	8218	8822	..
Category 4[2,4]	**MKDP**	16548	21744	18706	15370	15813	13613	12658	11 932	11339	10603	12050	..
Total substantiated incidents[4]	**MKDQ**	30 922	36406	33722	29880	29626	25196	23504	22034	20708	19 263	21355	..

1 See chapter text. Substantiated incidents to water, unless otherwise specified.
2 From 1999, categories 1-3 do not include all substantiated incidents to water. An additional category (Category 4) was introduced which includes all incidents which were substantiated, but which had no impact on the water environment. Therefore data are not comparable to previous years.

3 Data for all years refers to financial years.
4 Category 4 and Total substantiated incidents include incidents to other media (air, land) which did not involve the water environment.

Sources: Environment Agency;
South Environment Protection Agency;
Northern Ireland Environment Agency;

10.16 Bathing water:[1] by region

United Kingdom

Numbers and percentages

		Compliance with EC Bathing Water Directive coliform standards during the bathing season														% complying	
		Identified bathing waters							Numbers complying									
		2005	2006	2007	2008	2009	2010		2005	2006	2007	2008	2009	2010			2009	2010
Coastal bathing waters																		
Environment Agency Regions																		
United Kingdom	GPKA	559	561	567	587	587	587	GPKN	550	559	547	563	573	571	GPLA		98	97
North East	GPKB	55	55	55	54	54	54	GPKO	53	54	52	53	54	52	GPLB		100	96
North West	GPKC	34	33	32	33	33	30	GPKP	32	33	29	30	31	27	GPLC		94	90
Anglian	GPKE	39	39	39	38	38	39	GPKR	39	39	39	38	38	39	GPLE		100	100
Thames	GPKF	8	8	8	8	8	8	GPKS	8	8	8	8	8	8	GPLF		100	100
Southern	GPKG	79	78	81	81	81	82	GPKT	79	78	81	80	81	82	GPLG		100	100
South West	GPKH	190	191	190	191	191	191	GPKU	189	191	187	181	186	186	GPLH		97	97
England	GPKI	405	404	405	405	405	404	GPKV	400	403	396	390	398	394	GPLI		98	98
Wales	GPKJ	80	80	80	81	81	80	GPKW	80	79	78	80	81	80	GPLJ		100	100
Scotland	GPKL	58	61	59	77	77	79	GPKY	55	61	52	70	72	75	GPLL		94	95
Northern Ireland	GPKM	16	16	23	24	24	24	GPKZ	15	16	21	23	22	22	GPLM		92	92
Inland bathing waters																		
United Kingdom	JTIG	11	11	11	12	12	12	JTIH	11	10	11	11	12	12	JTII		100	100

1 See chapter text.

Sources: Environment Agency;
Scottish Environment Protection Agency;
Northern Ireland Environment Agency (NIEA)

10.17 Estimated abstractions from all surface and groundwater sources: by purpose[1]

England and Wales

Megalitres per day

		1997	1998	1999	2000	2001	2002	2003	2004	2005	2006	2007	2008
Public water supply	JZLA	16,820	16,765	16,255	16,990	16,231	16,938	16,920	17,210	17,370	17,004	16,381	16,241
Spray irrigation	JZLB	292	282	325	291	259	248	315	225	226	277	161	156
Agriculture (excl spray irrigation)[4]	JZLC	108	111	142	152	108	120	132	122	60	48	72	38
Electricity supply industry[2]	JZLD	33,307	34,587	29,490	31,546	32,263	35,447	31,378	30,568	30,021	32,160	32,485	30,588
Other industry[3]	JZLE	4,352	4,964	5,428	5,433	4,772	4,883	6,623	6,585	6,339	6,519	5,167	4,954
Fish farming, cress growing, amenity ponds	JYXG	4,211	5,495	4,867	4,709	4,657	3,215	3,077	4,068	3,654	3,622	3,412	2,850
Private water supply	JZLG	162	175	91	102	92	54	61	30	26	37	29	24
Other	JZLH	408	289	526	559	108	77	86	77	60	86	113	74
Total	JZLI	59,957	62,891	57,123	59,782	58,489	60,981	58,593	58,885	57,757	59,752	57,820	54,925

1 See chapter text.

Source: Environment Agency

2 Increased electricity supply abstraction from 2002 due to increased production from power station in Anglian Region and two new licences issued in Southern Region.

3 Three abstraction licences re-assigned to other industry from electricty supply in Midlands Region (2003)

4 Reduction in agricultural abstraction due to deregulation of licences with effect from 1 April 2005

10.18 Estimates of remaining recoverable oil and gas reserves

United Kingdom

Oil (Million tonnes)		1999	2000	2001	2002	2003	2004	2005	2006	2007	2008	2009
Reserves												
Proven	JKOV	665	630	605	593	571	533	516	479	452	408	378
Probable	JKOW	455	380	350	327	286	283	300	298	328	361	390
Proven plus Probable	JKOX	1,120	1,010	955	920	857	816	816	776	780	770	769
Possible	JKOY	545	480	475	425	410	512	451	478	399	360	343
Maximum	JKOZ	1,665	1,490	1,430	1,344	1,267	1,328	1,267	1,254	1,179	1,130	1,111
Range of undiscovered resources												
Lower	JKNY	250	225	205	272	323	396	346	438	379	454	397
Upper	JKNZ	2,600	2,300	1,930	1,770	1,826	1,830	1,581	1,637	1,577	1,561	1,477
Range of total reserves												
Lower[1]	JKOA	915	855	810	865	894	929	862	917	831	862	775
Upper[2]	JKOB	4,265	3,790	3,360	3,115	3,093	3,158	2,848	2,892	2,756	2,690	2,588
Expected level of reserves[3]												
Opening stocks	JKOC	1,535	1,370	1,235	1,160	1,192	1,180	1,212	1,162	1,215	1,159	1,223
Extraction[4]	JKOD	-137	-126	-117	-117	-106	-95	-85	-77	-77	-72	-68
Other volume changes	JKOE	-28	-9	42	149	94	127	35	130	21	136	10
Closing stocks	JKOF	1,370	1,235	1,160	1,192	1,180	1,212	1,162	1,215	1,159	1,223	1,165
Gas (billion cubic metres)												
Reserves												
Proven	JKOH	760	735	695	628	590	531	481	412	343	292	256
Probable	JKOI	500	460	445	369	315	296	247	272	304	309	308
Proven plus Probable	JKOJ	1,260	1,195	1,140	998	905	826	728	684	647	601	564
Possible	JKOK	490	430	395	331	336	343	278	283	293	306	276
Maximum	JKOL	1,750	1,630	1,535	1,329	1,241	1,169	1,006	967	940	907	840
Range of undiscovered resources												
Lower	JKOM	355	325	290	238	279	293	226	301	280	319	300
Upper	JKON	1,465	1,440	1,680	1,386	1,259	1,245	1,035	1,049	1,039	1,043	949
Range of total reserves												
Lower[1]	JKOO	1,115	1,060	985	866	869	824	707	713	623	611	556
Upper[2]	JKOP	3,215	3,065	3,215	2,714	2,500	2,415	2,041	2,016	1,979	1,950	1,789
Expected level of reserves[3]												
Opening stocks	JKOQ	1,780	1,615	1,520	1,430	1,235	1,184	1,120	954	985	927	920
Extraction[4]	JKOR	-99	-108	-104	-102	-102	-95	-86	-78	-71	-68	-57
Other volume changes	JKOS	-66	13	14	-93	51	31	-80	109	13	61	1
Closing stocks	JKOT	1,615	1,520	1,430	1,235	1,184	1,120	954	985	927	920	864

Sources: Office for National Statistics and Department of Energy and Climate Change

environment.accounts@ons.gsi.gov.uk

1 The lower end of the range of total reserves has been calculated as the sum of proven reserves and the lower end of the range of undiscovered reserves.

2 The upper end of the range of total reserves is the sum proven, probable and possible reserves and the upper end of the range of undiscovered reserves.

3 Expected reserves are the sum of proven reserves, probable reserves and the lower end of the range of undiscovered reserves.

4 Negative extraction is shown here for the purpose of the calculation only. Of itself, extraction should be considered as a positive value.

10.19 Municipal waste disposal: by method

United Kingdom

Thousand tonnes

		2000 /01	2001 /02	2002 /03	2003 /04	2004 /05	2005 /06	2006 /07	2007 /08	2008 /09	2009 /10
England											
Household											
Disposed	I6EB	22,270	22,327	22 092	20,927	19,873	18,658	17,799	16,553	15,189	14,268
Recycled/composted	I6EC	2,809	3,197	3,740	4,521	5,785	6,796	7,976	8,735	9,146	9,398
Total	I6ED	25 079	25,524	25,832	25,448	25,658	25,454	25,775	25,287	24,334	23,666
Non Household											
Disposed	I6EE	2,342	2,656	2,730	2,650	2,795	2,289	2,408	2,250	2,063	1,999
Recycled/composted	I6EF	636	724	832	1,016	1,167	1,003	961	969	936	877
Total	I6EG	2,978	3,380	3,562	3,666	3,962	3,292	3,369	3,219	2,999	2,876
Total Municipal Waste											
Disposed	I6EH	24,612	24,983	24,822	23,577	22,668	20,947	20,207	18,803	17,252	16,266
Recycled/composted	I6EI	3,445	3,921	4,572	5,537	6,952	7,799	8,937	9,703	10,082	10,275
Total	I6EJ	28, 057	28,905	29,394	29,114	29,619	28,745	29,144	28,506	27,334	26,541
Wales											
Household											
Disposed	I6EK	1,314	1,330	1,309	1,271	1,298	1,210	1,153	1,044	938	864
Recycled/composted	I6EL	90	126	179	252	286	332	419	499	534	586
Total	I6EM	1,404	1,456	1,488	1,522	1,585	1,542	1,572	1,543	1,472	1,451
Non Household											
Disposed	I6EN	223	244	238	227	213	204	132	150	140	130
Recycled/composted	I6EO	25	18	43	71	131	152	130	100	113	90
Total	I6EP	248	262	281	298	344	356	262	251	253	219
Total Municipal Waste											
Disposed	I6EQ	1,537	1,573	1,547	1,498	1,511	1,414	1,285	1,194	1,078	994
Recycled/composted	I6ER	115	144	222	323	418	484	549	599	646	676
Total	I6ES	1,652	1,718	1,769	1,820	1,928	1,898	1,834	1,794	1,724	1,670
Scotland											
Household											
Disposed	I6ET	2,405	2,472	2,477	2,375	2,276	2,221	2,127	2,022	1,878	1,757
Recycled/composted	I6EU	122	149	206	330	522	665	879	979	1,027	1,063
Total	I6EV	2,527	2,621	2,683	2,705	2,798	2,886	3,006	3,001	2,906	2,819
Non Household											
Disposed	I6EW	662	619	602	545	584	508	332	309	283	267
Recycled/composted	I6EX	22	27	60	66	125	265	99	103	100	111
Total	I6EY	684	646	663	611	709	773	431	412	382	378
Total local authority collected municipal waste											
Disposed	I6EZ	3,067	3,091	3,079	2,920	2,860	2,729	2,459	2,331	2,161	2,024
Recycled/composted	I6F2	145	176	267	397	647	930	978	1,082	1,127	1,174
Total	I6F3	3,211	3,267	3,345	3,317	3,506	3,658	3,437	3,414	3,288	3,197

		1999 /00	2001	2002	2003	2004 /05	2005 /06	2006 /07	2007 /08	2008 /09	2009 /10
Northern Ireland											
Household											
Disposed	I6F4	785	785	813	786	746	708	679	632	579	561
Recycled/composted	I6F5	94	94	90	112	173	230	260	296	303	311
Total	I6F6	879	879	902	898	919	937	939	928	880	875
Non Household											
Disposed	I6F7	..	..	119	116	114	111	108	117	116	103
Recycled/composted	I6F8	..	..	2	13	18	15	7	15	19	21
Total	I6F9	135	135	121	129	132	126	125	133	137	129
Total Municipal Waste											
Disposed	I6FA	..	..	932	902	860	813	792	755	695	664
Recycled/composted	I6FB	..	..	92	125	191	250	272	306	321	332
Total	I6FC	1,056	1,056	1,023	1,027	1,051	1,064	1,064	1,061	1,017	1,004

Sources: Department for Environment, Food and Rural Affairs 08459 335577;
Welsh Assembly Government 029 2046 6151;
Scottish Environment Protection Agency 01786 457700;
Department of the Environment 028 9054 0916

173

10.20 Amounts of different materials from household sources collected for recycling by collection method 2009/10

United Kingdom

Thousand tonnes

Household waste collected for recycling or composting	Paper & Card	Glass	Compost [4]	Scrap metals & white goods	Textiles	Cans	Plastics	Co-mingled	Other	Total
England [2]										
Kerbside collection	914	421	2,524	20	7	63	46	1,995	16	6,006
Bring site collection	150	288	17	2	35	7	17	38	7	561
Civic Amenity site collection	215	54	1,064	537	39	13	17	6	690	2,635
Private/ voluntary collection schemes [3]	22	4	112	1	37	2	0	2	93	273
Total	1,301	766	3,717	561	118	85	80	2,042	805	9,475
Wales										
Kerbside collection	61	32	135	1	1	7	8	102	-	347
Bring site collection	14	14	4	-	3	1	2	1	-	39
Civic Amenity site collection	15	5	57	38	2	-	3	8	59	188
Private/ voluntary collection schemes [3]	-	-	8	-	1	-	-	-	4	12
Total	90	51	204	39	7	8	13	111	63	586
Scotland										
Kerbside collection	91	39	231	2	1	3	3	141	12	523
Bring site & Civic Amenity site collection	37	48	81	34	15	2	3	22	179	420
Private/ voluntary collection schemes [4]	-	-	38	-	-	-	-	-	26	64
Total	128	87	350	36	15	5	6	163	216	1,006
Northern Ireland										
Kerbside collection	75	8	76	-	-	4	10	-	5	179
Bring site collection	1	9	-	-	1	-	-	-	1	11
Civic Amenity site collection	9	7	54	24	2	-	-	-	44	138
Total	85	22	118	23	3	4	10	1	30	301

Sources: Department for Environment Food and Rural affairs 020 7238 4908
Welsh Assembly Government 029 209466152
Scottish Environment Protection Agency 01786 457700
Department of the Environment 028 9054 0916

1 See chapter text

2 Total amount of household waste collected for recycling is greater than that sent for recycling as some material is subsequently rejected during sorting or by the reprocessor.

3 Includes household waste collected from municipal parks, community skips and other methods of capture for recycling/composting and a small quantity of collection rejects.

4 Includes street sweepings, street recycling bins, gully waste, community skips and household green waste collected by private/voluntary schemes.

10.21 Noise incidents[1] received by Environmental Health Officers[2]

England and Wales and Northern Ireland [3]   Number per million people

		2002/03	2003/04	2004/05	2005/06	2006/07	2007/08	2008/9	2009/10
Not controlled by the Environmental Protection									
Act 1990:		36	32	..	..	..	..	..	..
Road traffic	JZLJ	104	120	..	..	..	..	..	..
Aircraft	JZLK	18	21	..	..	..	..	..	..
Railway	JTHH								
Total	JUZR	158	173	..	..	..	..	..	..
Controlled by the Environmental Protection									
Act 1990:									
Industrial/commercial premises	JZLN	1,315	1,480	1,260	936	1,021	1,132	1,051	1,025
Industrial	EAC3	301	284	219	192	176	159	155	142
Commercial/leisure[4]	EAC4	1,014	1,196	1,041	744	845	973	896	883
Construction/demolition sites	SNLE	325	335	343	220	246	284	203	185
Domestic premises	JZLP	5,573	5,973	5,903	4,186	4,329	4,648	4,383	5,111
Vehicles, machinery and equipment in streets	JZLQ	377	346	330	180	205	211	168	207
Traffic	I4SR	..	..	..	116	154	139	72	69
Miscellaneous[5]	EAC2	..	..	433	267	414	443	268	328
Total	JZLR	7,590	8,134	8,269	5,905	6,369	6,857	6,145	6,925

Source: The Chartered Institute of Environmental Health;
www.cieh.org.uk

1 From 2004/05 Data reported is for incidents per million where previously complaints per million was reported.
2 See chapter text.
3 Before 2005/6 data is for England and Wales only.
4 Includes railway noise and airports (non aircraft).
5 From 2004/05 includes 'traffic' which consists of commercial vehicles, cars, motorbikes, fixed-wing aircraft in flight and helicopters in flight. From 2005/06 this data is recorded separately as 'traffic'.

10.22 Government revenues from environmental taxes

United Kingdom   £million

		1999	2000	2001	2002	2003	2004	2005	2006	2007	2008	2009	2010
Energy													
Duty on hydro carbon oils	GTAP	22,391	23,041	22,046	22,070	22,476	23,412	23,346	23,448	24,512	24,790	25,894	27,013
including													
Unleaded petrol [1,3]	GBHE	11,952	11,481	1,906	0	0	0	0	0	0	0	0	0
Leaded petrol/LRP [2]	GBHL	1,630	1,105	650	103	70	67	20	15	13	10	9	10
Ultra low sulphur petrol	ZXTK	0	968	10,117	12,624	12,098	12,160	11,688	11,274	11,313	11,114	10,549	10,775
Diesel[3]	GBHH	1,274	23	65	0	0	0	0	0	0	0	0	0
Ultra low sulphur diesel	GBHI	7,338	9,014	8,492	9,029	9,457	10,168	10,829	11,203	12,146	12,284	12,720	14,072
VAT on duty	CMYA	3,918	4,032	3,858	3,862	3,933	4,097	4,086	4,103	4,290	4,338	3,884	4,052
Fossil fuel levy	CIQY	104	56	86	32	0	0	0	0	0	0	0	0
Gas levy	GTAZ	-	-	-	-	-	-	-	-	-	-	0	0
Climate change levy	LSNT	-	-	585	825	828	756	747	711	690	717	693	672
Renewable energy obligations [4]	KIT9	0	0	0	195	345	373	369	450	520	496	470	472
Road vehicles													
Vehicle excise duty	CMXZ	4,873	4,606	4,102	4,294	4,720	4,763	4,762	5,010	5,384	5,524	5,630	5,713
Other environmental taxes													
Air passenger duty	CWAA	884	940	824	814	781	856	896	961	1,883	1,876	1,800	2,093
Landfill tax	BKOF	430	461	502	541	607	672	733	804	877	954	842	1,074
Aggregates levy	MDUQ	0	0	0	213	340	328	327	321	339	334	275	290
Total environmental taxes	JKVW	32,600	33,136	32,003	32,846	34,030	35,257	35,266	35,808	38,495	39,029	39,488	41,379
Environmental taxes as a % of:													
Total taxes and social contributions	JKVX	9.7	9.3	8.6	8.7	8.6	8.3	7.8	7.3	7.5	7.2	8.1	8.0
Gross domestic product	JKVY	3.5	3.4	3.1	3.1	3.0	2.9	2.8	2.7	2.7	2.7	2.8	2.8

Source: ONS, Department for Energy and Climate Change;
environment.accounts@ons.gsi.gov.uk

1 Unleaded petrol includes super unleaded petrol.
2 Lead Replacement Petrol (the alternative to 4-Starleaded petrol introduced in 2000) is lead-free.
3 Duty incentives have concentrated production on ultralow sulphur varieties.
4 Included for the first time following a review of environmental taxes.
See Environmental Accounts publication for more information.

Housing

Chapter 11

Housing

Permanent dwellings (Table 11.1, 11.3)

Local housing authorities include: the Commission for the New Towns and New Towns Development Corporations; Communities Scotland; and the Northern Ireland Housing Executive. The figures shown for housing associations include dwellings provided by housing associations other than the Communities Scotland and the Northern Ireland Housing Executive and include those provided or authorised by government departments for the families of police, prison staff, the Armed Forces and certain other services.

Mortgage possession actions by region (Table 11.6)

The table shows mortgage possession actions in the county courts of England and Wales and excludes a small number of mortgage actions in the High Court.

A claimant begins an action for an order for possession of a property by issuing a claim in the county court, either by using the Possession Claim Online system or locally through a county court. In mortgage possession cases, the usual procedure is for the claim being issued to be given a hearing date before a district judge. The court, following a judicial hearing, may grant an order for possession immediately. This entitles the claimants to apply for a warrant to have the defendant evicted. However, even where a warrant for possession is issued, the parties can still negotiate a compromise to prevent eviction.

Frequently the court grants the claimant possession but suspends the operation of the order. Provided the defendant complies with the terms of suspension, which usually require the defendant to pay the current mortgage instalments plus some of the accrued arrears, the possession order cannot be enforced.

The mortgage possession figures do not indicate how many houses have actually been repossessed through the courts. Repossessions can occur without a court order being made while not all court orders result in repossession.

A new mortgage pre-action protocol (MPAP), approved by the Master of the Rolls, was introduced for possession claims in the County Courts with effect from 19 November 2008. The MPAP gives clear guidance on what the courts expect lenders and borrowers to have done prior to a claim being issued.

Evidence from administrative records from Qtr4 2008 suggests that this date coincided with a fall of around 50% in the daily and weekly numbers of new mortgage repossession claims being issued in the courts.

It therefore seems highly likely that the launch of the MPAP has led to a fall in the number of new claims being issued since introduction of MPAP (19th November to 31st December 2008).

Mortgage possession orders are typically made (where necessary) around 8 weeks after the corresponding claims are issued. For this reason, the impact of the MPAP is yet to have visible effect on the statistics on possession orders made.

At this early stage is not clear to what extent the launch of the MPAP has led to a permanent fall in the numbers of new mortgage possession claims being issued, as opposed to some merely being postponed. This will become clearer as statistics for 2009 become available.

Households in Temporary Accommodation under homelessness provisions (Tables 11.7, 11.8, 11.9)

Comprises households in accommodation arranged by local authorities pending enquiries or after being accepted as owed a main homeless duty under the 1996 Act (includes residual cases awaiting re-housing under the 1985 Act). Excludes "homeless at home" cases. The data shown for Wales includes "homeless at home" cases.

11.1 Stock of Dwellings: by tenure and country [1,2]

Thousands

		1997	1998	1999	2000	2001	2002	2003	2004	2005	2006	2007	2008	2009	2010
England[3]															
Owner occupied	JUTY	14,111	14,308	14,518	14,701	14,838	14,942	15,088	15,210	15,312	15,369	15,396	..	..	..
Rented	JUUC	6,511	6,470	6,410	6,374	6,369	6,395	6,393	6,426	6,493	6,621	6,794	..	..	..
Local Authority	JUTZ	3,401	3,309	3,178	3,012	2,812	2,706	2,457	2,335	2,166	2,087	1,987	1,870	1,820	1,786
Privately	JUUA	2,125	2,121	2,086	2,089	2,133	2,197	2,285	2,389	2,525	2,669	2,856	..	..	..
Housing Associations	JUUB	985	1,040	1,146	1,273	1,424	1,492	1,651	1,702	1,802	1,865	1,951	2,056	2,128	2,180
All dwellings	JUUD	20,622	20,778	20,927	21,075	21,207	21,337	21,481	21,636	21,805	21,992	22,190	22,398	22,564	22,693
Wales[4]															
Owner occupied (r)	JUUE	909	908	926	914	923	950	936	954	961	975	978	975	955	941
Rented (r)	JUUI	334	343	333	353	352	332	353	343	344	339	344	357	383	403
Local Authority	JUUF	204	201	197	193	188	183	177	162	158	156	154	132	113	111
Privately (r)	JUUG	82	92	84	106	109	93	119	116	121	117	123	136	163	182
Housing Associations	JUUH	48	50	52	54	55	57	57	65	65	66	67	89	107	111
All dwellings	JUUJ	1,243	1,252	1,259	1,267	1,275	1,282	1,289	1,297	1,305	1,313	1,323	1,331	1,338	1,344
Scotland[5]															
Owner occupied	JUUK	1,366	1,400	1,435	1,472	1,446	1,479	1,514	1,544	1,555	1,570	1,587	1,590	1,612	..
Rented	JUUO	899	883	869	849	861	853	835	825	833	838	841	862	857	..
Local Authority	JUUL	630	608	583	557	553	531	416	389	374	362	347	263	326	..
Privately	JUUM	154	154	155	155	169	179	180	184	208	225	233	330	263	..
Housing Associations	JUUN	115	121	131	137	139	143	238	251	251	251	261	269	268	..
All dwellings	JUUP	2,266	2,283	2,303	2,322	2,307	2,332	2,349	2,369	2,389	2,408	2,427	2,452	2,469	..
Northern Ireland[6]															
Owner occupied	JUUQ	434	446	455	488	..	481	491	501	505	508	523	524	517	515
Rented	JUUU	183	180	180	185	..	187	188	183	193	198	190	207	220	228
Local Authority	JUUR	142	137	131	129	..	120	113	100	102	99	97	97	96	95
Privately	JUUS	26	27	32	37	..	47	54	61	68	76	69	83	97	105
Housing Associations	JUUT	15	16	17	19	..	20	21	22	22	23	24	26	28	28
All dwellings	JUUV	618	626	636	674	..	668	679	684	698	706	713	731	737	744
United Kingdom[7]															
Owner occupied	JUVY	16,751	16,996	17,279	17,494	17,677	17,834	18,018	18,201	18,323	18,484	18,457	..	..	..
Rented	JUWC	7,970	7,915	7,816	7,787	7,785	7,785	7,779	7,785	7,875	7,996	8,169	..	..	..
Local Authority	JUVZ	4,421	4,282	4,120	3,919	3,682	3,540	3,163	2,986	2,800	2,704	2,585	2,362	2,355	..
Privately	JUWA	2,402	2,413	2,361	2,393	2,466	2,533	2,649	2,759	2,934	3,087	3,281	..	..	..
Housing Associations	JUWB	1,147	1,220	1,335	1,475	1,637	1,712	1,967	2,040	2,140	2,205	2,303	2,440	2,531	..
All dwellings	JUWD	24,721	24,913	25,095	25,281	25,462	25,619	25,799	25,987	26,198	26,419	26,653	26,912	27,108	..

Sources: Communities and Local Government;
Welsh Government;
Scottish Executive;
Department for Social Development (Northern Ireland)

1 For detailed definitions of all tenures, see Definitions of housing terms in Housing Statistics home page.

2 April data for census years are based on census output.

3 Series from 1992 to 2001 for England has been adjusted so that 2001 total dwellings estimate matches the 2001 census. Estimates from 2002 are based on local authority and Registered Social Landlord dwelling counts, and the Labour force survey (LFS). Estimates may not be strictly comparable between periods.

4 As at 31 March each year. The tenure split between owner-occupied and privately rented dwellings has been calculated for 1997 onwards using information from the Labour Force Survey (LFS). These figures were revised in January 2011 following a re-weighting of the Labour Force Survey data.

5 Estimates up to 2000 are based on the 1991 Census. Estimates from 2001 onwards are based on the 2001 General Register of Scotland (GROS) dwelling counts and Scottish Household Survey (SHS) tenure splits are not strictly comparable.

6 To include estimates for vacant dwellings, stock figures in Northern Ireland Statistics 2006/07 table 1.3 have been apportioned according the % of occupied dwellings for each of the tenures given in table 1.4.

7 UK totals from 2002 are derived by summing country totals at 31st March. For 1991-2001 Scotland and Northern Ireland stock levels from the year before is added to the UK total. Data for earlier years are less reliable and definitions may not be consistent throughout the series. Components may not sum to totals due to rounding.

11.2 Type Of Accommodation by Tenure [1] 2009 Great Britain

(a) Type of accommodation by tenure
(b) Tenure by type of accommodation

Weighted Percentages

(a)	Detached House	Semi-detached house	Terraced House	All Houses	Purpose-built flat or maisonette	Converted flat maisonette/rooms	All flats
Owner-occupied							
Owned outright	37	34	21	92	6	2	8
Owned with mortgage	27	34	29	91	7	2	9
All owners	32	34	25	91	7	2	9
Rented from social Sector							
Council[3]	1	23	32	56	42	2	44
Housing association[4]	1	24	30	55	41	5	45
All rented from social sector	1	23	31	55	42	3	45
Rented privately[6]							
Unfurnished[5]	10	23	34	67	21	13	33
Furnished	5	17	23	44	32	24	56
Private renters[6]	9	22	32	63	22	15	37
All Tenures	23	31	27	81	15	4	19
(b)							
Owner-occupied							
Owned outright	50	35	25	36	13	14	13
Owned with mortgage	44	42	40	42	18	21	19
All owners	94	77	64	78	31	35	32
Rented from social Sector							
Council[3]	0	8	12	7	28	5	24
Housing association[4]	0	6	9	5	22	10	20
All rented from social sector	1	14	20	12	50	16	43
Rented privately[6]							
Unfurnished[5]	5	8	13	9	15	36	19
Furnished	0	1	2	1	4	13	6
Private renters[6]	5	9	15	10	19	50	25

Source: General Lifestyle Survey, Office for National Statistics

1 Results for 2009 include longitudinal data.

2 Tables for type of accommodation exclude households living in caravans.

3 Council includes local authorities.

4 Since 1996, housing associations are more correctly described as Registered Social Landlords (RSLs).

5 Unfurnished includes the answer 'partly furnished'.

6 Tenants whose accommodation goes with the job of someone in the household have been allocated to 'rented privately'. Squatters are also included.

11.3 Permanent dwellings completed:[1] by tenure and country

Numbers

	United Kingdom				England and Wales			
	All dwellings	Local authorities[2]	Private enterprise	Registered Social Landlords[3,4]	All dwellings	Local authorities[2]	Private enterprise	Registered Social Landlords[3,4]
	KAAD	KAAE	KAAF	KAAG	KAAH	KAAI	KAAJ	KAAK
1980	242,000	88,530	131,990	21,480	214,940	78,540	116,180	20,220
1981	206,630	68,330	118,590	19,700	179,790	58,410	104,020	17,360
1982	182,850	40,090	129,020	13,740	159,400	33,540	113,890	11,970
1983	209,030	39,170	153,040	19,700	181,400	31,640	134,900	14,870
1984	220,410	37,570	165,560	17,290	191,110	31,340	145,260	14,510
1985	207,470	30,420	163,400	13,650	178,290	24,360	142,020	11,910
1986	216,540	25,380	178,010	13,160	187,710	20,500	156,060	11,150
1987	226,230	21,830	191,250	13,150	198,740	17,430	169,900	11,410
1988	242,360	21,450	207,420	13,490	214,160	16,920	185,740	11,500
1989	221,460	19,320	187,540	14,600	190,990	15,330	163,340	12,310
1992/93	178,872	4,430	144,420	30,160	152,450	2,710	123,040	26,700
1993/94	185,960	3,590	146,820	36,670	157,810	1,730	122,780	33,310
1994/95	197,169	3,000	156,250	37,600	168,310	990	133,000	34,310
1995/96	198,212	3,040	156,940	38,550	164,580	960	130,900	32,740
1996/97	185,654	1,540	153,450	30,590	156,340	470	128,690	27,180
1997/98	190,748	1,520	160,680	28,550	157,990	320	134,330	23,340
1998/99	178,289	870	154,560	22,870	148,000	210	127,630	20,160
1999/00	183,982	320	160,490	23,170	150,510	60	132,330	18,120
2000/01	175,220	380	152,590	22,250	141590	230	124,030	17,330
2001/02	173,930	230	153,310	20,400	138140	130	123,190	14,810
2002/03	183,210	300	164,300	18,610	146050	210	131,980	13,860
2003/04	190,590	210	172,360	18,020	152260	210	137,960	14,090
2004/05	206,620	130	184,500	21,990	164380	130	147,120	17,140
2005/06	214,010	330	189,700	23,990	171660	330	152,820	18,510
2006/07	219,050	260	192,150	26,650	177010	250	154,670	22,100
2007/08	216,700	250	187,930	28,510	177430	230	153,770	23,450
2008/09	171,980	850	139,270	31,860	141230	520	114,510	26,200
2009/10[6]	146,730	680	113,640	32,410	119840	300	93,920	25,620

	Scotland				Northern Ireland [7]			
	All dwellings	Local authorities[2]	Private enterprise	Registered Social Landlords[3]	All dwellings	Local authorities[2]	Private enterprise	Registered Social Landlords[3]
	BLFI	BAEZ	BLFK	BLFO	BLGI	BAFA	BLGK	BLGO
1979	23,780	4,760	15,180	3,850	7,250	3,440	3,570	240
1980	20,611	7,488	12,242	881	6,456	2,563	3,568	325
1981	20,011	7,062	11,021	1,928	6,827	3,082	3,557	188
1982	16,423	3,733	11,523	1,167	7,033	3,032	3,606	395
1983	17,929	3,492	13,166	1,271	9,698	4,093	4,971	634
1984	18,838	2,647	14,115	2,076	10,464	3,594	6,177	693
1985	18,411	2,828	14,435	1,148	10,770	3,235	6,940	595
1986	18,637	2,301	14,870	1,466	10,197	2,580	7,082	535
	BLFI	BAEZ	BLFK	BLFO	BLGI	BAFA	BLGK	BLGO
1987	17,707	2,634	13,904	1,169	9,795	1,764	7,451	580
1988	18,272	2,815	14,179	1,278	9,931	1,715	7,511	705
1989	20,190	2,283	16,287	1,620	10,283	1,708	7,911	664
1992/93	18,990	770	15,620	2,600	7,559	992	5,759	808
1993/94	22,110	980	18,310	2,820	7,083	907	5,642	534
1994/95	21,810	1,130	17,890	2,790	7,212	877	5,859	476
1995/96	24,690	720	19,200	4,780	8,990	1,325	6,750	915
1996/97	20,700	240	17,490	2,960	9,166	860	7,373	933
1997/98	22,590	110	17,980	4,490	10,181	1,080	8,371	730
1998/99	20,660	120	18,780	1,750	9,638	538	8,140	960
1999/00	23,110	70	19,070	3,960	10,399	190	9,117	1,092

181

11.3 Permanent dwellings completed:[1] by tenure and country

	Scotland				Northern Ireland [7]			
	All dwellings	Local authorities[2]	Private enterprise	Registered Social Landlords[3]		All dwellings	Local authorities[2]	Private enterprise	Registered Social Landlords[3]
2000/01	22,110	110	18,200	3,800		11,668	44	10,512	1,112
2001/02	22,570	70	18,310	4,200		13,487	29	12,072	1,386
2002/03	22,750	90	18,940	3,720		14,415	2	13,387	1,026
2003/04	23,820	-	20,450	3,370		14,511	-	13,951	560
2004/05	26,470	-	22,440	4,020		15,768	-	14,940	828
2005/06	24,950	-	20,250	4,700		17,410	-	16,628	782
2006/07	24,250	10	21,010	3,230		17,797	-	16,470	1,327
2007/08	25,780	30	21,660	4,100		13,477	-	12,510	967
2008/09	21,020	340	16,110	4,580		9,722	-	8,650	1,072
2009/10[5]	17,150	380	11,190	5,580		9,745	-	8,532	1,213

1 See chapter text.

2 Including the Commission for the New Towns Development Corporations, Communities Scotland, the Northern Ireland Housing Executive.

3 Dwellings provided by housing associations other than Communities Scotland and the Northern Ireland Housing Trust and provided or authorised by government departments for families of police, prison staff, the armed forces and certain other services. In Northern Ireland this relates to Housing Association completions (new builds).

4 Includes non-registered social landlords

5 Revised

6 Provisional

7 Northern Ireland private enterprise completions are statistically adjusted to correct, as far as possible, the proven under recording of private sector completions in NI. This calculation has been revised for 2007/08, as such the figures and not comparable with previous years.

Sources: Communities and Local Government; Scottish Government; Welsh Government; Department for Social Development, Northern Ireland

11.4 Housebuilding completions: by number of bedrooms

Percentages

		1997 /98	1998 /99	1999 /00	2000 /01	2001[1] /02	2002[1] /03	2003[1] /04	2004[1] /05	2005[1] /06	2006[1] /07	2007[1] /08	2008[1] /09	2009[1] /10
England														
1 bedroom	JUWJ	7	7	7	7	7	6	8	10	10	11	11	13	13
2 bedrooms	JUWK	27	27	26	27	25	29	33	38	42	42	44	46	40
3 bedrooms	JUWL	38	36	35	34	31	30	29	28	27	27	26	24	27
4 or more bedrooms	JUWM	28	30	32	32	37	34	30	23	21	20	19	17	20
All houses and flats	JUWN	100	100	100	100	100	100	100	100	100	100	100	100	100
Wales[2]														
1 bedroom	JUWO	4	3	5	5	4	6	6	7	9	11	10	16	11
2 bedrooms	JUWP	24	21	19	18	19	18	20	21	27	28	30	33	33
3 bedrooms	JUWQ	46	46	43	42	39	35	37	35	35	33	33	30	36
4 or more bedrooms	JUWR	26	30	34	34	38	41	37	37	30	28	27	22	21
All houses and flats	JUWS	100	100	100	100	100	100	100	100	100	100	100	100	100

Sources: Communities and Local Government;
Welsh Government

1 Figures for 2001/02 onwards for England only are based on just NHBC figures, so there is some degree of variability owing to partial coverage.
2 Figures for all years for Wales are based on the reports of local authority building inspectors and the National House Building Council (NHBC). It does not include information from other private approved inspector.

11.5 County Court mortgage possession actions:[1] by region

Thousands

		1999	2000	2001	2002	2003	2004	2005	2006	2007	2008	2009	2010
Claims Issued													
England and Wales	JURS	77.8	70.1	65.5	63.0	65.4	77.0	114.7	131.2	137.7	142.7	93.5	75.4
North East	JURT	4.0	4.0	3.5	3.2	3.0	3.4	5.5	7.1	8.1	8.5	5.8	4.5
North West	JURU	14.0	12.6	12.0	11.0	9.8	10.4	15.3	19.2	21.7	23.1	15.1	12.1
Yorkshire and the Humber	JURV	8.8	7.7	7.0	6.1	5.8	6.6	10.1	12.0	13.8	14.7	10.1	8.5
East Midlands	JURW	6.5	5.7	5.2	4.7	4.8	5.7	8.6	10.2	10.8	11.4	7.3	6.1
West Midlands	JURX	8.5	8.0	7.4	6.8	7.2	8.6	12.2	14.8	16.2	16.5	10.0	8.3
East	JURY	6.8	6.2	5.6	5.4	6.4	7.8	11.2	12.0	12.4	12.8	8.4	6.7
London	JURZ	8.7	7.0	7.5	8.6	10.4	13.4	21.1	21.9	20.1	19.5	12.9	9.7
South East	JUSA	9.9	9.0	8.4	8.2	9.3	11.4	16.5	17.4	17.0	17.2	11.4	9.4
South West	JUSB	5.7	4.9	4.4	4.3	4.5	5.4	7.8	8.5	8.6	9.4	6.3	5.1
England	JUSC	72.9	65.1	61.0	58.3	61.2	72.7	108.3	123.0	128.5	133.0	87.3	70.4
Wales	JUSD	5.0	5.0	4.6	4.5	4.2	4.3	6.5	8.2	9.2	9.7	6.3	5.0
Northern Ireland	JUSE	1.9	1.7	1.6	1.6	1.7	2.2	2.6	2.5	..	..	..	..
Claims leading to													
Suspended orders made[2,3]													
England and Wales	JUSF	31.5	29.5	28.1	24.3	23.7	25.8	37.0	43.2	41.5	52.1	33.0	26.5
North East	JUSG	2.0	2.0	1.7	1.3	1.3	1.2	1.8	2.6	2.5	3.1	2.0	1.5
North West	JUSH	5.9	5.5	5.3	4.7	3.9	3.7	5.0	6.5	6.8	8.6	5.3	4.4
Yorkshire and the Humber	JUSI	3.8	3.4	3.3	2.5	2.2	2.3	3.4	4.2	4.1	5.4	3.3	2.8
East Midlands	JUSJ	2.7	2.4	2.3	1.8	1.8	2.0	2.8	3.3	3.4	4.0	2.4	2.1
West Midlands	JUSK	3.5	3.5	3.5	2.8	2.8	3.1	4.2	5.1	5.0	6.4	3.5	2.8
East	JUSL	2.7	2.5	2.3	2.1	2.3	2.6	3.7	3.9	3.5	4.6	3.0	2.4
London	JUSM	3.1	2.6	2.7	2.7	3.2	3.9	6.3	6.9	5.8	7.0	5.0	3.6
South East	JUSN	3.9	3.6	3.3	3.0	3.2	3.7	5.3	5.7	5.1	6.0	4.2	3.4
South West	JUSO	2.2	2.0	1.8	1.6	1.6	1.8	2.6	2.8	2.5	3.5	2.1	1.7
England	JUSP	29.6	27.4	26.1	22.5	22.1	24.3	35.0	40.6	38.7	48.4	30.7	24.7
Wales	JUSQ	2.0	2.1	2.0	1.8	1.7	1.5	2.1	2.6	2.8	3.7	2.3	1.8
Northern Ireland	JUSR	0.3	0.2	0.2	0.2	0.3	0.4	0.5	0.4	..	..	..	..
Claims leading to Outright													
Orders made													
England and Wales	JUSS	22.0	19.0	17.7	16.1	16.1	19.6	31.9	44.8	49.2	59.7	39.3	30.5
North East	JUST	1.2	1.1	1.1	0.9	0.8	0.8	1.4	2.4	3.0	3.7	2.8	2.1
North West	JUSU	4.1	3.8	3.6	3.1	2.6	2.6	4.0	6.3	7.5	9.8	6.5	5.0
Yorkshire and the Humber	JUSV	2.6	2.3	2.2	1.7	1.6	1.7	2.8	4.1	5.0	6.3	4.6	3.7
East Midlands	JUSW	2.0	1.5	1.5	1.3	1.2	1.5	2.5	3.7	4.0	5.3	3.2	2.8
West Midlands	JUSX	2.2	2.0	2.0	1.7	1.7	2.1	3.2	4.9	5.7	7.1	4.1	3.3
East	JUSY	1.9	1.6	1.4	1.3	1.5	2.0	3.2	4.4	4.4	5.4	3.6	2.7
London	JUSZ	2.4	1.7	1.8	2.1	2.7	3.7	6.5	8.1	7.7	7.7	4.8	3.4
South East	JUTA	2.5	2.1	1.9	1.8	2.1	2.8	4.5	5.6	6.0	6.5	4.6	3.5
South West	JUTB	1.7	1.2	1.0	1.0	1.0	1.4	2.2	2.8	3.0	3.8	2.6	2.1
England	JUTC	20.5	17.5	16.4	14.9	15.0	18.5	30.2	42.3	46.1	55.6	36.7	28.5
Wales	JUTD	1.4	1.5	1.3	1.2	1.0	1.1	1.7	2.7	3.0	4.0	2.6	2.0
Northern Ireland	JUTE	0.7	0.6	0.7	0.5	0.6	0.7	0.9	0.9	..	..	..	..

Sources: Ministry of Justice 020 3334 2747;
Northern Ireland Court Service: 028 9032 8594

Note: The mortgage Pre Action Protocol for possession claims relating to mortgage or home purchase arrears was introduced on 19th November 2008. It's introduction has coincided with a substantial fall in the number of new mortgage possession claims in 2008 quarter 4 and subsequently in the number of mortgage possession orders in 2009 quarter 1.

1 Includes all types of mortgage lender.
2 Where the court grants the claimant possession but suspends the operation of the order, provided the defendent complies with the terms of suspension, which usually require the defendent to pay the current mortgage plus some of the accrued arrears,the possession cannot be enforced.
3 Figures have been largely revised due to a change in the methodology as Orders are now recorded as claims leading to an Order.

11.6 Number of Mortgages Outstanding United Kingdom

		1999	2000	2001	2002	2003	2004	2005	2006	2007	2008	2009	2010
Mortgages[1] (Thousands)	JUTH	10,987	11,177	11,251	11,368	11,452	11,515	11,608	11,746	11,852	11,667	11,389	11,365
Arrears and repossessions[1] (Thousands)													
Loans in arrears at end-period													
By 6-12 months	JUTI	57	48	43	34	31	30	39	35	41	72	92	78
By over 12 months	JUTJ	30	21	20	17	13	11	15	16	15	30	68	62
Properties repossessed in period	JUTK	30	23	18	12	9	8	15	21	26	40	48	36

Source: Council of Mortgage Lenders

1. From Q1 2009 figures are grossed up to be representative of the entire first charge market mortgage market.
Earlier data relate to CML members only and so are not directly comparable with later figures.
2. There is also a discontinuity because in Q1 2009 around 490,000 "legacy loans" (those for which only a nominal balance is retained, for example for deed storage purposes) which had previously been reported were newly excluded, to bring reporting in line with our guidance notes. In Q3 2009 a further 100,000 such cases were identified and excluded from the data back to the start of 2009. Accordingly our estimate for the total number of mortgages up to and including 2008 is not comparable with estimates there after. It has not been possible to revise earlier estimates in line with this guidance.
The total number of arrears and possessions is not affected by this change.
3. As our figures cover first charge mortgage lending only and relate to the number of borrowers rather than individual loan accounts, they will be materially lower than, and not strictly comparable with, the aggregate MLAR figures published by the FSA.
4. Figures are subject to revision as better information about rates of growth and performance in different parts of the market is received, or lenders report for the first time or re-submit earlier figures.
5. Reporting lenders accounted for around 94% of the estimated total first-charge market in Q4 2010.

11.7 Households in Temporary Accommodation[1]: England

As at 31st March of each year

													Households	
		1998 /99	1999 /00	2000 /01	2001 /02	2002 /03	2003 /04	2004 /05	2005 /06	2006 /07	2007 /08	2008 /09	2009 /10[4]	2010 /11[4]
Bed and breakfast hotels	JUWF	6,570	8,680	10,860	12,710	12,440	7,090	6,780	5,150	4,310	3,840	2,450	2,050	2,750
Hostels/women's refuges	JUWG	9,840	10,300	10,610	9,570	10,060	10,780	10,280	9,010	7,640	6,450	5,170	4,240	4,250
Social sector accommodation[2]	JXVN	18,600	21,380	25,480	27,760	28,260	27,880	26,630	22,350	18,040	14,740	10,480	7,790	7,490
Private sector accommodation and other[3]	JXVO	21,570	24,810	28,250	30,170	38,290	51,930	57,390	59,870	57,140	52,480	45,910	37,240	33,750
All accommodation	JUWI	56,580	65,170	75,200	80,200	89,040	97,680	101,070	96,370	87,120	77,510	64,000	51,310	48,240

Sources: Department for Communities and Local Government;

1 Households in temporary accommodation arranged by the local authority pending enquiries, or after being accepted as owed a main duty under homelessness legislation. Excludes 'homeless at home' cases who have remained in their existing accommodation after acceptance but have the same rights to suitable alternative housing as those in accommodation arranged directly by authorities.
2 Local authorities' and Registered Social Landlords' own stock.
3 Includes private sector properties leased by social sector landlords, households placed directly with a private sector landlord and other accommodation.
From 2002 some self-contained B&B Annexe-style units, previously recorded under B&B have been more appropriately attributed to private sector accommodation.
4 Provisional

11.8 Households in Temporary Accommodation[1]: Wales

As at 31st March of each year

Households

		1998 /99	1999 /00	2000 /01	2001 /02	2002 /03	2003 /04	2004 /05	2005 /06	2006 /07	2007 /08	2008 /09	2009 /10
Bed and breakfast hotels	KI7W	43	85	80	78	78	123	302	691	761	593	378	282
Hostels/women's refuges	KI7X	180	164	185	157	151	194	232	311	310	448	407	477
Social sector accommodation[2]	KI7Y	73	275	233	312	375	397	453	356	460	614	574	445
Private sector accommodation and other[3]	KI7Z	166	183	313	193	209	163	285	401	587	806	938	1,090
All accommodation[4]	KI82	462	793	955	941	1,079	1,309	1,492	2,890	3,349	3,442	3,152	2,880

Source: Welsh Government

1 Households in temporary accommodation arranged by the local authority pending enquiries, or after being accepted as owed a main duty under homelessness legislation.
2 Local authorities' and Registered Social Landlords' own stock.
3 Includes private sector properties leased by social sector landlords, households placed directly with a private sector landlord and other accommodation.
4 Includes 'homeless at home' for Wales.

11.9 Households in Temporary Accommodation[1]: Scotland

As at 31st March of each year

Households

		2000 /01	2001 /02	2002 /03	2003 /04	2004 /05	2005 /06	2006 /07	2007 /08	2008 /09	2009 /10
Bed and breakfast hotels	KI83	502	569	898	1,190	1,516	1,494	1,528	1,609	1,748	1,787
Hostels/women's refuges	KI84	1,512	1,363	1,380	1,586	1,490	1,328	1,242	1,099	1,008	1,251
Social sector accommodation[2]	KI85	1,968	2,152	2,984	3,537	4,136	4,747	5,164	6,114	6,341	6,816
Private sector accommodation and other[3]	KI86	78	69	141	132	159	416	643	713	956	961
All accommodation	KI87	4,060	4,153	5,403	6,445	7,301	7,985	8,577	9,535	10,053	10,815

Source: Scottish Government

1 Households in temporary accommodation arranged by the local authority pending enquiries, or after being accepted as owed a main duty under homelessness legislation. Excludes 'homeless at home' cases who have remained in their existing accommodation after acceptance but have the same rights to suitable alternative housing as those in accommodation arranged directly by authorities.
2 Local authorities' and Registered Social Landlords' own stock.
3 Includes private sector properties leased by social sector landlords, households placed directly with a private sector landlord and other accommodation.
From 2002 some self-contained B&B Annexe-style units, previously recorded under B&B have been more appropriately attributed to private sector accommodation.
4. From 31st March 2008 there is a break in comparability in numbers in temporary accomodation in Glasgow. From this date, as a result of legacy case reviews of asylum applications undertaken by the home office, there was a significant increase in numbers recorded as homeless and in temporary accomodation.

Banking, insurance

Chapter 12

Banking, insurance

Bank lending to, and bank deposits from, UK residents (Tables 12.4 and 12.5)

These are series statistics based on the Standard Industrial Classification (SIC) 1992 (which was revised slightly in 2003).

Table 12.4. Until the third quarter of 2007, the analysis of lending covered loans, advances (including under reverse repos), finance leasing, acceptances and facilities (all in Sterling and other currencies) provided by reporting banks to their UK resident non-bank non-building society customers, as well as bank holdings of sterling and euro commercial paper issued by these resident customers. Following a review of statistical data collected, acceptances and holdings of sterling and euro commercial paper are no longer collected at the industry level detail with effect from fourth quarter 2007 data. Total lending therefore reflects loans and advances (including under reverse repos) only, from fourth quarter 2007 data.

Table 12.5 includes borrowing under sale and repo. Adjustments for transit items are not included. Figures for both tables are supplied by monthly reporting banks and grossed to cover quarterly reporters. Following the transition of building societies' statistical reporting from the Financial Services Authority to the Bank of England on 1st January 2008, both tables will include data reported by building societies from the first quarter of 2008 onwards. They exclude lending to building societies and to residents of the Channel Islands and Isle of Man.

Consumer credit (Table 12.12)

Figures for net lending refer to changes in amounts outstanding adjusted to remove distortions caused by revaluations of debt outstanding, such as write-offs. Class 3 loans are advanced under the terms of the Building Societies Act 1986.

A high proportion of credit advanced in certain types of agreement, notably on credit cards, is repaid within a month. This reflects use of such agreements as a method of payment rather than a way of obtaining credit. As from December 2006 the Bank of England has ceased to update the separate data on consumer credit provided by other specialist lenders, retailers and insurance companies previously contained in these tables. These categories have been merged into 'other consumer credit lenders'.

reporters. Following the transition of building societies' statistical reporting from the Financial Services Authority to the Bank of England on 1st January 2008, both tables will include data reported by building societies from the first quarter of 2008 onwards. They exclude lending to building societies and to residents of the Channel Islands and Isle of Man.

Consumer credit (Table 12.12)

Figures for net lending refer to changes in amounts outstanding adjusted to remove distortions caused by revaluations of debt outstanding, such as write-offs. Class 3 loans are advanced under the terms of the Building Societies Act 1986.

A high proportion of credit advanced in certain types of agreement, notably on credit cards, is repaid within a month. This reflects use of such agreements as a method of payment rather than a way of obtaining credit. As from December 2006 the Bank of England has ceased to update the separate data on consumer credit provided by other specialist lenders, retailers and insurance companies previously contained in these tables. These categories have been merged into 'other consumer credit lenders'.

12.1 Bank of England Balance Sheet

Liabilities and assets outstanding at end of period

		Liabilities						Assets				
	Notes in circulation	Reserve balances	Foreign currency public securities issued	Cash ratio deposits	Other liabilities	Short term open market operations	of which 1 week sterling reverse repo	Longer term sterling reverse repo	Ways and means advances to HMG	Bonds and other securities acquired via market transactions	Other assets	Total assets/ liabililties
	B55A	**B56A**	**B59A**	**B62A**	**B63A**	**B66A**	**B67A**	**B69A**	**B72A**	**B73A**	**B74A**	**B75A**
2010	53,165	139,699	3,891	2,445	47,104	0	0	16,800	370	13,836	215,298	246,304
2010 Jan	49,496	156,592	3,753	2,574	33,069	0	0	24,797	370	12,601	207,716	245,484
Feb	49,486	155,165	3,881	2,574	36,174	0	0	20,607	370	12,691	213,612	247,280
Mar	50,041	150,034	5,287	2,574	41,534	0	0	19,909	370	14,016	215,175	249,470
Apr	50,514	151,808	3,945	2,574	41,338	0	0	20,994	370	13,692	215,124	250,180
May	50,920	150,934	4,230	2,574	42,506	0	0	20,994	370	13,825	215,976	251,165
Jun	51,206	149,003	4,093	2,570	43,783	0	0	20,392	370	13,531	216,363	250,655
Jul	51,037	150,937	4,008	2,570	43,364	0	0	22,797	370	13,652	215,099	251,917
Aug	51,105	151,082	3,911	2,570	41,248	0	0	21,447	370	13,718	214,383	249,917
Sep	50,988	143,594	3,909	2,548	44,461	0	0	17,600	370	13,952	213,578	245,500
Oct	51,145	142,878	3,860	2,548	43,554	0	0	16,250	370	14,174	213,191	243,985
Nov	51,459	142,354	3,834	2,548	42,477	0	0	14,900	370	14,098	213,304	242,672
Dec	53,165	139,699	3,891	2,445	47,104	0	0	16,800	370	13,836	215,298	246,304
2011 Jan	51,776	138,664	3,804	2,444	46,216	0	0	14,702	370	13,320	214,511	242,903
Feb	51,542	138,015	3,783	2,444	45,857	0	0	14,102	370	13,273	213,896	241,642
Mar	51,793	134,006	5,049	2,444	49,287	0	0	13,042	370	14,284	214,884	242,580
Apr	53,240	132,054	3,706	2,444	49,084	0	0	12,875	370	14,025	213,259	240,529

Consolidated statement

12.1 Bank of England Balance Sheet

Liabilities and assets outstanding at end of period

Issue Department

	Liabilities					Assets		
	Notes in circulation	Short term open market operations	Of which 1 week sterling reverse repo	Longer term sterling reverse repo	Ways and means advances to HMG	Bonds and other securities acquired via market transactions	Other assets	Total assets and liabilities
	AEFA	**BL29**	**BL32**	**BL34**	**B54A**	**BL35**	**BL36**	**BL37**
2010	53,165	0	0	12,431	370	5,432	34,932	53,165
2010 Jan	49,496	0	0	19,712	370	5,439	23,975	49,496
Feb	49,486	0	0	17,093	370	5,439	26,585	49,486
Mar	50,041	0	0	16,386	370	5,309	27,976	50,041
Apr	50,514	0	0	17,675	370	5,309	27,160	50,514
May	50,920	0	0	17,675	370	5,309	27,566	50,920
Jun	51,206	0	0	18,306	370	5,418	27,112	51,206
Jul	51,037	0	0	11,182	370	5,418	34,067	51,037
Aug	51,105	0	0	9,832	370	5,418	35,485	51,105
Sep	50,988	0	0	5,100	370	5,603	39,915	50,988
Oct	51,145	0	0	12,524	370	5,603	32,648	51,145
Nov	51,459	0	0	11,174	370	5,603	34,312	51,459
Dec	53,165	0	0	12,431	370	5,432	34,932	53,165
2011 Jan	51,776	0	0	10,015	370	5,432	35,959	51,776
Feb	51,542	0	0	9,415	370	5,432	36,325	51,542
Mar	51,793	0	0	10,023	370	5,237	36,163	51,793
Apr	53,240	0	0	10,845	370	5,237	36,788	53,240

Banking Department

	Liabilities					Assets		
	Reserve balances	Foreign currency public securities issued	Cash ratio deposits	Other liabilities	Longer term sterling reverse repo	Bonds and other securities acquired via market transactions	Other assets	Total assets/ liabilities
	BL38	**BL43**	**BL44**	**BL45**	**B3J2**	**BL53**	**BL55**	**BL56**
2010	139,699	3,891	2,445	82,036	4,369	8,404	215,298	228,071
2010 Jan	156,592	3,753	2,574	57,044	5,085	7,163	207,716	219,964
Feb	155,165	3,881	2,574	62,759	3,514	7,252	213,612	224,379
Mar	150,034	5,287	2,574	69,510	3,523	8,707	215,175	227,405
Apr	151,808	3,945	2,574	68,499	3,319	8,384	215,124	226,826
May	150,934	4,230	2,574	70,072	3,319	8,516	215,976	227,811
Jun	149,003	4,093	2,570	70,894	2,086	8,112	216,363	226,561
Jul	150,937	4,008	2,570	77,431	11,615	8,233	215,099	234,947
Aug	151,082	3,911	2,570	76,733	11,615	8,300	214,383	234,297
Sep	143,594	3,909	2,548	84,376	12,500	8,349	213,578	234,427
Oct	142,878	3,860	2,548	76,202	3,726	8,571	213,191	225,488
Nov	142,354	3,834	2,548	76,789	3,726	8,495	213,304	225,525
Dec	139,699	3,891	2,445	82,036	4,369	8,404	215,298	228,071
2011 Jan	138,664	3,804	2,444	82,174	4,687	7,888	214,511	227,086
Feb	138,015	3,783	2,444	82,182	4,687	7,841	213,896	226,425
Mar	134,006	5,049	2,444	85,450	3,019	9,047	214,884	226,950
Apr	132,054	3,706	2,444	85,873	2,030	8,788	213,259	224,077

Source: Bank of England

12.2 Value of inter-bank clearings

United Kingdom

		2004	2005	2006	2007	2008	2009[4]	£ billion 2010
Bulk paper clearings								
Cheque and Credit Clearing Company								
Cheques[1]	**KCYY**	1 111	1 062	1 076	1 157	1 076	882	777
Euro Debits	**JT8O**	..	..	..	..	3	3	2
Credits	**KCYZ**	63	57	56	58	52	43	33
Inter-bank Cheque and Credit	**JT8P**	1 174	1 119	1 132	1 215	1 130	928	812
High-value clearings								
Faster Payments Scheme[3]	**JT8N**	..	..	..	..	33	101	162
CHAPS Sterling	**KCZB**	52 348	52 672	59 437	69 352	73 626	65 482	61 731
Electronic clearing (BACS) Standing Orders/Direct Credits[2]	**JT8J**	2 133	2 353	2 584	2 812	3 006	2 951	3 119
Direct Debits	**JT8L**	750	797	845	884	935	885	942
Euro Direct Credits	**JT8M**	..	..	..	..	5	5	4
Total Bacs	**KCZC**	2 883	3 150	3 429	3 696	3 946	3 840	4 064
Total all Inter-Bank Clearings	**JT8Q**	56 405	56 941	63 998	74 263	88 127	70 353	66 769

Source: APACS -The UK payments association: 020 7711 6223

1 Figures for 2004 - 2007 include Euro Debits.
2 Figures for 2004 - 2007 include Euro Direct Credits.
3 The UK Faster Payments Services was launched on 27th May 2008.
4 Figures revised.

12.3a Monetary Financial Institutions (Excluding Central Bank) Balance sheet, Liabilities and Assets

Amount outstanding at end of period

£ million

Sterling liabilities

	Sterling liabilities: (UK) Sight deposits				Sterling liabilities: (UK) Time deposit						Sterling liabilities	
	MFIs	UK Public sector	Other UK residents	Non-residents	MFIs	UK Public sector	Other UK residents	Of which cash ISAs	Of which SAYE	Non-residents	Notes outstanding and cash loaded cards	Accep-tances granted
	B3GL	B3MM	B3NM	B3OM	B3HL	B3PM	B3QM	B3SM	B3RM	B3TM	B3LM	B3XM
2011 Mar	133,653	10,483	896,596	132,042	228,814	13,526	1,027,702	180,947	..	..	5,735	829
Apr	129,239	12,112	883,995	123,880	237,464	16,363	1,039,084	188,127	..	..	5,940	852
Changes												
	B4GA	B4CF	B4BH	B4DD	B4HA	B4DF	B4CH	B4DH	B4FH	B4ED	B4IJ	B4BK
2011 Mar	6,963	-975	24,452	-428	10,086	-1,411	10,038	3,418	240	-8,286	-178	-66
Apr	-3,387	1,630	-11,934	-9,149	8,650	2,802	10,960	6,590	19	11,620	205	24

Sterling liabilities (continued)

	Sterling liabilities: (UK) under sale and repurchase agreements					Sterling liabilities					
	MFIs	UK Public sector	Other UK residents	Non-residents	CDs and other short term paper issued	Total sterling deposits	Sterling items in suspense and transmission	Net derivatives	Accrued amounts payable	Sterling capital and other internal funds	Total sterling liabilities
	B3IL	B3UM	B3VM	B3WM	B3YM	B3ZM	B3GN	B3HN	B3IN	B3JN	B3KN
2011 Mar	..	..	..	..	193,609	3,145,089	53,585	-9,838	28,220	500,041	3,722,831
Apr	..	..	..	..	193,483	3,149,012	52,377	-26,613	26,419	515,657	3,722,792
Changes											
	B4IA	B4EF	B4EH	B4FD	B4EJ	B4FJ	B4AK	B4GJ	B4CJ	B4DJ	B4JJ
2011 Mar	-20,667	61	-16,505	-2,678	-106	478	5,652	11,303	-2,412	1,947	16,790
Apr	-13,575	1,540	2,322	2,953	-126	4,328	-795	-16,775	-1,797	16,706	1,873

Foreign currency liabilities (including euro)

	Foreign currency liabilities: (UK) Sight and time deposits				Foreign currency liabilities: (UK) Sale and repurchase agreements			
	MFIs	UK Public sector	Other UK residents	Non-residents	MFIs	UK Public sector	Other UK residents	Non-residents
	B3JL	B3LN	B3MN	B3NN	B3KL	B3PN	B3QN	B3RN
2011 Mar	199,322	734	256,861	2,048,375	135,058	1,796	106,825	519,737
Apr	189,117	835	263,155	2,048,023	147,749	1,931	107,715	566,016
Changes								
	B4GB	B4FG	B4FI	B4GE	B4HB	B4GG	B4GI	B4HE
2011 Mar	-2,430	-1	3,275	8,526	-17,104	-4,297	-5,039	-35,815
Apr	-5,449	113	11,386	26,114	11,471	147	1,885	59,281

12.3b Monetary Financial Institutions (Excluding Central Bank) Balance sheet, Liabilities and Assets

Amount outstanding at end of period

	Foreign currency liabilities (including euro)(continued)								
	Accep-tances granted	CDs and other short term paper issued	Total foreign currency deposits	Items in suspense and transmission	Net deriv-atives	Accrued amounts payable	Capital and other internal funds	Total foreign currency liabilities	Total liabilities
	B3KQ	B3SN	B3TN	B3UN	B3VN	B3WN	B3XN	B3YN	B3ZN
2011 Mar	1,359	764,723	4,034,788	207,703	34,778	41,892	67,192	4,386,354	8,109,185
Apr	1,413	763,589	4,089,542	204,326	61,753	42,960	60,615	4,459,195	8,181,987
Changes									
	B4HM	B4CM	B4DM	B4GM	B4EM	B4AM	B4BM	B4FM	B4JM
2011 Mar	122	-8,697	-61,461	10,374	-22,277	849	10,348	-62,167	-45,377
Apr	70	8,442	113,460	-3,722	27,304	951	-6,011	131,982	133,855

Sterling Assets

	Sterling assets:with UK central bank		Market loans UK				Advances (UK)			
	Cash ratio deposits	Other	MFIs	MFIs CDs	MFIs comme-rcial paper	Non-residents	UK Public sector	Other UK residents	Non-residents	Notes and coin
	B3VO	B3WO	B3NL	B3OL	B3PL	B3XO	B3NP	B3OP	B3PP	B3UO
2011 Mar	2,445	135,684	354,518	17,543	121	139,998	7,663	1,950,628	90,953	8,721
Apr	2,445	133,332	360,761	17,662	152	138,779	7,636	1,948,795	89,135	10,045
Changes										
	B3YR	B3ZR	B4DC	B4JB	B4BC	B4BD	B4JE	B4JG	B4HC	B4II
2011 Mar	0	-5,885	17,008	558	1	-9,416	-253	-4,617	2,996	268
Apr	0	-2,352	6,282	119	32	-1,072	-24	1,965	-1,748	1,323

Sterling assets (continued)

	Sterling assets: (UK) Acceptances granted				Bills (UK)				Claims under sale and repurchase agreements (UK)			
	MFIs	UK Public sector	Other UK residents	Non-residents	Treasury bills	MFIs bills	Other UK residents	Non-residents	MFIs	UK Public sector	Other UK residents	Non-residents
	B3QL	B3YO	B3ZO	B3GP	B3HP	B3RL	B3IP	B3JP	B3SL	B3KP	B3LP	B3MP
2011 Mar	1	0	695	133	14,750	136	294	17,860	88,155	352	109,296	32,343
Apr	0	0	697	154	15,059	28	253	17,258	74,973	0	114,606	31,952
Changes												
	B4EC	B4FF	B3TR	B4GD	B4BA	B4IB	B4HG	B4IC	B4FA	B4BF	B4AH	B4CD
2011 Mar	0	0	-58	-8	1,923	5	54	..	-20,953	-103	-2,468	-67
Apr	0	0	3	21	309	-108	-42	..	-13,183	-352	5,952	-390

12.3c Monetary Financial Institutions (Excluding Central Bank) Balance sheet, Liabilities and Assets

	Sterling assets (continued)							£ million	
		Investments							
	British government securities	Other UK Public sector	MFIs	Other UK residents	Non-residents	suspense and collection	Accrued amount receivable	Other assets	Total sterling assets
	B3QP	**B3RP**	**B3TL**	**B3SP**	**B3TP**	**B3UP**	**B3VP**	**B3WP**	**B3XP**
2011 Mar	95,240	335	84,346	371,293	46,372	52,047	32,946	23,350	3,678,352
Apr	104,469	331	85,853	376,355	46,950	52,357	31,566	23,183	3,684,788
Changes									
	B4CA	**B4IE**	**B4CC**	**B4IG**	**B4JC**	**B4BJ**	**B4HI**	**B4JI**	**B4AJ**
2011 Mar	-2,366	-2	-1,176	13,842	-134	6,202	290	-106	-2,246
Apr	7,671	-3	908	3,997	736	311	-1,101	-167	8,348

	Foreign currency assets (including euro)										
	Market loans and advances					Claims under sale and repurchase agreements					
	MFIs	MFIs CDs etc.	UK public sector	Other UK residents	Non-residents	MFIs	UK public sector	Other UK residents	Non-residents	Acceptances granted	Bills
	B3UL	**B3VL**	**B3YP**	**B3ZP**	**B3GQ**	**B3WL**	**B3HQ**	**B3IQ**	**B3JQ**	**B4IP**	**B3LQ**
2011 Mar	196,145	5,059	147	284,652	1,969,198	139,890	1,364	172,837	635,900	1,359	50,827
Apr	192,193	5,277	68	279,175	1,981,391	150,856	854	181,888	666,477	1,413	61,160
Changes											
	B4EB	**B4AF**	**B4DG**	**B4DI**	**B4EE**	**B4FB**	**B4EG**	**B4EI**	**B4FE**	**B4HP**	**B4GL**
2011 Mar	-8,182	-318	62	13,745	22,838	-16,055	1	-9,858	-32,224	-32,224	122
Apr	-1,999	208	-77	61	38,951	12,318	-489	10,154	42,384	42,384	70

	Foreign currency assets (including euro)(continued)											
	Investments											
	British govt securities	Other public sector	MFIs	Other UK residents	Non-residents	Items in suspense & collection	Accrued amounts receivable	Other assets	Total foreign currency assets	Total assets	Holdings of own sterling acceptances	Holdings of own FC acceptances
	B3MQ	**B3NQ**	**B3XL**	**B3OQ**	**B3PQ**	**B3QQ**	**B3RQ**	**B3SQ**	**B3TQ**	**B3UQ**	**B3IM**	**B3JM**
2011 Mar	20	0	38,501	65,361	571,955	216,140	38,036	43,438	4,430,828	8,109,180	287	1,056
Apr	19	0	36,135	66,615	576,886	217,447	37,465	41,875	4,497,194	8,181,982	286	1,176
Changes												
	B4EA	**B4CG**	**B4AG**	**B4CI**	**B4DE**	**B4JL**	**B4FL**	**B4HL**	**B4IL**	**B4IM**	**B3VR**	**B3XR**
2011 Mar	-1	0	1,050	-2,387	-11,577	8,359	1,008	-4,470	-43,130	-45,377	4	104
Apr	-1	0	-2,197	2,239	8,515	5,343	41	-701	125,495	133,843	-1	155

Source: Bank of England

See Supplementary Information Also see footnotes in Bank of England Monetary and Financial Statistics Table B1.4

12.4a Industrial analysis of Monetary Financial Institution lending to UK residents[1]

Not seasonally adjusted

£ million

	UK residents	Agriculture, hunting and forestry	Fishing	Mining & quarrying	Manufacturing			
	Total				Total	Food, beverages & tobacco	Textiles and leather	Pulp, paper, publishing & printing

Total amounts outstanding (sterling & other currencies)

	TBSA	TBSC	TBSD	TBSE	TBSF	TBSG	TBSH	TBSI
2009	2,511,479	11,149	347	7,060	48,789	11,168	1,469	8,302
2010	2,544,731	11,556	313	7,250	46,091	10,169	1,194	7,506

of which in sterling

	TBUA	TBUC	TBUD	TBUE	TBUF	TBUG	TBUH	TBUI
2009	2,070,832	10,673	338	1,922	28,730	7,300	955	4,164
2010	2,082,339	11,180	306	2,295	26,796	6,881	762	3,779

Facilities granted

	TCAA	TCAC	TCAD	TCAE	TCAF	TCAG	TCAH	TCAI
2009	2,873,501	14,302	405	18,838	90,180	21,111	2,208	13,532
2010	2,911,176	14,656	381	23,255	89,598	20,643	1,672	12,211

of which in sterling

	TCCA	TCCC	TCCD	TCCE	TCCF	TCCG	TCCH	TCCI
2009	2,328,306		393	2,917	45,158	10,527	1,376	6,121
2010	2,334,646		375	3,293	43,752	10,793	1,010	5,546

	Manufacturing					Electricity, gas & water supply		
	Chemicals, man-made fibres, rubber & plastics	Non-metallic mineral products & metals	Machinery, equipment & transport equipment	Electrical, medical & optical equipment	Other manufacturing	Electricity, gas & heated water	Cold water purification & supply	Construction

Total amounts outstanding (sterling & other currencies)

	TBSJ	TBSK	TBSL	TBSM	TBSN	TBSO	TBSP	TBSQ
2009	..	6,756	7,697		4,852	8,021	3,518	26,333
2010	..	5,122	8,008		4,552	6,646	2,831	23,818

of which in sterling

	TBUJ	TBUK	TBUL	TBUM	TBUN	TBUO	TBUP	TBUQ
2009	2,662	4,017	4,141	1,926	3,565	5,922	3,485	25,611
2010	2,698	3,119	4,345	2,035	3,177	5,079	2,759	22,935

Facilities granted

	TCAJ	TCAK	TCAL	TCAM	TCAN	TCAO	TCAP	TCAQ
2009	..	11,350	14,668	6,054	7,583	15,668	7,233	39,142
2010	..	9,224	15,594	6,464	8,035	17,179	6,364	34,922

of which in sterling

	TCCJ	TCCK	TCCL	TCCM	TCCN	TCCO	TCCP	TCCQ
2009	4,702	6,278	7,821	2,998	5,336	9,651	6,413	36,495
2010	5,787	4,739	8,021	2,984	4,872	10,535	5,359	32,639

12.4b Industrial analysis of Monetary Financial Institution lending to UK residents[1]

Not seasonally adjusted continued

£ million

		Wholesale and retail trade					Real estate, renting, computer and other business activities		
	Total	Sale & repair of motor vehicles & fuel	Other wholesale trade	Other retail trade & repair	Hotels and restaurants	Transport, storage & communication	Total	Development, buying, selling, renting of real estate	Renting of machinery & equipment
Total Amounts outstanding (sterling & other currencies)									
	TBSR	TBSS	TBST	TBSU	TBSV	TBSW	TBSX	TBSY	TBTA
2009	47,438	11,260	15,639	20,539	..	29,600	300,783	249,284	7,766
2010	44,167	11,029	13,853	19,285	..	29,207	271,961	227,359	5,867
of which in sterling									
	TBUR	TBUS	TBUT	TBUU	TBUV	TBUW	TBUX	TBUY	TBVA
2009	40,314	10,881	10,313	19,119	31,742	21,805	285,896	242,599	6,596
2010	38,271	10,524	9,767	17,980	28,896	21,592	260,554	222,602	5,013
Facilities granted									
	TCAR	TCAS	TCAT	TCAU	TCAV	TCAW	TCAX	TCAY	TCBA
2009	73,035	14,217	24,918	33,900	38,110	46,893	359,495	288,737	9,774
2010	68,443	13,637	22,262	32,543	34,854	46,666	327,903	263,290	8,448
of which in sterling									
	TCCR	TCCS	TCCT	TCCU	TCCV	TCCW	TCCX	TCCY	TCDA
2009	56,678	13,066	15,400	28,212	35,707	30,632	332,384	276,677	7,811
2010	53,735	12,571	14,421	26,743	32,458	29,470	304,547	253,511	6,470

	Real estate, renting, computer and other business activities					Recreational, personal & community service activities		Financial intermediation (excl. insurance & pension funds)	
	Computer & related activities	Legal, accountancy, consultancy & other business activities	Public administration & defence	Education	Health & social work	Recreational, cultural & sporting activities	Personal & community services activities	Total	Financial leasing corporations
Total Amounts outstanding (sterling & other currencies)									
	TBTB	TBTC	TBTD	TBTE	TBTF	TBTH	TBTG	TBTI	TBTJ
2009	4,767		13,270	11,522	22,084	13,630	6,686	696,570	39,409
2010	3,682		11,148	11,798	22,529	11,591	5,928	652,805	36,298
of which in sterling									
	TBVB	TBVC	TBVD	TBVE	TBVF	TBVH	TBVG	TBVI	TBVJ
2009	3,137	33,564	12,140	11,371	21,684	12,409	6,100	412,975	28,856
2010	2,806	30,132	10,562	11,655	22,180	10,543	5,576	366,903	26,565
Facilities granted									
	TCBB	TCBC	TCBD	TCBE	TCBF	TCBH	TCBG	TCBI	TCBJ
2009	6,778	54,207	16,146	14,912	25,324	17,875	8,782	738,774	42,779
2010	5,621	50,543	14,138	14,907	26,727	15,351	8,054	694,531	40,248
of which in sterling									
	TCDB	TCDC	TCDD	TCDE	TCDF	TCDH	TCDG	TCDI	TCDJ
2009	4,189	43,707	14,892	14,663	24,618	15,200	7,757	432,099	31,605
2010	3,771	40,795	13,534	14,682	26,014	12,938	6,999	386,108	29,591

12.4c Industrial analysis of Monetary Financial Institution lending to UK residents[1]

Not seasonally adjusted

continued £ million

	Non-bank credit grantors, excl. credit unions	Credit unions	Factoring corporations	Mortgage & housing credit corporations	Investment & unit trusts excl. money market mutual funds	Money market mutual funds	Bank holding companies	Securities dealers (f)	Other financial intermediaries
	Financial intermediation (excl. insurance & pension funds)								

Amounts outstanding (sterling & other currencies)

Total

	TBTK	TBTL	TBTM	TBTN	TBTO	TBTP	TBTQ	TBTR	TBTS
2009	24,439	67	6,514	83,586	8,836	121	37,791	185,808	309,999
2010	18,506	2	7,589	73,504	18,394	140	40,962	174,597	282,814

of which in sterling

	TBVK	TBVL	TBVM	TBVN	TBVO	TBVP	TBVQ	TBVR	TBVS
2009	21,977	67	5,797	81,136	5,152	29	33,073	31,036	205,851
2010	16,479	1	6,956	71,309	6,314	57	35,968	24,419	178,835

Facilities granted

	TCBK	TCBL	TCBM	TCBN	TCBO	TCBP	TCBQ	TCBR	TCBS
2009	26,401	76	6,982	88,137	12,086	159	38,044	186,962	337,148
2010	19,763	12	8,028	76,342	20,493	140	41,215	175,746	312,545

of which in sterling

	TCDK	TCDL	TCDM	TCDN	TCDO	TCDP	TCDQ	TCDR	TCDS
2009	23,444	75	6,054	85,171	7,158	29	33,193	31,686	213,683
2010	17,264	11	7,296	73,924	7,395	57	36,080	24,737	189,753

	Insurance companies & pension funds	Fund management activities	Other	Total	Lending secured on dwellings inc. bridging finance	Other loans & activities
	Activities auxiliary to financial			Individuals and individual trusts		

Amounts outstanding (sterling & other currencies)

Loans & advances (including under repo & sterling commercial paper)

	TBPT	TBPU	TBPV	TBPW	TBPX	TBPY
2009	..	..	..	1,008,611	876,113	132,497
2010	..	..	..	1,131,932	1,002,795	129,137

Total

	TBTT	TBTU	TBTV	TBTW	TBTX	TBTY
2009	22,445	45,092	155,969	1,008,611	876,113	132,497
2010	21,735	48,967	152,909	1,131,932	1,002,795	129,137

of which in sterling

	TBVT	TBVU	TBVV	TBVW	TBVX	TBVY
2009	18,928	10,506	101,716	1,006,567	..	131,205
2010	17,753	14,585	71,752	1,130,166	..	128,051

Facilities granted

	TCBT	TCBU	TCBV	TCBW	TCBX	TCBY
2009	29,268	46,567	158,746	1,113,807	924,223	189,584
2010	28,122	51,160	157,517	1,236,449	1,051,655	184,794

of which in sterling

	TCDT	TCDU	TCDV	TCDW	TCDX	TCDY
2009	23,188	11,156	103,085	1,111,460	923,471	187,989
2010	21,145	15,412	73,032	1,234,426	1,050,976	183,451

1 See chapter text.

Source: Bank of England: 020 7601 3236

12.5a Industrial analysis of Monetary Financial Institution lending to UK residents[1]

£ million

	Total from UK residents	Agriculture, hunting and forestry	Fishing	Mining & quarrying	Manufacturing			
					Total	Food, beverages & tobacco	Textiles & leather	Pulp, paper, publishing & printing

Amounts outstanding (sterling & other currencies)

Deposit liabilities (including under repos)

	TDAA	TDAB	TDAC	TDAD	TDAE	TDAF	TDAG	TDAH
2009	2,312,141	5,076	202	7,483	44,808	3,207	1,283	4,192
2010	2,400,078	5,307	211	14,724	48,069	4,253	1,253	4,944
of which in sterling								
	TDCA	TDCB	TDCC	TDCD	TDCE	TDCF	TDCG	TDCH
2009	1,965,974	4,815	193	2,185	31,545	2,593	1,026	3,505
2010	2,046,846	5,132	200	2,872	33,960	3,221	865	3,651

	Manufacturing				Electricity, gas & water supply			
	Chemicals, man-made fibres, rubber & plastics	Non-metallic mineral products & metals	Machinery, equipment & transport equipment	Electrical, medical & optical equipment	Other manufacturing	Electricity, gas & heated water	Cold water purification & supply	Construction

Amounts outstanding (sterling & other currencies)

Deposit liabilities (including under repos)

	TDAI	TDAJ	TDAK	TDAL	TDAM	TDAN	TDAO	TDAP
2009	8,280	5,442	11,735	6,373	4,295	5,104	2,966	18,671
2010	9,146	4,889	11,636	7,319	4,627	6,092	3,118	17,928
of which in sterling								
	TDCI	TDCJ	TDCK	TDCL	TDCM	TDCN	TDCO	TDCP
2009	3,659	4,310	8,914	4,143	3,394	3,769	2,913	18,263
2010	6,866	3,919	7,802	4,371	3,266	3,987	3,101	17,439

	Wholesale and retail trade						Real estate, renting, computer and other business activities		
	Total	Sale & repair of motor vehicles & fuel	Other wholesale trade	Other retail trade & repair	Hotels and restaurants	Transport, storage & communication	Total	Development, buying, selling, renting of real estate	Renting of machinery and equipment

Amounts outstanding (sterling & other currencies)

Deposit liabilities (including under repos)

	TDAQ	TDAR	TDAS	TDAT	TDAU	TDAV	TDAW	TDAX	TDAY
2009	32,867	4,192	14,282	14,393	4,652	17,788	128,596	35,714	1,912
2010	33,036	5,509	14,789	12,738	5,082	19,479	131,867	35,422	2,125
of which in sterling									
	TDCQ	TDCR	TDCS	TDCT	TDCU	TDCV	TDCW	TDCX	TDCY
2009	28,259	3,864	10,952	13,443	4,578	14,088	111,148	34,944	1,608
2010	27,608	4,744	10,935	11,929	4,878	13,773	111,612	34,472	1,795

12.5b Industrial analysis of Monetary Financial Institution deposits from UK residents[1]

£ million

	Real estate, renting, computer and other business activities		Public administration & defence	Education	Health & social work	Recreational, personal & community service activities		Financial intermediation (excl. insurance & pension funds)	
	Computer & related activities	Legal, accountancy, consultancy & other business activities	Public administration & defence	Education	Health & social work	Recreational, cultural & sporting activities	Personal & community services activities	Total	Financial leasing corporations
Amounts outstanding (sterling & other currencies)									
Deposit liabilities (including under repos)									
	TDAZ	**TDBA**	**TDBB**	**TDBC**	**TDBD**	**TDBF**	**TDBE**	**TDBG**	**TDBH**
2009	9,862	81,107	58,082	11,199	15,287	17,562	16,488	700,405	4,979
2010	11,116	83,205	31,655	12,744	15,901	16,975	16,358	808,042	5,645
of which in sterling									
	TDCZ	**TDDA**	**TDDB**	**TDDC**	**TDDD**	**TDDF**	**TDDE**	**TDDG**	**TDDH**
2009	8,332	66,264	53,445	10,731	14,443	16,332	15,699	508,226	3,994
2010	9,405	65,941	26,924	12,175	15,209	15,813	15,762	618,153	4,793

	Financial intermediation (excl. insurance & pension funds)								
	Non-bank credit grantors, excl. credit unions	Credit unions	Factoring corporations	Mortgage & housing credit corporations	Investment & unit trusts excl. money market mutual funds	Money market mutual funds	Bank holding companies	Securities dealers	Other financial intermediaries
Amounts outstanding (sterling & other currencies)									
Deposit liabilities (including under repos)									
	TDBI	**TDBJ**	**TDBK**	**TDBL**	**TDBM**	**TDBN**	**TDBO**	**TDBP**	**TDBQ**
2009	8,607	514	841	115,986	34,202	498	67,519	128,854	338,404
2010	11,858	587	951	250,620	41,558	263	55,954	118,046	322,559
of which in sterling									
	TDDI	**TDDJ**	**TDDK**	**TDDL**	**TDDM**	**TDDN**	**TDDO**	**TDDP**	**TDDQ**
2009	6,865	514	756	114,230	25,660	303	48,377	37,320	270,208
2010	10,129	586	868	250,097	25,739	174	36,029	28,581	261,157

	Activities auxiliary to financial intermediation			
	Insurance companies & pension funds	Placed by fund managers	Other	Individuals & individual trusts
Amounts outstanding (sterling & other currencies)				
Deposit liabilities (including under repos)				
	TDBR	**TDBS**	**TDBT**	**TDBU**
2009	57,741	88,052	156,178	922,934
2010	53,523	97,241	110,949	951,776
of which in sterling				
	TDDR	**TDDS**	**TDDT**	**TDDU**
2009	48,986	42,947	114,725	918,685
2010	44,205	48,012	78,476	947,556

Source: Bank of England: 02076013236

1 See chapter text.

12.6 Public sector net cash requirement and other counterparts

Not seasonally adjusted

£ million

		2000	2001	2002	2003	2004	2005	2006	2007	2008	2009	2010
Public sector net cash requirement (surplus)	**ABEN**	-36,864	-2,019	18,010	37,160	41,915	41,278	33,916	31,089	125,369	205,186	..
Sales of public sector debt to M4 private sector	**IDH8**	13,639	7,716	-9,258	-32,438	-32,007	-11,257	-20,082	-16,293	..	..	..
M4 lending[1]	**AVBS**	111,202	82,574	107,553	127,820	156,084	158,087	218,445	238,491	270,461	135,507	-80,422
External and foreign currency finance of the public sector	**VQDC**	3,616	3,875	2,486	-13,441	-2,395	-30,708	-33,554	-38,366	-36,146	-21,179	..
Other external and foreign currency flows[2]	**AVBW**	7,178	-21,631	-25,132	-27,124	4,288	33,643	-874	-37,241	148,653	-159,956	..
Net non-deposit liabilities (increase)	**AVBX**	-31,050	-10,791	-25,130	-20,377	-67,401	-39,903	-29,964	-4,451	-172,812	-49,636	..
Money stock (M4)	**AUZI**	67,201	58,998	68,826	73,279	100,018	150,870	167,028	188,556	258,872	128,757	-29,755

Source: Bank of England: 020 7601 5468

1 Bank and building society lending, plus holdings of commercial bills by the Issue Department of the Bank of England.
2 Including sterling lending to non-residents sector.

12.7 Money stock and liquidity

£ million

		2000	2001	2002	2003	2004	2005	2006	2007	2008	2009	2010
Amounts outstanding at end-year												
Notes and coin in circulation with the M4 private sector[1]	**VQKT**	28,174	30,450	31,889	34,010	36,410	38,508	40,546	43,039	46,252	50,284	52,357
UK private sector sterling non-interest bearing sight deposits[2]	**AUYA**	45,867	50,548	45,594	51,274	50,845	55,208	54,800	62,051	72,664	124,126	..
Money stock (M2)[3]	**VQXV**	597,523	649,980	703,920	777,347	845,654	922,687	996,652	1,071,454	1,123,831	1,187,097	1,235,056
Money stock M4	**AUYM**	884,873	942,597	1,008,743	1,081,297	1,179,196	1,328,323	1,498,944	1,674,889	1,937,220	2,041,871	2,158,781
Changes during the year[4]												
Notes and coin in circulation with the M4 private sector[1]	**VQLU**	1,957	2,284	1,493	2,189	2,461	2,156	2,060	2,565	3,177	6,439	2,141
UK private sector sterling non-interest bearing sight deposits[2]	**AUZA**	3,533	4,914	-6,761	5,321	-227	5,699	-409	9,292	587	35,522	..
Money stock (M2)[3]	**AUZE**	39,123	52,813	53,698	72,255	68,901	78,428	72,764	65,042	48,558	..	..
Money stock M4	**AUZI**	67,201	58,998	68,826	73,279	100,018	150,870	167,028	188,556	258,872	128,757	-29,755

Source: Bank of England: 02076015468

1 The estimates of levels of coin in circulation include allowance for wastage, hoarding, etc.
2 Non-interest bearing deposits are confined to those with institutions included in the United Kingdom banks sector (See Table 12.3).

3 M2 comprises the UK non-monetary financial institutions and non-public sector, i.e. M4 private sector's holdings of notes and coin together with its sterling denominated retail deposits with UK monetary financial institutions.
4 As far as possible the changes exclude the effect of changes in the number of contributors to the series, and also of the introduction of new statistical returns. Changes are not seasonally adjusted.

12.8 Selected retail banks' base rate[1]

Operative between dates shown

Percentage rates

Date of change	New rate	Date of change	New rate	Date of change	New rate
1986 Jan-09	12.50	Oct-05	15.00	1999 Jan-07	6.00
Mar-19	11.50			Feb-04	5.50
Apr-08	11.00-11.50	1990 Oct-08	14.00	Apr-08	5.25
Apr-09	11.00			Jun-10	5.00
Apr-21	10.50	1991 Feb-13	13.50	Sep-08	5.00-5.25
May-23	10.00-10.50	Feb-27	13.00	Sep-10	5.25
May-27	10.00	Mar-22	12.50	Nov-04	5.50
Oct-14	10.00-11.00	Apr-12	12.00		
Oct-15	11.00	May-24	11.50	2000 Jan-13	5.75
		Jul-12	11.00	Feb-10	6.00
1987 Mar-10	10.50	Sep-04	10.50		
Mar-18	10.00-10.50			2001 Feb-08	5.75
Mar-19	10.00	1992 May-05	10.00	Apr-05	5.50
Apr-28	9.50-10.00	Sep-16[2]	12.00	May-10	5.25
Apr-29	9.50	Sep-17[2]	10.00-12.00	Aug-02	5.00
May-11	9.00	Sep-18	10.00	Sep-18	4.75
Aug-06	9.00-10.00	Sep-22	9.00	Oct-04	4.50
Aug-07	10.00	Oct-16	8.00-9.00	Nov-08	4.00
Oct-23	9.50-10.00	Oct-19	8.00		
Oct-29	9.50	Nov-13	7.00	2003 Feb-06	3.75
Nov-04	9.00-9.50			Jul-10	3.50
Nov-05	9.00	1993 Jan-26	6.00	Nov-06	3.75
Dec-04	8.50	Nov-23	5.50		
				2004 Feb-05	4.00
1988 Feb-02	9.00	1994 Feb-08	5.25	May-06	4.25
Mar-17	8.50-9.00	Sep-12	5.75	Jun-10	4.50
Mar-18	8.50	Dec-07	6.25	Aug-05	4.75
Apr-11	8.00				
May-17	7.50-8.00	1995 Feb-22	6.25-6.75	2005 Aug-04	4.50
May-18	7.50	Feb-03	6.75		
Jun-02	7.50-8.00	Dec-13	6.50	2006 Aug-03	4.75
Jun-03	8.00			Nov-09	5.00
Jun-06	8.00-8.50	1996 Jan-18	6.25		
Jun-07	8.50	Mar-08	6.00	2007 Jan-11	5.25
Jun-22	8.50-9.00	Jun-06	5.75	May-10	5.50
Jun-23	9.00	Oct-30	5.75-6.00	Jul-05	5.75
Jun-28	9.00-9.50	Oct-31	6.00	Dec-06	5.50
Jun-29	9.50				
Jul-04	9.50-10.00	1997 May-06	6.25	2008 Feb-07	5.25
Jul-05	10.00	Jun-06	6.25-6.50	Apr-10	5
Jul-18	10.00-10.50	Jun-09	6.50	Oct-08	4.5
Jul-19	10.50	Jul-10	6.75	Nov-06	3
Aug-08	10.50-11.00	Aug-07	7.00	Dec-04	2
Aug-09	11.00	Nov-06	7.25		
Aug-25	11.00-12.00			2009 Jan-08	1.5
Aug-26	12.00	1998 Jun-04	7.50	Feb-05	1
Nov-25	13.00	Oct-08	7.25	Mar-05	0.5
		Nov-05	6.75		
1989 May-24	14.00	Dec-10	6.25		

Source: Bank of England: 020 7601 3644

1 Data obtained from Barclays Bank, Lloyds/TSB Bank, HSBC Bank and
National Westminster Bank whose rates are used to compile this series.
2 Where all the rates did not change on the same day a spread is shown.

12.9 Average three month sterling money market rates[1]

Percentage rates

	1998	1999	2000	2001	2002	2003	2004	2005	2006	2007	2008	2009	2010	2011
Treasury bills:[2] KDMM														
January	6.8	5.28	5.72	5.49	3.83	3.8	3.92	4.66	4.39	5.3	5.12	0.9	0.49	0.51
February	6.88	5.04	5.83	5.46	3.87	3.5	4.01	4.69	4.38	5.34	5.02	0.72	0.49	0.54
March	6.95	4.92	5.86	5.23	3.97	3.47	4.13	4.77	4.4	5.33	4.88	0.6	0.51	0.56
April	7	4.9	5.92	5.12	3.97	3.45	4.2	4.7	4.42	5.43	4.83	0.63	0.51	..
May	7.01	4.93	5.95	4.98	3.95	3.44	4.4	4.66	4.5	5.55	4.95	0.53	0.50	..
June	7.29	4.76	5.85	4.99	3.98	3.47	4.61	4.62	4.54	5.67	5.11	0.5	0.48	..
July	7.22	4.76	5.83	5.01	3.84	3.31	4.67	4.46	4.53	5.77	5.08	0.44	0.50	..
August	7.19	4.85	5.81	4.72	3.77	3.4	4.71	4.41	4.75	5.79	4.95	0.4	0.50	..
September	6.94	5.12	5.78	4.43	3.79	3.52	4.69	4.4	4.84	5.69	4.74	0.38	0.50	..
October	6.54	5.23	5.75	4.16	3.75	3.65	4.68	4.4	4.94	5.61	3.68	0.43	0.51	..
November	6.31	5.2	5.68	3.78	3.8	3.81	4.66	4.42	5.01	5.5	1.99	0.47	0.49	..
December	5.72	5.46	5.62	3.83	3.84	3.83	4.68	4.43	5.08	5.3	1.29	0.36	0.49	..
Eligible bill: KDMY[3]														
January	7.28	5.63	5.9	5.64	3.91	3.87	3.94	4.75	..	..	..	..	..	..
February	7.24	5.28	6.01	5.56	3.92	3.65	4.06	4.78	..	..	..	..	..	..
March	7.25	5.11	5.98	5.37	3.99	3.54	4.19	4.88	..	..	..	..	..	..
April	7.24	5.02	6.05	5.21	4.04	3.52	4.28	4.84	..	..	..	..	..	..
May	7.2	5.08	6.09	5.06	4.01	3.52	4.42	4.8	..	..	..	..	..	..
June	7.42	4.94	6.03	5.08	4.04	3.45	4.68	4.76	..	..	..	..	..	..
July	7.49	4.89	5.97	5.07	3.94	3.39	4.75	4.57	..	..	..	..	..	..
August	7.4	4.94	5.97	4.82	3.86	3.42	4.85	4.51	..	..	..	..	..	..
September	7.2	5.16	5.95	4.57	3.86	3.59	4.83	..	..	..	..	..	..	..
October	6.91	5.42	5.92	4.26	3.82	3.69	4.79	..	..	..	..	..	..	..
November	6.52	5.43	5.88	3.85	3.84	3.88	4.78	..	..	..	..	..	..	..
December	6.05	5.59	5.78	3.88	3.71	3.9	4.77	..	..	..	..	..	..	..
Interbank rate: AMIJ														
January	7.48	5.8	6.06	5.76	3.98	3.91	3.99	4.8	4.54	5.45	5.61	2.28	0.60	0.78
February	7.46	5.43	6.15	5.69	3.98	3.69	4.1	4.82	4.52	5.52	5.61	2.08	0.60	0.78
March	7.48	5.3	6.15	5.47	4.06	3.58	4.23	4.92	4.53	5.5	5.86	1.83	0.60	0.78
April	7.44	5.23	6.21	5.33	4.11	3.58	4.33	4.88	4.57	5.61	5.9	1.48	0.60	0.80
May	7.41	5.25	6.23	5.17	4.08	3.57	4.46	4.83	4.65	5.72	5.79	1.3	0.66	..
June	7.63	5.12	6.14	5.19	4.11	3.57	4.73	4.78	4.69	5.83	5.9	1.21	0.71	..
July	7.71	5.07	6.11	5.19	3.99	3.42	4.79	4.59	4.68	5.98	5.8	1.03	0.75	..
August	7.66	5.18	6.14	4.93	3.92	3.45	4.89	4.53	4.9	6.34	5.76	0.8	0.75	..
September	7.38	5.32	6.12	4.65	3.93	3.63	4.87	4.54	4.98	6.58	5.87	0.62	0.76	..
October	7.14	5.94	6.08	4.36	3.9	3.73	4.83	4.53	5.09	6.21	6.18	0.56	0.75	..
November	6.89	5.78	6	3.93	3.91	3.91	4.82	4.56	5.18	6.36	4.4	0.6	0.75	..
December	6.38	5.97	5.89	3.99	3.95	3.95	4.81	4.59	5.25	6.35	3.21	0.61	0.76	..
Certificate of deposits: KOSA														
January	7.44	5.74	6.02	5.73	3.96	3.9	3.98	4.8	4.54	5.45	5.61	2.29	0.58	0.83
February	7.42	5.38	6.1	5.66	3.96	3.68	4.09	4.82	4.52	5.51	5.6	2.06	0.58	0.83
March	7.43	5.26	6.09	5.44	4.04	3.57	4.22	4.91	4.53	5.52	5.85	1.79	0.60	0.83
April	7.4	5.19	6.17	5.3	4.08	3.57	4.32	4.86	4.57	5.69	5.89	1.43	0.63	..
May	7.37	5.22	6.19	5.15	4.06	3.56	4.45	4.82	4.65	5.84	5.79	1.27	0.68	..
June	7.59	5.09	6.1	5.16	4.09	3.56	4.72	4.78	4.69	5.94	5.89	1.14	0.77	..
July	7.66	5.03	6.08	5.17	3.97	3.41	4.79	4.6	4.68	6.11	5.8	0.92	0.78	..
August	7.61	5.14	6.09	4.9	3.9	3.44	4.89	4.53	4.89	6.35	5.75	0.69	0.77	..
September	7.34	5.28	6.08	4.62	3.91	3.62	4.87	4.54	4.98	6.54	5.86	0.51	0.73	..
October	7.09	5.86	6.05	4.33	3.88	3.72	4.83	4.52	5.09	6.21	6.16	0.5	0.73	..
November	6.82	5.72	5.98	3.91	3.89	3.9	4.81	4.56	5.18	6.34	4.4	0.58	0.73	..
December	6.32	5.89	5.85	3.96	3.93	3.94	4.8	4.58	5.24	6.35	3.21	0.58	0.77	..
Local authority deposits: KDPX4														
January	7.43	5.76	6.03	5.73	3.85	3.87	3.91	..	..	..	..	..	..	..
February	7.4	5.38	6.09	5.62	3.88	3.61	4.08	..	..	..	..	..	..	..
March	7.4	5.27	6.08	5.39	4.01	3.55	4.12	..	..	..	..	..	..	..
April	7.38	5.17	6.12	5.26	4.05	3.54	4.31	..	..	..	..	..	..	..
May	7.34	5.19	6.14	5.13	4.06	3.54	4.45	..	..	..	..	..	..	..
June	7.56	5.07	6.09	5.1	4.05	3.57	4.75	..	..	..	..	..	..	..
July	7.64	5.01	6.04	5.12	3.95	3.39	4.82	..	..	..	..	..	..	..
August	7.55	5.11	6.06	4.86	3.87	3.43	4.92	..	..	..	..	..	..	..
September	7.35	5.19	6.05	4.58	3.88	3.61	4.9	..	..	..	..	..	..	..
October	7.08	5.83	6.03	4.29	3.86	3.71	4.85	..	..	..	..	..	..	..
November	6.85	5.64	5.96	3.82	3.87	3.9	4.84	..	..	..	..	..	..	..
December	6.35	5.88	5.8	3.87	3.93	3.92	4.82	..	..	..	..	..	..	..

Source: Bank of England: 020 7601 4444

1 A full definition of these series is given in Section 7 of the ONS Financial Statistics Explanatory Handbook.
2 Average rate of discount at weekly (Friday) tender.
3 This series discontinued at end of August 2005.
4 This series discontinued at end of December 2004.

12.10 Average foreign exchange rates[1]

	1998	1999	2000	2001	2002	2003	2004	2005	2006	2007	2008	2009	2010	2011
Sterling exchange rate index (1990 = 100)[2] AGBG														
January	104.7	99.6	108.5	104.4	106.9	104.0	102.4	102.1	102.7	..	..	..	..	..
February	104.7	100.8	108.4	104.1	107.4	102.4	104.8	103.3	102.8	..	..	..	..	..
March	106.8	102.8	108.4	105.0	106.5	100.6	105.0	103.2	102.1					
April	107.1	103.4	110.1	105.8	107.1	99.8	105.2	104.4	101.9					
May	103.4	104.2	108.5	106.6	105.3	97.9	104.6	103.6	104.1					
June	105.4	104.7	104.6	106.8	103.6	99.6	105.8	104.9	..	..	..	..	..	..
July	105.3	103.5	105.6	107.2	105.3	99.4	105.9	102.1						
August	104.6	103.3	107.4	105.1	105.4	99.0	105.2	102.8						
September	103.3	104.7	106.2	106.1	106.5	99.2	103.3	103.9						
October	100.7	105.4	109.2	105.8	106.7	99.8	102.2	103.1						
November	100.6	105.7	107.3	106.1	105.9	100.4	101.7	103.2						
December	100.4	106.7	106.4	106.5	105.5	100.3	103.2	103.3						
Effective Sterling exchange rate index (Jan 2005 = 100) BK67														
January	100.4	96.3	102.9	98.5	100.6	99.9	100.2	100	99.1	105.4	96.5	76.7	81.1	80.9
February	100.1	97.1	102.5	98.1	100.8	98.5	102.5	101	98.9	104.9	96	78.6	80.4	81.5
March	101.8	98.8	102.3	98.8	100.1	96.8	102.2	101.1	98.4	103.4	94.5	76.6	77.6	80.2
April	102.1	98.8	103.7	99.4	100.9	96.1	102.2	102	98.4	104.1	92.7	78.6	79.5	79.6
May	98.9	99.6	101.7	99.8	99.5	94.9	101.8	101	101.2	103.8	92.7	80.2	79.4	..
June	100.9	99.6	98.7	99.6	98.2	96.6	103.1	101.8	100.9	104.4	92.8	83.7	81.2	..
July	100.8	98.4	99.4	100.2	100.4	96.1	103.2	98.8	100.9	105.1	92.9	83.2	81.5	..
August	100.3	98.7	100.6	98.8	100.3	95.5	102.4	99.7	102.9	104.4	91.4	83.4	82.7	..
September	99.6	99.8	99.1	99.9	101.4	95.8	100.7	100.7	102.9	103.2	89.6	80.9	81.3	..
October	97.4	100.7	101.7	99.7	101.7	96.9	99.8	99.7	103.1	102.7	89.1	79.1	79.5	..
November	97.2	100.6	100.1	99.8	101.1	97.5	99.7	99.4	103.4	101.7	83.2	80.7	81.0	..
December	97.2	101.3	99.8	100.4	100.8	97.9	101.3	99.5	104.4	99.8	77.9	80.1	80.5	..
Sterling/US Dollar AUSS														
January	1.6	1.7	1.6	1.5	1.4	1.6	1.8	1.9	1.8	2	2	1.4	1.6	1.6
February	1.6	1.6	1.6	1.5	1.4	1.6	1.9	1.9	1.7	2	2	1.4	1.6	1.6
March	1.7	1.6	1.6	1.4	1.4	1.6	1.8	1.9	1.7	1.9	2	1.4	1.5	1.6
April	1.7	1.6	1.6	1.4	1.4	1.6	1.8	1.9	1.8	2	2	1.5	1.5	1.6
May	1.6	1.6	1.5	1.4	1.5	1.6	1.8	1.9	1.9	2	2	1.5	1.5	..
June	1.7	1.6	1.5	1.4	1.5	1.7	1.8	1.8	1.8	2	2	1.6	1.5	..
July	1.6	1.6	1.5	1.4	1.6	1.6	1.8	1.8	1.8	2	2	1.6	1.5	..
August	1.6	1.6	1.5	1.4	1.5	1.6	1.8	1.8	1.9	2	1.9	1.7	1.6	..
September	1.7	1.6	1.4	1.5	1.6	1.6	1.8	1.8	1.9	2	1.8	1.6	1.6	..
October	1.7	1.7	1.5	1.5	1.6	1.7	1.8	1.8	1.9	2	1.7	1.6	1.6	..
November	1.7	1.6	1.4	1.4	1.6	1.7	1.9	1.7	1.9	2.1	1.5	1.7	1.6	..
December	1.7	1.6	1.5	1.4	1.6	1.8	1.9	1.7	2	2	1.5	1.6	1.6	..
Sterling/Euro THAP														
January	1.5	1.4	1.6	1.6	1.6	1.5	1.4	1.4	1.5	1.5	1.3	1.1	1.1	1.2
February	1.5	1.5	1.6	1.6	1.6	1.5	1.5	1.4	1.5	1.5	1.3	1.1	1.1	1.2
March	1.6	1.5	1.6	1.6	1.6	1.5	1.5	1.4	1.5	1.5	1.3	1.1	1.1	1.2
April	1.5	1.5	1.7	1.6	1.6	1.5	1.5	1.5	1.4	1.5	1.3	1.1	1.1	1.1
May	1.5	1.5	1.7	1.6	1.6	1.4	1.5	1.5	1.5	1.5	1.3	1.1	1.2	..
June	1.5	1.5	1.6	1.6	1.6	1.4	1.5	1.5	1.5	1.5	1.3	1.2	1.2	..
July	1.5	1.5	1.6	1.6	1.6	1.4	1.5	1.5	1.5	1.5	1.3	1.2	1.2	..
August	1.5	1.5	1.6	1.6	1.6	1.4	1.5	1.5	1.5	1.5	1.3	1.2	1.2	..
September	1.5	1.5	1.6	1.6	1.6	1.4	1.5	1.5	1.5	1.5	1.3	1.1	1.2	..
October	1.4	1.5	1.7	1.6	1.6	1.4	1.4	1.5	1.5	1.4	1.3	1.1	1.1	..
November	1.4	1.6	1.7	1.6	1.6	1.4	1.4	1.5	1.5	1.4	1.2	1.1	1.2	..
December	1.4	1.6	1.6	1.6	1.6	1.4	1.4	1.5	1.5	1.4	1.1	1.1	1.2	..

Source: Bank of England: 020 7601 4444

1 Working day average. A full definition of these series is given in Section 7 of
the ONS Explanatory Handbook.
2 Series discontinued from 31 May 2006.

12.11 Average zero coupon yields [1]

Percentage rates

	1998	1999	2000	2001	2002	2003	2004	2005	2006	2007	2008	2009	2010	2011
Nominal Five Year Yield ZBRG														
January	6.18	4.30	6.28	5.07	4.90	4.15	4.61	4.43	4.11	5.06	4.31	2.79	2.98	2.54
February	6.10	4.46	6.13	5.04	4.94	3.85	4.63	4.53	4.17	5.08	4.33	2.66	2.91	2.77
March	6.09	4.69	5.89	4.86	5.22	3.93	4.56	4.73	4.33	5.00	4.04	2.41	2.85	2.59
April	5.93	4.66	5.80	4.96	5.21	4.09	4.80	4.54	4.48	5.20	4.27	2.59	2.85	2.70
May	5.95	4.95	5.82	5.14	5.22	3.85	5.01	4.31	4.67	5.32	4.64	2.69	2.52	..
June	6.04	5.28	5.61	5.25	5.05	3.72	5.15	4.17	4.69	5.59	5.17	2.91	2.34	..
July	6.12	5.49	5.58	5.26	4.88	3.98	5.07	4.16	4.69	5.55	4.93	3.08	2.25	..
August	5.80	5.75	5.65	5.03	4.54	4.36	4.96	4.23	4.74	5.25	4.56	2.91	1.99	..
September	5.32	6.00	5.65	4.90	4.31	4.46	4.83	4.12	4.67	5.02	4.37	2.74	1.90	..
October	4.94	6.25	5.46	4.74	4.36	4.73	4.65	4.26	4.76	4.95	4.12	2.64	1.79	..
November	4.92	5.86	5.33	4.55	4.38	4.91	4.58	4.29	4.73	4.64	3.53	2.79	2.02	..
December	4.51	5.90	5.14	4.88	4.34	4.71	4.43	4.21	4.80	4.57	3.02	2.81	2.35	..
Nominal Ten Year Yield ZBRH														
January	5.96	4.24	5.62	4.75	4.85	4.39	4.76	4.50	4.02	4.76	4.46	3.77	4.16	3.84
February	5.91	4.39	5.44	4.90	4.90	4.22	4.78	4.54	4.10	4.79	4.61	3.80	4.22	3.99
March	5.85	4.60	5.18	4.64	5.18	4.34	4.67	4.74	4.26	4.72	4.45	3.33	4.24	3.85
April	5.69	4.53	5.14	4.90	5.19	4.48	4.92	4.58	4.46	4.94	4.64	3.49	4.25	3.93
May	5.73	4.83	5.23	5.05	5.22	4.23	5.06	4.38	4.58	5.03	4.84	3.73	3.91	..
June	5.60	5.07	5.05	5.11	5.05	4.13	5.13	4.25	4.60	5.31	5.14	3.82	3.71	..
July	5.65	5.24	5.09	5.10	4.95	4.43	5.04	4.28	4.59	5.29	4.99	3.91	3.61	..
August	5.41	5.25	5.18	4.88	4.68	4.59	4.95	4.29	4.58	5.05	4.69	3.81	3.32	..
September	5.03	5.51	5.25	4.91	4.47	4.68	4.86	4.17	4.47	4.91	4.54	3.76	3.22	..
October	4.93	5.68	5.09	4.77	4.60	4.88	4.72	4.31	4.53	4.88	4.60	3.67	3.17	..
November	4.83	5.11	4.98	4.58	4.62	5.03	4.65	4.26	4.45	4.67	4.33	3.87	3.43	..
December	4.44	5.19	4.80	4.83	4.55	4.87	4.49	4.17	4.53	4.65	3.68	4.02	3.72	..
Nominal Twenty Year Yield ZBRI														
January	5.94	4.36	4.45	4.33	4.72	4.45	4.70	4.43	3.84	4.33	4.40	4.48	4.55	4.56
February	5.88	4.44	4.38	4.42	4.73	4.39	4.73	4.44	3.90	4.38	4.57	4.56	4.69	4.60
March	5.78	4.60	4.25	4.44	4.99	4.56	4.63	4.66	4.05	4.36	4.53	4.23	4.76	4.50
April	5.61	4.53	4.35	4.74	5.02	4.68	4.81	4.53	4.26	4.56	4.70	4.50	4.74	4.51
May	5.67	4.75	4.40	4.85	5.08	4.49	4.91	4.37	4.31	4.63	4.78	4.63	4.52	..
June	5.42	4.77	4.37	4.98	4.94	4.46	4.89	4.27	4.36	4.86	4.88	4.72	4.45	..
July	5.45	4.67	4.38	4.89	4.82	4.71	4.82	4.31	4.34	4.81	4.83	4.67	4.43	..
August	5.30	4.53	4.49	4.69	4.58	4.69	4.70	4.31	4.29	4.62	4.68	4.37	4.25	..
September	4.91	4.62	4.63	4.88	4.39	4.75	4.65	4.19	4.17	4.59	4.64	4.20	4.16	..
October	4.87	4.56	4.61	4.75	4.55	4.82	4.59	4.28	4.18	4.60	4.78	4.20	4.16	..
November	4.73	4.07	4.39	4.47	4.60	4.88	4.50	4.18	4.11	4.49	4.83	4.37	4.40	..
December	4.47	4.20	4.30	4.64	4.57	4.76	4.40	4.06	4.19	4.50	4.29	4.48	4.51	..
Real Ten Year Yield ZBRJ														
January	3.10	2.00	2.10	2.22	2.52	2.00	1.94	1.75	1.29	1.78	1.30	1.53	0.82	0.64
February	3.06	1.91	2.17	2.27	2.50	1.74	1.96	1.77	1.32	1.80	1.33	1.25	0.96	0.72
March	3.00	1.85	2.05	2.33	2.53	1.79	1.81	1.87	1.41	1.70	1.02	1.19	0.83	0.54
April	2.91	1.70	2.08	2.56	2.43	1.96	1.93	1.76	1.54	1.91	1.20	1.08	0.71	0.61
May	2.92	1.91	2.14	2.58	2.43	1.81	2.05	1.70	1.63	2.05	1.36	1.09	0.73	..
June	2.85	1.89	2.12	2.54	2.33	1.67	2.10	1.65	1.68	2.21	1.36	1.08	0.76	..
July	2.77	1.90	2.14	2.56	2.42	1.85	2.07	1.65	1.65	2.19	1.29	1.23	0.84	..
August	2.65	2.19	2.25	2.42	2.33	1.95	2.03	1.61	1.55	1.97	1.17	1.16	0.65	..
September	2.59	2.31	2.28	2.51	2.20	2.05	1.97	1.51	1.49	1.79	1.25	1.06	0.46	..
October	2.67	2.26	2.33	2.53	2.36	2.15	1.89	1.57	1.57	1.75	2.06	0.70	0.38	..
November	2.40	2.05	2.34	2.39	2.33	2.21	1.88	1.54	1.47	1.48	2.58	0.77	0.48	..
December	2.11	1.98	2.23	2.58	2.24	2.03	1.76	1.47	1.56	1.50	2.19	0.80	0.68	..
Real Twenty Year Yield ZBRK														
January	3.06	2.07	2.01	1.88	2.26	2.07	1.96	1.59	0.97	1.23	0.92	1.05	0.84	0.86
February	3.05	1.99	1.95	1.88	2.30	1.98	1.90	1.59	0.99	1.25	1.03	1.19	1.07	0.88
March	2.98	1.93	1.78	1.99	2.32	2.07	1.77	1.72	1.10	1.19	0.88	1.19	0.98	0.80
April	2.85	1.81	1.84	2.25	2.25	2.12	1.85	1.64	1.28	1.36	1.02	1.14	0.90	0.79
May	2.83	1.99	1.91	2.32	2.25	2.03	1.88	1.57	1.33	1.46	1.00	1.05	0.93	..
June	2.63	1.97	1.87	2.27	2.17	1.97	1.88	1.53	1.39	1.54	0.84	1.01	0.97	..
July	2.58	2.00	1.90	2.24	2.24	2.16	1.87	1.54	1.31	1.52	0.83	1.00	1.04	..
August	2.53	2.14	1.96	2.16	2.15	2.14	1.82	1.49	1.21	1.31	0.67	0.87	0.90	..
September	2.49	2.26	1.96	2.31	2.06	2.18	1.80	1.40	1.12	1.24	0.80	0.89	0.73	..
October	2.59	2.22	1.99	2.32	2.22	2.22	1.76	1.40	1.13	1.25	1.33	0.74	0.71	..
November	2.36	1.92	1.94	2.12	2.25	2.21	1.71	1.29	1.03	1.09	1.37	0.71	0.81	..
December	2.14	1.87	1.87	2.24	2.21	2.08	1.60	1.20	1.11	1.08	1.24	0.77	0.82	..

1 Working day average. Calculated using the Variable Roughness Penalty (VRP) model.

Source: Bank of England: 020 7601 4444

12.12 Consumer credit

United Kingdom												£ million
		2000	2001	2002	2003	2004	2005	2006	2007	2008	2009	2010
Total amount outstanding	VZRD	135,168	150,802	169,209	180,649	198,856	211,038	212,835	221,687	233,164	226,840	213,934
Total net lending	VZQC	15,969	19,673	23,443	22,401	25,337	19,666	13,054	13,471	10,854	-700	2,436
of which Credit cards	VZQS	6,686	6,229	7,579	8,710	9,998	6,166	1,951	2,251	4,092	2,326	2,025
Other	VZQT	9,284	13,445	15,867	13,692	15,340	13,499	11,102	11,221	6,762	-3,025	413
Other consumer credit lenders	BM59	2,640	3,554	5,811	6,954	5,796	8,112	3,489	7,135	7,205	901	3,370
Total gross lending	VZQG	160,744	177,452	196,451	207,255	221,318	217,467	207,460	204,632	192,863	170,304	175,255

Source: Office for National Statistics: 01633 456635

As from Dec 2006 the Bank of England has ceased to update the separate data on consumer credit provided by other specialist lenders, retailers and insurance companies previously contained in these tables. These categories have been merged into 'other consumer credit lenders'.

12.13 Investment trust, unit trust and property unit trust companies holdings at market values

											£ million
		2000	2001	2002	2003	2004	2005	2006	2007	2008	2009
Investment trusts											
Total assets	CBGW	63,728	58,100	40,368	50,564	50 312	56,296	52,190	58,911	42,476	50,476
Short term assets	CBGX	3,284	3,169	2,626	2,535	3,100	3,032	2,138	3,303	3,397	2,522
UK public sector securities[1]	LYGL	821	646	470	302	466	768	533	715	628	585
UK corporate securities:											
Ordinary shares	CBGY	33,456	30,338	19,475	23,292	23,941	25,037	22,870	23,034	14,366	17,646
Other[2]	CBGZ	1,654	1,516	946	1,079	1,270	673	1,071	1,259	813	665
Overseas securities:											
Corporate securities											
Ordinary shares	AHCC	21,355	19,476	14,453	20 294	18,967	23,065	21,659	25,795	18,385	23,865
Other[3]	CBHA	963	1,143	458	603	682	937	741	1,038	623	939
Government securities	AHBY	587	399	137	122	33	168	4	151	410	256
UK authorised unit trust units	AHBT	73	26	47	79	149	140	24	-	28	33
UK land and buildings	CBHB	316	375	532	498	39	117	252	154	142	141
Other UK and overseas assets[4]	AMSE	1,219	1,012	1,224	1,760	1,665	2,359	2,898	3,462	3,684	3,824
Total liabilities	CBHO	14,526	15,360	13,432	14,269	11,850	10,596	9,346	9,355	7,624	7,090
Unit trusts and property unit trusts											
Total assets	CBHR	235,485	215,308	202,758	262,031	286,962	377,230	452,773	497,124	430,903	512,374
Short term assets	CBHS	9,829	8,995	8,928	12,090	11,497	16,417	20,653	27,969	35,224	37,263
British government sterling securities	CBHT	4,693	4,690	7,077	9,125	9,768	25,181	31,603	32,120	33,466	29,331
UK corporate securities:											
Ordinary shares	RLIB	116,808	103,704	82,851	116,407	130 230	157,149	185,637	195,009	143,550	167,401
Other[2]	CBHU	14,654	16,318	21,152	23,972	22,467	29,293	29,876	30,626	30,174	36,646
Overseas securities:											
Corporate securities											
Ordinary shares	RLIC	79,601	71,329	63,152	75,074	81,034	105,443	127,409	142,211	113,667	150,863
Other[3]	CBHV	3,212	4,113	5,916	9,840	13,142	16,057	25,617	30,029	30,442	43,301
Government securities	CBHW	1,554	1,749	3,278	2,267	2,347	3,412	3,532	3,880	5,754	5,810
UK land and buildings	RLIE	3,488	2,078	4,026	5,125	5,909	9,623	12,781	12,480	8,518	7,248
Other UK and overseas assets[5]	CBHX	1,646	2,332	6,378	8,131	10,568	14,655	15,665	22,800	30,108	34,511
Total liabilities	RLLE	252,826	227,001	190,231	235,265	269,777	343,559	408,840	462,054	357,473	468,259

Source: National Statistics: 01633 456635

1 Includes British government securities, UK local authority securities and other UK public sector investments.
2 Includes UK corporate bonds and preference shares.
3 Includes overseas bonds and preference shares.
4 Includes UK open-ended investment companies, UK unauthorised unit trust units, overseas mutual funds, other UK fixed assets, overseas fixed assets, direct investment and other UK & overseas assets not elsewhere classified.
5 Includes British government foreign currency securities, UK local authority securities, other public sector investments, UK open-ended investment companies, UK unauthorised unit trust units, overseas mutual funds, other UK fixed assets, overseas fixed assets, direct investment and other UK & overseas assets not elsewhere classified.

12.14 Self-administered pension funds: holdings at market values

£ million

		2000	2001	2002	2003	2004	2005	2006	2007	2008	2009
Total net assets	AHVA	765,887	713,933	611,238	694,090	763,308	920,177	1,016,879	1,024,958	871,767	1,006,014
UK Short term assets:											
Balances with MFIs	JX5Q	19,923	17,162	15,079	16,103	16,216	17,789	22,823	25,974	20,133	23,054
Certificates of deposit	IX8H	2,515	1,374	1,109	2,063	1,678	2,649	4,932	8,156	6,480	2,269
Sterling Treasury bills	AHVE	229	861	771	206	69	80	19	299	548	1,702
Local authority debt	AHVF	294	296	365	276	337	270	221	205	323	210
Other short term assets	AHVG	7,656	5,758	4,773	6,442	17,494	31,104	35,938	41,443	42,093	98,752
Overseas short term assets	AHVH	1,667	852	1,168	1,107	844	855	1,613	2,867	2,922	1,352
UK public sector securities[1]	RYHC	93,418	84,352	85,271	89,450	88,283	95,220	106,057	115,015	99,840	111,346
UK corporate securities:											
Ordinary shares	AHVP	299,318	260,696	186,437	186,426	180,561	199,199	208,473	152,048	110,571	116,710
Other[2]	AHVQ	16,978	22,301	30,450	37,082	43,027	48,065	54,902	57,541	56,516	65,184
Overseas securities											
Corporate securities:											
Ordinary shares	AHVR	135,514	127,893	104,392	125,740	140,282	183,060	192,978	169,598	127,525	155,577
Other[3]	AHVS	12,736	11,781	11,386	12,475	15,996	20,502	31,536	45,470	48,222	58,653
Government securities	AHVT	19,206	20,383	16,031	16,340	15,075	19,037	21,776	22,434	21,527	16,900
Mutual funds[4]	JRS9	76,214	82,009	77,372	117,834	144,265	192,033	215,218	254,936	211,724	286,493
UK and overseas loans and mortgages	JRT4	16	20	144	35	44	9	42	417	518	1,768
UK and overseas fixed assets	JRT5	33,401	31,082	31,825	30,775	30,676	31,742	34,608	30,466	22,892	24,957
Other assets[5]	JF4A	52,810	50,555	46,438	57,390	85,007	107,759	123,621	145,065	131,842	121,418
Debtors net of creditors	AHWD	-3,748	-1,976	607	-438	-8,413	-17,518	-23,217	-30,796	-27,448	-76,472
LESS Borrowing	GQED	2,260	1,466	2,380	5,216	8,133	11,678	14,661	16,180	4,461	3,859

Source: National Statistcs: 01633 456635

1 Includes British government securities, UK local authority securities and
  other UK oublic sector investments.
2 Includes UK corporate bonds and preference shares.
3 Includes overseas bonds and preference shares.
4 Includes UK unit trust units, investment trust securities, open-ended investment
  compaines, other UK mutual funds and overseas mutual funds.
5 Includes investment in insurance managed funds and other UK and overseas
  assets not elsewhere classified.

12.15 Insurance companies: holdings at market values

£ million

		2000	2001	2002	2003	2004	2005	2006	2007	2008	2009
Long term insurance											
Total net assets	AHNA	936,175	920,123	859,312	913,118	965,870	1,119,818	1,225,747	1,317,716	1,137,693	1,224,498
UK short term assets:											
Balances with MFIs	JX2C	34,940	35,217	29,750	26,527	28,018	31,606	34,454	48,619	51,139	44,483
Certificates of deposit	AHND	11,731	14,049	15,910	19,344	18,733	14,200	17,256	15,177	11,401	8,177
Local authority debt	AHNF	83	-	-	-	-	-	-	-	-	-
Other short term assets	AHNG	16,168	15,738	14,258	10,959	11,285	15,743	15,653	22,516	29,821	31,878
Overseas short term assets	AHNH	3,490	2,865	3,172	4,539	3,820	12,063	9,385	13,394	17,976	11,363
UK public sector securities[1]	RYEK	118,040	121,126	133,076	145,136	159,317	164,753	163,918	160,326	168,527	169,363
UK corporate securities[2]	IFLE	463,377	429,926	375,993	388,430	389,692	440,825	460,021	453,911	348,943	371,148
Overseas corporate securities[3]	IFLJ	107,439	127,259	110,738	110,193	130,098	165,452	194,997	234,388	219,957	266,280
Overseas government securities	AHNS	18,004	21,285	19,762	20,561	20,161	16,065	21,078	25,787	29,053	24,601
Mutual funds[4]	IFLK	97,101	79,867	73,685	89,523	108,019	168,896	192,516	222,081	186,950	230,247
Other assets[5]	JX8I	80,152	81,657	81,444	93,314	98,688	99,038	114,797	119,912	100,524	89,035
Agents' and reinsurance balances (net)	AHNY	384	620	6,373	4,720	3,755	3,933	5,100	984	-7,820	-3,947
Debtors net of creditors	AHFZ	-3,617	4,734	8,315	15,460	8,805	2,439	10,941	13,047	-6,311	-7,264
LESS Borrowing	AHNI	11,133	14,221	13,164	15,617	14,536	15,224	14,369	12,426	12,467	10,866
General insurance											
Total net assets	AHMA	89,317	90,423	97,711	90,817	111,768	121,910	125,096	118,325	134,322	130,708
UK short term assets:											
Balances with MFIs	JX3H	5,817	7,034	10,309	12,683	18,051	9,116	9,327	8,949	9,871	10,227
Certificates of deposit	AHMD	1,300	3,687	4,800	3,486	6,808	8,402	7,708	8,264	7,775	2,002
Local authority debt	AHMF	-	-	-	3	-	-	-	-	-	-
Other short term assets	AHMG	748	594	1,566	1,905	1,448	4,144	2,303	4,223	5,901	6,226
Overseas short term assets	AHMH	1,174	1,016	1,536	2,088	3,142	4,929	5,531	4,387	4,273	3,889
UK public sector securities[1]	RYMV	14,832	15,120	18,406	19,658	19,800	19,880	19,368	16,108	18,444	17,034
UK corporate securities[2]	IFVU	16,541	15,888	13,646	13,924	18,604	20,719	21,944	22,447	22,590	23,539
Overseas corporate securities[3]	IFVZ	8,190	6,402	7,394	7,124	11,520	12,645	18,636	14,773	20,258	23,002
Overseas government securities	AHMS	6,849	7,134	7,156	5,720	6,662	7,341	8,035	4,869	8,505	7,204
Mutual funds[4]	IFWA	2,113	1,285	2,901	1,563	2,470	1,270	1,256	1,780	1,911	3,498
Other assets[5]	JX8M	32,934	37,251	30,769	25,379	31,266	39,409	41,259	45,394	48,012	47,802
Agents' and reinsurance balances (net)	AHMX	8,362	7,941	9,492	9,890	9,858	7,996	10,782	9,932	10,706	10,465
Debtors net of creditors	AHWY	-2,681	88	4,508	1,688	-628	786	-2,001	-4,204	-3,710	-8,578
LESS Borrowing	AHMI	6,889	13,066	14,772	14,306	17,256	14,790	19,052	18,597	20,214	15,602

Source: National Statistcs: 01633 456635

1 Includes British government securities, UK local authority securities and other UK public sector investments.
2 Includes UK corporate bonds, ordinary shares and preference shares.
3 Includes overseas bonds, ordinary shares and preference shares.
4 Includes UK unit trust units, investment trust securities, open-ended investment companies, other mutual funds and overseas mutual funds.
5 Includes UK and overseas loans, fixed assets, direct investment and other assets not elsewhere classified.

12.16 Individual insolvencies

United Kingdom   Numbers

		1999	2000	2001	2002	2003	2004	2005	2006	2007	2008	2009	2010 [7]
England and Wales													
Bankruptcies[1]	AIHW	21,611	21,550	23,477	24,292	28,021	35,898	47,291	62,956	64,480	67,428	74,670	59,194
Individual voluntary arrangements[2,3]	AIHI	7,195	7,978	6,298	6,295	7,583	10,752	20,293	44,332	42,165	39,116	47,641	50,716
Total	AIHK	28,806	29,528	29,775	30,587	35,604	46,651	67,584	107,288	106,645	106,544	134,142	135,089
Scotland													
Sequestrations[4]	KRHA	3,195	2,965	3,048	3,215	3,328	3,297	4,965	5,430	6,219	12,370	14,356	11,891
Protected Trust Deeds	GJ2I	2,144	2,801	3,779	5,174	5,452	6,024	6,881	8,208	7,595	7,542	9,126	8,438
Total	GJ2J	5,339	5,766	6,827	8,389	8,780	9,321	11,846	13,638	13,814	19,912	23,482	20,329
Northern Ireland													
Bankruptcies[5]	KRHB	401	349	292	334	517	666	821	1,035	898	1,079	1,237	1,321
Individual voluntary arrangements[3,6]	KJRK	172	267	176	207	318	449	633	774	440	559	722	1,002
Total	KRHD	573	616	468	541	835	1,115	1,454	1,809	1,338	1,638	1,959	2,323

1. Comprises receiving and administration orders under the Bankruptcy Act 1914 and bankruptcy orders under the Insolvency Act 1986. Orders later consolidated or rescinded are included in these figures.
2. Introduced under the Insolvency Act 1986.
3. For statistical purposes deeds of arrangement are now included with individual voluntary arrangements.
4. The sequestration figures included Low income and Low assest cases. These were introduced as a new route into bankruptcy under the Bankruptcy and Diligence etc (Scotland) Act 2007 wef 1 April 2008.

5. Comprises bankruptcy adjudication orders, arrangement protection orders and orders for the administration of estates of deceased insolvents. Orders later set aside or dismissed are included in these figures.
6. Introduced under the Insolvency Northern Ireland order 1989.
7. Provisional

Source: Insolvency Service: 020 7637 6504/6443

12.17 Company insolvencies

United Kingdom   Numbers

		1999	2000	2001	2002	2003	2004	2005	2006	2007	2008	2009	2010 [7]
England and Wales													
Compulsory liquidations	AIHR	5,209	4,925	4,675	6,231	5,234	4,584	5,233	5,418	5,165	5,494	5,643	4,793
Creditors' voluntary liquidations	AIHS	9,071	9,392	10,297	10,075	8,950	7,608	7,660	7,719	7,342	10,041	13,434	11,253
Total	AIHQ	14,280	14,317	14,972	16,306	14,184	12,192	12,893	13,137	12,507	15,535	19,077	16,044
Scotland													
Compulsory liquidations	KRGA	364	344	378	556	436	431	420	416	439	437	432	735
Creditors' voluntary liquidations	KRGB	208	239	224	232	195	190	149	133	100	87	152	306
Total	KRGC	572	583	602	788	631	621	569	549	539	524	584	1,041
Northern Ireland[1]													
Compulsory liquidations	KRGD	..	..	..	49	95	76	85	78	122	158	164	250
Creditors' voluntary liquidations	KRGE	..	..	..	53	47	45	53	50	42	51	83	132
Total	KRGF	..	..	..	102	142	121	138	128	164	209	247	382

Source: Insolvency Service: 020 7637 6504/6443

1. Prior to 2002, the quality of the statistics on company liquidations in Northern Ireland are not robust enough and have been removed from this table.
2. Provisional.
3. Including companies which had previously been in administration or other insolvency procedures.

12.18 Selected financial statistics[1]

£ million

| | Banks[4] | | | | | | Consumer credit[5] | | of which credit cards[5] | |
| | UK private sector deposits | | Lending to the private sector | | | | | | | |
	Unit trusts[3]	Net equity of households in life assurance and pension funds' reserves	Sterling (Not seasonally adjusted)	Other currencies	Sterling (Not seasonally adjusted)	Other currencies	Not seasonally adjusted	Seasonally adjusted	Not seasonally adjusted	Seasonally adjusted
Amount outstanding as at 31 Dec	AGXB		AEAS	AGAK	AECE	AECK	VZRD	VZRI	VZRE	VZRJ
2009	480,601		..	..	..	..	226,840	226,621	55,631	54,564
2010	578,062		..	..	..	..	213,934	213,623	59,692	58,540
							Net lending	Net lending	Net lending	Net lending
Transactions	AGXE	NBYD	AEAT	AEAZ	AECF		VZQC	RLMH	VZQS	VZQX
2007	3,870	65,070	162,298	71,345	213,349		13,471	13,010	2,251	2,041
2008	-2,151	19,930	219,067	-37,030	234,087		10,854	11,150	4,092	4,226
2009	29,561	20,408	143,201	3,141	150,157		-700	-720	2,326	2,286
2010	44693	22048	..	..	..		2436	2365	2025	1945
2009 Q1	5,627	1,518	70,297	-15,872	56,361		-677	-106	-804	612
Q2	7,741	12,894	-5,425	41,817	13,825		1,551	475	943	659
Q3	8,890	5,886	35,628	-12,883	45,929		-1,274	-539	520	390
Q4	7,303	110	42,701	-9,921	34,042		-300	-550	1,667	625
2010 Q1	4867	4225	..	..	..		-156	678	-945	722
Q2	13549	5817	..	..	..		1312	197	655	293
Q3	17818	5028	..	..	..		-517	104	756	495
Q4	8459	6978	..	..	..		1797	1386	1559	435
2011 Q1	4414	3463	..	..	..		68	963	-1295	453
2009 Apr	1,883	..	-6,967	45,101	-13,240		747	286	453	304
May	3,863	..	3,342	-1,887	25,212		291	71	65	181
Jun	1,995	..	-1,800	-1,397	1,853		514	118	425	175
Jul	2,448	..	14,522	-10,302	11,606		-926	-264	-102	87
Aug	2,692	..	-2,654	11,281	3,330		-903	-149	424	205
Sep	3,750	..	23,760	-13,862	30,993		555	-126	197	97
Oct	1,964	..	55,414	-3,633	41,536		-784	-472	-115	122
Nov	2,821	..	2,608	10,092	-6,133		191	-162	771	244
Dec	2,518	..	-15,321	-16,380	-1,361		293	84	1,010	260
2010 Jan	1,478	..	..	..	..		-141	251	-742	197
Feb	1,779	..	..	..	..		-111	236	-8	330
Mar	1,610	..	..	..	..		96	197	-195	172
Apr	8,314	..	..	..	..		543	-53	404	89
May	4,114	..	..	..	..		693	439	-42	137
Jun	2,672	..	..	..	..		76	-103	292	146
Jul	5,099	..	..	..	..		-484	118	114	204
Aug	7,663	..	..	..	..		-178	-155	585	115
Sep	3,457	..	..	..	..		148	128	57	177
Oct	5,402	..	..	..	..		138	499	-12	304
Nov	2,458	..	..	..	..		613	34	774	33
Dec	532	..					1056	807	796	69
2011 Jan	-4	..	..	..	..		-465	-335	-795	114
Feb	2446	..	..	..	..		478	782	-188	144
Mar	1972	..	..	..	..		54	516	-312	195
Apr	3329	..	..	..	..		1093	504	770	347

Source : Bank of England

1 For further details see Financial Statistics, Tables 1.2E, 3.2B, 4.2A, 4.3A, 4.3B, 5.2D, 6.2A, 10.5D.
2 Total administered by the Department for National Savings.
3 Including open ended investment companies (OEICs).
4 Monthly figures relate to calendar months.

12.19 Selected interest rates, exchange rates and security prices

	Selected retail banks' base rate	Average discount rate for 91 day Treasury bills	Inter bank 3 months bid rate	Inter bank 3 months offer rate	British government securities 20 years yield[1]	Exchange rate US spot
	ZCMG	AJNB	HSAJ	HSAK	AJLX	LUSS
2006 Feb	4.50	4.39	4.51	4.53	3.96	1.75
Mar	4.50	4.41	4.54	4.56	4.15	1.73
Apr	4.50	4.45	4.60	4.63	4.32	1.82
May	4.50	4.51	4.66	4.68	4.43	1.87
Jun	4.50	4.54	4.71	4.73	4.46	1.85
Jul	4.50	4.58	4.73	4.74	4.45	1.87
Aug	4.75	4.77	4.94	4.95	4.42	1.90
Sep	4.75	4.87	5.02	5.05	4.29	1.87
Oct	4.75	4.98	5.14	5.16	4.35	1.91
Nov	5.00	5.04	5.20	5.22	4.27	1.97
Dec	5.00	5.11	5.26	5.29	4.33	1.96
2007 Jan	5.25	5.37	5.54	5.55	4.51	1.96
Feb	5.25	5.31	5.48	5.50	4.59	1.96
Mar	5.25	5.38	5.56	5.58	4.52	1.96
Apr	5.25	5.47	5.66	5.70	4.72	2.00
May	5.50	5.59	5.76	5.78	..	1.98
Jun	5.50	5.77	5.93	5.98	..	2.01
Jul	5.75	5.75	6.00	6.02	..	2.03
Aug	5.75	5.77	6.55	6.65	4.80	2.02
Sep	5.75	5.61	6.18	6.28	4.74	2.04
Oct	5.75	5.57	6.17	6.25	4.74	2.08
Nov	5.75	5.44	6.53	6.58	4.59	2.06
Dec	5.50	5.24	5.95	5.95	4.59	1.99
2008 Jan	5.50	5.01	5.50	5.58	4.46	1.99
Feb	5.25	4.98	5.68	5.72	4.62	1.99
Mar	5.25	4.77	5.95	6.02	4.54	1.99
Apr	5.00	4.90	5.76	5.84	4.73	1.98
May	5.00	5.04	5.80	5.87	4.85	1.98
Jun	5.00	5.10	5.88	5.94	5.03	1.99
Jul	5.00	5.09	5.75	5.79	4.94	1.98
Aug	5.00	4.94	5.70	5.75	4.74	1.82
Sep	5.00	4.51	6.15	6.30	4.66	1.78
Oct	4.50	3.54	5.85	6.00	4.76	1.62
Nov	3.00	1.68	3.85	4.10	4.69	1.53
Dec	2.00	1.24	2.75	2.90	4.15	1.44
2009 Jan	0.50	0.49	0.50	0.70	..	1.60
Feb	0.50	0.49	0.50	0.70	..	1.52
Mar	0.50	0.51	0.50	0.70	..	1.52
Apr	0.50	0.50	0.50	0.70	..	1.53
May	0.50	0.49	0.60	0.75	..	1.45
Jun	0.50	0.49	0.65	0.85	..	1.50
Jul	0.50	0.50	0.65	0.85	..	1.57
Aug	0.50	0.49	0.65	0.85	..	1.54
Sep	0.50	0.51	0.65	0.85	..	1.58
Oct	0.50	0.51	0.65	0.85	..	1.60
Nov	0.50	0.49	0.65	0.84	..	1.56
Dec	0.50	0.50	0.70	0.85	..	1.57
2010 Jan	0.50	0.51	0.70	0.85		1.60
Feb	0.50	0.54	0.70	0.85		1.63
Mar	0.50	0.60	0.75	0.85		1.60
Apr	0.50		0.75	0.85		1.66
May	0.50		0.75	0.85		1.65

1 Average of working days.

Source: Bank of England

12.20 Mergers and acquisitions in the UK by UK companies: category of expenditure

£ million

	Number of companies acquired	Total[1]	Independent companies	Cash Subsidiaries	Issues of ordinary shares[2]	Issues of fixed interest securities[2]
	AIHA	DUCM	DWVW	DWVX	AIHD	AIHE
2005	769	25,134	13,425	8,510	2,768	431
2006	779	28,511	..	8,131	..	335
2007	869	26,778	13,671	6,507	4,909	1,691
2008	558	36,469	31,333	2,851	1,910	375
2009	286	12,195	2,937	709	8,435	114
2010	325	12,605	6,175	4,520	1,560	350
1999 Q4	104	3,737	2,795	580	250	112
2000 Q1	139	33,739	17,483	1,136	14,960	160
Q2	133	21,469	4,224	1,881	15,045	319
Q3	163	16,852	6,934	2,237	7,367	314
Q4	152	34,856	5,265	914	28,198	479
2001 Q1	131	6,181	2,606	2,255	982	338
Q2	108	4,890	1,679	2,214	555	442
Q3	129	16,079	3,457	1,526	10,649	447
Q4	124	1,844	747	709	170	218
2002 Q1	83	3,853	2,201	1,298	104	250
Q2	120	4,228	801	3,179	78	170
Q3	88	6,333	4,695	1,426	184	28
Q4	139	10,822	1,877	2,088	6,414	443
2003 Q1	107	3,857	1,003	1,892	609	353
Q2	122	3,753	1,437	1,713	258	345
Q3	153	4,700	2,495	1,919	153	133
Q4	176	6,369	4,021	1,659	647	42
2004 Q1	151	12,639	2,819	655	8,807	358
Q2	169	5,359	2,555	1,682	822	300
Q3	211	8,109	3,469	4,026	240	374
Q4	210	5,301	3,237	1,459	469	136
2005 Q1	166	3,516	1,334	1,918	166	98
Q2	215	8,983	4,869	2,715	1,285	114
Q3	211	7,287	4,106	1,878	1,207	96
Q4	177	5,348	3,116	1,999	110	123
2006 Q1	207	6,969	4,069	2,427	431	42
Q2	208	4,222	3,298	527	384	13
Q3	163	11,376	..	4,580	..	216
Q4	201	5,944	4,690	597	593	64
2007 Q1	191	5,649	2,824	276	2,407	142
Q2	212	10,122	3,605	4,361	1,874	282
Q3	258	7,846	5,545	833	358	1,110
Q4	208	3,161	1,697	1,037	270	157
2008 Q1	172	4,545	2,578	913	786	268
Q2	183	9,593	8,845	520	187	41
Q3	104	4,133	3,408	328	341	56
Q4	99	18,198	16,502	1,090	596	10
2009 Q1	88	8,206	332	128	7,699	47
Q2	59	729	130	150	437	12
Q3	62	1,886	1,409	214	254	9
Q4	77	1,374	1,066	217	45	46
2010 Q1	67	1,361	765	525	58	13
Q2	95	2,032	986	714	275	57
Q3	80	2,949	1,165	814	839	131
Q4	83	6,263	3,259	2,467	388	149
2011 Q1	60	1,163	497	412	235	19

Source: Office for National Statistics

Missing data for any series have been suppressed to avoid the disclosure of information relating to individual enterprises.

1 Includes deferred payments.
2 Issued to the vendor as payment.

Service industry

Chapter 13

Service industry

Annual Business Inquiry (Tables 13.1, 13.3 and 13.4)

The Annual Business Inquiry (ABI) estimates cover all UK businesses registered for Value Added Tax (VAT) and/or Pay As You Earn (PAYE). The businesses are classified to the 2007 Standard Industrial Classification (SIC(2007)) headings listed in the tables. The ABI obtains details on these businesses from the Office for National Statistics (ONS) Inter-Departmental Business Register (IDBR).

As with all its statistical inquiries, ONS is concerned to minimise the form-filling burden of individual contributors and as such the ABI is a sample inquiry. The sample was designed as a stratified random sample of about 66,600 businesses; the inquiry population is stratified by SIC(2007) and employment using the information from the register.

The inquiry results are grossed up to the total population so that they relate to all active UK businesses on the IDBR for the sectors covered.

The results meet a wide range of needs for government, economic analysts and the business community at large. In official statistics the inquiry is an important source for the national accounts and input-output tables, and also provides weights for the indices of production and producer prices. Additionally, inquiry results enable the UK to meet statistical requirements of the European Union.

Data from 1995 and 1996 were calculated on a different basis from those for 1997 and later years. In order to provide a link between the two data series, the 1995 and 1996 data were subsequently reworked to provide estimates on a consistent basis.

Revised ABI results down to SIC(2007) 4 digit class level for 1995–2007, giving both analysis and tabular detail, are available from the ONS website at: www.statistics.gov.uk, with further extracts and bespoke analyses available on request. This service replaces existing publications.

Retail trade: index numbers of value and volume (Table 13.2)

The main purpose of the Retail Sales Inquiry (RSI) is to provide up-to-date information on short period movements in the level of retail sales. In principle, the RSI covers the retail activity of every business classified in the retail sector (Division 52 of the 2007 Standard Industrial Classification (SIC(2007)) in Great Britain. A business will be classified to the retail sector if its main activity is one of the individual 4 digit SIC categories within Division 52. The retail activity of a business is then defined by its retail turnover, that is the sale of all retail goods (note that petrol, for example, is not a retail good).

The RSI is compiled from the information returned to the statutory inquiries into the distribution and services sector. The inquiry is addressed to a stratified sample of 5,000 businesses classified to the retail sector, the stratification being by 'type of store' (the individual 4 digit SIC categories within Division 52) and by size. The sample structure is designed to ensure that the inquiry estimates are as accurate as possible. In terms of the selection, this means that:

• each of the individual 4 digit SIC categories are represented – their coverage depending upon the relative size of the category and the variability of the data

• within each 4 digit SIC category the larger retailers tend to be fully enumerated with decreasing proportions of medium and smaller retailers

The structure of the inquiry is updated periodically by reference to the more comprehensive results of the Annual Business Inquiry (ABI). The monthly inquiry also incorporates a rotation element for the smallest retailers. This helps to spread the burden more fairly, as well as improving the representativeness between successive benchmarks.

13.1 Retail trade, except of motor vehicles and motor cycles[1]

United Kingdom

	£ million and percentages	
	2008	2009 [2]
Number of businesses	194,685	186,823
Total turnover[3]	349,098	347,824
Value Added Tax in total turnover	34,445	32,136
Retail turnover[3]	327,893	324,713
Non-retail turnover[3]	21,206	23,112
Other income		
Value of commercial insurance claims received	219	74
Subsidies received from UK government sources and the EC	2	6
Employment costs[4]	38,896	39,541
Gross wages and salaries	34,904	35,457
Redundancy and severance payments	186	204
Employers' National Insurance contributions	2,579	2,619
Contributions to pension funds	1,228	1,260
Stocks		
Increase during year	733	973
Value at end of year	26,595	25,944
Total turnover[4] divided by end-year stocks (Quotient)	12	12
Purchases of goods, materials and services[4]	247,833	247,887
Goods bought for resale without processing	205,346	205,576
Energy and water products for own consumption	3,527	3,508
Goods and materials	3,993	5,026
Hiring, leasing or renting of plant, machinery and vehicles	639	716
Commercial insurance premiums	929	935
Road transport services	3,013	2,594
Telecommunication services	538	560
Computer and related services	959	991
Advertising and marketing services	4,100	4,052
Other services	24,789	23,931
Taxes, duties and levies	6,676	6,794
National non-domestic (business) rates	5,194	5,390
Other amounts paid for taxes, duties and levies	1,482	1,404
Capital expenditure		
Cost of acquisitions	10,420	8,938
Proceeds from disposals	1,509	1,314
Net capital expenditure	8,911	7,624
Amount included in acquisitions for assets under finance leasing arrangements	322	393
Work of a capital nature carried out by own staff (included in acquisitions)	117	114
Gross margin		
Amount	108,732	109,880
As a percentage of adjusted turnover[5]	35	35
Approximate gross value added at basic prices	66,464	67,642

13.1 Retail trade, except of motor vehicles and motor cycles[1]

United Kingdom

	£ million	£ million
	2008	2009 [2]
Total turnover	349,098	..
Retail turnover	327,893	..
1 Fruit (including fresh, chilled, dried, frozen, canned and processed)	5,948	..
2 Vegetables (including fresh, chilled, dried, frozen, canned and processed)	10,130	..
3 Meat (including fresh, chilled, smoked, frozen, canned and processed)	17,186	..
4 Fish, crustaceans and molluscs (including fresh, chilled, frozen, canned and processed)	2,900	..
5 Bakery products and cereals (including rice and pasta products)	15,828	
6 Sugar,jam, honey, chocolate and confectionery (including ice-cream)	8,311	
7 Alcoholic drink	14,878	..
8 Non-alcoholic beverages (including tea, coffee, fruit drinks and vegetable drinks)	7,768	..
9 Tobacco (excluding smokers requisites, eg.pipes, lighters, etc)	10,496	..
10 Milk, cheese and eggs (including yoghurts and cream)	10,733	..
11 Oils and fats (including butter and margarine)	1,481	..
12 Food products not elsewhere classified (including sauces, herbs, spices and soups)	4,955	..
13 Pharmaceutical products	3,944	
14 National Health Receipts	11,259	..
15 Other medical products and therapeutic appliances and equipment	3,663	..
16 Other appliances, articles and products for personal care	12,633	..
17 Other articles of clothing, accessories for making clothing	3,073	..
18 Garments	34,152	..
19 Footwear (excluding sports shoes)	6,839	..
20 Travel goods and other personal effects not elsewhere classified	1,199	..
21 Household textiles (including furnishing fabrics, curtains, etc)	4,325	..
22 Household and personal appliances whether electric or not	6,627	..
23 Glassware, tableware and household utensils (including non-electric)	2,751	..
24 Furniture and furnishings	13,868	..
25 Audio and visual equipment (including radios, televisions and video recorders)	6,151	..
26 Recording material for pictures and sound (including audio and video tapes, blank and pre-recorded records, etc)	3,866	..
27 Information processing equipment (including printers, software, calculators and typewriters)	4,388	..
28 Decorating and DIY supplies	6,082	..
29 Tools and equipment for house and garden	3,208	..
30 Books	2,520	..
31 Newspapers and periodicals	4,027	..
32 Stationery and drawing materials and miscellaneous printed matter	4,496	..
33 Carpets and other floor coverings (excluding bathroom mats, rush and door mats)	3,358	..
34 Photographic and cinematographic equipment and optical instruments	2,252	..
35 Telephone and telefax equipment (including mobile phones)	3,559	..
36 Jewellery, silverware and plate; watches and clocks	5,036	..
37 Works of art and antiques (including furniture, floor coverings and jewellery)	1,292	..
38 Equipment and accessories for sport, camping, recreation and musical instruments	4,219	..
39 Spare part and accessories for all types of vehicle and sales of bicycles	1,026	..
40 Games, toys, hobbies (including video game software, video game computers that plug into the tv, video-games cassettes and CD-ROMs)	7,809	..
41 Other goods not elsewhere classified (including sale of new postage stamps and sales of liquid and solid fuels)	4,435	..
42 Non-durable household goods (including household cleaning, maintenance products) and paper products and other non-durable household goods	4,933	..
43 Natural or artificial plants and flowers	4,734	..
44 Pets and related products (including pet food)	3,625	..
45 Petrol, diesel, lubricating oil and other petroleum products	31,927	..

Source: Office for National Statistics

1 See chapter text.
2.Data for 2009 on this table are provisional.
2 Inclusive of VAT.
3 Exclusive of VAT.
4 Turnover is adjusted to takeout VAT.

13.2 Retail trade: index numbers of value and volume of sales[1]

Great Britain

Non-seasonally adjusted

		Sales in 2006 £ thousand	2000	2001	2002	2003	2004	2005	2006	2007	2008	2009	2010
Value													
All retailing	J5AH	292,109,664	81.4	85.0	88.4	90.8	95.1	96.4	100.0	103.9	107.9	108.7	111.5
Large	J5AI	219,416,835	76.3	80.7	84.8	89.1	93.7	95.6	100.0	104.8	109.9	111.8	116.7
Small	J5AJ	72,692,828	96.8	97.9	99.4	95.9	99.3	98.7	100.0	101.2	101.9	99.4	95.7
All retailing excluding automotive fuel	J43S	261,983,458	82.0	86.4	90.4	92.3	96.6	97.6	100.0	103.6	106.8	108.8	111.6
Predominantly food stores	EAFS	114,997,765	78.8	83.2	86.6	89.9	93.5	96.5	100.0	104.2	110.2	116.2	118.1
Predominantly non-food stores	EAFT	134,844,106	83.2	88.4	93.0	94.6	99.0	98.5	100.0	103.0	103.4	101.7	104.3
Non specialised predominantly non-food stores	EAGE	23,351,749	86.3	91.0	93.5	95.5	97.5	97.2	100.0	103.8	101.0	102.8	109.9
Textile, clothing, footwear and leather	EAFU	37,112,848	76.3	82.4	87.0	90.2	94.8	95.6	100.0	102.8	102.5	103.7	109.3
Household goods stores	EAFV	33,573,706	88.7	95.6	99.6	99.1	102.7	99.3	100.0	103.4	101.2	95.9	92.4
Other specialised non-food stores	EAFW	40,805,803	83.1	86.5	92.9	94.4	100.7	101.1	100.0	102.4	107.5	103.9	106.5
Non-store retailing	J596	12,141,587	99.2	95.3	97.4	88.9	98.1	97.9	100.0	104.2	111.2	118.3	131.2
Automotive fuel	J43H	30,126,206	76.3	72.5	71.1	78.3	82.6	85.5	100.0	107.1	117.6	107.5	110.4
Volume													
All retailing	J5DD	292,109,664	77.8	81.7	86.5	89.5	94.6	96.4	100.0	103.5	105.2	106.4	106.7
All retailing excluding automotive fuel	J448	261,983,458	77.0	81.2	86.4	89.1	94.7	97.1	100.0	103.5	105.7	107.4	109.0
Predominantly food stores	EAGW	114,997,765	84.3	86.7	90.0	92.7	96.2	98.4	100.0	101.0	100.9	102.1	100.7
Predominantly non-food stores	EAGX	134,844,106	70.8	76.8	83.4	86.9	93.6	96.1	100.0	105.3	108.9	110.0	113.0
Non specialised predominantly non-food stores	EAHI	23,351,749	74.9	80.0	84.5	88.4	92.7	95.0	100.0	105.8	106.0	109.6	117.8
Textile, clothing, footwear and leather	EAGY	37,112,848	60.5	68.3	76.3	81.3	88.6	92.8	100.0	105.4	110.3	118.6	125.3
Household goods stores	EAGZ	33,573,706	72.9	80.3	85.9	89.0	95.5	95.9	100.0	106.0	107.0	102.4	98.5
Other specialised non-food stores	EAHA	40,805,803	76.9	79.8	87.3	89.4	97.0	99.9	100.0	104.4	110.9	108.8	110.9
Non-store retailing	J5CL	12,141,587	85.7	83.7	88.0	82.2	93.1	95.6	100.0	106.7	117.2	128.0	142.8
Automotive fuel	J43V	30,126,206	87.8	87.9	88.6	94.1	94.3	90.1	100.0	103.8	100.0	98.0	87.1

Source: Office for National Statistics

1 See chapter text.

13.3 Wholesale and retail trade and repair of motor vehicles and motorcycles[1]

United Kingdom

Data for 2009 on this table are provisional.

£ million and percentages

	Wholesale and retail trade and repair of motor vehicles and motorcycles (SIC 2007 45.0)		Sale of motor vehicles (SIC 2007 45.1)		Maintenance and repair of motor vehicles (SIC 2007 45.2)		Sale of motor vehicle parts and accessories (SIC 2007 45.3)		Sale, maintenance and repair of motorcycles and related parts and accessories (SIC 2007 45.4)	
	2008	2009	2008	2009	2008	2009	2008	2009	2008	2009
Number of businesses	67,681	65,853	22,517	20,979	34,222	34,366	8,415	8,144	2,527	2,364
Total turnover	136,242	125,461	101,649	92,212	16,618	17,097	15,734	13,848	2,241	2,304
Motor trades turnover	132,866	122,165	99,721	90,759	16,019	16,491	14,885	12,625	2,241	2,289
Retail sales of:										
New cars	30,909	29,700	29,060	27,409	1,363	1,775	486	517	0	0
Other new motor vehicles and motorcycles	5,484	4,949	4,061	3,419	618	603	185	234	*	693
Sales to other dealers of:										
New cars	19,885	17,019	19,836	16,903	40	87	9	29	0	0
Other new motor vehicles and motorcycles	2,672	1,671	2,245	1,232	4	4	0	0	*	434
Gross sales of used motor vehicles and motorcycles	33,028	31,679	31,132	29,334	1,312	1,687	219	264	365	395
Turnover from sales of petrol, diesel, oil and other petroleum products	769	880	598	534	169	345	2	1	0	0
Other motor trades sales and receipts (including parts and accessories, workshop receipts)	40,119	36,266	12,789	11,928	12,513	11,990	13,985	11,580	832	767
Non-motor trades turnover	3,376	3,296	1,928	1,453	599	606	849	1,222	1	15
Purchases of goods, materials and services										
Total purchases	115,900	105,304	89,907	81,713	11,555	11,202	12,571	10,551	1,867	1,839
Energy, water and materials	2,634	2,316	1,147	754	917	933	533	598	37	31
Used motor vehicles and motorcycles	30,170	28,352	28,343	26,292	1,290	1,574	196	264	341	221
Parts used solely in repair and servicing activities	8,354	7,426	3,116	2,891	4,696	4,179	451	299	91	57
Other goods for resale	66,566	59,833	52,494	47,367	2,880	2,926	9,995	8,207	1,198	1,332
Hiring, leasing and renting of plant machinery and vehicles	227	205	77	71	99	68	50	63	2	3
Commercial insurance premiums	477	434	187	186	196	172	89	70	6	7
Road transport services	533	588	326	341	15	27	171	203	20	17
Telecommunication services	281	222	116	105	87	74	75	39	3	5
Computer and related services	335	325	216	210	52	46	61	63	7	6
Advertising and marketing services	1,991	1,621	1,712	1,354	126	129	114	102	38	35
Other services	4,331	3,982	2,172	2,142	1,197	1,072	838	643	124	124
Taxes, duties and levies										
Total taxes and levies	954	989	537	515	250	293	136	156	31	25
National (non-domestic business) rates	591	710	305	327	152	242	121	126	13	14
Other amounts paid for taxes, duties and levies	363	279	232	188	98	50	14	29	18	11
Capital expenditure										
Cost of acquisitions	2,089	1,393	1,293	832	455	370	319	173	22	18
Cost of disposals	1,034	739	680	515	274	172	60	43	20	8
Net capital expenditure	1,055	655	613	318	182	198	259	130	2	10
Work of a capital nature carried out by own staff (included in acquisitions)	9	7	9	5	0	0	0	2	0	0
Stocks										
Increase during year	504	-1,883	210	-1,842	45	58	206	-83	43	-16
Value at end of year	15,594	13,702	12,168	10,583	1,236	1,065	1,847	1,714	343	339
Total turnover divided by end-year stocks (Quotient)	9	9	8	9	13	16	9	8	7	7
Employment costs										
Total employment costs	10,954	10,477	5,679	5,230	3,099	3,012	1,968	2,042	208	193
Gross wages and salaries paid	9,693	9,233	5,010	4,582	2,766	2,702	1,729	1,774	188	175
National insurance and pension contributions	1,261	1,243	669	648	332	310	239	268	20	18
Gross margin										
Amount	31,546	27,895	17,878	13,794	7,733	8,461	5,292	4,973	643	667
As a percentage of adjusted turnover	23	22	18	15	47	49	34	36	29	29
Approximate gross value added at basic prices	20,768	18,256	11,947	8,652	5,048	5,971	3,368	3,195	405	438

1 See chapter text. Figures are exclusive of VAT.

Source: Office for National Statistics: 01633 456592

13.4 Accomodation and food service activities[1]

United Kingdom

Data for 2009 on this table are provisional.

£ million and percentages

	Accomodation (SIC 2007 55.0)		Hotels and similar accomodation (SIC 2007 55.1)		Holiday and other short stay accomodation (SIC 2007 55.2)	
	2008	2009	2008	2009	2008	2009
Number of businesses	15,726	15,120	10,179	9,681	2,973	3,329
Total turnover[2]	20,228	19,669	15,725	15,837	1,562	1,339
Taxesand levies[3]						
Total taxes and levies	667	652	558	568	33	32
National (non-domestic business) rates	652	628	548	549	30	29
Other amounts paid for taxes, duties and levies	16	24	11	19	2	3
Capital expenditure[3]						
Capital acquisitions	2,062	1,657	1,626	1,371	135	65
Capital disposals	152	101	72	46	38	16
Net capital expenditure	1,910	1,556	1,553	1,326	98	49
Work of a capital nature carried out by your own staff (included in acquisitions)	7	8	4	7	2	1
Stocks[3]						
Increase during year	-3	-38	5	-8	1	-4
Value at end of year	369	358	195	181	43	21
Purchases of goods and services[3]						
Total purchases	7,925	7,902	5,784	6,259	782	540
Energy, water and materials	2,730	2,761	2,141	2,287	147	158
Goods for resale	1,431	1,271	838	841	251	91
Hiring, leasing of plant, machinery etc.	97	92	56	63	5	3
Commercial insurance premiums	169	174	129	136	12	16
Road transport services	32	31	16	19	3	4
Telecommunication services	77	83	59	66	5	9
Computer and related services	104	112	81	94	7	6
Advertising and marketing services	467	375	292	249	54	41
Other services	2,778	2,954	2,144	2,474	293	207
Employment costs[3]						
Total employment costs	4,813	5,018	4,003	4,230	319	292
Gross wages and salaries paid	4,396	4,586	3,662	3,872	291	267
National insurance and pension contributions	418	433	341	359	28	26
Gross margin[4]						
Amount	16,033	15,866	12,664	12,943	1,108	1,088
As a percentage of turnover	92	92	94	94	81	92
Value added at basic prices[4]	9,587	9,303	7,752	7,572	582	644

13.4 Accomodation and food service activities[1]

United Kingdom

Data for 2009 on this table are provisional.

£ million and percentages

	Camping grounds, recreational vehicle parks and trailer parks (SIC 2007 55.2)		Other accomodation (SIC 2007 55.9)		Food and beverage serving activities (SIC 2007 56.0)	
	2008	2009	2008	2009	2008	2009
Number of businesses	1,728	1,704	846	406	120,779	113,593
Total turnover[2]	2,744	2,322	197	171	58,273	54,619
Taxesand levies[3]						
Total taxes and levies	72	50	4	2	1,449	1,462
National (non-domestic business) rates	71	49	3	2	1,362	1,316
Other amounts paid for taxes, duties and levies	1	1	1	1	87	147
Capital expenditure[3]						
Capital acquisitions	266	170	35	51	2,778	1,931
Capital disposals	*	38	*	1	439	422
Net capital expenditure	*	132	*	50	2,339	1,509
Work of a capital nature carried out by your own staff (included in acquisitions)	0	0	1	0	2	6
Stocks[3]						
Increase during year	-9	-27	0	0	47	42
Value at end of year	128	155	2	1	1,023	809
Purchases of goods and services[3]						
Total purchases	1,273	1,040	86	64	27,847	27,666
Energy, water and materials	412	304	30	12	11,272	10,779
Goods for resale	336	322	6	17	10,901	11,728
Hiring, leasing of plant, machinery etc.	32	26	4	0	264	309
Commercial insurance premiums	24	20	3	2	342	248
Road transport services	12	8	2	0	153	157
Telecommunication services	11	8	2	1	175	131
Computer and related services	14	9	2	2	101	114
Advertising and marketing services	117	84	4	1	424	456
Other services	308	244	34	29	5,108	4,625
Employment costs[3]						
Total employment costs	436	450	55	46	14,157	14,216
Gross wages and salaries paid	394	406	49	42	13,091	13,196
National insurance and pension contributions	42	44	6	4	1,066	1,020
Gross margin[4]						
Amount	2,085	1,692	175	143	40,526	37,394
As a percentage of turnover	86	82	96	89	80	77
Value added at basic prices[4]	1,158	990	95	97	22,713	20,597

13.4 Accomodation and food service activities[1]

United Kingdom

Data for 2009 on this table are provisional.

£ million and percentages

	Restaurants and mobile food service activities (SIC 2007 56.1)		Event catering and other food service activities (SIC 2007 56.2)		Beverage serving activities (SIC 2007 56.3)	
	2008	2009	2008	2009	2008	2009
Number of businesses	63,368	61,025	7,536	7,036	49,875	45,532
Total turnover[2]	25,744	25,077	8,471	7,576	24,057	21,966
Taxesand levies[3]						
Total taxes and levies	659	625	34	50	756	788
National (non-domestic business) rates	619	599	32	36	711	680
Other amounts paid for taxes, duties and levies	40	25	2	13	45	108
Capital expenditure[3]						
Capital acquisitions	1,122	1,179	98	70	1,558	682
Capital disposals	103	142	10	25	326	255
Net capital expenditure	1,019	1,036	88	45	1,231	427
Work of a capital nature carried out by your own staff (included in acquisitions)	0	5	0	0	1	1
Stocks[3]						
Increase during year	16	23	1	13	29	6
Value at end of year	449	300	146	123	428	386
Purchases of goods and services[3]						
Total purchases	12,181	12,456	3,729	3,458	11,937	11,752
Energy, water and materials	5,573	6,152	2,474	1,491	3,225	3,136
Goods for resale	3,919	4,376	547	1,328	6,435	6,025
Hiring, leasing of plant, machinery etc.	43	133	68	92	153	84
Commercial insurance premiums	138	98	36	24	168	126
Road transport services	94	89	25	15	34	54
Telecommunication services	85	48	25	19	66	65
Computer and related services	40	46	15	17	46	50
Advertising and marketing services	290	288	31	25	103	144
Other services	2,937	2,243	503	357	1,668	2,024
Employment costs[3]						
Total employment costs	6,228	6,490	2,954	2,864	4,974	4,862
Gross wages and salaries paid	5,794	5,988	2,692	2,632	4,605	4,575
National insurance and pension contributions	435	502	263	231	369	287
Gross margin[4]						
Amount	19,437	18,508	6,994	5,607	14,094	13,279
As a percentage of turnover	87	85	93	80	68	68
Value added at basic prices[4]	10,250	9,417	3,821	3,567	8,642	7,613

Source: Office for National Statistics: 01633 456592

1 See chapter text.
2 Inclusive of VAT.
3 Exclusive of VAT.
4 The total turnover figure used to calculate these data excludes VAT.
5 Includes figures for managed public houses owned by breweries.

Defence

Chapter 14

Defence

This section includes figures on Defence expenditure, on the size and role of the Armed Forces and on related support activities.

Much of the material in this section can be found in UK Defence Statistics 2010

Defence expenditure (Table 14.1)

UK Defence Expenditure - the move from cash to resource accounting

Up until financial year 1998/99, government expenditure was accounted for on a cash basis. In April 1999 the introduction of Resource Accounting and Budgeting (RAB) brought in an accruals -based accounting system, although government departments were still controlled on a cash basis. This transitional accounting regime remained for two financial years. Government expenditure has been accounted for on a resource basis only since 2001/02.

The main difference arising from the adoption of RAB is that costs are accounted for as they are incurred (the principle of accruals), rather than when payment is made (the principle of cash). This gives rise to timing differences in accounting between the cash and RAB systems and also to the recognition of depreciation, which expends the cost of an asset over its useful economic life, and the cost of capital charge, equivalent to an interest charge on the net assets held on the balance sheet. At the time that RAB was introduced the cost of capital charge was 6 per cent of the net value of assets; although this was reduced to 3.5 per cent in 2003/04.

The change from cash based accounting to resource (accruals) based accounting, and the two-stage introduction of RAB (outlined below) has affected the time series comparability of the data.

Please refer to UK Defence Statistics 2010 Chapter 1 – Resource Accounting and Budgeting section for a summary of the key events leading to the introduction of RAB. Back copies of this publication are available at www.dasa.mod.uk/applications/newWeb/www/index.php?page=67&pubType= 1&thiscontent=10&date

Control Regime

Under Resource Accounting, government departments are accountable for their spending against Resource and Capital Departmental Expenditure Limits (DELs). Spending against the Resource DEL includes current items, which are explained in the following two paragraphs. The Capital DEL, while part of the overall DEL, reflects investment spending that will appear on the department's balance sheet and be consumed over a number of years, net of the receipts from sale of assets. Departments are also responsible for Annually Managed Expenditure (AME). This spending is demand led (for example, payment of War Pensions) and therefore cannot be controlled by departments in the same way.

In Stage 1 of RAB, which was introduced at the start of financial year 2001/02, the Resource DEL covered current costs such as in year personnel costs, equipment, maintenance of land and buildings. Non-cash costs such as depreciation and the cost of capital charge fell within Annually Managed Expenditure (AME) and were not controlled to the same degree as DELs. This allowed departments an interim period to gain experience of managing the new non-cash costs and to review their holdings of stocks and fixed assets, which impact the non-cash costs, prior to the charge impacting on the more tightly controlled DELs.

Stage 2 of RAB was introduced at the start of the financial year 2003/04. This involved the movement of the primary non-cash costs (depreciation and the cost of capital charge) from AME into the Resource DEL, and reduced the cost of capital charge to 3.5 per cent of the net value of assets.

The change in definition of the DELs combined with volatile non-cash costs over the Stage 1 period make time series comparisons over the period 2001/02 - 2003/04 complex.

From 2006/07, the MOD has transferred ownership of fixed assets into two TLB's: Defence Estates (DE) for Land and Buildings: and Defence Equipment & Support (DE&S) for Plant and Machinery, Transport, IT and Communications equipment, and Single Use Military Equipment (SUME).

Factors affecting Cash to RAB data consistency

* There are timing differences as to when payments are recognised

* In financial year 2003/04 the rate of interest used to calculate the cost of capital charge was reduced from 6 per cent to 3.5 per cent.

* The discount rate for provisions was changed from 3.5 per cent real to 2.2 per cent real with effect from 1April 2005

* The discount rate for pension's liabilities was changed from 2.8 per cent real to 1.8 per cent real with effect from 1 April 2007

Changes to the 2009/10 MOD Accounts following introduction of International Financial Reporting Standards (IFRS)

In accordance with HM Treasury's timetable for the introduction of International Financial Reporting Standards (IFRS), the Department has prepared and published, for the first time, accounts based on IFRS as adapted and interpreted by HM Treasury in the Government Financial Reporting Manual (FReM). A break in series to Table 14.1 follows the 2008/09 outturn to denote the implementation of IFRS. Further details of the policies applied are provided at Note 1 to the Accounts - Statement of Accounting Policies.

Note 2 (Page 66) of the 2009/10 Accounts provides a reconciliation of the main changes /movements resulting from the MOD's adoption of IFRS. These include:

Construction Contracts - the year end balance in respect of the provision of security services to third parties is required to be accounted for as a receivable under IAS11 (previously accounted for as work-in-progress); the movement identified is based on updated information and includes an increase following the recalculation of related staff costs

Leases - a review of PFI contracts not meeting the criteria of a Service Concession Arrangement (IFRIC 12) and some other contracts, including the arrangement with Annington Homes for the provision of Service Families Accommodation, resulted in the £1.2 billion increase in the value of non current assets as property, plant and equipment were added to the Statement of Financial Position under finance leases (in accordance with IAS 17 - Leases)

Employee Benefits - in accordance with IAS 19 the accounts include an estimate of the value of unpaid overtime, outstanding non-consolidated pay and untaken leave balances as at year end. The initial assessment of the liability was £330 million and 83 per cent of this amount relates to untaken leave

Provisions - the £77 million movement is the increase in the value of the capitalised provisions for nuclear decommissioning. The increase results from the capitalisation of the movement following changes in the discount rate for provisions

Non-current Assets Held for Sale - the movement reflects the identification and valuation (fair value less costs of sale) of assets held for sale

Service Concession Arrangements - changes to the accounting treatment of some 32 PFI/PPP contracts assessed as Service Concession Arrangements under IFRIC 12 resulted in the net movements as a result of the differences between the depreciation, cost of capital charges and other charges applicable to the assets brought on to the Statement of Financial Position and the corresponding reduction in the service and financing charges

Table 14.1 provides a breakdown of MOD outturn in terms of resources consumed. This is distributed between the main personnel, fixed assets and other expenditure groups. The table also includes expenditure relating to conflict prevention and operations.

Resource DEL includes expenditure under the following headings:-

- **Equipment support**: internal and contracted out costs for equipment repair and maintenance.

- **Stock consumption**: consumption of armament, medical, dental, veterinary, oil, clothing, and general stores.

- **Property management**: estate and facilities management services and costs for building maintenance.

- **Movements**: cost of transportation of freight and personnel.

- **Accommodation and utilities**: charges include rent, rates, gas, electricity, water and sewerage costs.

- **Professional fees**: fees, such as legal costs paid to professional organisations

-**Fuel:** relates to fuel consumption by military vehicles, ships and aircraft.

- **Other Costs**: can include grants-in-aid, exchange rate movements, provisions, receipts, welfare, medical and legal costs, research and expensed development, rentals paid under operating leases, fixed assets and stock written off.

Expenditure on fixed asset categories in Capital DEL includes:-

-**Intangible assets**: comprise the development costs of major equipment projects and Intellectual Property Rights.

-**Single Use Military Equipment (SUME)**: are assets which only have a military use, such as tanks and fighter aircrafts. Dual use items that is those that also have a civilian use, are recorded under the other categories.

- **Assets under Construction**: largely consist of major weapons platforms under construction in the Defence Equipment & Support, and a smaller element of buildings under construction. Once construction is complete, those platforms will transfer to the relevant Top Level Budget holder as Single Use Military Equipment on their Balance Sheets.

-**Transport/Capital spares**: from 2004/05 transport has been recorded as a separate category and Capital Spares has been removed as a category, with the costs previously recorded here being incorporated into Transport or SUME.

- **Capital Income**: receipts for the sale of fixed assets. Redemption of QinetiQ preference shares refers to the proceeds received from the partial redemption of the redeemable preference shares during 2004/05.

Annual Managed Expenditure includes:

- **Other**: Under Stage 2 of RAB, this category now contains only demand led payments, such as cash release and cost of capital credit on nuclear provisions and QinetiQ loan repayments.

In order to give a single measure of spending on public services under full resource budgeting, the Defence Spending line is presented as the sum of the resource and capital budgets, net of depreciation and impairments. This reflects the resources required plus the net investment in them, but avoids double counting the writing down of the existing capital stock and the cash outlay on new assets. Control is exercised separately on gross Capital and Resource DEL.

Service personnel

(Tables 14.2, 14.3, 14.4, 14.6, 14.7, 14.9 and 14.10)

The Regular Forces consist entirely of volunteer members serving on a whole-time basis, figures for which include both trained and untrained personnel and exclude Gurkhas, Full-Time Reserve Service personnel, the Home Service battalions of the Royal Irish Regiment, mobilised reservists and Naval Activated Reservists.

Locally Entered Personnel are recruited outside the UK for whole-time service in special formations with special conditions of service and normally restricted locations. The Brigade of Gurkhas is an example.

The Regular Forces are supported by Reserves and Auxiliary Forces. There are both regular and volunteer Reserves. Regular Reserves consist of former Service personnel with a Reserve liability. Volunteer Reserves are open to both former personnel and civilians. The call out liabilities of the various reserve forces differ in accordance with their roles.

All three Services run cadet forces for young people and the Combined Cadet Force, which is found in certain schools where education is continued to the age of 17 or above, may operate sections for any or all of the Services.

FTRS (Full-Time Reserve Service) are personnel who fill Service posts for a set period on a full-time basis while being a member of one of the reserve Services, either as an ex-regular or as a volunteer. An FTRS reservist on:

Full Commitment (FC) fulfils the same range of duties and deployment liability as a Regular Service person

Limited Commitment (LC) serves at one location but can be detached for up to 35 days a year

Home Commitment (HC) is employed at one location and cannot be detached elsewhere

Each Service uses FTRS personnel differently:

The Naval Service predominantly uses FTRS to backfill gapped regular posts. However, they do have a small number of FTRS personnel that are not deployable for operations overseas. There is no distinction made in terms of fulfilling baseline Liability posts between FTRS Full Commitment (FC), Limited Commitment (LC) and Home Commitment (HC).

The Army employ FTRS(FC) and FTRS(LC) to fill Regular Army Liability (RAL) posts as a substitute for Regular personnel for set periods of time. FTRS(HC) personnel cannot be deployed to operations and are not counted against RAL.

The RAF consider that FTRS(FC) can fill regular RAF Liability posts but have identified separate liabilities for FTRS(LC) and FTRS(HC).

Operational Commitment Establishment (Reserve) (OCE(R)) FTRS(FC) personnel can be deployed either as a direct substitute for Regular Army personnel, or deployed into OCE(R) posts. While they are filling OCE(R) positions, FTRS(FC) personnel are not counted against Regular Army Liability. These are reported as **FTRS personnel serving against an additional requirement** along with non-deployable FTRS as defined above.

From 1 July 2009 some elements of the FTRS are excluded as described above.

Home Service battalions of the Royal Irish Regiment. Up until 1 July 1992, this was the Ulster Defence Regiment. The figures for the Territorial Army include Officer Training Corps and non-regular permanent staff.

The figures for cadet forces for each service include the Combined Cadet Force. Naval Service figures include officers and civilian instructors. The Army and Royal Air Force figures exclude officers and civilian instructors.

Intake of UK regular forces from civilian life: by service

(Table 14.2)

This table shows all intakes to UK Regular Forces, both trained and untrained, which comprises new entrants, re-entrants, direct trained entrants (including professionally qualified officers) and intake from the reserves. They exclude all movements within the Regular Forces; including flows from untrained to trained strength, transfers between Services and flows from ranks to officer due to promotion.

Formation of the armed forces

(Table 14.3)

This table shows the number of units which comprise the 'teeth' elements of the Armed Forces and excludes supporting units.

Outflow of UK regular forces: by service

(Table 14.4)

This table shows outflow from UK Regular Forces, both trained and untrained, including personnel leaving the Services, deaths, recalled reservists on release and outflow to the Home Service battalions of the Royal Irish Regiment (which disbanded on 31 March 2008). They do not include promotion from ranks to officers or flows between Services.

Civilian personnel

(Table 14.6)

In previous years, the Ministry of Defence civilian workforce definition has reflected the historical requirement to understand the number of civil servants being directly funded. However with changes in employment legislation and the requirement to plan the future of the civilian workforce there was a need to change the definition to a more inclusive one, better reflecting modern human resources methods and policies. In the longer term it will be used for skills planning, ensuring that the Ministry of Defence has a well-equipped workforce able to provide the best support to the UK Armed Forces.

In summary, the change over previous years is the addition of two further categories of individuals:

Casual personnel - those employed on a short-term casual contract;

Those not directly funded - personnel who are employed by the Ministry of Defence, but whose salaries are paid for by another Department/Agency etc. This includes personnel on loan to other government departments or working for NATO, as well as those on a career break or long term sickness absence.

These additions allow two levels of definition to be established:

Definition - Level 1 This includes permanent and casual personnel, Royal Fleet Auxiliaries, but excludes Trading Funds. This is generally used for internal reporting and planning.

Definition - Level 0 This contains all those at Level 1 plus Trading Funds and Locally Engaged Civilians. This is used for external reporting, including National Statistics publications CPS1 and UKDS, and Parliamentary business.

For more information on the revised civilian workforce definition, visit:
www.dasa.mod.uk/natstats/consultation/consultation.html

As from 1 April 2000 a new top level budget was formed in the Centre called Defence Logistics Organisation, replacing the top level budgets CinC Fleet Support, Quarter Master General and RAF Logistics Command.

At 1 April 2007, Chief of Defence Logistics and Defence Procurement Agency merged to form Defence Equipment & Support.

The QinetiQ portion of the Defence Evaluation and Research Agency was established as a private company in July 2001. The War Pensions Agency transferred from the Department of Work & Pensions in 2001. The Clyde Dockyards were contractorised in 2002.

Data on manually paid personnel before 1999 is not available, so estimates are used.

At 1 April 2008, the Rotary Wing and Components businesses of the trading fund, Defence Aviation Repair Agency (DARA) were aquired by the Vector Aerospace Corporation. In the region of 1,000 (FTE) DARA personnel transferred to the new company under TUPE terms.

At 1 April 2010 Corporate Science Innovation & Technology (CSIT) formally ceased to be a Top Level Budget (TLB) within the MOD Head Office, HQ and centrally managed expenditure budgetary area.

At 1 April 2011 the Defence Estates Top Level Budget (TLB) within the MOD Head Office, HQ and centrally managed expenditure budgetary area, formally ceased to be a TLB. Defence Infrastructure Organisation (DIO) TLB replaces the former Defence Estates TLB and includes TLB property and facilities management functions previously situated within other TLBs.

Totals and subtotals have been rounded separately and so may not appear to be the sums of their parts.

Family accommodation and defence land holdings

(Table 14.7)

In November 1996 most of the MOD's housing stock in England and Wales was sold to a private company, Annington Homes. The homes retained for use by Service families were leased back with the condition that the MOD releases a certain number of houses each year for disposal by Annington. The proceeds of the sale are being used to upgrade the housing stock

(Table 14.9)

Rates have been standardised to 2010 Armed Forces population age and gender structure. The data are presented for the Naval Service (Royal Navy and Royal Marines), the Army (including the Gurkhas), the Royal Air Force, and on a Tri-Service basis. Non-regular members of the UK Armed Forces who died whilst deployed on operations are included in the data presented.

Health

(Table 14.10)

The Services operate a number of hospitals in this country and in areas abroad where there is a significant British military presence. These hospitals take as patients, members of all three Services and their dependants. In addition, the hospitals in the UK take civilian patients under arrangements agreed with the National Health Service. Medical support is also supplied by service medical staff at individual units, ships and stations.

Defence services and the civilian community

The table also presents statistics of land and foreshore in the UK owned or leased by the Ministry of Defence or over which it has limited rights under grants or licences. Land declared as surplus to Defence requirements is also included.

Deployment of Service personnel

(Table 14.8)

Location data are based on the stationed location of the individual. Personnel deployed on operations to an area away from their stationed location are shown against their most recent stationed location. Naval Service personnel on sea service are included against the local authority containing the home port of their ship.

Prior to 2003, figures for UK distribution and global location are collated from separate sources and comparison is therefore not possible between the two sets of UK personnel figures. From 2001 the grouping of overseas locations has been changed to give a more relevant overview.

(Table 14.11)

Search & Rescue (SAR)

This table covers incidents attended by military Search and Rescue units. The Royal Air Force (RAF) and Royal Navy (RN) provide an essential service to the Search and Rescue (SAR) effort around the UK forming part of the national UK SAR coverage throughout the year for air, land and maritime operations. The military SAR teams' primary purpose is to recover aircrew from crashed military aircraft although, each year, over 90 per cent of callouts are to civilian incidents. The SAR force currently consists of 6 x RAF and 2 x RN SAR Sea King helicopter units and 4 RAF mountain rescue teams operating from bases around the UK. The Nimrod fixed-wing aircraft based at RAF Kinloss were withdrawn from service in March 2010.

The table also includes urgent medical incidents in which the military SAR facilities gave assistance (for example inter-hospital transfers).

More than one SAR unit may be called to the same incident; consequently the number of callouts is likely to be greater than the number of incidents.

Persons moved involves moving people from a hostile environment to a safe environment or to a medical facility to receive urgent medical attention. People assisted by RAF mountain rescue teams, but subsequently transported from the scene by helicopter, are recorded as having been rescued by the helicopter unit concerned.

Fisheries Protection

The Royal Navy Fishery Protection squadron operates within the British fishery limits under contract to the Department for Environment, Food and Rural Affairs. Boardings carried out by vessels of the Scottish Executive Environment and Rural Affairs Department and the Department of Agriculture for Northern Ireland are not included.

14.1 United Kingdom defence expenditure[1]

Inclusive of non-recoverable VAT at current prices (£ million)

		2003 /04	2004 /05	2005 /06	2006 /07	2007 /08	2008 /09	2009 /10
Defence Spending	C228	30,861	32,515	33,164	34,045	37,387	38,579	39,307
Departmental Expenditure Limits (DEL)	SNKJ	37,174	38,323	39,751	40,654	43,634	45,473	47,647
Resource DEL	E2XV	31,266	31,798	32,911	33,457	35,689	36,715	38,572
Expenditure on personnel	SNKK	10,435	10,996	11,255	11,204	11,474	11,723	12,231
of which: Armed forces	SNKL	7,974	8,047	8,263	8,423	8,646	8,937	9,481
of which: Civilians	SNKM	2,461	2,948	2,992	2,781	2,828	2,786	2,750
Depreciation/impairments	SNKN	6,313	5,808	6,587	6,609	6,247	6,894	8,340
Cost of capital	SNKO	2,770	3,026	3,106	3,242	3,371	3,626	3,828
Equipment support	SNKP	3,804	3,623	3,542	3,793	4,272	4,292	4,212
Stock consumption	SNKQ	1,060	1,079	1,039	1,140	1,071	1,181	1,112
Property management	SNKR	1,393	1,509	1,367	1,258	1,523	1,508	1,625
Movements	SNKS	491	711	729	774	858	975	929
Accommodation and utilities	SNKT	643	581	735	786	750	866	688
Professional fees	SNKU	549	565	553	482	471	391	308
Fuel	SNKV	161	239	369	416	537	695	482
Hospitality & Entertainment	I4SS	8	6	5	4	4	4	4
PFI Service Charges	I4ST	..	..	870	1,148	1,276	1,482	1,133
IT & Communications	I4SU	738	678	643	719	655	852	886
Research and Expensed Development	KN29	1,011	996	994	988	952	1,115	1,222
Rentals Paid Under Operating Leases	KN2A	214	229	56	138	152	148	254
Fixed Assets Written Off/Written On	KN2B	26	-86	-302	730	870	424	-95
Movement in Stock Related Provisions	KN2C	..	..	..	..	137	-250	322
Stock Written Off	KN2D	528	704	759	95	432	130	374
Other costs	KN2E	1,121	1,134	604	-69	637	659	716
Capital DEL	E2XW	5,908	6,525	6,840	7,197	7,945	8,758	9,075
Expenditure on fixed asset categories								
Intangible assets	SNKX	1,665	1,580	1,550	1,744	1,756	1,311	1,271
Land and buildings	SNKY	54	389	31	45	126	163	246
Single Use Military Equipment	SNKZ	90	434	402	404	657	552	504
Plant, machinery and vehicles	SNLA	78	124	64	32	36	30	299
IT and communications equipment	SNLB	183	134	180	206	361	336	347
Assets under construction	SNLC	3,931	4,335	4,879	5,099	5,450	6,515	6,277
Transport	E2XX	..	73	13	33	55	239	73
Capital spares	SNLD	581	..	..	..	..	..	..
Capital loan repayment	E2XY	-28	-25	-53	-8	-10	-65	-8
Capital Income	KN2F	-646	-519	-225	-358	-486	-323	-111
Other Costs	KN2G	..	..	..	..	..	..	176
Annually Managed Expenditure (AME)	SNLF	1,011	908	890	582	510	214	2,417
War pensions	SNLG	1,116	1,110	1,067	1,038	1,014	1,000	980
Other	SNLH	-105	-202	-177	-456	-504	-785	1,437

1 See chapter text. Where rounding has been used, totals and sub-totals have been rounded separately and so may not equal the sums of their rounded parts.

Sources: Ministry of Defence/DASA (Economic Statistics);
0117 913 4529/27

14.2 Intake to UK Regular Forces from civil life by Service and Sex[1]

Numbers

		2000 /01	2001 /02	2002 /03	2003 /04	2004 /05	2005 /06	2006 /07	2007 /08	2008 /09	2009[2] /10
All services:											
Male	KCJB	20,410	20,950	23,040	20,760	15,660	16,410	17,830	19,230	20,690	19,860
Female	KCJC	2,610	2,700	3,240	2,710	1,900	1,740	1,960	2,090	2,080	1,940
Total	KCJA	23,020	23,650	26,280	23,470	17,560	18,150	19,790	21,330	22,770	21,800
Naval service:											
Male	KCJE	3,990	4,270	4,420	3,530	3,240	3,480	3,300	3,400	3,590	3,760
Female	KCJF	630	740	800	580	460	460	460	470	410	390
Total	KCJD	4,620	5,010	5,220	4,120	3,690	3,940	3,770	3,860	4,000	4,150
Army:											
Male	KCJJ	13,450	13,620	15,060	13,930	10,780	11,740	13,160	13,390	13,500	13,210
Female	KCJK	1,320	1,240	1,550	1,260	910	990	1,140	1,150	1,020	970
Total	KCJI	14,770	14,850	16,610	15,190	11,690	12,730	14,300	14,540	14,510	14,180
Royal Air Force:											
Male	KCJM	2,980	3,070	3,550	3,290	1,640	1,190	1,370	2,450	3,600	2,890
Female	KCJN	660	720	890	870	530	290	360	480	660	580
Total	KCJL	3,630	3,780	4,450	4,160	2,180	1,480	1,720	2,930	4,260	3,470

1 See chapter text.
2 From 2009/10 Army intake figures include transfers from the
  Gurkhas to the UK Regular Forces.

Source: Ministry of Defence/DASA (Quad-Service): 0207 8078896

14.3 Formation of the United Kingdom armed forces[1]

At 1 April each year

Numbers

			2000	2001	2002	2003	2004	2005	2006	2007	2008	2009	2010
		Front Line Units											
Royal Navy													
Submarines	KCGA	Vessels	16	16	16	16	15	15	14 [3]	13 [4]	13	12 [6]	11 [2]
Destroyers and frigates	KCGC	"	32	32	32	31	31	28	25 [5]	25	25	24 [8]	23 [7]
Mine counter-measure	KCGE	"	21	23	22	22	19	16	16	16	16	16	16
Patrol ships and craft	KCGF	"	23	23	23	22	26	26	22 [10]	22	22 [11]	22	22
Fixed wing aircraft	KCGG	Squadrons	1	1	1	1	1	1	1	1	1	1	1
Helicopters[9]	KCGH	"	9	9	8	8	5	6	6	7	7	7	7
Royal Marines	KCGI	Commandos	3	3	3	3	3	3	3	3	3	3	3
Regular Army													
Royal Armoured Corps	KCGJ	Regiments	10	10	10	10	10	10	10	10	10	10	10
Royal Artillery [20]	KCGK	"	15	15	15	15	14	14	14	14	14	14	14
Royal Engineers	KCGL	"	11	11	11	11	11	11	11	11	11	11	12 [19]
Infantry	KCGM	Battalions	40	40	40	40	40	40	36	36	36	36	36
Royal Air Force													
Strike/attack	KCGP	Squadrons	5	5	5	5	5	5}					
Offensive support	KCGQ ZIZM	"	2	2	2	2	2	1}	13 [12]	13	11	11	10 [16]
Reconnaissance	KCGT	"	5	5	5	5	5	5}					
Air defence	KCGR	"	5	5	5	4	4	4}					
Maritime patrol	KCGU	"	3	3	3	3	3	3	3	2	2	2	2
Airborne early warning & ISTAR	KCGU	"	2	2	2	2	2	2	3	3	4	4	4
Air transport/Air refuelling	KCGV	"	8	9	9	9	9	9	8	8	8	8	8
Search and rescue	KCGX	"	2	2	2	2	2	2	2	2	2	2	2
RAF FP Wg	GHN7	HQs	..	4	4	4	4	4	6	6	7	7	8
RAF Ground based air defence[13,14]	GHN8	Squadrons	..	4	4	4	4	4	3	2	–	–	–
RAF Regiment Field[14]	GJ2F	"	..	6	6	6	6	6	6	6	7	7	8
RAF Regt (Jt CBRN)	I63Y	"	–	–	–	–	–	–	–	1	1	1	1
Tactical Provost Wg	GJ2G	HQs	–	–	–	–	–	–	1	1	1	1	1
Tactical Provost	GJ2H	Squadrons	–	–	–	–	–	–	2	1	1	1	1
Joint Helicopter Command													
Royal Navy Helicopter	JUAT	"	4	4	4	4	4	4	4	4	4	4	4
Army Aviation	JUAU	Regiments	5	5	5	5	5	5	5	5	5	5	5
Royal Air Force Helicopter	JUAV	Squadrons	5	5	5	5	5	5	5	5	6	6	6
Joint Force Harrier [15]													
Royal Navy	JUAW	"	3	3	3	3	2	1	1	2	2	2	1 [17]
Royal Air Force	JUAX	"	3	3	3	3	3	3	2	2	2	2	1 [18]

1. See chapter text.
2. HMS Trafalgar was withdrawn from service during the year.
3. HMS Spartan was withdrawn from service during the year.
4. HMS Sovereign was withdrawn from the service during the year.
5. HMS Cardiff, HMS Marlborough and HMS Grafton were withdrawn from service during the year.
6. HMS Superb was withdrawn from service during the year.
7. HMS Exeter and HMS Nottingham were withdrawn in 2010. HMS Daring entered service during 2010.
8. HMS Southampton was withdrawn from service during the year.
9. From 2000 excludes helicopters transferred to the Joint Helicopter command. OCUs/ OEUs excluded from 2005 onwards.
10. HMS Leeds Castle and the NI Squadron, consisting of HMS Brecon, HMS Cottlesmore and HMS Dulverton were withdrawn from service during the year.
11. HMS Clyde entered service during the year. HMS Dumbarton Castle was withdrawn from service.

12. From 2006, 4 Air Defence squadrons amalgamated with Strike/Attack, Offensive support and Reconnaissance to form multi-roled squadrons. One squadron moved from reconnaissance to ISTAR, and one squadron was disbanded.
13. Delivery of Ground Based Air Defence is now vested with the Army. The remaining 2 Squadrons were reroled on 1 April 08 to increase the numbers of FP WGS and field Regts.
14. In UKDS editions 2003 and 2004, Ground Based Air Defence and Field Squadrons for years 2001 to 2004 were also included under Regular Air Force.
15. Harrier aircraft were transferred to the Joint Force Harrier on 1 April 2000.
16. 43 Sqn was stood down on 1 July 2009.
17. With the reduction in the Joint Force Harrier force from 1 April 2010, the Fleet Air Arm Strike Wing is now counted as 1 Sqn.
18. 20 Sqn was disbanded 31 March 2010.
19. 101 Engr Regt (EOD) has now been 'regularised' under Op ENTIRETY, in order to support ongoing operations in Afghanistan.
20. Excludes 14th Regiment Artillery.

Source: MOD/DASA: 020 7218 0390

14.4 Outflow from United Kingdom regular forces: by Service and Sex[1]

		1998 /99	1999 /00	2000 /01	2001 /02	2002 /03	2003 /04	2004 /05	2005 /06	2006 /07	2007 /08	2008 /09	Numbers 2009 /10
All Services:													
Male	KDNA	24,500	23,870	22,520	22,360	21,770	21,200	21,330	21,290	23,000	22,510	19,940	17,110
Female	KDNB	2,970	2,750	2,430	2,350	2,340	2,200	2,100	1,980	2,160	2,170	1,940	1,470
Total	KDNC	27,470	26,620	24,950	24,710	24,100	23,400	23,430	23,260	25,160	24,690	21,880	18,580
Naval Service: [2]													
Male	KDND	4,920	5,160	4,480	5,110	4,680	4,230	4,150	4,000	3,830	3,870	3,970	3,400
Female	KDNE	610	630	550	690	620	540	490	480	490	470	460	340
Total	KDNF	5,530	5,800	5,040	5,800	5,300	4,770	4,630	4,490	4,320	4,340	4,430	3,740
Army: [2,3]													
Male	KDNI	15,320	14,620	13,900	13,290	13,420	13,500	13,990	13,240	14,660	14,230	12,210	11,120
Female	KDNJ	1,730	1,580	1,330	1,090	1,140	1,090	1,080	950	1,110	1,100	930	720
Total	KDNK	17,050	16,200	15,230	14,380	14,560	14,600	15,070	14,190	15,770	15,330	13,140	11,840
Royal Air Force: [2]													
Male	KDNL	4,250	4,080	4,140	3,960	3,670	3,470	3,200	4,050	4,500	4,420	3,770	2,590
Female	KDNM	640	540	540	570	580	570	530	540	560	610	550	410
Total	KDNN	4,890	4,620	4,680	4,530	4,250	4,040	3,730	4,590	5,070	5,020	4,320	3,000

1 See chapter text. Comprises all those who left the Regular Forces and includes deaths.

2 Due to ongoing validation of data from the new Personnel Administration System, Naval Service statistics from 1 October 2006, Army statistics from 1 April 2007 and RAF statistics from 1 May 2007 are provisional and subject to review.

3 Outflow figures up to and including 2008-09 include the net flow of between 100 and 200 personnel from the Regular Army to Long Term Absentee (LTA). Outflow figures for 2009/10 do not include this net flow to LTA.

Source: Ministry of Defence/DASA (Quad-Service): 0207 8078896

14.5 United Kingdom Defence: service manpower strengths

As at 1 April

Thousands

		2000	2001	2002	2003	2004	2005	2006	2007	2008	2009	2010
UK service personnel												
Full-time trained strength[1]	ZBTR	190.3	189.1	187.1	188.5	190.2	188.1	183.2	177.8	174.0	173.9	177.8
Trained Naval Service	ZBTS	38.9	38.5	37.5	37.6	37.5	36.4	35.6	34.9	35.1	35.0	35.5
UK regulars[2]	ZBTT	38.5	38.0	36.8	36.6	36.4	35.5	34.9	34.3	34.5	34.4	35.2
Full-time reserve service[3]	ZBTU	0.3	0.5	0.7	1.0	1.1	0.9	0.7	0.6	0.5	0.6	0.3
Trained Army	ZBTV	100.2	100.4	100.4	102.0	103.6	102.4	100.6	99.3	98.3	99.3	102.2
UK regulars[2]	ZBTW	96.5	96.3	96.0	97.6	99.4	98.5	96.8	95.4	93.8	94.6	98.0
Full-time reserve service[3]	ZBTX	0.5	0.7	0.9	1.0	0.7	0.4	0.5	0.7	0.9	1.1	0.6
Gurkhas	ZBTY	3.4	3.5	3.4	3.4	3.4	3.5	3.3	3.3	3.6	3.6	3.6
Trained Royal Air Force	ZBTZ	51.2	50.1	49.2	48.9	49.1	49.2	46.9	43.6	40.6	39.7	40.1
UK regulars[2]	ZBUA	51.0	49.8	48.9	48.5	48.7	48.8	46.6	43.2	40.3	39.3	40.1
Full-time reserve service[3]	ZBUB	0.2	0.3	0.3	0.4	0.4	0.4	0.3	0.3	0.4	0.4	–
Untrained UK regulars	ZBUC	21.6	21.5	23.0	24.2	22.5	18.3	17.5	17.5	18.4	20.1	18.4
Naval Service	ZBUD	4.3	4.4	4.9	5.0	4.5	4.4	4.5	4.5	4.0	3.9	3.6
Army	ZBUE	13.6	13.2	14.0	14.5	13.3	10.8	10.9	10.8	11.3	11.9	10.9
Royal Air Force	ZBUF	3.7	3.9	4.1	4.7	4.7	3.0	2.1	2.2	3.1	4.3	3.9
Locally Entered Personnel (excluding Gurkhas)	ZBUG	0.4	0.3	0.4	0.4	0.4	0.4	0.4	0.4	0.4	0.4	0.4
Royal Irish Regiment[4] **Home Service batallions**	ZBUH	4.2	3.8	3.6	3.5	3.4	3.2	3.1	2.1	–	–	–
Reserve personnel	ZBUI	294.8	284.2	273.4	259.7	246.7	235.6	..	..	..	..	..
Regular Reserves	ZBUJ	241.6	234.9	224.9	212.6	201.4	191.5	..	..	..	..	..
Naval Services	ZBUK	24.2	23.5	23.5	23.2	22.8	22.2	..	..	19.6	..	..
Army[5]	ZBUL	175.5	169.8	161.1	151.5	141.9	134.2	127.6	121.8	..	..	..
of which mobilised:	SNEO	0.3	0.2	0.3	0.4	0.1	0.2	0.3	0.1	–	..	..
Royal Air Force	ZBUM	41.9	41.5	40.2	37.7	36.4	35.0	34.4	33.4	..	..	..
of which mobilised:	SNEP	–	–	–	–	–	–	–	–	–	–	–
Volunteer Reserves	ZBUN	53.2	47.3	46.3	44.9	43.4	42.3	..	42.7	39.2	41.5	37.6
Royal Naval Reserve and Royal Marine Reserve	ZBUO	4.8	4.8	5.0	4.9	4.5	4.4	..	3.0	2.9	3.0	2.9
of which mobilised:	SNEQ	..	..	..	0.4	0.1	..	..	0.1	0.2	0.2	0.2
Territorial Army[2]	ZBUP	45.6	41.7	40.7	39.3	38.1	37.3	38.5	36.8	35.0	35.3	33.1
of which mobilised:	SNER	0.8	0.4	0.5	4.1	2.9	1.5	1.1	1.0	1.4	1.4	1.4
Royal Auxilliary Air Force	ZBUQ	2.7	1.6	1.5	1.5	1.4	1.4	1.4	1.3	1.3	1.4	1.5
of which mobilised:	SNES	–	–	0.1	0.8	–	..	0.1	0.2	0.1	0.2	0.1
Cadet Forces	ZBUR	154.5	151.0	152.3	155.6	155.6	153.1	..	150.5	150.4	153.8	157.3
Naval Service	ZBUS	24.1	23.8	23.8	23.2	22.6	21.9	..	18.2	18.6	19.0	17.9
Army[5]	ZBUT	77.4	75.4	75.8	78.7	80.5	80.9	81.7	81.9	82.7	84.9	86.4
Royal Air Force	ZBUU	53.0	51.8	52.7	53.7	52.5	50.3	51.0	50.4	49.5	50.1	53.0

1 Full time trained strength and trained requirement comprises trained UK Regular Forces, trained Gurkhas and Full Time Reserve Service Personnel (FTRS).

2 UK Regular Forces does not include Gurkhas, Full Time Reserve Service (FTRS) personnel and mobilised reservists.

3 From 1 July 2009 some elements of the FTRS are excluded. FTRS figures prior to 1 July 2009 include all Full Commitment, Limited Commitment and Home Commitment personnel.

4 The Royal Irish Regiment disbanded on 31 March 2008.

5 2008 Army Reserves data are as at 1 June.

Due to ongoing validation of the Joint Personnel Administration system, data are currently provisional and subject to review.

Source: Ministry of Defence/DASA (Quad-Service): 0207 8078896

14.6 United Kingdom defence: Civilian Manpower strengths[1]

As at 1 April

Thousands: Full-time Equivalent

		2000	2001	2002	2003	2004	2005	2006	2007	2008	2009	2010
Ministry of Defence civilians												
MOD Head Office, HQ and centrally managed expenditure[2,3]												
Non-industrial	KDQE	19.7	19.1	20.0	21.2	22.7	24.0	24.6	19.8	19.6	19.3	19.2
Industrial	KDQF	0.9	0.9	0.8	0.7	0.6	0.7	0.8	0.8	0.7	0.7	0.7
Defence Logistics Organisation[3]												
Non-industrial	ZBTJ	19.7	17.8	17.3	16.4	16.5	16.5	14.1	..	..	..	..
Industrial	ZBTK	11.5	8.4	6.3	4.4	4.3	4.1	3.9	..	..	..	..
Defence Equipment & Support[3]												
Non-industrial	I6P5	..	..	..	..	..	..	..	17.3	15.2	14.3	13.8
Industrial	I6P6	..	..	..	..	..	..	..	3.6	2.8	2.4	2.3
Naval Service												
Non-industrial	KYCW	3.0	3.0	2.9	2.7	2.9	2.6	2.3	2.3	1.8	1.8	1.9
Industrial	KYCX	1.0	0.9	0.8	0.8	0.8	0.7	0.6	0.6	0.5	0.5	0.6
Royal Fleet Auxiliary	EQS9	2.4	2.4	2.4	2.5	2.3	2.3	2.3	2.4	2.3	2.3	2.3
Army												
Non-industrial	KDQK	16.3	16.4	16.0	16.0	14.7	14.5	13.4	12.7	12.2	11.9	11.9
Industrial	KDQL	5.8	5.7	5.5	5.4	5.6	5.5	5.2	5.3	5.0	4.6	4.6
Royal Air Force												
Non-industrial	KDQM	7.1	7.0	7.1	7.0	7.3	7.0	6.7	6.0	5.7	5.7	5.8
Industrial	KDQN	4.5	4.4	4.3	4.4	4.4	4.0	4.0	3.0	3.0	2.8	2.8
Level 1 Total	C7PE	91.9	86.0	83.6	81.5	82.2	82.0	78.1	73.8	69.1	66.4	65.9
Non-industrial	C7PF	65.8	63.4	63.4	63.3	64.1	64.7	61.3	58.1	54.7	53.0	52.6
Industrial	C7PG	23.7	20.2	17.8	15.7	15.7	15.0	14.5	13.3	12.1	11.1	11.0
Royal Fleet Auxiliary	EQT2	2.4	2.4	2.4	2.5	2.3	2.3	2.3	2.4	2.3	2.3	2.3
Locally engaged overseas	KDQA	14.8	13.3	14.1	13.8	15.4	15.7	15.1	14.2	11.2	10.5	10.2
Non-industrial	KDQT	6.7	6.3	6.5	6.5	7.3	..	..	..	..	..	..
Industrial	KDQU	8.2	7.0	7.6	7.4	8.1	..	..	..	..	..	..
Trading funds	GQHI	14.5	18.8	12.4	12.2	11.4	10.8	10.7	10.1	9.2	9.6	9.7
Level 0 Total	C7PH	121.3	118.2	110.1	107.6	109.0	108.5	103.9	98.0	89.5	86.6	85.8

1 See chapter text. Industrials on temporary and geographic (T&G) promotion are classed as non-industrial. From 2004, personnel who cannot be correctly allocated to Top Level Budgets (TLBs) are included with the MOD Head Office, HQ and centrally managed.
2 The MOD Head Office, HQ and centrally managed expenditure budgetary area was formerly referred to as Centre.

3 At 1 April 2007, the Defence Logistics Organisation and the Defence Procurement Agency (formerly part of the MOD Head Office, HQ and centrally managed expenditure budgetary area) merged to form Defence Equipment & Support.

Source: Ministry of Defence/DASA (Quad Service): 0207 8078896

14.7 Family accommodation and defence land holdings

As at 1 April

Thousand hectares

		2000	2001	2002	2003	2004	2005	2006	2007	2008	2009[1]	2010[1]
Family accommodation (thousands)												
United Kingdom: Total	KDPA	64.8	59.2	55.8	53.8	52.8	51.9	51.8	51.1	51.2	49.9	49.1
Land holdings												
United Kingdom												
Land	KDPF	219.9	224.3	222.5	221.4	221.3	222.1	222.0	222.0	221.7	221.0	220.0
Foreshore	KDPH	18.6	18.6	18.6	18.6	18.6	18.6	18.6	18.6	18.6	18.0	18.0
Rights held[2]	KDPJ	124.8	124.8	124.9	131.1	131.1	124.9	124.9	124.9	133.1	133.0	133.0

1 Data for 2009 onwards have been rounded to the nearest thousand hectares, whereas data for previous years are rounded to the nearest hundred hectares.
2 'Rights held' are Land and Foreshore that are not owned by, or leased to MOD, but over which the Department has limited rights under grants and rights.

Sources: Ministry of Defence/Defence Estates Directorate of Operations;
Housing: 01480 52151
Ministry of Defence/Defence Estates: 0121 311 2140

14.8 Location of United Kingdom service personnel[1]

As at 1 April

Thousands

		2000	2001	2002	2003	2004	2005	2006	2007	2008	2009	2010
UK Service personnel, Regular Forces:												
UK distribution[2,3]												
In United Kingdom[4]	KDOB	170.3	172.0	..	..	..	169.7	167.3	161.4	158.7	162.7	166.1
England	KDOC	143.0	144.1	..	..	..	145.0	142.1	141.4	140.3	143.6	146.9
Wales	KDOD	3.2	2.6	..	..	..	2.9	3.3	2.6	2.6	2.7	2.9
Scotland	KDOE	15.1	14.5	..	..	..	13.2	13.5	12.6	12.0	12.0	12.1
Northern Ireland	KDOF	8.4	9.4	..	..	..	7.0	6.8	4.8	3.7	4.4	4.1
Global location[2,3]												
United Kingdom	MKCN	163.1	162.8	..	..	..	169.7	167.3	161.4	158.7	162.7	166.1
Overseas	KDOG	43.0	40.9	..	..	..	29.2	28.5	28.0	27.6	25.4	25.2
Mainland European States[4,5]	KDOI	8.2	8.6				27.0	26.6	26.2	26.0	23.4	23.3
Germany[6]	KDOH	19.5	17.3	..	..	..	22.2	22.0	21.7	21.7	19.1	19.1
Balkans	MKCO	..	..	..	..	..	0.1	–	0.1	–	–	–
Mediterranean[7,8]	KDOM	1.1	2.3				..	..	..	..	..	..
Gibraltar	KDOJ	0.6	0.5	..	..	..	0.4	0.3	0.3	0.3	0.3	0.3
Cyprus	KDOL	3.5	3.5	..	..	..	3.2	3.0	3.0	2.8	2.9	2.9
Far East/Asia[9]	MKCT	1.0	0.3	..	..	..	0.3	0.3	0.2	0.3	0.3	0.3
Africa[10]	MKCP	..	–	..	..	..	0.6	0.6	0.5	0.5	0.5	0.5
North America	MKCQ	..	2.5	..	..	..	0.7	0.7	0.7	0.7	0.8	0.8
Central/South America	MKCR	..	–	..	..	..	0.1	0.1	0.1	0.1	0.1	0.1
Falkland Islands	MKCS	..	0.8	..	..	..	0.3	0.3	0.3	0.1	0.3	0.2
Other locations, including unallocated	KDOQ	9.1	5.1	..	..	..	1.1	1.0	1.1	1.2	0.3	0.4
Locally entered service personnel:[11]												
United Kingdom	KDOS	2.1	2.3	2.6	2.6	2.6	2.5	2.6	2.8	3.0	3.2	3.0
Gibraltar	KDOT	0.3	0.4	0.4	0.4	0.4	0.4	0.4	0.4	0.4	0.4	0.4
Hong Kong	KDOV	–	–	–	–	–	–	–	–	–	–	–
Brunei	KDOW	0.8	0.8	0.8	0.8	0.7	0.8	0.8	0.8	0.8	0.7	0.7
India/Nepal	KDOX	0.5	0.4	0.3	0.4	0.4	0.3	0.3	0.1	–	–	–
Germany		..	..	..	..	..	..	..	..	..	..	0.1
Total	KDOK	3.7	3.9	4.2	4.1	4.1	4.1	4.0	4.1	4.1	4.3	4.2

1 See chapter text.
2 Prior to 2003, figures for UK distribution and global location are collated from seperate sources. Comparison is therefore not possible between the two sets of UK personnel figures.
3 Includes personnel within the UK whose location is unknown.
4 Includes the Balkans until 2002.
5 Post 2002 Mainland European States figure includes Germany, Balkans, Mediterranean, Gibraltar and Cyprus.
6 Prior to 1996, figures for the Federal Republic of Germany and Mainland European States were combined.

7 Includes Med Near East and Middle East until 2002.
8. Post 2002 Mediterranean figure is not shown separately but is included in Mainland European States figure.
9 Prior to 1997 figures include personnel serving in Hong Kong.
10 Post 2002 Africa figure includes Middle East.
11 Including trained Gurkhas.
Personnel deployed on operations and temporary assignments are shown against their permanent stationed location. As such figures for locations such as North Africa / Middle East & South Atlantic exclude large numbers of personnel deployed in those locations.

Source: Ministry of Defence/DASA (Quad-Service): 0207 8078772

14.9 United Kingdom regular forces: deaths[1]

Numbers and rates per thousand

		2000[2]	2001[3]	2002	2003	2004	2005	2006	2007	2008	2009
Deaths											
Total	SNIA	147	142	147	177	170	160	191	204	137	205
Male	SNIB	143	139	138	170	164	152	184	195	129	202
Female	SNIC	4	3	9	7	6	8	7	9	8	3
Rates per 100,000 strength[1]											
All	SNIH	72	71	75	84	82	81	98	106	73	107
Navy	SNII	63	79	73	90	93	71	86	72	109	56
Army	SNIJ	80	73	86	84	76	87	95	129	73	134
RAF	SNIK	64	52	52	72	65	72	88	71	36	53

1 Rates have been age and gender standardised to the 2010 Armed Forces population.
2 Rates for 2000 have been age and gender standardised to the 2009 Armed Forces population.
3 Rates for 2001 and onwards have been age and gender standardised to the 2010 Armed Forces population.

Source: Ministry of Defence/DASA (Health Information): 01225 467538

14.10 Strength of uniformed United Kingdom medical staff[1]

As at 1 April

Numbers

		2000	2001	2002	2003	2004	2005	2006	2007[6]	2008[7]	2009	2010
Qualified doctors:[2]												
Naval Service	KDMA	210	220	220	230	240	260	260	290	280	360	300
Army[3]	KDMB	460	470	490	550	600	610	650	550	600	490	490
Royal Air Force	KDMC	180	180	180	190	200	220	230	220	230	180	230
All Services	KDMD	860	870	890	970	1,040	1,090	1,140	1,060	1,110	1,040	1,020
Qualified dentists:[2]												
Naval Service	KDME	60	60	60	60	60	60	60	50	60	50	50
Army[3]	KDMF	140	150	140	150	150	150	140	130	130	110	110
Royal Air Force	KDMG	80	80	70	70	80	70	70	60	60	50	60
All Services	KDMH	280	290	280	270	290	280	270	240	250	220	210
Support staff:[4]												
Naval Service[5]	KDMI	1,000	1,030	1,010	1,060	1,110	1,110	1,120	1,130	1,280	1,150	1,110
Nursing services[5]	ZBTL	210	210	220	250	280	290	300	300	300	310	270
Support[5]	ZBTM	790	820	790	810	840	820	820	830	980	840	840
Army[3]	KDMJ	3,210	3,260	3,320	3,410	3,560	..	..	3,000	4,070	3,490	3,350
Nursing services[3,4,5]	ZBTN	570	610	650	710	770	770	800	790	960	950	800
Support[3]	ZBTO	2,640	2,650	2,670	2,700	2,800	..	..	2,210	3,110	2,540	2,540
Royal Air Force	KDMK	1,460	1,480	1,500	1,600	1,680	1,660	1,550	1,340	1,380	1,250	1,350
Nursing services[5]	ZBTP	400	420	450	470	480	510	480	490	440	460	520
Support	ZBTQ	1,060	1,070	1,050	1,130	1,200	1,160	1,070	850	940	790	820
All Services	KDML	5,760	5,800	5,930	6,180	6,440	..	..	..	..	..	..

1 Includes staff employed at units (including ships) and in hospitals.

2 The Medical and Dental Officers exclude Late Entry personnel. From 2007-10 'Qualified' Doctors refers to personnel who hold a basic registrable qualification but may not necessarily have completed their career directed professional training, and as such may not necessarily be fully trained in their speciality. From 2009-10, Dental Officers refers only to fully qualified Dentists.

3 Due to a change in source data, Army figures prior to 2005 cannot be verified.

4 'Support staff' from 2007 includes all medical support staff collated by the Defence Medical Services Dept (from 2009 onwards, HQ Surgeon General) in their tri-service manning return; trained and in-training. 2010 figures for Army Healthcare Assistants were not provided and so are not included in the 'Support' total shown. From 1999, 'Support Staff' figures are split so that nurses are separate from other support staff.

5 From 2007, includes trained and untrained.

6 Figures from 2007-2008 provided by Defence Medical Services Department. Figures from 2009-10 provided by HQ Surgeon General.

7 2008-10 support figures include all support staff both trained and untrained.

Source:DASA:0207 2181429/HQ Surgeon General, Pers Div, Manning (from 2009)

14.11 United Kingdom defence services and the civilian community[1]

Numbers

		2000	2001	2002	2003	2004	2005	2006	2007	2008	2009	2010
Military Search and rescue operations at home												
Call outs: total	**GPYC**	1,941	1,763	1,684	1,714	1,638	1,702	1,875	1,973	2,083	2,337	1,983
Royal Navy helicopters	**GPXO**	499	502	436	424	453	478	497	592	586	758	639
Royal Air Force helicopters	**GPXP**	1,278	1,115	1,122	1,173	1,079	1,114	1,258	1,258	1,377	1,479	1,282
Contractorised and other helicopters	**GPXQ**	–	–	–	–	–	–	1	–	–	–	–
Royal Air Force Nimrod aircraft[2]	**GPXR**	71	54	46	37	37	37	32	21	29	13	3
Other fixed wing aircraft[3]	**GPXS**	1	1	1	–	2	–	1	–	–	1	–
HM ships and auxilliary vessels[3]	**KCMG**	–	–	–	–	–	–	–	–	–	–	–
Royal Air Force mountain rescue teams	**KCMH**	92	91	79	80	67	73	86	102	91	86	59
Persons moved: total	**KCMI**	1,316	1,182	1,224	1,273	1,412	1,384	1,463	1,767	1,607	1,810	1,605
Persons moved by rescue service												
Royal Navy helicopters	**GPXT**	360	386	314	320	416	380	479	507	516	656	539
Royal Air Force helicopters	**GPXU**	934	781	900	922	978	907	968	1,219	1,062	1,135	1,047
Royal Air Force mountain rescue teams	**GPXV**	22	15	10	31	17	97	16	41	29	19	19
Other	**GPXW**	–	–	–	–	1	–	–	–	–	–	–
Persons moved by type of assistance												
Rescue[4]	**GPXX**	276	281	343	280	494	408	384	582	450	445	379
Medrescue[5]	**GPXY**	713	629	654	779	672	778	830	946	869	1,064	964
Medtransfer[5]	**GPXZ**	241	228	201	174	195	143	175	198	219	224	219
Recovery[7]	**GPYA**	29	36	21	25	33	31	43	24	40	44	21
Transfer[8]	**GPYB**	57	8	5	15	18	24	31	17	29	33	22
Search and rescue incidents: total	**KCMM**	1,781	1,608	1,544	1,600	1,504	1,584	1,703	1,803	1,941	2,191	1,901

Source: Ministry of Defence/DASA (Price Indices): 030 679 34524

		1999 /00	2000 /01	2001 /02	2002 /03	2003 /04	2004 /05	2005 /06	2006 /07	2007 /08	2008 /09	2009 /10
Fishery protection												
Vessels boarded	**KCMO**	1,716	1,603	1,464	1,375	1,709	1,747	1,371	1,335	1,309	1,102	1,201

Source: Fisheries Protection - Ministry of Defence

1 See chapter text.
2 Withdrawn from service in March 2010.
3 Not permanently on stand-by
4 Rescue: Moving an uninjured person from a hostile to a benign environment.
5 Medrescue: Moving an injured casualty from a hostile environment to a medical facility.
6 Medtransfer (formerly Medevac): Moving a sick person between medical facilities such as a hospital or occasionally to move transplant organs.
7 Recovery: Moving people declared dead on scene or confirmed dead on arrival by a qualified doctor.
8 Transfer (formerly Airlift): Moving military personnel, or their families, on compassionate grounds.

Population and vital statistics

Chapter 15

Population and Vital Statistics

This section begins with a summary of population figures for the United Kingdom and constituent countries for 1851 to 2031 and for Great Britain from 1801 (Table 15.1). Table 15.2 analyses the components of population change. Table 15.3 gives details of the national sex and age structures for years up to the present date, with projected figures up to the year 2026. Legal marital condition of the population is shown in Table 15.4. The distribution of population at regional and local levels is summarised in Table 15.5.

In the main, historical series relate to census information, while mid-year estimates, which make allowance for under-enumeration in the census, are given for the recent past and the present (from 1961 onwards).

Population
(Tables 15.1 - 15.3)

Figures shown in these tables relate to the population enumerated at successive censuses, (up to 1951), mid-year estimates (from 1961 to 2008) and population projections (up to 2031). Further information can be found on the National Statistics website www.ons.gov.uk.

Population projections are 2008-based and were published by the Office for National Statistics on 21st October 2009. Further information can be found at www.ons.gov.uk

Definition of resident population

The estimated resident population of an area includes all people who usually live there, whatever their nationality. Members of HM and US Armed Forces in England and Wales are included on a residential basis wherever possible. HM Forces stationed outside England and Wales are not included. Students are taken to be resident at their term time address.

The projections of the resident population of the United Kingdom and constituent countries were prepared by the National Statistics Centre for Demography within ONS, in consultation with the Registrars General, as a common framework for use in national planning in a number of different fields. New projections are made every second year on assumptions regarding future fertility, mortality and migration which seem most appropriate on the basis of the statistical evidence available at the time. The population projections in Tables 15.1 -15.3 are based on the estimates of the population of the United Kingdom at mid-2008 made by the Registrars General.

Marital condition (de jure): estimated population
(Table 15.4)

This table shows population estimates by marital status

Geographical distribution of the population
(Table 15.5)

The population enumerated in the censuses for 1911-1951, and the mid-year population estimates for later years, are provided for standard regions of the United Kingdom, for metropolitan areas, for broad groupings of local authority districts by type within England and Wales, and for some of the larger cities. Projections of future sub-national population levels are prepared from time to time by the Registrar General, but are not shown in this publication.

Migration into and out of the United Kingdom
(Tables 15.7 - 15.8)

A long-term international migrant is defined as a person who changes his or her country of usual residence for a period of at least a year,so that the country of destination effectively becomes the country of usual residence.

The main source of long-term international migration data is the International Passenger Survey (IPS). This is a continuous voluntary sample survey that provides information on passengers entering and leaving the UK by the principal air, sea and tunnel routes. Being a sample survey, the IPS is subject to some uncertainty; therefore it should be noted that long-term international migration estimates, in particular the difference between inflow and outflow, may be subject to large sampling errors. The IPS excludes routes between the Channel Islands and Isle of Man and the rest of the world.

The IPS data are supplemented with four types of additional information in order to provide a full picture of total long-term international migration, known as Long-Term International Migration or LTIM:

1. The IPS is based on intentions to migrate and intentions are liable to change. Adjustments are made for visitor switchers (those who intend to stay in the UK or abroad for less than one year but subsequently stay for longer and become migrants) and for migrant switchers (those who intend to stay in the UK or abroad for one year or more but then return earlier so are no longer migrants). These adjustments are primarily based on IPS data but for years prior to 2001, Home Office data on short-term visitors who were subsequently granted an extension of stay for a year or longer for other reasons have been incorporated.

2. Home Office data on applications for asylum and dependants of asylum seekers entering the UK are used to estimate inflows of asylum seekers and dependants not already captured by the I PS. In addition, Home Office data on removals and refusals are used to estimate outflows of failed asylum seekers not identified by the IPS.

3. Migration flows between the UK and the Irish Republic were added to the data to 2007 as the IPS did not cover this route until recently. These flows were obtained mainly from the Quarterly National Household Survey and were agreed between the Irish Central Statistics Office and ONS. From 2008 onwards, estimates of migration between the UK and Irish Republic come from the IPS.

4. Migration flows to and from Northern Ireland are added to the IPS data for Great Britain from 2008 onwards. These flows are obtained from the Irish Quarterly National Household Survey (from CSO Ireland) and health card registration data (from Northern Ireland Statistics Research Agency (NISRA)). These data are now deemed a better source for Northern Irish flows than IPS data. Prior to 2008, estimates of migration to and from Northern Ireland came from the IPS.

Grants for settlement in the United Kingdom
(Table 15.9)

This table presents in geographic regions, the statistics of individual countries of nationality, arranged alphabetically within each region. The figures are on a different basis from those derived from IPS (Tables 15.9 and 15.10) and relate only to people subject to immigration control. Persons granted settlement are allowed to stay indefinitely in the United Kingdom. They exclude temporary migrants such as students and generally relate only to non-EEA nationals. Settlement can occur several years after entry to the country.

Applications received for asylum in the United Kingdom, excluding dependants
(Table 15.10)

This table shows statistics of applications for asylum in the United Kingdom. Figures are shown for the main applicant nationalities by geographic region. The basis of assessing asylum applications, and hence of deciding whether to grant asylum in the United Kingdom, is the 1951 United Nations Convention on Refugees.

Marriages
(Table 15.11)
The figures in this table relate to marriages solemnised in England and Wales. They take no account of the growing trend towards marrying abroad.

Births
(Tables 15.14 –15.16)

For Scotland and Northern Ireland the number of births relate to those registered during the year. For England and Wales the figures up to and including 1930-32 are for those registered, while later figures relate to births occurring in each year.

All data for England and Wales and for Scotland include births occurring in those countries to mothers not usually resident in them. Data for Northern Ireland, and hence UK, prior to 1981 include births occurring in Northern Ireland to non-resident mothers; from 1981, such births are excluded.

Deaths
(Tables 15.18)

The figures relate to the number of deaths registered during each calendar year.

Infant and maternal mortality
(Table 15.19)

On 1 October 1992 the legal definition of a stillbirth was altered from a baby born dead after 28 completed weeks gestation or more, to one born after 24 completed weeks of gestation or more. The 258 stillbirths of 24 to 27 weeks gestation that which occurred between 1 October and 31 December 1992 are excluded from this table.

Life tables
(Table 15.21)

The current set of interim life tables are constructed from the estimated populations in 2007-2009 and corresponding data on births, infant deaths and deaths by individual age registered in those years.

Adoptions
(Table 15.22)

The figures shown within these tables relate to the date the adoption was entered in the Adopted Children Register. Figures based on the date of court order are available for England and Wales in the volume Marriage, divorce and adoption statistics 2007 (no. 35 in the FM2 series) available on the National Statistics website www.statistics.gov.uk or from the enquiry point in the ONS shown at the foot of the tables.

15.1 Population summary: by country and sex

Thousands

	United Kingdom			England and Wales			Wales	Scotland			Northern Ireland		
	Persons	Males	Females	Persons	Males	Females	Persons	Persons	Males	Females	Persons	Males	Females
Enumerated population: census figures													
1801	..	..	..	8,893	4,255	4,638	587	1,608	739	869	..	..	..
1851	22,259	10,855	11,404	17,928	8,781	9,146	1,163	2,889	1,376	1,513	1,442	698	745
1901	38,237	18,492	19,745	32,528	15,729	16,799	2,013	4,472	2,174	2,298	1,237	590	647
1911	42,082	20,357	21,725	36,070	17,446	18,625	2,421	4,761	2,309	2,452	1,251	603	648
1921 [1]	44,027	21,033	22,994	37,887	18,075	19,811	2,656	4,882	2,348	2,535	1,258	610	648
1931 [1]	46,038	22,060	23,978	39,952	19,133	20,819	2,593	4,843	2,326	2,517	1,243	601	642
1951	50,225	24,118	26,107	43,758	21,016	22,742	2,599	5,096	2,434	2,662	1,371	668	703
1961	52,709	25,481	27,228	46,105	22,304	23,801	2,644	5,179	2,483	2,697	1,425	694	731
Resident population: mid-year estimates													
	DYAY	BBAB	BBAC	BBAD	BBAE	BBAF	KGJM	BBAG	BBAH	BBAI	BBAJ	BBAK	BBAL
1973	56,223	27,332	28,891	49,459	24,061	25,399	2,773	5,234	2,515	2,719	1,530	756	774
1974	56,236	27,349	28,887	49,468	24,075	25,393	2,785	5,241	2,519	2,722	1,527	755	772
1975	56,226	27,361	28,865	49,470	24,091	25,378	2,795	5,232	2,516	2,716	1,524	753	770
1976	56,216	27,360	28,856	49,459	24,089	25,370	2,799	5,233	2,517	2,716	1,524	754	769
1977	56,190	27,345	28,845	49,440	24,076	25,364	2,801	5,226	2,515	2,711	1,523	754	769
1978	56,178	27,330	28,848	49,443	24,067	25,375	2,804	5,212	2,509	2,704	1,523	754	770
1979	56,240	27,373	28,867	49,508	24,113	25,395	2,810	5,204	2,505	2,699	1,528	755	773
1980	56,330	27,411	28,919	49,603	24,156	25,448	2,816	5,194	2,501	2,693	1,533	755	778
1981	56,357	27,412	28,946	49,634	24,160	25,474	2,813	5,180	2,495	2,685	1,543	757	786
1982	56,291	27,364	28,927	49,582	24,119	25,462	2,804	5,165	2,487	2,677	1,545	757	788
1983	56,316	27,371	28,944	49,617	24,133	25,484	2,803	5,148	2,479	2,669	1,551	759	792
1984	56,409	27,421	28,989	49,713	24,185	25,528	2,801	5,139	2,475	2,664	1,557	761	796
1985	56,554	27,489	29,065	49,861	24,254	25,606	2,803	5,128	2,470	2,658	1,565	765	800
1986	56,684	27,542	29,142	49,999	24,311	25,687	2,811	5,112	2,462	2,649	1,574	768	805
1987	56,804	27,599	29,205	50,123	24,371	25,752	2,823	5,099	2,455	2,644	1,582	773	809
1988	56,916	27,652	29,265	50,254	24,434	25,820	2,841	5,077	2,444	2,633	1,585	774	812
1989	57,076	27,729	29,348	50,408	24,510	25,898	2,855	5,078	2,443	2,635	1,590	776	814
1990	57,237	27,819	29,419	50,561	24,597	25,964	2,862	5,081	2,444	2,637	1,596	778	818
1991	57,439	27,909	29,530	50,748	24,681	26,067	2,873	5,083	2,445	2,639	1,607	783	824
1992	57,585	27,977	29,608	50,876	24,739	26,136	2,878	5,086	2,445	2,640	1,623	792	831
1993	57,714	28,039	29,675	50,986	24,793	26,193	2,884	5,092	2,448	2,644	1,636	798	837
1994	57,862	28,108	29,754	51,116	24,853	26,263	2,887	5,102	2,453	2,649	1,644	802	842
1995	58,025	28,204	29,821	51,272	24,946	26,326	2,889	5,104	2,453	2,650	1,649	804	845
1996	58,164	28,287	29,877	51,410	25,030	26,381	2,891	5,092	2,447	2,645	1,662	810	851
1997	58,314	28,371	29,943	51,560	25,113	26,446	2,895	5,083	2,442	2,641	1,671	816	856
1998	58,475	28,458	30,017	51,720	25,201	26,519	2,900	5,077	2,439	2,638	1,678	819	859
1999	58,684	28,578	30,106	51,933	25,323	26,610	2,901	5,072	2,437	2,635	1,679	818	861
2000	58,886	28,690	30,196	52,140	25,438	26,702	2,907	5,063	2,432	2,631	1,683	820	862
2001	59,113	28,832	30,281	52,360	25,574	26,786	2,910	5,064	2,434	2,630	1,689	824	865
2002	59,319	28,961	30,358	52,567	25,700	26,867	2,918	5,055	2,432	2,623	1,697	829	868
2003	59,552	29,104	30,448	52,792	25,837	26,955	2,929	5,057	2,435	2,623	1,703	833	870
2004	59,842	29,274	30,568	53,053	25,991	27,062	2,943	5,078	2,446	2,632	1,710	836	874
2005	60,235	29,493	30,742	53,416	26,193	27,224	2,950	5,095	2,456	2,639	1,724	844	880
2006	60,584	29,689	30,895	53,726	26,366	27,359	2,962	5,117	2,469	2,647	1,742	853	888
2007	60,986	29,918	31,068	54,082	26,570	27,512	2,976	5,144	2,486	2,659	1,759	862	897
2008	61,398	30,154	31,244	54,455	26,783	27,672	2,990	5,169	2,500	2,668	1,775	871	904
2009	61,792	30,374	31,418	54,809	26,980	27,829	2,999	5,194	2,515	2,679	1,789	879	910
2010	62,262	30,643	31,619	55,240	27,229	28,012	3,006	5,222	2,530	2,692	1,799	884	915
Resident population: projections (mid-year)[2]													
	C59J	C59K	C59L	C59M	C59N	C59O	C59P	C59Q	C59R	C59S	C59T	C59U	C59V
2011	62,649	30,842	31,807	55,601	27,412	28,189	3,024	5,233	2,537	2,695	1,815	892	923
2016	64,773	31,986	32,787	57,576	28,474	29,102	3,104	5,324	2,589	2,736	1,874	924	950
2021	66,958	33,134	33,824	59,620	29,547	30,073	3,187	5,411	2,635	2,776	1,927	952	975
2026	69,051	34,210	34,841	61,597	30,563	31,035	3,263	5,483	2,672	2,811	1,971	975	996
2031	70,933	35,162	35,772	63,397	31,473	31,924	3,326	5,532	2,696	2,835	2,005	992	1,012

1 Figures for Northern Ireland are estimated. The population at the Census of 1926 was
1,257 thousand (608 thousand males and 648 thousand females).
2 These projections are 2008-based. See chapter text for more detail.

Sources: Office for National Statistics: 01329 444661;
National Records of Scotland
Northern Ireland Statistics and Research Agency;

15.2 Population changes: by country

Thousands

	Population[1] at start of period	Average annual change				
		Overall annual change	Births	Deaths[2]	Natural change	Net migration and other changes
United Kingdom						
1901 - 1911	38,237	385	1,091	624	467	-82
1911 - 1921	42,082	195	975	689	286	-92
1921 - 1931	44,027	201	824	555	268	-67
1931 - 1951	46,038	213	793	603	190	22
1951 - 1961	50,225	258	839	593	246	12
1961 - 1971	52,807	312	962	638	324	-12
1971 - 1981	55,928	42	736	666	69	-27
1981 - 1991	56,357	108	757	655	103	5
1991 - 2001	57,439	161	731	631	100	61
2001 - 2007	59,113	312	710	591	119	193
2001 - 2008	59,113	326	722	588	134	193
2001 - 2009	59,113	335	730	586	144	191
2001 - 2010	59,113	350	737	582	155	195
2011 - 2021[3]	62,649	431	791	544	248	183
England and Wales						
1901 - 1911	32,528	354	929	525	404	-50
1911 - 1921	36,070	182	828	584	244	-62
1921 - 1931	37,887	207	693	469	224	-17
1931 - 1951	39,952	193	673	518	155	38
1951 - 1961	43,758	244	714	516	197	47
1961 - 1971	46,196	296	832	560	272	23
1971 - 1981	49,152	48	638	585	53	-5
1981 - 1991	49,634	111	664	576	89	23
1991 - 2001	50,748	155	647	556	92	63
2001 - 2007	52,360	287	634	520	114	173
2001 - 2008	52,360	299	644	517	127	172
2001 - 2009	52,360	306	652	515	137	169
2001 - 2010	52,360	320	658	512	147	173
2011 - 2021[3]	55,601	402	709	477	232	170
Scotland						
1901 - 1911	4,472	29	131	76	54	-25
1911 - 1921	4,761	12	118	82	36	-24
1921 - 1931	4,882	-4	100	65	35	-39
1931 - 1951	4,843	13	92	67	25	-12
1951 - 1961	5,096	9	95	62	34	-25
1961 - 1971	5,184	5	97	63	34	-30
1971 - 1981	5,236	-6	70	64	6	-11
1981 - 1991	5,180	-7	66	63	3	-10
1991 - 2001	5,083	-2	60	60	-1	-1
2001 - 2007	5,064	13	54	57	-3	16
2001 - 2008	5,064	15	55	57	-2	17
2011 - 2021[3]	5,233	18	58	52	5	12

15.2 Population changes: by country

Thousands

| | Population[1] at start of period | Overall annual change | Average annual change | | | |
			Births	Deaths[2]	Natural change	Net migration and other changes
Northern Ireland						
1901 - 1911	1,237	1	31	23	8	-6
1911 - 1921	1,251	1	29	22	7	-6
1921 - 1931	1,258	-2	28	19	9	-11
1931 - 1951	1,243	6	28	18	10	-4
1951 - 1961	1,371	6	30	15	15	-9
1961 - 1971	1,427	11	33	16	17	-6
1971 - 1981	1,540	-	28	17	11	-11
1981 - 1991	1,543	6	27	16	11	-5
1991 - 2001	1,607	8	24	15	9	-
2001 - 2007	1,689	12	22	14	8	4
2001 - 2008	1,689	12	23	14	8	4
2001-2009	1,689	12	23	15	8	4
2011 - 2021[3]	1,815	11	25	14	11	1

1 Census enumerated population up to 1951; mid-year estimates of resident population from 1961 to 2010 and mid-2008-based projections of resident population thereafter.
2 Including deaths of non-civilians and merchant seamen who died outside the country. These numbered 577,000 in 1911-1921 and 240,000 in 1931-1951 for England and Wales; 74,000 in 1911-1921 and 34,000 in 1931-1951 for Scotland; and 10,000 in 1911-1926 for Northern Ireland.
3 These projections are 2008-based. See chapter text for more detail

Sources:
Office for National Statistics: 01329 444661;
National Records of Scotland
Northern Ireland Statistics and Research Agency

15.3(a) Age distribution of the resident population: by sex and country

Thousands

		United Kingdom								
		Population enumerated in Census								
		1901	1931	1951	1981	1991 [2]	2001 [3]	2002	2003	2004
Persons: All ages	**KGUA**	38,237	46,038	50,225	56,357	57,439	59,113	59,319	59,552	59,842
Under 1	**KGUK**	938	712	773	730	790	663	661	680	705
1 - 4	**KABA**	3,443	2,818	3,553	2,726	3,077	2,819	2,752	2,704	2,685
5 - 9	**KGUN**	4,106	3,897	3,689	3,677	3,657	3,735	3,688	3,649	3,606
10 - 14	**KGUO**	3,934	3,746	3,310	4,470	3,485	3,890	3,914	3,895	3,866
15 - 19	**KGUP**	3,826	3,989	3,175	4,735	3,719	3,678	3,759	3,859	3,923
20 - 29	**KABB**	6,982	7,865	7,154	8,113	9,138	7,499	7,418	7,399	7,497
30 - 44	**KABC**	7,493	9,717	11,125	10,956	12,125	13,405	13,491	13,504	13,458
45 - 59	**KABD**	4,639	7,979	9,558	9,540	9,500	11,168	11,306	11,410	11,506
60 - 64	**KGUY**	1,067	1,897	2,422	2,935	2,888	2,884	2,892	2,949	3,027
65 - 74	**KBCP**	1,278	2,461	3,689	5,195	5,067	4,947	4,967	5,000	5,028
75 - 84	**KBCU**	470	844	1,555	2,677	3,119	3,296	3,344	3,399	3,431
85 and over	**KGVD**	61	113	224	603	873	1,130	1,127	1,104	1,111
School ages (5-15)	**KBWU**	..	..	7,649	9,086	7,818	8,381	8,370	8,333	8,252
Under 18	**KGUD**	..	..	13,248	14,472	13,120	13,357	13,309	13,257	13,216
Pensionable ages[5]	**KFIA**	2,387	4,421	6,828	10,035	10,557	10,845	10,915	11,012	11,118
Males: All ages	**KGWA**	18,492	22,060	24,118	27,412	27,909	28,832	28,961	29,104	29,274
Under 1	**KGWK**	471	361	397	374	403	338	338	349	362
1 - 4	**KBCV**	1,719	1,423	1,818	1,400	1,572	1,445	1,407	1,383	1,376
5 - 9	**KGWN**	2,052	1,967	1,885	1,889	1,871	1,913	1,890	1,869	1,846
10 - 14	**KGWO**	1,972	1,892	1,681	2,295	1,784	1,993	2,006	1,998	1,985
15 - 19	**KGWP**	1,898	1,987	1,564	2,424	1,905	1,879	1,936	1,990	2,019
20 - 29	**KBCW**	3,293	3,818	3,509	4,103	4,578	3,744	3,713	3,710	3,774
30 - 44	**KBCX**	3,597	4,495	5,461	5,513	6,045	6,645	6,685	6,693	6,666
45 - 59	**KBUU**	2,215	3,753	4,493	4,711	4,732	5,534	5,593	5,644	5,690
60 - 64	**KGWY**	490	894	1,061	1,376	1,390	1,412	1,414	1,440	1,479
65 - 74	**KBWL**	565	1,099	1,560	2,264	2,272	2,308	2,325	2,346	2,365
75 - 84	**KBWM**	196	335	617	922	1,146	1,308	1,338	1,369	1,392
85 and over	**KGXD**	23	36	70	141	212	312	315	312	321
School ages (5-15)	**KBWV**	..	..	3,895	4,666	4,001	4,294	4,290	4,272	4,231
Under 18	**KGWD**	..	..	6,753	7,430	6,711	6,845	6,822	6,798	6,778
Pensionable ages[4]	**KFIB**	785	1,471	2,247	3,327	3,630	3,928	3,978	4,028	4,078
Females: All ages	**KGYA**	19,745	23,978	26,107	28,946	29,530	30,281	30,358	30,448	30,568
Under 1[3]	**KGYK**	466	351	376	356	387	324	323	331	343
1 - 4	**KBWN**	1,724	1,397	1,735	1,327	1,505	1,375	1,345	1,321	1,309
5 - 9	**KGYN**	2,054	1,930	1,804	1,788	1,786	1,822	1,797	1,780	1,760
10 - 14	**KGYO**	1,962	1,854	1,629	2,175	1,701	1,897	1,908	1,897	1,881
15 - 19	**KGYP**	1,928	2,002	1,611	2,311	1,815	1,799	1,823	1,869	1,905
20 - 29	**KBWO**	3,690	4,047	3,644	4,009	4,560	3,755	3,705	3,689	3,723
30 - 44	**KBWP**	3,895	5,222	5,663	5,442	6,080	6,760	6,806	6,811	6,791
45 - 59	**KBWR**	2,424	4,226	5,065	4,829	4,769	5,634	5,713	5,766	5,816
60 - 64	**KGYY**	577	1,003	1,361	1,559	1,498	1,473	1,478	1,509	1,548
65 - 74	**KBWS**	713	1,361	2,127	2,931	2,795	2,640	2,642	2,654	2,663
75 - 84	**KBWT**	274	509	937	1,756	1,972	1,987	2,006	2,029	2,040
85 and over	**KGZD**	38	77	154	462	661	817	811	792	789
School ages (5-15)	**KBWW**	..	..	3,753	4,421	3,817	4,087	4,079	4,060	4,021
Under 18	**KGYD**	..	..	6,495	7,042	6,409	6,512	6,487	6,459	6,438
Pensionable ages[4]	**KFIC**	1,601	2,950	4,580	6,708	6,927	6,917	6,937	6,984	7,040

15.3(a) Age distribution of the resident population: by sex and country

Thousands

		United Kingdom							Projected population[1]		
		2005	2006	2007	2008	2009	2010	2011	2016	2021	2026
Persons: All ages	**KGUA**	60,235	60,584	60,986	61,398	61,792	62,262	62,649	64,773	66,958	69,051
Under 1	KGUK	716	732	756	788	784	795	775	787	801	795
1 - 4	KABA	2,712	2,764	2,838	2,912	2,994	3,063	3,108	3,111	3,190	3,199
5 - 9	KGUN	3,553	3,488	3,423	3,394	3,405	3,446	3,508	3,892	3,906	3,999
10 - 14	KGUO	3,818	3,750	3,703	3,657	3,612	3,567	3,500	3,515	3,898	3,912
15 - 19	KGUP	3,957	3,996	4,016	3,987	3,964	3,912	3,832	3,571	3,585	3,968
20 - 29	KABB	7,694	7,886	8,114	8,313	8,414	8,560	8,758	8,920	8,471	8,223
30 - 44	KABC	13,415	13,297	13,141	12,977	12,848	12,725	12,646	12,600	13,408	14,085
45 - 59	KABD	11,616	11,744	11,730	11,797	11,946	12,126	12,288	13,080	12,951	12,323
60 - 64	KGUY	3,114	3,240	3,485	3,641	3,719	3,764	3,746	3,442	3,840	4,300
65 - 74	KBCP	5,046	5,029	5,058	5,157	5,279	5,399	5,501	6,344	6,551	6,703
75 - 84	KBCU	3,420	3,416	3,424	3,441	3,458	3,494	3,540	3,829	4,360	5,130
85 and over	KGVD	1,174	1,243	1,298	1,335	1,369	1,411	1,447	1,682	1,995	2,413
School ages (5-15)	KBWU	8,156	8,037	7,914	7,814	7,771	7,750	7,739	8,077	8,543	8,692
Under 18	KGUD	13,171	13,115	13,108	13,116	13,117	13,140	13,120	13,375	13,978	14,269
Pensionable ages[5]	KFIA	11,232	11,344	11,563	11,794	12,007	12,228	12,178	12,493	12,906	13,457
Males: All ages	**KGWA**	29,493	29,689	29,918	30,154	30,374	30,643	30,842	31,986	33,134	34,210
Under 1	KGWK	367	374	388	403	402	407	397	403	410	407
1 - 4	KBCV	1,389	1,416	1,454	1,492	1,533	1,570	1,591	1,592	1,632	1,637
5 - 9	KGWN	1,818	1,783	1,749	1,735	1,742	1,762	1,795	1,989	1,995	2,043
10 - 14	KGWO	1,961	1,924	1,898	1,872	1,849	1,825	1,791	1,802	1,995	2,002
15 - 19	KGWP	2,030	2,060	2,069	2,049	2,035	2,013	1,966	1,831	1,841	2,034
20 - 29	KBCW	3,880	3,981	4,118	4,236	4,291	4,382	4,479	4,555	4,318	4,193
30 - 44	KBCX	6,652	6,592	6,521	6,450	6,397	6,338	6,311	6,353	6,812	7,180
45 - 59	KBUU	5,744	5,803	5,785	5,814	5,884	5,973	6,048	6,431	6,373	6,099
60 - 64	KGWY	1,523	1,585	1,703	1,780	1,818	1,840	1,824	1,673	1,864	2,078
65 - 74	KBWL	2,380	2,379	2,398	2,449	2,511	2,572	2,623	3,032	3,127	3,201
75 - 84	KBWM	1,400	1,413	1,432	1,452	1,472	1,501	1,535	1,716	1,988	2,355
85 and over	KGXD	350	379	403	422	439	460	482	610	778	982
School ages (5-15)	KBWV	4,184	4,119	4,051	3,999	3,978	3,965	3,961	4,134	4,369	4,445
Under 18	KGWD	6,754	6,724	6,719	6,719	6,717	6,730	6,719	6,848	7,154	7,301
Pensionable ages[4]	KFIB	4,130	4,171	4,233	4,323	4,422	4,533	4,639	5,358	5,893	6,158
Females: All ages	**KGYA**	30,742	30,895	31,068	31,244	31,418	31,619	31,807	32,787	33,824	34,841
Under 1[3]	KGYK	349	357	368	385	383	388	378	384	391	388
1 - 4	KBWN	1,323	1,349	1,383	1,420	1,462	1,493	1,517	1,519	1,558	1,562
5 - 9	KGYN	1,734	1,704	1,674	1,658	1,663	1,685	1,713	1,903	1,911	1,956
10 - 14	KGYO	1,856	1,826	1,805	1,785	1,763	1,742	1,709	1,714	1,903	1,911
15 - 19	KGYP	1,928	1,936	1,947	1,938	1,929	1,899	1,866	1,740	1,745	1,934
20 - 29	KBWO	3,814	3,905	3,996	4,076	4,123	4,178	4,278	4,366	4,153	4,031
30 - 44	KBWP	6,763	6,704	6,619	6,527	6,450	6,387	6,335	6,247	6,596	6,905
45 - 59	KBWR	5,872	5,941	5,945	5,983	6,061	6,152	6,240	6,649	6,579	6,223
60 - 64	KGYY	1,591	1,656	1,782	1,861	1,901	1,924	1,923	1,769	1,976	2,223
65 - 74	KBWS	2,666	2,650	2,660	2,708	2,768	2,827	2,878	3,312	3,424	3,503
75 - 84	KBWT	2,020	2,003	1,992	1,988	1,986	1,993	2,005	2,113	2,371	2,775
85 and over	KGZD	825	864	895	914	930	951	965	1,072	1,218	1,431
School ages (5-15)	KBWW	3,973	3,918	3,863	3,815	3,793	3,784	3,778	3,943	4,174	4,247
Under 18	KGYD	6,417	6,391	6,389	6,397	6,399	6,410	6,402	6,527	6,824	6,969
Pensionable ages[4]	KFIC	7,102	7,172	7,330	7,472	7,585	7,695	7,539	7,135	7,013	7,299

1 These projections are 2008-based. See chapter text for more detail

15.3(b) Age distribution of the resident population: by sex and country

		England										Projected population[1]	
		Estimated mid-year resident population											
		1991[2]	2002[4]	2003[4]	2004[4]	2005[4]	2006	2007	2008	2009	2010	2011	2026
Persons: All ages	KCCI	47,875	49,649	49,863	50,110	50,466	50,764	51,106	51,465	51,810	52,234	52 577	58,334
Under 1	KCCJ	660	558	576	597	606	620	641	667	664	675	657	682
1 - 4	KCCK	2,560	2,312	2,274	2,261	2,288	2,335	2,398	2,462	2,532	2,592	2,632	2,735
5 - 9	KCCL	3,019	3,084	3,054	3,018	2,974	2,919	2,868	2,848	2,863	2,903	2,959	3,402
10 - 14	KCCM	2,865	3,263	3,249	3,225	3,184	3,129	3,090	3,053	3,016	2,981	2,926	3,313
15 - 19	KCCN	3,067	3,117	3,206	3,264	3,298	3,335	3,354	3,330	3,312	3,266	3,199	3,354
20 - 29	KCEG	7,651	6,245	6,233	6,319	6,488	6,641	6,827	6,988	7,066	7,195	7,385	7,009
30 - 44	KCEH	10,147	11,345	11,367	11,335	11,315	11,224	11,102	10,973	10,874	10,775	10,711	12,003
45 - 59	KCEQ	7,920	9,438	9,520	9,590	9,675	9,777	9,759	9,813	9,941	10,099	10,235	10,392
60 - 64	KCEW	2,399	2,399	2,445	2,509	2,586	2,697	2,906	3,041	3,107	3,140	3,118	3,583
65 - 74	KCGD	4,222	4,129	4,155	4,175	4,190	4,171	4,193	4,276	4,380	4,487	4,572	5,541
75 - 84	KCJG	2,626	2,803	2,850	2,876	2,865	2,860	2,866	2,878	2,892	2,922	2,958	4,288
85 and over	KCKJ	739	956	936	942	995	1,055	1,102	1,135	1,163	1,198	1,226	2,032
School ages (5-15)	KCWX	6,439	6,984	6,959	6,893	6,815	6,715	6,615	6,537	6,508	6,499	6,495	7,375
Under 18	KCWY	10,840	11,117	11,087	11,060	11,031	10,992	10,992	11,004	11,012	11,045	11,035	12,130
Pensionable ages[5]	KEAA	8,827	9,110	9,188	9,273	9,370	9,463	9,646	9,842	10,022	10,211	10,164	11,207
Males: All ages	KEAB	23,291	24,287	24,415	24,561	24,756	24,924	25,119	25,323	25,515	25,758	25,932	28,952
Under 1	KEAC	336	286	296	306	310	317	329	342	340	346	337	349
1 - 4	KEAD	1,307	1,181	1,163	1,159	1,171	1,196	1,229	1,261	1,296	1,328	1,347	1,400
5 - 9	KEAE	1,545	1,581	1,564	1,545	1,521	1,492	1,464	1,456	1,464	1,483	1,513	1,738
10 - 14	KEAF	1,467	1,672	1,667	1,657	1,637	1,606	1,584	1,562	1,544	1,524	1,497	1,695
15 - 19	KECA	1,572	1,608	1,655	1,680	1,691	1,720	1,729	1,712	1,701	1,682	1,642	1,720
20 - 29	KECB	3,835	3,131	3,128	3,184	3,273	3,353	3,467	3,564	3,606	3,688	3,780	3,569
30 - 44	KECC	5,064	5,643	5,656	5,636	5,633	5,587	5,532	5,476	5,435	5,384	5,363	6,126
45 - 59	KECD	3,957	4,672	4,713	4,747	4,790	4,838	4,820	4,844	4,907	4,987	5,051	5,166
60 - 64	KECE	1,159	1,176	1,197	1,228	1,267	1,321	1,421	1,487	1,519	1,535	1,518	1,738
65 - 74	KECF	1,900	1,941	1,958	1,972	1,983	1,981	1,995	2,036	2,089	2,143	2,183	2,650
75 - 84	KECG	970	1,128	1,154	1,172	1,179	1,190	1,205	1,222	1,239	1,263	1,290	1,970
85 and over	KECH	181	269	267	274	298	324	344	361	375	393	411	832
School ages (5-15)	KECI	3,295	3,579	3,568	3,534	3,496	3,442	3,386	3,345	3,330	3,324	3,323	3,771
Under 18	KECJ	5,545	5,698	5,685	5,673	5,656	5,636	5,634	5,636	5,639	5,657	5,650	6,207
Pensionable ages[5]	KECK	3,050	3,338	3,378	3,419	3,461	3,494	3,544	3,619	3,703	3,798	3,885	5,137
Females: All ages	KEJV	24,584	25,362	25,448	25,549	25,710	25,840	25,987	26,141	26,295	26,476	26,645	29,382
Under 1	KEJW	324	273	280	291	296	303	312	326	324	329	321	333
1 - 4	KEJX	1,253	1,131	1,111	1,103	1,116	1,139	1,170	1,201	1,236	1,263	1,285	1,336
5 - 9	KEKP	1,474	1,503	1,490	1,474	1,453	1,427	1,403	1,392	1,399	1,420	1,445	1,664
10 - 14	KEKQ	1,399	1,591	1,582	1,568	1,547	1,523	1,507	1,491	1,473	1,457	1,429	1,617
15 - 19	KEKR	1,495	1,509	1,551	1,584	1,607	1,615	1,625	1,618	1,611	1,584	1,557	1,634
20 - 29	KEKS	3,816	3,114	3,105	3,134	3,215	3,288	3,360	3,424	3,460	3,508	3,606	3,440
30 - 44	KENR	5,083	5,702	5,711	5,698	5,682	5,637	5,570	5,498	5,439	5,391	5,348	5,877
45 - 59	KEOQ	3,964	4,766	4,807	4,843	4,885	4,939	4,939	4,969	5,034	5,112	5,184	5,226
60 - 64	KEOZ	1,239	1,222	1,248	1,281	1,319	1,376	1,485	1,554	1,588	1,605	1,600	1,846
65 - 74	KEQJ	2,323	2,187	2,197	2,204	2,206	2,191	2,198	2,239	2,291	2,344	2,388	2,891
75 - 84	KEQK	1,656	1,675	1,696	1,703	1,686	1,670	1,660	1,656	1,653	1,659	1,668	2,318
85 and over	KEQL	558	687	669	667	697	731	758	774	787	805	815	1,200
School ages (5-15)	KEQM	3,143	3,404	3,391	3,358	3,319	3,273	3,229	3,192	3,178	3,175	3,172	3,603
Under 18	KEQN	5,295	5,419	5,402	5,388	5,375	5,356	5,358	5,368	5,373	5,388	5,385	5,924
Pensionable ages[5]	KEQO	5,777	5,772	5,810	5,855	5,909	5,968	6,101	6,223	6,319	6,413	6,279	6,070

15.3(b) Age distribution of the resident population: by sex and country
Continued

Wales

		Estimated mid-year resident population										Projected population[1]	
		1991[2]	2002[4]	2003[4]	2004[4]	2005[4]	2006	2007	2008	2009	2010	2011	2026
Persons: All ages	KERY	2,873	2,918	2,929	2,943	2,950	2,962	2,976	2,990	2,999	3,006	3,024	3,263
Under 1	KFAC	38	30	31	32	32	33	34	35	35	35	35	35
1 - 4	KFBX	153	132	129	127	126	127	130	133	136	138	140	143
5 - 9	KFCA	186	183	180	178	175	172	167	163	161	161	163	183
10 - 14	KFCB	177	197	197	195	192	189	186	183	180	176	174	182
15 - 19	KFCC	187	190	196	199	200	202	204	203	201	199	194	186
20 - 29	KFCD	415	332	332	338	346	356	368	381	389	395	401	366
30 - 44	KFCE	583	610	608	605	599	590	579	567	556	546	544	619
45 - 59	KFCF	486	578	582	586	588	592	589	589	592	595	602	565
60 - 64	KFCG	154	156	161	166	171	177	188	197	200	203	203	216
65 - 74	KFCH	284	265	268	270	271	272	276	282	289	295	303	357
75 - 84	KFCI	164	185	187	188	186	186	185	185	185	186	188	283
85 and over	KFCK	45	59	59	60	63	67	70	72	74	77	79	128
School ages (5-15)	KFCL	397	419	417	413	407	401	393	385	379	374	373	402
Under 18	KFCM	662	659	654	651	646	641	637	634	629	625	623	653
Pensionable ages[5]	KFEB	573	589	595	602	608	615	627	639	650	661	661	728
Males: All ages	KFEI	1,391	1,413	1,422	1,431	1,437	1,442	1,451	1,459	1,466	1,471	1,480	1,610
Under 1	KFEJ	20	16	16	16	17	17	17	18	18	18	18	18
1 - 4	KFEK	78	68	66	65	65	65	67	68	70	71	72	73
5 - 9	KFEL	95	94	92	91	90	88	85	84	83	83	84	94
10 - 14	KFFA	91	101	101	100	99	97	96	94	92	91	89	93
15 - 19	KFFN	95	97	100	102	103	104	105	104	103	102	99	95
20 - 29	KFHA	207	164	165	169	174	179	186	193	198	202	205	188
30 - 44	KFHB	289	297	296	295	292	287	282	277	272	267	266	315
45 - 59	KFHW	242	285	287	288	289	291	289	288	289	291	293	275
60 - 64	KFQO	74	77	79	82	84	87	93	97	98	100	100	104
65 - 74	KFQV	128	125	126	128	129	130	132	135	139	142	146	171
75 - 84	KFUK	60	74	75	76	76	77	78	78	79	80	82	132
85 and over	KFUL	11	16	16	17	19	20	22	23	24	25	26	53
School ages (5-15)	KFUV	204	215	214	212	209	206	201	198	195	192	192	206
Under 18	KFVE	339	338	336	335	332	329	327	325	323	321	320	334
Pensionable ages[5]	KFVF	198	215	218	221	224	227	231	236	242	247	254	336
Females: All ages	KFVL	1,482	1,505	1,507	1,513	1,513	1,520	1,525	1,531	1,534	1,536	1,545	1,653
Under 1	KFYW	19	15	15	15	16	16	16	17	17	17	17	17
1 - 4	KFZJ	75	65	63	62	61	62	63	65	66	67	68	70
5 - 9	KGCK	91	89	88	87	85	84	81	79	78	78	79	90
10 - 14	KGCM	86	96	95	95	94	92	91	89	87	86	84	89
15 - 19	KGCN	91	93	95	96	97	98	99	98	98	96	95	91
20 - 29	KGCO	208	168	167	169	171	177	182	187	191	193	196	177
30 - 44	KGCP	294	313	312	311	307	303	297	291	284	279	278	304
45 - 59	KGGZ	244	293	295	298	299	301	300	301	303	305	308	290
60 - 64	KGIY	80	80	82	84	87	90	96	100	102	103	104	112
65 - 74	KGKR	156	140	141	142	142	143	144	147	150	153	157	186
75 - 84	KGTQ	104	111	112	112	110	108	107	107	106	106	106	151
85 and over	KGTZ	34	43	42	42	44	47	49	50	50	52	52	76
School ages (5-15)	KGVG	194	204	203	201	198	195	191	187	184	182	181	196
Under 18	KGVH	323	321	318	316	314	311	310	308	306	304	303	319
Pensionable ages[5]	KGVK	375	374	377	380	383	387	395	403	408	414	407	392

1 These projections are 2008-based. See chapter text for more detail

15.3(c) Age distribution of the resident population: by sex and country
continued

Thousands

		2001[3]	2002	2003	2004	2005	2006	2007	2008	2009	2010	2011	2026
						Scotland						Projected population[1]	
			Estimated mid-year resident population										
Persons: All ages	KGVP	5,064	5,055	5,057	5,078	5,095	5,117	5,144	5,169	5,194	5,222	5,233	5,483
Under 1	KHAQ	52	51	52	54	54	55	57	60	60	59	58	55
1 - 4	KHCT	224	217	212	210	211	213	218	223	229	234	235	226
5 - 9	KHDN	306	299	294	290	285	279	273	269	268	270	273	291
10 - 14	KHDQ	323	323	320	319	315	308	303	298	293	288	282	292
15 - 19	KHDT	318	319	324	328	327	329	330	327	326	324	316	303
20 - 29	KHDU	630	619	614	617	630	649	671	689	701	712	709	624
30 - 44	KHDV	1,163	1,158	1,150	1,140	1,124	1,107	1,086	1,065	1,049	1,036	1,027	1,068
45 - 59	KHFK	979	993	1,008	1,025	1,042	1,058	1,060	1,068	1,079	1,092	1,106	1,010
60 - 64	KHOZ	262	262	265	270	273	280	301	312	320	327	331	380
65 - 74	KHTU	447	449	452	455	457	456	457	463	470	474	480	614
75 - 84	KHUO	272	276	281	286	286	287	290	293	295	299	305	426
85 and over	KHUQ	89	88	86	85	91	95	98	100	104	107	110	193
School ages (5-15)	KHVV	694	687	679	672	664	653	642	631	623	618	614	642
Under 18	KIMT	1,098	1,086	1,074	1,067	1,059	1,050	1,047	1,046	1,042	1,038	1,029	1,044
Pensionable ages[5]	KIMU	944	950	958	968	975	983	1,001	1,017	1,033	1,047	1,045	1,161
Males: All ages	KIMV	2,434	2,432	2,435	2,446	2,456	2,469	2,486	2,500	2,515	2,530	2,537	2,672
Under 1	KIMW	26	26	26	28	28	28	29	30	31	30	30	28
1 - 4	KIMX	115	111	108	107	107	109	112	115	118	120	120	116
5 - 9	KIMY	156	153	151	149	146	143	140	138	137	138	139	148
10 - 14	KIMZ	166	165	164	163	161	157	155	152	150	148	145	149
15 - 19	KINA	161	163	166	168	168	169	169	168	167	166	161	155
20 - 29	KINB	311	308	306	309	317	327	339	350	356	362	361	318
30 - 44	KINC	563	560	556	550	542	534	524	515	509	504	502	540
45 - 59	KIND	483	490	496	503	511	517	517	520	524	528	534	486
60 - 64	KINE	125	125	126	129	131	135	146	152	156	160	161	178
65 - 74	KINR	200	202	204	207	208	208	210	213	217	220	224	288
75 - 84	KINS	103	106	108	111	112	113	116	118	120	122	126	193
85 and over	KINT	23	23	23	23	25	27	29	30	31	33	35	74
School ages (5-15)	KINU	356	352	348	344	340	334	328	322	319	317	314	328
Under 18	KINV	562	556	550	546	543	538	536	535	533	531	527	533
Pensionable ages[5]	KINW	327	331	336	341	345	349	354	361	368	375	385	520
Females: All ages	KINX	2,630	2,623	2,623	2,632	2,639	2,647	2,659	2,668	2,679	2,692	2,695	2,811
Under 1	KINY	26	25	25	26	26	27	28	29	29	29	28	27
1 - 4	KINZ	109	106	104	103	103	104	106	109	112	114	115	111
5 - 9	KIOA	149	146	143	141	139	136	134	132	131	132	133	142
10 - 14	KIOB	157	157	156	156	154	151	148	145	143	140	137	143
15 - 19	KIOC	156	156	158	160	159	160	160	160	159	158	155	148
20 - 29	KIOO	319	311	307	308	314	322	332	339	345	350	348	306
30 - 44	KIOP	600	598	595	590	583	573	562	550	540	532	526	529
45 - 59	KIOQ	496	504	512	521	531	541	542	548	556	564	572	525
60 - 64	KIOR	137	137	139	141	142	145	155	160	164	168	171	202
65 - 74	KIOS	246	247	248	248	249	247	247	250	253	254	256	326
75 - 84	KIOT	169	171	173	175	174	174	174	175	175	177	179	234
85 and over	KIOU	66	65	63	62	65	68	70	71	72	74	76	119
School ages (5-15)	KIOV	339	335	331	328	324	319	314	308	304	302	299	314
Under 18	KIOW	536	530	524	520	516	512	511	510	509	507	502	510
Pensionable ages[5]	KIOX	617	619	622	627	630	634	646	656	664	672	660	641

1 These projections are 2008-based. See chapter text for more detail
2 Data for mid 1991 for UK, Engand and Wales and Scotland are revised in light of the 2001 Census
3 Data for mid-2001 and mid-2002 revised in light of the local authority population studies
4 England & Wales population estimates for mid-2003 to mid-2005 were revised in August 2007 to take account of improved estimates of international migration
5 The pensionable age population is that over state retirement age. The 2011 figures take account of planned changes in retirement age from 65 for men and 60 for women at present to 65 for both sexes. This change will be phased in between April 2010 and March 2020.

15.3(c) Age distribution of the resident population: by sex and country
continued

Thousands

		Northern Ireland										Projected population[1]	
		Estimated mid-year resident population											
		2001[3]	2002	2003	2004	2005	2006	2007	2008	2009	2010	2011	2026
Persons: All ages	KIOY	1,689	1,697	1,703	1,710	1,724	1,742	1,759	1,775	1,789	1,799	1,815	1,971
Under 1	KIOZ	22	22	21	22	23	23	24	26	26	25	25	23
1 - 4	KIPA	93	91	89	87	88	89	91	94	97	99	101	94
5 - 9	KIPN	123	122	121	120	119	117	115	113	112	113	114	123
10 - 14	KIPP	132	131	129	128	126	125	124	123	122	121	119	126
15 - 19	KIPQ	130	132	133	133	132	131	128	127	125	123	124	125
20 - 29	KIPR	225	222	221	224	230	239	249	255	258	258	263	225
30 - 44	KIPS	376	378	378	378	377	375	374	371	369	368	364	394
45 - 59	KIPT	290	296	301	305	310	316	321	327	333	339	345	355
60 - 64	KIPU	74	75	78	81	84	87	90	91	92	93	94	121
65 - 74	KIPV	123	125	126	127	128	130	132	136	140	143	146	192
75 - 84	KIPW	77	79	81	82	83	83	84	85	86	88	89	132
85 and over	KIPX	23	24	24	24	25	26	27	28	29	30	32	60
School ages (5-15)	KIPY	282	281	278	274	271	268	265	262	260	258	257	274
Under 18	KIQL	451	447	443	437	435	432	432	433	433	432	433	442
Pensionable ages[5]	KIQM	262	266	271	275	280	284	290	296	302	308	309	361
Males: All ages	KIQN	824	829	833	836	844	853	862	871	879	884	892	975
Under 1	KIQO	11	11	11	11	12	12	13	13	13	13	13	12
1 - 4	KIQP	48	47	46	45	45	46	47	48	50	51	52	48
5 - 9	KIQQ	63	63	62	62	61	60	59	58	58	58	58	63
10 - 14	KIQR	68	67	66	65	64	64	63	63	63	62	61	64
15 - 19	KIQS	66	68	68	68	68	67	66	65	64	63	64	65
20 - 29	KIQT	113	111	111	112	116	121	126	129	131	130	134	118
30 - 44	KIQU	185	186	186	185	185	184	183	183	182	183	180	199
45 - 59	KIQV	144	147	149	151	153	156	158	161	164	167	170	173
60 - 64	KIQW	35	36	38	39	41	42	44	44	45	45	45	58
65 - 74	KIRJ	56	56	57	58	59	60	61	63	66	67	69	92
75 - 84	KIRK	30	31	31	32	32	33	33	34	35	36	37	60
85 and over	KIRL	6	6	7	7	7	8	8	8	9	9	10	23
School ages (5-15)	KIRM	145	144	142	141	139	138	136	134	133	132	132	140
Under 18	KIRN	231	229	227	225	223	222	222	222	222	221	222	226
Pensionable ages[5]	KIRO	92	94	95	97	99	101	103	106	109	112	116	165
Females: All ages	KIRP	865	868	870	874	880	888	897	904	910	915	923	996
Under 1	KIRQ	10	11	10	11	11	11	12	12	12	12	12	11
1 - 4	KIRR	45	44	43	42	43	43	44	46	47	48	49	46
5 - 9	KIRS	60	59	59	58	58	57	56	55	55	55	56	60
10 - 14	KIRT	65	64	63	62	62	61	60	60	60	59	58	61
15 - 19	KIRU	64	65	65	65	64	64	62	62	61	60	60	61
20 - 29	KISH	113	111	110	111	114	118	123	126	127	128	129	108
30 - 44	KISI	191	192	193	192	192	191	190	188	187	186	184	195
45 - 59	KISJ	146	149	152	154	157	160	163	165	169	172	176	182
60 - 64	KISK	38	39	40	42	43	45	46	47	47	48	48	63
65 - 74	KISL	68	68	68	69	69	69	70	72	74	76	77	100
75 - 84	KISM	47	48	49	50	50	51	51	51	51	52	52	72
85 and over	KISN	17	17	17	17	18	18	19	20	20	21	22	36
School ages (5-15)	KISO	138	137	135	134	132	130	129	127	126	125	125	134
Under 18	KISP	220	218	215	213	212	210	210	211	211	210	211	216
Pensionable ages[5]	KISQ	170	173	175	178	181	183	187	190	193	196	193	197

Sources: Office for National Statistics: www.ons.gov.uk
General Register Office for Scotland;
General Register Office (Northern Ireland);
Government Actuary's Department: www.gad.gov.uk

15.4 Marital condition (de jure): estimated population: by age and sex

England and Wales

		2001	2002[1]	2003[1]	2004[1]	2005[1]	2006[1]	2007[1]	2008[1]	2009[1]
All ages:										
Single	KRPL	12,270	12,407	12,549	12,714	12,891	13,077	13,280	13,471	13,644
Married	KRPM	11,090	11,040	10,992	10,939	10,922	10,879	10,853	10,854	10,862
Widowed	KRPN	733	729	726	722	719	716	715	714	712
Divorced	KRPO	1,482	1,524	1,570	1,617	1,661	1,694	1,722	1,744	1,763
Age groups:										
0 - 14: Single	KRPP	5,036	4,998	4,965	4,939	4,910	4,877	4,871	4,884	4,907
15 - 19: Single	KRPQ	1,645	1,699	1,750	1,778	1,792	1,822	1,832	1,814	1,803
Married	KRPR	5	5	4	3	2	2	2	2	2
Widowed	KRPS	1	1	1	0	0	0	0	0	0
Divorced	KRPT	1	1	1	0	0	0	0	0	0
20 - 24: Single	KRPU	1,501	1,531	1,569	1,634	1,695	1,743	1,815	1,856	1,866
Married	KRPV	74	73	74	75	73	67	64	61	57
Widowed	KRPW	1	1	1	1	1	1	1	1	0
Divorced	KRPX	3	3	3	3	3	3	3	2	2
25 - 34: Single	KRPY	2,227	2,228	2,229	2,244	2,291	2,342	2,385	2,452	2,524
Married	KRPZ	1,391	1,310	1,237	1,172	1,124	1,067	1,028	1,007	993
Widowed	KRQA	3	3	3	3	3	2	2	3	3
Divorced	KRQB	136	129	123	118	111	103	96	89	84
35 - 44: Single	KRQC	963	1,027	1,080	1,126	1,173	1,218	1,259	1,289	1,310
Married	KRQD	2,494	2,498	2,487	2,465	2,451	2,418	2,384	2,334	2,277
Widowed	KRQE	12	12	12	11	11	11	10	10	9
Divorced	KRQF	411	420	427	433	436	431	422	406	386
45 - 54: Single	KRQG	419	432	450	472	498	529	563	601	643
Married	KUAR	2,511	2,431	2,382	2,355	2,347	2,355	2,364	2,390	2,421
Widowed	KUBA	37	35	34	32	31	30	29	29	29
Divorced	KUBB	448	451	461	474	488	504	518	532	543
55 - 59: Single	KUBC	128	141	150	158	164	170	170	171	177
Married	KUBD	1,156	1,238	1,278	1,288	1,286	1,271	1,200	1,148	1,122
Widowed	KUBE	34	36	36	37	37	36	34	32	30
Divorced	KUBF	174	194	208	219	228	234	231	229	232
60 - 64: Single	KUBG	97	97	100	104	108	114	124	134	141
Married	KUBH	980	977	991	1,013	1,039	1,078	1,152	1,198	1,214
Widowed	KUBI	50	48	48	47	47	48	51	52	53
Divorced	KUBJ	125	131	138	146	156	168	186	201	210
65 - 74: Single	KUBK	155	154	153	152	151	149	150	153	156
Married	KUBL	1,569	1,581	1,595	1,606	1,614	1,610	1,619	1,651	1,690
Widowed	KUBM	188	183	178	174	170	165	162	160	159
Divorced	KUBN	139	148	158	168	178	186	196	208	222
75 and over: Single	KUBO	99	101	103	106	109	111	114	116	117
Married	KUBP	909	928	944	962	984	1,011	1,038	1,064	1,087
Widowed	KUBQ	407	411	414	417	419	422	425	427	429
Divorced	KUBR	44	48	51	56	61	66	72	77	83

1 Mid-2002 to Mid-2009 are revised to include marriages abroad.

15.4 Marital condition (de jure): estimated population: by age and sex

England and Wales
Continued+A1

		2001	2002[1]	2003[1]	2004[1]	2005[1]	2006[1]	2007[1]	2008[1]	2009[1]
All ages:										
Single	KUBS	10,917	11,034	11,166	11,310	11,494	11,674	11,857	12,052	12,234
Married	KVCC	11,150	11,093	11,033	10,981	10,944	10,894	10,856	10,818	10,794
Widowed	KVCD	2,745	2,709	2,669	2,628	2,588	2,548	2,512	2,477	2,444
Divorced	KVCE	1,975	2,030	2,087	2,144	2,197	2,243	2,288	2,325	2,357
Age groups:										
0 - 14: Single	KVCF	4,796	4,762	4,724	4,694	4,668	4,646	4,643	4,661	4,681
15 - 19: Single	KVCG	1,560	1,588	1,633	1,668	1,694	1,705	1,717	1,710	1,702
Married	KVCH	16	13	12	11	10	7	7	7	7
Widowed	KVCI	1	1	1	0	0	0	0	0	0
Divorced	KVCJ	1	1	0	0	0	0	0	0	0
20 - 24: Single	KVCK	1,390	1,427	1,460	1,493	1,542	1,595	1,640	1,693	1,717
Married	KVCL	178	170	166	163	157	147	136	127	117
Widowed	KVCM	1	1	1	2	2	1	1	1	1
Divorced	KVCN	8	8	8	8	8	7	6	6	5
25 - 34: Single	KVCO	1,770	1,787	1,809	1,844	1,905	1,960	2,002	2,049	2,112
Married	KVCP	1,768	1,670	1,583	1,504	1,451	1,385	1,327	1,283	1,248
Widowed	KVCQ	10	9	8	7	7	7	7	6	6
Divorced	KVCR	231	217	206	193	182	169	157	147	139
35 - 44: Single	KVEH	692	749	802	853	903	955	1,004	1,044	1,076
Married	KVEI	2,649	2,653	2,639	2,625	2,598	2,565	2,526	2,462	2,399
Widowed	KVEJ	36	35	34	32	31	30	29	27	26
Divorced	KVEK	558	570	579	588	590	585	574	554	529
45 - 54: Single	KVEL	256	271	288	310	334	364	398	436	478
Married	KVEM	2,548	2,477	2,428	2,402	2,391	2,399	2,415	2,440	2,465
Widowed	KVEN	111	105	99	96	92	90	87	85	83
Divorced	KVEO	557	565	576	591	609	630	653	676	696
55 - 59: Single	KVEP	74	81	86	91	96	102	104	108	114
Married	KVEQ	1,125	1,212	1,256	1,271	1,271	1,260	1,197	1,146	1,123
Widowed	KVER	112	115	114	111	109	106	98	92	87
Divorced	KVES	210	235	255	269	281	290	288	287	291
60 - 64: Single	KVET	62	61	62	63	65	69	75	80	86
Married	KVEU	906	910	932	958	988	1,029	1,110	1,158	1,177
Widowed	KVEV	178	172	167	163	160	159	162	162	159
Divorced	KVEW	151	158	169	180	193	210	234	254	268
65 - 74: Single	KMGN	130	126	123	120	117	113	111	111	112
Married	KMGO	1,322	1,336	1,356	1,374	1,389	1,393	1,411	1,449	1,494
Widowed	KMGP	697	675	655	634	611	584	563	551	541
Divorced	KMGQ	177	190	204	218	232	243	257	275	295
75 and over: Single	KMGR	188								
Married	KMGS	639	182	177	173	169	166	163	160	157
Widowed	KMGT	1,598	651	661	673	689	709	728	746	763
Divorced	KMGU	81	1,597	1,590	1,583	1,576	1,571	1,565	1,553	1,542

Source: Office for National Statistics; 01329 444661

15.5 Geographical distribution of the population

Thousands

		Population enumerated in Census					
		1911	1931	1951	1971	1991	2001
United Kingdom	KIUR	42,082	46,074	50,225	55,928	57,439	59,113
Great Britain	KISR	40,831	44,795	48,854	54,388	55,831	57,424
England	KKOJ	33,650	37,359	41,159	46,412	47,875	49,450
Standard Regions							
North	KKNA	2,729	2,938	3,009	3,152	3,073	3,028
Yorkshire and Humberside	KKNB	3,896	4,319	4,567	4,902	4,936	4,977
East Midlands	KKNC	2,467	2,732	3,118	3,652	4,011	4,190
East Anglia	KKND	1,191	1,231	1,381	1,688	2,068	2,181
South East.	KKNE	11,613	13,349	14,877	17,125	17,511	18,566
South West	KKNF	2,818	2,984	3,479	4,112	4,688	4,943
West Midlands	KKNG	3,277	3,743	4,423	5,146	5,230	5,281
North West	KKNH	5,659	6,062	6,305	6,634	6,357	6,285
Government Office Regions							
North East	JZBU	..	..	..	2,679	2,587	2,540
North West	JZBV	..	..	..	7,108	6,843	6,773
Yorkshire and The Humber	JZBX	..	..	..	4,902	4,936	4,977
East Midlands	JZBY	..	..	..	3,652	4,011	4,190
West Midlands	JZBZ	..	..	..	5,146	5,230	5,281
East	JZCB	..	..	..	4,454	5,121	5,400
London	JZCC	..	..	..	7,529	6,829	7,322
South East	JZCD	..	..	..	6,830	7,629	8,023
South West	JZCA	..	..	..	4,112	4,688	4,943
Wales	KKNI	2,421	2,593	2,599	2,740	2,873	2,910
Scotland	KGJB	4,761	4,843	5,096	5,236	5,083	5,064
Northern Ireland[4]	KGJC	1,251	1,280	1,371	1,540	1,607	1,689
Greater London	KKNJ	7,161	8,110	8,197	7,529	6,829	7,322
Inner London[2]	KISS	4,998	4,893	3,679	3,060	2,599	2,859
Outer London[2]	KITF	2,162	3,217	4,518	4,470	4,230	4,463
Metropolitan areas of England & Wales	KITG	9,716	10,770	11,365	11,862	11,085	10,888
Tyne and Wear	KGJN	1,105	1,201	1,201	1,218	1,124	1,087
West Yorkshire	KGJP	1,852	1,939	1,985	2,090	2,062	2,083
South Yorkshire	KGJO	963	1,173	1,253	1,331	1,289	1,266
West Midlands	KGJQ	1,780	2,143	2,547	2,811	2,619	2,568
Greater Manchester	KGJR	2,638	2,727	2,716	2,750	2,554	2,516
Merseyside	KGJS	1,378	1,587	1,663	1,662	1,438	1,368
Principal Metropolitan Cities[2]	KITH	3,154	3,906	3,915	3,910	3,415	3,344
Newcastle	KGJT	267	286	292	312	275	266
Leeds	KGJX	446	483	505	749	707	716
Sheffield	KGJV	455	512	513	579	520	513
Birmingham	KGKF	526	1,003	1,113	1,107	1,005	985
Manchester	KGKJ	714	766	703	554	433	423
Liverpool	KGKM	746	856	789	610	476	442
Other metropolitan districts[2]	KITI	6,562	6,864	7,450	7,952	7,670	7,544
Non-metropolitan districts of England & Wales	KITJ	19,194	21,072	24,196	29,761	32,834	31,239
Non-metropolitan cities[2,3]	KITK	..	..	..	4,715	..	..
Incl. Kingston-upon-Hull	KKNZ	278	314	299	288	263	250
Leicester	KKOA	227	239	285	285	281	283
Nottingham	KKNX	260	269	308	302	279	269
Bristol	KKNV	357	397	443	433	392	390
Plymouth	KITL	207	215	225	249	251	241
Stoke-on-Trent	KKOD	235	277	275	265	249	240
Cardiff	KKOB	182	224	244	291	297	310
Newport	IFX3	84	89	106	137	135	138
Industrial districts[2,3]	KITM	..	..	..	6,486	..	..
New Towns[2,3]	KITN	..	..	..	1,895	..	..
Resort, port and retirement districts[2,3]	KITO	..	..	..	3,184	..	..
Urban and mixed urban/rural districts[2,3]	KITP	..	..	..	8,821	..	..
Remoter, mainly rural districts[2,3]	KITQ	..	..	..	4,661	..	..
City of Edinburgh local government district	KGKU	320	439	467	478	436	449
City of Glasgow local government district	KGKT	784	1,088	1,090	983	629	579
Belfast[4]	KGKV	387	438	444	..	293	277

15.5 Geographical distribution of the population

Thousands

		Mid-year population estimate[1]								
		2002	2003	2004	2005	2006	2007	2008	2009	2010
United Kingdom	KIUR	59,319	59,552	59,842	60,235	60,584	60,986	61,398	61,792	62,262
Great Britain	KISR	57,622	57,850	58,132	58,511	58,843	59,227	59,623	60,003	60,463
England	KKOJ	49,649	49,863	50,110	50,466	50,764	51,106	51,465	51,810	52,234
Standard Regions										
North	KKNA	3,029	3,032	3,036	3,045	3,049	3,057	3,067	3,079	3,101
Yorkshire and Humberside	KKNB	5,002	5,029	5,067	5,111	5,146	5,182	5,217	5,258	5,301
East Midlands	KKNC	4,222	4,254	4,291	4,327	4,363	4,397	4,429	4,451	4,481
East Anglia	KKND	2,194	2,217	2,237	2,263	2,281	2,304	2,328	2,346	2,372
South East	KKNE	18,648	18,711	18,791	18,946	19,083	19,243	19,426	19,610	19,809
South West	KKNF	4,972	5,003	5,040	5,085	5,124	5,178	5,210	5,231	5,274
West Midlands	KKNG	5,294	5,310	5,324	5,347	5,362	5,378	5,408	5,431	5,455
North West	KKNH	6,288	6,308	6,324	6,342	6,355	6,367	6,378	6,403	6,441
Government Office Regions										
North East	JZBU	2,540	2,540	2,541	2,548	2,553	2,560	2,571	2,584	2,607
North West	JZBV	6,777	6,799	6,819	6,839	6,852	6,864	6,874	6,898	6,936
Yorkshire and The Humber	JZBX	5,002	5,029	5,067	5,111	5,146	5,182	5,217	5,258	5,301
East Midlands	JZBY	4,222	4,254	4,291	4,327	4,363	4,397	4,429	4,451	4,481
West Midlands	JZBZ	5,294	5,310	5,324	5,347	5,362	5,378	5,408	5,431	5,455
East	JZCB	5,430	5,468	5,500	5,551	5,593	5,649	5,717	5,767	5,832
London	JZCC	7,369	7,380	7,413	7,485	7,547	7,602	7,668	7,754	7,825
South East	JZCD	8,043	8,080	8,115	8,173	8,224	8,296	8,369	8,436	8,523
South West	JZCA	4,972	5,003	5,040	5,085	5,124	5,178	5,210	5,231	5,274
Wales	KKNI	2,918	2,929	2,943	2,950	2,962	2,976	2,990	2,999	3,006
Scotland	KGJB	5,055	5,057	5,078	5,095	5,117	5,144	5,169	5,194	5,222
Northern Ireland[4]	KGJC	1,697	1,703	1,710	1,724	1,742	1,759	1,775	1,789	1,799
Greater London	KKNJ	7,369	7,380	7,413	7,485	7,547	7,602	7,668	7,754	7,825
Inner London[2]	KISS	2,889	2,894	2,912	2,948	2,976	3,003	3,030	3,061	3,083
Outer London[2]	KITF	4,480	4,485	4,501	4,537	4,571	4,599	4,638	4,692	4,742
Metropolitan areas of England & Wales	KITG	13,628	13,665	13,707	13,775	13,826	13,878	13,949	14,033	14,135
Tyne and Wear	KGJN	1,087	1,086	1,085	1,088	1,090	1,092	1,096	1,106	1,120
West Yorkshire	KGJP	2,095	2,106	2,123	2,149	2,170	2,189	2,207	2,227	2,250
South Yorkshire	KGJO	1,270	1,274	1,280	1,288	1,293	1,300	1,307	1,317	1,328
West Midlands	KGJQ	5,294	5,310	5,324	5,347	5,362	5,378	5,408	5,431	5,455
Greater Manchester	KGJR	2,518	2,528	2,535	2,544	2,554	2,565	2,580	2,601	2,629
Merseyside	KGJS	1,364	1,361	1,360	1,359	1,356	1,353	1,350	1,351	1,353
Principal Metropolitan Cities[2]	KITH	3,358	3,372	3,398	3,443	3,473	3,502	3,530	3,574	3,627
Newcastle	KGJT	268	268	269	273	274	276	278	284	292
Leeds	KGJX	720	725	735	751	762	772	779	788	799
Sheffield	KGJV	514	515	520	526	530	535	540	547	556
Birmingham	KGKF	988	991	994	1,003	1,008	1,012	1,019	1,029	1,037
Manchester	KGKJ	426	432	439	447	456	465	473	484	499
Liverpool	KGKM	441	440	441	443	443	443	441	442	445
Other metropolitan districts[2]	KITI	10,270	10,292	10,309	10,332	10,353	10,376	10,419	10,459	10,508
Non-metropolitan districts of England & Wales	KITJ	31,374	31,553	31,732	31,960	32,154	32,399	32,633	32,816	33,074
Non-metropolitan cities[2,3]	KITK	..	..	..	..	..		..		
Incl. Kingston-upon-Hull	KKNZ	250	252	255	257	259	259	261	262	264
Leicester	KKOA	283	284	287	291	297	301	304	305	307
Nottingham	KKNX	272	276	281	286	290	292	297	301	307
Bristol	KKNV	390	393	398	408	414	421	426	433	441
Plymouth	KITL	242	242	245	248	251	254	256	257	259
Stoke-on-Trent	KKOD	240	239	240	240	240	238	239	239	240
Cardiff	KKOB	311	311	315	318	322	326	331	336	341
Newport	IFX3	138	139	139	139	139	139	140	140	141
Industrial districts[2,3]	KITM	..	..	..	..	..	..	..	..	..
New Towns[2,3]	KITN	..	..	..	..	..	..	..	..	..
Resort, port and retirement districts[2,3]	KITO	..	..	..	..	..	..	..	..	..
Urban and mixed urban/rural districts[2,3]	KITP	..	..	..	..	..	..	..	..	..
Remoter, mainly rural districts[2,3]	KITQ	..	..	..	..	..	..	..	..	..
City of Edinburgh local government district	KGKU	448	448	454	458	464	468	472	478	486
City of Glasgow local government district	KGKT	577	577	578	579	581	582	584	588	593
Belfast[4]	KGKV	274	272	269	268	267	268	268	268	269

1 Mid-2002 to mid-2008 population estimates for the UK and England & Wales have been updated to include the latest revised estimates that take into account improved estimates of international migration.

2 Details of the classification by broad area type are given in recent issues of the ONS annual reference volume Key Population and Vital Statistics; local and Health Authority areas (Series VS). The ten broad area types include all local authorities in England and Wales.

3 The breakdown on non-metropolitan districts by area type has not been provided from mid-2001 onwards. This is because the effect of boundary changes due to the major local government reorganisation of 1 April 1995 and 1 April 1996 (particularly in Wales) make the comparison of 2001 data for earlier years invalid.

4 The 1931 figures shown for Northern Ireland and the City of Belfast relate to the 1937 Census.

Sources: Office for National Statistics 01329 81331
National Records of Scotland
Northern Ireland Statististics and Research Agency

15.6 Population: by ethnic group and age, January - December 2010

United Kingdom

		0 to 4	5 to 9	10 to 14	15 to 19	20 to 24	25 to 29	30 to 34	35 to 44	45 to 59	60 to 74	75 and over	(=100%) 000's
White	British	6	5	6	6	7	6	5	14	21	16	8	49,277
	Other	5	4	4	4	8	13	12	17	16	11	6	3,336
Mixed	White and Black Caribbean	20	13	15	13	11	8	3	8	6	1	1	236
	White and Black African	24	15	12	10	4	7	4	9	11	3	0	114
	White and Asian	21	17	13	9	9	7	5	10	7	2	1	205
	Other Mixed	20	12	11	8	9	9	8	12	9	3	0	181
Asian	Indian	8	5	5	5	8	11	12	18	16	8	3	1,319
	Pakistani	13	11	9	8	9	10	10	15	9	4	2	1,054
	Bangladeshi	12	12	9	8	11	11	9	16	8	3	1	434
	Other Asian	9	7	8	7	8	8	11	20	16	4	2	577
Black	Black Caribbean	6	7	6	7	7	7	7	16	21	10	6	633
	Black African	12	10	9	8	8	9	9	20	13	3	1	919
	Black Other	10	9	8	11	12	4	7	19	13	5	3	65
	Chinese	5	3	3	6	19	15	9	14	18	6	3	271
	Other	9	7	6	6	8	11	12	20	14	6	1	946
	All[2]	6	6	6	6	7	7	6	14	20	15	7	61,378

1 Respondents in Northern Ireland who state that their ethnicity is white
  are not asked this question.
2 Includes those who did not state their ethnic origin and those in
  Northern Ireland who stated that their ethnicity was white.

Source: Office for National Statistics, Annual Population Survey

15.7 Long-Term International Migration
United Kingdom
England and Wales
Citizenship

Thousands

Year	All citizenships	British	Non-British	European Union[1]	European Union[1] 15	European Union[1] A8	Commonwealth[2] All[2]	Old	New[2]	Other foreign[3]
Inflow										
1991	**329**	110	219	53	53	:	85	26	59	82
1992	**268**	93	175	44	44	:	65	18	46	67
1993	**266**	86	179	44	44	:	70	23	47	65
1994	**315**	109	206	50	50	:	80	21	59	76
1995	**312**	84	228	61	61	:	85	27	58	82
1996	**318**	94	224	72	72	:	78	29	49	74
1997	**327**	90	237	71	71	:	90	31	59	76
1998	**391**	104	287	82	82	:	105	54	51	101
1999	**454**	115	338	66	66	:	123	55	68	150
2000	**479**	99	379	63	63	:	147	56	91	169
2001	**481**	110	370	58	58	:	149	65	84	164
2002	**516**	98	418	61	61	:	155	63	92	201
2003	**511**	100	411	66	66	:	167	62	105	177
2004	**589**	89	500	130	77	53	215	73	141	155
2005	**567**	98	469	152	73	76	180	62	117	137
2006	**596**	83	513	170	74	92	201	62	139	143
2007	**574**	74	500	195	77	112	174	45	129	131
2008	**590**	85	505	198	90	89	165	44	121	142
2009	**567**	96	471	167	82	68	171	30	141	132
Outflow										
1991	**285**	154	130	53	53	:	35	18	17	43
1992	**281**	155	126	38	38	:	31	18	13	57
1993	**266**	149	118	40	40	:	34	17	17	43
1994	**238**	125	113	42	42	:	31	14	17	40
1995	**236**	135	101	38	38	:	29	18	12	34
1996	**264**	156	108	44	44	:	32	17	14	32
1997	**279**	149	131	53	53	:	40	20	20	37
1998	**251**	126	126	49	49	:	33	20	13	44
1999	**291**	139	152	59	59	:	41	29	12	52
2000	**321**	161	160	57	57	:	47	32	15	55
2001	**309**	159	150	51	51	:	51	32	19	49
2002	**363**	186	177	54	54	:	58	42	16	64
2003	**363**	191	172	51	51	:	59	42	17	62
2004	**344**	196	148	43	39	3	53	33	19	52
2005	**361**	186	175	56	40	15	60	37	23	59
2006	**398**	207	192	66	44	22	66	42	24	60
2007	**341**	171	169	69	41	25	58	31	26	43
2008	**427**	173	255	134	54	69	66	35	31	55
2009	**368**	140	228	109	53	52	66	32	34	53
Balance										
1991	**+ 44**	- 44	+ 89	- 1	- 1	:	+ 50	+ 8	+ 42	+ 39
1992	**- 13**	- 62	+ 49	+ 5	+ 5	:	+ 34	-	+ 33	+ 10
1993	**- 1**	- 62	+ 62	+ 4	+ 4	:	+ 36	+ 6	+ 30	+ 22
1994	**+ 77**	- 16	+ 94	+ 9	+ 9	:	+ 49	+ 7	+ 42	+ 36
1995	**+ 76**	- 51	+ 127	+ 23	+ 23	:	+ 56	+ 9	+ 46	+ 48
1996	**+ 55**	- 62	+ 116	+ 28	+ 28	:	+ 47	+ 12	+ 35	+ 41
1997	**+ 48**	- 59	+ 107	+ 18	+ 18	:	+ 50	+ 11	+ 39	+ 38
1998	**+ 140**	- 22	+ 162	+ 33	+ 33	:	+ 72	+ 34	+ 38	+ 57
1999	**+ 163**	- 24	+ 187	+ 8	+ 8	:	+ 82	+ 26	+ 56	+ 98
2000	**+ 158**	- 62	+ 220	+ 6	+ 6	:	+ 100	+ 24	+ 76	+ 114
2001	**+ 171**	- 48	+ 220	+ 7	+ 7	:	+ 98	+ 33	+ 65	+ 115
2002	**+ 153**	- 88	+ 241	+ 7	+ 7	:	+ 97	+ 21	+ 77	+ 137
2003	**+ 148**	- 91	+ 239	+ 15	+ 15	:	+ 109	+ 20	+ 88	+ 115
2004	**+ 245**	- 107	+ 352	+ 87	+ 38	+ 49	+ 162	+ 40	+ 122	+ 104
2005	**+ 206**	- 88	+ 294	+ 96	+ 33	+ 61	+ 120	+ 25	+ 94	+ 78
2006	**+ 198**	- 124	+ 322	+ 104	+ 30	+ 71	+ 135	+ 20	+ 115	+ 83
2007	**+ 233**	- 97	+ 330	+ 127	+ 36	+ 87	+ 116	+ 13	+ 103	+ 88
2008	**+ 163**	- 87	+ 251	+ 63	+ 37	+ 20	+ 100	+ 9	+ 91	+ 87
2009	**+ 198**	- 44	+ 242	+ 58	+ 29	+ 16	+ 105	- 2	+ 107	+ 79

15.7 Long-Term International Migration

United Kingdom
England and Wales Citizenship

Thousands

Year	All citizenships	British	Non-British	European Union[1]	European Union[1] 15	European Union[1] A8	Commonwealth[2] All[2]	Old	New[2]	Other foreign[3]
England and Wales										
Inflow										
1991	**304**	98	207	50	50	:	81	25	57	76
1992	**251**	87	164	42	42	:	60	18	42	63
1993	**249**	80	170	40	40	:	67	22	45	62
1994	**292**	94	199	47	47	:	78	21	58	73
1995	**299**	79	220	59	59	:	83	25	58	79
1996	**300**	86	214	67	67	:	77	29	48	70
1997	**310**	85	226	69	69	:	86	29	57	71
1998	**370**	96	274	76	76	:	101	53	48	97
1999	**424**	101	323	63	63	:	117	51	65	143
2000	**446**	95	351	53	53	:	140	51	89	158
2001	**449**	99	350	56	56	:	139	59	79	156
2002	**485**	92	394	57	57	:	149	61	89	188
2003	**480**	93	387	61	61	:	159	58	101	167
2004	**549**	82	467	122	72	50	199	70	129	146
2005	**523**	87	436	143	66	74	167	56	111	126
2006	**549**	78	471	149	67	78	186	55	131	136
2007	**524**	65	460	175	68	101	163	43	120	122
2008	**528**	67	461	178	75	84	157	40	117	126
2009	**507**	83	424	142	69	58	160	25	135	122
Outflow										
1991	**253**	138	115	45	45	:	32	17	14	39
1992	**248**	135	113	34	34	:	29	17	12	49
1993	**244**	137	107	37	37	:	31	15	16	39
1994	**216**	113	103	36	36	:	29	13	16	38
1995	**216**	124	92	33	33	:	28	17	11	31
1996	**238**	141	97	39	39	:	28	16	12	30
1997	**244**	125	120	48	48	:	37	19	18	35
1998	**223**	107	116	44	44	:	31	19	12	41
1999	**273**	129	144	56	56	:	39	28	11	49
2000	**291**	141	151	55	55	:	44	30	14	52
2001	**282**	143	138	46	46	:	48	30	18	44
2002	**328**	168	159	47	47	:	52	38	14	60
2003	**333**	174	159	47	47	:	54	38	16	59
2004	**311**	175	135	41	37	3	48	31	17	46
2005	**328**	171	157	50	35	15	55	34	21	51
2006	**369**	192	177	60	38	22	62	39	22	55
2007	**307**	152	155	60	38	20	53	29	23	42
2008	**393**	157	235	126	49	65	59	32	27	50
2009	**328**	123	205	98	49	46	61	31	31	46
Balance										
1991	**+ 51**	- 40	+ 91	+ 5	+ 5	:	+ 50	+ 7	+ 42	+ 37
1992	**+ 4**	- 48	+ 51	+ 7	+ 7	:	+ 30	+ 1	+ 29	+ 14
1993	**+ 5**	- 57	+ 62	+ 3	+ 3	:	+ 36	+ 7	+ 30	+ 23
1994	**+ 77**	- 19	+ 96	+ 12	+ 12	:	+ 49	+ 8	+ 42	+ 35
1995	**+ 83**	- 45	+ 129	+ 25	+ 25	:	+ 55	+ 8	+ 47	+ 48
1996	**+ 62**	- 55	+ 117	+ 27	+ 27	:	+ 49	+ 12	+ 37	+ 41
1997	**+ 66**	- 40	+ 106	+ 21	+ 21	:	+ 49	+ 10	+ 39	+ 36
1998	**+ 147**	- 10	+ 157	+ 31	+ 31	:	+ 70	+ 34	+ 36	+ 56
1999	**+ 151**	- 28	+ 179	+ 7	+ 7	:	+ 77	+ 23	+ 54	+ 94
2000	**+ 154**	- 46	+ 200	- 2	- 2	:	+ 96	+ 22	+ 74	+ 105
2001	**+ 167**	- 45	+ 212	+ 10	+ 10	:	+ 90	+ 29	+ 61	+ 112
2002	**+ 158**	- 77	+ 234	+ 9	+ 9	:	+ 97	+ 22	+ 75	+ 128
2003	**+ 147**	- 81	+ 228	+ 14	+ 14	:	+ 105	+ 21	+ 84	+ 108
2004	**+ 238**	- 94	+ 332	+ 81	+ 35	+ 46	+ 151	+ 38	+ 112	+ 100
2005	**+ 195**	- 84	+ 279	+ 92	+ 31	+ 59	+ 112	+ 22	+ 90	+ 75
2006	**+ 180**	- 114	+ 294	+ 89	+ 29	+ 56	+ 124	+ 16	+ 109	+ 81
2007	**+ 217**	- 88	+ 305	+ 115	+ 30	+ 81	+ 110	+ 14	+ 97	+ 80
2008	**+ 135**	- 90	+ 225	+ 52	+ 26	+ 19	+ 97	+ 8	+ 89	+ 76
2009	**+ 179**	- 40	+ 219	+ 44	+ 20	+ 12	+ 99	- 5	+ 104	+ 76

The 2001-2007 estimates were revised in November 2009 following changes to source data. Therefore they may not agree with estimates published prior to this date.

1 Up to and including 2003, European Union estimates are only shown for the EU15 (Austria, Belgium, Denmark, Finland, France, Germany, Greece, the Irish Republic, Italy, Luxembourg, Netherlands, Portugal, Spain and Sweden). Between 2004 and 2006, European Union estimates are shown for the EU25 which includes the above countries plus the A8 group and Cyprus and Malta.

From 2007 European Union estimates are shown for the EU27, which is the EU25 plus Bulgaria and Romania. Unless stated otherwise, British citizens are excluded from all EU groupings and are shown separately.

2 From 2004 onwards, All and New Commonwealth exclude Malta and Cyprus.

3 From 2004 onwards, Other foreign excludes the eight central and eastern European member states that joined the EU in May 2004. From 2007 onwards, Other foreign excludes Bulgaria and Romania which joined the EU in January 2007.

15.8 Long-Term International Migration
United Kingdom
England and Wales
Country of last or next residence

Thousands

Year	All countries	European Union[1]	European Union 15[1]	European Union A8[1]	All Commonwealth countries[2]	Old Commonwealth	Australia	Canada	New Zealand	South Africa
United Kingdom										
Inflow										
1991	329	95	95	:	130	51	28	6	10	7
1992	268	89	89	:	96	38	20	4	8	6
1993	266	75	75	:	103	42	22	5	6	9
1994	315	95	95	:	112	42	19	6	8	9
1995	312	89	89	:	111	41	19	8	9	5
1996	318	98	98	:	112	48	22	7	9	11
1997	327	100	100	:	121	53	22	9	10	13
1998	391	109	109	:	148	84	38	9	16	20
1999	454	96	96	:	174	92	40	6	16	29
2000	479	89	89	:	189	85	35	10	18	22
2001	481	84	84	:	199	99	52	7	17	23
2002	516	90	90	:	188	86	38	8	13	28
2003	511	101	101	:	204	92	40	12	12	28
2004	589	153	98	54	249	96	39	7	13	37
2005	567	186	107	76	219	90	39	7	15	29
2006	596	210	110	93	219	80	40	7	12	21
2007	574	220	100	113	200	65	31	6	10	17
2008	590	224	114	89	196	68	29	10	9	20
2009	567	198	114	67	204	56	29	8	8	11
Outflow										
1991	285	95	95	:	101	68	38	15	9	7
1992	281	86	86	:	87	57	35	7	10	5
1993	266	88	88	:	92	61	38	9	10	4
1994	238	76	76	:	81	51	28	7	12	4
1995	236	76	76	:	81	58	33	7	12	6
1996	264	94	94	:	94	63	36	9	13	5
1997	279	92	92	:	100	65	35	9	13	8
1998	251	85	85	:	83	59	36	7	11	6
1999	291	103	103	:	101	80	53	8	12	7
2000	321	103	103	:	111	86	54	8	17	7
2001	309	95	95	:	114	88	54	10	16	8
2002	363	128	128	:	123	94	53	13	18	10
2003	363	123	123	:	131	104	62	7	21	14
2004	344	125	111	6	125	95	54	12	20	9
2005	361	138	118	17	128	99	51	12	22	13
2006	398	145	118	24	148	114	68	11	21	14
2007	341	131	98	25	127	94	58	8	17	11
2008	427	202	123	66	119	86	55	11	13	7
2009	368	144	88	50	127	88	57	11	14	6
Balance										
1991	+ 44	-	-	:	+ 29	- 17	- 10	- 10	+ 2	+ 1
1992	- 13	+ 3	+ 3	:	+ 9	- 19	- 15	- 3	- 2	+ 1
1993	- 1	- 14	- 14	:	+ 10	- 18	- 15	- 5	- 3	+ 5
1994	+ 77	+ 19	+ 19	:	+ 31	- 9	- 9	- 2	- 4	+ 5
1995	+ 76	+ 13	+ 13	:	+ 30	- 17	- 13	-	- 3	- 1
1996	+ 55	+ 5	+ 5	:	+ 17	- 15	- 14	- 2	- 4	+ 5
1997	+ 48	+ 9	+ 9	:	+ 21	- 12	- 13	-	- 4	+ 5
1998	+ 140	+ 24	+ 24	:	+ 65	+ 25	+ 3	+ 2	+ 5	+ 15
1999	+ 163	- 7	- 7	:	+ 73	+ 12	- 13	- 2	+ 5	+ 22
2000	+ 158	- 14	- 14	:	+ 78	- 1	- 18	+ 2	+ 1	+ 15
2001	+ 171	- 11	- 11	:	+ 85	+ 11	- 1	- 3	+ 1	+ 14
2002	+ 153	- 38	- 38	:	+ 65	- 8	- 15	- 5	- 6	+ 17
2003	+ 148	- 23	- 23	:	+ 74	- 12	- 23	+ 5	- 8	+ 14
2004	+ 245	+ 28	- 14	+ 47	+ 123	+ 2	- 16	- 4	- 7	+ 28
2005	+ 206	+ 48	- 11	+ 59	+ 91	- 9	- 12	- 5	- 8	+ 15
2006	+ 198	+ 65	- 8	+ 69	+ 72	- 34	- 28	- 4	- 9	+ 7
2007	+ 233	+ 88	+ 2	+ 88	+ 73	- 29	- 27	- 2	- 7	+ 6
2008	+ 163	+ 21	- 9	+ 23	+ 76	- 18	- 26	- 1	- 4	+ 14
2009	+ 198	+ 54	+ 26	+ 18	+ 77	- 32	- 27	- 3	- 6	+ 4

15.8 Long-Term International Migration

United Kingdom
England and Wales
Country of last or next residence

Thousands

Year	All countries	European Union[1]	European Union 15[1]	European Union A8[1]	All Commonwealth countries[2]	Old Commonwealth	Australia	Canada	New Zealand	South Africa
England and Wales										
Inflow										
1991	304	89	89	:	120	44	25	5	10	4
1992	251	85	85	:	87	35	19	4	7	5
1993	249	67	67	:	98	40	22	5	6	8
1994	292	86	86	:	108	40	18	6	8	8
1995	299	85	85	:	107	37	18	6	9	4
1996	300	89	89	:	108	45	21	6	9	9
1997	310	99	99	:	116	50	21	7	9	13
1998	370	101	101	:	139	79	36	8	16	20
1999	424	92	92	:	162	83	37	6	13	27
2000	446	77	77	:	182	80	33	6	18	22
2001	449	80	80	:	183	89	45	5	17	22
2002	485	84	84	:	179	82	36	7	12	27
2003	480	93	93	:	192	83	37	9	11	27
2004	549	144	92	51	231	91	37	7	12	35
2005	523	175	98	74	202	80	35	6	12	28
2006	549	190	104	79	203	71	34	7	11	19
2007	524	195	86	102	187	60	29	6	10	15
2008	528	199	95	84	183	61	27	6	8	19
2009	507	168	95	58	188	46	25	7	6	7
Outflow										
1991	253	87	87	:	89	58	34	11	8	5
1992	248	78	78	:	79	53	32	7	9	4
1993	244	82	82	:	85	56	36	8	9	3
1994	216	67	67	:	72	44	24	7	9	4
1995	216	69	69	:	74	54	30	7	11	6
1996	238	85	85	:	83	55	31	6	13	5
1997	244	78	78	:	90	58	32	6	12	8
1998	223	74	74	:	70	49	30	4	9	6
1999	273	96	96	:	95	75	49	7	11	7
2000	291	95	95	:	102	78	49	7	15	7
2001	282	89	89	:	104	79	48	8	15	8
2002	328	113	113	:	110	85	49	11	16	10
2003	333	115	115	:	117	92	56	5	18	13
2004	311	116	104	6	113	86	49	10	18	9
2005	328	126	106	17	116	90	47	10	20	13
2006	369	137	111	24	137	105	62	10	19	14
2007	307	119	90	20	112	83	50	7	15	11
2008	393	186	111	62	111	80	53	9	13	6
2009	328	128	78	43	115	79	50	10	13	6
Balance										
1991	+ 51	+ 2	+ 2	:	+ 32	- 14	- 9	- 6	+ 2	- 1
1992	+ 4	+ 8	+ 8	:	+ 8	- 18	- 13	- 3	- 2	+ 1
1993	+ 5	- 16	- 16	:	+ 14	- 15	- 14	- 3	- 3	+ 5
1994	+ 77	+ 18	+ 18	:	+ 36	- 4	- 6	- 1	- 2	+ 5
1995	+ 83	+ 16	+ 16	:	+ 33	- 17	- 11	- 1	- 2	- 2
1996	+ 62	+ 4	+ 4	:	+ 26	- 10	- 10	-	- 4	+ 4
1997	+ 66	+ 21	+ 21	:	+ 26	- 8	- 10	+ 1	- 3	+ 5
1998	+ 147	+ 26	+ 26	:	+ 69	+ 30	+ 5	+ 3	+ 7	+ 14
1999	+ 151	- 4	- 4	:	+ 68	+ 8	- 12	- 1	+ 2	+ 20
2000	+ 154	- 18	- 18	:	+ 80	+ 2	- 16	-	+ 3	+ 15
2001	+ 167	- 9	- 9	:	+ 79	+ 10	- 3	- 3	+ 1	+ 14
2002	+ 158	- 29	- 29	:	+ 69	- 4	- 13	- 4	- 4	+ 18
2003	+ 147	- 23	- 23	:	+ 75	- 9	- 19	+ 4	- 8	+ 13
2004	+ 238	+ 28	- 12	+ 45	+ 118	+ 5	- 12	- 3	- 6	+ 26
2005	+ 195	+ 49	- 8	+ 57	+ 85	- 10	- 12	- 4	- 8	+ 15
2006	+ 180	+ 52	- 7	+ 55	+ 66	- 34	- 28	- 4	- 8	+ 6
2007	+ 217	+ 76	- 4	+ 82	+ 75	- 23	- 21	- 1	- 5	+ 5
2008	+ 135	+ 12	- 16	+ 22	+ 71	- 20	- 25	- 3	- 4	+ 13
2009	+ 179	+ 41	+ 17	+ 14	+ 73	- 34	- 25	- 3	- 7	+ 1

15.8 Long-Term International Migration
United Kingdom
England and Wales
Country of last or next residence

Thousands

Year	New Commonwealth[2]	Other African Commonwealth	Indian sub-continent	Other Commonwealth[2]	Other foreign countries[3]	Remainder of Europe[3]	United States of America	Rest of America	Middle East	Other
United Kingdom										
Inflow										
1991	79	27	33	19	104	23	24	4	11	42
1992	57	17	23	17	84	21	18	5	8	32
1993	60	18	27	15	88	23	23	4	10	29
1994	71	23	27	20	108	26	29	5	12	36
1995	71	23	28	21	112	23	27	4	13	45
1996	64	19	27	18	109	20	32	4	14	39
1997	67	13	31	23	106	23	23	5	15	39
1998	64	20	27	17	134	32	37	4	13	48
1999	83	24	40	19	183	57	31	7	15	74
2000	104	30	50	24	200	50	24	12	30	85
2001	101	30	51	19	197	37	25	6	31	99
2002	102	41	46	15	237	47	29	7	33	122
2003	113	40	58	15	206	35	30	8	26	107
2004	152	45	90	17	187	18	27	9	29	104
2005	130	32	86	11	162	20	25	7	19	90
2006	139	23	102	14	167	21	23	8	21	93
2007	135	24	95	16	154	17	23	10	23	82
2008	128	31	80	17	171	14	28	12	30	87
2009	148	31	101	16	164	13	31	9	26	84
Outflow										
1991	33	9	10	14	88	12	35	5	14	23
1992	29	8	8	14	108	20	40	5	15	28
1993	31	8	9	14	86	12	36	5	11	22
1994	30	7	7	16	81	18	27	6	13	18
1995	23	5	6	12	80	12	30	3	10	25
1996	31	9	6	15	76	16	26	3	8	23
1997	35	7	9	18	88	21	28	2	13	22
1998	24	5	7	11	84	17	27	4	9	27
1999	21	3	5	14	87	16	33	4	10	24
2000	26	7	8	10	106	22	33	6	15	30
2001	26	5	11	10	100	24	28	4	9	34
2002	29	5	11	13	112	28	37	3	12	31
2003	27	6	11	10	109	35	27	6	7	34
2004	31	6	9	15	93	13	25	7	11	37
2005	29	6	16	7	95	17	24	8	11	34
2006	33	7	17	10	106	17	29	6	16	38
2007	33	5	18	9	83	15	18	7	11	31
2008	34	8	17	9	105	15	23	10	21	36
2009	39	8	23	8	97	11	27	5	15	39
Balance										
1991	+ 46	+ 18	+ 23	+ 5	+ 16	+ 11	− 10	− 1	− 3	+ 19
1992	+ 28	+ 9	+ 15	+ 3	− 25	−	− 22	−	− 7	+ 4
1993	+ 29	+ 10	+ 19	+ 1	+ 3	+ 12	− 13	− 1	− 1	+ 7
1994	+ 41	+ 16	+ 20	+ 4	+ 27	+ 9	+ 2	− 1	− 1	+ 18
1995	+ 47	+ 17	+ 22	+ 8	+ 32	+ 12	− 3	+ 1	+ 3	+ 20
1996	+ 33	+ 10	+ 20	+ 2	+ 33	+ 4	+ 7	+ 1	+ 5	+ 16
1997	+ 32	+ 6	+ 22	+ 5	+ 18	+ 2	− 5	+ 3	+ 2	+ 16
1998	+ 40	+ 14	+ 20	+ 6	+ 50	+ 15	+ 10	−	+ 4	+ 21
1999	+ 62	+ 22	+ 35	+ 5	+ 97	+ 41	− 2	+ 3	+ 5	+ 50
2000	+ 79	+ 23	+ 42	+ 14	+ 94	+ 28	− 10	+ 6	+ 15	+ 55
2001	+ 74	+ 25	+ 40	+ 10	+ 98	+ 13	− 3	+ 2	+ 21	+ 65
2002	+ 73	+ 36	+ 36	+ 2	+ 126	+ 19	− 9	+ 4	+ 21	+ 91
2003	+ 86	+ 34	+ 47	+ 5	+ 97	−	+ 3	+ 2	+ 19	+ 73
2004	+ 122	+ 39	+ 81	+ 2	+ 94	+ 5	+ 2	+ 2	+ 18	+ 68
2005	+ 101	+ 26	+ 70	+ 4	+ 67	+ 3	+ 1	− 1	+ 8	+ 56
2006	+ 106	+ 16	+ 85	+ 4	+ 61	+ 4	− 6	+ 3	+ 6	+ 55
2007	+ 103	+ 19	+ 77	+ 7	+ 72	+ 2	+ 4	+ 2	+ 12	+ 51
2008	+ 94	+ 23	+ 63	+ 8	+ 65	− 2	+ 5	+ 2	+ 9	+ 51
2009	+ 109	+ 23	+ 78	+ 8	+ 67	+ 2	+ 4	+ 4	+ 11	+ 46

15.8 Long-Term International Migration
United Kingdom
England and Wales
Country of last or next residence

Thousands

Year	New Commonwealth[2]	Other African Commonwealth	Indian sub-continent	Other Commonwealth[2]	Other foreign countries[3]	Remainder of Europe[3]	United States of America	Rest of America	Middle East	Other
England and Wales										
Inflow										
1991	76	26	32	18	95	20	21	4	10	39
1992	52	17	22	13	79	20	17	4	8	30
1993	58	17	27	14	84	22	21	3	10	28
1994	68	23	27	18	99	25	22	5	11	35
1995	70	22	27	20	107	23	23	4	13	44
1996	63	19	26	18	102	18	29	4	12	38
1997	66	13	30	23	96	22	20	5	14	35
1998	60	17	27	16	129	31	35	4	12	47
1999	79	23	38	18	170	56	25	7	14	68
2000	102	30	49	24	187	49	22	9	29	78
2001	94	28	48	17	187	35	22	6	29	95
2002	98	39	45	14	222	45	26	7	30	114
2003	108	39	55	15	196	32	29	7	25	102
2004	139	40	85	15	174	17	25	8	27	96
2005	121	30	81	10	147	18	21	7	17	83
2006	132	22	96	14	157	20	22	7	20	88
2007	126	23	88	16	143	15	21	9	21	77
2008	122	29	78	16	147	12	24	10	23	78
2009	143	30	97	16	150	12	26	9	24	79
Outflow										
1991	30	8	9	13	78	10	29	5	13	21
1992	27	7	7	12	91	17	31	5	13	25
1993	29	7	8	13	77	10	31	5	10	21
1994	28	7	6	15	77	16	26	6	12	17
1995	20	5	5	11	73	11	28	3	9	22
1996	27	8	5	14	70	14	25	3	7	21
1997	32	7	9	16	76	20	23	2	11	19
1998	21	4	7	10	78	14	25	4	8	27
1999	20	3	5	12	82	16	31	4	10	22
2000	24	6	8	10	95	21	29	5	12	28
2001	25	5	11	9	89	23	26	4	9	27
2002	24	5	10	10	104	27	34	3	11	30
2003	24	5	10	9	101	33	25	5	5	33
2004	27	6	9	12	82	12	22	7	8	33
2005	26	6	14	7	86	16	19	6	10	33
2006	32	6	16	10	95	16	25	5	15	33
2007	29	5	16	8	77	15	16	7	10	28
2008	31	8	15	8	95	15	20	9	19	31
2009	36	7	22	7	86	11	22	5	14	34
Balance										
1991	+ 45	+ 18	+ 23	+ 5	+ 17	+ 11	- 7	- 1	- 2	+ 17
1992	+ 25	+ 9	+ 15	+ 1	- 12	+ 3	- 14	- 1	- 5	+ 5
1993	+ 29	+ 10	+ 18	+ 1	+ 7	+ 12	- 10	- 1	-	+ 7
1994	+ 40	+ 17	+ 20	+ 3	+ 22	+ 9	- 3	- 1	- 1	+ 18
1995	+ 49	+ 18	+ 22	+ 9	+ 34	+ 13	- 6	+ 1	+ 3	+ 23
1996	+ 36	+ 11	+ 21	+ 3	+ 32	+ 4	+ 4	+ 1	+ 5	+ 18
1997	+ 34	+ 6	+ 21	+ 7	+ 20	+ 2	- 3	+ 2	+ 3	+ 16
1998	+ 39	+ 13	+ 20	+ 7	+ 51	+ 17	+ 10	-	+ 4	+ 20
1999	+ 59	+ 21	+ 33	+ 6	+ 88	+ 40	- 7	+ 3	+ 4	+ 47
2000	+ 79	+ 24	+ 41	+ 14	+ 92	+ 28	- 7	+ 4	+ 17	+ 50
2001	+ 69	+ 23	+ 38	+ 8	+ 98	+ 12	- 4	+ 2	+ 20	+ 68
2002	+ 73	+ 34	+ 35	+ 4	+ 118	+ 19	- 8	+ 4	+ 19	+ 84
2003	+ 84	+ 34	+ 44	+ 6	+ 94	- 1	+ 4	+ 3	+ 19	+ 70
2004	+ 112	+ 34	+ 76	+ 3	+ 92	+ 5	+ 3	+ 1	+ 19	+ 64
2005	+ 95	+ 24	+ 67	+ 3	+ 61	+ 1	+ 2	+ 1	+ 7	+ 50
2006	+ 100	+ 16	+ 80	+ 5	+ 62	+ 4	- 3	+ 1	+ 4	+ 55
2007	+ 97	+ 18	+ 72	+ 8	+ 66	-	+ 5	+ 2	+ 11	+ 49
2008	+ 91	+ 21	+ 62	+ 8	+ 52	- 3	+ 3	-	+ 4	+ 47
2009	+ 107	+ 22	+ 76	+ 9	+ 65	+ 2	+ 4	+ 4	+ 10	+ 45

The 2001-2007 estimates were revised in February 2010 following changes to source data. Therefore they may not agree with estimates published prior to this date.

1 European Union estimates are for the EU15 (Austria, Belgium, Denmark, Finland, France, Germany, Greece, the Irish Republic, Italy, Luxembourg, Netherlands, Portugal, Spain and Sweden) from 1991 - 2003, EU25 (EU15 and A8 groupings plus Malta and Cyprus) from 2004 - 2006, and for the EU27 (EU25 plus Bulgaria and Romania) from 2007. Estimates are also shown separately for the EU15 and the A8 (the Czech Republic, Estonia, Hungary, Latvia, Lithuania, Poland, Slovakia and Slovenia).

2 From 2004 onwards, All, New and Other Commonwealth excludes Malta and Cyprus.

3 From 2004 onwards, Other foreign and Remainder of Europe exclude the eight central and eastern European member states that joined the EU in May 2004.
From 2007 onwards, Other Foreign and Remainder of Europe exclude Bulgaria and Romania which joined the EU in January 2007.

15.9 Grants of settlement by country of nationality[1][2]

United Kingdom

Number of persons

Geographical region and country of nationality		2007	2008	2009	2010[7]	Geographical region and country of nationality		2007	2008	2009	2010[7]
All nationalities	KGFA	124,855	148, 935	194,780	241,190	**Africa (continued)**					
						Uganda	KGHL	530	665	920	1,500
Europe[1]						Zambia	KGHM	495	1,000	1,085	1,200
						Zimbabwe	KGHN	4,280	6,330	7,885	9,850
Accession States						Other Africa	KOSU	3,595	3,630	4,445	8,550
Bulgaria	KGFW	..	..	..	..						
Romania	KGGB	..	..	..	..	**Total Africa**	KGHO	34,050	40,405	47,730	64,875
Total Accession States	EL2O	..	..	..	..	**Asia**					
						Indian sub-continent					
Remainder of Europe						Bangladesh	KGHP	3,330	4,325	7,115	6,765
Albania	I4UK	1,220	1,250	1,185	1,080	India	KGHQ	14,865	22,885	37,260	37,435
Croatia	LQMA	175	175	180	250	Pakistan	KGHR	10,825	12,595	22,715	21,380
Russia	LQLX	1,310	1,255	1,740	1,795						
Serbia & Montenegro[3]	LQMC	1,400	1,520	1,580	2,760	Total Indian sub-continent	KGHS	29,020	39,805	67,090	65,580
Turkey	KGFT	2,545	3,670	3,450	5,580						
Ukraine	LQLY	865	845	1,160	1,370	Middle East					
Other former USSR[4]	LQLZ	855	935	1,025	1,215	Iran	KGHT	1,755	1,470	2,175	8,400
Other Europe	KOSO	290	305	255	290	Iraq	KGHU	7,020	4,310	4,720	7,065
						Isreal	KGHV	370	420	430	510
Remainder of Europe	EL2P	8,660	9,955	10,580	14,340	Jordan	KGHW	150	205	215	255
						Kuwait	KGHX	20	15	5	40
Total Europe[1]	KOSP	8,660	9,955	10,580	14,340	Lebanon	KGHY	450	380	450	615
						Saudi Arabia	KGHZ	30	40	70	45
Americas						Syria	KGIA	200	325	390	515
Argentina	KGGF	155	170	140	130	Yemen	KOSV	325	305	415	425
Barbados	KGGG	80	95	80	130	Other Middle East	KOSW	330	370	515	765
Brazil	KGGH	865	940	1,130	1,280						
Canada	KGGI	1,015	1,190	1,245	1,445	Total Middle East	KGIB	10,655	7,840	9,390	18,630
Chile	KGGJ	80	65	85	85						
Colombia	KGGK	590	655	700	845	**Remainder of Asia**					
Guyana	KGGM	140	350	475	550	Afghanistan	I4UL	3,165	2,915	5,090	5,405
Jamaica	KGGN	2,440	2,750	4,635	4,315	China[5]	KGIC	3,440	6,890	9,370	14,895
Mexico	KGGO	185	240	275	340	Hong Kong[6]	KOSX	785	1,040	690	585
Peru	KGGP	145	150	225	180	Indonesia	KGID	225	230	265	320
Trinidad and Tobago	KGGQ	405	505	535	575	Japan	KGIE	925	915	1,025	1,160
USA	KGGR	3,310	3,340	4,315	4,825	Malaysia	KGIF	1,635	2,190	1,645	1,665
Venezuela	KGGT	150	140	210	185	Nepal	I4UM	4,155	2,920	3,165	6,230
Other Americas	KOSR	885	995	1,065	1,300	Philippines	KGIG	8,485	11,290	10,000	9,935
						Singapore	KGIH	240	240	300	310
Total Americas	KGGU	10,435	11,590	15,120	16,185	South Korea	KOTE	565	740	815	865
						Sri Lanka	KGII	2,440	3,315	4,360	9,420
Africa						Thailand	KGIJ	1,605	1,740	2,655	3,030
Algeria	KGGV	750	905	915	1,525	Other Asia	KOSZ	625	710	885	2,405
Angola	KOSS	1,590	640	410	830						
Dem. Rep. of Congo	KOST	2,055	1,845	1,700	3,340	Total Remainder of Asia	KGIL	28,280	35,140	40,255	56,230
Egypt	KGGW	485	630	940	885						
Ethiopia	KGGX	635	640	625	1,520	**Total Asia**	KGIM	67,955	82,780	116,740	140,445
Ghana	KGGY	2,560	3,885	3,930	4,695						
Kenya	KGHA	1,575	1,890	1,895	2,415	**Oceania**					
Libya	KGHB	185	305	340	450	Australia	KGIN	2,215	2,625	2,890	3,295
Mauritius	KGHC	715	1,035	1,150	1,265	New Zealand	KGIO	1,280	1,335	1,405	1,540
Morocco	KGHD	360	420	525	630	Other Oceania	KOTA	125	80	70	205
Nigeria	KGHE	3,965	5,150	9,220	10,030						
Sierra Leone	KGHF	725	905	875	1,460	**Total Oceania**	KGIP	3,615	4,040	4,365	5,040
Somalia	KGHG	2,845	2,430	2,245	4,900						
South Africa	KGHH	5,805	6,960	7,145	7,530	British Overseas citizens	KGIQ	35	25	60	40
Sudan	KGHI	365	425	680	1,360	Nationality unknown	KGIS	100	135	185	275
Tanzania	KGHJ	360	495	575	625						
Tunisia	KGHK	175	220	225	310	**Grand Total**	KGFA	124,855	148,935	194,780	241,190

1 Excludes European Economic Area and Swiss nationals.

2 Data also excludes dependants of EEA and Swiss nationals in confirmed relationships granted permanent residence.

3 For the consistency of time series Serbia and Montenegro continue to be shown as one entity and includes: Federal Republic of Yugoslvia, Kosovo, Kosovo Resident - UN Issued Travel Documents, Republic of Montenegro, Republic of Serbia, Serbia & Montenegro and Yugoslavia.

4. Other former USSR contains grants for Amenia, Azerbaijan, Belarus, Georgia, Kazakhstan,Kyrgyzstan, Moldova, Tajikistan, Turkmenistan and Uzbekistan.

5 Includes Taiwan.

6 Hong Kong (Special Administrative Region of China) includes British overseas territories citizens and stateless persons from Hong Kong and British Nationals (overseas).

7 Provisional figures.

Source: Home Office: 020 8760 8291

Migrationstatsenquiries@homeoffice.gsi.gov.uk

15.10 Applications received for assylum in the United Kingdom, excluding dependants, by country of nationality - 2000 to 2010

Number of principal applicants

		2000 [2]	2001	2002	2003	2004	2005	2006	2007	2008	2009	2010 [5]
Europe												
Albania	LQME	1,490	1,065	1,150	595	295	175	155	165	160	210	175
Macedonia	PTDW	65	755	310	60	15	5	-	25	-	5	5
Moldova	VQHP	235	425	820	380	170	115	45	30	20	15	5
Russia	ZAEQ	1,000	450	295	280	190	130	115	80	50	65	70
Serbia & Montenegro [3]	ZAFA	6,070	3,230	2,265	815	290	155	70	-	..	:	:
Turkey	KEAW	3,990	3,695	2,835	2,390	1,230	755	425	210	195	185	155
Ukraine	ZAER	770	445	365	300	120	55	50	40	30	50	45
EU Accession States [4]	GH5T	5,985	3,455	4,455	875	370	130	95	25	5	15	15
Other Former USSR	ZAES	1,050	485	615	520	315	265	220	155	180	145	145
Other Europe	ZAEU	2,230	210	130	70	35	30	35	95	95	45	35
Total Europe	**KEAZ**	**22,880**	**14,215**	**13,235**	**6,295**	**3,025**	**1,810**	**1,210**	**825**	**740**	**735**	**650**
Americas												
Colombia	KEBZ	505	365	420	220	120	70	60	30	25	20	15
Ecuador	KYDB	445	255	315	150	35	10	15	10	15	5	5
Jamaica	PTDX	310	525	1,310	965	455	325	215	240	240	200	235
Other Americas	PTDY	155	170	240	230	130	100	95	115	130	140	175
Total Americas	**KECT**	**1,420**	**1,315**	**2,290**	**1,560**	**740**	**505**	**385**	**390**	**405**	**365**	**425**
Africa												
Algeria	KOTB	1,635	1,140	1,060	550	490	255	225	260	345	235	275
Angola	KECU	800	1,015	1,420	850	400	145	95	95	80	45	55
Burundi	PTDZ	620	610	700	650	265	90	35	25	15	20	10
Cameroon	VQHU	355	380	615	505	360	290	260	160	115	90	90
Congo	KEEH	485	540	600	320	150	65	45	25	25	35	30
Dem. Rep. of Congo	KEEH	1,030	1,370	2,215	1,540	1,475	1,080	570	370	335	205	190
Eritrea	PTEC	505	620	1,180	950	1,105	1,760	2,585	1,810	2,255	1,350	710
Ethiopia	KECW	415	610	700	640	540	385	200	90	130	105	95
Gambia	DMMA	50	65	130	95	100	90	110	100	125	210	245
Ghana	KECX	285	190	275	325	355	230	130	120	140	140	165
Ivory Coast	DMLZ	445	275	315	390	280	210	170	100	70	50	45
Kenya	KOTC	455	305	350	220	145	100	95	115	150	100	115
Liberia	C53K	55	115	450	740	405	175	50	40	20	15	15
Libya	GH5U	155	140	200	145	160	125	90	45	45	70	90
Nigeria	KECY	835	810	1,125	1,010	1,090	1,025	790	780	820	680	800
Rwanda	ZAEV	760	530	655	260	75	40	20	15	20	25	20
Sierra Leone	KOTD	1,330	1,940	1,155	380	230	135	125	85	55	80	80
Somalia	KECZ	5,020	6,420	6,540	5,090	2,585	1,760	1,845	1,615	1,345	930	585
Sudan	KEEE	415	390	655	930	1,305	885	670	330	265	215	575
Tanzania	DMMC	60	80	40	30	20	20	15	20	25	35	25
Uganda	KEEG	740	480	715	705	405	205	165	130	130	155	220
Zimbabwe	GRFS	1,010	2,140	7,655	3,295	2,065	1,075	1,650	1,800	3,165	5,600	1,445
Africa	PTEB	615	555	845	895	910	615	480	440	600	765	720
Total Africa	**KEEJ**	**18,185**	**20,840**	**29,710**	**20,605**	**15,045**	**10,885**	**10,500**	**8,630**	**10,270**	**11,160**	**6,600**
Middle East												
Iran	KEEK	5,610	3,420	2,630	2,875	3,455	3,150	2,375	2,210	2,270	1,835	1,865
Iraq	KEEL	7,475	6,680	14,570	4,015	1,695	1,415	945	1,825	1,850	845	380
Syria	GH5V	140	110	70	110	350	330	160	155	155	140	125
Other Middle East	ZAEX	930	810	725	735	730	595	660	755	620	465	355
Total Middle East	**KEGY**	**14,150**	**11,020**	**17,990**	**7,740**	**6,225**	**5,490**	**4,140**	**4,940**	**4,895**	**3,285**	**2,725**
Asia & Oceania												
Afghanistan	DMLY	5,555	8,920	7,205	2,280	1,395	1,580	2,400	2,500	3,505	3,330	1,595
Bangladesh	ZAEY	795	510	720	735	510	425	440	540	455	440	450
China	KEGZ	4,000	2,390	3,675	3,450	2,365	1,730	1,945	2,100	1,400	1,185	995
India	KEIL	2,120	1,850	1,865	2,290	1,405	940	680	510	715	615	525
Pakistan	KEIM	3,165	2,860	2,405	1,915	1,710	1,145	965	1,030	1,230	1,300	1,415
Sri Lanka	KEIN	6,395	5,510	3,130	705	330	395	525	990	1,475	1,115	1,355
Vietnam	VQIB	180	400	840	1,125	755	380	90	165	230	465	450
Other Asia	PTEE	1,025	1,040	910	650	375	320	275	740	535	385	485
Total Asia & Oceania	**KEJO**	**23,230**	**23,480**	**20,755**	**13,150**	**8,850**	**6,915**	**7,315**	**8,570**	**9,550**	**8,830**	**7,275**
Other & Nationality not known	KEJP	450	160	150	55	70	105	55	75	75	110	240
Grand Total	**KEJQ**	**80,315**	**71,025**	**84,130**	**49,405**	**33,960**	**25,710**	**23,610**	**23,430**	**25,930**	**24,485**	**17,915**

Sources: Home Office: 020 7035 4848;
Migrationstatsenquiries@homeoffice.gsi.gov.uk

1 Figures rounded to the nearest 5 (- =0, *+ 1 or 2)
2 May exclude some cases lodged at Local Enforcement Offices between January 1999 and March 2000.
3 Serbia (Inc Kosovo) and Montenegro counted separately under "Other Europe" from 2007.
4 EU Accession States: Bulgaria, Cyprus, Czech Republic, Estonia, Hungary, Latvia, Lithuania, Malta, Poland, Slovakia and Slovenia. Figures between 1998 and 2000 exclude Malta but include Cyprus (Northern part of).
5 Provisional figures.

15.11 Marriages by previous marital status and manner of solemnisation, 1981, 1991, 1999, 2001, 2005-2009

England and Wales

Year of marriage		Total marriages		Civil marriages		Religious marriages	
		Number	Percentage	Number	Percentage	Number	Percentage
2009[1,2]	**Total marriages**	**231,490**	**100.0**	**155,860**	**67.3**	**75,630**	**32.7**
	First marriage for both	150,600	65.1	88,680	38.3	61,920	26.7
	First marriage for one	44,230	19.1	35,460	15.3	8,770	3.8
	Remarriage for both	36,660	15.8	31,720	13.7	4,940	2.1
2008	**Total marriages**	**235,794**	**100.0**	**157,296**	**66.7**	**78,498**	**33.3**
	First marriage for both	149,204	63.3	85,323	36.2	63,881	27.1
	First marriage for one	46,712	19.8	37,238	15.8	9,474	4.0
	Remarriage for both	39,878	16.9	34,735	14.7	5,143	2.2
2007	**Total marriages**	**235,367**	**100.0**	**156,198**	**66.4**	**79,169**	**33.6**
	First marriage for both	146,216	62.1	82,351	35.0	63,865	27.1
	First marriage for one	47,669	20.3	37,941	16.1	9,728	4.1
	Remarriage for both	41,482	17.6	35,906	15.3	5,576	2.4
2006	**Total marriages**	**239,454**	**100.0**	**158,350**	**66.1**	**81,104**	**33.9**
	First marriage for both	145,995	61.0	81,288	33.9	64,707	27.0
	First marriage for one	50,061	20.9	39,549	16.5	10,512	4.4
	Remarriage for both	43,398	18.1	37,513	15.7	5,885	2.5
2005	**Total marriages**	**247,805**	**100.0**	**162,169**	**65.4**	**85,636**	**34.6**
	First marriage for both	148,405	59.9	80,941	32.7	67,464	27.2
	First marriage for one	53,108	21.4	41,631	16.8	11,477	4.6
	Remarriage for both	46,292	18.7	39,597	16.0	6,695	2.7
2001	**Total marriages**	**249,227**	**100.0**	**160,238**	**64.3**	**88,989**	**35.7**
	First marriage for both	148,642	59.6	77,048	30.9	71,594	28.7
	First marriage for one	55,943	22.4	44,601	17.9	11,342	4.6
	Remarriage for both	44,642	17.9	38,589	15.5	6,053	2.4
1999	**Total marriages**	**263,515**	**100.0**	**162,679**	**61.7**	**100,836**	**38.3**
	First marriage for both	155,027	58.8	74,244	28.2	80,783	30.7
	First marriage for one	59,540	22.6	46,435	17.6	13,105	5.0
	Remarriage for both	48,948	18.6	42,000	15.9	6,948	2.6
1991	**Total marriages**	**306,756**	**100.0**	**151,333**	**49.3**	**155,423**	**50.7**
	First marriage for both	192,238	62.7	64,614	21.1	127,624	41.6
	First marriage for one	63,159	20.6	44,643	14.6	18,516	6.0
	Remarriage for both	51,359	16.7	42,076	13.7	9,283	3.0
1981	**Total marriages**	**351,973**	**100.0**	**172,514**	**49.0**	**179,459**	**51.0**
	First marriage for both	227,713	64.7	71,530	20.3	156,183	44.4
	First marriage for one	67,048	19.0	51,628	14.7	15,420	4.4
	Remarriage for both	57,212	16.3	49,356	14.0	7,856	2.2

Source: Office for National Statistics

1. Figures for 2009 may not add precisely due to rounding.
2 Provisional

Note:
Percentages may not sum due to rounding.

15.12(a) Duration of marriage at divorce by age of wife at marriage
England and Wales

Numbers

Year of divorce	Age of wife at marriage	All durations	Duration of marriage (completed years)								
			0-2 years	0 years	1 year	2 years	3 years	4 years	5-9 years	5 years	6 years
2009	All ages	113,949	6,270	21	1,951	4,298	5,884	6,947	31,290	7,561	6,864
	Under 20	10,529	267	1	60	206	293	371	1,943	478	439
	20-24	39,231	1,540	1	472	1,067	1,516	1,813	8,350	2,065	1,889
	25-29	31,400	1,808	8	572	1,228	1,715	1,986	8,994	2,106	1,898
	30-44	29,021	2,184	7	683	1,494	1,981	2,389	10,610	2,554	2,307
	45 and over	3,768	471	4	164	303	379	388	1,393	358	331
2008	All ages	121,708	6,937	27	2,103	4,807	6,776	7,929	31,803	7,369	6,714
	Under 20	11,657	319	1	78	240	365	500	1,948	478	407
	20-24	42,578	1,685	10	463	1,212	1,798	2,103	8,401	2,043	1,879
	25-29	33,050	2,044	7	621	1,416	1,875	2,148	9,287	1,985	1,863
	30-44	30,642	2,379	7	741	1,631	2,349	2,751	10,819	2,512	2,304
	45 and over	3,781	510	2	200	308	389	427	1,348	351	261
2007	All ages	128,131	8,195	38	2,558	5,599	7,206	7,574	32,419	7,164	7,046
	Under 20	13,224	411	1	120	290	417	487	2,053	430	470
	20-24	45,806	2,039	7	623	1,409	1,905	1,977	8,481	1,928	1,814
	25-29	34,564	2,234	13	668	1,553	1,990	2,115	9,987	2,099	2,106
	30-44	30,808	2,942	11	929	2,002	2,521	2,591	10,617	2,403	2,366
	45 and over	3,729	569	6	218	345	373	404	1,281	304	290
2006	All ages	132,140	8,763	37	2,793	5,933	7,226	7,376	33,736	7,398	7,310
	Under 20	14,441	503	2	157	344	376	447	2,232	474	506
	20-24	48,396	2,240	9	668	1,563	1,975	1,997	8,954	1,967	1,901
	25-29	35,054	2,381	13	796	1,572	2,052	2,172	10,416	2,182	2,181
	30-44	30,613	3,087	6	966	2,115	2,441	2,424	10,858	2,473	2,437
	45 and over	3,636	552	7	206	339	382	336	1,276	302	285
2005	All ages	141,322	9,573	49	3,181	6,343	7,520	8,175	36,064	7,920	7,697
	Under 20	16,473	537	2	148	387	515	579	2,389	576	544
	20-24	52,884	2,469	15	783	1,671	2,025	2,203	9,961	2,083	2,016
	25-29	36,992	2,545	9	845	1,691	2,081	2,507	11,296	2,367	2,431
	30-44	31,213	3,413	17	1,171	2,225	2,540	2,554	11,025	2,545	2,406
	45 and over	3,760	609	6	234	369	359	332	1,393	349	300
2004	All ages	152,923	10,101	42	3,345	6,714	8,319	8,894	39,681	8,840	8,375
	Under 20	18,655	626	3	201	422	557	662	2,626	667	581
	20-24	59,356	2662	7	854	1,801	2,361	2,494	11,818	2,477	2,359
	25-29	39,459	2871	8	947	1,916	2,480	2,642	12,426	2,674	2,593
	30-44	31,631	3,353	15	1,122	2,216	2,542	2,724	11,356	2,679	2,515
	45 and over	3,822	589	9	221	359	379	372	1,455	343	327
2003	All ages	153,065	10,286	42	3,283	6,961	8,276	8,882	40,497	8,968	8,639
	Under 20	20,008	694	-	198	496	591	662	2,644	614	562
	20-24	60,883	2735	11	825	1,899	2,352	2,587	12,944	2,636	2,564
	25-29	38,628	2,954	9	903	2,042	2,554	2,715	12,663	2,778	2,716
	30-44	29,873	3,304	10	1,131	2,163	2,444	2,554	10,865	2,600	2,468
	45 and over	3,673	599	12	226	361	335	364	1,381	340	329
2002	All ages	147,735	10,239	31	3,326	6,882	8,325	8,780	39,730	8,823	8,370
	Under 20	19,828	684	3	184	497	623	597	2,589	591	541
	20-24	60,353	2,833	6	878	1,949	2,411	2,696	13,727	2,739	2,754
	25-29	36,387	2,903	8	906	1,989	2,581	2,778	12,269	2,795	2,602
	30-44	27,803	3,250	7	1,132	2,111	2,366	2,387	9,865	2,374	2,171
	45 and over	3,364	569	7	226	336	344	322	1,280	324	302
2001	All ages	143,818	10,190	36	3,413	6,741	8,206	8,591	39,079	8,632	8,329
	Under 20	20,218	738	3	225	510	634	560	2,676	574	498
	20-24	60,211	2,809	12	870	1,927	2,472	2,711	14,418	2,900	2,938
	25-29	34,759	3,041	10	973	2,058	2,571	2,737	11,728	2,648	2,600
	30-44	25,405	3,054	6	1,116	1,932	2,177	2,246	9,059	2,202	2,028
	45 and over	3,225	548	5	229	314	352	337	1,198	308	265

15.12(a) Duration of marriage at divorce by age of wife at marriage
England and Wales

Numbers

Year of divorce	Age of wife at marriage	Duration of marriage (completed years)								Not stated	Median duration
		7 years	8 years	9 years	10-14 years	15-19 years	20-24 years	25-29 years	30 years and over		
2009	**All ages**	**5,968**	**5,634**	**5,263**	**20,591**	**15,390**	**11,855**	**7,490**	**8,225**	7	**11.4**
	Under 20	355	357	314	1,177	1,092	1,337	1,484	2,565	-	..
	20-24	1,629	1,466	1,301	5,909	5,944	5,964	3,956	4,235	4	..
	25-29	1,679	1,648	1,663	6,704	4,926	2,983	1,299	985	-	..
	30-44	2,068	1,919	1,762	6,090	3,128	1,494	713	429	3	..
	45 and over	237	244	223	711	300	77	38	11	-	..
2008	**All ages**	**6,365**	**6,034**	**5,321**	**21,561**	**16,945**	**12,706**	**8,136**	**8,907**	8	**11.5**
	Under 20	358	363	342	1,174	1,274	1,526	1,749	2,800	2	..
	20-24	1,619	1,528	1332	6,315	6,881	6,511	4,247	4,632	5	..
	25-29	1,880	1,862	1697	7,075	5,204	2,945	1,389	1,082	1	..
	30-44	2,228	2,032	1,743	6,324	3,295	1,620	722	383	-	..
	45 and over	280	249	207	673	291	104	29	10	-	..
2007	**All ages**	**6,560**	**6,072**	**5,577**	**23,427**	**18,203**	**13,117**	**8,701**	**9,282**	7	**11.7**
	Under 20	423	395	335	1,240	1,542	1,929	2,099	3,045	1	..
	20-24	1,650	1,607	1482	7,397	7,930	6,757	4,498	4,820	2	..
	25-29	2,021	1,953	1808	7,777	5,240	2,802	1,377	1,039	3	..
	30-44	2,203	1,890	1755	6,343	3,219	1,526	686	362	1	..
	45 and over	263	227	197	670	272	103	41	16	-	..
2006	**All ages**	**6,769**	**6,249**	**6,010**	**24,606**	**18,735**	**13,472**	**8,764**	**9,449**	13	**11.6**
	Under 20	490	397	365	1,491	1,831	2,191	2,241	3,128	1	..
	20-24	1,751	1,681	1,654	8,443	8,470	6,949	4,415	4,947	6	..
	25-29	2,159	2,004	1,890	7,708	5,157	2,745	1,365	1,053	5	..
	30-44	2,107	1,939	1,902	6,263	3,034	1,483	717	305	1	..
	45 and over	262	228	199	701	243	104	26	16	-	..
2005	**All ages**	**7,343**	**6,801**	**6,303**	**26,310**	**20,310**	**14,268**	**9,241**	**9,852**	9	**11.6**
	Under 20	478	429	362	1,722	2,299	2,605	2,571	3,255	1	..
	20-24	2,007	1,920	1,935	9,570	9,450	7,368	4,636	5,200	2	..
	25-29	2,291	2,173	2,034	8,364	5,146	2,683	1,310	1,058	2	..
	30-44	2,266	2,040	1,768	5,965	3,161	1,526	699	326	4	..
	45 and over	301	239	204	689	254	86	25	13	-	..
2004	**All ages**	**7,900**	**7,683**	**6,883**	**28,984**	**21,515**	**15,431**	**9,705**	**10,293**	-	**11.5**
	Under 20	498	485	395	2133	2737	3103	2804	3407	-	..
	20-24	2,324	2,389	2,269	11471	10355	7893	4792	5510	-	..
	25-29	2,517	2,436	2,206	8671	5082	2823	1427	1037	-	..
	30-44	2,274	2,111	1,777	6064	3093	1539	639	321	-	..
	45 and over	287	262	236	645	248	73	43	18	-	..
2003	**All ages**	**8,228**	**7,686**	**6,976**	**29,751**	**20,863**	**14,974**	**9,627**	**9,907**	2	**11.3**
	Under 20	551	495	422	2,613	2,911	3,559	2,985	3,349	-	..
	20-24	2,569	2,622	2,553	12,281	10,413	7,534	4,708	5,327	2	..
	25-29	2,594	2,361	2,214	8,537	4,508	2,409	1,333	955	-	..
	30-44	2,232	1,965	1,600	5,679	2,811	1,391	564	261	-	..
	45 and over	282	243	187	641	220	81	37	15	-	..
2002	**All ages**	**8,020**	**7,564**	**6,953**	**28,592**	**19,784**	**13,989**	**9,106**	**9,190**	-	**11.1**
	Under 20	481	517	459	2,774	3,160	3,439	2,891	3,071	-	..
	20-24	2,795	2,770	2,669	12,516	9,810	6,845	4,480	5,035	-	..
	25-29	2,514	2,265	2,093	7,524	4,032	2,279	1,175	846	-	..
	30-44	1,985	1,796	1,539	5,249	2,577	1,355	523	231	-	..
	45 and over	245	216	193	529	205	71	37	7	-	..
2001	**All ages**	**7,909**	**7,463**	**6,746**	**28,176**	**18,603**	**13,318**	**8,986**	**8,667**	2	**10.9**
	Under 20	524	513	567	2,999	3,309	3,607	2,830	2,865	-	..
	20-24	2,925	2,943	2,712	12,875	9,251	6,432	4,505	4,736	2	..
	25-29	2,398	2,183	1,899	7,075	3,587	2,052	1,158	810	-	..
	30-44	1,810	1,612	1,407	4,721	2,270	1,157	475	246	-	..
	45 and over	252	212	161	506	186	70	18	10	-	..

15.12(b) Duration of marriage at divorce by age of wife at marriage

England and Wales

Numbers

Year of divorce	Age of wife at marriage	All durations	Duration of marriage (completed years)								
			0-2 years	0 years	1 year	2 years	3 years	4 years	5-9 years	5 years	6 years
2000	All ages	141,135	10,438	52	3,494	6,892	8,296	8,740	38,206	8,506	8,148
	Under 20	20,930	846	2	284	560	598	575	2,937	571	594
	20-24	59,874	2,954	8	925	2,021	2,631	2,978	14,663	3,014	3,021
	25-29	33,282	3,095	17	1,038	2,040	2,567	2,675	11,443	2,625	2,510
	30-44	23,912	2,971	14	1,012	1,945	2,159	2,179	8,082	2,032	1,779
	45 and over	3,137	572	11	235	326	341	333	1,081	264	244
1999	All ages	144,556	11,350	49	3,813	7,488	8,833	9,124	39,676	8,958	8,521
	Under 20	22,486	868	5	268	595	658	625	3,367	604	691
	20-24	62,853	3,445	15	1,125	2,305	2,965	3,366	16,221	3,440	3,404
	25-29	32,867	3,182	6	1,074	2,102	2,710	2,745	11,170	2,670	2,432
	30-44	23,270	3,197	14	1,082	2,101	2,147	2,076	7,898	1,982	1,735
	45 and over	3,080	658	9	264	385	353	312	1,020	262	259
1998	All ages	145,214	12,247	68	4,191	7,988	9,270	9,619	40,239	9,180	8,497
	Under 20	24,276	976	7	327	642	704	785	3,858	753	762
	20-24	64,453	4,000	16	1,303	2,681	3,475	3,737	17,413	3,800	3,586
	25-29	31,533	3,510	21	1,144	2,345	2,697	2,787	10,518	2,569	2,289
	30-44	22,076	3,162	18	1,140	2,004	2,062	2,027	7,478	1,801	1,631
	45 and over	2,876	599	6	277	316	332	283	972	257	229
1997	All ages	146,689	12,596	61	4,369	8,166	9,410	9,761	41,260	9,326	8,580
	Under 20	25,579	1,024	7	359	658	757	809	4,424	857	851
	20-24	66,167	4,412	10	1,449	2,953	3,773	4,114	18,226	3,917	3,736
	25-29	31,022	3,576	13	1,213	2,350	2,706	2,712	10,417	2,591	2,263
	30-44	21,017	2,958	20	1,073	1,865	1,879	1,818	7,241	1,719	1,513
	45 and over	2,904	626	11	275	340	295	308	952	242	217
1996	All ages	157,107	14,021	76	5,010	8,935	10,467	10,436	44,609	10,042	9,850
	Under 20	29,927	1,178	4	383	791	970	1,022	5,543	1,128	1,165
	20-24	71,123	5,289	20	1,744	3,525	4,236	4,392	20,221	4,408	4,417
	25-29	31,396	3,872	23	1,384	2,465	2,901	2,778	10,373	2,557	2,359
	30-44	21,640	3,018	15	1,197	1,806	2,008	1,919	7,480	1,702	1,691
	45 and over	3,021	664	14	302	348	352	325	992	247	218
1995	All ages	155,499	14,015	95	4,944	8,976	10,209	10,283	44,304	10,447	9,812
	Under 20	31,322	1,374	8	418	948	1,090	1,158	5,894	1,224	1,180
	20-24	71,360	5,634	28	1,948	3,658	4,375	4,477	20,360	4,748	4,457
	25-29	29,441	3,568	17	1,257	2,294	2,591	2,576	9,892	2,523	2,255
	30-44	20,506	2,817	26	1,034	1,757	1,842	1,792	7,208	1,684	1,707
	45 and over	2,870	622	16	287	319	311	280	950	268	213
1994	All ages	158,175	13,841	81	4,895	8,865	10,400	11,454	44,769	10,836	9,896
	Under 20	34,069	1,582	6	518	1,058	1,297	1,468	6,805	1,404	1,418
	20-24	73,291	5,689	19	1,956	3,714	4,518	5,106	21,102	4,975	4,681
	25-29	28,360	3,408	24	1,208	2,176	2,520	2,698	9,187	2,414	2,077
	30-44	19,686	2,574	17	959	1,598	1,749	1,838	6,807	1,806	1,523
	45 and over	2,769	588	15	254	319	316	344	868	237	197
1993	All ages	165,018	14,096	74	4,708	9,314	11,357	11,799	46,536	11,137	10,352
	Under 20	38,811	1,867	9	583	1,275	1,668	1,653	8,196	1,713	1,685
	20-24	76,853	6,163	12	2,045	4,106	5,066	5,470	21,731	5,194	4,901
	25-29	27,178	3,051	27	953	2,071	2,439	2,506	8,777	2,282	1,970
	30-44	19,357	2,419	18	878	1,523	1,832	1,827	6,920	1,722	1,562
	45 and over	2,819	596	8	249	339	352	343	912	226	234
1992	All ages	160,385	14,247	62	4,630	9,555	11,299	11,352	43,745	10,417	9,459
	Under 20	39,734	1,990	3	590	1,397	1,736	1,739	8,544	1,798	1,697
	20-24	74,701	6,208	19	1,949	4,240	5,159	5,510	20,464	4,952	4,469
	25-29	25,173	2,992	11	1,010	1,971	2,241	2,213	7,759	1,952	1,796
	30-44	18,011	2,430	16	832	1,582	1,822	1,631	6,054	1,476	1,275
	45 and over	2,766	627	13	249	365	341	259	924	239	222
1991	All ages	158,745	15,332	62	5,239	10,031	11,321	11,126	42,735	10,049	9,345
	Under 20	40,594	2,387	1	780	1,606	1,894	2,014	9,143	1,857	1,805
	20-24	74,050	6,863	17	2,271	4,575	5,308	5,292	19,926	4,808	4,493
	25-29	24,025	2,942	12	1,003	1,927	2,162	2,014	7,048	1,776	1,571
	30-44	17,359	2,486	16	892	1,578	1,640	1,556	5,765	1,390	1,269
	45 and over	2,717	654	16	293	345	317	250	853	218	207
1990	All ages	153,386	15,122	64	5,142	9,916	10,863	10,314	42,061	9,883	9,025
	Under 20	41,116	2,558	6	788	1,764	1,993	1,961	9,790	2,030	1,917
	20-24	71,489	6,919	20	2,312	4,587	5,115	4,981	19,248	4,702	4,265
	25-29	21,701	2,637	11	906	1,720	1,898	1,721	6,567	1,627	1,462
	30-44	16,387	2,378	16	866	1,496	1,533	1,386	5,608	1,297	1,214
	45 and over	2,693	630	11	270	349	324	265	848	227	167

15.12(b) Duration of marriage at divorce by age of wife at marriage

England and Wales Numbers

Year of divorce	Age of wife at marriage	Duration of marriage (completed years)								Not stated	Median duration
		7 years	8 years	9 years	10-14 years	15-19 years	20-24 years	25-29 years	30 years and over		
2000	All ages	7,778	7,183	6,591	27,459	17,870	12,907	9,017	8,196	6	10.7
	Under 20	566	604	602	3,230	3,413	3,556	3,003	2,770	2	..
	20-24	2,959	2,909	2,760	12,720	8,839	6,142	4,479	4,465	3	..
	25-29	2,356	2,046	1,906	6,521	3,192	1,995	1,078	715	1	..
	30-44	1,665	1,429	1,177	4,461	2,250	1,145	433	232	-	..
	45 and over	232	195	146	527	176	69	24	14	-	..
1999	All ages	7,861	7,338	6,998	27,384	18,072	12,888	9,349	7,871	9	10.5
	Under 20	620	722	730	3,532	3,886	3,874	3,040	2,633	3	..
	20-24	3,217	3,111	3,049	12,984	8,729	5,960	4,871	4,308	4	..
	25-29	2,205	2,044	1,819	6,209	3,127	1,950	1,053	720	1	..
	30-44	1,622	1,312	1,247	4,191	2,156	1,037	362	205	1	..
	45 and over	197	149	153	468	174	67	23	5	-	..
1998	All ages	7,785	7,757	7,020	26,698	17,934	12,675	9,056	7,468	8	10.2
	Under 20	740	823	780	3,986	4,364	4,020	3,075	2,508	-	..
	20-24	3,435	3,413	3,179	12,757	8,469	5,833	4,738	4,028	3	..
	25-29	2,026	1,955	1,679	5,599	2,955	1,851	896	716	4	..
	30-44	1,398	1,419	1,229	3,907	1,993	911	325	210	1	..
	45 and over	186	147	153	449	153	60	22	6	-	..
1997	All ages	8,324	7,935	7,095	26,215	18,027	13,148	9,058	7,202	12	10.0
	Under 20	923	894	899	4,197	4,648	4,284	2,957	2,476	3	..
	20-24	3,750	3,540	3,283	12,447	8,298	6,082	4,971	3,837	7	..
	25-29	2,065	1,918	1,580	5,353	2,881	1,860	834	681	2	..
	30-44	1,409	1,400	1,200	3,776	2,006	869	274	196	-	..
	45 and over	177	183	133	442	194	53	22	12	-	..
1996	All ages	9,092	8,171	7,454	27,332	19,321	14,236	9,511	7,165	9	9.9
	Under 20	1,120	1,116	1,014	5,084	5,507	4,867	3,294	2,461	1	..
	20-24	4,029	3,776	3,591	12,921	8,558	6,549	5,112	3,841	4	..
	25-29	2,168	1,734	1,555	5,119	2,998	1,882	805	665	3	..
	30-44	1,549	1,375	1,163	3,765	2,087	887	285	190	1	..
	45 and over	226	170	131	443	171	51	15	8	-	..
1995	All ages	8,822	7,965	7,258	27,365	18,943	14,483	8,925	6,962	10	9.6
	Under 20	1,161	1,176	1,153	5,768	5,604	5,009	3,072	2,350	3	..
	20-24	4,051	3,668	3,436	12,640	8,476	6,815	4,860	3,718	5	..
	25-29	2,023	1,664	1,427	4,781	2,832	1,796	711	692	2	..
	30-44	1,426	1,275	1,116	3,727	1,868	795	268	189	-	..
	45 and over	161	182	126	449	163	68	14	13	-	..
1994	All ages	8,881	7,900	7,256	28,073	19,200	14,891	8,801	6,739	7	9.8
	Under 20	1,403	1,327	1,253	6,458	6,077	5,101	3,050	2,230	1	14.6
	20-24	4,222	3,727	3497	12,808	8,351	7,303	4,777	3,633	4	10.1
	25-29	1,774	1,559	1,363	4,733	2,804	1,663	675	670	2	7.6
	30-44	1,315	1,144	1,019	3,693	1,785	761	278	201	-	7.1
	45 and over	167	143	124	381	183	63	21	5	-	5.5
1993	All ages	9,029	8,475	7,543	30,156	20,233	15,503	8,426	6,907	5	9.8
	Under 20	1,593	1,621	1,584	7,812	6,830	5,452	3,065	2,267	1	13.9
	20-24	4,311	3,892	3,433	13,538	8,796	7,909	4,434	3,743	3	10.0
	25-29	1,624	1,627	1,274	4,753	2,808	1,497	671	675	1	7.8
	30-44	1,328	1,177	1,131	3,667	1,648	588	242	214	-	7.0
	45 and over	173	158	121	386	151	57	14	8	-	5.4
1992	All ages	8,708	7,914	7,247	29,285	20,160	15,488	8,098	6,704	7	9.9
	Under 20	1,708	1,670	1,671	8,192	6,920	5,395	3,090	2,125	3	13.5
	20-24	4,090	3,694	3,259	12,837	8,721	8,038	4,067	3,694	3	10.0
	25-29	1,513	1,340	1,158	4,401	2,791	1,448	633	694	1	7.9
	30-44	1,219	1,059	1,025	3,477	1,552	570	289	186	-	6.9
	45 and over	178	151	134	378	176	37	19	5	-	5.6
1991	All ages	8,423	7,797	7,121	28,791	20,127	14,957	7,845	6,492	19	9.8
	Under 20	1,808	1,883	1,790	8,295	6,988	5,112	2,825	1,930	6	12.7
	20-24	3,902	3,506	3,217	12,304	8,775	7,924	4,066	3,581	11	9.9
	25-29	1,438	1,228	1,035	4,417	2,686	1,318	685	751	2	8.1
	30-44	1,118	1,033	955	3,355	1,521	553	261	222	-	7.0
	45 and over	157	147	124	420	157	50	8	8	-	5.7
1990	All ages	8,289	7,634	7,230	27,310	19,819	14,186	7,479	6,216	16	9.8
	Under 20	1,950	1,933	1,960	8,313	7,122	4,974	2,648	1,755	2	12.4
	20-24	3,767	3,380	3,134	11,542	8,786	7,500	3,897	3,490	11	9.8
	25-29	1,316	1,144	1,018	3,893	2,416	1,156	639	772	2	8.2
	30-44	1,101	1,016	980	3,163	1,330	514	283	191	1	7.0
	45 and over	155	161	138	399	165	42	12	8	-	6.0

15.12(c) Duration of marriage at divorce by age of wife at marriage

England and Wales

Continued

Year of divorce	Age of wife at marriage	All durations	Duration of marriage (completed years)								
			0-2 years	0 years	1 year	2 years	3 years	4 years	5-9 years	5 years	6 years
1989	All ages	150,872	15,231	56	5,420	9,755	10,372	10,116	42,108	9,569	8,928
	Under 20	42,612	2,915	11	980	1,924	2,059	2,144	10,798	2,209	2,199
	20-24	69,424	6,956	18	2,424	4,514	4,886	4,783	18,725	4,377	4,042
	25-29	20,369	2,468	8	887	1,573	1,651	1,580	6,189	1,476	1,360
	30-44	15,774	2,272	12	853	1,407	1,487	1,338	5,535	1,286	1,118
	45 and over	2,693	620	7	276	337	289	271	861	221	209
1988	All ages	152,633	15,003	88	5,403	9,512	10,213	10,376	42,617	9,730	9,080
	Under 20	44,693	3,151	7	1,055	2,089	2,296	2,472	11,676	2,374	2,424
	20-24	69,489	6,676	31	2,339	4,306	4,751	4,777	18,310	4,378	3,936
	25-29	20,267	2,298	16	854	1,428	1,525	1,543	6,167	1,464	1,331
	30-44	15,472	2,207	17	852	1,338	1,328	1,368	5,584	1,302	1,182
	45 and over	2,712	671	17	303	351	313	216	880	212	207
1987	All ages	151,007	14,549	..	..	..	10,248	10,626	43,150	10,262	9,626
	Under 20	46,097	3,387	..	..	..	2,554	2,755	12,428	2,823	2,628
	20-24	68,345	6,393	..	..	..	4,643	4,751	18,180	4,461	4,190
	25-29	19,049	2,045	..	..	..	1,449	1,449	6,088	1,420	1,353
	30-44	14,802	2,085	..	..	..	1,293	1,405	5,549	1,327	1,242
	45 and over	2,714	639	..	..	..	309	266	905	231	213
1986	All ages	153,903	14,596	..	..	..	11,683	12,358	42,187	10,656	9,329
	Under 20	48,621	3,735	..	..	..	3,239	3,618	12,978	3,204	2,863
	20-24	68,387	6,216	..	..	..	5,020	5,257	17,059	4,446	3,713
	25-29	18,990	1,955	..	..	..	1,504	1,561	5,845	1,369	1,296
	30-44	15,064	2,068	..	..	..	1,553	1,583	5,369	1,387	1,248
	45 and over	2,841	622	..	..	..	367	339	936	250	209
1985	All ages	160,300	14,662	..	..	..	16,929	14,185	41,537	10,942	9,352
	Under 20	52,858	4,034	..	..	..	5,320	4,481	13,455	3,471	3,008
	20-24	69,663	5,927	..	..	..	6,983	5,735	16,294	4,374	3,607
	25-29	18,689	1,748	..	..	..	1,894	1,720	5,620	1,408	1,269
	30-44	15,765	2,160	..	..	..	2,187	1,827	5,181	1,403	1,249
	45 and over	3,325	793	..	..	..	545	422	987	286	219
1984	All ages	144,501	1,336	..	..	..	15,296	13,868	40,866	10,434	8,830
	Under 20	49,610	304	..	..	..	5,084	4,577	13,821	3,452	2,994
	20-24	62,642	427	..	..	..	6,107	5,443	15,716	4,020	3,371
	25-29	16,811	183	..	..	..	1,707	1,737	5,477	1,329	1,118
	30-44	12,944	289	..	..	..	1,921	1,739	4,895	1,362	1,126
	45 and over	2,494	133	..	..	..	477	372	957	271	221
1983	All ages	147,479	1,528	..	..	..	15,706	13,863	42,041	10,413	8,785
	Under 20	52,547	389	..	..	..	5,529	4,866	15,084	3,693	3,129
	20-24	63,382	477	..	..	..	6,054	5,228	15,887	3,942	3,294
	25-29	16,351	196	..	..	..	1,723	1,654	5,362	1,270	1,130
	30-44	12,675	326	..	..	..	1,904	1,725	4,726	1,253	1,027
	45 and over	2,524	140	..	..	..	496	390	982	255	205
1982	All ages	146,698	1,712	..	..	..	15,190	13,360	42,499	10,126	8,984
	Under 20	54,067	484	..	..	..	5,580	5,003	15,957	3,720	3,283
	20-24	62,955	491	..	..	..	5,746	4,874	16,225	3,862	3,444
	25-29	15,714	247	..	..	..	1,671	1,581	5,188	1,235	1,116
	30-44	11,604	325	..	..	..	1,707	1,556	4,248	1,076	933
	45 and over	2,358	165	..	..	..	486	346	881	233	208
1981	All ages	145,713	1,859	..	..	..	14,318	12,463	43,808	10,413	9,511
	Under 20	54,424	550	..	..	..	5,489	4,889	16,870	4,042	3,560
	20-24	63,034	506	..	..	..	5,343	4,579	16,951	3,874	3,630
	25-29	15,281	264	..	..	..	1,553	1,382	5,227	1,281	1,168
	30-44	10,661	354	..	..	..	1,517	1,283	3,855	980	939
	45 and over	2,313	185	..	..	..	416	330	905	236	214
1980	All ages	148,301	1,576	..	..	..	13,645	13,296	45,152	10,918	9,745
	Under 20	55,946	433	..	..	..	5,378	5,378	18,047	4,348	3,870
	20-24	64,786	464	..	..	..	5,154	4,845	17,726	4,069	3,765
	25-29	15,060	198	..	..	..	1,456	1,506	4,824	1,210	1,109
	30-44	10,203	314	..	..	..	1,260	1,224	3,693	1,036	800
	45 and over	2,306	167	..	..	..	397	343	862	255	201

15.12(c) Duration of marriage at divorce by age of wife at marriage
England and Wales
Continued

Year of divorce	Age of wife at marriage	Duration of marriage (completed years)									Median duration
		7 years	8 years	9 years	10-14 years	15-19 years	20-24 years	25-29 years	30 years and over	Not stated	
1989	**All ages**	**8,392**	**7,887**	**7,332**	**26,281**	**19,418**	**13,575**	**7,333**	**6,419**	**19**	**9.7**
	Under 20	2,233	2,037	2,120	8,289	6,951	4,963	2,632	1,854	7	11.9
	20-24	3,698	3,538	3,070	10,775	8,890	7,051	3,758	3,590	10	9.8
	25-29	1,210	1,113	1,030	3,900	2,201	1,026	640	713	1	8.4
	30-44	1,094	1,054	983	2,885	1,226	491	286	253	1	7.0
	45 and over	157	145	129	432	150	44	17	9	-	5.8
1988	**All ages**	**8,784**	**7,906**	**7,117**	**26,545**	**20,132**	**13,723**	**7,476**	**6,548**	**-**	**9.7**
	Under 20	2,410	2,352	2116	8,648	7,126	4,896	2,571	1,857	-	11.5
	20-24	3,813	3,247	2936	10,753	9,646	7,074	3,915	3,587	-	10.1
	25-29	1,256	1,083	1033	3,962	2,046	1,180	698	848	-	8.7
	30-44	1,137	1,069	894	2,787	1,149	527	274	248	-	7.0
	45 and over	168	155	138	395	165	46	18	8	-	5.7
1987	**All ages**	**8,781**	**7,827**	**6,654**	**26,194**	**19,576**	**12,970**	**7,314**	**6,380**	**-**	**9.5**
	Under 20	2,592	2,324	2,061	8,925	7,019	4,820	2,472	1,737	-	11.0
	20-24	3,652	3,212	2,665	10,656	9,671	6,602	3,861	3,588	-	10.1
	25-29	1,196	1,127	992	3,723	1,791	1,021	694	789	-	8.5
	30-44	1,163	993	824	2,475	975	488	276	256	-	6.8
	45 and over	178	171	112	415	120	39	11	10	-	5.1
1986	**All ages**	**8,457**	**7,465**	**6,280**	**26,718**	**19,547**	**12,909**	**7,357**	**6,539**	**9**	**9.4**
	Under 20	2,616	2,313	1,982	9,208	6,946	4,810	2,317	1,766	4	10.4
	20-24	3,410	2,981	2509	10,953	9,857	6,376	3,986	3,661	2	10.3
	25-29	1,205	1,044	931	3,679	1,688	1,145	736	874	3	8.6
	30-44	1,034	969	731	2,477	940	541	301	232	-	6.4
	45 and over	192	158	127	401	116	37	17	6	-	5.4
1985	**All ages**	**7,932**	**6,884**	**6,427**	**27,087**	**19,460**	**12,463**	**7,388**	**6,576**	**13**	**8.9**
	Under 20	2,553	2,262	2,161	9,658	7,125	4,645	2,347	1,789	4	9.6
	20-24	3,114	2,705	2,494	11,276	9,665	6,122	4,016	3,638	7	10.0
	25-29	1,054	981	908	3,388	1,630	1,122	700	865	2	8.3
	30-44	1,015	781	733	2,348	935	538	315	274	-	6.0
	45 and over	196	155	131	417	105	36	10	10	-	4.8
1984	**All ages**	**7,854**	**7,105**	**6,643**	**27,336**	**19,108**	**12,516**	**7,528**	**6,637**	**10**	**10.1**
	Under 20	2,640	2,450	2,285	9,933	7,127	4,614	2,410	1,737	3	10.4
	20-24	3,060	2,687	2,578	11,723	9,412	6,154	3,942	3,711	7	11.5
	25-29	1,048	1,034	948	3,209	1,578	1,159	827	934	-	9.3
	30-44	911	793	703	2,093	884	545	328	250	-	6.8
	45 and over	195	141	129	378	107	44	21	5	-	6.0
1983	**All ages**	**8,072**	**7,662**	**7,109**	**28,432**	**19,103**	**12,579**	**7,529**	**6,661**	**37**	**10.1**
	Under 20	2,867	2,752	2,643	10,412	7,596	4,599	2,331	1,728	13	10.2
	20-24	3,111	2,916	2,624	12,764	8,987	6,227	4,045	3,699	14	11.6
	25-29	1,042	997	923	2,999	1,551	1,129	786	943	8	9.2
	30-44	846	825	775	1,899	865	587	355	286	2	7.1
	45 and over	206	172	144	358	104	37	12	5	-	5.9
1982	**All ages**	**8,444**	**7,747**	**7,198**	**28,737**	**18,855**	**12,585**	**7,199**	**6,517**	**44**	**10.1**
	Under 20	3,236	2,940	2,778	10,879	7,699	4,512	2,224	1,713	16	10.0
	20-24	3,188	2,936	2,795	13,312	8,606	6,298	3,821	3,559	23	11.5
	25-29	1,034	930	873	2,654	1,498	1,186	761	924	4	9.0
	30-44	817	803	619	1,586	940	552	375	314	1	7.3
	45 and over	169	138	133	306	112	37	18	7	-	5.8
1981	**All ages**	**8,522**	**8,098**	**7,264**	**28,242**	**18,499**	**12,435**	**7,301**	**6,763**	**25**	**10.1**
	Under 20	3,374	3,088	2,806	10,855	7,468	4,385	2,115	1,796	7	9.8
	20-24	3,186	3,196	3,065	13,263	8,477	6,332	3,932	3,635	16	11.5
	25-29	1,052	974	752	2,333	1,543	1,119	835	1,023	2	9.0
	30-44	726	669	541	1,479	902	559	409	303	-	7.4
	45 and over	184	171	100	312	109	40	10	6	-	6.0
1980	**All ages**	**9,014**	**8,069**	**7,406**	**28,620**	**18,541**	**12,684**	**7,419**	**7,368**	**-**	**10.1**
	Under 20	3,568	3,283	2,978	11,067	7,462	4,239	2,099	1,843	-	9.6
	20-24	3,420	3,237	3,235	13,455	8,430	6,623	4,016	4,073	-	11.4
	25-29	1,030	839	636	2,342	1,579	1,158	860	1,137	-	9.3
	30-44	812	572	473	1,434	944	608	419	307	-	7.6
	45 and over	184	138	84	322	126	56	25	8	-	6.0

Source: Office for National Statistics

15.13 Duration of marriage at divorce by husband at marriage

England and Wales

Numbers

Year of divorce	Age of husband at marriage	All durations	0-2 years	0 years	1 year	2 years	3 years	4 years	5-9 years	5 years	6 years
2009	All ages	113,949	6,270	21	1,951	4,298	5,884	6,947	31,290	7,561	6,864
	Under 20	3,066	74	-	24	50	75	114	543	129	98
	20-24	29,150	883	1	246	636	894	1,193	5,281	1,305	1,221
	25-29	35,305	1,746	4	553	1,189	1,702	1,991	9,186	2,188	1,912
	30-44	39,984	2,810	9	856	1,945	2,623	3,032	13,948	3,370	3,104
	45 and over	6,444	757	7	272	478	590	617	2,332	569	529
2008	All ages	121,708	6,937	27	2,103	4,807	6,776	7,929	31,803	7,369	6,714
	Under 20	3,364	91	-	29	62	98	130	564	125	125
	20-24	32,151	1,006	4	236	766	1,090	1,319	5,161	1,281	1,132
	25-29	37,895	1,978	9	604	1,365	1,889	2,278	9,594	2,013	1,972
	30-44	41,529	3,051	9	941	2,101	3,040	3,544	14,089	3,345	2,979
	45 and over	6,769	811	5	293	513	659	658	2,395	605	506
2007	All ages	128,131	8,195	38	2,558	5,599	7,206	7,574	32,419	7,164	7,046
	Under 20	4,036	132	-	36	96	122	146	611	131	151
	20-24	35,408	1,238	4	364	870	1,214	1,275	5,430	1,198	1,153
	25-29	39,546	2,202	13	659	1,530	1,986	2,109	10,074	2,129	2,133
	30-44	42,408	3,736	12	1,171	2,553	3,279	3,351	13,960	3,163	3,085
	45 and over	6,733	887	9	328	550	605	693	2,344	543	524
2006	All ages	132,140	8,763	37	2,793	5,933	7,226	7,376	33,736	7,398	7,310
	Under 20	4,115	140	-	49	91	119	132	630	142	143
	20-24	38,096	1,400	4	411	985	1,192	1,239	5,727	1,211	1,204
	25-29	40,683	2,304	10	724	1,570	2,054	2,176	10,907	2,285	2,295
	30-44	42,417	4,002	14	1,287	2,701	3,234	3,238	14,093	3,209	3,146
	45 and over	6,829	917	9	322	586	627	591	2,379	551	522
2005	All ages	141,322	9573	49	3,181	6,343	7,520	8,175	36,064	7,920	7,697
	Under 20	4,685	175	-	53	122	159	139	634	166	134
	20-24	42,354	1,516	5	497	1,014	1,308	1,415	6,526	1,328	1,309
	25-29	43,807	2,625	18	836	1,771	2,175	2,529	11,853	2,547	2,481
	30-44	43,631	4,287	13	1,472	2,802	3,250	3,466	14,547	3,270	3,219
	45 and over	6,845	970	13	323	634	628	626	2,504	609	554
2004	All ages	152,923	10,101	42	3,345	6,714	8,319	8,894	39,681	8,840	8,375
	Under 20	5,392	178	-	52	126	146	187	680	186	136
	20-24	47,794	1,680	7	552	1,121	1,475	1,538	7,762	1,572	1,540
	25-29	48,067	2,863	7	881	1,975	2,568	2,974	13,672	2,982	2,812
	30-44	44,701	4,428	19	1,507	2,902	3,468	3,531	15,035	3,505	3,299
	45 and over	6,969	952	9	353	590	662	664	2,532	595	588
2003	All ages	153,065	10,286	42	3,283	6,961	8,276	8,882	40,497	8,968	8,639
	Under 20	5,764	191	-	58	133	157	169	690	176	148
	20-24	50,015	1,720	4	483	1,233	1,484	1,658	8,685	1,675	1,718
	25-29	47,353	3,021	5	927	2,089	2,702	2,960	13,881	3,000	2,901
	30-44	43,173	4,386	17	1,456	2,913	3,362	3,459	14,702	3,519	3,328
	45 and over	6,760	968	16	359	593	571	636	2,539	598	544
2002	All ages	147,735	10,239	31	3,326	6,882	8,325	8,780	39,730	8,823	8,370
	Under 20	5,572	184	-	54	130	169	146	600	123	109
	20-24	50,028	1,739	5	481	1,253	1,529	1,717	9,494	1,814	1,928
	25-29	45,913	3,173	8	985	2,180	2,886	3,009	13,756	3,089	2,897
	30-44	39,977	4,218	9	1,460	2,749	3,125	3,349	13,589	3,216	2,930
	45 and over	6,245	925	9	346	570	616	559	2,291	581	506

15.13 Duration of marriage at divorce by husband at marriage
England and Wales

Numbers

Year of divorce	Age of husband at marriage	7 years	8 years	9 years	10-14 years	15-19 years	20-24 years	25-29 years	30 years and over	Not stated	Median duration
2009	**All ages**	**5,968**	**5,634**	**5,263**	**20,591**	**15,390**	**11,855**	**7,490**	**8,225**	7	**11.4**
	Under 20	106	108	102	316	296	343	429	876	-	..
	20-24	1,004	912	839	3,716	4,298	4,673	3,545	4,665	2	..
	25-29	1,732	1,719	1,635	7,059	5,566	4,022	2,124	1,907	2	..
	30-44	2,690	2,458	2,326	8,270	4,620	2,617	1,306	755	3	..
	45 and over	436	437	361	1,230	610	200	86	22	-	..
2008	**All ages**	**6,365**	**6,034**	**5,321**	**21,561**	**16,945**	**12,706**	**8,136**	**8,907**	8	**11.5**
	Under 20	113	90	111	321	342	407	501	909	1	..
	20-24	987	922	839	4,134	4,924	5,257	3,993	5,265	2	..
	25-29	1,910	1,908	1,791	7,677	6,168	4,089	2,233	1,984	5	..
	30-44	2,860	2,697	2,208	8,147	4,911	2,701	1,317	729	-	..
	45 and over	495	417	372	1,282	600	252	92	20	-	..
2007	**All ages**	**6,560**	**6,072**	**5,577**	**23,427**	**18,203**	**13,117**	**8,701**	**9,282**	7	**11.7**
	Under 20	139	108	82	353	425	516	661	1,070	-	..
	20-24	1,045	1,077	957	4,993	5,878	5,654	4,230	5,494	2	..
	25-29	2,003	1,961	1,848	8,330	6,392	4,045	2,396	2,009	3	..
	30-44	2,892	2,522	2,298	8,441	4,939	2,695	1,332	673	2	..
	45 and over	481	404	392	1,310	569	207	82	36	-	..
2006	**All ages**	**6,769**	**6,249**	**6,010**	**24,606**	**18,735**	**13,472**	**8,764**	**9,449**	13	**11.6**
	Under 20	145	106	94	370	463	569	666	1,025	1	..
	20-24	1,130	1,099	1,083	5,866	6,495	5,991	4,431	5,752	3	..
	25-29	2,199	2,085	2,043	8,483	6,388	4,053	2,268	2,044	6	..
	30-44	2,783	2,571	2,384	8,503	4,814	2,615	1,317	598	3	..
	45 and over	512	388	406	1,384	575	244	82	30	-	..
2005	**All ages**	**7,343**	**6,801**	**6,303**	**26,310**	**20,310**	**14,268**	**9,241**	**9,852**	9	**11.6**
	Under 20	116	125	93	445	575	734	761	1,062	1	..
	20-24	1,303	1,317	1,269	6,815	7,425	6,596	4,831	5,921	1	..
	25-29	2,437	2,267	2,121	9,377	6,742	4,049	2,313	2,142	2	..
	30-44	2,951	2,651	2,456	8,448	4,979	2,672	1,274	703	5	..
	45 and over	536	441	364	1,225	589	217	62	24	-	..
2004	**All ages**	**7,900**	**7,683**	**6,883**	**28,984**	**21,515**	**15,431**	**9,705**	**10,293**	-	**11.5**
	Under 20	127	120	111	596	710	894	849	1,152	-	..
	20-24	1,543	1,585	1,522	8,361	8,403	7,232	5,081	6,262	-	..
	25-29	2,699	2,699	2,480	10,158	6,893	4,251	2,510	2,178	-	..
	30-44	3,016	2,851	2,364	8,605	4,924	2,838	1,200	672	-	..
	45 and over	515	428	406	1,264	585	216	65	29	-	..
2003	**All ages**	**8,228**	**7,686**	**6,976**	**29,751**	**20,863**	**14,974**	**9,627**	**9,907**	2	**11.3**
	Under 20	127	122	117	705	798	1,064	902	1,087	1	..
	20-24	1,751	1,760	1,781	9,169	8,627	7,216	5,204	6,251	1	..
	25-29	2,781	2,745	2,454	10,243	6,314	3,938	2,330	1,964	-	..
	30-44	3,015	2,616	2,224	8,378	4,617	2,573	1,119	577	-	..
	45 and over	554	443	400	1,256	507	183	72	28	-	..
2002	**All ages**	**8,020**	**7,564**	**6,953**	**28,592**	**19,784**	**13,989**	**9,106**	**9,190**	-	**11.1**
	Under 20	130	115	123	741	875	1,005	899	953	-	..
	20-24	1,927	1,896	1,929	9,648	8,300	6,801	4,968	5,832	-	..
	25-29	2,760	2,645	2,365	9,594	5,843	3,593	2,193	1,866	-	..
	30-44	2,741	2,509	2,193	7,511	4,281	2,395	983	526	-	..
	45 and over	462	399	343	1,098	485	195	63	13	-	..

Source: Office for National Statistics

15.14(a) Births:[1] by country and sex

Thousands

	Live births				Rates				
	Total	Male	Female	Sex ratio[2]	Crude birth rate[3]	General fertility rate[4]	TFR[5]	Still-births[6]	Still-birth rate[6]
United Kingdom[7]									
1900 - 02	1,095	558	537	1,037	28.6	115.1	..	..	..
1910 - 12	1,037	528	508	1,039	24.6	99.4	..	..	..
1920 - 22	1,018	522	496	1,052	23.1	93.0	..	..	..
1930 - 32	750	383	367	1,046	16.3	66.5	..	..	..
1940 - 42	723	372	351	1,062	15.0	..	1.89	..	..
1950 - 52	803	413	390	1,061	16.0	73.7	2.21	..	..
1960 - 62	946	487	459	1,063	17.9	90.3	2.80	18.6	19.2
1970 - 72	880	453	427	1,064	15.8	82.5	2.36	11.3	12.7
1980 - 82	735	377	358	1,053	13.0	62.5	1.83	5.0	6.8
1990 - 92	790	405	385	1,051	13.8	63.7	1.81	3.6	4.6
2000 - 02	672	345	328	1,052	11.4	54.7	1.64	3.6	5.4
	BBCA	**KBCZ**	**KBCY**	**KMFW**	**KBCT**	**KBCS**	**KBCR**	**KBCQ**	**KMFX**
1997	727	372	354	1,051	12.6	59.6	1.72	3.9	5.3
1998	717	367	350	1,052	12.3	58.8	1.71	3.9	5.4
1999	700	359	341	1,056	11.9	57.3	1.68	3.7	5.3
2000	679	348	331	1,051	11.5	55.4	1.64	3.6	5.3
2001	669	343	326	1,050	11.3	54.3	1.63	3.6	5.3
2002	669	343	326	1,054	11.3	54.2	1.64	3.8	5.6
2003	696	357	339	1,052	11.7	56.2	1.71	4.0	5.7
2004	716	368	348	1,055	12.0	57.7	1.77	4.0	5.7
2005	723	370	353	1,050	12.0	57.8	1.78	4.0	5.3
2006	749	383	366	1,047	12.4	59.7	1.84	4.0	5.3
2007	772	397	376	1,056	12.7	61.5	1.90	4.0	5.2
2008	794	407	388	1,049	12.9	63.4	1.96	4.0	5.1
2009	790	405	385	1,052	12.8	63.2	1.94	4.1	5.2
England and Wales									
1900 - 02	932	475	458	1,037	28.6	114.7	..	..	..
1910 - 12	884	450	433	1,040	24.5	98.6	..	..	..
1920 - 22	862	442	420	1,051	22.8	91.1	..	27.0	..
1930 - 32	632	323	309	1,047	15.8	64.4	..	22.0	..
1940 - 42	607	312	295	1,057	15.6	61.3	1.81	16.0	..
1950 - 52	683	351	332	1,058	15.6	72.1	2.16	15.6	18.9
1960 - 62	812	418	394	1,061	17.6	88.9	2.77	9.7	12.5
1970 - 72	764	394	371	1,061	15.6	81.4	2.31	4.3	6.7
1980 - 82	639	328	311	1,053	12.9	61.8	1.81	3.2	4.5
1990 - 92	698	358	340	1,051	13.8	63.8	1.82	3.2	5.4
2000 - 02	598	307	292	1,052	11.4	55.2	1.65		
	BBCB	**KMFY**	**KMFZ**	**KMGA**	**KMGB**	**KMGC**	**KMGD**	**KMGE**	**KMGF**
1997	643	330	314	1,051	12.5	60.0	1.73	3.4	5.3
1998	636	326	310	1,051	12.3	59.2	1.72	3.4	5.3
1999	622	319	303	1,055	12.0	57.8	1.70	3.3	5.3
2000	604	310	295	1,050	11.6	55.9	1.65	3.2	5.3
2001	595	305	290	1,050	11.4	54.7	1.63	3.2	5.3
2002	596	306	290	1,055	11.3	54.7	1.65	3.4	5.6
2003	621	318	303	1,051	11.8	56.8	1.73	3.6	5.8
2004	640	328	311	1,054	12.1	58.2	1.78	3.7	5.7
2005	646	331	315	1,049	12.1	58.4	1.80	3.5	5.4
2006	670	342	327	1,047	12.5	60.2	1.86	3.6	5.4
2007	690	354	336	1,057	12.8	62.0	1.91	3.6	5.2
2008	709	363	346	1,050	13.0	63.8	1.97	3.6	5.1
2009	706	362	344	1,052	12.9	63.7	1.96	3.7	5.2
2010	723	371	352	1,053	13.1	65.4	2.00	3.7	5.1

15.14(b) Births:[1] by country and sex

Continued

Thousands

	Live births			Rates					
	Total	Male	Female	Sex ratio[2]	Crude birth rate[3]	General fertility rate[4]	TFR[5]	Stillbirths[6]	Stillbirth rate[6]
Scotland									
1900 - 02	132	67	65	1,046	29.5	120.6	..	..	..
1910 - 12	123	63	60	1,044	25.9	107.4	..	..	..
1920 - 22	125	64	61	1,046	25.6	105.9	..	..	..
1930 - 32	93	47	45	1,040	19.1	78.8	..	..	..
1940 - 42	89	46	43	1,051	18.5	73.7	..	4.0	..
1950 - 52	91	47	44	1,060	17.9	81.4	2.41	2.0	..
1960 - 62	102	53	50	1,060	19.7	97.8	2.98	2.2	20.8
1970 - 72	84	43	41	1,057	16.1	83.3	2.46	1.1	13.5
1980 - 82	68	35	33	1,051	13.1	62.2	1.80	0.4	6.3
1990 - 92	66	34	32	1,052	13.0	59.2	1.68	0.4	5.7
2000 - 02	52	27	26	1,046	10.3	48.6	1.48	0.3	5.6
	BBCD	**KMEU**	**KMEV**	**KMEW**	**KMEX**	**KMEY**	**KMEZ**	**KMFM**	**KMFN**
1997	59	31	29	1,055	11.7	54.4	1.58	0.3	5.3
1998	57	29	28	1,060	11.3	52.7	1.55	0.4	6.1
1999	55	28	27	1,050	10.9	50.9	1.51	0.3	5.2
2000	53	27	26	1,051	10.5	49.2	1.48	0.3	5.6
2001	53	27	26	1,041	10.4	48.8	1.49	0.3	5.7
2002	51	26	25	1,047	10.1	48.1	1.48	0.3	5.4
2003	52	27	26	1,054	10.4	49.4	1.54	0.3	5.6
2004	54	28	26	1,060	10.6	51.0	1.60	0.3	5.8
2005	54	28	26	1,068	10.7	51.5	1.62	0.3	5.3
2006	56	28	27	1,046	10.9	52.8	1.67	0.3	5.3
2007	58	30	28	1,057	11.2	54.8	1.73	0.3	5.6
2008	60	31	29	1,037	11.6	57.2	1.80	0.3	5.4
2009	59	30	29	1,044	11.4	56.6	1.77	0.3	5.3
2010	59	30	29	1,033	11.3	56.5	1.75	0.3	4.9
Northern Ireland[7]									
1900 - 02	..	..	..	..	..	..	..	..	..
1910 - 12	..	..	..	..	..	..	..	..	..
1920 - 22	31	16	15	1,048	24.2	105.9	..	..	..
1930 - 32	26	13	12	1,047	20.5	78.8	..	..	..
1940 - 42	27	14	13	1,078	20.8	73.7	..	..	..
1950 - 52	29	15	14	1,066	20.9	81.4	..	..	..
1960 - 62	31	16	15	1,068	22.5	111.5	3.47	0.7	22.0
1970 - 72	31	16	15	1,074	20.4	105.7	3.13	0.5	14.3
1980 - 82	28	14	13	1,048	18.0	87.5	2.59	0.2	8.4
1990 - 92	26	13	13	1,051	16.1	74.8	2.15	0.1	4.6
2000 - 02	22	11	11	1,054	12.8	58.8	1.78	0.1	5.0
	BBCE	**KMFO**	**KMFP**	**KMFQ**	**KMFR**	**KMFS**	**KMFT**	**KMFU**	**KMFV**
1997	24	12	12	1,048	14.4	66.4	1.93	0.1	5.4
1998	24	12	12	1,039	14.1	65.0	1.90	0.1	5.1
1999	23	12	11	1,084	13.7	62.9	1.86	0.1	5.7
2000	22	11	10	1,070	12.8	58.7	1.75	0.1	4.3
2001	22	11	11	1,058	13.0	59.7	1.80	0.1	5.1
2002	21	11	11	1,035	12.6	58.1	1.77	0.1	5.7
2003	22	11	10	1,081	12.7	59.0	1.81	0.1	5.0
2004	22	11	11	1,059	13.0	60.6	1.87	0.1	5.0
2005	22	11	11	1,032	12.9	60.4	1.87	0.1	4.0
2006	23	12	11	1,066	14.0	62.5	1.94	0.1	3.8
2007	24	13	12	1,049	13.9	65.1	2.02	0.1	4.2
2008	26	13	12	1,063	14.4	68.2	2.11	0.1	4.5
2009	25	13	12	1,057	13.9	66.4	2.04	0.1	4.8

1 See chapter text

2 Males per 1,000 females (calculated using whole numbers).

3 Rate per 1000 population (calculated using whole numbers).

4 Rate per 1000 women aged 15 - 44.

5 Total fertility rate is the average number of children which would be born to a woman if she experienced the age-specific rates of the period in question throughout her child-bearing life span. UK figures for the years 1970-72 and earlier are estimates.

6 On 1 October 1992 the legal definition of a stillbirth was changed from a baby born dead after 28 completed weeks gestation or more to one born dead after 24 completed weeks gestation or more. Between 1 October and 31 December 1992 in the UK there were 258 babies born dead between 24 and 27 completed weeks gestation (216 in England and Wales, 35 in Scotland and 7 in Northern Ireland). If these babies were included in the stillbirth figures given, the stillbirth rate would be 4.7 for the UK and England and Wales, while Scotland and Northern Ireland stillbirth rate would remain as stated.

7 From 1981, data for the United Kingdom and Northern Ireland have been revised to exclude births in Northern Ireland to non-residents of Northern Ireland.

Sources: Office for National Statistics: 01329 444410;
National Records of Scotland
Northern Ireland Statistics and Research Agency

15.15 Birth occurrence: inside and outside marriage by age of mother

Thousands

	Inside marriage						Outside marriage					
	All ages	Under 20	20-24	25-29	Over 30	Mean[1] age (Years)	All ages	Under 20	20-24	25-29	Over 30	Mean[1] age (Years)
United Kingdom[2,3]												
	KKEY	KKEZ	KKFY	KKFZ	KKGX	KKGY	KKGZ	KKIC	KKID	KKIE	KKIF	KKIG
1961	890	55	273	280	282	27.7	54	13	17	10	13	25.5
1971	828	70	301	271	185	26.4	74	24	25	13	12	23.8
1981	640	36	193	231	180	27.3	91	30	33	16	13	23.4
1988	589	16	144	234	195	28.2	198	51	76	42	29	24.1
1989	570	14	130	228	198	28.4	207	49	79	46	32	24.3
1990	576	13	121	233	209	28.6	223	51	83	53	37	24.5
1991	556	10	109	224	213	28.9	236	50	87	58	41	24.8
1992	540	9	98	216	218	29.1	241	46	86	62	46	25.1
1993	520	8	87	204	221	29.3	242	44	84	64	50	25.4
1994	510	7	78	194	231	29.6	240	41	80	65	55	25.7
1995	486	6	69	180	232	29.8	246	42	79	66	60	25.9
1996	473	6	61	170	237	30.1	260	45	80	69	66	26.0
1997	460	6	55	159	240	30.3	267	47	79	71	71	26.1
1998	447	6	51	149	243	30.5	270	49	77	70	74	26.2
1999	428	6	47	136	239	30.7	272	49	77	68	77	26.3
2000	411	5	44	126	237	30.9	268	47	77	66	78	26.4
2001	401	5	44	116	236	30.9	268	45	77	64	82	26.7
2002	397	5	44	109	239	31.1	272	44	80	62	85	26.7
2003	407	5	44	110	249	31.2	289	45	86	65	92	26.8
2004	413	4	44	110	255	31.3	303	47	90	69	97	26.9
2005	412	4	43	111	254	31.4	310	47	93	72	98	26.9
2006	422	3	43	115	260	31.4	327	48	99	78	102	26.9
2007	429	3	42	119	265	31.5	343	47	104	85	106	27.1
2008	434	3	41	123	266	31.5	361	48	110	93	110	27.0
2009	424	2	39	121	262	31.6	366	46	113	96	111	27.0
Great Britain												
	KKIH	KKII	KKIJ	KKIK	KKIL	KKIM	KKIN	KKIO	KKIP	KKIQ	KKIR	KKIS
1961	859	53	264	270	272	27.7	53	13	17	10	13	25.5
1971	797	68	293	261	176	26.4	73	24	25	13	12	23.8
1981	614	34	186	223	171	27.2	89	29	32	16	13	23.3
1987	574	17	147	227	184	28.0	174	46	66	36	25	23.4
1988	566	16	138	226	186	28.2	194	49	74	42	29	23.6
1989	549	13	125	220	190	28.4	202	48	77	45	32	24.2
1990	554	12	116	225	201	28.6	218	49	81	52	36	24.6
1991	535	10	105	216	205	28.9	231	48	85	57	41	24.8
1992	520	9	94	208	210	29.1	235	45	84	61	46	25.1
1993	500	7	84	196	213	29.3	236	42	82	62	49	25.4
1994	492	7	75	188	222	29.6	235	41	78	63	53	25.7
1995	468	6	66	173	223	29.8	240	40	77	65	59	25.9
1996	455	6	59	163	227	30.1	254	44	78	68	65	26.0
1997	442	6	53	152	231	30.3	261	46	76	69	69	26.2
1998	430	6	49	143	233	30.5	263	48	74	68	73	26.3
1999	412	6	46	131	230	30.7	265	48	74	67	76	26.4
2000	396	5	43	121	228	30.9	261	46	74	65	77	26.5
2001	386	5	43	112	227	30.9	261	44	75	62	80	26.6
2002	383	5	43	105	230	31.1	265	43	77	61	84	26.7
2003	393	4	43	106	239	31.2	281	44	83	64	90	26.9
2004	399	4	43	106	245	31.3	295	45	88	67	95	26.9
2005	398	4	42	107	245	31.4	302	45	90	70	97	26.9
2006	407	3	42	111	251	31.4	318	46	96	76	100	26.9
2007	414	3	41	114	255	31.5	334	46	101	83	104	27.1
2008	418	3	41	119	256	31.5	351	46	107	90	107	27.0
2009	409	2	38	117	252	31.6	356	45	109	94	108	27.1
2010	414	2	36	117	260	31.7	368	43	112	99	115	27.2

1 The mean ages presented in this table are unstandardised and therefore take no account of the age structure of the population.

2 From 1981, data for the United Kingdom have been revised to exclude births in Northern Ireland to non-residents of Northern Ireland.

3. 2010 data for Northern Ireland is not available, so no UK data available either.

Source: Office for National Statistics: 01329 444410;
National Records of Scotland
Northern Ireland Statistics and Research Agency

15.16(a) Live births: by age of mother and country

United Kingdom

Numbers

	All ages	Under 20	20 - 24	25 - 29	30 - 34	35 - 39	40 - 44	45 and over
	KMBZ	KMDV	KMDW	KMDX	KMDY	KMDZ	KMES	KMET
All live births [1,2]								
1997	726,622	52,851	133,257	229,429	212,162	84,508	13,731	618
1998	716,888	54,822	127,230	218,072	212,876	88,729	14,453	640
1999	699,976	54,921	124,036	204,808	208,986	91,272	15,210	695
2000	679,029	52,059	120,305	191,583	202,893	95,400	16,032	708
2001	669,123	50,157	121,664	179,776	202,017	97,379	17,271	831
2002	668,777	49,165	123,844	171,852	203,261	101,379	18,273	968
2003	695,549	49,874	129,867	175,473	210,071	109,038	20,233	933
2004	715,996	50,752	134,614	179,050	213,620	114,852	22,107	975
2005	722,549	50,396	135,891	183,513	211,076	116,902	23,518	1,176
2006	748,563	51,066	142,171	192,800	212,333	123,867	24,999	1,288
2007	772,245	50,515	145,725	204,276	214,020	129,599	26,663	1,420
2008	794,383	50,396	151,608	216,466	215,964	130,520	27,845	1,558
2009	790,204	48,567	151,312	217,460	214,789	128,065	28,244	1,747
Age-specific fertility rates[3]								
	KMBY	KMBR	KMBS	KMBT	KMBU	KMBV	KMBW	KMBX
1997	59.6	30.2	74.9	104.2	89.8	39.1	7.1	0.3
1998	58.8	30.8	73.6	101.4	90.4	40.0	7.4	0.3
1999	57.3	30.7	71.8	98.0	89.4	40.2	7.6	0.4
2000	55.4	29.2	68.7	93.9	87.7	41.0	7.8	0.4
2001	54.3	27.9	68.0	91.5	88.0	41.3	8.2	0.4
2002	54.2	27.0	68.0	91.3	89.7	42.6	8.4	0.5
2003	56.2	26.7	70.2	95.4	94.6	45.9	9.1	0.5
2004	57.7	26.7	71.5	97.3	99.2	48.6	9.7	0.5
2005	57.8	26.2	70.4	97.4	100.5	50.0	10.6	0.6
2006	59.7	26.4	72.0	100.1	104.6	53.4	10.6	0.6
2007	61.5	25.9	72.3	103.5	109.8	56.6	11.2	0.7
2008	63.4	26.0	73.5	107.9	113.1	58.2	12.4	0.7
2009	63.2	25.2	72.7	106.5	112.8	58.7	11.9	0.8

England and Wales

	All ages	Under 20	20 - 24	25 - 29	30 - 34	35 - 39	40 - 44	45 and over
All live births	KGSH	KGSA	KGSB	KGSC	KGSD	KGSE	KGSF	KGSG
1997	643,095	46,372	118,589	202,792	187,528	74,900	12,332	582
1998	635,901	48,285	113,537	193,144	188,499	78,881	12,980	575
1999	621,872	48,375	110,722	181,931	185,311	81,281	13,617	635
2000	604,441	45,846	107,741	170,701	180,113	84,974	14,403	663
2001	594,634	44,189	108,844	159,926	178,920	86,495	15,499	761
2002	596,122	43,467	110,959	153,379	180,532	90,449	16,441	895
2003	621,469	44,236	116,622	156,931	187,214	97,386	18,205	875
2004	639,721	45,094	121,072	159,984	190,550	102,228	19,884	909
2005	645,835	44,830	122,145	164,348	188,153	104,113	21,155	1,091
2006	669,601	45,509	127,828	172,642	189,407	110,509	22,512	1,194
2007	690,013	44,805	130,784	182,570	191,124	115,380	24,041	1,309
2008	708,711	44,691	135,971	192,960	192,450	116,220	24,991	1,428
2009	706,248	43,243	136,012	194,129	191,600	114,288	25,357	1,619
2010	723,165	40,591	137,312	199,233	202,457	115,841	25,973	1,758
Age-specific fertility rates[3]	KGSP	KGSI	KGSJ	KGSK	KGSL	KGSM	KGSN	KGSO
1997	60.0	30.2	76.0	104.3	89.8	39.4	7.3	0.3
1998	59.2	30.9	74.9	101.5	90.6	40.4	7.5	0.3
1999	57.8	30.9	73.0	98.3	89.6	40.6	7.7	0.4
2000	55.9	29.3	70.0	94.3	87.9	41.4	8.0	0.4
2001	54.7	28.0	69.0	91.7	88.0	41.5	8.4	0.5
2002	54.7	27.0	69.1	91.5	89.9	43.0	8.6	0.5
2003	56.8	26.9	71.1	95.8	94.9	46.4	9.3	0.5
2004	58.2	26.9	72.8	97.6	99.6	48.8	9.9	0.5
2005	58.3	26.3	71.6	97.9	100.7	50.3	10.8	0.6
2006	60.2	26.6	73.2	100.6	104.8	53.8	10.8	0.6
2007	62.0	26.0	73.5	104.0	110.2	56.9	11.4	0.7
2008	63.8	26.0	74.6	108.4	113.1	58.4	12.6	0.7
2009	63.7	25.3	73.9	107.2	113.1	59.0	12.1	0.8
2010	65.4	24.2	74.0	108.0	117.8	61.5	12.5	0.9

15.16 (b) Live births: by age of mother and country

Number

	All ages	Under 20	20 - 24	25 - 29	30 - 34	35 - 39	40 - 44	45 and over
Scotland								
All Live Births[1]	KGTH	KGTA	KGTB	KGTC	KGTD	KGTE	KGTF	KGTG
1997	59,440	4,835	10,607	18,782	17,455	6,740	936	19
1998	57,319	4,802	9,804	17,477	17,207	6,893	1,027	43
1999	55,147	4,755	9,440	16,011	16,722	7,034	1,096	41
2000	53,076	4,599	8,962	14,676	16,233	7,395	1,133	29
2001	52,527	4,444	9,121	13,763	16,206	7,701	1,224	40
2002	51,270	4,195	9,267	12,694	16,038	7,727	1,267	47
2003	52,432	4,155	9,626	12,725	16,085	8,310	1,432	39
2004	53,957	4,172	9,950	13,131	16,085	8,912	1,631	50
2005	54,386	4,171	10,008	13,229	15,962	9,179	1,694	66
2006	55,690	4,130	10,399	13,876	15,878	9,535	1,775	58
2007	57,781	4,305	10,913	14,917	15,622	10,035	1,849	83
2008	60,041	4,279	11,373	16,171	16,028	10,025	2,044	95
2009	59,046	3,990	11,188	16,178	15,835	9,695	2,045	95
2010	58,791	3,755	10,660	16,152	16,426	9,599	2,080	98
Age-specific fertility rates[3]	KGTP	KGTI	KGTJ	KGTK	KGTL	KGTM	KGTN	KGTO
1997	54.4	31.0	65.5	97.4	83.9	34.0	5.3	0.1
1998	52.7	30.6	62.8	94.3	83.2	34.1	5.7	0.3
1999	50.9	30.3	61.0	90.4	82.0	34.3	5.9	0.2
2000	49.2	29.3	57.6	86.5	81.3	35.6	6.0	0.2
2001	48.8	28.4	57.8	85.1	82.2	36.9	6.3	0.2
2002	48.1	26.8	58.3	83.3	83.6	37.1	6.4	0.3
2003	49.4	26.3	60.1	86.5	86.8	40.0	7.1	0.2
2004	51.0	26.1	61.8	89.4	90.3	43.3	7.9	0.3
2005	51.5	26.2	60.9	88.6	93.2	45.4	8.1	0.3
2006	52.8	25.8	61.9	90.2	97.1	47.8	8.4	0.3
2007	54.8	26.9	63.6	93.1	100.1	51.3	8.8	0.4
2008	57.2	26.8	65.3	98.1	105.4	53.1	10.2	0.5
2009	56.6	25.1	63.5	96.1	104.0	53.6	9.9	0.5
2010	56.5	23.8	60.1	93.6	106.0	55.2	10.2	0.5
Northern Ireland[4]	KMDM	KMDF	KMDG	KMDH	KMDI	KMDJ	KMDK	KMDL
All Live Births[2]								
1997	24,087	1,644	4,061	7,855	7,179	2,868	463	17
1998	23,668	1,735	3,889	7,451	7,170	2,955	446	22
1999	22,957	1,791	3,874	6,866	6,953	2,957	497	19
2000	21,512	1,614	3,602	6,206	6,547	3,031	496	16
2001	21,962	1,524	3,699	6,087	6,891	3,183	548	30
2002	21,385	1,502	3,619	5,779	6,691	3,203	565	26
2003	21,648	1,483	3,619	5,817	6,772	3,342	596	19
2004	22,318	1,486	3,592	5,935	6,985	3,712	592	16
2005	22,328	1,395	3,738	5,936	6,961	3,610	669	19
2006	23,272	1,427	3,944	6,282	7,048	3,823	712	36
2007	24,451	1,405	4,028	6,789	7,274	4,184	741	30
2008	25,631	1,426	4,264	7,335	7,486	4,275	810	35
2009	24,910	1,334	4,112	7,153	7,354	4,082	842	33
Age-specific fertility rates[2,3]	KMDU	KMDN	KMDO	KMDP	KMDQ	KMDR	KMDS	KMDT
1997	66.4	26.4	71.1	124.2	109.2	46.6	8.8	0.3
1998	65.0	27.8	69.6	119.0	108.4	47.2	8.2	0.4
1999	62.9	28.6	70.6	112.3	105.6	46.1	8.9	0.4
2000	58.7	25.6	66.0	103.9	100.4	46.2	8.5	0.3
2001	59.7	23.9	67.5	105.1	106.0	48.0	9.1	0.6
2002	58.1	23.3	66.0	102.9	104.2	48.2	9.2	0.5
2003	59.0	22.9	65.5	106.8	107.0	50.2	9.8	0.3
2004	60.6	23.0	62.8	109.8	112.6	56.1	9.5	0.3
2005	60.4	21.7	63.2	108.6	114.8	55.0	10.2	0.3
2006	62.5	22.5	63.6	112.0	119.2	58.2	10.8	0.6
2007	65.1	22.5	62.6	116.1	124.6	64.2	11.1	0.5
2008	68.2	23.0	65.6	120.5	131.1	67.0	12.6	0.6
2009	66.4	21.8	63.7	114.6	128.0	65.1	12.6	0.5

1 The 'All ages' figure for Scotland includes births to mothers whose age was not known. There were 66 such births in 1997, 66 in 1998, 48 in 1999, 49 in 2000, 28 in 2001, 35 in 2002, 60 in 2003 and 26 in 2004, 77 in 2005, 39 in 2006, 57 in 2007 and 20 in 2008.

2 From 1981 data for the United kingdom and Northern Ireland have been revised to exclude births in Northern Ireland to non residents .

3 The rates for women of all ages, under 20, and 45 and over are based upon the populations of women aged 15-44, 15-19 and 45 respectively.

4. 2010 data for Northern Ireland is not available, so no UK data is also available..

Sources: Office for National Statistics; 01329 444410
National Records of Scotland
Northern Ireland Statistics and Research Agency

15.17 Legal abortions[1]: by age for residents

	All ages	Under 15	15	16 - 19	20 - 24	25 - 29	30 - 34	35 - 39	40 - 44	45 and over	Numbers Not stated
England and Wales											
	C53Z	C542	C543	C544	C545	C546	C547	C548	C549	C54A	C54B
1987	156,191	907	2,858	35,167	49,256	31,243	18,960	12,639	4,757	390	14
1988	168,298	859	2,709	37,928	54,067	34,584	20,000	12,681	5,047	412	11
1989	170,463	803	2,580	36,182	54,880	36,604	21,284	12,713	5,020	388	9
1990	173,900	873	2,549	35,520	55,281	38,770	22,431	12,956	5,104	404	12
1991	167,376	886	2,272	31,130	52,678	38,611	23,445	13,035	4,901	408	10
1992	160,501	905	2,095	27,589	49,052	38,430	23,870	13,252	4,844	452	12
1993	157,846	964	2,119	25,806	46,846	38,139	24,690	13,885	4,889	494	14
1994	156,539	1,080	2,166	25,223	44,871	38,081	25,507	14,156	5,008	440	7
1995	154,315	946	2,324	24,945	43,394	37,254	25,759	14,352	4,868	457	16
1996	167,916	1,098	2,547	28,790	46,356	39,311	28,228	16,118	5,027	428	13
1997	170,145	1,020	2,414	29,947	44,960	40,159	28,892	16,858	5,413	482	0
1998	177,871	1,103	2,656	33,236	45,766	40,366	30,449	18,174	5,576	511	34
1999	173,701	1,066	2,537	32,807	45,004	38,492	29,139	18,341	5,755	502	58
2000	175,542	1,048	2,700	33,218	47,099	37,852	28,735	18,589	5,794	459	48
2001	176,364	1,066	2,592	33,431	48,267	36,506	28,782	19,146	6,094	456	24
2002	175,932	1,075	2,658	32,985	48,359	35,795	28,503	19,450	6,531	457	119
2003	181,582	1,171	2,796	32,985	51,201	36,018	28,749	19,868	7,032	500	0
2004	185,415	1,034	2,722	35,386	52,701	37,759	28,064	19,820	7,422	507	0
2005	186,416	1,083	2,703	35,313	53,342	38,330	27,836	19,782	7,459	568	0
2006	193,737	1,042	2,948	37,296	55,340	40,396	28,153	20,074	7,825	663	0
2007	198,499	1,171	3,205	39,579	56,963	41,704	27,257	19,976	7,915	729	0
2008	195,296	1,097	3,016	38,577	56,171	41,896	26,985	19,228	7,663	663	0
2009	189,100	1,047	2,776	36,244	54,749	40,634	26,701	18,817	7,395	737	0
2010	189,574	1,042	2,676	34,551	55,481	40,800	27,978	18,867	7,493	686	0
Scotland											
	C54C	C54D	C54E	C54F	C54G	C54H	C54I	C54J	C54K	C54L	EVH4
1986	9,611	74	236	2,526	2,984	1,740	1,080	702	247	22	0
1987	9,449	70	210	2,415	2,991	1,728	1,082	695	241	17	0
1988	10,111	65	217	2,526	3,299	1,965	1,105	662	257	15	0
1989	10,191	53	209	2,554	3,199	1,967	1,225	704	266	14	0
1990	10,198	54	185	2,536	3,235	2,061	1,157	698	253	19	0
1991	11,046	77	203	2,567	3,479	2,247	1,443	740	262	28	0
1992	10,791	73	173	2,368	3,383	2,283	1,444	798	252	17	0
1993	11,059	92	193	2,297	3,365	2,443	1,489	889	262	29	0
1994	11,371	78	214	2,311	3,480	2,427	1,640	876	315	30	0
1995	11,131	79	233	2,168	3,395	2,437	1,606	885	295	33	0
1996	11,957	87	234	2,360	3,569	2,595	1,798	957	330	27	0
1997	12,087	85	204	2,429	3,438	2,644	1,849	1,091	322	25	0
1998	12,458	73	213	2,703	3,419	2,740	1,801	1,148	339	22	0
1999	12,140	69	182	2,628	3,349	2,546	1,807	1,178	358	23	0
2000	11,976	93	181	2,606	3,348	2,400	1,765	1,174	381	28	0
2001	12,108	66	210	2,717	3,459	2,315	1,815	1,126	377	23	0
2002	11,839	80	194	2,646	3,446	2,165	1,731	1,166	382	29	0
2003	12,259	71	241	2,779	3,672	2,223	1,723	1,111	411	28	0
2004	12,414	104	207	2,899	3,687	2,260	1,660	1,182	383	32	0
2005	12,604	94	248	2,966	3,765	2,333	1,682	1,094	397	25	0
2006	13,108	91	273	3,085	3,967	2,432	1,614	1,205	413	28	0
2007	13,709	98	276	3,182	4,117	2,729	1,639	1,221	409	38	0
2008	13,846	94	248	3,144	4,290	2,752	1,651	1,211	426	30	0
2009	13,050	97	247	2,876	3,853	2,704	1,669	1,152	410	42	0
2010 [2]	12,785	89	223	2,746	3,940	2,579	1,640	1,133	398	37	0

Sources: Department of Health;
Notifications (to the Chief Medical Officer for Scotland) of abortions performed;
under the Abortion Act 1967: ISD Scotland

1 Refers to therapeutic abortions notified in accordance with the Abortion Act 1967.
2 Provisional.

15.18(a) Deaths: analysis by sex and age[1]

United Kingdom

Number

	All ages[2]	Under 1 year	1-4	4-9	10-14	15-19	20-24	25-34	35-44	45-54	55-64	65-74	75-84	85 and over
Males														
1900 - 02	340,664	87,242	37,834	8,429	4,696	7,047	8,766	19,154	24,739	30,488	37,610	39,765	28,320	6,563
1910 - 12	303,703	63,885	29,452	7,091	4,095	5,873	6,817	16,141	21,813	28,981	37,721	45,140	29,397	7,283
1920 - 22	284,876	48,044	19,008	6,052	3,953	5,906	6,572	13,663	19,702	29,256	40,583	49,398	34,937	7,801
1930 - 32	284,249	28,840	11,276	4,580	2,890	5,076	6,495	12,327	16,326	29,376	47,989	63,804	45,247	10,022
1940 - 42	314,643	24,624	6,949	3,400	2,474	4,653	4,246	11,506	17,296	30,082	57,076	79,652	59,733	12,900
1950 - 52	307,312	14,105	2,585	1,317	919	1,498	2,289	5,862	11,074	27,637	53,691	86,435	79,768	20,131
1960 - 62	318,850	12,234	1,733	971	871	1,718	1,857	3,842	8,753	26,422	63,009	87,542	83,291	26,605
1970 - 72	335,166	9,158	1,485	1,019	802	1,778	2,104	3,590	7,733	24,608	64,898	105,058	82,905	30,027
1980 - 82	330,495	4,829	774	527	652	1,999	1,943	3,736	6,568	19,728	54,159	105,155	98,488	31,936
1990 - 92	312,521	3,315	623	372	396	1,349	2,059	4,334	6,979	15,412	40,424	87,849	106,376	43,032
2000 - 02	289,452	2,079	377	239	334	1,082	1,563	4,432	7,268	15,449	32,435	67,034	98,608	58,553
	KHUA	KHUB	KHUC	KHUD	KHUE	KHUF	KHUG	KHUH	KHUI	KHUJ	KHUK	KHUL	KHUM	KHUN
1997	301,713	2,414	465	301	366	1,134	1,738	4,558	6,678	15,770	33,910	78,121	101,817	54,441
1998	299,655	2,315	465	297	361	1,145	1,651	4,782	6,893	15,836	33,673	75,608	101,066	55,563
1999	299,235	2,323	459	260	333	1,088	1,548	4,647	6,930	15,862	33,181	73,457	101,327	57,820
2000	291,337	2,136	390	263	305	1,068	1,595	4,491	7,168	15,458	32,661	69,707	98,398	57,697
2001	287,939	2,052	358	230	369	1,106	1,518	4,459	7,275	15,667	32,135	66,256	98,041	58,473
2002	289,081	2,050	382	224	327	1,071	1,575	4,345	7,362	15,221	32,509	65,140	99,386	59,489
2003	289,185	2,047	356	228	308	1,013	1,586	4,041	7,530	14,692	32,895	63,520	100,900	60,069
2004	278,918	2,033	345	206	282	975	1,484	3,831	7,454	14,510	31,660	60,760	98,466	56,912
2005	277,349	2,117	339	194	312	1,022	1,449	3,660	7,454	14,241	31,645	58,828	95,641	60,447
2006	274,201	2,078	328	213	299	1,008	1,482	3,712	7,485	14,406	32,012	56,319	92,532	62,327
2007	274,890	2,113	379	200	270	979	1,491	3,711	7,423	14,045	31,994	55,338	91,488	65,459
2008	276,745	2,123	319	211	218	955	1,487	3,718	7,519	14,420	31,406	55,445	90,367	68,557
2009	270,804	2,067	276	170	216	925	1,341	3,547	7,584	14,039	30,752	53,973	87,328	68,586
Females														
1900 - 02	322,058	68,770	36,164	8,757	5,034	6,818	8,264	18,702	21,887	25,679	34,521	42,456	34,907	10,099
1910 - 12	289,608	49,865	27,817	7,113	4,355	5,683	6,531	15,676	19,647	24,481	32,813	46,453	37,353	11,828
1920 - 22	274,772	35,356	17,323	5,808	4,133	5,729	6,753	14,878	18,121	24,347	34,026	48,573	45,521	14,203
1930 - 32	275,336	21,072	9,995	3,990	2,734	4,721	5,931	12,699	15,373	24,695	39,471	59,520	56,250	18,886
1940 - 42	296,646	17,936	5,952	2,743	2,068	4,180	5,028	11,261	14,255	23,629	42,651	70,907	71,377	24,658
1950 - 52	291,597	10,293	2,098	880	625	1,115	1,717	5,018	8,989	18,875	37,075	75,220	92,848	36,844
1960 - 62	304,871	8,887	1,334	627	522	684	811	2,504	6,513	16,720	36,078	73,118	105,956	51,117
1970 - 72	322,968	6,666	1,183	654	459	718	900	2,110	5,345	15,594	36,177	75,599	109,539	68,024
1980 - 82	330,269	3,561	585	355	425	733	772	2,099	4,360	12,206	32,052	72,618	117,760	82,743
1990 - 92	328,218	2,431	485	259	255	520	714	1,989	4,340	9,707	25,105	61,951	115,467	104,994
2000 - 02	318,220	1,601	289	193	215	457	562	1,903	4,448	10,304	20,602	47,457	101,897	128,292
1997	330,804	1,863	336	221	236	489	587	1,953	4,320	10,451	21,103	55,947	108,777	124,521
1998	327,938	1,744	339	221	233	511	554	2,015	4,316	10,441	20,819	54,048	106,704	125,993
1999	330,241	1,736	346	195	244	487	567	1,963	4,359	10,400	20,963	52,098	106,323	130,560
2000	319,242	1,677	288	181	215	468	573	1,975	4,488	10,477	20,620	49,138	102,052	127,090
2001	316,454	1,639	299	218	200	447	557	1,895	4,475	10,355	20,479	47,139	101,135	127,616
2002	318,964	1,488	280	181	229	456	556	1,838	4,380	10,081	20,707	46,094	102,504	130,170
2003	322,900	1,639	309	182	237	441	563	1,869	4,506	9,870	20,974	45,374	105,182	131,754
2004	305,873	1,626	279	160	201	480	572	1,765	4,486	9,463	20,500	43,118	100,775	122,448
2005	305,615	1,555	256	153	216	450	557	1,684	4,432	9,492	20,655	41,839	98,338	125,988
2006	298,024	1,659	303	151	201	437	520	1,604	4,434	9,475	20,855	40,290	92,877	125,218
2007	299,797	1,627	266	137	212	423	522	1,575	4,398	9,487	21,026	39,685	90,822	129,617
2008	302,952	1,622	296	158	161	430	544	1,667	4,446	9,680	21,060	39,496	89,459	133,933
2009	288,813	1,610	273	150	188	401	509	1,626	4,288	9,407	20,563	38,262	83,709	127,827

15.18(b) Deaths: analysis by sex and age[1]

continued

England and Wales

Numbers

	All ages[2]	Under 1 year	1-4	5-9	10-14	15-19	20-24	25-34	35-44	45-54	55-64	65-74	75-84	85 and over
Males														
1900 - 02	288,886	76,095	32,051	7,066	3,818	5,611	7,028	15,869	21,135	26,065	31,600	33,568	23,835	5,144
1910 - 12	257,253	54,678	24,676	5,907	3,348	4,765	5,596	13,603	18,665	24,820	32,217	38,016	24,928	6,036
1920 - 22	240,605	39,796	15,565	5,151	3,314	4,901	5,447	11,551	17,004	25,073	34,639	42,025	29,685	6,455
1930 - 32	243,147	23,331	9,099	3,844	2,435	4,354	5,580	10,600	14,041	25,657	41,581	54,910	39,091	8,624
1940 - 42	268,876	19,393	5,616	2,834	2,051	3,832	3,156	9,484	14,744	25,983	50,058	68,791	51,779	11,158
1950 - 52	266,879	11,498	2,131	1,087	778	1,248	1,947	4,990	9,489	23,815	46,948	75,774	69,496	17,677
1960 - 62	278,369	10,157	1,444	812	742	1,523	1,624	3,278	7,524	22,813	54,908	77,000	73,180	23,364
1970 - 72	293,934	7,818	1,259	860	677	1,524	1,788	3,079	6,637	21,348	56,667	92,389	73,365	26,522
1980 - 82	290,352	4,168	657	452	555	1,716	1,619	3,169	5,590	16,909	47,144	92,485	87,338	28,551
1990 - 92	275,550	2,926	545	325	338	1,157	1,757	3,717	6,057	13,258	34,977	77,063	94,672	38,757
2000 - 02	254,899	1,850	334	206	290	912	1,305	3,781	6,191	13,263	27,803	58,341	87,727	52,895
	KHVA	**KHVB**	**KHVC**	**KHVD**	**KHVE**	**KHVF**	**KHVG**	**KHVH**	**KHVI**	**KHVJ**	**KHVK**	**KHVL**	**KHVM**	**KHVN**
1997	266,164	2,160	421	268	327	970	1,468	3,915	5,718	13,565	29,110	68,275	90,659	49,308
1998	264,202	2,058	415	254	309	962	1,404	4,111	5,886	13,606	28,947	65,989	90,048	50,213
1999	263,166	2,080	408	221	289	905	1,265	3,978	5,918	13,633	28,532	64,017	89,963	51,957
2000	256,698	1,902	345	227	263	898	1,328	3,849	6,135	13,355	28,003	60,801	87,449	52,143
2001	253,608	1,818	329	192	320	927	1,276	3,830	6,184	13,424	27,599	57,638	87,238	52,833
2002	254,390	1,831	329	198	286	912	1,310	3,665	6,255	13,011	27,807	56,584	88,493	53,709
2003	254,433	1,827	310	203	263	852	1,348	3,478	6,440	12,697	28,291	55,064	89,596	54,064
2004	245,208	1,809	303	174	252	833	1,257	3,281	6,360	12,417	27,117	52,709	87,367	51,329
2005	243,870	1,877	297	166	272	856	1,217	3,146	6,362	12,158	27,292	51,019	84,661	54,547
2006	240,888	1,863	292	187	261	844	1,212	3,132	6,315	12,256	27,551	48,881	81,912	56,182
2007	240,787	1,889	339	182	226	797	1,218	3,138	6,264	11,893	27,508	47,830	80,573	58,930
2008	243,014	1,920	284	180	190	779	1,255	3,088	6,419	12,269	27,093	47,862	79,799	61,876
2009	238,062	1,856	245	147	195	778	1,121	2,974	6,473	11,975	26,607	46,748	77,068	61,875
Females														
1900 - 02	269,432	60,090	30,674	7,278	4,010	5,265	6,497	15,065	18,253	21,474	28,424	35,307	29,118	7,977
1910 - 12	242,079	42,642	23,335	5,883	3,519	4,522	5,256	12,742	16,363	20,611	27,571	38,489	31,363	9,782
1920 - 22	229,908	29,178	14,174	4,928	3,456	4,719	5,533	12,244	15,142	20,580	28,633	41,010	38,439	11,871
1930 - 32	233,915	16,929	8,013	3,338	2,293	3,969	5,039	10,716	13,022	21,190	33,798	50,844	48,531	16,234
1940 - 42	253,702	14,174	4,726	2,265	1,695	3,426	4,198	9,470	12,093	20,413	36,814	60,987	61,891	21,550
1950 - 52	252,176	8,367	1,727	732	520	893	1,365	4,131	7,586	16,161	31,875	65,087	81,154	32,579
1960 - 62	266,849	7,409	1,103	527	444	591	700	2,147	5,576	14,389	31,083	63,543	93,548	45,789
1970 - 72	284,181	5,677	1,020	562	396	620	806	1,814	4,585	13,417	31,222	65,817	96,952	61,293
1980 - 82	290,026	3,064	511	301	365	635	670	1,821	3,740	10,420	27,606	63,023	103,676	74,194
1990 - 92	288,851	2,161	420	227	217	455	625	1,718	3,765	8,347	21,466	53,783	101,752	93,914
2000 - 02	280,345	1,428	256	173	189	393	481	1,655	3,826	8,927	17,712	40,867	89,633	114,805
	KIVA	**KIVB**	**KIVC**	**KIVD**	**KIVE**	**KIVF**	**KIVG**	**KIVH**	**KIVI**	**KIVJ**	**KIVK**	**KIVL**	**KIVM**	**KIVN**
1997	291,888	1,664	300	183	206	428	503	1,711	3,734	9,055	18,053	48,553	96,009	111,489
1998	289,234	1,547	301	185	207	432	466	1,768	3,705	9,077	17,872	46,742	94,282	112,650
1999	290,366	1,555	308	168	219	399	484	1,707	3,773	8,999	17,949	44,958	93,360	116,487
2000	281,179	1,497	257	160	191	403	504	1,702	3,853	9,108	17,722	42,318	89,651	113,813
2001	278,890	1,449	272	198	171	386	472	1,665	3,858	8,984	17,608	40,639	89,036	114,152
2002	280,966	1,337	240	160	204	391	467	1,597	3,767	8,689	17,807	39,645	90,213	116,449
2003	284,718	1,479	278	159	209	370	485	1,636	3,884	8,554	18,001	39,001	92,694	117,968
2004	269,042	1,462	251	140	173	410	494	1,536	3,855	8,139	17,649	37,041	88,404	109,488
2005	269,123	1,371	222	134	189	379	478	1,481	3,805	8,175	17,797	35,913	86,309	112,870
2006	261,712	1,505	267	135	169	381	444	1,382	3,802	8,099	17,948	34,502	81,210	111,868
2007	263,265	1,456	235	121	192	357	453	1,360	3,787	8,072	18,166	33,903	79,411	115,752
2008	266,076	1,449	270	137	140	351	458	1,445	3,811	8,291	18,187	33,883	77,827	119,827
2009	253,286	1,456	240	132	165	328	429	1,395	3,649	7,999	17,746	32,743	72,856	114,148

15.18(c) Deaths: analysis by sex and age[1]

continued

Scotland

Numbers

	All ages[2]	Under 1 year	1-4	5-9	10-14	15-19	20-24	25-34	35-44	45-54	55-64	65-74	75-84	85 and over
Males														
1900 - 02	40,224	9,189	4,798	1,083	672	1,069	1,292	2,506	2,935	3,591	4,597	4,531	3,117	834
1910 - 12	35,981	7,510	3,935	962	595	826	910	1,969	2,469	3,325	4,356	5,113	3,182	813
1920 - 22	34,649	6,757	2,847	710	489	747	791	1,616	2,128	3,314	4,785	5,624	3,928	911
1930 - 32	32,476	4,426	1,771	610	365	568	706	1,352	1,848	2,979	5,095	6,906	4,839	1,010
1940 - 42	36,384	3,973	1,011	449	321	668	888	1,643	2,090	3,348	5,728	8,556	6,317	1,337
1950 - 52	32,236	1,949	349	175	105	200	265	693	1,267	3,151	5,574	8,544	8,094	1,871
1960 - 62	32,401	1,578	222	121	102	146	185	456	1,013	2,986	6,682	8,505	7,980	2,425
1970 - 72	32,446	944	168	119	93	178	233	396	875	2,617	6,641	10,176	7,383	2,624
1980 - 82	31,723	451	80	56	71	206	233	423	776	2,280	5,601	10,152	8,804	2,591
1990 - 92	29,421	287	57	34	40	137	230	485	744	1,730	4,402	8,611	9,311	3,353
2000 - 02	27,526	165	30	23	30	119	196	523	882	1,775	3,781	7,038	8,535	4,430
	KHWA	**KHWB**	**KHWC**	**KHWD**	**KHWE**	**KHWF**	**KHWG**	**KHWH**	**KHWI**	**KHWJ**	**KHWK**	**KHWL**	**KHWM**	**KHWN**
1997	28,305	186	32	22	27	114	208	521	788	1,794	3,876	7,909	8,791	4,037
1998	28,132	183	37	34	39	134	200	524	843	1,796	3,828	7,746	8,585	4,183
1999	28,605	161	31	23	33	138	215	545	818	1,820	3,773	7,569	8,908	4,571
2000	27,511	173	33	24	28	115	198	512	842	1,716	3,789	7,224	8,523	4,334
2001	27,324	155	22	27	35	131	179	510	902	1,820	3,751	6,950	8,433	4,409
2002	27,743	167	34	17	27	111	211	546	901	1,789	3,804	6,940	8,648	4,548
2003	27,832	146	35	15	31	122	186	469	893	1,634	3,787	6,797	8,994	4,723
2004	26,775	160	29	21	23	105	181	449	889	1,676	3,629	6,507	8,733	4,373
2005	26,522	159	33	19	30	106	150	385	882	1,654	3,478	6,352	8,691	4,583
2006	26,251	145	21	18	21	112	206	461	938	1,697	3,567	5,966	8,353	4,746
2007	26,895	154	25	13	31	127	207	461	908	1,685	3,572	6,082	8,547	5,083
2008	26,504	140	22	19	16	106	174	503	868	1,715	3,481	6,052	8,290	5,118
2009	25,828	142	21	14	13	105	149	448	884	1,628	3,312	5,810	8,061	5,241
Females														
1900 - 02	39,891	7,143	4,477	1,162	747	1,058	1,246	2,625	2,732	3,130	4,485	5,273	4,305	1,508
1910 - 12	36,132	5,854	3,674	981	618	836	910	2,149	2,473	2,909	3,960	5,636	4,588	1,552
1920 - 22	34,449	5,029	2,602	687	489	711	889	1,947	2,266	2,828	4,157	5,587	5,443	1,814
1930 - 32	32,377	3,319	1,602	527	339	568	666	1,508	1,812	2,731	4,380	6,630	6,178	2,117
1940 - 42	33,715	2,852	921	373	283	595	656	1,382	1,672	2,528	4,630	7,674	7,613	2,536
1950 - 52	31,525	1,432	284	115	84	185	293	714	1,127	2,188	4,204	8,157	9,310	3,431
1960 - 62	30,559	1,107	170	80	63	72	87	287	762	1,897	4,115	7,752	9,991	4,177
1970 - 72	30,978	694	118	69	46	73	74	231	608	1,769	4,036	7,823	10,112	5,324
1980 - 82	32,326	337	49	37	44	74	73	213	493	1,456	3,565	7,781	11,333	6,871
1990 - 92	31,747	190	45	20	29	49	72	218	458	1,093	2,966	6,630	11,079	8,898
2000 - 02	30,235	123	24	14	21	50	64	199	493	1,110	2,341	5,326	9,785	10,685
	KIWA	**KIWB**	**KIWC**	**KIWD**	**KIWE**	**KIWF**	**KIWG**	**KIWH**	**KIWI**	**KIWJ**	**KIWK**	**KIWL**	**KIWM**	**KIWN**
1997	31,189	130	23	28	21	43	71	199	496	1,128	2,480	5,985	10,164	10,421
1998	31,032	137	26	28	19	55	68	198	485	1,106	2,416	5,955	9,913	10,626
1999	31,676	115	26	20	17	65	58	201	467	1,128	2,431	5,837	10,198	11,113
2000	30,288	132	20	10	21	46	56	222	510	1,086	2,324	5,512	9,875	10,474
2001	30,058	135	20	16	21	47	71	189	480	1,111	2,361	5,235	9,695	10,677
2002	30,360	103	32	15	20	58	65	185	489	1,134	2,339	5,232	9,784	10,904
2003	30,640	119	24	18	20	57	64	181	489	1,062	2,446	5,194	9,977	10,989
2004	29,412	106	19	15	22	52	62	179	492	1,065	2,291	4,924	9,924	10,261
2005	29,225	125	27	11	18	55	58	163	506	1,073	2,316	4,841	9,620	10,412
2006	28,842	103	26	11	17	40	58	170	497	1,090	2,351	4,722	9,303	10,454
2007	29,091	118	26	11	14	50	52	166	490	1,124	2,311	4,732	9,083	10,914
2008	29,196	113	17	11	18	55	68	172	497	1,083	2,315	4,560	9,299	10,988
2009	28,028	93	20	11	19	47	64	184	508	1,111	2,251	4,395	8,625	10,700

15.18(d) Deaths: analysis by sex and age[1]
continued

Northern Ireland

	All ages[2]	Under 1 year	1-4	5-9	10-14	15-19	20-24	25-34	35-44	45-54	55-64	65-74	75-84	85 and over
Males														
1900 - 02	11,554	1,958	985	280	206	367	446	779	669	832	1,413	1,666	1,368	585
1910 - 12	10,469	1,697	841	222	152	282	311	569	679	836	1,148	2,011	1,287	434
1920 - 22	9,622	1,491	596	191	150	258	334	496	570	869	1,159	1,749	1,324	435
1930 - 32	8,626	1,083	406	126	90	154	209	375	437	740	1,313	1,988	1,317	388
1940 - 42	9,383	1,258	322	117	102	153	202	379	462	751	1,290	2,305	1,637	405
1950 - 52	8,197	658	105	55	36	50	77	179	318	671	1,169	2,117	2,178	583
1960 - 62	8,080	499	67	38	27	49	48	108	216	623	1,419	2,037	2,131	816
1970 - 72	8,786	396	58	40	32	76	83	115	221	643	1,590	2,493	2,157	881
1980 - 82	8,420	211	37	20	26	77	92	144	202	539	1,414	2,518	2,346	795
1990 - 92	7,550	102	21	13	18	55	73	132	178	423	1,044	2,175	2,393	922
2000 - 02	7,028	64	13	11	14	50	62	128	195	410	851	1,655	2,347	1,228
	KHXA	KHXB	KHXC	KHXD	KHXE	KHXF	KHXG	KHXH	KHXI	KHXJ	KHXK	KHXL	KHXM	KHXN
1997	7,244	68	12	11	12	50	62	122	172	411	924	1,937	2,367	1,096
1998	7,321	74	13	9	13	49	47	147	164	434	898	1,873	2,433	1,167
1999	7,464	82	20	16	11	45	68	124	194	409	876	1,871	2,456	1,292
2000	7,128	61	12	12	14	55	69	130	191	387	869	1,682	2,426	1,220
2001	7,007	79	7	11	14	48	63	119	189	423	785	1,668	2,370	1,231
2002	6,948	52	19	9	14	48	54	134	206	421	898	1,616	2,245	1,232
2003	6,920	74	11	10	14	39	52	94	197	361	817	1,659	2,310	1,282
2004	6,935	64	13	11	7	37	46	101	205	417	914	1,544	2,366	1,210
2005	6,957	81	9	9	10	60	82	129	210	429	875	1,457	2,289	1,317
2006	7,062	70	15	8	17	52	64	119	232	453	894	1,472	2,267	1,399
2007	7,208	70	15	5	13	55	66	112	251	467	914	1,426	2,368	1,446
2008	7,227	63	13	12	12	70	58	127	232	436	832	1,531	2,278	1,563
2009	6,914	69	10	9	8	42	71	125	227	436	833	1,415	2,199	1,470
Females														
1900 - 02	12,735	1,537	1,013	317	277	495	521	1,012	902	1,075	1,612	1,876	1,484	614
1910 - 12	11,397	1,369	808	249	218	325	365	785	811	961	1,282	2,328	1,402	494
1920 - 22	10,415	1,149	547	193	188	299	331	687	713	939	1,236	1,976	1,639	518
1930 - 32	9,044	824	380	125	102	184	226	475	539	774	1,293	2,046	1,541	535
1940 - 42	9,229	910	305	105	90	159	174	409	490	688	1,207	2,246	1,873	572
1950 - 52	7,896	494	87	33	21	37	59	173	276	526	996	1,976	2,384	834
1960 - 62	7,463	371	61	20	15	21	24	70	175	434	880	1,823	2,417	1,151
1970 - 72	7,809	295	45	23	17	25	20	65	152	408	919	1,959	2,475	1,407
1980 - 82	7,917	160	26	17	17	23	29	65	127	329	881	1,813	2,752	1,678
1990 - 92	7,620	80	20	12	9	16	17	53	117	267	672	1,538	2,636	2,182
2000 - 02	7,640	50	9	7	5	13	17	49	129	267	548	1,263	2,479	2,802
	KIXA	KIXB	KIXC	KIXD	KIXE	KIXF	KIXG	KIXH	KIXI	KIXJ	KIXK	KIXL	KIXM	KIXN
1997	7,727	69	13	10	9	18	13	43	90	268	570	1,409	2,604	2,611
1998	7,672	60	12	8	7	24	20	49	126	258	531	1,351	2,509	2,717
1999	8,199	66	12	7	8	23	25	55	119	273	583	1,303	2,765	2,960
2000	7,775	48	11	11	3	19	13	51	125	283	574	1,308	2,526	2,803
2001	7,506	55	7	4	8	14	14	41	137	260	510	1,265	2,404	2,787
2002	7,638	48	8	6	5	7	24	56	124	258	561	1,217	2,507	2,817
2003	7,542	41	7	5	8	14	14	52	133	254	527	1,179	2,511	2,797
2004	7,419	58	9	5	6	18	16	50	139	259	560	1,153	2,447	2,699
2005	7,267	59	7	8	9	16	21	40	121	244	542	1,085	2,409	2,706
2006	7,470	51	10	5	15	16	18	52	135	286	556	1,066	2,364	2,896
2007	7,441	53	5	5	6	16	17	49	121	291	549	1,050	2,328	2,951
2008	7,680	60	9	10	3	24	18	50	138	306	558	1,053	2,333	3,118
2009	7,499	61	13	7	4	26	16	47	131	297	566	1,124	2,228	2,979

1 See chapter text.

2 In some years the totals include a small number of persons whose age was not stated.

Sources: Office for National Statistics:
National Records of Scotland
Northern Ireland Statistics and Research Agency

15.19(a) Infant and maternal mortality [1]

(I) - By country. (II) - Infant mortality by country, type of death and sex

	United Kingdom			England and Wales [2]			Scotland			Northern Ireland			Maternal deaths per thousand live births [3]			
	Total	Males	Females	Total	Males	Females	Total	Males	Females	Total	Males	Females	UK	England and Wales	Scotland	Northern Ireland
1900 - 02	142	156	128	146	160	131	124	136	111	113	123	103	4.71	4.67	4.74	6.03
1910 - 12	110	121	98	110	121	98	109	120	97	101	110	92	3.95	3.67	5.65	5.28
1920 - 22	82	92	71	80	90	69	94	106	82	86	95	77	4.37	4.03	6.36	5.62
1930 - 32	67	75	58	64	72	55	84	94	73	75	83	66	4.54	4.24	6.40	5.24
1940 - 42	59	66	51	55	62	48	77	87	66	80	89	70	3.29	2.74	4.50	3.79
1950 - 52	30	34	26	29	33	25	37	42	32	40	45	36	0.88	0.79	1.09	1.09
1960 - 62	22	25	19	22	24	19	26	30	22	27	30	24	0.36	0.36	0.37	0.43
1970 - 72	18	20	16	18	20	15	19	22	17	22	24	20	0.17	0.17	0.17	0.12
1980 - 82	12	13	10	11	13	10	12	13	10	13	15	12	0.09	0.09	0.14	0.06
1990 - 92	7	8	6	7	8	6	7	8	6	7	8	6	0.07	0.07	0.10	-
2000-02	6	6	5	6	6	5	6	6	5	5	6	5	0.07	0.06	0.12	0.05
	KKAW	KKAX	KKAY	KKAZ	KKBW	KKBX	KKBY	KKBZ	KKCW	KKCX	KKCY	KKCZ	KKDW	KKDX	KKDY	KKDZ
1997	5.8	6.4	5.3	5.9	6.5	5.3	5.3	6.1	4.5	5.6	5.5	5.8	0.1	0.1	0.1	—
1998	5.7	6.3	5.0	5.7	6.4	5.0	5.6	6.2	4.9	5.6	6.1	5.1	0.1	0.1	0.1	0.0
1999	5.8	6.4	5.1	5.8	6.5	5.1	5.0	5.7	4.3	6.4	6.8	5.9	0.1	0.1	0.1	—
2000	5.6	6.1	5.1	5.6	6.1	5.1	5.7	6.4	5.1	5.0	5.4	4.6	0.1	0.1	0.2	—
2001	5.5	6.0	5.0	5.5	6.0	5.0	5.5	5.8	5.2	6.0	6.9	5.1	0.1	0.1	0.1	0.1
2002	5.3	6.0	4.6	5.3	6.0	4.6	5.3	6.4	4.1	4.6	4.7	4.5	0.1	0.1	0.1	0.1
2003	5.3	5.7	4.9	5.3	5.7	4.9	5.1	5.4	4.7	5.2	6.5	3.9	0.1	0.1	0.1	0.1
2004	5.1	5.5	4.6	5.1	5.5	4.6	4.9	5.8	4.0	5.3	5.4	5.2	0.1	0.1	0.1	0.0
2005	5.1	5.7	4.5	5.0	5.7	4.4	5.2	5.7	4.8	6.1	7.0	5.3	0.1	0.1	0.1	0.0
2006	5.0	5.4	4.5	5.0	5.4	4.6	4.5	5.1	3.8	5.1	5.7	4.4	0.1	0.1	0.1	0.1
2007	4.8	5.3	4.3	4.8	5.3	4.3	4.7	5.2	4.2	4.9	5.5	4.4	0.1	0.1	0.1	0.0
2008	4.7	5.2	4.2	4.8	5.3	4.2	4.2	4.6	3.8	4.7	4.7	4.7	0.1	0.1	0.1	0.0
2009	4.6	5.1	4.2	4.7	5.1	4.2	4.0	4.7	3.2	5.1	5.3	4.9	0.1	0.1	0.1	0.2

Deaths of Infants under 1 year of age per thousand live births

15.19 (b) Infant and maternal mortality [1]

continued

Deaths per thousand live births

		1998	1999	2000	2001	2002	2003	2004	2005	2006	2007	2008	2009
Total													
United Kingdom:													
Stillbirths[4]	KHNQ	5.4	5.3	5.3	5.3	5.6	5.7	5.7	5.3	5.3	5.2	5.1	5.2
Perinatal[4]	KHNR	8.3	8.2	8.2	8.0	8.3	8.5	8.4	8.0	7.9	7.7	7.5	7.6
Neonatal	KHNS	3.8	3.9	3.9	3.7	3.5	3.6	3.5	3.5	3.5	3.3	3.2	3.2
Post neonatal	KHNT	1.9	1.9	1.7	1.9	1.7	1.7	1.6	1.6	1.5	1.5	1.5	1.5
England and Wales:													
Stillbirths[4]	KHNU	5.3	5.3	5.3	5.3	5.6	5.8	5.7	5.4	5.4	5.2	5.1	5.2
Perinatal[4]	KHNV	8.2	8.2	8.2	8.0	8.3	8.6	8.4	8.0	8.0	7.7	7.6	7.6
Neonatal	KHNW	3.8	3.9	3.9	3.6	3.6	3.6	3.5	3.4	3.5	3.3	3.2	3.2
Post neonatal	KHNX	1.9	1.9	1.7	1.9	1.7	1.7	1.6	1.6	1.5	1.5	1.5	1.5
Scotland:													
Stillbirths[4]	KHNY	6.1	5.2	5.6	5.7	5.4	5.6	5.8	5.3	5.3	5.6	5.4	5.3
Perinatal[4]	KHNZ	8.7	7.6	8.4	8.5	7.6	8.0	8.1	7.7	7.4	7.8	7.4	7.4
Neonatal	KHOA	3.6	3.3	4.0	3.8	3.2	3.4	3.1	3.5	3.1	3.2	2.8	2.8
Post neonatal	KHOB	2.0	1.7	1.8	1.7	2.1	1.7	1.9	1.7	1.4	1.5	1.4	1.2
Northern Ireland[5]													
Stillbirths[4]	KHOC	5.1	5.7	4.3	5.1	5.7	5.0	5.0	4.0	3.8	4.2	4.5	4.8
Perinatal[4]	KHOD	8.1	10.0	7.2	8.4	8.7	8.0	8.0	8.1	6.9	6.9	7.4	7.8
Neonatal	KHOE	3.9	4.8	3.8	4.4	3.4	3.9	3.6	4.9	3.8	3.2	3.6	3.8
Post neonatal	KHOF	1.7	1.6	1.2	1.6	1.2	1.3	1.7	1.3	1.3	1.7	1.1	1.3
Males													
United Kingdom:													
Perinatal[4]	KHOG	8.8	8.7	8.7	8.6	8.9	8.8	8.8	8.3	8.2	8.1	7.9	7.9
Neonatal	KHOH	4.2	4.4	4.2	4.0	4.0	3.9	3.8	3.9	3.8	3.6	3.6	3.5
Infant mortality	KHOI	6.3	6.4	6.1	6.0	6.0	5.7	5.5	5.7	5.4	5.3	5.2	5.1
England and Wales:													
Perinatal[4]	KHOK	8.7	8.6	8.7	8.5	8.9	8.9	8.8	8.4	8.3	8.1	7.9	8.0
Neonatal	KHOL	4.3	4.3	4.2	3.9	4.0	3.8	3.8	3.8	3.8	3.6	3.6	3.5
Infant mortality	KHOM	6.4	6.5	6.1	6.0	6.0	5.7	5.5	5.7	5.4	5.3	5.3	5.1
Scotland:													
Perinatal[4]	KHOO	9.6	8.4	9.5	9.2	7.9	8.4	8.8	7.6	7.7	8.4	8.1	7.6
Neonatal	KHOP	4.0	3.8	4.5	4.0	3.7	3.6	3.6	3.8	3.4	3.5	3.0	3.3
Infant mortality	KHOQ	6.2	5.7	6.4	5.8	6.4	5.4	5.8	5.7	5.1	5.2	4.6	4.7
Northern Ireland:													
Perinatal[4]	KHOS	8.9	10.5	7.9	9.6	9.8	8.1	8.2	9.2	7.3	7.3	7.6	7.2
Neonatal	KHOT	4.4	5.5	4.2	5.2	3.7	4.6	3.7	5.5	4.6	3.4	3.7	4.0
Infant mortality	KHOU	6.1	6.8	5.4	6.9	4.7	6.5	5.4	7.0	5.7	5.5	4.7	5.3
Females													
United Kingdom:													
Perinatal[4]	KHOW	7.7	7.8	7.5	7.4	7.7	8.1	8.0	7.6	7.5	7.3	7.1	7.2
Neonatal	KHOX	3.3	3.4	3.5	3.3	3.1	3.3	3.1	3.1	3.1	3.0	2.9	2.9
Infant mortality	KHOY	5.0	5.1	5.1	5.0	4.6	4.9	4.6	4.5	4.5	4.3	4.2	4.2
England and Wales:													
Perinatal[4]	KHPA	7.7	7.8	7.6	7.3	7.7	8.2	8.0	7.6	7.6	7.4	7.2	7.2
Neonatal	KHPB	3.3	3.5	3.5	3.3	3.1	3.4	3.2	3.0	3.2	3.0	2.9	2.9
Infant mortality	KHPC	5.0	5.1	5.1	5.0	4.6	4.9	4.6	4.4	4.6	4.3	4.2	4.2
Scotland:													
Perinatal[4]	KHPE	7.9	6.7	7.2	7.8	7.2	7.7	7.3	7.9	7.1	7.3	6.7	7.2
Neonatal	KHPF	3.2	2.8	3.5	3.5	2.6	3.1	2.5	3.2	2.8	3.0	2.6	2.3
Infant mortality	KHPG	4.9	4.3	5.1	5.2	4.1	4.7	4.0	4.8	3.8	4.2	3.8	3.2
Northern Ireland:													
Perinatal[4]	KHPI	7.3	9.5	6.4	6.9	7.6	7.8	7.8	6.9	6.5	6.5	7.0	8.4
Neonatal	KHPJ	3.4	4.1	3.3	3.5	3.0	3.2	3.5	4.2	2.9	3.0	3.5	3.5
Infant mortality	KHPK	5.1	5.9	4.6	5.1	4.5	3.9	5.2	5.3	4.4	4.4	4.7	4.9

1 See chapter text.

2 From 1937 to 1956 death rates are based on the births to which they relate
  in the current and preceding years.

3 Deaths in pregnancy and childbirth.   4 Deaths per 1,000 live and stillbirths. See chapter introduction.

Sources: Office for National Statistics;
National Records of Scotland
Northern Ireland Statistics and Research Agency

15.20 Death rates by sex and age[1]

United Kingdom

Rates per 1,000 population

	All ages	0-4	5-9	10-14	15-19	20-24	25-34	35-44	45-54	55-64	65-74	75-84	85 and over
Males													
1900 - 02	18.4	57.0	4.1	2.4	3.7	5.0	6.6	11.0	18.6	35.0	69.9	143.6	289.6
1910 - 12	14.9	40.5	3.3	2.0	3.0	3.9	5.0	8.0	14.9	29.8	62.1	133.8	261.5
1920 - 22	13.5	33.4	2.9	1.8	2.9	3.9	4.5	6.9	11.9	25.3	57.8	131.8	259.1
1930 - 32	12.9	22.3	2.3	1.5	2.6	3.3	3.5	5.7	11.3	23.7	57.9	134.2	277.0
1940 - 42	..	..	..	..	..	..	..	..	..	..	..	..	..
1950 - 52	12.6	7.7	0.7	0.5	0.9	1.4	1.6	3.0	8.5	23.2	55.2	127.6	272.0
1960 - 62	12.5	6.4	0.5	0.4	0.9	1.1	1.1	2.5	7.4	22.2	54.4	123.4	251.0
1970 - 72	12.4	4.6	0.4	0.4	0.9	1.0	1.0	2.4	7.3	20.9	52.9	116.3	246.1
1980 - 82	12.1	3.2	0.3	0.3	0.8	0.9	0.9	1.9	6.3	18.2	46.7	107.1	224.9
1990 - 92	11.2	2.0	0.2	0.2	0.7	0.9	1.0	1.8	4.6	14.2	38.6	93.0	201.4
2000 - 02	10.0	1.4	0.1	0.2	0.6	0.9	1.1	1.7	4.0	10.4	29.0	75.4	188.2
	KHZA	KHZB	KHZC	KHZD	KHZE	KHZF	KHZG	KHZH	KHZJ	KHZK	KHZL	KHZM	KHZN
1997	10.6	1.5	0.2	0.2	0.6	1.0	1.0	1.7	4.1	11.8	33.9	83.2	196.7
1998	10.5	1.5	0.1	0.2	0.6	0.9	1.1	1.7	4.1	11.6	33.0	81.8	193.6
1999	10.5	1.5	0.1	0.2	0.6	0.9	1.0	1.7	4.1	11.2	32.2	80.9	195.7
2000	10.1	1.4	0.1	0.2	0.6	0.8	1.0	1.6	4.0	10.7	30.3	76.8	187.9
2001	10.0	1.3	0.1	0.2	0.6	0.8	1.0	1.6	4.1	10.4	28.7	74.8	187.2
2002	10.0	1.4	0.1	0.2	0.5	0.8	1.0	1.6	4.0	10.1	27.8	74.3	188.2
2003	9.9	1.4	0.1	0.1	0.5	0.8	1.0	1.6	3.9	9.9	27.0	73.6	191.7
2004	9.5	1.4	0.1	0.1	0.5	0.7	0.9	1.6	3.8	9.3	25.5	70.6	176.3
2005	9.5	1.4	0.1	0.1	0.5	0.7	0.9	1.6	3.7	9.3	24.8	68.7	187.8
2006	9.2	1.3	0.1	0.2	0.5	0.7	0.9	1.6	3.7	9.1	23.7	65.5	164.5
2007	9.2	1.3	0.1	0.1	0.5	0.7	0.9	1.6	3.6	9.0	23.1	63.9	162.5
2008	9.2	1.3	0.1	0.1	0.5	0.7	0.9	1.7	3.6	8.8	22.7	62.2	162.6
2009	8.9	1.2	0.1	0.1	0.5	0.6	0.9	1.7	3.4	8.6	21.5	59.3	156.2
Females													
1900 - 02	16.3	47.9	4.3	2.6	3.5	4.3	5.8	9.0	14.4	27.9	59.3	127.0	262.6
1910 - 12	13.3	34.0	3.3	2.1	2.9	3.4	4.4	6.7	11.5	23.1	50.7	113.7	234.0
1920 - 22	11.9	26.9	2.8	1.9	2.8	3.4	4.1	5.6	9.3	19.2	45.6	111.5	232.4
1930 - 32	11.5	17.7	2.1	1.5	2.4	2.9	3.3	4.6	8.3	17.6	43.7	110.1	246.3
1940 - 42	..	..	..	..	..	..	..	..	..	..	..	..	..
1950 - 52	11.2	6.0	0.5	0.4	0.7	1.0	1.4	2.3	5.3	12.9	35.5	98.4	228.8
1960 - 62	11.2	4.9	0.3	0.3	0.4	0.5	0.8	1.8	4.5	11.0	30.8	87.3	218.5
1970 - 72	11.3	3.6	0.3	0.2	0.4	0.4	0.6	1.6	4.5	10.5	27.5	76.7	196.1
1980 - 82	11.4	2.3	0.2	0.2	0.3	0.4	0.5	1.3	3.9	9.9	24.8	67.2	179.5
1990 - 92	11.1	1.5	0.1	0.2	0.3	0.3	0.4	1.1	2.9	8.4	22.1	58.7	157.2
2000-02	10.5	1.1	0.2	0.1	0.1	0.3	0.4	1.0	2.6	6.4	18.0	51.3	157.6
	KHZO	KHZP	KHZQ	KHZR	KHZS	KHZT	KHZU	KHZV	KHZW	KHZX	KHZY	KHZZ	KHZI
1996	11.1	1.2	0.1	0.1	0.3	0.3	0.5	1.1	2.7	7.3	21.0	56.4	159.4
1997	11.0	1.2	0.1	0.1	0.3	0.3	0.4	1.1	2.7	7.1	20.5	55.2	160.3
1998	11.0	1.2	0.1	0.1	0.3	0.3	0.4	1.0	2.7	7.0	20.2	54.1	159.8
1999	11.0	1.2	0.1	0.1	0.3	0.3	0.4	1.0	2.7	6.9	19.6	54.2	163.7
2000	10.5	1.1	0.1	0.1	0.3	0.3	0.5	1.0	2.7	6.6	18.5	51.6	155.8
2001	10.4	1.1	0.1	0.1	0.2	0.3	0.4	1.0	2.6	6.4	17.9	50.8	156.1
2002	10.5	1.0	0.1	0.1	0.2	0.3	0.4	1.0	2.6	6.2	17.4	51.1	160.3
2003	10.6	1.2	0.1	0.1	0.2	0.3	0.4	1.0	2.6	6.1	17.1	51.8	166.4
2004	10.0	1.1	0.1	0.1	0.2	0.3	0.4	1.0	2.4	5.8	16.2	49.3	155.2
2005	10.0	1.1	0.1	0.1	0.2	0.3	0.4	0.9	2.5	5.9	15.8	48.2	160.1
2006	9.6	1.1	0.1	0.1	0.2	0.3	0.4	0.9	2.4	5.7	15.2	46.4	144.9
2007	9.7	1.1	0.1	0.1	0.2	0.3	0.4	0.9	2.3	5.7	14.9	45.6	144.8
2008	9.7	1.1	0.1	0.1	0.2	0.3	0.4	1.0	2.3	5.7	14.6	45.0	146.6
2009	9.2	1.0	0.1	0.1	0.2	0.2	0.4	0.9	2.2	5.5	13.8	42.2	137.4

1 See Chapter Text

Sources: Office for National Statistics;
National Records of Scotland
Northern Ireland Statistics and Research Agency

15.21 Interim life tables, 2008-10

United Kingdom / England and Wales

Age(x)	UK Males l_x	UK Males e^0_x	UK Females l_x	UK Females e^0_x	E&W Males l_x	E&W Males e^0_x	E&W Females l_x	E&W Females e^0_x
0 years	100000.0	78.05	100000.0	82.12	100000.0	78.31	100000.0	82.33
5 years	99423.6	73.50	99511.4	77.52	99420.5	73.77	99509.2	77.74
10 years	99370.3	68.54	99466.4	72.56	99368.9	68.81	99464.1	72.77
15 years	99313.9	63.57	99417.8	67.59	99311.8	63.84	99416.2	67.80
20 years	99103.0	58.70	99311.4	62.66	99115.9	58.96	99317.4	62.87
25 years	98789.3	53.88	99189.5	57.73	98819.6	54.13	99202.3	57.94
30 years	98416.0	49.08	99024.3	52.83	98472.2	49.31	99041.6	53.03
35 years	97925.3	44.31	98780.1	47.95	98009.3	44.54	98807.0	48.15
40 years	97255.3	39.60	98418.9	43.12	97368.7	39.81	98459.6	43.31
45 years	96333.8	34.95	97856.2	38.35	96483.2	35.15	97913.8	38.53
50 years	95013.7	30.40	97004.5	33.66	95209.9	30.59	97085.1	33.84
55 years	93010.6	26.00	95628.3	29.11	93270.3	26.17	95747.0	29.28
60 years	89902.1	21.80	93565.0	24.69	90237.7	21.96	93731.2	24.85
65 years	85304.2	17.83	90468.9	20.44	85739.9	17.97	90716.7	20.59
70 years	78296.9	14.19	85752.7	16.42	78881.7	14.30	86127.6	16.54
75 years	68192.0	10.90	78404.6	12.71	68923.1	10.98	78942.0	12.80
80 years	53982.1	8.08	66960.4	9.42	54791.5	8.14	67667.0	9.49
85 years	35895.0	5.87	50035.8	6.72	36640.6	5.90	50798.8	6.77
90 years	18079.7	4.29	29526.6	4.65	18562.0	4.31	30152.1	4.67
95 years	6298.8	2.99	11529.6	3.18	6530.3	3.01	11866.5	3.20
100 years	1184.7	2.27	2466.1	2.25	1240.4	2.30	2564.8	2.26

Scotland / Northern Ireland

Age(x)	Scot Males l_x	Scot Males e^0_x	Scot Females l_x	Scot Females e^0_x	NI Males l_x	NI Males e^0_x	NI Females l_x	NI Females e^0_x
0 years	100000.0	75.75	100000.0	80.34	100000.0	76.96	100000.0	81.40
5 years	99483.1	71.14	99584.0	75.67	99372.5	72.44	99401.2	76.89
10 years	99421.4	66.18	99548.7	70.70	99295.1	67.50	99338.0	71.94
15 years	99377.6	61.21	99490.6	65.74	99223.9	62.54	99293.5	66.97
20 years	99078.3	56.38	99331.2	60.84	98817.4	57.79	99109.4	62.09
25 years	98649.7	51.62	99151.6	55.94	98313.0	53.07	98949.6	57.19
30 years	98045.1	46.92	98940.8	51.06	97811.3	48.33	98779.6	52.28
35 years	97246.8	42.28	98584.2	46.23	97297.4	43.57	98548.8	47.40
40 years	96257.6	37.69	98096.4	41.45	96591.3	38.87	98126.6	42.59
45 years	94985.8	33.16	97374.5	36.74	95561.4	34.26	97533.5	37.83
50 years	93277.8	28.72	96333.6	32.10	94001.1	29.79	96579.5	33.18
55 years	90709.9	24.46	94651.6	27.63	91889.7	25.41	95043.2	28.67
60 years	86931.6	20.41	92168.1	23.30	88613.7	21.26	92850.2	24.28
65 years	81350.1	16.62	88289.1	19.21	83979.5	17.28	89610.9	20.07
70 years	73010.7	13.22	82420.4	15.38	76700.9	13.67	84784.7	16.06
75 years	61667.3	10.17	73701.4	11.89	66219.5	10.42	77127.9	12.40
80 years	46844.7	7.57	60785.3	8.85	51706.7	7.62	65677.9	9.10
85 years	29403.7	5.57	43312.6	6.38	33467.4	5.40	48899.7	6.31
90 years	14045.8	4.07	24213.2	4.46	15684.3	3.80	27503.6	4.25
95 years	4512.3	2.82	8943.6	3.06	4516.3	2.76	9395.7	2.92
100 years	758.1	2.01	1747.4	2.18			1688.0	2.07

Note Column l x shows the number who would survive to exact **age**(x), out of 100 000 born, who were subject throughout their lives to the death rates experienced in the three-year period indicated.
Column **e0x** is 'the expectation of life', that is, the average future lifetime which would be lived by a person aged exactly x if likewise subject to the death rates experienced in the three-year period indicated. See introductory notes.

Source: Office for National Statistics

15.22(a)   Adoptions by date of entry in Adopted Children Register

Year	All ages		Under 1		1-4		5-9		10-14		15-17	
	Numbers	Percentage	Numbers	Percentage	Numbers	Percentage	Numbers	Percentage	Numbers	Percentage	Numbers	Percentage
United Kingdom												
2002	6239	100	313	5	2737	44	1937	31	999	16	253	4
2003	5426	100	212	4	2481	46	1716	32	789	15	228	4
2004	6116	100	274	5	2843	46	1856	30	847	14	269	4
2005	6139	100	242	4	3127	51	1757	29	798	13	228	4
2006	5538	100	216	4	2788	50	1608	29	696	13	226	4
2007	5224	100	163	3	2761	53	1400	27	672	13	205	4
2008	5580	100	129	2	3085	55	1388	25	706	13	272	5
2009	5296	100	108	2	3043	57	1375	26	558	11	212	4
Males	VOXU	**VOXV**	VOXW	**VOXX**	VOXY	**VOXZ**	VOYA	**VOYB**	VOYC	**VOYD**	VOYE	**VOYF**
2002	3140	100	176	6	1425	45	935	30	488	16	116	4
2003	2634	100	104	4	1224	46	844	32	351	13	111	4
2004	3051	100	145	5	1426	47	936	31	418	14	126	4
2005	3072	100	121	4	1566	51	910	30	370	12	106	3
2006	2708	100	97	4	1377	51	806	30	314	12	113	4
2007	2614	100	83	3	1392	53	714	27	314	12	103	4
2008	2770	100	59	2	1542	56	701	25	354	13	114	4
2009	2697	100	54	2	1598	59	700	26	256	9	89	3
Females	VOYG	**VOYH**	VOYI	**VOYJ**	VOYK	**VOYL**	VOYM	**VOYN**	VOYO	**VOYP**	VOYQ	**VOYR**
2002	3099	100	137	4	1312	42	1002	32	511	16	137	4
2003	2792	100	108	4	1257	45	872	31	438	16	117	4
2004	3065	100	129	4	1417	46	920	30	456	15	143	5
2005	3079	100	121	4	1561	51	847	28	428	14	122	4
2006	2831	100	119	4	1411	50	802	28	382	13	113	4
2007	2610	100	80	3	1369	52	686	26	358	14	102	4
2008	2810	100	70	2	1543	55	687	24	352	13	158	6
2009	2599	100	54	2	1445	56	675	26	302	12	123	5
England & Wales												
Persons	GQTP	**GQTQ**	GQTR	**GQTS**	GQTT	**GQTU**	GQTV	**GQTW**	GQTX	**GQTY**	GQTZ	**GQUA**
2002	5680	100	287	5	2532	45	1748	31	900	16	213	4
2003	4818	100	183	4	2260	47	1503	31	683	14	189	4
2004	5562	100	253	5	2,627	47	1651	30	786	14	245	4
2005	5565	100	222	4	2902	52	1555	28	683	12	199	4
2006	4980	100	197	4	2591	52	1406	28	585	12	195	4
2007	4637	100	151	3	2510	54	1206	26	576	12	171	4
2008	5065	100	120	2	2832	56	1239	24	628	12	246	5
2009	4725	101	91	2	2783	59	1184	25	480	10	187	4
2010	4550	102	95	2	2649	58	1140	25	470	10	196	4
Males												
2002	2871	100	160	6	1324	46	846	29	443	15	98	3
2003	2339	100	91	4	1115	48	737	32	301	13	95	4
2004	2777	100	132	5	1327	48	831	30	373	13	114	4
2005	2791	100	112	4	1461	52	808	29	320	11	90	3
2006	2446	100	95	4	1282	52	707	29	267	11	94	4
2007	2315	100	77	3	1253	54	618	27	270	12	89	4
2008	2522	100	53	2	1425	57	622	25	324	13	98	4
2009	2392	101	46	2	1448	61	599	25	214	9	85	4
2010	2302	102	53	2	1350	59	586	25	223	10	90	4
Females	GQUN	**GQUO**	GQUP	**GQUQ**	GQUR	**GQUS**	GQUT	**GQUU**	GQUV	**GQUW**	GQUX	**GQUY**
2002	2809	100	127	5	1208	43	902	32	457	16	115	4
2003	2479	100	92	4	1145	46	766	31	382	15	94	4
2004	2785	100	121	4	1300	47	820	29	413	15	131	5
2005	2774	100	110	4	1445	52	747	27	363	13	109	4
2006	2534	100	102	4	1310	52	699	28	318	13	101	4
2007	2322	100	74	3	1257	54	588	25	306	13	82	4
2008	2543	100	67	3	1407	55	617	24	304	12	148	6
2009	2333	100	45	2	1335	57	585	25	266	11	102	4
2010	2248	100	42	2	1299	58	554	25	247	11	106	5

15.22(b) Adoptions by date of entry in Adopted Children Register
Continued

Year	All ages		Under 1		1-4		5-9		10-14		15-17	
	Numbers	Percentage	Numbers	Percentage	Numbers	Percentage	Numbers	Percentage	Numbers	Percentage	Numbers	Percentage
Scotland												
Persons	GQUZ	**GQVA**	GQVB	**GQVC**	GQVD	**GQVE**	GQVF	**GQVG**	GQVH	**GQVI**	GQVJ	**GQVK**
2002	385	100	13	3	143	37	130	34	73	19	26	7
2003	468	100	25	5	153	33	170	36	88	19	32	7
2004	393	100	21	5	144	37	143	36	67	17	18	5
2005	439	100	18	4	162	37	155	35	81	18	23	5
2006	418	100	16	4	153	37	150	36	73	17	26	6
2007	440	100	9	2	198	45	141	32	65	15	27	6
2008	418	100	9	2	205	49	119	28	65	16	20	5
2009	455	100	16	4	217	48	145	32	58	13	19	4
2010	466	100	23	5	218	47	159	34	49	11	17	4
Males	GQVL	**GQVM**	GQVN	**GQVO**	GQVP	**GQVQ**	GQVR	**GQVS**	GQVT	**GQVU**	GQVV	**GQVW**
2002	193	100	8	4	75	39	60	31	37	19	13	7
2003	228	100	11	5	78	34	85	37	43	19	11	5
2004	200	100	13	7	67	34	77	39	34	17	9	5
2005	217	100	9	4	80	37	79	36	36	17	13	6
2006	194	100	2	1	72	37	78	40	25	13	17	9
2007	229	100	4	2	115	50	70	31	30	13	10	4
2008	200	100	6	3	97	49	62	31	24	12	11	6
2009	250	100	8	3	126	50	81	32	32	13	3	1
2010												
Females	GQVX	**GQVY**	GQVZ	**GQWA**	GRFK	**GRFL**	GRFM	**GRFN**	GRFO	**GRFP**	GRFQ	**GRFR**
2002	192	100	5	3	68	35	70	36	36	19	13	7
2003	240	100	14	6	75	31	85	35	45	19	21	9
2004	193	100	8	4	77	40	66	34	33	17	9	5
2005	222	100	9	4	82	37	76	34	45	20	10	5
2006	224	100	14	6	81	36	72	32	48	22	9	4
2007	211	100	5	2	83	39	71	34	35	17	17	8
2008	218	100	3	1	108	50	57	26	41	19	9	4
2009	205	100	8	4	91	44	64	31	26	13	16	8
2010	**250**	**100**	**17**	**7**	**117**	47	**81**	32	**23**	9	12	5
Northern Ireland												
Persons	VOYS	**VOYT**	VOYU	**VOYV**	VOYW	**VOYX**	VOYY	**VOYZ**	VOZA	**VOZB**	VOZC	**VOZD**
2002	174	100	13	7	62	36	59	34	26	15	14	8
2003	140	100	4	3	68	49	43	31	18	13	7	5
2004	161	100	4	2	70	43	61	38	20	12	6	4
2005	140	100	6	4	53	38	45	32	30	21	6	4
2006	141	100	3	2	44	31	51	36	38	27	5	4
2007	147	100	3	2	53	36	53	36	31	21	7	5
2008	97	100	0	-	48	49	30	31	13	13	6	6
2009	116	100	1	1	43	37	46	40	20	17	6	5
Males	VOZE	**VOZF**	VOZG	**VOZH**	VOZI	**VOZJ**	VOZK	**VOZL**	VOZM	**VOZN**	VOZO	**VOZP**
2002	76	100	8	11	26	34	29	38	8	11	5	7
2003	67	100	2	3	31	46	22	33	7	10	5	7
2004	74	100	1	1	32	43	28	38	10	14	3	4
2005	61	100	2	3	23	38	21	34	12	20	3	5
2006	68	100	-	-	24	35	20	29	22	32	2	3
2007	70	100	2	3	24	34	26	37	14	20	4	6
2008	48	100	0	-	20	42	17	35	6	13	5	10
2009	55	100	0	-	24	44	20	36	10	18	1	2
Females	VOZQ	**VOZR**	VOZS	**VOZT**	VOZU	**VOZV**	VOZW	**VOZX**	VOZY	**VOZZ**	VPAA	**VPVD**
2002	98	100	5	5	36	37	30	31	18	18	9	9
2003	73	100	2	3	37	51	21	29	11	15	2	3
2004	87	100	3	3	38	44	33	38	10	11	3	3
2005	79	100	4	5	30	38	24	30	18	23	3	4
2006	73	100	3	4	20	27	31	42	16	22	3	4
2007	77	100	1	1	29	38	27	35	17	22	3	4
2008	49	100	0	-	28	57	13	27	7	14	1	2
2009	61	100	1	2	19	31	26	43	10	16	5	8

Sources: Office for National Statistics: 01329 444410
Northern Ireland Statistics and Research Agency
National Records of Scotland

Health

Chapter 16

Health

Deaths: analysed by cause (Table 16.6)

All figures in this table for England and Wales represent the number of deaths occurring in each calendar year. All data for Scotland and Northern Ireland relate to the number of deaths registered during each calendar year. From 2001, all three constituent countries of the UK are coding their causes of death using the latest, tenth, revision of the International Statistical Classification of Diseases and Related Health Problems (ICD-10). All cause of death information from 2001 (also for 2000 for Scotland) presented in this table is based on the revised classification.

To assist users in assessing any discontinuities arising from the introduction of the revised classification, bridge-coding exercises were carried out on all deaths registered in 1999 in England and Wales and also in Scotland. For further information about ICD-10 and the bridge-coding carried out by The Office for National Statistics Quarterly 14 (2002), pages 75–83 or log on to the Office for National Statistics (ONS) website at: www.ons.gov.uk. For information on the Scottish bridge-coding exercise, consult the Annual Report of the General Register Office for Scotland or log on to their website at: www.groscotland.gov.uk. No bridge-coding exercise was conducted for Northern Ireland.

Neonatal deaths and homicide and assault

For England and Wales, neonatal deaths (those at age under 28 days) are included in the number of total deaths but excluded from the cause figures. This has particular impact on the totals shown for the chapters covered by the ranges P and Q, 'Conditions originating in the perinatal period' and 'Congenital malformations, deformations and chromosomal abnormalities'. These are considerably lower than the actual number of deaths because it is not possible to assign an underlying cause of death from the neonatal death certificate used in England and Wales. Also, for England and Wales only, the total number shown for Homicide and assault, X85–Y09, will not be a true representation because the registration of these deaths is often delayed by adjourned inquests.

Occupational ill health (Tables 16.8 and 16.9)

There are a number of sources of data on the extent of occupational or work-related ill health in Great Britain. For some potentially severe lung diseases caused by exposures which are highly unlikely to be found in a non-occupational setting, it is useful to count the number of death certificates issued each year. This is also true for mesothelioma, a cancer affecting the lining of the lungs and stomach, for which the number of cases with non-occupational causes is likely to be larger (although still a minority). Table 16.9 shows the number of deaths for mesothelioma and asbestosis (linked to exposure to asbestos), pneumoconiosis (linked to coal dust or silica), byssinosis (linked to cotton dust) and some forms of allergic alveolitis (including farmer's lung). For asbestos-related diseases the figures are derived from a special register maintained by HSE.

Most conditions which can be caused or made worse by work can also arise from other factors. The remaining sources of data on work-related ill health rely on attribution of individual cases of illness to work causes.

In The Health and Occupation Reporting Network (THOR), this is done by specialist doctors – either occupational physicians or those working in particular disease specialisms (covering musculoskeletal, psychological, respiratory, skin, audio logical and infectious disease). Table 16.8 presents data from THOR for the last three years. It should be noted that not all cases of occupational disease will be seen by participating specialists; for example, the number of deaths due to mesothelioma (shown in Table 16.9) is known to be greater than the number of cases reported to THOR.

Injuries at work (Table 16.10)

The Reporting of Injuries, Diseases and Dangerous Occurrences Regulations 1995 (RIDDOR) places a legal duty on employers to report injuries arising from work activity to the relevant enforcing authority, namely HSE, local authorities and the Office of Rail Regulation (ORR). These include injuries to employees, self-employed people and members of the public. From 12 September 2011 the reporting of all RIDDOR incidents will move to a predominantly online system.

While the enforcing authorities are informed about almost all relevant fatal workplace injuries, it is known that non-fatal injuries are substantially under-reported. Currently, it is estimated that just over half of all such injuries to employees are actually reported, with the self-employed reporting a much smaller proportion. These results are achieved by comparing reported non-fatal injuries (major as well as over-3-day), with results from the Labour Force Survey (LFS).

16.1 Ambulance Staff by Type: by country

					Headcount		
		2004	2005	2006	2007	2008	2009	2010
England								
Qualified ambulance staff:								
Total Amubulance Staff	JF83	26,902	28,180	28,648	28,471	28,771	30,303	31,126
Manager	JF85	789	773	614	598	678	684	685
Emergency care practitioner	JF87	..	..	438	646	688	728	755
Paramedic	JF89	7,536	8,311	8,222	8,241	8,934	9,755	10,287
Ambulance Technician	JF8B	..	..	6,902	7,543	6,589	6,048	5,959
Ambulance Personnel	JF8D	8,947	9,033	..	..	..	..	
Support to Ambulance Staff								
Trainee Ambulance Technician	JF8F	..	..	1,829	1,147	1,232	1,403	1,455
Trainee Ambulance Personnel	JF8H	2,047	2,201	..	..	..	..	..
Wales								
Qualified ambulance staff:								
Total Amubulance Staff	JF84	1,354	1,401	1,458	1,397	1,402	1,403	1429
Manager	JF86	144	136	125	99	89	83	70
Emergency care practitioner	JF88	..	..	..	2	4	3	13
Paramedic	JF8A	668	749	804	818	847	905	883
Ambulance Technician	JF8C	..	..	..	477	462	405	448
Ambulance Personnel	JF8E	385	385	489	..	..	..	..
Support to Ambulance Staff								
Trainee Ambulance Technician	JF8G	..	..	..	1	11	7	15
Trainee Ambulance Personnel	JF8I	157	131	40	..	..	..	..
Scotland								
Total Ambulance staff	JHQ3	2,779	2,883	..	3,655	3,681	3,836	3833
Paramedic	JHQ4	1,023	1,153	..	1,247	1,269	1,323	1391
Technician	JHQ5	982	899	..	1,010	989	1,051	1009
Driver/chauffeur	JHQ6	53	55	..	103	91	97	91
Care assistant	JHQ7	722	776	..	931	948	961	944
Other	JHQ8	-	- ..		364	384	404	398
Northern Ireland								
Total Ambulance staff	JHQ9	867	889	934	988	1,038	1,033	1025
Emergency Medical Technicians and Paramedics	JHR2	687	722	753	557	621	635	541
Other/Patient care services	JHR3	122	126	121	339	328	327	225
Ambulance officers	JHR4	45	28	48	79	89	71	80
Manager	JHR5	11	12	12	11	..	..	..

Sources: The NHS Information Centre for Health and Social Care;
Welsh Government;
ISD Scotland;
Department of Health, Social Services and Public Safety Northern Ireland

Note: In 2006 ambulance staff were collected under new, more detailed occupational codes. As a result, qualified totals and support to ambulance staff totals are not directly comparable with previous years.

1 Scottish ambulance service 2006 data is unavailable.
2 Includes EMDC/control from 2007, newly identified from Agenda for Change.

The specific information requested here can be found further into the report at -

http://www.isdscotland.org/Health-Topics/Workforce/Publications/2011-08-30/2011-08-30-Workforce-Report.pdf?22999209166
http://www.isdscotland.org/Health-Topics/Workforce/Publications/2011-08-30/All_Other_Staff_J2011.xls

16.2 Hospital and primary care services Scotland

			1999 /00	2000 /01	2001 /02	2002 /03	2003 /04	2004 /05
Hospital and community services In-patients:[1,2]								
Average available staffed beds	KDEA	Thousands	33.5	32.1	30.9	29.8	28.9	28.1
Average occupied beds:								
All departments	KDEB	"	26.9	25.8	25.1	24.2	23.2	22.5
Psychiatric and learning disability	KDEC	"	8.3	7.6	7.0	6.4	5.9	5.5
Discharges or deaths[3]	KDED	"	980	972	969	959	989	1003
Outpatients:[2,4]								
New cases	KDEE	"	2,766	2,749	2,728	2,731	2,750	2,718
Total attendances	KDEF	"	6,451	6,382	6,254	6,193	6,147	5,981
Medical and dental staff:[5,6]	JYXO	Numbers	9,273	9,325	9,644	10,256	10,407	10,658
Whole-time	KDEG	"	7,185	7,216	7,530	8,115	8,349	8,612
Part-time	KDEH	"	1,632	1,648	1,681	1,697	1,636	1,630
Honorary	JYXN	"	495	495	468	468	437	431
Professional and technical staff:[6,7]								
Whole-time	KDEI	"	11,261	11,261	11,705	12,265	12,942	13,258
Part-time	KDEJ	"	5,218	5,483	5,852	6,273	6,708	6,968
Nursing and midwifery staff:[6,8]								
Whole-time	KDEK	"	32,356	32,401	33,334	34,294	34,939	35,338
Part-time	KDEL	"	29,242	29,131	29,004	29,015	29,354	29,484
Administrative and clerical staff:[6,9]								
Whole-time	KDEM	"	14,541	14,710	15,361	16,200	17,260	17,806
Part-time	KDEN	"	7,456	7,677	8,075	8,630	9,307	9,943
Domestic, transport, etc, staff:[6,10]								
Whole-time	KDEO	"	7,972	7,848	7,625	7,768	8,234	8,305
Part-time	KDEP	"	12 424	12 272	11 522	11 915	12 588	12 324
Primary care services								
Primary Medical services								
General medical practitioners (GPs):[11]	JX4B	Numbers	4,072	4,253	4,346	4,360	4,447	4,456
Performer[12]	KDET	"	3,702	3,710	3,761	3,769	3,805	3,782
Performer salaried[13]	KDEU	"	88	99	108	114	155	188
Performer registrar	JX4C	"	283	261	283	284	281	282
Performer retainee[14]	JX4D	"	-	184	196	194	209	208
Expenditure on Primary Medical Services[15]	KDEW	£million	378	405	430	468	519	628
Pharmaceutical services[16]								
Prescriptions dispensed	KDEX	Millions	62	66	69	72	75	77
Payments to pharmacists (gross)	KDEY	£million	731	789	869	946	988	994
Average gross cost per prescription	KDEZ	£	11.7	12.0	12.6	13.2	13.2	12.9
Dental services								
Dentists on list[17]	KDFA	Numbers	1,808	1,808	1,844	1,869	1,882	1,900
Number of courses of treatment completed	KDFB	Thousands	3,338	3,389	3,359	3,420	3,359	3,375
Payments to dentists (gross)	KDFC	£million	161	163	165	172	170	174
Payments by patients	KDFD	"	49	51	52	55	53	54
Payments out of public funds	KDFE	"	112	112	113	118	117	120
Average gross cost per course	KDFF	£	38	38	38	40	40	40
General ophthalmic services Number of Eye Exams given[18,19]	KDFG	Thousands	850	861	877	907	920	935
Number of pairs of glasses supplied[20]	KDFH	"	494	439	463	458	450	457
Payments out of public funds for sight testing and dispensing[21]	KDFK	£ million	..	..	..	35	36	38

16.2   Hospital and primary care services Scotland

	2005 /06	2006 /07	2007 /08	2008 /09	2009 /10
Hospital and community services In-patients:[1,2]					
Average available staffed beds	27.4	26.9	26.3	25.8	24.9
Average occupied beds:				-	
All departments	22.1	21.7	21.0	20.6	19.9
Psychiatric and learning disability	5.2	4.9	4.6	4.3	4.1
Discharges or deaths[3]	1015	1037	1066	1091	1092
Outpatients:[2,4]					
New cases	2,762	2,827	2894	3,003	3,021
Total attendances	6,060	6,048	6093	6,271	6,233
Medical and dental staff:[5,6]	10,871	11,201	11,823	12,534	12,608
Whole-time	8,796	9,201	9,826	9,971	9,974
Part-time	1,670	1,607	1,597	2,257	2,435
Honorary	418	411	418	377	247
Professional and technical staff:[6,7]					
Whole-time	13,750	14,323	13,647	14,569	..
Part-time	7,440	7,990	8,313	8,788	..
Nursing and midwifery staff:[6,8]					
Whole-time	36,093	37,104	37,075	37,664	..
Part-time	29,688	29,995	30,270	30,301	..
Administrative and clerical staff:[6,9]					
Whole-time	18,434	18,907	18,192	18,163	..
Part-time	10,707	11,375	11,174	11,592	..
Domestic, transport, etc, staff:[6,10]					
Whole-time	8,516	8,697	10,206	10,625	..
Part-time	12 545	12 675	13,094	13,142	..
Primary care services					
Primary Medical services					
General medical practitioners (GPs):[11]	4,530	4,608	4,699	4,903	4,929
Performer[12]	3,761	3,767	3,782	3,778	3,800
Performer salaried[13]	298	366	430	475	510
Performer registrar	300	307	325	491	465
Performer retainee[14]	178	172	166	164	162
Expenditure on Primary Medical Services[15]	701	700	705	701	729
Pharmaceutical services[16]					
Prescriptions dispensed	79	82	85	88	..
Payments to pharmacists (gross)	1,064	1064	1095	1131	..
Average gross cost per prescription	13.2	13.0	12.9	12.8	..
Dental services					
Dentists on list[17]	1,936	2,009	2,099	2,204	2,313
Number of courses of treatment completed	3,348	3,387	3,401	3,548	3,686
Payments to dentists (gross)	179	188	199	220	231
Payments bypatients	54	46	47	50	52
Payments out of public funds	125	143	152	170	180
Average gross cost per course	41	42	43	45	
General ophthalmic services Number of Eye Exams given[18,19]	960	1,573	1,626	1,728	1,775
Number of pairs of glasses supplied[20]	457	443	451	468	474
Payments out of public funds forsight testing and dispensing[21]	39	66	79	86	91

Sources: ISD Scotland, NHS National Services Scotland; 0131 275 7777

1 Excludes joint user and contractual hospitals.

2 In year to 31 March.

3 Includes transfers out and emergency inpatients treated in day bed units.

4 Including attendances at accident and emergency consultant clinics.

5 As at 30 September. Figures exclude officers holding honorary locum appointments. Part-time includes maximum part-time appointments. There is an element of double counting of "heads" in this table as doctors can hold more than one contract. For example, they may hold contracts of different type, eg part time and honorary. Doctors holding two or more contracts of the same type, eg part time, are not double counted. Doctors, whose sum of contracts amounts to whole time, are classed as such. Figures have been revised due to coding changes.

6 The change in both collection and presentation of workforce data due to changes to staff groupings under Agenda for Change has inevitably meant that the amount of historical trend analysis of data is limited, though still available for some high level groupings.

7 As at 30 September. Comprises Therapeutic, Healthcare science, Technical and Pharmacy staff.

8 As at 30 September. Includes Health Care Assistants. Figures post 2003 have been amended due to a coding error resulting in some staff previously in this group being moved to the admin and clerical group.

9 As at 30 September. Comprises Senior Management and Administrative and Clerical staff. Figures for 2003 onwards have been amended due to the inclusion of some staff previously in the nursing and midwifery staff group

10 As at 30 September.Comprises Ambulance, Works, Ancillary and Trades.

11 Contracted GP's in post in Scottish general practices, at 1 October up to 2003/04 and 30 Sept for 2004/05 onwards. Excludes GP locums and GPs working only in Out of Hours services. The total may not equal the sum of the figures for individual GP designations as some GPs hold more than one contract. Source: www.isdscotland.org/workforce

12 For 2004/05 onwards this group comprised mainly of Provider (partner) GPs. Known prior to 2004/05 as Principal GPs.

13 Up to 2003/04 this group comprises salaried GPs plus associates, assistants and 'other' GPs. Terminology changed with the introduction of the new GMS contract in April 2004.

14 Data on the number of GP retainees not available prior to 2000.

15 Total expenditure on General Medical Services/Primary Medical Services Source: NHS Scotland Costs Book "R390" tables, www.isdscotland.org/costs Note, the contractual arrangements for payments to many general practices changed with the introduction of the new GMS contract in April 2004.

16 For prescriptions dispensed in calendar year by all community pharmacists (including stock orders), dispensing doctors and appliance suppliers. Gross total excludes patient charges.

17 Comprises of non-salaried GDS principal dentists only as at 31 March.

18 Figures represent sight tests paid for by health boards, hospital eye service referrals and GOD(s) ST (v) claimants.

19 Free NHS eye examinations were extended to all on 1st April 2006.

20 Does not include hospital eye service.

21 OPTIX, the electronic system for recording ophtalmic payment information, was introduced in 2002. Information for previous years is now not centrally available from ISD

Data next updated November 2011 -http://www.isdscotland.org/Health%2DTopics/Workforce/Trend/

16.3 Hospital and general health services

Northern Ireland

			1999	2000	2001	2002	2003	2004	2005	2006
Hospital services[1]										
In-patients:										
Beds available[2]	KDGA	Numbers	8,639	8,571	8,419	8,301	8,347	8,323	8,238	7,976
Average daily occupation of beds	KDGB	Percentages	82	82	83	84	84	84	84	83
Discharges or deaths[3]	KDGC	Thousands	332	333	328	327	332	337	296	295
Out-patients:[4]										
New cases	KDGD	"	984	994	997	992	1,014	1,027	1,040	1,081
Total attendances	KDGE	"	2,111	2,114	2,131	2,122	2,161	2,175	2,219	2,233
General health services										
Medical services[1]										
Doctors (principals) on the list[5,6]	KDGF	Numbers	1,054	1,066	1,073	1,076	1,076	1,078	1,084	1,100
Number of patients per doctor	KDGG	"	1,678	1,661	1,651	1,652	1,658	1,663	1,655	1,631
Gross Payments to doctors[7]	KDGH	£ thousand	78,604	82,471	84,664	88,194	96,894	..	..	..
Pharmaceutical services[8]										
Prescription forms dispensed	KDGI	Thousands	13,454	13,666	14,277	14,622	15,158	15,283	15,860	16,393
Number of prescriptions	KDGJ	"	23,249	23,985	24,705	25,501	26,656	27,401	28,417	29,599
Gross Cost[9]	KDGK	£ thousand	266,535	278,405	303,489	327,045	362,401	382,789	390,763	408,771
Charges[10]	KDGL	"	8,183	8,499	9,074	9,597	9,798	10,262	10,676	11,298
Net Cost[9]	KDGM	"	258,353	269,906	294,415	317,448	352,602	372,527	380,087	397,473
Average gross cost per prescription[9]	KDGN	£	11	12	12	13	14	14	14	14
Dental services[8,11]										
Dentists on the list[5]	KDGO	Numbers	632	661	673	689	696	720	722	751
Number of courses of paid treatment	KDGP	Thousands	1,086	1,113	1,126	1,123	1,107	1,086	1,084	1,064
Gross cost	KDGQ	£ thousand	58,712	61,237	64,454	66,201	66,910	67,294	69,480	65,172
Patients	KDGR	Thousands	14,358	15,302	16,041	930	919	907	910	900
Contributions (Net cost)	KDGS	£ thousand	44,354	46,152	48,413	49,376	50,282	50,498	52,308	50,068
Average gross cost per paid treatment	KDGT	£	54	55	57	59	60	62	64	61
Ophthalmic services[8]										
Number of sight tests given[12]	KDGU	Thousands	305	307	326	334	346	347	360	368
Number of optical appliances supplied[13]	KDGV	"	178	181	187	190	192	189	194	196
Cost of service (gross)[14]	KDGW	£ thousand	11,509	12,035	12,738	13,473	13,981	14,395	15,868	16,280
Health and social services[15]										
Medical and dental staff:										
Whole-time	KDGZ	Numbers	2,138	2,224	2,280	2,409	2,606	2,749	2,947	3,152
Part-time	KDHA	"	558	577	595	624	619	626	561	554
Nursing and midwifery staff:										
Whole-time	KDHB	"	9,864	9,906	9,804	10,221	10,709	11,116	11,395	11,454
Part-time	KDHC	"	7,180	7,486	7,774	8,354	8,665	8,850	9,015	9,072
Administrative and clerical staff:										
Whole-time	KDHD	"	7,138	7,280	7,447	7,820	8,188	8,676	8,878	8,938
Part-time	KDHE	"	2,708	2,946	3,112	3,349	3,579	3,828	4,160	4,221
Professional and technical staff:										
Whole-time	KDHF	"	3,495	3,634	3,752	3,968	4,155	4,518	4,685	4,758
Part-time	KDHG	"	1,221	1,278	1,362	1,491	1,605	1,724	1,822	2,021
Social services staff(excluding casual home helps):										
Whole-time	KDHH	"	2,875	3,011	3,120	3,280	3,454	3,709	3,773	3,889
Part-time	KDHI	"	844	862	906	978	1,093	1,197	1,289	1,417
Ancillary and other staff:										
Whole-time	KDHJ	"	3,465	3,498	3,467	3,421	3,413	3,469	3,722	3,833
Part-time	KDHK	"	4,684	4,502	4,917	5,118	5,410	5,580	5,486	5,892
Cost of services (gross)[14]	KDHL	£ thousand	1,422,920	1,576,657	1,639,283	1,868,538	2,113,453	..	..	..
Payments by recipients	KDHM	Thousands	65,533	71,411	78,478	88,860	87,999	..	..	..
Payments out of public funds	KDHN	£ thousand	1,357,387	1,505,246	1,560,805	1,779,678	2,025,454	..	..	..

16.3 Hospital and general health services
Northern Ireland

			2007	2008	2009	2010
Hospital services[1]						
In-patients:						
Beds available[2]	KDGA	Numbers	7,827	7,636	7274	6732
Average daily occupation of beds	KDGB	Percentages	83	82	82	83
Discharges or deaths[3]	KDGC	Thousands	306	311	300	295
Out-patients:[4]						
New cases	KDGD	"	1,115	1,149	1150	1148
Total attendances	KDGE	"	2,282	2,256	2231	2234
General health services						
Medical services[1]						
Doctors (principals) on the list[5,6]	KDGF	Numbers	1,127	1,148	1,156	1,160
Number of patients per doctor	KDGG	"	1,626	1,618	1,615	1,623
Gross Payments to doctors[7]	KDGH	£ thousand	..	..		
Pharmaceutical services[8]						
Prescription forms dispensed	KDGI	Thousands	17,280	17,910	19,241	20,411
Number of prescriptions	KDGJ	"	30,864	32,107	34,263	36,298
Gross Cost[9]	KDGK	£ thousand	425,440	445,184	470,049	490,670
Charges[10]	KDGL	"	11,943	10,243	4,447	0
Net Cost[9]	KDGM	"	413,497	434,940	465,603	490,670
Average gross cost per prescription[9]	KDGN	£	14	14	14	14
Dental services[8,11]						
Dentists on the list[5]	KDGO	Numbers	763	795	816	889
Number of courses of paid treatment	KDGP	Thousands	1,002	1,034	1,051	1,172
Gross cost	KDGQ	£ thousand	68,775	71,401	73,741	81,621
Patients	KDGR	Thousands	859	868	885	1,001
Contributions (Net cost)	KDGS	£ thousand	53,301	55,801	57,897	64,280
Average gross cost per paid treatment	KDGT	£	69	69	70	70
Ophthalmic services[8]						
Number of sight tests given[12]	KDGU	Thousands	385	404	413	425
Number of optical appliances supplied[13]	KDGV	"	200	210	212	219
Cost of service (gross)[14]	KDGW	£ thousand	16,970	18,468	19,638	19,823
Health and social services[15]						
Medical and dental staff:						
Whole-time	KDGZ	Numbers	3,250	3,278	3,301	3,294
Part-time	KDHA	"	587	603	599	618
Nursing and midwifery staff:						
Whole-time	KDHB	"	11,623	11,512	11,716	11,292
Part-time	KDHC	"	9,310	9,251	9,277	9,470
Administrative and clerical staff:						
Whole-time	KDHD	"	8,683	8,255	8,197	7,880
Part-time	KDHE	"	4,226	4,196	4,286	4,280
Professional and technical staff:						
Whole-time	KDHF	"	4,936	4,619	4,704	4,748
Part-time	KDHG	"	2,076	2,347	2,423	2,533
Social services staff(excluding casual home helps):						
Whole-time	KDHH	"	4,014	4,441	4,619	4,632
Part-time	KDHI	"	2,041	2,808	2,863	2,877
Ancillary and other staff:						
Whole-time	KDHJ	"	3,857	3,831	3,816	3,855
Part-time	KDHK	"	5,667	4,794	4,904	4,805
Cost of services (gross)[14]	KDHL	£ thousand	..	..	..	..
Payments by recipients	KDHM	Thousands	..	..	..	..
Payments out of public funds	KDHN	£ thousand	..	..	..	..

Sources: Business Services Organisation (BSO) Northern Ireland: 028 9053 2975;
Dept of Health, Social Services & Public Safety Northern Ireland: 028 9052 2509;
(Figures on Hospital Services: 028 9052 2800)

1 Financial Year.

2 Average available beds in wards open overnight during the year.

3 Includes transfers to other hospitals.

4 Includes consultant outpatient clinics and Accident and Emergency departments.

5 At beginning of period for Dentists. Doctors numbers at 2002 (Oct), 2003 (Nov), 2004, 2005 & 2006 (Oct).

6 From 2003 onwards (UPE's).

7 These costs refer to the majority of non-cash limited services: further expenditure under GMS is allocated through HSS Boards on a cash limited basis. Change between 2002 and 2003 is due to advance payments being made in relation to the new GMS contract introduced in April 2004.

8 From 1995 onwards figures are taken from financial year.

9 Gross cost is defined as net ingredient costs plus on-cost, fees and other payments.

10 Excludes amount paid by patients for pre-payment certificates.

11 Due to changes in the Dental Contract which came into force in October 1990 dentists are paid under a combination of headings relating to Capitation and Continuing Care patients. Prior to this, payment was simply on an item of service basis.

12 Excluding sight tests given in hospitals and under the school health service and in the home.

13 Relates to the number of vouchers supplied and excludes repair/replace spectacles.

14 Figures relate to the costs of the hospital, community health and personal social services,and have been estimated from financial year data.

15 Workforce figures are headcounts at 30th September and are taken from the Human Resources Management System.
 All workforce figures have been revised and now exclude Home Helps, Bank staff, staff on career breaks, Chairperson / Members of Boards and staff with a whole-time equivalent equal to or less than 0.03. The Ancillary and Other staff category includes Ancillary & General staff, Works & Maintenance staff and Ambulance staff for all years, and from 2008 also includes Generic staff who are multidisciplinary staff. Due to Agenda for Change, new grade codes were introduced (from 2007 onwards) which resulted in some staff moving between categories. Backward comparison of the workforce is therefore not advised due to variations in definitions.

Data used in this table can be found at - http://www.dhsspsni.gov.uk/index/stats_research/work_force/stats-hsc.htm

16.4 Health service workforce summary

England
As at 30 September each year

headcount

		2000	2001	2002	2003	2004
Total	JHR6	1,118,958	1,167,166	1,224,934	1,283,901	1,331,857
Total (excl bank)	KJ5S	1,066,458	1,109,131	1,161,483	1,212,585	1,260,860
Total HCHS medical and dental staff (incl HPCAs)	JX5A	71,688	73,846	77,031	80,851	86,996
Total HCHS non-medical staff	JX5B	919,252	962,528	1,013,199	1,063,846	1,101,797
Total GPs	JX5C	31,369	31,835	32,292	33,564	34,855
Total GP practice staff	JX5D	102,270	104,319	107,275	110,091	112,254
Professionally qualified clinical staff	JHR8	**554,053**	**575,796**	**604,187**	**634,346**	**661,476**
All doctors[2]	JHR9	**97,436**	**100,319**	**104,460**	**109,964**	**117,806**
Consultants (including directors of public health)	JHS3	24,401	25,782	27,070	28,750	30,650
Registrars	JHS4	12,730	13,220	13,770	14,619	16,823
Other doctors in training and equivalents	JHS5	19,192	19,572	21,145	22,701	24,874
Hospital practitioners and clinical assistants (non-dental specialties)[2]	JHS6	5,621	5,362	4,863	4,451	4,045
Other medical and dental staff	JHS7	9,744	9,910	10,183	10,330	10,604
GPs total	JX5E	31,369	31,835	32,292	33,564	34,855
GP Providers	JHT2	27,791	27,938	28,117	28,646	28,781
Other GPs	JHT3	802	864	1,085	1,712	2,742
GP registrars[5]	JHT4	1,659	1,883	1,980	2,235	2,562
GP retainers	JHT5	1,117	1,150	1,110	971	770
Total qualified nursing staff[3]	JHT6	**335,952**	**350,381**	**367,520**	**386,359**	**397,515**
Qualified nursing, midwifery & health visiting staff	JHT7	289,381	300,499	314,879	326,579	336,615
Bank nursing, midwifery & health visiting staff	JX5F	27,371	30,036	31,658	38,113	38,756
GP pratice nurses	JHT8	19,200	19,846	20,983	21,667	22,144
Total qualified scientific, therapeutic & technical staff	JHT9	**105,910**	**110,241**	**116,598**	**122,066**	**128,883**
Qualified Allied Health Professions	JHU2	54,788	57,001	59,415	62,189	65,515
Other qualified scientific, therapeutic & technical staff	JHU3	51,122	53,240	57,183	59,877	63,368
Qualified ambulance staff[4]	JHU4	**14,755**	**14,855**	**15,609**	**15,957**	**17,272**
Support to clinical staff	JHU5	**307,225**	**325,890**	**344,524**	**360,666**	**368,285**
Support to doctors & nursing staff	JHU6	232,007	243,979	255,305	265,549	271,389
Bank support to doctors & nursing staff	JX5G	25,129	27,999	31,793	33,203	32,241
Support to scientific, therapeutic & technical staff	JHU7	41,800	44,602	48,030	52,230	55,025
Support to ambulance staff	JHU8	8,289	9,310	9,396	9,684	9,630
NHS infrastructure support	JHU9	**173,733**	**179,783**	**189,274**	**199,808**	**211,489**
Central functions	JHV2	77,628	81,439	85,706	92,257	99,831
Hotel, property & estates	JHV3	70,849	70,920	71,274	72,230	73,932
Manager & senior manager	JHV4	25,256	27,424	32,294	35,321	37,726
Other non-medical staff or those with unknown classification	JHV5	877	1,224	657	657	497
Other GP pratice staff	JHV6	83,070	84,473	86,292	88,424	90,110

1.The new headcount methodology for 2010 data is not fully comparable with previous years data due to improvements that make it a more stringent count of absolute staff numbers. Further information on the headcount methodology is available in the Census publication.Headcount totals are unlikely to equal the sum of components.
2.In order to avoid double counting Hosptial Practitioners & Clinical Assistants (HPCAs) are excluded from the all doctors totals, as they are predominantly GPs that work part time in hospitals (applies to headcount data only).
3.Nursing and midwifery figures exclude students on training courses leading to a first qualification as a nurse or midwife.
4.In 2006 ambulance staff were collected under new, more detailed, occupation codes. As a result, qualified totals and support to ambulance staff totals are not directly comparable with previous years.
5.GP Registrar count from 2008 onwards represents an improvement in data collection processes and comparisons with previous years should be treated with caution

16.4 Health service workforce summary

England
As at 30 September each year

headcount

		2005	2006	2007	2008	2009	2010 [1]
Total	JHR6	1,366,030	1,338,779	1,331,109	1,368,693	1,431,996	1431557
Total (excl bank)	KJ5S	1,298,202	1,284,261	1,272,884	1,308,774	1,365,303	1370176
Total HCHS medical and dental staff (incl HPCAs)	JX5A	90,630	93,320	94,638	98,703	102,961	103,912
Total HCHS non-medical staff	JX5B	1,130,949	1,092,886	1,085,524	1,120,548	1,176,831	1,170,576
Total GPs	JX5C	35,944	36,008	36,420	37,720	40,269	39,409
Total GP practice staff	JX5D	112,094	119,642	117,375	114,483	114,268	119,655
Professionally qualified clinical staff	JHR8	**679,799**	**675,260**	**681,811**	**701,831**	**725,579**	**721,717**
All doctors[2]	JHR9	**122,987**	**126,251**	**128,210**	**133,662**	**140,897**	**141,326**
Consultants (including directors of public health)	JHS3	31,993	32,874	33,674	34,910	36,950	37,752
Registrars	JHS4	18,006	18,808	30,759	35,042	37,108	38,158
Other doctors in training and equivalents	JHS5	26,305	27,461	16,024	14,136	14,394	14,034
Hospital practitioners and clinical assistants (non-dental specialties) [2]	JHS6	3,587	3,077	2,848	2,761	2,333	2,148
Other medical and dental staff	JHS7	10,739	11,100	11,333	11,854	12,176	12,223
GPs total	JX5E	35,944	36,008	36,420	37,720	40,269	39,409
GP Providers	JHT2	29,340	27,691	27,342	27,347	27,613	27,036
Other GPs	JHT3	3,398	5,400	6,022	6,663	8,304	8,319
GP registrars[5]	JHT4	2,564	2,278	2,491	3,203	3,881	3,880
GP retainers	JHT5	642	639	565	507	471	419
Total qualified nursing staff[3]	JHT6	**404,161**	**398,335**	**399,597**	**408,160**	**417,164**	**410,615**
Qualified nursing, midwifery & health visiting staff	JHT7	344,677	343,184	340,859	346,377	353,570	352,104
Bank nursing, midwifery & health visiting staff	JX5F	36,580	31,354	35,878	39,735	41,659	37,186
GP pratice nurses	JHT8	22,904	23,797	22,860	22,048	21,935	21,325
Total qualified scientific, therapeutic & technical staff	JHT9	**134,534**	**134,498**	**136,976**	**142,558**	**149,596**	**151,607**
Qualified Allied Health Professions	JHU2	67,841	67,483	68,687	71,301	73,953	74,374
Other qualified scientific, therapeutic & technical staff	JHU3	66,693	67,015	68,289	71,257	75,643	77,296
Qualified ambulance staff[4]	JHU4	**18,117**	**16,176**	**17,028**	**17,451**	**17,922**	**18,450**
Support to clinical staff	JHU5	**376,219**	**357,877**	**346,596**	**355,010**	**377,617**	**380,605**
Support to doctors & nursing staff	JHU6	279,193	267,934	259,547	266,070	278,390	279,522
Bank support to doctors & nursing staff	JX5G	31,248	23,164	22,347	20,184	25,034	24,195
Support to scientific, therapeutic & technical staff	JHU7	55,715	54,307	53,259	55,689	59,831	62,726
Support to ambulance staff	JHU8	10,063	12,472	11,443	13,067	14,362	14,738
NHS infrastructure support	JHU9	**220,387**	**209,387**	**207,778**	**219,064**	**236,103**	**233,342**
Central functions	JHV2	105,565	101,860	100,177	105,354	115,818	116,846
Hotel, property & estates	JHV3	75,431	70,776	71,102	73,797	75,624	74,712
Manager & senior manager	JHV4	39,391	36,751	36,499	39,913	44,661	41,962
Other non-medical staff or those with unknown classification	JHV5	435	410	409	353	364	356
Other GP pratice staff	JHV6	89,190	95,845	94,515	92,436	92,333	98,330

Source: NHS Information Centre for Health and Social Care

16.5 Health service workforce summary
Wales

		Unit (a)	2006	2007	2008	2009	2010
					WTE and Numbers		
Directly employed NHS staff (b):							
Medical and dental staff (c):							
Hospital medical staff	JHV7	Wte	..	5,182	5,272	5,237	5,330
Of which consultants	JHV8	Wte	..	1,820	1,893	1,941	2,042
Community/Public health medical staff	JHV9	Wte	..	98	102	81	75
Hospital dental staff	JHW2	Wte	..	149	149	153	158
Of which consultants	JHW3	Wte	..	49	40	41	45
Community/Public health dental staff	JHW4	Wte	..	89	48	91	92
Total	JHW5	Wte	..	5,520	5,571	5,562	5,654
Nursing, midwifery and health visiting staff (d)	JHW6	Wte	27,901	28,060	27,806	28,199	28,168
of which qualified	JHW7	Wte	20,980	21,443	21,426	21,585	21,823
Scientific, therapeutic and technical staff	JHW8	Wte	10,242	10,654	10,843	11,202	11,483
Health care assistants and other support staff	JHW9	Wte	9,904	9,015	9,488	9,920	10,049
Administration and estates staff	JHX2	Wte	16,417	16,031	16,056	16,151	15,502
Ambulance staff	JHX3	Wte	1,444	1,377	1,398	1,403	1,429
Other (e)	JHX4	Wte	161	170	209	204	145
Unknown	JHX5	Wte	-	80	96	96	14
Total	JHX6	Wte	..	70,907	71,467	72,737	72,444
Family Practitioners:							
General medical practitioners (f)	JHX7	Number	1,882	1,936	1,940	1,940	1,991
GP Registrars	JHX8	Number	152	165	198	161	215
GP retainers	JHX9	Number	61	73	70	54	47
General dental practitioners (g)	JHY2	Number	..	1,141	1,247	1,293	1,310
Ophthalmic medical practitioners (h)	JHY3	Number	25	27	23	21	16
Ophthalmic opticians (h)	JHY4	Number	648	681	711	690	740

Source: Welsh Government

(a) Whole-time equivalent.

(b) At 30 September. The majority of the information on NHS staff has been obtained as a by-product of personnel systems. Some staff may be undergoing
    temporary regrading at the time and these staff are excluded from the figures.

(c) Excludes locum staff.

(d) Excludes pre-registration learners.

(e) Professional advisors and staff on general payments, eg Macmillan and Marie Curie nurses.

(f) At 30 September, except for 2009 which was counted at 1 October. All practitioners excluding GP registrars, GP Retainers and locums.

(g) Number of dental performers who have any NHS activity recorded against them via FP17 claim forms at any time in the year ending 31 March.

(h) Numbers at 31 December.

16.6 Deaths: by cause International Statistical Classification of Diseases, Injuries and Causes of Death[1]

Numbers

	ICD-10 code	England and Wales						
		2003	2004	2005	2006	2007	2008	2009
Total deaths		538,254	512,541	512,692	502,599	504,052	509,090	491,348
Deaths from natural causes	A00-R99	519,297	493,835	494,054	482,745	484,350	488,743	471,219
Certain infectious and parasitic diseases	A00-B99	4,763	5,009	6,141	7,632	8,169	6,499	5,750
Intestinal infectious diseases	A00-A09	1,063	1,382	2,221	3,630	4,225	2,690	1,861
Respiratory and other tuberculosis including late effects	A15-A19,B90	451	388	406	432	335	384	340
Meningococcal infection	A39	118	72	86	52	75	77	60
Viral hepatitis	B15-B19	209	197	205	205	223	218	258
AIDS (HIV - disease)	B20-B24	224	209	230	235	256	249	256
Neoplasms	C00-D48	139,360	138,062	138,454	138,777	140,080	141,143	140,497
Malignant neoplasms	C00-97	135,955	134,856	135,252	135,635	136,804	137,831	137,420
Malignant neoplasm of oesophagus	C15	6,427	6,298	6,490	6,495	6,424	6,609	6,645
Malignant neoplasm of stomach	C16	5,285	5,098	4,927	4,562	4,587	4,546	4,366
Malignant neoplasm of colon	C18	9,152	9,130	9,076	8,954	8,854	8,958	8,742
Malignant neoplasm of rectum and anus	C20-C21	3,982	3,917	3,995	3,870	3,795	3,872	3,788
Malignant neoplasm of pancreas	C25	6,242	6,294	6,509	6,584	6,845	6,929	7,146
Malignant neoplasm of trachea, bronchus and lung	C33-C34	28,765	28,328	28,792	29,332	29,660	30,326	30,018
Malignant neoplasm of skin	C43	1,585	1,597	1,622	1,649	1,825	1,847	1,858
Malignant neoplasm of breast	C50	11,276	11,031	11,121	11,011	10,727	10,779	10,440
Malignant neoplasm of cervix uteri	C53	951	957	911	831	820	830	830
Malignant neoplasm of prostate	C61	9,166	9,169	9,042	9,057	9,230	9,157	9,402
Leukaemia	C91-C95	3,916	3,828	3,910	3,859	3,935	3,924	3,990
Diseases of the blood and blood-forming organs and certain disorders involving the immune mechanism	D50-D89	1,065	1,014	1,096	1,013	1,029	952	1,026
Endocrine, nutritional and metabolic diseases	E00-E90	8,016	7,519	7,433	7,153	7,214	7,426	7,123
Diabetes mellitus	E10-E14	6,316	5,837	5,677	5,490	5,433	5,541	5,278
Mental and behavioural disorders	F00-F99	14,846	14,299	14,563	14,863	16,582	18,438	18,021
Vascular and unspecified dementia	F01,F03	13,401	12,756	12,995	13,289	14,948	16,610	16,424
Alcohol abuse (inc alcoholic psychosis)	F10	469	538	523	545	533	685	645
Drug dependence and non-dependent abuse of drugs	F11-F16,F18-F19	655	718	762	739	781	844	687
Diseases of the nervous system and sense organs	G00-H95	15,793	14,645	15,253	15,218	16,375	17,554	17,442
Meningitis (including meningococcal)	G00-G03	229	182	187	164	164	159	161
Alzheimer's disease	G30	5,055	4,821	4,914	4,901	5,697	6,231	6,194
Diseases of the circulatory system	I00-I99	205,508	190,603	183,997	174,637	170,338	168,238	159,779
Ischaemic heart diseases	I20-I25	99,790	92,528	88,271	82,619	79,910	76,985	72,170
Cerebrovascular diseases	I60-I69	57,808	52,899	50,772	48,389	46,597	46,446	43,595
Diseases of the respiratory system	J00-J99	75,138	69,213	72,517	68,599	68,974	71,751	67,559
Influenza	J10-J11	77	25	44	17	31	39	78
Pneumonia	J12-J18	34,400	30,649	31,443	28,674	28,152	28,929	26,741
Bronchitis, emphysema and other chronic obstructive pulmonary diseases	J40-J44	25,765	23,204	24,230	23,319	23,727	24,816	23,318
Asthma	J45-J46	1,284	1,243	1,186	1,082	1,033	1,071	1,018
Diseases of the digestive system	K00-K93	24,948	24,912	25,213	25,786	25,670	25,997	25,230
Gastric and duodenal ulcer	K25-K27	3,678	3,495	3,266	3,145	2,833	2,912	2,714
Chronic liver disease	K70,K73-K74	5,844	5,824	5,873	6,250	6,326	6,470	6,230
Diseases of the skin and subcutaneous tissue	L00-L99	1,661	1,670	1,788	1,812	1,822	1,895	1,849
Diseases of the musculo-skeletal system and connective tissue	M00-M99	4,634	4,393	4,378	4,238	4,304	4,398	4,141
Rheumatoid arthritis and juvenile arthritis	M05-M06,M08	907	794	835	743	734	753	653
Osteoporosis	M80-M81	1,583	1,478	1,416	1,390	1,509	1,420	1,288
Diseases of the genito-urinary system	N00-N99	9,120	9,397	10,231	10,722	11,301	11,886	11,998
Diseases of the kidney and ureter	N00-N29	4,135	4,024	3,967	3,988	4,386	4,381	4,371
Complications of pregnancy, childbirth and the puerperium	O00-O99	45	46	36	41	47	44	63
Certain conditions originating in the perinatal period (excluding neonatals)[1]	P00-P96	207	213	205	160	180	234	237
Congenital malformations, deformations and chromosomal abnormalities (excluding neonatals)[1]	Q00-Q99	1,299	1,274	1,292	1,214	1,235	1,139	1,261
Congenital malformations of the nervous system	Q00-Q07	142	116	123	117	124	118	133
Congenital malformations of the circulatory system	Q20-Q28	540	527	535	484	527	444	477
Symptoms, signs and abnormal clinical and laboratory findings not elsewhere classified	R00-R99	12,894	11,566	11,457	10,880	11,030	11,149	9,243
Senility without mention of psychosis (old age)	R54	11,394	9,905	9,785	9,169	9,195	9,320	7,531
Sudden infant death syndrome	R95	136	148	164	143	170	176	156
Deaths from external causes	V01-Y89	16,693	16,497	16,411	17,509	17,000	17,628	17,492
All accidents	V01-X59,Y85,Y86	10,979	10,735	11,053	11,824	11,883	12,306	12,017
Land transport accidents	V01-V89	2,943	2,693	2,697	2,990	2,919	2,626	2,221
Accidental falls	W00-W19	2,732	2,915	3,006	3,226	3,318	3,459	3,593
Accidental poisonings	X40-X49	835	927	910	1,072	1,207	1,429	1,537
Suicide and intentional self-harm	X60-X84,Y87.0	3,270	3,306	3,172	3,331	3,165	3,438	3,458
Homicide and assault[1]	X85-Y09,Y87.1	318	363	326	342	370	340	322
Event of undetermined intent	Y10-Y34, Y87.2	1,776	1,685	1,486	1,616	1,161	1,172	1,227

1 See chapter text

16.6 Deaths: by cause International Statistical Classification of Diseases, Injuries and Causes of Death[1]

Numbers

	ICD-10 code	Scotland 2003	2004	2005	2006	2007	2008	2009	2010[P]
Total deaths		58,472	56,187	55,747	55,093	55,986	55,700	53,856	53,967
Deaths from natural causes	A00-R99	56,161	53,759	53,535	52,856	53,683	53,439	..	..
Certain infectious and parasitic diseases	**A00-B99**	**660**	**688**	**719**	**791**	**949**	**936**	**838**	**811**
Intestinal infectious diseases	A00-A09	85	104	99	128	164	183	..	..
Respiratory and other tuberculosis including late effects	A15-A19,B90	59	52	49	43	41	46	49	33
Meningococcal infection	A39	5	8	4	6	8	4	5	3
Viral hepatitis	B15-B19	23	20	16	20	22	24	25	23
AIDS (HIV - disease)	B20-B24	33	16	31	19	21	18	17	18
Neoplasms	**C00-D48**	**15,412**	**15,336**	**15,408**	**15,360**	**15,570**	**15,525**	**15,484**	**15,595**
Malignant neoplasms	C00-C97	15,116	15,047	15,135	15,084	15,274	15,269	15,187	15,268
Malignant neoplasm of oesophagus	C15	776	801	798	765	786	831	746	811
Malignant neoplasm of stomach	C16	579	615	590	552	506	511	535	499
Malignant neoplasm of colon	C18	966	917	966	922	899	940	846	848
Malignant neoplasm of rectum and anus	C20-21	368	383	367	390	394	379	732	670
Malignant neoplasm of pancreas	C25	641	615	603	567	713	642	691	664
Malignant neoplasm of trachea, bronchus and lung	C33-34	3,893	3,923	4,009	4,062	4,115	4,080	4,147	4,018
Malignant neoplasm of skin	C43	146	151	158	158	164	171	185	194
Malignant neoplasm of breast	C50	1,149	1,093	1,151	1,112	1,067	1,050	1,010	1,029
Malignant neoplasm of cervix uteri	C53	120	102	127	92	105	102	107	99
Malignant neoplasm of prostate	C61	786	802	765	779	793	792	790	848
Leukaemia	C91-C95	367	352	351	362	348	366	387	..
Diseases of the blood and blood-forming organs and certain disorders involving the immune mechanism	D50-D89	148	111	118	113	111	85	113	87
Endocrine, nutritional and metabolic diseases	**E00-E90**	**958**	**972**	**988**	**1,018**	**980**	**991**	**873**	**990**
Diabetes mellitus	E10-E14	709	760	745	751	726	733	632	744
Mental and behavioural disorders	**F00-F99**	**2,637**	**2,670**	**2,454**	**2,817**	**3,117**	**3,362**	**3,327**	**3,270**
Vascular and unspecified dementia	F01,F03	1,997	1,955	1,835	2,101	2,446	2,590	2,585	..
Alcohol abuse (inc. alcoholic psychosis)	F10	356	421	343	378	321	342	312	297
Drug dependence and non-dependent abuse of drugs	F11-F16,F18-F19	228	238	217	293	310	395	410	..
Diseases of the nervous system and sense organs	**G00-H95**	**1,303**	**1,254**	**1,306**	**1,333**	**1,555**	**1,619**	**1,657**	**1,755**
Meningitis (including meningococcal)	G00-G03	19	25	18	15	16	20	9	13
Alzheimer's disease	G30	354	399	415	452	549	624	634	..
Diseases of the circulatory system	**I00-I99**	**22,102**	**20,837**	**20,060**	**18,771**	**18,579**	**17,849**	**16,769**	**16,521**
Ischaemic heart diseases	I20-I25	11,441	10,778	10,331	9,532	9,343	8,841	8,274	8,104
Cerebrovascular diseases	I60-I69	6,497	6,155	5,789	5,466	5,333	5,367	4,906	4,772
Diseases of the respiratory system	**J00-J99**	**7,454**	**6,743**	**7,093**	**7,183**	**7,362**	**7,443**	**7,125**	**6,878**
Influenza	J10-J11	15	3	11	2	5	10	62	11
Pneumonia	J12-J18	2,859	2,399	2,483	2,513	2,444	2,453	2,348	2,331
Bronchitis, emphysema and other chronic obstructive pulmonary diseases	J40-J44	3,014	2,752	2,857	2,848	2,901	2,848	2,986	..
Asthma	J45-J46	98	94	100	82	112	103	93	87
Diseases of the digestive system	**K00-K93**	**3,215**	**3,065**	**3,221**	**3,208**	**3,076**	**3,119**	**3,006**	**3,082**
Ulcer of the stomach, duodendum and jejunum	K25-K28	316	305	230	262	209	221	227	213
Chronic liver disease	K70,K73-K74	1,170	1,044	1,152	1,162	1,080	1,059	952	944
Diseases of the skin and subcutaneous tissue	L00-L99	131	131	127	130	131	159	157	150
Diseases of the musculo-skeletal system and connective tissue	M00-M99	369	350	326	354	395	351	344	340
Rheumatoid arthritis and osteoarthritis	M05-M06,M15-19	..	..	..	..	170	127	125	122
Diseases of the genito-urinary system	**N00-N99**	**1,056**	**965**	**1,063**	**1,112**	**1,149**	**1,279**	**1,269**	**1,328**
Diseases of the kidney and ureter	N00-N29	670	574	617	578	598	653	631	673
Complications of pregnancy, childbirth and the puerperium	O00-O99	7	6	4	7	8	5	6	2
Certain conditions originating in the perinatal period	P00-P96	149	151	164	139	157	134	123	118
Congenital malformations, deformations and chromasomal abnormalities	Q00-Q99	172	134	159	151	150	144	153	146
Congenital malformations of the nervous system	Q00-Q07	23	21	15	25	22	18	21	14
Congenital malformations of the circulatory system	Q20-Q28	63	53	58	46	47	46	49	42
Symptoms, signs and abnormal clinical and laboratory findings not elsewhere classified	R00-R99	388	346	325	369	394	438	414	696
Senility without mention of psychosis (old age)	R54	236	193	210	206	221	235	236	..
Sudden infant death syndrome	R95	43	28	20	27	31	22	23	17
Deaths from external causes	V01-Y89	2,311	2,428	2,212	2,237	2,303	2,261	2,198	2,198
All accidents	V01-X59,Y85,Y86	1,326	1,390	1,284	1,264	1,289	1,261	1,332	1,248
Land transport accidents	V01-V99	357	325	293	326	312	290	277	230
Accidental falls	W00-W19	668	690	676	642	658	634	685	675
Accidental poisonings	X40-X49	30	57	48	70	63	82	98	107
Intentional self-harm, assault and underteremined intent	X60-Y34,Y87	..	..	..	..	926	931	818	881

16.6 Deaths: by cause International Statistical Classification of Diseases, Injuries and Causes of Death[1]

Numbers

	ICD-10 code	Northern Ireland							
		2003	2004	2005	2006	2007	2008	2009	2010[P]
Total deaths		14,462	14,354	14,224	14,532	14,649	14,907	14413	14457
Deaths from natural causes	A00-R99	13,912	13,711	13,463	13,679	13,876	14,053		
Certain infectious and parasitic diseases	A00-B99	157	149	162	188	184	183	164	174
Intestinal infectious diseases	A00-A09	13	16	16	39	35	69	..	..
Respiratory and other tuberculosis including late effects	A15-A19,B90	11	13	4	7	10	6	8	..
Meningococcal infection	A39	4	5	1	1	3	2	2	..
Viral hepatitis	B15-B19	-	1	2	4	4	2	..	..
AIDS (HIV - disease)	B20-B24	2	-	5	-	-	-	1	..
Neoplasms	C00-D48	3,882	3,835	3,826	3,959	3,992	4,086	3992	4111
Malignant neoplasms	C00-C97	3,757	3,757	3,735	3,848	3,870	3,971	3885	4018
Malignant neoplasm of oesophagus	C15	154	138	162	161	161	176	185	..
Malignant neoplasm of stomach	C16	165	180	161	159	161	132	135	..
Malignant neoplasm of colon	C18	313	286	293	280	319	290	271	..
Malignant neoplasm of rectum and anus	C20-C21	103	94	99	99	96	106	166	..
Malignant neoplasm of pancreas	C25	173	152	173	194	205	228	214	..
Malignant neoplasm of trachea, bronchus and lung	C33-C34	810	837	824	850	863	927	906	..
Malignant neoplasm of skin	C43	40	36	43	48	56	57	45	..
Malignant neoplasm of breast	C50	291	320	307	300	311	312	308	..
Malignant neoplasm of cervix uteri	C53	31	37	20	29	16	28	21	..
Malignant neoplasm of prostate	C61	217	241	222	212	235	226	214	..
Malignant neoplasm of lymphatic, haematopoietic and related issues	C81-C96	280	278	296	285	264	290	260	
Diseases of the blood and blood-forming organs and certain disorders involving the immune mechanism	D50-D89	37	34	36	31	39	36	28	26
Endocrine , nutritional and metabolic diseases	E00-E90	246	248	302	281	299	254	319	291
Diabetes mellitus	E10-E14	190	189	224	197	210	181	229	203
Mental and behavioural disorders	F00-F99	341	370	408	418	514	575	525	569
Vascular and unspecified dementia	F01,F03	284	298	316	335	405	520	472	504
Alcohol abuse (inc. alcoholic psychosis)	F10	52	68	86	79	94	46	39	..
Drug dependence and non-dependent abuse of drugs	F11-F16,F18-F19	3	2	2	1	5	2	6	..
Diseases of the nervous system and sense organs	G00-H95	481	487	484	557	588	600	618	569
Meningitis (including meningococcal)	G00-G03	3	1	2	1	5	3	4	..
Alzheimer's disease	G30	224	251	207	265	291	293	541	279
Diseases of the circulatory system	I00-I99	5,448	5,272	5,002	4,879	4,838	4,752	4485	4476
Ischaemic heart diseases	I20-I25	2,843	2,775	2,708	2,556	2,494	2,410	2305	2234
Cerebrovascular diseases	I60-I69	1,531	1,435	1,307	1,326	1,325	1,329	1175	1239
Diseases of the respiratory system	J00-J99	2,082	1,950	1,921	1,982	1,992	2,096	2017	1886
Influenza	J10-J11	4	1	-	1	1	2	12	..
Pneumonia	J12-J18	1,025	909	895	895	859	900	820	..
Bronchitis, emphysema and other chronic obstructive pulmonary diseases	J40-J44	660	609	596	616	639	680	786	..
Asthma	J45-J46	32	44	32	35	28	31	23	..
Diseases of the digestive system	K00-K93	587	691	584	646	711	682	686	715
Gastric and duodenal ulcer	K25-K27	77	70	60	57	53	52	50	..
Chronic liver disease	K70,K73-K74	156	189	150	171	193	204	216	..
Diseases of the skin and subcutaneous tissue	L00-L99	15	19	20	21	26	24	38	..
Diseases of the musculo-skeletal system and connective tissue	M00-M99	93	66	95	79	76	85	84	..
Rheumatoid arthritis and juvenile arthritis	M05-M06,M08	26	15	28	36	25	18	26	..
Osteoporosis	M80-M81	16	10	12	11	12	15	..	..
Diseases of the genito-urinary system	N00-N99	327	364	351	359	381	400	367	..
Diseases of the kidney and ureter	N00-N29	225	252	210	219	232	246	201	..
Complications of pregnancy, childbirth and the puerperium	O00-O99	3	1	1	3	-	-	5	2
Certain conditions originating in the perinatal period	P00-P96	62	64	81	54	50	67	60	77
Congenital malformations, deformations and chromosomal abnormalities	Q00-Q99	69	61	82	84	61	74	82	85
Congenital malformations of the nervous system	Q00-Q07	12	10	10	9	8	16	15	..
Congenital malformations of the circulatory system	Q20-Q28	16	17	20	19	19	16	19	..
Symptoms, signs and abnormal clinical and laboratory findings not elsewhere classified	R00-R99	82	100	108	138	125	139	138	135
Senility without mention of psychosis (old age)	R54	63	70	71	98	95	107	..	..
Sudden infant death syndrome	R95	-	-	2	1	4	3	3	..
Deaths from external causes	V01-Y89	550	643	761	853	773	854	805	840
All accidents	V01-X59,Y85,Y86	364	448	492	525	499	525	512	..
Land transport accidents	V01-V89	120	161	175	184	172	147	127	..
Accidental falls	W00-W19	44	63	99	117	112	127	155	..
Accidental poisonings	X40-X49	30	17	40	22	37	63	59	..
Suicide and intentional self-harm	X60-X84,Y87.0	132	128	186	249	215	252	220	..
Homicide and assault	X85-Y09,Y87.1	30	32	32	30	30	40	31	..
Event of undetermined intent	Y10-Y34, Y87.2	12	18	27	42	27	30	40	..

Sources: Office for National Statistics;
General Register Office,Scotland;
Northern Ireland Statistics and Research Agency

16.7 Notifications of infectious diseases: by country

Numbers

		1998	1999	2000	2001	2002	2003	2004	2005	2006	2007	2008	2009	2010
United Kingdom														
Measles	KHQD	4,540	2,951	2,865	2,661	3,675	2,726	2,703	2,326	4,016	3,869	5,331	5,414	..
Mumps	KWNN	1,917	2,000	3,367	3,433	2,333	4,565	20,742	66,541	15,963	10,101	8,682	20,390	..
Rubella	KWNO	4,064	2,575	2,064	1,782	2,002	1,525	1,548	1,327	1,407	1,254	1,230	1,237	..
Whooping cough	KHQE	1,902	1,461	866	1,059	1,051	509	619	679	645	1,203	1,676	1,284	..
Scarlet fever	KHQC	4,708	2,956	2,544	2,320	2,749	3,252	2,642	2,075	2,653	2,477	3,983	4,957	..
Dysentery	KHQG	1,934	1,630	1,613	1,495	1,167	1,144	1,301	1,346	1,241	1,383	1,289	1,321	..
Food poisoning	KHQH	105,060	96,866	98,076	95,752	81,562	79,073	78,812	78,959	79,407	80,889	77,854	85,239	..
Typhoid and Paratyphoid fevers	KHQB	252	278	205	254	183	277	282	300	390	341	418	343	..
Hepatitis	KWNP	3,781	4,365	4,530	4,419	5,035	5,203	5,054	5,246	5,290	5,306	6,515	6,372	..
Tuberculosis	KHQI	6,605	6,701	7,100	7,204	7,239	6,978	7,259	8,017	8,083	7,461	7,878	7,803	..
Malaria	KWNQ	1,163	1,038	1,166	1,118	866	820	634	700	637	445	403	406	..
England and Wales[1]														
Measles	KHRD	3,728	2,438	2,378	2,250	3,187	2,488	2,356	2,089	3,705	3,670	5,088	5,191	..
Mumps	KWNR	1,587	1,691	2,162	2,741	1,997	4,204	16,367	56,256	12,841	7,196	7,827	18,629	..
Rubella	KWNS	3,208	1,954	1,653	1,483	1,660	1,361	1,287	1,155	1,221	1,082	1,096	1,130	..
Whooping cough	KHRE	1,577	1,139	712	888	883	409	504	594	550	1,089	1,512	1,155	..
Scarlet fever	KHRC	3,339	2,086	1,933	1,756	2,159	2,553	2,201	1,678	2,166	1,948	2,920	4,176	..
Dysentery	KHRG	1,813	1,538	1,494	1,388	1,087	1,047	1,203	1,237	1,122	1,217	1,166	1,218	..
Food poisoning	KHRH	93,932	86,316	86,528	85,468	72,649	70,895	70,311	70,407	70,603	72,382	68,962	74,974	..
Typhoid and Paratyphoid fevers	KHRB	243	276	204	250	175	275	280	298	386	334	410	340	..
Viral hepatitis	KWNT	3,183	3,424	3,541	3,388	3,859	4,004	3,932	4,109	4,007	3,857	4,756	4,979	..
Tuberculosis[2]	KHRJ	6,087	6,144	6,572	6,714	6,753	6,518	6,723	7,628	7,621	6,989	7,319	7,240	..
Malaria	KWNU	1,110	1,005	1,128	1,081	847	791	609	679	613	426	386	381	..
Meningitis	KHRO	2,072	2,094	2,432	2,623	1,545	1,472	1,267	1,381	1,494	1,251	1,181	1,219	..
Meningococcal septicaemia	KWNV	1,509	1,822	1,614	1,238	842	732	691	721	657	673	528	495	..
Ophthalmia neonatorum	KHRI	198	163	176	115	91	102	85	87	100	83	77	90	..
Scotland														
Measles	KHSE	700	434	395	315	399	181	257	186	259	168	219	172	..
Mumps	KWNW	251	216	199	155	259	181	3,595	5,698	2,917	2,741	720	1,129	..
Rubella	KWNX	745	548	349	234	292	130	222	141	153	146	106	93	..
Whooping cough	KHSF	225	214	93	106	99	60	87	51	67	98	134	104	..
Scarlet fever	KHSD	883	438	301	281	376	395	213	208	274	315	890	629	..
Dysentery	KHSH	103	82	95	85	73	83	90	103	112	156	107	95	..
Food poisoning	KHSI	9,186	8,517	9,263	8,640	7,693	6,910	6,835	6,918	7,335	7,186	7,625	8,813	..
Typhoid and Paratyphoid fevers	KHSB	6	2	1	3	4	2	2	1	3	4	7	3	..
Viral hepatitis	KWNY	490	863	943	1,008	1,165	1,159	1,063	1,002	1,235	1,397	1,684	1,311	..
Tuberculosis[3]	KHSL	457	496	469	442	418	422	463	389	414	409	502	503	..
Malaria	KWUC	30	20	27	24	17	28	20	20	18	15	15	20	..
Meningococcal infection	KWUD	313	329	301	256	175	117	147	139	140	150	120	122	..
Erysipelas	KHSC	66	64	41	39	41	28	28	17	25	20	23	13	..
Northern Ireland														
Measles	KHTD	112	79	92	96	89	57	90	56	52	31	24	51	58
Mumps	KHTR	79	93	1,006	537	77	180	780	4,556	205	164	135	632	209
Rubella	KHTQ	111	73	62	65	50	34	39	31	33	26	28	14	18
Whooping cough	KHTE	100	108	61	65	69	40	28	28	28	16	30	25	17
Scarlet fever	KHTC	486	432	310	283	214	304	228	186	213	214	173	207	152
Dysentery	KHTG	18	10	24	22	7	14	8	7	7	10	16	13	..
Food poisoning	KHTH	1,942	2,033	2,285	1,644	1,220	1,268	1,666	1,409	1,469	1,321	1,267	1,452	1,550
Typhoid and Paratyphoid fevers	KHTB	3	-	-	1	4	-	-	1	1	3	1	0	1
Infective hepatitis	KHTO	108	78	46	23	11	40	59	74	48	52	75	86	82
Tuberculosis	KHTI	61	61	59	48	68	38	73	68	48	63	57	53	60
Malaria	KWUE	23	13	11	13	2	1	5	2	6	4	2	5	6
Acute encephalitis/meningitis	KHTM	64	99	130	97	98	78	64	66	58	36	41	45	53
Meningococcal septicaemia	KWUF	87	145	123	90	98	76	82	66	75	42	33	46	44
Gastro-enteritis (children under 2 y	KHTP	1,371	1,121	1,205	1,106	882	867	697	736	718	762	758	612	1,045

Sources: Health Protection Scotland;
Communicable Disease Surveillance Centre (Northern Ireland);
Health Protection Agency,Centre for Infections,IM&T Dept: 020 8200 6868

1 The figures show the corrected number of notifications, incorporating revisons of diagnosis, either by the notifying medical practitioner or by the medical superintendent of the infectious diseases hospital. Cases notified in Port Health Authorities are included.
2 Formal notifications of new cases only. The figures exclude chemoprophylaxis.
3 Figures include cases of tuberculosis not notified before death.

16.8 Estimated number of cases of work-related disease reported by specialist physicians to THOR[1]

Numbers

	All physicians					Disease specialist					Occupational physicians				
	2005	2006	2007	2008	2009	2005	2006	2007	2008	2009	2005	2006	2007	2008	2009
Musculoskeletal disorders						MOSS					OPRA				
Upper limb	3,654	3,328	2,391	2,209	2,044	1,521	1,503	1,049	1,121	734	2,133	1,825	1,342	1,088	1,310
Spine/ back	1,761	1,348	1,243	1,139	708	447	392	297	227	208	1,314	956	946	912	500
Lower limb	441	406	487	225	328	122	158	150	125	134	319	248	337	100	194
Other	221	204	149	191	145	33	55	28	41	40	188	149	121	150	105
Total number of diagnoses	6,205	5,347	4,394	3,796	3,292	2,204	2,131	1,608	1,533	1,170	4,001	3,216	2,786	2,263	2,122
Total number of individuals[2]	5,932	5,160	4,226	3,646	3,154	2,064	2,036	1,521	1,469	1,060	3,868	3,124	2,705	2,177	2,094
Mental ill health						SOSMI					OPRA				
Stress/ anxiety/ depression	6,063	5,648	5,624	4,872	4,590	1,751	1,423	1,014	1,100	943	4,312	4,225	4,610	3,772	3,647
Other	912	908	806	594	581	702	660	507	397	410	210	248	299	197	171
Total number of diagnoses	6,975	6,556	6,430	5,466	5,171	2,453	2,083	1,521	1,497	1,353	4,522	4,473	4,909	3,969	3,818
Total number of individuals[2]	6,396	5,916	5,909	5,196	4,734	2,223	1,975	1,421	1,420	1,274	4,173	3,941	4,488	3,776	3,460
Respiratory disease						SWORD					OPRA				
Asthma	492	596	355	362	223	374	451	251	307	176	118	145	104	55	47
Malignant mesothelioma	762	653	885	647	519	754	637	884	633	519	8	16	1	14	-
Benign pleural disease	1,496	1,293	1,008	1,125	856	1,481	1,281	1,008	1,125	844	15	12	-	-	12
Other	906	564	592	574	653	620	506	419	481	539	286	58	173	93	114
Total number of diagnoses	3,656	3,106	2,840	2,708	2,251	3,229	2,875	2,562	2,546	2,078	427	231	278	162	173
Total number of individuals[2]	3,609	3,059	2,812	2,658	2,175	3,207	2,829	2,534	2,497	2,003	402	230	278	161	172
Skin disease						EPIDERM					OPRA				
Contact dermatitis	2,285	2,406	1,873	1,607	1,735	1,698	1,810	1,385	1,285	1,362	587	596	488	322	373
Skin neoplasia	434	760	623	407	490	434	760	623	407	490	-	-	-	-	
Other	361	390	224	202	230	176	295	155	115	162	185	95	69	87	68
Total number of diagnoses	3,080	3,556	2,720	2,216	2,455	2,308	2,865	2,163	1,807	2,014	772	691	484	409	441
Total number of individuals[2]	3,045	3,507	2,692	2,198	2,391	2,275	2,828	2,136	1,789	1,951	770	679	483	409	440
Audiological disease						OSSA					OPRA				
Sensor ineural hearing loss	315	264	..	..	..	53	28	..	..	..	262	236	..	..	..
Other	48	31	..	..	..	22	15	..	..	..	26	16	..	..	..
Total number of diagnoses	363	295	..	..	..	75	43	..	..	..	288	252	..	..	..
Total number of individuals[2]	340	280	..	..	..	54	28	..	..	..	286	252	..	..	..
Infections						SIDAW					OPRA				
Diarrhoeal diseases	1,429	1,408	..	..	..	1,396	1,408	..	..	..	33	-	..	..	..
Other	149	168	..	..	..	121	165	..	..	..	28	3	..	..	..
Total number of diagnoses	1,578	1,576	..	..	..	1,517	1,573	..	..	..	61	3	..	..	..
Total number of individuals[2]	1,578	1,576	..	..	..	1,517	1,573	..	..	..	61	3	..	..	..

Sources: Health and Safety Executive

1 THOR: The Health and Occupation Reporting Network (formerly know as ODIN) comprises of the following schemes: MOSS: Musculoskeletal Occupation Surveillance Scheme; SOSMI: Sur veillance of Occupational Stress and Mental Illness; SWORD: Surveillance or Work-related and Occupational Respirator y Disease; EPIDERM: Occupational Skin Disease Surveillance by Dermatologists; OSSA: Occupational Surveillance Scheme for Audiologists; SIDAW:Sur veillance of Infectious Disease at Work.
2 Individuals may have more than one diagnosis.

This information has been extracted from THOR tables located at - http://www.hse.gov.uk/statistics/tables/index.htm#thor

To find the dates of the latest and upcoming publications for HSE -http://www.hse.gov.uk/statistics/index.

16.9 Deaths due to occupationally related lung disease Great Britain

		1997	1998	1999	2000	2001	2002	2003	2004	2005	2006	2007	2008	2009
Asbestosis (without mesothelioma)[1,3]	KADY	191	165	171	186	233	234	235	266	301	324	320	366	411
Mesothelioma[2]	KADZ	1,367	1,541	1,615	1,633	1,862	1,868	1,887	1,978	2,049	2,059	2,176	2,263	2321
Pneumoconiosis (other than asbestosis)	KAEA	230	268	321	279	240	271	231	214	194	167	149	139	149
Byssinosis	KAEB	5	5	6	4	2	-	3	4	3	5	2	1	2
Farmer's lung and other occupational allergic alveolitis	KAEC	5	8	9	7	7	6	7	5	13	10	5	7	7
Total	KAED	1,798	1,987	2,122	2,109	2,344	2,373	2,362	2,467	2,548	2,562	2,617	2,756	2,890

Sources: Office for National Statistics;
Health and Safety Executive

1 By definition every case of asbestosis is due to asbestos; the association with mesothelioma is also very strong, though there is thought to be a low natural background incidence.
2 For the inclusion into the Mesothelioma register the cause of death on the death certificate must mention the word Mesothelioma.
3 For inclusion into the Asbestosis register the cause of death on the death certificate must mention the word Asbestosis.

Link used to obtain data: http://www.hse.gov.uk/statistics/tables/dc01.xls

This information has been extracted from the disease pages located at - http://www.hse.gov.uk/statistics/causdis/index.htm

To find the dates of the latest and upcoming publications for HSE - http://www.hse.gov.uk/statistics/index.

16.10 Injuries to workers: by industry and severity of injury

Great Britain
As reported to all enforcing authorities

Numbers

				Fatal					Major			
				2006 /07	2007 /08	2008 /09	2009 /10		2006 /07	2007 /08	2008 /09	2009 /10
		Section	SIC (92)									
Agriculture, hunting, forestry and fishing[3]	KSYS	A,B	01,02,05	36	46	25	38	KSZN	488	569	599	640
Energy and water supply industries	KSYT	C,E	10 -14,40/41	10	9	6	6	KSZO	397	402	361	351
Mining and quarrying	KSYU	C	,10 - 14	9	5	5	5	KSZP	196	201	148	166
Mining and quarrying of energy producing materials	KSON	CA	,10 - 12	7	3	2	4	KSZQ	117	129	105	111
Mining and quarrying except energy producing materials	KSOO	CB	13/14	2	2	3	1	KSZR	79	72	43	55
Electricity, gas and water supply	KSOP	E	40/41	1	4	1	1	KSZS	201	201	207	182
Manufacturing	KSOQ	D	15 - 37	36	33	33	25	KSZT	5,200	5,205	4,590	4,087
of food products; beverages and tobacco	KSOR	DA	15/16	3	2	2	6	KSZU	927	918	827	870
of textile and textile products	KSOS	DB	17/18	-	1	..	1	KSZV	131	101	89	77
of leather and leather products	KSOT	DC	19	-	-	..	-	KSZW	5	4	4	4
of wood and wood products	KSOU	DD	20	3	1	..	-	KSZX	228	271	205	191
of pulp, paper and paper products; publishing and printing	KSOV	DE	21/22	2	2	3	3	KSZY	340	321	271	240
of coke, refined petroleum products and nuclear fuel	KSOW	DF	23	1	-	1	-	KSZZ	23	9	14	12
of chemicals, chemical products and man-made fibres	KSOX	DG	24	2	2	..	1	KTAE	222	252	217	190
of rubber and plastic products	KSOY	DH	25	-	4	2	-	KTAF	368	383	283	256
of other non-metallic mineral products	KSOZ	DI	26	2	2	2	1	KTAG	268	291	225	182
of basic metals and fabricated metal products	KSYV	DJ	27/28	10	10	7	7	KTAH	1,206	1,226	1,132	881
of machinery and equipment not elsewhere classified	KSYW	DK	29	7	1	8	2	KTAI	322	368	317	263
of electrical and optical equipment	KSYX	DL	30 - 33	1	2	..	1	KTAJ	197	191	207	140
of transport equipment	KSYY	DM	34/35	3	2	2	1	KTAK	473	477	416	347
Manufacturing not elsewhere classified	KSYZ	DN	36/37	2	4	6	2	KTAL	490	393	371	425
Construction	KSZA	F	45	79	72	52	42	KTAM	4,457	4,415	3,937	3,120
Total service industries	KSZB	G-Q	50 - 99	86	73	63	41	KTAN	19,196	18,798	19,513	18,898
Wholesale and retail trade and repairs	KSZC	G	50 - 52	7	15	15	11	KTAO	3,671	3,505	3,486	3,291
Hotel and restaurants	KSZD	H	55	4	2	3	1	KTAP	1,099	1,198	1,225	1,148
Transport, storage and communication[4]	KSZE	I	60 - 64	34	21	20	13	KTAQ	3,362	3,468	3,386	3,142
Financial intermediation	KSZF	J	65 - 67	-	-	..	-	KTAR	277	289	306	262
Real estate, renting and business activities	KSZG	K	70 - 74	9	12	6	5	KTAS	2,489	2,356	2,330	2,118
Public administration and defence	KSZH	L	75	6	10	8	4	KTAT	3,438	2,246	2,171	2,214
Education	KSZI	M	80	4	2	1	2	KTAU	1,186	3,672	2,030	3,994
Health and social work	KSZJ	N	85	4	4	..	2	KTAV	2,428	5,038	3,043	6,461
Other community, social and personal services activities	KSZK	O-Q	90 - 99	18	10	10	5	KTAW	1,246	1,381	1,528	1,481
All industries	KSZM			247	233	179	152	KTAY	29,738	29,389	29,000	27,096

1 See chapter text.
2 Injuries causing incapacity for normal work for more than 3 days.
3 Excludes sea fishing.
4 Injuries arising from shore based services only. Excludes incidents reported under merchant shipping legislation.

The information used to populate this table can be found at - http://www.hse.gov.uk/statistics/tables/ridind.xls.

To find the dates of the latest and upcoming publications for HSE - http://www.hse.gov.uk/statistics/index.

General caveats on RIDDOR data
RIDDOR data needs to be interpreted with care because it is known that non-fatal injuries are substantially under-reported. Currently, it is estimated that just over half of all such injuries to employees are actually reported, with the self-employed reporting a much smaller proportion.

16.10 Injuries to workers: by industry and severity of injury
Great Britain
As reported to all enforcing authorities

Numbers

		Over[3] Days[2]				
		2006 /07	2007 /08	2008 /09	2009 /10	
Agriculture, hunting, forestry and fishing[3]	**KTAZ**	863	1,103	1,188	1096	A,B
Energy and water supply industries	**KTBH**	1,366	1,306	1,180	936	C,E
Mining and quarrying	**KTBI**	615	626	549	434	C
Mining and quarrying of energy producing materials	**KTBJ**	385	447	430	353	CA
Mining and quarrying except energy producing materials	**KTBK**	230	173	119	81	CB
Electricity, gas and water supply	**KTBL**	751	680	630	495	E
Manufacturing	**KTBM**	21,968	20,852	17,946	15120	D
of food products; beverages and tobacco	**KTBN**	5,281	4,866	4,401	4206	DA
of textile and textile products	**KTBO**	441	450	377	245	DB
of leather and leather products	**KTBP**	24	27	21	9	DC
of wood and wood products	**KTBQ**	702	720	564	508	DD
of pulp, paper and paper products; publishing and printing	**KTBR**	1,330	1,228	1,054	877	DE
of coke, refined petroleum products and nuclear fuel	**KTBS**	50	61	46	42	DF
of chemicals, chemical products and man-made fibres	**KTBT**	985	953	839	699	DG
of rubber and plastic products	**KTBU**	1,530	1,349	1,189	883	DH
of other non-metallic mineral products	**KTBV**	994	925	758	565	DI
of basic metals and fabricated metal products	**KTBW**	3,873	3,792	3,222	2461	DJ
of machinery and equipment not elsewhere classified	**KTBX**	1,387	1,475	1,202	966	DK
of electrical and optical equipment	**KTBY**	944	857	754	634	DL
of transport equipment	**KTBZ**	2,391	2,127	1,845	1537	DM
Manufacturing not elsewhere classified	**KTCA**	2,036	1,970	1,666	1440	DN
Construction	**KTCB**	7,915	8,188	7,379	6173	F
Total service industries	**KTCC**	83,687	79,726	78,499	72946	G-Q
Wholesale and retail trade and repairs	**KTCD**	14,206	9,954	13,520	12188	G
Hotel and restaurants	**KTCE**	4,102	4,134	4,332	4374	H
Transport, storage and communication[4]	**KTCF**	20,746	19,498	18,495	16639	I
Financial intermediation	**KTCG**	736	769	781	722	J
Real estate, renting and business activities	**KTCH**	7,227	6,597	6,665	6119	K
Public administration and defence	**KTCI**	16,565	11,480	10,288	9250	L
Education	**KTCJ**	2,989	9,590	5,132	9814	M
Health and social work	**KTCK**	14,133	19,693	15,223	29723	N
Other community, social and personal services activities	**KTCL**	2,983	4,052	4,058	3810	O-Q
All industries	**KTCN**	115,799	111,175	106,192	96271	

Sources: Health and Safety Executive (HSE)

1 See chapter text.
2 Injuries causing incapacity for normal work for more than 3 days.
3 Excludes sea fishing.
4 Injuries arising from shore based services only. Excludes incidents reported under merchant shipping legislation.

The information used to populate this table can be found at - http://www.hse.gov.uk/statistics/tables/ridind.xls.

To find the dates of the latest and upcoming publications for HSE - http://www.hse.gov.uk/statistics/index.

General caveats on RIDDOR data
RIDDOR data needs to be interpreted with care because it is known that non-fatal injuries are substantially under-reported. Currently, it is estimated that just over half of all such injuries to employees are actually reported, with the self-employed reporting a much smaller proportion.

Prices

Chapter 17

Prices

Producer price index numbers
(Tables 17.1 and 17.2)

The producer price indices (PPIs) were published for the first time in August 1983, replacing the former wholesale price indices. Full details of the differences between the two indices were given in an article published in British Business, 15 April 1983. The producer price indices are calculated using the same general methodology as that used by the wholesale price indices.

The high level index numbers in Tables 17.1 and 17.2 are constructed on a net sector basis. That is to say, they are intended to measure only transactions between the sector concerned and other sectors. Within-sector transactions are excluded. Index numbers for the whole of manufacturing are thus not weighted averages of sector index numbers.

The index numbers for selected industries in Tables 17.1 and 17.2 are constructed on a gross sector basis, that is, all transactions are included in deriving the weighting patterns, including sales within the same industry.

Producer Prices has implemented the change to the Standard Industrial Classification 2007 (SIC 2007). The most significant change to PPI output prices involves the reclassification of 'recovered secondary raw materials' and 'publishing'. These are no longer classified in the manufacturing sector, but are classified under services. In addition to this, a new SIC division, 'repair, installation and maintenance of machinery and equipment' has been created. Under SIC 2003 these activities were classified within the output of manufacturing, but as part of the specific industries where this activity took place.

Fundamental changes have been made to the classification of the PPI Trade surveys, Import Price indices (IPI) and Export Price Indices (EPI). As part of the reclassification project the classification of these trade surveys have become compliant with Eurostat's Short Term Statistics Regulation. The collection of IPI and EPI will now be on an SIC basis, a switch from the Standard International Trade Classification (SITC) and Combined Nomenclature (CN) previously used. PPI input prices are heavily dependant on IPI.

Further details are available from the Office for National Statistics website: www.ons.gov.uk.

Purchasing power of the pound
(Table 17.3)

Changes in the internal purchasing power of a currency may be defined as the 'inverse' of changes in the levels of prices; when prices go up, the amount which can be purchased with a given sum of money goes down. Movements in the internal purchasing power of the pound are based on the consumers' expenditure deflator (CED) prior to 1962 and on the general index of retail prices (RPI) from January 1962 onwards. The CED shows the movement in prices implied by the national accounts estimates of consumers' expenditure valued at current and at constant prices, while the RPI is constructed directly by weighting together monthly movements in prices according to a given pattern of household expenditure derived from the Expenditure and Food Survey. If the purchasing power of the pound is taken to be 100p in a particular month (quarter, year), the comparable purchasing power in a subsequent month (quarter, year) is:

$$100 \times \frac{\text{earlier period price index}}{\text{later period price index}}$$

where the price index used is the CED for years 1946–1961

Consumer prices index
(Table 17.4)

The CPI is the main UK domestic measure of consumer price inflation for macroeconomic purposes. It forms the basis for the Government's target for inflation that the Bank of England's Monetary Policy Committee (MPC) is required to achieve. From April 2011 the CPI is also being used for the indexation of benefits, tax credits and public service pensions. The uprating is based on the 12-month change in the September CPI.

Internationally, the CPI is known as the Harmonised Index of Consumer Prices (HICP). HICPs are calculated in each Member State of the European Union, according to rules specified in a series of European regulations developed by Eurostat in conjunction with the EU Member States. HICPs are used to compare inflation rates across the European Union. Since January 1999, the HICP has also been used by the European Central Bank (ECB) as the measure of price stability across the euro area.

The official CPI series starts in 1996 but estimates for earlier periods are available back to 1988. These estimates are broadly consistent with data from 1996 but should be treated with some caution.

A full description of how the CPI is compiled is given in the Consumer Price Indices Technical Manual at: www.ons.gov.uk/ons/guide-method/user-guidance/prices/cpi-and-rpi/index.html

Retail prices index
(Table 17.5)

The all items retail prices index (RPI) is the most long-standing general purpose measure of inflation in the UK. Historically the uses of the RPI include the indexation of various prices and incomes and the uprating of pensions, state benefits and index-linked gilts, as well as the revalorisation of excise duties. Please note, though, that from April 2011 the CPI is being used to uprate benefits, tax credits and public service pensions. RPI data are available back to 1947 but have been re-referenced on several occasions since then, generally accompanied by changes to the coverage and/or structure of the detailed sub-components.

A full description of how the RPI is compiled is given in the Consumer Price Indices Technical Manual at: www.ons.gov.uk/ons/guide-method/user-guidance/prices/cpi-and-rpi/index.html

Further details are available from the Office for National Statistics website: www.ons.gov.uk/ons/taxonomy/index.html?nscl=Price+Indices+and+Inflation

Tax and price index (TPI)
(Table 17.6)

The purpose and methodology of the TPI were described in an article in the August 1979 issue (No. 310) of Economic Trends. The TPI measures the change in gross taxable income needed for taxpayers to maintain their purchasing power, allowing for changes in retail prices. The TPI thus takes account of the changes to direct taxes (and employees' National Insurance (NI) contributions) faced by a representative cross-section of taxpayers as well as changes in the retail prices index (RPI).
When direct taxation or employees' NI contributions change, the TPI will rise by less than or more than the RPI according to the type of changes made. Between Budgets, the monthly increase in the TPI is normally slightly larger than that in the RPI, since all the extra income needed to offset any rise in retail prices is fully taxed.

Index numbers of agricultural prices
(Tables 17.7 and 17.8)

The indices of producer prices of agricultural products are currently based on the calendar year 2005. They are designed to provide short-term and medium-term indications of movements in these prices. All annual series are baseweighted Laspeyres type, using value weights derived from the Economic Accounts for Agriculture prepared for the Statistical Office of the European Union. Prices are measured exclusive of VAT. For Table 17.7, it has generally been necessary to measure the prices of materials (inputs) ex-supplier. For Table 17.8, it has generally been necessary to measure the prices received by producers (outputs) at the first marketing stage. The construction of the indices enables them to be combined with similar indices for other member countries of the EU to provide an overall indication of trends within the Union which appears in the Union's Eurostat series of publications.

Index numbers at a more detailed level and for earlier based series are available from the Department for Environment, Food and Rural Affairs, Room 309, Foss House, Kingspool 1–2 Peasholme Green, York, YO1 7PX, tel 01904 456561

17.1 Producer prices index (2005=100, SIC2007)

		Net sector input prices, including Climate Change Levy[1]				
		Materials and fuels purchased				
	All Manufacturing	Materials	Fuel	All manufacturing excluding food, beverages, tobacco & petroleum (NSA)	All manufacturing excluding food, beverages, tobacco & petroleum (SA)	Materials purchased by all manufacturing excluding food, beverages, tobacco & petroleum (NSA)
	6207000050	6207000010	6207000060	6207990050	6207998950	6207990010
SIC 2007						
	K646	**K644**	**K647**	**K655**	**K658**	**K653**
2007	113.0	112.0	122.8	109.8	109.8	108.4
2008	138.1	135.9	159.5	128.4	128.4	125.1
2009	132.9	129.4	167.9	130.5	130.5	126.5
2010	146.1	145.1	156.2	138.0	138.0	136.0
2009 Jan	130.1	122.8	202.2	132.5	131.9	125.1
Feb	130.6	123.9	196.7	131.4	131.3	124.5
Mar	132.6	127.0	188.3	132.3	130.8	126.3
Apr	130.0	126.3	166.0	129.2	129.1	125.3
May	130.9	127.6	162.6	129.0	128.5	125.4
Jun	131.5	129.1	155.2	127.7	128.0	124.8
Jul	130.5	128.1	154.1	127.7	127.8	124.9
Aug	133.3	131.4	152.5	128.8	129.9	126.3
Sep	133.4	131.5	152.7	130.3	131.4	127.9
Oct	137.1	134.5	162.0	132.4	133.0	129.3
Nov	137.3	134.9	161.1	132.1	132.1	129.0
Dec	137.9	135.5	161.8	132.8	132.5	129.7
2010 Jan	139.7	137.2	164.2	133.5	132.8	130.3
Feb	140.7	138.7	160.8	134.3	133.8	131.5
Mar	146.2	144.8	160.2	137.6	135.6	135.2
Apr	146.4	146.6	144.3	137.1	136.5	136.3
May	146.1	145.6	150.9	138.1	137.4	136.7
Jun	145.6	145.1	150.7	136.8	137.1	135.4
Jul	144.5	143.4	154.5	137.3	137.5	135.5
Aug	144.4	143.5	153.5	136.9	138.1	135.1
Sep	145.2	144.6	150.9	137.6	138.9	136.2
Oct	148.7	147.9	156.2	140.3	140.9	138.6
Nov	150.1	149.1	159.3	141.4	142.1	139.5
Dec	155.9	154.5	169.2	144.8	144.7	142.2
2011 Jan	159.5	158.9	166.1	147.5	146.7	145.5
Feb	161.7	161.4	164.5	148.7	148.4	147.0
Mar	167.9	167.9	168.0	151.8	150.2	150.1
Apr	172.6	173.2	166.5	153.8	153.1	152.5
May	169.6	169.9	166.3	153.5	152.6	152.2
Jun	170.3	170.6	167.2	154.3	154.5	153.0

17.1 Producer prices index (2005=100, SIC2007)

	Gross sector input prices, excluding Climate Change Levy						
	Manufacture of:						
	Textiles & textile products	Leather & related products	Wood & wood products	Pulp, paper and paper products	Coke & refined petroleum products	Chemicals, chemical products & man-made fibres	Rubber & plastic products
	6107131400	6107150000	6107160000	6107171800	6107190000	6107200000	6107220000
SIC 2007							
	K5VT	K5VU	K5VV	K5VW	K5VX	K5VY	K5W2
2007	103.2	104.7	113.1	105.1	121.3	107.5	107.4
2008	109.6	114.5	119.1	110.7	171.2	123.7	118.3
2009	113.5	120.0	120.3	113.8	131.4	128.7	121.6
2010	117.5	123.1	128.6	118.6	171.2	139.7	131.3
2009 Jan	114.0	120.6	120.9	114.6	99.2	128.8	120.6
Feb	113.8	120.4	120.2	114.3	105.5	127.8	120.0
Mar	114.3	120.7	120.4	114.2	112.6	128.6	121.0
Apr	113.4	120.3	118.7	113.1	116.8	127.5	120.3
May	113.3	120.5	118.6	113.2	125.5	127.0	119.9
Jun	112.4	120.0	118.2	112.8	138.1	125.3	118.8
Jul	112.4	118.6	118.8	112.7	134.4	126.6	120.4
Aug	112.8	118.7	119.2	112.4	146.4	129.0	122.0
Sep	113.3	119.8	120.3	112.9	140.3	130.0	123.4
Oct	114.1	120.1	122.5	115.0	150.1	130.8	124.1
Nov	114.0	120.0	122.5	114.8	154.6	131.0	124.3
Dec	113.7	120.5	123.0	115.2	153.3	131.8	124.9
2010 Jan	114.4	120.6	124.0	115.6	157.9	133.1	126.0
Feb	115.6	121.7	124.5	115.7	159.2	134.6	127.3
Mar	116.7	122.1	125.2	116.7	173.9	136.6	129.3
Apr	116.4	123.1	125.6	116.7	181.5	137.7	130.1
May	117.3	124.6	126.8	118.0	170.6	139.7	131.6
Jun	117.0	123.5	127.0	118.4	168.1	138.1	130.3
Jul	117.6	123.5	130.2	119.2	165.7	139.9	131.7
Aug	117.6	123.1	130.8	119.3	166.3	140.5	132.0
Sep	117.9	122.7	131.2	119.7	166.6	141.1	132.3
Oct	118.9	123.2	131.9	120.8	173.9	143.4	134.1
Nov	119.7	123.4	132.5	121.4	177.8	144.7	134.9
Dec	121.0	125.5	133.2	122.3	192.6	146.8	136.5
2011 Jan	123.8	126.6	134.6	123.5	203.7	151.8	140.3
Feb	123.5	127.5	134.9	123.9	211.2	150.0	139.0
Mar	125.1	129.9	135.6	125.2	231.0	152.4	141.1
Apr	127.7	131.8	136.2	126.0	248.0	156.1	144.2
May	128.0	132.5	137.2	126.3	231.3	157.4	145.6
Jun	128.6	132.6	137.5	127.2	232.5	157.9	145.9

17.1 Producer prices index (2005=100, SIC2007)

	Gross sector input prices, excluding Climate Change Levy					
	Manufacture of:					
	Other non-metallic mineral products	Basic metals & fabricated products	Computers, electronic & optical products	Machinery & equipment not elsewhere classified	Motor vehicles & other transport equipment	Other manufactured goods not elsewhere classified
	6107230000	6107242500	6107262700	6107280000	6107293000	6107313300
SIC 2007						
	K5W3	**K5W4**	**K5W5**	**K5W6**	**K5W7**	**K5W8**
2007	108.2	114.8	104.1	106.7	106.4	108.2
2008	124.8	127.4	110.7	114.9	113.1	115.9
2009	126.8	123.3	113.1	116.3	116.3	117.1
2010	128.9	133.6	118.0	121.1	121.1	123.1
2009 Jan	132.2	127.6	114.5	118.4	116.7	118.3
Feb	131.9	126.3	114.0	117.6	116.1	117.8
Mar	131.4	125.3	113.4	117.4	116.8	117.7
Apr	127.3	121.4	112.0	115.5	115.8	116.1
May	126.2	121.3	113.1	115.5	115.6	116.3
Jun	123.3	120.5	112.0	114.8	114.8	115.6
Jul	124.0	120.7	111.9	114.9	115.3	115.8
Aug	124.2	121.5	111.6	115.0	115.5	116.1
Sep	124.8	122.9	112.8	116.1	116.6	117.2
Oct	125.6	124.3	113.9	116.8	117.4	118.0
Nov	125.0	124.1	113.4	116.7	117.4	118.0
Dec	125.6	124.3	114.2	116.8	117.9	118.4
2010 Jan	126.0	124.8	114.5	117.2	118.5	118.9
Feb	127.0	125.4	115.0	117.7	118.9	119.4
Mar	128.8	129.7	117.0	119.6	120.5	121.3
Apr	126.7	132.8	117.8	120.6	120.9	122.4
May	128.7	135.1	118.8	121.7	121.6	123.6
Jun	128.5	134.8	119.1	121.9	121.6	123.5
Jul	129.7	136.1	119.4	122.4	121.3	124.1
Aug	128.8	135.8	118.3	122.0	121.2	123.8
Sep	129.0	135.8	118.6	122.0	121.5	124.1
Oct	130.3	136.8	119.0	122.5	122.3	124.9
Nov	130.9	137.0	119.1	122.3	122.3	125.2
Dec	132.9	138.6	119.7	123.0	123.1	126.2
2011 Jan	135.6	140.9	120.5	123.7	123.7	127.4
Feb	134.7	143.4	120.8	124.8	124.2	128.2
Mar	136.7	145.8	122.0	126.2	125.2	129.6
Apr	137.5	147.6	122.8	127.6	126.1	130.9
May	138.9	148.5	123.1	128.0	126.4	131.4
Jun	139.2	147.7	123.3	127.9	126.4	131.5

Source: Office for National Statistics;

1 The Climate Change Levy was introduced in April 2001. Further information on PPI is available from the National Statistics Website: www.statistics.gov.uk/ppi
2 A base weighted (2005=100) combination of the separate price indices for contractors' output in the six new work sectors
3 From Aug 2005 data is from the Regulated Mortgage Survey. From February 2002, data are based on a significantly enlarged return from the Survey of Mortgage Lenders, and are calculated through improved methodology. Annual and quarterly data prior to February 2002 are from the 5% Survey of Mortgage Lender and have been rebased to Feb 2002=100.
4 Indicates values which are considered less reliable than the remainder currently published mainly due to the lack of market coverage.
5 The Climate Change Levy was introduced in April 2001. Further information pm PPI is available from the National Statistics Website: www.statistics.goc.uk/ppi

Notes:
Producer Prices has implemented the change to the Standard Industrial Classification 2007 (SIC2007). For further information on changes and impact of the SIC2007 on prices can be found by following these links:
www.statistics.gov.uk/statbase/Product.asp?vlnk=15375
www.statistics.gov.uk/StatBase/Product.asp?vlnk=790&Pos=1&ColRank=1&Rank=208

More genaral information on UK SIC 2007, including correlation tables can be found by following this link:
www.statistics.gov.uk/statbase/Product.asp?vlnk=14012

Figures for the latest two months are provisional and the latest five months are subject to revisions in light of (a) late and revised respondent data and (b), for the seasonally adjusted series, revisions to seasonal adjustment factors which are re-estimated every month.

How to find this data from source -

http://www.communities.gov.uk/housing/housingresearch/housingstatistics/housingstatisticsby/housingmarket/housepriceindex/

17.2 Producer prices index of output (2005=100, SIC2007)

	Net sector output price		Gross sector output prices, not seasonally adjusted (selected sub-sections of industry)				
	Output of manufactured products	All manufacturing excluding food, beverages, tobacco & petroleum (NSA)	Food products, beverages & tobacco including duty	Textiles	Wearing apparel	Leather & related products	Wood & products of wood, cork except furniture
	7200700000	7200799000	7111101280	7112130000	7112140000	7112150000	7112160000
SIC 2007							
	JVZ7	K3BI	K65A	K37R	K37S	K37T	K37U
2007	104.4	102.9	..	102.4	101.5	102.9	111.4
2008	111.4	106.7	..	104.4	102.3	103.6	116.3
2009	113.2	109.4	121.4	107.5	102.2	104.1	118.9
2010	117.9	112.7	124.2	109.2	102.2	109.8	125.0
2009 Jan	111.6	108.8	120.4	106.5	102.9	102.5	118.8
Feb	111.6	108.8	120.6	107.0	101.9	102.1	118.4
Mar	111.7	108.9	120.8	107.4	102.1	103.5	118.9
Apr	112.4	109.1	121.1	107.4	102.2	104.0	118.8
May	112.7	109.1	121.5	107.7	102.2	104.3	118.7
Jun	113.1	108.9	122.0	107.7	102.2	104.6	118.6
Jul	113.3	109.1	121.7	107.6	102.2	103.6	118.4
Aug	113.4	109.2	121.3	107.5	102.2	104.2	118.4
Sep	113.9	109.6	121.6	107.6	102.2	104.1	119.3
Oct	114.3	110.1	121.2	107.7	102.2	104.9	119.3
Nov	114.7	110.2	121.7	107.7	102.3	105.4	119.5
Dec	115.2	110.8	122.2	107.6	102.3	105.9	119.9
2010 Jan	115.5	111.0	122.6	103.0	102.1	102.4	115.0
Feb	115.8	111.2	122.9	103.4	102.1	102.6	115.4
Mar	116.7	111.8	122.6	103.4	102.1	102.8	115.3
Apr	117.9	112.2	123.8	103.5	102.2	103.2	115.2
May	118.3	112.6	124.4	103.6	102.2	103.8	115.8
Jun	118.1	113.0	123.7	104.2	102.3	103.9	116.0
Jul	118.1	113.2	124.1	104.2	102.3	104.2	115.4
Aug	118.2	113.2	124.5	104.6	102.2	104.8	115.4
Sep	118.2	113.3	124.2	105.4	102.3	104.3	118.4
Oct	118.9	113.6	125.0	105.7	102.3	104.1	117.6
Nov	119.4	113.8	126.0	106.0	102.4	104.0	117.4
Dec	120.0	113.8	127.1	106.1	102.6	103.7	118.8
2011 Jan	121.3	114.7	128.8	113.5	102.2	114.1	128.2
Feb	121.9	114.7	129.9	113.5	102.3	116.0	129.0
Mar	123.2	115.3	131.0	114.1	102.3	121.7	129.5
Apr	124.5	116.2	132.8	115.5	103.9	124.4	129.8
May	124.7	116.4	133.3	115.9	104.6	123.6	131.4
Jun	124.8	116.6	133.7	116.6	104.2	123.8	131.8

1 The Climate Change Levy was introduced in April 2001. Further information on PPI is available from the National Statistics Website: www.statistics.gov.uk/ppi

2 A base weighted (2005=100) combination of the separate price indices for contractors' output in the six new work sectors

3 From Aug 2005 data is from the Regulated Mortgage Survey. From February 2002, data are based on a significantly enlarged return from the Survey of Mortgage Lenders, and are calculated through improved methodology. Annual and quarterly data prior to February 2002 are from the 5% Survey of Mortgage Lenders and have been rebased to Feb 2002=100.

4 Indicates values which are considered less reliable than the remainder currently published mainly due to the lack of market coverage.

5 The Climate Change Levy was introduced in April 2001. Further information pm PPI is available from the National Statistics Website: www.statistics.goc.uk/ppi

Notes:

Producer Prices has implemented the change to the Standard Industrial Classification 2007 (SIC2007). For further information on changes and impact of the SIC2007 on prices can be found by following these links:

www.statistics.gov.uk/statbase/Product.asp?vlnk=15375

www.statistics.gov.uk/StatBase/Product.asp?vlnk=790&Pos=1&ColRank=1&Rank=208

More genaral information on UK SIC 2007, including correlation tables can be found by following this link:

www.statistics.gov.uk/statbase/Product.asp?vlnk=14012

Figures for the latest two months are provisional and the latest five months are subject to revisions in light of (a) late and revised respondent data and (b), for the seasonally adjusted series, revisions to seasonal adjustment factors which are re-estimated every month.

How to find this data from source -

http://www.communities.gov.uk/housing/housingresearch/housingstatistics/housingstatisticsby/housingmarket/housepriceindex/

17.2 Producer prices index of output (2005=100, SIC2007)

Gross sector output prices, not seasonally adjusted (selected sub-sections of industry)

	Paper & Paper & products	Printing & recording services	Chemicals & chemical products	Rubber & plastic products	Other non-metallic mineral products	Basic metals	Computer, electronic & optical products
	7112170000	7112180000	7112200000	7112220000	7112230000	7112240000	7112260000
SIC 2007							
	K37V	**K37W**	**K37Z**	**K383**	**K384**	**K385**	**K387**
2007	104.6	100.8	105.6	104.2	108.5	120.4	95.8
2008	107.9	100.6	119.0	108.9	114.4	131.8	96.9
2009	109.6	101.4	125.0	110.7	118.9	119.7	98.2
2010	114.5	102.3	132.7	113.6	120.1	132.5	105.2
2009 Jan	109.8	101.2	123.3	110.5	119.1	126.3	98.1
Feb	109.8	100.8	123.5	110.7	119.5	124.5	97.6
Mar	109.7	101.1	124.0	111.0	119.5	122.6	96.2
Apr	109.8	100.8	124.5	110.7	119.3	117.7	96.5
May	110.0	101.0	124.7	110.4	118.9	117.5	96.8
Jun	109.6	101.5	123.1	109.8	118.2	117.6	97.0
Jul	109.1	101.6	123.8	110.1	118.4	117.1	97.0
Aug	108.4	101.2	126.1	110.4	118.3	117.7	97.1
Sep	108.5	101.1	126.6	110.8	118.7	118.1	98.1
Oct	109.6	102.4	126.4	111.1	119.0	119.8	100.9
Nov	110.0	102.2	126.8	111.5	118.8	119.0	100.6
Dec	110.4	102.1	127.3	111.5	119.2	119.1	102.9
2010 Jan	106.3	100.6	110.1	105.5	112.5	120.5	96.3
Feb	106.7	100.6	110.0	106.0	113.3	122.6	96.3
Mar	107.0	100.2	113.8	106.7	113.6	124.8	96.1
Apr	107.2	99.9	115.0	107.2	113.7	126.6	96.1
May	107.6	100.0	116.3	107.3	113.2	128.7	96.3
Jun	107.9	100.1	118.0	107.6	113.9	134.7	96.7
Jul	107.9	100.6	122.7	108.8	114.4	138.6	96.6
Aug	108.0	100.7	124.0	110.0	115.0	137.9	96.7
Sep	108.5	101.0	124.9	111.5	115.3	141.5	97.6
Oct	108.9	101.5	124.8	112.0	115.6	138.6	97.7
Nov	109.2	101.3	125.2	112.3	115.7	133.7	98.3
Dec	109.1	101.3	123.6	111.5	116.2	132.9	97.5
2011 Jan	120.1	103.1	142.0	116.1	121.7	140.2	103.3
Feb	120.5	103.1	140.4	117.0	122.1	144.4	103.1
Mar	122.2	103.3	141.8	117.9	122.3	147.2	103.0
Apr	123.4	103.3	144.5	118.8	122.8	150.0	102.8
May	123.8	103.4	145.1	119.5	123.1	151.9	102.7
Jun	125.0	103.6	145.3	119.8	123.3	149.8	102.9

17.2 Producer prices index of output (2005=100, SIC2007)

Gross sector output prices, not seasonally adjusted (selected sub-sections of industry)

	Electrical equipment	Machinery & equipment not elsewhere specified	Motor vehicles, trailers & semi trailers &	Other transport equipment	Furniture	Other manufactured goods	Quarterly construction output price index[2]	Monthly index of average price of new dwellings - at mortgage completion stage[3]
	7112270000	7112280000	7112290000	7112300000	7112310000	7112320000		
SIC 2007								
	K388	**K389**	**K38A**	**K38B**	**K38C**	**K38D**	**JYYC**	**FCBA**
2007	108.5	104.9	100.7	103.9	102.9	104.0	108.2	68.6
2008	112.3	109.1	104.6	106.1	105.6	108.0	109.1	64.4
2009	115.5	113.1	109.7	108.8	107.8	111.1	103.0	50.5
2010	121.3	114.8	111.3	111.1	110.1	114.6	99.2	58.3
2009 Jan	112.7	111.2	108.7	107.3	107.4	110.0	..	162.1
Feb	113.4	111.5	108.9	107.3	107.5	110.6	..	158.6
Mar	114.2	111.9	108.7	108.7	108.0	111.3	105.0	151.6
Apr	114.2	112.3	110.0	108.6	107.8	110.7	..	150.7
May	115.2	113.7	109.8	108.6	107.4	111.0	..	147.9
Jun	115.3	113.3	109.3	109.1	107.5	111.4	102.8	148.7
Jul	115.7	113.6	109.4	109.0	107.6	111.2	..	145.8
Aug	116.1	113.6	109.9	108.7	107.8	111.2	..	143.3
Sep	117.0	113.9	110.0	109.2	107.9	111.2	102.9	150.0
Oct	117.0	113.9	110.7	109.2	108.2	111.4	..	147.7
Nov	117.4	114.3	110.7	109.7	108.3	111.6	..	146.7
Dec	117.9	114.6	110.8	109.6	108.5	112.0	101.3	153.6
2010 Jan	110.2	107.4	102.1	105.7	104.4	106.0	..	158.7
Feb	110.7	107.7	102.2	105.1	104.4	106.6	..	151.0
Mar	111.3	108.0	102.5	105.3	104.6	107.0	99.9	153.5
Apr	112.3	108.6	102.9	105.4	104.5	107.2	..	162.5
May	112.3	108.8	104.5	105.6	104.7	107.6	..	157.9
Jun	112.4	109.1	104.7	105.7	104.8	107.9	99.3	162.0
Jul	112.8	109.1	105.2	106.2	105.5	108.5	..	159.6
Aug	112.8	109.5	105.3	106.4	106.5	108.9	..	155.6
Sep	113.3	109.9	105.9	106.0	106.4	109.2	98.5	158.4
Oct	113.3	109.6	106.0	106.7	107.1	109.2	..	153.8
Nov	113.5	110.2	106.7	107.4	107.1	108.9	..	159.6
Dec	112.9	111.2	107.7	107.6	107.2	109.2	98.9	165.3
2011 Jan	126.2	116.0	111.2	112.1	111.4	116.9	..	172.3
Feb	126.6	115.9	111.3	112.1	111.7	116.9	..	170.3
Mar	127.1	116.5	111.7	112.4	112.1	117.7	99.7	169.9
Apr	126.7	117.7	112.2	112.5	112.4	117.8	..	169.3
May	126.1	117.9	112.3	112.6	112.4	119.1		170.2
Jun	126.3	118.0	112.5	112.6	112.6	119.2		

Source: Office for National Statistics;
ONS (JYYC): 01633 456662

CLG (FCBA): 0303 444 2345

17.3 Internal purchasing power of the pound[1,2] United Kingdom

Pence

	1992	1993	1994	1995	1996	1997	1998	1999	2000	2001	2002	2003	2004	2005	2006	2007	2008	2009	2010
	CZVM	CBXX	DOFX	DOHR	DOLM	DTUL	CDQG	JKZZ	ZMHO	IKHI	FAUI	SEZH	C687	E9AO	GB4Y	HT4R	J5TL	JRT3	K9AD
1990	110	112	114	118	121	125	129	131	135	137	140	144	148	152	157	164	170	169	181
1991	104	105	108	112	114	118	122	124	128	130	132	136	140	144	148	155	161	160	171
1992	100	102	104	108	110	114	118	119	123	125	127	131	135	139	143	149	155	154	165
1993	98	100	102	106	109	112	116	118	121	123	125	129	133	136	141	147	153	152	162
1994	96	98	100	103	106	109	113	115	118	120	122	126	130	133	137	143	149	148	158
1995	93	94	97	100	102	106	109	111	114	116	118	122	125	129	133	139	144	143	153
1996	91	92	94	98	100	103	107	108	112	113	115	119	122	126	130	135	141	140	150
1997	88	89	92	95	97	100	103	105	108	110	112	115	119	122	126	131	136	136	145
1998	85	86	88	92	94	97	100	102	105	106	108	111	115	118	122	127	132	131	140
1999	84	85	87	90	92	95	98	100	103	105	107	110	113	116	120	125	130	129	138
2000	81	83	85	88	90	92	96	97	100	102	103	106	110	113	116	121	126	125	134
2001	80	81	83	86	88	91	94	95	98	100	102	105	108	111	114	119	124	123	132
2002	79	80	82	85	87	89	92	94	97	98	100	103	106	109	112	117	122	121	130
2003	76	78	79	82	84	87	90	91	94	96	97	100	103	106	109	114	118	118	126
2004	74	75	77	80	82	84	87	89	91	93	94	97	100	103	106	111	115	114	122
2005	72	73	75	78	80	82	85	86	89	90	92	94	97	100	103	108	112	111	119
2006	70	71	73	75	77	80	82	83	86	87	89	92	94	97	100	104	108	108	115
2007	67	68	70	72	74	76	79	80	82	84	85	88	90	93	96	100	104	103	111
2008	64	65	67	69	71	73	76	77	79	81	82	84	87	89	92	96	100	99	106
2009	65	66	67	70	71	74	76	77	80	81	82	85	87	90	93	97	101	100	107
2010	61	62	63	65	67	69	71	72	75	76	77	79	82	84	87	90	94	94	100

1 See chapter text. These figures are calculated by taking the inverse ratio of the respective annual averages of the Retail Prices Index (RPI).
2 To find the purchasing power of the pound in 1995, given that it was 100 pence in 1990, select the column headed 1990 and look at the 1995 row. The result is 85 pence.

Source: Office for National Statistics: 020 7533 5874

17.4 Consumer Prices Index:[1] detailed figures by division United Kingdom

Indices (2005=100)

	Food and non-alcoholic beverages	Alcoholic beverages and tobacco	Clothing and footwear	Housing, water, electricity gas & other fuels	Furniture, household equipment & routine maintenance	Health	Transport	Commun-ication	Recreation and culture	Education	Restaurants and hotels	Miscell-aneous goods and services	CPI (overall index)
Index level (2005=100)													
COICOP Division													
	CHZR	CHZS	CHZT	CHZU	CHZV	CHZW	CHZX	CHZY	CHZZ	CJUU	CJUV	CJUW	CHZQ
Weights 2011	118	42	62	129	61	24	159	26	147	18	120	94	1000
	D7BU	D7BV	D7BW	D7BX	D7BY	D7BZ	D7C2	D7C3	D7C4	D7C5	D7C6	D7C7	D7BT
2008	116.8	110.5	86.3	124.5	103.4	109.5	111.8	94.3	97.3	136.3	110.9	108.6	108.5
2009	123.2	115.3	79.6	129.9	106.7	112.5	112.7	95.2	98.5	146.7	113.6	111	110.8
2010	127.4	121.7	78.8	130.3	110	115.7	122.1	99.9	100.4	154.5	116.9	113.7	114.5
2010 Jan	124.3	119.5	75.2	130.7	107.3	114.6	118.2	97.6	99.9	152.2	114.7	112.2	112.4
Feb	125.7	119.1	76.8	129.7	108.5	114.5	118.9	97.9	99.9	152.2	115.3	112.2	112.9
Mar	126.0	120.0	78.1	129.9	110.2	114.6	120.3	98.0	100.1	152.2	115.8	112.4	113.5
Apr	126.4	122.6	79.9	129.7	108.4	114.7	121.9	100.8	100.2	152.2	116.4	113.3	114.2
May	126.3	122.4	80.2	129.9	109.7	114.7	122.7	100.6	100.0	152.2	116.8	113.5	114.4
Jun	126.2	121.9	78.4	129.9	110.5	115.0	123.1	101.6	100.5	152.2	117.0	114.2	114.6
Jul	127.4	121.9	74.6	130.0	108.4	115.9	124.0	101.7	100.2	152.2	117.2	113.6	114.3
Aug	127.6	121.8	76.6	130.0	109.5	116.5	125.6	100.9	100.4	152.2	117.3	114.1	114.9
Sep	127.6	122.5	81.5	130.3	111.4	116.6	121.3	99.4	100.3	156.7	117.6	114.4	114.9
Oct	128.2	123.5	80.9	130.4	110.3	117.5	121.8	100.3	100.9	160.2	117.8	114.5	115.2
Nov	130.2	123.1	82.5	130.8	112.1	117.2	121.8	100.0	100.7	160.2	118.0	114.4	115.6
Dec	132.2	122.0	81.0	132.6	113.5	117.0	126.1	99.8	101.1	160.2	118.3	114.9	116.8
2011 Jan	132.1	127.6	76.2	133.4	111.4	118.0	127.3	101.1	100.9	160.2	119.9	114.6	116.9
Feb	133.6	126.2	78.9	133.8	112.9	117.6	128.4	102.4	101.2	160.2	120.5	115.3	117.8
Mar	131.8	126.8	79.8	134.4	114.9	118.5	129.9	102.2	100.8	160.2	120.7	115.5	118.1
Apr	131.9	133.5	80.9	135.5	114.0	119.4	133.5	103.3	101.1	160.2	121.4	115.7	119.3
May	133.6	134.4	81.1	135.4	114.4	119.2	132.5	104.3	100.9	160.2	122.0	116.4	119.5
Jun	134.9	133.6	79.6	135.5	114.9	119.2	132.9	103.3	100.0	160.2	122.2	116.4	119.4
Jul	135.3	134.5	76.8	136	113.6	119.9	133.7	104.2	100	160.2	122.4	116.7	119.4
Aug	135.5	133.7	79.7	136.7	115.9	120.5	134.9	104.3	99.6	160.2	122.7	117.2	120.1
Percentage change on a year earlier													
	D7G8	D7G9	D7GA	D7GB	D7GC	D7GD	D7GE	D7GF	D7GG	D7GH	D7GI	D7GJ	D7G7
2008	9.1	3.9	-6.6	8.6	2.1	3.1	5.6	-2.6	-0.6	11.7	3.8	2.5	3.6
2009	5.4	4.4	-7.7	4.3	3.2	2.7	0.8	1	1.3	7.6	2.4	2.2	2.2
2010	3.4	5.5	-1	0.4	3.1	2.9	8.3	4.9	1.9	5.3	2.9	2.4	3.3
2010 Jan	1.9	6.2	-4.5	-0.3	5.1	3.7	11.0	4.1	3.6	5.2	2.2	2.0	3.5
Feb	1.3	4.2	-3.3	-1.0	3.7	3.4	10.6	4.6	2.4	5.2	2.4	1.6	3.0
Mar	2.1	4.7	-2.6	0.1	3.1	3.3	11.3	4.9	2.6	5.2	2.6	1.5	3.4
Apr	2.9	7.0	-0.6	0.2	2.5	2.5	11.0	5.6	2.4	5.2	2.9	2.2	3.7
May	1.8	5.1	-0.7	0.6	2.7	2.5	10.1	5.3	2.0	5.2	2.8	2.4	3.4
Jun	1.9	5.5	-1.4	0.5	2.4	2.6	8.9	6.4	1.8	5.2	2.9	3.0	3.2
Jul	3.4	5.2	-3.1	0.4	3.3	2.7	7.8	6.4	1.4	5.2	3.0	2.1	3.1
Aug	4.1	4.7	-1.7	0.3	2.8	2.7	7.5	5.7	1.4	5.2	3.0	2.4	3.1
Sep	5.1	5.2	0.9	0.5	2.9	2.6	5.4	4.4	1.1	6.4	3.2	2.5	3.1
Oct	4.5	6.3	0.7	0.5	2.7	2.9	5.8	3.9	1.5	5.3	3.1	3.0	3.2
Nov	5.5	6.5	2.1	0.7	3.5	2.9	5.1	3.9	1.1	5.3	3.2	2.9	3.3
Dec	6.1	5.8	1.5	2.0	2.5	3.2	6.5	3.5	1.5	5.3	3.5	2.9	3.7
2011 Jan	6.3	6.7	1.3	2.1	3.8	2.9	7.7	3.5	1.0	5.3	4.5	2.2	4.0
Feb	6.2	6.0	2.8	3.1	4.1	2.7	7.9	4.6	1.3	5.3	4.5	2.7	4.4
Mar	4.5	5.7	2.2	3.4	4.2	3.4	8.0	4.3	0.6	5.3	4.3	2.7	4.0
Apr	4.4	8.9	1.2	4.4	5.1	4.1	9.6	2.5	0.9	5.3	4.3	2.1	4.5
May	5.8	9.8	1.2	4.3	4.3	3.9	8.0	3.7	0.9	5.3	4.5	2.5	4.5
Jun	6.9	9.6	1.5	4.3	4.0	3.6	7.9	1.7	-0.5	5.3	4.5	1.9	4.2
Jul	6.2	10.3	3.1	4.6	4.8	3.5	7.8	2.5	-0.2	5.3	4.4	2.7	4.4
Aug	6.2	9.8	4	5.1	5.8	3.4	7.4	3.4	-0.8	5.3	4.6	2.8	4.5

1 See chapter text. Prior to 10 December 2003, the consumer prices index
(CPI) was published in the UK as the harmonised index of consumer prices
(HICP).

Source: Office for National Statistics: 020 7533 5874

17.5 Retail Prices Index[1] United Kingdom

Indices (13 January 1987=100)

	All items (RPI)	All items excluding mortgage interest payments (RPIX)	mortgage interest payments and depreciation	Housing	Food	Seasonal food[2]	Food and catering	Alcohol and tobacco	Housing and household expenditure	Personal expenditure	Travel and leisure	Consumer durables	All items excluding mortgage interest payments and indirect taxes (RPIY)[3]
Weights													
	CZGU	CZGY	DOGZ	CZGX	CZGV	CZGW	CBVV	CBVW	CBVX	CBVY	CBVZ	CBWA	
2001	1000	954	914	795	884	982	169	97	362	96	276	125	
2002	1000	964	924	801	886	980	166	99	363	94	278	126	
2003	1000	961	919	797	891	983	160	98	365	92	285	126	
2004	1000	961	914	791	889	981	160	97	367	93	283	121	
2005	1000	950	901	776	890	981	159	96	387	89	269	122	
2006	1000	950	906	778	895	983	155	96	392	90	267	117	
2007	1000	945	895	762	895	981	152	95	408	83	262	109	
2008	1000	940	885	746	889	980	158	86	417	83	256	104	
2009	1000	959	909	764	882	979	168	90	416	80	246	106	
2010	1000	966	911	763	888	981	159	91	403	81	266	105	
2011	1000	968	914	762	882	980	165	88	408	82	257	106	
Annual averages													
	CHAW	CHMK	CHON	CHAZ	CHAY	CHAX	CHBS	CHBT	CHBU	CHBV	CHBW	CHBY	CBZW
2001	173.3	171.3	169.5	163.7	178.0	174.3	162.2	216.9	180.0	135.7	172.0	105.0	163.7
2002	176.2	175.1	172.5	166.0	181.1	177.2	164.8	222.3	184.6	133.2	174.2	101.9	167.5
2003	181.3	180.0	176.2	168.9	186.7	182.4	167.9	228.0	194.3	133.2	177.0	99.8	172.0
2004	186.7	184.0	179.1	170.9	192.8	187.9	170.0	233.6	207.4	131.5	178.1	97.7	175.5
2005	192.0	188.2	182.6	173.7	198.7	193.3	172.9	239.8	219.4	131.0	179.2	95.3	179.4
2006	198.1	193.7	187.8	178.3	205.2	199.5	176.9	247.1	231.8	131.7	181.1	94.0	184.8
2007	206.6	199.9	193.3	183.2	213.9	207.9	184.3	256.2	248.1	132.9	183.8	93.3	190.8
2008	214.8	208.5	201.9	191.3	221.2	216.0	198.5	266.7	258.6	132.4	189.0	91.6	199.2
2009	213.7	212.6	207.2	196.3	218.3	214.6	207.6	276.7	247.4	131.4	191.2	90.7	204.8
2010	223.6	222.7	217	206.5	228.8	224.5	214.1	289.9	253.8	138.2	207.6	94.4	211.9
Monthly figures													
2010 Jan	217.9	217.1	211.6	200.8	223	218.9	209.8	284.3	250	129.7	200.5	89.3	206.5
Feb	219.2	218.4	212.8	202.1	224.2	220.1	211.4	284.3	250.5	133.5	201.7	91.9	208
Mar	220.7	219.9	214.3	203.9	225.9	221.7	212	286.3	251.7	136.1	203.4	94.2	209.5
Apr	222.8	222	216.4	205.9	228.1	223.8	212.9	290.7	252.1	138.7	207.3	94.1	210.9
May	223.6	222.8	217.2	206.7	229.2	224.6	212.6	291	253.1	139	208.8	94.8	211.8
June	224.1	223.3	217.6	207.2	229.7	225.1	212.6	290.6	254.4	138	209.5	95.2	212.4
July	223.6	222.7	216.9	206.4	228.8	224.5	214.4	290.6	253.7	134.8	209	91.9	211.8
Aug	224.5	223.6	217.7	207.2	229.8	225.5	214.6	290.6	254.5	137.4	209.8	93.5	212.8
Sep	225.3	224.4	218.5	208	230.7	226.3	214.9	291.6	255.8	142.5	208.1	96.9	213.6
Oct	225.8	224.9	219	208.6	231.1	226.8	215.6	293	255.4	142.2	209.6	95.7	214
Nov	226.8	225.9	220.2	209.8	232	227.8	217.8	293.1	256.3	144	210	97.4	215
Dec	228.4	227.5	221.9	211.8	233.4	229.2	220.1	292.5	258.1	142.5	212.9	97.6	216.9
2011 Jan	229	228.2	222.6	212.5	234	229.9	221.4	301.8	257.7	138.8	214.4	93.5	214.3
Feb	231.3	230.5	225.1	215.3	236.3	232.2	223.3	300.9	259	145.5	216.7	97.7	216.6
Mar	232.5	231.7	226.4	216.7	238	233.5	221.9	302	260.1	147.8	219	99.7	217.8
Apr	234.4	233.7	228.5	218.8	240.2	235.6	222.4	312.3	260.4	149.9	221.9	99.8	219.3
May	235.2	234.5	229.4	219.7	240.7	236.3	224.6	313.9	260.6	150.4	222.4	100.2	220.1
June	235.2	234.5	229.4	219.7	240.5	236.3	226.2	313.3	261	149	221.8	99.3	220.2
July	234.7	233.9	228.8	218.9	239.8	235.8	226.8	314.4	260.9	146.1	220.8	96.9	219.8

1 See chapter text.

2 Seasonal food is defined as items of food the prices of which show significant

seasonal variations. These are fresh fruit and vegetables, fresh fish, eggs and home-killed lamb.

3 There are no weights available for RPIY.

Source: Office for National Statistics: 020 7533 5874

17.6 Tax and Price Index[1] United Kingdom

Indices and percentages

Tax and Price Index: (January 1988=100)
DQAB

	1997	1998	1999	2000	2001	2002	2003	2004	2005	2006	2007	2008	2009	2010	2011
January	143.6	147.1	150.5	152.7	156.7	156.5	161.4	166.9	172.1	175.9	183.3	190.7	188.6	194.7	205.5
February	144.2	147.9	150.8	153.7	157.6	157.0	162.3	167.6	172.8	176.7	184.8	192.3	189.8	196.0	207.7
March	144.6	148.4	151.2	154.6	157.8	157.7	163.0	168.4	173.7	177.4	186.1	192.9	189.7	197.4	208.8
April	143.8	149.7	151.2	155.7	156.3	158.6	164.9	168.9	174.1	178.3	186.3	192.2	188.5	199.5	209.2
May	144.4	150.6	151.7	156.3	157.4	159.1	165.2	169.7	174.5	179.5	187.1	193.4	189.7	200.3	210.0
June	145.0	150.5	151.7	156.7	157.6	159.1	165.0	170.0	174.7	180.3	188.2	195.1	190.2	200.8	210.0
July	145.0	150.1	151.1	156.1	156.5	158.8	165.0	170.0	174.7	180.3	187.0	194.8	190.2	200.3	209.5
August	146.0	150.8	151.5	156.1	157.2	159.3	165.4	170.6	175.1	181.0	188.2	195.5	191.3	201.2	210.9
September	146.9	151.5	152.3	157.3	157.8	160.6	166.3	171.3	175.6	181.9	188.9	196.7	192.2	201.9	..
October	147.1	151.6	152.6	157.2	157.5	160.9	166.4	171.8	175.8	182.2	189.8	196.0	192.9	202.4	..
November	147.2	151.5	152.8	157.7	156.8	161.2	166.5	172.2	176.1	176.1	182.8	190.6	194.3	193.4	203.4	..
December	147.6	151.5	153.4	157.8	156.6	161.5	167.3	173.1	176.6	184.4	191.8	191.2	194.8	204.9	..

Retail Prices Index: (January 1988=100)
CHAW

	1997	1998	1999	2000	2001	2002	2003	2004	2005	2006	2007	2008	2009	2010	2011
January	154.4	159.5	163.4	166.6	171.1	173.3	178.4	183.1	188.9	193.4	201.6	209.8	210.1	217.9	229.0
February	155.0	160.3	163.7	167.5	172.0	173.8	179.3	183.8	189.6	194.2	203.1	211.4	211.4	219.2	231.3
March	155.4	160.8	164.1	168.4	172.2	174.5	179.9	184.6	190.5	195.0	204.4	212.1	211.3	220.7	232.5
April	156.3	162.6	165.2	170.1	173.1	175.7	181.2	185.7	191.6	196.5	205.4	214.0	211.5	222.8	234.4
May	156.9	163.5	165.6	170.7	174.2	176.2	181.5	186.5	192.0	197.7	206.2	215.1	212.8	223.6	235.2
June	157.5	163.4	165.6	171.1	174.4	176.2	181.3	186.8	192.2	198.5	207.3	216.8	213.4	224.1	235.2
July	157.5	163.0	165.1	170.5	173.3	175.9	181.3	186.8	192.2	198.5	206.1	216.5	213.4	223.6	234.7
August	158.5	163.7	165.5	170.5	174.0	176.4	181.6	187.4	192.6	199.2	207.3	217.2	214.4	224.5	236.1
September	159.3	164.4	166.2	171.7	174.6	177.6	182.5	188.1	193.1	200.1	208.0	218.4	215.3	225.3	..
October	159.5	164.5	166.5	171.6	174.3	177.9	182.6	188.6	193.3	200.4	208.9	217.7	216.0	225.8	..
November	159.6	164.4	166.7	172.1	173.6	178.2	182.7	189.0	193.6	201.1	209.7	216.0	216.6	226.8	..
December	160.0	164.4	167.3	172.2	173.4	178.5	183.5	189.9	194.1	202.7	210.9	212.9	218.0	228.4	..

Percentage changes on one year earlier[1]

Tax and Price Index[1]

	1997	1998	1999	2000	2001	2002	2003	2004	2005	2006	2007	2008	2009	2010	2011
January	1.4	2.4	2.3	1.5	2.6	−0.1	3.1	3.4	3.1	2.2	4.2	4.0	−1.1	3.2	5.5
February	1.3	2.6	2.0	1.9	2.5	−0.4	3.4	3.3	3.1	2.3	4.6	4.1	−1.3	3.3	6.0
March	1.1	2.6	1.9	2.2	2.1	−0.1	3.4	3.3	3.1	2.1	4.9	3.7	−1.7	4.1	5.8
April	1.5	4.1	1.0	3.0	0.4	1.5	4.0	2.4	3.1	2.4	4.5	3.2	−1.9	5.8	4.9
May	1.7	4.3	0.7	3.0	0.7	1.1	3.8	2.7	2.8	2.9	4.2	3.4	−1.9	5.6	4.8
June	2.0	3.8	0.8	3.3	0.6	1.0	3.7	3.0	2.8	3.2	4.4	3.7	−2.5	5.6	4.6
July	2.5	3.5	0.7	3.3	0.3	1.5	3.9	3.0	2.8	3.2	3.7	4.2	−2.4	5.3	4.6
August	2.7	3.3	0.5	3.0	0.7	1.3	3.8	3.1	2.6	3.4	4.0	3.9	−2.1	5.2	4.8
September	2.7	3.1	0.5	3.3	0.3	1.8	3.5	3.0	2.5	3.6	3.8	4.1	−2.3	5.0	..
October	2.9	3.1	0.7	3.0	0.2	2.2	3.4	3.2	2.3	3.6	4.2	3.3	−1.6	4.9	..
November	2.9	2.9	0.9	3.2	−0.6	2.8	3.3	3.4	2.3	3.8	4.3	1.9	−0.5	5.2	..
December	2.8	2.6	1.3	2.9	−0.8	3.1	3.6	3.5	2.0	4.4	4.0	−0.3	1.9	5.2	..

Retail Prices Index - CZBH

	1997	1998	1999	2000	2001	2002	2003	2004	2005	2006	2007	2008	2009	2010	2011
January	2.8	3.3	2.4	2.0	2.7	1.3	2.9	2.6	3.2	2.4	4.2	4.1	0.1	3.7	5.1
February	2.7	3.4	2.1	2.3	2.7	1.0	3.2	2.5	3.2	2.4	4.6	4.1	0.0	3.7	5.5
March	2.6	3.5	2.1	2.6	2.3	1.3	3.1	2.6	3.2	2.4	4.8	3.8	−0.4	4.4	5.3
April	2.4	4.0	1.6	3.0	1.8	1.5	3.1	2.5	3.2	2.6	4.5	4.2	−1.2	5.3	5.2
May	2.6	4.2	1.3	3.1	2.1	1.1	3.0	2.8	2.9	3.0	4.3	4.3	−1.1	5.1	5.2
June	2.9	3.7	1.3	3.3	1.9	1.0	2.9	3.0	2.9	3.3	4.4	4.6	−1.6	5.0	5.0
July	3.3	3.5	1.3	3.3	1.6	1.5	3.1	3.0	2.9	3.3	3.8	5.0	−1.4	4.8	5.0
August	3.5	3.3	1.1	3.0	2.1	1.4	2.9	3.2	2.8	3.4	4.1	4.8	−1.3	4.7	5.2
September	3.6	3.2	1.1	3.3	1.7	1.7	2.8	3.1	2.7	3.6	3.9	5.0	−1.4	4.6	..
October	3.7	3.1	1.2	3.1	1.6	2.1	2.6	3.3	2.5	3.7	4.2	4.2	−0.8	4.5	..
November	3.7	3.0	1.4	3.2	0.9	2.6	2.5	3.4	2.4	3.9	4.3	3.0	0.3	4.7	..
December	3.6	2.8	1.8	2.9	0.7	2.9	2.8	3.5	2.2	4.4	4.0	0.9	2.4	4.8	..

1 See chapter text.

Source: Office for National Statistics: 020 7533 5874

17.7 Index of purchase prices of the means of agricultural production[1]
United Kingdom

Annual averages							Indices (2005=100)		
		2003	2004	2005	2006	2007	2008	2009	2010
Goods and services currently consumed[2]	C3FU	93.0	100.3	100.0	104.0	115.4	145.8	133.0	139.1
Seeds	C3FV	104.0	130.1	100.0	92.5	100.1	111.6	112.1	110.3
Energy, lubricants	C3FW	73.9	79.8	100.0	112.2	117.9	158.2	130.4	147.1
Fuels for heating	C3FX	65.8	74.5	100.0	116.5	127.9	173.1	138.9	170.7
Motor fuel	C3FY	71.1	77.7	100.0	109.5	111.1	160.4	123.3	145.4
Electricity	C3FZ	87.2	89.3	100.0	119.2	135.6	143.4	149.8	141.2
Fertilisers and soil improvers	C3G3	82.0	91.0	100.0	105.7	119.8	272.5	189.8	182.4
Straight nitrogen	C3G4	75.5	87.2	100.0	108.3	112.0	225.0	151.4	158.5
Compound fertilisers	C3G5	87.1	94.2	100.0	103.4	128.1	330.0	231.8	211.5
Other fertiliser (mainly lime and chalk)	C3G6	99.8	99.8	100.0	103.5	108.4	113.6	113.9	107.6
Fungicides	JT6Q	96.6	98.9	100.0	101.6	102.9	105.3	106.9	103.3
Insecticides	JT6R	88.0	88.2	100.0	106.2	111.1	113.3	126.7	124.0
Herbicides	JT6S	92.1	95.9	100.0	103.3	104.8	107.0	107.4	105.0
Plant protection products	C3G7	94.0	96.9	100.0	102.5	104.2	106.4	108.5	105.6
Feed wheat	C3G9	109.0	122.5	100.0	114.7	159.8	216.3	159.4	175.6
Feed barley	JT6U	106.5	114.6	100.0	111.5	161.8	194.6	134.0	155.8
Feed oats	JT6V	89.4	99.2	100.0	108.2	130.9	164.7	116.5	103.9
Soya bean meal	JT6W	107.7	112.2	100.0	95.8	116.4	174.7	193.8	188.5
White fish meal	C3GE	102.0	95.0	100.0	144.2	137.2	138.6	174.8	252.2
Field beans	JT6X	99.5	117.1	100.0	96.9	171.0	205.2	157.8	176.1
Field Peas	JT6Y	103.3	103.3	103.3	103.3	103.3	103.3	103.3	103.3
Dried Sugar Beet Pulp	JT6Z	100.0	100.0	100.0	100.0	100.0	100.0	100.0	100.0
All straight feedstuffs	C3GG	104.9	112.2	100.0	106.4	142.9	184.0	156.2	173.5
Compound feedstuffs for:	C3GI	99.7	106.1	100.0	103.2	119.7	154.6	149.8	151.2
Cattle and calves	C3GJ	98.6	104.2	100.0	101.4	116.4	151.6	147.3	145.0
Pigs	C3GK	101.0	107.3	100.0	105.5	122.7	151.6	147.0	154.6
Poultry	C3GL	100.6	108.0	100.0	104.9	123.6	162.2	155.7	159.7
Sheep	C3GM	98.1	104.6	100.0	99.8	112.2	141.9	141.9	137.8
Maintenance and repair of plant	C3GN	89.1	94.0	100.0	105.8	109.9	116.3	121.5	126.9
Maintenance and repair of buildings	C3GO	91.4	95.9	100.0	106.3	114.1	122.3	122.0	130.4
Veterinary services	C3GP	97.9	100.7	100.0	106.9	108.4	104.0	104.7	118.8
Other goods and services	C3GQ	91.5	96.2	100.0	102.6	108.2	113.5	115.4	123.3
Goods and services contributing to investment in agriculture	C3GR	93.0	100.3	100.0	104.0	115.4	145.8	133.0	139.1
Machinery and other equipment	C3GT	91.6	92.5	100.0	104.5	110.3	117.5	122.1	125.3
Machinery and plant for cultivation	C3GU	90.2	94.8	100.0	101.4	106.3	113.6	117.1	122.2
Machinery and plant for harvesting	C3GV	90.1	89.2	100.0	107.7	115.8	125.1	130.2	132.5
Farm machinery and installations	C3GW	97.0	97.2	100.0	100.9	102.8	104.6	109.3	112.4
Tractors	C3GX	102.7	97.6	100.0	101.4	102.9	105.5	110.7	115.5
Other vehicles	C3GY	106.9	104.5	100.0	97.8	95.7	90.8	91.7	96.8
Buildings	C3GZ	90.7	95.5	100.0	105.9	113.0	120.3	120.6	126.9
Engineering and soil improvement operations	C3H2	93.6	96.4	100.0	102.1	107.3	112.1	118.2	119.8
All means of Agricultural Production	JT72	93.6	99.6	100.0	103.8	114.2	139.9	129.9	135.7

1 See chapter text.

2 The sum of the percentages of categories included does not add up to 100% due to the exclusion of some minor categories.

Source: Department for Environment, Food and Rural Affairs: 01904 456561

17.8 Index of producer prices of agricultural products[1] United Kingdom

Annual averages						Indices (2005=100)		
		2003	2004	2005	2006	2007	2008	2009	2010

		2003	2004	2005	2006	2007	2008	2009	2010
Wheat for :									
breadmaking	C3H9	109.5	117.0	100.0	106.7	176.6	210.3	162.1	182.8
other milling	C3HA	112.3	121.5	100.0	113.6	188.5	206.9	152.8	190.3
feeding	C3HB	108.4	122.9	100.0	114.3	158.2	216.2	159.8	174.8
Barley for :									
feeding	C3HC	106.6	112.7	100.0	111.3	162.7	189.9	133.1	158.6
malting	C3HD	105.8	98.4	100.0	109.5	187.6	205.7	128.9	162.7
Oats for :									
milling	C3HE	87.1	92.7	100.0	111.7	141.6	167.3	125.0	155.2
feeding	C3HF	88.6	98.8	100.0	108.4	129.7	167.8	116.4	104.3
Potatoes									
early	C3HH	91.8	127.3	100.0	134.5	104.2	142.1	106.8	144.5
Main crop	C3HI	94.1	131.0	100.0	130.9	149.1	155.0	124.4	141.0
Industrial crops	C3HJ	108.6	106.8	100.0	106.7	108.2	152.4	132.0	138.3
Oilseed rape (non set-aside)	C3HK	123.7	117.1	100.0	119.8	143.9	232.9	183.4	199.0
Sugar beet	C3HL	95.7	98.6	100.0	96.2	74.8	77.3	83.2	81.3
Fresh vegetables	C3HM	104.1	95.6	100.0	109.1	122.1	117.5	113.9	131.9
Cauliflowers	C3HN	97.3	82.6	100.0	105.1	130.7	107.7	114.3	128.4
Lettuce	C3HO	108.4	93.9	100.0	109.4	107.1	119.1	107.9	129.9
Tomatoes	C3HP	116.4	89.3	100.0	109.9	110.8	117.7	103.8	133.7
Carrots	C3HQ	90.3	83.7	100.0	107.6	123.4	128.2	129.5	117.6
Cabbage	C3HR	95.5	92.0	100.0	103.8	139.6	124.6	124.0	131.3
Beans	C3HS	100.8	109.1	100.0	137.5	153.7	138.9	123.5	141.8
Onions	C3HT	118.7	115.3	100.0	129.3	165.4	131.2	133.3	211.5
Mushrooms	C3HU	119.2	112.5	100.0	95.7	84.5	84.6	87.2	127.1
Fresh fruit	C3HV	111.9	98.4	100.0	104.1	107.4	126.4	124.6	129.6
Dessert apples	C3HW	110.7	104.4	100.0	105.7	121.5	130.9	131.4	140.8
Dessert pears	C3HX	102.7	102.2	100.0	108.6	106.0	134.0	149.7	131.3
Cooking apples	C3HY	135.8	121.3	100.0	111.5	122.9	155.1	127.5	129.1
Strawberries	C3HZ	111.3	87.8	100.0	96.5	101.5	112.9	122.1	130.4
Raspberries	C3I2	101.8	96.6	100.0	111.5	100.5	119.6	120.9	123.6
Seeds (excluding cereal seeds)	C3I3	73.8	80.4	100.0	100.2	118.3	126.4	126.4	126.4
Flowers and plants	C3I4	101.9	99.9	100.0	103.4	110.1	115.1	116.7	138.2
Other crop products	C3I5	81.6	86.2	100.0	100.5	113.3	119.4	119.5	119.9
Crop Products	JT6M	102.7	107.0	100.0	109.6	133.7	153.7	131.1	149.2
Animals and animal products	C3I6	98.6	101.2	100.0	101.0	108.5	136.0	139.4	141.1
Animals for slaughter	C3I7	98.6	101.2	100.0	103.5	105.5	133.2	146.0	146.2
Calves	C3I8	135.3	137.1	100.0	117.0	132.6	155.0	193.6	158.2
Clean cattle	C3I9	93.1	99.0	100.0	108.3	109.9	141.7	151.2	144.0
Clean pigs	C3IA	99.3	99.6	100.0	101.0	104.1	121.7	140.2	136.4
Sows and boars	C3IB	83.1	99.1	100.0	101.5	80.9	126.4	151.7	132.7
Sheep	JT6O	108.0	107.1	100.0	102.0	90.6	116.0	143.8	156.4
Ewes and rams	C3ID	127.1	125.1	100.0	106.6	104.2	120.5	183.7	221.6
All poultry	C3IE	98.4	100.7	100.0	98.6	107.1	134.6	138.7	142.1
Chickens	C3IF	98.2	101.3	100.0	98.1	106.0	130.8	135.8	140.3
Turkeys	C3IG	103.7	101.0	100.0	99.4	114.6	157.6	157.7	155.3
Cows' milk	C3IH	97.6	100.0	100.0	97.2	112.3	140.4	128.4	133.5
Eggs	C3II	104.7	109.9	100.0	104.0	118.3	140.4	144.7	137.8
Wool (clip)	C3IK	117.5	116.3	100.0	36.4	77.7	78.9	71.4	107.5
Total of all products	JT6P	100.3	103.6	100.0	104.5	118.8	143.3	136.0	144.4

1 See chapter text.

2 The sum of the percentages of all the categories does not add up to 100% due to the exclusion of some minor categories.

Source: Department for Environment, Food and Rural Affairs: 01904 455249

17.9 Harmonised Indices of Consumer Prices (HICPs)

International comparisons: EU countries
percentage change over 12 months

Percent

		2008	2009	2010	2010 Jul	2010 Aug	2010 Sep	2010 Oct	2010 Nov	2010 Dec	2011 Jan	2011 Feb	2011 Mar	2011 Apr	2011 May	2011 Jun	2011 Jul
European Union countries																	
United Kingdom[1]	D7G7	3.6	2.2	3.3	3.1	3.1	3.1	3.2	3.3	3.7	4.0	4.4	4.0	4.5	4.5	4.2	4.4
Austria	D7SK	3.2	0.4p	1.7	1.7	1.6	1.7	2.0	1.8	2.2	2.5	3.1	3.3	3.7	3.7	3.7	3.8
Belgium	D7SL	4.5	–	2.3	2.4	2.4	2.9	3.1	3.0	3.4	3.7	3.5	3.5	3.3	3.1	3.4	4.0
Bulgaria	GHY8	12.0	2.5	3.0	3.2	3.2	3.6	3.6	4.0	4.4	4.3	4.6	4.6	3.3	3.4	3.5	3.4
Cyprus	D7RO	4.4	0.2	2.6	2.7	3.4	3.6	3.2	1.7	1.9	3.0	3.1	3.2	3.5	4.1	4.5	3.5
Czech Republic	D7RP	6.3	0.6	1.2	1.6	1.5	1.8	1.8	1.9	2.3	1.9	1.9	1.9	1.6	2.0	1.9	1.9
Denmark	D7SM	3.6	1.1	2.2	2.1	2.3	2.5	2.4	2.5	2.8	2.6	2.6	2.5	2.8	3.1	2.9	3.0
Estonia	D7RQ	10.6	0.2	2.7	2.8	2.8	3.8	4.5	5.0	5.4	5.1	5.5	5.1	5.4	5.5	4.9	5.3
Finland	D7SN	3.9	1.6	1.7	1.3	1.3	1.4	2.3	2.4	2.8	3.1	3.5	3.5	3.4	3.4	3.4	3.7
France	D7SO	3.2	0.1	1.7	1.9	1.6	1.8	1.8	1.8	2.0	2.0	1.8	2.2	2.2	2.2	2.3	2.1
Germany	D7SP	2.8	0.2	1.2	1.2	1.0	1.3	1.3	1.6	1.9	2.0	2.2	2.3	2.7	2.4	2.4	2.6
Greece	D7SQ	4.2	1.3	4.7	5.5	5.6	5.7	5.2	4.8	5.2	4.9	4.2	4.3	3.7	3.1	3.1	2.1
Hungary	D7RR	6.0	4.0	4.7	3.6	3.6	3.7	4.3	4.0	4.6	4.0	4.2	4.6	4.4	3.9	3.5	3.1
Ireland	D7SS	3.1	−1.7	−1.6	−1.2	−1.2	−1.0	−0.8	−0.8	−0.2	0.2	0.9	1.2	1.5	1.2	1.1	1.0
Italy	D7ST	3.5	0.8	1.6	1.8	1.8	1.6	2.0	1.9	2.1	1.9	2.1	2.8	2.9	3.0	3.0	2.1
Latvia	D7RS	15.3	3.3	−1.2	−0.7	−0.4	0.3	0.9	1.7	2.4	3.5	3.8	4.1	4.3	4.8	4.7	4.2
Lithuania	D7RT	11.1	4.2	1.2	1.7	1.8	1.8	2.6	2.5	3.6	2.8	3.0	3.7	4.4	5.0	4.8	4.6
Luxembourg	D7SU	4.1	–	2.8	2.9	2.5	2.6	2.9	2.5	3.1	3.4	3.9	4.0	4.0	3.8	3.8	3.2
Malta	D7RU	4.7	1.8	2.0	2.5	3.0	2.4	2.2	3.4	4.0	3.3	2.7	2.8	2.4	2.5	3.1	2.2
Netherlands	D7SV	2.2	1.0p	0.9	1.3	1.2	1.4	1.4	1.4	1.8	2.0	2.0	2.0	2.2	2.4	2.5	2.9
Poland	D7RV	4.2	4.0	2.7	1.9	1.9	2.5	2.6	2.6	2.9	3.5	3.3	4.0	4.1	4.3	3.7	3.6
Portugal	D7SX	2.7	−0.9	1.4	1.9	2.0	2.0	2.3	2.2	2.4	3.6	3.5	3.9	4.0	3.7	3.3	3.0
Romania	GHY7	7.9	5.6	6.1	7.1	7.6	7.7	7.9	7.7	7.9	7.0	7.6	8.0	8.4	8.5	8.0	4.9
Slovakia	D7RW	3.9	0.9	0.7	1.0	1.1	1.1	1.0	1.0	1.3	3.2	3.5	3.8	3.9	4.2	4.1	3.8
Slovenia	D7RX	5.5	0.9	2.1	2.3	2.4	2.1	2.1	1.6	2.2	2.3	2.0	2.4	2.0	2.4	1.6	1.1
Spain	D7SY	4.1	−0.3	2.0	1.8	1.6	2.8	2.5	2.3	2.9	3.0	3.4	3.3	3.5	3.4	3.0	3.0
Sweden	D7SZ	3.3	1.9	1.9	1.4	1.1	1.5	1.6	1.7	2.1	1.4	1.2	1.4	1.8	1.7	1.5	1.6
EICP2 EU 27 average[3]	GJ2E	3.7	1.0	2.1	2.1	2.0	2.2	2.3	2.3	2.7	2.8	2.9	3.1	3.3	3.2	3.1	2.9

Note: Further information on HICP is available from the National Statistics
Website: www.statistics.gov.uk/hicp.

1 Published as the Consumer Prices Index (CPI) in the UK. (UK 2005=100, others 1996=100)
2 The EICP (European Index of Consumer Prices)is the official EU aggregate. It covers 15 member states until April 2004, 25 member states from May 2004, and 27 members from Jan 2007, the new member states being Integrated using a chain index formula. The EU 25 annual average for 2004 is calculated from the EU 15 average from January to April and the EU 25 averages from May to December.
3. The coverage of the European Union was extended to include Cyprus, Czech Republic, Estonia, Hungary, Latvia, Lithuania, Malta, Poland, Slovakia and Slovenia from 1 May 2004 and Bulgaria and Romania from 1 Jan 2007.

Production

Chapter 18

Production

Annual Business Survey
(Table 18.1)

The Annual Business Survey (ABS) estimates cover all UK businesses registered for Value Added Tax (VAT) and/or Pay As You Earn (PAYE) classified to the 2007 Standard Industrial Classification (SIC (2007)) headings listed in the tables. The ABS obtains details on these businesses from the Office for National Statistics (ONS) Inter-Departmental Business Register (IDBR).

As with all its statistical inquiries, ONS is concerned to minimise the form-filling burden of individual contributors and as such the ABS is a sample inquiry. The sample was designed as a stratified random sample of about 66,300 businesses; the inquiry population is stratified by SIC (2007) and employment using the information from the register.

The inquiry results are grossed up to the total population so that they relate to all active UK businesses on the IDBR for the sectors covered.

The results meet a wide range of needs for government, economic analysts and the business community at large. In official statistics the inquiry is an important source for the national accounts and input-output tables, and also provides weights for the indices of production and producer prices. Inquiry results also enable the UK to meet statistical requirements of the European Union.

Revised ABS results down to SIC (2007) 4 digit class level for 2008-2009, giving both analysis and tabular detail, are available from the ONS website at: www.ons.gov.uk with further extracts and bespoke analyses available on request.

Import penetration and export sales ratios
(Table 18.2)

The ratios were first introduced in the August 1977 edition of Economic Trends in an article entitled 'The Home and Export Performance of United Kingdom Industries'. The article described the conceptual and methodological problems involved in measuring such variables as import penetration.

The industries are now grouped according to the 2007 Standard Industrial Classification at 2-digit level.

Table 18.2a lists total UK manufacturers' sales, and tables 18.2b to 18.2e list the four different sets of ratios defined as follows:

Ratio 1: percentage ratio of imports to home demand

Ratio 2: percentage ratio of imports to home demand plus exports

Ratio 3: percentage ratio of exports to total manufacturers' sales

Ratio 4: percentage ratio of exports to total manufacturers' sales plus imports

Home demand is defined as total manufacturers' sales plus imports minus exports. This is only an approximate estimate as different sources are used for the total manufacturers' sales and the import and export data. Total manufacturers' sales are determined by the Products of the European Community Inquiry and import and export data are provided by HM Revenue & Customs (HMRC).

Ratio 1 is commonly used to describe the import penetration of the home market. Allowance is made for the extent of a domestic industry's involvement in export markets by using Ratio 2; this reduces as exports increase.

Similarly, Ratio 3 is the measure normally used to relate exports to total sales by UK producers and Ratio 4 makes an allowance for the extent to which imports of the same product are coming into the UK.

PRODCOM 2008 estimates are now aligned with the NACE Rev 2 (2007). As many of the product descriptions for 2007 have been merged or split leading to the new PRODCOM List for 2008, PRODCOM 2008 estimates cannot be comprehensively compared with those of 2007 and previous years.

The PRODCOM 2007 estimates in table 22.2 of the Annual Abstract of Statistics will not be updated. However, PRODCOM 2008 and 2009 five-digit SIC2007 estimates, in the revised structure, are currently available in Microsoft Excel format on the ONS website at:
http://www.ons.gov.ukstatbase/Product.asp?vlnk=15281

PRODCOM 2008 and 2009 estimates at two-digit level, aligned with the NACE Rev 2, are published in Table 18.2 of Chapter 18.

Number of local units in manufacturing industries
(Table 18.3)

The table shows the number of local units (sites) in manufacturing by employment size band. The classification breakdown is at division level (two digit) as classified to SIC(2003) held on the Inter-Departmental Business Register (IDBR). This register became fully operational in 1995 and combines information on VAT traders and PAYE employers in a statistical register comprising 2.1 million enterprises (businesses) representing nearly 99 per cent of economic activity.
UK Business: Activity, Size and Location 2007 provides further details and contains detailed information regarding enterprises in the UK including size, classification, and local units in the UK including size, classification and location.

For further information on the IDBR see the ONS website at: www.ons.gov.uk/idbr

Production of primary fuels
(Table 18.4)

This table shows indigenous production of primary fuels. It includes the extraction or capture of primary commodities and the generation or manufacture of secondary commodities. Production is always gross; that is, it includes the quantities used during the extraction or manufacturing process. Primary fuels are coal, natural gas (including colliery methane), oil, primary electricity (that is, electricity generated by hydro, nuclear wind and tide stations and also electricity imported from France through the interconnector) and renewables (includes solid renewables such as wood, straw and waste and gaseous renewables such as landfill gas and sewage gas). The figures are presented on a common basis expressed in million tonnes of oil equivalent. Estimates of the gross calorific values used for converting the statistics for the various fuels to these are given in the Digest of UK Energy Statistics available at:
www.decc.gov.uk/en/content/cms/statistics/publications/dukes/dukes.aspx

Total inland energy consumption
(Table 18.5)

This table shows energy consumption by fuel and final energy consumption by fuel and class of consumer. Primary energy consumption covers consumption of all primary fuels (defined above) for energy purposes. This measure of energy consumption includes energy that is lost by converting primary fuels into secondary fuels (the energy lost burning coal to generate electricity or the energy used by refineries to separate crude oil into fractions) in addition to losses in distribution. The other common way of measuring energy consumption is to measure the energy content of the fuels supplied to consumers. This is called final energyconsumption. It is net of fuel used by the energy industries, conversion, transmission and distribution losses. The figures are presented on a common basis, measured as energy supplied and expressed in million tonnes of oil equivalent. Estimates of the gross calorific values used for converting the statistics for the various fuels to these are given in the Digest of UK Energy Statistics available at:
www.decc.gov.uk/ en/content/cms/statistics/publications/dukes/dukes.aspx

So far as practicable the user categories have been grouped on the basis of the SIC(2003) although the methods used by each of the supply industries to identify end users are slightly different. Chapter 1 of the Digest of UK Energy Statistics gives more information on these figures.

Coal
(Table 18.6)

Since 1995, aggregate data on coal production have been obtained from the Coal Authority. In addition, main coal producers provide data in response to an annual Department of Energy and Climate Change (DECC) inquiry which covers production (deepmined and opencast), trade, stocks and disposals. HM Revenue & Customs (HMRC) also provides trade data for solid fuels. DECC collects information on the use of coal from the UK Iron and Steel Statistics Bureau and consumption of coal for electricity generation is covered by data provided by the electricity generators.

Gas
(Table 18.7)

Production figures, covering the production of gas from the UK Continental Shelf offshore and onshore gas fields and gas obtained during the production of oil, are obtained from returns made under the DECC's Petroleum Production Reporting System. Additional information is used on imports and exports of gas and details from the operators of gas terminals in the UK to complete the picture.

It is no longer possible to present information on fuels input into the gas industry and gas output and sales in the same format as in previous editions of this table. As such, users are directed to Chapter 4 of the 2002 edition of the Digest of UK Energy Statistics, where more detailed information on gas production and consumption in the UK is available.

DECC carry out an annual survey of gas suppliers to obtain details of gas sales to the various categories of consumer. Estimates are included for the suppliers with the smallest market share, since the DECC inquiry covers only the largest suppliers (that is, those known to supply more than 1,750 GWh per year).

Electricity
(Tables 18.8–18.10)

Tables 18.8 to 18.10 cover all generators and suppliers of electricity in the UK. The relationship between generation, supply, availability and consumption is as follows:

Electricity generated

less electricity used on works

equals electricity supplied (gross)

less electricity used in pumping at pumped storage stations.

equals electricity supplied (net)

plus imports (net of exports) of electricity

equals electricity available

less losses and statistical differences

equals electricity consumed

In Table 18.8 'major power producers' are those generating companies corresponding to the old public sector supply system:
• AES Electric Ltd.
• Baglan Generation Ltd.
• Barking Power Ltd.
• British Energy plc
• Centrica Energy
• Coolkeeragh ESB Ltd.
• Corby Power Ltd.
• Coryton Energy Company Ltd.
• Derwent Cogeneration Ltd.
• Drax Power Ltd.
• EDF Energy plc
• E.ON UK plc
• Energy Power Resources Ltd.
• Gaz De France
• GDF Suez Teesside Power Ltd
• Immingham CHP
• International Power plc
• Magnox Electric Ltd.
• Premier Power Ltd.
• RGS Energy Ltd.
• Rocksavage Power Company Ltd.
• RWE Npower plc
• Scottish Power plc
• Scottish and Southern Energy plc
• Seabank Power Ltd.
• SELCHP Ltd.
• Spalding Energy Company Ltd.
• Uskmouth Power Company Ltd.
• Western Power Generation Ltd.

Additionally, from 2007, the following major wind farm companies are included as 'major power producers':

• Airtricity
• Cumbria Wind Farms
• Fred Olsen
• H G Capital
• Renewable Energy Systems
• Vattenfall Wind

In Table 18.10 all fuels are converted to the common unit of million tonnes of oil equivalent, that is, the amounts of oil which would be needed to produce the output of electricity generated from those fuels.

More detailed statistics on energy are given in the Digest of United Kingdom Energy Statistics 2009. Readers may wish to note that the production and consumption of fuels are presented using commodity balances. A commodity balance shows the flows of an individual fuel through from production to final consumption, showing its use in transformation and energy industry own use.

Oil and oil products
(Tables 18.11–18.13)

Data on the production of crude oil, condensates and natural gases given in Table 19.11 are collected by DECC direct from the operators of production facilities and terminals situated on UK territory, either onshore or offshore, that is, on the UK Continental Shelf. Data are also collected from the companies on their trade in oil and oil products. These data are used in preference to the foreign trade as recorded by HMRC in Overseas Trade Statistics.

Data on the internal UK oil industry (that is, on the supply, refining and distribution of oil and oil products in the UK) are collected by the UK Petroleum Industry Association. These data, reported by individual refining companies and wholesalers and supplemented where necessary by data from other sources, provide the contents of Tables 19.12 and 19.13. The data are presented in terms of deliveries to the inland UK market. This is regarded as an acceptable proxy for actual consumption of products. The main shortcoming is that, while changes in stocks held by companies in central storage areas are taken into account, changes in the levels of stocks further down the retail ladder (such as stocks held on petrol station forecourts) are not. This is not thought to result in a significant degree of difference in the data.

Iron and steel
(Tables 18.14–18.16)
Iron and steel industry
The general definition of the UK iron and steel industry is based on groups 271 'ECSC iron and steel', 272 'Tubes', and 273 'Primary Transformation' of the UK SIC(92), except those parts of groups 272 and 273 which cover cast iron pipes, drawn wire, cold formed sections and Ferro alloys.

The definition excludes certain products which may be made by works within the industry, such as refined iron, finished steel castings, steel tyres, wheels, axles and rolled rings, open and closed die forgings, colliery arches and springs. Iron foundries and steel stockholders are also considered to be outside of the industry.

Statistics

The statistics for the UK iron and steel industry are compiled by the Iron and Steel Statistics Bureau (ISSB) Ltd from data collected from UK steel producing companies, with the exception of trade data which is based on HMRC data.

'Crude steel' is the total of usable ingots, usable continuously cast semi-finished products and liquid steel for castings.

'Production of finished products' is the total production at the mill of that product after deduction of any material which is immediately scrapped

'Deliveries' are based on invoiced tonnages and will include deliveries made to steel stockholders and service centres by the UK steel industry.

For more detailed information on definitions etc please contact ISSB Ltd. on 020 7343 3900.

Fertilisers
(Table 18.17)

Table 18.17 gives the quantity of the fertiliser nutrients nitrogen (N), phosphate (P2O5) and potash (K2O) used by UK farmers during the growing season, or fertiliser year, which is taken as the year ending in June. The nitrogen usage is shown divided between the quantity used as a single-nutrient fertiliser and that used in compound fertilisers. The total quantity of compound fertiliser product is also given.

Minerals
(Table 18.18)

Table 18.18 gives, separately for Great Britain and Northern Ireland, the production of minerals extracted from the ground. The figures for chemicals and metals are estimated from the quality of the ore which is extracted. The data come from an annual census of the quarrying industry, which, for Great Britain, is conducted by ONS for Communities and Local Government and Business, Innovation and Skills (BIS) –formally known as Business, Enterprise and Regulatory Reform (BERR)

Building materials
(Table 18.19)

Table 18.19 gives the production and deliveries of a number of building materials, including bricks, concrete blocks, sand and gravel, slate, cement, concrete roofing tiles and ready mixed cement. The data come from surveys conducted by the ONS and Trade Associations on behalf of BIS.

Construction
(Tables 18.20–18.21)

Figures for the construction industry are based on SIC(2003).

The value of output represents the value of construction work done during the quarter in Great Britain and is derived from returns made by private contractors and public authorities with their own direct labour forces. The series (and the accompanying index of the volume of output) include estimates of the output of small firms and self-employed workers not recorded in the regular quarterly output inquiry.

The new orders statistics are collected from private contractors and analysed by the principal types of construction work involved. The series includes speculative work for eventual sale or lease undertaken on the initiative of the respondent where no formal contract or order is involved.

Engineering turnover and orders
(Tables 18.22–18.23)

The figures represent the output of UK-based manufacturers classified to Subsections DK and DL of the SIC(2003). They are derived from the monthly production inquiry (MPI) and include estimates for non-responders and for establishments which are not sampled.

**Drink and tobacco
(Tables 18.24–18.25)**

Data for these tables are derived by HMRC from the systems for collecting excise duties.
Alcoholic drinks and tobacco products become liable for duty when released for consumption in the
UK. Figures for releases include both home-produced products and commercial imports. Production
figures are also available for potable spirits distilled and beer brewed in the UK.

**Alcoholic drink
(Table 18.24)**

The figures for imported ad other spirits released for home consumption include gin and other
UK produced spirits for which a breakdown is not available.

Since June 1993 beer duty has been charged when the beer leaves the brewery or other registered
premises. Previously duty was chargeable at an earlier stage (the worts stage) in the brewing process
and an allowance was made for wastage. Figures for years prior to 1994 include adjustments to bring
them into line with current data. The change in June 1993 also led to the availability of data on the
strength; a series in hectolitres of pure alcohol is shown from 1994.

Made wine with alcoholic strength from 1.2 per cent to 5.5 per cent is termed 'coolers'. Included in
'coolers' are alcoholic lemonade and similar products of appropriate strength. From 28 April 2002
duty on spirit-based 'coolers' (ready to drink products) is charged at the same rate as spirits per litre
of alcohol. Made wine coolers include only wine based 'coolers' from this period.

**Tobacco products
(Table 18.25)**

Releases of cigarettes and other tobacco products tend to be higher in the period before a Budget.
Products may then be stocked, duty paid, before being sold.

18.1 Production and construction[1]: summary table

United Kingdom

Standard Industrial Classfication 2007: Estimates for all firms

Standard Industrial Classification (Revised 2007) Section Division	Description	Year	Total turnover £ million	Approximate gross value added at basic prices £ million	Total purchases of goods, materials and services £ million	Total employment costs £ million	Total net capital expenditure £ million
B-F	Production and Construction	2008	900,629	307,352	575,445	133,821	38,900
		2009	805,887	268,208	511,256	125,417	34,118
B-E	Production industries	2008	677,230	222,540	437,677	93,852	31,168
		2009	616,350	197,609	396,188	89,082	29,068
B	Mining and quarrying	2008	61,172	34,159	27,122	3,757	5,662
		2009	47,959	23,023	25,038	3,652	5,582
05	Mining of coal and lignite	2008	816	384	458	282	123
		2009	864	345	537	313	116
06	Extraction of crude petroleum and natural gas	2008	49,255	28,830	20,562	1,475	5,047
		2009	37,366	18,980	18,661	1,699	5,012
07	Mining of metal ores	2008	-	-	-	-	-
		2009	-	-	-	-	-
08	Other mining and quarrying	2008	4,864	1,762	3,016	742	302
		2009	3,372	1,059	2,152	577	116
09	Mining support service activities	2008	6,238	3,183	3,086	1,258	191
		2009	6,358	2,639	3,689	1,063	338
C	Manufacturing	2008	500,246	149,441	332,630	81,226	11,625
		2009	448,517	130,227	293,911	76,285	9,484
10	Manufacture of food products	2008	66,052	18,309	48,111	9,489	1,497
		2009	67,789	18,498	49,135	9,507	1,369
11	Manufacture of beverages	2008	*	*	9,543	2,032	917
		2009	19,004	5,382	9,901	2,114	642
12	Manufacture of tobacco products	2008	*	*	901	224	41
		2009	10,132	1,677	1,022	203	62
13	Manufacture of textiles	2008	5,628	2,096	3,583	1,281	97
		2009	5,020	1,860	3,100	1,153	78
14	Manufacture of wearing apparel	2008	2,925	930	2,001	515	14
		2009	2,700	681	1,966	443	12
15	Manufacture of leather and related products	2008	745	279	473	163	9
		2009	761	244	503	157	13
16	Manufacture of wood and of products of wood and cork, except furniture; manufacture of articles of straw and plaiting materials	2008	7,817	2,811	5,021	1,626	133
		2009	6,938	2,059	4,796	1,352	186
17	Manufacture of paper and paper products	2008	10,794	2,760	8,058	1,810	221
		2009	10,475	2,688	7,767	1,829	134
18	Printing and reproduction of recorded media	2008	13,465	6,477	6,992	3,589	537
		2009	11,402	5,084	6,279	3,425	434
19	Manufacture of coke and refined petroleum products	2008	39,320	1,420	27,002	596	359
		2009	31,192	1,294	20,419	702	374
20	Manufacture of chemicals and chemical products	2008	41,858	10,243	31,907	4,552	1,121
		2009	33,796	9,491	23,731	4,429	644
21	Manufacture of basic pharmaceutical products and pharmaceutical preparations	2008	15,402	7,566	7,834	2,839	609
		2009	16,261	7,828	8,566	2,724	523
22	Manufacture of rubber and plastic products	2008	21,872	8,126	14,421	4,719	638
		2009	20,161	6,813	13,220	4,302	423

18.1 Production and construction[1]: summary table

United Kingdom

Standard Industrial Classfication 2007: Estimates for all firms

Standard Industrial Classification (Revised 2007) Section Division	Description	Year	Total turnover	Approximate gross value added at basic prices	Total purchases of goods, materials and services	Total employment costs	Total net capital expenditure
			£ million	£ million	£ million	£ million	£ million
23	Manufacture of other non-metallic mineral products	2008	14,333	4,547	9,690	3,189	725
		2009	13,206	3,673	9,179	2,864	323
24	Manufacture basic metals	2008	21,337	5,639	15,780	2,962	416
		2009	15,706	3,225	12,053	2,694	232
25	Manufacture of fabricated metal products, except machinery and equipment	2008	34,266	14,221	20,125	8,556	652
		2009	29,015	12,062	16,615	7,647	545
26	Manufacture of computer, electronic and optical products	2008	21,343	8,620	13,077	4,570	376
		2009	19,128	7,210	11,807	4,100	308
27	Manufacture of electrical equipment	2008	13,467	4,351	9,167	2,755	224
		2009	12,917	4,104	8,615	2,739	139
28	Manufacture of machinery and equipment n.e.c	2008	36,932	13,120	24,043	7,215	495
		2009	31,343	10,730	19,875	6,796	535
29	Manufacture of motor vehicles, trailers and semi-trailers	2008	50,553	9,999	40,646	5,780	1,252
		2009	38,564	5,991	32,067	4,968	1,161
30	Manufacture of other transport equipment	2008	23,275	9,198	14,877	5,307	567
		2009	25,540	8,043	17,725	5,331	604
31	Manufacture of furniture	2008	8,266	3,091	5,186	1,890	108
		2009	6,824	2,528	4,299	1,609	168
32	Other manufacturing	2008	8,963	3,465	5,601	2,052	160
		2009	8,487	3,803	4,551	1,997	242
33	Repair and installation of machinery and equipment	2008	14,110	5,602	8,589	3,515	457
		2009	12,156	5,260	6,719	3,200	333
D	Electricity, gas, steam and air conditioning supply	2008	86,790	23,627	63,763	4,521	6,919
		2009	91,425	29,191	63,819	4,937	8,179
E	Water supply, sewerage, waste management, and remediation activities	2008	29,022	15,314	14,163	4,349	6,963
		2009	28,448	15,168	13,419	4,208	5,823
36	Water collection, treatment and supply	2008	11,162	8,233	3,413	1,578	4,874
		2009	11,745	8,670	3,248	1,588	4,029
37	Sewerage	2008	2,473	1,931	684	388	*
		2009	2,449	1,936	686	376	*
38	Waste collection, treatment and disposal activities; materials recovery	2008	15,279	5,094	10,013	2,353	*
		2009	14,159	4,511	9,434	2,204	*
39	Remediation activities and other waste management services	2008	108	56	52	30	7
		2009	96	51	50	39	10
F	Construction	2008	223,399	84,812	137,768	39,969	7,731
		2009	189,537	70,599	115,068	36,335	5,050
41	Construction of buildings	2008	91,608	30,994	59,926	11,856	5,838
		2009	78,884	27,479	48,247	10,243	3,299
42	Civil engineering	2008	47,644	14,701	32,974	9,119	763
		2009	41,826	12,044	29,646	8,139	1,145
43	Specialised construction activities	2008	84,147	39,117	44,867	18,995	1,130
		2009	68,827	31,076	37,176	17,953	606

1 See chapter text.

Source: Office for National Statistics: 01633 456592

18.1 Production and construction[1]: summary table

United Kingdom

Standard Industrial Classfication 2007: Estimates for all firms

Standard Industrial Classification (Revised 2007) Section Division	Description	Total net capital expenditure- acquisitions	Total net capital expenditure - disposals	Total stocks and work in progress - value at end of year	Total stocks and work in progress - value at beginning of year	Total stocks and work in progress - increase during year
		£ million	£ million	£ million	£ million	£ million
B-F	Production and Construction	46,735	7,835	99,523	95,954	3,569
		40,547	6,429	105,152	109,988	-4,836
B-E	Production industries	34,756	3,587	55,181	51,224	3,958
		32,265	3,197	53,343	54,536	-1,194
B	Mining and quarrying	5,849	186	1,434	1,152	282
		5,810	228	1,420	1,401	19
05	Mining of coal and lignite	132	10	94	68	26
		*	*	112	93	19
06	Extraction of crude petroleum and natural gas	5,131	84	737	578	159
		*	*	832	774	58
07	Mining of metal ores	-	-	-	-	-
		-	-	-	-	-
08	Other mining and quarrying	366	65	380	316	65
		152	36	269	303	-33
09	Mining support service activities	219	28	223	191	32
		405	67	207	231	-24
C	Manufacturing	14,566	2,941	50,972	48,050	2,921
		11,835	2,351	47,515	50,091	-2,576
10	Manufacture of food products	1,832	335	4,408	3,923	485
		1,705	336	4,478	4,469	9
11	Manufacture of beverages	*	*	4,750	4,246	504
		*	*	5,079	4,734	346
12	Manufacture of tobacco products	*	*	206	159	47
		*	*	285	206	79
13	Manufacture of textiles	139	42	813	780	34
		107	29	598	650	-53
14	Manufacture of wearing apparel	26	12	522	518	4
		21	9	397	444	-46
15	Manufacture of leather and related products	10	1	121	113	9
		14	1	141	152	-11
16	Manufacture of wood and of products of wood and cork, except furniture; manufacture of articles of straw and plaiting materials	200	67	779	797	-18
		210	24	516	597	-81
17	Manufacture of paper and paper products	281	60	873	841	32
		232	98	768	793	-25
18	Printing and reproduction of recorded media	715	178	692	691	1
		569	136	450	490	-41
19	Manufacture of coke and refined petroleum products	384	26	1,359	1,785	-427
		390	16	1,806	1,353	453
20	Manufacture of chemicals and chemical products	1,448	327	4,122	3,829	293
		878	234	3,522	4,064	-543
21	Manufacture of basic pharmaceutical products and pharmaceutical preparations	665	56	2,019	2,011	8
		594	70	1,984	1,853	131
22	Manufacture of rubber and plastic products	811	174	2,021	1,831	190
		536	113	1,781	1,912	-131

18.1 Production and construction[1]: summary table

United Kingdom

Standard Industrial Classfication 2007: Estimates for all firms

Standard Industrial Classification (Revised 2007) Section Division	Description	Total net capital expenditure- acquisitions	Total net capital expenditure - disposals	Total stocks and work in progress - value at end of year	Total stocks and work in progress - value at beginning of year	Total stocks and work in progress - increase during year
		£ million	£ million	£ million	£ million	£ million
23	Manufacture of other non-metallic mineral products	888 / 458	162 / 135	1,572 / 1,456	1,606 / 1,716	-34 / -260
24	Manufacture basic metals	455 / 280	39 / 49	2,585 / 2,097	2,529 / 2,522	56 / -424
25	Manufacture of fabricated metal products, except machinery and equipment	960 / 674	308 / 129	3,223 / 2,810	3,154 / 3,174	69 / -364
26	Manufacture of computer, electronic and optical products	507 / 397	131 / 89	2,719 / 2,724	2,348 / 2,822	370 / -98
27	Manufacture of electrical equipment	296 / 217	72 / 78	1,353 / 1,408	1,292 / 1,589	61 / -181
28	Manufacture of machinery and equipment n.e.c	861 / 721	367 / 186	4,270 / 3,793	4,031 / 4,556	239 / -763
29	Manufacture of motor vehicles, trailers and semi-trailers	1,434 / 1,329	182 / 168	3,509 / 2,764	3,365 / 3,212	145 / -448
30	Manufacture of other transport equipment	641 / 686	74 / 82	5,176 / 5,441	4,524 / 5,230	652 / 211
31	Manufacture of furniture	131 / 195	23 / 26	714 / 644	709 / 669	5 / -25
32	Other manufacturing	233 / 317	73 / 75	1,293 / 1,147	1,185 / 1,277	107 / -130
33	Repair and installation of machinery and equipment	527 / 417	69 / 84	1,872 / 1,426	1,784 / 1,607	88 / -181
D	Electricity, gas, steam and air conditioning supply	7,109 / 8,639	190 / 460	2,100 / 3,615	1,546 / 2,274	554 / 1,341
E	Water supply, sewerage, waste management, and remediation activities	7,233 / 5,982	270 / 158	676 / 792	476 / 770	200 / 22
36	Water collection, treatment and supply	4,922 / 4,057	48 / 28	169 / 136	101 / 169	68 / -33
37	Sewerage	* / *	33 / *	32 / 13	22 / 13	10 / 1
38	Waste collection, treatment and disposal activities; materials recovery	* / *	186 / *	472 / 636	348 / 585	123 / 51
39	Remediation activities and other waste management services	9 / 12	2 / 2	3 / 7	4 / 4	-1 / 3
F	Construction	11,979 / 8,282	4,247 / 3,232	44,341 / 51,809	44,730 / 55,451	-389 / -3,642
41	Construction of buildings	9,049 / 5,733	3,212 / 2,434	37,779 / 45,462	38,228 / 48,524	-449 / -3,062
42	Civil engineering	1,086 / 1,409	323 / 265	3,247 / 3,269	3,211 / 3,394	36 / -125
43	Specialised construction activities	1,844 / 1,139	713 / 533	3,315 / 3,078	3,291 / 3,534	25 / -456

1 See chapter text.

Source: Office for National Statistics: 01633 456592

18.2 Manufacturers' sales: by industry[1]

United Kingdom
Standard Industrial Classification 2003

£ million

Industry	SIC (03)		2004	2005	2006	2007
Other mining and quarrying						
Quarrying of stone for construction	KSPF	14,110	..	..	..	..
Quarrying of limestone, gypsum and chalk	KSPG	14,120	..	..	..	..
Quarrying of slate	KSPH	14,130	..	..	..	..
Operation of gravel and sand pits	KSPJ	14,210	..	..	..	..
Mining of clays and kaolin	KSPK	14,220	..	..	..	..
Mining of chemical and fertilizer minerals	KSPL	14,300	..	..	..	..
Production of salt	KSPM	14,400	..	..	..	..
Other mining and quarrying not elsewhere classified	KSPN	14,500	46	52	42	37
Manufacture of food products and beverages						
Production and preserving of meat	KSPO	15,110	3,927	4,166	4,319	4,320
Production and preserving of poultry meat	KSPP	15,120	..	2,064	2,197	2,432
Bacon and ham production	KSPQ	15,131	1,364	1,465	1,543	1,466
Other meat and poultry meat processing	KSPR	15,139	3,993	4,174	3,976	4,189
Processing and preserving of fish and fish products	KSPS	15,200	1,741	1,802	1,873	1,805
Processing and preserving of potatoes	KSPT	15,310	1,233	..	1,286	1,336
Fruit and vegetable juice	KSPU	15,320	567	586	712	775
Processing and preserving of fruit and vegetables not elsewhere classified	KSPV	15,330	2,474	2,544	2,582	2,637
Crude oils and fats	KSPW	15,410	399	446	372	397
Refined oils and fats	KSPX	15,420	914	889	831	820
Margarine and similar edible fats	KSPY	15,430	..	..	417	..
Operation of dairies	KTEH	15,510	5,460	5,640	5,882	6,110
Ice cream	KSPZ	15,520	..	467	432	438
Grain mill products	KSQA	15,610	2,786	2,595	2,732	2,911
Starches and starch products	KSQB	15,620	380	429	352	400
Prepared feeds for farm animals	KSPI	15,710	2,419	2,151	2,365	2,685
Prepared pet foods	KSQC	15,720	1,214	..	1,251	1,339
Bread; fresh pastry goods and cakes	KSQD	15,810	4,407	4,186	4,367	4,596
Rusks and biscuits; preserved pastry goods and cakes	KSQE	15,820	..	3,211	3,089	..
Sugar	KSQF	15,830	1,133	1,077	1,056	1,045
Cocoa; chocolate and sugar confectionery	KSQG	15,840	3,384	3,175	3,623	3,609
Macaroni, noodles, couscous and similar farinaceous products	KSQH	15,850	..	..	468	..
Processing of tea and coffee	KSQI	15,860	1,420	1,502	1,636	..
Condiments and seasonings	KSQJ	15,870	1,129	1,129	1,235	1,217
Homogenised food preparations and dietetic foods	KSQK	15,880	..	42	47	35
Manufacture of other food products not elsewhere classified	KSQL	15,890	2,200	2,300	2,401	2,519
Distilled potable alcoholic beverages	KSQM	15,910	2,216	..	..	..
Production of ethyl alcohol from fermented materials	KSQN	15,920	..	..	..	..
Wines	KSQO	15,930	52	..	..	..
Cider and other fruit wines	KSQP	15,940	..	458	453	..
Other non-distilled fermented beverages	KSQQ	15,950	-	-	-	..
Beer	KSQR	15,960	4,072	3,805	3,896	3,578
Malt	KSQS	15,970	255	239	242	..
Mineral waters and soft drinks	KSQT	15,980	..	3,021	3,241	3,273
Manufacture of tobacco products						
Tobacco products	KSQU	16,000	1,838	1,718	1,875	1,626
Manufacture of textiles						
Preparation and spinning of textile fibres	KSQV	17,100	486	433	398	386
Textile weaving	KSQW	17,200	690	626	593	578
Finishing of textiles	KSQX	17,300	472	490	476	468
Soft furnishings	KSQY	17,401	576	564	635	646
Canvas goods, sacks etc	KSQZ	17,402	101	80	100	..
Household textiles	KSRA	17,403	654	643	645	686
Carpets and rugs	KSRB	17,510	690	711	770	773
Cordage, rope, twine and netting	KSRC	17,520	76	84	76	85

18.2 Manufacturers' sales: by industry[1]

United Kingdom
Standard Industrial Classification 2003
continued

£ million

Industry		SIC (03)	2004	2005	2006	2007
Manufacture of textiles continued						
Nonwovens and articles made from nonwovens, except apparel	KSRD	17,530	149	150	160	169
Lace	KSRE	17,541	16	19	15	..
Narrow fabrics	KSRF	17,542	145	133	124	110
Other textiles not elsewhere classified	KSRG	17,549	435	468	453	382
Knitted and crocheted fabrics	KSRH	17,600	197	..	..	..
Knitted and crocheted hosiery	KSRI	17,710	230	..	..	..
Knitted and crocheted pullovers, cardigans and similar	KSRJ	17,720	219	193	176	155
Manufacture of wearing apparel; dressing and dyeing of fur						
Leather clothes	KSRK	18,100	7	5	2	4
Workwear	KSRL	18,210	263	225	220	198
Men's outerwear	KSRM	18,221	249	182	158	167
Other women's outerwear	KSRN	18,222	792	632	622	541
Men's underwear	KSRO	18,231	171	..	102	63
Women's underwear	KSRP	18,232	392	350	368	..
Hats	KSRQ	18,241	35	..	31	28
Other wearing apparel and accessories	KSRR	18,249	315	280	276	265
Dressing/dyeing of fur; articles of fur	KSRS	18,300	4	4	3	3
Tanning and dressing of leather; manufacture of luggage, handbags, saddlery, harness and footwear						
Tanning and dressing of leather	KSRT	19,100	..	..	..	200
Luggage, handbags and the like, saddlery and harness	KSRU	19,200	140	128	127	132
Footwear	KSRV	19,300	250	227	212	217
Manufacture of wood and of products of wood and cork, except furniture; manufacture of articles of straw and plaiting materials						
Sawmilling and planing of wood, impregnation of wood	KSRW	20,100	752	786	834	994
Veneer sheets	KSRX	20,200	801	790	838	874
Builders' carpentry and joinery	KSRY	20,300	3,209	3,500	3,683	3,950
Wooden containers	KSRZ	20,400	413	438	453	513
Other products of wood	KSSA	20,510	380	408	373	437
Articles of cork, straw and plaiting materials	KSSB	20,520	6	5	5	6
Manufacture of pulp, paper and paper products						
Paper and paperboard	KSSC	21,120	2,775	2,787	2,798	2,759
Corrugated paper and paperboard, sacks and bags	KSSD	21,211	551	513	543	603
Cartons, boxes, cases and other containers	KSSE	21,219	3,100	2,899	2,881	3,050
Household and sanitary goods and toilet requisites	KSSF	21,220	2,071	..	1,628	1,661
Paper stationery	KSSG	21,230	580	581	555	..
Wallpaper	KSSH	21,240	184	..	102	..
Manufacture of printed labels	EQ2T	21,251	481	461	463	492
Manufacture of unprinted labels	EQ2U	21,252	49	..	..	..
Manufacture of other articles of paper and paperboard not elsewhere classified	EQ2V	21,259	292	228	203	380
Publishing, printing and reproduction of recorded media						
Publishing of books	KSSJ	22,110	3,247	3,118	3,201	3,458
Publishing of newspapers	KSSK	22,120	4,320	4,135	4,241	4,120
Publishing of journals and periodicals	KSSL	22,130	7,303	7,632	7,544	7,304
Publishing of sound recordings	KSSM	22,140	..	296	266	296
Other publishing	KSSN	22,150	549	576	588	598
Printing of newspapers	KSSO	22,210	235	..	..	193
Printing not elsewhere classified	KSSP	22,220	9,148	8,859	8,576	8,993
Bookbinding and finishing	KSSQ	22,230	414	422	365	353
Composition and plate-making	KSSR	22,240	346	..	344	350
Other activities related to printing	KSSS	22,250	819	712	652	687
Reproduction of sound recording	KSST	22,310	209	242	128	65
Reproduction of video recording	KSSU	22,320	272	197	123	..
Reproduction of computer media	KSSV	22,330	..	26	..	6
Manufacture of chemicals and chemical products						
Industrial gases	KSSW	24,110	528	525	565	599
Dyes and pigments	KSSX	24,120	936	1,019	1,044	1,047
Other inorganic basic chemicals	KSSY	24,130	1,090	1,165	1,169	1,211
Other organic basic chemicals	KSSZ	24,140	5,825	5,740	7,169	7,101
Fertilizers and nitrogen compounds	KSTA	24,150	786	863	846	945

18.2 Manufacturers' sales: by industry[1]

United Kingdom
Standard Industrial Classification 2003
continued

£ million

Industry	SIC (03)	2004	2005	2006	2007
Manufacture of chemicals and chemical products continued					
Plastics in primary forms **KSTB**	24,160	3,740	3,783	3,577	3,549
Synthetic rubber in primary forms **KSTC**	24,170	..	..	..	464
Pesticides and other agro-chemical products **KSTD**	24,200	470	433	424	393
Paints, varnishes and similar coatings, printing ink and mastic **KSTE**	24,300	2,776	2,673	2,706	2,822
Basic pharmaceutical products **KSTF**	24,410	734	895	1,057	797
Pharmaceutical preparations **KSTG**	24,420	8,761	9,568	9,731	10,960
Soap and detergents, cleaning and polishing preparations **KSTH**	24,510	1,805	1,661	1,646	1,753
Perfumes and toilet preparations **KSTI**	24,520	2,171	1,769	1,848	1,888
Explosives **KSTJ**	24,610	110	120	..	..
Glues and gelatines **KSTK**	24,620	400	438	460	382
Essential oils **KSTL**	24,630	..	504	564	..
Photographic chemical material **KSTM**	24,640	250	260	247	218
Prepared unrecorded media **KSTN**	24,650	..	..	31	27
Other chemical products not elsewhere classified **KSTO**	24,660	1,992	1,969	2,079	2,085
Man-made fibres **KSTP**	24,700	587	482	616	577
Manufacture of rubber and plastic products					
Rubber tyres and tubes **KSTQ**	25,110	569	..	551	..
Retreading and rebuilding of rubber tyres **KSTR**	25,120	99	..	..	..
Other rubber products **KSTS**	25,130	1,549	1,529	1,554	1,624
Plastic plates, sheets, tubes and profiles **KSTT**	25,210	3,755	4,202	4,348	4,389
Plastic packing goods **KSTU**	25,220	..	..	..	..
Builders' ware of plastic **KSTV**	25,230	4,478	4,393	4,344	4,230
Other plastic products **KSTW**	25,240	3,414	3,259	3,386	3,647
Manufacture of other non-metallic mineral products					
Flat glass **KSTX**	26,110	..	..	..	..
Shaping and processing of flat glass **KSTY**	26,120	1,026	1,044	1,050	1,084
Hollow glass **KSTZ**	26,130	638	632	560	525
Glass fibres **KSUA**	26,140	322	357	358	381
Manufacturing and processing of other glass including technical glassware **KSUB**	26,150	253	177	131	117
Ceramic household and ornamental articles **KSUC**	26,210	..	..	..	268
Ceramic sanitary fixtures **KSUD**	26,220	..	180	179	..
Ceramic insulators and insulating fittings **KSUE**	26,230	..	22	25	31
Other technical ceramic products **KSUF**	26,240	21	20	21	22
Other ceramic products **KSUG**	26,250	..	..	..	..
Refractory ceramic products **KSUH**	26,260	335	331	334	332
Ceramic tiles and flags **KSUI**	26,300	97	98	91	92
Bricks, tiles and construction products in baked clay **KSUJ**	26,400	656	650	652	614
Cement **KSUK**	26,510	763	..	860	963
Lime **KSUL**	26,520	..	78	..	..
Plaster **KSUM**	26,530	125	131	158	152
Concrete products for construction purposes **KSUN**	26,610	2,278	2,209	2,183	2,234
Plaster products for construction purposes **KSUO**	26,620	392	427	..	..
Ready mixed concrete **KSUP**	26,630	1,017	898	1,257	1,502
Mortars **KSUQ**	26,640	143	147	..	..
Fibre cement **KSUR**	26,650	85	96	..	101
Other articles of concrete, plaster and cement **KSUS**	26,660	116	100	87	81
Cutting, shaping and finishing of stone **KSUT**	26,700	386	..	435	453
Abrasive products **KSUU**	26,810	167	180	171	143
Other non-metallic mineral products not elsewhere classified **KSUV**	26,820	718	759	793	..
Manufacture of basic metals					
Cast iron tubes **KSUW**	27,210	164	178	211	199
Steel tubes **KSUX**	27,220	1,053	1,254	1,498	1,690
Cold drawing **KSUY**	27,310	141	146	133	142

18.2 Manufacturers' sales: by industry[1]

United Kingdom
Standard Industrial Classification 2003
continued

£ million

Industry	SIC (03)	2004	2005	2006	2007
Manufacture of basic metals continued					
Cold rolling of narrow strip	KSUZ	27,320	124	116	120	140
Cold for ming or folding	KSVA	27,330	..	..	..	..
Wire drawing	KSVB	27,340	..	235	..	259
Precious metals production	KSVD	27,410	247	280	302	322
Aluminium production	KSVE	27,420	1,781	1,781	2,343	2,339
Lead, zinc and tin production	KSVF	27,430	..	305	454	522
Copper production	KSVG	27,440	786	685	..	652
Other non-ferrous metal production	KSVH	27,450	638	755	981	1,306
Casting of iron	KSVI	27,510	433	438	396	371
Casting of steel	KSVJ	27,520	109	135	139	149
Casting of light metals	KSVK	27,530	323	303	337	396
Casting of other non-ferrous metals	KSVL	27,540	262	226	215	205
Manufacture of fabricated metal products, except machinery and equipment					
Metal structures and parts of structures	KSVM	28,110	5,386	5,917	6,189	7,328
Builders' carpentry and joinery of metal	KSVN	28,120	1,009	1,202	1,163	1,259
Tanks, reservoirs and containers of metal	KSVO	28,210	294	313	373	421
Central heating radiators and boilers	KSVP	28,220	652	805	..	..
Steam generators, except central heating hot water boilers	KSVQ	28,300	..	..	..	..
Forging, pressing, stamping and roll for ming of metal	KSVR	28,400	1,965	2,056	2,057	2,135
Treatment and coating of metals	KSVS	28,510	1,163	1,274	1,345	1,335
General mechanical engineering	KSVT	28,520	2,798	2,933	3,429	3,732
Cutlery	KSVU	28,610	25	21	24	23
Tools	KSVV	28,620	805	755	735	757
Locks and hinges	KSVW	28,630	597	566	547	567
Steel drums and similar containers	KSVX	28,710	122	138	127	118
Light metal packaging	KSVY	28,720	1,079	1,093	1,176	1,194
Wire products	KSVZ	28,730	500	534	630	665
Fasteners, screw machine products, chain and spring	KSWA	28,740	623	618	581	606
Other fabricated metal products not elsewhere classified	KSWB	28,750	1,662	1,618	1,689	1,714
Manufacture of machinery and equipment not elsewhere classified					
Engines and turbines, except aircraft, vehicles and cycle engines	KSWC	29,110	2,307	2,446	2,614	2,773
Pumps	KSWD	29,121	1,157	1,220	1,233	1,412
Compressors	KSWE	29,122	1,177	1,086	1,240	1,333
Taps and valves	KSWF	29,130	1,164	1,237	1,269	1,423
Bearings, gears, gearing and driving elements	KSWG	29,140	863	936	976	1,021
Furnaces and furnace bur ners	KSWH	29,210	269	258	253	277
Lifting and handling equipment	KSWI	29,220	2,948	3,101	3,165	3,261
Non-domestic cooling and ventilation equipment	KSWJ	29,230	2,827	2,794	2,943	3,275
Other general purpose machinery not elsewhere classified	KSWK	29,240	2,003	2,192	2,347	2,474
Agricultural tractors	KSWL	29,310	739	658	698	748
Other agricultural and forestry machinery	KSWM	29,320	510	497	547	565
Manufacture of portable hand held power tools	EQ2W	29,410	146	148	..	..
Manufacture of other metal working machine tools	EQ2X	29,420	529	544	553	622
Manufacture of other machine tools n.e.c.	EQ2Y	29,430	271	252	300	296
Machinery for metallurgy	KSWO	29,510	71	81	77	87
Machinery for mining	KSWP	29,521	540	824	..	818
Earth-moving equipment	KSWQ	29,522	..	1,287	1,429	1,854
Equipment for concrete crushing and screening and roadworks	KSWR	29,523	..	..	..	940
Machinery for food, beverage and tobacco processing	KSWS	29,530	683	644	647	774
Machinery for textile, apparel and leather production	KSWT	29,540	106	94	93	91
Machinery for paper and paperboard production	KSWU	29,550	200	160	..	135
Other special purpose machinery not elsewhere classified	KSWV	29,560	1,721	1,614	1,584	1,707
Weapons and ammunition	KSWW	29,600	2,094	107	94	73

18.2 Manufacturers' sales: by industry[1]

United Kingdom
Standard Industrial Classification 2003

£ million

Industry	SIC (03)	2004	2005	2006	2007
Manufacture of machinery and equipment not elsewhere classified continued					
Electric domestic appliances	KSYR	29,710	2,047	1,706	1,724	1,741
Non-electric domestic appliances	KSWX	29,720	487	445	468	478
Manufacture of office machinery and computers					
Office machinery	KSWY	30,010	367	446	412	313
Computers and other information processing equipment	KSWZ	30,020	4,042	3,635	2,224	1,546
Manufacture of electrical machinery and apparatus not elsewhere classified					
Electric motors, generators and transformers	KSXA	31,100	2,142	2,318	2,642	2,756
Electricity, distribution and control apparatus	KSXB	31,200	2,410	2,398	2,426	2,682
Insulated wire and cable	KSXC	31,300	989	928	1,103	1,093
Accumulators, primary cells and batteries	KSXD	31,400	318	267	207	260
Lighting equipment and electric lamps	KSXE	31,500	1,090	1,104	1,049	1,100
Electrical equipment for engines and vehicles not elsewhere classified	KSXF	31,610	924	871	799	850
Other electrical equipment not elsewhere classified	KSXG	31,620	1,670	1,773	1,887	1,865
Manufacture of radio, television and communication equipment and apparatus					
Electronic valves and tubes and other electronic components	KSXH	32,100	2,995	2,710	2,450	2,304
Telegraph and telephone apparatus and equipment	KSXI	32,201	941	883	1,005	828
Radio and electronic capital goods	KSXJ	32,202	1,707	1,755	..	1,730
Television and radio receivers, sound or video recording etc	KSXK	32,300	2,502	2,017	2,143	2,092
Manufacture of medical, precision and optical instruments, watches and clocks					
Medical and surgical equipment and orthopaedic appliances	KSXL	33,100	2,262	2,510	2,599	2,771
Instruments and appliances for measuring, checking, testing etc	KSXM	33,200	4,841	4,956	5,131	5,731
Industrial process control equipment	KSXN	33,300	709	820	835	1,028
Optical instruments and photographic equipment	KSXO	33,400	958	949	952	1,005
Watches and clocks	KSXP	33,500	52	53	42	39
Manufacture of motor vehicles, trailers and semi-trailers					
Motor vehicles	KSXQ	34,100	22,485	23,914	22,645	25,543
Bodies (coachwork) for motor vehicles (excluding caravans)	KSXR	34,201	..	702	722	714
Trailers and semi-trailers	KSXS	34,202	1,118	1,186	1,039	1,131
Caravans	KSXT	34,203	593	..	..	..
Parts and accessories for motor vehicles and their engines	KSXU	34,300	9,678	9,531	9,324	9,428
Manufacture of other transport equipment					
Building and repairing of ships	KSXV	35,110	1,552	465	492	480
Building and repairing of pleasure and sporting boats	KSXW	35,120	640	768	813	873
Railway and tramway locomotives and rolling stock	KSXX	35,200	2,103	..	1,317	..
Aircraft and spacecraft	KSXY	35,300	11,904	9,552	9,709	10,667
Motorcycles	KSXZ	35,410	..	..	..	..
Bicycles	KSYA	35,420	54	49	45	25
Invalid carriages	KSYB	35,430	..	..	106	109
Other transport equipment not elsewhere classified.	KSYC	35,500	83	..	..	..
Manufacture of furniture; manufacturing not elsewhere classified					
Chairs and seats	KSYD	36,110	2,871	2,885	2,801	2,849
Other office and shop furniture	KSYE	36,120	1,046	1,099	1,108	1,220
Other kitchen furniture	KSYF	36,130	970	940	1,047	1,158
Other furniture	KSYG	36,140	1,884	1,775	1,875	2,091
Mattresses	KSYH	36,150	591	542	546	523
Striking of coins and medals	KSYI	36,210	..	..	..	..
Jewellery and related articles not elsewhere classified	KSYJ	36,220	385	338	444	434
Musical instruments	KSYK	36,300	43	42	31	32
Sports goods	KSYL	36,400	336	326	293	311
Games and toys	KSYM	36,500	354	354	322	352
Imitation jewellery	KSYN	36,610	25	31	35	37
Brooms and brushes	KSYO	36,620	130	..	110	127
Miscellaneous stationers' goods	KSYP	36,631	..	174	177	159
Other manufacturing not elsewhere classified	KSYQ	36,639	390	423	419	447

1 See chapter text. PRODCOM data is published on the ONS website in the PRA and PRQ series of reports.

Source: Office for National Statistics: 01633 456746

18.3 Number of local units in manufacturing industries

United Kingdom

Standard Industrial Classification 2003 Division by Employment Sizeband

Numbers

Division	0 -4	5 - 9	10-19	20 -49	50 -99	100 -249	250 -499	500+	Total
15/16 Food products; beverages and tobacco	3,895	2,070	1,360	1,090	550	500	240	175	9,880
17 Textiles and textile products	2,860	830	545	420	195	105	20	5	4,980
18 Wearing apparel; dressing and dyeing of fur	2,455	690	380	235	80	25	5	0	3,870
19 Leather and leather products	430	140	80	65	25	15	0	0	755
20 Wood and wood products	5,485	1,480	965	545	160	70	15	0	8,720
21 Pulp, paper and paper products	940	275	255	320	165	160	35	5	2,155
22 Publishing, printing and reproduction of recorded media	20,065	3,895	2,330	1,490	550	325	95	50	28,800
23 Coke, refined petroleum products and nuclear fuel	160	50	25	20	20	15	15	10	315
24 Chemicals, chemical products and man-made fibres	1,885	580	495	530	335	245	110	55	4,235
25 Rubber and plastic products	3,015	1,330	1,180	1,020	500	330	70	15	7,460
26 Other non-metallic mineral products	3,515	1,020	670	565	265	180	40	10	6,265
27 Basic metals	800	270	230	250	145	100	30	15	1,840
28 Fabricated metal products, except machinery and equipment	17,420	4,940	3,480	2,475	850	335	60	15	29,575
29 Machinery and equipment not elsewhere classified	7,085	2,205	1,755	1,420	535	365	105	55	13,525
30 Office machinery and computers	775	140	75	75	30	25	10	10	1,140
31 Electrical machinery and apparatus not elsewhere classified	2,880	735	640	595	245	180	50	20	5,345
32 Radio, television and communication equipment and apparatus	1,695	365	250	270	105	90	35	15	2,825
33 Medical, precision and optical instruments, watches and clocks	2,935	880	710	580	255	140	55	15	5,570
34 Motor vehicles, trailers and semi-trailers	1,775	505	360	350	190	160	75	60	3,475
35 Other transport equipment	1,750	390	285	195	120	110	50	55	2,955
36/37 Manufacturing not elsewhere classified	12,750	3,170	1,640	985	315	180	45	15	19,100
Total manufacturing (15/37)	94,570	25,960	17,710	13,495	5,635	3,655	1,160	600	162,785

1 The data in this table is taken from the NS publication, UK Business: Activity, Size and Location 2008.
The count of units refers to local units, i.e. individual sites, rather than whole businesses. All counts have been rounded to avoid disclosure.

Source: Office for National Statistics: 01633 812293

18.4 Production of primary fuels[1]

United Kingdom

Million tonnes of oil equivalent

		1998	1999	2000	2001	2002	2003	2004	2005	2006	2007	2008	2009	2010
Coal	**HFZQ**	25.8	23.2	19.6	20.0	18.8	17.6	15.6	12.7	11.4	10.7	11.3	11.0	11.5
Petroleum[2]	**HGCY**	145.3	150.2	138.3	127.8	127.0	116.2	104.5	92.9	84.0	83.9	78.6	74.7	69.0
Natural Gas[3]	**HGDB**	90.2	99.1	108.4	105.9	103.6	103.0	96.4	88.2	80.0	72.1	69.7	59.7	57.2
Primary electricity[4]	**HGDN**	24.0	22.9	20.2	21.2	20.6	20.4	18.7	19.0	17.9	14.9	13.0	16.5	15.1
Renewable energy[5]	**HGDO**	2.1	2.2	2.3	2.5	2.8	3.0	3.1	3.7	4.0	4.4	4.5	5.0	5.3
Total Production	**HGDP**	287.2	297.7	288.7	277.4	272.9	260.3	238.4	216.5	197.2	186.0	177.0	167.0	158.1

1 See chapter text.
2 Includes crude oil, natural gas liquids and feedstocks.
3 Includes colliery methane.
4 Nuclear, natural flow hydro-electricity and generation at wind stations.
5 Includes solar and geothermal heat, solid renewable sources (wood, waste, etc), and gaseous renewable sources (landfill gas, sewage gas).

Source: Department of Energy and Climate Change: 0300 068 5060

18.5 Total inland energy consumption

United Kingdom
Heat supplied basis

Million tonnes of oil equivalent

		1998	1999	2000	2001	2002	2003	2004	2005	2006	2007	2008	2009	2010
Inland energy consumption of primary fuels and equivalents[1]	**KLWA**	230.8	230.6	233.9	236.3	229.7	232.2	233.6	235.9	233.3	227.7	225.6	211.5	218.5
Coal[2]	**KLWB**	40.9	36.7	38.8	41.0	37.5	40.6	39.1	39.8	43.5	41.0	38.0	31.5	32.2
Petroleum[3]	**KLWC**	76.0	75.2	75.9	75.4	74.0	73.5	75.3	77.9	77.4	76.4	75.1	71.1	70.7
Primary electricity	**KLWD**	25.0	24.2	21.4	22.1	21.3	20.6	19.4	19.8	18.5	15.4	13.9	16.7	15.4
Natural gas	**KLWE**	86.9	92.5	95.6	95.4	94.2	94.5	96.6	94.3	89.4	90.2	93.0	86.0	93.2
Renewables and waste	**GYUY**	2.1	2.2	2.3	2.5	2.8	3.1	3.5	4.2	4.4	4.7	5.5	6.2	7.0
less Energy used by fuel producers and losses in conversion and distribution	**KLWF**	74.7	74.1	74.5	75.4	73.1	73.8	73.6	76.2	76.2	73.2	71.4	68.0	68.3
Total consumption by final users[1]	**KLWG**	155.9	156.5	159.4	160.9	156.5	158.1	159.9	159.6	157.0	154.3	154.0	143.4	150.1
Final energy consumption by type of fuel														
Coal (direct use)	**KLWH**	3.7	3.5	2.7	2.7	2.2	2.1	2.0	1.7	1.6	1.8	1.8	1.7	1.7
Coke and breeze	**KLWI**	0.9	0.9	0.8	0.8	0.7	0.7	0.6	0.6	0.5	0.5	0.5	0.3	0.3
Other solid fuel[4]	**KLWJ**	0.7	0.6	0.6	0.5	0.5	0.4	0.4	0.4	0.4	0.4	0.4	0.4	0.4
Coke oven gas	**KLWK**	0.4	0.2	0.2	0.2	0.1	0.1	0.1	0.1	0.1	0.1	0.1	0.0	0.1
Natural gas (direct use)	**KLWL**	55.9	55.1	57.1	57.8	55.2	56.7	57.1	55.4	52.6	50.0	51.1	45.8	51.6
Electricity	**KLWM**	27.1	27.8	28.3	28.6	28.7	28.9	29.1	30.0	29.7	29.5	29.4	27.7	28.2
Petroleum (direct use)[5]	**KLWN**	66.1	65.1	66.3	67.1	66.1	66.8	68.6	69.4	69.8	69.5	67.3	64.0	63.8
Renewables[6]	**GYVA**	0.9	0.7	0.7	0.7	0.7	0.7	0.7	0.8	1.0	1.2	2.0	2.2	2.6
Heat	**JT3J**	..	2.5	2.5	2.3	2.1	1.8	1.3	1.3	1.2	1.3	1.5	1.2	1.3
Final energy consumption by class of consumer														
Agriculture	**KLWP**	1.4	1.3	1.2	1.3	1.2	0.9	0.9	1.0	0.9	0.9	1.0	0.9	1.0
Iron and steel industry	**KLWQ**	4.0	3.8	2.2	2.3	2.0	1.9	1.9	1.8	1.9	1.8	1.6	1.2	1.3
Other industries	**KLWR**	30.5	30.5	33.3	33.2	31.8	32.1	31.0	30.5	29.6	28.8	29.2	25.4	26.2
Railways[7]	**KLWS**	1.3	1.4	1.4	1.4	1.4	1.4	1.0	1.0	1.0	1.0	1.0	1.0	1.0
Road transport	**KLWT**	41.0	41.4	41.1	41.1	41.9	41.8	42.2	42.5	42.7	43.3	42.2	40.8	41.0
Water transport	**KLWU**	1.2	1.1	1.0	0.8	0.7	1.2	1.2	1.4	1.8	1.6	1.8	1.6	1.5
Air transport	**KLWV**	10.2	11.0	12.0	11.8	11.7	11.9	12.9	13.9	14.0	13.9	13.5	12.8	12.3
Domestic	**KLWW**	46.1	46.1	46.9	48.2	47.5	48.3	49.3	47.8	46.6	44.9	45.5	43.0	48.5
Public administration	**KLWX**	8.1	8.2	8.1	8.0	7.0	6.7	7.2	7.1	6.6	6.3	6.4	5.7	5.8
Commercial and other services	**KLWY**	12.0	11.8	12.2	12.8	11.3	11.8	12.2	12.7	12.0	11.8	11.9	11.1	11.6

1 Includes heat sold from 1999.
2 Includes net trade and stock change in other solid fuels.
3 Refinery throughput of crude oil, plus net foreign trade and stock change in petroleum products. Petroleum products not used as fuels
 (chemical feed-stock, industrial and white spirits, lubr icants, bitumen and wax) are excluded.
4 Includes briquettes, ovoids, Phur nacite, Coalite, etc., and wood, waste etc., used for heat generation.
5 Includes manufactured liquid fuels from 1994.
6 Predominantly used for renewable heat: includes liquid biofuels from 2006, consumption of renewable electricity is included under 'Electricity'.
7 Includes fuel used at transport premises.

Source: Department of Energy and Climate Change: 0300 068 5060

18.6 Coal: supply and demand[1]

United Kingdom   Million tonnes

		1997	1998	1999	2000	2001	2002	2003	2004	2005	2006	2007	2008	2009	2010
Supply															
Production of deep-mined coal	KLXA	30.3	25.7	20.9	17.2	17.3	16.4	15.6	12.5	9.6	9.4	7.7	8.1	7.5	7.4
Production of opencast coal	KLXB	16.7	14.3	15.3	13.4	14.2	13.1	12.1	12.0	10.4	8.6	8.9	9.5	9.9	10.4
Total	KLXC	47.0	40.0	36.2	30.6	31.5	29.5	27.7	24.5	20.0	18.0	16.6	17.6	17.4	17.8
Recovered slurry, fines, etc	KLXD	1.5	1.1	0.9	0.6	0.4	0.4	0.5	0.6	0.5	0.4	0.5	0.4	0.5	0.6
Imports	KLXE	19.8	21.2	20.3	23.4	35.5	28.7	31.9	36.2	44.0	50.5	43.4	43.9	38.2	26.5
Total	KLXF	68.3	62.3	57.4	54.6	67.4	58.6	60.1	61.3	64.5	68.9	60.5	61.9	56.1	44.9
Change in stocks at collieries and opencast sites	KSOL	0.6	-0.2	0.6	-3.6	0.0	0.9	-0.9	-0.4	-0.1	-0.3	-0.1	0.2	0.5	0.1
Total supply	KLXI	68.9	62.1	58.0	51.0	67.4	59.5	59.2	60.9	64.4	68.6	60.4	62.1	56.6	45.0
Home consumption															
Total home consumption	KLXW	63.1	63.2	55.7	59.9	63.9	58.6	63.0	60.5	61.9	67.6	63.0	58.4	48.9	51.5
Overseas shipments and bunkers	KLXX	1.1	1.0	0.8	0.7	0.5	0.5	0.5	0.6	0.5	0.4	0.5	0.6	0.6	0.7
Total consumption and shipments	KLXY	64.2	64.2	56.5	60.6	64.4	59.1	63.5	61.1	62.4	68.0	63.5	59.0	49.5	52.2
Change in distributed stocks[2]	KLXZ	4.6	-1.2	0.6	-2.4	3.5	-1.4	-2.4	0.5	1.9	1.9	-3.0	3.0	6.2	-7.2
Balance[3]	KLYA	0.1	-0.9	0.9	-7.2	-0.5	1.8	-1.9	-0.7	0.1	-1.3	-0.1	0.1	0.9	0.0
Stocks at end of year															
Distributed[2]	KLYB	15.4	14.2	14.8	12.4	15.9	14.5	12.1	12.6	14.5	16.4	13.4	16.4	22.6	15.4
At collieries and opencast sites	KSOM	4.8	4.6	5.2	1.6	1.6	2.5	1.6	1.2	1.1	0.8	0.7	0.9	1.4	1.5
Total stocks	KLYE	20.2	18.8	20.0	14.0	17.5	17.0	13.7	13.8	15.6	17.2	14.1	17.3	24.0	16.9

1 See chapter text. Figures relate to periods of 52 weeks. For 1998, figures
relate to 52 weeks estimate for period ended 26 December 1998.
2 Excludes distributed stocks held in merchant yards etc., mainly for the domestic
market, and stocks held by the industrial sector.
3 This is the balance between supply and consumption, shipments and changes
in known distributed stocks.

Source: Department of Energy and Climate Change: 0300 068 5044

18.7 Fuel input and gas output: gas consumption[1,2]

United Kingdom

Giga-watt hours

Analysis of gas consumption		2000	2001	2002	2003	2004	2005	2006	2007	2008	2009	2010
Transformation sector	I77I	349,454	336,525	351,856	344,410	362,668	354,146	333,431	379,518	402,236	382,061	395,625
Electricity generation	I77G	324,563	312,939	329,847	324,580	340,824	331,658	311,408	355,878	376,810	359,303	371,736
Heat generation[3]	I77H	24,891	23,586	22,009	19,830	21,844	22,488	22,023	23,640	25,426	22,758	23,890
Energy industry use total	I77N	77,941	91,451	91,260	88,918	88,468	87,161	81,859	76,025	72,280	69,065	69,462
Oil and gas extraction	I77J	65,555	78,457	79,364	76,848	77,753	73,372	69,252	64,230	61,292	61,110	61,124
Petroleum refineries	KIKN	3,641	4,189	3,350	2,773	3,076	5,163	5,161	5,206	4,971	3,916	4,255
Coal extraction and coke manufacture	I77K	224	211	196	187	150	114	112	91	95	89	87
Blast furnaces	I77L	712	375	222	539	728	941	611	719	718	450	641
Other	I77M	7,792	8,210	8,128	8,570	6,761	7,572	6,723	5,779	5,204	3,499	3,355
Final consumption total	I77F	678,142	683,753	653,151	669,457	673,860	652,024	620,035	591,274	603,461	540,643	608,683
Iron and steel industry	KIKR	8,953	8,502	8,791	10,327	9,715	8,453	8,391	7,323	6,920	5,037	5,826
Other industries	KIKS	174,488	171,341	156,375	155,890	144,238	142,988	136,150	126,028	131,768	111,372	116,138
Domestic	KIKT	369,909	379,426	376,372	386,486	396,411	381,879	366,928	352,868	359,554	332,499	389,595
Public administration	KIKU	44,552	46,232	42,998	44,362	51,934	50,319	45,803	42,444	42,565	37,084	38,390
Commercial	I77D	36,216	37,098	36,224	39,537	37,595	38,197	34,273	33,098	33,358	29,305	31,758
Agriculture	KIKV	1,522	2,329	2,346	2,324	2,355	2,261	2,013	1,998	2,161	1,860	1,969
Miscellaneous	KIKW	28,166	27,452	19,265	20,510	21,591	20,014	18,564	17,286	17,552	15,485	16,507
Non energy use	I77E	14,336	11,373	10,780	10,021	10,021	7,913	7,913	10,228	9,583	8,001	8,499
Total gas consumption	I77O	1,105,537	1,111,729	1,096,267	1,102,785	1,124,996	1,093,331	1,035,325	1,046,817	1,077,977	991,769	1,073,770

Source: Department of Energy and Climate Change: 0300 068 5044

1 See chapter text. The breakdown of consumption by industrial users is made according to the 2003 Standard Industrial Classification.
2 Natural gas plus colliery methane.
3 Heat generation data are not available before 1999. For earlier years gas used to generate heat for sale is allocated to final consumption by the sector producing the heat.

18.8 Electricity: generation, supply and consumption[1]

United Kingdom   Gigawatt-hours

		1998	1999	2000	2001	2002	2003	2004	2005	2006	2007	2008	2009	2010
Electricity generated														
Major power producers: total	KLUA	333,764	336,608	341,783	353,066	353,994	362,600	358,313	362,212	361,232	361,410	355,324	342,483	347,704
Conventional thermal and other[2]	AWLC	134,009	118,762	131,062	132,744	126,694	146,382	139,105	140,405	157,638	144,411	126,400	104,312	107,511
Combined cycle gas turbine stations	KJCS	93,832	114,620	117,935	123,846	132,016	121,076	131,182	130,689	117,669	140,011	160,109	151,454	160,517
Nuclear stations	KLUC	99,486	95,133	85,063	90,093	87,848	88,686	79,999	81,618	75,451	63,028	52,486	69,098	62,140
Hydro-electric stations:														
Natural flow	KLUE	4,237	4,431	4,331	3,215	3,927	2,568	3,908	3,826	3,693	4,144	4,224	4,294	2,703
Pumped storage	KLUF	1,624	2,902	2,694	2,422	2,652	2,734	2,649	2,930	3,853	3,859	4,089	3,685	3,150
Renewables other than hydro	KLUG	576	761	698	738	856	1,154	1,471	2,744	2,928	5,957	8,016	9,640	11,683
Other generators: total	KLUH	28,938	31,543	35,285	31,721	33,252	35,609	35,616	36,148	36,050	35,371	33,369	34,257	33,423
Conventional thermal and other[2]	AWLD	19,091	19,419	19,094	16,621	15,788	17,244	14,419	13,407	12,486	13,090	11,786	11,345	10,963
Combined cycle gas turbine stations	KJCT	5,428	7,141	10,859	8,979	10,577	10,879	11,852	11,792	11,430	12,073	11,522	10,790	10,190
Hydro-electric stations (natural flow)	KLUK	881	905	755	840	860	660	936	1,096	900	946	944	968	900
Renewables other than hydro	KILA	3,538	4,078	4,577	5,283	6,028	6,825	8,408	9,853	11,235	9,262	9,117	11,155	11,370
All generating companies: total	KLUL	362,702	368,151	377,068	384,787	387,246	398,209	393,929	398,360	397,282	396,781	388,693	376,740	381,128
Conventional thermal and other[2]	AWYH	153,100	138,181	150,156	149,365	142,482	163,626	153,524	153,812	170,124	157,501	138,186	115,657	118,474
Combined cycle gas turbine stations	KJCU	99,260	121,761	128,794	132,825	142,593	131,955	143,034	142,481	129,099	152,084	171,631	162,244	170,707
Nuclear stations	KLUN	99,486	95,133	85,063	90,093	87,848	88,686	79,999	81,618	75,451	63,028	52,486	69,098	62,140
Hydro-electric stations:														
Natural flow	KLUP	5,118	5,336	5,086	4,055	4,787	3,228	4,844	4,922	4,593	5,089	5,168	5,262	3,606
Pumped storage	KLUQ	1,624	2,902	2,694	2,422	2,652	2,734	2,649	2,930	3,853	3,859	4,089	3,685	3,150
Renewables other than hydro	KLUR	4,114	4,839	5,275	6,021	6,884	7,979	9,879	12,597	14,164	15,219	17,133	20,794	23,053
Electricity used on works: Total	KLUS	17,408	16,706	16,304	17,394	17,126	18,136	17,032	17,873	18,503	17,690	16,268	16,499	15,803
Major generating companies	KLUT	16,140	15,461	14,952	16,066	15,746	16,747	15,582	16,265	17,031	16,099	14,674	14,761	14,381
Other generators	KLUU	1,268	1,245	1,352	1,328	1,380	1,389	1,451	1,608	1,472	1,591	1,595	1,738	1,422
Electricity supplied (gross)														
Major power producers: total	KLUV	317,624	321,147	326,831	336,999	338,248	345,854	342,732	345,947	344,201	345,311	340,650	327,722	333,323
Conventional thermal and other[2]	AWYI	127,788	112,919	124,828	126,434	120,495	139,137	132,240	133,513	149,223	136,729	119,528	98,736	101,889
Combined cycle gas turbine stations	KJCV	93,005	112,768	116,110	121,344	129,384	118,546	128,983	128,179	115,695	137,657	157,417	148,907	157,818
Nuclear stations	KLUX	90,590	87,672	78,334	82,985	81,090	81,911	73,682	75,173	69,237	57,249	47,673	62,762	56,475
Hydro-electric stations:														
Natural flow	KLUZ	4,225	4,409	4,316	3,203	3,914	2,559	3,901	3,821	3,680	4,114	4,209	4,279	2,694
Pumped storage	KLVA	1,569	2,804	2,603	2,340	2,562	2,641	2,559	2,776	3,722	3,846	4,075	3,672	3,139
Renewables other than hydro	KLVB	447	574	640	692	802	1,059	1,367	2,486	2,643	5,717	7,749	9,365	11,308
Other generators: total	KLVC	27,670	30,298	33,933	30,393	31,873	34,220	34,165	34,539	34,578	33,779	31,774	32,519	32,002
Conventional thermal and other[2]	AWYJ	18,250	18,643	18,499	15,996	15,211	16,711	13,986	13,026	12,132	12,730	11,454	11,011	10,635
Combined cycle gas turbine stations	KJCW	5,157	6,785	10,318	8,531	10,049	10,336	11,260	11,204	10,859	11,470	10,947	10,251	9,682
Hydro-electric stations (natural flow)	KLVF	869	894	743	829	849	653	919	930	885	930	927	950	883
Renewables other than hydro	KIKZ	3,393	3,977	4,374	5,037	5,764	6,519	7,999	9,380	10,702	8,650	8,446	10,307	10,802
All generating companies: total	KLVG	345,294	351,445	360,764	367,392	370,121	380,074	376,897	380,486	378,779	379,091	372,425	360,241	365,324
Conventional thermal and other[2]	AWYK	146,038	131,562	143,327	142,430	135,706	157,136	146,226	146,539	161,355	149,459	130,982	109,747	112,524
Combined cycle gas turbine stations	KJCX	98,162	119,553	126,428	129,875	139,433	128,882	140,243	139,383	126,554	149,127	168,364	159,159	167,500
Nuclear stations	KLVI	90,590	87,672	78,334	82,985	81,090	81,911	73,682	75,173	69,237	57,249	47,673	62,762	56,475
Hydro-electric stations:														
Natural flow	KLVK	5,094	5,303	5,059	4,032	4,763	3,212	4,820	4,750	4,566	5,043	5,136	5,229	3,577
Pumped storage	KLVL	1,569	2,804	2,603	2,340	2,562	2,641	2,559	2,776	3,722	3,846	4,075	3,672	3,139
Renewables other than hydro	KLVM	3,840	4,551	5,014	5,729	6,566	7,578	9,366	11,866	13,345	14,367	16,195	19,672	22,110
Electricity used in pumping														
Major power producers	KLVN	2,594	3,774	3,499	3,210	3,463	3,546	3,497	3,707	4,918	5,071	5,371	4,843	4,212
Electricity supplied (net): Total	KLVO	342,700	347,671	357,266	364,182	366,657	376,528	373,399	376,780	373,861	374,019	367,053	355,398	361,112
Major power producers	KLVP	315,030	317,373	323,332	333,789	334,785	342,308	339,235	342,240	339,283	340,240	335,279	322,879	329,111
Other generators	KLVQ	27,670	30,298	33,933	30,393	31,873	34,220	34,165	34,539	34,578	33,779	31,774	32,519	32,002
Net imports	KGEZ	12,468	14,244	14,174	10,399	8,414	2,160	7,490	8,321	7,517	5,215	11,022	2,861	2,663
Electricity available	KGIZ	355,168	361,915	371,440	374,581	375,072	378,687	380,889	385,101	381,378	379,233	378,076	358,259	363,776
Losses in transmission etc	KGKW	29,818	29,862	31,146	32,077	30,963	32,070	33,175	27,901	27,514	26,784	27,631	27,272	26,830
Electricity consumption: Total	KGKX	325,350	332,053	340,294	342,504	344,109	346,617	347,714	357,199	353,863	352,449	350,444	330,989	336,945
Fuel industries	KGKY	8,406	8,037	9,703	8,625	10,060	9,752	8,142	7,850	7,997	9,186	7,709	7,668	8,206
Final users: total	KGKZ	316,944	324,016	330,593	333,879	334,049	336,865	339,572	349,349	345,866	343,263	342,735	323,321	328,739
Industrial sector	KGLZ	108,443	112,250	115,286	112,495	110,816	109,926	112,092	116,699	115,533	114,406	115,073	101,444	104,920
Domestic sector	KGMZ	109,410	110,308	111,842	115,337	120,014	123,001	124,200	125,711	124,704	123,076	119,800	118,541	118,681
Other sectors	KGNZ	99,091	101,457	103,465	106,047	103,219	103,938	103,280	106,939	105,629	105,781	107,862	103,336	105,138

1 See chapter text.

2 Includes electricity supplied by gas turbines and oil engines and plants producing
electricity from renewable resources other than hydro.

Source: Department of Energy and Climate Change: 0300 068 5050

18.9 Electricity: plant capacity and demand

United Kingdom
At end of December

Megawatts

		2000	2001	2002	2003	2004	2005	2006	2007	2008	2009	2010
Major power producers:[1]												
Total declared net capability	GUFY	72,193	73,382	70,369	71,471	73,293	73,941	74,996	75,979	76,782	77,675	83,197
Conventional steam stations	GUFZ	34,835	34,835	30,687	31,867	31,982	32,292	33,608	33,734	32,423	32,431	32,439
Combined cycle gas turbine stations	GUGA	19,349	20,517	21,800	22,037	23,783	24,263	24,859	24,854	26,578	27,269	32,209
Nuclear stations[2]	GUGB	12,486	12,486	12,240	11,852	11,852	11,852	10,969	10,979	10,979	10,858	10,865
Gas turbines and oil engines	GUGC	1,291	1,291	1,433	1,537	1,495	1,356	1,444	1,445	1,456	1,560	1,560
Hydro-electric stations:												
Natural flow	GUGD	1,327	1,348	1,304	1,273	1,276	1,273	1,294	1,293	1,392	1,395	1,391
Pumped storage	GUGE	2,788	2,788	2,788	2,788	2,788	2,788	2,726	2,744	2,744	2,744	2,744
Renewables other than hydro	GUGF	117	117	117	117	117	117	96	929	1,210	1,418	1,989
Other generators:												
Total capacity of own generating plant[3]	GUGG	6,258	6,296	6,336	6,793	6,829	7,422	7,407	6,763	6,664	7,091	7,011
Conventional steam stations[4]	GUGH	3,544	3,464	3,325	3,480	3,275	3,269	3,059	2,924	2,722	2,813	2,757
Combined cycle gas turbine stations	GUGI	1,709	1,777	1,854	1,927	1,968	2,182	2,106	2,076	2,015	1,945	1,890
Hydro-electric stations (natural flow)	GUGJ	158	160	162	129	132	120	123	126	127	131	133
Renewables other than hydro	GUGK	847	895	995	1,257	1,454	1,852	2,118	1,637	1,800	2,203	2,231
All generating companies: Total capacity[3]	GUGL	78,451	79,678	76,705	78,264	80,122	81,363	82,403	82,742	83,446	84,766	90,208
Conventional steam stations[4]	GUGM	38,379	38,299	34,012	35,347	35,257	35,561	36,667	36,658	35,145	35,244	35,196
Combined cycle gas turbine stations	GUGN	21,058	22,294	23,654	23,964	25,751	26,445	26,965	26,930	28,593	29,214	34,099
Nuclear stations	GUGO	12,486	12,486	12,240	11,852	11,852	11,852	10,969	10,979	10,979	10,858	10,865
Gas turbines and oil engines	GUGP	1,291	1,291	1,433	1,537	1,495	1,356	1,444	1,445	1,456	1,560	1,560
Hydro-electric stations:												
Natural flow	GUGQ	1,485	1,508	1,466	1,402	1,408	1,393	1,417	1,419	1,519	1,526	1,524
Pumped storage	GUGR	2,788	2,788	2,788	2,788	2,788	2,788	2,726	2,744	2,744	2,744	2,744
Renewables other than hydro	GUGS	964	1,012	1,112	1,374	1,571	1,969	2,214	2,567	3,010	3,620	4,220
Major power producers:[1]												
Simultaneous maximum load met[5]	GUGT	58,452	58,589	61,717	60,501	61,013	61,697	59,071	61,527	60,289	60,231	60,893
System load factor[6] **(percentages)**	GUGU	67	69	65	67	67	66	69	66	68	64	65

1 See chapter text.

2 Nuclear generators are now included under "major power producers" only.

3 Capacity figures for other generators are as at end-December of the previous year.

4 For other generators, conventional steam stations cover all types of stations not separately listed.

5 Maximum load in year to end of March.

6 The average hourly quantity of electricity available during the year ending March expressed as a percentage of the maximum demand.

Source: Department of Energy and Climate Change : 0300 068 5050

18.10 Electricity: fuel used in generation

United Kingdom
At end of December[1]

Million tonnes of oil equivalent

		1997	1998	1999	2000	2001	2002	2003	2004	2005	2006	2007	2008	2009	2010
Major power producers:[1]	**KGPS**	71.5	74.9	73.6	74.4	77.4	75.8	77.5	76.8	78.2	78.7	76.0	74.2	70.2	70.9
total all fuels															
Coal	**FTAJ**	27.7	28.7	24.5	27.8	30.6	28.6	31.6	30.4	31.7	35.0	32.0	29.0	23.8	24.8
Oil[2]	**FTAK**	1.4	0.9	0.8	0.8	0.8	0.7	0.7	0.6	0.9	1.0	0.7	1.1	1.0	0.6
Gas	**KGPT**	19.3	20.3	24.2	24.4	23.8	25.0	24.5	26.2	25.4	23.9	27.5	29.6	28.2	29.4
Nuclear[3]	**FTAL**	23.0	23.4	22.2	19.6	20.8	20.1	20.0	18.2	18.4	17.1	14.0	11.9	15.2	13.9
Hydro (natural flow)	**FTAM**	0.3	0.4	0.4	0.4	0.3	0.3	0.2	0.3	0.3	0.3	0.4	0.4	0.4	0.2
Other fuels used by UK companies	**KGPU**	0.2	0.2	0.2	0.2	0.3	0.3	0.4	0.5	0.8	0.7	0.9	1.2	1.3	1.7
Net imports	**KGPV**	1.4	1.1	1.2	1.2	0.9	0.7	0.2	0.6	0.7	0.6	0.4	0.9	0.2	0.2
Other generators:	**KGPW**	6.7	7.1	7.3	8.0	7.6	8.0	8.7	8.4	9.2	9.0	8.8	8.3	8.6	8.4
total all fuels															
Transport under takings															
Gas	**KGPX**	0.2	0.2	0.2	0.2	0.2	0.2	0.0	0.0	0.0	0.0	0.0	0.0	0.0	0.0
Under takings in industrial sector															
Coal	**KGPY**	1.2	1.2	1.0	0.9	1.0	1.0	1.0	0.9	0.9	0.9	0.9	1.0	0.9	0.8
Oil	**KGPZ**	0.8	0.7	0.7	0.8	0.6	0.6	0.5	0.5	0.4	0.5	0.5	0.5	0.5	0.5
Gas	**KGQM**	2.2	2.5	2.7	3.3	2.9	3.2	3.4	3.1	3.1	2.9	3.1	2.8	2.7	2.5
Hydro (natural flow)	**KGQO**	0.1	0.1	0.1	0.1	0.1	0.1	0.1	0.1	0.1	0.1	0.1	0.1	0.1	0.1
Other fuels	**KGQP**	2.2	2.4	2.6	2.8	2.7	3.0	3.7	3.8	4.7	4.7	4.2	4.0	4.5	4.4
All generating companies:	**KGQQ**	78.2	82.0	80.9	82.4	84.9	83.8	86.2	85.2	87.4	87.7	84.8	82.5	78.8	79.3
total fuels															
Coal	**KGQR**	28.3	29.9	25.5	28.7	31.6	29.6	32.5	31.3	32.6	35.9	32.9	30.0	24.7	25.6
Oil	**KGQS**	2.0	1.5	1.5	1.5	1.4	1.3	1.2	1.1	1.3	1.4	1.2	1.6	1.5	1.2
Gas	**KGQT**	21.7	23.0	27.1	27.9	26.9	28.4	27.9	29.3	28.5	26.8	30.6	32.4	30.9	32.0
Nuclear[3]	**KGQU**	22.0	23.4	22.2	19.6	20.8	20.1	20.0	18.2	18.4	17.1	14.0	11.9	15.2	13.9
Hydro (natural flow)	**KGQV**	0.4	0.4	0.5	0.4	0.3	0.4	0.3	0.4	0.4	0.4	0.4	0.4	0.5	0.3
Other fuels used by UK companies[4]	**KGQW**	2.4	2.6	2.9	3.0	3.0	3.2	4.0	4.3	5.5	5.4	5.2	5.3	5.8	6.1
Net imports	**KGQX**	1.4	1.1	1.2	1.2	0.9	0.7	0.2	0.6	0.7	0.6	0.4	0.9	0.2	0.2

1 See chapter text.

2 Includes oil used in gas turbine and diesel plant for lighting up coal fired boilers and Orimulsion.

3 Nuclear generators are now included under "major power producers" only.

4 Main fuels included are coke oven gas, blast furnace gas, waste products from chemical processes and sludge gas.

Source: Department of Energy and Climate Change: 0300 068 5050

18.11 Indigenous petroleum production, refinery receipts, imports and exports of oil[1]

Thousand tonnes

		1997	1998	1999	2000	2001	2002	2003	2004	2005	2006	2007	2008	2009	2010
Total indigenous petroleum production[2]	KMBA	128,234	132,633	137,099	126,245	116,678	115,944	106,073	95,374	84,721	76,578	76,575	71,665	68,199	62,962
Crude petroleum:[3]															
Refinery receipts total	KMBB	97,023	93,797	88,286	88,013	83,343	84,784	84,585	89,821	86,135	83,214	81,477	80,740	75,225	73,200
Foreign trade[4]															
Imports	KMBF	49,994	47,958	44,869	54,386	53,551	56,968	54,177	62,517	58,885	59,443	57,357	60,041	54,387	54,587
Exports	AXRB	79,400	84,610	91,797	92,917	86,930	87,144	74,898	64,504	54,099	50,195	50,999	48,401	45,202	42,196
Net imports	AXRC	−29406	−36652	−46928	−38,531	−33378	−30176	−20720	−1987	4,786	9,249	6,357	11,640	9,185	12,391
Petroleum products															
Foreign trade															
Imports[4]	BHMI	8,705	11,418	13,896	14,212	17,234	14,900	16,472	18,545	22,512	26,828	25,093	24,186	22,407	24,210
Exports[4]	AXRD	26,755	24,375	21,730	20,677	19,088	23,444	23,323	30,495	29,722	29,009	30,017	28,791	25,733	26,065
Net imports[4]	AXRE	−18049	−12957	−7834	−6465	−1854	−8544	−6851	−11950	−7210	−2181	−4924	−4604	−3326	−1,855
International marine bunkers	BHMK	2,961	3,080	2,329	2,079	2,274	1,913	1,764	2,085	2,055	2,348	2,371	2,594	2,490	2,139

1 See chapter text. The term 'indigenous' is used in this table to cover oil produced on the UK Continental Shelf. This includes small amounts produced onshore.
2 Crude oil plus condensates and petroleum gases derived at onshore treatment plants.
3 Includes process (partly refined) oils.
4 Foreign trade as recorded by the petroleum industry and may differ from figures published in Overseas Trade Statistics.

Source: Department of Energy and Climate Change : 0300 068 5038

18.12 Throughput of crude and process oils and output of refined products from refineries[1]

United Kingdom

Thousand tonnes

		1998	1999	2000	2001	2002	2003	2004	2005	2006	2007	2008	2009	2010
Throughput of crude and process oils	KMAU	93,797	88,285	88,014	83,343	84,784	84,585	89,821	86,135	83,213	81,477	80,740	75,225	73,200
less: Refinery fuel:	KMAA	6,177	5,538	5,252	5,059	5,677	5,456	5,417	5,602	4,879	4,682	4,752	4,399	4,478
Losses	KMAB	1,004	1,552	1,632	1,233	788	56	7	372	374	199	315	332	328
Total output of refined products	KMAC	86,616	81,195	81,130	77,051	78,319	79,073	84,411	80,161	77,960	76,596	75,673	70,494	68,394
Gases:														
Butane and propane	KMAE	1,962	1,976	1,919	1,764	2,139	2,281	2,152	2,184	2,104	2,259	2,248	2,113	2,247
Other petroleum	KMAF	394	361	289	272	537	715	520	427	661	517	449	445	517
Naphtha	KMAG	2,316	2,430	3,082	3,428	3,154	3,503	3,168	3,019	2,733	2,561	1,863	1,529	1,596
Aviation spirit	KMAH	–	16	30	101	28	26	31	32	25				
Motor spirit	KMAJ	27,166	25,230	23,445	21,455	22,944	22,627	24,589	22,620	21,443	21,313	20,319	20,404	19,918
Industrial and white spirit	KMAK	135	129	122	121	121	104	100	136	107	70	55	61	66
Kerosene:														
Aviation turbine fuel	KMAL	7,876	7,249	6,484	5,910	5,365	5,277	5,615	5,167	6,261	6,176	6,549	6,022	5,781
Burning oil	KMAM	3,442	3,553	3,078	3,088	3,506	3,521	3,613	3,325	3,374	2,968	3,092	2,830	2,570
Gas/diesel oil	KMAN	27,542	25,755	28,229	26,748	28,343	27,380	28,646	28,486	26,037	26,391	26,761	25,393	24,837
Fuel oil	KMAO	11,125	10,446	10,296	10,179	8,507	9,495	11,308	10,155	11,280	10,433	10,496	7,964	6,912
Lubricating oil	KMAP	1,125	907	702	656	509	576	1,136	936	617	547	514	530	412
Bitumen	KMAQ	2,172	1,644	1,438	1,707	1,918	1,925	2,196	1,912	1,749	1,628	1,485	1,338	1,276
Petroleum wax	KMAR	59	261	437	416	430	460	94	98	16	12	8	0	0
Petroleum coke	KMAS	678	648	657	513	441	612	633	660	606	676	662	660	705
Other products	KMAT	623	590	921	693	377	571	610	1,004	947	1,045	1,172	1,205	1,557

1 See chapter text. Crude and process oils comprise all feedstocks, other than distillation benzines, for treatment at refinery plants. Refinery production does not cover further treatment of finished products for special grades such as in distillation plant for the preparation of industrial spirits.

Source: Department of Energy and Climate Change: 0300 068 5038

18.13 Deliveries of petroleum products for inland consumption

United Kingdom   Thousand tonnes

		1998	1999	2000	2001	2002	2003	2004	2005	2006	2007	2008	2009	2010
Total (including refinery fuel)	**KMCA**	78,438	77,974	77,196	76,413	76,233	77,154	79,066	80,946	79,812	77,428	76,119	71,962	71,691
Total (excluding refinery fuel)	**KMCB**	72,261	72,436	71,944	71,354	70,557	71,697	73,649	75,345	74,933	72,747	71,367	67,563	67,213
Butane and propane	ECAQ	2,369	2,249	2,070	2,097	2,553	3,017	3,115	3,315	3,127	2,827	3,178	3,088	2,932
Other Petroleum Gases (includes Ethane)	ECAR	1,752	2,041	1,886	2,077	2,181	2,114	1,918	2,021	1,920	1,815	1,801	1,583	1,523
Naphtha	ECAS	2,882	3,100	2,344	1,592	1,592	2,332	2,029	1,916	2,278	1,608	818	1,011	1,061
Aviation spirit	KMCI	36	45	52	59	50	46	49	52	46	33	30	22	21
Motor spirit:														
Retail deliveries:														
Leaded Premium / Lead Replacement Petrol[2]	KMCK	4,595	2,629	1,462	838	401	183	74	21	18	15	11	11	11
Super Premium Unleaded[2]	KMCL	409	474	403	420	706	861	810	772	698	796	1,028	855	650
Premium Unleaded	KMCM	16,432	18,306	19,008	19,100	19,167	18,291	17,795	17,111	16,725	15,994	15,029	14,328	13,802
Total Retail Deliveries	**ECAT**	21,436	21,409	20,873	20,358	20,274	19,335	18,679	17,904	17,442	16,806	16,068	15,194	14,463
Commercial consumers:														
Leaded Premium / Lead Replacement Petrol[2]	KMCO	91	61	44	34	19	19	14	2	2	1	1	0	0
Super Premium Unleaded[2]	KMCP	4	6	6	9	17	22	26	44	63	24	40	4	109
Premium Unleaded	KMCQ	318	311	480	538	499	542	765	782	637	764	570	564	417
Total Commercial Consumers	**ECAU**	413	378	530	581	535	583	805	828	702	789	611	568	526
Total Motor spirit	**BHOD**	21,848	21,787	21,403	20,940	20,808	19,918	19,484	18,732	18,144	17,594	16,678	15,762	14,988
Industrial and white spirits	KMCS	179	174	170	151	157	147	281	284	156	167	148	174	224
Kerosene:														
Aviation turbine fuel	BHOE	9,241	9,939	10,806	10,614	10,519	10,765	11,637	12,497	12,641	12,574	12,216	11,533	11,116
Burning oil	KMCT	3,574	3,633	3,839	4,236	3,578	3,569	3,950	3,869	4,016	3,629	3,693	3,732	4,012
Gas/diesel oil:														
Derv fuel:														
Retail Deliveries	ECAV	6,602	7,137	7,181	7,846	8,153	9,057	9,517	10,679	11,453	12,342	12,870	12,614	13,251
Commercial Consumers	ECAW	8,541	8,371	8,451	8,213	8,774	8,655	8,997	8,757	8,693	8,723	7,743	7,443	7,623
Total Derv fuel	**BHOI**	15,143	15,508	15,632	16,059	16,926	17,712	18,514	19,436	20,146	21,065	20,613	20,057	20,873
Other gas/diesel oil (includes Mdf)	ECAX	7,909	7,455	7,576	6,959	6,099	6,326	6,030	6,762	6,526	6,109	5,967	5,353	5,228
Fuel oil	BHOK	3,105	2,701	2,119	2,578	1,722	1,540	2,064	2,207	2,251	2,209	2,455	1,919	1,790
Lubricating oils	BHOL	813	790	801	846	829	868	914	750	713	672	514	510	578
Bitumen	BHOM	1,967	1,928	1,975	1,934	2,002	1,959	1,991	1,906	1,610	1,563	1,741	1,381	1,370
Petroleum wax	KMCU	18	37	32	33	51	57	50	72	48	39	46	34	37
Petroleum coke	KMCV	887	660	776	702	893	880	1,146	1,042	925	544	919	865	825
Miscellaneous products	KMCW	538	388	463	476	596	449	476	484	389	299	550	539	634

1 See chapter text.

2 With effect from 2007, deliveries of Lead Replacement Petrol are now included with Super Premium Unleaded.

Source: Department of Energy and Climate Change: 0300 068 5038

18.14 Iron and steel:[1] summary of steel supplies, deliveries and stocks

United Kingdom

Supply, disposal and consumption -(Finished product weight -Thousand tonnes)		2000	2001	2002	2003	2004	2005	2006	2007	2008	2009	2010
UK producers' home deliveries	KLTA	7,255	6,762	6,506	6,227	7,064	6,246	6,758	6,482	6,142	4,173	4,690
Imports excluding steelworks receipts	KLTB	6,387	6,978	6,793	6,893	7,272	6,298	7,385	7,847	6,915	3,763	5,201
Total deliveries to home market (a)	KLTC	13,642	13,740	13,299	13,120	14,336	12,544	14,143	14,329	13,057	7,936	9,891
Total exports (producers, consumers, merchants)	KLTD	7,446	6,512	6,320	7,008	7,466	8,414	8,201	9,134	8,657	6,092	5,828
Exports by UK producers	KLTE	7,163	6,182	5,594	6,202	6,277	6,627	6,852	7,658	7,408	5,186	4,767
Derived consumers' and merchants' exports (b)	KLTF	283	330	708	806	1,189	1,787	1,349	1,476	1,249	906	1,061
Net home disposals (a)-(b)	KLTG	13,359	13,410	12,591	12,314	13,147	10,757	12,794	12,853	11,808	7,030	8,830
Estimated home consumption	KLTI	13,359	13,410	12,591	12,114	13,147	10,757	12,794	12,853	11,808	7,030	8,830
Stocks -(Finished product weight - Thousand tonnes)												
Producers -ingots & semis	KLTJ	727	705	690	706	765	869	790	725	688	798	638
-finished steel	KLTK	1,039	981	932	917	901	947	876	862	607	552	703
Estimated home consumption -(Crude steel equivalent -Million tonnes)												
Crude steel production[2]	KLTN	15.15	13.54	11.53	13.13	13.77	13.23	13.9	14.39	13.52	10.07	9.71
Producers' stock change	KLTO	..	..	..	..	..	0.18	–	-0.08	-0.30	0.15	-0.19
Re-usable material	KLTP	..	..	..	..	..	..	–	..	..		
Total supply from home sources	KLTQ	15.48	13.68	11.61	13.13	13.77	13.2	13.9	14.47	13.82	9.92	9.9
Total imports[3]	KLTR	8.43	9.11	9.86	9.32	10.31	9.82	10.3	10.38	8.92	4.80	6.91
Total exports[3]	KLTS	8.61	7.53	7.39	8.65	9.15	8.93	10.4	10.28	9.73	6.90	6.67
Net home disposals	KLTT	15.3	15.26	14.08	14.2	14.99	13.09	14.7	14.57	13.01	7.82	10.14
Estimated home consumption	KLTV	15.3	15.26	14.08	14.2	14.99	13.09	14.7	14.57	13.01	7.82	10.14

1 See chapter text. The figures relate to periods of 52 weeks.
2 Includes liquid steel for castings only up to 2003.
3 Based on HM Customs Statistics, reflecting total trade rather than producers' trade.

Source: International and Steel Statistics Bureau: 020 7343 3900

18.15 Iron and steel:[1] iron ore, manganese ore, pig iron and iron and steel scrap

United Kingdom

Thousand tonnes

		2004	2005	2006	2007	2008	2009	2010
Iron ore[2]	KLOF	16,013	15,991	16,539	16,607	15,338	11,171	10,572
Manganese ore[2]	KLOG	6	3	6	3	4	20	0
Pig iron (and blast furnace ferro-alloys)								
Average number of furnaces in blast during period	KLOH	6	6	7	7	6	4	5
Production								
Steelmaking iron	KLOI	10,180	10,189	10,696	10,960	10,137	7,671	7,233
In blast furnaces: total	KLOL	10,180	10,189	10,696	10,960	10,137	7,671	7,233
In steel works	KLOM	10,180	10,189	10,696	10,960	10,137	7,671	7,233
Consumption of pig iron: total	KLOO	10,180	10,189	10,696	10,960	10,137	7,671	7,233
Iron and steel scrap								
Steelworks and steel foundries								
Circulating scrap	KLOQ	1,787	1,737	1,669	1,658	1,589	1,115	1,256
Purchased receipts	KLOR	3,371	2,779	3,171	3,425	3,429	2,146	2,507
Consumption	KLOS	5,123	4,531	4,811	5,144	4,888	3,459	3,713
Stocks (end of period)	KLOT	242	228	257	196	326	128	178

1 See chapter text. The figures relate to periods of 52 weeks.
2 Consumption.

Source: International and Steel Statistics Bureau: 020 7343 3900

18.16 Iron and steel:[1] furnaces and production of steel

United Kingdom				Number and thousand tonnes		
		2006	2007	2008	2009	2010
Steel furnaces (numbers[2])	KLPA	..	..	..		
Oxygen converters	KLPC	..	..	..		
Electric	KLPD	..	..	..		
Production of crude steel	KLPF	13905	14,392	13,521	10,075	9,708
by process						
Oxygen converters	KLPH	11203	11,362	10,478	7,955	7,323
Electric	KLPI	2702	3,030	3,043	2,120	2,385
by cast method						
Cast to ingot	KLPK	206	201	224	136	153
Continuously cast	KLPL	13698	14,191	13,296	9,938	9,555
Steel for castings	KLPM	..	..	..		
by quality						
Non alloy steel	KLPN	..	13,613	12,695	9,681	9,201
Stainless and other alloy steel	KLPO	760	779	826	394	507
Production of finished steel products (All quantities)[3]						
Rods and bars for reinforcement (in coil and lengths)	KLPP	902	1,113	1,109	801	792
Wire rods and other rods and bars in coil	KLPQ	962	869	803	778	874
Hot rolled bars in lengths	KLPR	1249	1,350	1,252	644	884
Bright steel bars[4]	KLPS	226	239	226	102	158
Light sections other than rails	KLPT	149	162	157	156	127
Heavy sections	KGQZ	1527	1,436	1,425	897	1,069
Hot rolled plates, sheets and strip in coil and lengths	KLPW	6010	5,639	4,969	3,924	4,733
Cold rolled plates and sheets in coil and lengths	KLPX	2726	2,520	2,315	1,922	2,200
Cold rolled strip[4]	KLPZ	98	81	73	39	45
Tinplate	KLQW	421	443	462	396	468
Other coated sheet	KLQX	1773	1,661	1,472	1,136	1,278
Tubes and pipes[4]	KLQY	993	991	842	515	638
Forged bars[4]	KLQZ	..	..	..		

1 See chapter text. The figures relate to periods of 52 weeks.
2 Includes steel furnaces at steel foundries, only up to 2003.

Source: International and Steel Statistics Bureau: 020 7343 3900

18.17 Fertilisers

Years ending 30 June											Thousand tonnes		
		1999	2000	2001	2002	2003	2004	2005	2006	2007	2008	2009	2010
Nutrient Content													
Nitrogen (N):													
Straight	KGRM	819	819	714	751	664	662	691	631	656	744	733	771
Compounds	KGRN	465	449	448	446	467	463	370	372	352	292	180	245
Phosphate (P2O5)	KGRO	347	317	279	283	282	278	259	235	224	215	129	184
Potash (K2O)	KGRP	451	409	369	391	375	375	352	325	317	325	208	251
Compounds - total product	KGRQ	3,013	2,851	2,471	2,511	2,558	2,550	2,221	2,134	2,039	1,827	1,116	1,529

Source: Agricultural Industries Confederation: 01733 385230

18.18 Minerals: production[1]

United Kingdom
Thousand tonnes

		1998	1999	2000	2001	2002	2003	2004	2005	2006	2007	2008	2009
Great Britain													
Limestone	**KLEA**	85,382	82,714	80,810	83,492	88,013	84,445	86,846	81,830	82,598	83,482	74,324	58,092
Sandstone	**KLEB**	13,545	11,870	12,056	11,897	11,788	11,665	11,929	11,609	11,827	11,978	9,558	8,542
Igneous rock	**KLEC**	39,838	45,294	44,633	45,053	44,544	45,305	46,193	45,992	47,867	50,684	47,009	38,860
Clay/shale	**KLED**	12,230	11,355	10,838	10,426	10,306	10,680	11,164	10,898	10,432	10,104	8,459	5,310
Industrial sand	**KLEE**	4,662	4,092	4,095	3,848	3,833	4,073	5,011	4,146	5,174	4,909	4,777	3,755
Chalk	**KLEF**	9,934	9,667	9,213	8,205	8,587	8,066	7,997	7,105	7,376	7,565	5,874	4,047
Fireclay	**KLEG**	577	545	595	459	491	528	402	395	228	338	180	129
Barium sulphate	**KLEH**	64	59	54	70	56	..	..	62	44	54	46	..
Calcium fluoride	**KLEI**	52	46	21	46	22	..	..	44	133	..	..	49
Lead	**KLEK**	1	1	..	1	..	..	..	1	4	..	..	..
Iron ore: crude	**KLEN**	2	1	1	1	1	–	..	–	–	..	..	..
Iron ore: iron content	**KLEO**	1	1	1	..	..	–	..	–	–	..	..	..
Calcspar	**KLEP**	15	..	..	12	..	–	..	–	..	..	..	..
China clay	**KILC**	2,866	2,841	2,779	2,804	2,467	2,378	2,148	1,908	..	1,821	1,321	988
Chert and flint	**KLER**	..	6	..	2	2	..	2	2	..	1	1	1
Fuller's earth	**KLES**	111	83	103	..	33	19	11	..	–	..	..	..
Salt[2]	**I8AV**	..	..	..	..	..	..	..	5,770	5,224	5,320	5,287	5,855
Dolomite	**KLEY**	15,632	13,698	13,069	14,314	12,946	..	..	11,514	12,100	7,622	5,510	3,164
Gypsum	**KLEZ**	..	..	..	..	..	..	1,686	..	..	..	..	..
Slate[3]	**KLFA**	425	361	479	551	742	832	901	928	865	1,428	1,058	683
Soapstone and talc	**KLFB**	5	6	5	5	6	6	4	6	4	3	2	3
Sand and gravel (land-won)	**KLFC**	73,016	74,785	74,877	74,599	69,889	68,090	73,061	69,368	66,268	66,724	59,506	55,709
Sand and gravel (marine dredged)	**KLFD**	12,952	13,424	14,356	13,611	12,832	12,131	12,996	13,024	13,974	13,777	12,621	9,592
Northern Ireland													
Sand and gravel	**KLFG**	5,300	5,517	5,073	6,194	5,512	4,894	5,084	5,803	5,150	8,086	7,134	4,855
Basalt and igneous rock (other than granite)	**KLFH**	6,107	7,861	9,480	6,448	6,681	6,051	6,844	7,112	6,087	8,225	6,481	5,757
Limestone	**KLFI**	3,892	4,219	3,538	4,746	4,514	4,887	5,634	5,588	6,385	5,904	3,739	3,972
Sandstone[4]	**KLFJ**	6,584	3,615	2,844	8,070	6,574	6,594	6,915	7,076	6,211	4,828	2,697	3,793
Others[5]	**KLFN**	473	1,579	3,098	753	242	1,055	1,266	2,090	1,698	2,468	2,931	1,998

1 See chapter text.

Source: Office for National Statistics: 01633 812082

2 Includes rock salt, salt from brine and salt in brine.

3 Roofing and vertically hanging slates, includes 'true' slate and stone slates produced from thinly bedded sandstones and limestones. Also includes 'true' and stone slates sold as sawn slabs for decorative cladding.

4 Prior to 1993 the 'Sandstone' heading was called 'Grit and conglomerate'. The new heading is all encompassing and was confirmed as correct with the Geological Survey in Norther n Ireland.

5 Rock salt, Chalk, Dolomite, Fireclay and Granite.

18.19 Building materials and components[1]

Great Britain   Monthly averages or calendar months

	Building bricks (millions)		Concrete blocks (000 sq m)		Concrete roofing tiles (000 sq m of roof covered)		Slate[2] (tonnes)		Cement[3] (000 tonnes)		RMX[4] (000 cu m)	Sand and gravel (000 tonnes)
	Production	Deliveries	Production	Deliveries	Production	Deliveries	Production	Deliveries	Production	Deliveries	Deliveries	Deliveries
	BLDA	QXIH	BLDM	QXII	BLDN	QXIJ	BLDQ	QXIK	QXIM	QXIL	BLDP	BLDS
2001	230	235	7,327	7,376	2,069	2,036	7,760	7,852	924	888	1,917	8,121
2002	229	235	7,623	7,612	2,085	2,033	7,913	7,972	924	897	1,883	7,126
2003	231	245	7,973	8,032	1,786	1,783	6,591	6,543	935	923	1,857	6,896
2004	239	236	8,021	7,905	1,728	1,617	..	..	950	923	1,905	6,779
2005	229	214	7,500	7,463	2,143	2,041	..	..	935	917	1,869	6,708
2006	209	200	7,292	7,251	1,978	2,010	..	..	956	935	1,919	6,491
2007	206	201	7,496	7,395	1,963	1,984	..	..	991	970	1,962	6,293
2008	161	150	5,645	5,595	1,674	1,660	..	..	839	828	1,671	6,221
2009	101	116	4,200	4,220	1,173	1,301	..	5,626	635	623	1,172	4,874
2010	112	124	4,469	4,313	1,485	1,429	4,843	4,854	657	647	1,170	4,544
2008 Q4	97	111	3,829	4,086	1,301	1,283	..	..	713	691	1,394	5,628
2009 Q1	96	96	4,031	3,883	1,221	1,094	..	5,242	587	594	1,194	4,877
Q2	125	128	4,488	4,397	1,018	1,312	5,418	6,011	668	657	1,212	5,120
Q3	107	128	4,257	4,641	1,193	1,482	5,271	5,655	666	666	1,209	4,959
Q4	77	110	4,022	3,958	1,260	1,316	5,540	5,597	619	574	1,074	4,538
2010 Q1	95	112	4,205	4,024	1,376	1,168	5,297	4,873	575	581	1,109	4,570
Q2	125	144	4,985	4,918	1,654	1,641	5,452	5,682	719	718	1,273	4,647
Q3	118	135	5,057	4,781	1,594	1,608	4,412	4,737	734	732	1,277	4,704
Q4	112	103	3,629	3,530	1,315	1,298	4,211	4,127	599	558	1,020	4,256
2011 Q1	119	128	4,661	4,265	1,607	1,360	4,855	4,784	660	681	1,276	4,717
2009 Apr	114	121	4,580	4,447	..	..	..	..	618	637	..	..
May	122	126	4,158	4,144	..	..	..	..	711	629	..	..
Jun	140	137	4,725	4,600	..	..	..	..	675	704	..	..
Jul	106	141	4,740	4,863	..	..	..	..	705	697	..	..
Aug	84	107	3,417	4,264	..	..	..	..	637	606	..	..
Sep	131	137	4,614	4,797	..	..	..	..	656	696	..	..
Oct	120	137	4,740	4,818	..	..	..	..	758	696	..	..
Nov	71	111	4,372	4,072	..	..	..	..	667	605	..	..
Dec	41	83	2,954	2,984	..	..	..	..	..	..	..	..
2010 Jan	62	58	3,342	3,003	..	..	..	..	400	397	..	..
Feb	96	120	4,341	4,100	..	..	..	..	601	595	..	..
Mar	126	159	4,931	4,969	..	..	..	..	725	752	..	..
Apr	126	141	4,814	4,948	..	..	..	..	675	684	..	..
May	136	152	4,790	4,765	..	..	..	..	732	703	..	..
Jun	114	140	5,353	5,040	..	..	..	..	750	767	..	..
Jul	120	144	5,266	4,970	..	..	..	..	804	766	..	..
Aug	107	129	4,711	4,614	..	..	..	..	688	688	..	..
Sep	128	133	5,195	4,759	..	..	..	..	711	741	..	..
Oct	144	143	4,295	4,372	..	..	..	..	741	702	..	..
Nov	118	117	3,999	4,092	..	..	..	..	687	662	..	..
Dec	72	48	2,593	2,126	..	..	..	..	368	310	..	..
2011 Jan	83	95	3,924	3,591	..	..	..	..	521	570	..	..
Feb	126	130	4,664	4,220	..	..	..	..	669	668	..	..
Mar	148	160	5,394	4,984	..	..	..	..	789	805	..	..
Apr	139	132	4,356	4,289	..	..	..	..	725	652	..	..

1 See chapter text.
2 Excluding slate residue used as fill.
3 United Kingdom; Great Britain from January 2002
4 United Kingdom; RMX stands for ready mixed concrete.

Sources: Department for Business,Innovation and Skills (BIS); (formerly BERR)
Email: materialstats@bis.gsi.gov.uk
Tel: 020 7215 3092

18.20 Volume of construction output by all agencies[1,2] by type of work at constant 2005 prices (seasonally adjusted)

Great Britain

£ millions

| | New Housing | | Infrastr-ucture | Other New Work | | | All New Work | Housing | | | Non Housing R&M | All Repair and Maintenance | All work |
| | Public | Private | | Excluding Infrastructure | | | | Public | Private | Total | | | |
				Public	Private Industrial	Private Commercial							
	K5FU	K5FW	K5FX	K5G3	K5G5	K5G6	K5FV	K5FY	K5FZ	K5G2	K5FD	K5G7	K5G8
2007	2,928	17,991	6,990	6,429	5,563	29,436	69,337	6,143	10,772	16,915	21,980	38,895	108,233
2008	2,709	14,562	8,071	7,461	4,505	30,013	67,321	6,312	11,143	17,455	22,257	39,712	107,034
2009	2,861	10,912	9,287	9,933	3,076	22,964	58,940	6,094	9,842	15,940	19,869	35,808	94,833
2010	4,243	12,179	11,169	13,210	3,482	22,801	67,082	6,267	10,194	16,459	17,494	33,954	101,036
2007 Q1	734	4,642	1,619	1,624	1,465	7,142	17,224	1,594	2,689	4,283	5,509	9,792	27,017
Q2	741	4,545	1,713	1,591	1,461	7,215	17,267	1,518	2,684	4,202	5,443	9,645	26,912
Q3	732	4,483	1,792	1,600	1,362	7,376	17,346	1,484	2,634	4,118	5,426	9,544	26,890
Q4	721	4,321	1,866	1,614	1,275	7,703	17,500	1,547	2,765	4,312	5,602	9,914	27,414
2008 Q1	697	4,166	2,007	1,739	1,314	8,009	17,933	1,514	2,790	4,304	5,802	10,106	28,039
Q2	681	3,761	2,064	1,843	1,142	7,458	16,949	1,638	2,797	4,435	5,797	10,232	27,181
Q3	682	3,480	2,086	1,911	1,084	7,524	16,767	1,606	2,720	4,326	5,483	9,809	26,577
Q4	649	3,155	1,914	1,968	965	7,022	15,672	1,554	2,836	4,390	5,175	9,565	25,237
2009 Q1	627	2,915	2,084	2,129	825	6,363	14,943	1,461	2,566	4,027	5,052	9,079	24,022
Q2	653	2,808	2,231	2,317	758	5,960	14,718	1,497	2,421	3,919	4,796	8,714	23,432
Q3	736	2,552	2,288	2,543	717	5,459	14,295	1,626	2,570	4,196	5,203	9,399	23,694
Q4	839	2,616	2,721	2,922	781	5,139	15,018	1,480	2,254	3,735	4,861	8,595	23,613
2010 Q1	921	2,608	2,820	2,994	796	5,329	15,467	1,608	2,280	3,888	4,302	8,190	23,657
Q2	1,044	3,124	2,903	3,310	854	5,611	16,846	1,575	2,500	4,074	4,429	8,504	25,350
Q3	1,121	3,246	2,780	3,458	972	5,996	17,573	1,562	2,725	4,286	4,455	8,741	26,314
Q4	1,157	3,201	2,666	3,448	860	5,865	17,196	1,522	2,689	4,211	4,308	8,519	25,715
2011 Q1	1,079	2,996	2,887	3,291	909	5,382	16,545	1,531	2,443	3,974	4,555	8,529	25,074

1 Classified to construction in the Standard Industrial Classification 2007.
2 Construction output underwent significant development during 2008/09 resulting in a new monthly survey from 2010.

Sources: Office for National Statistics; 01633 456344

18.21 Value of new orders obtained by contractors for new work[1] at current prices

Great Britain

£ millions

	New housing[3]			Other new work					
	Public and housing association	Private	All new housing	Infrastructure	Public[5]	Private industrial[5]	Private commercial[5]	All other work	All new work
	K5G9	K5GA	K5GB	K5GC	K5GD	K5GE	K5GF	K5GG	K5GH
2007	3,733	16,037	19,769	6,965	11,393	5,836	32,115	56,309	76,078
2008	3,081	9,200	12,283	7,897	14,672	4,346	23,353	50,267	62,550
2009	3,107	6,393	9,500	11,032	14,709	2,654	12,886	41,280	50,780
2010	3,549	10,273	13,822	9,205	13,630	2,233	14,210	39,279	53,100
2007 Q1	1,338	4,280	5,618	2,110	2,618	1,574	7,499	13,802	19,420
Q2	886	4,327	5,213	1,881	2,956	1,491	9,400	15,727	20,940
Q3	713	3,841	4,553	1,501	3,076	1,324	7,999	13,900	18,453
Q4	796	3,589	4,385	1,473	2,743	1,447	7,217	12,880	17,265
2008 Q1	992	3,217	4,210	2,220	3,588	1,267	7,066	14,141	18,351
Q2	829	2,732	3,562	2,379	3,498	942	6,268	13,087	16,648
Q3	709	1,778	2,487	1,695	4,123	1,166	5,832	12,816	15,303
Q4	551	1,473	2,024	1,603	3,463	971	4,187	10,223	12,248
2009 Q1	765	1,422	2,186	2,474	2,793	554	3,297	9,117	11,303
Q2	638	1,668	2,306	3,265	4,091	738	3,433	11,527	13,833
Q3	907	1,456	2,363	3,089	4,405	630	2,926	11,050	13,413
Q4[3]	797	1,847	2,645	2,204	3,420	732	3,230	9,586	12,231
2010 Q1	1,333	2,294	3,627	3,350	3,712	492	3,348	10,902	14,529
Q2	738	2,182	2,920	2,533	3,465	603	3,586	10,187	13,106
Q3	544	2,913	3,457	1,501	2,882	526	3,650	8,559	12,016
Q4	934	2,884	3,818	1,821	3,571	612	3,626	9,631	13,449
2011 Q1	1,190	2,699	3,889	1,970	2,837	525	3,095	8,427	12,315

Sources: Office for National Statistics: 01633 456344

1 Classified to construction in the Standard Industrial Classification 2007.
2 Including the value of speculative building when work starts on site.
3 Excluding orders for home improvement work.
4 Construction new orders underwent significant development during 2008/09 resulting in a new quarterley survey from 2010.
5 Excluding infrastructure.

18.22 Total engineering[1]

Values at current prices

£ million

	Turnover			New Orders		
	Export	Home	Total	Export	Home	Total
	JWO5	JWO6	JWO7	JWO8	JWO9	JWP2
2005	28,328.2	61,088.9	89,417.2	29,263.1	50,471.2	79,734.0
2006	31,570.6	62,715.9	94,287.4	28,845.7	46,964.1	75,809.6
2007	33,202.3	67,167.5	100,370.1	32,938.0	52,618.8	85,556.6
2008	33,929.2	68,053.8	101,983.0	30,512.2	54,571.6	85,084.4
2009	29,994.1	56,556.9	86,550.6	26,189.2	44,661.1	70,850.7
2010	37,532.0	61,679.2	99,211.2	35,537.8	54,997.3	90,535.1
2006 Q1	7,682.9	15,277.3	22,960.7	6,959.8	11,961.3	18,921.0
Q2	7,792.9	15,784.4	23,577.6	7,289.9	11,812.9	19,102.7
Q3	7,609.4	15,957.3	23,566.6	6,995.7	11,129.3	18,124.9
Q4	8,485.4	15,696.9	24,182.5	7,600.3	12,060.6	19,661.0
2007 Q1	8,282.8	16,603.9	24,886.4	8,726.8	12,596.4	21,323.2
Q2	8,491.7	16,349.6	24,841.6	8,693.7	12,280.6	20,974.2
Q3	8,064.4	17,149.3	25,213.8	8,108.5	13,463.0	21,571.4
Q4	8,363.4	17,064.7	25,428.3	7,409.0	14,278.8	21,687.8
2008 Q1	8,142.2	17,060.6	25,203.3	7,687.2	14,276.8	21,964.2
Q2	8,770.8	17,362.6	26,133.1	8,176.6	13,830.9	22,007.5
Q3	8,394.8	17,295.0	25,689.6	7,371.0	14,296.0	21,667.3
Q4	8,621.4	16,335.6	24,957.0	7,277.4	12,167.9	19,445.4
2009 Q1	7,396.6	14,414.2	21,810.7	6,415.1	10,982.5	17,398.1
Q2	7,065.8	13,824.1	20,889.9	6,452.2	10,589.0	17,041.3
Q3	7,094.7	14,005.9	21,100.4	6,328.2	11,271.4	17,599.5
Q4	8,437.0	14,312.7	22,749.6	6,993.7	11,818.2	18,811.8
2010 Q1	8,405.6	14,561.7	22,967.3	8,184.8	13,131.0	21,315.8
Q2	9,268.8	15,326.0	24,594.8	9,293.0	14,418.4	23,711.4
Q3	9,498.2	16,005.1	25,503.3	8,595.8	13,589.2	22,185.0
Q4	10,359.4	15,786.4	26,145.8	9,464.2	13,858.7	23,322.9
2011 Q1	10,070.8	15,094.9	25,165.7	10,334.9	12,833.8	23,168.7
2010 Jan	2,312.3	4,220.1	6,532.4	2,454.9	3,959.9	6,414.8
Feb	2,669.1	4,592.6	7,261.7	2,605.9	4,052.8	6,658.7
Mar	3,424.2	5,749.0	9,173.2	3,124.0	5,118.3	8,242.3
Apr	2,891.9	4,940.1	7,832.0	2,981.8	4,205.1	7,186.9
May	3,026.2	4,850.2	7,876.4	2,959.2	4,036.4	6,995.6
Jun	3,350.7	5,546.7	8,897.4	3,351.1	6,177.6	9,528.7
Jul	3,022.8	5,444.3	8,467.1	2,787.6	4,652.0	7,439.6
Aug	2,928.1	5,102.8	8,030.9	2,757.7	4,302.1	7,059.8
Sep	3,542.1	5,489.8	9,031.9	3,046.2	4,676.8	7,723.0
Oct	3,429.2	5,380.9	8,810.1	2,974.1	4,361.9	7,336.0
Nov	3,524.4	5,544.7	9,069.1	2,935.9	4,835.7	7,771.6
Dec	3,396.0	4,897.0	8,293.0	3,543.6	4,696.1	8,239.7
2011 Jan	3,061.3	4,575.9	7,637.2	3,480.8	4,038.0	7,518.8
Feb	3,184.7	4,726.6	7,911.3	3,057.0	4,013.0	7,070.0
Mar	3,824.8	5,792.4	9,617.2	3,797.1	4,782.8	8,579.9
Apr	3,245.8	4,717.7	7,963.5	3,392.8	4,028.0	7,420.8
May	3,429.0	5,218.0	8,647.0	3,501.6	3,869.4	7,371.0

Source: Office for National Statistics : 01633 646659

1 The data for tables 4.5 - 4.7 (and published in the Turnover and Orders in Production and Services Industries) Standard
are based on SIC 2007 (the Industrial Classification for 2007). The change is a result of the SIC 2003 based MPI survey
(which provided figures up to the April edition of the Monthly Digest) becoming part of the SIC 2007 based Monthly Business
Survey (MBS). This is part of an ONS wide project to convert all data series to the latest SIC. This means that the three
engineering tables: 4.5 Total engineering (SIC 03 29-33); 4.6 Manufacture of machinery and equipment not elsewhere classified
(SIC 03 29); 4.7 Manufacture of electrical and optical equipment (SIC 03 30-33) have been replaced with: 4.5 Total engineering
(SIC 07 25-28) ;4.6 Manufacture of fabricated metal products and machinery and equipment n.e.c. (SIC 07 25, 28);
4.7 Manufacture of electrical and optical equipment (SIC 07 26-27). Please note these new tables do not include
Orders on Hand.

18.23 Manufacture of fabricated metal products and machinery and equipment n.e.c.[1]

Values at current prices

£ million

	Turnover			New Orders		
	Export	Home	Total	Export	Home	Total
	JWM9	JWN2	JWN3	JWN4	JWN5	JWN6
2005	14,918.4	38,926.9	53,845.3	15,150.1	28,998.0	44,147.7
2006	17,288.6	40,598.9	57,887.9	14,977.7	29,110.8	44,088.3
2007	18,628.0	45,697.2	64,325.5	17,322.7	32,001.5	49,324.0
2008	20,022.2	46,615.9	66,638.5	16,445.4	36,125.6	52,571.6
2009	16,407.4	37,694.8	54,102.1	14,092.0	26,752.2	40,844.4
2010	22,257.5	42,731.1	64,988.6	21,727.5	34,866.8	56,594.3
2006 Q1	4,126.6	9,791.1	13,917.9	3,708.9	7,217.7	10,926.5
Q2	4,345.6	10,191.8	14,537.7	3,820.7	7,098.8	10,919.5
Q3	4,226.6	10,393.8	14,620.3	3,545.4	7,017.0	10,562.4
Q4	4,589.8	10,222.2	14,812.0	3,902.7	7,777.3	11,679.9
2007 Q1	4,565.3	11,147.5	15,712.7	4,540.4	7,387.5	11,927.9
Q2	4,761.8	11,208.4	15,970.4	4,501.0	7,453.5	11,954.4
Q3	4,551.0	11,762.1	16,313.1	4,245.6	8,915.3	13,160.9
Q4	4,749.9	11,579.2	16,329.3	4,035.7	8,245.2	12,280.8
2008 Q1	4,920.2	11,586.7	16,507.3	4,337.7	9,049.0	13,386.9
Q2	5,340.0	11,958.4	17,298.4	4,470.1	9,120.8	13,591.0
Q3	4,968.4	12,009.0	16,977.3	4,004.0	10,027.5	14,031.7
Q4	4,793.6	11,061.8	15,855.5	3,633.6	7,928.3	11,562.0
2009 Q1	3,975.4	9,812.2	13,787.6	3,238.9	6,990.6	10,229.9
Q2	3,776.4	9,349.0	13,125.4	3,620.6	6,259.2	9,879.8
Q3	3,866.1	9,359.6	13,225.5	3,398.0	6,789.5	10,187.4
Q4	4,789.5	9,174.0	13,963.6	3,834.5	6,712.9	10,547.3
2010 Q1	4,838.8	9,902.9	14,741.7	4,810.6	8,203.9	13,014.5
Q2	5,567.2	10,577.9	16,145.1	5,852.1	9,155.6	15,007.7
Q3	5,622.2	11,313.3	16,935.5	5,113.6	8,520.7	13,634.3
Q4	6,229.3	10,937.0	17,166.3	5,951.2	8,986.6	14,937.8
2011 Q1	6,076.8	10,542.2	16,619.0	6,673.6	8,353.1	15,026.7
2010 Jan	1,312.3	2,894.3	4,206.6	1,437.7	2,401.6	3,839.3
Feb	1,526.6	3,112.7	4,639.3	1,547.1	2,511.5	4,058.6
Mar	1,999.9	3,895.9	5,895.8	1,825.8	3,290.8	5,116.6
Apr	1,731.7	3,412.8	5,144.5	1,783.6	2,610.7	4,394.3
May	1,788.7	3,349.1	5,137.8	1,881.0	2,539.9	4,420.9
Jun	2,046.8	3,815.8	5,862.6	2,187.5	4,003.8	6,191.3
Jul	1,820.0	3,833.0	5,653.0	1,681.5	3,060.0	4,741.5
Aug	1,693.2	3,575.0	5,268.2	1,597.0	2,547.2	4,144.2
Sep	2,109.2	3,904.5	6,013.7	1,835.2	2,917.7	4,752.9
Oct	2,082.5	3,811.1	5,893.6	1,889.9	2,905.6	4,795.5
Nov	2,149.8	3,858.7	6,008.5	1,842.7	2,974.0	4,816.7
Dec	1,992.6	3,265.3	5,257.9	2,211.7	3,115.7	5,327.4
2011 Jan	1,823.9	3,191.5	5,015.4	2,197.6	2,625.8	4,823.4
Feb	1,944.0	3,303.8	5,247.8	2,054.6	2,593.5	4,648.1
Mar	2,308.9	4,046.9	6,355.8	2,421.4	3,133.8	5,555.2
Apr	1,921.6	3,438.3	5,359.9	2,212.1	2,746.7	4,958.8
May	2,086.9	3,856.1	5,943.0	2,311.6	2,593.3	4,904.9

Source: Office for National Statistics : 01633 646659

1 The data for tables 4.5 - 4.7 (and published in the Turnover and Orders in Production and Services Industries) Standard are based on SIC 2007 (the Industrial Classification for 2007). The change is a result of the SIC 2003 based MPI survey (which provided figures up to the April edition of the Monthly Digest) becoming part of the SIC 2007 based Monthly Business Survey (MBS). This is part of an ONS wide project to convert all data series to the latest SIC. This means that the three engineering tables: 4.5 Total engineering (SIC 03 29-33); 4.6 Manufacture of machinery and equipment not elsewhere classified (SIC 03 29); 4.7 Manufacture of electrical and optical equipment (SIC 03 30-33) have been replaced with: 4.5 Total engineering (SIC 07 25-28) ;4.6 Manufacture of fabricated metal products and machinery and equipment n.e.c. (SIC 07 25, 28); 4.7 Manufacture of electrical and optical equipment (SIC 07 26-27). Please note these new tables do not include Orders on Hand.

18.24 Alcoholic drink[1]

United Kingdom

			1999	2000	2001	2002	2003	2004	2005	2006	2007	2008	2009 [4]
		Thousand hectolitres of alcohol											
Spirits[2]													
Production	KMEA	"	4705	4210	4368	4508	4553	4081	4365	4485	5498	6072	4261
Released for home consumption													
Home produced whisky	KMEE	"	323	314	321	321	318	319	301	283	286	289	258
Spirit-based Ready-to-drink[3]	SNET	"	..	..	..	105	124	114	84	65	52	42	31
Imported and other	KMEG	"	596	615	647	689	744	792	822	767	832	816	802
Total	KMEH	"	919	929	968	1115	1187	1226	1206	1114	1170	1147	1091
Beer		Thousand hectolitres											
Production	BFNK	"	57854	55279	56802	56672	58014	57461	56255	53768	51341	49611	45141
Released for home consumption	BAYL	"	58917	57007	58234	59384	60301	59194	57572	55751	53465	51498	46722
Production	JYXJ	Thousand hectolitres of pure alcohol	2364	2299	2358	2352	2414	2433	2338	2250	2160	2062	1891
Released for home consumption	JYXK		2428	2382	2429	2473	2515	2499	2398	2335	2247	2145	1953
Wine of fresh grapes													
Released for home consumption		Thousand hectolitres											
Fortified	KMEM		316	289	287	325	296	298	306	302	305	324	219
Still table	KMEN	"	8391	8864	9534	10319	10647	11768	12117	11655	12559	12402	11729
Sparkling	KMEO	"	576	543	515	578	640	676	721	715	838	757	731
Total	KMEP	"	9284	9696	10336	11222	11584	12742	13143	12672	13702	13483	12680
Made-wine													
Released for home consumption													
Still	JTI9	"	413	428	360	366	338	351	334	316	343	374	390
Sparkling	JTJ2	"	3	3	4	2	1	1	–	1	5	7	2
Coolers[3]	KJDD		1802	2800	3712	1606	423	508	597	528	720	611	597
Total made wine	JTJ3	"	2218	3232	4075	1974	762	859	931	844	1068	993	989
Cider and perry													
Released for home consumption	KMER	"	6022	6006	5911	5939	5876	6139	6377	7523	8046	8412	9404

1 See chapter text.
2 Potable spirits distilled.
3 Made wine with alcoholic strength 1.2% to 5.5%. Includes alcoholic lemonade of appropriate strength and similar products. From 28 April 2002, duty on spirit-based "coolers" is charged at the same rate as spirits per litre of alcohol. Coolers for calendar year 2002 includes only wine based "coolers".

Sources: HM Revenue & Customs UK Trade Infor mation website:;
http://www.uktradeinfo.com/index.cfm?task=bulletins

18.25 Tobacco products: released for home consumption[1]

United Kingdom

Thousand kilogrammes

	Million Cigarettes			Other tobacco products			Total tobacco products other than cigarettes
	Home-produced	Imported	Total	Cigars	Hand-rolling	Other[2]	
	LUQN	**LUQO**	**LUQP**	**LUQQ**	**LUQR**	**LUQS**	**LUQT**
2005	45922	4322	50244	758	3189	499	4445
2006	44392	4570	48962	689	3454	439	4581
2007	41955	3794	45749	602	3644	398	4643
2008	42053	3680	45733	546	4154	381	5081
2009 [3]	43989	3586	47575	534	5076	397	6007
2009 Apr	6902	665	7567	107	801	51	959
May	1056	7	1063	18	149	18	185
Jun	2757	239	2996	39	316	30	385
Jul	3701	320	4021	34	440	32	506
Aug	3495	296	3791	43	410	30	483
Sep	4114	291	4405	44	473	35	552
Oct	3479	283	3761	42	368	33	443
Nov [3]	3339	283	3622	50	427	37	515
Dec [3]	4771	395	5166	45	546	42	633

1 See chapter text.
2 Excluding snuff.
3 Provisional.

Sources: HM Revenue and Customs Statistical Bulletins at;
http://www.uktradeinfo.com/index.cfm?task=bulletins

National accounts

Chapter 19

National accounts

The tables are based on those in The Blue Book 2011 Edition. The Blue Book presents the full set of economic accounts for the United Kingdom. The accounts are based on the European System of Accounts 1995 (ESA 95), a system of national accounts that all European Union members have agreed to use. ESA 95 is fully compliant with the System of National Accounts 1993 (SNA93), which was unanimously approved by the Statistical Commission of the United Nations, and is used by statistical offices throughout the world.

The Blue Book contains an introduction which provides an overview of the accounts and an explanation of the underlying framework. A detailed description of the structure of the accounts and the methods used to derive the figures is provided in a separate Office for National Statistics (ONS) publication United Kingdom National Accounts: Concepts, Sources and Methods (TSO 1998). Further information on the financial accounts is given in the Financial Statistics Explanatory Handbook.

Brief definitions of some national accounting terms used in this chapter are included here. Current prices (or, more precisely, current price estimates) describe values during the period of the observation. Hence, in a time series, they will describe changes to price and to volume. Chain volume measures exclude the effects of price change. Basic prices do not include taxes and subsidies on products, whereas these are included in market prices.

Gross Domestic Product and Gross National Income (Tables 19.1, 19.2, 19.3)

Table 19.1 shows three of the most important economic aggregates: Gross Domestic Product (GDP), Gross National Income (GNI) and Gross National Disposable Income (GNDI). In all three cases 'gross' denotes that depreciation (or consumption) of fixed capital is ignored. GDP is the total value of the UK's output. GNI is GDP plus primary incomes received from the rest of the world minus primary incomes paid to the rest of the world. Primary income comprises taxes on production and imports, property income and compensation of employees. These measures are given as current price estimates and chained volume measures. GNDI equals GNI plus net current transfers to the rest of the world. Transfers are unrequited payments such as taxes, social benefits and remittances.

There are three different approaches to measuring GDP: output, income and expenditure. Table 19.2 shows the various money flows which are used in these different approaches, and those that are used to measure GNI at current prices. The output approach to measuring GDP takes the gross value added for the entire economy (that is, the value of the UK's output minus the goods and services consumed in the productive process) to give gross value added at basic prices. This figure is then adjusted to include taxes and exclude subsidies on products. This gives gross value added at market prices for the UK, which is equivalent to GDP.

The expenditure approach to GDP shows consumption expenditure by households and government, gross capital formation and expenditure on UK exports. The sum of these items overstates the amount of income generated in the UK by the value of imported goods and services. This item is therefore subtracted to produce GDP at market prices.

The income approach to GDP shows gross operating surplus, mixed income and compensation of employees (previously known as income from employment). Production taxes less subsidies are added to produce the total of the income-based components at market prices.

Table 19.2 also shows the primary incomes received from the rest of the world, which are added to GDP, and primary incomes payable to non-resident units, which are deducted from GDP, to arrive at GNI. Primary income comprises compensation of employees, taxes less subsidies on production, and property and entrepreneurial income. The data in Table 19.2 are in current prices. This means that changes between years will be driven by a combination of price effects and changes in the volume of production. The second of these components is often referred to as 'real growth'.

Table 19.3 shows the expenditure approach to the chained volume measure of GDP, that is to say the effects of price change have been removed. In chained volume series, volume measures for each year are produced in prices of the previous year. These volume measures are then 'chain-linked' together to produce a continuous time series.

Industrial analysis
(Tables 19.4, 19.5)

The analysis of gross value added by industry at current prices shown in Table 19.4 reflects the estimates based on the 2007 Standard Industrial Classification (SIC2007). The table is based on current price data reconciled through the input–output process for 2002 to 2008.

Table 19.5 shows chained volume measures of gross value added by industry. These indices are based on basic price measures. Chained volume measures of gross value added provides a lead economic indicator. The analysis of gross value added is estimated in terms of change and expressed in index number form.

Sector analysis – Distribution of income accounts and capital account
(Tables 19.6 to 19.13)

The National Accounts accounting framework includes the sector accounts which provide, by institutional sector, a description of the different stages of the economic process, from the income generated by production and its distribution and re-distribution to different economic units, and finally, capital accumulation and financing. Tables 19.6 to 19.12 show the 'allocation of primary income account' and the 'secondary distribution of income account' for the non-financial corporations, financial corporations, government and households sectors. Additionally, Table 19.12 shows the 'use of income account' for the households sector and Table 19.13 provides a summary of the capital account. The full sequence of accounts is shown in The Blue Book.

The allocation of primary income account shows the resident units and institutional sectors as recipients rather than producers of primary income. The balancing item of this account is the gross balance of primary income (B.5g) for each sector and, if the gross balance is aggregated across all sectors of the economy, the result is Gross National Income.

The secondary distribution of income account describes how the balance of income for each sector is allocated by redistribution; through transfers such as taxes on income, social contributions and benefits, and other current transfers. The balancing item of this account is Gross Disposable Income (GDI). For the households sector, the chained volume measure of GDI is shown as real household disposable income.

Table 19.12 shows, for the household sector, the use of disposable income where the balancing item is saving (B.8g). For the non-financial corporations sector the balancing item of the secondary distribution of income account, gross disposable income (B.6g), is equal to saving (B.8g).

The summary capital account (Table 19.13) brings together the saving and investment of the sectors of the economy. It shows saving, capital transfers, gross capital formation and net acquisition of non-financial assets for each of these.

Households' and non-profit institutions serving households' consumption expenditure at current market prices and chained volume measures
(Tables 19.14 to 19.17)

Households' and non-profit institutions serving households' (NPISH) final consumption expenditure is a major component of the expenditure measure of GDP. In Table 19.2 this expenditure is given at current market prices, broken down by the type of good or service purchased. Table 19.3 supplies the same breakdown in chain volume measures. Household final consumption expenditure includes the value of income-in-kind and imputed rent of owner-occupied dwellings. It includes expenditure on durable goods (for instance motor cars) which, from the point of view of the individual might more appropriately be treated as capital expenditure. The purchase of land and dwellings (including costs incurred in connection with the transfer of their ownership) and expenditure on major improvements by occupiers are treated as personal capital expenditure. Other goods and services purchased by the household sector (with the exception of goods and services that are to be used in self-employment) are treated as final consumption expenditure. The most detailed figures are published quarterly in Consumer Trends

Change in inventories (previously known as value of physical increase in stocks and work in progress)
(Table 19.18)

This table gives a broad analysis by industry of the value of entries less withdrawals and losses of inventories (stocks), and analysis by asset for manufacturing industry.

Gross fixed capital formation
(Table 19.19 to 19.22)

Gross fixed capital formation is the total value of the acquisition less disposal of fixed assets, and improvements to land.

19.1 United Kingdom national and domestic product[1]

Main aggregates

At current prices and chained volume measures, reference year 2008

Indices (2008=100) and £ million

		2001	2002	2003	2004	2005	2006	2007	2008	2009	2010
INDICES (2008=100)											
VALUES AT CURRENT PRICES											
Gross domestic product at current market prices ("money GDP")	YBEU	71.2	75	79.5	83.9	87.5	92.7	98	100	97.2	101.7
Gross value added at current basic prices	YBEX	70.7	74.5	79	83.4	87	92.2	97.6	100	97.9	101.3
CHAINED VOLUME MEASURES											
Gross domestic product at market prices	YBEZ	85.3	87.5	90.6	93.3	95.2	97.7	101.1	100	95.6	97.3
Gross national disposable income at market prices	YBFP	84.3	87.5	90.6	93.2	94.7	96.4	100.5	100	94.6	96
Gross value added at basic prices	CGCE	85.3	87.3	90.5	93	95.1	97.5	101	100	95.4	97.1
PRICES											
Implied deflator of GDP at market prices	YBGB	83.6	85.7	87.7	89.9	91.8	94.8	97	100	101.7	104.5
VALUES AT CURRENT PRICES (£ million)											
Gross measures (before deduction of fixed capital consumption) at current market prices											
Gross Domestic Product ("money GDP")	YBHA	1021625	1075368	1139441	1202370	1254292	1328597	1405796	1433870	1393854	1458452
Employment, property and entrepreneurial income from the rest of the world (receipts less payments)	YBGG	9425	18503	17770	18029	21886	9512	21369	33136	20397	23039
Subsidies (receipts) less taxes (payments) on products from/to the rest of the world	-QZOZ	-3920	-2890	-2596	-1234	-4260	-4496	-4731	-4906	-4238	-5186
Other subsidies on production from/to the rest of the world	-IBJL	582	519	592	592	3408	3221	2952	3051	3411	3032
Gross National Income (GNI)	ABMX	1027712	1091500	1155207	1219759	1275323	1336830	1425387	1465152	1413417	1479337
Current transfers from the rest of the world (receipts less payments)	-YBGF	-3182	-6500	-7835	-9645	-11052	-10610	-11804	-11912	-14290	-17937
Gross National Disposable Income	NQCO	1024530	1085000	1147372	1210114	1264271	1326220	1413583	1453240	1399127	1461400
Adjustment to current basic prices											
Gross Domestic Product (at current market prices)	YBHA	1021625	1075368	1139441	1202370	1254292	1328597	1405796	1433870	1393854	1458452
Adjustment to current basic prices (less taxes plus subsidies on products)	-NQBU	-114232	-118469	-124738	-132001	-137410	-144657	-153194	-149986	-136922	-157334
Gross Value Added (at current basic prices)	ABML	907393	956899	1014703	1070369	1116882	1183940	1252602	1283884	1256932	1301118
Net measures (after deduction of fixed capital consumption) at current market prices	-NQAE	-115796	-121914	-125603	-135067	-138272	-147323	-154297	-151370	-159862	-164006
Net domestic product	NHRK	905829	953454	1013838	1067303	1116020	1181274	1251499	1282500	1233992	1294446
Net national income	NSRX	911916	969586	1029604	1084692	1137051	1189507	1271090	1313782	1253555	1315331
Net national disposable income	NQCP	908734	963086	1021769	1075047	1125999	1178897	1259286	1301870	1239265	1297394
CHAINED VOLUME MEASURES											
(Reference year 2008, £ million)											
Gross measures (before deduction of fixed capital consumption) at market prices											
Gross Domestic Product	ABMI	1222650	1255142	1299381	1337782	1365685	1401290	1449861	1433871	1371163	1395312
Terms of trade effect ("Trading gain or loss")	YBGJ	-1764	5106	8274	8337	280	2495	2016	-1	-2023	-2961
Real gross domestic income	YBGL	1220886	1260248	1307655	1346119	1365965	1403785	1451877	1433870	1369140	1392351
Real employment, property and entrepreneurial income from the rest of the world (receipts less payments)	YBGI	11246	21691	20400	20210	23866	10066	22122	33136	20036	21984
Subsidies (receipts) less taxes (payments) on production from/to the rest of the world	-QZPB	-4678	-3388	-2980	-1383	-4646	-4758	-4898	-4906	-4163	-4948
Other subsidies on production from/to the rest of the world	-IBJN	695	608	680	664	3716	3408	3056	3051	3351	2893
Gross National Income (GNI)	YBGM	1228158	1279184	1325782	1365637	1388923	1412542	1472183	1465151	1388364	1412280
Real current transfers from the rest of the world (receipts less payments)	-YBGP	-3797	-7621	-8995	-10813	-12054	-11227	-12220	-11912	-14037	-17115
Gross National Disposable Income	YBGO	1224364	1271562	1316786	1354824	1376871	1401315	1459964	1453239	1374327	1395165
Adjustment to basic prices											
Gross Domestic Product (at market prices)	ABMI	1222650	1255142	1299381	1337782	1365685	1401290	1449861	1433871	1371163	1395312
Adjustment to basic prices (less taxes plus subsidies on products)	-NTAQ	-127762	-133997	-137875	-144020	-144884	-149352	-153669	-149983	-145769	-149232
Gross Value Added (at basic prices)	ABMM	1095181	1121184	1161561	1193753	1220787	1251874	1296131	1283863	1225399	1246080
Net measures (after deduction of fixed capital consumption) at market prices	-CIHA	-123867	-129469	-130493	-138887	-139711	-146702	-149893	-144846	-150107	-149928
Net national income at market prices	YBET	1092303	1137185	1181327	1212271	1234697	1251939	1310714	1313781	1242226	1262352
Net national disposable income at market prices	YBEY	1088519	1129564	1172330	1201458	1222647	1240710	1298495	1301869	1228189	1245237

1 See chapter text.

Source: Office for National Statistics: 01633 456713

19.2 United Kingdom gross domestic product and national income[1]

Current prices

£million

		2001	2002	2003	2004	2005	2006	2007	2008	2009	2010
Gross domestic product: Output											
Gross value added, at basic prices											
Output of goods and services	KN26	1860987	1939727	2040249	2140984	2258356	2398550	2537820	2630445	2590111	..
less inter mediate consumption	-KN25	-953594	-982828	-1025546	-1070614	-1141474	-1214609	-1285218	-1346562	-1333179	..
Total Gross Value Added	ABML	907393	956899	1014703	1070369	1116882	1183940	1252602	1283884	1256932	1301118
Value added taxes (VAT) on products	QYRC	67097	71059	77335	81544	83425	87758	92017	91952	79900	95964
Other taxes on products	NSUI	52844	53946	54813	58308	59167	62865	66786	63186	62729	67934
less subsidies on products	-NZHC	-5709	-6536	-7410	-7851	-5182	-5966	-5609	-5152	-5707	-6564
Gross Domestic Product at market prices	YBHA	1021625	1075368	1139441	1202370	1254292	1328597	1405796	1433870	1393854	1458452
Gross domestic product: Expenditure											
Final consumption expenditure											
Actual individual consumption											
Household final consumption expenditure	ABPB	647370	680649	714512	749607	784149	819164	862242	878024	858242	900204
Final consumption expenditure of NPISH	ABNV	25111	26422	27668	29197	30824	32408	34324	35767	35863	37702
Individual government final consumption expenditure	NNAQ	119718	132003	143649	147751	159195	172489	181762	194621	206913	212764
Total actual individual consumption	NQEO	792199	839074	885829	926555	974168	1024061	1078328	1108412	1101018	1150670
Collective government final consumption expenditure	NQEP	74891	80553	88962	103177	109078	112637	113392	120945	120436	125303
Total final consumption expenditure	ABKW	867090	919627	974791	1029732	1083246	1136698	1191720	1229357	1221454	1275973
Households and NPISH	NSSG	672481	707071	742180	778804	814973	851572	896566	913791	894105	937906
Central government	NMBJ	118778	130348	142658	152274	161329	173416	178058	191348	199649	207349
Local government	NMMT	75831	82208	89953	98654	106944	111710	117096	124218	127700	130718
Gross capital formation											
Gross fixed capital formation	NPQX	171785	180533	186759	200430	209722	227172	250036	241364	209253	217108
Changes in inventories	ABMP	6327	3026	4242	4890	4405	5172	6224	1711	-11651	6832
Acquisitions less disposals of valuables	NPJO	396	215	-37	-36	-377	285	465	561	429	638
Total gross capital formation	NQFM	178506	183776	190965	205285	213750	232630	256725	243634	198035	224577
Exports of goods and services	KTMW	276775	280454	290207	303612	331067	379091	374032	422864	395588	436796
less imports of goods and services	-KTMX	-300747	-308488	-316522	-336255	-373771	-419822	-416681	-461988	-421225	-476480
External balance of goods and services	KTMY	-23972	-28034	-26315	-32643	-42704	-40731	-42649	-39124	-25637	-39684
Statistical discrepancy between expenditure components and GDP	RVFD										
Gross Domestic Product at market prices	YBHA	1021625	1075368	1139441	1202370	1254292	1328597	1405796	1433870	1393854	1458452
Gross domestic product: Income											
Operating surplus, gross											
Non-financial corporations											
Public non-financial corporations	NRJT	6754	6631	7152	6860	8473	9628	10114	8043	9496	8810
Private non-financial corporations	NRJK	182932	187332	197893	216750	224811	244309	257995	255260	233436	246074
Financial corporations	NQNV	13699	27198	33065	33654	34323	39098	43643	57758	65816	52898
Adjustment for financial services	-NSRV										
General government	NMXV	9796	10289	10807	11312	11927	12634	13231	13963	14675	15500
Households and non-profit institutions serving households	QWLS	53000	55647	60983	65752	67494	69807	77768	74878	57744	72098
Total operating surplus, gross	ABNF	266181	287097	309900	334328	347028	375476	402751	409902	381167	395380
Mixed income	QWLT	60638	66316	72316	73335	78487	80432	82898	86376	81424	81047
Compensation of employees	HAEA	564253	586843	615995	646006	677517	713513	751858	770969	776872	799974
Taxes on production and imports	NZGX	137507	143117	150665	158704	162298	171454	180335	178207	166823	191829
less subsidies	-AAXJ	-6953	-8009	-9436	-10005	-11039	-12280	-12047	-11584	-12431	-12819
Statistical discrepancy between income components and GDP	RVFC	0	3	1	3	-2	-2	2	1	-8	3041
Gross Domestic Product at market prices	YBHA	1021625	1075368	1139441	1202370	1254292	1328597	1405796	1433870	1393854	1458452
Gross Domestic Product at market prices	YBHA	1021625	1075368	1139441	1202370	1254292	1328597	1405796	1433870	1393854	1458452
Compensation of employees											
receipts from the rest of the world	KTMN	1087	1121	1116	931	974	938	984	1046	1176	1097
less payments to the rest of the world	-KTMO	-1021	-1054	-1057	-1425	-1584	-1896	-1718	-1761	-1435	-1486
Total	KTMP	66	67	59	-494	-610	-958	-734	-715	-259	-389
less Taxes on products paid to the rest of the world											
plus Subsidies received from the rest of the world	-QZOZ	-3920	-2890	-2596	-1234	-4260	-4496	-4731	-4906	-4238	-5186
Other subsidies on production	-IBJL	582	519	592	592	3408	3221	2952	3051	3411	3032
Property and entrepreneurial income											
receipts from the rest of the world	HMBN	137447	120543	122069	137380	185640	237505	291614	262842	169313	162366
less payments to the rest of the world	-HMBO	-128088	-102107	-104358	-118857	-163144	-227035	-269511	-228991	-148657	-138938
Total	HMBM	9359	18436	17711	18523	22496	10470	22103	33851	20656	23428
Gross National Income at market prices	ABMX	1027712	1091500	1155207	1219759	1275323	1336830	1425387	1465152	1413417	1479337

Source: Office for National Statistics: 01633 456492

19.3 United Kingdom gross domestic product[1]

Chained volume measures, reference year 2008

£ million

		2001	2002	2003	2004	2005	2006	2007	2008	2009	2010
Gross domestic product: expenditure approach											
Final consumption expenditure											
Actual individual consumption											
Household final consumption expenditure	**ABPF**	748122	781860	807653	832690	851338	867082	890872	878024	846961	855302
Final consumption expenditure of non-profit institutions serving households	**ABNU**	37037	36615	36266	36441	36334	36421	36582	35767	34487	35803
Individual government final consumption expenditure	**NSZK**	166421	172082	176681	181706	185163	188485	191998	194621	188270	191930
Total actual individual consumption	**YBIO**	950375	989940	1020298	1050668	1072795	1091991	1119538	1108412	1069718	1083035
Collective government final consumption expenditure	**NSZL**	98783	103486	111027	115879	118881	120132	118558	120945	127111	128260
Total final consumption expenditure	**ABKX**	1049625	1093862	1131451	1166570	1191701	1212138	1238115	1229353	1196821	1211287
Gross capital formation											
Gross fixed capital formation	**NPQR**	195509	202615	204883	215291	220497	234572	253562	241364	209051	214486
Changes in inventories	**ABMQ**	7989	1862	5044	5345	4925	4200	7798	1710	-12474	4940
Acquisitions less disposals of valuables	**NPJP**	457	236	-42	-41	-412	312	489	561	418	604
Total gross capital formation	**NPQU**	199328	200670	208248	218872	223272	237272	260714	243635	196996	220028
Gross domestic final expenditure	**YBIK**	1248470	1293540	1338724	1384657	1414155	1449024	1499124	1472988	1393817	1431315
Exports of goods and services	**KTMZ**	322079	328327	334505	351734	378960	423242	417578	422864	382886	406457
Gross final expenditure	**ABME**	1572158	1623417	1674822	1738028	1794294	1872175	1917438	1895852	1776703	1837772
less imports of goods and services	**-KTNB**	-348298	-366783	-373815	-398915	-428270	-471768	-467579	-461988	-405540	-440151
Statistical discrepancy between expenditure components and GDP	**GIXS**	0	0	0	-1	0	-1	0	1	0	-2312
Gross Domestic Product at market prices	**ABMI**	1222650	1255142	1299381	1337782	1365685	1401290	1449861	1433871	1371163	1395312
of which External balance of goods and services	**KTNC**	-26219	-38456	-39310	-47181	-49310	-48526	-50001	-39124	-22654	-33694

1 See chapter text.

Source: Office for National Statistics: 01633 455644

19.4 Gross value added at current basic prices: by industry[1,2]

United Kingdom

£million

		2002	2003	2004	2005	2006	2007	2008	2009	2010
A Agriculture	KKD5	8993	9882	10055	7915	8440	8648	9096	8030	7569
B-F Production and Construction										
B-E Production										
B Mining and quarrying	KKD7	19724	18768	19815	23001	26547	27337	32489	25876	28804
C Manufacturing										
CA Food products, beverages and tobacco	KKE5	20984	21648	22147	22039	21869	22544	22139	22465	23608
CB Textiles, wearing apparel and leather products	KKE7	4882	4450	4278	4225	4315	4439	4220	4089	4085
CC Wood, paper products and printing	KKE9	10625	10736	10588	10798	11262	11859	11672	11500	11488
CD Coke and refined petroleum products	KKF3	1073	1070	1048	1055	1161	1091	854	805	714
CE Chemicals and chemical products	KKF5	10638	10624	10138	10853	11749	11806	10915	10610	9667
CF Basic pharmaceutical products and preparations	KKF7	4875	4921	5545	6230	6951	7304	9632	11199	10841
CG Rubber, plastic and other non-metallic mineral products	KKF9	11297	11222	10867	10364	10420	10648	9832	9127	8808
CH Basic metals and metal products	KKG3	17342	17096	16942	18216	17679	18590	18415	16609	16236
CI Computer, electronic and optical products	KKG5	8970	8593	8286	8600	9167	9791	9674	8776	9607
CJ Electrical equipment	KKG7	5208	5078	4778	4655	4578	4552	4364	4027	4043
CK Machinery and equipment n. e. c.	KKG9	8408	8544	8392	8124	8322	8534	8643	8455	8681
CL Transport equipment	KKH3	14326	14155	14099	13793	13812	13474	11473	10240	12854
CM Other manufacturing and repair	KKH5	9511	9014	9317	9272	9544	10079	9724	8837	9979
C Total manufacturing	KKE3	128139	127151	126425	128224	130829	134711	131557	126739	130611
D Electricity, gas, steam and air conditioning supply	KKH7	13794	14039	13696	13701	17217	17869	18409	21146	17259
E Water supply, sewerage, waste mgmt and remediation	KKH9	9624	10494	11415	12349	13672	14707	15175	15173	14887
B-E Total production	KKJ5	171281	170452	171351	177275	188265	194624	197630	188934	191561
F Construction	KKI3	66938	72619	79311	82634	88287	96897	97873	87373	90685
B-F Total production and construction	KKD9	238219	243071	250662	259909	276552	291521	295503	276307	282246
G-T Services										
G-I Distribution, transport, hotels and restaurants										
G Wholesale, retail, repair of motor vehicles and m/cycles	KKI5	113177	119069	126337	129357	135244	142041	139782	137682	140171
H Transportation and storage	KKI9	51714	53356	54582	57151	59213	62529	64189	61870	60232
I Accommodation and food service activities	KKJ3	28028	29242	30932	31989	33966	35517	36672	35228	36936
G-I Total distribution, transport, hotels and restaurants	KKI7	192919	201667	211851	218497	228423	240087	240643	234780	237339
J Information and communication										
JA Publishing, audiovisual and broadcasting activities	KKK3	18136	18741	19216	19520	19589	20657	21358	21074	24591
JB Telecommunications	KKK5	20885	22213	23002	23155	23215	24142	24451	23534	25582
JC IT and other information service activities	KKK7	20498	23374	26496	27273	28967	32515	33345	32491	36105
J Total information and communication	KKJ9	59519	64328	68714	69948	71771	77314	79154	77099	86278
K Financial and insurance	KKK9	63263	71383	75481	80039	91478	99013	113877	126894	115161
L Real estate	KKL3	79307	86462	92971	95519	98003	110307	108054	90415	119691
M-N Professional and support										
M Professional, scientific and technical activities										
MA Legal, accounting, mgmt, architect, engineering etc	KKL9	50060	53251	56375	60016	65854	70095	71959	70378	63740
MB Scientific research and development	KKM3	3747	3952	4199	4686	5057	4746	4268	4321	4510
MC Other professional, scientific and technical activities	KKM5	13509	14043	14554	16225	17243	17706	18582	17755	19371
M Total professional, scientific and technical activities	KKL5	67316	71246	75128	80927	88154	92547	94809	92454	87621
N Administrative and support service activities	KKM7	45196	47477	50086	53166	55813	58743	58040	56101	59155
M-N Total professional and support	KKL7	112512	118723	125214	134093	143967	151290	152849	148555	146776
O-Q Government, health and education										
O Public admin, defence, compulsory social security	KKM9	47298	51449	55312	59889	62154	63403	65243	68037	68756
P Education	KKN5	58740	62360	65891	70367	75306	79537	83398	85677	88152
Q Human health and social work activities										
QA Human health activities	KKN9	45689	50570	55939	59286	63746	65654	67452	70669	75354
QB Residential care and social work activities	KKO3	18020	19681	20811	22216	23515	24687	26966	28660	29576
Q Total human health and social work activities	KKN7	63709	70251	76750	81502	87261	90341	94418	99329	104930
O-Q Total government, health and education	KKN3	169747	184060	197953	211758	224721	233281	243059	253043	261838
R-T Other services										
R Arts, entertainment and recreation	KKO5	15680	17105	18143	18914	19677	19572	19571	19405	21225
S Other service activities	KKO9	12225	13170	14377	15092	15609	16280	16242	17089	16446
T Activities of households as employers, undiff. goods	KKP3	4515	4852	4948	5198	5299	5289	5836	5315	6549
R-T Total other services	KKO7	32420	35127	37468	39204	40585	41141	41649	41809	44220
G-T Total service industries	KKJ7	709687	761750	809652	849058	898948	952433	979285	972595	1011303
B.1g All industries	ABML	956899	1014703	1070369	1116882	1183940	1252602	1283884	1256932	1301118

1 See chapter text. Components may not sum to totals as a result of rounding

2 Because of differences in the annual and monthly production inquiries, estimates
of current price output and gross value added by industry derived
from the current price Input-Output Supply and Use Tables are not consistent
with the equivalent measures of chained volume measures growth given
in 19.5. These differences do not affect GDP totals.

Source: Office for National Statistics: 01633 456771

19.5 Gross value added at basic prices: by industry[1,2,3,4]
Chained volume indices

United Kingdom

	Weight per 1000 [1]			Indices (2008=100)			
	2008			2001	2002	2003	2004
A Agriculture	7.1	**L2KL**	L2KL	79.2	89.2	87.6	86.4
B-F Production and Construction							
B-E Production							
B Mining and quarrying	25.3	**L2KR**	L2KR	148.3	148.2	141	129.8
C Manufacturing							
CA Food products, beverages and tobacco	17.2	**KN3D**	KN3D	100.5	103.6	101.6	103.2
CB Textiles, wearing apparel and leather products	3.3	**KN3E**	KN3E	123.7	116.7	115.5	103.2
CC Wood, paper products and printing	9.1	**KN3F**	KN3F	106	109	107.8	107.6
CD Coke and refined petroleum products	0.7	**KN3G**	KN3G	106.1	111.2	109.8	115.7
CE Chemicals and chemical products	8.5	**KN3H**	KN3H	97.7	96.5	94.5	98
CF Basic pharmaceutical products and preparations	7.5	**KN3I**	KN3I	79.3	84.9	89.5	91.6
CG Rubber, plastic and other non-metallic mineral products	7.7	**KN3J**	KN3J	100.1	97.8	100	101.8
CH Basic metals and metal products	14.3	**KN3K**	KN3K	98.7	94.1	95.3	98.7
CI Computer, electronic and optical products	7.5	**KN3L**	KN3L	130.1	109.8	105.9	110.5
CJ Electrical equipment	3.4	**KN3M**	KN3M	111.6	102.1	96.4	97.2
CK Machinery and equipment n. e. c.	6.7	**KN3N**	KN3N	93.8	89.2	88.8	91.7
CL Transport equipment	8.9	**KN3O**	KN3O	91.3	90.3	94.3	97.8
CM Other manufacturing and repair	7.6	**KN3P**	KN3P	103.1	98.3	96.7	98.4
C Total manufacturing	102.5	**L2KX**	L2KX	101.1	98.6	98.4	100.4
D Electricity, gas, steam and air conditioning supply	14.3	**L2MW**	L2MW	95.1	95.9	97.7	99.2
E Water supply, sewerage, waste mgmt and remediation	11.8	**L2N2**	L2N2	87.3	91.7	96	97.2
B-E Total production	153.9	**L2KQ**	L2KQ	104.3	102.7	102.4	103.3
F Construction	76.2	**L2N8**	L2N8	88.3	93.2	97.6	102.6
B-F Total production and construction		**L2KP**	L2KP	99.5	99.8	100.9	103
G-T Services							
G-I Distribution, transport, hotels and restaurants							
G Wholesale, retail, repair of motor vehicles and m/cycles	108.9	**L2NE**	L2NE	84.9	89.5	91.6	95.4
H Transportation and storage	50	**L2NI**	L2NI	93.3	92.9	94.4	96
I Accommodation and food service activities	28.6	**L2NQ**	L2NQ	85.6	87.8	90.3	92
G-I Total distribution, transport, hotels and restaurants	187.4	**L2ND**	L2ND	87.1	90.1	92.1	95.1
J Information and communication							
JA Publishing, audiovisual and broadcasting activities	16.6	**L2NU**	L2NU	103.7	102	100.6	98.7
JB Telecommunications	19	**L2NZ**	L2NZ	62.4	66.2	71.9	77.8
JC IT and other information service activities	26	**L2O3**	L2O3	71.9	71.1	78.1	82.5
J Total information and communication	61.7	**L2NT**	L2NT	75.7	76.8	81.3	84.8
K Financial and insurance	88.7	**L2O6**	L2O6	65.9	78.6	84.3	86.5
L Real estate	84.2	**L2OC**	L2OC	86.8	88.8	92.5	93.8
M-N Professional and support							
M Professional, scientific and technical activities							
MA Legal, accounting, mgmt, architect, engineering etc	56	**L2OJ**	L2OJ	63.8	61.3	66.3	69.4
MB Scientific research and development	3.3	**L2OQ**	L2OQ	57.4	62.5	69.1	83.7
MC Other professional, scientific and technical activities	14.5	**L2OS**	L2OS	93.3	90.8	94	95.1
M Total professional, scientific and technical activities	73.8	**L2OI**	L2OI	68.1	66	70.9	74.3
N Administrative and support service activities	45.2	**L2OX**	L2OX	78.1	75.6	78.3	82.1
M-N Total professional and support	119.1	**L2OH**	L2OH	71.8	69.6	73.7	77.3
O-Q Government, health and education							
O Public admin, defence, compulsory social security	50.8	**L2P8**	L2P8	81.5	83.3	93.7	95.6
P Education	65	**L2PA**	L2PA	97	98.8	99.5	99.9
Q Human health and social work activities							
QA Human health activities	52.5	**L2PD**	L2PD	76.9	79.8	83.2	86.7
QB Residential care and social work activities	21	**L2PF**	L2PF	86.1	90.1	94	97.5
Q Total human health and social work activities	73.5	**L2PC**	L2PC	79.2	82.4	85.9	89.5
O-Q Total government, health and education	189.3	**L2P7**	L2P7	85.4	87.8	92.4	94.5
R-T Other services							
R Arts, entertainment and recreation	15.2	**L2PJ**	L2PJ	90.4	93.9	100.6	103.9
S Other service activities	12.7	**L2PP**	L2PP	96.1	96.8	92.7	93
T Activities of households as employers, undiff. goods	4.5	**L2PT**	L2PT	109.3	111.6	113.6	114.5
R-T Total other services	32.4	**L2PI**	L2PI	94.3	96.6	98.6	100.4
G-T Total service industries	762.8	**L2NC**	L2NC	81.3	83.8	87.5	90.2
B.1g All industries	1 000.0	**CGCE**	CGCE	85.3	87.3	90.5	93

1 The weights shown are in proportion to total gross value added (GVA) in 2008 and are used to combine the industry output indices to calculate the totals. For 2007 and earlier, totals are calculated using the equivalent weights for the previous year (e.g. totals for 2007 use 2006 weights). Weights may not sum to totals due to rounding.

2 As GVA is expressed in index number for m, it is inappropriate to show as a statistical adjustment any divergence from the other measures of GDP. Such an adjustment does, however, exist implicitly.

3 See footnote 2 to Table 19.4.

Weights may not sum to totals due to rounding.

19.5 Gross value added at basic prices: by industry[1,2,3,4]
Chained volume indices

United Kingdom

			2005	2006	2007	2008	2009	2010
							Indices (2008=100)	
A Agriculture	L2KL	L2KL	92.2	89.3	86.1	100	84.8	83.6
B-F Production and Construction								
B-E Production								
B Mining and quarrying	L2KR	L2KR	118.7	109.7	107	100	91	86.4
C Manufacturing								
CA Food products, beverages and tobacco	KN3D	KN3D	104	103	102.4	100	98.4	101.8
CB Textiles, wearing apparel and leather products	KN3E	KN3E	101	101.6	99.8	100	90.3	93.3
CC Wood, paper products and printing	KN3F	KN3F	105.8	104.4	104	100	93.1	92.2
CD Coke and refined petroleum products	KN3G	KN3G	108.5	102.2	101.5	100	94	92.2
CE Chemicals and chemical products	KN3H	KN3H	97.4	98.7	100.6	100	86.3	82.4
CF Basic pharmaceutical products and preparations	KN3I	KN3I	98.1	103.3	98.9	100	106	100.6
CG Rubber, plastic and other non-metallic mineral products	KN3J	KN3J	100.6	104.9	104.5	100	86.3	86.5
CH Basic metals and metal products	KN3K	KN3K	99.6	102	104.3	100	80.5	84.3
CI Computer, electronic and optical products	KN3L	KN3L	105.1	106	106.5	100	94.1	88.5
CJ Electrical equipment	KN3M	KN3M	95.5	100.1	102.2	100	77.8	85.5
CK Machinery and equipment n. e. c.	KN3N	KN3N	93.4	98.4	100.9	100	79.4	95.5
CL Transport equipment	KN3O	KN3O	97	98.1	101.4	100	88.9	111.2
CM Other manufacturing and repair	KN3P	KN3P	98.6	101.7	103.9	100	93.7	96.2
C Total manufacturing	L2KX	L2KX	100.2	101.9	102.7	100	90.4	93.8
D Electricity, gas, steam and air conditioning supply	L2MW	L2MW	98.9	98.7	99.5	100	95.2	98.6
E Water supply, sewerage, waste mgmt and remediation	L2N2	L2N2	101.6	98.8	101.8	100	91.9	90.4
B-E Total production	L2KQ	L2KQ	102.4	102.4	102.9	100	91	92.8
F Construction	L2N8	L2N8	100	100.8	102.9	100	86.5	93.6
B-F Total production and construction	L2KP	L2KP	101.6	101.9	102.9	100	89.5	93
G-T Services								
G-I Distribution, transport, hotels and restaurants								
G Wholesale, retail, repair of motor vehicles and m/cycles	L2NE	L2NE	94.7	98	103	100	95.4	96.9
H Transportation and storage	L2NI	L2NI	97.6	98.1	101.7	100	91.4	89.5
I Accommodation and food service activities	L2NQ	L2NQ	94.7	98.9	102.6	100	95.5	97.5
G-I Total distribution, transport, hotels and restaurants	L2ND	L2ND	95.4	98.2	102.6	100	94.3	95
J Information and communication								
JA Publishing, audiovisual and broadcasting activities	L2NU	L2NU	94.8	97	100.8	100	92.1	106.5
JB Telecommunications	L2NZ	L2NZ	86.6	89.9	98.3	100	103.7	111.2
JC IT and other information service activities	L2O3	L2O3	87.1	90.7	98.4	100	94.3	106.3
J Total information and communication	L2NT	L2NT	88.9	92.1	99	100	96.6	107.8
K Financial and insurance	L2O6	L2O6	89.4	95.7	101.5	100	95.1	89.9
L Real estate	L2OC	L2OC	97.5	99.7	100.6	100	104.2	103.5
M-N Professional and support								
M Professional, scientific and technical activities								
MA Legal, accounting, mgmt, architect, engineering etc	L2OJ	L2OJ	76.2	84.7	97.1	100	91.8	85.3
MB Scientific research and development	L2OQ	L2OQ	91.6	97.2	102.3	100	94.1	103.2
MC Other professional, scientific and technical activities	L2OS	L2OS	100.6	98.4	100.9	100	90.1	96.1
M Total professional, scientific and technical activities	L2OI	L2OI	81.1	87.7	98	100	91.6	88.2
N Administrative and support service activities	L2OX	L2OX	88.1	93.2	101	100	87.7	100.4
M-N Total professional and support	L2OH	L2OH	83.7	89.8	99.2	100	90.1	92.8
O-Q Government, health and education								
O Public admin, defence, compulsory social security	L2P8	L2P8	97.1	96.1	95.7	100	104.2	102.8
P Education	L2PA	L2PA	102.5	101.5	101.3	100	101.1	100.8
Q Human health and social work activities								
QA Human health activities	L2PD	L2PD	90.6	93.3	97.9	100	104.9	109.2
QB Residential care and social work activities	L2PF	L2PF	100.2	101.9	103.4	100	100.3	103.9
Q Total human health and social work activities	L2PC	L2PC	93.1	95.5	99.4	100	103.6	107.7
O-Q Total government, health and education	L2P7	L2P7	97.2	97.6	99	100	102.9	104
R-T Other services								
R Arts, entertainment and recreation	L2PJ	L2PJ	102.4	104.1	108	100	97.6	99.7
S Other service activities	L2PP	L2PP	96.8	102.7	98.6	100	103.9	97.7
T Activities of households as employers, undiff. goods	L2PT	L2PT	120.4	115.4	102.5	100	91.6	106.7
R-T Total other services	L2PI	L2PI	101.9	104.6	103.4	100	99.2	99.9
G-T Total service industries	L2NC	L2NC	93.2	96.3	100.5	100	97.4	98.5
B.1g All industries	CGCE	CGCE	95.1	97.5	101	100	95.4	97.1

1 The weights shown are in proportion to total gross value added (GVA) in 2008 and are used to combine the industry output indices to calculate the totals. For 2007 and earlier, totals are calculated using the equivalent weights for the previous year (e.g. totals for 2007 use 2006 weights). Weights may not sum to totals due to rounding.

2 As GVA is expressed in index number for m, it is inappropriate to show as a statistical adjustment any divergence from the other measures of GDP. Such an adjustment does, however, exist implicitly.

3 See footnote 2 to Table 19.4.

Weights may not sum to totals due to rounding.

19.6 Non-financial corporations[1] Allocation of primary income account[2]

United Kingdom. ESA95 sector S.11										£million
		2001	2002	2003	2004	2005	2006	2007	2008	2009	2010
Resources											
Operating surplus, gross	NQBE	189686	193963	205045	223610	233284	253937	268109	263303	242932	254884
Property income, received											
Interest	EABC	13177	9330	9727	14141	17380	25391	30521	24566	7399	6920
Distributed income of corporations	EABD	37478	30550	50263	42964	46687	43893	38953	47124	62606	55915
Reinvested earnings on direct foreign investment	HDVR	22950	26893	12492	22713	33199	36511	50609	37890	13665	26928
Attributed property income of insurance policy-holders	FAOF	333	300	398	368	582	545	309	365	363	299
Rent	FAOG	117	118	120	122	122	124	123	126	132	130
Total	FAKY	74102	67229	73067	80463	98125	106678	120666	109895	84283	90307
Total resources	FBXJ	263788	261192	278112	304073	331409	360615	388775	373198	327215	345191
Uses											
Property income, paid											
Interest	EABG	30661	28871	29395	34812	39078	43572	55018	52806	31877	24428
Distributed income of corporations	NVCS	103881	85619	89102	93788	104875	108471	109167	114025	113829	105286
Reinvested earnings on direct foreign investment	HDVB	1699	1614	3955	6325	4983	15452	15051	3656	-1445	-621
Rent	FBXO	1955	1939	1603	1221	1268	1265	1273	1204	1213	1212
Total	FBXK	138196	118043	124055	136146	150204	168760	180509	171691	145474	130305
Balance of primary incomes, gross	NQBG	125592	143149	154057	167927	181205	191855	208266	201507	181741	214886
Total uses	FBXJ	263788	261192	278112	304073	331409	360615	388775	373198	327215	345191
After deduction of fixed capital consumption	-DBGF	-68362	-70547	-72598	-75559	-77277	-80365	-83243	-86127	-90888	-94636
Balance of primary incomes, net	FBXQ	57230	72602	81459	92368	103928	111490	125023	115380	90853	120250

1 See chapter text.
2 Before deduction of fixed capital formation.

Source: Office for National Statistics: 01633 456621

19.7 Non-financial corporations[1] Secondary distribution of income account

United Kingdom. ESA95 sector S.11										£ million
		2001	2002	2003	2004	2005	2006	2007	2008	2009	2010
Resources											
Balance of primary incomes, gross	NQBG	125592	143149	154057	167927	181205	191855	208266	201507	181741	214886
Social contributions											
Imputed social contributions	NSTJ	3598	3932	4206	4121	4392	4560	4824	5763	6809	4399
Current transfers other than taxes, social contributions and benefits											
Total	NRJB	3836	5543	6123	6550	7261	7476	4007	5682	5290	5714
Total resources	FCBR	133026	152624	164386	178598	192858	203891	217097	212952	193840	224999
Uses											
Current taxes on income, wealth etc.											
Taxes on income	FCBS	23177	24038	23702	27366	33618	37184	38403	40845	33542	35641
Social benefits other than social transfers in kind	NSTJ	3598	3932	4206	4121	4392	4560	4824	5763	6809	4399
Current transfers other than taxes, social contributions and benefits											
Net non-life insurance premiums	FCBY	3714	5396	5999	6522	7261	7476	4007	5682	5290	5714
Total, other current transfers	FCBX	4220	5876	6461	6973	7749	7953	4495	6170	5778	6202
Gross Disposable Income	NRJD	102031	118778	130017	140138	147099	154194	169375	160174	147711	178757
Total uses	FCBR	133026	152624	164386	178598	192858	203891	217097	212952	193840	224999
After deduction of fixed capital consumption	-DBGF	-68362	-70547	-72598	-75559	-77277	-80365	-83243	-86127	-90888	-94636
Disposable income, net	FCCF	33669	48231	57419	64579	69822	73829	86132	74047	56823	84121

1 See chapter text.

Source: Office for National Statistics: 01633 456621

19.8 General government[1] Allocation of primary income account

United Kingdom. ESA95 sector S.13 Unconsolidated

£ million

	2001	2002	2003	2004	2005	2006	2007	2008	2009	2010
Resources										
Operating surplus, gross	9796	10289	10807	11312	11927	12634	13231	13963	14675	15500
Taxes on production and imports, received										
Taxes on products										
Value added tax (VAT)	63522	68251	74595	79755	81426	85591	89698	89682	78307	93711
Taxes and duties on imports excluding VAT										
Import duties	-	-	-	-	-	-	-	-	..	
Taxes on imports excluding VAT and import duties	-	-	-	-	-	..	..	..	..	
Taxes on products excluding VAT and import duties	50744	52002	52858	56138	56906	60536	64374	60550	60084	65001
Total taxes on products	114266	120253	127453	135893	138332	146127	154072	150232	138391	158712
Other taxes on production	17565	18113	18517	18853	19706	20831	21532	23069	24194	27931
Total taxes on production and imports, received	131831	138366	145970	154746	158038	166958	175604	173301	162585	186643
less Subsidies, paid										
Subsidies on products	-3954	-4674	-5311	-5126	-5182	-5966	-5609	-5152	-5707	-6564
Other subsidies on production	-662	-954	-1434	-1562	-2449	-3093	-3486	-3381	-3313	-3223
Total	-4616	-5628	-6745	-6688	-7631	-9059	-9095	-8533	-9020	-9787
Property income, received										
Total Interest	7359	6683	7131	6838	6471	7465	8544	10166	7626	5846
Distributed income of corporations	4710	3290	3027	2794	2900	2566	3118	3305	2214	1245
Property income attributed to insurance policy holders	24	18	19	19	27	25	20	24	24	20
Rent										
from sectors other than general government	1919	1901	1565	1182	1229	1226	1233	1164	1174	1172
Total	14012	11892	11742	10833	10627	11282	12915	14659	11038	8283
Total resources	151023	154919	161774	170203	172961	181815	192655	193390	179278	200639
Uses										
Property income, paid										
Total interest	27911	25410	26913	26973	29376	30976	34792	36501	30173	45316
Total	27911	25410	26913	26973	29376	30976	34792	36501	30173	45316
Balance of primary incomes, gross	123112	129509	134861	143230	143585	150839	157863	156889	149105	155323
Total uses	151023	154919	161774	170203	172961	181815	192655	193390	179278	200639
After deduction of fixed capital consumption	-9796	-10289	-10807	-11312	-11927	-12634	-13231	-13963	-14675	-15500
Balance of primary incomes, net	113316	119220	124054	131918	131658	138205	144632	142926	134430	139823

1 See chapter text.

Source: Office for National Statistics: 0207 014 2122

19.9 General government[1] Secondary distribution of income account

United Kingdom. ESA95 sector S.13 Unconsolidated

£ million

		2001	2002	2003	2004	2005	2006	2007	2008	2009	2010
Resources											
Balance of primary incomes, gross	NMZH	123112	129509	134861	143230	143585	150839	157863	156889	149105	155323
Current taxes on income, wealth etc.											
Taxes on income	NMZJ	147264	142842	144234	154127	172498	192600	199851	207597	185160	191342
Other current taxes	NVCM	22068	23664	26016	28001	29443	30908	32697	34032	34888	35847
Total	NMZL	169332	166506	170250	182128	201941	223508	232548	241629	220048	227189
Social contributions											
Actual social contributions											
Employers' actual social contributions	NMZM	38460	38780	45067	49490	52852	56040	60736	64924	63507	65874
Employees' social contributions	NMZN	28725	29568	34376	39062	41836	44391	44091	45570	44072	45406
Social contributions by self- and non-employed persons	NMZO	2183	2318	2595	2727	2825	2930	2861	3053	2879	2576
Total	NMZP	69368	70666	82038	91279	97513	103361	107688	113547	110458	113856
Imputed social contributions	NMZQ	7577	8348	6456	6218	7383	7289	7894	7911	8741	9589
Total	NMZR	76945	79014	88494	97497	104896	110650	115582	121458	119199	123445
Other current transfers											
Non-life insurance claims	NMZS	265	320	276	338	328	349	262	374	345	359
Current transfers within general government	NMZT	72522	77592	85224	94720	101369	110407	113108	117867	124622	132444
Current international cooperation	NMZU	4568	3112	3570	3673	3726	3674	3684	4996	5522	3179
Miscellaneous current transfers											
from sectors other than general government	NMZX	460	502	562	721	728	606	556	508	515	597
Other current transfers	NNAA	77815	81526	89632	99452	106151	115036	117610	123745	131004	136579
Total resources	NNAB	447204	456555	483237	522307	556573	600033	623603	643721	619356	642536
Uses											
Social benefits other than social transfers in kind	NNAD	129591	136801	146066	154313	161422	167045	178407	190187	210806	220725
Other current transfers											
Net non-life insurance premiums	NNAE	265	320	276	338	328	349	262	374	345	359
Current transfers within general government	NNAF	72522	77592	85224	94720	101369	110407	113108	117867	124622	132444
Current international cooperation	NNAG	2190	2362	2433	3080	3255	3632	3930	4292	5011	5683
Miscellaneous current transfers											
to sectors other than general government	NNAI	22131	27351	30275	31178	34355	34695	35878	36301	40364	42419
Of which: GNP based four th own resource	NMFH	3858	5335	6772	7549	8732	8521	8323	8423	10555	10819
Other current transfers	NNAN	97108	107625	118208	129316	139307	149083	153178	158834	170342	180905
Gross Disposable Income	NNAO	219603	211253	218121	237754	254822	282830	290907	293553	237019	239670
Total uses	NNAB	447204	456555	483237	522307	556573	600033	623603	643721	619356	642536
After deduction of fixed capital consumption	-NMXO	-9796	-10289	-10807	-11312	-11927	-12634	-13231	-13963	-14675	-15500
Disposable income, net	NNAP	209807	200964	207314	226442	242895	270196	277676	279590	222344	224170

1 See chapter text.

19.10 Households and non-profit institutions serving households[1] Allocation of primary income account

United Kingdom. ESA95 sectors S.14 and S.15

£million

		2001	2002	2003	2004	2005	2006	2007	2008	2009	2010
Resources											
Operating surplus, gross	**QWLS**	53000	55647	60983	65752	67494	69807	77768	74878	57744	72098
Mixed income, gross	**QWLT**	60638	66316	72316	73335	78487	80432	82898	86376	81424	81047
Compensation of employees											
Wages and salaries	**QWLW**	491862	508771	526814	548875	569632	597548	632122	649858	648904	661379
Employers' social contributions	**QWLX**	72457	78139	89240	96637	107275	115007	119002	120396	127709	138206
Total	**QWLY**	564319	586910	616054	645512	676907	712555	751124	770254	776613	799585
Property income											
Interest	**QWLZ**	31956	26658	27251	34805	40332	43764	55077	50796	9772	9325
Distributed income of corporations	**QWMA**	50496	42517	41042	46828	49241	51397	53406	48551	48019	50750
Attributed property income of insurance policy holders	**QWMC**	53277	52104	54999	54623	64028	66649	71684	75123	66374	63497
Rent	**QWMD**	105	106	108	110	110	110	110	115	115	117
Total	**QWME**	135834	121385	123400	136366	153711	161920	180277	174585	124280	123689
Total resources	**QWMF**	813791	830258	872753	920965	976599	1024714	1092067	1106093	1040061	1076419
Uses											
Property income											
Interest	**QWMG**	33752	30490	31975	43738	50858	55982	74601	67407	7479	5534
Rent	**QWMH**	215	216	220	224	224	226	225	233	239	239
Total	**QWMI**	33967	30706	32195	43962	51082	56208	74826	67640	7718	5773
Balance of primary incomes, gross	**QWMJ**	779824	799552	840558	877003	925517	968506	1017241	1038453	1032343	1070646
Total uses	**QWMF**	813791	830258	872753	920965	976599	1024714	1092067	1106093	1040061	1076419
After deduction of											
fixed capital consumption	**-QWLL**	-32908	-36043	-36903	-42509	-43257	-48584	-51904	-44914	-47375	-46716
Balance of primary incomes, net	**QWMK**	746916	763509	803655	834494	882260	919922	965337	993539	984968	1023930

1 See chapter text.

Source:Office for National Statistics: 01633 451559

19.11 Households and non-profit institutions serving households[1]
Secondary distribution of income account

United Kingdom. ESA95 sectors S.14 and S.15   £million

Resources		2001	2002	2003	2004	2005	2006	2007	2008	2009	2010
Balance of primary incomes, gross	QWMJ	779824	799552	840558	877003	925517	968506	1017241	1038453	1032343	1070646
Imputed social contributions	RVFH	502	530	505	498	506	514	518	524	524	528
Social benefits other than social transfers in kind	QWML	171055	182030	193573	198972	212540	226994	227926	252054	277534	287196
Other current transfers											
Non-life insurance claims	QWMM	11723	17327	13891	17479	17199	19802	14080	20025	18548	19204
Miscellaneous current transfers	QWMN	29080	33041	34687	34845	37840	38729	40518	39654	41648	43550
Total	QWMO	40803	50368	48578	52324	55039	58531	54598	59679	60196	62754
Total resources	QWMP	992184	1032480	1083214	1128797	1193602	1254545	1300283	1350710	1370597	1421124
Uses											
Current taxes on income, wealth etc											
Taxes on income	QWMQ	111888	112171	113087	119591	130200	139685	151528	155284	146111	146064
Other current taxes	NVCO	21166	22788	25174	27077	28421	29833	31586	32885	33699	34611
Total	QWMS	133054	134959	138261	146668	158621	169518	183114	188169	179810	180675
Social contributions											
Actual social contributions											
Employers' actual social contributions	QWMT	60296	64805	77571	85297	94487	102133	105252	105678	111115	123166
Employees' social contributions	QWMU	60599	62458	66490	70264	77929	83203	83411	89181	83428	85874
Social contributions by self and non-employed	QWMV	2183	2318	2595	2727	2825	2930	2861	3053	2879	2576
Total	QWMW	123078	129581	146656	158288	175241	188266	191524	197912	197422	211616
Imputed social contributions	QWMX	12161	13334	11669	11340	12788	12874	13750	14718	16594	15040
Total	QWMY	135239	142915	158325	169628	188029	201140	205274	212630	214016	226656
Social benefits other than social transfers in kind	QWMZ	977	1006	987	987	1000	1010	1014	1020	1020	1024
Other current transfers											
Net non-life insurance premiums	QWNA	11723	17327	13891	17479	17199	19802	14080	20025	18548	19204
Miscellaneous current transfers	QWNB	11081	11458	11930	12462	13442	13286	14405	13771	14060	14381
Total	QWNC	22804	28785	25821	29941	30641	33088	28485	33796	32608	33585
Gross Disposable Income[2]	QWND	700110	724815	759820	781573	815311	849789	882396	915095	943143	979184
Total uses	QWMP	992184	1032480	1083214	1128797	1193602	1254545	1300283	1350710	1370597	1421124
After deduction of fixed capital consumption	-QWLL	-32908	-36043	-36903	-42509	-43257	-48584	-51904	-44914	-47375	-46716
Disposable income, net	QWNE	667202	688772	722917	739064	772054	801205	830492	870181	895768	932468

1 See chapter text.
2 Gross household disposable income revalued by the implied households
and NPISH's final consumption expenditure deflator. For more details see
United Kingdom National Accounts (*the Blue book*).

Source:Office for National Statistics: 01633 451559

19.12 Households and non-profit institutions serving households[1]
Use of disposable income account

United Kingdom. ESA95 sectors S.14 and S.15   £million and percentages

Resources		2001	2002	2003	2004	2005	2006	2007	2008	2009	2010
Disposable income, gross	QWND	700110	724815	759820	781573	815311	849789	882396	915095	943143	979184
Adjustment for the change in net equity											
of households in pension funds	NSSE	16038	17784	21377	26386	30881	29343	38871	27842	26547	35105
Total resources	NSSF	716148	742599	781197	807959	846192	879132	921267	942937	969690	1014289
Uses											
Final consumption expenditure											
Individual consumption expenditure	NSSG	672481	707071	742180	778804	814973	851572	896566	913791	894105	937906
Saving, gross	NSSH	43667	35528	39017	29155	31219	27560	24701	29146	75585	76383
Total uses	NSSF	716148	742599	781197	807959	846192	879132	921267	942937	969690	1014289
Saving ratio (percentages)	RVGL	6.1	4.8	5	3.6	3.7	3.1	2.7	3.1	7.8	7.5

1 See chapter text.

Source:Office for National Statistics: 01633 451559

19.13 The sector accounts: key economic indicators[1]

United Kingdom

£million

		2001	2002	2003	2004	2005	2006	2007	2008	2009	2010
Net lending/borrowing by:											
Non-financial corporations	EABO	-6657	14749	28670	39532	37967	40086	38279	31231	50880	61215
Financial corporations	NHCQ	-21706	4062	11011	17533	7110	2649	23611	52755	46332	17706
General government	NNBK	7634	-20163	-40965	-41707	-40341	-35020	-38331	-70457	-151967	-150151
Households and NPISH's	NSSZ	985	-16120	-15632	-38188	-35899	-49834	-55821	-30040	38084	32757
Rest of the world	NHRB	19744	17469	16914	22826	31164	42120	32260	16512	16679	33018
Private non-financial corporations											
Gross trading profits											
Continental shelf profits	CAGD	17112	16038	15331	16029	19299	22352	23309	27851	21256	32926
Others	CAED	153311	160468	172079	188092	192831	209067	220310	209870	196111	198987
Rental of buildings	FCBW	11904	13818	14709	15288	16882	17005	19233	22353	21317	22562
less Holding gains of inventories	-DLQZ	605	-2992	-4226	-2659	-4201	-4115	-4857	-4814	-5248	-8401
Gross operating surplus	NRJK	182932	187332	197893	216750	224811	244309	257995	255260	233436	246074
Households and NPISH											
Household gross disposable income	QWND	700110	724815	759820	781573	815311	849789	882396	915095	943143	979184
Implied deflator of household and NPISH individual consumption expenditure indicies (2003=100)	YBFS	85.8	86.4	88	89.6	91.8	94.3	96.7	100	101.4	105.3
Real household disposable income:											
Chained volume measures (Reference year 2003)	RVGK	816438	838455	863663	872030	887943	901557	912788	915095	929792	930323
Indices (2003=100)	OSXR	89.2	91.6	94.4	95.3	97	98.5	99.7	100	101.6	101.7
Gross saving	NSSH	43667	35528	39017	29155	31219	27560	24701	29146	75585	76383
Households total resources	NSSJ	835866	874602	924846	955710	1005387	1051621	1103029	1137558	1176603	1227053
Saving ratio (percentages)	RVGL	6.1	4.8	5	3.6	3.7	3.1	2.7	3.1	7.8	7.5

1 See chapter text.

Source: Office for National Statistics: 01633 456660

19.14 Household final consumption expenditure: by purpose[1]
Current market prices

United Kingdom £million

		2001	2002	2003	2004	2005	2006	2007	2008	2009	2010
Durable goods											
Furnishings, household equipment and routine maintenance of the house	LLIJ	18929	20115	21208	21216	21674	21992	23092	22414	20032	20082
Health	LLIK	2110	2399	2719	2513	2420	2801	2969	3034	3135	2872
Transport	LLIL	36565	37100	37997	39024	38422	38238	40247	36652	36977	38888
Communication	LLIM	630	630	732	684	728	760	717	761	839	714
Recreation and culture	LLIN	16477	16473	17065	19211	20210	21846	22647	23444	22887	24047
Miscellaneous goods and services	LLIO	3930	4428	4540	4976	4828	5394	5140	5108	4761	5521
Total durable goods	UTIA	78641	81145	84261	87624	88282	91031	94812	91413	88631	92124
Semi-durable goods											
Clothing and footwear	LLJL	35071	37600	39819	41775	43120	46027	47424	48271	47040	49760
Furnishings, household equipment and routine maintenance of the house	LLJM	11855	13062	13572	13046	12964	13717	14200	13146	13015	13269
Transport	LLJN	3064	3339	3745	3396	3832	3849	3820	4176	4244	3879
Recreation and culture	LLJO	22746	24944	26638	27487	26683	27046	29156	28680	26305	26822
Miscellaneous goods and services	LLJP	2378	2769	3295	3498	3320	3475	3335	2998	3812	4831
Total semi-durable goods	UTIQ	75114	81714	87069	89202	89919	94114	97935	97271	94416	98561
Non-durable goods											
Food & drink	ABZV	60814	62360	64712	66362	69547	72202	75706	79790	81185	83401
Alcohol & tobacco	ADFL	24782	25707	26973	28359	28511	28658	29258	29885	29906	31532
Housing, water, electricity, gas and other fuels	LLIX	23008	23382	24175	28502	32136	36504	38570	45215	44753	46919
Furnishings, household equipment and routine maintenance of the house	LLIY	3034	3263	3388	3564	3609	3813	3772	3770	4088	4061
Health	LLIZ	3877	4105	4057	4285	4371	4513	4715	4765	4949	5070
Transport	LLJA	19836	19457	20345	22579	24695	25846	28090	30665	27884	32503
Recreation and culture	LLJB	12952	13316	13155	14105	14615	15594	15793	16143	14889	14884
Miscellaneous goods and services	LLJC	10265	11654	12989	13503	13726	14763	15383	15101	14586	14681
Total non-durable goods	UTII	158568	163244	169794	181259	191210	201893	211287	225334	222240	233051
Total goods	UTIE	312323	326103	341124	358085	369411	387038	404034	414018	405287	423736
Services											
Clothing and footwear	LLJD	771	790	776	720	770	838	893	1021	1044	910
Housing, water, electricity, gas and other fuels	LLJE	93341	99226	107626	115230	121335	127209	137300	144296	150927	166446
Furnishings, household equipment and routine maintenance of the house	LLJF	5108	5293	5621	5731	5976	6037	6021	6439	5916	7695
Health	LLJG	4425	4630	4896	5279	5648	6192	6901	6435	7005	7254
Transport	LLJH	37489	39972	41752	43898	47402	50223	53607	53422	53160	54598
Communication	LLJI	13442	14095	15076	15097	16144	15726	16415	15877	15826	17152
Recreation and culture	LLJJ	21772	24029	25578	27180	29215	30782	32651	32636	33155	34393
Education	ADIE	10143	10645	10806	10944	11408	12213	12987	13163	13451	13837
Restaurants and hotels	ADIF	68150	72565	74886	77153	79922	82060	84974	86353	82092	87391
Miscellaneous goods and services	LLJK	71355	73120	74456	78351	84958	89457	94247	90875	80868	78759
Total services	UTIM	325996	344365	361473	379583	402778	420737	445996	450517	443444	468435
Final consumption expenditure in the UK by resident and non-resident households **(domestic concept)**	ABQI	638319	670468	702597	737668	772189	807775	850030	864535	848731	892171
Final consumption expenditure outside the UK by UK resident households	ABTA	22351	23967	25984	27547	29026	30388	31701	33286	29063	29203
less Final consumption expenditure in the UK by households resident in the rest of the world	CDFD	-13300	-13786	-14069	-15608	-17066	-18999	-19489	-19797	-19552	-21170
Final consumption expenditure by UK resident households in the UK and abroad (national concept)	ABPB	647370	680649	714512	749607	784149	819164	862242	878024	858242	900204

1. Additional detail is published in Consumer Trends and table A7 of UK Economic Accounts, available from the ONS website
http://www.ons.gov.uk/ons/publications/all-releases.html?definition=tcm%3A77-23619

Source:Office for National Statistics: 01633 455889

19.15 Household final consumption expenditure: by purpose[1] Chained volume measures, reference year 2005

United Kingdom

£ million

		2001	2002	2003	2004	2005	2006	2007	2008	2009	2010
Durable goods											
Furnishings, household equipment and routine maintenance of the house	LLME	19390	20658	21902	21935	22367	22855	23626	22414	19357	18803
Health	LLMF	2188	2436	2749	2544	2448	2864	3000	3034	3124	2832
Transport	LLMG	37561	37757	37956	38054	37511	37381	39166	36652	37860	36490
Communication	LLMH	571	565	653	619	676	706	695	761	833	678
Recreation and culture	LLMI	6918	7507	8656	10801	13058	16033	19247	23444	24910	27653
Miscellaneous goods and services	LLMJ	4594	5189	5180	5616	5503	5892	5425	5108	4519	4911
Total durable goods	UTIC	65473	68450	72100	75949	79195	84333	90485	91413	90603	91367
Semi-durable goods											
Clothing and footwear	LLNG	24187	28016	30886	34079	37102	41284	44214	48271	51015	54500
Furnishings, household equipment and routine maintenance of the house	LLNH	10555	11839	12613	12249	12612	13656	14163	13146	12795	12709
Transport	LLNI	3413	3678	4072	3641	4034	3948	3903	4176	4110	3607
Recreation and culture	LLNJ	18184	20622	23180	24933	24964	26038	28429	28680	26749	27375
Miscellaneous goods and services	LLNK	2284	2729	3289	3595	3427	3587	3379	2998	3769	4824
Total semi-durable goods	UTIS	57897	66178	73244	77998	81783	88291	93933	97271	98438	103015
Non-durable goods											
Food & drink	ADIP	73741	75128	77111	78579	81167	82276	82534	79790	76986	76627
Alcohol & tobacco	ADIS	29028	29574	29992	31203	30973	30317	30215	29885	28701	29087
Housing, water, electricity, gas and other fuels	LLMS	40282	40291	41002	46036	47186	45487	44596	45215	41632	44270
Furnishings, household equipment and routine maintenance of the house	LLMT	3084	3322	3536	3877	3940	4026	3900	3770	3809	3670
Health	LLMU	3907	4130	4060	4315	4448	4611	4756	4765	4871	4909
Transport	LLMV	28389	28818	29032	30536	30818	30650	32371	30665	30142	29249
Recreation and culture	LLMW	14572	14849	14381	15210	15680	16350	16345	16143	14322	13721
Miscellaneous goods and services	LLMX	10025	11664	13235	14095	14464	15322	15635	15101	14202	13949
Total non-durable goods	UTIK	202303	207784	212693	223375	228151	229026	230370	225334	214665	215482
Total goods	UTIG	317481	336404	353846	373219	385673	399890	414189	414018	403706	409864
Services											
Clothing and footwear	LLMY	959	959	913	824	847	891	920	1021	1022	872
Housing, water, electricity, gas and other fuels	LLMZ	129700	132532	137511	138463	138322	140063	142740	144296	144610	146423
Furnishings, household equipment and routine maintenance of the house	LLNA	7110	6975	7036	6816	6807	6611	6292	6439	5808	7395
Health	LLNB	5781	5759	5855	6175	6297	6599	7084	6435	6716	6713
Transport	LLNC	48694	50224	50676	51404	53272	54378	55846	53422	51668	51663
Communication	LLND	12546	13051	13879	13998	15331	14875	16019	15877	15651	16185
Recreation and culture	LLNE	28233	29450	30350	31501	32666	32948	33646	32636	31902	31866
Education	ADMJ	17240	17128	16159	15621	15522	15525	14508	13163	12480	12190
Restaurants and hotels	ADMK	86694	88762	89128	89557	89403	88453	88342	86353	80131	83473
Miscellaneous goods and services	LLNF	84947	88851	88781	89254	92002	91918	94337	90875	86745	84068
Total services	UTIO	420461	432611	439447	442922	450212	451886	459717	450517	436733	440848
Final consumption expenditure in the UK by resident and non-resident households (domestic concept)	ABQJ	733190	765392	790906	815148	835256	851605	873882	864535	840439	850712
Final consumption expenditure outside the UK by UK resident households *less Final consumption expenditure in the UK*	ABTC	30627	32663	32840	35235	34807	35813	37327	33286	25932	25140
by households resident in the rest of the world	CCHX	-15360	-15738	-15767	-17202	-18386	-19950	-19888	-19797	-19410	-20550
Final consumption expenditure by UK resident households in the UK and abroad (national concept)	ABPF	748122	781860	807653	832690	851338	867082	890872	878024	846961	855302

1 See chapter text. Additional detail is published in Consumer Trends and table A7 of UK Economic Accounts, available from the National Statistics websitehttp://www.ons.gov.uk/ons/publications/all-releases.html?definition=tcm%3A77-23619

Source:Office for National Statistics: 01633 455889

19.16 Individual consumption expenditure: by households, NPISHs and general government[1]

Current market prices United Kingdom. Classified by function (COICOP/COPNI/COFOG)[2]   £ million

		2001	2002	2003	2004	2005	2006	2007	2008	2009	2010
FINAL CONSUMPTION EXPENDITURE OF HOUSEHOLDS											
Food and non-alcoholic beverages	ABZV	60814	62360	64712	66362	69547	72202	75706	79790	81185	83401
Food	ABZW	53596	54990	56993	58221	60907	63165	66530	70519	71621	73506
Non-alcoholic beverages	ADFK	7218	7370	7719	8141	8640	9037	9176	9271	9564	9895
Alcoholic beverages and tobacco	ADFL	24782	25707	26973	28359	28511	28658	29258	29885	29906	31532
Alcoholic beverages	ADFM	10360	11148	11710	13062	13146	13034	13596	14146	14159	14510
Tobacco	ADFN	14422	14559	15263	15297	15365	15624	15662	15739	15747	17022
Clothing and footwear	ADFP	35842	38390	40595	42495	43890	46865	48317	49292	48084	50670
Clothing	ADFQ	31070	33181	35007	36518	37758	40185	41440	42195	41124	43116
Footwear	ADFR	4772	5209	5588	5977	6132	6680	6877	7097	6960	7554
Housing, water, electricity, gas and other fuels	ADFS	116349	122608	131801	143732	153471	163713	175870	189511	195680	213365
Actual rentals for housing	ADFT	25634	27141	30005	32878	33975	35486	39532	42055	43303	47796
Imputed rentals for housing	ADFU	59566	63397	68567	73067	77440	80707	86265	91054	96593	107612
Maintenance and repair of the dwelling	ADFV	11418	12072	12623	13804	13734	13737	13719	13904	13297	13057
Water supply and miscellaneous dwelling services	ADFW	5078	5304	5599	5884	6366	6905	7517	7455	7741	8202
Electricity, gas and other fuels	ADFX	14653	14694	15007	18099	21956	26878	28837	35043	34746	36698
Furnishings, household equipment and routine maintenance of the house	ADFY	38926	41733	43789	43557	44223	45559	47085	45769	43051	45107
Furniture, furnishings, carpets and other floor coverings	ADFZ	14139	15268	16387	16186	16241	16559	17527	16454	15057	14663
Household textiles	ADGG	4479	4961	5271	4787	4476	4699	5188	5051	5333	5543
Household appliances	ADGL	5698	5732	5589	6117	6357	6385	6290	6308	5770	6358
Glassware, tableware and household utensils	ADGM	4350	4588	4608	4332	4653	4759	4492	4292	4058	4070
Tools and equipment for house and garden	ADGN	2912	3338	3618	3536	3591	3947	4396	3966	3337	3256
Goods and services for routine household maintenance	ADGO	7348	7846	8316	8599	8905	9210	9192	9698	9496	11217
Health	ADGP	10412	11134	11672	12077	12439	13506	14585	14234	15089	15196
Medical products, appliances and equipment	ADGQ	5987	6504	6776	6798	6791	7314	7684	7799	8084	7942
Out-patient services	ADGR	2454	2449	2591	2923	3145	3567	4188	3639	3889	4123
Hospital services	ADGS	1971	2181	2305	2356	2503	2625	2713	2796	3116	3131
Transport	ADGT	96954	99868	103839	108897	114351	118156	125764	124915	122265	129868
Purchase of vehicles	ADGU	36565	37100	37997	39024	38422	38238	40247	36652	36977	38888
Operation of personal transport equipment	ADGV	38031	39587	41279	43956	48213	50242	53332	56699	54700	60127
Transport services	ADGW	22358	23181	24563	25917	27716	29676	32185	31564	30588	30853
Communication	ADGX	14072	14725	15808	15781	16872	16486	17132	16638	16665	17866
Postal services	CDEF	1022	1057	1040	1098	1165	1131	1149	1083	1067	1026
Telephone & telefax equipment	ADWO	630	630	732	684	728	760	717	761	839	714
Telephone & telefax services	ADWP	12420	13038	14036	13999	14979	14595	15266	14794	14759	16126
Recreation and culture	ADGY	73947	78762	82436	87983	90723	95268	100247	100903	97236	100146
Audio-visual, photographic and information processing equipment	ADGZ	17490	17921	18385	20894	21443	22129	22040	22370	20471	21257
Other major durables for recreation and culture	ADHL	4935	4809	5314	5544	5843	6244	6548	6919	7408	7853
Other recreational items and equipment; flower garden and pets	ADHZ	21236	23585	24906	24942	24763	25518	28683	28765	27578	28554
Recreational and cultural services	ADIA	20083	22317	23798	25225	26810	28533	30065	30289	30485	31526
Newspapers, books and stationery	ADIC	10203	10130	10033	11378	11864	12844	12911	12560	11294	10956
Package holidays[3]	ADID	0	0	0	0	0	0	0	0	0	0
Education											
Education services	ADIE	10143	10645	10806	10944	11408	12213	12987	13163	13451	13837
Restaurants and hotels	ADIF	68150	72565	74886	77153	79922	82060	84974	86353	82092	87391
Catering services	ADIG	58783	62797	64893	67275	69418	71091	73024	73878	70330	73874
Accommodation services	ADIH	9367	9768	9993	9878	10504	10969	11950	12475	11762	13517
Miscellaneous goods and services	ADII	87928	91971	95280	100328	106832	113089	118105	114082	104027	103792
Personal care	ADIJ	15113	16903	18615	19819	20084	21122	21734	21369	21111	21675
Personal effects not elsewhere classified	ADIK	5633	6370	6740	7026	6870	7794	7410	7245	7520	9225
Social protection	ADIL	8963	9131	9427	9475	9948	10569	10962	12117	13098	13791
Insurance	ADIM	21046	22007	20917	21683	23217	23106	24837	22169	23659	21922
Financial services not elsewhere classified	ADIN	31035	31693	33240	35316	39289	43289	45612	43664	31458	30204
Other services not elsewhere classified	ADIO	6138	5867	6341	7009	7424	7209	7550	7518	7181	6975

19.16 Individual consumption expenditure: by households, NPISHs and general government[1]

Current market prices United Kingdom. Classified by function (COICOP/COPNI/COFOG)[2]

£ million

		2001	2002	2003	2004	2005	2006	2007	2008	2009	2010
Final consumption expenditure in the UK by resident and non-resident households **(domestic concept)**	**ABQI**	638319	670468	702597	737668	772189	807775	850030	864535	848731	892171
Final consumption expenditure outside the UK by UK resident households	**ABTA**	22351	23967	25984	27547	29026	30388	31701	33286	29063	29203
less Final consumption expenditure in the UK by households resident in the rest of the world	**CDFD**	-13300	-13786	-14069	-15608	-17066	-18999	-19489	-19797	-19552	-21170
Final consumption expenditure by UK resident households in the UK and abroad (national concept)	**ABPB**	647370	680649	714512	749607	784149	819164	862242	878024	858242	900204
FINAL CONSUMPTION EXPENDITURE OF UK RESIDENT HOUSEHOLDS Final consumption expenditure of UK resident households in the UK and abroad	**ABPB**	647370	680649	714512	749607	784149	819164	862242	878024	858242	900204
FINAL INDIVIDUAL CONSUMPTION EXPENDITURE OF NPISH											
Final individual consumption expenditure of NPISH	**ABNV**	25111	26422	27668	29197	30824	32408	34324	35767	35863	37702
FINAL INDIVIDUAL CONSUMPTION EXPENDITURE OF OF GENERAL GOVERNMENT											
Health	**IWX5**	57895	63219	69838	76027	81733	89403	94233	101562	109958	112717
Recreation and culture	**IWX6**	6687	7370	7797	4974	5550	5801	5852	6048	6207	6215
Education	**IWX7**	35282	39045	40361	41891	45070	48632	51992	55330	58371	60902
Social protection	**IWX9**	19441	22369	25383	24859	26842	28653	29685	31681	32377	32930
Housing	**QYXO**	–	–	–	–	–	–	–	–	–	–
Final individual consumption expenditure of general government	**NNAQ**	119718	132003	143649	147751	159195	172489	181762	194621	206913	212764
Total, individual consumption expenditure/ actual individual consumption	**NQEO**	792199	839074	885829	926555	974168	1024061	1078328	1108412	1101018	1150670

1 See chapter text.

Source:Office for National Statistics: 01633 455889

2 "Purpose" or "function" classifications are designed to indicate the "soci-economic objectives" that institutional units aim to achieve through various kinds of outlays. COICOP is the Classification of Individual Consumption by Purpose and applies to households. COPNI is the Classification of the Purposes of Non-Profit Institutions Serving Households and COFOG the Classification of the Functions of Government. The introduction of ESA95 coincides with the redefinition of these classifications and data will be available on a consistent basis for all European Union member states.

3 Package holidays data are dispersed between components (transport etc).

19.17 Individual consumption expenditure: by households, NPISHs and general government[1] Chained volume measures, reference year 2005

United Kingdom. Classified by function (COICOP/COPNI/COFOG)[2]

£ million

		2001	2002	2003	2004	2005	2006	2007	2008	2009	2010
FINAL CONSUMPTION EXPENDITURE OF HOUSEHOLDS											
Food and non-alcoholic beverages	ADIP	73741	75128	77111	78579	81167	82276	82534	79790	76986	76627
Food	ADIQ	65957	67156	68708	69565	71581	72626	73132	70519	67834	67700
Non-alcoholic beverages	ADIR	7858	8043	8452	9022	9574	9643	9415	9271	9152	8927
Alcoholic beverages and tobacco	ADIS	29028	29574	29992	31203	30973	30317	30215	29885	28701	29087
Alcoholic beverages	ADIT	10639	11467	11882	13413	13719	13438	13986	14146	13461	13611
Tobacco	ADIU	18882	18437	18387	17881	17288	16911	16232	15739	15240	15476
Clothing and footwear	ADIW	24984	28854	31720	34878	37936	42172	45135	49292	52037	55372
Clothing	ADIX	21174	24525	26984	29695	32353	35840	38509	42195	44834	47497
Footwear	ADIY	3831	4340	4746	5191	5587	6345	6630	7097	7203	7875
Housing, water, electricity, gas and other fuels	ADIZ	170304	173295	179148	184195	184957	185403	187346	189511	186242	190693
Actual rentals for housing	ADJA	33525	34418	37005	38048	37899	38486	40354	42055	41448	41977
Imputed rentals for housing	ADJB	84570	86365	88792	88988	88921	89431	90298	91054	92383	93737
Maintenance and repair of the dwelling	ADJC	14243	14630	14876	15870	15422	15054	14417	13904	12831	12100
Water supply and miscellaneous dwelling services	ADJD	7548	7704	7833	7821	7692	7809	8001	7455	7359	7713
Electricity, gas and other fuels	ADJE	29967	29314	29368	33049	35361	34767	34276	35043	32221	35166
Furnishings, household equipment and routine maintenance of the house	ADJF	39724	42598	44968	44754	45632	47132	48002	45769	41769	42577
Furniture, furnishings, carpets and other floor coverings	ADJG	15360	16523	17644	17316	17182	17412	18102	16454	14655	13890
Household textiles	ADJH	3711	4229	4584	4172	4070	4479	5079	5051	5320	5463
Household appliances	ADJI	5031	5150	5182	5784	6127	6438	6289	6308	5455	5773
Glassware, tableware and household utensils	ADJJ	4121	4364	4431	4208	4697	4885	4543	4292	3957	3819
Tools and equipment for house and garden	ADJK	2679	3131	3572	3557	3697	4029	4436	3966	3265	3081
Goods and services for routine household maintenance	ADJL	9060	9354	9704	9901	10006	9955	9563	9698	9117	10551
Health	ADJM	11826	12331	12680	13028	13180	14072	14833	14234	14711	14454
Medical products, appliances and equipment	ADJN	6095	6564	6805	6858	6895	7475	7756	7799	7995	7741
Out-patient services	ADJO	2899	2807	2916	3299	3394	3702	4226	3639	3787	3947
Hospital services	ADJP	2926	3016	2991	2897	2922	2904	2849	2796	2929	2766
Transport	ADJQ	118656	120990	122269	123866	125702	126399	131308	124915	123780	121009
Purchase of vehicles	ADJR	37561	37757	37956	38054	37511	37381	39166	36652	37860	36490
Operation of personal transport equipment	ADJS	54083	55991	55714	56260	57704	57160	58609	56699	56215	55132
Transport services	ADJT	26649	27095	28331	29314	30493	31839	33436	31564	29705	29387
Communication	ADJU	13117	13616	14533	14616	16007	15582	16714	16638	16484	16863
Postal services	CCGZ	1443	1486	1418	1454	1486	1329	1223	1083	979	889
Telephone & telefax equipment	ADQF	570	565	653	618	676	706	695	761	833	678
Telephone & telefax services	ADQG	11250	11713	12559	12651	13929	13597	14808	14794	14672	15296
Recreation and culture	ADJV	62150	66888	71924	78879	83799	89923	97013	100903	97883	100615
Audio-visual, photographic and information processing equipment	ADJW	6814	7598	8752	11219	13324	15702	18241	22370	23351	26145
Other major durables for recreation and culture	ADJX	5584	5324	5714	5770	6009	6413	6679	6919	7159	7250
Other recreational items and equipment; flowers, gardens and pets	ADJY	17965	20650	22888	23607	23881	25158	28514	28765	27079	27774
Recreational and cultural services	ADJZ	26163	27406	28278	29258	29983	30521	30933	30289	29353	29234
Newspapers, books and stationery	ADKM	11959	11639	11168	12425	12888	13544	13423	12560	10941	10212
Package holidays[3]	ADMI										
Education											
Education services	ADMJ	17240	17128	16159	15621	15522	15525	14508	13163	12480	12190
Restaurants and Hotels	ADMK	86694	88762	89128	89557	89403	88453	88342	86353	80131	83473
Catering services	ADML	74536	76525	77040	78099	77870	76921	76163	73878	68316	70127
Accommodation services	ADMM	12217	12290	12135	11489	11565	11562	12191	12475	11815	13346
Miscellaneous goods and services	ADMN	101059	107875	110306	112540	115348	116678	118768	114082	109235	107752
Personal care	ADMO	15981	17972	19833	21267	21463	22123	22205	21369	20618	20649
Personal effects not elsewhere classified	ADMP	6178	7052	7355	7686	7571	8358	7719	7245	7260	8659
Social protection	ADMQ	13065	12562	12251	11666	11553	11655	11467	12117	12522	12778
Insurance	ADMR	27808	29101	26712	26294	26622	25031	25787	22169	22600	19727
Financial services not elsewhere classified	ADMS	31089	34327	36355	37255	39693	41655	43673	43664	39206	39301
Other services not elsewhere classified	ADMT	9467	8519	8821	9148	9066	8159	8067	7518	7029	6638

19.17 Individual consumption expenditure: by households, NPISHs and general government[1] Chained volume measures, reference year 2005

United Kingdom. Classified by function (COICOP/COPNI/COFOG)[2]

£ million

		2001	2002	2003	2004	2005	2006	2007	2008	2009	2010
Final consumption expenditure in the UK by resident and non-resident households (domestic concept)	ABQJ	733190	765392	790906	815148	835256	851605	873882	864535	840439	850712
Final consumption expenditure outside the UK by UK resident households	ABTC	30627	32663	32840	35235	34807	35813	37327	33286	25932	25140
less Final consumption expenditure in the UK by households resident in the rest of the world	CCHX	-15360	-15738	-15767	-17202	-18386	-19950	-19888	-19797	-19410	-20550
Final consumption expenditure by UK resident households in the UK and abroad (national concept)	ABPF	748122	781860	807653	832690	851338	867082	890872	878024	846961	855302
FINAL CONSUMPTION EXPENDITURE OF UK RESIDENT HOUSEHOLDS											
Final consumption expenditure of UK resident households in the UK and abroad	ABPF	748122	781860	807653	832690	851338	867082	890872	878024	846961	855302
FINAL INDIVIDUAL CONSUMPTION EXPENDITURE OF NPISH Final individual consumption expenditure of NPISH	ABNU	37037	36615	36266	36441	36334	36421	36582	35767	34487	35803
FINAL INDIVIDUAL CONSUMPTION OF GENERAL GOVERNMENT											
Health	K4CP	78495	81420	84488	88076	91063	94279	98295	101562	100932	104918
Recreation and culture	K4CQ	5108	5479	5623	5830	6170	6237	6144	6048	5790	5686
Education	K4CR	47338	50161	52971	55972	55945	55729	55647	55330	51651	51712
Social protection	K4CS	28661	30152	31347	32404	32355	32456	31963	31681	29897	29614
Housing	QYXN	–	–	–	–	–	–	–	–	–	–
Final individual consumption expenditure of general government	NSZK	166421	172082	176681	181706	185163	188485	191998	194621	188270	191930
Total, individual consumption expenditure/ actual individual consumption	YBIO	950375	989940	1020298	1050668	1072795	1091991	1119538	1108412	1069718	1083035

1 See chapter text.

Source:Office for National Statistics: 01633 455889

2 "Purpose" or "function" classifications are designed to indicate the "socio-economic objectives" that institutional units aim to achieve through various kinds of outlays. COICOP is the Classification of Individual Consumption by Purpose and applies to households. COPNI is the Classification of the Purposes of Non-Profit Institutions Serving Households (NPISH) and COFOG the Classification of the Functions of Government. The introduction of ESA95 coincides with the redefinition of these classifications and data will be available on a consistent basis for all European Union member states.

3 Package holidays data are dispersed between components (transport etc).

19.18 Change in inventories[1,2]
Chained volume measures, reference year 2008

United Kingdom   £ million

	Manufacturing industries					Distributive trades				
	Mining and quarrying FADO	Materials and fuel FBID	Work in progress FBIE	Finished goods FBIF	Total DHBH	Electricity, gas and water supply FADP	Wholesale[3] FAJM	Retail[3] FBYH	Other industries[4] DLWV	Change in inventories ABMQ
2001	587	-1301	1067	996	762	-737	4731	3448	-804	7989
2002	181	-301	-143	773	329	88	401	3541	-2678	1862
2003	-32	-917	-327	-34	-1278	-320	345	4716	1610	5044
2004	-304	100	-1076	-587	-1563	-388	-37	2489	5147	5345
2005	-382	1089	604	415	2109	-299	-2581	2550	3527	4925
2006	-30	-519	-903	403	-1018	555	1396	2100	1197	4200
2007	82	585	-119	521	987	110	620	2823	3175	7798
2008	340	-238	-722	-311	-1269	152	-1288	1249	2525	1710
2009	-557	-403	-81	-1118	-1601	2130	-1876	-87	-10481	-12474
2010	194	1817	-444	2011	3385	75	-111	-1248	2643	4940

1 See chapter text. Estimates are given to the nearest £ million but cannot be regarded as accurate to this degree.

2 Components may not sum to totals due to rounding.

3 Wholesaling and retailing estimates exclude the motor trades.

4 Quarterly alignment adjustment included in this series.

Source: Office for National Statistics: 01633 455644

19.19 Gross fixed capital formation at current purchasers' prices:
by broad sector and type of asset[1,2]

United Kingdom. Total economy   £ million

		2001	2002	2003	2004	2005	2006	2007	2008	2009	2010
Private sector											
New dwellings, excluding land	DFDF	29725	35277	40664	47918	51390	54870	58660	52237	39071	40307
Other buildings and structures	EQBU	34946	30534	30784	32118	35668	40949	47937	50499	41015	39425
Transport equipment	EQBV	14896	17070	15440	13035	12634	13836	13468	12981	11560	16150
Other machinery and equipment and cultivated assets	EQBW	52115	51352	49740	49187	49153	50319	55672	54021	44973	46410
Intangible fixed assets	EQBX	12924	13590	14321	14468	14716	15124	15816	16415	15863	16050
Costs associated with the transfer of ownership of non-produced assets	EQBY	10463	13427	13444	19227	18495	22933	26031	15055	11469	14190
Total	EQBZ	155069	161251	164393	175951	182056	198031	217582	201208	163951	172533
Public non-financial corporations											
New dwellings, excluding land	KNG2	1634	1937	980	722	4124	3299	3657	4096	4379	4577
Other buildings and structures	DEES	947	1165	490	233	1766	1045	1114	779	1020	652
Transport equipment	DEEP	87	56	28	30	280	103	95	222	231	416
Other machinery and equipment and cultivated assets	DEEQ	319	398	227	163	13790	563	793	1539	1774	1699
Intangible fixed assets	DLXJ	196	274	133	112	615	429	489	660	772	797
Costs associated with the transfer of ownership of non-produced assets	DLXQ	-2254	-2764	-5674	-5440	-2675	-2375	-2032	-1106	-262	
Total	FCCJ	3183	3830	1857	1260	20575	5440	6148	7296	8177	8141
General government											
New dwellings, excluding land	KNG3	78	69	55	103	53	9	3	15	1	-8
Other buildings and structures	EQCH	10184	11493	16026	17619	20410	20220	22517	28155	30955	29148
Transport equipment	EQCI	602	577	736	1063	669	496	548	518	607	649
Other machinery and equipment and cultivated assets	EQCJ	2312	2932	3167	3903	-14388	2519	2821	3829	5159	6037
Intangible fixed assets	EQCK	358	381	525	531	348	457	417	342	402	608
Total	NNBF	13533	15452	20509	23219	7091	23701	26306	32860	37125	36434
Total gross fixed capital formation	NPQX	171785	180533	186759	200430	209722	227172	250036	241364	209253	217108

1 See chapter text.

2 Components may not sum to totals due to rounding.

Source: Office for National Statistics: 01633 455644

19.20 Gross fixed capital formation at current purchasers' prices: by type of asset[1,2]

United Kingdom. Total economy

£ million

		2001	2002	2003	2004	2005	2006	2007	2008	2009	2010
Tangible fixed assets											
New dwellings, excluding land	DFDK	31023	36782	41487	48525	54434	57192	61112	55449	42683	43931
Other buildings and structures	DLWS	46077	43192	47300	49970	57844	62215	71567	79433	72990	69225
Transport equipment	DLWZ	15584	17703	16204	14128	13582	14435	14110	13721	12398	17215
Other machinery and equipment and cultivated assets	DLXI	54041	53851	52250	52465	47832	52555	58345	58126	50434	52565
Total	EQCQ	147430	152359	158125	165875	174415	187243	206074	207993	179977	184518
Intangible fixed assets	DLXP	13478	14245	14979	15110	15678	16009	16723	17417	17038	17456
Costs associated with the transfer of ownership of non-produced assets	DFBH	10877	13929	13656	19444	19629	23920	27238	15954	12238	15134
Total gross fixed capital formation	NPQX	171785	180533	186759	200430	209722	227172	250036	241364	209253	217108

1 See chapter text.

2 Components may not sum to totals due to rounding.

Source: Office for National Statistics: 01633 455644

19.21 Gross fixed capital formation: by broad sector and type of asset[1,2,3] Chained volume measures, reference year 2008

United Kingdom. Total economy

£ million

		2001	2002	2003	2004	2005	2006	2007	2008	2009	2010
Private sector											
New dwellings, excluding land	DFDP	42025	46314	49745	54867	54711	56941	59423	52237	40362	40755
Other buildings and structures	EQCU	37123	31740	32175	32530	36011	41183	48052	50499	45293	43424
Transport equipment	EQCV	16089	18569	16714	14040	13438	14546	14155	12981	10381	13912
Other machinery and equipment and cultivated assets	EQCW	45318	46929	46385	47571	48681	50524	56540	54021	47253	47914
Intangible fixed assets	EQCX	14753	14621	15431	15580	15544	15758	16129	16415	15362	15270
Costs associated with the transfer of ownership of non-produced assets	EQCY	19175	21865	19303	26589	23858	25972	26132	15055	14232	16558
Total	EQCZ	173918	177994	178088	187997	190429	203294	219316	201208	172882	177833
Public non-financial corporations											
New dwellings, excluding land	KNG7	2198	2458	1174	855	4772	3696	3785	4096	−2724	−2911
Other buildings and structures	DEEX	1324	1564	647	289	2125	1197	1199	779	1076	697
Transport equipment	DEEU	93	57	27	30	284	103	93	222	230	384
Other machinery and equipment and cultivated assets	DEEV	262	340	199	147	13043	582	817	1539	1687	1598
Intangible fixed assets	EQDE	245	336	159	127	687	464	506	660	762	770
Total	EQDG	1182	1490	1102	1477	21620	5754	6424	7296	1031	538
General government											
New dwellings and transfer costs	KNG8	89	77	59	111	57	9	3	15	–	-9
Other buildings and structures	EQDI	13953	15199	20346	21368	23021	21600	23137	28155	29676	29697
Transport equipment	EQDJ	439	373	444	518	582	522	496	518	536	534
Other machinery and equipment and cultivated assets	EQDK	1760	2356	2566	3251	-13162	2611	3061	3829	4548	5339
Intangible fixed assets	EQDL	241	249	596	580	371	482	431	342	378	554
Total	EQDN	17973	19616	24982	26376	9850	25304	26987	32860	35137	36115
Total gross fixed capital formation	NPQR	195509	202615	204883	215291	220497	234572	253562	241364	209051	214486

1 See chapter text.

2 For the years before 2003, the total differs from the sum of their components

3 Components may not sum to totals due to rounding.

Source: Office for National Statistics: 01633 455644

19.22 Gross fixed capital formation: by type of asset[1,2,3]
Chained volume measures, reference year 2008

United Kingdom. Total economy

£ million

		2001	2002	2003	2004	2005	2006	2007	2008	2009	2010
Tangible fixed assets											
New dwellings, excluding land	**DFDV**	42852	47526	49782	54746	58044	59068	61630	55449	44119	44450
Other buildings and structures	**EQDP**	52401	48503	53167	54188	61158	63979	72388	79433	76045	73818
Transport equipment	**DLWJ**	16186	18548	16762	14332	14009	14909	14533	13721	11147	14831
Other machinery and equipment and cultivated assets	**DLWM**	47867	50320	49496	51461	48278	54260	61150	58126	48756	49867
Total	**EQDS**	159969	165215	170195	175292	182117	192345	209507	207993	184799	187948
Intangible fixed assets	**EQDT**	14962	15032	15988	16083	16388	16531	16923	17417	16502	16593
Costs associated with the transfer of ownership of non-produced assets	**DFDW**	19879	22625	19587	26875	25305	27141	27386	15954	7750	9944
Total gross fixed capital formation	**NPQR**	195509	202615	204883	215291	220497	234572	253562	241364	209051	214486

1 See chapter text.

2 For the years before 2003, the total differs from the sum of their components.

3 Components may not sum to totals due to rounding

Source: Office for National Statistics: 01633 455644

Education

Chapter 20

Education

Educational establishments in the UK are administered and financed in several ways. Most schools are controlled by local authorities, which are part of the structure of local government, but some are 'assisted', receiving grants direct from central government sources and being controlled by governing bodies who have a substantial degree of autonomy. Completely outside the public sector are non.maintained schools run by individuals, companies or charitable institutions.

For the purposes of UK education statistics, schools fall under the following broad categories:

Mainstream state schools
(In Northern Ireland, grant-aided mainstream schools)

These schools work in partnership with other schools and local authorities and they receive funding from local authorities. Since 1 September 1999, the categories (typically in England) are:

Community – schools formerly known as 'county' plus some former grant-maintained (GM) schools

Foundation – most former GM schools

Voluntary Aided – schools formerly known as 'aided' and some former GM schools

Voluntary Controlled – schools formerly known as 'controlled'

Non-maintained mainstream schools

These consist of:

(a) Independent schools

Schools which charge fees and may also be financed by individuals, companies or charitable institutions. These include Direct Grant schools, where the governing bodies are assisted by departmental grants and a proportion of the pupils attending them do so free or under an arrangement by which local authorities meet tuition fees. City Technology Colleges (CTCs) and Academies (applicable in England only) are also included as independent schools.

(b) Non-maintained schools
Run by voluntary bodies who may receive some grant from central government for capital work and for equipment, but their current expenditure is met primarily from the fees charged to local authorities for pupils placed in schools.

Special schools

Special schools provide education for children with Special Educational Needs (SEN) (in Scotland, Record of Needs or a Coordinated Support Plan), who cannot be educated satisfactorily in an ordinary school. Maintained special schools are run by local authorities, while non-maintained special schools are financed as described at (b) above.

Pupil Referral Units

Pupil Referral Units (PRUs) operate in England and Wales and provide education outside of a mainstream or special school setting, to meet the needs of difficult or disruptive children.

Schools in Scotland are categorised as Education Authority, Grant-aided, Opted-out/Self-governing (these three being grouped together as 'Publicly funded' schools), Independent schools and Partnership schools.

The home government departments dealing with education statistics are:

Department for Education (DfE)
Department for Business, Innovation and Skills (BIS)
Welsh Government (WG)
Scottish Government (SG)
Northern Ireland Department of Education (DENI)
Northern Ireland Department for Employment and Learning (DELNI)

Each of the home education departments in Great Britain, along with the Northern Ireland Department of Education, have overall responsibility for funding the schools sectors in their own country.

Up to March 2001, further education (FE) courses in FE sector colleges in England and in Wales were largely funded through grants from the respective FE funding councils. In April 2001, however, the Learning and Skills Council (LSC) took over the responsibility for funding the FE sector in England, and the National Council for Education and Training for Wales (part of Education and Learning Wales – ELWa) did so for Wales. The Apprenticeships, Skills, Children and Learning Act 2009 received Royal Assent on 12 November 2009 for the dissolution of the Learning and Skills Council by 2010 and the transfer of its functions on 1 April 2010 to local authorities and two new agencies: the Young People's Learning Agency (YPLA) and the Skills Funding Agency. The YPLA champions young people's learning by providing financial support to young learners; by funding academies, general FE and sixth form colleges and other 16 to 19 providers; and supporting local authorities to secure sufficient education and training places for all 16 to 19 year olds in England. The Skills Funding Agency funds further education colleges and training providers in England to deliver adult skills and apprenticeships. In Wales, the National Council – ELWa, funds FE provision made by FE institutions via a third party or sponsored arrangements. The Scottish Further Education Funding Council (SFEFC) funds FE colleges in Scotland, while the Department for Employment and Learning funds FE colleges in Northern Ireland.

From 1 April 2012, funding for the education and training of 3 to 19 year olds in England will become the responsibility of the Education Funding Agency (EFA), which will be a new executive agency of the Department for Education. The EFA will directly fund academies, free schools, university technology colleges, studio schools and 16 to 19 providers. It will distribute funding to local authorities for them to pass on to their maintained schools and it will also be responsible for the distribution of capital funding.

Higher education (HE) courses in higher education establishments are largely publicly funded through block grants from the HE funding councils in England and Scotland, the Higher Education Council – ELWa in Wales, and the Department for Employment and Learning in Northern Ireland. In addition, some designated HE (mainly HND/HNC Diplomas and Certificates of HE) is also funded by these sources. The FE sources mentioned above fund the remainder.

Statistics for the separate systems obtained in England, Wales, Scotland and Northern Ireland are collected and processed separately in accordance with the particular needs of the responsible departments. Since 1994/95 the Higher Education Statistics Agency (HESA) has undertaken the data collection for all higher education institutions (HEIs) in the UK. This includes the former Universities Funding Council (UFC) funded UK universities previously collected by the Universities Statistical Record. There are some structural differences in the information collected for schools, FE and HE in each of the four home countries and in some tables the GB/UK data presented are amalgamations from sources that are not entirely comparable.

Stages of education

There are five stages of education: early years, primary, secondary, FE and HE, and education is compulsory for all children between the ages of 5 (4 in Northern Ireland) and 16. The non-compulsory fourth stage, FE, covers non-advanced education, which can be taken at further (including tertiary) education colleges, HE institutions (HEIs) and increasingly in secondary schools. The fifth stage, HE, is study beyond GCE A levels and their equivalent which, for most full-time students, takes place in universities and other HEIs.

Early years education

Children under 5 attend a variety of settings including state nursery schools, nursery classes within primary schools and, in England and Wales, reception classes within primary schools, as well as s ettings outside the state sector such as voluntary pre-schools or privately run nurseries. In recent years there has been a major expansion of early years education, and the Education Act 2002 extended the National Curriculum for England to include the foundation stage. The foundation stage was introduced in September 2000, and covered children's education from the age of 3 to the end of the reception year, when most are just 5 and some almost 6 years old. The Early Years Foundation Stage (EYFS), came into force in September 2008, and is a single regulatory and quality framework for the provision of learning, development and care for children in all registered early years settings between birth and the academic year in which they turn 5.

Children born in Scotland between March and December are eligible for early years education at the time the Pre-School Education and Day Care Census is carried out. In Scotland, early years education is called ante-pre-school education for those aged 3 to 4 years old, and pre-school education for those aged 4.

Primary education

The primary stage covers three age ranges: nursery (under 5), infant (5 to 7 or 8) and junior (up to 11 or 12) but in Scotland and Northern Ireland there is generally no distinction between infant and junior schools. Most public sector primary schools take both boys and girls in mixed classes. It is usual to transfer straight to secondary school at age 11 (in England, Wales and Northern Ireland) or 12 (in Scotland), but in England some children make the transition via middle schools catering for various age ranges between 8 and 14. Depending on their individual age ranges middle schools are classified as either primary or secondary.

Secondary education

Public provision of secondary education in an area may consist of a combination of different types of school, the pattern reflecting historical circumstance and the policy adopted by the local authority. Comprehensive schools largely admit pupils without reference to ability or aptitude and cater for all the children in a neighbourhood, but in some areas they co.exist with grammar, secondary modern or technical schools. In 2005/06, 88 per cent of secondary pupils in England attended comprehensive schools while all secondary schools in Wales are comprehensive schools.

The majority of education authority secondary schools in Scotland are comprehensive in character and offer six years of secondary education; however, in remote areas there are several two-year and four-year secondary schools.

In Northern Ireland, post-primary education is provided by grammar schools and non-selective secondary schools.

In England, the Specialist Schools Programme helps schools, in partnership with private sector sponsors and supported by additional government funding, to establish distinctive identities through their chosen specialisms and achieve their targets to raise standards. Specialist schools have a special focus on their chosen subject area but must meet the National Curriculum requirements and deliver a broad and balanced education to all pupils. Any maintained secondary school in England can apply to be designated as a specialist school in one of ten specialist areas: arts, business & enterprise, engineering, humanities, languages, mathematics & computing, music, science, sports and technology. Schools can also combine any two specialisms.

Academies, operating in England, are publicly funded independent local schools that provide free education. They are all-ability schools established by sponsors from business, faith or voluntary groups working with partners from the local community.

Academies benefit from greater freedoms to help innovate and raise standards. These include freedom from local authority control, ability to set pay and conditions for staff, freedom from following the National Curriculum and the ability to change the lengths of terms and school days.

The Academies Programme was first introduced in March 2000 with the objective of replacing poorly performing schools. Academies were established and driven by external sponsors, to achieve a transformation in education performance.

The Academies Programme was expanded through legislation in the Academies Act 2010. This enables all maintained primary, secondary and special schools to apply to become an Academy. The early focus is on schools rated outstanding by Ofsted and the first of these new academies opened in September 2010. These schools do not have a sponsor but instead are expected to work with underperforming schools to help raise standards.

Special schools

Special schools (day or boarding) provide education for children who require specialist support to complete their education, for example because they have physical or other difficulties. Many pupils with special educational needs are educated in mainstream schools. All children attending special schools are offered a curriculum designed to overcome their learning difficulties and to enable them to become self-reliant. Since December 2005, special schools have also been able to apply for the Special Educational Needs (SEN) specialism, under the Specialist Schools Programme. They can apply for a curriculum specialism, but not for both the SEN and a curriculum specialism.

Further education

The term further education may be used in a general sense to cover all non.advanced courses taken after the period of compulsory education, but more commonly it excludes those staying on at secondary school and those in higher education, that is, courses in universities and colleges leading to qualifications above GCE A Level, Scottish Certificate of Education (SCE) Higher Grade, GNVQ/NVQ level 3, and their equivalents. Since 1 April 1993, sixth form colleges in England and Wales have been included in the further education sector.

Higher education

Higher education is defined as courses that are of a standard that is higher than GCE A level, the Higher Grade of the SCE/National Qualification, GNVQ/NVQ level 3 or the Edexcel (formerly BTEC) or SQA National Certificate/Diploma. There are three main levels of HE course:

(i) Postgraduate courses leading to higher degrees, diplomas and certificates (including postgraduate certificates of education (PGCE) and professional qualifications) which usually require a first degree as entry qualification.

(ii) Undergraduate courses which include first degrees, first degrees with qualified teacher status, enhanced first degrees, first degrees obtained concurrently with a diploma, and intercalated first degrees (where first degree students, usually in medicine, dentistry or veterinary medicine, interrupt their studies to complete a one-year course of advanced studies in a related topic).

(iii) Other undergraduate courses which include all other higher education courses, for example HNDs and Diplomas in HE.

As a result of the Further and Higher Education Act 1992, former polytechnics and some other HEIs were designated as universities in 1992/93. Students normally attend HE courses at HEIs, but some attend at FE colleges. Some also attend institutions which do not receive public grant (such as the University of Buckingham) and these numbers are excluded from the tables. However, the University of Buckingham is included in Tables 20.6 and 20.7.

20.1 Number of schools by type and establishments of further and higher education

Academic years

Numbers

		2003 /04	2004 /05	2005 /06	2006 /07	2007 /08	2008 /09	2009 /10
United Kingdom:								
Public sector mainstream								
Nursery[1]	KBFK	3,438	3,425	3,349	3,326	3,273	3,209	3,166
Primary	KBFA	22,509	22,343	22,156	21,968	21,768	21,568	21,427
Secondary[2,3]	KBFF	4,281	4,261	4,244	4,232	4,209	4,183	4,149
of which Admissions Policy								
Comprehensive		..	..	..	..	3,304	3,247	3,156
Selective		..	..	..	..	233	233	233
Modern		..	..	..	..	172	169	160
City Technology Colleges (CTCs)		..	..	..	..	5	3	3
Academies		..	..	..	..	83	133	203
Not Applicable		..	..	..	..	412	398	394
of which Middle deemed secondary		..	..	..	..	243	231	225
of which Specialist schools[4]		..	..	..	..	2,799	2,981	2,857
Non-maintained mainstream	KBFU	2,498	2,445	2,455	2,486	2,527	2,547	2,570
Special schools	KBFP	1,465	1,436	1,416	1,391	1,378	1,378	1,373
of which maintained	KPVX	1,362	1,329	1,311	1,285	1,264	1,264	1,253
of which non-maintained	KPGO	103	107	105	106	114	114	120
Pupil referral units	KXEP	457	478	481	489	506	511	452
ALL SCHOOLS[8]		..	..	..	..	33,661	33,396	33,137
England:								
Public sector mainstream								
Nursery	KBAK	468	456	453	446	445	438	428
Primary	KBAA	17,762	17,642	17,504	17,361	17,205	17,064	16,971
Secondary[2,3]	KBAF	3,435	3,416	3,405	3,399	3,383	3,361	3,333
of which Admissions Policy								
Comprehensive		..	..	..	..	2,704	2,648	2,559
Selective		..	..	..	..	164	164	164
Modern		..	..	..	..	172	169	160
City Technology Colleges (CTCs)		..	..	..	..	5	3	3
Academies		..	..	..	..	83	133	203
Not Applicable		..	..	..	..	255	244	244
of which Middle deemed secondary		..	..	..	..	243	231	225
of which Specialist schools[4]		..	..	..	..	2,799	2,981	2,857
Non-maintained mainstream	KBAU	2,304	2,252	2,263	2,286	2,329	2,358	2,378
Special schools	KBAP	1,148	1,122	1,105	1,078	1,065	1,058	1,054
maintained	KPGT	1,078	1,049	1,033	1,006	993	985	979
non maintained	KPGU	70	73	72	72	72	73	75
Pupil referral units	KXEQ	426	447	449	448	455	458	452
ALL SCHOOLS		..	..	..	..	24,882	24,737	24,616
Wales:								
Public sector mainstream								
Nursery	KBBK	34	34	33	31	28	28	25
Primary	KBBA	1,588	1,572	1,555	1,527	1,509	1,478	1,462
Secondary[3,5]	KBBF	227	227	224	224	222	223	223
Non-maintained mainstream	KBBU	60	58	56	66	66	60	64
Special (maintained)	KBBP	43	43	43	44	44	44	43
Pupil referral units[8]	KZBF	31	31	32	41	51	53	..
ALL SCHOOLS[8]		..	..	..	..	1,920	1,886	1,817

20.1 Number of schools by type and establishments of further and higher education

Academic years

Numbers

		2003 /04	2004 /05	2005 /06	2006 /07	2007 /08	2008 /09	2009 /10
Scotland:								
Public sector mainstream								
Nursery[2]	KBDK	2,836	2,836	2,763	2,750	2,702	2,645	2,615
Primary	KBDA	2,248	2,217	2,194	2,184	2,169	2,153	2,128
Secondary	KBDF	386	386	385	381	378	376	374
Non-maintained mainstream	KBDU	117	118	117	116	115	113	114
Special schools	KBDP	227	226	223	224	226	234	235
of which maintained	KYCZ	194	192	190	190	184	193	190
of which non-maintained	KYDA	33	34	33	34	42	41	45
ALL SCHOOLS		..	..	..	..	5,590	5,521	5,466
Northern Ireland:								
Grant aided mainstream								
Nursery[6]	KBEK	100	99	100	99	98	98	98
Primary[7]	KBEA	911	912	903	896	885	873	866
Secondary	KBEF	233	232	230	228	226	223	219
of which								
Grammar		..	..	..	..	69	69	69
Other (Secondary intermediate)						157	154	150
Non-maintained mainstream	KBEU	17	17	19	18	17	16	14
Special (maintained)	KBEP	47	45	45	45	43	42	41
ALL SCHOOLS		..	..	..	..	1,269	1,252	1,238

1 Nursery schools figures for Scotland prior to 1998/99 only include data for Local Authority pre-schools. Data thereafter include partnership pre-schools. From 2005/06, figures exclude pre-school education centres not in partnership with the Local Authority.

2 Time series revised to show State-funded secondary schools (i.e. including CTCs and Academies, previously included in the 'Non-maintained mainstream' category).

3 Excludes sixth form colleges in England and Wales which were reclassified as further education colleges on 1 April 1993.

4 Operational from September of the first year shown.

5 All secondary schools are classed as Comprehensive.

6 Excludes voluntary and private pre-school education centres.

7 From 1995/96, includes Preparatory Departments in Grammar Schools.

8 The 2009/10 data does not include Pupil referal units in Wales.

Sources: Department for Education;
Department for Children, Schools and Families;
Welsh Government;
Scottish Government;
Northern Ireland Department of Education;
Northern Ireland Department for Employment and Learning;
020 778 38455

20.2 Full-time and part-time pupils in school[1] by age and gender[2]

United Kingdom

All schools at January[3]

Thousands

		2000	2001	2002	2003	2004	2005	2006	2007	2008	2009	2010
Age at previous 31 August[4]												
Number (thousands) England	KBIA	8,346	8,374	8,369	8,367	8,335	8,274	8,216	8,149	8,102	8,071	8,064
Wales	KBIB	512	512	511	509	506	501	495	490	485	479	476
Scotland	KBIC	874	882	876	874	866	851	850	845	829	818	815
Northern Ireland[2]	KBID	349	348	346	345	341	337	333	329	326	323	322
United Kingdom	KBIE	10,081	10,116	10,102	10,095	10,048	9,963	9,893	9,813	9,742	9,691	9,677
Male and Female												
2-4 [5]	KBIF	1,184	1,187	1,180	1,189	1,145	1,138	1,130	1,139	1,160	1,181	1,203
5[6]-10	KBIG	4,629	4,597	4,537	4,489	4,403	4,378	4,321	4,264	4,212	4,163	4,154
11	KBIH	783	771	783	791	784	758	756	739	730	744	725
12-14	KBII	2,256	2,297	2,320	2,343	2,355	2,369	2,344	2,309	2,265	2,236	2,221
15	KBIK	705	732	737	751	775	764	777	786	783	757	754
16	KBIL	285	287	298	290	314	304	304	314	320	329	327
17	KBIM	213	219	223	217	238	226	235	234	242	249	259
18	KBIN	27	27	23	24	32	27	26	28	30	32	30
19 and over		..	..	..	..	..	..	..	..	..	..	5
Males												
14	KBIO	381	384	391	401	394	402	407	404	391	389	379
15	KBIP	359	374	377	384	394	390	397	401	401	387	385
16	KBIQ	138	139	145	140	150	146	146	150	154	160	160
17	KBIR	101	105	107	104	112	107	111	110	114	119	124
18	KBIS	14	15	13	13	17	14	15	15	16	17	16
19 and over		..	..	..	..	..	..	..	..	..	..	3
Females												
14	KBIT	364	365	373	384	378	384	388	385	373	372	363
15	KBIU	346	358	360	368	379	375	380	385	382	370	369
16	KBIV	147	148	153	150	161	159	159	164	165	169	167
17	KBIW	111	114	116	113	124	119	123	124	128	131	134
18	KBIX	13	12	11	11	15	12	12	13	14	15	14
19 and over		..	..	..	..	..	..	..	..	..	..	2

1 From 1 April 1993 excludes 6th form colleges in England and Wales which were reclassified as further education colleges.

2 In Northern Ireland, a gender split is not collected by age but is available by year group and so this is used as a proxy.

3 In Scotland, as at the previous September.

4 1 July for Northern Ireland and 31 December for non-maintained primary and secondary schools pupils in Scotland and age at census date in January for pre-school education in Scotland.

5 Includes the so-called "rising 5s" (i.e. those pupils who become 5 during the autumn term).

6 In Scotland, includes some 4-year-olds.

Sources: Department for Education;
Department for Business,Innovation and Skills;
Welsh Government;
Scottish Government;
Northern Ireland Department of Education;
Northern Ireland Department for Employment and Learning;
020 778 38455

20.3 Number of pupils and teachers and pupil: pupil teacher ratios: by school type

At January

	Pupil: teacher ratio within schools[1]				
	1995/96 [3]	2000/01	2007/08 [4,5]	2008/09	2009/10
United Kingdom					
Public sector mainstream					
Nursery schools	21.3	23.1	17.3	17.5	17.3
Primary schools[6]	22.7	22.3	20.9	20.7	20.7
Secondary schools[7,8]	16.1	16.5	15.6	15.4	15.3
Pupil Referral Units (PRUs)	..	..	4.1	3.7	3.2
Non-maintained mainstream schools	10.3	9.7	9.2	9.2	9.4
Special schools					
Maintained	6.3	6.3	5.8	5.8	5.8
Non-maintained	.	.	4.6	4.5	6.2
All schools[9]	**18.0**	**17.9**	**16.5**	**16.4**	**16.2**
England					
Public sector mainstream					
Nursery schools	19.2	17.7	16.3	16.5	16.2
Primary schools	23.2	22.9	21.6	21.4	21.3
Secondary schools[7,8]	16.6	17.1	16.1	15.9	15.7
Pupil Referral Units (PRUs)	4.3	4.4	4.1	3.7	3.2
Non-maintained mainstream schools	10.2	9.7	9.2	9.2	9.4
Special schools					
Maintained	6.7	6.6	6.1	6.2	6.1
Non-maintained	4.6	4.8	5.1	5	5.1
All schools	**18.2**	**18.1**	**16.8**	**16.5**	**16.4**
Wales					
Public sector mainstream					
Nursery schools	19.5	17.3	15.4	15.4	15.1
Primary schools	22.5	21.5	19.9	19.9	20.1
Secondary schools[7]	16.0	16.6	16.5	16.5	16.5
Pupil Referral Units (PRUs)	..	..	..	..	..
Non-maintained mainstream schools	10.1	9.6	8.4	8.5	8.2
Special schools (maintained)	6.7	6.8	6.3	6.5	6.5
All schools[9]	**18.7**	**18.4**	**17.5**	**17.5**	**17.6**
Scotland					
Public sector mainstream					
Nursery schools	24.3	28.5	..	..	..
Primary schools	19.5	19.0	16.0	16.0	15.8
Secondary schools	12.9	13.0	11.7	11.8	11.9
Non-maintained mainstream schools	11.0	10.1	9.8	9.6	9.6
Special schools					
Maintained	4.8	4.2	3.3	3.3	3.4
Non-maintained	3.7	3.3	3.2	3.0	..
All schools	**15.5**	**15.4**	**12.8**	**12.9**	**12.6**
Northern Ireland					
Grant-aided sector mainstream					
Nursery schools	24.1	24.4	25.0	25.4	26.3
Primary schools[6]	20.7	20.1	20.6	20.3	21.1
Secondary schools	14.8	14.5	14.5	14.5	15.0
Non-maintained mainstream schools	10.9	9.3	7.3	7.1	6.9
Special schools (maintained)	6.7	5.9	6.0	6.0	6.1
All schools	**17.2**	**16.6**	**16.7**	**16.6**	**17.2**

1 The within-schools PTR is calculated by dividing the total full-time equivalent (FTE) number of pupils on roll in schools by the total FTE number of **qualified teachers** employed in schools.

2 The within-schools PAR is calculated by dividing the total FTE number of pupils on roll in schools by the total FTE number of **all teachers** and support staff employed in schools, excluding administrative and clerical staff.

3 Nursery schools figures for Scotland exclude pre-school education centres and are not therefore directly comparable with figures from 1999/00.

4 Since 2003/04, data on teacher numbers in Northern Ireland have been compiled on a new, improved basis. Pupil/teacher ratios in Northern Ireland from 2003/04 are not comparable with previous years.

5 Excluding nursery school figures for Scotland as FTE pupil numbers are not available.

6 Includes preparatory departments attached to grammar schools in Northern Ireland.

7 Excludes sixth form colleges in England and Wales which were reclassified as further education colleges from 1 April 1993.

8 For 2007/08, State-funded secondary schools (i.e. including City Technology Colleges (CTCs) and Academies in England, which were previously included under 'Non-maintained').

9 Excludes Pupil Referral Units as information on teachers is not collected for Wales.

Sources: Department for Education;
Department for Business, Innovation and Skills;
Welsh Government;
Scottish Government;
Northern Ireland Department of Education;
Northern Ireland Department for Employment and Learning;
020 778 38455

20.4 Full-time and part-time pupils with Special Educational Needs (SEN) or equivalent[1], 2009/10[2]

United Kingdom

Thousands and percentages

	United Kingdom	England[3]	Wales	Scotland	Northern Ireland
All schools					
Total pupils	9677.8	8064.3	476.4	814.7	322.5
SEN pupils with statements	252.6	220.9	14.1	4.0	13.6
Incidence (%) [4]	2.6	2.7	3.0	0.5	4.2
State-funded schools[5]					
Nursery[6]					
Total pupils[7]	152.5	37.5	1.7	107.4	5.9
SEN pupils with statements[8]	0.8	0.3	-	0.4	0.1
Incidence (%)[4]	0.5	0.7	1.0	0.4	1.1
Placement (%)[9]	0.3	0.1	0.1	11.1	0.5
Primary[10]					
Total pupils	4882.1	4093.7	257.4	367.1	163.8
SEN pupils without statements	857.0	759.1	50.3	18.6	28.9
SEN pupils with statements	67.5	57.3	4.4	1.3	4.5
SEN Pupils with statements-incidence (%)[4]	1.4	1.4	1.7	0.4	2.8
SEN Pupils with statements-placement (%)[9]	26.7	25.9	31.0	32.7	33.5
Secondary[12]					
Total pupils	3906.7	3252.1	203.9	302.9	147.8
SEN pupils without statements	709.6	639.2	34.6	17.1	18.8
SEN pupils with statements	74.4	63.6	5.4	0.6	4.8
SEN Pupils with statements - incidence (%)[4]	1.9	2.0	2.7	0.2	3.2
SEN Pupils[4] with statements - placement (%)[9]	29.5	28.8	38.3	14.4	35.3
Special[13,14]					
Total pupils	101.5	86.3	4.1	6.7	4.4
SEN pupils with statements	93.6	84.2	4.0	1.3	4.2
Incidence (%)[4]	92.3	97.6	96.0	19.9	93.7
Placement (%)[9]	37.1	38.1	27.9	33.5	30.7
Pupil referral units[13]					
Total pupils	13.2	13.2	..	..	..
SEN pupils with statements	1.7	1.7	..	..	..
Incidence (%)[4]	12.8	12.8	..	..	..
Placement (%)[9]	0.7	0.8	..	..	..
Other schools					
Independent[12]					
Total pupils	616.3	576.9	9.2	29.5	0.7
SEN pupils with statements	9.9	9.5	0.4	0.1	..
Incidence (%)[4]	1.6	1.6	4.1	0.2	..
Placement (%)[9]	3.9	4.3	2.7	1.7	..
Non-maintained special[13]					
Total pupils	5.5	4.5	..	1.0	..
SEN pupils with statements	4.6	4.4	..	0.3	..
Incidence (%)[4]	84.4	97.0	..	26.4	..
Placement (%)[9]	1.8	2.0	..	6.5	..

1 Scotland no longer has Special Educational Needs as the Education (Additional Support for Learning) (Scotland) Act 2004 (the Act) replaces the system for assessment and recording of children and young people with special educational needs. Nursery schools include the number of children registered for pre-school education with Additional Support Needs with a Coordinated Support Plan. Primary and secondary schools include pupils with a Record of Needs or a Coordinated Support Plan, including some who also had an individualised educational Programme (IEP).

2 Pupil numbers are not compiled on the same basis as those in table 20.2 (Full-time and part-time pupils in schoold by age and gender).

3 Includes new codes for recording SEN status following the introduction of a new SEN Code of Practice from January 2002.

4 Incident of pupils - the number of pupils with statements within each school type expressed as a proportion of the total number of pupils on roll in each school type.

5 Grant-Aided schools in Northern Ireland.

6 Includes pupils in Voluntary and Private Pre-School Centres in Northern Ireland funded under the Pre-School Expansion Programme which began in 1998/99.

7 In Scotland, pre-school registrations for places funded by the local authority, in centres providing pre-school education as a local authority centre or in partnership with the local authority only. Children are counted once for each centre they are registered with. Figures are not directly comparable with previous years.

8 For Scotland, number of children registered for pre-school education and Additional Support Needs with a Coordinated Support Plan are likely to be an undercount as only centres that returned the full census form were asked about Coordinated Support Plans, and of those who were asked, not all completed them. Out of 2,702 centres,713 did not provide this information.

9 Placement of pupils - the number of pupils with statements within each school type expressed as a proportion of the number of pupils with statements in all schools.

10 Includes nursery classes (except for Scotland, where they are included with Nursery schools) and reception classes in Primary schools.

11 For Scotland, those with IEP only used for the 'without statement' category.

12 City Technology Colleges (CTCs) and Acadamies in England, previously included with Independent schools are included with State-funded secondary schools, therefore figures are not directly comparable with previous years.

13 England and Wales figures exclude dually registered pupils,where applicable.

14 Including general and hospital special schools.

Sources: Department for Education;
Welsh Government; Scottish Government;
Northern Ireland Department of Education;
Northern Ireland Department for Employment and Learning;
020 778 38455

20.5 GCE, GCSE and SCE/NQ[1] and vocational qualifications obtained by pupils and students

United Kingdom

Percentages and thousands

| | Pupils in their last year of compulsory education[2] | | | | | Pupils/students in education[3] | |
| | | | | | | % achieving GCE A Levels and equivalent[4,5] | |
	5 or more grades A*-C[6]	.1-4 grades A*-C[6]	Grades D-G[7] only	No graded results	Total (=100%) (Thousands)	2 or more passes[8]	Population aged 17 (thousands)
2000/01							
All	51	24.1	19.4	5.5	729.7	37.4	717.9
Males	45.7	24.6	23.1	6.5	372.1	33.4	366.6
Females	56.5	23.6	15.5	4.4	357.6	41.6	351.3
2001/02							
All	52.5	23.7	18.4	5.4	732.5	37.4	739
Males	47.2	24.3	22	6.4	374	33	379.8
Females	58	23.1	14.6	4.3	358.5	42	359.2
2002/03							
All	53.5	23.1	18.2	5.2	750.2	38.4	771.2
Males	48.3	23.6	21.8	6.3	382.7	33.9	397.2
Females	58.8	22.7	14.4	4.1	367.6	43.2	374
2003/04							
All	54.2	22.7	18.8	4.4	772	39.2	769.5
Males	49.2	23.1	22.4	5.3	392.6	34.7	395.8
Females	59.3	22.2	15	3.4	379.4	44	373.7
2004/05							
All	57	22.1	17.9	3	759.1	38.3	788.5
Males	52.1	22.8	21.4	3.7	385.5	33.8	405.2
Females	62.1	21.4	14.2	2.3	373.5	43.1	383.4
2005/06							
All	59	21.4	16.9	2.7	773.8	37.3	807.3
Males	54.3	22.1	20.3	3.3	394.2	32.7	415.5
Females	63.9	20.6	13.5	2.1	379.6	42.1	391.8
2006/07							
All	61.3	20.1	17	1.6	778.2	45.2	791.6
Males	56.9	20.6	20.5	2.1	395.8	39.5	407.8
Females	65.8	19.5	13.4	1.2	382.4	51.2	383.8
2007/08							
All	64.4	-	-	-	-	46.3	806.1
Males	60.0	-	-	-	-	41.2	415.7
Females	69.0	-	-	-	-	51.9	390.4
2008/09							
All	68.7	-	-	-	-	48.7	811.0
Males	64.5	-	-	-	-	43.6	418.0
Females	73.2	-	-	-	-	54.2	393.0

Sources: Department for Education;
Department for Business, Innovation and Skills;
Welsh Government;
Scottish Government;
Northern Ireland Department of Education;
Northern Ireland Department for Employment and Learning;
020 778 38455

1 From 1999/00, National Qualifications (NQ) were introduced in Scotland but are not all shown until 2000/01. NQs include Intermediate Standard Grades, 1 & 2 and Higher Grades. The figures for Higher Grades combine the new NQ Higher and the old SCE Higher and include Advanced Highers.

2 Pupils aged 15 at the start of the academic year, pupils in Year S4 in Scotland. From 2004/05, pupils at the end of Key Stage 4 in England.

3 Pupils in schools and students in further education institutions generally aged 16-18 at the start of the academic year in England, Wales and Northern Ireland as a percentage of the 17 year old population. Data from 2002/03 for Wales and Northern Ireland however, relate to schools only. Pupils in Scotland generally sit Highers one year earlier than those sitting A levels in the rest of the UK, and the figures relate to the results of the pupils in Year S5/S6.

4 Figures, other than for Scotland, include Vocational Certificates of Education (VCE) and, previously, Advanced level GNVQ which is equivalent to 2 GCE A level or AS equivalents.

5 2 AS levels or 2 Highers/1 Advanced Higher or 1 each in Scotland, count as 1 A level pass.

6 Standard Grades 1-3/Intermediate 2 A-C/Intermediate 1 A in Scotland, count as 1 A level pass.

7 Grades D-G at GCSE and Scottish Standard Grades 4-6/Intermediate 1 B and C/Access 3 (pass).

8 3 or more SCE/NQ Higher Grades/2 or more Advanced Highers/1 Advanced Higher with 2 or more Higher Passes in Scotland.

20.6 Students[1,2] obtaining higher education qualifications[3,4], 2008/09

| United Kingdom | (i) By level, gender and subject group | | | | | Thousands |
| | Postgraduate | | | | | Total |
	PhD & equivalent	Masters and other	Total	First Degree	Sub-degree[5]	Higher Education
All						
Medicine & Dentistry	2.0	4.3	6.3	9.1	0.3	15.6
Subjects Allied to Medicine	1.0	12.6	13.6	31.4	35.4	80.4
Biological Sciences	2.6	7.4	10.0	30.7	5.4	46.1
Vet. Science, Agriculture & related	0.2	1.2	1.4	3.0	1.7	6.1
Physical Sciences	2.3	4.5	6.8	13.5	2.5	22.8
Mathematical and Computer Sciences	1.2	8.7	9.9	20.0	6.6	36.5
Engineering & Technology	2.4	11.6	13.9	20.8	6.8	41.5
Architecture, Building & Planning	0.2	6.1	6.4	8.9	4.7	20.0
Social Studies[6]	1.8	27.8	29.6	47.8	16.6	94.0
Business & Administrative Studies	0.8	45.2	46.0	47.2	14.8	108.0
Mass Communication & Documentation	0.1	4.5	4.6	9.7	1.4	15.8
Languages	0.9	5.4	6.4	20.9	5.1	32.5
Historical and Philosophical Studies	1.1	5.1	6.2	16.4	2.5	25.0
Creative Arts & Design	0.4	8.1	8.5	34.6	7.4	50.5
Education[7]	0.6	34.2	34.8	15.0	23.6	73.3
Combined, general	-	0.2	0.2	4.6	1.3	6.2
All subjects	**17.7**	**186.9**	**204.6**	**333.7**	**136.1**	**674.4**
Males						
Medicine & Dentistry	0.9	1.7	2.6	3.6	-	6.3
Subjects Allied to Medicine	0.4	3.5	3.9	6.3	4.9	15.1
Biological Sciences	1.0	2.4	3.4	11.1	2.2	16.7
Vet. Science, Agriculture & related	0.1	0.6	0.7	0.9	0.7	2.3
Physical Sciences	1.4	2.5	3.9	7.7	1.4	13.0
Mathematical and Computer Sciences	1.0	6.6	7.5	15.0	5.0	27.5
Engineering & Technology	1.9	9.2	11.1	17.4	6.2	34.7
Architecture, Building & Planning	0.2	3.7	3.8	6.3	3.3	13.4
Social Studies[6]	0.9	11.7	12.7	18.1	5.4	36.1
Business & Administrative Studies	0.5	23.9	24.4	23.5	6.7	54.7
Mass Communication & Documentation	0.1	1.5	1.5	4.1	0.7	6.4
Languages	0.4	1.7	2.1	5.9	2.0	10.0
Historical and Philosophical Studies	0.6	2.5	3.1	7.6	1.1	11.8
Creative Arts & Design	0.2	3.0	3.3	13.3	3.1	19.6
Education[7]	0.2	9.5	9.7	2.1	5.9	17.7
Combined, general	-	0.1	0.1	1.8	0.5	2.4
All subjects	**9.7**	**84.0**	**93.7**	**144.8**	**49.2**	**287.7**
Females						
Medicine & Dentistry	1.1	2.6	3.7	5.5	0.2	9.3
Subjects Allied to Medicine	0.6	9.1	9.7	25.1	30.5	65.3
Biological Sciences	1.6	5.0	6.6	19.6	3.2	29.4
Vet. Science, Agriculture & related	0.1	0.6	0.8	2.1	1.0	3.8
Physical Sciences	0.9	2.0	2.8	5.8	1.2	9.8
Mathematical and Computer Sciences	0.3	2.1	2.4	5.0	1.6	9.0
Engineering & Technology	0.5	2.3	2.9	3.4	0.6	6.8
Architecture, Building & Planning	0.1	2.5	2.6	2.6	1.4	6.6
Social Studies[6]	0.9	16.0	16.9	29.8	11.3	57.9
Business & Administrative Studies	0.3	21.3	21.6	23.7	8.1	53.4
Mass Communication & Documentation	0.1	3.0	3.1	5.6	0.7	9.4
Languages	0.6	3.8	4.3	15.0	3.1	22.4
Historical and Philosophical Studies	0.5	2.6	3.1	8.8	1.4	13.3
Creative Arts & Design	0.2	5.1	5.3	21.4	4.2	30.9
Education[7]	0.4	24.7	25.1	12.9	17.6	55.6
Combined, general	-	0.2	0.2	2.8	0.8	3.8
All subjects	**7.9**	**102.9**	**110.9**	**188.9**	**86.9**	**386.7**

Sources: Department for Education; Department for Business, Innovation and Skills

1 Includes students on Open University courses. The field "gender" has changed to be consistent with the MIAP common data definitions coding frame. Students of indeterminate gender are now included in total figures but not in separate breakdowns. "Indeterminate" means unable to be classified as either male or female and is not related in any way to trans-gender.
2 Includes students qualifying on all modes of study.
3 Excludes qualifications from the private sector, except the University of Buckingham who returned data to HESA in 2008/09.
4 Includes higher education qualifications in higher education institutions in the United Kingdom only. Higher education qualifications in further education institutions are excluded.
5 Excludes students who successfully completed courses for which formal qualifications are not awarded.
6 Including Law.
7 Including ITT and INSET.
8 Government Office Region by location of study.

20.7 Students[1,2] obtaining higher education qualifications[3,4], 2008/09

| United Kingdom | (ii) By level, gender and Government Office Region (GOR)[5] | | | | | Thousands |

		Postgraduate					Total Higher Education
		PhD & equivalent	Masters and other	Total	First Degree	Sub-degree[5]	
All							
United Kingdom		**17.7**	**186.9**	**204.6**	**333.7**	**136.1**	**674.4**
	North East	0.7	8.8	9.4	17.1	11.0	37.5
	North West	1.6	18.0	19.7	37.7	16.1	73.5
	Yorkshire and the Humber	1.6	14.0	15.6	32.2	9.6	57.3
	East Midlands	1.2	11.2	12.4	24.6	8.3	45.2
	West Midlands	1.0	15.3	16.3	25.5	11.3	53.2
	East	1.6	10.3	11.9	17.3	8.5	37.8
	London	3.4	45.8	49.2	51.5	21.9	122.6
	South East	2.6	20.9	23.5	45.7	25.9	95.1
	South West	1.0	9.4	10.4	24.5	9.2	44.1
	England	14.6	153.8	168.4	276.1	121.8	566.3
	Wales	0.7	10.2	10.9	18.4	5.3	34.6
	Scotland	1.8	19.5	21.3	30.7	7.4	59.4
	Northern Ireland	0.4	3.4	3.9	8.4	1.7	14.0
Males							
United Kingdom		**9.7**	**84.0**	**93.7**	**144.8**	**49.2**	**287.7**
	North East	0.4	4.0	4.4	7.8	4.7	16.9
	North West	0.9	7.9	8.8	16.2	5.3	30.3
	Yorkshire and the Humber	0.9	6.4	7.4	14.5	3.4	25.2
	East Midlands	0.7	5.1	5.7	11.1	2.8	19.7
	West Midlands	0.5	7.0	7.5	11.2	3.8	22.5
	East	0.9	4.7	5.6	7.5	3.0	16.2
	London	1.8	20.5	22.2	22.1	7.5	51.8
	South East	1.4	9.5	10.8	19.4	9.1	39.4
	South West	0.5	3.7	4.3	10.8	3.5	18.6
	England	8.0	68.8	76.8	120.7	43.2	240.7
	Wales	0.4	5.0	5.4	7.9	2.5	15.7
	Scotland	1.0	9.0	10.0	13.0	3.0	26.1
	Northern Ireland	0.2	1.3	1.5	3.2	0.5	5.2
Females							
United Kingdom		**7.9**	**102.9**	**110.9**	**188.9**	**86.9**	**386.7**
	North East	0.3	4.7	5.0	9.2	6.3	20.5
	North West	0.7	10.2	10.9	21.5	10.8	43.2
	Yorkshire and the Humber	0.7	7.6	8.2	17.7	6.2	32.1
	East Midlands	0.5	6.1	6.6	13.4	5.4	25.5
	West Midlands	0.5	8.3	8.8	14.3	7.5	30.6
	East	0.7	5.7	6.4	9.8	5.4	21.6
	London	1.6	25.3	27.0	29.5	14.3	70.8
	South East	1.2	11.5	12.7	26.3	16.8	55.8
	South West	0.4	5.7	6.1	13.7	5.7	25.5
	England	6.6	85.0	91.6	155.4	78.6	325.7
	Wales	0.3	5.2	5.5	10.6	2.8	18.9
	Scotland	0.8	10.5	11.3	17.7	4.4	33.4
	Northern Ireland	0.2	2.1	2.4	5.2	1.2	8.8

Sources: Department for Education; Department for Business, Innovation and Skills

1 Includes students on Open University courses. The field "gender" has changed to be consistent with the MIAP common data definitions coding frame. Students of indeterminate gender are now included in total figures but not in separate breakdowns. "Indeterminate" means unable to be classified as either male or female and is not related in any way to trans-gender.
2 Includes students qualifying on all modes of study.
3 Excludes qualifications from the private sector, except the University of Buckingham who returned data to HESA in 2008/09.
4 Includes higher education qualifications obtained in higher education institutions in the United Kingdom only. Higher education qualifications in further education institutions are excluded.
5 Government Office Region by location of study.

20.8 Students in higher[1] education by level, mode of study,[2] gender and age,[3] 2008/09[4,5]

United Kingdom (home and overseas students)

Thousands

	Postgraduate level						First degree		Other undergraduate		Total higher education students[6]	
	PhD and equivalent		Masters and others		Total postgraduate							
	Full-time	Part-time	Full-time	Part-time	Full-time	Part-time	Full-time	Part-time	Full-time	Part-time	Full-time	Part-time
All												
Age under 16	-	-	-	-	-	-	-	-	-	0.6	-	0.6
16	-	-	-	-	-	-	0.3	0.1	0.5	5.0	0.9	5.1
17	-	-	-	-	-	-	10.2	0.2	4.2	3.2	14.4	3.4
18	-	-	-	-	-	-	189.4	1.8	20.5	8.3	210.0	10.1
19	-	-	0.1	0.1	0.1	0.1	253.9	5.1	25.1	13.0	279.2	18.2
20	0.1	-	2.4	0.5	2.4	0.5	263.2	8.4	20.5	14.2	286.0	23.2
21	0.7	-	20.9	2.2	21.6	2.2	163.8	10.9	13.8	13.7	199.1	26.9
22	3.1	0.1	32.7	5.3	35.9	5.4	79.4	10.5	10.7	13.8	125.9	29.6
23	5.2	0.2	30.6	8.0	35.8	8.2	42.0	8.9	8.5	14.1	86.3	31.2
24	6.6	0.3	24.0	9.6	30.5	9.9	25.0	8.2	6.7	14.2	62.3	32.2
25	6.3	0.4	18.3	10.2	24.6	10.6	17.9	7.6	5.5	14.3	48.0	32.5
26	5.5	0.6	13.4	10.6	18.9	11.2	13.9	7.4	4.9	14.0	37.7	32.6
27	4.7	0.7	10.6	10.9	15.4	11.6	11.2	7.2	4.3	14.2	30.8	33.0
28	3.8	0.7	8.5	10.9	12.3	11.7	9.1	7.1	3.9	14.4	25.3	33.2
29	3.2	0.8	7.0	10.7	10.2	11.5	7.6	6.6	3.4	13.4	21.1	31.5
30+	19.4	19.2	41.5	171.0	60.9	190.2	67.2	124.2	41.7	299.1	169.8	613.5
Unknown	-	-	-	0.8	0.1	0.8	-	0.1	-	1.9	0.1	2.8
All ages	58.6	23.1	210.1	250.7	268.7	273.8	1,154.0	214.6	174.1	471.3	1,596.9	959.7
Males												
Age under 16	-	-	-	-	-	-	-	-	-	0.3	-	0.3
16	-	-	-	-	-	-	0.1	0.1	0.2	2.0	0.4	2.0
17	-	-	-	-	-	-	4.4	0.1	1.9	1.4	6.4	1.5
18	-	-	-	-	-	-	83.4	0.7	9.2	4.5	92.6	5.2
19	-	-	0.1	-	0.1	-	114.6	2.4	11.4	7.2	126.0	9.7
20	-	-	1.2	0.1	1.2	0.1	119.2	4.2	8.9	7.4	129.4	11.7
21	0.4	-	9.7	0.8	10.1	0.8	79.2	5.5	5.9	6.7	95.2	13.0
22	1.8	-	15.3	1.8	17.1	1.8	40.4	5.1	4.4	6.2	62.0	13.2
23	3.0	0.1	14.4	2.8	17.4	2.9	21.3	4.1	3.5	5.7	42.3	12.8
24	3.6	0.1	11.7	3.5	15.3	3.6	12.4	3.6	2.7	5.5	30.3	12.7
25	3.4	0.2	9.2	3.8	12.6	4.0	8.4	3.2	2.2	5.4	23.2	12.6
26	2.8	0.3	6.8	3.9	9.7	4.2	6.5	3.0	1.9	5.0	18.0	12.2
27	2.4	0.3	5.5	4.1	7.9	4.5	5.0	2.9	1.6	5.1	14.5	12.4
28	2.0	0.4	4.5	4.3	6.5	4.7	4.0	2.8	1.4	5.1	11.9	12.6
29	1.7	0.4	3.8	4.4	5.4	4.8	3.3	2.6	1.2	4.9	10.0	12.2
30+	11.0	9.7	22.2	72.3	33.2	82.1	22.4	46.0	12.1	102.0	67.7	230.1
Unknown	-	-	-	0.2	-	0.2	-	-	-	0.8	0.1	1.0
All ages	32.1	11.6	104.4	102.2	136.5	113.8	524.7	86.5	68.7	175.3	729.9	375.5
Females												
Age under 16	-	-	-	-	-	-	-	-	-	0.3	-	0.3
16	-	-	-	-	-	-	0.2	0.1	0.3	3.0	0.5	3.0
17	-	-	-	-	-	-	5.7	0.1	2.3	1.8	8.0	1.9
18	-	-	-	-	-	-	106.0	1.1	11.3	3.8	117.4	4.9
19	-	-	0.1	-	0.1	-	139.4	2.7	13.7	5.8	153.2	8.5
20	-	-	1.2	0.4	1.2	0.4	143.9	4.3	11.5	6.8	156.7	11.5
21	0.3	-	11.2	1.4	11.5	1.4	84.5	5.5	7.9	7.0	104.0	13.9
22	1.3	-	17.4	3.5	18.7	3.5	38.9	5.4	6.2	7.5	63.9	16.4
23	2.2	0.1	16.2	5.1	18.4	5.2	20.7	4.8	4.9	8.3	44.0	18.4
24	3.0	0.2	12.3	6.1	15.2	6.2	12.6	4.6	4.0	8.7	31.9	19.5
25	3.0	0.2	9.1	6.4	12.1	6.6	9.4	4.4	3.3	8.9	24.8	19.9
26	2.7	0.3	6.6	6.6	9.2	7.0	7.4	4.3	3.0	9.0	19.7	20.3
27	2.3	0.4	5.1	6.7	7.4	7.1	6.2	4.4	2.7	9.1	16.3	20.6
28	1.8	0.4	4.0	6.6	5.8	7.0	5.1	4.3	2.5	9.3	13.4	20.7
29	1.5	0.4	3.2	6.3	4.7	6.8	4.3	4.0	2.2	8.5	11.2	19.3
30+	8.4	9.5	19.3	98.6	27.7	108.1	44.8	78.2	29.5	197.1	102.0	383.4
Unknown	-	-	-	0.5	-	0.6	-	-	-	1.2	0.1	1.8
All ages	26.5	11.5	105.7	148.5	132.2	160.0	629.3	128.1	105.5	296.1	867.0	584.2

1 Higher Education Statistics Agency (HESA) higher education institutions include Open University students. Part-time figures include those writing up at home and on sabbaticals. The field "gender" has changed to be consistent with the MIAP common data definitions coding frame. Students of "indeterminate gender" are now included in total figures but not in seperate breakdowns. "Indeterminate" means unable to be classified as either male or female and is not related in any way to trans-gender.

2 Full-time includes sandwich. Part-time comprises both day and evening, including block release and open/distance learning.

3 Ages as at 31 August 2008 (1 July for Northern Ireland and 31 December for Scotland).

4 Figures for higher education (HE) institutions are based on the HESA 'standard registration' count. Figures for FE institutions are whole year enrolments.

5 FE institution figures for England include Learning and Skills Council (LSC) funded students only.

6 Includes data for HE students in FE institutions in Wales which cannot be split by level.

Sources: Department for Education; Department for Business, Innovation and Skills;
Welsh Government; Scottish Government; Northern Ireland Department of Education;
Northern Ireland Department for Employment and Learning; 020 778 38455

20.9 Students in higher[1] education by level, mode of study[2], gender and subject group[3], 2008/09[3,4]

United Kingdom (home and overseas students)

Thousands

| | Postgraduate level | | | | | | First degree | | Other undergraduate | | Total higher education[5] | |
| | PhD and equivalent | | Masters and others | | Total Postgraduate | | | | | | | |
	Full-time	Part-time	Full-time	Part-time	Full-time	Part-time	Full-time	Part-time	Full-time	Part-time	Full-time	Part-time
All persons												
Medicine & Dentistry	4.3	2.4	3.6	8.3	7.9	10.7	44.3	0.1	0.5	0.4	**52.6**	**11.2**
Subjects Allied to Medicine	2.8	2.1	9.1	36.2	12.0	38.3	90.3	25.3	54.8	74.4	**157.1**	**138.1**
Biological Sciences	9.3	2.2	9.0	8.6	18.3	10.8	111.1	19.6	4.8	7.6	**134.2**	**38.0**
Vet. Science, Agriculture & related	0.7	0.1	1.5	1.2	2.2	1.4	11.5	0.5	3.7	4.7	**17.4**	**6.6**
Physical Sciences	8.7	0.7	5.7	3.3	14.4	4.0	53.2	8.4	1.5	4.7	**69.1**	**17.1**
Mathematical and Computing Sciences	4.7	1.0	14.5	6.6	19.2	7.6	75.3	13.1	8.2	12.8	**102.6**	**33.5**
Engineering & Technology	8.6	1.4	18.2	10.8	26.8	12.2	77.7	11.9	8.7	17.1	**113.2**	**41.2**
Architecture, Building & Planning	0.8	0.4	5.7	8.6	6.5	9.0	29.6	8.5	4.7	8.6	**40.8**	**26.1**
Social Sciences (inc Law)	6.3	2.3	32.6	23.4	39.0	25.7	165.6	28.7	11.7	35.1	**216.2**	**89.5**
Business & Administrative Studies	2.6	2.2	52.0	50.1	54.6	52.2	154.9	19.7	18.0	43.8	**227.6**	**115.7**
Mass Communication & Documentation	0.4	0.3	5.6	3.4	5.9	3.6	34.9	1.7	2.5	1.5	**43.4**	**6.9**
Languages	3.3	1.2	7.0	4.7	10.3	5.9	75.9	10.2	3.5	25.4	**89.8**	**41.5**
Historical and Philosophical Studies	3.2	1.9	5.5	5.9	8.7	7.8	52.3	13.1	0.8	11.4	**61.8**	**32.3**
Creative Arts & Design	1.5	1.0	10.3	5.9	11.8	6.9	122.2	5.7	17.7	7.0	**151.7**	**19.6**
Education[6]	1.4	4.0	29.0	66.7	30.4	70.6	44.6	10.8	10.0	51.8	**85.0**	**133.2**
Other subjects[7]	-	-	0.1	2.1	0.1	2.1	4.0	29.0	3.2	92.4	**7.3**	**123.5**
Unknown[5,8]	-	-	0.7	4.8	0.7	4.8	6.7	8.3	19.9	72.6	**27.3**	**85.8**
All subjects	**58.6**	**23.1**	**210.1**	**250.7**	**268.7**	**273.8**	**1,154.0**	**214.6**	**174.1**	**471.3**	**1,596.9**	**959.7**
of which overseas students	28.8	5.9	120.1	28.9	148.8	34.8	144.9	9.3	15.5	21.0	309.2	65.0
Males												
Medicine and Dentistry	1.8	1.2	1.4	3.8	3.1	5.0	18.6	0.1	0.1	0.1	**21.8**	**5.1**
Subjects Allied to Medicine	1.2	0.7	3.2	9.6	4.4	10.4	20.1	4.2	6.7	11.0	**31.2**	**25.5**
Biological Sciences	3.4	0.8	3.3	2.6	6.7	3.4	42.4	5.4	2.8	2.2	**51.8**	**11.0**
Vet. Science, Agriculture & related	0.3	0.1	0.7	0.6	1.0	0.6	3.3	0.2	1.5	2.5	**5.8**	**3.3**
Physical Sciences	5.5	0.4	3.1	1.9	8.6	2.3	31.5	4.9	0.8	2.5	**40.8**	**9.6**
Mathematical and Computing Sciences	3.5	0.8	11.6	5.1	15.0	5.9	57.4	9.7	6.8	8.6	**79.2**	**24.2**
Engineering & Technology	6.7	1.1	14.8	8.6	21.4	9.7	64.9	10.7	7.7	15.4	**94.1**	**35.8**
Architecture, Building & Planning	0.5	0.3	3.4	5.3	3.9	5.6	20.4	6.6	3.5	6.4	**27.8**	**18.6**
Social Sciences (inc Law)	3.2	1.1	14.2	9.1	17.4	10.2	64.5	9.6	3.9	9.4	**85.9**	**29.2**
Business & Administrative Studies	1.6	1.4	29.1	26.8	30.6	28.2	80.0	9.0	8.2	19.6	**118.8**	**56.8**
Mass Communication & Documentation	0.2	0.1	1.9	1.1	2.1	1.3	15.7	0.8	1.5	0.7	**19.3**	**2.7**
Languages	1.4	0.5	2.2	1.4	3.6	1.9	22.5	2.7	1.8	10.1	**27.9**	**14.7**
Historical and Philosophical Studies	1.8	1.1	2.7	3.0	4.5	4.0	25.1	5.5	0.4	4.0	**30.0**	**13.6**
Creative Arts & Design	0.8	0.5	4.0	2.2	4.7	2.7	47.6	2.0	7.7	2.1	**60.1**	**6.8**
Education[6]	0.5	1.6	8.6	18.6	9.0	20.1	7.0	1.3	2.4	13.5	**18.4**	**35.0**
Other subjects[7]	-	-	-	0.9	-	0.9	1.5	11.0	1.7	35.4	**3.3**	**47.3**
Unknown[5,8]	-	-	0.3	1.6	0.3	1.6	2.4	2.9	11.3	31.9	**13.9**	**36.4**

20.9 Students in higher[1] education by level, mode of study[2], gender and subject group[3], 2008/09[3,4]

United Kingdom (home and overseas students)

Thousands

	Postgraduate level						First degree		Other undergraduate		Total higher education[5]	
	PhD and equivalent		Masters and others		Total Postgraduate							
	Full-time	Part-time	Full-time	Part-time	Full-time	Part-time	Full-time	Part-time	Full-time	Part-time	Full-time	Part-time
All subjects	32.1	11.6	104.4	102.2	136.5	113.8	524.7	86.5	68.7	175.3	729.9	375.5
of which overseas students	16.6	3.4	66.3	16.3	83.0	19.7	72.8	4.9	8.6	9.9	164.4	34.5
Females												
Medicine & Dentistry	2.5	1.2	2.2	4.5	4.7	5.7	25.7	-	0.4	0.3	**30.8**	**6.0**
Subjects Allied to Medicine	1.6	1.4	5.9	26.6	7.6	28.0	70.3	21.2	48.1	63.5	**126.0**	**112.6**
Biological Sciences	5.9	1.4	5.7	6.0	11.6	7.4	68.7	14.2	2.0	5.4	**82.4**	**27.0**
Vet. Science, Agriculture & related	0.4	0.1	0.8	0.7	1.2	0.7	8.2	0.3	2.2	2.2	**11.6**	**3.3**
Physical Sciences	3.3	0.3	2.6	1.4	5.8	1.7	21.7	3.6	0.7	2.2	**28.3**	**7.5**
Mathematical and Computing Sciences	1.2	0.2	3.0	1.5	4.2	1.7	17.9	3.4	1.4	4.2	**23.4**	**9.3**
Engineering & Technology	1.9	0.3	3.5	2.2	5.4	2.5	12.8	1.2	0.9	1.7	**19.1**	**5.4**
Architecture, Building & Planning	0.3	0.1	2.3	3.3	2.6	3.4	9.2	1.8	1.2	2.2	**13.0**	**7.5**
Social Sciences (inc Law)	3.1	1.2	18.4	14.3	21.5	15.5	101.0	19.1	7.8	25.7	**130.4**	**60.3**
Business & Administrative Studies	1.1	0.8	23.0	23.2	24.0	24.0	75.0	10.7	9.8	24.2	**108.8**	**58.9**
Mass Communication & Documentation	0.2	0.1	3.6	2.3	3.8	2.4	19.3	0.9	1.1	0.8	**24.1**	**4.2**
Languages	1.9	0.7	4.8	3.3	6.7	4.0	53.4	7.5	1.7	15.3	**61.9**	**26.8**
Historical and Philosophical Studies	1.4	0.8	2.8	2.9	4.2	3.7	27.2	7.6	0.5	7.4	**31.8**	**18.8**
Creative Arts & Design	0.7	0.5	6.4	3.7	7.1	4.2	74.6	3.7	10.0	4.9	**91.6**	**12.8**
Education[6]	0.9	2.4	20.4	48.1	21.3	50.5	37.6	9.4	7.6	38.2	**66.5**	**98.1**
Other subjects[7]	-	-	0.1	1.2	0.1	1.2	2.5	18.0	1.5	57.0	**4.0**	**76.3**
Unknown[5,8]	-	-	0.4	3.3	0.4	3.3	4.4	5.4	8.6	40.7	**13.4**	**49.4**
All subjects	26.5	11.5	105.7	148.5	132.2	160.0	629.3	128.1	105.5	296.1	867.0	584.2
of which overseas students	12.2	2.5	53.7	12.6	65.9	15.2	72.1	4.4	6.9	11.1	144.9	30.6

Sources: Department for Education;
Department for Business, Innovation and Skills;
Welsh Government;
Scottish Government;
Northern Ireland Department of Education;
Northern Ireland Department for Employment and Learning;
020 778 38455

1 Higher Education Statistics Agency (HESA) higher education institutions include Open University students. Part-time figures include those writing up at home and on sabbaticals. The field "gender" has changed to be consistent with the MIAP common data definitions coding frame. Students of "indeterminate gender" are now included in total figures but not in separate breakdowns. "Indeterminate" means unable to be classified as either male or female and is not related in any way to trans-gender.
2 Full-time includes sandwich. Part-time comprises both day and evening, including block release and open/distance learning.
3 Figures for higher education (HE) institutions are based on the HESA 'standard registration' count. Figures for FE institutions are whole year enrolments.
4 Further education (FE) institution figures for England include Learning and Skills Council (LSC) funded students only.
5 Includes data for higher education students in further education institutions in Wales which cannot be split by level.
6 Including ITT and INSET.
7 Includes Combined and general categories.
8 Includes data for higher education students in further education institutions in England, which cannot be split by subject group.

20.10 Qualified teachers: by type of school and gender[1]

United Kingdom   **(i) Full-time teachers**   **Thousands**

	1990/91	1995/96[2]	2000/01[3,4]	2006/07	2007/08[5]	Total of which	England & Wales[1]	Scotland	Northern Ireland[12]
							2008/09		
All									
Public sector mainstream									
Nursery[6,7] and Primary	208.8	211.8	211.2	207.0	206.6	206.0	176.6	22.2	7.2
Secondary[9]	233.1	222.1	225.7	234.4	232.0	228.0	194.5	24.0	9.5
Non-maintained mainstream	44.9 [9]	48.6 [9]	52.3	58.7	62.0	66.0	63.2	2.7	0.1
All Special	19.0	17.2	16.5	20.5	20.6	20.7	17.9	2.2	0.7
All schools[10]	**505.7**	**499.7**	**505.7**	**520.6**	**521.1**	**520.8**	**452.2**	**51.2**	**17.4**
Males									
Public sector mainstream									
Nursery[11] and Primary	37.7	35.5	32.1	30.7	30.6	30.6	27.6	1.8	1.3
Secondary[8]	120.7	107.9	102.9	99.9	97.6	95.1	81.7	10.0	3.5
Non-maintained mainstream	20.6 [9]	21.1 [9]	21.3	23.9	25.2	26.8	25.7	1.1	-
All Special	5.9	5.4	5.0	6.1	6.1	6.0	5.4	0.5	0.1
All schools[10]	**184.9**	**169.8**	**161.3**	**160.6**	**159.5**	**158.6**	**140.3**	**13.3**	**4.9**
Females									
Public sector mainstream									
Nursery[11] and Primary	171.1	176.3	179.1	174.6	174.3	173.8	149.0	18.9	6.0
Secondary[8]	112.3	114.2	122.8	134.5	134.4	132.9	112.9	14.0	6.0
Non-maintained mainstream	24.3 [9]	27.4 [9]	30.9	34.8	36.8	39.2	37.5	1.7	0.1
All Special	13.1	11.8	11.6	14.4	14.6	14.7	12.5	1.6	0.5
All schools[10]	**320.8**	**329.9**	**344.4**	**358.3**	**360.0**	**360.6**	**311.8**	**36.2**	**12.5**

           (ii) Full-time equivalent (FTE) of part-time teachers   **Thousands**

	1990/91[*]	1995/96[2]	2000/01[3,4]	2006/07	2007/08	Total of which	England & Wales[1]	Scotland	Northern Ireland[12]
							2008/09		
All									
Public sector mainstream									
Nursery[6,7] and Primary	..	19.1	21.9	31.1	33.0	33.9	30.2	3.0	0.7
Secondary[8]	..	17.7	16.7	22.1	23.0	23.8	21.2	2.0	0.6
Non-maintained mainstream	..	8.9 [9]	10.2	11.8	12.1	12.5	12.1	0.4	-
All Special	..	1.5	1.6	2.1	2.2	2.2	1.9	0.3	0.1
All schools[10]	**30.0**	**47.2**	**50.4**	**67.1**	**70.2**	**72.4**	**65.4**	**5.8**	**1.3**

Sources: Department for Education; Welsh Government; Scottish Government; Northern Ireland Department of Education

1 Public sector teachers numbers in England & Wales have been provided from the 618G survey and gender split has been calculated by using the proportions from the Database of Teacher Records (DTR).
2 Includes 1994/95 data for Northern Ireland.
3 Includes 1999/00 pre-school data for Scotland.
4 Includes 2001/02 data for Northern Ireland.
5 Includes revised data.
6 From 2005/06, data for Scotland include only centres providing pre-school education as a local authority centre or in partnership with the local authority. Figures are not therefore directly comparable with previous years.
7 From 2005/06, for Scotland pre-school education centres, the total full-time equivalent (FTE) of General Teaching Council of Scotland (GTC) registered staff has been provided within the 'full-time' section because information on full-time/part-time split is not available. Teachers are counted once for each centre they work for, so the number of teachers contains some double counting. However, as each centre calculates the teacher's FTE as the time they spend working in that centre, the FTE should not be double-counted. Full-time/part-time figures for 2004/05 are estimates based on the headcount of all GTC registered staff.
8 From 1993/94 excludes sixth form colleges in England and Wales which were reclassified as further education colleges on 1 April 1993.
9 Figures refer to Great Britain.
10 Excludes Pupil Referral Units (PRUs).
11 For Scotland pre-school education centres FTE staff, a gender split is not available. Gender figures for 2004/05 are estimates based on the headcount of all GTC registered staff.
12 From 2008/09 onwards Northern Ireland data excludes all temporary teachers.

Crime and Justice

Chapter 21

Crime and Justice

There are differences in the legal and judicial systems of England and Wales, Scotland and Northern Ireland which make it impossible to provide tables covering the UK as a whole in this section. These differences concern the classification of offences, the meaning of certain terms used in the statistics, the effects of the several Criminal Justice Acts and recording practices.

Recorded crime statistics
(Table 21.3)

Crimes recorded by the police provide a measure of the amount of crime committed. For a variety of reasons, many offences are either not reported to the police or not recorded by them. The changes in the number of offences recorded do not necessarily provide an accurate reflection of changes in the amount of crime committed.

The recorded crime statistics include all indictable and triable-either-way offences together with a few summary offences which are closely linked to these offences. The revised rules changed the emphasis of measurement more towards one crime per victim, and also increased the coverage of offences.

In order to further improve the consistency of recorded crime statistics and to take a more victim-oriented approach to crime recording, the National Crime Recording Standard (NCRS) was introduced across all forces in England, Wales and Northern Ireland from 1 April 2002. Some police forces implemented the principles of NCRS in advance of its introduction across all forces. The NCRS had the effect of increasing the number of offences recorded by the police and data before and after 2002/03 are not directly comparable.

For a variety of reasons many offences are either not reported to the police or not recorded by them. The changes in the number of offences recorded do not necessarily provide an accurate reflection of changes in the amount of crime committed.

Similarly, the Scottish Crime Recording Standard (SCRS) was introduced by the eight Scottish police forces with effect from 1 April 2004. This means that no corroborative evidence is required initially to record a crime-related incident as a crime if the victim perceived it as a crime. Again, the introduction of this new recording standard was expected to increase the numbers of minor crimes recorded by the police, such as minor crimes of vandalism and minor thefts and offences of petty assault and breach of the peace. However, it was expected that the SCRS would not have much impact on the figures for the more serious crimes such as serious assault, sexual assault, robbery or housebreaking.

The Sexual Offences Act 2003 introduced in May 2004 altered the definition and coverage of sexual offences. In particular, it redefined indecent exposure as a sexual offence, which is likely to account for much of the increase in sexual offences.

The Sexual Offences (Scotland) Act 2009 introduced in 1 December 2010 repealed a number of common law crimes including rape, clandestine injury to women and sodomy and replaced them with new statutory sexual offences. The Act created a number of new "protective" offences, which criminalise sexual activity with children and mentally disordered persons. Protective offences are placed into categories concerning young children (under 13) and older (13-15 years). The new legislation may result in some increases in Group 2 crimes. For example, the offences of voyeurism or indecent communication towards an adult would previously have been classified as breach of the peace. It is likely that the effect will be to change the distribution of these crimes among the sub classifications. For example, some crimes previously categorised as lewd and libidinous practices will now be classified as sexual assault. The standard breakdown provided in response to information requests on sexual offences has had to be revised to accommodate these changes. Details of changes are provided below.

Offences committed before 1 December 2010:

Rape & attempted rape includes:

- Rape
- Assault with intent to rape

Indecent assault includes:

- Indecent assault

Lewd and indecent behaviour includes:

- Public indecency

'Other' includes:

- Incest
- Unnatural crimes
- Prostitution
- Procuration and other sexual offences

Offences committed on or after 1 December 2010:

Rape & attempted rape includes:

- Rape
- Attempted rape

Sexual assault includes:

- Contact sexual assault (13-15 years old or adult 16+)
- other sexually coercive conduction (adult 16+)
- Sexual offences against children under 13
- Sexual activity with children aged 13-15
- Other sexual offences involving children aged 13-15
- Lewd and libidinous practices

Prostitution

- Offences relating to prostitution

'Other' includes:

- Incest
- Unnatural crimes
- Public indecency
- Sexual exposure
- Procuration and other sexual offences

Further information is available from Crime in England and Wales 2007/2008 (Home Office, Sian Nicholas, Chris Kershaw and Alison Walker, editors).

Court proceedings and police cautions
(Tables 21.4 to 21.8, 21.12 to 21.16, 21.19 to 21.21)

The statistical basis of the tables of court proceedings is broadly similar in England and Wales, Scotland and Northern Ireland; the tables show the number of persons found guilty, recording a person under the heading of the principal offence of which they were found guilty, excluding additional findings of guilt at the same proceedings. A person found guilty at a number of separate court proceedings is included more than once.

The statistics on offenders cautioned in England and Wales cover only those who, on admission of guilt, were given a formal caution by, or on the instructions of, a senior police officer as an alternative to prosecution. Written warnings by the police for motor offences and persons paying fixed penalties for certain motoring offences are excluded. Formal cautions are not issued in Scotland. There are no statistics on cautioning available for Northern Ireland.

The Crime and Disorder Act 1998 created provisions in relation to reprimands and final warnings, new offences and orders which have been implemented nationally since 1 June 2000. They replace the system of cautioning for offenders aged under 18. Reprimands can be given to first-time offenders for minor offences. Any further offending results in either a final warning or a charge.

For persons proceeded against in Scotland, the statistics relate to the High Court of Justiciary, the sheriff courts and the district courts. The High Court deals with serious solemn (that is, jury) cases and has unlimited sentencing power. Sheriff courts are limited to imprisonment of 3 years for solemn cases, or 3 months (6 months when specified in legislation for second or subsequent offences and 12 months for certain statutory offences) for summary (that is, non-jury) cases. District courts deal only with summary cases and are limited to 60 days imprisonment and level 4 fines. Stipendiary magistrates sit in Glasgow District Court and have the summary sentencing powers of a sheriff.

In England and Wales, indictable offences are offences which are:

• triable only on indictment. These offences are the most serious breaches of the criminal law and must be tried at the Crown Court. 'Indictable-only' offences include murder, manslaughter, rape and robbery
• triable either way. These offences may be tried at the Crown Court or a magistrates' court

The Criminal Justice Act 1991 led to the following main changes in the sentences available to the courts in England and Wales:

• introduction of combination orders
• introduction of the 'unit fine scheme' at magistrates' courts
• abolishing the sentence of detention in a young offender institution for 14-year-old boys and changing the minimum and maximum sentence lengths for 15 to 17-year-olds to 10 and 12 months respectively, and
• abolishing partly suspended sentences of imprisonment and restricting the use of a fully suspended sentence

(The Criminal Justice Act 1993 abolished the 'unit fine scheme' in magistrates' courts, which had been introduced under the Criminal Justice Act 1991.

A charging standard for assault was introduced in England and Wales on 31 August 1994 with the aim of promoting consistency between the police and prosecution on the appropriate level of charge to be brought.

The Criminal Justice and Public Order Act 1994 created several new offences in England and Wales, mainly in the area of public order, but also including male rape (there is no statutory offence of male rape in Scotland, although such a crime may be charged as serious assault). The Act also:

• extended the provisions of section 53 of the Children and Young Persons Act 1993 for 10 to 13-year-olds
• increased the maximum sentence length for 15 to 17-year-olds to 2 years
• increased the upper limit from £2,000 to £5,000 for offences of criminal damage proceeded against as if triable only summarily
• introduced provisions for the reduction of sentences for early guilty pleas, and
• increased the maximum sentence length for certain firearm offences

 Provisions within the Crime (Sentences) Act 1997 (as amended by the Powers of Criminal Courts Sentencing Act 2000) in England and Wales, and the Crime and Punishment (Scotland) Act 1997 in Scotland, included:

• an automatic life sentence for a second serious violent or sexual offence unless there are exceptional circumstances (this provision has not been enacted in Scotland)
• a minimum sentence of 7 years for an offender convicted for a third time of a class A drug trafficking offence unless the court considers this to be unjust in all the circumstances, and
• in England and Wales, the new section 38A of the Magistrates' Courts' Act 1980 extending the circumstances in which a magistrates' court may commit a person convicted of an offence triable-either-way to the Crown Court for sentence – it was implemented in conjunction with section 49 of the Criminal Procedure and Investigations Act 1996, which involves the magistrates' courts in asking defendants to indicate a plea before the mode of trial decision is taken and compels the court to sentence, or commit for sentence, any defendant who indicates a guilty plea.

Under the Criminal Justice and Court Service Act 2000 new terms were introduced for certain orders. Community rehabilitation order is the new name for a probation order. A community service order is now known as a community punishment order. Finally, the new term for a combination order is community punishment and rehabilitation order. In April 2000 the secure training order was replaced by the detention and training order. Section 53 of the Children and Young Persons Act 1993 was repealed on 25 August 2000 and its provisions were transferred to sections 90 to 92 of the Powers of Criminal Courts (Sentencing) Act 2000. Reparation and action plan orders were implemented nationally from 1 June 2000. The drug treatment and testing order was introduced in England, Scotland and Wales from October 2000. The referral order was introduced in England, Scotland and Wales from April 2000. Youth rehabilitation orders came into effect in November 2009 as part of the Criminal Justice and Immigration Act 2008. These changes are now reflected in Table 21.8.

Following the introduction of the Libra case management system during 2008, offenders at magistrates' courts can now be recorded as sex 'Not Stated'. In 2008 one per cent of offenders sentenced were recorded as sex 'Not Stated' as well as 'Male', 'Female', or 'Other'. Amendments to the data tables have been made to accommodate this new category.

The system of magistrates' courts and Crown courts in Northern Ireland operates in a similar way to that in England and Wales. A particularly significant statutory development, however, has been the Criminal Justice (NI) Order 1996 which introduced a new sentencing regime into Northern Ireland, largely replicating that which was introduced into England and Wales by the Criminal Justice Acts of 1991 and 1993. The order makes many changes to both community and custodial sentences, while introducing new orders such as the combination order, the custody probation order, and orders for release on licence of sexual offenders.

Expenditure on penal establishments in Scotland
(Table 21.18)

The results shown in this table are reported on a cash basis for financial years 1996/97 to 2000/01 in line with funding arrangements. Financial year 2001/02 is reported on a resource accounting basis in line with the introduction of resource budgeting. Capital charges were introduced with resource accounting and budgeting.

The Sexual Offences (Scotland) Act 2009 introduced in 1 December 2010 repealed a number of common law crimes including rape, clandestine injury to women and sodomy and replaced them with new statutory sexual offences. The Act created a number of new "protective" offences, which criminalise sexual activity with children and mentally disordered persons. Protective offences are placed into categories concerning young children (under 13) and older (13-15 years). The new legislation may result in some increases in Group 2 crimes. For example, the offences of voyeurism or indecent communication towards an adult would previously have been classified as breach of the peace. It is likely that the effect will be to change the distribution of these crimes among the sub classifications. For example, some crimes previously categorised as lewd and libidinous practices will now be classified as sexual assault. The standard breakdown provided in response to information requests on sexual offences has had to be revised to accommodate these changes.

21.1 Police forces strength:[1] by country and sex

As at 31 March

Numbers

		1999	2000	2001	2002	2003	2004	2005	2006	2007	2008	2009	2010	2011
England and Wales														
Regular police (FTE)														
Strength:														
Men	KERB	103,956	101,801	102,139	104,483	107,371	110,544	111,119	110,003	108,775	107,528	107,648	106,746	102,577
Women	KERC	19,885	20,155	21,174	22,784	25,139	27,925	29,940	31,520	33,117	34,333	36,121	36,988	36,532
Seconded:[2][3]														
Men	KERD	2,017	1,965	1,914	2,031	1,689	1,811	1,514	1,545	422	432	438	423	391
Women	KERE	238	249	292	305	251	284	222	203	60	70	66	78	85
Special constables strength:[4]														
Men	KERH	10,860	9,623	8,630	8,014	7,718	7,645	8,074	8,829	9,327	9,719	9,544	10,629	12,669
Women	KERI	5,624	4,724	4,108	3,584	3,319	3,343	3,844	4,350	4,694	4,828	4,707	4,876	5,752
Scotland														
Regular police														
Strength:[5]														
Men	KERK	12,287	12,069	12,237	12,184	12,214	12,239	12,309	12,364	12,232	12,011	12,328	12,367	12,141
Women	KERL	2,238	2,290	2,573	2,696	2,846	2,826	3,122	3,334	3,479	3,601	3,991	4,288	4,386
Central service:[6]														
Men	KERM	88	95	87	116	131	166	195	171	153	219	180	194	203
Women	KERN	9	13	10	12	17	29	29	25	28	44	37	47	39
Seconded:[7]														
Men	KERO	85	130	140	133	166	192	216	200	195	196	291	289	279
Women	KERP	12	18	14	18	24	30	31	27	28	30	69	64	53
Additional regular police:														
Men	HFVM	85	80	83	80	79	88	79	85	107	106	129	131	131
Women	HFVN	6	4	5	12	10	13	21	15	12	14	24	29	32
Special constables Strength:														
Men	KERS	1229	981	924	812	711	773	718	888	886	884	..	..	..
Women	KERT	422	355	336	307	280	328	437	432	471	510	..	..	..
Northern Ireland														
Regular police[8][9]														
Strength:														
Men	KERU	7,406	6,844	6,227	6,057	6,171	6,108	6,016	5,992	5,949	5,761	5,669	5,548	5,371
Women	KERV	987	966	1,009	1,080	1,266	1,418	1,547	1,534	1,600	1,653	1,735	1,837	1,922
Reserve[10]														
Strength:														
Men	KERW	3,199	2,962	2,629	2,223	1,983	1,824	1,431	1,424	1,212	1,119	930	774	597
Women	KERX	641	607	556	510	453	485	410	402	400	382	345	311	283

1 Figures for England and Wales are as 31 March. Figures prior to 2003 are based on full-time equivalent strength excluding career break or maternity/paternity leave and those from 2003 are full-time equivalent strength figures that have been rounded to the nearest whole number.

Figures for Scotland are as at 31 March. From 1999 to 2003 the figures are based on a headcount strength. From 2004 onwards the figures are based on full-time equivalent strength. The figures exclude those on career breaks.

From 1999, figures for Northern Ireland reflect the position at the end of the financial year, ie 1999 and 2000 figures are as at 31 March 2000 and 31 March 2001 respectively. Prior to this figures were as at 31 December.

2 Figures exclude secondments outside the police service in England and Wales (eg to the private sector or to law enforcement agencies overseas).

3 From 31 March 2007 onwards details of officers seconded to NCIS and NCS will no longer appear following the launch of the Serious Organised Crime Agency (SOCA) in April 2006.

4 Special constable figures are given as a headcount measure.

5 'Strength' is police officers in force.

6 Instructors at Training Establishments, etc, formerly shown as secondments.

7 Includes Scottish Crime and Drug Enforcement Agency and Scottish Police Services Authority.

8 Does not include officers on secondment.

9 Also includes student officers.

10 Includes part-time reserve and full-time reserve,
FTR - 515 as at 31 March 2009 (481 males and 34 females).
Con PT - 760 as at 31 March 2009 (449 males and 311 females).
FTR - 382 as at 31 March 2010 (362 males and 20 females).
Con PT - 703 as at 31 March 2010 (412 males and 291 females).

Sources: Home Office: 020 7035 0289;
The Scottish Government Justice Analytical Services: 0131 244 2635
The Police Service of Northern Ireland: 0845 6008000 ext 240

21.2 Prison population[1] international comparisons with other EU countries and selected other countries 2003-2009

Thousands

Country	2003	2004	2005	2006	2007	2008	2009	% change 2008-2009	Rate per 100,000 population in 2009
England & Wales[2]	72,992	75,057	76,896	79,085	80,692	83,406	84,116	1%	153
Northern Ireland[3]	1,160	1,274	1,301	1,433	1,468	1,507	1,468	-3%	82
Scotland[3]	6,524	6,805	6,792	7,111	7,291	7,741	7,928	2%	153
Austria	7,816	9,000	8,767	8,780	8,887	7,899	8,423	7%	101
Belgium[4]	9,308	9,245	9,375	9,635	10,008	9,858	10,159	3%	94
Bulgaria[5]	9,422	10,066	10,871	11,436	11,058	10,271	9,408	-8%	124
Cyprus[6]	355	546	536	599	673	671	700	4%	88
Czech Republic[7]	17,277	18,343	18,937	18,578	18,901	20,502	21,734	6%	207
Denmark	3,577	3,762	4,132	3,759	3,406	3,451	3,881	12%	70
Estonia[5]	4,352	4,576	4,565	4,411	4,327	3,467	3,656	5%	273
Finland[7]	3,463	3,535	3,883	3,477	3,370	3,457	3,231	-7%	60
France[8]	57,440	56,271	56,595	55,754	60,677	62,843	61,787	-2%	96
Germany[9]	81,176	81,166	80,410	78,581	75,719	75,056	73,592	-2%	90
Greece[10]	8,555	8,760	9,589	10,113	11,120	11,798	11,080	-6%	98
Hungary[7]	16,507	16,543	15,720	14,821	14,353	14,736	15,373	4%	153
Ireland[11]	2,986	3,083	3,022	3,080	3,305	3,523	4,009	14%	89
Italy[7]	56,845	56,068	59,523	39,005	48,693	58,127	64,791	11%	107
Latvia[5]	8,366	8,179	7,646	6,965	6,548	6,548	6,873	5%	304
Lithuania[5]	11,070	8,063	8,125	8,137	8,079	7,866	8,000	2%	239
Luxembourg	498	548	693	756	745	674	679	1%	136
Malta[12]	278	277	298	346	387	412	480	17%	116
Netherlands	18,242	20,075	21,826	20,463	18,103	16,416	15,676	-5%	95
Poland[2]	80,692	79,344	82,656	87,669	90,199	84,549	85,598	1%	225
Portugal[7]	13,835	13,152	12,889	12,636	11,587	10,830	11,099	2%	104
Romania[7]	42,815	39,031	36,700	34,038	29,390	26,212	26,716	2%	124
Slovakia[7]	8,873	9,422	8,897	8,249	7,986	8,166	9,316	14%	172
Slovenia	1,099	1,126	1,132	1,301	1,336	1,317	1,360	3%	66
Spain	55,244	59,224	61,269	64,120	66,400	71,778	76,509	7%	164
Sweden[13]	6,755	7,332	7,054	7,175	6,770	6,853	7,286	6%	78
European Union 27	607,522	609,873	620,099	601,513	611,478	619,934	634,928	2%	127
Croatia[5]	2,732	2,803	3,022	3,485	3,833	4,290	4,734	10%	107
Iceland	112	115	119	119	115	140	175	25%	55
Norway	2,914	2,975	3,097	3,164	3,280	3,278	3,285	0%	68
Russian Federation[5]	877,393	847,004	763,115	823,451	871,693	883,170	887,723	1%	626
Switzerland[14]	5,214	5,977	6,137	5,888	5,715	5,780	6,084	5%	79
Turkey[15]	64,051	71,148	54,296	67,795	85,865	99,416	113,493	14%	157
Ukraine[16]	198,386	193,489	179,519	165,716	154,055	145,946	146,394	0%	320
Australia[17]	23,555	24,171	25,353	25,790	27,224	27,615	29,317	6%	134
Brazil[18]	308,304	336,358	361,402	401,236	422,590	451,429	473,626	5%	243
Canada[19]	35,868	34,155	34,365	35,436	37,326	38,348	39,132	2%	117
Japan[7]	73,734	76,413	79,052	81,255	83,518	80,523	78,952	-2%	62
Korea (Rep. of)[3]	58,945	57,184	52,403	46,721	46,313	46,684	49,467	6%	102
Mexico[7]	182,530	193,889	205,821	210,140	212,841	219,754	224,749	2%	204
New Zealand[3]	6,059	6,556	7,100	7,595	7,959	7,763	8,287	7%	192
South Africa[9]	189,748	187,640	187,394	150,302	161,639	165,840	165,230	0%	335
U.S.A.[17]	2,082,728	2,129,802	2,183,152	2,245,189	2,296,133	2,308,561	2,297,400	0%	748

Sources: Ministries responsible for prisons, national prison administrations, national statistical offices, Council of Europe Annual Penal Statistics (SPACE), World Prison Population List (Roy Walmsley) and World Prison Brief (International Centre for Prison Studies)

1 At 1 September: number of prisoners, including pre-trial detainees/remand prisoners.
2 At 31 August.
3 Annual averages. Countries calculate these on the basis of daily, weekly or monthly figures.
4 At 1 March.
5 At 1 January.
6 At 1 September (2003-08), August (2009).
7 At 31 December.
8 Metropolitan and overseas departments and territories.
9 At 31 March.
10 At 1 September (2003, 05-06, 08-09), December (2004), November (2007).

11 At 1 September (2003-08), 9 October (2009).
12 At 1 September (2003-06), annual average (2007-08), 22 June (2009).
13 At 1 October.
14 At first Wednesday in September.
15 At 1 September (2003-08), 31 August (2009).
16 At 1 September (2003-07, 09), 31 December (2008).
17 At 30 June.
18 At December.
19 Annual averages by financial year (e.g. 2009 = 1 April 2008 - 31 March 2009).
20 Based on estimates of national population.

21.3 Recorded crime statistics by offence group[1,2]

England and Wales

		2002/03 [3]	2003/04	2004/05	2005/06	2006/07	2007/08	2008/09	2009/10	Thousands 2010/11
Violence against the person	**LQMP**	845.1	967.2	1,048.1	1,059.6	1,046.2	961.4	903.5	871.4	822.0
Sexual offences [4]	**LQMQ**	58.9	62.5	62.9	62.1	57.5	53.6	51.4	54.4	55.0
Burglary	**LQMR**	890.1	820.0	680.4	645.1	622.0	583.7	581.6	540.7	522.6
Robbery	**LQMS**	110.3	103.7	91.0	98.2	101.4	84.8	80.1	75.1	76.2
Offences against vehicles [5]	**I8RM**	1,074.7	985.0	820.1	792.8	765.0	656.5	591.9	494.9	449.7
Other theft offences	**I8RN**	1,336.9	1,327.9	1,247.6	1,226.2	1,180.8	1,121.2	1,080.0	1,037.3	1,078.7
Fraud and forgery [6]	**LQMU**	331.1	319.6	280.1	232.8	199.7	155.4	163.2	152.2	145.8
Criminal damage	**LQMV**	1,120.6	1,218.5	1,197.5	1,184.3	1,185.0	1,036.4	936.4	806.6	701.0
Drug offences	**LQYT**	143.3	143.5	145.8	178.5	194.2	229.9	243.5	235.6	232.2
Other offences	**LQYU**	64.0	65.7	64.0	75.6	75.7	69.4	71.2	70.1	66.9
Total	**LQYV**	5,975.0	6,013.8	5,637.5	5,555.2	5,427.6	4,952.3	4,702.7	4,338.4	4,150.1

1 See chapter text.

2 Data includes the 43 police forces in England and Wales together with the British Transport Police.

3 The National Crime Recording Standard (NCRS) was introduced in England and Wales from 1 April 2002.
These figures are not directly comparable with those for earlier years.

4 The Sexual Offences Act 2003, introduced in May 2004, altered the definitions and coverage of sexual offences.

5 Includes aggravated vehicle taking, theft of and from a vehicle and interfering with a motor vehicle.

6 The Fraud Act 2006 was introduced in January 2007. Figures before and after that date are not directly comparable.

Source: Home Office: 020 7035 0293

21.4 Offenders found guilty: by offence group[1, 2, 3]

England and Wales
Magistrates' courts and the Crown Court

Thousands

		2000	2001	2002	2003	2004	2005	2006	2007	2008[6]	2009	2010
All ages[4]												
Indictable offences												
Violence against the person:	KJEJ	35.3	35.3	37.7	38.0	39.1	40.9	41.9	42.0	41.5	43.5	44.8
Murder	KESB	0.3	0.3	0.3	0.3	0.4	0.4	0.4	0.4	0.4	0.4	0.3
Manslaughter	KESC	0.2	0.3	0.3	0.2	0.3	0.3	0.2	0.2	0.2	0.2	0.2
Wounding	KESD	33.5	33.5	35.7	35.9	36.9	38.6	39.8	39.8	39.3	41.2	42.4
Other offences of violence against the person	KESE	1.3	1.2	1.4	1.6	1.6	1.6	1.5	1.5	1.5	1.7	1.9
Sexual offences	KESF	3.9	4.0	4.4	4.4	4.8	4.8	4.9	5.1	5.1	5.1	5.8
Burglary	KESG	26.2	24.8	26.7	25.7	24.3	23.0	23.0	23.8	23.9	23.0	23.9
Robbery	KESH	5.9	6.8	7.7	7.3	7.5	7.1	8.1	8.8	8.5	8.6	8.5
Theft and handling stolen goods	KESI	128.0	127.0	127.3	119.1	110.6	103.8	99.0	106.0	110.9	112.0	121.8
Fraud and forgery	KESJ	19.2	18.3	18.1	18.0	18.1	18.5	18.2	19.9	19.8	21.0	21.0
Criminal damage	KESK	10.3	10.7	11.0	11.2	11.7	11.7	12.7	12.5	9.6	7.9	7.8
Drug offences	KBWX	44.6	45.6	49.0	51.2	39.2	39.1	39.6	44.6	52.9	56.8	62.0
Other offences (excluding motoring)	KESL	44.5	44.0	48.0	51.4	54.5	53.1	50.0	45.3	40.1	47.7	51.6
Motoring offences	KESM	7.6	7.7	8.2	8.7	8.0	6.6	5.9	5.4	4.5	3.6	3.4
Total	KESA	**325.5**	**324.2**	**338.3**	**335.1**	**317.8**	**308.5**	**303.2**	**313.3**	**316.9**	**329.2**	**350.6**
Summary offences												
Summary assaults	KESO	37.4	37.7	40.7	45.6	53.4	60.4	64.5	68.9	67.7	67.4	69.6
Offences against Public Order	JW94	29.8	28.6	29.0	31.0	33.5	32.6	34.9	38.7	37.0	36.2	37.0
FirearmsActs	JW95	0.4	0.3	0.3	0.3	0.5	0.8	0.6	0.7	0.5	0.4	0.4
Interference with a motor vehicle	JW96	2.6	2.6	2.6	2.6	2.5	2.4	2.3	2.3	1.9	1.8	1.6
Stealing or unauthorised taking of a conveyance	JW97	7.0	6.9	7.2	6.6	5.9	5.2	4.8	4.6	3.9	3.8	3.5
Social Security Offences	JW98	6.5	7.5	6.8	7.0	6.9	6.3	4.0	3.3	3.4	2.8	4.9
Intoxicating Liquor Laws:												
Drunkenness	KESR	27.2	26.2	26.9	27.7	21.1	16.1	15.7	17.4	18.9	19.8	19.4
Education Acts	KEST	5.1	5.6	5.8	5.8	6.5	6.4	7.4	8.4	8.5	8.9	9.3
Summary offences of criminal Criminal Damage - £5,000 or less	KESW	28.0	26.9	28.3	29.8	31.5	31.1	30.2	32.1	33.3	33.2	32.4
Offences by prostitutes	KESX	3.4	2.8	2.7	2.6	1.7	1.1	0.7	0.5	0.5	0.5	0.3
TV licence evasion	KETC	105.7	83.8	96.6	79.9	89.3	105.0	115.5	121.0	122.0	148.9	142.4
Motoring offences (summary)	KETA	607.5	583.3	595.8	662.6	707.9	667.1	622.5	611.1	552.2	564.6	523.4
Other summary non-motoring offences	JX2K	237.5	213.2	240.3	254.6	270.1	241.6	215.0	193.6	196.5	191.0	172.8
Total	KESN	**1,098.2**	**1,025.5**	**1,083.0**	**1,156.1**	**1,230.7**	**1,175.9**	**1,118.2**	**1,102.6**	**1,046.3**	**1,079.3**	**1,016.8**
Persons aged 10 to under 18[5]												
Indictable offences												
Violence against the person:	KETF	6.4	6.9	6.9	6.6	6.9	7.4	7.5	7.7	7.4	6.8	6.4
Wounding	KBXC	6.3	6.8	6.8	6.5	6.8	7.3	7.4	7.6	7.3	6.7	6.3
Other offences of violence against the person	KCAA	0.1	0.1	0.1	0.1	0.1	0.1	0.1	0.1	0.1	0.1	0.1
Sexual offences	KETG	0.5	0.5	0.6	0.4	0.6	0.6	0.5	0.5	0.5	0.5	0.6
Burglary	KETH	6.8	6.3	6.4	5.8	5.9	6.0	6.2	6.1	5.4	5.4	5.1
Robbery	KETI	2.2	2.8	2.8	2.6	3.0	3.1	3.7	4.1	3.6	3.6	3.4
Theft and handling stolen goods	KETJ	21.0	20.6	18.4	16.5	16.8	17.1	16.3	18.2	16.0	14.6	13.6
Fraud and forgery	KETK	1.0	1.0	0.9	0.8	0.8	0.7	0.6	0.7	0.5	0.6	0.5
Criminal damage	KETL	2.6	2.9	2.9	2.9	3.2	3.3	3.7	3.6	2.6	1.9	1.8
Drug offences	KCAB	3.7	4.3	5.0	5.1	4.5	4.6	4.5	5.3	6.4	6.3	5.9
Other offences (excluding motoring)	KETM	4.4	4.3	4.4	4.3	4.6	4.5	4.1	4.2	3.5	4.1	4.0
Motoring	KETN	0.6	0.7	0.8	0.8	0.7	0.6	0.5	0.4	0.3	0.3	0.2
Total	KETE	**49.2**	**50.3**	**49.1**	**46.0**	**47.0**	**47.8**	**47.6**	**50.9**	**46.3**	**44.0**	**41.5**
Summary offences												
Summary assaults	JW99	6.3	6.8	7.3	7.9	9.5	11.0	12.0	13.0	11.8	10.5	9.9
Offences against Public Order	JW9A	4.4	4.5	4.3	4.6	5.3	5.4	6.0	6.8	6.2	5.4	4.9
Firearms Acts	JW9B	0.2	0.1	0.1	0.1	0.2	0.3	0.2	0.2	0.2	0.1	0.1
Interference with a motor vehicle	JW9N	1.1	1.0	1.0	1.0	0.9	0.9	0.8	0.7	0.6	0.5	0.4
Stealing or unauthorised taking of a conveyance	JW9P	3.4	3.5	3.5	3.0	2.6	2.4	2.0	1.8	1.4	1.3	1.0
Criminal Damage - £5,000 or less	KETS	6.7	6.9	7.0	7.2	8.3	8.8	8.6	9.2	8.7	7.2	6.3
Intoxicating liquor laws Drunkenness	JW9E	1.9	1.9	1.8	2.0	1.9	1.5	1.5	1.7	1.8	1.6	1.2
Motoring offences (summary)	KCAC	14.5	16.7	17.1	17.8	17.0	14.8	12.1	9.9	7.7	6.5	5.0
Other summary non-motoring offences	JX3D	3.8	3.8	3.3	2.8	3.3	3.2	3.0	3.2	3.8	4.6	3.7
Total	KETO	**42.2**	**45.2**	**45.4**	**46.6**	**49.2**	**48.3**	**46.1**	**46.6**	**42.1**	**37.6**	**32.4**

1 See chapter text.

2 Data provided on the principal offence basis.

3 Every effort is made to ensure that the figures presented are accurate and complete. However, it is important to note that these data have been extracted from large administrative data systems generated by the courts and police forces. As a consequence, care should be taken to ensure data collection processes and their inevitable limitations are taken into account when those data are used.

4 Includes 'Companies', etc.

5 Figures for persons aged 10 to under 18 are included in the totals above.

6 2008 figures exclude data for Cardiff magistrates' court for April, July and August 2008.

Source: Justice Statistics Analytical Services

21.5 Offenders cautioned: by offence group[1, 2, 3]

England and Wales

Thousands

		2000	2001	2002	2003	2004	2005	2006	2007	2008	2009	2010
All ages[4]												
Indictable offences												
Violence against the person	KELB	19.9	19.6	23.6	28.8	36.6	51.0	57.3	52.3	37.9	27.3	21.9
Wounding	KCAF	19.3	18.9	22.9	27.9	35.4	49.6	55.7	50.8	36.3	25.6	20.2
Other violence against the person	KCAG	0.6	0.6	0.7	0.9	1.2	1.4	1.5	1.6	1.6	1.7	1.7
Sexual offences	KELC	1.3	1.2	1.2	1.3	1.5	1.7	1.9	1.9	1.7	1.5	1.4
Burglary	KELD	6.6	6.4	5.8	5.6	5.6	6.5	7.7	7.0	5.4	4.4	3.5
Robbery	KELE	0.6	0.5	0.4	0.4	0.5	0.6	0.7	0.6	0.4	0.2	0.2
Theft and handling stolen goods	KELF	67.6	63.5	54.2	54.5	61.9	67.6	72.4	72.8	64.0	60.7	47.5
Fraud and forgery	KELG	6.2	5.8	5.3	5.5	6.0	6.9	8.0	8.6	8.3	7.2	6.1
Criminal damage	KELH	3.2	3.4	3.1	3.7	5.5	7.2	9.0	8.8	7.9	6.4	5.1
Drug offences	KCAI	41.1	39.4	44.9	45.7	32.6	34.4	37.4	43.1	47.0	43.8	40.7
Other offences	KELI	4.4	4.2	4.4	5.3	6.0	6.9	9.4	10.0	8.6	8.0	7.2
All offenders cautioned	KELA	150.9	143.9	142.9	150.7	156.3	182.9	203.8	205.1	181.2	159.5	133.5
Summary offences												
Summary assaults	KELK	17.2	18.2	17.3	19.8	26.1	40.8	64.6	72.6	69.5	64.2	54.3
Offences against Public Order	JW9W	13.4	13.0	12.7	15.1	15.4	15.3	18.5	20.6	19.0	17.3	14.3
Firearms Acts	JW9X	0.6	0.4	0.3	0.2	0.8	1.1	1.0	1.1	0.6	0.4	0.2
Interference with a motor vehicle	JW9Y	0.5	0.5	0.5	0.5	0.4	0.5	0.6	0.6	0.4	0.3	0.2
Stealing or unauthorised taking of a conveyance	JW9Z	4.3	4.4	3.9	3.7	3.3	3.2	3.3	3.2	2.6	2.1	1.6
Social Security Offences	JWA2	0.0	0.0	0.0	0.0	0.0	0.0	0.0	0.0	0.0	0.0	0.0
Intoxicating Liquor Laws:												
Drunkenness	KELN	18.1	16.6	16.2	18.1	13.5	8.6	5.8	6.1	8.0	6.0	5.2
Education Acts	KELP	0.0	0.0	0.0	0.1	0.1	0.1	0.1	0.1	0.1	0.0	0.0
Offences by prostitutes	KELT	1.2	0.7	1.4	0.9	1.2	0.9	0.8	0.6	0.6	0.5	0.9
TV licence evasion	KELY	0.0	0.0	0.0	0.0	0.0	0.0	0.0	0.0	0.0	0.0	0.0
Other summary non-motoring offences	JX6L	32.8	32.1	30.0	32.7	38.7	45.5	51.5	53.0	46.0	40.2	32.5
Total	KELJ	88.1	85.9	82.4	91.1	99.5	116.0	146.2	157.8	146.7	131.1	109.3
Persons aged 10 to under 18[5]												
Indictable offences												
Violence against the person:	KEMB	8.3	8.7	9.3	11.0	13.6	16.5	16.6	13.9	9.4	6.8	4.9
Wounding	KCAP	8.2	8.6	9.3	10.9	13.5	16.4	16.5	13.8	9.4	6.8	4.9
Other violence against the person	KCCE	0.1	0.1	0.1	0.1	0.1	0.1	0.1	0.1	0.1	0.0	0.0
Sexual offences	KEMC	0.5	0.5	0.4	0.5	0.5	0.6	0.6	0.7	0.5	0.4	0.4
Burglary	KEMD	5.4	5.3	4.6	4.4	4.2	4.6	5.0	4.5	3.2	2.5	1.8
Robbery	KEME	0.5	0.5	0.4	0.4	0.4	0.5	0.6	0.5	0.3	0.2	0.2
Theft and handling stolen goods	KEMF	36.9	35.2	28.1	28.3	33.1	36.8	39.4	39.7	30.1	26.6	15.6
Fraud and forgery	KEMG	1.5	1.3	1.1	1.0	1.0	1.1	1.3	1.4	1.2	0.8	0.6
Criminal damage	KEMH	2.1	2.3	1.9	2.3	3.1	3.9	4.7	4.5	3.5	2.4	1.7
Drug offences	KCCF	7.9	8.5	9.5	9.6	8.3	7.8	7.1	8.1	8.5	7.5	6.2
Other offences	KEMI	1.3	1.3	1.3	1.4	1.6	1.6	1.9	2.0	1.6	1.3	1.0
Total	KEMA	64.3	63.5	56.6	58.7	65.9	73.4	77.1	75.2	58.3	48.5	32.4
Summary offences												
Summary assaults	JWA3	6.4	6.9	6.2	6.8	8.8	12.2	16.2	16.8	14.2	11.3	8.3
Offences against Public Order	JWA5	4.0	4.1	3.8	4.6	5.8	6.2	7.4	7.3	5.8	4.5	3.4
Firearms Acts	JWA4	0.4	0.3	0.2	0.1	0.4	0.6	0.5	0.6	0.3	0.1	0.1
Interference with a motor vehicle	JWA6	0.4	0.4	0.4	0.4	0.3	0.3	0.3	0.3	0.2	0.2	0.1
Stealing or unauthorised taking of a conveyance	JWA7	3.5	3.7	3.3	3.1	2.6	2.3	2.0	1.7	1.3	1.0	0.6
Criminal Damage - £5,000 or less	KEMN	14.4	15.2	12.6	14.3	17.1	19.8	21.9	21.7	15.1	10.5	6.2
Intoxicating liquor laws:												
Drunkenness	JWA8	2.3	2.3	2.1	2.4	2.5	1.9	1.5	1.6	1.5	1.4	0.9
Other summary non-motoring offences	JX6M	1.9	1.7	1.4	1.5	1.6	2.1	2.1	2.2	1.6	1.3	1.0
Total	KEMJ	33.2	34.5	29.9	33.3	39.1	45.5	52.0	52.1	39.9	30.2	20.6

1 See chapter text.

2 Data are on the principal offence basis.

3 Every effort is made to ensure that the figures presented are accurate and complete. However, it is important to note that these data have been extracted from large administrative data systems generated by police forces. As a consequence, care should be taken to ensure data collection processes and their inevitable limitations are taken into account when those data are used.

4 Includes 'Companies', etc.

5 Figures for persons aged 10 to under 18 are included in the totals above.

Source: Justice Statistics Analytical Services in the Ministry of Justice 020 3334 3737

21.6 Offenders found guilty: by offence group[1, 2, 3]

England and Wales
Magistrates' Courts and the Crown Court

Thousands

		2000	2001	2002	2003	2004	2005	2006	2007	2008 [4]	2009	2010
Males												
Indictable offences												
All ages	KEFA	276.5	275.5	287.1	283.4	268.4	261.3	258.4	266.9	267.7	277.6	296.8
10 and under 15 years	KEFB	8.7	9.0	8.8	8.0	8.5	8.6	8.3	8.5	7.7	6.5	5.5
15 and under 18 years	KEFC	33.8	34.4	33.7	31.4	31.8	32.0	32.5	35.0	31.9	30.8	30.3
18 and under 21 years	KEFD	49.9	48.2	46.6	43.8	39.9	38.5	39.0	40.5	38.3	39.8	41.5
21 years and over	KEFE	184.0	183.9	198.0	200.2	188.2	182.2	178.7	182.9	189.8	200.4	219.5
Summary offences												
All ages	KEFF	881.0	826.6	866.4	937.1	990.0	931.2	877.7	851.5	778.5	770.8	718.8
10 and under 15 years	KEFG	5.8	6.2	6.1	6.1	6.7	7.2	7.0	7.3	6.3	5.1	4.4
15 and under 18 years	KEFH	32.2	34.5	34.6	35.3	36.4	34.6	32.3	31.8	28.2	25.4	21.9
18 and under 21 years	KEFI	93.0	92.2	94.7	99.9	98.2	89.4	85.1	80.5	76.6	76.2	66.6
21 years and over	KEFJ	750.0	693.6	731.0	795.8	848.7	800.1	753.4	731.8	667.4	664.0	625.8
Females												
Indictable offences												
All ages	KEFK	47.7	47.4	50.0	50.2	48.4	46.1	43.7	45.3	46.4	49.0	51.1
10 and under 15 years	KEFL	1.5	1.6	1.6	1.6	1.7	1.7	1.7	1.8	1.6	1.4	1.1
15 and under 18 years	KEFM	5.2	5.3	5.1	4.9	5.0	5.5	5.1	5.5	4.9	5.0	4.4
18 and under 21 years	KEFN	7.5	7.0	6.9	6.2	5.7	5.3	4.8	4.6	4.7	5.0	5.1
21 years and over	KEFO	33.5	33.5	36.5	37.5	35.9	33.6	32.1	33.4	35.3	37.6	40.5
Summary offences												
All ages	KEFP	208.3	190.2	208.7	210.5	231.2	236.6	233.9	244.2	242.0	265.9	254.1
10 and under 15 years	KEFQ	0.9	0.9	1.1	1.2	1.4	1.6	1.6	1.8	1.7	1.5	1.3
15 and under 18 years	KEFR	3.3	3.6	3.6	4.0	4.6	4.9	5.2	5.7	5.5	5.2	4.4
18 and under 21 years	KEFS	11.8	11.1	11.6	12.6	13.0	13.5	14.2	14.9	16.5	18.3	16.1
21 years and over	KEFT	192.3	174.7	192.4	192.7	212.1	216.6	212.9	221.9	218.3	240.9	232.4
Not stated[5]												
Indictable offences												
All ages		-	-	-	-	-	-	-	-	1.9	1.9	1.9
10 and under 15 years		-	-	-	-	-	-	-	-	0.0	0.0	0.0
15 and under 18 years		-	-	-	-	-	-	-	-	0.2	0.2	0.2
18 and under 21 years		-	-	-	-	-	-	-	-	0.2	0.2	0.2
21 years and over		-	-	-	-	-	-	-	-	1.4	1.5	1.6
Summary offences												
All ages		-	-	-	-	-	-	-	-	18.7	34.7	37.0
10 and under 15 years		-	-	-	-	-	-	-	-	0.1	0.1	0.0
15 and under 18 years		-	-	-	-	-	-	-	-	0.3	0.3	0.3
18 and under 21 years		-	-	-	-	-	-	-	-	1.7	2.8	2.4
21 years and over		-	-	-	-	-	-	-	-	16.6	31.5	34.2
Companies, etc												
Indictable offences	KEFU	1.3	1.3	1.2	1.4	1.1	1.1	1.0	1.1	0.9	0.7	0.8
Summary offences	KEFV	8.8	8.6	7.9	8.6	9.4	8.1	6.6	6.9	7.2	7.9	7.0

1 See chapter text.

2 These data are on the principal offence basis.

3 Every effort is made to ensure that the figures presented are accurate and complete. However, it is important to note that these data have been extracted from large administrative data systems generated by the courts and police forces. As a consequence, care should be taken to ensure data collection processes and their inevitable limitations are taken into account when those data are used.

4 Excludes data for Cardiff magistrates' court for April, July and August 2008.

5 Following the introduction of the Libra case management system during 2008, offenders at magistrates' courts can now be recorded as sex 'Not Stated'.

Source: Justice Statistics Analytical Services
the Ministry of Justice: 020 3334 3737

21.7 Persons cautioned by the police: by age and gender[1, 3, 4]

England and Wales

Thousands

		2000	2001	2002	2003	2004	2005	2006	2007	2008	2009	2010
Males												
Indictable offences												
All ages	**KEGA**	109.7	103.8	104.4	109.8	110.0	129.9	147.6	148.5	133.4	114.9	98.6
10 and under 15 years[4]	**KEGB**	20.3	19.7	16.7	16.9	18.7	21.0	21.7	19.7	14.6	10.9	7.0
15 and under 18 years[4]	**KEGC**	25.0	24.5	23.3	24.1	25.9	28.0	30.2	30.0	24.5	20.2	15.5
18 and under 21 years	**KEGD**	20.1	18.5	18.9	19.4	16.7	19.8	22.9	23.7	21.7	19.2	16.9
21 years and over	**KEGE**	44.3	41.2	45.6	49.4	48.7	61.1	72.8	75.1	72.5	64.6	59.2
Summary offences												
All ages	**KEGF**	69.6	68.0	63.8	70.9	76.0	87.6	112.0	120.2	112.4	100.7	83.9
10 and under 15 years[4]	**KEGG**	12.0	12.7	10.3	10.9	12.6	15.5	17.9	17.9	12.4	8.8	5.5
15 and under 18 years[4]	**KEGH**	14.8	15.2	13.3	15.1	17.2	18.6	21.3	21.3	16.8	13.3	9.3
18 and under 21 years	**KEGI**	11.9	11.0	11.0	12.4	12.3	12.2	15.0	16.4	16.6	15.5	13.2
21 years and over	**KEGJ**	30.9	29.0	29.2	32.5	33.9	41.2	57.8	64.6	66.6	63.1	55.9
Females												
Indictable offences												
All ages	**KEGK**	41.2	40.1	38.5	41.0	46.3	53.0	56.2	56.6	47.8	44.7	35.0
10 and under 15 years[4]	**KEGL**	10.0	10.1	8.4	8.6	10.6	12.2	12.5	12.5	9.0	8.0	4.2
15 and under 18 years[4]	**KEGM**	9.0	9.3	8.3	9.1	10.6	12.2	12.7	13.0	10.2	9.3	5.8
18 and under 21 years	**KEGN**	5.2	4.9	4.8	4.9	5.2	5.8	6.2	6.3	5.6	5.3	4.5
21 years and over	**KEGO**	17.0	15.9	17.0	18.4	19.9	22.8	24.7	24.8	23.1	22.0	20.6
Summary offences												
All ages	**KEGP**	18.5	18.0	18.6	20.2	23.5	28.5	34.2	37.6	34.4	30.5	25.4
10 and under 15 years[4]	**KEGQ**	2.8	2.9	2.7	3.0	3.9	5.1	5.6	5.6	4.4	3.3	2.3
15 and under 18 years[4]	**KEGR**	3.7	3.8	3.6	4.3	5.4	6.2	7.1	7.3	6.2	4.9	3.5
18 and under 21 years	**KEGS**	2.5	2.3	2.4	2.7	2.9	3.3	4.1	4.7	4.5	4.3	3.7
21 years and over	**KEGT**	9.6	9.0	9.8	10.2	11.3	13.9	17.4	20.0	19.1	18.0	15.9

1 See chapter text.

2 These data are on the principal offence basis.

3 Every effort is made to ensure that the figures presented are accurate and complete. However, it is important to note that these data have been extracted from large administrative data systems generated by police forces. As a consequence, care should be taken to ensure data collection processes and their inevitable limitations are taken into account when those data are used.

4 From 1 June 2000 the Crime and Disorder Act 1998 came into force nationally and removed the use of cautions for persons under 18 and replaced them with reprimands and warnings. These are included in the totals.

Source: Justice Statistics Analytical Services
in the Ministry of Justice 020 3334 3737

21.8 Sentence or order passed on persons sentenced for indictable offences: by gender[1]

England and Wales
Magistrates' Courts and the Crown Court

Percentages and thousands

		2000	2001	2002	2003	2004	2005	2006	2007	2008	2009	2010
Males												
Sentence or order												
Absolute discharge	KEJB	0.6	0.6	0.8	0.9	0.8	0.7	0.7	0.7	0.6	0.5	0.5
Conditional discharge	KEJC	14.1	13.4	12.4	13.0	12.2	11.9	11.4	12.2	11.4	10.6	11.0
Fine	KEJF	25.7	24.5	23.9	24.0	20.9	19.4	17.5	16.2	16.0	17.4	17.6
Community rehabilitation order	KEJD	10.1	10.7	10.6	10.1	9.5	5.6	0.8	0.5	0.4	0.3	0.1
Supervision order	KEJE	2.4	2.3	2.1	1.8	2.0	2.1	2.3	2.4	1.9	1.6	0.3
Community punishment order	KEJG	9.5	9.0	8.6	8.3	8.8	6.3	1.2	0.5	0.4	0.4	0.1
Attendance centre order	KEJH	1.5	1.2	0.7	0.6	0.6	0.6	0.6	0.6	0.5	0.5	0.1
Community punishment and rehabilitation order	KIJW	3.6	2.6	2.6	2.6	2.8	2.1	0.6	0.4	0.4	0.4	0.1
Curfew order	LUJP	0.5	0.7	1.1	1.6	2.7	2.3	1.3	1.3	1.4	1.5	0.5
Reparation order	SNFI	0.7	1.3	0.8	0.4	0.4	0.5	0.6	0.6	0.6	0.5	0.3
Action plan order	SNFJ	0.9	1.7	1.1	0.7	0.8	0.8	0.8	0.8	0.7	0.5	0.0
Drug treatment and testing order	SNFK	0.1	1.2	1.4	1.9	2.3	1.6	0.1	0.0	0.0	0.0	-
Referral order	SNFL	-	-	3.0	4.0	4.4	5.2	5.2	5.5	5.0	4.7	4.2
Community order[2]	GN7P	-	-	-	-	-	8.7	19.9	20.4	20.7	21.9	21.8
Youth rehabilitation order		-	-	-	-	-	-	-	-	-		2.8
Suspended sentence order	KEJL	0.7	0.6	0.5	0.5	0.6	1.7	6.7	8.6	8.9	9.3	9.7
Imprisonment												
Sec 90-92	LUJQ	0.2	0.2	0.2	0.2	0.2	0.2	0.2	0.1	0.2	0.1	0.1
Detention and training order	LUJR	1.4	1.9	1.8	1.5	1.6	1.6	1.7	1.5	1.5	1.3	1.0
Young offender institution	KEJK	5.2	4.5	4.2	3.6	3.8	3.7	3.7	3.8	3.6	3.7	3.3
Unsuspended imprisonment	KEJM	19.9	20.0	20.9	20.6	21.5	21.3	20.5	19.9	21.6	21.4	21.2
Other sentence or order	KEJN	3.1	3.4	3.3	3.5	4.1	3.9	4.4	3.9	4.4	3.5	5.1
Total number of males (thousands) = 100 per cent	KEJA	277.1	274.6	285.6	282.3	267.5	259.4	257.6	265.8	266.9	276.0	294.7
Females												
Sentence or order												
Absolute discharge	KEKB	0.6	0.6	0.9	1.0	0.8	0.8	0.8	0.8	0.7	0.6	0.7
Conditional discharge	KEKC	24.9	23.9	22.0	22.5	21.8	20.7	20.0	20.8	20.0	19.6	20.2
Fine	KEKF	20.1	18.6	17.9	18.5	16.7	15.2	12.8	12.1	11.9	13.7	13.7
Community rehabilitation order	KEKD	19.6	19.1	19.2	17.0	15.4	9.0	1.4	0.5	0.4	0.3	0.1
Supervision order	KEKE	2.8	2.7	2.1	2.1	2.1	2.4	2.6	2.6	2.0	1.6	0.4
Community punishment order	KEKG	7.5	7.3	6.8	6.6	7.6	6.1	1.6	0.4	0.2	0.1	0.0
Attendance centre order	KEKH	0.8	0.6	0.4	0.3	0.3	0.3	0.3	0.3	0.3	0.2	0.0
Community punishment and rehabilitation order	KIJX	3.0	2.1	2.1	1.8	1.9	1.5	0.5	0.2	0.2	0.2	0.1
Curfew order	LUJT	0.4	0.6	0.8	1.4	2.2	2.3	1.2	1.1	1.1	1.1	0.4
Reparation order	SNFX	0.8	1.6	0.8	0.4	0.5	0.5	0.5	0.6	0.6	0.7	0.4
Action plan order	SNFZ	1.0	2.0	1.2	0.8	0.8	1.0	0.9	0.9	0.7	0.6	0.0
Drug treatment and testing order	SNGA	0.1	1.4	1.7	2.4	3.2	2.1	0.2	0.0	0.0	-	-
Referral order	SNGB	-	-	3.9	5.1	5.6	6.7	6.8	7.0	6.2	6.0	5.0
Community order[2]	GN7Q	-	-	-	-	-	9.9	23.2	24.5	25.4	26.9	27.2
Youth rehabilitation order	KO27	-	-	-	-	-	-	-	-	-		2.2
Suspended sentence order	KEKL	1.3	1.2	1.1	1.0	1.3	2.5	7.8	9.6	10.1	10.8	10.9
Imprisonment												
Sec 90-92	LUJU	0.1	0.1	0.1	0.1	0.1	0.1	0.0	0.0	0.0	0.1	0.0
Detention and training order	LUJV	0.6	0.8	0.8	0.7	0.7	0.8	0.7	0.8	0.7	0.6	0.4
Young offender institution	KEKK	2.2	2.0	1.9	1.7	1.4	1.6	1.5	1.4	1.3	1.3	1.1
Unsuspended imprisonment	KEKM	11.5	12.1	12.7	12.8	13.3	12.7	12.8	12.4	13.5	12.3	12.3
Other sentence or order	KEKN	2.9	3.5	3.4	3.8	4.2	3.8	4.3	3.7	4.7	3.3	4.9
Total number of females (thousands) = 100 per cent	KEKA	47.8	47.3	49.9	50.2	48.3	46.1	43.9	45.4	46.3	48.9	50.9

21.8 Sentence or order passed on persons sentenced for indictable offences: by gender[1]

England and Wales
Magistrates' Courts and the Crown Court

Percentages and thousands

		2000	2001	2002	2003	2004	2005	2006	2007	2008	2009	2010
Not stated[4]												
Sentence or order												
Absolute discharge	KEKB	-	-	-	-	-	-	-	-	0.8	0.6	0.4
Conditional discharge	KEKC	-	-	-	-	-	-	-	-	17.5	13.6	13.3
Fine	KEKF	-	-	-	-	-	-	-	-	26.1	31.0	34.2
Community rehabilitation order	KEKD	-	-	-	-	-	-	-	-	0.3	0.5	-
Supervision order	KEKE	-	-	-	-	-	-	-	-	1.8	0.8	0.5
Community punishment order	KEKG	-	-	-	-	-	-	-	-	0.4	0.4	0.1
Attendance centre order	KEKH	-	-	-	-	-	-	-	-	0.2	0.6	0.2
Community punishment and rehabilitation order	KIJX	-	-	-	-	-	-	-	-	0.6	0.5	0.2
Curfew order	LUJT	-	-	-	-	-	-	-	-	1.2	1.6	0.6
Reparation order	SNFX	-	-	-	-	-	-	-	-	0.8	0.6	0.3
Action plan order	SNFZ	-	-	-	-	-	-	-	-	0.6	0.5	0.1
Drug treatment and testing order	SNGA	-	-	-	-	-	-	-	-	-	-	-
Referral order	SNGB	-	-	-	-	-	-	-	-	5.6	4.9	3.8
Community order[2]	GN7Q	-	-	-	-	-	-	-	-	19.9	21.6	21.1
Youth rehabilitation order	KO27	-	-	-	-	-	-	-	-	-	-	2.6
Suspended sentence order	KEKL	-	-	-	-	-	-	-	-	4.9	5.4	6.1
Imprisonment												
Sec 90-92	LUJU	-	-	-	-	-	-	-	-	-	-	-
Detention and training order	LUJV	-	-	-	-	-	-	-	-	1.0	1.1	1.1
Young offender institution	KEKK	-	-	-	-	-	-	-	-	1.3	1.8	1.1
Unsuspended imprisonment	KEKM	-	-	-	-	-	-	-	-	11.0	10.0	7.7
Other sentence or order	KEKN	-	-	-	-	-	-	-	-	6.0	4.4	6.8
Total number of persons where sex (thousands) = 100 per cent	KEKA	-	-	-	-	-	-	-	-	1.7	1.7	1.8

Source: Justice Statistics Analytical Services
in the Ministry of Justice 020 3334 3737

1 See chapter text. Every effort is made to ensure that the figures presented are accurate and complete. However, it is important to note that these data have been extracted from large administrative data systems generated by police forces. As a consequence care should be taken to ensure data collection processes and their inevitable limitations are taken into account when those data are used.

2 The community order was introduced on 4 April 2005 and applies to offences committed on or after that date.

3 Excludes data for Cardiff magistrates' court for April, July and August 2008.

4 Following the introduction of the Libra case management system during 2008, offenders at magistrates' courts can now be recorded as sex 'Not Stated'.

21.9 Persons sentenced to life imprisonment and immediate custody: by gender and age

England and Wales

Number of persons

		2000	2001	2002	2003	2004	2005	2006	2007	2008	2009	2010
Life imprisonment[1]												
Males												
All ages	I28G	446	484	536	489	548	594	531	471	495	401	364
Aged 10-17	I28D	19	28	21	11	15	27	16	23	24	22	17
Aged 18-20	I28E	9	27	21	47	24	50	46	70	54	57	39
Aged 21 and over	I28F	418	429	494	431	509	517	469	378	417	322	308
Females												
All ages	I28K	21	19	19	24	22	31	16	21	28	20	20
Aged 10-17	I28H	2	1	1	-	1	1	-	3	1	1	2
Aged 18-20	I28I	1	3	2	4	2	4	2	3	2	1	2
Aged 21 and over	I28J	18	15	16	20	19	26	14	15	25	18	16
All persons												
All ages	I28O	467	503	555	513	570	625	547	492	523	421	384
Aged 10-17	I28L	21	29	22	11	16	28	16	26	25	23	19
Aged 18-20	I28M	10	30	23	51	26	54	48	73	56	58	41
Aged 21 and over	I28N	436	444	510	451	528	543	483	393	442	340	324
Immediate custody[2]												
Males												
All ages	JF7E	97,841	97,728	102,240	98,371	97,020	91,954	86,239	85,245	88,826	90,420	91,664
Aged 10-17	JF7F	6,949	7,119	6,865	5,765	5,866	5,463	5,669	5,273	4,939	4,485	3,877
Aged 18-20	JF7G	17,315	16,855	16,269	14,418	13,793	13,237	12,802	13,117	12,354	12,978	12,296
Aged 21 and over	JF7H	73,577	73,754	79,106	78,188	77,361	73,254	67,768	66,855	71,533	72,957	75,491
Females												
All ages	JF7I	7,879	8,042	8,812	8,786	8,732	8,231	7,783	7,722	8,284	8,059	8,150
Aged 10-17	JF7J	444	448	529	424	443	498	453	466	442	378	256
Aged 18-20	JF7K	1,116	1,063	1,071	969	817	875	841	793	782	803	734
Aged 21 and over	JF7L	6,319	6,531	7,212	7,393	7,472	6,858	6,489	6,463	7,060	6,878	7,160
All persons												
All ages	JF7M	105,720	105,770	111,052	107,157	105,752	100,185	94,022	93,007	97,464	98,809	100,110
Aged 10-17	JF7N	7,393	7,567	7,394	6,189	6,309	5,961	6,122	5,743	5,403	4,890	4,159
Aged 18-20	JF7O	18,431	17,918	17,340	15,387	14,610	14,112	13,643	13,919	13,180	13,837	13,073
Aged 21 and over	JF7P	79,896	80,285	86,318	85,581	84,833	80,112	74,257	73,345	78,881	80,082	82,878

1 Includes detention under the Powers of Criminal Courts (Sentencing) Act 2000, Secs 90-92 (Children and Young Persons Act 1933,
(Secs 53(1) and (2) prior to August 2000) (persons aged 10-17), custody for life under the Powers of Criminal Courts (Sentencing) Act 2000,
Secs 93 and 94 (1) (persons aged 18-20), mandatory life sentences under the Powers of Criminal Courts (Sentencing) Act 2000,
Sec 109 (persons aged 18 and over) and immediate prisonment (persons aged 21 and over). Indeterminate sentences for
Criminal Courts (Sentencing) Act 2000, Sec 109 (persons aged 18 and over) and immediate prisonment (persons aged 21 and over).
Indeterminate sentences for public protection under the Criminal Justice Act 2003 are excluded.
2 Excludes life and indeterminate sentences.

Source: Justice Statistics Analytical Services on the Ministry of Justice 020 3334 3737

21.10 Prison receptions and population in custody

England and Wales

Numbers[1]

		2002	2003	2004	2005	2006	2007	2008	2009	2010
Receptions										
Type of inmate:										
Untried	**KEDA**	58,708	58,696	54,556	55,455	55,809	55,305	57,417	55,207	-
Convicted, unsentenced	**KEDB**	53,301	53,246	50,115	49,104	47,995	43,566	44,773	37,003	-
Sentenced	**KEDE**	94,807	93,495	95,161	92,452	90,038	91,736	100,348	94,964	-
Immediate custodial sentence	**KEDF**	93,615	92,245	93,326	90,414	88,134	90,261	98,820	93,621	-
Young offenders	**KEDG**	20,236	18,179	18,264	17,819	17,985	19,022	19,489	17,745	-
Up to 12 months	**KEDH**	12,891	11,850	11,855	11,610	11,526	12,295	12,654	11,097	-
12 months up to 4 years	**KEDJ**	6,355	5,412	5,426	5,243	5,317	5,530	5,573	5,475	-
4 years up to and including life	**KEDL**	990	917	983	966	1,142	1,197	1,262	1,173	-
Adults	**KFBO**	73,379	74,066	75,062	72,595	70,149	71,239	79,331	75,877	-
Up to 12 months	**KEDV**	47,870	48,962	49,814	48,190	45,768	46,706	52,331	48,540	-
12 months up to 4 years	**KEDW**	18,313	17,968	17,988	17,397	16,970	17,233	19,061	19,804	-
4 years up to and including life	**KEDX**	7,196	7,136	7,260	7,008	7,411	7,300	7,939	7,533	-
Committed in default of payment of a fine	**KEDY**	1,192	1,250	1,835	1,876	1,904	1,475	1,528	1,343	-
Young offenders	**KEEA**	110	116	155	162	118	92	101	73	-
Adults	**KAFQ**	1,082	1,134	1,680	1,714	1,786	1,383	1,427	1,270	-
Non-criminal prisoners	**KEDM**	2,674	3,142	3,669	3,668	4,734	3,888	3,836	4,282	-
Immigration Act 1971	**KEDN**	2,093	2,457	3,041	3,093	4,073	3,347	3,466	-	-
Others	**KEDO**	581	685	628	575	661	541	370	-	-
Population (30 June)[2]										
Total in prison service establishments	**KFBQ**	71,218	73,656	74,488	76,191	77,982	79,735	83,195	83,454	85,002
Untried	**KEDQ**	7,877	7,896	7,716	8,084	8,064	8,387	8,750	8,933	8,487
Convicted, unsentenced	**KEDR**	5,204	5,177	4,779	4,780	5,003	4,457	4,690	4,523	4,517
Total sentenced	**KEDU**	57,306	59,438	60,976	62,258	63,493	65,602	68,235	68,488	71,000
Total Immediate custodial sentence	**KFBR**	57,272	59,392	60,924	62,180	63,404	65,534	68,125	68,375	70,871
Young offenders	**KFBS**	8,855	8,559	8,306	8,290	8,470	9,254	9,357	9,133	8,602
Determinate sentence	**I7IJ**	8,695	8,392	8,143	8,097	8,084	8,573	8,527	8,394	7,885
Indeterminate sentence	**I7IL**	160	167	163	193	386	681	830	739	717
Recalls		0	0	0	0	0	0	0	0	574
Adults	**KFCO**	48,417	50,833	52,618	53,890	54,934	56,280	58,768	59,242	61,695
Determinate sentence	**I7IK**	43,430	45,579	47,187	48,201	48,045	47,480	48,216	47,460	44,502
Indeterminate sentence	**I7IM**	4,987	5,254	5,431	5,689	6,889	8,800	10,552	11,782	12,417
Recalls		0	0	0	0	0	0	0	0	4,776
Committed in default of payment of a fine	**KFCS**	34	46	52	78	89	68	110	113	129
Young offenders	**KFEW**	0	3	5	2	5	4	6	5	5
Adults	**KFEX**	34	43	47	76	84	64	104	108	124
Non-criminal prisoners	**KEEB**	831	1,145	1,017	1,069	1,422	1,289	1,520	1,510	998
Immigration Act 1971	**KEEC**	759	1,079	957	996	1,366	1,218	1,473	1,465	963
Others	**KEED**	72	66	60	73	56	71	47	45	35
Accommodation[2]	**I7IQ**	64,232	66,104	67,576	69,443	70,585	73,618	73,452	74,849	77,855

Source: Ministry of Justice

1 Due to the introduction of a new prison IT system the 2010 prison population data is now taken from a different source and recalls are shown separately
(they were previously included in the relevant sentence length band). See OMCS 2010 for more details.
2 In use Certified Normal Accommodation at 30 June every year.

21.11 Prison population under immediate custodial sentence by age and offence (2005 to 2010)

England and Wales

Numbers

	Total	15 - 17	18 - 20	21 - 24	25 - 29	30 - 39	40 - 49	50 - 59	60 and over
At 30 June 2005									
Offences									
Males									
Total	**58,707**	**1,782**	**5,595**	**9,937**	**10,969**	**16,843**	**8,731**	**3,256**	**1,594**
Violence against the person	14,541	366	1,493	2,553	2,553	4,015	2,402	840	319
Sexual offences	6,147	65	186	397	505	1,436	1,552	1,084	922
Robbery	8,035	422	1,307	1,819	1,705	2,035	649	83	15
Burglary	7,844	285	719	1,559	1,947	2,570	669	78	17
Theft, handling, fraud and forgery	4,997	240	433	858	1,074	1,449	650	238	55
Drugs offences	9,429	76	491	1,332	1,834	3,263	1,741	544	148
Other offences	7,079	310	870	1,306	1,245	1,902	987	360	99
Offence not known	635	18	96	113	106	173	81	29	19
Females									
Total	**3,479**	**55**	**269**	**614**	**680**	**1,073**	**585**	**179**	**24**
Violence against the person	638	23	68	109	85	190	114	40	9
Sexual offences	39	0	2	3	4	12	8	7	3
Robbery	343	16	59	61	82	102	20	3	0
Burglary	239	4	18	50	62	79	23	3	0
Theft, handling, fraud and forgery	583	4	35	105	119	202	88	27	3
Drugs offences	1,234	3	54	195	255	366	268	84	9
Other offences	374	5	30	84	68	117	56	14	0
Offence not known	29	0	3	7	5	5	8	1	0
At 30 June 2006									
Offences									
Males									
Total	**59,898**	**1,814**	**5,716**	**9,612**	**11,349**	**16,828**	**9,349**	**3,511**	**1,719**
Violence against the person	15,537	381	1,563	2,616	2,977	4,109	2,609	935	348
Sexual offences	6,561	67	213	452	560	1,497	1,683	1,118	971
Robbery	8,100	486	1,413	1,739	1,674	1,975	706	91	16
Burglary	7,563	275	707	1,363	1,838	2,554	715	97	15
Theft, handling, fraud and forgery	5,147	200	451	830	1,093	1,598	707	214	54
Drugs offences	9,484	68	492	1,232	1,913	3,153	1,829	623	174
Other offences	7,129	327	835	1,326	1,231	1,838	1,040	406	129
Offence not known	378	12	43	55	64	105	60	28	10
Females									
Total	**3,506**	**50**	**271**	**551**	**707**	**1,094**	**604**	**189**	**39**
Violence against the person	678	11	75	111	101	205	118	48	9
Sexual offences	37	1	3	2	2	8	13	5	3
Robbery	315	17	48	67	76	86	18	2	0
Burglary	228	7	13	39	63	80	24	2	0
Theft, handling, fraud and forgery	671	3	30	97	171	232	106	24	7
Drugs offences	1,163	4	62	168	217	354	253	88	17
Other offences	385	7	36	61	72	120	67	19	3
Offence not known	30	1	5	5	4	9	5	1	0

21.11 Prison population under immediate custodial sentence by age and offence (2005 to 2010)

England and Wales

Numbers

	Total	15 - 17	18 - 20	21 - 24	25 - 29	30 - 39	40 - 49	50 - 59	60 and over
At 30 June 2007									
Offences									
Males									
Total	**62,188**	**1,827**	**6,354**	**9,860**	**11,653**	**16,606**	**10,092**	**3,823**	**1,973**
Violence against the person	16,929	402	1,772	2,927	3,183	4,337	2,846	1,063	399
Sexual offences	7,287	73	276	487	675	1,555	1,909	1,202	1,112
Robbery	8,437	495	1,558	1,855	1,716	1,928	774	96	14
Burglary	7,723	281	817	1,334	1,865	2,492	812	109	13
Theft, handling, fraud and forgery	4,844	194	426	677	1,044	1,478	711	246	67
Drugs offences	9,569	71	546	1,285	1,858	3,002	1,908	689	210
Other offences	7,051	294	908	1,237	1,242	1,731	1,087	401	152
Offence not known	348	17	51	59	69	83	47	18	5
Females									
Total	**3,345**	**56**	**280**	**475**	**662**	**1,011**	**610**	**202**	**49**
Violence against the person	687	20	99	113	111	170	117	47	11
Sexual offences	48	0	1	3	7	16	15	4	2
Robbery	311	13	54	53	78	82	27	2	1
Burglary	197	2	11	28	56	76	23	1	0
Theft, handling, fraud and forgery	601	7	29	68	128	211	111	37	10
Drugs offences	1,044	3	42	124	201	335	230	90	19
Other offences	423	9	45	75	76	115	77	20	6
Offence not known	35	2	0	10	5	6	10	2	0
At 30 June 2008									
Offences									
Males									
Total	**64,600**	**1,876**	**6,454**	**10,373**	**12,144**	**17,056**	**10,564**	**3,995**	**2,139**
Violence against the person	18,159	486	1,843	3,162	3,405	4,603	3,078	1,130	452
Sexual offences	7,569	74	300	513	729	1,552	1,997	1,204	1,200
Robbery	8,437	472	1,517	1,904	1,760	1,883	783	106	12
Burglary	7,733	315	831	1,294	1,793	2,521	854	108	16
Theft, handling, fraud and forgery	5,098	151	379	663	1,107	1,681	780	256	80
Drugs offences	9,992	106	672	1,437	1,929	2,994	1,914	726	215
Other offences	7,380	264	878	1,360	1,370	1,772	1,119	453	162
Offence not known	232	8	34	40	51	49	38	11	3
Females									
Total	**3,524**	**57**	**303**	**523**	**698**	**1,033**	**654**	**201**	**55**
Violence against the person	771	19	99	139	129	188	140	45	12
Sexual offences	47	0	0	7	7	10	15	6	2
Robbery	295	13	43	46	83	89	20	1	1
Burglary	203	5	15	23	52	70	33	5	0
Theft, handling, fraud and forgery	757	6	39	96	167	252	133	50	14
Drugs offences	990	5	56	145	180	289	219	74	22
Other offences	438	9	51	66	75	127	88	19	4
Offence not known	24	1	1	2	5	7	6	2	0

21.11 Prison population under immediate custodial sentence by age and offence (2005 to 2010)

England and Wales

Numbers

	Total	15 - 17	18 - 20	21 - 24	25 - 29	30 - 39	40 - 49	50 - 59	60 and over
					Age				
At 30 June 2009									
Offences									
Males									
Total	**64,993**	**1,517**	**6,593**	**10,798**	**12,004**	**16,779**	**10,930**	**4,091**	**2,281**
Violence against the person	19,108	366	1,949	3,408	3,604	4,750	3,345	1,188	497
Sexual offences	7,919	77	295	572	830	1,498	2,096	1,279	1,272
Robbery	8,715	440	1,611	2,053	1,810	1,873	790	123	14
Burglary	7,678	248	909	1,370	1,650	2,498	865	122	15
Theft, handling, fraud and forgery	4,592	125	325	641	926	1,501	723	253	96
Drugs offences	9,803	82	643	1,437	1,881	2,937	1,924	693	208
Other offences	6,888	175	818	1,266	1,236	1,656	1,144	416	178
Offence not known	291	4	42	52	67	65	43	15	3
Females									
Total	**3,382**	**42**	**253**	**478**	**676**	**981**	**653**	**237**	**63**
Violence against the person	839	15	101	137	136	205	172	57	15
Sexual offences	54	0	3	7	5	14	16	7	1
Robbery	334	10	45	58	83	96	36	5	1
Burglary	207	3	13	31	66	56	35	3	0
Theft, handling, fraud and forgery	665	3	26	69	135	225	137	55	16
Drugs offences	893	4	42	110	183	270	177	85	23
Other offences	378	7	23	64	68	108	78	25	6
Offence not known	13	0	0	2	1	7	3	0	0
At 30 June 2010									
Offences									
Males									
Total	**67,450**	**1,162**	**6,337**	**11,358**	**12,350**	**17,539**	**11,600**	**4,540**	**2,564**
Violence against the person	19,349	306	1,820	3,479	3,721	4,864	3,376	1,284	499
Sexual offences	9,221	57	399	818	982	1,763	2,319	1,417	1,466
Robbery	8,562	283	1,451	2,113	1,787	1,923	843	141	21
Burglary	6,706	201	838	1,219	1,320	2,164	826	116	22
Theft, handling, fraud and forgery	4,771	80	323	629	963	1,560	794	297	125
Drugs offences	10,235	63	579	1,537	1,983	3,097	2,028	730	218
Other offences	7,805	167	829	1,428	1,422	1,959	1,294	517	189
Offence not known	801	5	98	135	172	209	120	38	24
Females									
Total	**3,421**	**23**	**286**	**480**	**665**	**992**	**661**	**260**	**54**
Violence against the person	898	10	114	138	147	228	171	75	15
Sexual offences	83	0	7	9	10	26	20	8	3
Robbery	272	5	40	41	74	87	21	4	0
Burglary	151	0	10	23	32	56	27	3	0
Theft, handling, fraud and forgery	623	1	23	75	137	189	135	51	12
Drugs offences	829	1	39	104	172	254	168	77	14
Other offences	479	4	39	85	77	124	101	41	8
Offence not known	86	2	14	5	16	28	18	1	2

1 The data presented in this table are drawn from administrative IT systems. Where figures in the table have been rounded to the nearest whole number, the rounded components do not always add to the totals, which are calculated and rounded independently. Reconciliation exercises with published Home Office figures may demonstrate differences due to rounded components.

2 Excludes persons committed in default of payment of a fine.

Source: Ministry of Justice

21.12 Crimes and offences recorded by the police: by crime group[1]

Scotland

		2001/02	2002/03	2003/04	2004[4]/05	2005/06	2006/07	2007/08	2008/09	2009/10	2010/11
Non-sexual crimes of violence against the person	BEBC	15.7	16.1	15.1	14.7	13.8	14.1	12.9	12.6	11.2	11.4
Serious assault, etc[2]	KAFS	7.5	7.6	7.5	7.8	7.2	7.5	6.9	6.6	5.7	5.6
Robbery	KAFU	4.6	4.6	4.2	3.7	3.6	3.6	3.1	3.0	2.5	2.6
Other	KAFV	3.5	3.8	3.5	3.2	3.0	3.0	3.0	3.0	3.0	3.3
Crimes involving indecency	BEBD	6.0	6.6	6.8	7.3	6.6	6.7	6.6	6.3	6.5	6.5
Rape & Attempted Rape	OXBQ	0.8	0.9	1.0	1.1	1.2	1.1	1.1	1.0	1.0	1.1
Sexual Assault		2.9	3.3	3.3	3.5	3.4	3.5	3.5	3.3	3.4	3.2
Prostitution		1.2	1.1	1.2	1.4	0.7	0.7	0.5	0.5	0.4	0.4
Other Indecency		1.2	1.3	1.3	1.4	1.3	1.4	1.5	1.5	1.6	1.8
Crimes involving dishonesty	BEBE	242.8	224.8	211.0	210.4	187.8	183.7	166.7	167.8	153.3	155.9
Housebreaking[3]	KAGB	45.5	40.6	36.4	35.0	31.3	30.6	25.4	25.5	23.8	25.0
Theft by opening lockfast places	KAGC	8.2	7.8	7.4	7.9	8.3	7.4	6.4	7.0	5.1	4.1
Theft from a motor vehicle (OLP)	EPI4	32.7	30.4	26.8	20.4	16.5	16.1	15.2	13.6	10.2	9.5
Theft of a motor vehicle	KAGD	23.1	20.9	17.6	15.6	14.0	15.0	12.1	11.6	9.3	8.7
Shoplifting	KAGE	31.6	28.3	27.9	28.5	28.2	28.8	29.2	32.0	30.3	29.7
Other theft	KAGF	76.0	73.2	72.5	77.6	72.1	70.2	64.6	64.4	61.0	64.7
Fraud	KAGG	17.4	15.8	15.3	18.3	11.1	9.3	8.4	8.3	8.3	9.0
Other	KAGH	8.4	7.9	7.0	7.1	6.3	6.4	5.3	5.4	5.3	5.3
Fire-raising, vandalism, etc	BEBF	95.0	97.7	103.8	128.5	127.9	129.7	118.0	109.4	93.4	82.0
Fire-raising	KAGJ	2.9	3.8	4.2	4.7	4.9	5.0	4.6	4.7	4.2	4.0
Vandalism, etc	KAGK	92.0	93.8	99.6	123.9	123.0	124.8	113.4	104.8	89.2	78.1
Other crimes	BEBG	66.8	73.2	77.5	77.2	81.9	84.9	81.3	81.3	73.7	67.2
Crimes against public justice	KAGM	20.9	22.7	25.8	25.6	27.7	32.1	31.4	29.5	26.9	26.3
Handling offensive weapons	KAFT	9.0	9.4	9.3	9.5	9.6	10.1	9.0	9.0	7.0	6.3
Drugs	KAGN	36.8	40.9	42.3	41.8	44.2	42.4	40.7	42.5	39.4	34.3
Other	KAGO	0.1	0.2	0.2	0.2	0.3	0.4	0.3	0.3	0.3	0.3
Total crimes	KAGQ	426.2	418.3	414.2	438.1	417.8	419.3	385.5	377.4	338.0	323.1
Miscellaneous offences	BEBH	163.4	169.6	181.0	214.3	219.5	232.4	224.3	226.8	231.0	210.2
Minor assault	KAGS	55.4	55.0	57.4	73.7	72.3	78.2	73.5	74.1	72.2	70.8
Breach of the peace	KAGT	72.7	74.7	77.9	90.0	89.6	93.4	90.3	91.2	85.2	56.5
Drunkenness	KAGU	7.8	7.3	7.5	7.2	7.0	6.7	6.7	6.0	5.7	5.8
Other	KAGV	27.6	32.6	38.2	43.4	50.6	54.2	53.7	55.4	67.9	77.1
Motor vehicle offences	BEBI	362.5	350.1	435.0	424.3	380.5	375.1	347.8	333.5	332.7	320.3
Dangerous and careless driving	KAGX	12.2	12.7	12.0	13.1	13.0	13.6	13.0	11.5	11.1	9.8
Drink driving	KAGY	11.5	11.8	11.6	11.1	11.3	11.7	10.7	9.8	8.5	7.6
Speeding	KAGZ	126.8	117.2	199.2	210.1	167.7	162.9	137.2	117.3	113.5	114.1
Unlawful use of a motor vehicle	KAHA	94.6	99.5	99.5	76.7	75.1	73.1	73.7	68.6	63.3	53.8
Vehicle defect offences	KAHB	45.5	46.5	37.2	27.0	23.9	21.2	22.3	25.6	26.7	21.9
Other	KAHC	77.9	66.9	75.4	86.3	89.4	92.6	90.8	100.7	109.7	113.1
Total offences	KAHD	532.0	524.1	615.9	638.6	600.0	607.4	572.1	560.3	563.7	530.4
Total crimes and offences	BEBB	952.4	937.8	1030.1	1076.7	1017.7	1026.6	957.6	937.7	901.8	853.5

1 See chapter text.
2 Includes murder, attempted murder, culpable homicide and serious assault.
3 Includes dwellings, non-dwellings and other premises.
4 The introduction of the Scottish Crime Recording Standard on 1 April 2004 has increased the number of minor crimes recorded, such as minor crimes of theft, vandalism, petty assault and breach of the peace.

21.13 Persons with a charge proved: by crime group[1]

Scotland

Numbers

		2001 /02	2002 /03	2003 /04	2004 /05	2005 /06	2006 /07	2007 /08	2008 /09	2009 /10	2010 /11[1]
Non-sexual crimes of violence	KEHC	**2,092**	**2,381**	**2,595**	**2,427**	**2,458**	**2,461**	**2,749**	**2,655**	**2,460**	**2,517**
Homicide	KEHD	103	99	131	143	111	121	136	114	116	116
Serious assault and attempted murder	KEHE	1,171	1,360	1,474	1,374	1,560	1,495	1,731	1,707	1,507	1,406
Robbery	KEHG	627	682	689	610	512	529	548	561	532	519
Other violence	KEHH	191	240	301	300	275	316	334	273	305	476
Crimes of indecency	KEHI	**614**	**562**	**666**	**810**	**853**	**866**	**790**	**947**	**837**	**766**
Rape and attempted rape	HFVU	67	55	58	70	61	59	49	41	54	36
Sexual assault	KEHJ	307	282	297	270	262	259	259	285	260	280
Prostitution		110	99	126	225	282	299	228	229	165	160
Other	KEHL	130	126	185	245	248	249	254	392	358	290
Crimes of dishonesty	KEHM	**21,513**	**21,661**	**19,847**	**19,654**	**18,007**	**18,398**	**17,753**	**17,450**	**15,971**	**15,606**
Housebreaking	KEHN	2,672	2,751	2,508	2,372	2,074	2,025	1,867	1,860	1,604	1,536
Theft by opening lockfast place	KEHO	1,478	1,448	1,288	1,194	951	911	944	863	722	663
Theft of motor vehicle	KEHP	1,319	1,337	1,098	975	847	851	776	733	572	482
Shoplifting	KEHQ	8,366	8,826	8,123	8,427	8,162	8,548	8,457	8,287	8,098	7,842
Other theft	KEHR	4,278	3,894	3,652	3,666	3,289	3,430	3,258	3,113	2,765	2,849
Fraud	KEHS	1,479	1,459	1,443	1,354	1,243	1,179	1,159	1,220	953	903
Other	KEHT	1,921	1,946	1,735	1,666	1,441	1,454	1,292	1,374	1,257	1,331
Fire-raising, vandalism, etc	KEHU	**4,051**	**4,212**	**4,759**	**5,025**	**5,000**	**5,438**	**5,392**	**4,375**	**3,836**	**3,351**
Fire-raising	KEHV	125	147	169	192	192	251	224	244	190	158
Vandalism, etc	KEHW	3,926	4,065	4,590	4,833	4,808	5,187	5,168	4,131	3,646	3,193
Other crime	KEHX	**13,831**	**13,964**	**15,454**	**16,804**	**16,979**	**19,864**	**20,266**	**19,786**	**19,090**	**18,684**
Crime against public justice	KFBK	5,265	5,058	5,291	5,771	5,764	7,218	8,043	8,704	8,351	8,491
Handling an offensive weapon	KEHF	2,633	2,771	2,875	3,447	3,500	3,550	3,422	3,541	2,866	2,473
Drugs offences	KFBL	5,913	6,111	7,258	7,555	7,606	8,893	8,533	7,303	7,683	7,500
Other	KFBM	20	24	30	31	109	203	268	238	190	220
Total crimes	KEHB	**42,101**	**42,780**	**43,321**	**44,720**	**43,297**	**47,027**	**46,950**	**45,213**	**42,194**	**40,924**
Miscellaneous offences	KEHZ	**30,144**	**32,052**	**34,536**	**37,488**	**39,668**	**42,272**	**41,301**	**35,745**	**32,854**	**30,410**
Common assault	KEIA	10,823	11,745	12,317	13,574	14,427	15,443	15,502	15,137	14,148	13,640
Breach of the peace	KEIB	13,950	14,384	15,050	16,172	16,894	18,104	17,494	16,003	14,077	11,003
Drunkenness	KEIC	374	370	418	311	293	261	235	129	146	160
Other	KEID	4,997	5,553	6,751	7,431	8,054	8,464	8,070	4,476	4,483	5,607
Motor vehicle offences	KEIE	**44,844**	**47,994**	**50,661**	**47,524**	**45,239**	**45,114**	**45,356**	**44,931**	**45,980**	**44,064**
Dangerous and careless driving	KEIF	3,319	3,628	4,118	3,810	3,621	3,774	3,967	3,696	3,404	3,162
Drink/drug driving	KEIG	6,538	9,508	8,158	8,001	7,970	8,066	7,820	7,222	6,232	5,347
Speeding	KEIH	9,684	9,809	12,675	13,521	12,252	13,395	14,156	13,589	14,357	12,945
Unlawful use of vehicle	KEII	18,553	19,192	19,563	16,696	14,712	13,450	13,609	12,741	12,175	11,034
Vehicle defect offences	KEIJ	1,252	1,510	1,859	1,791	1,652	1,707	1,414	1,483	1,662	1,723
Other	KEIK	5,498	4,347	4,288	3,705	5,032	4,722	4,390	6,200	8,150	9,853
Total offences	KEHY	**74,988**	**80,046**	**85,197**	**85,012**	**84,907**	**87,386**	**86,657**	**80,676**	**78,834**	**74,474**
Total crimes and offences	KEHA	**117,089**	**122,826**	**128,518**	**129,732**	**128,204**	**134,413**	**133,607**	**125,889**	**121,028**	**115,398**

1 Figures for some categories dealt with by the high court - including homicide, rape and major drug cases may be underestimated slightly due to late recording of disposals

Source: Scottish Government Justice Department: 0131 244 2227

21.14 Persons with a charge proved: by type of court[1,2]

Scotland

Numbers

		2001 /02	2002 /03	2003 /04[2]	2004 /05	2005 /06	2006 /07	2007 /08	2008 /09	2009 /10	2010 /11
Court procedure											
High Court[3]	**KEIQ**	1,125	1,194	1,217	974	885	908	861	804	757	682
Sheriff Court	**KEIU**	68,966	76,817	76,619	77,195	75,989	80,503	79,980	73,898	65,585	61,458
District Court[4,5]	**KEIV**	43,939	41,516	47,144	47,891	47,358	48,319	47,569	46,632	50,448	49,243
Total called to court[6]	**KEIZ**	**117,089**	**122,826**	**128,518**	**129,732**	**128,204**	**134,413**	**133,607**	**125,889**	**121,028**	**115,398**

1 See chapter text.
2 All figures are now reported as financial years.
3 Including cases remitted to the High Court from the Sheriff Court.
4 District Court figures from 2002/03 include the Stipendiary Magistrate Court.
5 Figures for 2007/08 includes Justice of the Peace courts in Lothian & Borders from 10 March 2008.
6 Includes court type not known.

Source: Scottish Government Justice Department: 0131 244 2229

21.15 Persons with charge proved: by main penalty[1,2]

Scotland

Thousands

		2001 /02	2002 /03	2003 /04	2004 /05	2005 /06	2006 /07	2007 /08	2008 /09	2009 /10	2010 /11
Main penalty											
Restriction of liberty order	**ZBRE**	166	656	879	1,097	1,136	1,179	1,155	1,143	931	816
Supervised attendance order[3]	**ZBRF**	11	13	18	33	99	112	129	198	247	276
Drug Treatment & testing order	**OEWA**	286	409	610	713	758	865	822	885	808	806
Absolute discharge[4]	**KEXA**	415	385	435	403	401	413	430	412	522	455
Admonition or caution	**KEXB**	11,702	12,360	12,934	13,744	14,175	15,967	16,084	16,399	15,687	16,412
Probation	**KEXC**	7,708	8,451	8,137	8,623	8,785	8,614	9,002	9,912	8,893	7,902
Remit to children's hearing	**KEXD**	158	230	196	221	260	313	259	209	175	170
Community service order	**KEXE**	4,323	4,719	4,298	4,849	5,183	5,286	5,601	5,784	5,471	5,302
Fine	**KEXF**	76,217	78,540	84,327	83,237	80,723	83,445	82,019	72,840	71,452	66,442
Compensation order	**KEXG**	1,142	1,347	1,767	1,695	1,471	1,375	1,325	1,153	1,039	1,083
Insanity, hospital, guardianship order	**KYAN**	103	101	129	95	115	65	20	16	15	18
Prison	**KEXI**	11,437	12,427	11,959	12,306	12,155	13,489	13,593	13,900	13,013	13,099
Young offenders' institution	**KEXJ**	3,407	3,162	2,801	2,685	2,903	3,245	3,142	3,017	2,753	2,157
Other custody	**KEXM**	14	25	24	20	24	24	26	21	22	12
Total persons with charge proved[5]	**KEXO**	**117,089**	**122,826**	**128,518**	**129,732**	**128,204**	**134,413**	**133,607**	**125,889**	**121,028**	**115,390**

1 See chapter text.
2 All figures are now reported as financial years.
3 Of first instance.
4 Includes a small number of court cautions and dog-related disposals.
5 Includes a small number of sentence unknown.

Source: Scottish Government Justice Department: 0131 244 2229

21.16 Persons with charge proved by main penalty:
by gender and age
Scotland

Numbers

	2001 /02	2002 /03	2003 /04	2004 /05	2005 /06	2006 /07	2007 /08	2008 /09	2009 /10	2010 /11
Total[1,2,3]	116,745	122,471	128,051	129,234	127,843	134,113	133,352	125,875	121,024	115,378
Males										
Total[4]	100,874	104,311	107,931	108,459	107,804	113,511	112,787	106,295	101,601	96,886
Under 21	23,780	24,076	23,550	23,205	24,185	25,639	24,525	20,535	17,327	15,117
21 to 30	38,441	39,405	40,052	39,336	38,079	40,404	41,222	38,896	37,312	35,109
Over 30	38,362	40,811	44,324	45,912	45,537	47,466	47,040	46,864	46,962	46,659
Females										
Total[4]	15,871	18,160	20,120	20,775	20,039	20,602	20,565	19,580	19,423	18,492
Under 21	2,746	2,845	2,944	2,909	2,937	3,264	3,306	2,830	2,511	2,223
21 to 30	6,200	6,843	7,494	7,652	7,387	7,401	7,387	7,313	7,009	6,558
Over 30	6,854	8,468	9,680	10,214	9,715	9,935	9,872	9,437	9,903	9,709
Custody	14,858	15,614	14,784	15,010	15,082	16,758	16,761	16,938	15,788	15,267
Males										
Total[4]	13,884	14,610	13,684	13,809	13,939	15,583	15,486	15,585	14,509	13,966
Under 21	3,185	2,979	2,620	2,521	2,803	3,070	2,986	2,856	2,600	2,000
21-30	6,626	7,145	6,726	6,478	6,030	6,684	6,864	6,715	6,151	6,052
Over 30	4,072	4,486	4,338	4,809	5,106	5,829	5,636	6,014	5,758	5,914
Females										
Total[4]	974	1,004	1,100	1,201	1,143	1,175	1,275	1,353	1,279	1,301
Under 21	237	218	211	191	125	200	182	182	175	169
21-30	463	499	542	611	563	592	615	682	580	586
Over 30	274	287	347	399	455	383	478	489	524	546
Community Sentence	12,494	14,245	13,942	15,315	15,973	16,077	16,709	17,921	16,350	15,550
Males										
Total[4]	10,538	11,952	11,623	12,820	13,355	13,566	13,886	14,955	13,484	12,927
Under 21	3,677	4,012	3,583	3,914	4,158	4,486	4,471	4,608	3,640	3,439
21-30	3,969	4,511	4,435	4,831	4,920	4,878	4,935	5,303	5,037	4,670
Over 30	2,890	3,429	3,605	4,075	4,277	4,202	4,480	5,044	4,807	4,818
Females										
Total[4]	1,956	2,293	2,319	2,495	2,618	2,511	2,823	2,966	2,866	2,623
Under 21	480	498	478	529	532	633	667	593	559	451
21-30	894	1,071	987	1,042	1,126	926	1,092	1,176	1,013	1,015
Over 30	582	723	854	924	960	952	1,064	1,197	1,294	1,157
Financial Penalty	77,037	79,562	85,647	84,468	81,862	84,541	83,104	73,980	72,487	67,508
Males										
Total[4]	67,188	68,016	72,573	71,134	69,505	72,051	71,057	63,241	61,480	57,311
Under 21	14,026	13,997	14,389	13,765	14,029	14,646	13,597	9,886	8,462	7,066
21-30	24,941	24,663	25,771	24,840	23,884	25,214	25,791	23,102	22,258	20,343
Over 30	27,947	29,340	32,409	32,524	31,589	32,189	31,669	30,253	30,760	29,901
Females										
Total[4]	9,849	11,546	13,074	13,334	12,357	12,490	12,047	10,739	11,007	10,197
Under 21	1,318	1,437	1,549	1,494	1,507	1,572	1,569	1,206	1,061	909
21-30	3,665	4,019	4,572	4,611	4,254	4,253	4,140	3,754	3,818	3,378
Over 30	4,805	6,087	6,952	7,229	6,596	6,663	6,338	5,779	6,128	5,908
Other Sentence	12,356	13,050	13,678	14,441	14,926	16,737	16,778	17,036	16,399	17,053
Males										
Total[4]	9,264	9,733	10,051	10,696	11,005	12,311	12,358	12,514	12,128	12,682
Under 21	2,892	3,088	2,958	3,005	3,195	3,437	3,471	3,185	2,625	2,612
21-30	2,905	3,086	3,120	3,187	3,245	3,628	3,632	3,776	3,866	4,044
Over 30	3,453	3,556	3,972	4,504	4,565	5,246	5,255	5,553	5,637	6,026
Females										
Total[4]	3,092	3,317	3,627	3,745	3,921	4,426	4,420	4,522	4,271	4,371
Under 21	711	692	706	695	773	859	888	849	716	694
21-30	1,178	1,254	1,393	1,388	1,444	1,630	1,540	1,701	1,598	1,579
Over 30	1,193	1,371	1,527	1,662	1,704	1,937	1,992	1,972	1,957	2,098

1 Includes people wih sentence unknown.
2 Excludes people with gender unknown.
3 Excludes companies.
4 Includes people with age unknown.

Source: Scottish Government Justice Department: 0131 244 2229

21.17 Penal establishments: average daily population and receptions

Scotland

Numbers

		2000/01	2001/02	2002/03	2003/04	2004/05	2005/06	2006/07	2007/08	2008/09	2009/10	2010/11
Average daily population												
Male	KEPB	5,676	5,925	6,171	6,293	6,444	6,521	6,833	7,005	7,415	7,539	7,419
Female	KEPC	207	257	282	314	332	334	353	371	412	424	435
Total	**KEPA**	**5,883**	**6,182**	**6,452**	**6,606**	**6,776**	**6,856**	**7,187**	**7,376**	**7,826**	**7,963**	**7,853**
Analysis by type of custody												
Remand	KEPD	881	996	1,207	1,237	1,223	1,250	1,572	1,561	1,679	1,522	1,474
Untried	JTT6	771	862	1,055	1,074	1,035	1,032	1,329	1,306	1,415	1,170	1,112
Convicted awaiting sentence	JTT7	109	134	152	163	188	218	243	255	264	352	362
Young offenders	JTT8	220	262	273	256	261	285	361	355	334	305	262
Adults	JTT9	661	734	933	981	962	965	1,211	1,206	1,344	1,217	1,212
Persons under sentence: total[1]	KEPE	5,001	5,186	5,245	5,369	5,553	5,605	5,615	5,815	6,148	6,441	6,379
Adult prisoners	KEPF	4,346	4,303	4,378	4,474	4,600	4,553	4,432	4,517	4,878	5,119	5,110
Young offenders	KEPI	655	595	569	539	544	607	621	658	657	690	576
Young offenders (fine defaulters)[2]	JTU2	9	7	7	6	5	5	4	2	1	1	1
Adult (fine defaulters)[2]	JTU3	55	46	49	49	46	43	41	26	10	8	8
Persons recalled from supervision/licence	KEPN	145	196	236	293	351	397	515	611	600	622	682
Others	KEPO	36	36	6	7	5	1	-	-	-	-	-
Persons sentenced by court martial	KEPP	-	-	-	-	1	-	-	-	1	-	1
Civil prisoners	KEPQ	1	2	1	1	1	1	1	1	-	1	-
Receptions to penal establishments												
Remand	KEPR	14,062	15,668	18,595	18,385	18,538	19,105	22,811	22,136	22,300	20,635	21,026
Male	KEPS	13,042	14,325	16,881	16,601	16,786	17,374	20,809	19,966	20,054	18,790	19,133
Female	KEPT	1,020	1,343	1,714	1,784	1,752	1,731	2,002	2,170	2,246	1,845	1,893
Persons under sentence: total[1]	KEPU	19,136	20,328	20,955	20,438	19,653	19,488	20,427	18,227	16,562	15,813	14,880
Male	KEPV	17,953	19,032	19,567	19,021	18,267	18,171	19,039	17,011	15,429	14,689	13,773
Female	KEPW	1,183	1,296	1,388	1,417	1,386	1,317	1,388	1,216	1,133	1,124	1,107
Imprisoned: Adults:												
directly	KEPX	8,943	9,785	10,602	10,518	10,628	10,758	11,702	11,847	12,369	11,898	11,409
in default of fine[2]	KEPY	6,450	6,772	6,834	6,776	6,081	5,450	5,272	3,211	1,322	1,152	1,097
Sentenced to young offenders' institution:												
directly	KEQA	2,436	2,391	2,225	2,004	1,948	2,162	2,287	2,354	2,265	2,143	1,700
in default of fine[2]	KEQB	1,116	1,194	1,074	876	726	771	698	403	185	180	153
Persons recalled from supervision/licence	JYYD	191	186	220	264	270	347	468	412	421	440	521
Persons sentenced by court martial	KEQH	2	2	3	1	6	-	-	2	1	-	2
Civil prisoners	KEQI	10	8	11	12	6	4	4	11	4	12	22

1 Includes persons recalled from supervision/licence or categorised as 'other'.

2 Includes in default of compensation orders.

Source: The Scottish Government Justice Directorate: 0131 244 8740

21.18 Expenditure on penal establishments[1]

Scotland

Years ended 31 March

£ thousands

		2000 /01	2001 /02	2002 /03	2003 /04	2004 /05	2005 /06	2006 /07	2007 /08	2008 /09	2009 /10
Departmental Expenditure											
Manpower and Associated Services	KPHC	160,242	172,490	168,593	169,784	181,931	200,742	199,854	206,298	214,346	187,968
Prisoner and Associated Costs	KPHD	23,501	24,652	23,363	51,070	42,767	28,582	41,821	29,408	29,793	29,422
Capital Expenditure	KPHE	24,283	24,955	36,519	34,617	72,812	70,406	81,818	53,564	100,231	87,902
Gross Expenditure	KPHF	208,026	222,097	228,475	255,471	297,510	299,730	323,493	289,270	344,370	305,292
Less Receipts:-	KPHG	8,380	8,194	3,485	3,298	3,312	2,872	2,178	2,034	2,579	2,419
Net Departmental Expenditure	KPHH	199,646	213,903	224,990	252,173	294,198	296,858	321,315	287,236	341,791	302,873
plus Annually Managed Expenditure Capital Charges	DSJI	..	31,341	40,432	41,728	48,497	52,840	41,816	59,498	89,656	84,519
Total Net Expenditure	DSNX	199,646	245,244	265,422	293,901	342,695	349,698	363,131	346,734	431,447	387,392

1 See chapter text.

Source: The Scottish Executive Justice Department: 0131 244 2227

21.19 Recorded crime

Northern Ireland

Thousands

	1998 /99	1999 /00	2000 /01	2001 /02	2002 /03	2003 /04	2004 /05	2005 /06	2006 /07	2007 /08	2008 /09	2009 /10	2010 /11
Violence Against the Person	18.7	21.7	21.6	26.4	28.7	29.2	29.7	31.3	32.3	30.1	29.9	30.3	29.8
Sexual Offences	1.6	1.3	1.2	1.4	1.4	1.7	1.7	1.7	1.7	1.7	1.8	1.8	1.9
Burglary	15.3	15.9	15.7	17.0	18.5	16.3	13.3	12.7	11.5	11.6	12.3	12.5	11.8
Robbery	1.4	1.4	1.8	2.2	2.5	2.0	1.5	1.7	1.6	1.1	1.3	1.3	1.3
Theft	35.4	37.0	36.9	41.7	41.9	35.7	31.1	29.5	27.8	24.7	26.2	26.6	25.4
Fraud and forgery	6.8	7.6	7.8	8.2	8.1	5.9	4.8	4.8	4.2	2.7	3.6	3.3	3.0
Criminal Damage	27.7	31.2	32.3	40.0	36.6	32.4	31.4	34.8	36.3	30.9	28.4	26.4	25.0
Drug Offences	1.4	1.7	1.5	1.1	1.9	2.6	2.6	2.9	2.4	2.7	3.0	3.1	3.5
Other Miscellaneous Offences	0.9	1.2	1.3	1.7	2.8	2.1	2.0	3.8	3.4	2.8	3.5	3.8	3.2
Total	**109.1**	**119.1**	**119.9**	**139.8**	**142.5**	**128.0**	**118.1**	**123.2**	**121.1**	**108.5**	**110.1**	**109.1**	**105.0**

1 See chapter text

Source: The Police Service of Northern Ireland

21.20 Prisons and Young Offenders Centres

Northern Ireland
Receptions and average population

Thousands

		1997	1998	1999	2000	2001	2002	2003	2004	2005	2006	2007	2008	2009
Receptions:														
Reception of untried prisoners	**KEOA**	2,188	2,284	2,497	2,197	1,922	2,337	2,439	2,440	2,776	3,193	2,929	2,905	3,082
Reception of sentenced prisoners:														
Imprisonment under sentence of immediate custody[1]	**KEOB**	1,062	949	963	1,001	791	916	1,032	975	966	1,075	1,123	1,227	1,183
Imprisonment in default of payment of a fine	**KEOC**	1,513	1,530	1,423	1,261	1,090	990	1,143	1,296	1,437	1,569	1,425	1,504	1,270
Total	**KEOD**	2,575	2,479	2,386	2,262	1,881	1,906	2,175	2,271	2,403	2,644	2,548	2,731	2,453
Reception into Young Offender Centres:														
Detention under sentence of immediate custody	**KEOE**	331	347	346	282	252	315	268	287	222	229	247	239	142
Detention in default of payment of a fine	**KEOF**	366	385	417	389	303	250	310	351	377	382	299	238	124
Total	**KEOG**	697	732	763	671	555	565	578	638	599	611	546	477	266
Other receptions[2]:	**KEOL**	42	70	38	56	58	57	117	106	134	24	38	72	91
Daily average population:														
Unconvicted[3]	**KEON**	376	383	377	317	272	347	393	456	450	531	531	513	511
Convicted[4]	**KEOP**	1,256	1,124	867	751	638	679	767	818	851	902	935	976	954
Total	**KEOM**	**1,632**	**1,507**	**1,244**	**1,068**	**910**	**1,026**	**1,160**	**1,274**	**1,301**	**1,433**	**1,466**	**1,490**	**1,465**

1 Includes those detained under Section 73 of the Children and Young Persons (NI) Act 1968.
2 Non-criminal prisoners including those imprisoned for non-pament of maintenance, non-payment of debt, contempt of court or are being held under the terms of an Immigration Act.
3 Prisoners on remand or awaiting trial and prisoners committed by civil process.
4 Includes those sentenced to immediate custody and fine defaulters.

Source: Department of Justice Northern Ireland: 028 9052 7534
The Northern Ireland Prison Population in 2009.

Transport and communications

Chapter 22

Transport and communication

Road data (Tables 22.4 & 22.5)

The Department for Transport has undertaken significant development work over the last two years to improve its traffic estimates and measurement of traffic flow on particular stretches of the road network. This work has previously been outlined in a number of publications (Road Traffic Statistics: 2001 SB(02)23, Traffic in Great Britain Q4 2002 Data SB(03)5 and Traffic in Great Britain Q1 2003 SB(03)6).

The main point to note is that figures for 1993 to 2004 have been calculated on a different basis from years prior to 1993. Therefore, figures prior to 1993 are not directly comparable with estimates for later years. Estimates on the new basis for 1993 and subsequent years were first published by the Department on 8 May 2003 in Traffic in Great Britain Q1 2003 SB(03)6. A summary of the main methodological changes to take place over the last couple of years appears below.

Traffic estimates are now disaggregated for roads in urban and rural areas rather than between built-up and non built-up roads. Built-up roads were defined as those with a speed limit of 40 mph or lower. This created difficulties in producing meaningful disaggregated traffic estimates because an increasing number of clearly rural roads were subject to a 40 mph speed limit for safety reasons. The urban/rural split of roads is largely determined by whether roads lie within the boundaries of urban areas with a population of 10,000 or more with adjustments in some cases for major roads at the boundary.

Traffic estimates are based on the results of many 12-hour manual counts in every year, which are grossed up to estimates of annual average daily flows using expansion factors based on data from automatic traffic counters on similar roads. These averages are needed so that traffic in off-peak times, at weekends and in the summer and winter months (when only special counts are undertaken) can be taken into account when assessing the traffic at each site. For this purpose roads are now sorted into 22 groupings (previously there were only seven) and this allows a better match of manual count sites with our automatic count sites. These groupings are based on a detailed analysis of the results from all the individual automatic count sites and take into account regional groupings, road category (that is, both the urban/rural classification of the road and the road class) and traffic flow levels. The groupings range from lightly trafficked, rural minor roads in holiday areas such as Cornwall and Devon, to major roads in central London.

With the increasing interest in sub-regional statistics, we have undertaken a detailed study of traffic counts on minor roads carried out in the last ten years. This has been done in conjunction with a Geographic Information System to enable us to establish general patterns of minor road traffic in each local authority. As a result of this, we have been able to produce more reliable estimate of traffic levels in each authority in our base year of 1999. This in turn has enabled us to produce better estimates of traffic levels back to 1993, as well as more reliable estimates for 1999 onwards.

The Department created a database for major roads based on a Geographic Information System and Ordnance Survey data. This was checked by local authorities and discussed with government regional offices and the Highways Agency to ensure that good local knowledge supplemented the available technical data.

Urban major and minor roads, from 1993 onwards, are defined as being within an urban area with a population of more than 10,000 people, based on the 2001 urban settlements. The definition for urban settlement can be found on the CLG web site at:
www.communities.gov.uk/planningandbuilding/planningbuilding/planningstatistics/urbanrural.

Rural major and minor roads, from 1993 onwards, are defined as being outside an urban settlement.

New vehicle registrations (Table 22.8)

Special concession group
Various revisions to the vehicle taxation system were introduced on 1 July 1995 and on 29 November 1995. Separate taxation classes for farmers' goods vehicles were abolished on 1 July 1995; after this date new vehicles of this type were registered as Heavy Goods Vehicles (HGVs). The total includes 5,900 vehicles registered between 1 January and 30 June in the (now abolished) agricultural and special machines group in classes which were not eligible to register in the special concession group. The old agricultural and special machines taxation group was abolished at end June 1995. The group includes agricultural and mowing machines, snow ploughs and gritting vehicles. Electric vehicles are also included in this group and are no longer exempt from Vehicle Excise Duty (VED). Steam propelled vehicles were added to this group from November 1995.

Other licensed vehicles
Includes three wheelers, pedestrian controlled vehicles, general haulage and showmen's tractors and recovery vehicles. Recovery vehicle tax class introduced January 1988.

Special vehicles group
The special vehicles group was created on 1 July 1995 and consists of various vehicle types over 3.5 tonnes gross weight but not required to pay VED as heavy goods vehicles. The group includes mobile cranes, work trucks, digging machines, road rollers and vehicles previously taxed as showman's goods and haulage. The figure shown for 1995 covers the period from 1 July to 31 December only.

National Travel Survey data (Tables 22.1 & 22.11)
The National Travel Survey (NTS) is designed to provide a databank of personal travel information for Great Britain. It has been conducted as a continuous survey since July 1988, following ad hoc surveys since the mid-1960s. The survey is designed to identify long-term trends and is not suitable for monitoring short-term trends.

In 2006, a weighting strategy was introduced to the NTS and applied retrospectively to data back to 1995. The weighting methodology adjusts for non-response bias and also adjusts for the drop-off in the number of trips recorded by respondents during the course of the travel week. All results now published for 1995 onwards are based on weighted data, and direct comparisons cannot be made to earlier years or previous publications.

During 2008, over 8,000 households provided details of their personal travel by filling in travel diaries over the course of a week. The drawn sample size from 2002 was nearly trebled compared with previous years following recommendations in a National Statistics Review of the NTS. This enables most results to be presented on a single year basis from 2002.

Travel included in the NTS covers all trips by British residents within Great Britain for personal reasons, including travel in the course of work.

A trip is defined as a one-way course of travel having a single main purpose. It is the basic unit of personal travel defined in the survey.

A round trip is split into two trips, with the first ending at a convenient point about half-way round as a notional stopping point for the outward destination and return origin.

A stage is that portion of a trip defined by the use of a specific method of transport or of a specific ticket (a new stage being defined if either the mode or ticket changes). The main mode of a trip is that used for the longest stage of the trip. With stages of equal length, the mode of the latest stage is used. Walks of less than 50 yards are excluded.

Travel details provided by respondents include trip purpose, method of travel, time of day and trip length. The households also provided personal information, such as their age, sex, working status, driving licence holding, and details of the cars available for their use.

Because estimates made from a sample survey depend on the particular sample chosen, they generally differ from the true values of the population. This is not usually a problem when considering large samples (such as all car trips in Great Britain), but it may give misleading information when considering data from small samples even after weighting.

The most recent editions of all NTS publications are available on the DfT website at: www.dft.gov.uk/transtat/personaltravel. Bulletins of key results are published annually. The most recent bulletin is National Travel Survey: 2005.

Households with regular use of cars (Table 22.11)

The mid-year estimates of the percentage of households with regular use of a car or van are based on combined data from the NTS, the Expenditure and Food Survey (previously the Family Expenditure Survey) and the General Household Survey. The method for calculating these figures was changed slightly in 2006, to incorporate weighted data from the NTS and the GHS. Figures since have also been revised to incorporate weighted data. Results by area type are based on weighted data from the NTS only.

Continuing Survey of Road Goods Transport (Tables 22.2, 22.17 & 22.18)

The estimates are derived from the Continuing Survey of Road Goods Transport (CSRGT) which in 2005 was based on an average weekly returned sample of some 330 HGVs. The samples are drawn from the computerised vehicle licence records held by the Driver and Vehicle Licensing Agency. Questionnaires are sent to the registered keepers of the sampled vehicles asking for a description of the vehicle and its activity during the survey week. The estimates are grossed to the vehicle population,, and at the overall national level have a 2 per cent margin of error (at 95 per cent confidence level). Further details and results are published in Road Freight Statistics 2005, and previously in Transport of Goods by Road in Great Britain.

Methodological changes

A key component of National Statistics outputs is a programme of quality reviews carried out at least every five years to ensure that such statistics are fit for purpose and that their quality and value continue to improve. A quality review of the Department for Transport's road freight surveys, including the CSRGT, was carried out in 2003. A copy of the report can be accessed at: www.statistics.gov.uk/nsbase/methods_quality/quality_review/downloads/NSQR30FinalReport.doc

The quality review made a number of recommendations about the CSRGT. The main methodological recommendation was that, to improve the accuracy of survey estimates, the sample strata should be amended to reflect current trends in vehicle type, weight and legislative groups. These new strata are described more fully in Appendix C of the survey report. For practical and administrative reasons, changes were also made to the sample selection methodology (see Appendix B of the report). These changes have resulted in figures from 2004 not being fully comparable with those for 2003 and earlier years. Detailed comparisons should therefore be made with caution.

Railways: permanent way and rolling stock (Table 22.21)

1) Locomotives - locos owned by Northern Ireland Railways (NIR), does not include those from the Republic of Ireland Railway System.

2) Diesel electric etc rail motor vehicles - powered passenger carrying vehicles, includes diesel electric (DE) power cars and all Construcciones y Auxiliar de Ferocarriles (CAF) vehicles. (Note: only 16 of the CAF sets were delivered to NIR at the time.)

3) Loco hauled coaches - NIR owned De Dietrich plus Gatwick but not including gen van.

4) Rail car trailers - 80 class and 450 class trailers. Not CAF, they are all powered.

5) Rolling stock for maintenance and repair - a 'standalone' figure - may or may not be included in the above totals. Anything listed as 'repair' or 'workshop' in the motive power sheets is included. Also, those CAF vehicles not yet delivered at the time.

6) The information is a 'snapshot' taken from the motive power sheets at end of March, together with any other known information.

Activity at civil aerodromes (Table 22.26)

Figures exclude Channel Island and Isle of Man airports. 'Other' covers local pleasure flights, scheduled service, positioning flights and non-transport charter flights for reward (for example: aerial survey work, crop dusting and delivery of empty aircraft). 'Non-commercial' covers test and training flights, private, aeroclub, military and official flights, and business aviation, etc.

22.1 Trips per person per year: by sex, main mode and trip purpose[1], 2010

Great Britain

trips / thousands

Purpose	All persons					
	Walk	Car	Bus & Coach	Rail[2]	Other[3]	All modes
Commuting	16	100	14	12	8	150
Business	2	23	1	2	1	29
Education	22	20	10	2	5	59
Escort education	17	28	1	-	-	47
Shopping	43	125	18	2	5	193
Other escort	9	79	2	-	1	91
Other personal business	21	65	7	2	3	98
Social / entertainment	38	148	13	5	9	213
Holiday / day trip	2	29	2	2	4	39
Other including just walk	40	-	-	0	0	41
All purposes (= 100 %)	210	618	68	27	38	960
Unweighted base (trips in thousands)	76	216	23	8	13	336

Purpose	Males					
	Walk	Car	Bus & Coach	Rail[2]	Other[3]	All modes
Commuting	15	118	13	15	12	172
Business	2	28	1	2	1	34
Education	22	19	11	2	7	61
Escort education	9	18	-	-	-	27
Shopping	43	111	13	1	5	173
Other escort	7	76	2	-	1	85
Other personal business	20	62	6	2	3	93
Social / entertainment	38	144	12	5	10	210
Holiday / day trip	3	28	2	2	5	39
Other including just walk	39	-	0	0	0	39
All purposes (= 100 %)	197	604	60	30	45	935
Unweighted base (trips in thousands)	34	103	10	5	8	159

Purpose	Females					
	Walk	Car	Bus & Coach	Rail[2]	Other[3]	All modes
Commuting	17	83	14	10	4	128
Business	2	18	1	1	1	23
Education	23	20	10	2	4	57
Escort education	25	38	2	-	1	66
Shopping	43	139	23	3	5	212
Other escort	10	82	2	-	1	96
Other personal business	22	68	8	1	3	103
Social / entertainment	38	152	13	5	9	216
Holiday / day trip	2	30	2	2	3	39
Other including just walk	41	1	-	0	0	42
All purposes (= 100 %)	223	632	75	24	31	984
Unweighted base (trips in thousands)	42	113	13	4	5	177

Source: National Travel Survey
Telephone: 020 79443097

1. Main mode is that used for the longest part of the trip
2. Includes London Underground
3. Includes bicycles, motorcycles, other private (including school buses), taxi minicabs and other public transport (air, ferries and light rail).

22.2 Domestic freight transport: by mode

Great Britain

percentage

		1999	2000	2001	2002	2003	2004 [5,6]	2005 [7]	2006	2007 [8]	2008 [9]	2009 [10]
Goods moved (billion tonnes kilometres)												
Petroleum products												
Road[1]	ZBZP	5.0	6.4	5.8	5.2	5.5	5.7	5.5	5.6	5.1	6.5	4.8
Rail[2]	ZBZQ	1.5	1.4	1.2	1.2	1.2	1.2	1.2	1.5	1.6	1.5	1.4
Water[3]	ZBZR	48.6	52.7	43.5	51.7	46.9	46.9	47.2	37.8	36.4	36.4	36.4
of which : coastwise	ZBZS	33.3	26.0	23.1	24.2	23.3	26.6	30.3	22.7	25.0	26.5	27.1
Pipeline[9]	ZBZT	11.6	11.4	11.5	10.9	10.5	10.7	10.8	10.8	10.2	10.2	10.2
All modes	ZBZU	66.7	71.9	62.0	69.0	64.1	64.5	64.7	55.8	53.3	54.6	52.8
Coal and coke												
Road[1]	ZBZV	2.2	1.5	2.1	1.5	1.5	1.2	1.5	1.3	1.6	1.0	1.0
Rail[2]	ZBZW	4.8	4.8	6.2	5.7	5.8	6.7	8.3	8.8	7.7	7.9	6.2
Water[3]	ZBZX	0.5	0.2	0.5	0.3	0.5	0.3	0.4	0.5	0.5	0.5	0.3
All modes	ZBZY	7.5	6.5	8.8	7.5	7.9	8.5	10.2	10.4	9.8	9.5	7.5
Other traffic												
Road[1]	ZBZZ	150.5	151.5	150.6	152.7	154.7	155.6	156.4	159.7	166.4	156.0	137.6
Rail[2]	ZCAA	11.9	11.9	12.0	11.7	11.9	12.5	12.2	11.8	11.9	11.2	11.4
Water[3]	ZCAB	9.6	14.6	14.8	15.2	13.5	12.3	13.3	13.5	13.9	12.7	11.9
All modes	ZCAC	172.0	178.0	177.4	179.6	180.0	180.4	181.9	185.0	192.2	179.9	161.0
All traffic												
Road[1]	KCTA	157.7	159.4	158.5	159.4	161.7	162.5	163.4	166.7	173.1	163.5	143.5
Rail[2]	KCTB	18.2	18.1	19.4	18.5	18.9	20.4	21.7	21.9	21.2	20.6	19.1
Water[3]	ZCAD	58.7	67.4	58.8	67.2	60.9	59.5	60.9	51.9	50.8	49.7	48.6
Pipeline	KCTE	11.6	11.4	11.5	10.9	10.5	10.7	10.8	10.8	10.2	10.2	10.2
All modes	KCTF	246.2	256.3	248.2	256.0	252.0	253.0	256.8	251.3	255.3	244.0	221.3
Percentage of all traffic												
Road[1]	ZCAE	64.0	62.0	64.0	62.0	64.0	64.0	64.0	66.0	68.0	67.0	65.0
Rail[2]	ZCAF	7.0	7.0	8.0	7.0	7.0	8.0	8.0	9.0	8.0	8.0	9.0
Water[3]	ZCAG	24.0	26.0	24.0	26.0	24.0	23.0	24.0	21.0	20.0	20.0	22.0
Pipeline	ZCAH	5.0	4.0	5.0	4.0	4.0	4.0	4.0	4.0	4.0	4.0	5.0
All modes	ZCAI	100.0	100.0	100.0	100.0	100.0	100.0	100.0	100.0	100.0	100.0	100.0
Goods lifted (million tonnes)												
Petroleum products												
Road[1]	ZCAJ	61.0	75.0	74.0	59.0	64.0	67.0	70.0	69.0	71.0	80.0	61.0
Rail[2]	ZCAK	..	..	..	..	..	..	..	..	..	..	..
Water[3]	ZCAL	72.0	72.0	60.0	67.0	64.0	63.0	66.0	57.0	56.0	58.0	55.0
of which : coastwise	ZCAM	52.0	40.0	34.0	36.0	35.0	38.0	42.0	34.0	35.0	36.0	36.0
Pipeline[9]	ZCAN	155.0	151.0	151.0	146.0	141.0	158.0	168.0	159.0	146.0	147.0	147.0
All modes[4]	ZCAO	288.0	298.0	285.0	272.0	269.0	288.0	304.0	285.0	274.0	285.0	263.0
Coal and coke												
Road[1]	ZCAP	28.0	22.0	21.0	17.0	22.0	14.0	21.0	17.0	24.0	15.0	10.0
Rail[2]	ZCAQ	36.0	35.0	40.0	34.0	35.0	43.0	48.0	49.0	43.0	47.0	38.0
Water[3]	ZCAR	3.0	3.0	3.0	2.0	2.0	1.0	2.0	2.0	2.0	2.0	1.0
All modes	ZCAS	75.0	60.0	64.0	53.0	59.0	67.0	72.0	68.0	69.0	63.0	49.0
Other traffic												
Road[1]	ZCAT	1,575.0	1,596.0	1,587.0	1,658.0	1,667.0	1,782.0	1,777.0	1,854.0	1,906.0	1,773.0	1,484.0
Rail[2]	ZCAU	61.0	60.0	55.0	53.0	54.0	57.0	58.0	59.0	59.0	56.0	49.0
Water[3]	ZCAV	70.0	62.0	68.0	70.0	67.0	63.0	65.0	66.0	68.0	63.0	54.0
All modes	ZCAW	1,706.0	1,718.0	1,710.0	1,781.0	1,788.0	1,902.0	1,901.0	1,980.0	2,032.0	1,892.0	1,587.0
All traffic												
Road[1]	KCTG	1,664.0	1,693.0	1,682.0	1,734.0	1,753.0	1,863.0	1,868.0	1,940.0	2,001.0	1,868.0	1,556.0
Rail[2]	KCTH	97.0	96.0	94.0	87.0	89.0	1,006.0	1,057.0	1,087.0	1,028.0	103.0	87.0
Water[3]	ZCAX	144.0	137.0	131.0	139.0	133.0	127.0	133.0	126.0	126.0	123.0	110.0
Pipeline	KCTK	155.0	151.0	151.0	146.0	141.0	158.0	168.0	159.0	146.0	147.0	147.0
All modes	KCTL	2,060.0	2,077.0	2,058.0	2,106.0	2,116.0	2,249.0	2,275.0	2,333.0	2,376.0	2,241.0	1,900.0

22.2 Domestic freight transport: by mode
Great Britain

percentage

		1999	2000	2001	2002	2003	2004 [5,6]	2005 [7]	2006	2007 [8]	2008 [9]	2009 [10]
Percentage of all traffic												
Road [1]	**ZCAY**	81.0	82.0	82.0	82.0	83.0	83.0	82.0	83.0	84.0	83.0	82.0
Rail [2]	**ZCAZ**	5.0	5.0	5.0	4.0	4.0	4.0	5.0	5.0	4.0	5.0	5.0
Water [3]	**ZCBA**	7.0	7.0	6.0	7.0	6.0	6.0	6.0	5.0	5.0	5.0	6.0
Pipeline	**ZCBB**	8.0	7.0	7.0	7.0	7.0	7.0	7.0	7.0	6.0	7.0	8.0
All modes	**ZCBC**	100.0	100.0	100.0	100.0	100.0	100.0	100.0	100.0	100.0	100.0	100.0

1 All goods vehicles, including those up to 3.5 tonnes gross vehicle weight.
2 Figures for rail are for financial years (e.g. 1999 will be 1999/00).
3 Figures for water are for UK traffic.
4 Excludes rail.
5 For road data see footnote 2 Table 4.4.
6 Break in the rail goods lifted series; increase largely due to changes in data collection method.
7 Break in the rail goods lifted series; figures from 2005/06 onwards include some of the tonnes lifted by GB Railfreight.
8 Break in the rail goods lifted series; coal data was not supplied by GB Railfreight prior to 2007/08.
9 Some pipeline data based on estimates – this survey is currently under review by DECC to improve data quality.
10 Pipeline figures are not currently available for 2009. Figures for 2008 have been used to generate totals for all modes.

Sources:
Road - DfT
Rail - ORR
Pipeline - DECC

Rail: 020 7944 2419
Road: 020 7944 3180
Pipeline: 020 7215 2718

22.3 Passenger transport by mode

Great Britain

		1999	2000	2001	2002	2003	2004	2005	2006	2007	2008	2009 [5]
Billion passenger kilometres												
Road												
Buses and coaches	**GRXK**	46	47	47	47	47	37	36	.. [4]	37	39	37
Cars, vans and taxis	**GRXG**	642	640	654	677	673	678	675	682	685	678	680
Motor cycles	**GRXH**	5	5	5	5	6	6	6	6	6	5	6
Pedal cycles	**GRXI**	4	4	4	4	5	4	4	5	4	5	5
All road	**GRXJ**	697	695	710	733	731	736	733	746	732	727	727
Rail [1]	**KCTN**	46	47	48	48	50	51	52	56	59	61	61
Air [2]	**KCTM**	7	8	8	8	9	10	10	10	10	9	8
All modes [3]	**GRXM**	751	750	765	790	790	787	783	..	801	797	797
Percentages												
Road												
Buses and coaches	**GRXN**	6	6	6	6	6	6	6	..	6	5	5
Cars, vans and taxis	**GRXO**	86	85	85	86	85	85	85	85	84	85	85
Motor cycles	**GRXP**	1	1	1	1	1	1	1	1	1	1	1
Pedal cycles	**GRXQ**	1	1	1	1	1 -		1	1	1	1	1
All road	**GRXR**	93	93	93	93	93	92	92	92	91	91	91
Rail [1]	**ZCBJ**	6	6	6	6	6	6	6	7	7	8	8
Air [2]	**ZCBK**	1.0	1.0	1.0	1.0	1.0	1.2	1.2	1.3	1.2	1.1	1.1
All modes [3]	**GRXU**	100	100	100	100	100	100	100	100	100	100	100

Sources: Bus & coach: 020 7944 3076;
Car,m/cycle & pedal cycle: 020 7944 3097;
Rail: 020 7944 3076;
Air :020 7944 3088;
Rail : ORR Air : CAA

Note: Bus and coach data not available at time of going to press and rail data for 2008 excludes urban metros.

1 Financial years. National Rail, urban metros and modern trams.
2 UK airlines, domestic passengers uplifted on scheduled and non-scheduled flights.
3 Excluding travel by water.
4 This figure is unavailable due to concerns over the quality of the non-local bus element of the series.
5 Provisional

22.4 Motor vehicle traffic: by road class: 1999-2009
Great Britain

Billion vehicle kilometres

		1999	2000 [1]	2001 [2]	2002	2003	2004	2005	2006	2007	2008	2009
Motorways	**JSZV**	87.8	88.4	90.8	92.6	93.0	96.6	97.0	99.4	100.6	100.1	99.5
Rural 'A' roads [3]												
Trunk [5]	**JSZW**	64.7	64.2	65.9	64.6	61.5	59.7	58.0	59.2	58.6	58.6	58.1
Principal [5]	**JSZX**	66.0	65.8	67.4	71.8	77.7	81.6	83.3	84.4	84.9	84.2	83.8
All rural 'A' roads	**JSZY**	130.7	130.0	133.3	136.4	139.3	141.3	141.3	143.6	143.5	142.8	142.0
Urban 'A' roads [4]												
Trunk [5]	**JSZZ**	14.0	14.0	7.6	7.4	6.7	6.0	5.5	5.6	5.4	5.5	5.5
Principal [5]	**JTAA**	67.9	67.7	74.2	74.8	75.1	76.8	76.2	76.9	75.9	74.6	75.0
All urban 'A' roads	**JTAB**	81.9	81.7	81.8	82.2	81.7	82.8	81.7	82.5	81.3	80.1	80.4
All Major Roads	**I45C**	300.4	300.0	305.9	311.2	314.0	320.7	320.1	325.5	325.4	323.0	321.9
Minor roads												
Minor rural roads	**JTAC**	61.3	61.5	61.6	64.5	64.4	65.9	66.8	69.3	72.0	72.2	70.1
Minor urban roads	**JTAD**	105.3	105.5	106.9	110.8	111.9	112.0	112.5	112.7	115.5	113.7	112.0
All minor roads	**JTAE**	166.6	167.0	168.5	175.3	176.4	177.9	179.3	182.0	187.5	185.9	182.2
All roads	**JTAF**	**467.0**	**467.1**	**474.4**	**486.5**	**490.4**	**498.6**	**499.4**	**507.5**	**513.0**	**508.9**	**504.0**

Source: DfT National Road Traffic Survey
Telephone: 020 7944 3095

1 The decline in the use of cars and taxis in 2000 was due to the fuel dispute.

2 Figures affected by the impact of Foot and Mouth disease during 2001.

3 Rural roads; Major and minor roads, from 1993 onwards, are defined as being outside an urban area. (see definition below).

4 Urban roads; Major and minor roads, from 1993 onwards, are defined as within an urban area with a population of 10,000 or more. These are based on the 2001 urban settlements. The definition for 'urban settlement' is in Urban and Rural area definitions: a user guide which can be found on the Department for Communities and Local Government web site at: http:/www.communities.gov.uk/publications/planningandbuilding/urbanrural

5 Figures for trunk and principal 'A' roads in England, from 2001 onwards are affected by the detrunking programme.

Email: roadtraff.stats@dft.gsi.gov.uk

Notes & definitions (http://www.dft.gov.uk/pgr/statistics/datatablespublications/roads/traffic/#technical)

22.5 Public road length:[1] by road type

Great Britain

Kilometres

		1999	2000	2001	2002	2003	2004	2005	2006	2007	2008	2009
Trunk motorway	JSZD	3,404	3,422	3,431	3,433	3,432	3,478	3,466	3,503	3,518	3,518	3,519
Principal motorway	JSZE	45	45	45	45	46	46	54	53	41	41	41
Rural 'A' roads[2]:												
Trunk[3]	JSZF	10,611	10,627	10,607	9,973	9,027	8,641	8,239	8,277	8,258	8,213	8,179
Principal[3]	JSZG	24,852	24,866	24,915	25,559	26,498	26,889	27,312	27,336	27,346	27,372	27,460
All rural 'A' roads	JSZH	35,463	35,493	35,522	35,532	35,525	35,530	35,550	35,612	35,603	35,586	35,639
Urban 'A' roads[4]:												
Trunk[3]	JSZI	1,087	1,074	762	705	587	506	444	446	425	420	417
Principal[3]	JSZJ	10,019	10,040	10,370	10,436	10,539	10,632	10,663	10,696	10,714	10,685	10,714
All urban 'A' roads	JSZK	11,106	11,114	11,132	11,141	11,127	11,138	11,107	11,143	11,139	11,105	11,131
Minor rural roads[5]:												
B roads	JSZL	24,579	24,570	24,562	24,554	24,547	24,640	24,639	24,574	24,795	24,685	24,663
C roads	JSZM	73,500	73,593	73,688	73,783	73,878	73,363	73,581	73,548	73,480	73,582	73,571
Unclassified	JSZN	111,350	111,568	111,787	112,006	112,231	109,561	109,426	115,250	115,365	115,032	114,646
All minor rural roads	JSZO	209,429	209,731	210,037	210,343	210,656	207,565	207,646	213,371	213,641	213,299	212,880
Minor urban roads[5]:												
B roads	JSZP	5,626	5,630	5,633	5,638	5,641	5,538	5,550	5,445	5,470	5,476	5,479
C roads	JSZQ	11,009	11,031	11,054	11,076	11,098	10,859	10,878	10,921	10,942	10,992	11,242
Unclassified	JSZR	113,432	113,772	114,114	114,456	114,816	113,520	113,757	114,355	114,524	114,450	114,499
All minor urban roads	JSZS	130,068	130,432	130,802	131,169	131,556	129,917	130,186	130,721	130,936	130,918	131,220
All major roads	GG5B	50,018	50,074	50,130	50,152	50,130	50,192	50,176	50,310	50,302	50,250	50,329
All minor roads[5]	JSZT	339,496	340,163	340,838	341,512	342,212	337,482	337,832	344,092	344,577	344,217	344,099
All roads	JSZU	389,515	390,237	390,969	391,663	392,342	387,674	388,008	394,402	394,879	394,467	394,428

Sources: National Road Traffic Survey;
Department for Transport 0207 944 3095

1. A number of minor revisions have been made to the lengths of major roads from 1993 onwards.
2. Rural roads: Major and minor roads, from 1993 onwards, are defined as being outside an urban area.
3. Figures for trunk and principal 'A' roads in England, from 2001 onwards, are affected by the detrunking programme.
4. Urban roads: Major and minor roads, from 1993 onwards, are defined as within an urban area with a population of 10,000 or more. These are based on the 2001 urban settlements. The definition for 'urban settlement' is in 'Urban and rural area definitions: a user guide which can be found on the Communities and Local Government web site at: http://www.communities.gov.uk/publications/planningandbuilding/urbanrural
5. New information from 2004 and from 2006 has enabled better estimates of minor road lengths to be made.

453

22.6 Road traffic: by type of vehicle Great Britain

Great Britain

Billion vehicle kilometres

		1998	1999	2000[1]	2001[2]	2002	2003	2004	2005	2006	2007[3]	2008	2009
Cars and taxis	JTAH	370.6	377.4	376.8	382.8	392.9	393.1	398.1	397.2	402.6	404.1	401.7	400.7
Motor cycles etc.	JTAI	4.1	4.5	4.6	4.8	5.1	5.6	5.2	5.4	5.2	5.6	5.1	5.2
Larger buses and coaches	JTAJ	5.2	5.3	5.2	5.2	5.2	5.4	5.2	5.2	5.4	5.7	5.2	5.2
Light vans[4]	JTAK	50.8	51.6	52.3	53.7	55.0	57.9	60.8	62.6	65.2	68.2	68.1	66.6
Goods vehicles[5]:													
2 axles rigid	JTAL	11.1	11.6	11.7	11.5	11.6	11.7	11.7	11.5	11.3	11.1	10.7	6.2
3 axles rigid	JTAM	1.9	1.7	1.7	1.8	1.8	1.8	1.9	1.9	1.9	2.0	2.0	1.2
4 or more axles rigid	JTAN	1.6	1.5	1.5	1.5	1.5	1.6	1.6	1.7	1.7	1.8	1.9	1.0
3 and 4 axles artic	JTAO	3.0	3.0	2.7	2.5	2.3	2.2	2.2	2.0	1.9	1.8	1.6	0.9
5 axles artic	JTAP	7.3	7.2	6.7	6.4	6.4	6.2	6.5	6.4	6.6	6.6	6.5	3.6
6 or more axles artic	JTAQ	2.9	3.3	4.1	4.5	4.8	5.0	5.4	5.5	5.7	6.1	6.0	3.5
All	JTAR	27.7	28.1	28.2	28.1	28.3	28.5	29.4	29.0	29.1	29.4	28.7	16.4
All motor vehicles	JURA	458.5	467.0	467.1	474.4	486.5	490.4	498.6	499.4	507.5	513.0	508.9	504.0
Pedal cycles	JURB	4.0	4.1	4.2	4.2	4.4	4.5	4.2	4.4	4.6	4.2	4.7	5.0

Sources: National Road Traffic Survey;
Department for Transport 0207 944 3095

1 The decline in the use of cars and taxis in 2000 was due to the fuel dispute.
2 Figures affected by the impact of Foot and Mouth disease during 2001.
3 Data for 'Light vans' and 'Larger buses and coaches' for 2007 have been revised.
4 Not exceeding 3,500 kgs gross vehicle weight.
5 Over 3,500 kgs gross vehicle weight.

22.7 Motor vehicles licensed by tax class: by method of propulsion, 2009

By taxation class

Thousand

	Petrol	Diesel	Gas/petroleum	Gas bi-fuel/Gas diesel	Hybrid-electric	Other[1]	All
Private and light goods	19,734	10,494	29	34	61	-	30,352
ow: body type cars	19,570	7,386	26	24	61	-	27,067
Motorcycles, scooters and mopeds	1,157	1	-	0	0	1	1,160
Bus	1	111	-	0	0	0	112
Goods	1	414	-	0	0	0	415
Special vehicles group	12	66	1	1	-	-	80
Other non-exempt vehicles							
Exempt vehicles	1,300	786	2	1	1	49	2,139
ow: former Special concessionary group	18	289	-	0	0	8	315
Total All Vehicles	22,205	11,872	32	36	61	51	34,258

Source - DVLA Licensed Vehicles Database
Telephone: 020-7944-3077

1. Other comprises electricity, steam, new fuel technologies, electric diesel and fuel cells.

22.8 New vehicle registrations by taxation class
Great Britain

Thousands

		1998	1999	2000	2001	2002	2003	2004	2005	2006	2007	2008	2009
Cars	BMAA	2,123.5	2,100.4	2,174.9	2,426.4	2,528.9	2,497.1	2,437.5	2,266.2	2,241.7	2,539.0	2,188.0	1,959.0
Other Vehicles	BMAE	244.5	241.6	254.9	278.0	286.9	323.5	347.2	337.0	338.4	348.0	296.4	..
Motor Cycles, Scooters and Mopeds	BMAL	143.3	168.4	182.9	177.5	162.3	157.3	133.7	132.1	131.9	143.0	138.4	112.0
Goods	BBJY	49.1	48.3	50.4	49.0	44.9	48.4	48.0	51.3	47.9	41.2	47.0	27.0
Buses	BBJZ	7.4	8.0	7.5	7.1	7.7	8.4	8.1	8.9	7.6	9.1	8.3	7.0
Other Vehicles[1]	I8B3	157.0	174.0	176.0	169.0	192.0	189.0	204.0	218.0	219.0	265.0	290.0	266.0
All Vehicles	BBKD	2,740.3	2,765.8	2,870.9	3,136.6	3,229.5	3,231.9	3,185.3	3,021.4	2,913.6	2,996.9	2,672.2	2,371.0

Source: Department for Transport: 0207 944 3077

1 Includes three wheelers, special machines, special concessionary, special vehicles and crown and exempt vehicles.

22.9 Driving test pass rates: by sex and type of vehicle licence
Great Britain

Percentages

		1989 /90	1991 /92	1998 /99	2001 /02	2002 /03	2003 /04	2004 /05	2005 /06	2006 /07	2007 /08	2008 /09	2009 /10	2010 /11
Males														
Motorcycle	JTRB	72	69	69	67	66	67	66	66	67	68	68	70	69
Car	JTRC	58	57	51	47	47	46	46	46	46	47	49	49	50
Bus	JTTG	-	-	48	46	44	46	46	43	43	50	51	51	52
Lorry	JTTH	-	-	52	50	50	49	47	45	46	46	49	51	52
All males	JTTI	-	-	-	50	49	48	47	47	48	49	50	49	50
Females														
Motorcycle	JTTJ	68	63	63	55	54	53	53	52	54	56	55	70	70
Car	JTTK	47	46	42	40	40	40	39	40	41	41	42	43	43
Bus	JTTL	-	-	47	40	40	45	46	47	49	53	55	58	62
Lorry	JTTM	-	-	50	47	46	48	45	45	47	48	52	55	54
All females	JTTN	-	-	-	41	40	40	40	40	41	42	42	43	43
All														
Motorcycle	JTTO	-	-	68	66	65	65	64	64	65	67	66	70	70
Car	JTTP	-	-	46	43	43	43	42	42	43	44	45	46	46
Bus	JTTQ	-	-	48	45	44	46	44	43	44	50	52	52	54
Lorry	JTTR	-	-	52	56	49	49	46	45	46	46	49	51	52
All persons	JTTS	-	-	-	46	45	44	43	44	44	45	47	46	46

Source: Driving Standards Agency - info.rsis@dsa.gov.uk

22.10 Full car driving licence holders by sex and age[1]

Great Britain

Percentages and millions

	All aged 17+	17-20	21-29	30-39	40-49	50-59	60-69	70 and over	Estimated number of licence holders (millions)
All adults									
1975/76	48	28	59	67	60	50	35	15	19.4
1985/86	57	33	63	74	71	60	47	27	24.3
1989/91	64	43	72	77	78	67	54	32	27.8
1992/94	67	48	75	82	79	72	57	33	29.3
1995/97[2]	69	43	74	81	81	75	63	38	30.3
1998/00	71	41	75	84	83	77	67	39	31.4
	GB9O	C98J	C98K	C98L	C98M	C98N	C98O	C98P	C98Q
2005	72	32	66	82	84	82	74	51	33.3
2006	72	34	67	82	84	82	76	50	33.7
2007	71	38	66	81	83	82	75	52	33.8
2008	72	36	64	82	83	83	78	53	34.5
2009	72	36	65	80	84	83	78	54	34.7
2010	73	35	63	81	84	83	79	57	35.3
Males									
1975/76	69	36	78	85	83	75	58	32	13.4
1985/86	74	37	73	86	87	81	72	51	15.1
1989/91	80	52	82	88	89	85	78	58	16.7
1992/94	81	54	83	91	88	88	81	59	17.0
1995/97[2]	81	50	80	88	89	89	83	65	17.2
1998/00	82	44	80	89	91	88	83	65	17.4
	GB9P	C98R	C98S	C98T	C98U	C98V	C98W	C98X	C98Y
2005	81	37	69	86	90	90	88	73	18.1
2006	81	37	71	86	89	91	90	76	18.4
2007	80	41	69	86	88	90	87	75	18.4
2008	81	38	67	87	89	91	90	75	18.7
2009	80	37	67	84	89	91	90	76	18.8
2010	80	35	66	86	90	90	89	78	19.0
Females									
1975/76	29	20	43	48	37	24	15	4	6.0
1985/86	41	29	54	62	56	41	24	11	9.2
1989/91	49	35	64	67	66	49	33	15	11.1
1992/94	54	42	68	73	70	57	37	16	12.2
1995/97[2]	57	36	67	74	73	62	45	21	13.1
1998/00	60	38	69	78	76	67	53	22	14.0
	GB9Q	C98Z	C992	C993	C994	C995	C996	C997	C998
2005	63	27	62	77	79	73	61	35	15.2
2006	63	31	63	78	79	74	63	31	15.3
2007	63	34	62	76	78	74	63	36	15.4
2008	65	35	61	78	78	75	67	36	15.8
2009	65	35	62	76	79	75	67	37	16.0
2010	66	34	60	77	79	77	69	41	16.3

Source: National Travel Survey, Department for Transport 0207 944 3097

1 See chapter text.
2 Figures for 1995 onwards are based on weighted data.

22.11 Household car availability

Great Britain

Percentages/number

	No car/van	One car/van	Two or more cars/vans	Cars/van per household	Unweighted sample size
2002	27	44	29	1.08	8,849
2003	27	43	31	1.10	9,196
2004	26	44	30	1.10	8,991
2005	25	43	32	1.15	9,453
2006	25	44	32	1.15	9,261
2007	25	43	32	1.14	9,278
2008	25	43	32	1.14	8,924
2009	25	43	32	1.14	9,128
2010	25	42	33	1.16	8,775

	No car/van	One car/van	Two or more cars/vans	Cars/vans per household
Government Office Regions, 2009/10[2]				
Great Britain	25	43	32	1.15
North East	31	40	28	1.03
North West	26	43	30	1.10
Yorkshire and The Humber	26	43	31	1.12
East Midlands	20	42	38	1.29
West Midlands	25	42	33	1.17
East of England	16	45	39	1.33
London	43	42	16	0.76
South East	18	40	42	1.35
South West	18	44	38	1.29
England	25	42	33	1.16
Wales	21	44	34	1.26
Scotland	30	43	27	1.03
Northern Ireland				

	No car/van	One car/van	Two or more cars/vans	Cars/vans per household
Area type, 2009/10[2]				
London	43	42	16	0.76
Metropolitan areas	32	42	25	0.99
Other urban areas with population:				
Over 250,000	26	44	30	1.11
25,000 - 250,000	24	44	32	1.15
10,000 - 25,000	22	45	34	1.21
3,000 - 10,000	17	43	40	1.32
Rural areas	9	37	53	1.61
All areas	25	43	32	1.15

Source: National Travel Survey
Telephone: 020 7944 3097

1. Figures for 1995 onwards are based on weighted data.

2. Two survey years combined, e.g. 2009 and 2010. A survey year runs from mid-January to mid-January.

22.12 Vehicles with current licences[1]
Northern Ireland

Numbers

		1998	1999	2000	2001 [3]	2002	2003 [4]	2004	2005	2006	2007	2008	2009	2010
Private light goods, etc	KNKA	584,706	608,316	615,180	644,968	666,731	711,913	737,198	765,061	800,969	840,621	857,044	873,562	877,034
Motorcycles, Scooters and mopeds	KNKB	11,663	13,087	14,116	15,205	17,598	23,820	24,533	25,998	27,083	28,150	28,180	28,080	26,771
Public road passenger vehicles[2]:														
Taxis,buses,coaches	KNKD	..	..	..	..	..	..	..	..	..	..	..		
Buses,coaches (9 seats or more)	KNKE	2,175	2,204	2,266	2,315	2,322	2,353	2,378	2,566	2,670	2,865	2,951	2,987	3,035
Total	KNKC	2,175	2,204	2,266	2,315	2,322	2,353	2,378	2,566	2,670	2,865	2,951	2,987	3,035
General (HGV) goods vehicles:	KNKF	18,312	17,075	17,864	19,415	20,244	22,100	23,062	23,517	24,806	25,785	25,136	24,534	23,863
Agricultural tractors and engines,etc[3]	KNKM	5,906	5,505	5,048	4,901	5,731	7,503	8,674	9,584	10,586	12,817	14,326	15,526	17,059
Other	KNKN	1,193	1,446	1,287	1,366	1,347	1,671	1,794	1,898	2,039	2,125	2,232	2,244	2,180
Vehicles exempt from duty:														
Government owned	KNKP	3,785	4,032	3,822	6,427	6,383	6,172	6,116	6,367	7,315	9,655	6,902	7,215	7,488
Other:														
Ambulances	KNKQ	425	417	452	318	299	325	355	355	388	378	390	426	477
Fire engines	KNKR	285	286	290	181	174	170	178	179	166	155	142	122	125
Other exempt[4]	KNKS	66,981	68,277	70,405	72,209	73,648	76,715	78,973	81,874	82,655	85,738	87,093		
Total	KNKO	71,476	73,012	74,969	79,135	80,504	83,382	85,622	88,775	90,524	95,926	94,527	89,209	92,449
Total	KNKT	695,431	720,645	730,730	767,305	794,477	852,742	883,261	917,399	958,677	1,008,289	1,024,396	1,043,905	1,050,481

Source: Driver and Vehicle Agency: 028 7034 6903

1 Licences current at 31 December.

2 Tax class change from 'Hackney' to 'Bus' with effect from July 2005. Only Vehicles with 9 or more seats are included in 'Bus' class. Vehicles with 8 seats or less previously recorded in ' Hackney ' class moved into 'Private Light Goods' class.

3 Taxation classes have been revised

4 New Tax Class 36 introduced.

22.13 New vehicle registrations

Northern Ireland

Numbers

		1998	1999	2000	2001	2002	2003	2004	2005	2006	2007	2008	2009	2010
Private cars	KNLA	91,141	89,078	84,973	88,592	83,402	87,506	85,190	86,366	91,224	97,346	78,864	75594	71838
Motorcycles	KNLB	4,307	5,310	6,010	5,591	5,596	6,804	4,601	4,648	4,289	4,477	3,985	3403	2528
Public road passenger vehicles	KNLC	486	568	565	451	439	609	467	621	677	629	677	477	486
Goods vehicles:														
General haulage vehicles:														
Under 3.5 tonnes	KNLH	10,107	11,054	12,617	13,274	12,007	11,492	11,090	12,300	13,457	13,855	11,451	9139	7807
3.5 tonnes and over	KNLJ	3,572	3,697	3,502	4,534	3,669	4,059	3,987	3,768	4,080	3,676	2,923	2797	2546
Agricultural tractors[1]	KNLM	971	987	1,313	301	1	9	2	2	8	-	1	3	0
Vehicles exempt from duty	KNLR	10,718	11,081	10,789	12,126	12,515	11,907	12,881	13,987	13,031	14,083	14,846	13683	15449
General haulage and special types	JTAG	..	..	..	..	15	12	11	16	32	46	16	26	25
Total	KNLS	121,302	121,777	119,769	124,869	117,644	122,398	118,229	121,708	126,798	134,112	112,763	105122	100679

Source: Driver and Vehicle Agency : 028 7034 6903

1 Agricultural tractors driven on public roads. From April 2001 tractors were exept.

22.14 Local bus services: passenger journeys by area: 1999/00-2010/11

Millions

		1999 /00	2000 /01	2001 /02	2002 /03	2003 /04	2004 /05	2005 /06	2006 /07	2007 /08	2008 /09	2009 /10	2010 /11
Great Britain	ZCET	4,376	4,420	4,455	4,550	4,681	4,587	4,664	4,890	5,137	5,244	5,188	5,160
London	KILS	1,294	1,347	1,422	1,527	1,692	1,802	1,881	1,993	2,160	2,228	2,238	2,269
English Metropolitan Counties	KILT	1,213	1,203	1,196	1,182	1,162	1,066	1,037	1,060	1,075	1,080	1,073	1,055
English other areas	KILU	1,297	1,292	1,263	1,255	1,233	1,137	1,158	1,236	1,283	1,317	1,292	1,284
England	ZCER	3,804	3,842	3,881	3,964	4,087	4,005	4,077	4,290	4,519	4,626	4,604	4,609
Scotland	KILV	455	458	466	471	478	461	468	482	498	493	467	438
Wales	KILW	117	119	108	115	116	121	120	118	120	125	117	113

Source: DfT Public Service Vehicle Survey, Transport for London Tel: 020 7944 3094

1 Break in the local bus series (outside London) due to changes in the estimation methodology from 2004/05

2 Deregulation of the bus market took place in October 1986

Bus Statistics (http://www.dft.gov.uk/pgr/statistics/datatablespublications/public/bus/)

22.15 Local bus fares (at current prices[2]): by area: 1999 - 2011

Current Prices

March (2005=100)

		1999	2000	2001	2002	2003	2004	2005	2006	2007	2008	2009	2010	2011
Great Britain	KNEU	78.3	80.9	84.1	86.4	89.2	93.4	100.0	107.9	110.4	113.4	123.1	129.0	135.2
London	KNEP	83.3	83.2	83.9	81.5	81.8	86.9	100.0	105.7	116.6	111.2	120.0	135.2	144.5
English Metropolitan Counties	KILD	75.8	79.1	83.3	87.3	90.3	94.7	100.0	111.9	113.6	121.6	136.5	137.6	146.4
English other areas	KILE	74.9	78.4	82.7	86.6	90.8	95.3	100.0	107.8	102.0	106.7	113.9	115.6	119.4
England	ZCEP	77.0	79.6	82.9	85.3	88.0	92.7	100.0	108.3	110.2	112.8	122.5	128.8	135.7
Scotland	KILF	87.5	89.6	92.2	93.5	96.1	97.1	100.0	105.1	111.4	116.7	126.5	129.5	132.2
Wales	KILG	75.3	80.3	84.7	88.6	91.6	95.8	100.0	105.0	111.5	117.5	125.3	128.7	130.1

Source: Fares survey - Department for Transport 0207 944 4139

1 Index as at March.
2 Not adjusted for inflation.

22.16 Road accident casualties: by road user type and severity
Great Britain

Numbers

		1999	2000	2001	2002	2003	2004	2005	2006	2007	2008	2009
Child pedestrians[1]:												
Killed	ZCDH	107	107	107	79	74	77	63	71	57	57	37
Killed or seriously injured	KIJS	3,457	3,226	3,144	2,828	2,381	2,339	2,134	2,025	1,899	1,784	1,660
All severities	ZCDI	16,876	16,184	15,819	14,231	12,544	12,234	11,250	10,131	9,527	8,648	7,983
Adult pedestrians[2]:												
Killed	ZCDJ	760	750	712	688	695	589	604	602	585	515	463
Killed or seriously injured	KIJT	6,221	6,112	5,745	5,644	5,422	5,005	4,847	4,894	4,900	4,724	4,295
All severities	ZCDK	24,806	24,481	23,463	23,258	22,531	21,404	20,725	19,774	19,676	19,013	18,248
Child pedal cyclists[1]:												
Killed	ZCDL	36	27	25	22	18	25	20	31	13	12	14
Killed or seriously injured	KIJU	950	758	674	594	595	577	527	503	522	417	458
All severities	ZCDM	7,290	6,260	5,451	4,809	4,769	4,682	4,286	3,765	3,633	3,306	3,204
Adult pedal cyclists[2]:												
Killed	ZCDN	135	98	111	107	95	109	127	115	122	103	90
Killed or seriously injured	KIJV	2,172	1,954	1,951	1,801	1,776	1,697	1,787	1,898	1,994	2,101	2,225
All severities	ZCDO	14,834	13,630	12,974	11,712	11,643	11,366	11,637	11,911	12,050	12,546	13,420
Motorcyclists[3] and passengers:												
Killed	ZCDP	547	605	583	609	693	585	569	599	588	493	472
Killed or seriously injured	ZCDQ	6,908	7,374	7,305	7,500	7,652	6,648	6,508	6,484	6,737	6,049	5,822
All severities	BMDH	26,192	28,212	28,810	28,353	28,411	25,641	24,824	23,326	23,459	21,550	20,703
Car drivers and passengers:												
Killed	ZCDS	1,687	1,665	1,749	1,747	1,769	1,671	1,675	1,612	1,432	1,257	1,059
Killed or seriously injured	ZCDT	20,368	19,719	19,424	18,728	17,291	16,144	14,617	14,254	12,967	11,968	11,112
All severities	ZCDU	205,735	206,799	202,802	197,425	188,342	183,858	178,302	171,000	161,433	149,188	143,412
Bus/coach drivers and passengers:												
Killed	ZCDV	11	15	14	19	11	20	9	19	12	6	14
Killed or seriously injured	KCUZ	611	578	562	551	500	488	363	426	455	432	370
All severities	ZCDW	10,252	10,088	9,884	9,005	9,068	8,820	7,920	7,253	7,079	6,929	6,317
LGV drivers and passengers:												
Killed	ZCDX	65	66	64	70	72	62	54	52	58	43	36
Killed or seriously injured	ZCDY	867	813	811	780	765	631	587	564	494	445	417
All severities	ZCDZ	7,124	7,007	7,304	7,007	6,897	6,166	6,048	5,914	5,340	4,913	4,743
HGV drivers and passengers:												
Killed	ZCEA	52	55	54	63	44	47	55	39	52	23	14
Killed or seriously injured	ZCEB	540	571	500	524	429	406	395	383	363	240	189
All severities	ZCEC	3,484	3,597	3,388	3,178	3,061	2,883	2,843	2,530	2,476	1,930	1,519
All road users[4]:												
Killed	BMDC	3,423	3,409	3,450	3,431	3,508	3,221	3,201	3,172	2,946	2,538	2,222
Killed or seriously injured	ZCEE	42,545	41,564	40,560	39,407	37,215	34,351	32,155	31,845	30,720	28,572	26,912
All severities	BMDA	320,310	320,283	313,309	302,605	290,607	280,840	271,017	258,404	247,780	230,905	222,146

Source: Department for Transport 0207 944 6595

1 Casualities aged 0 - 15.

2 Casualities aged 16 and over.

3 Includes mopeds and scooters.

4 Includes other motor or non-motor vehicle users, and unknown road user type and casualty age.

22.17 Freight transport by road: goods moved by goods vehicles over 3.5 tonnes[1]

Great Britain

Billion tonne kilometres

		1998	1999	2000	2001	2002	2003	2004[2,3]	2005[3]	2006	2007	2008	2009
By mode of working													
Mainly public haulage	KNND	114.3	110.9	113.0	114.7	110.6	114.3	110.8	109.7	112.1	115.6	102.9	81.4
Mainly own account	KNNC	37.6	38.3	37.5	34.7	39.2	37.4	41.4	43.0	43.5	45.9	48.9	50.3
All modes	KNNB	151.9	149.2	150.5	149.4	149.8	151.7	152.2	152.7	155.6	161.5	151.7	131.7
By gross weight of vehicle													
Rigid vehicles:													
Over 3.5 tonnes to 17 tonnes	ZCIL	17.8	17.9	15.8	13.1	11.9	10.1	9.1	8.1	7.2	5.8	5.5	5.5
Over 17 tonnes to 25 tonnes	ZCIM	4.2	4.3	4.8	5.7	6.3	6.8	7.9	8.3	8.6	9.5	8.3	7.6
Over 25 tonnes	ZCIN	14.7	15.3	15.4	15.6	17.3	18.3	18.9	20.3	20.8	22.5	20.3	17.5
All rigids	ZCIO	36.6	37.5	36.0	34.5	35.6	35.2	35.9	36.7	36.6	37.8	34.1	30.6
Articulated vehicles:													
Over 3.5 tonnes to 33 tonnes	ZCIP	14.4	14.0	14.0	12.8	9.9	8.8	7.0	6.3	6.1	5.6	5.2	4.8
Over 33 tonnes	ZCIQ	100.9	97.7	100.4	102.1	104.4	107.7	109.4	109.7	112.9	118.1	112.5	96.3
All articulated vehicles	ZCIR	115.3	111.7	114.4	114.9	114.3	116.5	116.4	116.0	119.0	123.7	117.6	101.2
All vehicles													
Over 3.5 tonnes to 25 tonnes	ZCIS	22.5	22.7	21.3	19.3	18.7	17.3	17.3	16.7	16.3	15.7	14.1	13.8
Over 25 tonnes	KNNG	129.4	126.5	129.2	130.1	131.1	134.4	134.9	136.0	139.3	145.8	137.6	117.9
All weights	ZCIT	151.9	149.2	150.5	149.4	149.8	151.7	152.2	152.7	155.6	161.5	151.7	131.7
By commodity													
Food, drink and tobacco	ZCIU	42.5	41.5	44.3	41.4	43.1	42.2	41.7	40.6	42.0	45.1	43.7	43.6
Wood, timber and cork	ZCIV	3.6	3.8	3.7	3.9	3.8	4.1	4.5	4.7	4.1	3.3	4.0	3.9
Fertiliser	ZCIW	1.2	1.4	1.2	1.2	1.2	1.2	0.8	1.1	0.8	0.9	1.3	1.7
Crudeminerals	ZCIX	13.3	12.7	12.4	13.0	13.9	13.8	14.1	14.8	15.4	16.0	13.3	10.2
Ores	ZCIY	1.1	1.3	1.2	1.2	1.1	1.2	1.4	1.7	1.4	1.8	1.8	1.3
Crude materials	ZCIZ	2.6	2.6	2.6	2.3	2.7	2.3	3.3	2.4	2.7	2.6	2.3	2.1
Coal and coke	ZCJA	2.0	2.2	1.5	2.1	1.5	1.5	1.2	1.5	1.3	1.6	1.0	1.0
Petrol and petroleum products	ZCJB	5.2	5.0	6.4	5.8	5.2	5.5	5.7	5.5	5.7	5.1	6.5	4.8
Chemicals	ZCJC	7.9	7.4	6.8	7.2	6.5	6.8	6.3	7.6	6.2	7.0	6.1	5.2
Building materials	ZCJD	10.7	10.6	10.6	11.7	10.9	12.0	12.1	10.9	11.5	11.6	11.0	8.5
Iron and steel products	ZCJE	7.7	6.8	6.8	5.7	5.3	5.4	5.4	5.2	4.7	6.4	4.1	3.4
Other metal products	ZCJF	1.7	1.7	1.7	1.4	1.5	1.5	1.9	2.1	2.1	2.0	1.8	1.8
Machinery and transport equipment	ZCJG	9.1	8.7	9.1	8.9	8.5	8.7	8.9	9.3	9.4	9.5	8.9	7.3
Miscellaneous manufactures	ZCJH	15.9	15.7	15.1	15.4	16.2	15.8	16.3	15.5	16.3	16.4	12.6	11.1
Miscellaneous articles	ZCJI	27.5	27.9	27.1	28.2	28.4	29.5	28.8	29.8	31.7	32.2	33.3	25.9
All commodities	ZCJJ	151.9	149.2	150.5	149.4	149.8	151.7	152.2	152.7	155.6	161.5	151.7	131.7

Source: Department for Transport
Telephone: 020 7944 3180

1 Rigid vehicles or articulated vehicles (tractive unit and trailer) with gross vehicle weight over 3.5 tonnes.
2 Figures for 2004 onwards are not fully comparable with those for 2003 and earlier years. Detailed comparisons should therefore be made with caution.
3 There have been minor revisions to some data in 2004 and 2005

22.18 Freight transport by road: goods lifted by goods vehicles over 3.5 tonnes[1]

Great Britain

Million tonnes

		1999	2000	2001	2002	2003	2004 [2,3]	2005 [2]	2006	2007	2008	2009
By mode of working												
Mainly public haulage	ZCJK	991	1,038	1,052	1,019	1,053	1,101	1,079	1,127	1,145	986	723
Mainly own account	ZCJL	576	556	529	608	590	643	667	685	724	748	699
All modes	ZCJM	1,567	1,593	1,581	1,627	1,643	1,744	1,746	1,813	1,869	1,734	1,422
By gross weight of vehicle												
Rigid vehicles:												
Over 3.5 tonnes to 17 tonnes	ZCJN	254	229	203	188	159	160	135	130	109	103	95
Over 17 tonnes to 25 tonnes	ZCJO	86	87	86	90	100	113	118	120	130	122	106
Over 25 tonnes	ZCJP	408	424	443	491	506	539	559	598	629	532	391
All rigids	ZCJQ	748	741	733	768	765	812	812	849	868	757	592
Articulated vehicles:												
Over 3.5 tonnes to 33 tonnes	ZCJR	113	107	97	81	69	60	51	50	50	46	41
Over 33 tonnes	ZCJS	706	746	751	778	809	872	883	914	952	931	790
All articulated vehicles	ZCJT	819	852	848	859	878	932	934	964	1,001	977	830
All vehicles												
Over 3.5 tonnes to 25 tonnes	ZCJU	346	325	294	283	265	277	257	256	245	230	207
Over 25 tonnes	ZCJV	1,221	1,268	1,287	1,343	1,378	1,467	1,489	1,557	1,624	1,504	1,215
All weights	ZCJW	1,567	1,593	1,581	1,627	1,643	1,744	1,746	1,813	1,869	1,734	1,422
By commodity												
Food, drink and tobacco	ZCJX	333	346	321	339	333	351	339	360	373	370	372
Wood, timber and cork	ZCJY	28	26	28	28	32	42	36	30	29	35	32
Fertiliser	ZCJZ	11	10	9	11	12	7	14	7	9	22	20
Crude minerals	ZCKA	297	308	298	333	327	364	370	380	390	317	216
Ores	ZCKB	20	16	16	17	21	22	23	19	22	24	16
Crude materials	ZCKC	20	18	20	21	19	25	22	23	23	20	16
Coal and coke	ZCKD	28	22	21	17	22	14	21	17	24	15	10
Petrol and petroleum products	ZCKE	61	75	74	59	64	67	70	69	71	80	61
Chemicals	ZCKF	47	49	50	41	47	46	53	48	48	45	38
Building materials	ZCKG	159	165	165	167	165	185	169	180	175	177	126
Iron and steel products	ZCKH	48	49	44	39	41	43	42	41	47	33	26
Other metal products	ZCKI	17	16	14	14	16	19	19	21	20	20	20
Machinery and transport equipment	ZCKJ	67	69	70	68	66	70	76	79	83	75	68
Miscellaneous manufactures	ZCKK	91	97	97	105	98	111	109	112	113	95	82
Miscellaneous articles	ZCKL	340	328	353	367	379	378	384	426	440	406	318
All commodities	ZCKM	1,567	1,593	1,581	1,627	1,643	1,744	1,746	1,813	1,869	1,734	1,422

Source: Continuing Survey of Road Goods Transport, DfT
Telephone: 020 7944 3180

1 Rigid vehicles or articulated vehicles (tractive unit and trailer) with gross vehicle weight over 3.5 tonnes.
2 Figures for 2004 onwards are not fully comparable with those for 2003 and earlier years.
  Detailed comparisons should therefore be made with caution. See Notes and Definitions.
3 There have been minor revisions to some data for 2004 and 2005

22.19 Rail systems summary

		1998/99	1999/00	2000/01	2001/02	2002/03	2003/04	2004/05	2005/06	2006/07	2007/08	2008/09	2009/10
Passenger journeys (millions)													
National Rail network[1]	ZCKN	892	931	957	960	976	1,012	1,040	1,076	1,145	1,218	1,266	1,258
London Underground	KNOE	866	927	970	953	942	948	976	970	1,040	1,096	1,089	1,059
Docklands Light Railway	ZCKO	28	31	38	41	46	48	50	54	64	67	68	69
Glasgow Underground	ZCKP	15	15	14	14	13	13	13	13	13	14	14	13
Tyne and Wear Metro[2]	ZCKQ	34	33	33	33	37	38	37	36	38	40	41	41
Blackpool trams[3]	EL9L	4	4	4	5	4	4	4	4	3	3	2	2
Manchester Metrolink[4]	ZCKS	13	14	17	18	19	19	20	20	20	20	21	20
Midland Metro[5]	ZCKR	-	5	5	5	5	5	5	5	5	5	5	5
Croydon Tramlink[6]	GEOE	-	-	15	18	19	20	22	23	25	27	27	26
Sheffield Supertram	ZCKT	10	11	11	11	12	12	13	13	14	15	15	15
Nottingham NET[7]	C3MI	-	-	-	-	-	-	8	10	10	10	10	9
All rail	ZCKU	1,862	1,971	2,065	2,059	2,072	2,119	2,188	2,224	2,377	2,515	2,558	2,516
All light rail	GENZ	104	113	138	146	154	160	172	177	192	201	203	199
Passenger revenue (£ million at													
National Rail network	KNDL	3,089	3,368	3,413	3,548	3,663	3,901	4,158	4,493	5,012	5,555	6,004	6,179
London Underground	KNOA	977	1,058	1,129	1,151	1,138	1,161	1,241	1,309	1,417	1,525	1,615	1,635
Docklands Light Railway	ZCKV	27	28	37	41	44	45	47	53	60	67	67	77
Glasgow Underground	ZCKW	9	10	10	10	10	10	11	11	12	13	15	14
Tyne and Wear Metro	ZCKX	30	31	31	32	35	38	38	39	39	34	43	42
Blackpool trams	EL9M	6	6	6	6	6	5	5	5	5	4	4	3
Manchester Metrolink	ZCKZ	21	22	24	26	26	25	26	26	26	24	24	24
Midland Metro	ZCKY	-	3	4	5	6	6	6	7	7	5	7	7
Croydon Tramlink	GEOF	-	-	16	16	18	19	21	22	21	17	19	17
Sheffield Supertram	ZCLA	8	9	9	10	13	11	13	12	14	12	16	16
Nottingham NET	C3MJ	-	-	-	-	-	..	7	8	8	8	9	8
All rail	ZCLB	4,167	4,534	4,679	4,844	4,959	5,220	5,573	5,985	6,621	7,263	7,822	8,021
All light rail	GEOA	101	108	137	145	158	158	174	183	192	183	203	207
Passenger kilometres (millions)													
National Rail network	KNDZ	36,280	38,472	38,179	39,141	39,678	40,906	41,705	43,146	46,154	48,930	50,613	51,101
London Underground	KNOI	6,716	7,171	7,470	7,451	7,367	7,340	7,606	7,586	7,947	8,352	8,646	8,457
Docklands Light Railway	ZCLC	144	172	200	207	232	235	245	257	301	326	318	365
Glasgow Underground	ZCLD	47	47	46	44	43	43	43	42	42	46	45	42
Tyne and Wear Metro	ZCLE	238	230	229	238	275	284	283	279	295	313	319	327
Blackpool trams	EL9N	..	13	13	15	14	11	12	11	10	9	7	7
Manchester Metrolink	ZCLG	117	126	152	161	167	169	204	206	208	210	221	206
Midland Metro	ZCLF	-	50	56	50	50	54	52	54	51	51	50	50
Croydon Tramlink	GEOG	-	-	96	99	100	105	112	117	128	141	144	134
Sheffield Supertram	ZCLH	35	37	38	39	40	42	44	44	42	44	45	103
Nottingham NET	C3MK	-	-	-	-	-	2	37	42	43	44	42	38
All rail	ZCLI	43,577	46,318	46,479	47,446	47,965	49,191	50,343	51,784	55,221	58,466	60,450	60,829
All light rail	GEOB	581	675	830	854	920	945	1,033	1,052	1,120	1,185	1,191	1,271
Route kilometres open for passenger traffic (numbers)													
National Rail network[8]	ZCLJ	15,038	15,038	15,042	15,042	15,042	14,883	14,328	14,356	14,353	14,484	14,494	14,482
London Underground	ZCLK	392	408	408	408	408	408	408	408	408	408	408	400
Docklands Light Railway	ZCLM	22	26	26	26	26	26	26	30	31	32	33	33
Glasgow Underground	ZCLN	11	11	11	11	11	11	11	10	10	10	10	10
Tyne and Wear Metro	ZCLO	59	59	59	78	78	78	78	78	78	78	78	78
Blackpool trams	EL9O	18	18	18	18	18	18	18	18	18	18	18	18
Manchester Metrolink	ZCLQ	31	39	39	39	39	39	39	39	39	42	39	39
Midland Metro	ZCLP	-	20	20	20	20	20	20	20	20	20	20	20
Croydon Tramlink	GEOH	-	-	28	28	28	28	28	28	28	28	28	28
Sheffield Supertram	ZCLR	29	29	29	29	29	29	29	29	29	29	29	29
Nottingham NET	C3ML	-	-	-	-	-	14	14	15	14	14	14	14
All rail	ZCLS	15,600	15,648	15,680	15,699	15,699	15,554	14,999	15,032	15,028	15,186	15,171	15,151
All light rail	GEOC	170	202	230	249	249	263	263	268	267	294	269	269

22.19 Rail systems summary

		1998 /99	1999 /00	2000 /01	2001 /02	2002 /03	2003 /04	2004 /05	2005 /06	2006 /07	2007 /08	2008 /09	2009 /10
Stations served (numbers)													
National Rail network	ZCLT	2,499	2,503	2,508	2,508	2,508	2,507	2,508	2,510	2,520	2,516	2,516	2,516
London Underground	KNOO	269	274	274	274	274	274	274	274	273	268	270	270
Docklands Light Railway	ZCLU	29	34	34	34	34	34	34	38	34	39	40	40
Glasgow Underground	ZCLV	15	15	15	15	15	15	15	15	15	15	15	15
Tyne and Wear Metro	ZCLW	46	46	46	58	58	58	58	59	59	60	60	60
Blackpool trams	EL9P	124	124	124	124	124	124	124	124	121	121	121	117
Manchester Metrolink	ZCLY	26	36	36	36	37	37	37	37	37	37	37	37
Midland Metro	ZCLX	-	23	23	23	23	23	23	23	23	23	23	23
Croydon Tramlink	GEOI	-	-	38	38	38	38	38	39	39	38	39	39
Sheffield Supertram	ZCLZ	47	47	47	48	48	48	48	48	48	48	48	48
Nottingham NET	C3MM	-	-	-	-	-	23	23	23	23	23	23	23
All rail	ZCLL	3,055	3,102	3,146	3,145	3,159	3,181	3,182	3,190	3,192	3,188	3,192	3,188
All light rail	GSOC	287	325	363	376	377	400	400	406	399	404	406	402

Sources: Department for Transport: 0207 944 3076/8874;
Network Rail, former Rail track,ORR, TfL, light rail operators and PTEs

1 Franchised train operating companies from Feb 1996 after privatisation.
2 Tyne & Wear Metro extension to Sunderland opened in March 2002.
3 Blackpool Trams shown as a self-contained system.
4 Transfer of 20 stations from the rail network to Manchester Metrolink.
5 Midland Metro opened in 1999.
6 Croydon Tramlink opened in 2000.
7 Nottingham Express Transit opened in March 2004.
8 Break in series due to change in methodology.

22.20 National railways freight: 1998/99-2008/09

Great Britain

Billion tonne kilometres

		1998[1] /99	1999 /00	2000 /01	2001 /02	2002 /03	2003 /04	2004 /05	2005 /06	2006 /07	2007 /08	2008 /09
Freight moved by commodity												
Coal	ZCGG	4.5	4.8	4.8	6.2	5.7	5.8	6.7	8.3	8.6	7.7	7.9
Metals	ZCGH	2.1	2.2	2.1	2.4	2.7	2.6	2.6	2.2	2.0	1.8	1.5
Construction	ZCGI	2.1	2.0	2.4	2.8	2.5	2.7	2.9	2.9	2.7	2.8	2.7
Oil and petroleum	ZCGJ	1.6	1.5	1.4	1.2	1.2	1.2	1.2	1.2	1.5	1.6	1.5
Other traffic	ZCGK	7.1	7.6	7.4	6.7	6.6	6.8	7.0	7.1	7.1	7.2	7.0
All traffic	VOXD	17.3	18.2	18.1	19.4	18.5	18.9	20.4	21.7	21.9	21.2	20.6

											Million	tonnes
		1998 /99	1999[2] /00	2000 /01	2001 /02	2002 /03	2003 /04	2004[3] /05	2005[4] /06	2006 /07	2007[5] /08	2008 /09
Freight lifted by commodity												
Coal	ZCGL	45.3	35.9	35.3	39.5	34.0	35.2	43.3	47.6	48.7	43.3	46.6
Metals	ZCGM	..	..	..	..	..	..	..	..	..	..	..
Construction	ZCGN	..	..	..	..	..	..	..	..	..	..	..
Oil and petroleum	ZCGO	..	..	..	..	..	..	..	..	..	..	..
Other traffic	ZCGP	56.8	60.6	60.3	54.5	53.0	53.7	56.8	57.7	59.5	59.1	56.1
All traffic	VOXE	102.1	96.5	95.6	93.9	87.0	88.9	100.1	105.3	108.2	102.4	102.7

Source: Rail: ORR 0207 944 8874

1 There is a break in the series between 1998-99 and 1999-00 due to a change in the source data.
2 Break in series from 1999/2000.
3 Break in series with most of the increase due to changes in the data collection method.
4 Break in the series from 2005/06 as some GB Railfreight tonnes lifted now included.
5 Break in series from 2007/08 as GB Railfreight coal data now included.

22.21 Railways: permanent way and rolling stock

Northern Ireland
At end of year

		1998	1999	2000	2001	2002	2003	2004	2005	2006	2007	2008	2009	2010
Length of road open for traffic[1] (Km)	KNRA	335	335	356	334	334	334	299	299	299	299	299	299	299
Length of track open for traffic (Km)														
Total	KNRB	526	526	547	480	480	480	445	445	445	445	445	445	445
Running lines	KNRC	484	484	505	464	464	464	427	427	427	427	427	427	427
Sidings (as single track)	KNRD	42	42	42	16	16	16	18	18	18	18	18	18	18
Locomotives														
Diesel-electrics	KNRE	5	6	6	6	6	5	6	5	5	5	5	5	5
Passenger carrying vehicles														
Total	KNRF	120	105	105	106	100	100	102	124	125	128	130	130	130
Rail motor vehicles:														
Diesel-electric,etc	KNRG	28	30	30	29	28	28	28	70	85	84	84	84	84
Trailer carriages:														
Total locomotive hauled	KNRH	38	21	21	25	22	22	22	22	22	22	22	22	22
Ordinary coaches	KNRI	36	19	19	23	20	20	20	20	20	20	20	20	20
Restaurant cars	KNRJ	2	2	2	2	2	2	2	2	2	2	2	2	2
Rail car trailers	KNRK	54	54	54	52	50	50	52	32	18	22	24	24	24
Rolling stock for maintenance and repair	KNRT	26	18	18	18	18	39	46	48	48	48	48	48	48

Sources: Department for Regional Development;
Northern Ireland: 02890 540981

1 The total length of railroad open for traffic irrespective of the number of tracks comprising the road.

22.22 Operating statistics of railways

Northern Ireland

		Unit	1998	1999	2000	2001	2002	2003	2004	2005	2006	2007	2008	2009	2010
Maintenance of way and works															
Material used:															
Ballast	KNSA	Thousand m²	38.5	40.0	47.0	80.0	40.0	130.0	70.0	90.0	30.0	15.0	10.0	35.0	10.0
Rails	KNSB	Thousand tonnes	2.5	3.0	3.5	2.5	1.0	4.5	1.0	3.2	1.0	1.0	0.1	1.4	1.2
Sleepers	KNSC	Thousands	32.0	30.0	40.0	50.0	5.0	40.0	28.0	45.0	2.0	5.0	2.0	2.0	2.0
Track renewed	KNSD	Km	22.5	7.0	29.0	15.0	5.0	25.8	2.0	29.0	1.0	-	..	6.0	1.0
New Track laid	KPGD	Km	-	-	21.0	-	-	-	-	-	-	-	..	–	0.0
Engine kilometres															
Total[1]	KNSE	Thousand Km	4,100	4,100	4,100	4,056	4,056	4,170	4,110	3,610	3,900	3,900	3,900	3,900	3,900
Train kilometres:															
Total	KNSF	"	3,670	3,670	3,670	3,626	3,626	3,704	3,610	3,610	3,900	3,900	3,900	3,900	3,900
Coaching	KNSG	"	3,666	3,666	3,666	3,622	3,622	3,700	3,610	3,610	3,900	3,900	3,900	3,900	3,900
Freight	KNSH	"	4	4	4	4	4	4	-	-	-	-	..	..	..

Sources: Department for Regional Development;
Northern Ireland: 02890 540981

1 Including shunting, assisting, light, departmental, maintenance and repair.

22.23 Main output of United Kingdom airlines

		1999	2000	2001	2002	2003	2004	2005	2006	2007	2008	2009	2010
											Available tonne kilometres (millions)		
All services	KNTA	42,002	43,379	42,370	40,550	42,784	43,883	48,186	50,391	54,181	53,348	49,150	47168
Percentage growth on previous year	KNTB	5.0	3.6	-2.4	-4.3	5.5	2.6	9.8	4.4	7.5	-1.6	-7.9	-4
Scheduled services	KNTC	31,815	32,938	31,866	30,433	31,513	32,422	36,937	38,590	40,971	41,241	39,207	38059
Percentage growth on previous year	KNTD	6.9	3.5	-3.3	-4.5	3.6	2.9	13.9	4.5	6.2	0.7	-5.1	-2.9
Non-scheduled services	KNTE	10,186	10,440	10,505	10,117	11,271	11,461	11,249	11,801	13,209	12,077	9,944	9109
Percentage growth on previous year	KNTF	-0.7	4.1	0.6	-3.7	11.4	1.7	-1.8	4.3	11.9	-8.6	-17.7	-8.4

Source: Civil Aviation Authority: 0207 453 6246

22.24 Air traffic between the United Kingdom and abroad[1]

Thousands

		1999	2000	2001	2002	2003	2004	2005	2006	2007	2008	2009	2010
Flights													
United Kingdom airlines													
Scheduled services	KNUA	480.9	520.3	536.7	531.3	517.7	546.5	584.2	596.3	621.9	601.7	550.5	519.1
Non-scheduled services	KNUB	212.6	216.2	208.5	218.6	211.0	198.6	200.6	209.6	207.1	193.4	172.6	159.5
Overseas airlines[2]													
Scheduled services	KNUC	467.6	467.6	496.8	487.5	487.0	544.2	584.5	629.5	656.9	686.7	700.2	657.3
Non-scheduled services	KNUD	31.7	31.7	26.0	36.7	27.1	28.8	33.7	28.4	27.2	24.3	21.9	16
Total	KNUE	1,192.8	1,235.8	1,268.0	1,274.1	1,242.8	1,318.1	1,403.0	1,463.8	1,513.1	1,506.1	1,445.2	1351.9
Passengers carried													
United Kingdom airlines													
Scheduled services	KNUF	50,148.5	54,522.8	53,591.7	54,360.0	56,476.7	63,216.1	69,106.2	72,196.4	76,959.9	76,636.5	71,586.9	69005.4
Non-scheduled services	KNUG	32,603.8	33,185.9	34,009.1	33,935.7	33,385.6	32,195.7	30,179.4	29,725.5	28,524.0	25,906.9	21,774.2	20566.2
Overseas airlines[2]													
Scheduled services	KNUH	46,628.0	46,627.9	51,107.8	51,317.6	54,504.0	60,278.0	67,634.9	74,670.8	79,820.1	83,176.7	84,321.0	81055.7
Non-scheduled services	KNUI	4,156.5	4,156.5	3,966.1	3,956.3	3,947.1	4,068.3	4,169.1	4,107.7	3,803.3	3,417.0	3,049.5	2094.6
Total	KNUJ	133,536.8	138,493.1	142,674.7	143,569.6	148,313.4	159,758.1	171,089.6	180,700.4	189,107.3	189,137.1	180,731.6	172722

Source: Civil Aviation Authority: 0207 453 6246

1 Excludes travel to and from the Channel Islands.
2 Includes airlines of overseas UK Territories.

22.25 Operations and traffic on scheduled services: revenue traffic

United Kingdom airlines[1]

		Unit	1999	2000	2001	2002	2003	2004
All services								
Aircraft stage flights:								
Number	KNFA	Numbers	835,031.0	878,582.0	921,556.0	911,518.0	895,095.0	926,498.0
Average length	KNFB	Kilometres	1,134.0	1,156.0	1,138.0	1,149.0	1,215.0	1,227.0
Aircraft-kilometres flown	KNFC	Millions	947.0	1,016.0	1,049.0	1,047.0	1,088.0	1,137.0
Passengers uplifted	KNFD	"	65.0	70.0	70.0	72.0	76.0	83.0
Seat-kilometres used	KNFE	"	160,336.0	170,469.0	158,651.0	156,494.0	164,806.0	173,722.0
Cargo uplifted:[2]	KNFF	Tonnes	860,291.0	897,184.0	742,705.0	768,736.0	800,645.0	842,912.0
Tonne-kilometres used:								
Passenger	KNFH	Millions	15,518.0	16,507.0	15,258.0	15,035.0	15,419.0	15,580.0
Freight	KNFI	"	4,925.0	5,160.0	4,548.0	4,941.0	5,187.0	5,297.0
Mail	KNFJ	"	153.0	179.0	102.0	57.0	55.0	75.0
Total	KNFG	"	20,596.0	21,846.0	19,908.0	20,032.0	20,660.0	20,952.0
Domestic services								
Aircraft stage flights:								
Number	KNFK	Numbers	354,864.0	353,525.0	365,881.0	359,400.0	345,954.0	373,858.0
Average length	KNFL	Kilometres	337.0	344.0	350.0	350.0	357.0	360.0
Aircraft-kilometres flown	KNFM	Millions	120.0	121.0	128.0	126.0	123.0	135.0
Passengers uplifted	KNFN	"	17.0	18.0	18.0	20.0	21.0	22.0
Seat-kilometres used	KNFO	"	7,184.0	7,542.0	7,645.0	8,322.0	8,904.0	9,263.0
Cargo uplifted:[2]	KNFP	Tonnes	25,964.0	24,644.0	19,498.0	16,755.0	17,248.0	14,862.0
Tonne-kilometres used:								
Passenger	KNFR	Millions	610.0	640.0	649.0	703.0	738.0	757.0
Freight	KNFS	"	6.0	6.0	4.0	4.0	3.0	3.0
Mail	KNFT	"	4.0	4.0	4.0	3.0	3.0	3.0
Total	KNFQ	"	620.0	650.0	656.0	709.0	744.0	762.0
International services								
Aircraft stage flights:								
Number	KNFU	Numbers	480,167.0	525,057.0	555,675.0	552,118.0	549,141.0	552,640.0
Average length	KNFV	Kilometres	1,723.0	1,704.0	1,656.0	1,670.0	1,758.0	2,148.0
Aircraft-kilometres flown	KNFW	Millions	827.0	895.0	921.0	921.0	965.0	1,002.0
Passengers uplifted	KNFX	"	48.0	52.0	52.0	52.0	56.0	61.0
Seat-kilometres used	KNFY	"	153 153.0	162 927.0	151 006.0	148 172.0	155 903.0	164 459.0
Cargo uplifted:[2]	KNFZ	Tonnes	834,327.0	872,540.0	723,206.0	751,975.0	783,397.0	828,051.0
Tonne-kilometres used:								
Passenger	KNJX	Millions	14,908.0	15,867.0	14,610.0	14,332.0	14,681.0	14,824.0
Freight	KNJY	"	4,919.0	5,154.0	4,544.0	4,937.0	5,184.0	5,294.0
Mail	KNJZ	"	149.0	176.0	98.0	54.0	51.0	72.0
Total	KNJW	"	19,976.0	21,197.0	19,252.0	19,322.0	19,916.0	20,190.0

1 Includes services of British Airwaysand other UK private companies.
2 Cargo has re-defined as freight and mail.

22.25 Operations and traffic on scheduled services: revenue traffic

United Kingdom airlines[1]

		Unit	2005	2006	2007	2008	2009	2010
All services								
Aircraft stage flights:								
Number	KNFA	Numbers	1,016,354.0	1,037,729.0	1,052,799.0	1,056,298.0	1,001,504.0	978,269.0
Average length	KNFB	Kilometres	1,304.0	1,349.0	1,400.0	1,427.9	1,441.3	1,440.1
Aircraft-kilometres flown	KNFC	Millions	1,325.0	1,400.0	1,474.0	1,508.3	1,443.5	1,408.8
Passengers uplifted	KNFD	"	94.0	98.0	102.0	104.7	102.5	101.5
Seat-kilometres used	KNFE	"	200,460.0	213,442.0	227,720.0	232,591.6	230,588.3	225,649.3
Cargo uplifted:[2]	KNFF	Tonnes	921,412.0	946,365.0	941,421.0	979,791.0	900,668.0	929,136.0
Tonne-kilometres used:								
Passenger	KNFH	Millions	15,044.0	16,090.0	17,246.0	17,717.7	17,474.4	17,096.7
Freight	KNFI	"	5,998.0	6,213.0	6,199.0	6,283.8	5,863.7	6,071.5
Mail	KNFJ	"	90.0	99.0	112.0	99.0	88.6	95.0
Total	KNFG	"	21,133.0	22,402.0	23,557.0	24,100.5	23,426.7	23,263.3
Domestic services								
Aircraft stage flights:								
Number	KNFK	Numbers	394,069.0	399,438.0	383,591.0	369,499.0	341,207.0	329,341.0
Average length	KNFL	Kilometres	374.0	371.0	367.0	469.0	360.8	350.4
Aircraft-kilometres flown	KNFM	Millions	147.0	148.0	140.0	173.3	123.1	115.4
Passengers uplifted	KNFN	"	23.0	23.0	22.0	21.0	19.5	18.2
Seat-kilometres used	KNFO	"	9,795.0	9,800.0	9,449.0	8,951.5	8,326.3	7,710.9
Cargo uplifted:[2]	KNFP	Tonnes	10,015.0	8,498.0	7,099.0	6,125.0	5,202.0	4,670.0
Tonne-kilometres used:								
Passenger	KNFR	Millions	784.0	759.0	733.0	720.2	644.8	596.7
Freight	KNFS	"	3.0	2.0	2.0	1.8	1.6	1.3
Mail	KNFT	"	-	1.0	1.0	0.1	0.7	0.5
Total	KNFQ	"	787.0	762.0	735.0	722.1	647.1	598.5
International services								
Aircraft stage flights:								
Number	KNFU	Numbers	622,285.0	638,291.0	669,208.0	686,799.0	660,027.0	648,928.0
Average length	KNFV	Kilometres	1,893.0	1,960.0	1,993.0	1,994.4	2,000.5	1,993.1
Aircraft-kilometres flown	KNFW	Millions	1,178.0	1,251.0	1,333.0	1,371.0	1,320.4	1,293.4
Passengers uplifted	KNFX	"	71.0	75.0	80.0	83.8	82.9	83.3
Seat-kilometres used	KNFY	"	190 666.0	203 642.0	218 271.0	223 640.1	222 262.0	217,938.4
Cargo uplifted:[2]	KNFZ	Tonnes	911,398.0	937,868.0	934,323.0	973,665.0	895,466.0	924,465.0
Tonne-kilometres used:								
Passenger	KNJX	Millions	14,260.0	15,331.0	16,513.0	16,997.5	16,829.6	16,500.0
Freight	KNJY	"	5,995.0	6,383.0	6,197.0	6,282.0	5,862.1	6,070.3
Mail	KNJZ	"	90.0	99.0	111.0	98.9	88.6	95.0
Total	KNJW	"	20,345.0	21,813.0	22,822.0	23,378.4	22,780.3	22,665.3

Source: Civil Aviation Authority: 0207 453 6246

1 Includes services of British Airwaysand other UK private companies.
2 Cargo has re-defined as freight and mail.

22.26 Activity at civil aerodromes

United Kingdom[1]

Thousands and tonnes

		2000	2001	2002	2003	2004	2005	2006	2007	2008	2009	2010
Movement of civil aircraft (thousands)												
Commercial												
Transport	**KNQC**	2,045	2,095	2,094	2,160	2,277	2,406	2,451	2,494	2,407	2,195	2,069
Other[2]	**KNQD**	159	150	120	117	116	120	129	124	113	96	99
Total	**KNQB**	2,204	2,245	2,214	2,277	2,393	2,526	2,580	2,609	2,520	2,291	2,168
Non-commercial[3]	**KNQE**	1,186	1,207	1,100	1,186	1,135	1,129	1,059	1,033	964	912	758
Total	**KNQA**	3,390	3,452	3,314	3,463	3,528	3,655	3,639	3,637	3,484	3,203	2,926
Passengers handled												
Terminal	**KNQG**	179,885	181,231	188,761	199,950	215,681	228,214	235,139	240,722	235,359	218,126	210,642
Transit	**KNQH**	1,167	1,087	1,054	990	950	984	1,016	963	735	519	513
Total	**KNQF**	181,052	182,318	189,815	200,940	216,631	229,198	236,155	241,685	236,094	218,645	211,155
Commercial freight handled[4] (tonnes)												
Set down	**KNQJ**	1,174,635	1,093,142	1,124,026	1,172,552	1,267,411	1,282,724	1,277,177	1,316,359	1,274,539	1,120,886	1,255,342
Picked up	**KNQK**	1,139,292	1,052,379	1,071,407	1,035,680	1,103,539	1,080,620	1,038,261	1,009,414	1,007,616	926,974	1,069,441
Total	**KNQI**	2,313,927	2,145,521	2,195,433	2,208,232	2,370,950	2,363,344	2,315,438	2,325,773	2,282,155	2,047,860	2,324,783
Mail handled												
Set down	**KNQM**	101,743	98,690	90,738	86,415	108,481	102,344	91,535	102,027	111,002	96,183	92,444
Picked up	**KNQN**	123,352	117,389	99,747	93,096	112,424	110,576	98,391	105,755	123,014	112,001	113,592
Total	**KNQL**	225,095	216,079	190,485	179,511	220,905	212,920	189,926	207,790	234,016	208,184	206,036

Source: Civil Aviation Authority: 0207 453 6258

1 Figures exclude Channel Island and Isle of Man Airports.
2 Local pleasure flights for reward (eg aerial survey work, crop dusting and delivery of empty aircraft) and empty positioning flights.
3 Test and Training flights, Other flights by Air Transport Operators, Aero-club, Private, Official, Military & Business Aviation.
4 With effect from 2001, passengers, freight and mail handled exclude traffic carried on air taxi operations.

Government
finance

Chapter 23

Government Finance

Public sector (Tables 23.1 to 23.3 and 23.6)

In Table 23.1 the term public sector describes the consolidation of central government, local government and public corporations. General government is the consolidated total of central government and local government. The table shows details of the key public sector finances' indicators, consistent with the European System of Accounts 1995 (ESA95), by sub-sector.

The concepts in Table 23.1 are consistent with the format for public finances in the Economic and Fiscal Strategy Report (EFSR), published by HM Treasury on 11 June 1998, and the Budget. The public sector current budget is equivalent to net saving in national accounts plus capital tax receipts. Net investment is gross capital formation, plus payments less receipts of investment grants, less depreciation. Net borrowing is net investment less current budget. Net borrowing differs from the net cash requirement (see below) in that it is measured on an accruals basis whereas the net cash requirement is mainly a cash measure which includes some financial transactions.

Table 23.2 shows the public sector key fiscal balances. The table shows the component detail of the public sector key fiscal balance by economic category. The tables are consistent with the Budget.

Table 23.3 shows public sector net debt. Public sector net debt consists of the public sector's financial liabilities at face value, minus its liquid assets – mainly foreign currency exchange reserves and bank deposits. General government gross debt (consolidated) in Table 23.3 is consistent with the definition of general government gross debt reported to the European Commission under the requirements of the Maastricht Treaty.

More information on the concepts in Table 23.1, 23.2 and 23.3 can be found in a guide to monthly public sector finance statistics, GSS Methodology Series No 12, the ONS First Releases Public Sector Finances and Financial Statistics Explanatory Handbook.

Table 23.6 shows the taxes and National Insurance contributions paid to central government, local government, and to the institutions of the European Union. The table is the same as Table 11.1 of the National Accounts Blue Book. More information on the data and concepts in the table can be found in Chapter 11 of the Blue Book.

Consolidated Fund and National Loans Fund (Tables 23.4, 23.5 and 23.7)

The central government embraces all bodies for whose activities a Minister of the Crown, or other responsible person, is accountable to Parliament. It includes, in addition to the ordinary government departments, a number of bodies administering public policy, but without the substantial degree of financial independence which characterises the public corporations. It also includes certain extra-budgetary funds and accounts controlled by departments.

The government's financial transactions are handled through a number of statutory funds or accounts. The most important of these is the Consolidated Fund, which is the government's main account with the Bank of England. Up to 31 March 1968 the Consolidated Fund was virtually synonymous with the term 'Exchequer', which was then the government's central cash account. From 1 April 1968 the National Loans Fund, with a separate account at the Bank of England, was set up by the National Loans Act 1968. The general effect of this Act was to remove from the Consolidated Fund most of the government's domestic lending and the whole of the government's borrowing transactions, and to provide for them to be brought to account in the National Loans Fund.

Revenue from taxation and miscellaneous receipts, including interest and dividends on loans made from votes, continue to be paid into the Consolidated Fund.

After meeting the ordinary expenditure on Supply Services and the Consolidated Fund Standing Services, the surplus or deficit of the Consolidated Fund (Table 23.4), is payable into or met by the National Loans Fund. Table 23.4 also provides a summary of the transactions of the National Loans Fund. The service of the National Debt, previously borne by the Consolidated Fund, is now met from the National Loans Fund which receives:

• interest payable on loans to the nationalised industries, local authorities and other bodies, whether the loans were made before or after 1 April 1968 and

• the profits of the Issue Department of the Bank of England, mainly derived from interest on government securities, which were formerly paid into the Exchange Equalisation Account.

The net cost of servicing the National Debt after applying these interest receipts and similar items is a charge on the Consolidated Fund as part of the standing services. Details of National Loans Fund loans outstanding are shown in Table 23.5. Details of borrowing and repayments of debt, other than loans from the National Loans Fund, are shown in Table 23.7.

Income tax (Table 23.10, 23.11)

Following the introduction of Independent Taxation from 1990/91, the Married Couple's Allowance was introduced. It is payable in addition to the Personal Allowance and between 1990/91 and 1992/93 went to the husband unless the transfer condition was met. The condition was that the husband was unable to make full use of the allowance himself and, in that case, he could transfer only part or all of the Married Couple's Allowance to his wife. In 1993/94 all or half of the allowance could be transferred to the wife if the couple had agreed beforehand. The wife has the right to claim half the allowance. The Married Couple's Allowance, and allowances linked to it, were restricted to 20 per cent in 1994/95 and to 15 per cent from 1995/96. From 2000/01 only people born before 6 April 1935 are entitled to Married Couple's Allowance.

The age allowance replaces the single allowance, provided the taxpayer's income is below the limits shown in the table. From 1989/90, for incomes in excess of the limits, the allowance is reduced by £1 for each additional £2 of income until the ordinary limit is reached (before it was £2 for each £3 of additional income). The relief is due where the taxpayer is aged 65 or over in the year of assessment.

The additional Personal Allowance could be claimed by a single parent (or by a married man if his wife was totally incapacitated) who maintained a resident child at his or her own expense. Widow's Bereavement Allowance was due to a widow in the year of her husband's death and in the following year provided the widow had not remarried before the beginning of that year. Both the additional Personal Allowance and the Widow's Bereavement Allowance were abolished from April 2000.

The Blind Person's Allowance may be claimed by blind persons (in England and Wales, registered as blind by a local authority) and surplus Blind Person's Allowance may be transferred to a husband or wife. Relief on life assurance premiums is given by deduction from the premium payable. From 1984/85, it is confined to policies made before 14 March 1984.

From 1993/94 until 1998/99 a number of taxpayers with taxable income in excess of the lower rate limit only paid tax at the lower rate. This was because it was only their dividend income and (from 1996/97) their savings income which took their taxable income above the lower rate limit but below the basic rate limit, and such income was chargeable to tax at the lower rate and not the basic rate.

In 1999/2000 the 10 per cent starting rate replaced the lower rate and taxpayers with savings or dividend income at the basic rate of tax are taxed at 20 per cent and 10 per cent respectively. Before 1999/2000 these people would have been classified as lower rate taxpayers.

Rateable values (Table 23.12)

Major changes to local government finance in England and Wales took effect from 1 April 1990. These included the abolition of domestic rating (replaced by the Community Charge, then replaced in 1993 by the Council Tax), the revaluation of all non-domestic properties, and the introduction of the Uniform Business Rate. Also in 1990, a new classification scheme was introduced which has resulted in differences in coverage. Further differences are caused by legislative changes which have changed the treatment of certain types of property. There was little change in the total rateable value of non-domestic properties when all these properties were re-valued in April 1995. Rateable values for offices fell and there was a rise for all other property types shown in the table.

With effect from 1 April 2000, all non-domestic properties were re-valued. Overall there was an increase in rateable values of over 25 per cent compared with the last year of the 1995 list. The largest proportionate increase was for offices and cinemas, with all property types given in the table showing rises.

The latest revaluation affecting all non-domestic properties took effect from 1 April 2010. In this revaluation the overall increase in rateable values between 1 April of the first year of the new list and the same day on the last year of the 2005 list was 21 per cent. The largest proportionate increase was for offices and educational properties, with all property types in the table showing rises.

Local authority capital expenditure and receipts (Table 23.16)

Authorities finance capital spending in a number of ways, including use of their own revenue funds, borrowing or grants and contributions from elsewhere. Until 31 March 2004, the capital finance system laid down in Part 4 of the Local Government and Housing Act 1989 (the '1989 Act') provided the framework within which authorities were permitted to finance capital spending from sources other than revenue - that is by the use of borrowing, long-term credit or capital receipts.

Until 31 March 2004, capital spending could be financed by:

• revenue resources – either the General Fund Revenue Account, the Housing Revenue Account (HRA) or the Major Repairs Reserve – but an authority could not charge council tenants for spending on general services, or spending on council houses to local taxpayers

• borrowing or long-term credit as authorised by the credit approvals issued by central government. Credit approvals were normally accompanied by an element of Revenue Support Grant (RSG) covering most of the costs of borrowing

• grants received from central government

• contributions or grants from elsewhere – including the National Lottery and non-departmental public bodies (NDPBs) such as Sport England, English Heritage and Natural England, as well as private sector partners, capital receipts (that is, proceeds from the sale of land, buildings or other fixed assets) and sums set aside as Provision for Credit Liabilities (PCL). This required the use of a credit approval, unless the authority was debt-free

From 1 April 2004, capital spending can be financed in the same ways, except that central government no longer issues credit approvals to allow authorities to finance capital spending by borrowing. However, it continues to provide financial support in the usual way, via RSG or HRA subsidy, towards some capital spending financed by borrowing that is Supported Capital Expenditure (Revenue). Authorities are now free to finance capital spending by self-financed borrowing within limits of affordability set, having regard to the 2003 Act and the CIPFA Prudential Code. The concept of PCL has not been carried forward into the new system, although authorities that were debt-free and had a negative credit ceiling at the end of the old system could still spend amounts of PCL built up under the old rules.

In 2009/10 capital receipts remained well below the 2007/08 level, at £1.4 billion. This reflects a drop in the sale of assets by local authorities. The in-year capital receipts of £1.4 billion were more than offset by the use of £1.6 billion of capital receipts to finance expenditure.

In 2009/10 capital expenditure of £5 billion (about 23 per cent) was financed by self-financed borrowing, an increase of 18 per cent from the amount financed in 2008/09.

In 2009/10 government grants accounted for 34 per cent of the total financing. Financing by government grant in 2007/08 was affected by the grant of £1.7 billion paid by the Department for Transport to the Greater London Authority (GLA) in respect of Metronet liabilities; this caused government grants to account for 34 per cent of the total financing for 2007/08.

Local authority financing for capital expenditure (Table 23.16, 23.17)

Capital spending by local authorities is mainly for buying, constructing or improving physical assets such as:
• buildings – schools, houses, libraries and museums, police and fire stations
• land – for development, roads, playing fields
• vehicles, plant and machinery – including street lighting and road signs

It also includes grants and advances made to the private sector or the rest of the public sector for capital purposes, such as advances to Registered Social Landlords Local authority capital expenditure more than doubled between 2001/02 and 2007/08.

The underlying trend in capital expenditure shows an increase of 8 per cent from 2008/09 to 2009/10. The exceptional event was the payment by the Greater London Authority (Transport for London) of £1.7 billion to Metronet in 2007/08.

New construction, conversion and renovation forms the major part of capital spending. The largest increases in capital expenditure in 2008/09 were in police (44 per cent), and education (22 per cent). Capital expenditure on transport increased by 14 per cent, allowing for the Greater London Authority's grant payment via TfL in respect of Metronet in 2007/08. Between 2004/05 and 2008/09 capital expenditure on transport had risen from 20 per cent to 24 per cent of the total, while capital expenditure on housing has fallen from 28 per cent to 25 per cent of the total.

The largest percentage increase in capital expenditure in 2009/10 was in transport (24 per cent). Capital expenditure on housing and police fell by 8 per cent and 11 per cent respectively. Between 2005/06 and 2009/10 capital expenditure on transport has risen from 21 per cent to 28 per cent of the total, while capital expenditure on housing has fallen from 27 per cent to 21 per cent of the total.

23.1 Sector analysis of key fiscal balances[1]

United Kingdom
Not seasonally adjusted

£ million[2]

		1999/00	2000/01	2001/02	2002/03	2003/04	2004/05	2005/06	2006/07	2007/08	2008/09	2009/10	2010/11
Surplus on current budget[3]													
Central Government	ANLV	24,401	26,756	13,812	-8,121	-17,559	-17,757	-13,498	-5,829	-6,025	-48,360	-105,655	-100,097
Local government	NMMX	-4,507	-3,790	-3,909	-4,960	-3,245	-3,135	-5,257	-2,526	-2,661	-4,078	-4,084	-3,474
General Government	ANLW	20,012	22,624	10,833	-11,864	-19,112	-21,252	-19,072	-9,498	-10,437	-52,623	-109,518	-107,748
Public corporations	IL6M	934	763	1,269	508	1,663	1,966	4,538	3,587	3,933	15,983	25,285	29,026
Public sector	ANMU	20,994	23,433	12,144	-11,323	-17,418	-19,249	-13,953	-5,021	-4,810	-36,797	-84,481	-72,458
Net investment[4]													
Central government	ANNS	9,493	8,947	14,234	18,231	19,570	20,798	20,002	27,140	32,827	44,062	51,605	37,662
Local government	ANNT	-832	-1,882	-1,824	-3,595	-682	1,756	416	-452	-2,315	-11	-886	-174
General Government	ANNV	8,238	7,305	13,336	15,566	18,116	21,227	20,017	25,708	28,988	43,475	45,626	36,085
Public corporations	JSH6	-2,789	-2,018	-1,419	-1,750	-2,492	-639	3,202	-653	-863	-6,516	-7,513	523
Public sector	ANNW	5,434	5,125	11,902	13,804	15,623	20,574	23,257	25,750	29,411	36,655	43,377	37,823
Net borrowing[5]													
Central government	NMFJ	-14,908	-17,809	422	26,352	37,129	38,555	33,476	33,132	39,079	92,031	151,946	140,533
Local government	NMOE	3,134	2,490	2,081	1,078	99	3,924	5,613	2,074	346	4,067	3,198	3,300
General Government	NNBK	-11,774	-15,319	2,503	27,430	37,228	42,479	39,089	35,206	39,425	96,098	155,144	143,833
Public corporations	IL6E	-3,723	-2,781	-2,688	-2,258	-4,155	-2,605	-1,336	-4,240	-4,796	-22,499	-32,798	-28,503
Public sector	ANNX	-15,494	-18,307	-243	25,128	33,041	39,823	37,409	30,861	33,935	73,755	127,823	110,777
Net cash requirement													
Central government[6]	RUUX	-10,664	-37,251	3,366	24,214	42,717	37,454	35,908	36,891	29,621	162,513	197,715	137,716
Local government	ABEG	979	-611	-423	-2,715	-2,712	1,270	4,153	58	-723	4,401	4,958	773
General Government	RUUS	-9,685	-37,862	2,943	21,499	40,005	38,724	40,061	36,949	28,898	166,914	202,673	138,489
Public corporations	IL6F	1,712	1,541	1,159	3,095	-1,539	-242	396	-1,792	-1,753	21,958	-103,675	-139,241
Public sector	RURQ	-8,053	-36,521	4,014	24,535	38,421	38,439	40,376	35,032	26,972	188,141	99,316	-748
Public sector debt													
Public sector net debt	BKQK	344,352	311,143	314,257	346,034	381,502	422,065	461,671	497,806	621,898	2,038,432	2,187,559	2,235,092
Public sector net debt (£ billion)	RUTN	344	311	314	346	382	422	462	498	622	2,107	2,225	2,250
Public sector net debt as a percentage of GDP	RUTO	35.6	30.7	29.7	30.8	32.1	34	35.3	35.9	43.1	150.4	154.5	149.6
Excluding financial interventions													
Net debt	HF6W	344.4	311.1	314.3	346	381.5	422.1	461.7	497.8	527.2	606.8	760.3	905.3
Net debt as a % GDP	HF6X	35.6	30.7	29.7	30.8	32.1	34	35.3	35.9	36.5	43.3	52.8	60.2

Source: Office for National Statistics: 01633 456673

1 National accounts entities as defined under the European System of
Accounts 1995 (ESA95) consistent with the latest national accounts. See chapter text.
2 Unless otherwise stated.
3 Net saving plus capital taxes
4 Gross capital for mation plus payments less receipts of investment grants less depreciation.
5 Net investment less surplus on current budget. A version of General government net borrowing is reported to the European Commission under the requirements
of the Maastricht Treaty.
6 Central government net cash requirement (own account).

23.2 Public sector transactions and fiscal balances[1]

United Kingdom

£ million

		1998 /99	1999 /00	2000 /01	2001 /02	2002 /03	2003 /04	2004 /05	2005 /06	2006 /07	2007 /08	2008 /09	2009 /10	2010 /11
Current receipts														
Taxes on income and wealth	ANSO	123,875	133,668	144,091	145,081	143,194	145,445	160,363	179,697	193,880	207,826	206,151	183,533	194,718
Taxes on production	NMYE	115,227	125,098	129,270	133,043	139,829	148,831	155,132	159,449	170,122	176,106	167,756	169,766	190,886
Other current taxes[2]	MJBC	17,688	18,916	19,696	21,569	23,194	25,794	27,422	28,808	30,317	31,889	33,216	33,929	34,611
Taxes on capital	NMGI	1,804	2,054	2,236	2,383	2,370	2,521	2,941	3,276	3,618	3,890	26,552	2,431	2,723
Social contributions	ANBO	54,746	56,935	62,068	63,162	63,529	75,148	80,923	85,489	90,564	95,324	97,313	97,049	97,529
Gross operating surplus	ANBP	16,822	17,022	16,756	16,966	17,161	18,436	18,674	21,595	22,851	24,888	35,560	41,996	45,530
Interest and dividends from private sector and Rest of World	ANBQ	5,283	4,345	6,206	4,879	4,586	4,649	6,053	6,726	6,492	10,602	46,345	50,741	46,006
Rent and other current transfers[3]	ANBS	891	1,037	2,036	2,427	2,470	2,036	1,964	1,969	1,864	1,763	999	1,815	24
Total current receipts	ANBT	336,336	359,076	382,362	389,510	396,331	422,861	453,471	487,009	519,708	551,996	589,180	580,451	611,657
Current expenditure														
Current expenditure on goods and services[4]	GZSN	159,443	172,299	185,875	198,935	217,512	236,606	255,961	274,005	287,696	300,825	318,507	330,793	340,694
Subsidies	NMRL	4,164	4,215	4,412	4,504	6,043	6,787	7,461	8,138	8,837	9,608	8,010	9,650	9,347
Social benefits	ANLY	106,585	105,555	108,010	118,269	122,636	130,799	136,848	142,294	147,074	157,842	172,969	188,650	196,307
Net current grants abroad[5]	GZSI	-1,018	-461	-380	-2,075	-824	-1,352	-637	-64	108	-87	-1,347	976	3,234
Other current grants	NNAI	15,199	19,106	21,676	23,932	27,555	30,369	32,502	34,079	34,886	37,110	36,156	41,638	41,513
Interest and dividends paid to private sector and Rest of World	ANLO	29,289	25,297	26,400	22,495	21,453	22,822	24,955	26,938	29,251	35,079	71,531	70,637	77,124
Total current expenditure	ANLT	313,662	326,011	345,993	366,060	394,375	426,010	457,029	485,326	507,784	540,292	605,814	642,343	668,186
Saving, gross plus capital taxes	ANSP	22,674	33,065	36,369	23,450	1,956	-3,149	-3,558	1,683	11,924	11,704	-16,634	-61,892	-56,529
Depreciation	-ANNZ	-12,436	-12,763	-13,107	-13,571	-14,460	-14,942	-15,608	-16,436	-17,252	-17,964	-19,828	-21,657	-22,744
Surplus on current budget	ANMU	10,423	20,994	23,433	12,144	-11,323	-17,418	-19,249	-13,953	-5,021	-4,810	-36,797	-84,481	-72,458
Net investment														
Gross fixed capital formation[6]	ANSQ	14,061	14,149	13,283	17,308	20,125	21,079	25,644	27,929	28,971	33,886	41,654	47,180	44,696
Less depreciation	-ANNZ	-12,436	-12,763	-13,107	-13,571	-14,460	-14,942	-15,608	-16,436	-17,252	-17,964	-19,828	-21,657	-22,744
Increase in inventories and valuables	ANSR	231	-472	-126	-10	-74	2,011	-234	-166	79	-98	57	364	222
Capital grants to private sector and Rest of World	ANSS	4,942	4,304	3,875	7,958	7,564	10,142	11,046	12,452	15,365	14,779	40,649	18,584	16,134
Capital grants from private sector and Rest of World	-ANST	-367	-427	-756	-989	-1,091	-1,352	-972	-1,202	-1,413	-1,192	-25,877	-1,094	-485
Total net investment	-ANNW	5,955	5,434	5,125	11,902	13,804	15,623	20,574	23,257	25,750	29,411	36,655	43,377	37,823
Net borrowing[7]	-ANNX	-4,468	-15,494	-18,307	-243	25,128	33,041	39,823	37,409	30,861	33,935	73,755	127,823	110,777
Financial transactions determining net cash requirement														
Net lending to private sector and Rest of World	ANSU	171	2,212	3,174	2,674	2,736	2,641	925	874	-889	-4,835	-7,671	-29,736	-51,769
Net acquisition of UK company securities	ANSV	704	-310	949	-394	765	355	521	655	-2,271	-3,238	55,983	53,528	-28,774
Accounts receivable/payable	ANSW	803	8,393	-17,163	2,210	-2,779	9,031	2,453	2,688	9,903	-8,538	28,862	14,743	-1,778
Adjustment for interest on gilts	ANSX	-2,446	-1,294	-2,630	-361	-1,444	-1,187	-2,304	-2,749	-1,279	-4,584	-4,359	2,051	-5,967
Other financial transcations[8]	ANSY	-909	-1,560	-2,544	128	129	-5,460	-2,979	1,499	-1,293	14,232	41,571	-69,093	-23,237
Public sector net cash requirement	RURQ	-6,145	-8,053	-36,521	4,014	24,535	38,421	38,439	40,376	35,032	26,972	188,141	99,316	-748

Source: Office for National Statistics: 01633 456673

1 See chapter text.
2 Includes domestic rates, council tax, community charge, motor vehicle duty paid by household and some licence fees.
3 ESA95 transactions D44, D45, D74, D75 and D72-D71: includes rent of land, oil royalties, other property income and fines.
4 Includes non-trading capital consumption.
5 Net of current grants received from abroad.
6 Including net acquisition of land.
7 Net investment less surplus on current budget.
8 Includes statistical discrepancy, finance leasing and similar borrowing, insurance technical reserves and some other minor adjustments.

23.3 Public sector net debt[1]

United Kingdom

£ million

		2001 /02	2002 /03	2003 /04	2004 /05	2005 /06	2006 /07	2007 /08	2008 /09	2009 /10	2010 /11
Central government sterling gross debt:											
British government stock											
Conventional gilts	BKPK	200,833	206,119	232,877	261,373	287,481	306,489	320,622	426,107	608,511	697,968
Index linked gilts	BKPL	70,417	75,966	78,982	86,749	98,654	113,090	132,404	154,038	178,170	220,631
Total	BKPM	271,250	282,085	311,859	348,122	386,135	419,579	453,026	580,145	786,681	918,599
Sterling Treasury bills	BKPJ	9,700	15,000	19,300	20,350	19,100	15,600	17,569	43,748	62,866	63,174
National savings	ACUA	62,275	63,087	66,522	68,504	73,365	78,885	84,764	97,231	98,804	98,820
Tax instruments	ACRV	478	376	407	350	308	353	428	1,121	819	679
Other sterling debt [2]	BKSK	28,276	32,711	35,032	32,279	36,481	41,261	39,348	57,534	40,206	34,360
Central government sterling gross debt total	BKSL	371,979	393,259	433,120	469,605	515,389	555,678	595,135	779,779	989,376	1,115,632
Central government foreign currency gross debt:											
US$ bonds	BKPG	2,107	0	1,632	1,587	1,730	1,530	1,509	0	0	0
ECU/Euro Treasury notes	EYSV	1,225	0	0	0	0	0	0	0	0	0
Other foreign currency debt	BKPH	243	172	105	57	1	0	0	0	0	0
Central government foreign currency gross debt total	BKPI	3,575	172	1,738	1,644	1,731	1,530	1,509	0	0	0
Central government gross debt total	BKPW	375,554	393,431	434,858	471,249	517,120	557,208	596,644	779,779	989,376	1,115,632
Local government gross debt total	EYKP	52,566	51,353	50,547	53,300	60,114	62,425	66,371	67,301	68,226	70,656
less											
Central government holdings of local government debt	EYKZ	-47,530	-44,836	-41,540	-42,339	-46,664	-47,956	-50,364	-50,508	-50,889	-52,848
Local government holdings of central government debt	EYLA	-29	-184	-510	-62	-62	0	-81	-2,960	-2,689	-2,077
General government gross debt (consolidated)	BKPX	380,561	399,764	443,355	482,148	530,508	571,677	612,570	793,612	1,004,024	1,131,363
Public corporations gross debt	EYYD	8,859	18,660	13,895	14,875	14,687	14,430	13,804	13,669	10,518	10,405
less:											
Central government holdings of public corporations debt	EYXY	-4,308	-4,171	-5,188	-5,740	-5,631	-4,984	-5,092	-4,879	-5,617	-5,604
Local government holdings of public corporations debt	EYXZ	-122	-121	-120	-121	-112	-103	-104	-107	-153	-155
Public corporations holdings of central government debt	BKPZ	-4,638	-4,928	-4,780	-5,080	-2,822	-2,255	-4,119	-3,947	-3,352	-3,301
Public corporations holdings of local government debt	EYXV	-60	-50	-84	-138	-79	-198	-39	-33	-63	-150
Public sector gross debt (consolidated)	BKQA	380,292	409,154	447,078	485,944	536,551	578,567	715,043	2,865,505	3,126,829	3,163,700
Public sector liquid assets:											
Official reserves	AIPD	28,055	26,387	25,266	25,813	27,835	26,631	29,561	31,527	44,652	52,969
Central government deposits [3]	BKSM	2,802	2,900	3,879	3,868	5,212	6,171	5,439	5,242	4,351	5,783
Other central government	BKSN	10,743	8,141	7,077	3,044	8,498	11,369	14,834	37,352	45,822	20,433
Local government deposits [3]	BKSO	13,698	14,797	16,797	18,718	20,993	23,740	28,327	21,781	18,182	19,201
Other local government short term assets	BKQG	5,990	6,061	5,573	5,057	5,381	4,709	4,946	4,142	4,250	5,322
Public corporations deposits [3]	BKSP	2,336	2,133	2,813	3,411	2,375	3,746	2,366	1,781	2,203	1,923
Other public corporations short term assets	BKSQ	1,180	1,586	2,845	2,457	2,453	2,378	2,254	2,166	2,284	2,170
Public sector liquid assets total	BKQJ	64,804	62,005	64,250	62,368	72,747	78,744	91,040	823,718	935,861	924,603
Public sector net debt	BKQK	314,257	346,034	381,502	422,065	461,671	497,806	621,898	2,038,432	2,187,559	2,235,092
as percentage of GDP[4]	RUTO	29.7	30.8	32.1	34	35.3	35.9	43.1	150.4	154.5	149.6

Source: Office for National Statistics: 01633 456673

1 See chapter text.
2 Including overdraft with Bank of England.
3 Bank and building society deposits.
4 Gross domestic product at market prices from 12 months centred on the end of the month.

23.4(a) Central government surplus on current budget and net borrowing

United Kingdom, years ending 31 March

	Current Receipts									
	Taxes on production	of which	Taxes on income and wealth				Compulsory social contributions	Interest and dividends	Other receipts[3]	Total
	Total	VAT	Total	Income and capital gains tax[1]	Other[2]	Other taxes				
	NMBY	NZGF	NMCU	LIBR	LIBP	LIQR	AIIH	LIQP	LIQQ	ANBV
2000	129,138	59,998	140,002	105,459	34,543	8,651	60,252	8,281	6,624	352,948
2001	131,997	63,525	147,281	112,165	35,116	9,370	63,125	8,664	7,161	367,598
2002	138,663	68,258	142,814	112,440	30,374	9,569	63,410	7,386	7,228	369,070
2003	145,782	74,603	144,234	113,621	30,525	10,118	71,540	7,864	7,203	387,319
2004	154,582	79,755	154,127	120,725	33,402	10,862	79,224	7,739	7,247	414,294
2005	157,856	81,426	172,498	131,689	40,809	11,481	84,459	7,662	7,517	441,671
2006	166,760	85,591	192,600	141,714	50,886	12,262	89,550	7,903	7,593	476,902
2007	175,360	89,706	199,851	153,477	46,562	13,213	93,210	9,369	7,744	498,758
2008	173,167	89,732	207,589	156,975	50,542	12,892	98,319	10,215	7,959	510,347
2009	163,041	78,307	185,148	147,316	37,832	12,215	94,615	7,500	7,996	472,268
2010	186,341	93,530	191,161	147,143	43,993	12,828	97,857	5,614	8,741	503,492
2000/01	129,536	60,746	144,263	110,324	33,939	8,646	62,068	9,044	6,890	360,447
2001/02	133,199	64,735	145,185	111,688	33,497	9,458	63,162	7,855	7,046	365,905
2002/03	140,032	69,087	143,273	112,373	30,883	9,588	63,529	7,918	7,232	371,808
2003/04	148,651	76,633	145,558	115,233	30,254	10,309	75,148	7,795	7,166	395,143
2004/05	154,964	79,979	160,490	124,477	36,013	10,950	80,923	7,495	7,302	422,562
2005/06	159,263	81,507	179,960	134,918	45,042	11,760	85,559	7,761	7,539	452,017
2006/07	169,918	87,740	194,198	146,478	47,720	12,520	90,916	7,969	7,613	483,334
2007/08	175,859	89,896	208,014	158,781	49,341	13,264	95,437	9,986	7,759	510,231
2008/09	167,655	85,350	200,777	153,714	47,071	12,651	96,596	9,710	8,049	496,109
2009/10	170,091	83,616	182,494	144,389	38,076	12,328	97,361	6,764	8,153	478,760
2010/11	190,695	97,226	194,381	149,363	45,022	12,793	97,771	5,682	8,745	510,793
2005 Q1	37,280	19,526	53,955	44,003	9,952	2,723	22,529	2,103	1,868	120,557
2005 Q2	39,221	20,146	35,024	26,726	8,298	2,865	20,289	1,713	1,899	101,084
2005 Q3	40,450	20,736	43,615	32,760	10,855	3,175	20,546	1,963	1,854	111,560
2005 Q4	40,905	21,018	39,904	28,200	11,704	2,718	21,095	1,883	1,896	108,470
2006 Q1	38,687	19,607	61,417	47,232	14,185	3,002	23,629	2,202	1,890	130,903
2006 Q2	41,577	21,301	37,343	28,779	8,564	3,116	21,613	1,827	1,899	107,444
2006 Q3	42,725	22,152	49,653	35,611	14,042	3,073	21,624	1,761	1,878	120,749
2006 Q4	43,771	22,531	44,187	30,092	14,095	3,071	22,684	2,113	1,926	117,806
2007 Q1	41,845	21,756	63,015	51,996	11,019	3,260	24,995	2,268	1,910	137,335
2007 Q2	43,921	22,369	39,150	30,688	8,588	3,311	22,354	2,135	1,970	112,873
2007 Q3	44,775	22,849	51,207	37,952	13,208	3,438	22,560	2,158	1,921	126,046
2007 Q4	44,819	22,732	46,479	32,841	13,747	3,204	23,301	2,808	1,943	122,504
2008 Q1	42,344	21,946	71,178	57,300	13,798	3,311	27,222	2,885	1,925	148,808
2008 Q2	45,528	24,235	39,460	30,339	9,121	3,299	23,784	2,365	1,973	116,333
2008 Q3	43,258	22,533	53,073	38,688	14,391	3,278	23,597	2,593	2,050	127,662
2008 Q4	42,037	21,018	43,878	30,648	13,232	3,004	23,716	2,372	2,011	117,544
2009 Q1	36,832	17,564	64,366	54,039	10,327	3,070	25,499	2,380	2,015	134,570
2009 Q2	40,188	19,058	35,933	28,858	7,075	3,022	23,086	1,967	2,056	106,595
2009 Q3	41,807	20,200	43,837	35,402	8,435	3,222	22,583	1,518	1,863	115,426
2009 Q4	44,214	21,485	41,012	29,017	11,995	2,901	23,447	1,635	2,062	115,677
2010 Q1	43,882	22,873	61,712	51,112	10,571	3,183	28,245	1,644	2,172	141,062
2010 Q2	49,200	23,429	37,017	29,386	7,631	3,215	23,112	1,196	2,138	116,172
2010 Q3	46,462	23,677	48,921	36,650	12,273	3,371	22,993	1,480	2,192	125,650
2010 Q4	46,797	23,551	43,511	29,995	13,518	3,059	23,507	1,294	2,239	120,608
2011 Q1	48,236	26,569	64,932	53,332	11,600	3,148	28,159	1,712	2,176	148,363

23.4(a) Central government surplus on current budget and net borrowing

United Kingdom, years ending 31 March

	Taxes on production	of which	Taxes on income and wealth				Compulsory social contributions	Interest and dividends	Other receipts[3]	Total
				Income and capital gains						
	Total	VAT	Total	tax[1]	Other[2]	Other taxes				
	NMBY	NZGF	NMCU	LIBR	LIBP	LIQR	AIIH	LIQP	LIQQ	ANBV
2009 Jan	12,236	5,952	32,080	24,059	8,021	972	8,103	623	673	54,687
2009 Feb	11,725	5,296	18,918	17,559	1,359	931	8,240	599	672	41,085
2009 Mar	12,827	6,316	13,368	12,421	947	1,167	9,173	1,158	670	38,363
2009 Apr	13,214	6,104	15,077	10,202	4,875	1,055	7,582	834	685	38,447
2009 May	13,027	6,125	9,431	8,552	879	955	7,546	546	685	32,190
2009 Jun	13,946	6,829	11,425	10,104	1,321	1,012	7,862	587	686	35,518
2009 Jul	14,118	6,934	21,049	14,680	6,369	1,059	7,541	460	622	44,849
2009 Aug	13,689	6,556	11,657	10,919	738	997	7,425	380	622	34,770
2009 Sep	14,004	6,710	11,131	9,803	1,328	1,166	7,569	678	619	35,167
2009 Oct	14,880	7,532	16,915	9,538	7,377	1,020	7,601	693	687	41,796
2009 Nov	14,517	7,065	10,897	9,365	1,532	929	7,624	502	687	35,156
2009 Dec	14,339	6,888	13,200	10,114	3,086	952	8,179	440	688	37,798
2010 Jan	14,543	7,859	27,385	19,919	7,466	967	8,035	326	724	51,980
2010 Feb	14,033	7,050	18,464	16,875	1,589	1,031	8,840	416	725	43,509
2010 Mar	15,369	7,964	15,834	14,318	1,516	1,185	10,834	902	723	44,847
2010 Apr	18,580	7,802	14,936	9,607	5,329	1,089	7,515	394	712	43,226
2010 May	14,978	7,512	10,458	9,543	915	1,042	7,526	367	714	35,085
2010 Jun	15,628	8,115	11,623	10,236	1,387	1,084	8,027	435	712	37,509
2010 Jul	15,431	7,750	24,145	15,490	8,655	1,147	7,631	366	729	49,449
2010 Aug	15,323	7,684	12,549	11,326	1,223	1,060	7,637	371	730	37,670
2010 Sep	15,708	8,243	12,229	9,834	2,395	1,164	7,695	743	733	38,272
2010 Oct	15,373	7,594	19,457	9,963	9,494	1,035	7,656	436	745	44,702
2010 Nov	15,933	8,048	10,824	9,334	1,490	1,004	7,657	407	745	36,570
2010 Dec	15,500	7,909	13,232	10,698	2,534	1,020	8,196	451	749	39,148
2011 Jan	15,642	8,772	32,637	24,154	8,483	946	8,502	384	726	58,837
2011 Feb	15,511	8,312	17,258	15,928	1,330	1,051	9,201	370	726	44,117
2011 Mar	17,083	9,485	15,037	13,250	1,787	1,151	10,456	958	724	45,409
2011 Apr	16,694	8,884	15,643	9,811	5,832	1,215	7,964	406	764	42,686
2011 May	16,329	8,766	11,142	9,841	1,301	1,392	7,837	506	765	37,971

23.4(b) Central government surplus on current budget and net borrowing

United Kingdom, years ending 31 March

continued

	Current expenditure				Saving, gross plus capital taxes	Depreciation	Surplus on current budget	Net investment	Net borrowing
Interest	Net Social Benefits	Other	Total						
NMFX	GZSJ	LIQS	ANLP	ANPM	NSRN	ANLV	ANNS	NMFJ
2000	25,679	96,611	200,263	322,553	30,395	5,038	25,357	-9,279	16,078
2001	23,141	103,598	214,236	340,975	26,623	5,050	21,573	-12,846	8,727
2002	20,867	107,799	239,447	368,113	957	5,132	-4,175	-15,924	-20,099
2003	22,101	115,456	263,081	399,999	-12,680	5,902	-18,582	-20,612	-39,194
2004	22,971	122,021	281,640	427,471	-13,177	5,998	-19,175	-18,094	-37,269
2005	25,652	126,132	301,017	453,273	-11,602	6,108	-17,710	-18,026	-35,736
2006	27,284	130,415	323,807	481,899	-4,997	6,269	-11,266	-24,577	-35,843
2007	31,099	139,593	332,666	504,925	-6,167	6,533	-12,700	-26,712	-39,412
2008	32,484	147,761	350,256	529,489	-19,142	6,905	-26,047	-39,443	-65,490
2009	26,873	165,125	368,398	560,873	-88,605	7,232	-95,837	-50,109	-145,946
2010	42,820	172,120	387,109	602,464	-98,972	7,587	-106,559	-39,036	-145,595
2000/01	25,958	97,675	205,077	328,710	31,737	4,981	26,756	-8,947	17,809
2001/02	22,000	104,904	220,190	347,094	18,811	4,999	13,812	-14,234	-422
2002/03	20,962	109,466	244,547	375,732	-3,924	5,360	-9,284	-17,933	-27,217
2003/04	22,298	117,280	267,496	406,051	-10,908	5,932	-16,840	-19,014	-35,854
2004/05	23,950	122,624	287,806	434,964	-12,402	6,039	-18,441	-19,713	-38,154
2005/06	25,970	127,374	306,504	460,311	-8,294	6,137	-14,431	-18,575	-33,006
2006/07	28,215	131,698	324,042	484,390	-1,056	6,324	-7,380	-26,107	-33,487
2007/08	30,801	140,838	339,371	511,237	-1,006	6,614	-7,620	-32,217	-39,837
2008/09	31,036	152,776	352,629	536,669	-40,560	6,985	-47,545	-43,829	-91,374
2009/10	30,906	167,165	376,448	575,039	-96,279	7,331	-103,610	-46,634	-150,244
2010/11	43,742	172,802	388,308	605,173	-94,380	7,483	-101,863	-36,766	-138,629
2005 Q1	6,289	29,681	75,068	111,156	9,401	1,520	7,881	-7,434	447
2005 Q2	6,262	30,201	75,127	111,742	-10,658	1,522	-12,180	584	-11,596
2005 Q3	6,208	31,101	75,274	112,649	-1,089	1,529	-2,618	-4,585	-7,203
2005 Q4	6,893	35,149	75,548	117,726	-9,256	1,537	-10,793	-6,591	-17,384
2006 Q1	6,607	30,923	80,555	118,194	12,709	1,549	11,160	-7,983	3,177
2006 Q2	6,481	31,870	82,844	121,300	-13,856	1,559	-15,415	-6,153	-21,568
2006 Q3	6,582	32,976	80,413	120,083	666	1,573	-907	-4,810	-5,717
2006 Q4	7,614	34,646	79,995	122,322	-4,516	1,588	-6,104	-5,631	-11,735
2007 Q1	7,538	32,206	80,790	120,685	16,650	1,604	15,046	-9,513	5,533
2007 Q2	7,619	34,360	84,824	127,515	-14,642	1,623	-16,265	-3,976	-20,241
2007 Q3	7,234	35,376	83,718	126,437	-391	1,641	-2,032	-5,952	-7,984
2007 Q4	8,708	37,651	83,334	130,288	-7,784	1,665	-9,449	-7,271	-16,720
2008 Q1	7,240	33,451	87,495	126,997	21,811	1,685	20,126	-15,018	5,108
2008 Q2	8,692	36,647	89,619	134,972	-18,639	1,710	-20,349	-5,708	-26,057
2008 Q3	8,074	37,577	85,774	131,484	-3,822	1,742	-5,564	-9,328	-14,892
2008 Q4	8,478	40,086	87,368	136,036	-18,492	1,768	-20,260	-9,389	-29,649
2009 Q1	5,792	38,466	89,868	134,177	393	1,765	-1,372	-19,404	-20,776
2009 Q2	7,373	40,740	95,004	143,138	-36,543	1,793	-38,336	-7,893	-46,229
2009 Q3	4,632	41,655	91,163	137,730	-22,304	1,823	-24,127	-8,948	-33,075
2009 Q4	9,076	44,264	92,363	145,828	-30,151	1,851	-32,002	-13,864	-45,866
2010 Q1	9,825	40,506	97,918	148,343	-7,281	1,864	-9,145	-15,929	-25,074
2010 Q2	11,532	42,141	97,987	151,750	-35,578	1,887	-37,465	-7,131	-44,596
2010 Q3	10,162	43,356	95,018	148,617	-22,967	1,909	-24,876	-7,684	-32,560
2010 Q4	11,301	46,117	96,186	153,754	-33,146	1,927	-35,073	-8,292	-43,365
2011 Q1	10,747	41,188	99,117	151,052	-2,689	1,760	-4,449	-13,659	-18,108

23.4(b) Central government surplus on current budget and net borrowing

United Kingdom, years ending 31 March

continued

| | Current expenditure | | | | Saving, gross plus capital | | Surplus on | | |
| | Interest | Net Social Benefits | Other | Total | taxes | Depreciation | current budget | Net investment | Net borrowing |
	NMFX	GZSJ	LIQS	ANLP	ANPM	NSRN	ANLV	ANNS	NMFJ
2009 Jan	2,538	13,564	28,666	44,768	9,919	546	9,373	-6,286	3,087
2009 Feb	2,193	12,095	27,873	42,161	-1,076	546	-1,622	-5,212	-6,834
2009 Mar	1,026	12,807	33,329	47,162	-8,799	545	-9,344	-8,032	-17,376
2009 Apr	2,684	13,421	32,869	48,974	-10,527	572	-11,099	-1,560	-12,659
2009 May	2,991	13,635	30,598	47,224	-15,034	572	-15,606	-3,499	-19,105
2009 Jun	1,696	13,624	31,537	46,857	-11,339	573	-11,912	-7,027	-18,939
2009 Jul	2,408	14,361	29,991	46,760	-1,911	497	-2,408	-2,454	-4,862
2009 Aug	1,307	13,519	29,962	44,788	-10,018	497	-10,515	-2,762	-13,277
2009 Sep	905	13,761	31,210	45,876	-10,709	495	-11,204	-4,085	-15,289
2009 Oct	3,354	13,908	30,426	47,688	-5,892	557	-6,449	-2,560	-9,009
2009 Nov	3,012	16,114	29,558	48,684	-13,528	557	-14,085	-2,922	-17,007
2009 Dec	2,698	14,241	32,379	49,318	-11,520	557	-12,077	-8,549	-20,626
2010 Jan	3,818	13,915	30,738	48,471	3,509	599	2,910	-2,855	55
2010 Feb	3,600	12,543	31,058	47,201	-3,692	599	-4,291	-4,362	-8,653
2010 Mar	2,391	14,012	36,122	52,525	-7,678	598	-8,276	-8,795	-17,071
2010 Apr	3,640	13,930	33,943	51,513	-8,287	582	-8,869	-1,603	-10,472
2010 May	4,034	14,033	32,513	50,580	-15,495	582	-16,077	-3,183	-19,260
2010 Jun	3,838	14,175	31,531	49,544	-12,035	582	-12,617	-2,506	-15,123
2010 Jul	3,965	14,652	30,452	49,069	380	594	-214	-2,348	-2,562
2010 Aug	3,851	14,200	30,500	48,551	-10,881	594	-11,475	-2,013	-13,488
2010 Sep	2,333	14,519	34,066	50,918	-12,646	595	-13,241	-3,476	-16,717
2010 Oct	3,881	14,364	30,579	48,824	-4,122	611	-4,733	-2,430	-7,163
2010 Nov	4,329	16,785	31,828	52,942	-16,372	611	-16,983	-2,338	-19,321
2010 Dec	3,064	15,017	33,779	51,860	-12,712	612	-13,324	-3,654	-16,978
2011 Jan	4,113	14,074	31,243	49,430	9,407	587	8,820	-2,401	6,419
2011 Feb	4,092	12,957	31,616	48,665	-4,548	587	-5,135	-3,236	-8,371
2011 Mar	2,542	14,157	36,258	52,957	-7,548	586	-8,134	-8,022	-16,156
2011 Apr	4,699	15,126	34,699	54,524	-11,838	633	-12,471	-1,299	-13,770
2011 May	4,393	14,764	32,556	51,713	-13,742	633	-14,375	-2,711	-17,086

Source: Office for National Statistics; HM Treasury

1 Includes capital gains tax paid by households. Includes income tax and capital gains tax paid by corporations.

2 Mainly comprises corporation tax and petroleum revenue tax.

3 Includes receipts from the spectrum.

23.5 National Loans Fund: assets and liabilities

United Kingdom
At 31 March each year

£ million

		2001	2002	2003	2004	2005	2006	2007	2008	2009	2010	2011
NATIONAL LOANS FUND[2]												
Total assets	**KQKD**	425,956	434,545	448,006	108,243	94,227	83,228	82,872	89,765	394,715	351,023	282,406
Total National Loans Fund loans outstanding[3]	**KQKE**	51,038	50,251	47,719	2,963	2,910	2,964	3,022	2,971	2,853	3,163	3,360
Loans to Public Corporations:												
Royal Mail Group plc	**KQKF**	500	500	550	500	500	500	500	500	500	830	1,100
Civil Aviation Authority	**KQKQ**	93	10	9	8	8	11	10	9	8	13	11
British Railways Board	**KQKS**	481	..	..	..	..	..	..	..	..	..	..
British Waterways Board	**KQKU**	17	16	15	15	15	11	10	8	7	6	5
New Towns - Development Royal Mint	**KQLP**	5	15	11	16	18	23	15	8	7	0	27
Harbour Authorities	**KQLV**	0	0	0	0	0	0	0	0	0	0	0
Ordnance Survey	**GPVF**	14	12	11	10	9	8	7	7	6	6	3
Registers of Scotland	**KZBB**	4	4	4	4	3	3	3	3	3	3	3
East of Scotland Water Authority	**KZBC**	268	258	248	238	223	213	203	203	201	193	193
North of Scotland Water Authority	**KZBD**	237	237	232	232	227	227	227	227	227	227	227
West of Scotland Water Authority	**KZBE**	412	412	412	402	402	402	377	357	352	342	337
Loans to local authorities	**KQLY**	47,239	47,093	44,640	41,468	42,103	47,124	48,111	50,753	-	-	-
Loans to private sector: Housing associations	**KGVS**	1	..	..	..	..	..	..	..	..	..	..
Loans within central government: New Towns - Development Corporations and Commission	**KQLD**	8	8	8	8	8	8	8	8	8	8	8
Scottish Homes	**KQLF**	162	150	138	101	-	..	..	..	..	..	..
Housing Corporation (England)	**KQLH**	3	2	2	1	1	1	1	1	-	-	-
Welsh Development Agency	**KQLN**	0	0	0	..	..	..	..	..	..	..	..
Development Board for Rural Wales	**KQLO**	4	4	4	4	4	4	4	4	4	4	4
Northern Ireland Exchequer	**KGVW**	1,533	1,474	1,380	1,372	1,441	1,504	1,608	1,589	1,486	1,479	1,402
Married quarters for Armed Forces	**KGVX**	58	56	55	53	52	50	48	46	44	42	40
Other assets: Exchange Equalisation Account - Advances o/s	**KGVZ**	5,680	831	30	670	910	2,005	1,805	1,330	760	3,960	9,160
Subscriptions and contributions to international financial organisations: International Monetary Fund	**KGXE**	9,497	9,495	9,294	8,697	8,616	8,814	8,271	8,881	11,196	10,762	10,581
Borrowing included in public sector net debt but not brought to account by 31March	**KGXF**	406	418	467	..	..	..	..	..	..	..	..
Other NLF Assets	**GLX9**	..	..	..	18,546	18,792	20,735	20,859	25,180	36,261	38,892	47,323
Debt Management Account advances outstanding	**GPVG**	35,000	35,000	28,000	35,000	20,000	-	..	-	292,000	242,000	157,000
Consolidated Fund liability	**KCYI**	324,336	338,550	362,497	395,161	436,345	483,836	519,312	571,228	730,371	920,794	1,061,388
Total liabilities National Loans Fund - Gross liabilities outstanding	**KCYJ**	425,956	434,545	448,006	503,405	530,572	567,064	602,184	660,994	11,250,856	1,271,817	1,343,794

1 See Chapter text.
2 From 2003-04 the NLF Account has been prepared on an Accruals basis.
The figures from 2004 onwards reflect this accounting change.
3 Restated from 2004 onward. PWLB advances no longer included with NLF loans.

Source: HM Treasury: 0207 270 4761

23.6(a) Taxes paid by UK residents to general government and the European Union[1]

Total economy sector S.1

£ million

		1999 /00	2000 /01	2001 /02	2002 /03	2003 /04	2004 /05	2005 /06	2006 /07	2007 /08	2008 /09
Generation of income											
Uses											
Taxes on products and imports											
Value added tax (VAT)											
Paid to central government	NZGF	58,688	60,746	64,735	69,087	76,633	79,979	81,505	87,739	89,891	85,350
Paid to the European Union	FJKM	3,451	4,172	3,592	2,518	2,574	1,905	1,964	2,288	2,571	2,455
Total	QYRC	62,127	64,908	68,322	71,599	79,201	81,869	83,421	89,855	92,433	..
Taxes and duties on imports excluding VAT											
Paid to EU: import duties	FJWE	2,049	2,103	2,024	1,893	1,957	2,207	2,264	2,332	2,462	2,667
Taxes on products excluding VAT and import duties											
Paid to central government											
Customs and Excise revenue											
Beer	GTAM	2,848	2,798	2,907	2,952	3,084	3,099	3,092	3,068	3,034	..
Wines, cider, perry & spirits	GTAN	3,652	3,814	4,068	4,430	4,526	4,790	4,784	4,846	5,181	..
Tobacco	GTAO	7,796	7,638	7,639	8,046	8,092	8,113	7,952	8,146	8,006	..
Hydrocarbon oils	GTAP	22,510	22,630	21,916	22,147	22,780	23,313	23,438	23,585	24,905	..
Betting, gaming & lottery	CJQY	1,500	1,517	1,317	977	898	876	884	958	961	..
Air passenger duty	CWAA	882	956	802	804	799	872	906	1,114	1,949	..
Insurance premium tax	CWAD	1,511	1,751	1,921	2,189	2,313	2,353	2,349	2,317	2,314	..
Landfill tax	BKOF	456	475	501	545	639	673	754	837	898	..
Other	ACDN	-	-	-	-	-	-	-	-	-	..
Fossil fuel levy	CIQY	84	52	92	9	-	-	-	-	-	-
Gas levy	GTAZ	-	-	-	-	-	-	-	-	-	..
Stamp duties	GTBC	6,898	8,165	6,983	7,549	7,544	8,966	10,918	13,386	14,123	..
Camelot payments to National Lottery											
Distribution Fund	LIYH	1,593	1,542	1,520	1,382	1,311	1,354	1,397	1,366	1,349	..
Hydro-benefit	LITN	38	44	44	44	43	40	-	-	-	..
Aggregates Levy	MDUQ	-	-	-	293	341	326	323	327	340	..
Climate change levy	LSNT	-	-	822	813	816	750	741	711	705	..
Renewable energy obligations	EP89	-	-	-	265	375	368	381	389	..	..
Other taxes and levies	GCSP	-	-	-	-	-	-	-	-	-	..
Total paid to central government	NMBV	49,768	51,382	50,551	52,486	53,664	56,183	57,965	61,268	64,434	58,989
Paid to the European Union											
Sugar levy	GTBA	46	43	27	25	19	24	24	-	-	-
Total paid to the European Union	FJWG	46	43	27	25	19	24	24	-	-	..
Total taxes on products excluding VAT & import duties	QYRA	49,814	51,425	50,578	52,511	53,643	55,989	57,945	61,050	64,415	..
Total taxes on products and imports	NZGW	113,990	118,436	120,924	126,003	134,801	140,065	143,630	153,236	159,313	
Production taxes other than on products											
Paid to central government											
Consumer Credit Act fees	CUDB	156	171	157	200	211	223	189	234	328	..
National non-domestic rates	CUKY	14,353	15,154	16,252	16,728	16,902	17,206	18,147	19,168	19,584	21,072
Old style non-domestic rates	NSEZ	123	132	131	136	140	146	193	326	372	..
Levies paid to CG levy-funded bodies	LITK	234	213	215	190	194	218	239	244	256	..
Motor vehicle duties paid by businesses	EKED	1,559	1,230	751	736	787	802	850	869	880	..
Regulator fees	GCSQ	86	105	95	94	101	88	74	71	75	..
Total	NMBX	16,511	17,005	17,601	18,084	18,360	18,802	19,793	20,912	21,484	22,990
Paid to local government											
Old style non-domestic rates	NMYH	144	150	161	176	181	167	187	207	229	245
Total production taxes other than on products	NMYD	16,655	17,155	17,762	18,260	18,541	18,969	19,980	21,119	21,713	23,440
Total taxes on production and imports, paid											
Paid to central government	NMBY	124,727	129,536	133,199	140,152	148,753	154,962	159,281	169,874	175,806	167,483
Paid to local government	NMYH	144	150	161	176	181	167	187	207	229	245
Paid to the European Union	FJWB	5,546	6,318	5,643	4,436	4,550	4,136	4,252	4,620	5,033	5,122
Total	NZGX	130,645	135,591	138,686	144,263	153,367	159,094	163,486	174,793	181,032	..

23.6(b) Taxes paid by UK residents to general government and the European Union[1]

Total economy sector S.1

Continued

£ million

		1999 /00	2000 /01	2001 /02	2002 /03	2003 /04	2004 /05	2005 /06	2006 /07	2007 /08	2008 /09
Secondary distribution of income											
Uses											
Current taxes on income, wealth etc											
Taxes on income											
Paid to central government											
Household income taxes	DRWH	96,977	106,866	108,526	110,407	112,356	121,273	130,555	141,226	152,194	144,443
Petroleum revenue tax	DBHA	853	1,518	1,310	958	1,179	1,284	2,016	2,155	1,680	2,567
Windfall tax	EYNK	-	-	-	-	-	-	-	-	-	-
Other corporate taxes	BMNX	1,842	3,458	3,302	2,657	3,974	4,445	5,539	7,006	8,029	..
Total	NMCU	133,994	144,263	145,185	143,256	145,487	160,490	179,960	194,198	208,122	200,815
Other current taxes											
Paid to central government											
Motor vehicle duty paid by households	CDDZ	3,296	3,039	3,540	3,600	3,902	3,935	4,100	4,270	4,513	4,684
Old style domestic rates	NSFA	117	108	109	104	129	227	235	247	272	284
Licences	NSNP	8	2	-	-	-	-	-	-	-	-
National non-domestic rates paid by non-market sectors	BMNY	1,002	997	1,065	1,013	1,008	1,093	1,221	1,274	1,313	1,362
Passport fees	E8A6	89	113	139	153	198	237	285	346	..	..
Television licence fee	DH7A	2,286	2,064	2,183	2,287	2,391	2,508	2,623	2,734	..	..
Total	NMCV	6,798	6,323	7,036	7,157	7,633	8,019	8,484	8,902	9,374	9,519
Paid to local government											
Old style domestic rates	NMHK	68	76	80	85	92	111	149	157	173	..
Council tax	NMHM	12,918	14,155	15,371	16,809	18,911	20,190	21,227	22,299	23,398	..
Total	NMIS	12,986	14,231	15,451	16,894	19,016	20,335	21,375	22,497	23,677	24,729
Total	NVCM	19,784	20,554	22,487	24,051	26,649	28,354	29,859	31,399	33,051	34,446
Total current taxes on income, wealth etc											
Paid to central government	NMCP	140,792	150,586	152,215	150,447	153,191	168,509	188,444	203,400	217,662	210,532
Paid to local government	NMIS	12,986	14,231	15,451	16,894	19,016	20,335	21,375	22,497	23,677	24,729
Total	NMZL	153,778	164,817	167,666	167,341	172,207	188,844	209,819	225,897	241,339	235,261
Social contributions											
Actual social contributions											
Paid to central government											
(National Insurance Contributions)											
Employers' compulsory contributions	CEAN	31,705	35,212	35,816	35,476	41,459	44,864	47,425	50,356	54,030	55,952
Employees' compulsory contributions	GCSE	23,289	24,772	25,130	25,701	31,013	33,088	35,181	37,426	39,250	..
Self- and non-employed persons' compulsory contributions	NMDE	1,941	2,084	2,216	2,352	2,676	2,744	2,852	2,956	3,032	3,112
Total	AIIH	56,935	62,068	63,162	63,529	75,148	80,923	85,559	90,916	95,437	96,961
Capital account											
Changes in liabilities and net worth											
Other capital taxes											
Paid to central government											
Inheritance tax	GILF	2,016	2,181	2,346	2,323	2,486	2,874	3,226	3,508	3,814	..
Tax on other capital transfers	GILG	38	55	37	47	35	48	50	50	50	..
Development land tax and other	GCSV	-	-	-	-	-	-	-	-	-	..
Total	NMGI	2,054	2,236	2,383	2,370	2,521	2,941	3,276	3,618	3,890	23,783
Total taxes and compulsory social contributions											
Paid to central government	GCSS	324,736	344,015	350,642	355,995	379,465	406,928	436,107	467,323	492,501	..
Paid to local government	GCST	13,130	14,381	15,612	17,070	19,195	20,498	21,563	22,663	23,800	..
Paid to the European Union	FJWB	5,546	6,318	5,643	4,436	4,550	4,136	4,252	4,620	5,033	5,122
Total	GCSU	343,412	364,714	371,897	377,501	403,258	431,975	462,356	495,079	520,614	504,909
Total taxes and social contributions as percentage of GDP	GDWM	36	37	36	35	35	36	36	37	37	..

Sources: HM Treasury;
Office for National Statistics

1 See chapter text.

23.7 Borrowing and repayment of debt[1]

United Kingdom
Years ending 31 March

£ million

		1999 /00	2000 /01	2001 /02	2002 /03	2003 /04	2004 /05
Borrowing							
Government securities: new issues	KQGA	26,426.5	25,789.8	43,433.4	54,068.9	53,220.9	57,290.5
National savings securities:							
National savings certificates	KQGB	1,962.7	3,086.2	2,580.7	2,434.3	1,940.4	1,696.4
Capital bonds	KQGC	35.4	29.0	40.9	107.3	65.0	25.2
Income bonds	KQGD	653.4	760.5	625.6	484.8	415.3	426.6
Deposit bonds	KQGE	..	..	..	..	-	..
British savings bonds	KQGF	..	..	..	..	-	..
Premium savings bonds	KQGG	3,449.4	3,296.0	3,859.6	4,604.5	7,530.1	5,737.8
Residual Account	JT3F	..	..	..	..	..	..
Save As You Earn	KQGH	5.0	0.3	..	..	..	..
Yearly plan	KQGI	..	..	..	..	-	..
National savings stamps and gift tokens	KQGJ	..	..	..	..	-	..
National Savings Bank Investments	KQGK	901.6	955.3	864.9	1,012.4	809.9	817.5
Children's Bonus Bonds	KGVO	58.5	53.4	45.0	54.0	51.7	66.8
Direct Saver Account	KNE3	..	..	..	..	..	..
NS&I Main Account	KNE4						
First Option Bonds	KIAR	34.3	..	..	..	-	..
Pensioners Guaranteed Income Bond	KJDW	590.7	687.2	603.5	662.9	274.2	323.9
Treasurer's account	KWNF	13.6	12.5	15.2	19.4	13.9	11.1
Individual Savings Account	ZAFC	257.8	265.9	397.8	405.6	335.4	276.4
Fixed Rate Savings Bonds	ZAFD	175.9	284.7	192.7	193.0	82.0	86.3
Guaranteed Equity Bonds	ECPU	..	..	27.2	274.8	227.9	317.1
Easy Access Savings Account	C3OM	..	..	..	..	126.9	903.5
Certificate of tax deposit	KQGL	121.4	76.5	77.6	59.6	145.2	114.8
Certificate of tax deposit - monies returned	KNE5	..	..	..	..	..	..
Nationalised industries', etc temporary deposits	KQGM	40,343.3	56,106.6	62,150.0	55,395.1	47,958.6	25,022.0
Sterling Treasury bills (net receipt)	KQGO	..	..	..	..	-	..
ECU Treasury bills (net receipt)	KQGP	..	..	..	..	-	..
ECU Treasury notes (net receipt)	KDZZ	721.1	..	..	..	-	..
Ways and means (net receipt)	KQGQ	5,599.0	12,126.0	12,095.3	3,899.9	22,700.2	..
Other debt: payable in sterling:							
Interest free notes	KQGR	373.5	972.7	1,427.2	754.0	1,213.2	662.3
Other debt: payable in external currencies	KHCY	..	..	..	..	1,792.5	..
Total receipts	KHCZ	81,723.0	104,503.0	128,437.0	124,430.0	138,903.0	93,778.0
Repayment of debt							
Government securities: redemptions	KQGS	19,815.8	33,722.2	43,642.3	42,109.9	35,087.4	25,130.1
Statutory sinking funds	KQGT	2.0	2.0	1.9	1.9	1.8	1.8
Terminable annuities:							
National Debt Commissioners	KQGU	..	..	..	..	-	..
National savings securities:							
National savings certificates	KQGV	2,405.2	4,546.8	4,177.7	4,146.7	2,769.1	1,979.6
Capital bonds	KQGW	324.2	375.0	175.9	155.9	116.9	121.1
Income bonds	KQGX	1,686.3	857.0	933.8	1,144.2	977.1	879.5
Deposit bonds	KQGY	70.2	71.1	45.4	369.9	4.4	..
Yearly Plan	KQGZ	141.8	18.4	4.5	3.0	2.0	..
British savings bonds	KQHA	..	..	..	..	-	..
Premium savings bonds	KQHB	1,923.8	1,872.6	1,942.9	2,343.3	2,967.4	3,492.4
Direct Saver Account	KNE6	..	..	..	..	..	..
NS&I Main Account	KNE7	..	..	..	..	..	..
Residual Account	JT3G	..	..	..	..	..	..
Save As You Earn	KQHC	34.5	22.9	8.0	.	0.5	..
National savings stamps and gift tokens	KQHD	..	..	..	..	-	1.2
National Savings Bank Investments (repayments)	KQHE	1,886.3	1,654.1	1,415.8	1,350.1	1,342.7	1,554.0
Children's Bonus Bonds	KGVQ	69.3	95.0	114.5	92.6	79.8	84.5
First Option Bonds	KIAS	298.1	225.2	111.6	77.4	62.2	33.4
Pensioners Guaranteed Income Bond	KPOB	935.3	2,003.8	1,640.4	703.9	538.5	445.0
Treasurer's account	KWNG	16.4	13.9	16.5	16.9	14.2	16.2
Individual Savings Account	ZAFE	12.3	39.9	70.3	105.9	157.6	202.2
Fixed Rate Savings Bonds	ZAFF	2.8	62.1	110.1	133.6	153.1	92.1
Guaranteed Equity Bonds	JUWE	..	..	..	3.9	3.3	..
Easy Access Savings Account	C3ON	..	..	..	..	126.9	189.3
Certificates of tax deposit	KQHF	159.9	120.1	91.4	161.5	113.1	171.9

23.7 Borrowing and repayment of debt[1]

United Kingdom
Years ending 31 March

£ million

		1999 /00	2000 /01	2001 /02	2002 /03	2003 /04	2004 /05
Tax reserve certificates	**KQHG**	..	..	..	..	-	..
Nationalised industries', etc temporary deposits	**KQHH**	41,089.4	56,004.0	63,127.9	55,695.6	47,757.7	25,949.5
Debt to the Bank of England	**KPOC**	..	..	..	..	-	..
Sterling Treasury bills (net repayment)	**KQHJ**	3,014.8	6,194.2	..	..	-	..
ECU Treasury bills (net repayment)	**KJEG**	2,492.9		..	..	-	..
ECU Treasury notes (net repayment)	**KSPA**	..	1,391.9	1,359.6	1,453.1	-	..
Ways and means (net repayment)	**KQHK**	..	..	..	..	-	9,760.2
Other debt: payable in sterling:							
Interest free notes	**KQHL**	246.4	458.2	1,723.3	1,393.3	990.5	300.4
Other	**KQHM**	..	..	..	..	-	..
Other debt : payable in external currencies	**KQHN**	98.1	1,835.6	2,838.1	1,960.3	47.0	46.5
Total payments	**KQHO**	76,726.0	111,586.0	123,552.0	113,426.0	93,313.0	70,451.0
Net borrowing	**KQHP**	4,997.3	..	4,884.7	11,004.4	45,590.1	23,327.3
Net repayment	**KHDD**	..	7,083.4	..	..	-	..

Note: the table excludes transactions in treasury bills issued for the Special
Liquidity scheme
1 See chapter text.

23.7 Borrowing and repayment of debt[1]

United Kingdom
Years ending 31 March

		2005 /06	2006 /07	2007 /08	2008 /09	2009 /10	£ million 2010 /11
Borrowing							
Government securities: new issues	KQGA	80,668.9	66,233.4	64,197.4	276,504.4	352,475.9	167,903.8
National savings securities:							
National savings certificates	KQGB	1,206.8	1,464.7	2,524.9	3,390.9	1,051.7	2,072.1
Capital bonds	KQGC	34.3	20.7	31.6	0.0	0.0	0.0
Income bonds	KQGD	567.5	593.5	1,502.6	3,213.2	1,437.1	678.4
Deposit bonds	KQGE	..	..	..	..		
British savings bonds	KQGF	..	..	..	..		
Premium savings bonds	KQGG	7,817.5	8,432.5	6,573.2	8,472.2	6,578.0	2,693.8
Residual Account	JT3F	..	..	..	343.3	29.7	27.5
Save As You Earn	KQGH	..	..	..	..		
Yearly plan	KQGI	..	..	..	..		
National savings stamps and gift tokens	KQGJ	..	..	..	..		
National Savings Bank Investments	KQGK	643.6	558.4	535.7	1,071.8	481.4	164.5
Children's Bonus Bonds	KGVO	59.5	54.1	54.1	46.8	34.1	12.2
Direct Saver Account	KNE3	..	..	..		65.3	1,297.9
NS&I Main Account	KNE4					0.0	6,420.1
First Option Bonds	KIAR	..	..	..	..		
Pensioners Guaranteed Income Bond	KJDW	142.7	216.4	371.3	0.3	0.0	0.0
Treasurer's account	KWNF	10.9	11.6	2.4	-	0.0	0.0
Individual Savings Account	ZAFC	261.3	1,015.1	1,394.2	835.0	375.1	243.2
Fixed Rate Savings Bonds	ZAFD	51.2	69.5	347.4	4,327.6	5,777.4	60.3
Guaranteed Equity Bonds	ECPU	81.4	62.1	56.0	99.9	79.8	0.0
Easy Access Savings Account	C3OM	608.6	513.2	933.4	3,763.5	836.2	268.0
Certificate of tax deposit	KQGL	110.6	100.2	163.7	1,301.7	507.3	383.5
Certificate of tax deposit - monies returned	KNE5	..	..	..	..	218.8	10.4
Nationalised industries', etc temporary deposits	KQGM	22,039.1	35,224.0	51,365.0	60,200.9	78,442.6	63,527.7
Sterling Treasury bills (net receipt)	KQGO	..	..	..	..		
ECU Treasury bills (net receipt)	KQGP	..	..	..	..		
ECU Treasury notes (net receipt)	KDZZ	..	..	..	..		
Ways and means (net receipt)	KQGQ	..	23,428.0	12,810.5	-	0.0	4,513.0
Other debt: payable in sterling:							
Interest free notes	KQGR	1,858.9	1,049.9	97.2	822.8	2,317.2	594.0
Other debt: payable in external currencies	KHCY	..	..	..	..		
Total receipts	KHCZ	116,163.0	139,047.0	142,961.0	364,394.0	450,707.6	250,870.4
Repayment of debt							
Government securities: redemptions	KQGS	17,456.5	62,406.9	32,940.2	37,503.6	150,276.4	53,445.7
Statutory sinking funds	KQGT	0.4	..	..	..		
Terminable annuities:							
National Debt Commissioners	KQGU	..	..	..	..		
National savings securities:							
National savings certificates	KQGV	1,107.4	1,172.1	1,201.9	1,240.2	1,829.1	954.3
Capital bonds	KQGW	159.2	137.4	184.0	229.0	225.9	130.1
Income bonds	KQGX	724.6	719.2	712.8	2,145.1	2,119.9	1,065.7
Deposit bonds	KQGY	..	..	..	..		
Yearly Plan	KQGZ	..	0.8	4.9	19.3	0.0	0.0
British savings bonds	KQHA	..	..	..	..		
Premium savings bonds	KQHB	3,289.2	4,279.8	4,952.3	4,613.9	5,718.2	3,759.3
Direct Saver Account	KNE6	..	..	..	..	15.9	407.1
NS&I Main Account	KNE7	..	..	..	..		3,861.6
Residual Account	JT3G	..	..	..	14.9	28.9	50.0
Save AsYou Earn	KQHC	0.5	0.5	1.6	10.1	0.0	0.0
National savings stamps and gift tokens	KQHD	..	..	..	..		
National Savings Bank Investments (repayments)	KQHE	1,153.3	1,172.4	976.8	1,058.2	1,106.6	703.0
Children's Bonus Bonds	KGVQ	95.8	105.7	108.5	106.1	106.9	82.7
First Option Bonds	KIAS	36.1	25.6	26.6	25.2	37.8	16.8
Pensioners Guaranteed Income Bond	KPOB	428.6	452.7	543.1	1,343.0	683.3	123.9
Treasurer's account	KWNG	18.3	11.7	47.1	18.6	0.0	0.0
Individual Savings Account	ZAFE	194.1	193.6	274.9	822.2	997.8	433.9
Fixed Rate Savings Bonds	ZAFF	105.0	77.2	104.2	246.8	1,164.9	2,672.1
Guaranteed Equity Bonds	JUWE	0.2	3.7	365.9	370.3	330.3	86.8
Easy Access Savings Account	C3ON	400.6	509.7	544.6	1,507.3	2,016.9	1,150.8
Certificates of tax deposit	KQHF	152.1	56.0	88.0	608.8	1,028.4	533.2

23.7 Borrowing and repayment of debt[1]

United Kingdom
Years ending 31 March

£ million

		2005 /06	2006 /07	2007 /08	2008 /09	2009 /10	2010 /11
Tax reserve certificates	**KQHG**	..	..	..	.. ..	..	
Nationalised industries', etc temporary deposits	**KQHH**	21,943.1	35,686.5	48,265.0	55,847.8	78,523.6	63,413.8
Debt to the Bank of England	**KPOC**	..	..	..	.. ..	..	
Sterling Treasury bills (net repayment)	**KQHJ**	..	..	..	.. ..	..	
ECU Treasury bills (net repayment)	**KJEG**	..	..	..	.. ..	..	
ECU Treasury notes (net repayment)	**KSPA**	..	..	..	.. ..	..	
Ways and means (net repayment)	**KQHK**	36,207.3	..	..	3,161.7	27,040.3	0.0
Other debt: payable in sterling:							
Interest free notes	**KQHL**	222.3	586.4	474.4	1,092.9	975.0	2,030.3
Other	**KQHM**	..	..	..	..		
Other debt : payable in external currencies	**KQHN**	98.9	52.4	-	..		
Total payments	**KQHO**	83,794.0	107,650.0	91,817.0	111,985.0	274,226.1	134,921.1
Net borrowing	**KQHP**	32,369.3	31,397.0	51,143.8	252,409.3	176,481.5	115,949.3
Net repayment	**KHDD**	..	..	..	..		

Source: HM Treasury: 0207 270 4761

Note: the table excludes transactions in treasury bills issued for the Special
Liquidity scheme
1 See chapter text.

23.8 Central government net cash requirement on own account (receipts and outlays on a cash basis)

£ million

	Cash receipts								Cash outlays				Own account net cash requirement
	HM Revenue and Customs												
	Total paid over[1]	Income tax[2]	Corpora-tion tax[2]	NICs[3]	V.A.T.[4]	Interest and dividends	Other receipts[5]	Total	Interest payments	Net acquisition of company securities[6]	Net departmental outlays[7]	Total	
	1	2	3	4	5	6	7	8	9	10	11	12	13
	MIZX	RURC	ACCD	ABLP	EYOO	RUUL	RUUM	RUUN	RUUO	ABIF	RUUP	RUUQ	RUUX
2000	305,547	103,118	33,003	59,274	58,509	9,009	46,078	360,634	23,890	-251	297,933	321,572	-39,062
2001	316,517	111,874	33,520	62,973	60,282	8,611	24,643	349,771	23,132	-661	324,633	347,104	-2,667
2002	315,987	111,559	28,866	63,992	63,000	6,954	25,310	348,251	19,343	0	347,612	366,955	18,704
2003	325,138	113,712	28,489	69,360	67,525	7,335	25,329	357,802	20,348	-39	379,418	399,727	41,925
2004	347,514	121,493	31,160	77,026	71,907	6,855	25,137	379,506	21,027	0	400,631	421,658	42,152
2005	372,567	130,818	37,820	83,612	73,012	6,549	26,341	405,457	22,434	0	421,021	443,455	37,998
2006	401,362	140,616	47,108	87,156	76,103	6,640	28,115	436,117	25,834	-347	448,131	473,618	37,501
2007	422,465	149,968	43,912	96,656	80,301	8,251	30,083	460,799	25,537	-2,340	470,169	493,366	32,567
2008	428,380	157,500	46,487	98,504	80,709	9,354	30,556	468,290	26,033	19,714	544,720	590,467	122,177
2009	384,875	147,425	35,402	95,053	68,637	6,666	31,282	422,823	29,304	41,809	548,810	619,923	197,100
2010	411,846	147,768	41,174	95,884	80,851	5,274	34,062	451,182	34,029	0	569,599	603,628	152,458
2000/01	309,726	108,414	32,421	60,614	58,501	8,715	46,772	365,213	23,798	-81	304,245	327,962	-37,251
2001/02	314,959	111,028	32,041	63,168	61,026	7,843	25,001	347,803	22,126	-683	329,726	351,169	3,366
2002/03	317,174	111,102	29,268	64,553	63,451	7,425	24,725	349,324	19,687	-39	353,890	373,538	24,214
2003/04	331,133	116,194	28,077	72,457	69,075	7,172	25,348	363,653	21,251	0	385,119	406,370	42,717
2004/05	355,917	125,202	33,641	78,098	73,026	6,633	25,074	387,624	21,810	0	403,268	425,078	37,454
2005/06	382,067	133,519	41,829	85,522	72,856	6,393	27,022	415,482	23,121	-347	428,616	451,390	35,908
2006/07	406,337	147,134	44,308	87,274	77,360	6,754	27,359	440,450	26,279	0	451,062	477,341	36,891
2007/08	431,800	152,591	46,383	100,411	80,601	9,000	31,205	472,005	25,390	-2,340	478,576	501,626	29,621
2008/09	416,512	155,704	43,077	96,884	78,439	8,724	28,008	453,244	25,947	32,250	557,560	615,757	162,513
2009/10	382,331	141,774	35,805	95,516	70,160	6,201	32,326	420,858	32,189	29,273	557,111	618,573	197,715
2010/11	419,580	151,604	42,016	96,509	83,486	5,559	38,584	463,723	36,607	0	564,832	601,439	137,728
2000 Q1	84,955	32,523	8,856	15,502	14,593	2,915	4,527	92,397	4,555	-148	73,814	78,221	-14,176
2000 Q2	71,699	22,831	4,997	14,991	14,290	1,753	18,343	91,795	7,492	0	71,815	79,307	-12,488
2000 Q3	75,188	26,391	7,256	14,777	14,294	1,799	16,727	93,714	4,597	-103	73,311	77,805	-15,909
2000 Q4	73,705	21,373	11,894	14,004	15,332	2,542	6,481	82,728	7,246	0	78,993	86,239	3,511
2001 Q1	89,134	37,819	8,274	16,842	14,585	2,621	5,221	96,976	4,463	22	80,126	84,611	-12,365
2001 Q2	72,882	24,620	5,966	15,923	15,008	2,120	5,587	80,589	6,969	0	80,187	87,156	6,567
2001 Q3	77,727	27,340	7,322	15,800	14,707	1,958	6,631	86,316	4,754	-683	76,620	80,691	-5,625
2001 Q4	76,774	22,095	11,958	14,408	15,982	1,912	7,204	85,890	6,946	0	87,700	94,646	8,756
2002 Q1	87,576	36,973	6,795	17,037	15,329	1,853	5,579	95,008	3,457	0	85,219	88,676	-6,332
2002 Q2	74,585	24,145	5,793	16,649	15,779	1,688	5,472	81,745	6,254	0	84,027	90,281	8,536
2002 Q3	78,319	27,737	7,138	15,720	15,171	1,797	7,516	87,632	3,682	0	85,156	88,838	1,206
2002 Q4	75,507	22,704	9,140	14,586	16,721	1,616	6,743	83,866	5,950	0	93,210	99,160	15,294
2003 Q1	88,763	36,516	7,197	17,598	15,780	2,324	4,994	96,081	3,801	-39	91,497	95,259	-822
2003 Q2	76,531	25,184	5,869	17,760	16,529	1,547	6,240	84,318	7,053	0	95,376	102,429	18,111
2003 Q3	81,637	28,919	7,262	17,404	17,047	1,728	6,901	90,266	4,167	0	93,496	97,663	7,397
2003 Q4	78,207	23,093	8,161	16,598	18,169	1,736	7,194	87,137	5,327	0	99,049	104,376	17,239
2004 Q1	94,758	38,998	6,785	20,695	17,330	2,161	5,013	101,932	4,704	0	97,198	101,902	-30
2004 Q2	82,029	25,114	7,110	20,601	18,039	1,546	5,791	89,366	5,140	0	98,121	103,261	13,895
2004 Q3	87,673	31,464	8,045	18,585	17,707	1,549	7,474	96,696	5,192	0	98,424	103,616	6,920
2004 Q4	83,054	25,917	9,220	17,145	18,831	1,599	6,859	91,512	5,991	0	106,888	112,879	21,367
2005 Q1	103,161	42,707	9,266	21,767	18,449	1,939	4,950	110,050	5,487	0	99,835	105,322	-4,728
2005 Q2	86,274	28,884	7,766	20,941	17,342	1,469	6,592	94,335	5,568	0	105,729	111,297	16,962
2005 Q3	94,524	32,042	9,765	22,007	18,188	1,611	7,430	103,565	5,836	0	105,215	111,051	7,486
2005 Q4	88,608	27,185	11,023	18,897	19,033	1,530	7,369	97,507	5,543	0	110,242	115,785	18,278

23.8 Central government net cash requirement on own account (receipts and outlays on a cash basis)

£ million

	Cash receipts								Cash outlays				Own account net cash requirement
	Total paid over[1]	HM Revenue and Customs								Net acquisition of company securities[6]	Net departmental outlays[7]		
		Income tax[2]	Corpora-tion tax[2]	NICs[3]	V.A.T.[4]	Interest and dividends	Other receipts[5]	Total	Interest payments			Total	
	1	2	3	4	5	6	7	8	9	10	11	12	13
	MIZX	**RURC**	**ACCD**	**ABLP**	**EYOO**	**RUUL**	**RUUM**	**RUUN**	**RUUO**	**ABIF**	**RUUP**	**RUUQ**	**RUUX**
2006 Q1	112,661	45,408	13,275	23,677	18,293	1,783	5,631	120,075	6,174	-347	107,430	113,257	-6,818
2006 Q2	91,224	30,604	7,882	22,211	18,021	1,497	6,459	99,180	5,298	0	117,434	122,732	23,552
2006 Q3	100,664	35,891	12,958	20,798	18,731	1,428	8,403	110,495	8,628	0	108,129	116,757	6,262
2006 Q4	96,813	28,713	12,993	20,470	21,058	1,932	7,622	106,367	5,734	0	115,138	120,872	14,505
2007 Q1	117,636	51,926	10,475	23,795	19,550	1,897	4,875	124,408	6,619	0	110,361	116,980	-7,428
2007 Q2	96,004	29,417	8,015	25,932	20,123	1,864	8,204	106,072	5,959	-2,340	121,026	124,645	18,573
2007 Q3	107,134	37,488	12,465	24,165	19,301	1,986	9,934	119,054	6,486	0	114,418	120,904	1,850
2007 Q4	101,691	31,137	12,957	22,764	21,327	2,504	7,070	111,265	6,473	0	124,364	130,837	19,572
2008 Q1	126,971	54,549	12,946	27,550	19,850	2,646	5,997	135,614	6,472	0	118,768	125,240	-10,374
2008 Q2	97,153	34,333	8,509	23,517	20,087	2,252	8,154	107,559	6,449	0	131,441	137,890	30,331
2008 Q3	108,990	39,286	12,742	24,801	21,235	2,266	9,143	120,399	6,566	-255	150,477	156,788	36,389
2008 Q4	95,266	29,332	12,290	22,636	19,537	2,190	7,262	104,718	6,546	19,969	144,034	170,549	65,831
2009 Q1	115,103	52,753	9,536	25,930	17,580	2,016	3,449	120,568	6,386	12,536	131,608	150,530	29,962
2009 Q2	85,699	31,277	6,362	22,727	16,102	1,892	9,626	97,217	8,534	-2,021	145,058	151,571	54,354
2009 Q3	93,410	35,562	8,049	23,574	16,847	1,357	9,721	104,488	7,577	0	133,158	140,735	36,247
2009 Q4	90,663	27,833	11,455	22,822	18,108	1,401	8,486	100,550	6,807	31,294	138,986	177,087	76,537
2010 Q1	112,559	47,102	9,939	26,393	19,103	1,551	4,493	118,603	9,271	0	139,909	149,180	30,577
2010 Q2	94,699	34,346	7,148	22,894	19,881	1,049	8,869	104,617	6,963	0	147,380	154,343	49,727
2010 Q3	107,569	37,462	11,267	23,907	20,564	1,370	11,556	120,495	10,789	0	136,851	147,640	27,156
2010 Q4	97,019	28,858	12,820	22,690	21,303	1,304	9,144	107,467	7,006	0	145,459	152,465	44,998
2011 Q1	120,293	50,938	10,781	27,018	21,738	1,836	9,015	131,144	11,849	0	135,142	146,991	15,847

Sources: HM Revenue & Customs; Office for National Statistics

Relationships between columns 1+6+7=8; 9+10+11=12; 12-8=13

1 Comprises payments into the Consolidated Fund and all payovers of NICS excluding those for Northern Ireland.

2 Income tax includes capital gains tax and is net of any tax credits treated by HM Revenue and Customs as tax deductions.

3 UK receipts net of personal pension rebates; gross of Statutory Maternity Pay and Statutory Sick Pay.

4 Payments into Consolidated Fund.

5 Including some elements of expenditure not separately identified.

6 Mainly comprises privatisation proceeds.

7 Net of certain receipts, and excluding on-lending to local authorities and public corporations.

23.9 HM Revenue and Customs taxes and duties

£ million

		Net receipts by HM Revenue and Customs					Payments into Consolidated Fund[6]	Advance cor- poration tax
	Total[1,6]	Income tax and Capital gains tax[2,3]	Corpor- ation tax[4]	Inheritance tax[6]	Stamp duties	Petroleum revenue tax[5]		
	MDXD	RURC	ACCD	ACCH	ACCI	ACCJ	ACAB	ACCN
2000	148,231	103,118	33,003	2,203	8,367	1,540	145,975	-445
2001	156,638	111,874	33,520	2,374	7,344	1,526	151,159	-295
2002	151,166	111,559	28,866	2,364	7,431	946	146,418	-219
2003	153,003	113,712	28,489	2,400	7,256	1,146	144,533	-71
2004	165,564	121,493	31,160	2,861	8,884	1,166	153,699	-32
2005	183,481	130,818	37,820	3,134	9,912	1,799	170,130	-73
2006	206,851	140,616	47,108	3,507	13,070	2,546	192,715	-21
2007	213,705	149,968	43,912	3,804	14,635	1,387	200,127	0
2008	219,318	157,500	46,487	3,169	9,497	2,663	202,283	0
2009	193,358	147,425	35,402	2,343	7,141	1,047	171,509	0
2010	202,082	147,768	41,174	2,632	9,099	1,349	182,469	0
2000/01	152,741	108,414	32,421	2,223	8,165	1,518	149,085	-449
2001/02	153,719	111,028	32,041	2,357	6,983	1,310	149,114	-188
2002/03	151,233	111,102	29,268	2,356	7,549	958	145,899	-182
2003/04	155,498	116,194	28,077	2,504	7,544	1,179	145,555	-74
2004/05	172,017	125,202	33,641	2,924	8,966	1,284	158,974	-33
2005/06	191,540	133,519	41,829	3,258	10,918	2,016	178,707	-84
2006/07	210,535	147,134	44,308	3,545	13,392	2,155	195,598	-4
2007/08	218,601	152,591	46,383	3,824	14,124	1,680	205,681	0
2008/09	212,187	155,704	43,077	2,837	7,999	2,567	193,539	0
2009/10	188,792	141,774	35,805	2,386	7,903	923	167,703	0
2010/11	206,810	151,604	42,016	2,717	8,932	1,465	183,694	0
2005 Q1	55,047	42,707	9,266	708	1,971	395	51,656	-6
2005 Q2	39,965	28,884	7,766	799	2,285	231	36,762	-7
2005 Q3	46,288	32,042	9,765	839	2,858	784	43,353	-8
2005 Q4	42,181	27,185	11,023	788	2,795	389	38,359	-52
2006 Q1	63,106	45,408	13,275	832	2,976	612	60,233	-17
2006 Q2	42,814	30,604	7,882	874	3,089	365	39,406	-2
2006 Q3	53,944	35,891	12,958	887	3,419	789	47,921	0
2006 Q4	46,987	28,713	12,993	914	3,586	780	45,155	-2
2007 Q1	66,790	51,926	10,475	870	3,298	221	63,116	0
2007 Q2	42,352	29,417	8,015	937	3,727	256	38,704	0
2007 Q3	55,460	37,488	12,465	1,054	3,998	455	52,463	0
2007 Q4	49,103	31,137	12,957	943	3,611	455	45,844	0
2008 Q1	71,686	54,549	12,946	890	2,787	514	68,670	0
2008 Q2	46,490	34,333	8,509	808	2,572	267	41,394	0
2008 Q3	56,375	39,286	12,742	787	2,239	1,320	51,626	0
2008 Q4	44,767	29,332	12,290	684	1,899	562	40,593	0
2009 Q1	64,555	52,753	9,536	558	1,290	418	59,926	0
2009 Q2	40,179	31,277	6,362	552	1,621	367	34,109	0
2009 Q3	46,273	35,562	8,049	617	1,979	66	39,869	0
2009 Q4	42,351	27,833	11,455	616	2,251	196	37,605	0
2010 Q1	59,989	47,102	9,939	601	2,053	294	56,120	0
2010 Q2	44,416	34,346	7,148	667	2,133	101	36,581	0
2010 Q3	52,619	37,462	11,267	716	2,522	634	50,833	0
2010 Q4	45,058	28,858	12,820	648	2,391	320	38,935	0
2011 Q1	64,717	50,938	10,781	686	1,886	410	57,345	0

1 The total is not always equal to the sum of the individual taxes due to rounding.

2 Income tax and Capital gains tax combined.

3 Figures for income tax treat payments of the personal tax credits as negative tax to the extent that the credits are less than or equal to the tax liability of the family. Payments exceeding this liability are treated as public expenditure.

4 Including net advance corporation tax receipts shown separately in the final column.

5 Including net advance petroleum revenue tax.

6 Payments into the consolidated fund are not directly comparable to receipts Over the year payments into the consolidated fund will always be lower than total receipts because the public expenditure element of payments of tax being recorded in receipts. Because the public expenditure element of payments of tax credits (both personal and company) are deducted from the payments into the consolidated fund but have no impact on receipts. In addition, there is a timing difference between payments taking value and hence paid over to the consolidated fund and being recorded in receipts.

Sources: HM Revenue and Customs;
National Statistics

23.10 Income tax: allowances and reliefs[1]

United Kingdom

£

		1999 /00	2000 /01	2001 /02	2002 /03	2003 /04	2004 /05	2005 /06	2006 /07	2007 /08	2008 /09	2009 /10	2010 /11	2011 /12
Personal allowances														
Personal allowance	KDZP	4,335	4,385	4,535	4,615	4,615	4,745	4,895	5,035	5,225	6,035	6,475	6,475	7,475
Married couple's (both partners under 65)[2]	KDZR	1,970	..	..	..	..	..	..	..	..	..	..	..	..
Age allowance:														
Personal (aged 65-74)	KSOH	5,720	5,790	5,990	6,100	6,610	6,830	7,090	7,280	7,550	9,030	9,490	9,490	9,940
Personal (aged 75 or over)	KSOI	5,980	6,050	6,260	6,370	6,720	6,950	7,220	7,420	7,690	9,180	9,640	9,640	10,090
Married couple's (either partner between 65-74 but neither partner 75 or over)[2,3]	KEDI	5,125	5,185	5,365	5,465	5,565	5,725	5,905	6,065	6,285	6,535	..	..	..
Married couple's (either partner 75 or over)[2]	KEIY	5,195	5,255	5,435	5,535	5,635	5,795	5,975	6,135	6,365	6,625	6,965	6,965	7,295
Minimum married couple's allowance	C58D	1,970	2,000	2,070	2,110	2,150	2,210	2,280	2,350	2,440	2,540	2,670	2,670	2,800
Income limit[4]	KEOO	16 800	17 000	17 600	17 900	18 300	18 900	19 500	20 100	20 900	21 800	22 900	22 900	24,000
Additional personal allowance[2]	KEPG	1,970	..	..	..	..	..	..	..	..	..	..	..	..
Income limit for personal allowance													100,000	100,000
Widow's bereavement allowance	KEPH	1,970	..	..	..	..	..	..	..	..	..	..	..	..
Blind person's allowance														
Single or married (one spouse blind)	KSOJ	1,380	1,400	1,450	1,480	1,510	1,560	1,610	1,660	1,730	1,800	1,890	1,890	1,980
Married (both spouses blind)	KSOK	2,760	2,800	2,900	2,960	3,020	3,120	3,220	3,320	3,460	3,600	3,780	3,780	3,960
Life Assurance Relief														
Percentage of gross premium	KFDR	13 or Nil	13 or Nil	13 or Nil	13 or Nil	13 or Nil	13 or Nil	13 or Nil	13 or Nil	13 or Nil	13 or Nil	13 or Nil	13 or Nil	13 or Nil

Source: HM Revenue & Customs: 0207 147 3045

1 See chapter text.

2 The allowance was restricted to 20 per cent in 1994-95, 15 per cent from 1995-96 and 10 per cent from 1999-00.

3 In the 2009-10 tax year all Married Couples Allowance claimants in this category will become 75 at some point during the year and will therefore be entitled to the higher amount of allowance, for those aged 75 and over.

4 If the total income, less allowable deductions of a taxpayer aged 65 or over exceeds the limit, the age-related allowances are reduced by £1 for each £2 of income over the aged income level until the basic levels of the personal and married couple's allowances are reached.

23.11 Rates of Income tax

United Kingdom

	2001/02		2002/03		2003/04		2004/05	
	Bands of taxable income (£)[1]	Rate of tax - Percentages	Bands of taxable income (£)[1]	Rate of tax - Percentages	Bands of taxable income (£)[1]	Rate of tax - Percentages	Bands of taxable income (£)[1]	Rate of tax - Percentages
Starting rate[2]	1-1 880	10	1-1 920	10	1-1 960	10	1-2020	10
Basic rate[3]	1 881 - 29,400	22	1 921 - 29,900	22	1 961 - 30,500	22	2 021 - 31,400	22
Higher rate4	over 29,400	40	over 29,900	40	over 30,500	40	over 31,400	40

	2005/06		2006/07		2007/08		2008/09	
	Bands of taxable income (£)[1]	Rate of tax - Percentages	Bands of taxable income (£)[1]	Rate of tax - Percentages	Bands of taxable income (£)[1]	Rate of tax - Percentages	Bands of taxable income (£)[1]	Rate of tax - Percentages
Starting rate[2]	1-2090	10	1-2150	10	1-2230	10	1-2230	10
Basic rate[3]	2091 - 32,400	22	2 151 - 33,300	22	2231 - 34,600	22	2231 - 34,800	20
Higher rate[4]	over 31,400	40	over 33,300	40	over 34,600	40	over 34,800	40

	2009/10		2010/11		2011/12	
	Bands of taxable income (£)[1]	Rate of tax - Percentages	Bands of taxable income (£)[1]	Rate of tax - Percentages	Bands of taxable income (£)[1]	Rate of tax - Percentages
Starting rate[2]	1-2440	-	1-2440	-	1-2560	-
Basic rate[3]	0 - 37,400	20	0 - 37,400	20	0 - 35,000	20
Higher rate[4]	over 37,400	40	37,401 - 150,000	40	35,001 - 150,000	40
Additional rate	Not applicable		over 150,000	50	over 150 000	50

Source: HM Revenue & Customs: 020 7147 3045

1 Taxable income is defined as gross income for income tax purposes less any allowances and reliefs available at the taxpayer's marginal rate.

2 From 2008-09 there is a 10 per cent starting rate for savings income only. If non-savings income is above this limit then the 10 per cent starting rate for savings does not apply.

3 The basic rate of tax on dividends is 10% and savings income is 20%

4 The higher rate of tax on dividends is 32.5%.

23.12 Rateable Values[1]

England and Wales
At 1 April each year

		1999	2000	2001	2002	2003	2004	2005	2006	2007	2008	2009	2010
Number of properties (Thousands)													
Commercial	KMIN	1,219	1,223	1,230	1,234	1,236	1,239	1,234	1,245	1,258	1,267	1,279	1,296
Shops and cafes	KMIO	484	478	476	473	469	466	462	459	457	456	455	456
Offices	KMIP	258	261	269	273	279	284	287	296	304	311	320	332
Other	KMIQ	477	484	485	487	488	490	485	490	497	500	504	509
On-licensed premises	KMIR	60	61	61	60	60	60	66	65	65	64	63	63
Entertainment and recreational:	KMIS	80	79	79	80	80	80	78	79	81	81	83	85
Cinemas	KMIT	1	1	1	1	1	1	1	1	1	1	1	1
Theatres and music-halls	KMIU	1	1	1	1	1	1	1	1	1	1	1	1
Other	KMIV	79	76	76	77	77	78	76	78	80	80	81	84
Public utility	KMIW	9	8	8	8	8	8	8	8	8	8	7	7
Educational and cultural	KMIX	41	41	42	42	42	43	45	45	45	45	45	46
Miscellaneous	KMIY	61	67	70	70	72	74	74	77	80	81	83	84
Industrial	KMIZ	250	250	251	250	250	250	252	251	252	249	246	247
Total	KMIH	1,720	1,729	1,740	1,745	1,749	1,754	1,756	1,771	1,788	1,796	1,806	1,828
Value of assessments (£ million)													
Commercial	KMHG	19,652	26,320	27,255	27,622	27,713	27,878	33,013	33,548	33,566	33,427	33,728	40,955
Shops and cafes	KMHH	5,840	6,801	6,972	6,953	6,863	6,845	8,257	8,311	8,289	8,251	8,321	9,952
Offices	KMHI	5,575	8,625	9,191	9,388	9,555	9,591	10,840	11,034	10,904	10,724	10,794	13,730
Other	KMHJ	8,237	10,894	11,092	11,281	11,295	11,441	13,916	14,203	14,373	14,452	14,613	17,274
On-licensed premises	KMHK	997	1,311	1,347	1,345	1,334	1,320	1,667	1,652	1,615	1,589	1,567	1,829
Entertainment and recreational	KMHL	1,045	1,310	1,369	1,430	1,416	1,362	1,467	1,483	1,481	1,478	1,466	1,675
Cinemas	KMHM	45	79	92	104	106	96	117	115	110	101	102	104
Theatres and music-halls	KMHN	20	24	25	26	26	26	34	35	35	35	36	43
Other	KMHO	980	1,207	1,252	1,300	1,284	1,240	1,316	1,333	1,337	1,342	1,328	1,529
Public utility	KMHP	3,361	3,828	3,411	3,460	3,444	3,410	3,680	3,668	3,668	3,656	3,471	4,210
Educational and cultural	KMHQ	1,672	1,829	1,872	1,902	1,895	1,904	2,359	2,411	2,407	2,397	2,417	3,052
Miscellaneous	KMHR	1,439	2,142	2,172	2,220	2,218	2,022	2,582	2,646	2,687	2,694	2,697	3,572
Industrial	KMHS	5,463	6,249	6,202	6,157	6,034	5,935	6,651	6,575	6,453	6,314	6,122	6,827
Total	KMHA	33,649	42,985	43,626	44,136	44,053	43,831	51,419	51,983	51,878	51,555	51,468	62,121

Source: HM Revenue & Customs: 0207 147 2941

1 See chapter text.

23.13 Revenue expenditure of local authorities

£ million

	2006/07 outturn	2007/08[10] outturn	2008/09[10] outturn	2009/10[11] outturn	2010/11[11] budget
England					
Education[1]	37,942	40,135	42,148	44,473	45,966
Highways and Transport	5,316	5,634	5,679	6,531	6,661
Social care[2]	18,108	18,587	19,604	20,968	20,857
Housing (excluding HRA)[3]	14,963	15,841	16,964	19,990	19,373
Cultural, environmental and planning	9,658	10,143	10,474	11,064	10,959
of which:					
Cultural	3,129	3,188	3,297	3,465	3,391
Environmental	4,524	4,836	5,087	5,308	5,510
Planning and development	2,005	2,120	2,091	2,290	2,057
Police	11,542	11,704	11,555	12,028	12,165
Fire	2,193	2,233	2,104	2,177	2,284
Courts	62	70	73	71	
Central services	3,430	3,596	3,846	3,690	3,664
Other	128	369	643	266	86
Net current expenditure	103,341	108,341	113,018	121,259	121,994
Capital financing	2,993	3,008	2,971	3,702	3,861
Capital Expenditure charged to Revenue Account	1,103	1,096	1,706	1,964	1,993
Interest receipts	-1,481	-1,862	-1,926	-780	-424
Pension Interest Costs and expected return on Pension assets	4,534	4,808	7,042	7,670	-
Other non-current expenditure[4]	3,350	3,448	3,654	2,003	-
Specific grants outside Aggregate External Finance (AEF)	-19,643	-20,762	-21,772	-24,742	-24,869
Revenue expenditure	88,172	92,384	98,107	103,404	105,790
Specific and special grants inside AEF	-41,741	-44,485	-42,920	-45,767	45,737
Area Based Grant (ABG)	n/a	n/a	-35,050	-3,314	4,679
Net revenue expenditure	46,432	47,899	52,137	54,323	55,373
Appropriation to/from reserves (excluding pension reserves)	974	1,497	248	-308	10
Appropriation to/from Pension Reserves	-6,025	-5,595	-6,395		
Other adjustments	16	2	2	1	-4
Budget requirement	47,421	49,398	52,387	54,016	55,380
Police grant	-3,936	-4,028	-4,136	-4,253	-4,374
Revenue support grant	-3,378	-3,105	-2,854	-4,501	-3,122
Redistributed business rates	-17,506	-18,506	-20,506	-19,515	-21,516
General Greater London Authority Grant	-38	-38	-48	-48	-48
Other items	-111	-111	-85	-65	-65
Council tax requirement	22,453	23,608	24,759	25,633	26,254
Scotland					
Net revenue expenditure on general fund	10,708	11,023	11,981	12,369	12,099

1 Includes mandatory student awards and inter-authority education recoupment.
2 Includes supported employment.
3 Includes mandatory rent allowances and rent rebates.
4 Includes:
(i) Gross expenditure on council tax benefit.
(ii) Expenditure on council tax reduction scheme.
(iii) Discretionary (non-domestic) rate relief.
(iv) Flood defence payments to the Environment Agency.
(v) Bad debt provision.
5 Service expenditure is shown excluding that financed by sales, fees and charges, but including that financed by specific and special government grants.
6 Includes housing benefit and private sector costs such as provision for the homeless. Includes rent rebates granted to HRA tenants which is 100% grant funded. Excludes council owned housing.

7 Includes cemeteries and crematoria, community safety, environmental health, consumer protection, waste collection/disposal and central services to the public such as birth registration and elections.
8 Excludes council tax benefit expednditure funded by the specific grant from the Department for Work and Pensions.
9 Includes agricultural services, coastal and flood defence and community councils. Also includes central administrative costs of corporate management, democratic representation and certain costs, such as those relating to back year or additional pension contributions which should not be allocated to individual services, capital expenditure charged to the revenue account and is net of any interest expected to accrue on balances.
10 Produced on a Financial Reporting Standard 17 (FRS17) basis
11 Produced on a non-FRS17 and PFI off balance sheet basis.

23.13 Revenue expenditure of local authorities

£ million

	2005/06 outturn	2006/07 outturn	2007/08 outturn	2008/09 outturn	2009/10 outturn	2010/11 outturn	2011/12 budget
Wales[5]							
Education	2,213.0	2,325.6	2,427.5	2,427.5	2,550.4	2,584.3	2,576.0
Personal social services	1,253.6	1,302.9	1,348.8	1,348.8	1,418.0	1,461.1	1,440.3
Housing[6]	716.7	759.4	878.2	878.2	985.3	999.5	965.4
Local environmental services[7]	353.9	356.4	393.0	393.0	419.6	423.9	419.1
Roads and transport	283.3	296.4	329.8	329.8	325.3	330.7	316.3
Libraries, culture, heritage, sport and recreation	259.9	267.4	285.8	285.8	296.0	288.2	264.5
Planning, economic development and community development	115.2	113.6	164.7	164.7	152.4	159.0	134.0
Council tax benefit and administration[8]	32.1	31.7	31.5	31.5	32.4	31.3	30.2
Debt financing costs: counties	278.0	289.0	320.5	320.5	316.4	321.3	325.6
Central administrative and other revenue expenditure: counties[9]	207.4	217.3	198.0	198.0	190.1	205.9	302.7
Total county and county borough council expenditure	5,713.1	5,959.8	6,377.8	6,377.8	6,685.8	6,805.3	6,774.2
Total police expenditure	601.4	623.3	642.6	642.6	670.9	666.6	663.0
Total fire expenditure	142.1	138.2	145.0	145.0	150.1	148.0	149.0
Total national park expenditure	15.8	17.8	18.0	18.3	16.1	16.0	16.2
Gross revenue expenditure	6,472.4	6,739.1	7,183.3	7,183.6	7,522.9	7,636.0	7,602.4
less specific and special government grants				1,809.0	1,987.2	2,019.6	1,825.7
(except council tax benefit grant)	-1,529.7	-1,630.2	-1,809.0				
Net revenue expenditure	4,942.7	5,108.9	5,374.3	5,374.6	5,535.7	5,616.4	5,776.7
Putting to (+)/drawing from (-) reserves	24.6	97.0	14.0	14.0	23.9	135.8	-21.6
Budget requirement	4,967.3	5,205.9	5,388.4	5,388.6	5,559.6	5,752.2	5,755.1
Plus discretionary non-domestic rate relief	2.6	2.5	2.4	2.4	2.6	2.8	3.1
less revenue support grant	-2,951.8	-3,061.6	-3,104.6	3,104.6	3,191.7	3,282.4	4,414.9
less police grant	-217.0	-225.0	-230.5	230.5	236.3	242.2	245.7
less re-distributed non-domestic rates income	-730.0	-791.0	-868.0	868.0	894.0	935.0	787.0
Council tax requirement	1,071.2	1,130.8	1,187.9	1,187.9	1,240.2	1,295.4	1,343.3
of which:							
Paid by council tax benefit grant from the Department for Work and Pensions	177.2	184.6	194.8	194.8	218.6	230.9	195.5
Paid directly by council tax payers	894.0	946.2	993.1	993.1	1,021.6	1,064.5	1,147.8

Sources: Communities and Local Government: 0207 944 4158;
Scottish Government, Statistical Support for Local Government: 0131 245 7034;
Welsh Assembly Government: 02920 825355

23.14 Financing of revenue expenditure England and Wales

England and Wales
Years ending 31 March

£ million

		1999 /00	2000 /01	2001 /02	2002 /03	2003 /04	2004 /05	2005 /06	2006 /07	2007 /08	20081 /09	2009 /10	2010 /11	2011 /12 [1]
England[2]														
Revenue expenditure[3]														
Cash £m	**KRTN**	53,651	57,329	61,952	65,898	75,244	79,303	84,422	88,172	92,384	98,107	103,404	104,342	
Government grants														
Cash £m	**KRTO**	26,421	27,809	31,469	32,634	41,777	45,258	45,838	49,093	51,656	53,008	57,883	57,791	..
Percentage of revenue expenditure	**KRTP**	49	49	50	50	56	57	54	56	56	54	55	55	..
Redistributed business rates[4]														
Cash £m	**KRTQ**	13,619	15,407	15,144	16,639	15,611	15,004	18,004	17,506	18,506	20,506	19,515	21,516	..
Percentage of revenue expenditure	**KRTR**	25	27	24	25	21	19	21	20	20	22	19	21	..
Council tax														
Cash £m	**KRTS**	13,278	14,200	15,246	16,648	18,946	20,299	21,315	22,453	23,608	24,759	25,633	26,254	..
Percentage of revenue expenditure	**KRTT**	25	25	25	25	25	26	25	25	26	25	25	25	..
Wales														
Gross revenue expenditure[5]	**ZBXH**	3,424	3,605	4,350	4,709	5,243	5,786	6,128	6,472	6,739	7,184	7,523	7,636	7,602
General government grants[6]	**ZBXI**	2,093	2,234	2,345	2,541	2,743	2,817	2,987	3,169	3,287	3,335	3,428	3,525	3,628
Specific government grants[7]	**ZBXG**	80	94	601	779	1,005	1,381	1,473	1,530	1,630	1,809	1,987	2,020	1,826
Share of redistributed business rates	**ZBXJ**	656	638	697	643	660	672	672	730	791	868	894	935	787
Council tax income[8]	**ZBXK**	596	670	716	776	861	924	1,012	1,071	1,131	1,188	1,240	1,295	1,343
Other[9]	**ZBXL**	-1	-31	-10	-30	-25	-8	-16	-27	-99	-16	-26	-139	19

1 Budget estimates.
2 Produced on a non-Financial Reporting Standard 17 (FRS17) basis.
3 The sum of government grants, business rates and local taxes does not normally equal revenue expenditure because of the use of reserves.
4 1993-94 to 2003-04 includes City of London Offset.
5 Gross revenue expenditure is total local authority expenditure on services, plus capital charges, but net of any income from sales, fees, and charges and other non-grant sources. It includes expenditure funded by specific grants. The figures have been adjusted to account for FRS17 pension costs.
6 Includes all unhypothecated grants, namely revenue support grant, police grant, council tax reduction scheme grant, transitional grant and the adjustment to reverse the transfer.
7 Comprises specific and supplementary grants,excluding police grant.
8 This includes community council precepts, and income covered by charge/council tax benefit grant, but excludes council tax reduction scheme.

Sources: Communities and Local Government: 0207 944 4158;
Welsh Government 02920 825355

23.15 Capital expenditure and income

England

£ million

Financial year	Central government grants[1]	Other grants and contributions[2]	Use of usable capital receipts	BCA/SCE(R)Single Capital Pot	BCA/SCE(R)Separate Programme Element	Other borrowing and credit arrangements not supported by central government
	KRVM	I4V9	I4VA	I4VB	I4VC	I4VD
1999/00	1,161	571	1,599	1,051	1,250	..
2000/01	1,298	762	1,592	2,271	945	..
2001/02	2,027	757	1,975	1,173	1,378	..
2002/03	2,474	716	2,426	2,281	935	..
2003/04	2,642	869	1,988	2,583	1,326	..
2004/05	3,196	1,080	2,647	2,959	704	1,061
2005/06	3,909	1,377	2,812	2,932	947	2,251
2006/07	4,083	1,344	2,628	2,734	630	2,291
2007/08	7,007	2,019	2,665	2,296	630	3,186
2008/09	5,733	1,978	2,040	2,257	759	4,224
2009/10	7,494	1,266	1,603	2,181	748	5,002

Financial year	Use of other resources[3]	Revenue financing of capital expenditure, of which:			Total resources used
		Housing revenue account	Major repairs reserve	General Fund	
	I4VE	I4VF	I4VG	I4VH	I4VI
1999/00	231	327	..	808	6,998
2000/01	304	218	..	896	8,288
2001/02	387	1,505	..	825	10,028
2002/03	375	175	1,465	825	11,672
2003/04	262	212	1,388	1,055	12,326
2004/05	..	187	1,440	1,130	14,404
2005/06	..	238	1,327	1,004	16,797
2006/07	..	240	1,337	1,185	16,472
2007/08	..	208	1,180	1,204	20,395
2008/09	..	228	1,224	1,789	20,233
2009/10	..	247	1,377	1,908	21,826

Source: Department for Communities and Local Government: 0303 444 2121

1 2007-08 includes an exceptional item, £1.7 billion grant from DfT to GLA (TfL) for the £1.7 billion payment to Metronet.

2 Includes grants and contributions for private developers, Non-Departmental Public Bodies, National Lottery and European Structural Fund.

3 Use of monies set aside as provision for credit liabilities to finance capital expenditure (debt free authorities).

23.16 Local authority capital expenditure and receipts

England
Final outrun: Year ending 31 March

£ million

		2003 /04	2004 /05	2005 /06	2006 /07	2007 /08	2008 /09	2009 /10
Expenditure[1]								
Education	**KRUD**	2,780	3,087	3,492	3,442	3,711	4,542	5,392
Personal Social Services	**KRUE**	260	285	387	364	411	300	288
Transport[2]	**KRUC**	2,552	2,906	3,461	3,480	5,916	4,735	5,851
Housing[3]	**KRUB**	3,485	3,987	4,534	4,507	5,008	4,901	4,514
Arts and libraries	**GEKZ**	196	227	329	296	321	356	647
Agriculture and fisheries	**GELA**	72	66	93	96	85	82	13
Sport and recreation	**KRUH**	263	305	424	415	446	496	598
Other[4]	**GELB**	2,056	2,725	3,218	3,052	3,342	3,427	3,165
Fire and rescue	**GELC**	68	81	96	126	169	167	189
Police[5]	**GELD**	513	561	606	531	550	794	704
Magistrates courts	**GELE**	37	46	1	-	-	-	
Total	**KRUR**	12,282	14,276	16,641	16,307	19,958	19,801	21,361
Receipts[6]								
Education	**KRUT**	221	210	217	261	272	102	167
Personal social services	**KRUV**	74	75	85	85	100	45	37
Transport	**KRUU**	92	101	87	130	301	41	126
Housing	**KRUS**	3,622	3,193	2,179	1,769	1,696	487	486
Arts and libraries	**GELF**	5	10	7	10	13	5	19
Agriculture and fisheries	**GELG**	53	45	63	65	69	39	23
Sport and recreation	**KRUX**	7	11	48	51	78	23	7
Other[4]	**GELH**	1,145	931	987	1,172	1,316	523	492
Fire and rescue	**GELI**	18	6	8	9	20	17	7
Police	**GELJ**	78	71	96	117	126	70	63
Magistrates court	**GELK**	6	8	1	-	..	1	0
Total[7]	**KRVB**	5,322	4,661	3,777	3,671	3,992	1,353	1,427

Source: Department for Communities and Local Government: 0303 444 2121

1 Includes aquisition of share and loan capital.

2 For 2007-08 Transport includes an exceptional item, the payment by the GLA (TfL) of £1.7 billion to Metronet.

3 For 2007-08 Housing includes an exceptional item, Liverpool's transfer of its housing stock to a registered social landlord which had the effect of
its housing stock to a registered social landlord which had the effect of
increasing expenditure in 2007-08 by £500million.

4 Environmental services, consumer protection and employment services.

5 For 2008-09 Police includes a one-off acquisition of land and existing buildings by the Metropolitan Police.

6 Includes disposal of share and loan capital and disposal of other investments.

7 In 2008-09 capital receipts fell to £1.4 billion, a year on year decrease of 66%. This fall reflects the effect of the economic climate over that period on local
This fall reflects the effect of the economic climate over that period on local
authority sales of assets.

23.17 Local authority capital expenditure and receipts

Wales
Final outrun: Year ending 31 March

£ million

		2004 /05	2005 /06	2006 /07	2007 /08	2008 /09	2009 /10
Expenditure							
Education	**IY8Q**	143.8	161.1	185.8	189.8	199.1	213.6
Social Services	**IY8R**	16.8	20.5	18.7	18.5	28.4	25.4
Transport	**IY8S**	141.2	203.4	214.0	237.6	134.6	146.1
Housing	**IY8T**	242.3	257.5	267.0	247.1	224.0	217.1
Local environmental services	**IY8U**	272.8	298.3	354.9	409.7	325.1	263.8
law, order and protective services	**IY8V**	43.4	41.5	36.5	43.1	71.6	61.7
Total expenditure	**IY8W**	860.3	982.3	1,077.0	1,145.9	982.8	927.7
Receipts							
Education	**IY8X**	10.2	4.6	6.1	12.2	14.7	3.6
Social Services	**IY8Y**	1.3	0.2	3.7	1.5	..	..
Transport	**IY8Z**	1.2	4.5	0.8	0.4	10.2	9.3
Housing	**IY92**	147.7	88.2	75.1	54.9	38.5	7.3
Local environmental services	**IY93**	55.3	69.5	131.1	100.0	103.4	40.6
law, order and protective services	**IY94**	1.2	1.4	1.1	4.2	16.0	2.7
Total receipts	**IY95**	216.8	168.5	218.0	173.2	185.6	66.6

Source: Welsh Assembly Government:029 2082 5355

23.18 Expenditure of local authorities

Scotland
Years ending 31 March

£ thousand

		1999 /00	2000 /01	2001 /02	2002 /03	2003 /04
Out of revenue:[1]Total	**KQTA**	10,447,706	10,951,402	11,558,721	9,324,680	13,658,834
General Fund Services:	KQTB	7,429,626	7,884,168	8,428,217	5,756,415	10,139,679
Education	KQTC	2,855,945	3,037,780	3,283,827	3533 853	3,872,786
Libraries,museums and galleries	KQTD	131,696	134,174	138,318	152,308	160,540
Social work	KQTE	1,519,191	1,632,843	1,793,732	2,173,752	2,400,652
Law, order and protective services	KQTF	1,006,000	1,047,034	1,088,791	1,130,693	1,226,067
Roads and Transport[2]	KQTG	527,018	564,738	506,326	601,454	611,721
Environmental services	KQTH	373,050	393,333	414,975	484,177	525,556
Planning	KQTI	198,285	194,771	223,414	265,315	282,572
Leisure and recreation	KQTJ	375,579	387,115	401,904	426,495	472,120
Other services	KQTL	435,155	465,612	572,136	515,661	585,425
Other general fund expenditure[3]	KQTM	7,707	26,768	4,794	6,560	2,240
Housing	KQTN	1,821,380	1,886,189	1,954,444	2,224,209	2,295,005
Trading services:	KQTO	87,321	80,355	61,899	74,062	92,782
Passenger transport	KQTR	336	162	343	427	441
Ferries	KQTS	9,709	10,005	9,650	11,493	11,768
Harbours,docks and piers	KQTT	15,923	13,604	10,912	12,222	13,405
Road bridges	KQTV	8,231	8,606	6,914	7,267	11,235
Slaughterhouses	KQTW	4	..	..	..	..
Markets	KQTX	14,106	23,844	16,657	17,995	14,824
Other trading services	KQTY	39,012	24,134	17,423	24,658	41,109
Loan charges:[4]Total	KQTZ	1,109,379	1,100,690	1,114,161	1,269,994	1,131,368
Allocated to :						
General Fund services	KMHV	701,515	708,822	739,351	738,870	772,852
Housing	KMHW	402,936	386,512	369,943	525,201	348,180
Trading services	KMHX	4,928	5,356	4,867	5,923	10,336
On capital works:[4]Total	KQUA	816,473	802,672	929,631	972,049	1,052,310
General Fund Services:	KQUB	557,119	538,843	610,485	662,869	767,122
Education	KQUC	136,508	127,781	143,268	157,439	172,227
Libraries, museums and galleries	KQUD	10,261	5,834	8,683	19,018	12,043
Social work	KQUE	22,097	21,539	31,359	30,116	31,966
Law, order and protective services	KQUF	37,132	35,761	39,901	53,268	65,477
Roads and Transport	KQUG	108,500	117,485	147,975	147,357	200,278
Environmental services	KQUH	14,936	17,944	16,396	17,957	20,567
Planning	KQUI	52,045	47,684	33,312	40,241	36,496
Leisure and recreation	KQUJ	52,365	44,516	39,240	50,558	71,486
Administrative buildings and equipment	KQUK	35,824	34,633	53,189	68,438	48,896
Other services	KQUL	87,451	85,666	97,162	78,477	107,686
Housing	KQUM	255,019	255,189	300,054	284,418	261,715
Trading Services:	KQUN	4,335	8,640	19,092	24,762	23,473
Ferries	KQUR	1,030	23	467	1	111
Harbours,docks and piers	KQUS	1,389	6,192	15,898	20,361	19,503
Airports	KQUT	..	607	663	1,031	609
Shipping, Airports, Transport piers & Ferry Terminals	J96X	..	..	..	..	..
Road bridges	KQUU	600	964	882	2,386	2,395
Slaughterhouses	KQUV	12	..	40	116	82
Other trading services	KMHY	1,304	854	1,142	867	773

1 Gross expenditure less inter-authority and inter-account transfers.
2 Including general fund support for transport (LA and NON-LA).
3 General fund contributions to Housing and Trading services (excluding transport),are also included in the expenditure figures for these services.
4 Expenditure out of loans, government grants and other capital receipts.
5 Figures for 2009-10 have been adjusted to exclude expenditure financed through PPP/PFI for past years.

23.18 Expenditure of local authorities

Scotland

Years ending 31 March

£ thousand

		2004 /05	2005 /06	2006 /07	2007 /08	2008 /09	2009 /10[5]
Out of revenue:[1]Total	KQTA	14,527,867	15,746,429	15,986,751	16,578,249	17,403,497	18,139,334
General Fund Services:	KQTB	10,964,598	12,021,453	12,143,056	12,653,585	13,255,975	13,662,114
Education	KQTC	4,180,675	4,406,876	4,596,832	4,747,148	4,869,127	4,818,152
Libraries,museums and galleries	KQTD	161,650	168,953	164,976	163,185	170,177	171,315
Social work	KQTE	2,621,134	2,808,040	2,994,486	3,192,214	3,408,851	3,559,328
Law, order and protective services	KQTF	1,306,085	1,501,854	1,469,644	1,506,432	1,631,037	1,646,531
Roads and Transport[2]	KQTG	635,329	673,167	625,341	633,828	678,922	674,525
Environmental services	KQTH	581,220	635,475	670,308	708,736	757,555	789,900
Planning	KQTI	299,182	351,617	366,803	372,445	437,261	514,080
Leisure and recreation	KQTJ	494,237	520,612	543,047	547,132	572,111	597,672
Other services	KQTL	681,288	948,167	702,554	782,035	730,934	889,716
Other general fund expenditure[3]	KQTM	3,798	6,692	9,065	430	0	895
Housing	KQTN	2,459,146	2,609,228	2,740,592	2,788,537	2,976,629	3,097,399
Trading services:	KQTO	106,445	103,461	102,336	100,104	110,042	100,677
Passenger transport	KQTR	282	353	355	315	397	248
Ferries	KQTS	13,759	14,308	18,483	21,907	23,872	25,018
Harbours,docks and piers	KQTT	12,407	11,995	8,495	8,312	276	-1,013
Road bridges	KQTV	13,276	12,366	16,279	22,005	17,189	16,894
Slaughterhouses	KQTW	..	..	..	..	..	..
Markets	KQTX	15,353	17,447	16,793	18,461	20,250	18,467
Other trading services	KQTY	51,368	46,992	41,931	29,104	48,058	41,063
Loan charges:[4]Total	KQTZ	997,678	1,012,287	1,000,767	1,036,023	1,060,851	1,279,144
Allocated to :							
General Fund services	KMHV	772,648	792,404	782,002	806,806	854,918	1,072,286
Housing	KMHW	212,440	210,856	214,395	201,297	197,776	199,196
Trading services	KMHX	12,590	9,027	4,370	27,920	8,157	7,662
On capital works:[4]Total	KQUA	1,264,031	1,572,281	1,952,249	2,182,509	2,554,081	2,424,018
General Fund Services:	KQUB	1,006,150	1,160,818	1,462,620	1,652,425	1,850,660	1,723,958
Education	KQUC	199,387	310,054	402,865	464,827	479,258	418,540
Libraries, museums and galleries	KQUD	24,796	22,762	24,210	29,963	39,583	42,579
Social work	KQUE	33,450	37,877	50,327	65,449	63,233	66,375
Law, order and protective services	KQUF	65,154	51,146	60,287	68,680	101,062	83,779
Roads and Transport	KQUG	258,071	308,366	418,987	484,669	479,769	471,763
Environmental services	KQUH	40,773	55,020	43,104	101,325	121,267	121,342
Planning	KQUI	61,544	76,043	66,063	121,596	124,060	171,613
Leisure and recreation	KQUJ	74,116	83,681	98,275	136,029	167,505	173,766
Administrative buildings and equipment	KQUK	64,414	84,569	113,896	..	..	..
Other services	KQUL	184,445	131,300	184,606	179,887	274,923	174,201
Housing	KQUM	241,107	382,697	454,838	507,905	680,657	678,125
Trading Services:	KQUN	16,774	28,766	34,791	22,179	22,764	21,935
Ferries	KQUR	608	195	547	..	..	..
Harbours,docks and piers	KQUS	12,024	12,899	5,855	..	..	..
Airports	KQUT	572	663	798	..	..	..
Shipping, Airports, Transport piers & Ferry Terminals	J96X	..	..	..	18,654	14,018	2,273
Road bridges	KQUU	442	12,106	22,865	-	0	0
Slaughterhouses	KQUV	-	-	-	-	..	..
Other trading services	KMHY	3,128	2,903	4,726	3,525	8,746	19,662

1 Gross expenditure less inter-authority and inter-account transfers.

2 Including general fund support for transport (LA and NON-LA).

3 General fund contributions to Housing and Trading services (excluding transport),are also included in the expenditure figures for these services.

4 Expenditure out of loans, government grants and other capital receipts.

5 Figures for 2009-10 have been adjusted to exclude expenditure financed through PPP/PFI for past years.

Source: Scottish Government,Local Government Finance Statistics: 0131 244 7033

23.19 Income of local authorities: classified according to source

Scotland
Years ending 31 March

£ thousand

		1998 /99	1999 /00	2000 /01	2001 /02	2002 /03	2003 /04	2004 /05	2005 /06	2006 /07	2007 /08	2008 /09	2009 /10
Revenue account													
Non-Domestic Rates[1]	KQXA	1,437,646	1,440,522	1,662,691	1,553,926	1,718,104	1,804,423	1,895,941	1,897,073	1,883,769	1,859,727	1,962,800	2,165,100
Council tax	KPUC	1,146,366	1,193,693	1,273,316	1,363,399	1,459,212	1,532,071	1,614,808	1,720,305	1,811,577	1,889,913	1,908,972	1,909,627
Government grants													
General Revenue Funding [2]	KQXC	3,483,815	3,537,043	3,440,842	3,935,328	4,557,867	5,037,140	5,266,054	5,567,902	5,777,204	6,169,645	7,425,884	7,756,689
Council tax rebate grants	KPUD	274,940	275,789	279,459	285,131	293,606	307,733	344,899	354,067	359,159	354,030	351,165	368,381
Other grants and subsidies	KQXI	1,642,045	1,778,216	1,891,839	2,061,297	2,141,543	2,479,311	2,823,820	2,940,137	3,147,497	3,310,712	2,602,219	2,723,587
Sales	KQXJ	39,595	43,660	49,826	..	..	..	..	..	..	..	..	..
Fees and charges[3]	KQXK	1,668,223	1,682,385	1,776,455	1,789,428	1,954,337	1,785,672	1,845,161	1,951,315	2,039,217	2,125,114	2,253,653	2,277,743
Other income	KQXL	324,932	398,894	453,458	490,574	712,423	515,897	709,226	1,003,925	961,693	875,369	766,126	672,925
Capital account													
Sale of fixed assets	KQXM	335,037	303,582	149,504	165,016	207,388	222,844	355,069	366,302	451,353	513,913	229,805	229,397
Revenue contributions to capital	KQXP	204,982	213,564	210,912	147,760	239,778	212,533	219,593	247,693	199,749	173,668	196,836	166,141
Transfer from special funds	KMHZ	26,959	125,365	27,317	37,087	39,650	52,619	82,991	72,195	20,935	15,711	26,036	39,638
Other receipts[4]	KMGV	45,028	39,014	45,351	90,360	75,846	114,745	130,575	261,872	595,722	826,145	742,231	874,318

1 This is the Distributable Amount of Non-Domestic Rates.
2 Revenue Support Grant re-named General Revenue Funding from 2008-09.
3 From 2001-02 onwards, fees & charges incorporates sales.
4 Figures include public sector contributions from 2001-02 onwards.

Source: Scottish Government,Local Government Finance Statistics: 0131 244 7033

23.20 Income of local authorities from government grants[1]

Scotland
Year ending 31 March

£ thousand

		1999 /00	2000 /01	2001 /02	2002 /03	2003 /04	2004 /05	2005 /06	2006 /07	2007 /08	2008 /09	2009 /10
General fund services	KQYA	818,537	935,452	1,032,591	952,692	1,029,338	1,207,912	1,358,190	1,524,829	1,503,002	1,041,117	1,069,140
Education	KQYB	225,668	324,340	380,726	251,333	217,743	287,226	327,905	439,678	418,636	96,477	84,211
Libraries,museums and galleries	KQYC	507	634	1,137	5,359	1,517	763	818	1,394	1,523	1,869	881
Social work	KQYD	71,611	78,611	86,533	114,591	205,229	240,665	236,774	222,551	222,741	122,999	130,509
Law, order and protective services	KQYE	382,246	401,485	423,636	445,275	476,681	512,501	597,322	601,593	569,637	594,770	624,872
Roads and Transport[2]	KQYF	68,429	57,702	49,900	57,664	27,280	35,038	31,704	49,295	62,799	41,773	30,752
Environmental services	KQYG	71	301	2,272	5,407	18,120	39,971	45,338	55,173	59,112	7,219	5,621
Planning and Economic Development	KQYH	4,311	4,375	20,351	19,434	21,517	20,767	31,293	33,750	41,068	97,250	122,999
Leisure and recreation	KQYI	1,491	2,377	3,322	2,968	3,732	5,830	6,256	9,194	12,796	15,532	10,469
Other services	KQYK	64,203	65,627	64,714	50,661	57,519	65,151	80,780	112,201	114,690	63,228	58,826
Housing	KQYL	959,276	956,239	1,028,529	1,188,626	1,449,616	1,614,976	1,580,504	1,622,049	1,805,354	1,560,883	1,654,212
Trading services	KQYM	403	148	177	225	357	932	1,443	619	2,356	219	235
Grants not allocated to specific services[3]	KMGY	3,537,043	3,440,842	3,935,328	4,557,867	5,037,140	5,266,054	5,567,902	5,777,204	6,169,645	7,425,884	7,756,689
Total	KMGZ	5,315,259	5,332,681	5,996,625	6,699,410	7,516,451	8,089,874	8,508,039	8,924,701	9,480,357	10,028,103	10,480,276

1 Including grants for capital works.
2 Decrease in general fund services in 2008-09 is due to the rolling-up of ring-fenced grants into General Revenue Funding.
3 General revenue funding.

Source: Scottish Government,Local Government Finance Statistics: 0131 244 7033

23.21 Expenditure of local authorities

Northern Ireland
Years ending 31 March

£ thousand

		1997/98	1998/99	1999/00	2000/01	2001/02	2002/03	2003/04	2004/05	2005/06	2006/07	2007/08	2008/09[1]	2009/10
Libraries,museums and art galleries	**KQVB**	13,928	14,571	19,900	23,097	24,181	32,728	30,062	30,481	33,516	28,655	31,557	36,527	35,549
Environmental health services:														
Refuse collection and disposal	**KQVC**	56,246	56,360	62,226	65,289	73,336	90,148	94,715	102,633	113,768	121,879	136,181	142,071	151,332
Public baths	**KQVD**	2,585	2,634	1,750	1,724	1,423	..	..	..	..	..	.. ..		
Parks, recreation grounds,etc	**KQVE**	115,302	118,396	158,304	170,999	184,406	194,224	193,617	205,734	221,298	198,314	213,780	265,720	257,522
Other sanitary services	**KQVF**	39,682	42,923	44,214	45,552	48,784	52,075	55,349	59,906	66,294	68,641	74,624	86,428	87,000
Housing (grants and small dwellings acquisition)	**KQVG**	545	358	37	28	27	12	21	18	10	15	17	8	15
Trading services:														
Cemeteries	**KQVI**	5,626	5,887	5,973	6,151	6,538	7,208	7,980	8,455	8,520	7,752	8,726	9,125	9,353
Other trading services (including markets, fairs and harbours)	**KQVJ**	7,016	10,779	9,366	7,209	7,769	18,281	17,489	18,776	19,596	15,240	17,498	27,711	21,115
Miscellaneous	**KQVK**	63,375	161,790	86,649	89,881	98,244	79,645	114,971	105,031	128,304	141,717	160,606	263,230	183,563
Total expenditure	**KQVA**	304,305	413,698	388,419	409,930	444,708	474,321	490,619	531,034	591,306	582,213	642,991	830,820	745,450
Total loan charges	**KQVL**	34,823	26,413	..	..	..	..	..	..	..	..	..	..	..

Source: Department of the Environment for Northern Ireland: 028 9025 6086

1. The overall expenditure figure for 2008/2009 is much higher than 2009/2010 substantially due to the Capital Finance Reserve of one particular council.

Agriculture

Chapter 24

Agriculture

Input and Output (Tables 24.1 and 24.2)

For both tables, output is net of VAT collected on the sale of non-edible products. Figures for total output include subsidies on products, that is, payments that have the purpose of influencing production, their prices or remuneration of the factors of production. Unspecified crops include turf, other minor crops and arable area payments for fodder maize. Eggs include the value of duck eggs and exports of eggs for hatching. Landlords' expenses are included within farm maintenance, miscellaneous expenditure and depreciation of buildings and works. Also included within 'Other farming costs' are livestock and crop costs, water costs, insurance premia, bank charges, professional fees, rates, and other farming costs.

Non-subsidy payments

Payments other than subsidies on products from which farmers can benefit as a consequence of engaging in agriculture. This includes:
• environment and countryside management schemes
• organic farming schemes
• support schemes for less favoured areas
• Single Payment Scheme
• animal disease compensation attributable to income
• other payments

Compensation of employees and interest charges

Total compensation of employees excludes the value of work done by farm labour on own account capital formation in buildings and work. 'Interest' relates to interest charges on loans for current farming purposes and buildings, less interest on money held on short-term deposit.

Rent

Rent paid (after deductions) is the rent paid on all tenanted land including 'conacre' land in Northern Ireland, less landlords' expenses and the benefit value of dwellings on that land. Rent received (after deductions) is the rent received by farming landowners from renting of land to other farmers, less landlords' expenses and the benefit value of dwellings on that land. Total net rent is the net rent flowing out of the agricultural sector paid to non-farming landowners, including that part of tenanted land in Northern Ireland.

Agricultural censuses and surveys
(Tables 24.3, 24.5 and 24.13)

For tables 24.3 and 24.5, the coverage includes all main and minor holdings for each country up until 2008. From 2009 onwards, the data for England relate to commercial holdings only. The term 'commercial' covers all English holdings which have more than 5 hectares of agricultural land, 1 hectare of orchards, 0.5 hectares of vegetables or 0.1 hectares of protected crops, or more than 10 cows, 50 pigs, 20 sheep, 20 goats or 1,000 poultry. These thresholds are specified in the EU Farm Structure Survey Regulation EC 1166/2008. All data in table 24.13 relate to commercial holdings only for England.

Estimated quantity of crops and grass harvested
(Table 24.4)

The estimated yield of sugar beet is obtained from production figures supplied by British Sugar plc in England and Wales. In Great Britain, potato yields are estimated in consultation with the Potato Council Limited.

Forestry
(Table 24.6)

Statistics for state forestry are from Forestry Commission and Forest Service management information systems. For private forestry in Great Britain, statistics on new planting and restocking are based on records of grant aid and estimates of planting undertaken without grant aid, and softwood production is estimated from a survey of the largest timber harvesting companies. Hardwood production is estimated from deliveries of roundwood to primary wood processors and others, based on surveys of the UK timber industry, data provided by trade associations and estimates provided by the Expert Group on Timber and Trade Statistics.

Average weekly earnings and hours of agricultural and horticultural workers
(Tables 24.11 and 24.12)

Before 1998, data were collected from a monthly postal survey, which mainly covered male full-time workers. Between 1998 and 2002 the survey collected information on an annual basis via a telephone survey. The survey was reviewed in 2002 and it was concluded that the frequency of the survey should be increased to four times per year to enable the production of more representative annual estimates. The annual sample size has been retained and has been split between four quarterly telephone surveys.

From April 2009, publication of quarterly results ceased. In 2009 results were published on an annual basis, for the 12 months ending in September, using data from the four quarterly data collections. In 2010 the intention was to run surveys in March and September with larger sample sizes than the quarterly surveys. However, following the announcement of the intention to abolish the Agricultural Wages Board (AWB) the September 2010 survey was subsequently cancelled so all 2010 figures are point-in-time estimates as at March 2010. The minimum wage and other terms and conditions of employment for workers employed in agriculture are set by the Agricultural Wages Board.

The Agricultural Wages Board is an independent body with a statutory obligation to set minimum wages for workers employed in agriculture in England and Wales. It was established by the Agricultural Wages Act (1948).. The Board also has powers to decide other terms and conditions of employment, e.g. holidays and sick pay. It produces a legally binding Order which is enforced by Defra. The Order is made annually and normally comes into force on 1 October.

As at autumn 2011 the future of the Survey of Earnings and Hours of Agricultural and Horticultural Workers is under review.

The survey covers seven main categories of workers and provides data which are used by the AWB when considering wage claims and in considering the cost of labour in agriculture and horticulture.

Data on earnings represents the total earnings for workers aged 20 and over. Figures include all payments-in-kind, valued where applicable in accordance with the Agricultural Wages Order. Part-time workers are defined as those working less than 39 basic hours per week. Casual workers are those employed on a temporary basis.

Results can be found on the Department for Environment, Food and Rural Affairs (DEFRA) website at: www.defra.gov.uk/statistics/foodfarm/farmmanage/earningshours/

Fisheries
(Table 24.15)
Figures show the number of registered and licensed fishing vessels based on information provided by the Registry of Shipping and Seamen and licence registers maintained by the Marine and Fisheries Agency for England and Wales, the Scottish Government and the Department of Agriculture and Rural Development in Northern Ireland.

Estimated average household food consumption – 'Family Food' Expenditure and Food Survey (Table 24.16)
In 2008 the Expenditure and Food Survey (EFS) was renamed as the Living Costs and Food Survey (LCFS) when it became part of the Integrated Household Survey (IHS). The Expenditure and Food Survey started in April 2001, having been preceded by the National Food Survey (NFS) and the Family Expenditure Survey (FES). Both surveys were brought into one to provide value for money without compromising data quality. The EFS was effectively a continuation of the FES extended to record quantities of purchases. This extension is now known as the Family Food Module of the LCFS. Estimates from the NFS prior to 2000 have been adjusted by aligning estimates for the year 2000 with corresponding estimates from the FES. From 2006 the survey moved onto a calendar year basis (from the previous financial year basis) in preparation for its integration to the Integrated Household Survey from January 2008.

The Living Costs and Food Survey is a voluntary sample survey of private households throughout the UK. The basic unit of the survey is the household which is defined as a group of people living at the same address and sharing common catering arrangements. The survey is continuous, interviews being spread evenly over the year to ensure that seasonal effects are covered. Each household member over the age of seven keeps a diary of all their expenditure over a two-week period. A simplified version of the diary is used by those aged between seven and 15. The diaries record expenditure and quantities of purchases of food and drink rather than consumption of food and drink. Items of food and drink are defined as either household or eating out and are recorded in the form the item was purchased not how it was consumed. 'Household' covers all food that is brought into the household. 'Eating out' covers all food that never enters the household, for example restaurant meals, school meals and snacks eaten away from home.

In 2008 the Living Costs and Food Survey collected the diaries of 13,890 people within 5,845 households across the UK. The response rate for 2008 was 51 per cent in Great Britain and 54 per cent in Northern Ireland.

24.1 Production and income account at current prices[1]

United Kingdom

£ million

Output[3]		1999	2000	2001	2002	2003	2004	2005	2006	2007	2008	2009	2010[2]
1.Total cereals:	C5X5	1620.2	1621.4	1348.3	1534.7	1491.3	1707.3	1434.4	1506.9	1947.7	3149.9	2300.4	2259.3
Wheat	KFKA	1105.2	1124.8	836.6	1095.1	1000.8	1232.3	1018.3	1066.4	1324.8	2241.6	1549.6	1682.9
Rye	VQBG	1.8	22.0	5.6	1.2	1.4	1.6	1.3	1.4	2.3	1.9	1.8	1.7
Barley	KFKB	474.6	432.1	465.7	392.3	445.7	433.1	379.5	383.8	555.4	816.3	675.7	510.4
Oats and summer cereal mixtures	KFKC	37.9	41.7	39.8	45.2	42.5	39.5	34.4	54.4	64.5	88.9	70.9	62.7
Other cereals	VQBH	0.8	0.9	0.6	0.9	0.8	0.9	0.9	0.8	0.8	1.3	2.4	1.5
2.Total industrial crops	VQBI	783.3	699.4	774.3	860.0	813.1	799.0	815.3	735.2	769.2	1164.8	1099.3	1341.9
Oilseeds	VQBJ	225.0	143.8	177.1	220.1	314.2	266.2	278.3	318.4	426.6	628.2	486.0	724.2
Oilseed rape	KFKG	194.8	139.0	171.5	217.4	303.8	256.7	261.2	310.4	422.3	617.9	468.9	701.6
Other oil seeds	KIBT	30.1	4.8	5.6	2.6	10.4	9.5	17.0	8.0	4.3	10.4	17.1	22.6
Sugar beet	KFKH	279.7	252.1	256.4	282.9	279.7	278.1	279.0	178.2	161.5	208.3	246.3	197.6
Other industrial crops	VQBK	278.7	303.4	340.8	357.0	219.2	254.7	258.1	238.5	181.1	328.2	367.1	420.1
Fibre plants	VQBL	2.3	1.3	1.7	1.0	1.8	1.2	0.9	0.9	0.4	1.0	0.3	0.7
Hops	KFKI	12.1	10.4	9.0	7.2	6.1	5.7	5.4	4.4	4.4	4.4	4.4	4.4
Others[4]	VQBM	264.2	291.7	330.1	348.8	211.4	247.8	251.8	233.2	176.2	322.9	362.4	415.0
3.Total forage plants	VQBO	161.6	160.0	201.6	182.5	214.2	228.6	230.3	234.5	238.3	291.9	317.0	326.1
4.Total vegetables and horticultural products	VQBP	1667.5	1561.1	1612.6	1591.1	1672.6	1625.1	1694.5	1762.0	1850.2	1904.0	1952.1	2231.8
5.Total potatoes (including seeds)	KFKO	769.4	478.4	701.8	504.8	547.9	695.2	531.0	637.6	683.3	767.4	667.0	780.2
6.Total fruit	KFKQ	256.9	232.2	238.8	251.2	310.3	315.8	388.1	382.8	467.4	545.6	579.5	575.2
7.Other crop products including seeds	VQBQ	42.0	37.7	37.5	25.5	31.6	31.0	52.0	47.9	43.2	44.6	57.7	50.0
8.Total crop output (Sum 1 to 7)	VQBR	5300.9	4790.1	4914.8	4949.9	5080.9	5401.9	5145.6	5306.7	5999.4	7868.1	6972.9	7564.4
9.Total livestock production	VQBS	4326.7	4358.1	4277.9	4572.9	4813.9	4813.9	4908.8	5095.8	5231.6	6580.0	7170.6	7302.4
Primarily for meat	KFLA	3929.5	3964.4	3651.3	3866.3	4083.8	4156.6	4299.3	4364.3	4432.2	5502.1	5852.3	6097.5
Cattle	KFKU	1145.2	1093.7	955.3	1145.8	1227.1	1279.2	1465.7	1561.3	1623.2	2071.4	2138.9	2141.4
Pigs	KFKW	784.8	800.2	748.4	687.2	671.1	680.0	676.9	685.2	736.3	865.4	968.4	981.6
Sheep	VQBT	574.8	616.8	438.0	613.4	696.4	725.7	685.9	709.0	640.6	796.7	965.4	977.4
Poultry	KFXX	1275.8	1301.1	1354.6	1262.3	1328.0	1306.0	1299.9	1233.2	1248.6	1578.3	1590.2	1799.1
Other animals	KFKY	148.9	152.6	154.9	157.7	161.2	165.7	170.9	175.5	183.5	190.3	189.4	198.0
Gross fixed capital formation	KFLI	397.3	393.8	626.6	706.7	730.0	657.3	609.5	731.5	799.5	1077.9	1318.3	1204.9
Cattle	KUJZ	206.9	192.9	371.3	392.2	447.7	337.4	360.9	447.3	492.9	784.5	895.1	698.9
Pigs	LUKB	6.9	5.6	5.3	7.4	7.0	7.6	6.2	7.9	5.3	6.4	8.7	8.9
Sheep	LUKA	56.7	63.9	122.5	177.5	145.8	176.4	111.5	145.8	152.5	124.9	229.9	318.1
Poultry	LUKC	126.8	131.4	127.5	129.5	129.5	135.9	130.8	130.5	148.7	162.2	184.6	179.0
10.Total livestock products	KFLF	2963.1	2711.4	3088.2	2834.3	3030.7	3037.7	3009.5	2918.1	3285.9	4018.6	3711.8	3960.5
Milk	KFLB	2662.0	2385.8	2742.6	2466.3	2628.5	2610.4	2592.5	2497.2	2823.4	3446.8	3124.2	3324.8
Eggs	KFLC	254.0	280.3	307.1	314.5	336.4	378.3	349.4	361.7	410.1	520.2	530.9	561.2
Raw wool	KFLD	21.4	22.7	17.2	19.1	20.8	20.1	19.5	11.5	11.6	10.4	13.7	25.2
Other animal products	KFLE	25.7	22.6	21.2	34.5	45.1	28.9	48.1	47.7	40.8	41.2	42.9	49.3
11.Total livestock output (9+10)	VQBV	7289.8	7069.5	7366.1	7407.2	7844.6	7851.6	7918.3	8013.9	8517.5	10598.6	10882.4	11262.9
12.Total other agricultural activities	LUOS	726.1	638.1	632.2	644.2	632.5	718.3	639.3	623.6	680.3	792.3	869.8	925.6
Agricultural services	LUKD	609.6	587.0	604.0	601.4	592.3	636.2	630.7	622.6	679.9	792.1	869.6	925.5
Leasing out quota	VQBW	116.5	51.2	28.1	42.8	40.2	82.0	8.6	0.9	0.4	0.2	0.2	0.2
13.Total inseparable non-agricultural activities	LUOT	430.4	488.3	624.1	559.9	592.3	637.3	678.4	684.3	762.5	813.5	913.7	986.4
14.Gross output at market prices (8+11+12+13)	LUOV	13747.1	12965.7	13533.4	13561.2	14150.2	14609.2	14381.6	14628.5	15960.6	20073.7	19640.0	20715.8
15.Total subsidies (less taxes) on product	LUOU	2213.6	2011.7	1749.7	1941.8	1976.1	2167.5	212.0	84.8	59.5	54.7	33.9	25.1
16.Output at basic prices (14+15) of which transactions within the agricultural industry	KFLT	15960.7	14977.3	15283.1	15503.0	16126.3	16776.7	14593.6	14713.3	16020.1	20128.4	19673.9	20740.9
Feed wheat	LUNQ	64.4	40.1	41.1	41.9	70.1	103.8	85.9	83.4	100.0	133.5	109.8	95.5
Feed barley	LUNR	147.9	137.8	148.9	144.6	149.2	148.6	136.1	142.0	177.9	207.2	156.2	185.7
Feed oats	LUNS	14.5	12.6	12.5	11.7	11.8	13.5	11.9	15.3	19.2	23.5	19.8	19.2
Fodder maize		85.7	79.1	98.2	92.2	118.7	117.6	130.9	151.0	146.3	152.7	179.4	196.7
Seed potatoes	LUNT	29.0	6.9	13.8	12.0	4.1	9.2	12.5	15.9	8.5	12.6	15.7	15.5
Straw	LUNU	232.9	258.6	291.2	306.5	177.0	209.0	210.4	191.0	137.4	266.5	301.8	354.0
Contract work	LUNV	609.6	587.0	604.0	601.4	592.3	636.2	630.7	622.6	679.9	792.1	869.6	925.5
Leasing of quota	LUNW	116.5	51.2	28.1	42.8	40.2	82.0	8.6	0.9	0.4	0.2	0.2	0.2
Total capital formation in livestock	LUNX	397.3	393.8	626.6	706.7	730.0	657.3	609.5	731.5	799.5	1077.9	1318.3	1204.9

24.1 Production and income account at current prices[1]

United Kingdom

£ million

		1999	2000	2001	2002	2003	2004	2005	2006	2007	2008	2009	2010[2]
Intermediate consumption													
17.Seeds	KFME	542.8	468.2	510.1	485.8	466.7	619.9	661.9	579.5	608.4	703.6	690.0	637.4
18.Energy	VQDO	621.9	697.9	683.4	647.0	600.0	669.1	778.8	831.1	897.0	1166.5	1096.6	1204.9
Electricity	VQDQ	221.7	230.2	240.1	234.8	204.8	209.7	235.2	258.5	274.0	340.6	341.3	355.0
Fuels	VQDV	400.2	467.8	443.2	412.2	395.2	459.4	543.6	572.7	623.0	825.9	755.2	849.9
19.Fertilisers	KFMM	785.8	765.8	843.3	831.3	773.2	770.9	810.6	812.1	810.9	1514.2	1210.0	1131.3
20.Pesticides	KFMN	621.0	579.4	526.2	531.2	501.1	576.1	547.2	517.6	570.7	690.2	715.2	755.9
21.Veterinary expenses	KCPC	270.0	255.8	241.2	250.1	253.4	279.1	280.3	284.5	302.4	338.1	361.0	400.7
22.Animal feed	KFMB	2346.6	2244.3	2509.4	2360.9	2512.8	2676.7	2447.0	2574.9	3022.7	3896.1	3611.1	4015.4
Compounds	LUNY	1402.4	1283.3	1398.2	1376.9	1348.2	1449.6	1318.0	1425.7	1702.5	2185.8	2087.6	2248.2
Straights	LUNZ	631.7	691.4	810.4	693.6	814.8	843.5	764.2	757.6	876.8	1193.5	1058.3	1270.0
Feed purchased from other farms	LUOA	312.5	269.5	300.8	290.4	349.8	383.5	364.8	391.7	443.4	516.9	465.1	497.1
23.Total maintenance[5]	VQDW	1013.4	939.0	980.3	960.7	970.1	1016.4	998.8	1016.8	1084.8	1217.6	1282.2	1338.2
Materials	KFMO	698.2	651.5	660.1	636.2	641.3	662.9	653.1	655.0	695.5	744.8	797.9	826.5
Buildings	KCPB	315.2	287.5	320.2	324.4	328.8	353.6	345.7	361.8	389.3	472.8	484.3	511.7
24.Agricultural services	LUOE	609.6	587.0	604.0	601.4	592.3	636.2	630.7	622.6	679.9	792.1	869.6	925.5
FISIM		120.3	110.5	102.8	86.3	84.0	86.5	102.0	105.0	111.5	137.0	120.7	132.2
25.Other goods and services[5,6]	VQDX	2265.6	2083.3	2031.9	2062.5	2123.4	2363.0	2346.4	2318.2	2380.5	2582.8	2667.5	2777.0
26.Total intermediate consumption (Sum 17 to 25)	KCPM	9196.8	8731.3	9032.6	8817.1	8877.0	9694.0	9603.5	9662.4	10468.7	13038.1	12623.8	13318.8
27.Gross value added at market prices (14-26)	LUOG	4550.3	4234.4	4500.8	4744.1	5273.2	4915.2	4778.1	4966.0	5491.9	7035.6	7016.2	7397.0
28.Gross value added at basic prices (16-26)	JT3Z	6763.9	6246.0	6250.5	6685.9	7249.3	7082.7	4990.1	5050.8	5551.4	7090.3	7050.1	7422.1
29.Total consumption of Fixed Capital	KCPS	2436.7	2493.9	2598.2	2581.6	2645.3	2529.8	2658.9	2681.2	2717.3	3070.4	3260.0	3273.6
Equipment	KCPR	1316.7	1266.5	1261.6	1259.9	1203.5	1189.9	1204.5	1199.0	1212.8	1267.9	1391.1	1451.7
Buildings[5,7]	LUOH	700.6	690.5	685.8	688.8	691.6	673.3	675.0	684.6	695.9	709.0	719.6	715.7
Livestock	VQEA	419.3	537.0	650.8	632.9	750.1	666.7	779.3	797.6	808.7	1093.5	1149.3	1106.2
Cattle	LUOI	208.2	281.1	348.4	353.2	441.2	363.6	489.6	499.4	503.3	745.5	709.8	662.0
Pigs	LUOK	7.7	8.0	6.1	7.8	7.7	8.6	7.3	7.3	6.1	6.8	8.1	8.1
Sheep	LUOJ	69.6	120.1	169.5	141.5	173.0	167.3	150.7	161.7	156.8	187.9	267.0	269.5
Poultry	LUOL	133.8	127.8	126.8	130.4	128.3	127.2	131.6	129.2	142.5	153.3	164.3	166.5
30.Net value added at market prices (27-29)	KCPT	2113.6	1740.4	1902.6	2162.4	2628.0	2385.3	2119.3	2284.8	2774.5	3965.2	3756.2	4123.4
31.Net value added at basic prices (28-29)	JT42	4327.2	3752.1	3652.3	4104.2	4604.1	4552.9	2331.2	2369.6	2834.0	4020.0	3790.1	4148.5
32.Compensation of employees[8]	LUOR	1942.6	1851.4	1859.0	1835.7	1830.9	1898.5	1953.8	1973.9	2004.6	2064.5	2136.1	2203.1
33.Other taxes on production	VQEB	-92.3	-92.1	-84.9	-91.4	-82.8	-95.7	-101.8	-98.3	-101.0	-102.8	-106.5	-114.5
34.Other subsidies on production	VQEC	470.1	462.1	695.7	723.4	782.1	777.7	2818.2	2902.9	2953.9	3230.9	3587.6	3433.3
Animal disease compensation	LUOM	11.9	19.1	13.0	24.5	24.6	18.5	20.1	17.0	21.3	25.8	20.8	20.6
Set-aside	LUON	170.0	127.3	180.1	142.5	176.7	129.5	..	..	..	..	..	..
Agri-environment schemes[9]	ZBXC	128.5	140.3	164.1	196.4	222.9	257.0	293.8	383.1	466.5	493.5	482.8	511.9
Other including Single Payment Scheme[10]	VQED	159.6	175.4	338.5	360.2	358.1	372.6	2504.2	2502.8	2466.1	2711.7	3084.0	2900.9
35.Net value added at factor cost	LUOQ	4705.0	4122.0	4263.2	4736.2	5303.4	5234.9						
36.Rent	KCPV	238.9	222.6	314.7	297.0	311.3	284.4	267.5	286.5	305.3	350.2	356.6	434.2
Paid[11]	ZBXE	321.0	300.6	410.7	383.1	408.4	388.1	352.2	373.9	401.9	444.9	446.1	523.1
Received[12]	ZBXF	-82.1	-78.1	-96.1	-86.0	-97.1	-103.7	-84.7	-87.5	-96.6	-94.7	-89.4	-88.9
37.Interest[13]	KCPU	465.3	481.3	421.3	368.6	346.3	399.4	422.2	412.8	469.7	367.2	167.3	179.0
Total income from farming (35-32-36-37)	KCQB	2058.2	1566.7	1668.2	2234.9	2814.8	2652.5	2404.1	2501.0	2907.4	4366.2	4611.2	4651.0

1 See chapter text.

2 Provisional.

3 Output is net of VAT collected on the sale of non-edible products. Figures for total output include subsidies on products, but not other subsidies.

4 Includes straw and minor crops.

5 Landlords' expenses are included within 'Total maintenance', 'Other goods and services' and 'Total consumption of Fixed Capital of buildings'.

6 Includes livestock and crop costs, water costs, insurance premiums, bank charges, professional fees, rates and other far ming costs.

7 A more empirically based methodology for calculating landlords' consumption of fixed capital was introduced in 2000. The new series has been linked with the old one using a smoothing procedure for the transition year of 1996.

8 Excludes the value of work done by far m labour on own account capital formation in buildings and works.

9 Includes Environmentally and Nitrate Sensitive Areas, Countryside Stewardship and other management schemes, and Moorland, Habitat, Farm Woodland and Organic Farming Schemes.

10 Land area based schemes which replaced the Hill Livestock Compensatory - Allowance Scheme in 2001. These are Tir Mynydd in Wales, Less Favoured Area Compensatory Scheme in Northern Ireland, Less Favoured Areas Support Scheme in Scotland and Hill Farm Allowance in England.

11 Rent paid on all tenanted land (including 'conacre' land in Northern Ireland) less landlords' expenses, landlords' consumption of fixed capital and the benefit value of dwellings on that land.

12 Rent received by farming landowners from renting of land to other farmers less landlords' expenses. This series starts in 1996 following a revision to the methodology of calculating net rent.

13 Interest charges on loans for current farming purposes and buildings and works less interest on money held on short term deposit.

Source: Department for Environment, Food and Rural Affairs: 01904 455 080

24.2 Output and input volume indices[1]

United Kingdom

Indices (2005=100)

		1999	2000	2001	2002	2003	2004	2005	2006	2007	2008	2009	2010
Outputs[2]													
1. Total cereals:	VQAN	103.4	111.9	89.8	108.8	102.3	104.4	100.0	99.0	91.1	114.6	102.0	99.4
Wheat	LUKH	99.1	111.4	78.1	107.0	96.3	103.8	100.0	98.9	88.7	114.7	94.4	99.7
Rye	VQAO	121.1	115.8	121.1	105.3	100.0	100.0	100.0	100.0	100.0	100.0	100.0	115.8
Barley	LUKI	117.1	114.4	120.4	111.2	115.9	105.0	100.0	95.7	93.1	111.1	119.3	93.8
Oats and summer cereal mixtures	LUKJ	101.1	120.3	116.6	141.8	140.5	117.3	100.0	137.6	134.5	147.8	140.3	129.1
Other cereals	VQAP	78.4	95.2	71.0	104.5	102.7	98.9	100.0	100.0	85.3	97.6	154.1	127.6
2. Total industrial crops:	VQAQ	113.6	96.6	90.2	102.1	105.7	102.1	100.0	93.3	84.1	97.6	99.4	100.9
Oil seeds	VQAR	99.5	59.6	59.8	73.9	91.4	83.4	100.0	97.3	106.6	105.1	103.5	121.2
Oilseed rape	VQAS	89.9	60.4	60.8	76.9	92.9	84.8	100.0	99.6	111.0	108.9	105.5	123.1
Other oil seeds	LUKN	338.2	47.7	42.5	18.2	65.4	59.1	100.0	56.4	22.0	33.2	60.6	80.4
Sugar beet	C5X4	121.8	104.5	95.9	110.0	105.5	104.1	100.0	85.2	77.5	88.0	97.3	75.1
Other industrial crops	VQAU	126.8	133.1	121.6	129.6	122.5	124.1	100.0	96.5	61.1	101.4	103.2	99.3
Fibre plants	VQAV	439.9	315.1	218.4	127.0	212.1	143.4	100.0	102.4	50.8	77.4	20.8	59.9
Hops	LUKP	181.5	161.4	152.2	152.6	116.9	116.9	100.0	82.5	82.5	82.5	82.5	82.5
Others[3]	VQAW	124.5	131.9	120.6	129.0	122.3	124.1	100.0	96.7	60.7	101.7	103.8	99.7
3.Total forage plants	VQAX	34.6	83.3	100.3	97.4	95.6	93.5	100.0	98.2	90.2	100.7	114.7	107.8
4.Total vegetables and horticultural													
Products:	VQAY	106.9	104.4	101.0	100.4	97.7	99.9	100.0	94.5	93.5	95.5	93.8	96.5
Fresh vegetables	LUKX	114.9	108.1	104.5	95.5	95.0	96.0	100.0	98.5	93.8	96.2	100.6	103.0
Plants and flowers	LUKZ	97.1	99.6	96.6	106.1	100.8	104.4	100.0	89.6	93.4	94.9	86.0	88.9
5.Total potatoes (including seeds)	LUKW	122.2	101.6	114.7	112.1	102.0	107.3	100.0	94.7	90.8	97.0	109.7	103.5
6.Total fruit	LUKY	72.8	67.3	71.3	67.2	73.9	87.6	100.0	100.8	118.6	123.0	128.8	128.2
7.Other crop products including seeds	VQAZ	82.3	80.9	81.9	55.8	67.1	68.5	100.0	90.2	81.4	86.2	89.8	80.4
8.Total crop output	VQBA	101.2	101.1	94.8	101.2	98.6	100.9	100.0	96.2	92.4	104.6	102.2	101.5
9.Total livestock production	VQBB	106.8	101.4	96.0	99.5	97.0	97.7	100.0	98.4	99.3	99.8	96.6	99.3
Mainly for meat processing	LULH	105.4	100.7	92.8	96.8	95.6	96.1	100.0	97.5	97.8	97.2	94.5	97.7
Cattle	LULC	86.7	84.1	74.5	86.4	89.1	87.9	100.0	95.9	98.1	96.4	94.3	97.5
Pigs	LULE	152.6	129.8	118.0	112.7	99.7	100.7	100.0	99.8	105.0	103.9	100.4	105.3
Sheep	LULD	115.8	111.3	79.9	91.0	92.7	98.6	100.0	99.8	99.3	96.6	93.5	86.5
Poultry	LULF	100.4	100.2	105.5	103.2	101.9	101.1	100.0	96.8	92.4	94.3	91.4	100.1
Other animals	LULG	100.4	100.4	100.1	100.3	99.7	99.6	100.0	99.5	99.8	99.5	99.6	99.6
Gross fixed capital formation	LULR	114.5	102.0	118.1	118.2	107.4	109.2	100.0	103.9	108.9	116.7	110.3	110.9
Cattle	LULN	115.4	102.4	118.7	113.3	111.8	104.2	100.0	101.0	103.6	123.4	105.6	100.6
Pigs	LULP	185.7	125.4	106.8	158.8	126.9	117.2	100.0	121.1	110.9	125.1	123.1	124.1
Sheep	LULO	126.8	86.0	133.8	149.2	102.7	127.5	100.0	118.7	131.7	92.6	111.4	131.0
Poultry	LULQ	102.9	106.5	102.0	101.6	100.6	104.3	100.0	98.7	105.5	108.0	129.4	129.4
10.Total livestock products	LULM	100.9	98.2	99.8	101.1	102.2	99.8	100.0	98.7	96.5	95.2	94.4	98.0
Milk	LULI	103.2	100.4	101.7	102.7	103.9	100.7	100.0	99.1	97.2	95.0	94.0	96.3
Eggs	LULJ	87.8	86.8	93.2	93.0	91.1	98.4	100.0	96.5	94.2	100.2	101.2	113.5
Raw wool	LULK	118.2	113.7	94.5	98.2	96.0	97.5	100.0	90.4	83.4	80.3	73.9	72.5
Other animal products	LULL	68.3	57.6	50.8	80.3	100.1	60.6	100.0	100.1	79.3	65.0	68.7	73.9
11.Total livestock output	VQBC	104.4	100.1	97.4	100.1	99.0	98.5	100.0	98.5	98.2	98.0	95.7	98.8
12.Total other agricultural activities	VQBD	120.8	104.0	102.9	104.8	102.6	114.2	100.0	95.6	102.3	116.8	125.7	131.1
Agricultural services	VQBE	102.6	96.8	99.6	99.2	97.7	102.9	100.0	96.8	103.6	118.4	127.4	132.9
Leasing out quota	VQBF	1470.7	627.4	339.0	507.6	463.0	917.7	100.0	10.2	4.2	2.4	1.9	1.6
13.Total inseparable non-agricultural													
Activities	LULX	78.5	86.1	107.2	93.2	95.2	97.9	100.0	96.3	101.7	102.6	115.4	118.7
14.Gross output at market prices	VQEG	102.8	100.0	97.1	100.4	98.8	100.0	100.0	97.4	96.4	101.6	100.2	102.0
15.Total subsidies (less taxes) on product	VQEE	99.1	92.2	79.3	91.1	91.8	91.8	100.0	92.0	87.0	82.5	85.6	89.6
16.Output at basic prices	LULY	102.9	99.5	95.2	99.6	98.4	99.4	100.0	97.4	96.3	101.4	100.1	101.9
of which transactions within the													
agricultural industry													
Feed wheat	LULZ	67.4	46.4	44.3	47.7	75.3	102.1	100.0	90.2	78.3	80.9	78.8	66.4
Feed barley	LUMA	100.7	100.2	107.7	114.3	107.4	96.9	100.0	97.8	86.2	80.7	83.7	90.6
Feed oats	LUMB	112.7	103.0	107.2	105.6	113.8	113.6	100.0	114.3	114.6	109.5	113.8	115.6
Fodder Maize		14.7	79.5	98.7	92.7	90.7	89.8	100.0	104.8	111.7	116.6	124.6	125.2
Seed potatoes	LUMC	107.5	76.2	83.7	83.6	33.1	50.2	100.0	105.3	40.4	58.3	53.8	51.3
Straw	LUMD	132.0	140.5	126.1	134.6	126.4	127.8	100.0	95.5	55.8	98.5	100.6	95.9
Contract work	LUME	102.6	96.8	99.6	99.2	97.7	102.9	100.0	96.8	103.6	118.4	127.4	132.9
Leasing of quota	LUMF	1470.7	627.4	339.0	507.6	463.0	917.7	100.0	10.2	4.2	2.4	1.9	1.6
Total capital formation in livestock	LUMG	114.4	101.9	118.1	118.2	107.4	109.2	100.0	103.9	108.9	116.8	110.4	110.9
Intermediate Consumption													
17.Seeds	LUMO	121.0	108.1	107.3	91.5	88.8	82.1	100.0	108.0	121.7	116.6	113.1	109.0
Cereals	LUMM	102.0	92.1	90.8	88.5	77.8	81.4	..	..	..	..	..	..
Other	LUMN	99.2	98.6	103.5	101.1	100.4	99.0	..	..	..	..	..	..
18.Energy	VQEH	133.7	122.2	123.7	122.9	104.5	107.7	100.0	95.3	98.2	94.5	113.1	110.7
Electricity	VQEI	132.2	122.3	132.4	134.9	109.7	105.9	100.0	92.9	87.5	95.2	120.4	123.3
Fuels	VQEJ	134.5	122.1	119.5	117.0	102.0	108.5	100.0	96.4	103.3	94.3	110.3	105.8
19.Fertilisers	VQEK	128.1	120.9	112.3	114.7	110.2	107.0	100.0	94.2	95.4	84.5	74.5	84.7
20.Pesticides	LUMQ	109.8	108.3	101.7	103.8	98.0	107.6	100.0	93.6	101.6	120.4	122.5	133.0
21.Veterinary expenses	LUMW	98.7	94.7	90.6	94.7	92.4	98.9	100.0	94.9	99.7	117.1	124.1	121.5
22.Animal feed	LUML	90.1	94.0	98.8	96.2	99.7	101.3	100.0	100.1	98.9	100.5	100.0	106.9
Compounds	LUMH	109.3	100.5	103.4	102.7	102.6	103.7	100.0	104.8	108.1	107.4	105.9	112.8
Straights	LUMI	80.6	89.7	96.0	88.6	97.7	99.7	100.0	92.6	86.3	92.5	92.0	102.0
Feed purchased from other farms	LUMJ	49.8	79.7	87.9	89.6	93.8	96.3	100.0	99.1	93.7	93.0	96.0	95.4

24.2 Output and input volume indices[1]
United Kingdom

Indices (2005=100)

		1999	2000	2001	2002	2003	2004	2005	2006	2007	2008	2009	2010
23.Total maintenance[4]	VQEL	120.7	109.5	112.1	105.9	107.5	108.2	100.0	96.9	101.0	107.0	109.0	108.7
Materials	LUMU	137.9	126.4	125.0	115.6	109.7	108.9	100.0	95.7	101.3	103.0	104.3	104.2
Buildings	LUMT	92.8	82.1	90.7	89.3	103.6	107.0	100.0	99.0	100.6	114.1	117.3	116.6
24.Agricultural services	VQEM	102.6	96.8	99.6	99.2	97.7	102.9	100.0	96.8	103.6	118.4	127.4	132.9
FISIM		110.2	106.4	99.2	99.7	98.4	94.6	100.0	99.8	99.0	101.3	104.7	112.5
25.Other goods and services[4,5]	VQEO	113.3	100.9	94.5	94.6	100.1	106.4	100.0	95.8	93.6	97.2	99.8	97.5
26.Total intermediate consumption	LUNE	108.5	103.0	102.0	100.2	100.5	103.1	100.0	97.6	99.2	101.5	102.9	106.0
27.Gross value added at market prices	LUNF	92.0	94.0	87.7	100.2	95.3	94.2	100.0	97.1	91.2	101.7	95.4	95.0
Gross value added at basic prices		94.6	93.8	85.4	97.7	94.5	93.7	100.0	97.0	91.0	101.4	95.2	94.8
28.Total consumption of Fixed Capital	LUNN	108.4	107.0	105.1	100.5	99.8	98.9	100.0	96.7	96.3	99.9	94.3	95.3
Equipment	LUNI	110.7	108.1	105.7	103.8	102.3	101.4	100.0	98.1	97.7	99.8	102.4	103.2
Buildings[4,6]	LUNG	109.9	105.3	106.4	108.8	105.9	103.5	100.0	102.0	104.5	105.0	105.4	105.0
Livestock	VQES	102.6	108.7	104.4	88.2	90.6	90.8	100.0	90.4	87.8	95.3	78.3	80.0
Cattle	LUNJ	95.6	108.5	93.8	82.5	87.9	88.4	100.0	85.8	81.4	91.2	67.7	72.3
Pigs	LUNL	171.8	146.5	99.5	143.1	114.8	114.5	100.0	97.4	101.5	110.3	98.2	98.2
Sheep	LUNK	110.3	116.0	140.0	91.3	90.4	91.2	100.0	100.6	98.7	102.7	96.1	85.7
Poultry	LUNM	108.0	102.9	100.9	101.8	99.1	97.1	100.0	97.0	100.3	101.0	108.6	116.3
29.Net value added at market prices	LUNO	74.2	79.2	68.6	99.4	90.1	88.8	100.0	97.6	85.9	102.1	95.3	93.8

Source: Department for Environment, Food and Rural Affairs: 01904 455080

1 See chapter text.

2 Output is net of VAT collected on the sale of non-edible products. Figures for total output include subsidies on products, but not other subsidies.

3 Includes straw and minor crops.

4 Landlords' expenses are included within 'Total maintenance', 'Other goods and services' and 'Total consumption of Fixed Capital of buildings'.

5 Includes livestock and crop costs, water costs, insurance premiums, bank charges, professional fees, rates, and other farming costs.

6 A more empirically based methodology for calculating landlords' depreciation was introduced in 2000. The new series has been linked with the old one using a smoothing procedure for the transition year of 1996.

24.3 Agriculture land-use

United Kingdom Area at the June Survey

Thousand hectares

Crop areas (thousand hectares)	2000	2001	2002	2003	2004	2005	2006	2007	2008	2009	2010	2011
Total area of arable crops (1)	4 493	4 283	4 398	4 301	4 413	4 251	4 231	4 271	4 565	4 437	4 441	4 497
of which: wheat[2]	2 086	1 635	1 996	1 836	1 990	1 867	1 836	1 830	2 080	1 775	1 939	1968
barley	1 128	1 245	1 101	1 076	1 007	938	881	898	1 032	1 143	921	968
oats	109	112	126	121	108	90	121	129	135	129	124	109
rye, mixed corn and triticale	..	..	..	..	..	..	25	27	27	28	29	28
oilseed rape	332	404	357	460	498	519	568	674	598	570	642	705
linseed	71	31	12	32	29	45	36	13	16	28	44	36
potatoes	166	165	158	145	148	137	140	140	144	144	138	146
sugar beet (not for stockfeeding)	173	177	169	162	154	148	130	125	120	114	118	113
peas for harvesting dry and field beans	208	276	249	235	242	239	231	161	148	228	210	155
maize	104	129	121	119	118	131	137	146	153	163	164	165
Total area of horticultural crops	172	173	176	176	175	170	166	169	170	170	169	176
of which: vegetables grown outdoors	119	120	124	125	125	121	119	121	122	125	121	129
orchard fruit[3]	28	28	26	25	24	23	23	23	24	22	24	24
soft fruit & wine grapes	10	9	9	9	9	9	10	10	10	10	10	10
outdoor plants and flowers	14	14	15	14	15	14	12	13	13	11	12	11
glasshouse crops	2	2	2	2	2	2	2	2	2	2	2	2

1 Includes crops grown on set-aside land for England for 2006 and 2007.
2 Figures for England from 2009 onwards relate to commercial holdings only.
3 Includes non-commercial orchards.

24.4 Estimated quantity of crops and grass harvested[1]

United Kingdom

Thousand tonnes

		1999	2000	2001	2002	2003	2004	2005	2006	2007	2008	2009	2010
Agricultural crops													
Wheat	BADO	14867	16704	11580	15973	14288	15473	14863	14755	13221	17 227	14 076	14 878
Barley (Winter and Spring)	BADP	6581	6492	6660	6128	6370	5816	5495	5239	5079	6144	6 668	5 252
Oats	BADQ	541	640	621	753	749	627	528	728	712	784	744	685
Sugar beet[2]	BADR	10584	9079	8335	9557	9168	9042	8687	7400	6733	7641	8457	6484
Potatoes	BADS	7131	6178	6674	6921	6058	6246	5979	5727	5564	6145	6396	6045
Horticultural crops													
Field vegetables													
Brussels sprouts	BADT	72.5	78.5	67.3	54.8	42.7	55.8	45.1	46.1	44.8	43.3	43.6	42.9
Cabbage (including savoys and spring greens)	BADU	283.6	269.1	254.3	282.1	244.0	222.3	263.3	256.0	217.5	234.4	233.8	248.4
Cauliflowers	BADV	191.7	172.4	156.1	107.4	116.5	126.3	168.3	133.2	123.7	122.1	108.5	109.35
Carrots	BADW	617.6	673.2	725.8	760	718.4	676.1	710.0	711.9	726.7	710.3	718.7	747.9
Turnips and swedes	BADX	117.5	123.3	132.1	141.8	103.9	96.9	103.1	114.9	100.9	108.2	106.0	98.9
Beetroot	BADY	69.5	63.4	67.1	68.6	56.3	53.1	51.0	57.3	56.8	55.0	55.2	57.3
Onions, dry bulb	BADZ	342	391.4	392.7	374.9	283.4	373.6	340.9	413.6	358.8	303.8	354.9	364.47
Peas, green for market (in pod weight)	BAEA	7	7	6.7	6.2	7.2	5.9	5.9	5.9	5.9	5.9	5.9	5.9
Peas, green for processing (shelled weight)	BAEB	152	143.1	184.5	161	169.3	131.1	130.1	124.4	97.8	152.5	168.4	156.2
Lettuce	BAEC	151.8	155.2	135.8	123.9	109.9	125.6	140.9	131.7	126.4	109	110.6	126.6
Protected crops													
Tomatoes	BAED	107.6	116.6	113	109.1	100.9	75.6	78.5	84.1	83.6	85.6	86.8	89.8
Cucumbers	BAEE	83.8	83.8	79.8	71.5	73.6	77	61.4	59.9	56.5	49.4	57.7	64.6
Lettuce	BAEF	20.6	19.9	18.7	20.9	16	16.6	10.4	8.1	8.2	7.8	6.8	7.3
Fruit													
Dessert apples	BFCD	97.8	133.9	101.3	104.4	84.0	69.0	92.2	118	129.3	106.2	121.1	124.7
Cooking apples	BFCE	85.9	112.4	107.5	107.4	95.3	78.2	100.1	111.5	136.9	124.5	107.5	103.0
Soft fruit	BFCF	60.1	65.9	65.6	64.6	67.1	79.9	86	105.4	107.7	124.1	150.6	145.7
Pears	BFBQ	26.3	22.7	26.6	38.5	34.2	22.7	23.4	28.4	20.6	19.8	20.5	32.8

1 See chapter text.

2 Figures are adjusted to constant 16% sugar content.

Source: Agricultural Departments:01904 455 332

24.5 Cattle , sheep, pigs and poultry on agricultural holdings[1]

United Kingdom

At June each year

Thousands

		2000	2001	2002	2003	2004	2005	2006	2007	2008	2009	2010
Total cattle and calves[1]	**BFCG**	11 135	10 602	10 345	10 508	10 588	10 770	10 579	10 304	10 107	10 025	10 112
of which:												
dairy cows[2]	**BFCH**	2 336	2 251	2 227	2 191	2 129	1 998	1 979	1 954	1 909	1 857	1 847
beef cows[3]	**BFCI**	1 842	1 708	1 657	1 698	1 736	1 751	1 737	1 698	1 670	1 626	1 657
Total sheep and lambs	**BFCM**	42 264	36 716	35 834	35 812	35 817	35 416	34 722	33 946	33 131	31 445	31 084
of which:												
ewes and shearlings	**CKUQ**	20 449	17 921	17 630	17 580	17 630	16 935	16 637	16 064	15 616	14 636	14 740
lambs under one year old	**BFCP**	20 857	17 769	17 310	17 322	17 238	17 488	17 058	16 855	16 574	15 892	15 431
Total pigs	**BFCQ**	6 482	5 845	5 588	5 046	5 159	4 862	4 933	4 834	4 714	4 540	4 460
of which:												
sows in pig and other sows for breeding	**CKUU**	537	527	483	442	449	403	401	398	365	379	360
gilts in pig	**CKUR**	73	71	74	73	66	67	67	57	55	48	67
Total fowls	**KPSV**	169 773	179 880	168 996	178 800	181 759	173 909	173 081	167 667	166 200	152 753	163 867
of which:												
table fowls including broilers	**CKUT**	105 689	112 531	105 137	116 738	119 888	111 475	110 672	109 794	109 859	98 754	105 309
laying and breeding fowl	**CKUV**	48 815	51 345	49 869	48 547	47 936	49 034	47 530	47 719	44 321	42 663	47 107
turkeys, ducks, geese and all other poultry	**JT3R**	15 269	16 004	13 991	13 514	13 935	13 400	14 879	10 154	12 019	11 335	11 451

1 Cattle figures in this table are based on all agricultural holdings.
2 Dairy cows are defined as female dairy cows over 2 years old with offspring.
3 Beef cows are defined as female beef cows over 2 years old with offspring.

Sources: Department for Environment, Food and Rural Affairs;
Farming Statistics :01904 455 332

24.6 Forestry[1]

United Kingdom

Woodland area[2] - (Thousand hectares)		1980	1990	2000	2004	2005	2006	2007	2008	2009	2010	2011
United Kingdom	C5OF	2 175	2 400	2 793	2 816	2 825	2 829	2 837	2 841	2 841	2845	3079
England[3]	C5OG	948	958	1 103	1 114	1 119	1 121	1 124	1 127	1 128	1130	1297
Wales[3]	C5OI	241	248	289	286	286	285	285	285	284	284	304
Scotland[3]	C5OH	920	1 120	1 318	1 330	1 334	1 337	1 341	1 342	1 341	1343	1390
Northern Ireland	C5OJ	67	74	83	86	85	86	87	87	88	88	88
Forestry Commission/Forest Service	C5OK	946	956	886	842	838	832	827	821	814	809	870
Other[5]	C5OL	1 230	1 443	1 907	1 974	1 987	1 997	2 010	2 020	2 027	2037	2209
Conifer	C5OM	1 372	1 576	1 663	1 651	1 647	1 642	1 640	1 635	1 628	1625	1724
Broadleaved[6]	C5ON	804	824	1 131	1 165	1 178	1 187	1 197	1 207	1 213	1220	1355

		1998 /99	1999 /00	2000 /01	2001 /02	2002 /03	2003 /04	2004 /05	2005 /06	2006 /07	2007 /08	2008 /09	2009 /10	2010 /11
New Planting[7] - (Thousand hectares)														
United Kingdom	C5OO	17	17.9	18.7	14.4	13.5	12.4	11.9	8.7	10.7	7.5	6.4	5.4	8.6
England	C5OP	5.1	5.9	5.9	5.4	5.9	4.6	5.3	3.7	3.2	2.6	2.5	2.3	2.5
Wales	C5OR	0.6	0.7	0.4	0.3	0.3	0.5	0.5	0.5	0.4	0.2	0.1	0.1	0.7
Scotland	C5OQ	10.5	10.4	11.7	8	6.7	6.8	5.7	4	6.6	4.2	3.4	2.7	5.1
Northern Ireland	C5OS	0.7	0.8	0.7	0.7	0.6	0.5	0.4	0.6	0.5	0.6	0.3	0.2	0.3
Forestry Commission/Forest Service	C5OT	0.2	0.3	0.3	0.8	0.9	0.2	0.1	0.3	0.2	0.2	0.9	0.7	0.8
Other[8]	C5OU	16.8	17.6	18.4	13.6	12.6	12.1	11.8	8.4	10.4	7.4	5.4	4.6	7.8
Conifer	C5OV	6.6	6.5	4.9	3.9	3.7	2.9	2.1	1.1	2.1	0.9	1.2	0.5	1.6
Broadleaved	C5OW	10.4	11.4	13.8	10.5	9.8	9.5	9.8	7.6	8.5	6.7	5.1	4.8	7.1
Restocking[7] - (Thousand hectares)														
United Kingdom	C5OX	14.1	15.2	15.3	13.9	14.5	14.9	16.1	15.9	19	18.9	16.1	15.1	14.1
England	C5OY	4.1	3.9	4	3.4	3.4	3.2	2.8	3.2	2.8	3.5	3.5	2.8	4
Wales	C5P2	3	2.6	2.2	1.9	1.9	1.8	1.8	2.8	3	2.3	2.2	2.1	2.1
Scotland	C5OZ	6.3	8	8	7.8	8.5	8.9	10.4	9	12.4	12.6	9.6	9.5	6.9
Northern Ireland	C5P3	0.7	0.6	1.1	0.9	0.7	1.1	1	0.9	0.8	0.5	0.8	0.7	1
Forestry Commission/Forest Service	C5P4	8.5	8.8	8.9	9.2	9.1	9.9	10.6	10.4	11	10.4	9.2	7.1	10
Other[8]	C5P5	5.6	6.4	6.4	4.7	5.3	5	5.5	5.5	8	8.5	6.9	8	4.1
Conifer	C5P6	11.3	11.9	12.3	11.5	12	12.1	13	12.5	15.3	14.8	12.1	11.5	10.3
Broadleaved	C5P7	2.8	3.3	3	2.4	2.5	2.8	3	3.4	3.6	4.1	4	3.6	3.8

		2000	2001	2002	2003	2004	2005	2006	2007	2008	2009	2010
Wood Production (volume - Thousand green tonnes[9])												
United Kingdom	C5P8	8080	8140	8250	8880	9040	9080	8936	9462	8862	9096	10249
Softwood total	C5PA	7430	7500	7630	8320	8520	8490	8499	9022	8432	8560	9718
Forestry Commission/Forest Service	C5PB	4850	4600	4650	4820	4890	4580	4627	4693	4458	5213	4695
Non-Forestry Commission/Forest Service[10]	C5PC	2580	2900	2980	3500	3630	3910	4309	4769	4404	3883	5553
Hardwood[11]	C5PD	650	630	620	560	510	590	438	440	431	536	532

Source: Forest Service Agency;Forestry Commission: 0131 314 6171

1 See chapter text.

2 Areas as at 31 March.

3 For England, Wales and Scotland, 1980 woodland area figures are the published results from the 1979-1982
Census of Woodlands and Trees and figures for 1990 are adjusted to reflect subsequent changes.
From 1998 on-wards they are based on results from the 1995-1999 National Inventory of Woodlands and Trees,
adjusted to reflect subsequent changes.

4 The apparent fall in woodland cover in 2001 is due to the reclassification of Forestry Commission open land within the forest

5 Includes private woodland and non-Forestry Commission / Forest Service public woodland.

6 Broadleaved includes coppice. For data based on1979-82 Census, all scrub and
other non-plantation woodland have been assumed to be broadleaved.

7 Figures shown are for the areas of new planting and restocking in the year to31 March.

8 Includes grant aided planting on non-Forestry Commission/ Forest Service woodland
and estimates for areas planted without the aid of grants.

9 Figures have been rounded to the nearest10 thousand green tonnes.

10 Before 2006 only softwood figures used.

11 Hardwood is timber from broadleaved species. Most hardwood production comes from
non-FC/FS woodland; the figures are estimates based on reported deliveries to wood processing industries.

24.7 Sales for food of agricultural produce and livestock
United Kingdom

			1999	2000	2001	2002	2003	2004	2005	2006	2007	2008	2009	2010
Milk[1]:														
Utilised for liquid consumption	KCQO	Million litres	6889	6793	6748	6825	6753	6693	6652	6734	6724	6678	6626	6756
Utilised for manufacture	KCQP	"	6973	6532	6752	6883	7140	6724	6490	6266	6085	5840	5699	6082
Total available for domestic use[2]	KCQQ	"	14234	13749	13957	14141	14321	13894	13809	13325	13146	12816	12845	13174
Hen eggs in shell	KCQR	Million dozens	738	712	753	747	730	773	772	743	720	754	751	826
Animals slaughtered:														
Cattle and calves:														
Cattle	KCQS	Thousands	2217	2275	2072	2184	2188	2290	2302	2583	2603	2570	2451	2672
Calves	KCQT	"	75	152	92	98	87	103	111	51	46	44	43	62
Total	KCQU	"	2292	2427	2164	2282	2275	2393	2413	2634	2649	2614	2494	2734
Sheep and lambs	KCQV	"	19116	18442	12964	14993	15095	15492	16284	16414	15804	16697	15600	14295
Pigs:														
Clean pigs	MBGD	"	14350	12370	10446	10260	9133	9150	8971	8900	9274	9192	8824	9441
Sows and boars	KCQZ	"	379	321	180	314	241	240	202	196	210	235	206	108
Total	KCRA	"	14728	12692	10626	10575	9374	9390	9173	9097	9484	9427	9030	9549
Poultry[3]	KCRB	Millions	863	844	867	862	882	881	903	886	874	862	868	933

Note: The figures for cereals and for animals slaughtered relate to periods of 52 weeks

1 Data to 1994 sourced from the Milk Marketing Boards. Data from 1995 sourced from surveys run by the agricultural departments. 1994 includes two months of data sourced from the surveys run by the agricultural departments.

2 The totals of liquid consumption and milk used for manufacture may not add up to the total available for domestic use because of adjustments for dairy wastage, stock changes and other uses, such as far mhouse consumption, milk fed to stock and on farm waste.

3 Total fowls, ducks, geese and turkeys.

Source: Department for Environment, Food and Rural Affairs: 01904 455 332

24.8 Estimates of producers of organic and in-conversion livestock[1]
United Kingdom

At January each year

Thousand head

		2003	2004	2005	2006	2007	2008	2009	2010
Cattle	IDR8	126.8	174.8	214.3	244.8	250.4	319.6	331.2	350.1
Sheep[2]	IDR9	n/a	n/a	691	747.3	863.1	1178.3	884.8	981.2
Pigs[3]	IDS2	48.8	43.7	30	32.9	50.4	71.2	49.4	47.4
Poultry	IDS3	2166.2	2431.6	3439.5	4421.3	4440.7	4362.9	3958.7	3870.9
Goats	IDS4	0.7	0.5	0.5	0.6	0.5	0.4	0.1	0.1
Other Livestock	IDS5	1.0	1.2	1.5	4.3	3.4	4.4	3.3	4.4

1 Certification bodies record production data at various times of the year so figures should be treated with care as they will not represent an exact snap-shot of organic livestock farming.

2 We are currently unable to provide historical data for sheep as we are investigating some inconsistencies in the historical data and will publish these results as soon as they are available.

3 Please note that the 2009 total pigs figure has been revised in the light of more up to date data being available.

Sources: Department for Environment, Food and Rural Affairs;
Organic Statistics Team: 01904 455407

24.9 Producers of organic and in-conversion livestock, Organic producers, growers, processors and importers

United Kingdom

Number of businesses

	2003	2004	2005	2006	2007	2008	2009	2010
Producers and growers								
North East	103	104	129	161	173	179	167	160
North West	289	289	311	332	367	367	333	315
Yorkshire & Humberside	254	271	279	319	356	330	308	302
East Midlands	406	401	416	446	487	449	422	408
West Midlands	455	452	478	520	556	555	507	494
Eastern	483	485	508	556	574	551	529	515
South West	1354	1378	1532	1732	1961	2002	1988	1953
South East (inc. London)	856	877	901	939	1042	1041	1024	984
England	4200	4257	4554	5005	5516	5474	5278	5131
Wales	719	755	800	835	953	1230	1176	1166
Scotland	856	809	792	911	860	889	820	737
Northern Ireland	183	217	267	292	302	303	293	253
United Kingdom	5958	6038	6413	7043	7631	7896	7567	7287

Source: Organic certifier bodies collated by Defra Statistics

(a) Processers can include abattoirs, bakers, storers and wholesalers.
The recorded location depends on the address registered with the
Certifier Bodies and so larger businesses may be recorded at their
headquarters.

24.10 Organic and in-conversion land and land use

United Kingdom

Thousand hectares

		2003	2004	2005	2006	2007	2008	2009	2010
Land, in-conversion									
North East	IDS6	6.8	4.6	6.6	6.9	4.8	9.8	6.5	4.0
North West	IDS7	2.6	2.5	3.2	1.8	3.3	3.8	3.4	2.4
Yorkshire and Humberside	IDS8	1.7	1.3	2.3	3.4	4.1	3.8	2.7	0.9
East Midlands	IDS9	1.6	1.2	2.4	2.1	3.1	3.7	3.1	1.0
West Midlands	IDT2	3.7	2.4	3.2	4	5.7	8.2	5.7	2.1
Eastern	IDT3	3	2.4	2.6	3.6	5.3	4.8	4.1	1.4
South West	IDT4	10.8	9.1	22	31.6	48.2	46.5	34.7	13.6
South East (including London)	IDT5	6.5	5.4	10.7	13.2	14.6	10.4	7.3	4.3
England	IDT6	36.8	28.8	53.2	66.5	89	91.1	67.6	29.8
Wales	IDT7	8	8.6	12.8	15.4	30.9	49.5	36.8	4.0
Scotland	IDT8	20.4	13.7	16.7	35.2	34.8	6.2	12	12.6
Northern Ireland	IDT9	0.8	1.6	3.2	4	3.2	2.3	3	4.4
United Kingdom	IDU2	66	52.7	86	121.1	157.9	149.1	119.4	50.8
Land, fully organic									
North East	IDU3	20.5	25.3	29.3	22.6	25.8	25.6	26.8	30.6
North West	IDU4	19.9	19.8	18.9	19.4	20.4	21.2	19.8	20.0
Yorkshire and Humberside	IDU5	8.1	8.6	9	9	9.6	10.9	11.9	13.8
East Midlands	IDU6	16.1	13.4	13.2	12.5	13.2	12.2	14.4	16.3
West Midlands	IDU7	25.5	26.8	27	26.3	28.2	29.7	32	35.4
Eastern	IDU8	9.7	10.3	11.8	10.8	12.7	13.2	14.2	17.3
South West	IDU9	86.2	90.5	94	93.4	106.3	123.9	140.4	174.6
South East (including London)	IDV2	34.3	34.9	35.2	35.8	42.5	47.2	51.6	54.1
England	IDV3	220.2	229.6	238.4	229.9	258.7	284	311.2	362.0
Wales	IDV4	50.2	55.6	58	63.5	65.1	75.1	88.6	118.8
Scotland	IDV5	351.9	331.6	231.2	200.1	193.1	225.1	209.3	176.3
Northern Ireland	IDV6	6.6	5	6.3	5.1	7.3	10.1	10.3	10.4
United Kingdom	IDV7	629	621.8	533.9	498.6	524.3	594.4	619.3	667.6

		2002	2003	2004	2005	2006	2007	2008	2009	2010
Land, in-conversion										
Cereals	IDV8	11.2	7.0	4.1	10.3	11.9	13.2	9.9	6.5	2.2
Other Crops	IDV9	6.5	1.9	2.7	3.5	3.4	3.5	2.5	2.1	0.7
Fruit and Nuts	IDW2	0.4	0.2	0.2	0.2	0.2	0.4	0.4	0.3	0.2
Vegetables (including potatoes)	IDW3	3.0	1.9	1.3	1.3	2.1	2.6	2.0	1.6	0.5
Herbs and ornamentals	IDW4	0.1	0.1	0.0	0.2	0.1	0.1	0.6	0.8	1.0
Temporary pasture	IDW5	18.1	12.7	10.4	15.9	22.9	34.2	31.0	19.6	7.3
Set aside	IDW6	3.5	2.3	1.3	1.4	1.1	0.0	0.0	0.0	0.0
Permanent pasture[1]	IDW7	159.1	38.1	27.2	47.5	72.1	93.6	96.0	82.7	35.7
Woodland	IDW8	1.1	0.7	0.6	3.5	4.2	5.6	2.7	2.6	1.9
Non cropping	IDW9	0.2	0.3	2.9	1.1	2.3	3.3	1.9	1.1	0.7
Other	IDX2	0.4	0.3	1.7	1.1	0.2	0.3	0.3	0.1	0.2
Unknown	IDX3	0.8	0.5	0.1	0.1	0.8	1.1	1.7	2.0	0.5
Total	IDX4	204.3	66.0	52.7	86.0	121.1	157.9	149.1	119.4	50.8
Land, fully organic										
Cereals	IDX5	25.7	35.4	35.1	37.4	35.5	38.4	47.3	53.4	54.7
Other Crops	IDX6	14.1	7.5	10.2	7.3	6.8	7.8	8.7	9.1	10.2
Fruit and Nuts	IDX7	1.5	1.4	1.5	1.5	1.6	1.6	1.5	1.9	2.0
Vegetables (including potatoes)	IDX8	9.7	11.7	12.7	12.4	13.5	14.3	17.7	17.3	17.4
Herbs and ornamentals	IDX9	0.2	0.2	0.2	0.6	0.6	0.5	4.9	4.9	5.2
Temporary pasture	IDY2	58.9	77.3	80.3	82.0	79.8	90.9	98.8	106.6	117.5
Set aside	IDY3	3.4	4.6	4.6	2.3	1.3	0.0	0.0	0.0	0.0
Permanent pasture[1]	IDY4	413.9	481.3	467.8	380.9	350.5	358.4	398.3	413.0	443.3
Woodland	IDY5	5.6	4.8	5.2	3.3	4.0	5.9	3.2	4.6	6.2
Non cropping	IDY6	1.4	0.9	1.3	2.4	4.0	4.7	4.4	5.7	5.5
Other	IDY7	0.2	3.0	2.4	3.2	0.4	0.4	1.0	1.5	1.7
Unknown	IDY8	2.4	0.8	0.4	0.4	0.6	1.4	8.6	1.1	3.9
Total	IDY9	536.9	629.0	621.8	533.9	498.6	524.3	594.4	619.3	667.6

Note: DEFRA have recalculated the basis on which these data are collected to make it clearer that they are a yearly average, not a snapshot.

1 Includes rough grazing.

Sources: Department for Environment, Food and Rural Affairs
Organic Statistics Team: 01904 455558

24.11 Average weekly and hourly earnings and hours of full-time male agricultural workers[1]

England and Wales:
At September each year

		2004	2005	2006	2007	2008	2009	2010
Average weekly earnings (£) 95% confidence interval	**LQML**	331.26 (+/-£12.46)	357.64 (+/-£13.62)	340.60 (+/-£22.05)	352.33 (+/-£13.62)	356.13 (+/-£18.97)	404.05 (+/-£19.93)	389.57 (+/-£10.71)
Average weekly hours worked 95% confidence interval	**LQMM**	46.2 (+/-1.2)	48.4 (+/-1.4)	46.1 (+/-2.4)	47.0 (+/-1.4)	46.6 (+/-2.3)	49.4 (+/-2.1)	47.5 (+/-0.9)
Average earnings/hours (£) 95% confidence interval	**LQMN**	7.16 (+/-£0.17)	7.40 (+/-£0.17)	7.39 (+/-£0.21)	7.50 (+/-£0.16)	7.64 (+/-£0.16)	8.19 (+/-£0.17)	8.20 (+/-£0.11)
Number of workers in the sample		311	299	248	279	283	231	138

1 See chapter text.

Source: Department for Environment, Food and Rural Affairs: 01904 455332

24.12 Average weekly and hourly earnings and hours of agricultural workers[1] :by type , aged 20 and over

England and Wales: At September 2010

	Full-time		Part-time		Casual		Managers
	Male	Female	Male	Female	Male	Female	
Average weekly earnings (£) 95% confidence interval	389.57 (+/-£10.71)	319.63 (+/-£14.19)	170.37 (+/-£12.86)	151.02 (+/-£10.16)	220.16 (+/-£18.01)	169.10 (+/-£28.20)	596.46 (+/-£28.12)
Average weekly hours worked 95% confidence interval	47.5 (+/-0.9)	42.8 (+/-1.1)	22.3 (+/-1.5)	21.8 (+/-1.2)	33.0 (+/-3.4)	26.2 (+/-3.9)	..
Average earnings/hour (£) 95% confidence interval	8.20 (+/-£0.11)	7.48 (+/-£0.16)	7.65 (+/-£0.24)	6.93 (+/-£0.13)	7.13 (+/-£0.22)	6.47 (+/-£0.23)	..
Number of workers in the sample	138	59	48	70	41	29	69

1 See chapter text.

Source: Department for Environment, Food and Rural Affairs: 01904 455332

24.13 Workers employed in agriculture[1]: by type

United Kingdom
At June each year

Thousands

		2000	2001	2002	2003	2004	2005	2006	2007	2008	2009	2010
Total labour force on commercial holdings (incl. farmers and spouses)[1]		516	514	507	491	501	494	491	481	483	464	466
Farmers, business partners, directors and spouses		318	318	319	313	315	311	313	305	302	289	295
	Full time	165	163	160	155	151	149	146	141	140	137	134
	Part time[2]	153	155	160	158	164	162	167	165	161	152	161
Salaried managers		11	12	12	11	14	15	14	15	14	11	11
Other workers		188	184	175	166	171	169	164	161	167	164	160
Full time		83	81	76	69	66	66	63	61	64	63	64
	Male	73	71	64	60	57	56	53	51	54	52	..
	Female	10	10	11	10	9	10	10	10	11	11	..
Part time (b)		42	40	38	36	38	39	39	43	43	42	39
	Male	23	22	21	20	22	23	23	27	27	27	..
	Female	19	18	17	16	16	16	16	16	16	16	..
Seasonal, casual or gang labour		63	62	62	61	66	64	62	57	60	59	56
	Male	45	45	45	44	48	45	43	40	42	42	40
	Female	17	17	17	17	18	18	19	17	18	17	17

1 See chapter text. Figures for England relate to commercial holdings only.
2 Part time is defined as less than 39 hours per week in England and Wales, less than 38 hours per week in Scotland and less than 30 hours per week in Northern Ireland.

24.14 Summary of UK fishing industry

United Kingdom

£ million (unless otherwise stated)

		2001	2002	2003	2004	2005	2006	2007	2008	2009	2010
GDP for fishing[1] current price gross value added at basic prices	QTUF	368	366	368	380	394	439	505	518	525	546
Output index (chain volume measures) 2005 =100	EWAC	128.7	124.7	112.1	103.4	102.8	100.0	104.0	103.5	104.6	107.6
GDP for agriculture, forestry and fishing Current price gross value added at basic prices	QTOP	8,334	9,008	9,807	10,670	7,530	7,788	8,628	9,715	9,034	9,310
Output index (chain volume measures) 2005 =100	GDQA	84.0	93.8	92.3	92.2	99.2	100.0	95.2	95.0	90.4	87.2
GDP at market prices Current price GDP at market prices	YBHA	1,021,828	1,075,564	1,139,746	1,202,956	1,254,058	1,328,363	1,404,845	1,445,580	1,394,989	1,455,397
Chain volume measures index 2005 =100	YBEZ	88.1	90.0	92.5	95.2	97.3	100.0	102.7	102.6	100.8	98.9
Percentage contribution of GVA from fishing to GVA for agriculture , hunting, forestry & fishing Current prices		4.5%	4.4%	4.1%	3.8%	3.5%	5.0%	5.1%	4.8%	4.3%	5.9%

		2001	2002	2003	2004	2005	2006	2007	2008	2009	2010
Fleet size at end of year[2] number of vessels	I3TC	7,721	7,578	7,096	7,022	6,716	6,752	6,763	6,573	6,500	6,477
Employment Number of fishermen	I3TD	14,958	14,205	13,122	13,453	12,831	12,934	12,871	12,614	12,212	12,703
Total landings by UK vessels[3] quantity ('000 tonnes)	I3TE	737.8	685.5	639.7	653.7	715.7	619.6	613.9	588.2	581.0	606.3
value	I3TF	574.4	545.6	528.3	513.0	574.6	614.3	646.3	635.6	674.4	719.3
Imports quantity ('000 tonnes)	I3TG	626.6	621.4	631.5	671.3	720.4	753.3	747.9	781.7	720.6	703.0
value[4]	I3TH	1,435.1	1,438.7	1,439.0	1,474.0	1,696.0	1,920.6	1,993.9	2,210.1	2,177.2	2,250.4
Exports quantity ('000 tonnes)	I3TI	391.0	389.1	479.5	477.8	461.4	415.6	466.9	415.8	479.7	516.4
value[4]	I3TJ	744.6	762.2	891.0	886.0	939.0	942.2	982.0	1,009.4	1,166.1	1,342.7

		2001	2002	2003	2004	2005	2006	2007	2008	2009	2010
Household consumption ('000 tonnes)[5]	I3TK	482	479	485	492	523	537	525	515	508	no data
Population ('000 persons)	I3TL	59,113	59,319	59,552	59,842	60,235	60,584	60,986	61,398	61,792	62,262
Consumer expenditure on fish	I3TM	2,857	2,870	2,917	3,090	3,275	3,525	3,674	3,685	3,765	no data
on food	I3TN	66,332	67,955	70,395	71,924	73,998	76,701	79,341	68,282	71,162	no data
Fish as a % of food[6]	I3TO	4.3%	4.2%	4.1%	4.3%	4.4%	4.6%	4.6%	5.4%	5.3%	no data
Landed Price index 1987 =100	I3TP	103.8	103.1	105.7	109.3	123.8	134.4	136.2	141.1	141.7	152.2
Retail Price Index[7]	I3TQ	101.6	104.6	103.5	101.7	102.3	108.5	115.7	124.0	130.3	138.3

1 GDP for fish includes landings abroad.
2 The number of vessels excludes those registered in the Channel Islands and the Isle of Man.
3 The quantity of landed fish is expressed in terms of liveweight. The figures relate to landings both into the UK and abroad.
4 Imports are valued at cost, including insurance and freight terms whereas exports are valued at free on board terms.

5 Data are derived from the National Food Survey prior to 2001, and from the Expenditure and Food Survey from 2001 onwards. Figures for 2001 onwards are based on financial year data.
6 Including non-alcoholic beverages.
7 The fish component of the RPI which includes canned and processed fish. The index is calculated on a monthly basis with January 1987 =100.

Source: Fisheries Statistics Unit: 020 7979 8503

24.15 Fishing fleet[1]

United Kingdom
At December each year

Numbers

By size		1999	2000	2001	2002	2003	2004	2005	2006	2007	2008	2009	2010
10m and under	KSNF	5409	5273	5227	5287	5113	5092	4833	4896	4521	4520	4435	4442
10.01 -12.19m	KSNG	577	547	536	514	486	465	449	445	446	439	430	415
12.20 -17.00m	KSNH	468	467	442	409	405	393	387	384	378	379	372	366
17.01 -18.29m	KSNI	154	131	143	129	121	115	112	111	110	106	102	99
18.30 -24.38m	KSNJ	414	406	405	322	271	257	253	244	245	247	248	245
24.39 -30.48m	KSNK	224	219	218	185	156	147	143	139	121	125	126	119
30.49 -36.58m	KSNL	80	77	75	65	63	60	55	56	44	41	43	43
over 36.58m	KSNM	122	122	123	122	120	112	109	97	88	79	73	71
Total over 10m	KSNN	2039	1969	1942	1746	1622	1549	1508	1476	1432	1416	1394	1358
Total UK fleet[2]	KSNO	7448	7242	7169	7033	6735	6641	6341	6372	5953	5936	5829	5800
By segment													
Pelagic gears	KSNP	46	44	47	45	42	31	23	16	..	..	..	
Beam trawl	KSNQ	114	111	116	113	162	102	96	93	..	..	..	
Demersal, Seines and Nephrops	JZCI	1235	1208	1158	969	853	852	812	785	..	..	..	
Lines and Nets	KSNR	172	165	146	136	118	123	114	111	..	..	..	
Shellfish: mobile	KSNS	243	211	229	228	191	166	155	151	..	..	..	
Shellfish: fixed	KSNT	301	297	301	304	307	253	236	230	..	..	..	
Distant water	KSNU	12	13	11	10	8	10	10	8	..	..	..	
Under10m	KSNV	5916	5769	5713	5773	5587	5395	4276	4131	..	..	..	
Other : Mussel Dredgers	JZCJ	2	2	7	15	15	13	7	6	..	..	..	
Total UK fleet[3]	13TC	8041	7820	7728	7593	7283	7022	6716	6752	6763	6573	6500	6477

1 See chapter text.
2 Excluding Channel Islands and Isle of Man.
3 Including Channel Islands and Isle of Man.

Source: Fisheries Statistics Unit: 020 7979 8503

24.16 Estimated household food consumption[1]

Grammes per person per week

		Great Britain					2001 /02	2002 /03
		1997	1998	1999	2000			
Liquid wholemilk[2] (ml)	KPQM	712	693	634	664	VQEW	599	555
Fully skimmed (ml)	KZBH	158	164	167	164	VQEX	160	166
Semi skimmed (ml)	KZBI	978	945	958	975	VQEZ	931	919
Other milk and cream (ml)	KZBJ	248	243	248	278	VQFA	333	350
Cheese	KPQO	109	104	104	110	VQFB	112	112
Butter	KPQP	38	39	37	39	VQFC	42	37
Margarine	KPQQ	26	26	20	21	VQFD	13	13
Low and reduced fat spreads	KZBK	77	69	71	68	VQFE	72	70
All other oils and fats (ml for oils)	KPQR	62	62	58	58	VQFF	70	70
Eggs (number)	KPQS	2	2	2	2	VQFG	2	2
Preserves and honey	KPQT	41	38	33	33	VQFH	35	34
Sugar	KPQU	128	119	107	105	VQFI	112	111
Beef and veal	KPQV	110	109	110	124	VQFJ	118	118
Mutton and lamb	KPQW	56	59	57	55	VQFK	51	51
Pork	KPQX	75	76	69	68	VQFL	61	61
Bacon and ham, uncooked	KPQY	72	76	68	71	VQFM	68	69
Bacon and ham, cooked (including canned)	KPQZ	41	40	39	41	VQFN	45	45
Poultry uncooked	JZCH	221	218	201	214	VQFO	206	199
Cooked poultry (not purchased in cans)	KYBP	33	33	35	39	VQFQ	43	44
Other cooked and canned meats	KPRB	52	49	48	51	VQFR	54	59
Offals	KPRC	7	5	5	5	VQFS	6	6
Sausages, uncooked	KPRD	63	60	58	60	VQFT	66	66
Other meat products	KPRE	209	216	221	239	VQFU	313	319
Fish, fresh and processed (including shellfish)	KPRF	70	70	70	67			
Canned fish	KPRG	31	29	31	32			
Fish and fish products, frozen	KPRH	46	46	42	44			
Fish, fresh chilled or frozen						VQAI	51	48
Other fish and fish products						VQAJ	105	106
Potatoes (excluding processed)	KPRI	745	715	673	707	VQFY	647	617
Fresh green vegetables	KPRJ	251	246	245	240	VQAK	229	231
Other fresh vegetables	KPRK	497	486	500	492	VQAL	502	505
Frozen potato products	KYBQ	106	111	113	120			
Other frozen vegetables	KPRL	94	88	87	80			
Potato products not frozen	JZCF	90	89	86	82			
Canned beans	KPRM	122	118	112	114			
Other canned vegetables (excl. potatoes)	KPRN	104	99	92	97			
Other processed vegetables (excl. potatoes)	LQZH	52	54	59	54			
All processed vegetables						VQAM	620	613
Apples	KPRO	179	181	169	180	VQGN	175	172
Bananas	KPRP	195	198	202	206	VQGO	203	208
Oranges	KPRQ	62	63	50	54	VQGP	55	62
All other fresh fruit	KPRR	276	274	290	304	VQGS	318	351
Canned fruit	KPRS	44	37	38	38	VQGT	40	39
Dried fruit, nuts and fruit and nut products	KPRT	35	34	30	35	VQGU	39	41
Fruit juices (ml)	KPRU	277	304	284	303	VQGX	327	333
Flour	KPRV	54	55	56	67	VQGY	55	61
Bread	KPRW	746	742	717	720	VQGZ	769	756
Buns, scones and teacakes	KPRX	43	41	40	43	VQHA	37	41
Cakes and pastries	KPRY	93	88	87	89	VQHB	139	122
Biscuits	KPRZ	138	137	132	141	VQHC	166	174
Breakfast cereals	KPSA	135	136	134	143	VQHE	133	132
Oatmeal and oat products	KPSB	16	11	13	15	VQHF	12	13
Other cereals and cereal products	JZCG	293	270	284	291	VQHG	345	366
Tea	KPSC	36	35	32	34	VQHK	34	34
Instant coffee	KPSD	11	12	11	11	VQHL	13	12
Canned soups	KPSE	70	71	67	71	VQHM	79	80
Pickles and sauces	KPSF	92	96	91	107	VQHN	121	123

1 See chapter text.

2 Including also school and welfare milk (pre-2001-02)

24.16 Estimated household food consumption[1]

		United Kingdom							Grammes per person per week
		2003 /04	2004 /05	2005 /06	2006	2007	2008	2009	2010
Liquid wholemilk[2] (ml)	VQEW	585	484	460	477	420	410	412	352
Fully skimmed (ml)	VQEX	154	158	159	163	173	158	165	172
Semi skimmed (ml)	VQEZ	926	975	1008	974	982	987	991	985
Other milk and cream (ml)	VQFA	358	366	385	395	397	392	427	389
Cheese	VQFB	113	110	116	116	119	111	116	118
Butter	VQFC	35	35	38	40	41	40	39	40
Margarine	VQFD	12	11	20	18	19	22	24	23
Low and reduced fat spreads	VQFE	71	68	55	57	53	51	48	49
All other oils and fats (ml for oils)	VQFF	68	68	70	69	68	72	71	71
Eggs (number)	VQFG	2	2	2	2	2	2	2	2
Preserves and honey	VQFH	33	34	35	34	33	34	35	36
Sugar	VQFI	102	99	94	92	92	93	90	90
Beef and veal	VQFJ	119	123	120	128	126	111	112	114
Mutton and lamb	VQFK	49	50	53	54	55	45	46	44
Pork	VQFL	56	56	52	55	54	55	54	53
Bacon and ham, uncooked	VQFM	70	70	68	66	64	63	68	70
Bacon and ham, cooked (including canned)	VQFN	47	43	44	45	45	45	43	43
Poultry uncooked	VQFO	200	197	212	207	208	207	205	201
Cooked poultry (not purchased in cans)	VQFQ	48	49	48	48	43	44	41	41
Other cooked and canned meats	VQFR	60	58	56	53	50	51	51	48
Offals	VQFS	7	5	5	5	5	5	6	5
Sausages, uncooked	VQFT	70	67	64	65	65	62	65	66
Other meat products	VQFU	335	330	323	315	316	311	309	331
Fish, fresh and processed (including shellfish)									
Canned fish									
Fish and fish products, frozen									
Fish, fresh chilled or frozen	VQAI	45	42	45	47	43	43	41	38
Other fish and fish products	VQAJ	111	115	122	123	122	118	117	113
Potatoes (excluding processed)	VQFY	600	570	587	565	537	535	514	501
Fresh green vegetables	VQAK	228	225	235	221	224	203	201	192
Other fresh vegetables	VQAL	505	536	567	566	566	557	552	565
Frozen potato products									
Other frozen vegetables									
Potato products not frozen									
Canned beans									
Other canned vegetables (excl. potatoes)									
Other processed vegetables (excl. potatoes)									
All processed vegetables	VQAM	611	597	608	601	594	599	597	592
Apples	VQGN	171	173	179	180	178	162	163	156
Bananas	VQGO	211	217	225	226	230	219	205	204
Oranges	VQGP	64	57	59	55	59	49	45	47
All other fresh fruit	VQGS	343	358	392	394	389	360	348	348
Canned fruit	VQGT	40	38	36	39	35	32	29	30
Dried fruit, nuts and fruit and nut products	VQGU	40	46	51	53	51	52	51	52
Fruit juices (ml)	VQGX	322	280	350	366	340	325	302	296
Flour	VQGY	52	55	60	54	54	63	58	58
Bread	VQGZ	728	695	701	692	677	659	656	634
Buns, scones and teacakes	VQHA	44	47	46	45	44	43	47	45
Cakes and pastries	VQHB	120	117	122	120	115	111	111	108
Biscuits	VQHC	163	165	165	165	163	170	169	162
Breakfast cereals	VQHE	134	131	135	135	130	130	133	133
Oatmeal and oat products	VQHF	12	14	19	17	19	20	21	21
Other cereals and cereal products	VQHG	360	354	378	378	387	386	393	402
Tea	VQHK	31	31	33	30	30	30	29	28
Instant coffee	VQHL	13	13	13	14	13	14	15	15
Canned soups	VQHM	77	76	82	79	79	76	78	76
Pickles and sauces	VQHN	121	120	125	128	129	130	132	131

1 See chapter text.

2 Including also school and welfare milk (pre-2001-02)

Sources: Living Costs and Food Survey;
Department for Environment Food and Rural Affairs;
Office for National Statistics: 01904 455359